THE
DOLPHIN
READER

THE
DOLPHIN
READER

DOUGLAS HUNT

University of Missouri

HOUGHTON MIFFLIN COMPANY   BOSTON

DALLAS   GENEVA, ILLINOIS   LAWRENCEVILLE, NEW JERSEY

PALO ALTO

ACKNOWLEDGMENTS

ROGER ANGELL: "In the Country," from *Late Innings* by Roger Angell. Copyright © 1982 by Roger Angell. Reprinted by permission of Simon & Schuster, Inc.
JAMES BALDWIN: "Fifth Avenue, Uptown: A Letter from Harlem," from *Nobody Knows My Name* by James Baldwin. Copyright © 1960 by James Baldwin. Reprinted by permission of Doubleday & Company, Inc.
JOHN BERGER: "An Independent Woman," from *Pig Earth* by John Berger. Copyright © 1979 by John Berger. Reprinted by permission of Pantheon Books, a division of Random House, Inc.

Acknowledgments continue following Author/Title Index.

COVER ILLUSTRATION BY STEVE HARVARD.

Printed in the U.S.A.

Library of Congress Catalog Card Number: 85-80766

ISBN: 0-395-35789-6

BCDEFGHIJ- FG -89876

BRIEF
CONTENTS

Note: See also the annotated table of contents, which starts on page xi. An asterisk (*) denotes fiction.

ANNOTATED CONTENTS

Note: An asterisk (*) denotes fiction.

promises of impossibilities. The wise man of the Stoics would, no doubt, be a grander object than a steam engine. But there are steam engines.

words will express it? What image or idiom will make it
clearer? Is this image fresh enough to have effect?

PREFACE

Composition readers are among my favorite books, but not for teaching composition. They generally include a miscellaneous collection of fine essays, and I read them with the same sort of pleasure with which I read *The New Yorker*, or *The Atlantic* or *Harper's*. Whether the nominal arrangement is rhetorical or thematic, they are essentially anthologies, filled with essays that are wonderful individually but are as disengaged from one another as strangers in an elevator. A thematic reader will have a dozen essays collected as an "Education" unit, but the teacher may find that no two have enough in common to provoke the sort of discussion and debate that can give students substantial issues to write about. A decade of using such readers has shown me that teaching from them is like trying to start a fire by rubbing one stick together.

The Dolphin Reader is first and foremost an attempt to solve this problem. Each of its twelve units explores a theme interesting to all thoughtful people, and each selection contributes substantially—though not always *gravely*, I'm glad to say—to the exploration. This is not an anthology of literary masterpieces (though it includes a number of those). It is an invitation to hard thinking and thoughtful writing. The great challenge has been to draw writers as diverse as Plato, Martin Luther King, Jr., Jane Jacobs, and Gretel Ehrlich into a conversation. The great pleasure has been to imagine the contributions that students will make to the conversation.

As the thematic units developed, it became clear that they would be richer for the addition of fiction that mirrored their themes. The selection of stories was particularly difficult, but the result was an unexpected bonus. *The Dolphin Reader* contains, dispersed among its thematic units, a brief introduction to fiction that illustrates all the principal elements: point of view, setting, character, symbol, and irony. The writers represented include "classics" like Nathaniel Hawthorne and Ernest Hemingway, contemporaries like Alice Munro and Evan S. Connell, and important international figures like Nadine Gordimer and Gabriel García Márquez.

The apparatus in *The Dolphin Reader* is as unobtrusive as editorial and typographical ingenuity could make it. We have glossed what seemed necessary, but not what is easily findable in the dictionary. The only unfamiliar elements of the apparatus are the annotated table of contents, the end-of-unit commentaries and questions, and the browser's index. All of these are designed primarily as maps to help students find their way to interesting and useful selections. What we had to communicate to the teacher we put into *The Guide to the Dolphin Reader*.

I can't begin to thank all the people whose thoughts helped to shape *The Dolphin Reader*, but I do especially want to thank the following colleagues, whose comments both informed and heartened me: Michael Allen, Wooster College (OH); John P. Bodnar, Prince George's Community College (MD); Neil Daniel, Texas Christian University; Kitty Chen Dean, Nassau County Community College (NY); John Dick, University of Texas, El Paso; C.R. Embry, Truckee Meadows Community College (NV); Patricia Hampl, University of Minnesota; Muriel Harris, Purdue University; Michael Johnson, University of Kansas; Nancy C. Martinez, University of New Mexico; and Linda Peterson, Yale University.

Special thanks go to Melody Daily, whose assistance on the *Guide to the Dolphin Reader* made an impossible task a pleasure, and to W. Raymond Smith, whose biographical notes on our authors testify to his energy and ingenuity. Above all, thanks to my editors at Houghton Mifflin, who were helpful, supportive, and brave.

                                                    DOUG HUNT

Introduction: About Essays and Essayists

Ask most people what an essay is, and they will tell you what it is not: not a whole book, not a short story, not a poem, not a play. A more positive definition is difficult because the essay resembles other forms of writing and mingles with them freely. A poem looks like a poem, with plenty of white space on the page and lines of irregular length; and a play looks like a play. Flannery O'Connor begins "Revelation" like this:

> The doctor's waiting room, which was very small, was almost full when the Turpins entered and Mrs. Turpin, who was very large, made it look even smaller by her presence. . . . Her bright little black eyes took in all the patients as she sized up the seating situation.

We hear the machinery of fiction—setting, character, and point of view—humming smoothly in the background, and we settle down to read a short story. But very often we are well into an essay before we recognize it for what it is. It may look like just another letter, textbook chapter, book review, encyclopedia entry, lecture, or magazine article. Indeed, it probably *will* be one of these things: Martin Luther King, Jr.'s "Letter from Birmingham Jail"—a widely admired essay—was an open letter addressed to eight clergymen. W.E.B. DuBois's "Jacob and Esau" was a commencement address. Joan Didion's "Georgia O'Keeffe" was a column for *The Saturday Evening Post*, written, as columns always are, against a deadline and specification of length. The essay was once a leisurely literary form; today it has put on street clothes and sensible shoes and got itself a job.

But beneath even the most modern exterior, every essayist is a good deal like Montaigne, the Frenchman who christened the form four hundred years ago. He called his writings *essais* (French for "attempts") because they were not reports of objective truth but explorations of his own attitudes and thoughts on such subjects as cannibals, war, women, and hatred. Essayists in every era have been drawn to subjects where the facts do not speak for themselves, but must be measured against some personal frame of reference. The writer of a news story often gives us bare information: the journalistic formula is "who, what, where, when, why, and how?" But the essayist reserves a good deal of attention for other questions: "So what? Why should I care? What does this tell us about how

1

we should live, or about how we do?" These are "moral" questions, not in the sermonizing sense, but in a broader sense. They are concerned with our *mores*—the customs, habits, and preoccupations that give life its shape. Some essayists state a "moral" thesis at the outset, as Russell Lynes does in "The New Snobbism": ". . . snobbery has emerged in a whole new set of guises, for it is as indigenous to man's nature as ambition and a great deal easier to exercise." Others, like C.S. Lewis in "The Inner Ring," provide a ladder on which we climb toward the thesis, rung by rung. Still others, like Annie Dillard and Edward Hoagland, seem to accumulate meaning as they wander through a series of anecdotes and observations. Finally, though, we see that the writer has led us to a statement of values.

Questions of value must always be referred to the individual head and heart. They cannot be approached in a purely objective way. As G.K. Chesterton once pointed out, we can learn a good deal about entomology without being insects, but if we want to understand humanity, we have to be human ourselves and project our understanding from the inside out. Facts, figures, charts, diagrams, quantifiable experiments—these can sometimes be useful, but they can't tell us how we should react on the day that the Supreme Court orders the desegregation of public schools, or men land on the moon, or the United States invades Cambodia, or a professional football team signs a quarterback for seven million dollars. They can't help us sort out the enigma of our own identities. They certainly can't help us order our minds when we face some personal tragedy. To think well about such things, a person needs a *perspective,* a considered opinion large enough to hold the particular event in its jaws. Perspective transforms an article into an essay.

This talk about perspective sounds obscure enough to need an example. Samuel Johnson—the eighteenth-century essayist—was half-blind and scarred from infancy by a skin disease, and for the first half of his life was poor and nearly friendless. The weight of this personal experience was behind his grim observation that "human life is everywhere a state in which much is to be endured and little to be enjoyed." Everywhere Johnson looked he saw lives following a familiar trajectory—rising from unhappiness to the pursuit of some unreachable pleasure and sinking once more into unhappiness. His essays and sometimes even his individual sentences are shaped by this trajectory. "Hope is itself a species of happiness," he once began, and then let the air out of the balloon by adding, ". . . perhaps, the chief happiness which this world affords." This pessimism goes further than most of us are willing to be taken, but the perspective it provided made Johnson a formidable essayist and conversationalist. No one could size up a situation more quickly.

When he had to explain the significance of the Great Pyramid, he pronounced it "a monument to the insufficiency of human enjoyments," evidence that even the Pharaohs were unhappy and had to "amuse the tediousness" of life by forcing slaves to lay stone upon stone for no reason. When he heard that a friend had remarried, he said that it was "the triumph of hope over experience"—one of the better lines in the history of black humor. When he wrote an essay on the dangers of affectation, he compared the pleasure of an inflated reputation to the ice palace raised by the Empress of Russia: "It was for a time splendid and luminous, but the first sunshine melted it away."

If Johnson's perspective had been *merely* internal and emotional, he might have been an obscure depressive instead of a famous writer. The world has plenty of people in it who have been driven to despair: one bleat more would hardly have been worth noting. But by reading and thinking, Johnson had connected his private experience with two of the great traditions of Western thought: Stoicism and Christianity, duty and faith. Through Marcus Aurelius and St. Paul, he had reached an understanding of life, and he honed his understanding in discussions that were sometimes long and loud. (Johnson was never afraid of an argument. After a long night at a tavern, he said to James Boswell, "Well, we had a good talk." Boswell answered, "Yes, you tossed and gored several persons.") Thus his perspective was both personal and universal. He had his own statement to make about human misery, but it was a statement enlarged by reading, talk, and observation till it became, as Boswell said, "true, evident, and actual wisdom." In their time Johnson's essays were read and admired everywhere that English was spoken. Today they are out of fashion; but if you blow the dust off one of the old volumes and read it patiently, you can learn a good deal about the human condition.

Not every essayist is so gloomy, thank goodness, or writes from a conviction about life that is as sweeping, but we can see in Johnson's case one of the defining characteristics of the essay: that the writer uses a particular topic (like the Great Pyramid) as a way of expressing an insight of general interest (the insufficiency of human enjoyments). Assign three competent encyclopedists the task of describing the Grand Canyon in 500 words, and you'll get three articles that are more or less interchangeable. Ask three essayists what they did on their summer vacations and, if you are very, very lucky, you'll get "In the Country," "The Way to Rainy Mountain," and "Once More to the Lake." Roger Angell will show you how devotion to a game enriches people's lives, Scott Momaday will reflect on the fate of his Kiowa ancestors, and E.B. White will remind you of the sweetness of life and its shortness. An essayist approaches a topic the way a carpenter approaches an old barn, estimating the board feet it will provide toward some project already forming in his or her mind.

No insight, no essay: this is an uncomfortable truth for people of ordinary humility. When you sit down to write an essay, you may wish that you had traveled as extensively as Jan Morris or grown up in China like Pearl Buck. You may wish that you had H.D.F. Kitto's depth of scholarship or Richard Selzer's experience as a physician. You may even wish for a moment that you had led a life as miserable as Johnson's. Then, when it came to insight, you would have some cards to play.

In fact, all of us have three good cards. First, our lives—however ordinary they may seem to us—are unlike the lives of others. Our experiences touch at different points on the large issues that affect all lives. Perhaps you grew up in a small prairie town and have seen issues of race and class from an angle no New Yorker ever knew. Perhaps you attended a parochial school and watched the sisters react to feminism. Perhaps you have been a victim and have a statement to make on crime, or a technophile irritated by the technophobes around you. Whatever you are, it is one card you have to play.

Your second card is that you live in an astonishingly communicative culture. The airwaves are crowded with songs, advertisements, soap operas, news programs. The campus is buzzing with conversations about movies, books, politics, sex, teachers, and fashion. And, of course, there are the library and the bookstore. Some of the ideas floating in this great flood of words will surely be useful; some will not. Writing about status or friendship with an insight from a deodorant commercial is setting to sea in a very small boat. If you are trying to explain the curious popularity of stabbings and shootings on television, you're not likely to get a large enough frame of reference from a *People* magazine story. Even a large idea is useless as a tool until you see how it fits into the vast conversations that are going on around you. Here, I hope, is one way that *The Dolphin Reader* can be of practical help. The selections are not chosen solely because they are classics or because they have achieved some special brilliance of execution, but because they actively contribute to one of these perennial conversations. All the essays in the Progress section, for instance, are part of a familiar argument: X claims that technology is creating more problems than it is solving; Y claims that X is a hypocritical romantic who wouldn't dream of giving up his blow dryer or computer or nuclear deterrent; Z says that both have a point, but both need to define their terms more carefully. A political debate on defense or energy policy is often little more than a remote branch of this conversation. The discussion of whether to take a camping vacation or fly to San Francisco may be another. So may a professorial dispute over the relative merits of Henry James and Tom Robbins. The Progress section explores still other branches, but, more important, it traces the conversation to its trunk. Grasp the trunk, and you can shake all the branches. Get a sense of the tug-of-war that connects writers as diverse as Thomas Babington Macaulay, E.B. White, and Alice Bloom, and you'll soon find a way to get your hands on the rope.

Your third card is time. Listen to the "man-on-the-street" interviews on the local news if you need to be reminded how hard it is to talk extemporaneously on a subject more complex than the weather. A very few people sound coherent and informed; most mumble whatever banalities and catch phrases come readily to mind and are embarrassed, I'm sure, when they hear the broadcast. Some of our best writers interview terribly. Bruce Lee of *Newsweek* once interviewed E.B. White and found him polite, dull, and uncommunicative. The next day White sent Lee two typed pages of crisp answers to the interview questions and a short note of apology: "I do not have the gift of oral expression, and am almost helpless except when running paper through a typewriter. . . ." Writing gives you time to draft, revise, attack the topic from a different angle, ask for opinions and advice, read what other people have said. If you ransack your brain at first and don't *find* an insight you can apply to your topic, you have time to *make* one (never as much time as you would like, of course). This opportunity—or necessity—of furnishing the mind is one of the rewards of writing an essay. Cardinal Newman once wrote that a university education "gives a man a clear conscious view of his own opinions and judgments, a truth in developing them, an eloquence in expressing them, and a force in urging them." That's a rather grand goal even for the whole of an education, but every hour spent struggling with an essay should bring you a little closer to it.

THE EVOLUTION OF AN ESSAY

That struggle, that *essaying* to clarify the writer's views, should really be included in the definition of an essay. Try to imagine essays in this expanded form. John McPhee's "A Sense of Where You Are," for example, would balloon out from its seventeen printed pages and encompass interviews with basketball players and coaches, hundreds of pages of notes transcribed, topics written on notecards and pinned to a bulletin board, pages scissored to ribbons and rearranged, and twelve-hour days of very slow and meticulous drafting. It would be a subject for a long book with few readers, and we won't undertake it here.

We can, however, examine the evolution of a short "comment" written by E.B. White. Comments are unsigned essays in miniature: in *The New Yorker* they are written using the "editorial *we*," a practice that tends to make the writer sound like a Siamese twin. White began writing comments in 1927, and so had more than forty years of experience with them by 1969. Nonetheless, when the magazine asked him to comment on the moon landing that year, it was a particularly difficult assignment. The deadline pressure was intense: Neil Armstrong took his small step to the lunar surface at 10:56 P.M. on July 27, and the television broadcast of the moon walk lasted until 1:00 A.M.; White, who lived on a farm in Maine, had to cable his comment to New York in time for a press run at noon.

There were other difficulties. He was a little out of sympathy with the topic. The general response to the moon landing was a burst of pride, but White was not inclined to sound a fanfare in honor of the technological advance. Much of his best writing aims to "keep Man in a mood of decent humility." One of the observations on the pages he mailed to Bruce Lee was this:

> I am pessimistic about the human race because it is too ingenious for its own good. Our approach to nature is to beat it into submission. We would stand a better chance of survival if we accommodated ourselves to this planet and viewed it appreciatively instead of skeptically and dictatorially. Never dictate to a swamp, or assume that it has no merit until drained.

He didn't share the nationalistic pride that the landing stirred in many Americans. Having seen nationalism cause two world wars, he was an advocate of the United Nations. These concerns were clearly on his mind when he sat down to run a first draft through the typewriter.

> Planning a trip to the moon differs in no essential respect from planning a trip to the beach. You have to decide what to take along, what to leave behind. Should the thermos jug go? The child's rubber horse? The dill pickles? These are sometimes fateful decisions on which the success or failure of the whole outing turns. Something goes along that spoils everything because it is always in the way. Something gets left behind that spoils everything because it is desperately needed for comfort or safety. The men who had to decide what to take along to the moon must have pondered long and hard, drawn up many a list. We're not sure they planned well, when they included

the little telescoped flagpole and the American flag, artificially stiffened so that it would fly to the breeze that didn't blow. As we watched the Stars and Stripes planted on the surface of the moon, we experienced the same sensations of pride that must have filled the hearts of millions of Americans. But the emotion soon turned to   This was our great chance, and we muffed it. The men who stepped out onto the surface of the moon are in a class by themselves—pioneers of what is universal. They saw the earth whole—just as it is, a round ball in a   But they colored the moon red, white, and blue—good colors all—but out of place in that setting. The moon still influences the tides, and the tides lap on every shore, right around the globe. The moon still belongs to lovers, and lovers are everywhere—not just in America. What a pity we couldn't have planted some emblem that precisely expressed this unique, this incredible occasion, even if it were nothing more than a white banner, with the legend: "At last!"

Judged as a finished product by a writer of White's caliber, this is a dismal performance. Over the years, I've offered several right arms in exchange for a fragment of White's talent, so it reassures me to see that his first draft sounds flat and sometimes awkward. But of course he never imagined that this draft would be good. Notice, for instance, that he twice began sentences that he couldn't end. *What* exactly did our emotions turn to? A round ball in a *what*? Having no adequate answers, White left spaces and went on. His aim here was to discover the general shape of the comment, to see what he had to say. He may not have found the results very encouraging. The comparison to the family outing in the first seven sentences attempted to reduce the event to human scale, keeping us in a "mood of decent humility," but it was far-fetched. If White was going to get his readers to accept the analogy, he'd have to come up with some details that make moon-trip planning seem more ordinary and domestic. And didn't the passage about "experiencing the same sensations of pride" sound like a press release from NASA? Readers would surely be suspicious of a writer who parroted the official good cheer, then turned sharply around to say that we had "muffed" our chance. The draft had an un-charitable tone. It was a self-righteous condemnation of the space program at its moment of triumph. It had some good parts—the stiffened flag, the windless moon, the association of the moon with tides and lovers—but principally it helped White see what he should be thinking about. What *did* "our" emotions turn to? What did they start out as? Was he being a spoilsport?

In writing the second draft, White reconsidered both the moon landing and the paragraph, measuring them against his own values

of charity, humility, and good humor. He kept the first seven
sentences, but changed the rest substantially:

> The men who drew up the moon list for the astronauts planned long
> and hard and well. (Should the vacuum cleaner go to suck up moondust
> and save the world?) Among the items they sent along, of course,
> was the little jointed flagpole and the flag that could be stiffened to
> the breeze that didn't blow. It is traditional among explorers to plant
> the flag. Yet the two men who stepped out on the surface of the
> moon were in a class by themselves: they were of a new race of
> men, those who had seen the earth whole. When, following instructions,
> they colored the moon red, white, and blue, they were stepping out
> of character—or so it seemed to us who watched, trembling with
> awe and admiration and pride. This was the last scene in the long
> book of nationalism, and they followed the book. But the moon still
> holds the key to madness, which is universal, still controls the tides,
> that lap on every shore everywhere, and blesses lovers that kiss in
> every land, under no particular banner. What a pity we couldn't have
> played the scene as it should have been played; planting, perhaps, a
> simple white handkerchief, symbol of the common cold, that, like
> the moon, belongs to all and recognizes no borders.

This draft was *truer* than the first—truer to White's feelings and
to the event. It had been silly to say that the planners "muffed"
the moon trip. Now he gave them their due, acknowledging that
they planned "long and hard and well." However much White
may have wished that they had not brought along the flag, they
had reasons for doing so: the precedent of former explorers, the
"long book of nationalism." And if planting the flag was a mistake,
the astronauts certainly couldn't be blamed; they were "following
instructions." By making these changes, White avoided the sourness
of the first draft. By adding madness to the list of the things
associated with the moon in the next-to-last sentence, he went
beyond the moon-spoon-June-croon formula of sentimental songs.

But the most important revision was in the last sentence. James
Thurber once noted that the challenge of writing a comment is
"to make something that was ground out sound as if it were
dashed off." The closing sentence of the first draft, with its talk
about "this unique, this incredible occasion" and its "white banner
with the legend: 'At last!',", labored under the burden of its serious
political intent. By converting the banner to a handkerchief White
lightened the tone, retained the political note, and kept us "in a
mood of decent humility"—all in one seemingly effortless phrase.

He must have felt encouraged at this point in the evolution of
his paragraph, but he also saw some flaws. The addition of the
vacuum cleaner made the analogy between the family outing and

the moon trip a little more credible, but the "save the world" part of the sentence was a feeble joke. And the final sentence, good as it was, trailed loosely off and lost some of its impact. At this point White typed a draft to correct these faults.

> Planning a trip to the moon differs in no essential respect from planning a trip to the beach. You have to decide what to take along, what to leave behind. Should the thermos jug go? The child's rubber horse? The dill pickles? These are the sometimes fateful decisions on which the success or failure of the whole outing turns. Something goes along that spoils everything because it is always in the way; something gets left behind that is desperately needed for comfort or for safety. The men who drew up the moon list for the astronauts planned long and hard and well. (Should the vacuum cleaner go to suck up moondust?) Among the items they sent along, of course, was the little jointed flagpole and the flag that could be stiffened to the breeze that did not blow. (It is traditional among explorers to plant the flag.) Yet the two men who stepped out on the surface of the moon were in a class by themselves and should have been equipped accordingly: they were of the new breed of men, those who had seen the earth whole. When, following instructions, they colored the moon red, white, and blue, they were fumbling with the past—or so it seemed to us who watched, trembling with awe and admiration and pride. This was the last chapter in the long book of nationalism, one that could well have been omitted. But the moon still holds the key to madness, which is universal, still controls the tides that lap on shores everywhere, and guards lovers that kiss in every land, under no banner but the sky. What a pity we couldn't have forsworn our little Iwo Jima scene and planted instead a banner acceptable to all—a simple white handkerchief, perhaps, symbol of the common cold, which, like the moon, affects us all.

This paragraph had a finished look, and White, considering it finished, cabled it to *The New Yorker*. When the heat of composition cooled, however, he began to see faults. His attempt to absolve the astronauts of blame by saying that they were "following instructions" was shaky ethically and awkward stylistically. The expression about coloring the moon red, white, and blue was flashy nonsense. The talk about "trembling" with pride was over-blown and hackneyed; the reader would doubt that a generally level-headed writer spends much time trembling. The lead, the first seven sentences, was a mistake. The whole comparison to the family outing was unconvincing, inappropriate, belittling; and with the last sentences in the paragraph now doing all that is necessary to "keep Man in a mood of decent humilty," it was superfluous. Time was very short, but even now White wasn't content to mend faults. An enthusiastic sailor, he remembered the doctrine of freedom of the seas. He found a way to add impact to the last sentence. He took the paragraph through three more drafts. Then he sent another cable saying that the comment was "no good as is" and offering to dictate over the phone "a shorter one on the same theme but different in tone." Here is the result as it appeared on page one of *The New Yorker*:

> The moon, it turns out, is a great place for men. One-sixth gravity must be a lot of fun, and when Armstrong and Aldrin went into their bouncy little dance, like two happy children, it was a moment not only of triumph but of gaiety. The moon, on the other hand, is a poor place for flags. Ours looked stiff and awkward, trying to float on the breeze that does not blow. (There must be a lesson here somewhere.) It is traditional, of course, for explorers to plant the flag, but it struck us, as we watched with awe and admiration and pride, that our two fellows were universal men, not national men, and should have been equipped accordingly. Like every great river and every great sea, the moon belongs to none and belongs to all. It still holds the key to madness, still controls the tides that lap on shores everywhere, still guards the lovers that kiss in every land under no banner but the sky. What a pity that in our moment of triumph we couldn't have forsworn the familiar Iwo Jima scene and planted instead a device acceptable to all: a limp white handkerchief, perhaps, symbol of the common cold, which, like the moon, affects us all, unites us all.

This is certainly not the best comment White ever wrote, but like all his comments it is compact and lively. Of the 305 words of the original draft, 15 survive to the final draft. This is a fairly low survival rate, but hardly unique. The journalist James Fallows estimates his survival rate for a long essay at about one percent. Joan Didion, the novelist and essayist, says that there is a point in the writing of a new piece where she sits in a room "literally papered with false starts." What is important here is not the survival rate but the rethinking. It isn't merely White's *recording* of his reaction to the moon landing that changes from first draft to last: the reaction itself changes to something more generous and complete.

READING WITH A WRITER'S EYE

Occasionally, we can retrace a writer's steps by examining a series of drafts like White's, but there is always guesswork involved. We would rather hear about the writing process directly from the writer. The About Writing section of *The Dolphin Reader* allows you to do that. In it you will find writers talking shop: describing how they work, telling about turning points in their attitudes toward writing, bitterly criticizing the prose of other writers, or enthusiastically expressing admiration. Essays like these, as well as the sort of interviews published in *The Paris Review* and *The Writer*, give us glimpses of the writer at work, but they are merely glimpses. Despite 2500 years of interest and two decades of intense research, we can't say precisely how a writer works or how a person becomes a writer.

We *can* say, however, from the testimony of innumerable writers, that reading good prose is one of the keys. You will have heard this so often that I'm afraid you won't hear it properly now. Writers who emphasize the importance of "reading good prose" don't mean relaxing over a good book or getting a mandatory exposure to culture. They mean *devouring* good prose, drawing from it interest, excitement, and a fully conscious appreciation of the writer's craftsmanship. The best writer I know is also the widest-ranging reader, equally likely to be worked up over a children's book or a philosophical treatise, equally inclined to adapt a phrase from *The Wind in the Willows* or from the *Tractatus Logico-Philosophicus*. The selections in *The Dolphin Reader* will please him: they range from direct narrative to complex argument. One way you can improve your own writing is to observe the skill of writers in this wide range, trying to see in the finished work the lines of its construction, just as an art student will carefully examine a painting to find the artist's brush strokes.

The narratives in *The Dolphin Reader* (both fiction and non-fiction) were chosen to give you a good look at the tools available to the storyteller. Ernest Hemingway's "Indian Camp," for instance, uses dialogue so economically that it has become a model not only for fiction writers but for reporters who must capture a whole character in a few sentences of quotation. In "Which New Era Would That Be?," Nadine Gordimer uses particularly clever shifts in point of view to dramatize the gap between races in South Africa, and Roger Angell uses a more elaborate dual perspective to make "In the Country" something larger than a report on semi-pro baseball. The symbols in stories by José Donoso, William Faulkner, and Nathaniel Hawthorne are so varied that they could form the basis for a seminar on symbolism. Alice Walker, Alice Munro, and William Manchester portray memorable characters memorably. Flannery O'Connor and John Steinbeck use setting brilliantly as an aid to characterization. And so, element by element, *The Dolphin Reader* can serve as a sourcebook for those who want to write narratives or simply to appreciate how they work.

The line between the narrative and the "essay proper" is not always easy to draw, since some narratives are very pointed and some essays include memorable storytelling. It is a line worth tracing, though, before you set out to write one or the other. Perhaps the best tests are *purpose* and *authorial presence*. The narrative's purpose is to give us an experience, not to deliver a message. In *The Dolphin Reader*, for instance, you'll find several stories that have racism as a theme, and in every case the writer clearly opposes it, but the story will suffer if we read it merely as a statement of liberal views. When Flannery O'Connor created Mrs. Turpin, she didn't intend her to be simply a specimen of racism, any more than a parent wants a daughter to be simply a specimen of childhood. The writer of stories (fiction or nonfiction) is creating a new world, inhabited by characters who should have lives of their own. Because she wants us to enter this new world with a minimum of interference from the actual world in which we are sitting as we read, she doesn't remind us that she herself is present, trundling the scenery in from the wings and moving the actors back and forth on the stage. She certainly doesn't harass us with instructions about how we should interpret her story. She is like the ideal companion at the movies; she drives the car, pays for the ticket, and never breathes a word until the show is over. She hopes—almost—that we will forget the story *has* a maker.

As we move across the middle ground between story and essay, we find that the writer's purpose is changing, that what once had been theme has taken on a more argumentative edge and become thesis. The writer no longer wants us to forget his presence and experience the story in itself. He wants to convince us of something and will very likely address us face to face. Garrison Keillor's introduction to *Happy To Be Here* is close to the borderline: it contains a strong narrative, but is finally an essay. It tells the story of Keillor's struggle with his "shelf novel," and in that story Keillor figures only as a comic character. But Keillor doesn't stay in character. At several points he steps out of the narrative to talk to us directly to make sure we don't miss his point. The most important of these asides begins with a discussion of "*The New Yorker*'s great infield of Thurber, Liebling, Perelman, and White":

> They were my heroes: four older gentlemen, one blind, one fat, one delicate, and one a chicken rancher, and in my mind they took the field against the big mazumbos of American Literature, and I cheered for them. I cheer for them now, all dead except Mr. White, and still I think (as I thought then) that it is more worthy in the eyes of God and better for us as a people if a writer make three pages sharp and funny about the lives of geese than to make three hundred flat and flabby about God or the American people.

Keillor takes the podium here, dismisses the actors, brings down the curtain, and tells us what is on his mind. He has a statement to make about the value of humor and modesty. If we aren't moved to consider the statement, the essay is a failure no matter how much the story may have amused us. Whether it is his failure or ours might be disputed.

When an essay uses narrative, then, it puts it in harness and makes it pull the plow, and some writers are dismayed by the lack of freedom this situation creates. But as an essayist you enjoy many compensating freedoms, notably in what the textbooks call *voice* and *tone*. As E.B. White once said, "The essayist arises in the morning and, if he has work to do, selects his garb from an unusually extensive wardrobe: he can pull on any sort of shirt, be any sort of person, according to his mood or his subject matter—philosopher, scold, jester, raconteur, confidant, pundit, devil's advocate, enthusiast." Consider, for instance, the opening sentences of Harry Crews's essay "Pages from the Life of a Georgia Innocent":

> Not very long ago I went with my twelve-year-old boy to a Disney movie, one of those things that show a farm family, poor but God knows honest, out there on the land building character through hunger and hard work. The hunger and hard work seemed to be a hell of a lot of fun. The deprivation was finally so rewarding you could hardly stand it.

Clearly, this is not the voice of the pundit or the enthusiast. The writer has taken on a distinct character—mocking, relaxed, earthy. He writes like a man who wears blue jeans and is not too delicate to drink beer out of a can. If you read the whole essay, you'll see how well this voice suits the content.

But compare the opening sentence of Cynthia Ozick's "We Are the Crazy Lady":

> A long, long time ago, in another century—1951, in fact—when you, dear younger readers, were most likely still in your nuclear-family playpen (where, if female, you cuddled a rag-baby to your potential titties, or, if male, let down virile drool over your plastic bulldozer), the Famous Critic told me never, never to use a parenthesis in the very first sentence.

Here is a writer introducing herself as a very different person: witty, urbane, ingenious enough to construct an opening sentence that comments humorously on itself. Crews's sentences are short and relaxed; he seems to take the first word that comes to mind. Ozick's sentence is a grammarian's nightmare, full of interruptions

and asides, chutes and ladders, ambushes. She teases with a fairy
tale opening. She gets a smile by matching the formal adjective
and the colloquial noun ("potential titties," "virile drool"). She
separates herself from her readers by reminding them that she is
a generation older. Her style, as she tells us elsewhere, is her cabin
and her shell—tight, highly polished, brilliant enough to keep the
reader at a distance, on guard. The two voices are so distinct that
reading them is like traveling in two different countries.

Even when the writer's purpose is largely informative and he
chooses not to introduce himself directly to the reader, we often
find a distinctive voice and tone. Here, for example, is a passage
in which H.D.F. Kitto comments on the relatively tiny Greek city-
state, or *polis*:

> To think on this scale is difficult for us, who regard a state of ten
> million as small, and are accustomed to states which, like the U.S.A.
> and the U.S.S.R., are so big that they have to be referred to by their
> initials; but when the adjustable reader has become accustomed to
> the scale, he will not commit the vulgar error of confusing size with
> significance. The modern writer is sometimes heard to speak with
> splendid scorn of "those petty Greek states, with their interminable
> quarrels." Quite so; Plataea, Sicyon, Aegina and the rest are petty,
> compared with modern states. The Earth itself is petty, compared with
> Jupiter—but then, the atmosphere of Jupiter is mainly ammonia, and
> that makes a difference.

Kitto was a classical scholar of the first rank; he was also a writer
who never forgot his audience. Periodically he reaches out from
the page to jab, tickle, scold, or conspire. In the passage above,
after the very English joke about countries that go by initials, he
grabs "the modern reader" by the lapels and gives him a good
shaking. We stand to one side, like schoolchildren watching a
classmate being punished, and think how often we have committed
the same "vulgar error" that has earned this punishment. By the
time Kitto puts the poor fellow down, we are probably more
"adjustable readers" and certainly more alert ones.

Rarely will you find yourself in a situation where you want to
assume precisely the voice of Kitto, Crews, or Ozick. But as E.B.
White once pointed out, we form our styles by the unconscious
imitation of prose we consciously admire. The wider the range of
styles you admire, the more options available to you as a writer.
The voice and style you adopt will depend partly on your identity,
partly on the writing situation and the audience. When he addressed
the prisoners of Cook County Jail, Clarence Darrow assumed the
voice and diction of the plain fellow who delivers simple truths

in simple sentences. To dazzle with a style like Ozick's would obviously have been wrong. But when he later published the lecture, he wrote an introduction very different in tone:

> Realizing the force of the suggestion that the truth should not be spoken to all people, I have caused these remarks to be printed on rather good paper and in a somewhat expensive form. In this way the truth does not become cheap and vulgar, and is only placed before those whose intelligence and affluence will prevent their being influenced by it.

Since no one reads introductions, this bit of irony has gone largely unnoticed.

Writing in the academic world often requires an understated, scholarly voice like Daniel Boorstin's or Margaret Mead's. It seems sometimes to require the artificial voice of the specialist. This is unfortunate, since a person whose attention is absorbed by the effort of *sounding* like an historian, anthropologist, or economist may be too preoccupied to write well. But a good mind can express the special insights of a discipline without clanking around in the armor of its special jargon. John Kenneth Galbraith, as subtle an economist as you will find, says that there is no important insight in economics that cannot be expressed in plain English. The best academic writers manage, sometimes against terrible odds, to maintain a human voice.

The selections in *The Dolphin Reader* illustrate a variety of voices, styles, and tactics. "The New Snobbism," besides making me smile even while I write this sentence, could be a textbook illustration of classification as a mode of development. "On a Greek Holiday" would do equally well as a model for comparison/contrast. The formal diction, elaborate sentences, and weighty allusions of "Letter from Birmingham Jail" show us what a writer can do to add gravity to a public statement. Tom Wolfe's firecracker style is King's turned on its head—a blend of parody, hyperbole, and red pepper. Henry David Thoreau, Annie Dillard, and E.B. White are all masters of description. Those of you who relish a good metaphor or simile should have a field day with this book. I think immediately of Johnson's comparison of an imposter to a man in a leaky boat, Patricia Hampl's discovery that middle C is the belly button of the piano, and William Manchester's description of Mencken's hands lying in his lap "like weapons put to rest." If you take pains to admire what is good in the essays collected here, you'll surely begin to assimilate some of the technical skills that help make a writer.

But I don't want to end this introduction with a suggestion that you treat *The Dolphin Reader* as a collection of museum pieces. Outside the composition classroom, no one picks up an essay hoping to find examples of extended metaphor or stipulative definition. We read writers who have something to say to us, and we ourselves aren't worth reading until we find our own insights and messages. The principal purpose of *The Dolphin Reader* is to help you in that search. Francis Bacon long ago identified the spirit in which a writer ought to read—"not to contradict, or to believe, but to weigh and consider." Three centuries later another scientist, Charles Darwin, perfected a method of aggressive reading. When Darwin read a book, he noted on the back flyleaf the page number of any passage that struck him as particularly interesting or provocative. When he had finished the book, he broke its spine, tore out the interesting pages, put them into a box, and threw the rest away. I hope you will use *The Dolphin Reader* almost as ungently, ransacking it for the parts that can trigger something in your own writing.

No one can predict where these will be or what state of mind will allow you to find them. The best discoveries come partly by chance. I spent, for instance, a dreadful morning in committee meetings last spring listening to people explain what is wrong with the university. A distinguished professor of humanities said that the problem was the shift from a culture of readers to a culture of viewers. A science professor with a reputation for severity said that it was a damnable tendency to accept fluff in place of substance. A sociologist said that it was a failure to recognize the demographic characteristics of the new student. The president of the student body said that it was a lack of leadership roles for students. By noon, exhausted and confused, I took a solitary walk to the bookstore, and found myself thumbing through a copy of Tom Wolfe's *The Pump House Gang*. Buried in the introduction was a discussion of "statuspheres" that turned the day around. Suddenly I saw our morning's work from a fresh perspective, saw each of us isolated in a bubble of defensive pride, busily dabbing at the speck in other eyes rather than considering the log in our own. Under such circumstances, a person might serve the institution better by unlimbering a typewriter at once and shaping the insight into an essay, but the devil caught me by the sleeve and led me back to the committee room. Still, somebody *should* write this essay—and several others that have slipped through our fingers these last few centuries.

Perhaps you will.

NATURE AND
CIVILIZATION

EDWARD HOAGLAND

Dogs, and the Tug of Life

It used to be that you could tell just about how poor a family 1
was by how many dogs they had. If they had one, they were
probably doing all right. It was only American to keep a dog to
represent the family's interests in the intrigues of the back alley;
not to have a dog at all would be like not acknowledging one's
poor relations. Two dogs meant that the couple were dog lovers,
with growing children, but still might be members of the middle
class. But if a citizen kept three, you could begin to suspect he
didn't own much else. Four or five irrefutably marked the household
as poor folk, whose yard was also full of broken cars cannibalized
for parts. The father worked not much, fancied himself a hunter;
the mother's teeth were black. And an old bachelor living in a
shack might possibly have even more, but you knew that if one
of them, chasing a moth, didn't upset his oil lamp some night and
burn him up, he'd fetch up in the poorhouse soon, with the dogs
shot. Nobody got poor feeding a bunch of dogs, needless to say,
because the more dogs a man had, the less he fed them. Foraging
as a pack, they led an existence of their own, but served as evidence
that life was awfully lonesome for him and getting out of hand.
If a dog really becomes a man's best friend his situation is desperate.

That dogs, low-comedy confederates of small children and ragged 2
bachelors, should have turned into an emblem of having made it
to the middle class—like the hibachi, like golf clubs and a second
car—seems at the very least incongruous. Puppies which in the
country you would have to carry in a box to the church fair to
give away are bringing seventy-five dollars apiece in some of the
pet stores, although in fact dogs are in such oversupply that one
hundred and fifty thousand are running wild in New York City
alone.

There is another line of tradition about dogs, however. Show 3
dogs, toy dogs, foxhounds for formal hunts, Doberman guard dogs,
bulldogs as ugly as a queen's dwarf. An aristocratic Spanish lady
once informed me that when she visits her Andalusian estate each
fall the mastiffs rush out and fawn about her but would tear to
pieces any of the servants who have accompanied her from Madrid.
In Mississippi it was illegal for a slave owner to permit his slaves
to have a dog, just as it was to teach them how to read. A "negro

Originally published in Harper's, February 1975.

dog" was a hound trained by a bounty hunter to ignore the possums, raccoons, hogs and deer in the woods that other dogs were supposed to chase, and trail and tree a runaway. The planters themselves, for whom hunting was a principal recreation, whooped it up when a man unexpectedly became their quarry. They caught each other's slaves and would often sit back and let the dogs do the punishing. Bennet H. Barrow of West Feliciana Parish in Louisiana, a rather moderate and representative plantation owner, recounted in his diary of the 1840s, among several similar incidents, this for November 11, 1845: In "5 minutes had him up & a going, And never in my life did I ever see as excited beings as R & myself, ran ½ miles & caught him dogs soon tore him naked, took him Home Before the other negro(es) at dark & made the dogs give him another over hauling." Only recently in Louisiana I heard what happened to two Negroes who happened to be fishing in a bayou off the Blind River, where four white men with a shotgun felt like fishing alone. One was forced to pretend to be a scampering coon and shinny up a telephone pole and hang there till he fell, while the other impersonated a baying, bounding hound.

   Such memories are not easy to shed, particularly since childhood,   4
the time when people can best acquire a comradeship with animals, is also when they are likely to pick up their parents' fears. A friend of mine hunts quail by jeep in Texas with a millionaire who brings along forty bird dogs, which he deploys in eight platoons that spell each other off. Another friend though, will grow apprehensive at a dinner party if the host lets a dog loose in the room. The toothy, mysterious creature lies dreaming on the carpet, its paws pulsing, its eyelids open, the nictitating membranes twitching; how can he be certain it won't suddenly jump up and attack his legs under the table? Among Eastern European Jews, possession of a dog was associated with the hard-drinking *goyishe*[1] peasantry, traditional antagonists, or else with the gentry, and many carried this dislike to the New World. An immigrant fleeing a potato famine or the hunger of Calabria[2] might be no more equipped with the familiar British-German partiality to dogs—a failing which a few rugged decades in a great city's slums would not necessarily mend. The city had urbanized plenty of native farmers' sons as well, and so it came about that what to rural America had been the humblest, most natural amenity—friendship with a dog—has been trans-

---

1. Non-Jewish, i.e., Gentile.
2. Region in southern Italy, forming the toe of the peninsular "boot"; severe economic hardship and natural disasters forced large-scale emigration from Calabria in the late nineteenth and early twentieth centuries.

mogrified into a piece of the jigsaw of moving to the suburbs: there to cook outdoors, another bit of absurdity to the old countryman, whose toilet was outdoors but who was pleased to be able to cook and eat his meals inside the house.

There are an estimated forty million dogs in the United States (nearly two for every cat). Thirty-seven thousand of them are being destroyed in humane institutions every day, a figure which indicates that many more are in trouble. Dogs are hierarchal beasts, with several million years of submission to the structure of a wolf pack in their breeding. This explains why the Spanish lady's mastiffs can distinguish immediately between the mistress and her retainers, and why it is about as likely that one of the other guests at the dinner party will attack my friend's legs under the table as that the host's dog will, once it has accepted his presence in the room as proper. Dogs need leadership, however; they seek it, and when it's not forthcoming quickly fall into difficulties in a world where they can no longer provide their own.

"Dog" is "God" spelled backwards—one might say, way backwards. There's "a dog's life," "dog days," "dog-sick," "dog-tired," "dog-cheap," "dog-eared," "doghouse," and "dogs" meaning villains or feet. Whereas a wolf's stamina was measured in part by how long he could go without water, a dog's is becoming a matter of how long he can *hold* his water. He retrieves a rubber ball instead of coursing deer, chases a broom instead of hunting marmots. His is the lowest form of citizenship: that tug of life at the end of the leash is like the tug at the end of a fishing pole, and then one doesn't have to kill it. On stubby, amputated-looking feet he leads his life, which if we glance at it attentively is a kind of cutout of our own, all the more so for being riskier and shorter. Bam! A member of the family is dead on the highway, as we expected he would be, and we just cart him to the dump and look for a new pup.

Simply the notion that he lives on four legs instead of two has come to seem astonishing—like a goat or cow wearing horns on its head. And of course to keep a dog is a way of attempting to bring nature back. The primitive hunter's intimacy, telepathy, with the animals he sought, surprising them at their meals and in their beds, then stripping them of their warm coats to expose a frame so like our own, is all but lost. Sport hunters, especially the older ones, retain a little of it still; and naturalists who have made up their minds not to kill wild animals nevertheless appear to empathize primarily with the predators at first, as a look at the tigers, bears, wolves, mountain lions on the project list of an organization such as the World Wildlife Fund will show. This is as it should be, these creatures having suffered from our brotherly envy before.

But in order to really enjoy a dog, one doesn't merely try to train him to be semihuman. The point of it is to open oneself to the possibility of becoming partly a dog (after all, there are plenty of sub- or semi-human beings around whom we don't wish to adopt). One wants to rediscover the commonality of animal and man— to see an animal eat and sleep that hasn't forgotten how to enjoy doing such things—and the directness of its loyalty.

The trouble with the current emphasis on preserving "endangered 8 species" is that, however beneficial to wildlife the campaign works out to be, it makes all animals seem like museum pieces, worth saving for sentimental considerations and as figures of speech (to "shoot a sitting duck"), but as a practical matter already dead and gone. On the contrary, some animals are flourishing. In 1910 half a million deer lived in the United States, in 1960 seven million, in 1970 sixteen million. What has happened is that now that we don't eat them we have lost that close interest.

Wolf behavior prepared dogs remarkably for life with human 9 beings. So complete and complicated was the potential that it was only a logical next step for them to quit their packs in favor of the heady, hopeless task of trying to keep pace with our own community development. The contortions of fawning and obeisance which render group adjustment possible among such otherwise forceful fighters—sometimes humping the inferior members into the shape of hyenas—are what squeezes them past our tantrums, too. Though battling within the pack is mostly accomplished with body checks that do no damage, a subordinate wolf bitch is likely to remain so in awe of the leader that she will cringe and sit on her tail in response to his amorous advances, until his female co-equal has had a chance to notice and dash over and redirect his attention. Altogether, he is kept so busy asserting his dominance that this top-ranked female may not be bred by him, finally, but by the male which occupies the second rung. Being breadwinners, dominant wolves feed first and best, just as we do, so that to eat our scraps and leavings strikes a dog as normal procedure. Never-theless, a wolf puppy up to eight months old is favored at a kill, and when smaller can extract a meal from any pack member— uncles and aunts as well as parents—by nosing the lips of the adult until it regurgitates a share of what it's had. The care of the litter is so much a communal endeavor that the benign sort of role we expect dogs to play within our own families toward children not biologically theirs comes naturally to them.

For dogs and wolves the tail serves as a semaphore of mood 10 and social code, but dogs carry their tails higher than wolves do, as a rule, which is appropriate, since the excess spirits that used to go into lengthy hunts now have no other outlet than backyard negotiating. In addition to an epistolary anal gland, whose message-carrying function has not yet been defined, the anus itself, or stool when sniffed, conveys how well the animal has been eating—in effect, its income bracket—although most dog foods are sorrily monotonous compared to the hundreds of tastes a wolf encounters, perhaps dozens within the carcass of a single moose. We can speculate on a dog's powers of taste because its olfactory area is proportionately fourteen times larger than a man's, its sense of smell at least a hundred times as keen.

The way in which a dog presents his anus and genitals for   11
inspection indicates the hierarchal position that he aspires to, and other dogs who sniff his genitals are apprised of his sexual condition. From his urine they can undoubtedly distinguish age, build, state of sexual activity and general health, even hours after he's passed by. Male dogs dislike running out of urine, as though an element of potency were involved, and try to save a little; they prefer not to use a scent post again until another dog has urinated there, the first delight and duty of the ritual being to stake out a territory, so that when they are walked hurriedly in the city it is a disappointment to them. The search is also sexual, because bitches in heat post notices about. In the woods a dog will mark his drinking places, and watermark a rabbit's trail after chasing it, as if to notify the next predator that happens by exactly who it was that put such a whiff of fear into the rabbit's scent. Similarly, he squirts the tracks of bobcats and of skunks with an aloof air unlike his brisk and cheery manner of branding another dog's or fox's trail, and if he is in a position to do so, will defecate excitedly on a bear run, leaving behind his best effort, which no doubt he hopes will strike the bear as a bombshell.

The chief complaint people lodge against dogs is their extraordinary   12
stress upon lifting the leg and moving the bowels. Scatology did take up some of the slack for them when they left behind the entertainments of the forest. The forms of territoriality replaced the substance. But apart from that, a special zest for life is characteristic of dogs and wolves—in hunting, eating, relieving themselves, in punctiliously maintaining a home territory, a pecking order and a love life, and educating the resulting pups. They grin and grimace and scrawl graffiti with their piss. A lot of inherent strategy goes into these activities: the way wolves spell each other off, both when hunting and in their governess duties around the den, and often "consult" as a pack with noses together and tails wagging before flying in to make a kill. (Tigers, leopards, house

cats base their social relations instead upon what ethologists call "mutual avoidance.") The nose is a dog's main instrument of discovery, corresponding to our eyes, and so it is that he is seldom offended by organic smells, such as putrefaction, and sniffs intently for the details of illness, gum bleeding and diet in his master and his fellows, and for the story told by scats, not closing off the avenue for any reason—just as we rarely shut our eyes against new information, even the tragic or unpleasant kind.

Though dogs don't see as sharply as they smell, trainers usually rely on hand signals to instruct them, and most firsthand communication in a wolf pack also seems to be visual—by the expressions of the face, by body english and the cant of the tail. A dominant wolf squares his mouth, stares at and "rides up" on an inferior, standing with his front legs on its back, or will pretend to stalk it, creeping along, taking its muzzle in his mouth, and performing nearly all of the other discriminatory pranks and practices familiar to anybody who has a dog. In fact, what's funny is to watch a homely mutt as tiny as a shoebox spin through the rigmarole which a whole series of observers in the wilderness have gone to great pains to document for wolves. 13

Dogs proffer their rear ends to each other in an intimidating fashion, but when they examine the region of the head it is a friendlier gesture, a snuffling between pals. One of them may come across a telltale bone fragment caught in the other's fur, together with a bit of mud to give away the location of bigger bones. On the same impulse, wolves and free-running dogs will sniff a wanderer's toes to find out where he has been roaming. They fondle and propitiate with their mouths also, and lovers groom each other's fur with tongues and teeth adept as hands. A bitch wolf's period in heat includes a week of preliminary behavior and maybe two weeks of receptivity—among animals, exceptionally long. Each actual copulative tie lasts twenty minutes or a half an hour, which again may help to instill affection. Wolves sometimes begin choosing a mate as early as the age of one, almost a year before they are ready to breed. Dogs mature sexually a good deal earlier, and arrive in heat twice a year instead of once—at any season instead of only in midwinter, like a wolf, whose pups' arrival must be scheduled unfailingly for spring. Dogs have not retained much responsibility for raising their young, and the summertime is just as perilous as winter for them because, apart from the whimsy of their owners, who put so many of them to sleep, their nemesis is the automobile. Like scatology, sex helps fill the gulf of what is gone. 14

The scientist David Mech has pointed out how like the posture 15 of a wolf with a nosehold on a moose (as other wolves attack its hams) are the antics of a puppy playing tug-of-war at the end of a towel. Anybody watching a dog's exuberance as it samples bites of long grass beside a brook, or pounds into a meadow bristling with the odors of woodchucks, snowshoe rabbits, grouse, a doe and buck, field mice up on the seedheads of the weeds, kangaroo mice jumping, chipmunks whistling, weasels and shrews on the hunt, a plunging fox, a porcupine couched in a tree, perhaps can begin to imagine the variety of excitements under the sky that his ancestors relinquished in order to move indoors with us. He'll lie down with a lamb to please us, but as he sniffs its haunches, surely he must remember atavistically that this is where he'd start to munch.

There is poignancy in the predicament of a great many animals: 16
as in the simple observation which students of the California condor have made that this huge, most endangered bird prefers the carrion meat of its old standby, the deer, to all the dead cows, sheep, horses and other substitutes it sees from above, sprawled about. Animals are stylized characters in a kind of old saga—stylized because even the most acute of them have little leeway as they play out their parts. (*Rabbits*, for example, I find terribly affecting, imprisoned in their hop.) And as we drift away from any cognizance of them, we sacrifice some of the intricacy and grandeur of life. Having already lost so much, we are hardly aware of what remains, but to a primitive snatched forward from an earlier existence it might seem as if we had surrendered a richness comparable to all the tapestries of childhood. Since this is a matter of the imagination as well as of animal demographics, no Noah projects, no bionomic discoveries on the few sanctuaries that have been established are going to reverse the swing. The very specialists in the forefront of finding out how animals behave, when one meets them, appear to be no more intrigued than any ordinary Indian was.

But we continue to need—as aborigines did, as children do—   17
a parade of morality tales which are more concise than those that politics, for instance, later provides. So we've had Aesop's and medieval and modern fables about the grasshopper and the ant, the tiger and Little Black Sambo, the wolf and the three pigs, Br'er Rabbit and Br'er Bear, Goldilocks and her three bears, Pooh Bear, Babar and the rhinos, Walt Disney's animals, and assorted humbler scary bats, fat hippos, funny frogs and eager beavers. Children have a passion for clean, universal definitions, and so it is that animals have gone with children's literature as Latin has with religion. Through them they first encountered death, birth, their own maternal feelings, the gap between beauty and cleverness,

or speed and good intentions. The animal kingdom boasted the powerful lion, the mothering goose, the watchful owl, the tardy tortoise, Chicken Little, real-life dogs that treasure bones, and mink that grow posh pelts from eating crawfish and mussels.

In the cartoons of two or three decades ago, Mouse doesn't get 18 along with Cat because Cat must catch Mouse or miss his supper. Dog, on the other hand, detests Cat for no such rational reason, only the capricious fact that dogs don't dote on cats. Animal stories are bounded, yet enhanced, by each creature's familiar lineaments, just as a parable about a prince and peasant, a duchess and a milkmaid, a blacksmith and a fisherman, would be. Typecasting, like the roll of a metered ode, adds resonance and dignity, summoning up all of the walruses and hedgehogs that went before: the shrewd image of Br'er Rabbit to assist his suburban relative Bugs Bunny behind the scenes. But now, in order to present a tale about the contest between two thieving crows and a scarecrow, the storyteller would need to start by explaining that once upon a time crows used to eat a farmer's corn if he didn't defend it with a mock man pinned together from old clothes. Crows are having a hard go of it and may soon receive game-bird protection.

One way childhood is changing, therefore, is that the nonhuman 19 figures—"Wild Things" or puppet monsters—constructed by the best of the new artificers, like Maurice Sendak or the *Sesame Street* writers, are distinctly humanoid, ballooned out of faces, torsos met on the subway. The televised character Big Bird does not resemble a bird the way Bugs Bunny remained a rabbit—though already he was less so than Br'er or Peter Rabbit. Big Bird's personality, her confusion, haven't the faintest connection to an ostrich's. Lest she be confused with an ostrich, her voice has been slotted unmistakably toward the prosaic. Dr. Seuss did transitional composites of worldwide fauna, but these new shapes—a beanbag like the *Sesame Street* Grouch or Cookie Monster or Herry Monster, and the floral creations in books—have been conceived practically from scratch by the artist ("in the night kitchen," to use a Sendak phrase), and not transferred from the existing caricatures of nature. In their conversational conflicts they offer him a fresh start, which may be a valuable commodity, whereas if he were dealing with an alligator, it would, while giving him an old-fashioned boost in the traditional manner, at the same time box him in. A chap called Alligator, with that fat snout and tail, cannot squirm free of the solidity of actual alligators. Either it must stay a heavyweight or else play on the sternness of reality by swinging over to impersonate a cream puff and a Ferdinand.

Though animal programs on television are popular, what with 20 the wave of nostalgia and "ecology" in the country, we can generally say about the animal kingdom, "The King is dead, long live the King." Certainly the talent has moved elsewhere. Those bulbous Wild Things and slant-mouthed beanbag puppets derived from the denizens of Broadway—an argumentative night news vendor, a lady on a traffic island—have grasped their own destinies, as characters on the make are likely to. It was inevitable they would. There may be a shakedown to remove the elements that would be too bookish for children's literature in other hands, and another shakedown because these first innovators have been more city-oriented than suburban. New authors will shift the character sources away from Broadway and the subway and the ghetto, but the basic switch has already been accomplished—from the ancient juxtaposition of people, animals, and dreams blending the two, to people and monsters that grow solely out of people by way of dreams.

Which leaves us in the suburbs, with dogs as a last link. Cats   21
are too independent to care, but dogs are in an unenviable position, they hang so much upon our good opinion. We are coming to *have* no opinion; we don't pay enough attention to form an opinion. Though they admire us, are thrilled by us, heroize us, we regard them as a hobby or a status symbol, like a tennis racquet, and substitute leash laws for leadership—expect them not simply to learn English but to grow hands, because their beastly paws seem stranger to us every year. If they try to fondle us with their handyjack mouths, we read it as a bite; and like used cars, they are disposed of when the family relocates, changes its "bag," or in the scurry of divorce. The first reason people kept a dog was to acquire an ally on the hunt, a friend at night. Then it was to maintain an avenue to animality, as our own nearness began to recede. But as we lose our awareness of all animals, dogs are becoming a bridge to nowhere. We can only pity their fate.

KONRAD LORENZ

The Language of Animals

Animals do not possess a language in the true sense of the word.   1
In the higher vertebrates, as also in insects, particularly in the socially living species of both great groups, every individual has

From *King Solomon's Ring* (1952).

a certain number of innate movements and sounds for expressing feelings. It has also innate ways of reacting to these signals whenever it sees or hears them in a fellow-member of the species. The highly social species of birds such as the jackdaw or the greylag goose, have a complicated code of such signals which are uttered and understood by every bird without any previous experience. The perfect coordination of social behaviour which is brought about by these actions and reactions conveys to the human observer the impression that the birds are talking and understanding a language of their own. Of course, this purely innate signal code of an animal species differs fundamentally from human language, every word of which must be learned laboriously by the human child. Moreover, being a genetically fixed character of the species—just as much as any bodily character—this so-called language is, for every individual animal species, ubiquitous in its distribution. Obvious though this fact may seem, it was, nevertheless, with something akin to naïve surprise that I heard the jackdaws in northern Russia "talk" exactly the same, familiar "dialect" as my birds at home in Altenberg. The superficial similarity between these animal utterances and human languages diminishes further as it becomes gradually clear to the observer that the animal, in all these sounds and movements expressing its emotions, has in no way the conscious intention of influencing a fellow-member of its species. This is proved by the fact that even geese or jackdaws reared and kept singly make all these signals as soon as the corresponding mood overtakes them. Under these circumstances the automatic and even mechanical character of these signals becomes strikingly apparent and reveals them as entirely different from human words.

In human behaviour, too, there are mimetic signs which automatically transmit a certain mood and which escape one, without or even contrary to one's intention of thereby influencing anybody else: the commonest example of this is yawning. Now the mimetic sign by which the yawning mood manifests itself is an easily perceived optical and acoustical stimulus whose effect is, therefore, not particularly surprising. But, in general, such crude and patent signals are not always necessary in order to transmit a mood. On the contrary, it is characteristic of this particular effect that it is often brought about by diminutive sign stimuli which are hardly perceptible by conscious observation. The mysterious apparatus for transmitting and receiving the sign stimuli which convey moods is age-old, far older than mankind itself. In our own case, it has doubtless degenerated as our word-language developed. Man has no need of minute intention-displaying movements to announce his momentary mood: he can say it in words. But jackdaws or dogs are obliged to "read in each other's eyes" what they are about to do in the next moment. For this reason, in higher and social animals, the transmitting, as well as the receiving apparatus of "mood-convection" is much better developed and more highly specialized than in us humans. All expressions of animal emotions, for instance, the "Kia" and "Kiaw" note of the jackdaw, are therefore not comparable to our spoken language, but only to those expressions such as yawning, wrinkling the brow and smiling, which are expressed unconsciously as innate actions and also understood by a corresponding inborn mechanism. The "words" of the various animal "languages" are merely interjections.

Though man may also have numerous gradations of unconscious ³ mimicry, no George Robey or Emil Jannings would be able, in this sense, to convey, by mere miming, as the greylag goose can, whether he was going to walk or fly, or to indicate whether he wanted to go home or to venture further afield, as a jackdaw can do quite easily. Just as the transmitting apparatus of animals is considerably more efficient than that of man, so also is their receiving apparatus. This is not only capable of distinguishing a large number of signals, but, to preserve the above simile, it responds to much slighter transmissions than does our own. It is incredible, what minimal signs, completely imperceptible to man, animals will receive and interpret rightly. Should one member of a jackdaw flock that is seeking for food on the ground fly upwards merely to seat itself on the nearest apple-tree and preen its feathers, then none of the others will cast so much as a glance in its direction; but, if the bird takes to wing with intent to cover a longer distance, then it will be joined, according to its authority as a member of the flock, by its spouse or also a larger group of jackdaws, in spite of the fact that it did not emit a single "Kia."

In this case, a man well versed in the ways and manners of ⁴ jackdaws might also, by observing the minutest intention-displaying movements of the bird, be able to predict—if with less accuracy than a fellow-jackdaw—how far that particular bird was going to fly. There are instances in which a good observer can equal and even surpass an animal in its faculty of "understanding" and anticipating the intentions of its fellow, but in other cases he cannot hope to emulate it. The dog's "receiving set" far surpasses our own analogous apparatus. Everybody who understands dogs knows with what almost uncanny certitude a faithful dog recognizes in its master whether the latter is leaving the room for some reason uninteresting to his pet, or whether the longed-for daily walk is pending. Many dogs achieve even more in this respect. My Alsatian Tito, the great-great-great-great-great-grandmother of the dog I

now possess, knew, by "telepathy," exactly which people got on
my nerves, and when. Nothing could prevent her from biting,
gently but surely, all such people on their posteriors. It was particularly dangerous for authoritative old gentlemen to adopt towards
me, in discussion, the well-known "you are, of course, too young"
attitude. No sooner had the stranger thus expostulated, than his
hand felt anxiously for the place in which Tito had punctiliously
chastised him. I could never understand how it was that this
reaction functioned just as reliably when the dog was lying under
the table and was therefore precluded from seeing the faces and
gestures of the people round it: how did she know who I was
speaking to or arguing with?

This fine canine understanding of the prevailing mood of a   5
master is not really telepathy. Many animals are capable of perceiving
the smallest movements, withheld from the human eye. And a
dog, whose whole powers of concentration are bent on serving
his master and who literally "hangs on his every word" makes
use of this faculty to the utmost. Horses too have achieved considerable feats in this field. So it will not be out of place to speak
here of the tricks which have brought some measure of renown
to certain animals. There have been "thinking" horses which could
work out square roots, and a wonder-dog Rolf, an Airedale terrier,
which went so far as to dictate its last will and testament to its
mistress. All these "counting," "talking" and "thinking" animals
"speak" by knocking or barking sounds, whose meaning is laid
down after the fashion of a Morse code. At first sight, their performances are really astounding. You are invited to set the examination yourself and you are put opposite the horse, terrier or
whatever animal it is. You ask, how much is twice two; the terrier
scrutinizes you intently and barks four times. In a horse, the feat
seems still more prodigious for he does not even look at you. In
dogs, who watch the examiner closely, it is obvious that their
attention is concentrated upon the latter and not, by any means,
on the problem itself. But the horse has no need to turn his eyes
towards the examiner since, even in a direction in which the
animal is not directly focusing, it can see, by indirect vision, the
minutest movement. And it is you yourself who betray, involuntarily
to the "thinking" animal, the right solution. Should one not know
the right answer oneself, the poor animal would knock or bark
on desperately, waiting in vain for the sign which would tell him
to stop. As a rule, this sign is forthcoming, since few people are
capable, even with the utmost self-control, of withholding an unconscious and involuntary signal. That it is the human being who
finds the solution and communicates it was once proved by one

of my colleagues in the case of a dachshund which had become quite famous and which belonged to an elderly spinster. The method was perfidious: It consisted in suggesting a wrong solution of all the problems not to the "counting" dog, but to his mistress. To this end, my friend made cards on one side of which a simple problem was printed in fat letters. The cards, however, unknown to the dog's owner, were constructed of several layers of transparent paper on the last of which another problem was inscribed in such a manner as to be visible from behind, when the front side was presented to the animal. The unsuspecting lady, seeing, in looking-glass writing, what she imagined to be the problem to be solved, transmitted involuntarily to the dog a solution which did not correspond to that of the problem on the front of the card, and was intensely surprised when, for the first time in her experience, her pet continued to give wrong answers. Before ending the séance, my friend adopted different tactics and presented mistress and dog with a problem, which, for a change, the dog could answer and the lady could not: He put before the animal a rag impregnated with the smell of a bitch in season. The dog grew excited, wagged his tail and whined—he knew what he was smelling and a really knowledgeable dog owner might have known, too, from observing his behaviour. Not so the old lady. When the dog was asked what the rag smelled of, he promptly morsed *her* answer: "Cheese!"

The enormous sensitivity of many animals to certain minute 6 movements of expression, as, for example, the above described capacity of the dog to perceive the friendly or hostile feelings which his master harbours for another person, is a wonderful thing. It is therefore not surprising that the naïve observer, seeking to assign to the animal human qualities, may believe that a being which can guess even such inward unspoken thoughts, must, still more, understand every word that the beloved master utters; now an intelligent dog does understand a considerable number of words, but, on the other hand, it must not be forgotten that the ability to understand the minutest expressional movements is thus acute in animals for the very reason that they lack true speech.

As I have already explained, all the innate expressions of emotion, 7 such as the whole complicated "signal code" of the jackdaw, are far removed from human language. When your dog nuzzles you, whines, runs to the door and scratches it, or puts his paws on the wash basin under the tap, and looks at you imploringly, he does something that comes far nearer to human speech than anything that a jackdaw or goose can ever "say," no matter how clearly "intelligible" and appropriate to the occasion the finely differentiated expressional sounds of these birds may appear. The dog wants to

make you open the door or turn on the tap, and what he does
has the specific and purposeful motive of influencing you in a
certain direction. He would never perform these movements if you
were not present. But the jackdaw or goose merely gives unconscious
expression to its inward mood and the "Kia" or "Kiaw," or the
warning sound escapes the bird involuntarily; when in a certain
mood, it must utter the corresponding sound, whether or not there
is anybody there to hear it.

The intelligible actions of the dog described above are not innate   8
but are individually learned and governed by true insight. Every
individual dog has different methods of making himself understood
by his master and will adapt his behaviour according to the situation.
My bitch Stasie, the great-grandmother of the dog I now possess,
having once eaten something which disagreed with her, wanted
to go out during the night. I was at that time overworked, and
slept very soundly, so that she did not succeed in waking me and
indicating her requirements, by her usual signs; to her whining
and nosing I had evidently only responded by burying myself still
deeper in my pillows. This desperate situation finally induced her
to forget her normal obedience and to do a thing which was strictly
forbidden her: she jumped on my bed and then proceeded literally
to dig me out of the blankets and roll me on the floor. Such an
adaptability to present needs is totally lacking in the "vocabulary"
of birds: they never roll you out of bed.

Parrots and large corvines are endowed with "speech" in still   9
another sense: they can imitate human words. Here, an association
of thought between the sounds and certain experiences is sometimes
possible. This imitating is nothing other than the so-called mocking
found in many song birds. Willow warblers, red-backed shrikes
and many others are masters of this art. Mocking consists of sounds,
learned by imitation, which are not innate and are uttered only
while the bird is singing; they have no "meaning" and bear no
relation whatsoever to the inborn "vocabulary" of the species.
This also applies to starlings, magpies and jackdaws, who not only
"mock" birds' voices but also successfully imitate human words.
However, the talking of big corvines and parrots is a somewhat
different matter. It still bears that character of playfulness and lack
of purpose which is also inherent in the mocking of smaller birds
and which is loosely akin to the play of more intelligent animals.
But a corvine or a parrot will utter its human words independently
of song and it is undeniable that these sounds may occasionally
have a definite thought association.

Many grey parrots, as well as others, will say "good morning"   10
only once a day and at the appropriate time. My friend Professor

Otto Koehler possessed an ancient grey parrot which, being addicted to the vice of feather-plucking, was nearly bald. This bird answered to the name of "Geier" which in German means vulture. Geier was certainly no beauty but he redeemed himself by his speaking talents. He said "good morning" and "good evening" quite aptly and, when a visitor stood up to depart, he said, in a benevolent bass voice "Na, auf Wiedersehen." But he only said this if the guest really departed. Like a "thinking" dog, he was tuned in to the finest, involuntarily given signs; what these signs were, we never could find out and we never once succeeded in provoking the retort by staging a departure. But when the visitor really left, no matter how inconspicuously he took his leave, promptly and mockingly came the words "Na, auf Wiedersehen!"

The well-known Berlin ornithologist, Colonel von Lukanus, also possessed a grey parrot which became famous through a feat of memory. Von Lukanus kept, among other birds, a tame hoopoe named "Höpfchen." The parrot, which could talk well, soon mastered this word. Hoopoes unfortunately do not live long in captivity, though grey parrots do; so, after a time, "Höpfchen" went the way of all flesh and the parrot appeared to have forgotten his name, at any rate, he did not say it any more. Nine years later, Colonel von Lukanus acquired another hoopoe and, as the parrot set eyes on him for the first time, he said at once, and then repeatedly, "Höpfchen" . . . "Höpfchen". . . .

In general, these birds are just as slow in learning something new as they are tenacious in remembering what they have once learned. Everyone who has tried to drum a new word into the brain of a starling or a parrot knows with what patience one must apply oneself to this end, and how untiringly one must again and again repeat the word. Nevertheless, such birds can, in exceptional cases, learn to imitate a word which they have heard seldom, perhaps only once. However, this apparently only succeeds when a bird is in an exceptional state of excitement; I myself have seen only two such cases. My brother had, for years, a delightfully tame and lively blue-fronted Amazon parrot named Papagallo, which had an extraordinary talent for speech. As long as he lived with us in Altenberg, Papagallo flew just as freely around as most of my other birds. A talking parrot that flies from tree to tree and at the same time says human words, gives a much more comical effect than one that sits in a cage and does the same thing. When Papagallo, with loud cries of "Where's the Doc?" flew about the district, sometimes in a genuine search for his master, it was positively irresistible.

Still funnier, but also remarkable from a scientific point of view, was the following performance of the bird; Papagallo feared nothing and nobody, with the exception of the chimney-sweep. Birds are very apt to fear things which are up above. And this tendency is associated with the innate dread of the bird of prey swooping down from the heights. So everything that appears against the sky, has for them something of the meaning of "bird of prey." As the black man, already sinister in his darkness, stood up on the chimney stack and became outlined against the sky, Papagallo fell into a panic of fear and flew, loudly screaming, so far away that we feared he might not come back. Months later, when the chimney-sweep came again, Papagallo was sitting on the weathercock, squabbling with the jackdaws who wanted to sit there too. All at once, I saw him grow long and thin and peer down anxiously into the village street; then he flew up and away, shrieking in raucous tones, again and again, "the chimney-sweep is coming, the chimney-sweep is coming." The next moment, the black man walked through the doorway of the yard!

Unfortunately, I was unable to find out how often Papagallo 14 had seen the chimney-sweep before and how often he had heard the excited cry of our cook which heralded his approach. It was, without a doubt, the voice and intonation of this lady which the bird reproduced. But he had certainly not heard it more than three times at the most and, each time, only once and at an interval of months.

The second case known to me in which a talking bird learned 15 human words after hearing them only once or very few times, concerns a hooded crow. Again it was a whole sentence which thus impressed itself on the bird's memory. "Hansl," as the bird was called, could compete in speaking talent with the most gifted parrot. The crow had been reared by a railwayman, in the next village, and it flew about freely and had grown into a well-proportioned, healthy fellow, a good advertisement for the rearing ability of its foster-father. Contrary to popular opinion, crows are not easy to rear and, under the inadequate care which they usually receive, mostly develop into those stunted, half-crippled specimens which are so often seen in captivity. One day, some village boys brought me a dirt-encrusted hooded crow whose wings and tail were clipped to small stumps. I was hardly able to recognize, in this pathetic being, the once beautiful Hansl. I bought the bird, as, on principle, I buy all unfortunate animals that the village boys bring me and this I do partly out of pity and partly because amongst these stray animals there might be one of real interest. And this one certainly was! I rang up Hansl's master who told me that the bird had actually been missing some days and begged me to adopt him till the next moult. So, accordingly, I put the crow in the pheasant pen and gave it concentrated food, so that, in the imminent new moult, it would grow good new wing and tail feathers. At this time, when the bird was, of necessity, a prisoner, I found out that Hansl had a surprising gift of the gab and he gave me the opportunity of hearing plenty! He had, of course, picked up just what you would expect a tame crow to hear that sits on a tree, in the village street, and listens to the "language" of the inhabitants.

I later had the pleasure of seeing this bird recover his full plumage 16 and I freed him as soon as he was fully capable of flight. He returned forthwith to his former master, in Wordern, but continued, a welcome guest, to visit us from time to time. Once he was missing for several weeks and, when he returned, I noticed that he had, on one foot, a broken digit which had healed crooked. And this is the whole point of the history of Hansl, the hooded crow. For we know just how he came by this little defect. And from whom do we know it? Believe it or not, Hansl told us himself! When he suddenly reappeared, after his long absence, he knew a new sentence. With the accent of a true street urchin, he said, in lower Austrian dialect, a short sentence which, translated into broad Lancashire, would sound like "Got 'im in t'bloomin' trap!" There was no doubt about the truth of this statement. Just as in the case of Papagallo, a sentence which he had certainly not heard often, had stuck in Hansl's memory because he had heard it in a moment of great apprehension, that is, immediately after he had been caught. How he got away again, Hansl unfortunately did not tell us.

In such cases, the sentimental animal lover, crediting the creature 17 with human intelligence, will take an oath on it that the bird understands what he says. This, of course, is quite incorrect. Not even the cleverest "talking" birds which, as we have seen, are certainly capable of connecting their sound-expressions with particular occurrences, learn to make practical use of their powers, to achieve purposefully even the simplest object. Professor Koehler, who can boast of the greatest successes in the science of training animals, and who succeeded in teaching pigeons to count up to six, tried to teach the above-mentioned, talented grey parrot "Geier" to say "food" when he was hungry and "water" when he was dry. This attempt did not succeed, nor, so far, has it been achieved by anybody else. In itself, the failure is remarkable. Since, as we have seen, the bird is able to connect his sound utterances with certain occurrences, we should expect him, first of all, to connect them with a purpose; but this, surprisingly, he is unable to do. In all other cases, where an animal learns a new type of behaviour, it does so to achieve some purpose. The most curious types of behaviour may be thus acquired, especially with the object of influencing the human keeper. A most grotesque habit of this kind was learned by a Blumenau's parakeet which belonged to Prof. Karl von Frisch. The scientist only let the bird fly freely when he had just watched it have an evacuation of the bowels, so that, for the next ten minutes, his well-kept furniture was not endangered. The parakeet learned very quickly to associate these facts and, as he was passionately fond of leaving his cage, he would force out a minute dropping with all his might, every time Prof. von Frisch came near the cage. He even squeezed desperately when it was impossible to produce anything, and really threatened to do himself an injury by the violence of his straining. You just had to let the poor thing out, every time you saw him!

Yet the clever "Geier," much cleverer than that little parakeet, [18] could not even learn to say "food" when he was hungry. The whole complicated apparatus of the bird's syrinx and brain that makes imitation and association of thought possible, appears to have no function in connection with the survival of the species. We ask ourselves vainly what it is there for!

I only know one bird that learned to use a human word when [19] he wanted a particular thing and who thus connected a sound-expression with a purpose, and it is certainly no coincidence that it was a bird of that species which I consider to have the highest mental development of all, namely the raven. Ravens have a certain innate call-note which corresponds to the "Kia" of the jackdaw and has the same meaning, that is, the invitation to others to fly with the bird that utters it. In the raven, this note is a sonorous, deep-throated, and, at the same time, sharply metallic "krack-rackrack." Should the bird wish to persuade another of the same species which is sitting on the ground to fly with it, he executes the same kind of movements as described in the chapter on jackdaws: he flies, from behind, close above the other bird and, in passing it, wobbles with his closely folded tail, at the same time emitting a particularly sharp "krackrackrackrack" which sounds almost like a volley of small explosions.

My raven Roah, so named after the call-note of the young raven, [20] was, even as a mature bird, a close friend of mine and accompanied me, when he had nothing better to do, on long walks and even on skiing tours, or on motorboat excursions on the Danube. Particularly in his later years he was not only shy of strange people, but also had a strong aversion to places where he had once been frightened or had had any other unpleasant experience. Not only did he hesitate to come down from the air to join me in such places, but he could not bear to see me linger in what he considered to be a dangerous spot. And, just as my old jackdaws tried to make their truant children leave the ground and fly after them, so Roah bore down upon me from behind, and, flying close over my head, he wobbled with his tail and then swept upwards again, at the same time looking backwards over his shoulder to see if I was following. In accompaniment to this sequence of movements—which, to stress the fact again, is entirely innate—Roah, instead of uttering the above described call-note, said his own name, with human intonation. The most peculiar thing about this was that Roah used the human word for me only. When addressing one of his own species, he employed the normal innate call-note. To suspect that I had unconsciously trained him would obviously be wrong; for this could only have taken place if, by pure chance, I had walked up to Roah at the very moment when he happened to be calling his name, and, at the same time, to be wanting my company. Only if this rather unlikely coincidence of three factors had repeated itself on several occasions, could a corresponding association of thought have been formed by the bird, and that certainly was not the case. The old raven must, then, have possessed a sort of insight that "Roah" was my call-note! Solomon was not the only man who could speak to animals, but Roah is, so far as I know, the only animal that has ever spoken a human word to a man, in its right context—even if it was only a very ordinary call-note.

SHEILA BURNFORD

Pas Devant le Chien

I bought a little electric heater for my workroom: pale turquoise with a slatted metal grille; and it very cleverly came on when the room grew cold, then switched off at the desired dialed warmth. The first afternoon I plugged it in it was resting quietly when Jonny wandered in, looking for someone to distract after a boring homework session with the nervous system of a frog. She lolled over my desk for some minutes, snapping the jaws of a stapler round the blotting paper, then: "What are you doing?" she asked. It was perfectly obvious what I was doing: sitting at a desk, writing a letter with a leaking ball-point pen. I have been campaigning against this barren, bootless type of question for years in the family,

From *Fields of Noon* (1964).

mainly with success, but with Jonny it seems to have deteriorated into a kind of verbal Snakes and Ladders[1], the rules undefined, yet each of us knowing perfectly clearly who has scored. My move: "I am walking down an up escalator, playing the bagpipes," I said, and licked a stamp squashingly, quite a feat in itself. "As you will, Mother," said Jonny equably, "although most people would think you were sitting at a desk, writing a letter with a leaking ball-point pen." She was going to play it cool. She leaned over my shoulder to read the letter—another habit I detest. "Dear Hermione," she started, and at that fatal moment the heater's fan purred into life.

"What's that?" she asked. Fair enough, it *could* be mistaken for a loudspeaker. "A heater," I said, and added, generously, "it heats the room." "Big news," said Jonny, "but how does it turn itself on like that?" She is seventeen, lives in a land of thermostats and passed physics last year. "There's a little man inside," I explained; "he lies on a tiny chaise longue, lightly dressed; and when he feels chilly he turns up the heat; and when he is all nice and warm again he turns it off. He is very sensitive."

"Oh, really?" said Jonny coldly.

If only she had retired now, chastened, to her frog; if only I hadn't—but I did: I leaned over and looked down into the grille with a fond smile, and I waved a tiny, intimate wave. And then heaven help me, I opened the door to the dial at the back, and lifted my tenant out. "Isn't he adorable?" I said, and smoothed back his hair as he sat on the palm of my hand.

"Ugh," said Jonny, then suddenly lunged and snatched him from me. She suspended him distastefully—by his arms, I suppose— between forefingers and thumbs, then twirled him rapidly round and round in the manner that expert grocers use to close paper bags. "How do you like *that*, you sensitive little man?" she asked, then threw him up to the ceiling and watched him fall, unmoved. I grabbed, but she pinned him down with a foot, then ground him very thoroughly into the carpet. "We don't want him to multiply, do we?" she said with a smugness that spurred me on down the fatal path. I gathered up the tiny remains, rearranged them, then restored him with a finger dipped in a cup of cold tea, ignoring Jonny's ostentatious wiping of the carpet. "Here's a leg," she said, smiling evilly as she handed it over—"and it's not his wooden one either," she added quickly, forestalling me. I screwed

1. A popular children's board game, in which players roll dice and land on squares marked with snakes and ladders while trying to reach the hundredth square as quickly as possible.

the leg back on with a hairpin, outwardly nonchalant. "You see,"
I said triumphantly, "he's as good as new again—"

"I'd like to shake his little hand—" said Jonny; but she moved   6
towards me with such a predatory look that I swiftly popped him
back into the Tom Tiddler's ground of the heater. She kneeled
beside me and peered into the grille. "He looks shocked," she said
accusingly, "you put that leg on backwards—"

I was just about to make a tacit admission of defeat by saying   7
that I had no further use for him anyway, and then returning to
my letter, when a third head thrust its way in between us, and
a third pair of eyes stared intently down the grille. We had forgotten
all about him: he had followed Jonny in, and must have witnessed
the whole terrible scene from his lair under the table—stout, immensely respectable and elderly, a most dogged dog, he had taken
everything to his zealous heart. He has a loosely fitting coat with
a lot of surplus material, several folds of which were now puckered
into deep thoughtful furrows all over his face. His honest eyes
shone with the sincerity of his belief, his ears fairly quivered with
anticipation: something lived in that new cage—it had been taken
out, made much of, massacred, restored—*and put back in again.*
He could not yet see it, but with application, resolution and vigilance
he would: today, tomorrow, it mattered not. He would wait. He
had plenty of time.

Our hearts sank under his solid weight of purpose. We knew
it too well. A small example: throughout the day he sleeps at the
top of the stairs; they are narrow, he is not; for nine years he has
been trodden on, tripped over, cursed, threatened, dragged away,
prodded, Hoovered[2]; he has many breakfasts and countless cups
of coffee spilt over him on Sundays. He is there at this very
moment. "I must return to my frog," said Jonny uneasily; and
left me, well and truly hoist.

An hour later he was still staring in, his absorption fanned into   9
white-hot intensity at excitingly irregular intervals. I turned the
switch off, but silence was apparently even more suspenseful. I
unplugged it and shoved it under a loveseat; as much of him as
could immediately manage disappeared after, his voluminous white
knickerbockers heaved, the seat teetered drunkenly for a minute,
then settled down, panting audibly and wagging a long feathered
tail. Even Jonny was appalled when she saw what we had done:
it was as bad as some well-meaning but confused adult searching
the night skies with field glasses for airborne reindeer on Christmas
Eve, she said pointedly. I thought that probably the parent had

2. Vacuumed (from the Hoover brand name).

been driven into understandable confusion by the constant asking
of idiotic questions by its children. Score equal.

We locked the heater into a cupboard: he lay like a Landseer   10
with his nose to the crack, whining. We unscrewed the back and
showed him the exposed innards: he settled down to his vigil
wearing the heater on the front half of his head. We lured him
down to his dinner and tried smuggling it out in a suitcase during
his absence, but he tracked it out to the garage, and flopped as
possessively on the suitcase as though it had a recent headstone
at one end. We climbed a ladder and thrust it through the attic
trapdoor in the ceiling: he threw his head back and howled below.
We could not settle down to anything. At midnight we threw in
the sponge, put the heater in his basket and went to bed, leaving
him gazing rapturously into its depths.

His whiskers were wilted with sleeplessness next morning, his   11
eyes drooping halfway down his face—but the same fanatic light
still burned as bright as ever in their depths. I was torn between
compassion and a strong desire to short-circuit the heater and
shock him back to his senses. But Jonny thought this should only
be done as a last resort. She suggested that as I had tenanted the
little turquoise home in the first place I was technically the landlady:
I should now use the same convincing powers to evict my tenant.
So I plucked the poor little man out, not once but a dozen times,
and we took turns in disposing of him under the watchful eyes
of the dog: he was thrown out of the window, buried, drowned
in breakfast cereal, flushed away, posted, and returned to the
milkman in an empty bottle. Jonny finally made a sandwich out
of him and took him to school for lunch. Each method was attended
to its tragic end by the dog, who would then reel back to his post
at the source.

I spent a profitless day with the sleep-starved victim of my   12
pedantic folly. I borrowed a long-playing bear that tinkled Brahms'
Lullaby when a knob in its stomach was pressed; I sat it on the
heater, then drew the blinds and tiptoed into cover—hoping he
might drop off so that I could snatch the heater, and he would
wake up and think he had dreamed the whole thing. This made
me think, when I woke myself up later, of a friend who is a retired
psychiatrist and has a pack of decidedly neurotic poodles. I rang
him up, long distance too, and explained our problem. *Very,* very
interesting, he said, after a long expensive pause, it was a classic
case of Canine Fixation. The patient's suspense must be relieved:
attempting to relieve it by the negation of nonexistence was a
negative approach: *positive* substitution was indicated. In other
words, he explained in bright kindly tones, murdering little male

thermostats meant nothing to a dog, we must install instead a *real* little tenant in our heater. He said that he was sorry, sizewise, that he was not able to move in himself, it sounded cozy; but he thought that there must be plenty of tenant material at the Bottom of the Garden if we inquired around, or knocked on the doors of a few toadstools—with this present cold spell as an added inducement there must be many who would be only too delighted to move into a heated apartment. We might consider Lilliput[3] too . . . ideal recruiting ground . . . probably direct jet service there nowadays . . . I promised to send him a postcard if there was, and hung up discouraged: if this was a *professional* reaction—

When Jonny returned late that afternoon Old Faithful had been   13
without sleep for twenty-four hours—twenty-two more than his usual daily quota—and he looked it: disheveled, sagging, reeling in his tracks. So was I. I was ready to give my brand-new heater away—it was by now too battered to return—or hurl it into the lake, pound it to pieces with a sledge hammer— But Jonny, refreshed after an eight-hour absence, pointed out that the results of sudden heater-deprivation might be even more traumatic: he might spend the rest of his life keening round the house like some hairy banshee, looking for it. The Poodle Doctor's idea of a genuine occupant really added up— "Then wing off to Never-Never Land[4] with him and find one," I said querulously, "and before you go pour me a long, strong drink." "Do you mind if I take the car instead?" she said. "The nursery window's stuck."

She returned within an hour, modestly triumphant. "We'll leave   14
Him in the car until H Hour," she said. H Hour was 6:30—Old Faithful's dinnertime. At 6:29 he dragged himself away from the heater to fortify himself for the night watch. His bowl, well greased on the underside, awaited him on the skiddy kitchen tiles, its contents mixed into a glutinous delaying paste. Jonny tore out to the car and then upstairs. Ten minutes later he lurched through the doorway, heading blearily for the heater. I unscrewed the back, and he watched with polite interest. Then Jonny inserted her hand and slowly drew out a fat, placid hamster, clutching a peanut in its pink hand. It gazed benignly down on the astounded furrowed face below, and crammed the peanut into its bulging cheeks. The dog was enchanted; in a quivering ecstasy he watched Jonny open

---

3. The imaginary country inhabited by tiny people in Jonathan Swift's *Gulliver's Travels*.

4. In J.M. Barrie's play *Peter Pan*, a country inhabited by Indians, Mermaids, and Pirates. Peter Pan, a half-magical boy, takes the Darling children there; they leave by flying through the open nursery window.

the door of a neat green cage with a kind of treadwheel inside. He rested his head on the table, his nose against the bars, his besotted eyes following the hamster as it waddled around, inspecting the larder, doing a few press-ups on the bars. He positively doted when it scratched its ear. It curled up in a corner in a snug ball, yawned hugely, and fell asleep. A minute later there was another cavernous yawn, and the dog slowly folded into a vast inanimate heap under the table.

It has been the most successful substitution. Godot[5], the hamster,   15
sleeps most of the day, leaving the dog free to get his own head down at the top of the stairs, or check the dustbins, etc. In the evening he delights the dog with a performance of acrobatics. Last thing at night he has a run round the workroom, and does some intrepid mountaineering up the loose sliding terrain of his infatuated owner. The heater heats, turning itself on and off, untenanted, ignored.

Yesterday Jonny came into the kitchen when I was frying some   16
bacon and eggs, the dog in hopeful attendance. "What are you doing?" she asked. "I am mixing some cement for. . . ." I started automatically, then caught her eye: *"Pas devant le chien—'*[6] she said with a priggish wag of her finger. "I am frying two eggs and four rashers of bacon in a frying pan," I said humbly.

5. The allusion is to Samuel Beckett's play *Waiting for Godot*, in which two characters wait hopefully for Godot, who never arrives.
6. "Not in front of the dog."

BRIGID BROPHY

The Menace of Nature

So? Are you just back? Or are you, perhaps, staying on there   1
for the extra week? By "there" I mean, of course, one of the few spots left where the machine has not yet gained the upper hand; some place as yet unstrangled by motorways and unfouled by concrete mixers; a place where the human spirit can still—but for how much longer?—steep itself in natural beauty and recuperate after the nervous tension, the sheer stress, of modern living.

Well (I assume you're *enough* recuperated to stand this infor-   2
mation?): I think you've been piously subscribing to a heresy. It's

First published in *New Statesman* in 1965.

a heresy I incline offhand to trace, with an almost personally piqued sense of vendetta, to the old heresiarch himself, the sometimes great, often bathetic but never cogently thoughtful poet, William Wordsworth. Since the day he let the seeds of heresy fall (on, no doubt, the Braes of the Yarrow or the Banks of Nith), the thing has spread and enlarged itself into one of the great parroted, meaningless (but slightly paranoid) untruths of our age.

I am not trying to abolish the countryside. (I *state* this because it   3
is true; I emphasise it because I don't want the lynch mob outside my window.) I'm not such a pig as to want the country built on or littered up with bottles and plastic bags merely because it doesn't appeal to *me*. As it happens, my own taste for countryside, though small, is existent. I've found the country very pleasant to be driven through in a tolerably fast car by someone whose driving I trust and whose company I like. But I admit that landscape as such bores me—to the extent that I have noticed myself in picture galleries automatically pausing to look at "Landscape with Ruins" or "Bandits in a Landscape" but walking straight past the pure landscapes at a speed which is obviously trying to simulate the effect of being driven past in a car.

I'm not, however, out to dissuade *you* from spending your holiday   4
as a sort of legalised bandit in the landscape. Neither am I anti-holiday. Holidays have been sniped at lately as things everyone feels an obligation to enjoy but no one really does. Yet I suspect there would be fewer dissatisfied holiday-makers if social pressure didn't try to limit our choice to "Landscape" or "Landscape with Seascape." You can be made to feel quite guiltily antisocial in the summer months if you are, like me, constitutionally unable either to relax or to take a suntan. Indeed, relaxation is becoming this decade's social *sine qua non,* like Bridge in the 'thirties. They'll scarcely let you have a *baby* these days if you can't satisfy them beforehand you're adept at relaxing. But on the in some ways more private question of having a holiday, constitutional urbanites are still free, if only they can resist being shamed onto the beaches, to opt out of a rest and settle for the change which even the proverb allows to be as good as it. By simply exchanging their own for a foreign city, they are released from the routine of earning their daily bread and washing up after it, but don't suffer the disorientation, the uncorseted discomfort, which overtakes an ur-banite cast up on a beach with no timetable to live by except the tides.

Still, it isn't in the holidays but during the rest of the year that   5
the great rural heresy does its damage. How many, for example, of the middle-class parents who bring up their children in London do so with unease or even apology, with a feeling that they are

selfishly depriving the children of some "natural heritage" and sullying their childhood with urban impurities? Some parents even let this guilt drive them out to the suburbs or further, where they believe they cancel the egocentricity of their own need or desire for the town by undergoing the martyrdom of commuting. This parental masochism may secure the child a rural heritage (though parents should enquire, before moving, whether their child has the rural temperament and *wants* the rural heritage) but it deprives him of the cultural one; he gains the tennis club but is condemned to the tennis club light-opera society's amateur production of *No, No, Nanette* because the trains don't run late enough to bring him home after Sadler's Wells.[1]

The notion that "nature" and "nature study" are somehow   6
"nice" for children, regardless of the children's own temperament, is a sentimental piety—and often a hypocritical one, like the piety which thinks Sunday School nice for *them* though we don't go to church ourselves. (In fact, it is we middle-aged who may need fresh air and exercise; the young are cat-like enough to remain lithe without.) Historically, it is not inept to trace the supposed affinity between children and "nature" to Wordsworth's time. It was about that time that there settled on England, like a drizzle, the belief that sex is *not* "nice" for children. Children's sexual curiosity was diverted to "the birds and the bees" and gooseberry bushes; and birds, bees and bushes—in other words, "nature"—have remained "suitable" for children ever since.

If the romantic belief in children's innocence is now exploded,   7
its numinous energy has only gone to strengthen the even more absurd romantic belief in the innocence of landscape's, as opposed to man-created, beauty. But I reject utterly the imputation that a brook is purer than Bach or a breeze more innocent than *As You Like It*. I warn you I shall be suspicious of this aesthetic faculty of yours that renders you so susceptible to the beauty of Snowdon[2] if it leaves you unable to see anything in All Souls', Langham Place; and I shall be downright sceptical of it if (I am making allowance for your sensibility to run exclusively in that landscape groove which mine leaves out) you doat on the Constable country

---

1. Theater in London, primarily used by visiting theatrical companies.
2. The references in the last sentence in the paragraph are: *Snowdon*, highest mountain in Wales, in a district noted for scenic beauty; *All Soul's, Langham Place*, church in London built 1822–25 by John Nash; *Constable country*, rural areas in southern Great Britain painted by the famous landscape painter John Constable (1776–1837); *a 74*, a bus; *the V.&A.*, the Victoria & Albert Museum in London, where a number of Constables are hung.

but feel it vaguely impure to take a 74 to the V. & A. to see a Constable.

You'll protest you feel no such impurity. Yet didn't you read 8 the first paragraph of this article without taking so much as a raised eyebrow's worth of exception? Didn't you let the assumption pass that the city is corrupt? Weren't you prepared to accept from me, as you have from a hundred august authorities—sociologists, physicians, psychologists—that *idée reçue*[3] about the nervous tension and stress of modern urban life? But what in heaven's name is this stressful modern urban life being compared with? Life in a medieval hamlet? Will no one take into account the symptoms into which the stress of *that* erupted—the epidemics of dancing madness and flagellation frenzy? Or life in a neolithic cave—whose stress one can only imagine and flinch at?

The truth is that the city is a device for *reducing* stress—by giving 9 humans a freer choice of escapes from the pressure (along with the weather) of their environment. The device doesn't always work perfectly: traffic jams *are* annoying; the motor car does maim and must be prevented from doing so: but the ambulance which arrives so mercifully quick is also powered by a motor. The city is one of the great indispensable devices of civilisation (itself only a device for centralising beauty and transmitting it as a heritage). It is one of the cardinal simple brilliant inventions, like currency. Like currency, it is a medium of exchange and thereby of choice—whereas the country is a place where one is under the thumb of chance, constrained to love one's neighbour not out of philanthropy but because there's no other company.

What's more, in the eighteenth century the city was suddenly 10 upgraded from a device of civilisation to a manifestation of it. The city became an art form. (The form had been discovered, but not very consciously remarked, earlier. It was discovered, like many art forms, by accident—often, as at Venice and Bruges, an accident of water.) We are in dire danger now of clogging up our cities as devices and at the same time despoiling them as works of art; and one of the biggest villains in this process is our rural heresy.

Most western European beings have to live in cities, and all but 11 the tiny portion of them who are temperamental rustics would do so contentedly, without wasting energy in guilt, and with an appreciative eye for the architecturescapes round them, had they not been told that liking the country is purer and more spiritual. Our cities run to squalor and our machines run amok because our citizens' minds are not on the job of mastering the machines

3. An idea generally accepted by everyone.

and using them to make the cities efficient and beautiful. Their
eyes are blind to the Chirico-esque[4] handsomeness of the M1,
because their hearts are set on a rustic Never-Never Land. Rustic
sentimentality makes us build our suburban villas to mimic cottages,
and then pebble-dash their outside walls in pious memory of the
holiday we spent sitting agonised on the shingle. The lovely terraced
façades of London are being undermined, as by subsidence, by
our yearning, our sickly nostalgia, for a communal country childhood
that never existed. We neglect our towns for a fantasy of going
"back" to the land, back to our "natural" state. But there isn't
and never was a natural man. We are a species that doesn't occur
wild. No pattern in his genes instructs man on what pattern to
build his nest. Instead, if he's fortunate, the Muses whisper to him
the ground-plan of an architectural folly. Even in his cave, he
frescoed the walls. All that is infallibly natural to our species is to
make things that are artificial. We are *homo artifex, homo faber,*[5]
homo Fabergé. Yet we are so ignorant of our own human nature
that our cities are falling into disrepair and all we worry about is
their encroachment on "nature."

For, as I said at the start, the rural fantasy is paranoid. A glance   12
at history shews that it is human life which is frail, and civilisation
which flickers in constant danger of being blown out. But the
rural fantasy insists that every plant is a delicate plant. The true
paranoid situation is on the other foot. I wouldn't wish to do (and
if we live at sensibly high densities there's no need to do) either,
but were I forced either to pull down a Nash terrace or to build
over a meadow, I'd choose the latter. If you don't like what you've
put up on the meadow, you can take it away again and the
meadow will re-seed itself in a year or two; but human semen is
lucky if it engenders an architectural genius a century. The whole
Wordsworthian fallacy consists in gravely underestimating the
toughness of plants. In fact, no sooner does civilisation admit a
crack—no sooner does a temple of Apollo lapse into disuse—than
a weed forces its wiry stem through the crack and urges the blocks
of stone further apart. During the last war, the bomber engines
were hardly out of earshot before the loosestrife[6] leapt up on the

---

4. The allusion is to Giorgio de Chirico, an early twentieth-century Italian painter
whose mysterious, symbolic work influenced surrealist painters. The M1 is a major
northbound highway out of London.
5. Very freely translatable either as "man the craftsman, man the builder, man the
perfumed" or as "man the tool-user, man the engineer, man the jeweler." Fabergé
is the name of both an international manufacturer of fragrances and a brilliant
Russian goldsmith, known especially for his Imperial Easter eggs.
6. A wild flowering plant.

bombed site. Whether we demolish our cities in a third world war or just let them tumble into decay, the seeds of the vegetable kingdom are no doubt waiting to seize on the rubble or sprout through the cracks. *Aux armes, citoyens*[7]. To your trowels and mortar. Man the concrete mixers. The deep mindless silence of the countryside is massing in the Green Belt, ready to move in.

7. "To arms, citizens"—a call to battle (the third line of the French national anthem, *La Marseillaise*, written at the time of the French Revolution, 1792).

E. B. WHITE

Twins

On a warm, miserable morning last week we went up to the   1
Bronx Zoo to see the moose calf and to break in a new pair of black shoes. We encountered better luck than we had bargained for. The cow moose and her young one were standing near the wall of the deer park below the monkey house, and in order to get a better view we strolled down to the lower end of the park, by the brook. The path there is not much travelled. As we approached the corner where the brook trickles under the wire fence, we noticed a red deer getting to her feet. Beside her, on legs that were just learning their business, was a spotted fawn, as small and perfect as a trinket seen through a reducing glass. They stood there, mother and child, under a gray beech whose trunk was engraved with dozens of hearts and initials. Stretched on the ground was another fawn, and we realized that the doe had just finished twinning. The second fawn was still wet, still unrisen. Here was a scene of rare sylvan splendor, in one of our five favorite boroughs, and we couldn't have asked for more. Even our new shoes seemed to be working out all right and weren't hurting much.

The doe was only a couple of feet from the wire, and we sat   2
down on a rock at the edge of the footpath to see what sort of start young fawns get in the deep fastnesses of Mittel Bronx. The mother, mildly resentful of our presence and dazed from her labor, raised one forefoot and stamped primly. Then she lowered her head, picked up the afterbirth, and began dutifully to eat it, allowing it to swing crazily from her mouth, as though it were a bunch of withered beet greens. From the monkey house came the loud,

First published in *The New Yorker*, June 12, 1948.

insane hooting of some captious primate, filling the whole woodland
with a wild hooroar. As we watched, the sun broke weakly through,
brightened the rich red of the fawns, and kindled their white spots.
Occasionally a sightseer would appear and wander aimlessly by,
but of all who passed none was aware that anything extraordinary
had occurred. "Looka the kangaroos!" a child cried. And he and
his mother stared sullenly at the deer and then walked on.

In a few moments the second twin gathered all his legs and all   3
his ingenuity and arose, to stand for the first time sniffing the
mysteries of a park for captive deer. The doe, in recognition of
his achievement, quit her other work and began to dry him, running
her tongue against the grain and paying particular attention to
the key points. Meanwhile the first fawn tiptoed toward the shallow
brook, in little stops and goes, and started across. He paused mid-
stream to make a slight contribution, as a child does in bathing.
Then, while his mother watched, he continued across, gained the
other side, selected a hiding place, and lay down under a skunk-
cabbage leaf next to the fence, in perfect concealment, his legs
folded neatly under him. Without actually going out of sight, he
had managed to disappear completely in the shifting light and
shade. From somewhere a long way off a twelve-o'clock whistle
sounded. We hung around awhile, but he never budged. Before
we left, we crossed the brook ourself, just outside the fence, knelt,
reached through the wire, and tested the truth of what we had
once heard: that you can scratch a new fawn between the ears
without starting him. You can indeed.

LEWIS THOMAS

Ponds

Large areas of Manhattan are afloat. I remember when the new   1
Bellevue Hospital was being built, fifteen years ago; the first stage
was the most spectacular and satisfying, an enormous square lake.
It was there for the two years, named Lake Bellevue, while the
disconsolate Budget Bureau went looking for cash to build the
next stage. It was fenced about and visible only from the upper
windows of the old hospital, but pretty to look at, cool and blue

Originally published in *The New England Journal of Medicine.* Collected in *The Medusa
and the Snail* (1979).

in midsummer, frozen gleaming as Vermont in January. The fence, like all city fences, was always broken, and we could have gone down to the lake and used it, but it was known to be an upwelling of the East River. At Bellevue there were printed rules about the East River: if anyone fell in, it was an emergency for the Infectious-Disease Service, and the first measures, after resuscitation, were massive doses of whatever antibiotics the hospital pharmacy could provide.

But if you cleaned the East River you could have ponds all over town, up and down the East Side of Manhattan anyway. If you lifted out the Empire State Building and the high structures nearby, you would have, instantly, an inland sea. A few holes bored in the right places would let water into the subways, and you'd have lovely underground canals all across to the Hudson, uptown to the Harlem River, downtown to the Battery, a Venice underground, without pigeons.

It wouldn't work, though, unless you could find a way to keep out the fish. New Yorkers cannot put up with live fish out in the open. I cannot explain this, but it is so.

There is a new pond, much smaller than Lake Bellevue, on First Avenue between Seventieth and Seventy-first, on the east side of the street. It emerged sometime last year, soon after a row of old flats had been torn down and the hole dug for a new apartment building. By now it is about average size for Manhattan, a city block long and about forty feet across, maybe eight feet deep at the center, more or less kidney-shaped, rather like an outsized suburban swimming pool except for the things floating, and now the goldfish.

With the goldfish, it is almost detestable. There are, clearly visible from the sidewalk, hundreds of them. The neighborhood people do not walk by and stare into it through the broken fence, as would be normal for any other Manhattan pond. They tend to cross the street, looking away.

Now there are complaints against the pond, really against the goldfish. How could people do such a thing? Bad enough for pet dogs and cats to be abandoned, but who could be so unfeeling as to abandon goldfish? They must have come down late at night, carrying their bowls, and simply dumped them in. How could they?

The ASPCA[1] was called, and came one afternoon with a rowboat. Nets were used, and fish taken away in new custodial bowls, some to Central Park, others to ASPCA headquarters, to the fish pond.

1. American Society for the Prevention of Cruelty to Animals.

But the goldfish have multiplied, or maybe those people with their bowls keep coming down late at night for their furtive, unfeeling dumping. Anyway, there are too many fish for the ASPCA, for which this seems to be a new kind of problem. An official stated for the press that the owners of the property would be asked to drain the pond by pumping, and then the ASPCA would come back with nets to catch them all.

You'd think they were rats or roaches, the way people began   8
to talk. Get those goldfish out of that pond, I don't care how you do it. Dynamite, if necessary. But get rid of them. Winter is coming, someone said, and it is deep enough so that they'll be swimming around underneath the ice. Get them out.

It is this knowledge of the East River, deep in the minds of all   9
Manhattan residents, more than the goldfish themselves, I think. Goldfish in a glass bowl are harmless to the human mind, maybe even helpful to minds casting about for something, anything, to think about. But goldfish let loose, propagating themselves, worst of all *surviving* in what has to be a sessile eddy of the East River, somehow threaten us all. We do not like to think that life is possible under some conditions, especially the conditions of a Manhattan pond. There are four abandoned tires, any number of broken beer bottles, fourteen shoes and a single sneaker, and a visible layer, all over the surface, of that grayish-green film that settles on all New York surfaces. The mud at the banks of the pond is not proper country mud but reconstituted Manhattan landfill, ancient garbage, fossilized coffee grounds and grapefruit rind, the defecation of a city. For goldfish to be swimming in such water, streaking back and forth mysteriously in small schools, feeding, obviously feeding, looking as healthy and well-off as goldfish in the costliest kind of window-box aquarium, means something is wrong with our standards. It is, in some deep sense beyond words, insulting.

I thought I noticed a peculiar sort of fin on the under-surface   10
of two of the fish. Perhaps, it occurs to me now in a rush of exultation, in such a pond as this, with all its chemical possibilities, there are contained some mutagens, and soon there will be schools of mutant goldfish. Give them just a little more time, I thought. And then, with the most typically Manhattan thought I've ever thought, I thought: The ASPCA will come again, next month, with their rowboat and their nets. The proprietor will begin pumping out the pond. The nets will flail, the rowboat will settle, and then the ASPCA officials will give a sudden shout of great dismay. And with a certain amount of splashing and grayish-greenish spray, at all the edges of the pond, up all the banks of ancient New York landfill mud, crawling on their new little feet, out onto the sidewalks,

up and down and across the street, into doorways and up the fire escapes, some of them with little suckers on their little feet, up the sides of buildings and into open windows, looking for something, will come the goldfish.

It won't last, of course. Nothing like this ever does. The mayor will come and condemn it in person. The Health Department will come and recommend the purchase of cats from out of town because of the constitutional boredom of city cats. The NIH will send up teams of professionals from Washington with a new kind of antifish spray, which will be recalled four days later because of toxicity to cats.   11

After a few weeks it will be finished anyway, like a lot of New York events. The goldfish will dive deep and vanish, the pond will fill up with sneakers, workmen will come and pour concrete over everything, and by next year the new building will be up and occupied by people all unaware of their special environmental impact. But what a time it was.   12

HARRY CREWS

Pages from the Life of a Georgia Innocent

Not very long ago I went with my twelve-year-old boy to a Disney movie, one of those things that show a farm family, poor but God knows honest, out there on the land building character through hunger and hard work. The hunger and hard work seemed to be a hell of a lot of fun. The deprivation was finally so rewarding you could hardly stand it. The farm was full of warm, fuzzy, furry, damp-nosed creatures: bawling calves and braying mules and dogs that were treated like people. There was a little pain here and there but just so much as would teach important lessons to all of us. It sometimes even brought a tear to the eye, but not a real tear because the tear only served to prove that a family out in the middle of nowhere scratching in the earth for survival didn't have it so bad after all. Somebody was forever petting and stroking the plump little animals, crooning to them, as they were raised for strange, unstated reasons, but surely not to be castrated and slaughtered and skinned and eaten. They were, after all, friends.   1

Originally published in *Esquire*, July 1976.

If somebody got sick, he'd just pop into an old, rattling but   2
trustworthy pickup truck and go off to town, where a kindly doctor
would receive him immediately into his office and effect an instant
cure by looking down his throat and asking him to say Ah. No
mention was made of payment.

As my boy and I came out of the movie, blinking in the sunlight,   3
it occurred to me that Disney and others—the folks who bring
you *The Waltons*, say, or *The Little House on the Prairie*—had managed
to sell this strange vision of poverty and country life not only to
suburbanites, while the suburbanites stuffed themselves with malt
balls and popcorn, but also to people in little towns throughout
the South who had proof in their daily lives to the contrary.

All fantasy. Now there is nothing wrong with fantasy. I love it,   4
even live off it at times. But driving home, the reality behind the
fantasy began to go bad on me. It seemed immoral and dangerous
to show so many smiles without an occasional glimpse of the skull
underneath.

As we were going down the driveway, my boy, Byron, said: 5
"That was a great movie, huh, Dad?"

"Yeah," I said. "Great."   6

"I wish I could've lived in a place like that," he said.   7

"No, you don't," I said. "You just think you do."   8

My grandmother in Bacon County, Georgia, raised biddies: tiny   9
cheeping bits of fluff that city folk allow their children to squeeze
to death at Easter. But city children are not the only ones who
love biddies; hawks love them, too. Hawks like to swoop into the
yard and carry off one impaled on their curved talons. Perhaps
my grandmother, in her secret heart, knew that hawks even then
were approaching the time when they would be on the endangered-
species list. Whether she did or not, I'm sure she often felt she
and her kind were already on the list. It would not do.

I'll never forget the first time I saw her get rid of a hawk.   10
Chickens, as everybody knows, are cannibals. Let a biddy get a
spot of blood on it from a scrape or a raw place and the other
biddies will simply eat it alive. My grandmother penned up all
the biddies except the puniest one, already half pecked to death
by the other cute little bits of fluff, and she set it out in the open
yard by itself. First, though, she put arsenic on its head. I—about
five years old and sucking on a sugar-tit—saw the hawk come in
low over the fence, its red tail fanned, talons stretched, and nail
the poisoned biddy where it squatted in the dust. The biddy never
made a sound as it was carried away. My gentle grandmother
watched it all with satisfaction before she let her other biddies out
of the pen.

Another moment from my childhood that comes instantly to 11
mind was about a chicken, too; a rooster. He was boss cock of
the whole farm, a magnificent bird nearly two feet tall. At the
base of a chicken's throat is its craw, a kind of pouch into which
the bird swallows food, as well as such things as grit, bits of rock
and shell. For reasons I don't understand they sometimes become
crawbound. The stuff in the craw does not move; it remains in
the craw and swells and will ultimately cause death. That's what
would have happened to the rooster if the uncle who practically
raised me hadn't said one day: "Son, we got to fix him."

He tied the rooster's feet so we wouldn't be spurred and took 12
out his castrating knife, honed to a razor's edge, and sterilized it
over a little fire. He soaked a piece of fine fishing line and a needle
in alcohol. I held the rooster on its back, a wing in each hand.
With the knife my uncle split open the craw, cleaned it out, then
sewed it up with the fishing line. The rooster screamed and screamed.
But it lived to be cock of the walk again.

Country people never did anything worse to their stock than 13
they sometimes were forced to do to themselves. We had a man
who farmed with us, a man from up north somewhere who had
drifted down into Georgia with no money and a mouth full of
bad teeth. Felix was his name and he was good with a plow and
an ax, a hard worker. Most of the time you hardly knew he was
on the place, he was so quiet and well-mannered. Except when
his teeth began to bother him. And they bothered him more than
a little. He lived in a shedlike little room off the side of the house.
The room didn't have much in it: a ladder-back chair, a kerosine
lamp, a piece of broken glass hanging on the wall over a pan of
water where he shaved as often as once a week, a slat-board bed,
and in one corner a chamber pot—which we called a slop jar—
for use in the middle of the night when nature called. I slept in
a room on the other side of the wall from him. I don't remember
how old I was the night of his terrible toothache, but I do remember
I was still young enough to wear a red cotton gown with five
little pearl buttons down the front my grandmother had made
for me.

When I heard him kick the slop jar, I knew it was his teeth. I 14
just didn't know how bad it was. When the ladder-back chair
splintered, I knew it was a bad hurt, even for Felix. A few times
that night I managed to slip off to sleep only to be jarred awake
when he would run blindly into the thin wall separating us. He
groaned and cursed, not loudly but steadily, sometimes for as long
as half an hour. Ordinarily, my mother would have fixed a hot
poultice for his jaw or at least tried to do *something*, but he was
a proud man and when he was really dying from his teeth, he

preferred to suffer, if not in silence, at least by himself. The whole house was kept awake most of the night by his thrashing and groaning, by the wash pan being knocked off the shelf, by his broken shaving mirror being broken again, and by his blind charges into the wall.

See, our kindly country dentist would not have gotten out of 15 his warm bed for anything less than money. And Felix didn't have any money. Besides, the dentist was in town ten miles away and we didn't have a rattling, trustworthy old truck. The only way we had to travel was two mules. And so there was nothing for Felix to do but what he was doing and it built practically no character at all. Looking back on it now, I can see that it wasn't even human. The sounds coming through the wall sure as hell weren't human anyway. On a Georgia dirt farm, pain reduced everything—man and beast alike—to the lowest common denominator. And it was pretty low and pretty common. Not something you'd want to watch while you ate malt balls and popcorn.

I was huddled under the quilts shaking with dread—my nerves 16 were shot by the age of four and so they have remained—when I heard Felix kick open the door to his room and thump down the wooden steps in his heavy brogan work shoes, which he'd not taken off all night. I couldn't imagine where he was going but I knew I wanted to watch whatever was about to happen. The only thing worse than my nerves is my curiosity, which has always been untempered by pity or compassion, a serious character failing in most societies but a sanity-saving virtue in Georgia when I was a child.

It was February and I went out the front door barefoot onto 17 the frozen ground. I met Felix coming around the corner of the house. In the dim light I could see the craziness in his eyes, the same craziness you see in the eyes of a trapped fox when it has not quite been able to chew through its own leg. Felix headed straight for the well, with me behind him, shaking in my thin cotton gown. He took the bucket from the nail on the rack built over the open wall and sent it shooting down hard as he could to break the inch of ice that was over the water. As he was drawing the bucket up on the pulley, he seemed to see me for the first time.

"What the hell, boy! What the hell!" His voice was as mad as 18 his eyes and he either would not or could not say anything else. He held the bucket and took a mouthful of the freezing water. He held it a long time, spat it out, and filled his mouth again.

He turned the bucket loose and let it fall again into the well 19 instead of hanging it back on the nail where it belonged. With his cheeks swelling with water he took something out of the back pocket of his overalls. As soon as I saw what he had I knew beyond all belief and good sense what he meant to do, and suddenly I was no longer cold but stood on the frozen ground in a hot passion waiting to see him do it, to see if he *could* do it.

He had a piece of croker sack about the size of a half-dollar in [20] his left hand and a pair of wire pliers in his right. He spat the water out and reached way back in his rotten mouth and put the piece of sack over the tooth. He braced his feet against the well and stuck the pliers in over the sackcloth. He took the pliers in both hands and immediately a forked vein leapt in his forehead. The vein in his neck popped big as a pencil. He pulled and twisted and pulled and never made a sound.

It took him a long time and finally as he fought with the pliers [21] and with himself his braced feet slipped so that he was flat on his back when the blood broke from his mouth, followed by the pliers holding a tooth with roots half an inch long. He got slowly to his feet, sweat running off his face, and held the bloody tooth up between us.

He looked at the tooth and said in his old, recognizable voice: [22] *"Huh now, you sumbitch!"*

LOREN EISELEY

The Brown Wasps

There is a corner in the waiting room of one of the great Eastern [1] stations where women never sit. It is always in the shadow and overhung by rows of lockers. It is, however, always frequented— not so much by genuine travelers as by the dying. It is here that a certain element of the abandoned poor seeks a refuge out of the weather, clinging for a few hours longer to the city that has fathered them. In a precisely similar manner I have seen, on a sunny day in midwinter, a few old brown wasps creep slowly over an abandoned wasp nest in a thicket. Numbed and forgetful and frost-blackened, the hum of the spring hive still resounded faintly in their sodden tissues. Then the temperature would fall and they would drop away into the white oblivion of the snow. Here in

First published in *Gentry* (a literary quarterly), Winter 1956–57.

the station it is in no way different save that the city is busy in
its snows. But the old ones cling to their seats as though these
were symbolic and could not be given up. Now and then they
sleep, their gray old heads resting with painful awkwardness on
the backs of the benches.

Also they are not at rest. For an hour they may sleep in the   2
gasping exhaustion of the ill-nourished and aged who have to
walk in the night. Then a policeman comes by on his round and
nudges them upright.

"You can't sleep here," he growls.   3

A strange ritual then begins. An old man is difficult to waken.   4
After a muttered conversation the policeman presses a coin into
his hand and passes fiercely along the benches prodding and ges-
turing toward the door. In his wake, like birds rising and settling
behind the passage of a farmer through a cornfield, the men totter
up, move a few paces and subside once more upon the benches.

One man, after a slight, apologetic lurch, does not move at all.   5
Tubercularly thin, he sleeps on steadily. The policeman does not
look back. To him, too, this has become a ritual. He will not have
to notice it again officially for another hour.

Once in a while one of the sleepers will not awake. Like the   6
brown wasps, he will have had his wish to die in the great droning
center of the hive rather than in some lonely room. It is not so
bad here with the shuffle of footsteps and the knowledge that
there are others who share the bad luck of the world. There are
also the whistles and the sounds of everyone, everyone in the
world, starting on journeys. Amidst so many journeys somebody
is bound to come out all right. Somebody.

Maybe it was on a like thought that the brown wasps fell away   7
from the old paper nest in the thicket. You hold till the last, even
if it is only to a public seat in a railroad station. You want your
place in the hive more than you want a room or a place where
the aged can be eased gently out of the way. It is the place that
matters, the place at the heart of things. It is life that you want,
that bruises your gray old head with the hard chairs; a man has
a right to his place.

But sometimes the place is lost in the years behind us. Or   8
sometimes it is a thing of air, a kind of vaporous distortion above
a heap of rubble. We cling to a time and place because without
them man is lost, not only man but life. This is why the voices,
real or unreal, which speak from the floating trumpets at spiritualist
seances are so unnerving. They are voices out of nowhere whose
only reality lies in their ability to stir the memory of a living person
with some fragment of the past. Before the medium's cabinet both

the dead and the living revolve endlessly about an episode, a place, an event that has already been engulfed by time.

This feeling runs deep in life; it brings stray cats running over 9 endless miles, and birds homing from the ends of the earth. It is as though all living creatures, and particularly the more intelligent, can survive only by fixing or transforming a bit of time into space or by securing a bit of space with its objects immortalized and made permanent in time. For example, I once saw, on a flower pot in my own living room, the efforts of a field mouse to build a remembered field. I have lived to see this episode repeated in a thousand guises, and since I have spent a large portion of my life in the shade of a nonexistent tree, I think I am entitled to speak for the field mouse.

One day as I cut across the field which at that time extended 10 on one side of our suburban shopping center, I found a giant slug feeding from a runnel of pink ice cream in an abandoned Dixie cup. I could see his eyes telescope and protrude in a kind of dim, uncertain ecstasy as his dark body bunched and elongated in the curve of the cup. Then, as I stood there at the edge of the concrete, contemplating the slug, I began to realize it was like standing on a shore where a different type of life creeps up and fumbles tentatively among the rocks and sea wrack. It knows its place and will only creep so far until something changes. Little by little as I stood there I began to see more of this shore that surrounds the place of man. I looked with sudden care and attention at things I had been running over thoughtlessly for years. I even waded out a short way into the grass and the wild-rose thickets to see more. A huge black-belted bee went droning by and there were some indistinct scurryings in the underbrush.

Then I came to a sign which informed me that this field was 11 to be the site of a new Wanamaker suburban store. Thousands of obscure lives were about to perish, the spores of puffballs would go smoking off to new fields, and the bodies of little white-footed mice would be crunched under the inexorable wheels of the bull-dozers. Life disappears or modifies its appearances so fast that everything takes on an aspect of illusion—a momentary fizzing and boiling with smoke rings, like pouring dissident chemicals into a retort. Here man was advancing, but in a few years his plaster and bricks would be disappearing once more into the in-satiable maw of the clover. Being of an archaeological cast of mind, I thought of this fact with an obscure sense of satisfaction and waded back through the rose thickets to the concrete parking lot. As I did so, a mouse scurried ahead of me, frightened of my steps if not of that ominous Wanamaker sign. I saw him vanish

in the general direction of my apartment house, his little body
quivering with fear in the great open sun on the blazing concrete.
Blinded and confused, he was running straight away from his
field. In another week scores would follow him.

I forgot the episode then and went home to the quiet of my   12
living room. It was not until a week later, letting myself into the
apartment, that I realized I had a visitor. I am fond of plants and
had several ferns standing on the floor in pots to avoid the noon
glare by the south window.

As I snapped on the light and glanced carelessly around the   13
room, I saw a little heap of earth on the carpet and a scrabble of
pebbles that had been kicked merrily over the edge of one of the
flower pots. To my astonishment I discovered a full-fledged burrow
delving downward among the fern roots. I waited silently. The
creature who had made the burrow did not appear. I remembered
the wild field then, and the flight of the mice. No house mouse,
no *Mus domesticus,* had kicked up this little heap of earth or sought
refuge under a fern root in a flower pot. I thought of the desperate
little creature I had seen fleeing from the wild-rose thicket. Through
intricacies of pipes and attics, he, or one of his fellows, had climbed
to this high green solitary room. I could visualize what had occurred.
He had an image in his head, a world of seed pods and quiet, of
green sheltering leaves in the dim light among the weed stems.
It was the only world he knew and it was gone.

Somehow in his flight he had found his way to this room with   14
drawn shades where no one would come till nightfall. And here
he had smelled green leaves and run quickly up the flower pot
to dabble his paws in common earth. He had even struggled half
the afternoon to carry his burrow deeper and had failed. I examined
the hole, but no whiskered twitching face appeared. He was gone.
I gathered up the earth and refilled the burrow. I did not expect
to find traces of him again.

Yet for three nights thereafter I came home to the darkened   15
room and my ferns to find the dirt kicked gaily about the rug and
the burrow reopened, though I was never able to catch the field
mouse within it. I dropped a little food about the mouth of the
burrow, but it was never touched. I looked under beds or sat
reading with one ear cocked for rustlings in the ferns. It was all
in vain; I never saw him. Probably he ended in a trap in some
other tenant's room.

But before he disappeared I had come to look hopefully for his   16
evening burrow. About my ferns there had begun to linger the
insubstantial vapor of an autumn field, the distilled essence, as it
were, of a mouse brain in exile from its home. It was a small

dream, like our dreams, carried a long and weary journey along pipes and through spider webs, past holes over which loomed the shadows of waiting cats, and finally, desperately, into this room where he had played in the shuttered daylight for an hour among the green ferns on the floor. Every day these invisible dreams pass us on the street, or rise from beneath our feet, or look out upon us from beneath a bush.

Some years ago the old elevated railway in Philadelphia was   17
torn down and replaced by a subway system. This ancient El with its barnlike stations containing nut-vending machines and scattered food scraps had, for generations, been the favorite feeding ground of flocks of pigeons, generally one flock to a station along the route of the El. Hundreds of pigeons were dependent upon the system. They flapped in and out of its stanchions and steel work or gathered in watchful little audiences about the feet of anyone who rattled the peanut-vending machines. They even watched people who jingled change in their hands, and prospected for food under the feet of the crowds who gathered between trains. Probably very few among the waiting people who tossed a crumb to an eager pigeon realized that this El was like a food-bearing river, and that the life which haunted its banks was dependent upon the running of the trains with their human freight.

I saw the river stop.   18

The time came when the underground tubes were ready; the   19
traffic was transferred to a realm unreachable by pigeons. It was like a great river subsiding suddenly into desert sands. For a day, for two days, pigeons continued to circle over the El or stand close to the red vending machines. They were patient birds, and surely this great river which had flowed through the lives of unnumbered generations was merely suffering from some momentary drought.

They listened for the familiar vibrations that had always heralded   20
an approaching train; they flapped hopefully about the head of an occasional workman walking along the steel runways. They passed from one empty station to another, all the while growing hungrier. Finally they flew away.

I thought I had seen the last of them about the El, but there   21
was a revival and it provided a curious instance of the memory of living things for a way of life or a locality that has long been cherished. Some weeks after the El was abandoned workmen began to tear it down. I went to work every morning by one particular station, and the time came when the demolition crews reached this spot. Acetylene torches showered passersby with sparks, pneumatic drills hammered at the base of the structure, and a blind man who, like the pigeons, had clung with his cup to a

stairway leading to the change booth, was forced to give up his place.

It was then, strangely, momentarily, one morning that I witnessed   22
the return of a little band of the familiar pigeons. I even recognized
one or two members of the flock that had lived around this particular
station before they were dispersed into the streets. They flew bravely
in and out among the sparks and the hammers and the shouting
workmen. They had returned—and they had returned because the
hubbub of the wreckers had convinced them that the river was
about to flow once more. For several hours they flapped in and
out through the empty windows, nodding their heads and watching
the fall of girders with attentive little eyes. By the following morning
the station was reduced to some burned-off stanchions in the
street. My bird friends had gone. It was plain, however, that they
retained a memory for an insubstantial structure now compounded
of air and time. Even the blind man clung to it. Someone had
provided him with a chair, and he sat at the same corner staring
sightlessly at an invisible stairway where, so far as he was concerned,
the crowds were still ascending to the trains.

I have said my life has been passed in the shade of a nonexistent   23
tree, so that such sights do not offend me. Prematurely I am one
of the brown wasps and I often sit with them in the great droning
hive of the station, dreaming sometimes of a certain tree. It was
planted sixty years ago by a boy with a bucket and a toy spade
in a little Nebraska town. That boy was myself. It was a cottonwood
sapling and the boy remembered it because of some words spoken
by his father and because everyone died or moved away who was
supposed to wait and grow old under its shade. The boy was
passed from hand to hand, but the tree for some intangible reason
had taken root in his mind. It was under its branches that he
sheltered; it was from this tree that his memories, which are my
memories, led away into the world.

After sixty years the mood of the brown wasps grows heavier   24
upon one. During a long inward struggle I thought it would do
me good to go and look upon that actual tree. I found a rational
excuse in which to clothe this madness. I purchased a ticket and
at the end of two thousand miles I walked another mile to an
address that was still the same. The house had not been altered.

I came close to the white picket fence and reluctantly, with great   25
effort, looked down the long vista of the yard. There was nothing
there to see. For sixty years that cottonwood had been growing
in my mind. Season by season its seeds had been floating farther
on the hot prairie winds. We had planted it lovingly there, my
father and I, because he had a great hunger for soil and live things

growing, and because none of these things had long been ours to
protect. We had planted the little sapling and watered it faithfully,
and I remembered that I had run out with my small bucket to
drench its roots the day we moved away. And all the years since
it had been growing in my mind, a huge tree that somehow stood
for my father and the love I bore him. I took a grasp on the picket
fence and forced myself to look again.

A boy with the hard bird eye of youth pedaled a tricycle slowly   26
up beside me.

"What'cha lookin' at?" he asked curiously.   27

"A tree," I said.   28

"What for?" he said.   29

"It isn't there," I said, to myself mostly, and began to walk   30
away at a pace just slow enough not to seem to be running.

"What isn't there?" the boy asked. I didn't answer. It was   31
obvious I was attached by a thread to a thing that had never been
there, or certainly not for long. Something that had to be held in
the air, or sustained in the mind, because it was part of my orientation
in the universe and I could not survive without it. There was more
than an animal's attachment to a place. There was something else,
the attachment of the spirit to a grouping of events in time; it
was part of our morality.

So I had come home at last, driven by a memory in the brain   32
as surely as the field mouse who had delved long ago into my
flower pot or the pigeons flying forever amidst the rattle of nut-
vending machines. These, the burrow under the greenery in my
living room and the red-bellied bowls of peanuts now hovering
in midair in the minds of pigeons, were all part of an elusive world
that existed nowhere and yet everywhere. I looked once at the
real world about me while the persistent boy pedaled at my heels.

It was without meaning, though my feet took a remembered   33
path. In sixty years the house and street had rotted out of my
mind. But the tree, the tree that no longer was, that had perished
in its first season, bloomed on in my individual mind, unblemished
as my father's words. "We'll plant a tree here, son, and we're not
going to move any more. And when you're an old, old man you
can sit under it and think how we planted it here, you and me,
together."

I began to outpace the boy on the tricycle.   34

"Do you live here, Mister?" he shouted after me suspiciously.   35
I took a firm grasp on airy nothing—to be precise, on the bole of
a great tree. "I do," I said. I spoke for myself, one field mouse,
and several pigeons. We were all out of touch but somehow permanent. It was the world that had changed.

ANNIE DILLARD

The Fixed

I have just learned to see praying mantis egg cases. Suddenly 1
I see them everywhere; a tan oval of light catches my eye, or I
notice a blob of thickness in a patch of slender weeds. As I write
I can see the one I tied to the mock orange hedge outside my
study window. It is over an inch long and shaped like a bell, or
like the northern hemisphere of an egg cut through its equator.
The full length of one of its long sides is affixed to a twig; the
side that catches the light is perfectly flat. It has a dead straw,
deadweed color, and a curious brittle texture, hard as varnish, but
pitted minutely, like frozen foam. I carried it home this afternoon,
holding it carefully by the twig, along with several others—they
were light as air. I dropped one without missing it until I got
home and made a count.

Within the week I've seen thirty or so of these egg cases in a 2
rose-grown field on Tinker Mountain, and another thirty in weeds
along Carvin's Creek. One was on a twig of tiny dogwood on the
mud lawn of a newly built house. I think the mail-order houses
sell them to gardeners at a dollar apiece. It beats spraying, because
each case contains between one hundred twenty-five to three
hundred fifty eggs. If the eggs survive ants, woodpeckers, and
mice—and most do—then you get the fun of seeing the new
mantises hatch, and the smug feeling of knowing, all summer
long, that they're out there in your garden devouring gruesome
numbers of fellow insects all nice and organically. When a mantis
has crunched up the last shred of its victim, it cleans its smooth
green face like a cat.

In late summer I often see a winged adult stalking the insects 3
that swarm about my porch light. Its body is a clear, warm green;
its naked, triangular head can revolve uncannily, so that I often
see one twist its head to gaze at me as it were over its shoulder.
When it strikes, it jerks so suddenly and with such a fearful clatter
of raised wings, that even a hardened entomologist like J. Henri
Fabre[1] confessed to being startled witless every time.

Excerpted from Chapter 4 of *Pilgrim at Tinker Creek* (1974).
1. Noted French observer of the behavior of insects (1823–1915).

Adult mantises eat more or less everything that breathes and is 4
small enough to capture. They eat honeybees and butterflies, including monarch butterflies. People have actually seen them seize
and devour garter snakes, mice, and even *hummingbirds*. Newly
hatched mantises, on the other hand, eat small creatures like
aphids and each other. When I was in elementary school, one of
the teachers brought in a mantis egg case in a Mason jar. I watched
the newly hatched mantises emerge and shed their skins; they
were spidery and translucent, all over joints. They trailed from
the egg case to the base of the Mason jar in a living bridge that
looked like Arabic calligraphy, some baffling text from the Koran
inscribed down the air by a fine hand. Over a period of several
hours, during which time the teacher never summoned the nerve
or the sense to release them, they ate each other until only two
were left. Tiny legs were still kicking from the mouths of both.
The two survivors grappled and sawed in the Mason jar; finally
both died of injuries. I felt as though I myself should swallow the
corpses, shutting my eyes and washing them down like jagged
pills, so all that life wouldn't be lost.

When mantises hatch in the wild, however, they straggle about 5
prettily, dodging ants, till all are lost in the grass. So it was in
hopes of seeing an eventual hatch that I pocketed my jackknife
this afternoon before I set out to walk. Now that I can see the
egg cases, I'm embarrassed to realize how many I must have missed
all along. I walked east through the Adams' woods to the cornfield,
cutting three undamaged egg cases I found at the edge of the field.
It was a clear, picturesque day, a February day without clouds,
without emotion or spirit, like a beautiful woman with an empty
face. In my fingers I carried the thorny stems from which the egg
cases hung like roses; I switched the bouquet from hand to hand,
warming the free hand in a pocket. Passing the house again,
deciding not to fetch gloves, I walked north to the hill by the
place where the steers come to drink from Tinker Creek. There
in the weeds on the hill I found another eight egg cases. I was
stunned—I cross this hill several times a week, and I always look
for egg cases here, because it was here that I had once seen a
mantis laying her eggs.

It was several years ago that I witnessed this extraordinary pro- 6
cedure, but I remember, and confess, an inescapable feeling that
I was watching something not real and present, but a horrible
nature movie, a "secrets-of-nature" short, beautifully photographed
in full color, that I had to sit through unable to look anywhere
else but at the dimly lighted EXIT signs along the walls, and that
behind the scenes some amateur moviemaker was congratulating

himself on having stumbled across this little wonder, or even on having contrived so natural a setting, as though the whole scene had been shot very carefully in a terrarium in someone's greenhouse.

I was ambling across this hill that day when I noticed a speck ⁊ of pure white. The hill is eroded; the slope is a rutted wreck of red clay broken by grassy hillocks and low wild roses whose roots clasp a pittance of topsoil. I leaned to examine the white thing and saw a mass of bubbles like spittle. Then I saw something dark like an engorged leech rummaging over the spittle, and then I saw the praying mantis.

She was upside-down, clinging to a horizontal stem of wild rose ⁸ by her feet which pointed to heaven. Her head was deep in dried grass. Her abdomen was swollen like a smashed finger; it tapered to a fleshy tip out of which bubbled a wet, whipped froth. I couldn't believe my eyes. I lay on the hill this way and that, my knees in thorns and my cheeks in clay, trying to see as well as I could. I poked near the female's head with a grass; she was clearly undisturbed, so I settled my nose an inch from that pulsing abdomen. It puffed like a concertina, it throbbed like a bellows; it roved, pumping, over the glistening, clabbered surface of the egg case testing and patting, thrusting and smoothing. It seemed to act so independently that I forgot the panting brown stick at the other end. The bubble creature seemed to have two eyes, a frantic little brain, and two busy, soft hands. It looked like a hideous, harried mother slicking up a fat daughter for a beauty pageant, touching her up, slobbering over her, patting and hemming and brushing and stroking.

The male was nowhere in sight. The female had probably eaten ⁹ him. Fabre says that, at least in captivity, the female will mate with and devour up to seven males, whether she has laid her egg cases or not. The mating rites of mantises are well known: a chemical produced in the head of the male insect says, in effect, "No, don't go near her, you fool, she'll eat you alive." At the same time a chemical in his abdomen says, "Yes, by all means, now and forever yes."

While the male is making up what passes for his mind, the ¹⁰ female tips the balance in her favor by eating his head. He mounts her. Fabre describes the mating, which sometimes lasts six hours, as follows: "The male, absorbed in the performance of his vital functions, holds the female in a tight embrace. But the wretch has no head; he has no neck; he has hardly a body. The other, with her muzzle turned over her shoulder continues very placidly to gnaw what remains of the gentle swain. And, all the time, that masculine stump, holding on firmly, goes on with the business!

. . . I have seen it done with my own eyes and have not yet recovered from my astonishment."

I watched the egg-laying for over an hour. When I returned the next day, the mantis was gone. The white foam had hardened and browned to a dirty suds; then, and on subsequent days, I had trouble pinpointing the case, which was only an inch or so off the ground. I checked on it every week all winter long. In the spring the ants discovered it; every week I saw dozens of ants scrambling over the sides, unable to chew a way in. Later in the spring I climbed the hill every day, hoping to catch the hatch. The leaves of the trees had long since unfolded, the butterflies were out, and the robins' first broods were fledged; still the egg case hung silent and full on the stem. I read that I should wait for June, but still I visited the case every day. One morning at the beginning of June everything was gone. I couldn't find the lower thorn in the clump of three to which the egg case was fixed. I couldn't find the clump of three. Tracks ridged the clay, and I saw the lopped stems: somehow my neighbor had contrived to run a tractor-mower over that steep clay hill on which there grew nothing to mow but a few stubby thorns. 11

So. Today from this same hill I cut another three undamaged cases and carried them home with the others by their twigs. I also collected a suspiciously light cynthia moth cocoon. My fingers were stiff and red with cold, and my nose ran. I had forgotten the Law of the Wild, which is, "Carry Kleenex." At home I tied the twigs with their egg cases to various sunny bushes and trees in the yard. They're easy to find because I used white string; at any rate, I'm unlikely to mow my own trees. I hope the woodpeckers that come to the feeder don't find them, but I don't see how they'd get a purchase on them if they did. 12

Night is rising in the valley; the creek has been extinguished for an hour, and now only the naked tips of trees fire tapers into the sky like trails of sparks. The scene that was in the back of my brain all afternoon, obscurely, is beginning to rise from night's lagoon. It really has nothing to do with praying mantises. But this afternoon I threw tiny string lashings and hitches with frozen hands, gingerly, fearing to touch the egg cases even for a minute because I remembered the Polyphemus moth.[2] 13

I have no intention of inflicting all my childhood memories on anyone. Far less do I want to excoriate my old teachers who, in 14

2. Polyphemus, in classical mythology, was a one-eyed giant (a Cyclops) whom the hero Odysseus blinded. (*Odyssey*, Book 9). A Polyphemus moth has a large eyespot on each hind wing.

their bungling, unforgettable way, exposed me to the natural world, a world covered in chitin, where implacable realities hold sway. The Polyphemus moth never made it to the past; it crawls in that crowded, pellucid pool at the lip of the great waterfall. It is as present as this blue desk and brazen lamp, as this blackened window before me in which I can no longer see even the white string that binds the egg case to the hedge, but only my own pale, astonished face.

Once, when I was ten or eleven years old, my friend Judy   15
brought in a Polyphemus moth cocoon. It was January; there were doily snowflakes taped to the schoolroom panes. The teacher kept the cocoon in her desk all morning and brought it out when we were getting restless before recess. In a book we found what the adult moth would look like; it would be beautiful. With a wingspread of up to six inches, the Polyphemus is one of the few huge American silk moths, much larger than, say, a giant or tiger swallowtail butterfly. The moth's enormous wings are velveted in a rich, warm brown, and edged in bands of blue and pink delicate as a watercolor wash. A startling "eyespot," immense, and deep blue melding to an almost translucent yellow, luxuriates in the center of each hind wing. The effect is one of a masculine splendor foreign to the butterflies, a fragility unfurled to strength. The Polyphemus moth in the picture looked like a mighty wraith, a beating essence of the hardwood forest, alien-skinned and brown, with spread, blind eyes. This was the giant moth packed in the faded cocoon. We closed the book and turned to the cocoon. It was an oak leaf sewn into a plump oval bundle; Judy had found it loose in a pile of frozen leaves.

We passed the cocoon around; it was heavy. As we held it in   16
our hands, the creature within warmed and squirmed. We were delighted, and wrapped it tighter in our fists. The pupa began to jerk violently, in heart-stopping knocks. Who's there? I can still feel those thumps, urgent through a muffling of spun silk and leaf, urgent through the swaddling of many years, against the curve of my palm. We kept passing it around. When it came to me again it was hot as a bun; it jumped half out of my hand. The teacher intervened. She put it, still heaving and banging, in the ubiquitous Mason jar.

It was coming. There was no stopping it now, January or not.   17
One end of the cocoon dampened and gradually frayed in a furious battle. The whole cocoon twisted and slapped around in the bottom of the jar. The teacher fades, the classmates fade, I fade: I don't remember anything but that thing's struggle to be a moth or die trying. It emerged at last, a sodden crumple. It was a male; his long antennae were thickly plumed, as wide as his fat abdomen.

His body was very thick, over an inch long, and deeply furred. A gray, furlike plush covered his head; a long, tan furlike hair hung from his wide thorax over his brown-furred, segmented abdomen. His multijointed legs, pale and powerful, were shaggy as a bear's. He stood still, but he breathed.

He couldn't spread his wings. There was no room. The chemical that coated his wings like varnish, stiffening them permanently, dried, and hardened his wings as they were. He was a monster in a Mason jar. Those huge wings stuck on his back in a torture of random pleats and folds, wrinkled as a dirty tissue, rigid as leather. They made a single nightmare clump still wracked with useless, frantic convulsions. [18]

The next thing I remember, it was recess. The school was in Shadyside, a busy residential part of Pittsburgh. Everyone was playing dodgeball in the fenced playground or racing around the concrete schoolyard by the swings. Next to the playground a long delivery drive sloped downhill to the sidewalk and street. Someone— it must have been the teacher—had let the moth out. I was standing in the driveway, alone, stock-still, but shivering. Someone had given the Polyphemus moth his freedom, and he was walking away. [19]

He heaved himself down the asphalt driveway by infinite degrees, unwavering. His hideous crumpled wings lay glued and rucked on his back, perfectly still now, like a collapsed tent. The bell rang twice; I had to go. The moth was receding down the driveway, dragging on. I went; I ran inside. The Polyphemus moth is still crawling down the driveway, crawling down the driveway hunched, crawling down the driveway on six furred feet, forever. [20]

JOSÉ DONOSO

Paseo

I

This happened when I was very young, when my father and Aunt Mathilda, his maiden sister, and my uncles Gustav and Armand were still living. Now they are all dead. Or I should say, I prefer to think they are all dead: it is too late now for the questions they did not ask when the moment was right, because events seemed to freeze all of them into silence. Later they were able to construct [1]

First published in English in *TriQuarterly*, 1969. In Spanish, *paseo* means "a walk, a stroll, a promenade."

a wall of forgetfulness or indifference to shut out everything, so that they would not have to harass themselves with impotent conjecture. But then, it may not have been that way at all. My imagination and my memory may be deceiving me. After all, I was only a child then, with whom they did not have to share the anguish of their inquiries, if they made any, nor the result of their discussions.

What was I to think? At times I used to hear them closeted in the library, speaking softly, slowly, as was their custom. But the massive door screened the meaning of their words, permitting me to hear only the grave and measured counterpoint of their voices. What was it they were saying? I used to hope that, inside there, abandoning the coldness which isolated each of them, they were at last speaking of what was truly important. But I had so little faith in this that, while I hung around the walls of the vestibule near the library door, my mind became filled with the certainty that they had chosen to forget, that they were meeting only to discuss, as always, some case in jurisprudence relating to their specialty in maritime law. Now I think that perhaps they were right in wanting to blot out everything. For why should one live with the terror of having to acknowledge that the streets of a city can swallow up a human being, leaving him without life and without death, suspended as it were, in a dimension more dangerous than any dimension with a name?

One day, months after, I came upon my father watching the street from the balcony of the drawing room on the second floor. The sky was close, dense, and the humid air weighed down the large, limp leaves of the ailanthus trees. I drew near my father, eager for an answer that would contain some explanation.

"What are you doing here, Papa?" I murmured.

When he answered, something closed over the despair on his ⁵ face, like the blow of a shutter closing on a shameful scene.

"Don't you see? I'm smoking . . ." he replied.

And he lit a cigarette.

It wasn't true. I knew why he was peering up and down the street, his eyes darkened, lifting his hand from time to time to stroke his smooth chestnut whiskers: it was in hope of seeing them reappear, returning under the trees of the sidewalk, the white bitch trotting at heel.

Little by little I began to realize that not only my father but all of them, hiding from one another and without confessing even to themselves what they were doing, haunted the windows of the house. If someone happened to look up from the sidewalk he would surely have seen the shadow of one or another of them posted beside a curtain, or faces aged with grief spying out from behind the window panes.

In those days the street was paved with quebracho wood, and under the ailanthus trees a clangorous streetcar used to pass from time to time. The last time I was there neither the wooden pavements nor the streetcars existed any longer. But our house was still standing, narrow and vertical like a little book pressed between the bulky volumes of new buildings, with shops on the ground level and a crude sign advertising knitted undershirts covering the balconies of the second floor.

When we lived there all the houses were tall and slender like our own. The block was always happy with the games of children playing in the patches of sunshine on the sidewalks, and with the gossip of the servant girls on their way back from shopping. But our house was not happy. I say it that way, "it was not happy" instead of "it was sad," because that is exactly what I mean to say. The word "sad" would be wrong because it has too definite a connotation, a weight and a dimension of its own. What took place in our house was exactly the opposite: an absence, a lack, which because it was unacknowledged was irremediable, something that, if it weighed, weighed by not existing.

My mother died when I was only four years old, so the presence of a woman was deemed necessary for my care. As Aunt Mathilda was the only woman in the family and she lived with my uncles Armand and Gustav, the three of them came to live at our house, which was spacious and empty.

Aunt Mathilda discharged her duties towards me with that propriety which was characteristic of everything she did. I did not doubt that she loved me, but I could never feel it as a palpable experience uniting us. There was something rigid in her affections, as there was in those of the men of the family. With them, love existed confined inside each individual, never breaking its boundaries to express itself and bring them together. For them to show affection was to discharge their duties to each other perfectly, and above all not to inconvenience, never to inconvenience. Perhaps to express love in any other way was unnecessary for them now, since they had so long a history together, had shared so long a past. Perhaps the tenderness they felt in the past had been expressed to the point of satiation and found itself stylized now in the form of certain actions, useful symbols which did not require further elucidation. Respect was the only form of contact left between those four isolated individuals who walked the corridors of the house which, like a book, showed only its narrow spine to the street.

I, naturally, had no history in common with Aunt Mathilda.

How could I, if I was no more than a child then who could not understand the gloomy motivations of his elders? I wished that their confined feeling might overflow and express itself in a fit of rage, for example, or with some bit of foolery. But she could not guess this desire of mine because her attention was not focused on me: I was a person peripheral to her life, never central. And I was not central because the entire center of her being was filled up with my father and my uncles. Aunt Mathilda was born the only woman, an ugly woman moreover, in a family of handsome men, and on realizing that for her marriage was unlikely, she dedicated herself to looking out for the comfort of those three men, by keeping house for them, by taking care of their clothes and providing their favorite dishes. She did these things without the least servility, proud of her role because she did not question her brothers' excellence. Furthermore, like all women, she possessed in the highest degree the faith that physical well-being is, if not principal, certainly primary, and that to be neither hungry nor cold nor uncomfortable is the basis for whatever else is good. Not that these defects caused her grief, but rather they made her impatient, and when she saw affliction about her she took immediate steps to remedy what, without doubt, were errors in a world that should be, that had to be, perfect. On another plane, she was intolerant of shirts which were not stupendously well-ironed, of meat that was not of the finest quality, of the humidity that owing to someone's carelessness had crept into the cigar-box.

After dinner, following what must have been an ancient ritual in the family, Aunt Mathilda went upstairs to the bedrooms, and in each of her brothers' rooms she prepared the beds for sleeping, parting the sheets with her bony hands. She spread a shawl at the foot of the bed for that one, who was subject to chills, and placed a feather pillow at the head of this one, for he usually read before going to sleep. Then, leaving the lamps lighted beside those enormous beds, she came downstairs to the billiard room to join the men for coffee and for a few rounds, before, as if bewitched by her, they retired to fill the empty effigies of the pajamas she had arranged so carefully upon the white, half-opened sheets.

But Aunt Mathilda never opened my bed. Each night, when I went up to my room, my heart thumped in the hope of finding my bed opened with the recognizable dexterity of her hands. But I had to adjust myself to the less pure style of the servant girl who was charged with doing it. Aunt Mathilda never granted me that mark of importance because I was not her brother. And not to be "one of my brothers" seemed to her a misfortune of which

many people were victims, almost all in fact, including me, who
after all was only the son of one of them.

Sometimes Aunt Mathilda asked me to visit her in her room
where she sat sewing by the tall window, and she would talk to
me. I listened attentively. She spoke to me about her brothers'
integrity as lawyers in the intricate field of maritime law, and she
extended to me her enthusiasm for their wealth and reputation,
which I would carry forward. She described the embargo on a
shipment of oranges, told of certain damages caused by miserable
tugboats manned by drunkards, of the disastrous effects that arose
from the demurrage of a ship sailing under an exotic flag. But
when she talked to me of ships her words did not evoke the
hoarse sounds of ships' sirens that I heard in the distance on
summer nights when, kept awake by the heat, I climbed to the
attic, and from an open window watched the far-off floating lights,
and those blocks of darkness surrounding the city that lay forever
out of reach for me because my life was, and would ever be,
ordered perfectly. I realize now that Aunt Mathilda did not hint
at this magic because she did not know of it. It had no place in
her life, as it had no place in the life of anyone destined to die
with dignity in order afterward to be installed in a comfortable
heaven, a heaven identical to our house. Mute, I listened to her
words, my gaze fastened on the white thread that, as she stretched
it against her black blouse, seemed to capture all of the light from
the window. I exulted at the world of security that her words
projected for me, that magnificent straight road which leads to a
death that is not dreaded since it is exactly like this life, without
anything fortuitous or unexpected. Because death was not terrible.
Death was the final incision, clean and definitive, nothing more.
Hell existed, of course, but not for us. It was rather for chastising
the other inhabitants of the city and those anonymous seamen
who caused the damages that, when the cases were concluded,
filled the family coffers.

Aunt Mathilda was so removed from the idea of fear that, since
I now know that love and fear go hand in hand, I am tempted
to think that in those days she did not love anyone. But I may
be mistaken. In her rigid way she may have been attached to her
brothers by a kind of love. At night, after supper, they gathered
in the billiard room for a few games. I used to go in with them.
Standing outside that circle of imprisoned affections, I watched
for a sign that would show me the ties between them did exist,
and did, in fact, bind. It is strange that my memory does not bring
back anything but shades of indeterminate grays in remembering

the house, but when I evoke that hour, the strident green of the
table, the red and white of the balls and the little cube of blue
chalk become inflamed in my memory, illumined by the low lamp
whose shade banished everything else into dusk. In one of the
family's many rituals, the voice of Aunt Mathilda rescued each of
the brothers by turn from the darkness, so that they might make
their plays.

"Now, Gustav . . ."

And when he leaned over the green table, cue in hand, Uncle   20
Gustav's face was lit up, brittle as paper, its nobility contradicted
by his eyes, which were too small and spaced too close together.
Finished playing, he returned to the shadow, where he lit a cigar
whose smoke rose lazily until it was dissolved in the gloom of
the ceiling. Then his sister said: "All right, Armand . . ."

And the soft, timid face of Uncle Armand, with his large sky-
blue eyes concealed by gold-rimmed glasses, bent down underneath
the light. His game was generally bad because he was "the baby,"
as Aunt Mathilda sometimes referred to him. After the comments
aroused by his play he took refuge behind his newspaper and
Aunt Mathilda said: "Pedro, your turn . . ."

I held my breath when I saw him lean over to play, held it
even more tightly when I saw him succumb to his sister's command.
I prayed, as he got up, that he would rebel against the order
established by his sister's voice. I could not see that this order was
in itself a kind of rebellion, constructed by them as a protection
against chaos, so that they might not be touched by what can be
neither explained nor resolved. My father, then, leaned over the
green cloth, his practiced eye gauging the exact distance and positions
of the billiards. He made his play, and making it, he exhaled in
such a way that his mustache stirred about his half-opened mouth.
Then he handed me his cue so I might chalk it with the blue cube.
With this minimal role that he assigned to me, he let me touch
the circle that united him with the others, without letting me take
part in it more than tangentially.

Now it was Aunt Mathilda's turn. She was the best player. When
I saw her face, composed as if from the defects of her brothers'
faces, coming out of the shadow, I knew that she was going to
win. And yet . . . had I not seen her small eyes light up that face
so like a brutally clenched fist, when by chance one of them
succeeded in beating her? That spark appeared because, although
she might have wished it, she would never have permitted herself
to let any of them win. That would be to introduce the mysterious
element of love into a game that ought not to include it, because

affection should remain in its place, without trespassing on the strict reality of a carom shot.

II

I never did like dogs. One may have frightened me when I was very young, I don't know, but they have always displeased me. As there were no dogs at home and I went out very little, few occasions presented themselves to make me uncomfortable. For my aunt and uncles and for my father, dogs, like all the rest of the animal kingdom, did not exist. Cows, of course, supplied the cream for the dessert that was served in a silver dish on Sundays. Then there were the birds that chirped quite agreeably at twilight in the branches of the elm tree, the only inhabitant of the small garden at the rear of the house. But animals for them existed only in the proportion in which they contributed to the pleasure of human beings. Which is to say that dogs, lazy as city dogs are, could not even dent their imagination with a possibility of their existence.

Sometimes, on Sunday, Aunt Mathilda and I used to go to Mass early to take communion. It was rare that I succeeded in concentrating on the sacrament, because the idea that she was watching me without looking generally occupied the first place of my conscious mind. Even when her eyes were directed to the altar, or her head bowed before the Blessed Sacrament, my every movement drew her attention to it. And on leaving the church she told me with sly reproach that it was without doubt a flea trapped in the pews that prevented me from meditating, as she had suggested, that death is the good foreseen end, and from praying that it might not be painful, since that was the purpose of masses, novenas and communions.

This was such a morning. A fine drizzle was threatening to turn into a storm, and the quebracho pavements extended their shiny fans, notched with streetcar rails, from sidewalk to sidewalk. As I was cold and in a hurry to get home I stepped up the pace beside Aunt Mathilda, who was holding her black mushroom of an umbrella above our heads. There were not many people in the street since it was so early. A dark-complexioned gentleman saluted us without lifting his hat, because of the rain. My aunt was in the process of telling me how surprised she was that someone of mixed blood had bowed to her with so little show of attention, when suddenly, near where we were walking, a streetcar applied its brakes with a screech, making her interrupt her monologue. The conductor looked out through his window:

"Stupid dog!" he shouted.

We stopped to watch.

A small white bitch escaped from between the wheels of the streetcar and, limping painfully, with her tail between her legs, took refuge in a doorway as the streetcar moved on again.

"These dogs," protested Aunt Mathilda. "It's beyond me how   30
they are allowed to go around like that."

Continuing on our way, we passed by the bitch huddled in the corner of a doorway. It was small and white, with legs which were too short for its size and an ugly pointed snout that proclaimed an entire genealogy of misalliances: the sum of unevenly matched breeds which for generations had been scouring the city, searching for food in the garbage cans and among the refuse of the port. She was drenched, weak, trembling with cold or fever. When we passed in front of her I noticed that my aunt looked at the bitch, and the bitch's eyes returned her gaze.

We continued on our way home. Several steps further I was on the point of forgetting the dog when my aunt surprised me by abruptly turning around and crying out: "Psst! Go away!"

She had turned in such absolute certainty of finding the bitch following us that I trembled with the mute question which arose from my surprise: How did she know? She couldn't have heard her, since she was following us at an appreciable distance. But she did not doubt it. Perhaps the look that had passed between them of which I saw only the mechanics—the bitch's head raised slightly toward Aunt Mathilda, Aunt Mathilda's slightly inclined toward the bitch—contained some secret commitment? I do not know. In any case, turning to drive away the dog, her peremptory "psst" had the sound of something like a last effort to repel an encroaching destiny. It is possible that I am saying all this in the light of things that happened later, that my imagination is embellishing with significance what was only trivial. However, I can say with certainty that in that moment I felt a strangeness, almost a fear of my aunt's sudden loss of dignity in condescending to turn around and confer rank on a sick and filthy bitch.

We arrived home. We went up the stairs and the bitch stayed down below, looking up at us from the torrential rain that had just been unleashed. We went inside, and the delectable process of breakfast following communion removed the white bitch from my mind. I have never felt our house so protective as that morning, never rejoiced so much in the security derived from those old walls that marked off my world.

In one of my wanderings in and out of the empty sitting rooms,   35
I pulled back the curtain of a window to see if the rain promised

to let up. The storm continued. And, sitting at the foot of the stairs still scrutinizing the house, I saw the white bitch. I dropped the curtain so that I might not see her there, soaked through and looking like one spellbound. Then, from the dark outer rim of the room, Aunt Mathilda's low voice surprised me. Bent over to strike a match to the kindling wood already arranged in the fireplace, she asked: "Is it still there?"

"What?"

I knew what.

"The white bitch . . ."

I answered yes, that it was.

III

It must have been the last storm of the winter, because I remember   40 quite clearly that the following days opened up and the nights began to grow warmer.

The white bitch stayed posted on our doorstep scrutinizing our windows. In the mornings, when I left for school, I tried to shoo her away, but barely had I boarded the bus when I would see her reappear around the corner or from behind the mailbox. The servant girls also tried to frighten her away, but their attempts were as fruitless as mine, because the bitch never failed to return.

Once, we were all saying goodnight at the foot of the stairs before going up to bed. Uncle Gustav had just turned off the lights, all except the one on the stairway, so that the large space of the vestibule had become peopled with the shadowy bodies of furniture. Aunt Mathilda, who was entreating Uncle Armand to open the window of his room so a little air could come in, suddenly stopped speaking, leaving her sentence unfinished, and the movements of all of us, who had started to go up, halted.

"What is the matter?" asked Father, stepping down one stair.

"Go on up," murmured Aunt Mathilda, turning around and gazing into the shadow of the vestibule.

But we did not go up.   45

The silence of the room was filled with the sweet voice of each object: a grain of dirt trickling down between the wallpaper and the wall, the creaking of polished woods, the quivering of some loose crystal. Someone, in addition to ourselves, was where we were. A small white form came out of the darkness near the service door. The bitch crossed the vestibule, limping slowly in the direction of Aunt Mathilda, and without even looking at her, threw herself down at her feet.

It was as though the immobility of the dog enabled us to move again. My father came down two stairs. Uncle Gustav turned on the light. Uncle Armand went upstairs and shut himself in his room.

"What is this?" asked my father.

Aunt Mathilda remained still.

"How could she have come in?" she asked aloud.   50

Her question seemed to acknowledge the heroism implicit in having either jumped walls in that lamentable condition, or come into the basement through a broken pane of glass, or fooled the servants' vigilance by creeping through a casually opened door.

"Mathilda, call one of the girls to take her away," said my father, and went upstairs followed by Uncle Gustav.

We were left alone looking at the bitch. She called a servant, telling the girl to give her something to eat and the next day to call a veterinarian.

"Is she going to stay in the house?" I asked.

"How can she walk in the street like that?" murmured Aunt   55
Mathilda. "She has to get better so we can throw her out. And she'd better get well soon because I don't want animals in the house."

Then she added: "Go upstairs to bed."

She followed the girl who was carrying the dog out.

I sensed that ancient drive of Aunt Mathilda's to have everything go well about her, that energy and dexterity which made her sovereign of immediate things. Is it possible that she was so secure within her limitations that for her the only necessity was to overcome imperfections, errors not of intention or motive, but of condition? If so, the white bitch was going to get well. She would see to it because the animal had entered the radius of her power. The veterinarian would bandage the broken leg under her watchful eye, and protected by rubber gloves and an apron, she herself would take charge of cleaning the bitch's pustules with disinfectant that would make her howl. But Aunt Mathilda would remain deaf to those howls, sure that whatever she was doing was for the best.

And so it was. The bitch stayed in the house. Not that I saw her, but I could feel the presence of any stranger there, even though confined to the lower reaches of the basement. Once or twice I saw Aunt Mathilda with the rubber gloves on her hands, carrying a vial full of red liquid. I found a plate with scraps of food in a passage of the basement where I went to look for the bicycle I had just been given. Weakly, buffered by walls and floors, at times the suspicion of a bark reached my ears.

One afternoon I went down to the kitchen. The bitch came in,   60
painted like a clown with red disinfectant. The servants threw her out without paying her any mind. But I saw that she was not

hobbling any longer, that her tail, limp before, was curled up like a feather, leaving her shameless bottom in plain view.

That afternoon I asked Aunt Mathilda: "When are you going to throw her out?"

"Who?" she asked.

She knew perfectly well.

"The white bitch."

"She's not well yet," she replied.

Later I thought of insisting, of telling her that surely there was nothing now to prevent her from climbing the garbage cans in search of food. I didn't do it because I believe it was the same night that Aunt Mathilda, after losing the first round of billiards, decided that she did not feel like playing another. Her brothers went on playing, and she, ensconced in the leather sofa, made a mistake in calling their names. There was a moment of confusion. Then the thread of order was quickly picked up again by the men, who knew how to ignore an accident if it was not favorable to them. But I had already seen.

It was as if Aunt Mathilda were not there at all. She was breathing at my side as she always did. The deep, silencing carpet yielded under her feet as usual and her tranquilly crossed hands weighed on her skirt. How is it possible to feel with the certainty I felt then the absence of a person whose heart is somewhere else? The following nights were equally troubled by the invisible slur of her absence. She seemed to have lost all interest in the game and left off calling her brothers by their names. They appeared not to notice it. But they must have, because their games became shorter and I noticed an infinitesimal increase in the deference with which they treated her.

One night, as we were going out of the dining room, the bitch appeared in the doorway and joined the family group. The men paused before they went into the library so that their sister might lead the way to the billiard room, followed this time by the white bitch. They made no comment, as if they had not seen her, beginning their game as they did every night.

The bitch sat down at Aunt Mathilda's feet. She was very quiet. Her lively eyes examined the room and followed the players' strategies as if all of that amused her greatly. She was fat now and had a shiny coat. Her whole body, from her quivering snout to her tail ready to waggle, was full of an abundant capacity for fun. How long had she stayed in the house? A month? Perhaps more. But in that month Aunt Mathilda had forced her to get well, caring for her not with displays of affection but with those hands of hers which could not refrain from mending what was broken.

The leg was well. She had disinfected, fed and bathed her, and
now the white bitch was whole.

In one of his plays Uncle Armand let the cube of blue chalk   70
fall to the floor. Immediately, obeying an instinct that seemed to
surge up from her picaresque past, the bitch ran toward the chalk
and snatched it with her mouth away from Uncle Armand, who
had bent over to pick it up. Then followed something surprising:
Aunt Mathilda, as if suddenly unwound, burst into a peal of
laughter that agitated her whole body. We remained frozen. On
hearing her laugh, the bitch dropped the chalk, ran towards her
with tail waggling aloft, and jumped up onto her lap. Aunt Mathilda's
laugh relented, but Uncle Armand left the room. Uncle Gustav
and my father went on with the game: now it was more important
than ever not to see, not to see anything at all, not to comment,
not to consider oneself alluded to by these events.

I did not find Aunt Mathilda's laugh amusing, because I may
have felt the dark thing that had stirred it up. The bitch grew calm
sitting on her lap. The cracking noises of the balls when they hit
seemed to conduct Aunt Mathilda's hand first from its place on
the edge of the sofa, to her skirt, and then to the curved back of
the sleeping animal. On seeing that expressionless hand reposing
there, I noticed that the tension which had kept my aunt's features
clenched before, relented, and that a certain peace was now softening
her face. I could not resist. I drew closer to her on the sofa, as if
to a newly kindled fire. I hoped that she would reach out to me
with a look or include me with a smile. But she did not.

IV

When I arrived from school in the afternoon, I used to go directly
to the back of the house and, mounting my bicycle, take turn after
turn around the narrow garden, circling the pair of cast-iron benches
and the elm tree. Behind the wall, the chestnut trees were beginning
to display their light spring down, but the seasons did not interest
me, for I had too many serious things to think about. And since
I knew that no one came down into the garden until the suffocation
of midsummer made it imperative, it seemed to be the best place
for meditating about what was going on inside the house.

One might have said that nothing was going on. But how could
I remain calm in the face of the entwining relationship which had
sprung up between my aunt and the white bitch? It was as if Aunt
Mathilda, after having resigned herself to an odd life of service
and duty, had found at last her equal. And as women-friends do,
they carried on a life full of niceties and pleasing refinements.
They ate bonbons that came in boxes wrapped frivolously with
ribbons. My aunt arranged tangerines, pineapples and grapes in

tall crystal bowls, while the bitch watched her as if on the point of criticizing her taste or offering a suggestion.

Often when I passed the door of her room, I heard a peal of laughter like the one which had overturned the order of her former life that night. Or I heard her engage in a dialogue with an interlocutor whose voice I did not hear. It was a new life. The bitch, the guilty one, slept in a hamper near her bed, an elegant, feminine hamper, ridiculous to my way of thinking, and followed her everywhere except into the dining room. Entrance there was forbidden her, but waiting for her friend to come out again, she followed her to the billiard room and sat at her side on the sofa or on her lap, exchanging with her from time to time complicitory glances.

How was it possible? I used to ask myself: why had she waited   75
until now to go beyond herself and establish a dialogue? At times she appeared insecure about the bitch, fearful that, in the same way she had arrived one fine day, she might also go, leaving her with all this new abundance weighing on her hands. Or did she still fear for her health? These ideas, which now seem to clear, floated blurred in my imagination while I listened to the gravel of the path crunching under the wheels of my bicycle. What was not blurred, however, was my vehement desire to become gravely ill, to see if I might also succeed in harvesting some kind of relationship. Because the bitch's illness had been the cause of everything. If it had not been for that, my aunt might have never joined in league with her. But I had a constitution of iron, and furthermore it was clear that Aunt Mathilda's heart did not have room for more than one love at a time.

My father and my uncles did not seem to notice any change. The bitch was very quiet and, abandoning her street ways, seemed to acquire manners more worthy of Aunt Mathilda. But still, she had somehow preserved all the sauciness of a female of the streets. It was clear that the hardships of her life had not been able to cloud either her good humor or her taste for adventure which, I felt, lay dangerously dormant inside her. For the men of the house it proved easier to accept her than to throw her out, since this would have forced them to revise their cannons of security.

One night, when the pitcher of lemonade had already made its appearance on the console table of the library, cooling that corner of the shadow, and the windows had been thrown open to the air, my father halted abruptly at the doorway of the billiard room.

"What is that?" he exclaimed, looking at the floor.

The three men stopped in consternation to look at a small, round pool on the waxed floor.

"Mathilda!" called Uncle Gustav.   80

She went to look and then reddened with shame. The bitch

had taken refuge under the billiard table in the adjoining room. Walking over to the table my father saw her there, and changing direction sharply, he left the room, followed by his brothers.

Aunt Mathilda went upstairs. The bitch followed her. I stayed in the library with a glass of lemonade in my hand, and looked out at the summer sky, listening to some far-off siren from the sea, and to the murmur of the city stretched out under the stars. Soon I heard Aunt Mathilda coming down. She appeared with her hat on and with her keys chinking in her hand.

"Go up and go to bed," she said. "I'm going to take her for a walk on the street so that she can do her business."

Then she added something strange: "It's such a lovely night." And she went out.   85

From that night on, instead of going up after dinner to open her brothers' beds, she went to her room, put her hat tightly on her head and came downstairs again, chinking her keys. She went out with the bitch without explaining anything to anyone. And my uncles and my father and I stayed behind in the billiard room, and later we sat on the benches of the garden, with all the murmuring of the elm tree and the clearness of the sky weighing down on us. These nocturnal walks of Aunt Mathilda's were never spoken of by her brothers. They never showed any awareness of the change that had occurred inside our house.

In the beginning Aunt Mathilda was gone at the most for twenty minutes or half an hour, returning to take whatever refreshment there was and to exchange some trivial commentary. Later, her sorties were inexplicably prolonged. We began to realize, or I did at least, that she was no longer a woman taking her dog out for hygienic reasons: outside there, in the streets of the city, something was drawing her. When waiting, my father furtively eyed his pocket watch, and if the delay was very great Uncle Gustav went up to the second floor pretending he had forgotten something there, to spy for her from the balcony. But still they did not speak. Once, when Aunt Mathilda stayed out too long, my father paced back and forth along the path that wound between the hydrangeas. Uncle Gustav threw away a cigar which he could not light to his satisfaction, then another, crushing it with the heel of his shoe. Uncle Armand spilled a cup of coffee. I watched them, hoping that at long last they would explode, that they would finally say something to fill the minutes that were passing by one after another, getting longer and longer and longer without the presence of Aunt Mathilda. It was twelve-thirty when she arrived.

"Why are you all waiting up for me?" she asked, smiling.

She was holding her hat in her hand, and her hair, ordinarily

so well-groomed, was mussed. I saw that a streak of mud was
soiling her shoes.

"What happened to you?" asked Uncle Armand.   90

"Nothing," came her reply, and with it she shut off any right
of her brothers to meddle in those unknown hours that were now
her life. I say they were her life because, during the minutes she
stayed with us before going up to her room with the bitch, I
perceived an animation in her eyes, an excited restlessness like
that in the eyes of the animal: it was as though they had been
washed in scenes to which even our imagination lacked access. •
Those two were accomplices. The night protected them. They belonged to the murmuring sound of the city, to the sirens of the
ships which, crossing the dark or illuminated streets, the houses
and factories and parks, reached my ears.

Her walks with the bitch continued for some time. Now we said
good night immediately after dinner, and each one went up to
shut himself in his room, my father, Uncle Gustav, Uncle Armand
and I. But no one went to sleep before she came in, late, sometimes
terribly late, when the light of dawn was already striking the top
of our elm. Only after hearing her close the door of her bedroom
did the pacing with which my father measured his room cease,
or was the window in one of his brothers' rooms finally closed
to exclude that fragment of the night which was no longer dangerous.

Once I heard her come up very late, and as I thought I heard
her singing softly, I opened my door and peeked out. When she
passed my room, with the white bitch nestled in her arms, her
face seemed to me surprisingly young and unblemished, even
though it was dirty, and I saw a rip in her skirt. I went to bed
terrified, knowing this was the end.

I was not mistaken. Because one night, shortly after, Aunt Mathilda took the dog out for a walk after dinner, and did not return.

We stayed awake all night, each one in his room, and she did   95
not come back. No one said anything the next day. They went—
I presume—to their office, and I went to school. She wasn't home
when we came back and we sat silently at our meal that night.
I wonder if they found out something definite that very first day.
But I think not, because we all, without seeming to, haunted the
windows of the house, peering into the street.

"Your aunt went on a trip," the cook answered me when I
finally dared to ask, if only her.

But I knew it was not true.

Life continued in the house just as if Aunt Mathilda were still
living there. It is true that they used to gather in the library for
hours and hours, and closeted there they may have planned ways

of retrieving her out of that night which had swallowed her.
Several times a visitor came who was clearly not of our world, a
plainclothesman perhaps, or the head of a stevedore's union come
to pick up indemnification for some accident. Sometimes their
voices rose a little, sometimes there was a deadened quiet, sometimes
their voices became hard, sharp, as they fenced with the voice I
did not know. But the library door was too thick, too heavy for
me to hear what they were saying.

Translated by Lorraine O'Grady Freeman

WILLIAM FAULKNER

The Bear

He was ten. But it had already begun, long before that day when   1
at last he wrote his age in two figures and he saw for the first
time the camp where his father and Major de Spain and old
General Compson and the others spent two weeks each November
and two weeks again each June. He had already inherited then,
without ever having seen it, the tremendous bear with one trap-
ruined foot which, in an area almost a hundred miles deep, had
earned for itself a name, a definite designation like a living man.

He had listened to it for years: the long legend of corncribs
rifled, of shotes and grown pigs and even calves carried bodily
into the woods and devoured, of traps and deadfalls overthrown
and dogs mangled and slain, and shotgun and even rifle charges
delivered at point-blank range and with no more effect than so
many peas blown through a tube by a boy—a corridor of wreckage
and destruction beginning back before he was born, through which
sped, not fast but rather with the ruthless and irresistible deliberation
of a locomotive, the shaggy tremendous shape.

It ran in his knowledge before he ever saw it. It looked and
towered in his dreams before he even saw the unaxed woods
where it left its crooked print, shaggy, huge, red-eyed, not malevolent
but just big—too big for the dogs which tried to bay it, for the
horses which tried to ride it down, for the men and the bullets
they fired into it, too big for the very country which was its
constricting scope. He seemed to see it entire with a child's complete
divination before he ever laid eyes on either—the doomed wilderness

First published in *The Saturday Evening Post*, May 9, 1942.

whose edges were being constantly and punily gnawed at by men with axes and plows who feared it because it was wilderness, men myriad and nameless even to one another in the land where the old bear had earned a name, through which ran not even a mortal animal but an anachronism, indomitable and invincible, out of an old dead time, a phantom, epitome and apotheosis of the old wild life at which the puny humans swarmed and hacked in a fury of abhorrence and fear, like pygmies about the ankles of a drowsing elephant; the old bear solitary, indomitable and alone, widowered, childless and absolved of mortality—old Priam reft of his old wife and having outlived all his sons.[1]

Until he was ten, each November he would watch the wagon containing the dogs and the bedding and food and guns and his father and Tennie's Jim, the Negro, and Sam Fathers, the Indian, son of a slave woman and a Chickasaw chief, depart on the road to town, to Jefferson, where Major de Spain and the others would join them. To the boy, at seven and eight and nine, they were not going into the Big Bottom to hunt bear and deer, but to keep yearly rendezvous with the bear which they did not even intend to kill. Two weeks later they would return, with no trophy, no head and skin. He had not expected it. He had not even been afraid it would be in the wagon. He believed that even after he was ten and his father would let him go too, for those two November weeks, he would merely make another one, along with his father and Major de Spain and General Compson and the others, the dogs which feared to bay it and the rifles and shotguns which failed even to bleed it, in the yearly pageant of the old bear's furious immortality.

Then he heard the dogs. It was in the second week of his first   5
time in the camp. He stood with Sam Fathers against a big oak beside the faint crossing where they had stood each dawn for nine days now, hearing the dogs. He had heard them once before, one morning last week—a murmur, sourceless, echoing through the wet woods, swelling presently into separate voices which he could recognize and call by name. He had raised and cocked the gun as Sam told him and stood motionless again while the uproar, the invisible course, swept up and past and faded; it seemed to him that he could actually see the deer, the buck, blond, smoke-colored, elongated with speed, fleeing, vanishing, the woods, the gray solitude, still ringing even when the cries of the dogs had died away.

1. In Greek mythology, Priam was the King of Troy during the Trojan War. He was husband to Hecuba and father of fifty children—all of whom were killed in the course of the war. Priam was killed when Troy fell to the Greeks.

"Now let the hammers down," Sam said.

"You knew they were not coming here too," he said.

"Yes," Sam said. "I want you to learn how to do when you didn't shoot. It's after the chance for the bear or the deer has done already come and gone that men and dogs get killed."

"Anyway," he said, "it was just a deer."

Then on the tenth morning he heard the dogs again. And he readied the too-long, too-heavy gun as Sam had taught him, before Sam even spoke. But this time it was no deer, no ringing chorus of dogs running strong on a free scent, but a moiling yapping an octave too high, with something more than indecision and even abjectness in it, not even moving very fast, taking a long time to pass completely out of hearing, leaving even then somewhere in the air that echo, thin, slightly hysterical, abject, almost grieving, with no sense of a fleeing, unseen, smoke-colored, grass-eating shape ahead of it, and Sam, who had taught him first of all to cock the gun and take position where he could see everywhere and then never move again, had himself moved up beside him; he could hear Sam breathing at his shoulder and he could see the arched curve of the old man's inhaling nostrils.

"Hah," Sam said. "Not even running. Walking."

"Old Ben!" the boy said. "But up here!" he cried. "Way up here!"

"He do it every year," Sam said. "Once. Maybe to see who in camp this time, if he can shoot or not. Whether we got the dog yet that can bay and hold him. He'll take them to the river, then he'll send them back home. We may as well go back, too; see how they look when they come back to camp."

When they reached the camp the hounds were already there, ten of them crouching back under the kitchen, the boy and Sam squatting to peer back into the obscurity where they huddled, quiet, the eyes luminous, glowing at them and vanishing, and no sound, only that effluvium of something more than dog, stronger than dog and not just animal, just beast, because still there had been nothing in front of that abject and almost painful yapping save the solitude, the wilderness, so that when the eleventh hound came in at noon and with all the others watching—even old Uncle Ash, who called himself first a cook—Sam daubed the tattered ear and the raked shoulder with turpentine and axle grease, to the boy it was still no living creature, but the wilderness which, leaning for the moment down, had patted lightly once the hound's temerity.

"Just like a man," Sam said. "Just like folks. Put off as long as she could having to be brave, knowing all the time that sooner or later she would have to be brave once to keep on living with herself, and knowing all the time beforehand what was going to happen to her when she done it."

That afternoon, himself on the one-eyed wagon mule which did not mind the smell of blood nor, as they told him, of bear, and with Sam on the other one, they rode for more than three hours through the rapid, shortening winter day. They followed no path, no trail even that he could see; almost at once they were in a country which he had never seen before. Then he knew why Sam had made him ride the mule which would not spook. The sound one stopped short and tried to whirl and bolt even as Sam got down, blowing its breath, jerking and wrenching at the rein while Sam held it, coaxing it forward with his voice, since he could not risk tying it, drawing it forward while the boy got down from the marred one.

Then, standing beside Sam in the gloom of the dying afternoon, he looked down at the rotted overturned log, gutted and scored with claw marks and, in the wet earth beside it, the print of the enormous warped two-toed foot. He knew now what he had smelled when he peered under the kitchen where the dogs huddled. He realized for the first time that the bear which had run in his listening and loomed in his dreams since before he could remember to the contrary, and which, therefore, must have existed in the listening and dreams of his father and Major de Spain and even old General Compson, too, before they began to remember in their turn, was a mortal animal, and that if they had departed for the camp each November without any actual hope of bringing its trophy back, it was not because it could not be slain, but because so far they had had no actual hope to.

"Tomorrow," he said.

"We'll try tomorrow," Sam said. "We ain't got the dog yet."

"We've got eleven. They ran him this morning."   20

"It won't need but one," Sam said. "He ain't here. Maybe he ain't nowhere. The only other way will be for him to run by accident over somebody that has a gun."

"That wouldn't be me," the boy said. "It will be Walter or Major or—"

"It might," Sam said. "You watch close in the morning. Because he's smart. That's how come he has lived this long. If he gets hemmed up and has to pick out somebody to run over, he will pick out you."

"How?" the boy said. "How will he know—" He ceased. "You mean he already knows me, that I ain't never been here before, ain't had time to find out yet whether I—" He ceased again,

looking at Sam, the old man whose face revealed nothing until
it smiled. He said humbly, not even amazed, "It was me he was
watching. I don't reckon he did need to come but once."

The next morning they left the camp three hours before daylight.   25
They rode this time because it was too far to walk, even the dogs
in the wagon; again the first gray light found him in a place which
he had never seen before, where Sam had placed him and told
him to stay and then departed. With the gun which was too big
for him, which did not even belong to him, but to Major de Spain,
and which he had fired only once—at a stump on the first day,
to learn the recoil and how to reload it—he stood against a gum
tree beside a little bayou whose black still water crept without
movement out of a cane-brake and crossed a small clearing and
into cane again, where, invisible, a bird—the big woodpecker
called Lord-to-God by Negroes—clattered at a dead limb.

It was a stand like any other, dissimilar only in incidentals to
the one where he had stood each morning for ten days; a territory
new to him, yet no less familiar than that other one which, after
almost two weeks, he had come to believe he knew a little—the
same solitude, the same loneliness through which human beings
had merely passed without altering it, leaving no mark, no scar,
which looked exactly as it must have looked when the first ancestor
of Sam Fathers' Chickasaw predecessors crept into it and looked
about, club or stone ax or bone arrow drawn and poised; different
only because, squatting at the edge of the kitchen, he smelled the
hounds huddled and cringing beneath it and saw the raked ear
and shoulder of the one who, Sam said, had had to be brave once
in order to live with herself, and saw yesterday in the earth beside
the gutted log the print of the living foot.

He heard no dogs at all. He never did hear them. He only heard
the drumming of the woodpecker stop short off and knew that
the bear was looking at him. He never saw it. He did not know
whether it was in front of him or behind him. He did not move,
holding the useless gun, which he had not even had warning to
cock and which even now he did not cock, tasting in his saliva
that taint as of brass which he knew now because he had smelled
it when he peered under the kitchen at the huddled dogs.

Then it was gone. As abruptly as it had ceased, the woodpecker's
dry, monotonous clatter set up again, and after a while he even
believed he could hear the dogs—a murmur, scarce a sound even,
which he had probably been hearing for some time before he even
remarked it, drifting into hearing and then out again, dying away.
They came nowhere near him. If it was a bear they ran, it was
another bear. It was Sam himself who came out of the cane and

crossed the bayou, followed by the injured bitch of yesterday. She
was almost at heel, like a bird dog, making no sound. She came
and crouched against his leg, trembling, staring off into the cane.
   "I didn't see him," he said. "I didn't, Sam!"
   "I know it," Sam said. "He done the looking. You didn't hear   30
him neither, did you?"
   "No," the boy said. "I—"
   "He's smart," Sam said. "Too smart." He looked down at the
hound, trembling faintly and steadily against the boy's knee. From
the raked shoulder a few drops of fresh blood oozed and clung.
"Too big. We ain't got the dog yet. But maybe someday. Maybe
not next time. But someday."

   So I must see him, he thought. *I must look at him.* Otherwise, it
seemed to him that it would go on like this forever, as it had gone
on with his father and Major de Spain, who was older than his
father, and even with old General Compson, who had been old
enough to be a brigade commander in 1865. Otherwise, it would
go on so forever, next time and next time, after and after and
after. It seemed to him that he could see the two of them, himself
and the bear, shadowy in the limbo from which time emerged,
becoming time; the old bear absolved of mortality and himself
partaking, sharing a little of it, enough of it. And he knew now
what he had smelled in the huddled dogs and tasted in his saliva.
He recognized fear. *So I will have to see him,* he thought, without
dread or even hope. *I will have to look at him.*
   It was in June of the next year. He was eleven. They were in
camp again, celebrating Major de Spain's and General Compson's
birthdays. Although the one had been born in September and the
other in the depth of winter and in another decade, they had met
for two weeks to fish and shoot squirrels and turkey and run
coons and wildcats with the dogs at night. That is, he and Boon
Hoggenbeck and the Negroes fished and shot squirrels and ran
the coons and cats, because the proved hunters, not only Major
de Spain and old General Compson, who spent those two weeks
sitting in a rocking chair before a tremendous iron pot of Brunswick
stew, stirring and tasting, with old Ash to quarrel with about how
he was making it and Tennie's Jim to pour whisky from the
demijohn into the tin dipper from which he drank it, but even
the boy's father and Walter Ewell, who were still young enough,
scorned such, other than shooting the wild gobblers with pistols
for wagers on their marksmanship.
   Or, that is, his father and the others believed he was hunting   35
squirrels. Until the third day he thought that Sam Fathers believed

that too. Each morning he would leave the camp right after breakfast. He had his own gun now, a Christmas present. He went back to the tree beside the little bayou where he had stood that morning. Using the compass which old General Compson had given him, he ranged from that point; he was teaching himself to be a better-than-fair woodsman without knowing he was doing it. On the second day he even found the gutted log where he had first seen the crooked print. It was almost completely crumbled now, healing with unbelievable speed, a passionate and almost visible relinquishment, back into the earth from which the tree had grown.

He ranged the summer woods now, green with gloom; if anything, actually dimmer than in November's gray dissolution, where, even at noon, the sun fell only in intermittent dappling upon the earth, which never completely dried out and which crawled with snakes— moccasins and water snakes and rattlers, themselves the color of the dappled gloom, so that he would not always see them until they moved, returning later and later, first day, second day, passing in the twilight of the third evening the little log pen enclosing the log stable where Sam was putting up the horses for the night.

"You ain't looked right yet," Sam said.

He stopped. For a moment he didn't answer. Then he said peacefully, in a peaceful rushing burst as when a boy's miniature dam in a little brook gives way, "All right. But how? I went to the bayou. I even found that log again. I—"

"I reckon that was all right. Likely he's been watching you. You never saw his foot?"

"I," the boy said—"I didn't—I never thought—"   40

"It's the gun," Sam said. He stood beside the fence, motionless— the old man, the Indian, in the battered faded overalls and the frayed five-cent straw hat which in the Negro's race had been the badge of his enslavement and was now the regalia of his freedom. The camp—the clearing, the house, the barn and its tiny lot with which Major de Spain in his turn had scratched punily and evanescently at the wilderness—faded in the dusk, back into the immemorial darkness of the woods. *The gun,* the boy thought. *The gun.*

"Be scared," Sam said. "You can't help that. But don't be afraid. Ain't nothing in the woods going to hurt you unless you corner it, or it smells that you are afraid. A bear or a deer, too, has got to be scared of a coward the same as a brave man has got to be."

The gun, the boy thought.

"You will have to choose," Sam said.

He left the camp before daylight, long before Uncle Ash would   45
wake in his quilts on the kitchen floor and start the fire for breakfast.

He had only the compass and a stick for snakes. He could go
almost a mile before he would begin to need the compass. He sat
on a log, the invisible compass in his invisible hand, while the
secret night sounds, fallen still at his movements, scurried again
and then ceased for good, and the owls ceased and gave over to
the waking of day birds, and he could see the compass. Then he
went fast yet still quietly; he was becoming better and better as
a woodsman, still without having yet realized it.

He jumped a doe and a fawn at sunrise, walked them out of
the bed, close enough to see them—the crash of undergrowth, the
white scut, the fawn scudding behind her faster than he had
believed it could run. He was hunting right, upwind, as Sam had
taught him; not that it mattered now. He had left the gun; of his
own will and relinquishment he had accepted not a gambit, not
a choice, but a condition in which not only the bear's heretofore
inviolable anonymity but all the old rules and balances of hunter
and hunted had been abrogated. He would not even be afraid,
not even in the moment when the fear would take him completely—
blood, skin, bowels, bones, memory from the long time before it
became his memory—all save that thin, clear, quenchless, immortal
lucidity which alone differed him from this bear and from all the
other bear and deer he would ever kill in the humility and pride
of his skill and endurance, to which Sam had spoken when he
leaned in the twilight on the lot fence yesterday.

By noon he was far beyond the little bayou, farther into the
new and alien country than he had ever been. He was traveling
now not only by the compass but by the old, heavy, biscuit-thick
silver watch which had belonged to his grandfather. When he
stopped at last, it was for the first time since he had risen from
the log at dawn when he could see the compass. It was far enough.
He had left the camp nine hours ago; nine hours from now, dark
would have already been an hour old. But he didn't think that.
He thought, *All right. Yes. But what?* and stood for a moment,
alien and small in the green and topless solitude, answering his
own question before it had formed and ceased. It was the watch,
the compass, the stick—the three lifeless mechanicals with which
for nine hours he had fended the wilderness off; he hung the
watch and compass carefully on a bush and leaned the stick beside
them and relinquished completely to it.

He had not been going very fast for the last two or three hours.
He went no faster now, since distance would not matter even if
he could have gone fast. And he was trying to keep a bearing on
the tree where he had left the compass, trying to complete a circle
which would bring him back to it or at least intersect itself, since

direction would not matter now either. But the tree was not there,
and he did as Sam had schooled him—made the next circle in
the opposite direction, so that the two patterns would bisect somewhere, but crossing no print of his own feet, finding the tree at
last, but in the wrong place—no bush, no compass, no watch—
and the tree not even the tree, because there was a down log
beside it and he did what Sam Fathers had told him was the next
thing and the last.

As he sat down on the log he saw the crooked print—the
warped, tremendous, two-toed indentation which, even as he
watched it, filled with water. As he looked up, the wilderness
coalesced, solidified—the glade, the tree he sought, the bush, the
watch and the compass glinting where a ray of sunlight touched
them. Then he saw the bear. It did not emerge, appear; it was
just there, immobile, solid, fixed in the hot dappling of the green
and windless noon, not as big as he had dreamed it, but as big
as he had expected it, bigger, dimensionless against the dappled
obscurity, looking at him where he sat quietly on the log and
looked back at it.

Then it moved. It made no sound. It did not hurry. It crossed   50
the glade, walking for an instant into the full glare of the sun;
when it reached the other side it stopped again and looked back
at him across one shoulder while his quiet breathing inhaled and
exhaled three times.

Then it was gone. It didn't walk into the woods, the undergrowth.
It faded, sank back into the wilderness as he had watched a fish,
a huge old bass, sink and vanish back into the dark depths of its
pool without even any movement of its fins.

He thought, *It will be next fall.* But it was not next fall, nor the
next nor the next. He was fourteen then. He had killed his buck,
and Sam Fathers had marked his face with the hot blood, and in
the next year he killed a bear. But even before that accolade he
had become as competent in the woods as many grown men with
the same experience; by his fourteenth year he was a better woodsman than most grown men with more. There was no territory
within thirty miles of the camp that he did not know—bayou,
ridge, brake, landmark tree and path. He could have led anyone
to any point in it without deviation, and brought them out again.
He knew game trails that even Sam Fathers did not know; in his
thirteenth year he found a buck's bedding place, and unbeknown
to his father he borrowed Walter Ewell's rifle and lay in wait at
dawn and killed the buck when it walked back to the bed, as
Sam had told him how the old Chickasaw fathers did.

But not the old bear, although by now he knew its footprint

better than he did his own, and not only the crooked one. He could see any one of the three sound ones and distinguish it from any other, and not only by its size. There were other bears within those thirty miles which left tracks almost as large, but this was more than that. If Sam Fathers had been his mentor and the back-yard rabbits and squirrels at home his kindergarten, then the wilderness the old bear ran was his college, the old male bear itself, so long unwifed and childless as to have become its own ungendered progenitor, was his alma mater. But he never saw it.

He could find the crooked print now almost whenever he liked, fifteen or ten or five miles, or sometimes nearer the camp than that. Twice while on stand during the three years he heard the dogs strike its trail by accident; on the second time they jumped it seemingly, the voices high, abject, almost human in hysteria, as on that first morning two years ago. But not the bear itself. He would remember that noon three years ago, the glade, himself and the bear fixed during that moment in the windless and dappled blaze, and it would seem to him that it had never happened, that he had dreamed that too. But it had happened. They had looked at each other, they had emerged from the wilderness old as earth, synchronized to that instant by something more than the blood that moved the flesh and bones which bore them, and touched, pledged something, affirmed something more lasting than the frail web of bones and flesh which any accident could obliterate.

Then he saw it again. Because of the very fact that he thought of nothing else, he had forgotten to look for it. He was still-hunting with Walter Ewell's rifle. He saw it cross the end of a long blowdown, a corridor where a tornado had swept, rushing through rather than over the tangle of trunks and branches as a locomotive would have, faster than he had ever believed it could move, almost as fast as a deer even, because a deer would have spent most of that time in the air, faster than he could bring the rifle sights up to it, so that he believed the reason he never let off the shot was that he was still behind it, had never caught up with it. And now he knew what had been wrong during all the three years. He sat on a log, shaking and trembling as if he had never seen the woods before nor anything that ran them, wondering with incredulous amazement how he could have forgotten the very thing which Sam Fathers had told him and which the bear itself had proved the next day and had now returned after three years to reaffirm.

And he now knew what Sam Fathers had meant about the right dog, a dog in which size would mean less than nothing. So when he returned alone in April—school was out then, so that the sons of farmers could help with the land's planting, and at last his father had granted him permission, on his promise to be back in

four days—he had the dog. It was his own, a mongrel of the sort
called by Negroes a fyce, a ratter, itself not much bigger than a
rat and possessing that bravery which had long since stopped being
courage and had become foolhardiness.

It did not take four days. Alone again, he found the trail on
the first morning. It was not a stalk; it was an ambush. He timed
the meeting almost as if it were an appointment with a human
being. Himself holding the fyce muffled in a feed sack and Sam
Fathers with two of the hounds on a piece of plowline rope, they
lay down wind of the trail at dawn of the second morning. They
were so close that the bear turned without even running, as if in
surprised amazement at the shrill and frantic uproar of the released
fyce, turning at bay against the trunk of a tree, on its hind feet;
it seemed to the boy that it would never stop rising, taller and
taller, and even the two hounds seemed to take a sort of desperate
and despairing courage from the fyce, following it as it went in.

Then he realized that the fyce was actually not going to stop.
He flung, threw the gun away, and ran; when he overtook and
grasped the frantically pinwheeling little dog, it seemed to him
that he was directly under the bear.

He could smell it, strong and hot and rank. Sprawling, he looked
up to where it loomed and towered over him like a cloudburst
and colored like a thunderclap, quite familiar, peacefully and even
lucidly familiar, until he remembered: This was the way he had
used to dream about it. Then it was gone. He didn't see it go. He
knelt, holding the frantic fyce with both hands, hearing the abased
wailing of the hounds drawing farther and farther away, until Sam
came up. He carried the gun. He laid it down quietly beside the
boy and stood looking down at him.

"You've done seed him twice now with a gun in your hands,"   60
he said. "This time you couldn't have missed him."

The boy rose. He still held the fyce. Even in his arms and clear
of the ground, it yapped frantically, straining and surging after the
fading uproar of the two hounds like a tangle of wire springs. He
was panting a little, but he was neither shaking nor trembling
now.

"Neither could you!" he said. "You had the gun! Neither did
you!"

"And you didn't shoot," his father said. "How close were you?"
"I don't know, sir," he said. "There was a big wood tick inside
his right hind leg. I saw that. But I didn't have the gun then."

"But you didn't shoot when you had the gun," his father said.   65
"Why?"

But he didn't answer, and his father didn't wait for him to, rising and crossing the room, across the pelt of the bear which the boy had killed two years ago and the larger one which his father had killed before he was born, to the bookcase beneath the mounted head of the boy's first buck. It was the room which his father called the office, from which all the plantation business was transacted; in it for the fourteen years of his life he had heard the best of all talking. Major de Spain would be there and sometimes old General Compson, and Walter Ewell and Boon Hoggenbeck and Sam Fathers and Tennie's Jim, too, because they, too, were hunters, knew the woods and what ran them.

He would hear it, not talking himself but listening—the wilderness, the big woods, bigger and older than any recorded document of white man fatuous enough to believe he had bought any fragment of it or Indian ruthless enough to pretend that any fragment of it had been his to convey. It was of the men, not white nor black nor red, but men, hunters with the will and hardihood to endure and the humility and skill to survive, and the dogs and the bear and deer juxtaposed and reliefed against it, ordered and compelled by and within the wilderness in the ancient and unremitting contest by the ancient and immitigable rules which voided all regrets and brooked no quarter, the voices quiet and weighty and deliberate for retrospection and recollection and exact remembering, while he squatted in the blazing firelight as Tennie's Jim squatted, who stirred only to put more wood on the fire and to pass the bottle from one glass to another. Because the bottle was always present, so that after a while it seemed to him that those fierce instants of heart and brain and courage and wiliness and speed were concentrated and distilled into that brown liquor which not women, not boys and children, but only hunters drank, drinking not of the blood they had spilled but some condensation of the wild immortal spirit, drinking it moderately, humbly even, not with the pagan's base hope of acquiring thereby the virtues of cunning and strength and speed, but in salute to them.

His father returned with the book and sat down again and opened it. "Listen," he said. He read the five stanzas aloud, his voice quiet and deliberate in the room where there was no fire now because it was already spring. Then he looked up. The boy watched him. "All right," his father said. "Listen." He read again, but only the second stanza this time, to the end of it, the last two lines, and closed the book and put it on the table beside him. " 'She cannot fade, though thou hast not thy bliss, for ever wilt thou love, and she be fair,' " he said.

"He's talking about a girl," the boy said.

"He had to talk about something," his father said. Then he said,   70
"He was talking about truth. Truth doesn't change. Truth is one
thing. It covers all things which touch the heart—honor and pride
and pity and justice and courage and love. Do you see now?"

He didn't know. Somehow it was simpler than that. There was
an old bear, fierce and ruthless, not merely just to stay alive, but
with the fierce pride of liberty and freedom, proud enough of that
liberty and freedom to see it threatened without fear or even alarm;
nay, who at times even seemed deliberately to put that freedom
and liberty in jeopardy in order to savor them, to remind his old
strong bones and flesh to keep supple and quick to defend and
preserve them. There was an old man, son of a Negro slave and
an Indian king, inheritor on the one side of the long chronicle of
a people who had learned humility through suffering, and pride
through the endurance which survived the suffering and injustice,
and on the other side, the chronicle of a people even longer in
the land than the first, yet who no longer existed in the land at
all save in the solitary brotherhood of an old Negro's alien blood
and the wild and invincible spirit of an old bear. There was a boy
who wished to learn humility and pride in order to become skillful
and worthy in the woods, who suddenly found himself becoming
so skillful so rapidly that he feared he would never become worthy
because he had not learned humility and pride, although he had
tried to, until one day and as suddenly he discovered that an old
man who could not have defined either had led him, as though
by the hand, to that point where an old bear and a little mongrel
dog showed him that, by possessing one thing other, he would
possess them both.

And a little dog, nameless and mongrel and many-fathered,
grown, yet weighing less than six pounds, saying as if to itself, "I
can't be dangerous, because there's nothing much smaller than I
am; I can't be fierce, because they would call it just noise; I can't
be humble, because I'm already too close to the ground to genuflect;
I can't be proud, because I wouldn't be near enough to it for
anyone to know who was casting that shadow, and I don't even
know that I'm not going to heaven, because they have already
decided that I don't possess an immortal soul. So all I can be is
brave. But it's all right. I can be that, even if they still call it just
noise."

That was all. It was simple, much simpler than somebody talking
in a book about a youth and a girl he would never need to grieve
over, because he could never approach any nearer her and would
never have to get any farther away. He had heard about a bear,
and finally got big enough to trail it, and he trailed it four years

and at last met it with a gun in his hands and he didn't shoot. Because a little dog— But he could have shot long before the little dog covered the twenty yards to where the bear waited, and Sam Fathers could have shot at any time during that interminable minute while Old Ben stood on his hind feet over them. He stopped. His father was watching him gravely across the spring-rife twilight of the room; when he spoke, his words were as quiet as the twilight, too, not loud, because they did not need to be because they would last, "Courage, and honor, and pride," his father said, "and pity, and love of justice and of liberty. They all touch the heart, and what the heart holds to becomes truth, as far as we know truth. Do you see now?"

Sam, and Old Ben, and Nip, he thought. And himself too. He had been all right too. His father had said so. "Yes, sir," he said.

Thinking About Nature and Civilization

Asking whether humans live in nature or in civilization is in some ways like asking whether they walk on their left feet or on their right. Since Darwin's time, we have become accustomed to viewing ourselves as trousered apes, bundles of animal instincts over which civilization has cast a thin veneer. On the other hand, we realize what an enormous barrier of self-consciousness and acculturation this thin veneer becomes when we try to find the "natural" self beneath. As Brigid Brophy says, "there is no such thing as a natural man. We are a species that doesn't occur wild." The question is not whether we belong to nature or civilization, but how we can deal with our dual citizenship and maintain a sane balance.

The problem must be nearly as old as our species, but as life has become more urban, more regulated, more a thing of clocks and concrete, the clash between nature and civilization has consumed more of our attention. The Industrial Revolution was spreading factories across the English countryside and converting London into a feverish commercial center when William Wordsworth wrote one of his most memorable poems:

> The world is too much with us, late and soon,
> Getting and spending, we lay waste our powers
> Little we see in Nature that is ours;
> We have given our hearts away, a sordid boon!
> The Sea that bares her bosom to the moon,
> The winds that will be blowing at all hours,
> And are up-gathered now like sleeping flowers,
> For this, for everything, we are out of tune;
> It moves us not—Great God! I'd rather be
> A Pagan suckled on a creed outworn;
> So might I, standing on this pleasant lee,
> Have glimpses that would make me less forlorn;
> Have sight of Proteus rising from the sea;
> And hear old Triton blow his wreathéd horn.

Wordsworth's call for communion with nature, tightly laced into the sonnet form and adorned with classical allusions, distills a tension between the natural and the synthetic, the spontaneous and the planned. Every selection in Nature and Civilization reflects the same sort of tension and draws from it energy, insight, or humor.

Dogs, as Edward Hoagland points out, are one of the few links left between the city dweller and nature, so they get a great deal of attention here. Besides the many dogs in Hoagland's own essay, there are clever ones in Konrad Lorenz's essay on animal intelligence, a brave one in William Faulkner's "The Bear," a neurotic one in Sheila Burnford's "Pas Devant le Chien," and a mysterious one in José Donoso's "Paseo."

The essays by Hoagland, Lorenz, Burnford, and Loren Eiseley—remarkably diverse as they are in tone—all share a sort of binocular vision: one eye is on animal nature, one on human, and the result is a clearer definition of both. Brigid Brophy, Lewis Thomas, and E.B. White all look at humans in their unnatural habitat: the city. Harry Crews and William Faulkner take us out of civilized life for a time, to be disenchanted or uplifted. Annie Dillard explores the regions where nature and civilization intertwine: the field where praying mantis eggs are swept up by the mower, the city school where children pass a cocoon from hand to hand till it comes prematurely to life and death.

QUESTIONS

1. Think about times when you lived for a while (perhaps on vacation) closer to or further from nature than you presently do. How did you react to the situation? How do your reactions compare with those of Brophy, for instance, to city life or Crews to country life?

2. If you could design a way of life that best balances nature and civilization, what would it be?

3. From your personal observation, how "human" can the thinking of animals be? Or, to put it another way, how much of an animal's perception of the world can we understand by analogy to our own perceptions?

4. Where, if anywhere, would you draw the line between the human experience of life and an animal's experience? What are the consequences of drawing this line? Is your line the same as Lorenz's? Brophy's? Burnford's? Faulkner's?

5. Where in popular culture, in the classroom, or in everyday life do you find the balance between nature and civilization gone awry? Has it drifted toward a blind worship of nature, or toward an indifference to it? Where do you find nature and civilization well balanced?

6. Where have you got an especially strong sense of civilization's encroachment on nature or nature's counterattack on civilization?

7. Wordsworth (and a great many of his contemporaries) clearly believed that nature had a healing power for the human spirit. Brigid Brophy thinks this notion is "one of the great parroted, meaningless (but slightly paranoid) untruths of our age." With whom do you agree?

PROGRESS

THOMAS BABINGTON MACAULAY

Francis Bacon

The chief peculiarity of Bacon's philosophy seems to us to have 1
been this, that it aimed at things altogether different from those
which his predecessors had proposed to themselves. This was his
own opinion. "Finis scientiarum," says he, "a nemine adhuc bene
positus est."[1] ... The more carefully his works are examined, the
more clearly, we think, it will appear that this is the real clue to
his whole system, and that he used means different from those
used by other philosophers, because he wished to arrive at an end
altogether different from theirs.

What then was the end which Bacon proposed to himself? It 2
was, to use his own emphatic expression, "fruit." It was the mul-
tiplying of human enjoyments and the mitigating of human sufferings. It was "the relief of man's estate." It was "commodis
humanis inservire."[2] It was "efficaciter operari ad sublevanda vitæ
humanæ incommoda."[3] It was "dotare vitam humanam novis
inventis et copiis."[4] It was "genus humanum novis operibus et
potestatibus continuo dotare."[5] This was the object of all his speculations in every department of science, in natural philosophy, in
legislation, in politics, in morals.

Two words form the key of the Baconian doctrine, Utility and 3
Progress. The ancient philosophy disdained to be useful, and was
content to be stationary. It dealt largely in theories of moral perfection, which were so sublime that they never could be more
than theorists; in attempts to solve insoluble enigmas; in exhortations
to the attainment of unattainable frames of mind. It could not
condescend to the humble office of ministering to the comfort of
human beings. All the schools contemned that office as degrading;
some censured it as immoral. Once indeed Posidonius, a distinguished writer of the age of Cicero and Cæsar, so far forgot himself
as to enumerate, among the humbler blessings which mankind
owed to philosophy, the discovery of the principle of the arch,

Excerpted from an essay first published in *The Edinburgh Review*, July, 1837. Francis
Bacon (1561–1626) was a lawyer, courtier, statesman, philosopher, and masterful
writer in both Latin and English.
1. "Until now, no one has properly established the purpose of the sciences."
2. "to contribute to human comforts"
3. "to work effectually to remove the discomforts of human life"
4. "to enrich human life with inventions and goods"
5. "constantly to offer new works and powers to mankind"

and the introduction of the use of metals. This eulogy was considered as an affront, and was taken up with proper spirit. Seneca vehemently disclaims these insulting compliments. Philosophy, according to him, has nothing to do with teaching men to rear arched roofs over their heads. The true philosopher does not care whether he has an arched roof or any roof. Philosophy has nothing to do with teaching men the uses of metals. She teaches us to be independent of all material substances, of all mechanical contrivances. The wise man lives according to nature. Instead of attempting to add to the physical comforts of his species, he regrets that his lot was not cast in that golden age when the human race had no protection against the cold but the skins of wild beasts, no screen from the sun but a cavern. To impute to such a man any share in the invention or improvement of a plough, a ship, or a mill, is an insult. "In my own time," says Seneca, "there have been inventions of this sort, transparent windows, tubes for diffusing warmth equally through all parts of a building, short-hand, which has been carried to such a perfection that a writer can keep pace with the most rapid speaker. But the inventing of such things is drudgery for the lowest slaves; philosophy lies deeper. It is not her office to teach men how to use their hands. The object of her lessons is to form the soul. *Non est, inquam, instrumentorum ad usus necessarios opifex.*"[6] If the *non* were left out, this last sentence would be no bad description of the Baconian philosophy, and would, indeed, very much resemble several expressions in the Novum Organum. "We shall next be told," exclaims Seneca, "that the first shoemaker was a philosopher!" For our own part, if we are forced to make our choice between the first shoemaker and the author of the three books On Anger, we pronounce for the shoemaker. It may be worse to be angry than to be wet. But shoes have kept millions from being wet; and we doubt whether Seneca ever kept anybody from being angry.

It is very reluctantly that Seneca can be brought to confess that any philosopher had ever paid the smallest attention to anything that could possibly promote what vulgar people would consider as the well-being of mankind. He labors to clear Democritus from the disgraceful imputation of having made the first arch, and Anacharsis from the charge of having contrived the potter's wheel. He is forced to own that such a thing might happen; and it may also happen, he tells us, that a philosopher may be swift of foot. But it is not in his character of philosopher that he either wins a race or invents a machine. No, to be sure. The business of a

4

6. "She is not, I say, a maker of pragmatic tools."

philosopher was to declaim in praise of poverty with two millions sterling out at usury, to meditate epigrammatic conceits about the evils of luxury, in gardens which moved the envy of sovereigns, to rant about liberty, while fawning on the insolent and pampered freedmen of a tyrant, to celebrate the divine beauty of virtue with the same pen which had just before written a defence of the murder of a mother by a son.

From the cant of this philosophy, a philosophy meanly proud of its own unprofitableness, it is delightful to turn to the lessons of the great English teacher. We can almost forgive all the faults of Bacon's life when we read that singularly graceful and dignified passage: "Ego certe, ut de me ipso, quod res est, loquar, et in iis quæ nunc edo, et in iis quæ in posterum meditor, dignitatem ingenii et nominis mei, si qua sit, sæpius sciens et volens projicio, dum commodis humanis inserviam; quique architectus fortasse in philosophia et scientiis esse debeam, etiam operarius, et bajulus, et quidvis demum fio, cum haud pauca quæ omnino fieri necesse sit, alii autem ob innatam superbiam subterfugiant, ipse sustineam et exsequar."[7] This *philanthropia*, which, as he said in one of the most remarkable of his early letters, "was so fixed in his mind, as it could not be removed," this majestic humility, this persuasion that nothing can be too insignificant for the attention of the wisest, which is not too insignificant to give pleasure or pain to the meanest, is the great characteristic distinction, the essential spirit of the Baconian philosophy. We trace it in all that Bacon has written on Physics, on Laws, on Morals. And we conceive that from this peculiarity all the other peculiarities of his system directly and almost necessarily sprang.

The spirit which appears in the passage of Seneca to which we have referred tainted the whole body of the ancient philosophy from the time of Socrates downwards, and took possession of intellects with which that of Seneca cannot for a moment be compared. It pervades the dialogues of Plato. It may be distinctly traced in many parts of the works of Aristotle. Bacon has dropped hints from which it may be inferred that, in his opinion, the prevalence of this feeling was in a great measure to be attributed to the influence of Socrates. Our great countryman evidently did not consider the revolution which Socrates effected in philosophy

7. "But, to say how things stand in my own case, both with respect to my present work and my future projects, I often set aside the dignity of my intellect and reputation, if there is any, to improve human comforts; and being one who should, perhaps, be an architect in philosophy and the sciences, I become a common laborer, a hod-carrier, anything that is needed; many essential tasks that others shrink from because of their innate pride, I shoulder and see through to the end."

as a happy event, and constantly maintained that the earlier Greek speculators, Democritus in particular, were, on the whole, superior to their more celebrated successors.

Assuredly if the tree which Socrates planted and Plato watered   7 is to be judged of by its flowers and leaves, it is the noblest of trees. But if we take the homely test of Bacon, if we judge of the tree by its fruits, our opinion of it may perhaps be less favorable. When we sum up all the useful truths which we owe to that philosophy, to what do they amount? We find, indeed, abundant proofs that some of those who cultivated it were men of the first order of intellect. We find among their writings incomparable specimens both of dialectical and rhetorical art. We have no doubt that the ancient controversies were of use, in so far as they served to exercise the faculties of the disputants; for there is no controversy so idle that it may not be of use in this way. But, when we look for something more, for something which adds to the comforts or alleviates the calamities of the human race, we are forced to own ourselves disappointed. We are forced to say with Bacon that this celebrated philosophy ended in nothing but disputation, that it was neither a vineyard nor an olive ground, but an intricate wood of briars and thistles, from which those who lost themselves in it brought back many scratches and no food.

We readily acknowledge that some of the teachers of this unfruitful   8 wisdom were among the greatest men that the world has ever seen. If we admit the justice of Bacon's censure, we admit it with regret, similar to that which Dante felt when he learned the fate of those illustrious heathens who were doomed to the first circle of Hell:—

> *"Gran duol mi prese al cuor quando lo 'ntesi,*
> *Perocché gente di molto valore*
> *Conobbi che 'n quel limbo eran sospesi."*[8]

But in truth the very admiration which we feel for the eminent   9 philosophers of antiquity forces us to adopt the opinion that their powers were systematically misdirected. For how else could it be that such powers should effect so little for mankind? A pedestrian may show as much muscular vigor on a treadmill as on the highway road. But on the road his vigor will assuredly carry him forward; and on the treadmill he will not advance an inch. The ancient

---

8. *"Grief smote my heart to think, as thus he ended,*
   What souls I knew, of great and soveran
   Virtue, who in that Limbo dwelt suspended." [translation by Dorothy L. Sayers]

philosophy was a treadmill, not a path. It was made up of revolving questions, of controversies which were always beginning again. It was a contrivance for having much exertion and no progress. We must acknowledge that more than once, while contemplating the doctrines of the Academy and the Portico, even as they appear in the transparent splendor of Cicero's incomparable diction, we have been tempted to mutter with the surly centurion in Persius, "Cur quis non prandeat hoc est?"[9] What is the highest good, whether pain be an evil, whether all things be fated, whether we can be certain of anything, whether we can be certain that we are certain of nothing, whether a wise man can be unhappy, whether all departures from right be equally reprehensible, these, and other questions of the same sort, occupied the brains, the tongues, and the pens of the ablest men in the civilized world during several centuries. This sort of philosophy, it is evident, could not be progressive. It might indeed sharpen and invigorate the minds of those who devoted themselves to it; and so might the disputes of the orthodox Lilliputians and the heretical Blefuscudians about the big ends and the little ends of eggs. But such disputes could add nothing to the stock of knowledge. The human mind accordingly, instead of marching, merely marked time. It took as much trouble as would have sufficed to carry it forward; and yet remained on the same spot. There was no accumulation of truth, no heritage of truth acquired by the labor of one generation and bequeathed to another, to be again transmitted with large additions to a third. Where this philosophy was in the time of Cicero, there it continued to be in the time of Seneca, and there it continued to be in the time of Favorinus. The same sects were still battling, with the same unsatisfactory arguments, about the same interminable questions. There had been no want of ingenuity, of zeal, of industry. Every trace of intellectual cultivation was there, except a harvest. There had been plenty of ploughing, harrowing, reaping, threshing. But the garners contained only smut and stubble.

The ancient philosophers did not neglect natural science; but they did not cultivate it for the purpose of increasing the power and ameliorating the condition of man. The taint of barrenness had spread from ethical to physical speculations. Seneca wrote largely on natural philosophy, and magnified the importance of that study. But why? Not because it tended to assuage suffering, to multiply the conveniences of life, to extend the empire of man over the material world; but solely because it tended to raise the mind above low cares, to separate it from the body, to exercise

10

9. "Should a man miss his dinner for *this?*"

its subtilty in the solution of very obscure questions. Thus natural philosophy was considered in the light merely of a mental execise. It was made subsidiary to the art of disputation; and it consequently proved altogether barren of useful discoveries.

There was one sect which, however absurd and pernicious some of its doctrines may have been, ought, it should seem, to have merited an exception from the general censure which Bacon has pronounced on the ancient schools of wisdom. The Epicurean, who referred all happiness to bodily pleasure, and all evil to bodily pain, might have been expected to exert himself for the purpose of bettering his own physical condition and that of his neighbors. But the thought seems never to have occurred to any member of that school. Indeed, their notion, as reported by their great poet, was, that no more improvements were to be expected in the arts which conduce to the comfort of life:—

> *"Ad victum quæ flagitat usus*
> *Omnia jam ferme mortalibus esse parata."*[10]

This contented despondency, this disposition to admire what has been done, and to expect that nothing more will be done, is strongly characteristic of all the schools which preceded the school of Fruit and Progress. Widely as the Epicurean and the Stoic differed on most points, they seem to have quite agreed in their contempt for pursuits so vulgar as to be useful. The philosophy of both was a garrulous, declaiming, canting, wrangling philosophy. Century after century they continued to repeat their hostile war cries, Virtue and Pleasure; and in the end it appeared that the Epicurean had added as little to the quantity of pleasure as the Stoic to the quantity of virtue. It is on the pedestal of Bacon, not on that of Epicurus, that those noble lines ought to be inscribed:—

> *"O tenebris tantis tam clarum extollere lumen*
> *Qui primus potuisti, illustrans commoda vitæ."*[11]

. . . .

The difference between the philosophy of Bacon and that of his predecessors cannot, we think, be better illustrated than by comparing his views on some important subjects with those of Plato. We select Plato, because we conceive that he did more than any other person towards giving to the minds of speculative men that bent which they retained till they received from Bacon a new impulse in a diametrically opposite direction.

11

12

13

10. "Mortals have almost everything necessary for life provided to them."
11. "O, you, who first were able from such darkness to lift up a light, illuminating the comforts of life."

It is curious to observe how differently these great men estimated 14 the value of every kind of knowledge. Take Arithmetic for example. Plato, after speaking slightly of the convenience of being able to reckon and compute in the ordinary transactions of life, passes to what he considers as a far more important advantage. The study of the properties of numbers, he tells us, habituates the mind to the contemplation of pure truth, and raises us above the material universe. He would have his disciples apply themselves to this study, not that they may be able to buy or sell, not that they may qualify themselves to be shopkeepers or travelling merchants, but that they may learn to withdraw their minds from the ever-shifting spectacle of this visible and tangible world, and to fix them on the immutable essences of things.

Bacon, on the other hand, valued this branch of knowledge, 15 only on account of its uses with reference to that visible and tangible world which Plato so much despised. He speaks with scorn of the mystical arithmetic of the later Platonists, and laments the propensity of mankind to employ, on mere matters of curiosity, powers the whole exertion of which is required for purposes of solid advantage. He advises arithmeticians to leave these trifles, and to employ themselves in framing convenient expressions, which may be of use in physical researches.

The same reasons which led Plato to recommend the study of 16 arithmetic led him to recommend also the study of mathematics. The vulgar crowd of geometricians, he says, will not understand him. They have practice always in view. They do not know that the real use of the science is to lead men to the knowledge of abstract, essential, eternal truth. Indeed, if we are to believe Plutarch, Plato carried this feeling so far that he considered geometry as degraded by being applied to any purpose of vulgar utility. Archytas, it seems, had framed machines of extraordinary power on mathematical principles. Plato remonstrated with his friend, and declared that this was to degrade a noble intellectual exercise into a low craft, fit only for carpenters and wheelwrights. The office of geometry he said, was to discipline the mind, not to minister to the base wants of the body. His interference was successful, and from that time, according to Plutarch, the science of mechanics was considered as unworthy of the attention of a philosopher.

Archimedes in a later age imitated and surpassed Archytas. But 17 even Archimedes was not free from the prevailing notion that geometry was degraded by being employed to produce anything useful. It was with difficulty that he was induced to stoop from speculation to practice. He was half ashamed of those inventions which were the wonder of hostile nations, and always spoke of them slightingly as mere amusements, as trifles in which a math-

ematician might be suffered to relax his mind after intense application
to the higher parts of his science.

The opinion of Bacon on this subject was diametrically opposed   18
to that of the ancient philosophers. He valued geometry chiefly,
if not solely, on account of those uses, which to Plato appeared so
base. And it is remarkable that the longer Bacon lived the stronger
this feeling became. When in 1605 he wrote the two books on
the Advancement of Learning, he dwelt on the advantages which
mankind derived from mixed mathematics; but he at the same
time admitted that the beneficial effect produced by mathematical
study on the intellect, though a collateral advantage, was "no less
worthy than that which was principal and intended." But it is
evident that his views underwent a change. When, near twenty
years later, he published the De Augmentis, which is the Treatise
on the Advancement of Learning, greatly expanded and carefully
corrected, he made important alterations in the part which related
to mathematics. He condemned with severity the high pretensions
of the mathematicians, "delicias et fastum mathematicorum." Assuming the well-being of the human race to be the end of knowledge,
he pronounced that mathematical science could claim no higher
rank than that of an appendage or an auxiliary to other sciences.
Mathematical science, he says, is the handmaid of natural philosophy; she ought to demean herself as such; and he declares
that he cannot conceive by what ill chance it has happened that
she presumes to claim precedence over her mistress. He predicts—
a prediction which would have made Plato shudder—that as more
and more discoveries are made in physics, there will be more and
more branches of mixed mathematics. Of that collateral advantage
the value of which, twenty years before, he rated so highly, he
says not one word. This omission cannot have been the effect of
mere inadvertence. His own treatise was before him. From that
treatise he deliberately expunged whatever was favorable to the
study of pure mathematics, and inserted several keen reflections
on the ardent votaries of that study. This fact, in our opinion,
admits of only one explanation. Bacon's love of those pursuits
which directly tend to improve the condition of mankind, and his
jealousy of all pursuits merely curious, had grown upon him, and
had, it may be, become immoderate. He was afraid of using any
expression which might have the effect of inducing any man of
talents to employ in speculations, useful only to the mind of the
speculator, a single hour which might be employed in extending
the empire of man over matter. If Bacon erred here, we must
acknowledge that we greatly prefer his error to the opposite error
of Plato. We have no patience with a philosophy which, like those

Roman matrons who swallowed abortives in order to preserve their shapes, takes pains to be barren for fear of being homely.

Let us pass to astronomy. This was one of the sciences which 19 Plato exhorted his disciples to learn, but for reasons far removed from common habits of thinking. "Shall we set down astronomy," says Socrates, "among the subjects of study?" "I think so," answers his young friend Glaucon: "to know something about the seasons, the months, and the years is of use for military purposes, as well as for agriculture and navigation." "It amuses me," says Socrates, "to see how afraid you are, lest the common herd of people should accuse you of recommending useless studies." He then proceeds, in that pure and magnificent diction which, as Cicero said, Jupiter would use if Jupiter spoke Greek, to explain, that the use of astronomy is not to add to the vulgar comforts of life, but to assist in raising the mind to the contemplation of things which are to be perceived by the pure intellect alone. The knowledge of the actual motions of the heavenly bodies Socrates considers as of little value. The appearances which make the sky beautiful at night are, he tells us, like the figures which a geometrician draws on the sand, mere examples, mere helps to feeble minds. We must get beyond them; we must neglect them; we must attain to an astronomy which is as independent of the actual stars as geometrical truth is independent of the lines of an ill-drawn diagram. This is, we imagine, very nearly, if not exactly, the astronomy which Bacon compared to the ox of Prometheus, a sleek, well-shaped hide, stuffed with rubbish, goodly to look at, but containing nothing to eat. He complained that astronomy had, to its great injury, been separated from natural philosophy, of which it was one of the noblest provinces, and annexed to the domain of mathematics. The world stood in need, he said, of a very different astronomy, of a living astronomy, of an astronomy which should set forth the nature, the motion, and the influences of the heavenly bodies, as they really are.

On the greatest and most useful of all human inventions, the 20 invention of alphabetical writing, Plato did not look with much complacency. He seems to have thought that the use of letters had operated on the human mind as the use of the go-cart in learning to walk, or of corks in learning to swim, is said to operate on the human body. It was a support which, in his opinion, soon became indispensable to those who used it, which made vigorous exertion first unnecessary, and then impossible. The powers of the intellect would, he conceived, have been more fully developed without this delusive aid. Men would have been compelled to exercise the understanding and the memory, and, by deep and assiduous meditation, to make truth thoroughly their own. Now, on the contrary, much knowledge is traced on paper, but little is engraved in the soul. A man is certain that he can find information at a moment's notice when he wants it. He therefore suffers it to fade from his mind. Such a man cannot in strictness be said to know anything. He has the show without the reality of wisdom. These opinions Plato has put into the mouth of an ancient king of Egypt. But it is evident from the context that they were his own; and so they were understood to be by Quintilian. Indeed, they are in perfect accordance with the whole Platonic system.

Bacon's views, as may easily be supposed, were widely different.   21
The powers of the memory, he observes, without the help of writing, can do little towards the advancement of any useful science. He acknowledges that the memory may be disciplined to such a point as to be able to perform very extraordinary feats. But on such feats he sets little value. The habits of his mind, he tells us, are such that he is not disposed to rate highly any accomplishment, however rare, which is of no practical use to mankind. As to these prodigious achievements of the memory, he ranks them with the exhibitions of rope-dancers and tumblers. "The two performances," he says, "are of much the same sort. The one is an abuse of the powers of the body; the other is an abuse of the powers of the mind. Both may perhaps excite our wonder; but neither is entitled to our respect."

To Plato, the science of medicine appeared to be of very disputable   22
advantage. He did not indeed object to quick cures for acute disorders, or for injuries produced by accidents. But the art which resists the slow sap of a chronic disease, which repairs frames enervated by lust, swollen by gluttony, or inflamed by wine, which encourages sensuality by mitigating the natural punishment of the sensualist, and prolongs existence when 'the intellect has ceased to retain its entire energy, had no share of his esteem. A life protracted by medical skill he pronounced to be a long death. The exercise of the art of medicine ought, he said, to be tolerated, so far as that art may serve to cure the occasional distempers of men whose constitutions are good. As to those who have bad constitutions, let them die; and the sooner the better. Such men are unfit for war, for magistracy, for the management of their domestic affairs, for severe study and speculation. If they engage in any vigorous mental exercise, they are troubled with giddiness and fulness of the head, all which they lay to the account of philosophy. The best thing that can happen to such wretches is to have done with life at once. He quotes mythical authority in support of this doctrine;

and reminds his disciples that the practice of the sons of Æsculapius[12], as described by Homer, extended only to the cure of external injuries.

Far different was the philosophy of Bacon. Of all the sciences, [23] that which he seems to have regarded with the greatest interest was the science which, in Plato's opinion, would not be tolerated in a well-regulated community. To make men perfect was no part of Bacon's plan. His humble aim was to make imperfect men comfortable. The beneficence of his philosophy resembled the beneficence of the common Father, whose sun rises on the evil and the good, whose rain descends for the just and the unjust. In Plato's opinion man was made for philosophy; in Bacon's opinion philosophy was made for man; it was a means to an end; and that end was to increase the pleasures and to mitigate the pains of millions who are not and cannot be philosophers. That a valetudinarian who took great pleasure in being wheeled along his terrace, who relished his boiled chicken and his weak wine and water, and who enjoyed a hearty laugh over the Queen of Navarre's tales[13], should be treated as a *caput lupinum*[14] because he could not read the *Timæus*[15] without a headache, was a notion which the humane spirit of the English school of wisdom altogether rejected. Bacon would not have thought it beneath the dignity of a philosopher to contrive an improved garden chair for such a valetudinarian, to devise some way of rendering his medicines more palatable, to invent repasts which he might enjoy, and pillows on which he might sleep soundly; and this though there might not be the smallest hope that the mind of the poor invalid would ever rise to the contemplation of the ideal beautiful and the ideal good. As Plato had cited the religious legends of Greece to justify his contempt for the more recondite parts of the art of healing, Bacon vindicated the dignity of that art by appealing to the example of Christ, and reminded men that the great Physician of the soul did not disdain to be also the physician of the body.

When we pass from the science of medicine to that of legislation, [24] we find the same difference between the systems of these two great men. Plato, at the commencement of the Dialogue on Laws, lays it down as a fundamental principle that the end of legislation is to make men virtuous. It is unnecessary to point out the

12. Machaon and Pudalirius, physicians to the Greek army in the Trojan War.
13. Her *Heptameron* was a sixteenth-century pot-boiler.
14. An outlaw.
15. A dialogue by Plato.

extravagant conclusions to which such a proposition leads. Bacon well knew to how great an extent the happiness of every society must depend on the virtue of its members; and he also knew what legislators can and what they cannot do for the purpose of promoting virtue. The view which he has given of the end of legislation, and of the principal means for the attainment of that end, has always seemed to us eminently happy, even among the many happy passages of the same kind with which his works abound. "Finis et scopus quem leges intueri atque ad quem jussiones et sanctiones suas dirigere debent, non alius est quam ut cives feliciter degant. Id fiet si pietate et religione recte instituti, moribus honesti, armis adversus hostes externos tuti, legum auxilio adversus seditiones et privatas injurias muniti, imperio et magistratibus obsequentes, copiis et opibus locupletes et florentes fuerint."[16] The end is the well-being of the people. The means are the imparting of moral and religious education; the providing of everything necessary for defence against foreign enemies; the maintaining of internal order; the establishing of a judicial, financial, and commercial system, under which wealth may be rapidly accumulated and securely enjoyed.

Even with respect to the form in which laws ought to be drawn, there is a remarkable difference of opinion between the Greek and the Englishman. Plato thought a preamble essential; Bacon thought it mischievous. Each was consistent with himself. Plato, considering the moral improvement of the people as the end of legislation, justly inferred that a law which commanded and threatened, but which neither convinced the reason, nor touched the heart, must be a most imperfect law. He was not content with deterring from theft a man who still continued to be a thief at heart, with restraining a son who hated his mother from beating his mother. The only obedience on which he set much value was the obedience which an enlightened understanding yields to reason, and which a virtuous disposition yields to precepts of virtue. He really seems to have believed that, by prefixing to every law an eloquent and pathetic exhortation, he should, to a great extent, render penal enactments superfluous. Bacon entertained no such romantic hopes; and he well knew the practical inconveniences of the course which Plato

25

---

16. "The purpose and scope the laws should attend to and direct provisions and punishments toward is, simply that the people should live happily. This will happen if citizens are trained in proper piety and religion, are morally sound, protected by arms from all external enemies, fortified by law against seditions and private injuries, obedient to the government and magistrates, rich in power and resources, and flourishing in health."

recommended. "Neque nobis," says he, "prologi legum qui inepti olim habiti sunt, et leges introducunt disputantes non jubentes, utique placerent, si priscos mores ferre possemus. . . . Quantum fieri potest prologi evitentur, et lex incipiat a jussione."[17]

Each of the great men whom we have compared intended to illustrate his system by a philosophical romance; and each left his romance imperfect. Had Plato lived to finish the Critias, a comparison between that noble fiction and the new Atlantis would probably have furnished us with still more striking instances than any which we have given. It is amusing to think with what horror he would have seen such an institution as Solomon's House[18] rising in his republic: with what vehemence he would have ordered the brew houses, the perfume houses, and the dispensatories to be pulled down; and with what inexorable rigor he would have driven beyond the frontier all the Fellows of the College, Merchants of Light and Depredators, Lamps and Pioneers.

To sum up the whole, we should say that the aim of the Platonic philosophy was to exalt man into a god. The aim of the Baconian philosophy was to provide man with what he requires while he continues to be man. The aim of the Platonic philosophy was to raise us far above vulgar wants. The aim of the Baconian philosophy was to supply our vulgar wants. The former aim was noble; but the latter was attainable. Plato drew a good bow; but, like Acestes in Virgil, he aimed at the stars: and therefore, though there was no want of strength or skill, the shot was thrown away. His arrow was indeed followed by a track of dazzling radiance, but it struck nothing:—

> "*Volans liquidis in nubibus arsit arundo*
> *Signavitque viam flammis, tenuisque recessit*
> *Consumta in ventos.*"[19]

Bacon fixed his eye on a mark which was placed on the earth and within bowshot, and hit it in the white. The philosophy of Plato began in words and ended in words, noble words indeed, words such as were to be expected from the finest of human intellects exercising boundless dominion over the finest of human

26

27

17. "Nor do we at all approve of preambles to the laws, which long ago were thought inappropriate, and which present the laws disputing rather than commanding, if only we could support the ancient practices . . . So far as possible, shun preambles, and let the law begin with a command."
18. The seat of government for the utopia described by Bacon in his *New Atlantis*.
19. "*The shaft, as it sped among the streaming clouds, took fire,*
   Blazing a trail in the sky, then burnt itself and vanished
   Into the air" [translated by C. Day Lewis]

languages. The philosophy of Bacon began in observations and ended in arts.

The boast of the ancient philosophers was that their doctrine 28 formed the minds of men to a high degree of wisdom and virtue. This was indeed the only practical good which the most celebrated of those teachers even pretended to effect; and undoubtedly, if they had effected this, they would have deserved far higher praise than if they had discovered the most salutary medicines or constructed the most powerful machines. But the truth is that, in those very matters in which alone they professed to do any good to mankind, in those very matters for the sake of which they neglected all the vulgar interests of mankind, they did nothing, or worse than nothing. They promised what was impracticable; they despised what was practicable; they filled the world with long words and long beards; and they left it as wicked and as ignorant as they found it.

An acre in Middlesex is better than a principality in Utopia. The 29 smallest actual good is better than the most magnificent promises of impossibilities. The wise man of the Stoics would, no doubt, be a grander object than a steam engine. But there are steam engines. And the wise man of the Stoics is yet to be born. A philosophy which should enable a man to feel perfectly happy while in agonies of pain would be better than a philosophy which assuages pain. But we know that there are remedies which will assuage pain; and we know that the ancient sages liked the toothache just as little as their neighbors. A philosophy which should extinguish cupidity would be better than a philosophy which should devise laws for the security of property. But it is possible to make laws which shall, to a very great extent, secure property. And we do not understand how any motives which the ancient philosophy furnished could extinguish cupidity. We know indeed that the philosophers were no better than other men. From the testimony of friends as well as of foes, from the confessions of Epictetus and Seneca, as well as from the sneers of Lucian and the fierce invectives of Juvenal, it is plain that these teachers of virtue had all the vices of their neighbors, with the additional vice of hypocrisy. Some people may think the object of the Baconian philosophy a low object, but they cannot deny that, high or low, it has been attained. They cannot deny that every year makes an addition to what Bacon called "fruit." They cannot deny that mankind have made, and are making, great and constant progress in the road which he pointed out to them. Was there any such progressive movement among the ancient philosophers? After they had been declaiming eight hundred years, had they made the world better than when they began? Our belief is that, among the philosophers themselves, instead of a progressive improvement there was a progressive degeneracy. An abject superstition which Democritus or Anaxagoras would have rejected with scorn added the last disgrace to the long dotage of the Stoic and Platonic schools. Those unsuccessful attempts to articulate which are so delightful and interesting in a child shock and disgust us in an aged paralytic; and in the same way, those wild mythological fictions which charm us, when we hear them lisped by Greek poetry in its infancy, excite a mixed sensation of pity and loathing, when mumbled by Greek philosophy in its old age. We know that guns, cutlery, spyglasses, clocks, are better in our time than they were in the time of our fathers, and were better in the time of our fathers than they were in the time of our grandfathers. We might, therefore, be inclined to think that, when a philosophy which boasted that its object was the elevation and purification of the mind, and which for this object neglected the sordid office of ministering to the comforts of the body, had flourished in the highest honor during many hundreds of years, a vast moral amelioration must have taken place. Was it so? Look at the schools of this wisdom four centuries before the Christian era and four centuries after that era. Compare the men whom those schools formed at those two periods. Compare Plato and Libanius[20]. Compare Pericles[21] and Julian[22]. This philosophy confessed, nay boasted, that for every end but one it was useless. Had it attained that one end?

Suppose that Justinian[23], when he closed the schools of Athens, had called on the last few sages who still haunted the Portico, and lingered round the ancient plane trees, to show their title to public veneration: suppose that he had said: "A thousand years have elapsed since, in this famous city, Socrates posed Protagoras and Hippias[24]; during those thousand years a large proportion of the ablest men of every generation has been employed in constant efforts to bring to perfection the philosophy which you teach; that philosophy has been munificently patronized by the powerful; its professors have been held in the highest esteem by the public; it has drawn to itself almost all the sap and vigor of the human intellect: and what has it effected? What profitable truth has it taught us which we should not equally have known without it?

30

20. A sophist of the fourth century A.D.
21. The enlightened leader of Athenian democracy in Plato's era.
22. Roman emperor who persecuted the Christians in the fourth century A.D.
23. Roman emperor of the sixth century A.D.
24. Characters in Plato's *Protagoras*.

What has it enabled us to do which we should not have been equally able to do without it?" Such questions, we suspect, would have puzzled Simplicius and Isidore[25]. Ask a follower of Bacon what the new philosophy, as it was called in the time of Charles the Second, has effected for mankind, and his answer is ready: "It has lengthened life; it has mitigated pain; it has extinguished diseases; it has increased the fertility of the soil; it has given new securities to the mariner; it has furnished new arms to the warrior; it has spanned great rivers and estuaries with bridges of form unknown to our fathers; it has guided the thunderbolt innocuously from heaven to earth; it has lighted up the night with the splendor of the day; it has extended the range of the human vision; it has multiplied the power of the human muscles; it has accelerated motion; it has annihilated distance; it has facilitated intercourse, correspondence, all friendly offices, all dispatch of business; it has enabled man to descend to the depths of the sea, to soar into the air, to penetrate securely into the noxious recesses of the earth, to traverse the land in cars which whirl along without horses, and the ocean in ships which run ten knots an hour against the wind. These are but a part of its fruits, and of its first fruits. For it is a philosophy which never rests, which has never attained, which is never perfect. Its law is progress. A point which yesterday was invisible is its goal to-day, and will be its starting post to-morrow."

25. Neo-Platonists of Justinian's era.

ADAM SMITH

Division of Labor

The greatest improvement in the productive powers of labour, and the greater part of the skill, dexterity, and judgment with which it is any where directed, or applied, seem to have been the effects of the division of labour. 1

The effects of the division of labour, in the general business of society, will be more easily understood, by considering in what manner it operates in some particular manufactures. It is commonly supposed to be carried furthest in some very trifling ones; not 2

Excerpted from the first chapter of *The Wealth of Nations* (1776).

perhaps that it really is carried further in them than in others of more importance: but in those trifling manufactures which are destined to supply the small wants of but a small number of people, the whole number of workmen must necessarily be small; and those employed in every different branch of the work can often be collected into the same workhouse, and placed at once under the view of the spectator. In those great manufactures, on the contrary, which are destined to supply the great wants of the great body of the people, every different branch of the work employs so great a number of workmen, that it is impossible to collect them all into the same workhouse. We can seldom see more, at one time, than those employed in one single branch. Though in such manufactures, therefore, the work may really be divided into a much greater number of parts, than in those of a more trifling nature, the division is not near so obvious, and has accordingly been much less observed.

To take an example, therefore, from a very trifling manufacture; but one in which the division of labour has been very often taken notice of, the trade of the pin-maker; a workman not educated to this business (which the division of labour has rendered a distinct trade), nor acquainted with the use of the machinery employed in it (to the invention of which the same division of labour has probably given occasion), could scarce, perhaps, with his utmost industry, make one pin in a day, and certainly could not make twenty. But in the way in which this business is now carried on, not only the whole work is a peculiar trade, but it is divided into a number of branches, of which the greater part are likewise peculiar trades. One man draws out the wire, another straights it, a third cuts it, a fourth points it, a fifth grinds it at the top for receiving the head; to make the head requires two or three distinct operations; to put it on, is a peculiar business, to whiten the pins is another; it is even a trade by itself to put them into the paper; and the important business of making a pin is, in this manner, divided into about eighteen distinct operations, which, in some manufactories, are all performed by distinct hands, though in others the same man will sometimes perform two or three of them. I have seen a small manufactory of this kind where ten men only were employed, and where some of them consequently performed two or three distinct operations. But though they were very poor, and therefore but indifferently accommodated with the necessary machinery, they could, when they exerted themselves, make among them about twelve pounds of pins in a day. There are in a pound upwards of four thousand pins of a middling size. Those ten persons, therefore, could make among them upwards of forty-eight thousand pins in a day. Each person, therefore, making a tenth part of forty-eight thousand pins, might be considered as making four thousand eight hundred pins in a day. But if they had all wrought separately and independently, and without any of them having been educated to this peculiar business, they certainly could not each of them have made twenty, perhaps not one pin in a day; that is, certainly, not the two hundred and fortieth, perhaps not the four thousand eight hundredth part of what they are at present capable of performing, in consequence of a proper division and combination of their different operations.

In every other art and manufacture, the effects of the division   4
of labour are similar to what they are in this very trifling one; though, in many of them, the labour can neither be so much subdivided, nor reduced to so great a simplicity of operation. The division of labour, however, so far as it can be introduced, occasions, in every art, a proportionable increase of the productive powers of labour. The separation of different trades and employments from one another, seems to have taken place, in consequence of this advantage. This separation too is generally carried furthest in those countries which enjoy the highest degree of industry and im-provement; what is the work of one man in a rude state of society, being generally that of several in an improved one. In every improved society, the farmer is generally nothing but a farmer; the man-ufacturer, nothing but a manufacturer. The labour too which is necessary to produce any one complete manufacture, is almost always divided among a great number of hands. How many different trades are employed in each branch of the linen and woollen manufactures, from the growers of the flax and the wool, to the bleachers and smoothers of the linen, or to the dyers and dressers of the cloth!

This great increase of the quantity of work, which, in consequence   5
of the division of labour, the same number of people are capable of performing, is owing to three different circumstances; first, to the increase of dexterity in every particular workman; secondly, to the saving of the time which is commonly lost in passing from one species of work to another; and lastly, to the invention of a great number of machines which facilitate and abridge labour, and enable one man to do the work of many.

First, the improvement of the dexterity of the workman necessarily   6
increases the quantity of the work he can perform; and the division of labour, by reducing every man's business to some one simple operation, and by making this operation the sole employment of

his life, necessarily increases very much the dexterity of the workman. A common smith, who, though accustomed to handle the hammer, has never been used to make nails, if upon some particular occasion he is obliged to attempt it, will scarce, I am assured, be able to make above two or three hundred nails in a day, and those too very bad ones. A smith who has been accustomed to make nails, but whose sole or principal business has not been that of a nailer, can seldom with his utmost diligence make more than eight hundred or a thousand nails in a day. I have seen several boys under twenty years of age who had never exercised any other trade but that of making nails, and who, when they exerted themselves, could make, each of them, upwards of two thousand three hundred nails in a day. The making of a nail, however, is by no means one of the simplest operations. The same person blows the bellows, stirs or mends the fire as there is occasion, heats the iron, and forges every part of the nail: In forging the head too he is obliged to change his tools. The different operations into which the making of a pin, or of a metal button, is subdivided, are all of them much more simple, and the dexterity of the person, of whose life it has been the sole business to perform them, is usually much greater. The rapidity with which some of the operations of those manufactures are performed, exceeds what the human hand could, by those who had never seen them, be supposed capable of acquiring.

Secondly, the advantage which is gained by saving the time 7 commonly lost in passing from one sort of work to another, is much greater than we should at first view be apt to imagine it. It is impossible to pass very quickly from one kind of work to another, that is carried on in a different place, and with quite different tools. A country weaver, who cultivates a small farm, must lose a good deal of time in passing from his loom to the field, and from the field to his loom. When the two trades can be carried on in the same workhouse, the loss of time is no doubt much less. It is even in this case, however, very considerable. A man commonly saunters a little in turning his hand from one sort of employment to another. When he first begins the new work he is seldom very keen and hearty; his mind, as they say, does not go to it, and for some time he rather trifles than applies to good purpose. The habit of sauntering and of indolent careless application, which is naturally, or rather necessarily acquired by every country workman who is obliged to change his work and his tools every half hour, and to apply his hand in twenty different ways almost every day of his life; renders him almost always slothful and lazy, and incapable of any vigorous application even on the most pressing occasions. Independent, therefore, of his deficiency in point of dexterity, this cause alone must always reduce considerably the quantity of work which he is capable of performing.

Thirdly, and lastly, every body must be sensible how much 8 labour is facilitated and abridged by the application of proper machinery. It is unnecessary to give any example. I shall only observe, therefore, that the invention of all those machines by which labour is so much facilitated and abridged, seems to have been originally owing to the division of labour. Men are much more likely to discover easier and readier methods of attaining any object, when the whole attention of their minds is directed towards that single object, than when it is dissipated among a great variety of things. But in consequence of the division of labour, the whole of every man's attention comes naturally to be directed towards some one very simple object. It is naturally to be expected, therefore, that some one or other of those who are employed in each particular branch of labour should soon find out easier and readier methods of performing their own particular work, wherever the nature of it admits of such improvement. A great part of the machines made use of in those manufactures in which labour is most subdivided, were originally the inventions of common work-men, who, being each of them employed in some very simple operation, naturally turned their thoughts towards finding out easier and readier methods of performing it. Whoever has been much accustomed to visit such manufactures, must frequently have been shewn very pretty machines, which were the inventions of such workmen, in order to facilitate and quicken their own particular part of the work. In the first fire-engines, a boy was constantly employed to open and shut alternately the communication between the boiler and the cylinder, according as the piston either ascended or descended. One of those boys, who loved to play with his companions, observed that, by tying a string from the handle of the valve which opened this communication to another part of the machine, the valve would open and shut without his assistance, and leave him at liberty to divert himself with his play-fellows. One of the greatest improvements that has been made upon this machine, since it was first invented, was in this manner the discovery of a boy who wanted to save his own labour.

All the improvements in machinery, however, have by no means 9 been the inventions of those who had occasion to use the machines. Many improvements have been made by the ingenuity of the makers of the machines, when to make them became the business of a peculiar trade; and some by that of those who are called philosophers or men of speculation, whose trade it is not to do any thing, but to observe every thing; and who, upon that account, are often capable of combining together the powers of the most distant and dissimilar objects. In the progress of society, philosophy or speculation becomes, like every other employment, the principal or sole trade and occupation of a particular class of citizens. Like every other employment too, it is subdivided into a great number of different branches, each of which affords occupation to a peculiar tribe or class of philosophers; and this subdivision of employment in philosophy, as well as in every other business, improves dexterity, and saves time. Each individual becomes more expert in his own peculiar branch, more work is done upon the whole, and the quantity of science is considerably increased by it.

It is the great multiplication of the productions of all the different 10 arts, in consequence of the division of labour, which occasions, in a well-governed society, that universal opulence which extends itself to the lowest ranks of the people. Every workman has a great quantity of his own work to dispose of beyond what he himself has occasion for; and every other workman being exactly in the same situation, he is enabled to exchange a great quantity of his own goods for a great quantity, or, what comes to the same thing, for the price of a great quantity of theirs. He supplies them abundantly with what they have occasion for, and they accommodate him as amply with what he has occasion for, and a general plenty diffuses itself through all the different ranks of the society.

Observe the accommodation of the most common artificer or 11 day-labourer in a civilized and thriving country, and you will perceive that the number of people of whose industry a part, though but a small part, has been employed in procuring him this accommodation, exceeds all computation. The woollen coat, for example, which covers the day-labourer, as coarse and rough as it may appear, is the produce of the joint labour of a great multitude of workmen. The shepherd, the sorter of the wool, the wool-comber or carder, the dyer, the scribbler, the spinner, the weaver, the fuller, the dresser, with many others, must all join their different arts in order to complete even this homely production. How many merchants and carriers, besides, must have been employed in transporting the materials from some of those workmen to others who often live in a very distant part of the country! how much commerce and navigation in particular, how many ship-builders, sailors, sail-makers, rope-makers, must have been employed in order to bring together the different drugs made use of by the dyer, which often come from the remotest corners of the world! What a variety of labour too is necessary in order to produce the tools of the meanest of those workmen! To say nothing of such complicated machines as the ship of the sailor, the mill of the fuller, or even the loom of the weaver, let us consider only what a variety of labour is requisite in order to form that very simple machine, the shears with which the shepherd clips the wool. The miner, the builder of the furnace for smelting the ore, the feller of the timber, the burner of the charcoal to be made use of in the smelting-house, the brick-maker, the brick-layer, the workmen who attend the furnace, the mill-wright, the forger, the smith, must all of them join their different arts in order to produce them. Were we to examine, in the same manner, all the different parts of his dress and household furniture, the coarse linen shirt which he wears next his skin, the shoes which cover his feet, the bed which he lies on, and all the different parts which compose it, the kitchen-grate at which he prepares his victuals, the coals which he makes use of for that purpose, dug from the bowels of the earth, and brought to him perhaps by a long sea and a long land carriage, all the other utensils of his kitchen, all the furniture of his table, the knives and forks, the earthen or pewter plates upon which he serves up and divides his victuals, the different hands employed in preparing his bread and his beer, the glass window which lets in the heat and the light, and keeps out the wind and the rain, with all the knowledge and art requisite for preparing that beautiful and happy invention, without which these northern parts of the world could scarce have afforded a very comfortable habitation, together with the tools of all the different workmen employed in producing those different conveniencies; if we examine, I say, all these things, and consider what a variety of labour is employed about each of them, we shall be sensible that without the assistance and co-operation of many thousands, the very meanest person in a civilized country could not be provided, even according to, what we very falsely imagine, the easy and simple manner in which he is commonly accommodated. Compared, indeed, with the more extravagant luxury of the great, his accommodation must no doubt appear extremely simple and easy; and yet it may be true, perhaps, that the accommodation of an European prince does not always so much exceed that of an industrious and frugal peasant, as the accommodation of the latter exceeds that of many an African king, the absolute master of the lives and liberties of ten thousand naked savages.

HENRY DAVID THOREAU

The Fitness of a Man's Building His Own House

Near the end of March, 1845, I borrowed an axe and went 1
down to the woods by Walden Pond, nearest to where I intended
to build my house, and began to cut down some tall, arrowy white
pines, still in their youth, for timber. It is difficult to begin without
borrowing, but perhaps it is the most generous course thus to
permit your fellow-men to have an interest in your enterprise.
The owner of the axe, as he released his hold on it, said that it
was the apple of his eye; but I returned it sharper than I received
it. It was a pleasant hillside where I worked, covered with pine
woods, through which I looked out on the pond, and a small
open field in the woods where pines and hickories were springing
up. The ice in the pond was not yet dissolved, though there were
some open spaces, and it was all dark-colored and saturated with
water. There were some slight flurries of snow during the days
that I worked there; but for the most part when I came out on
to the railroad, on my way home, its yellow sand-heap stretched
away gleaming in the hazy atmosphere, and the rails shone in
the spring sun, and I heard the lark and pewee and other birds
already come to commence another year with us. They were pleasant
spring days, in which the winter of man's discontent was thawing
as well as the earth, and the life that had lain torpid began to
stretch itself. One day, when my axe had come off and I had cut
a green hickory for a wedge, driving it with a stone, and had
placed the whole to soak in a pond-hole in order to swell the
wood, I saw a striped snake run into the water, and he lay on
the bottom, apparently without inconvenience, as long as I stayed
there, or more than a quarter of an hour; perhaps because he had
not yet fairly come out of the torpid state. It appeared to me that
for a like reason men remain in their present low and primitive
condition; but if they should feel the influence of the spring of
springs arousing them, they would of necessity rise to a higher
and more ethereal life. I had previously seen the snakes in frosty
mornings in my path with portions of their bodies still numb and

Excerpted from "Economy," the opening chapter of *Walden* (1854).

inflexible, waiting for the sun to thaw them. On the 1st of April it rained and melted the ice, and in the early part of the day, which was very foggy, I heard a stray goose groping about over the pond and cackling as if lost, or like the spirit of the fog.

So I went on for some days cutting and hewing timber, and also studs and rafters, all with my narrow axe, not having many communicable or scholar-like thoughts, singing to myself,—

> *Men say they know many things;*
> *But lo! they have taken wings,—*
> *The arts and sciences,*
> *And a thousand appliances:*
> *The wind that blows*
> *Is all that anybody knows.*

I hewed the main timbers six inches square, most of the studs on two sides only, and the rafters and floor timbers on one side, leaving the rest of the bark on, so that they were just as straight and much stronger than sawed ones. Each stick was carefully mortised or tenoned by its stump, for I had borrowed other tools by this time. My days in the woods were not very long ones; yet I usually carried my dinner of bread and butter, and read the newspaper in which it was wrapped, at noon, sitting amid the green pine boughs which I had cut off, and to my bread was imparted some of their fragrance, for my hands were covered with a thick coat of pitch. Before I had done I was more the friend than the foe of the pine tree, though I had cut down some of them, having become better acquainted with it. Sometimes a rambler in the wood was attracted by the sound of my axe, and we chatted pleasantly over the chips which I had made.

By the middle of April, for I made no haste in my work, but rather made the most of it, my house was framed and ready for the raising. I had already bought the shanty of James Collins, an Irishman who worked on the Fitchburg Railroad, for boards. James Collins' shanty was considered an uncommonly fine one. When I called to see it he was not at home. I walked about the outside, at first unobserved from within, the window was so deep and high. It was of small dimensions, with a peaked cottage roof, and not much else to be seen, the dirt being raised five feet all around as if it were a compost heap. The roof was the soundest part, though a good deal warped and made brittle by the sun. Doorsill there was none, but a perennial passage for the hens under the door-board. Mrs. C. came to the door and asked me to view it from the inside. The hens were driven in by my approach. It was dark, and had a dirt floor for the most part, dank, clammy, and aguish, only here a board and there a board which would not bear removal. She lighted a lamp to show me the inside of the roof and the walls, and also that the board floor extended under the bed, warning me not to step into the cellar, a sort of dust hole two feet deep. In her own words, they were "good boards overhead, good boards all around, and a good window,"—of two whole squares originally, only the cat had passed out that way lately. There was a stove, a bed, and a place to sit, an infant in the house where it was born, a silk parasol, gilt-framed looking-glass, and a patent new coffee-mill nailed to an oak sapling, all told. The bargain was soon concluded, for James had in the meanwhile returned. I to pay four dollars and twenty-five cents to-night, he to vacate at five to-morrow morning, selling to nobody else meanwhile: I to take possession at six. It were well, he said, to be there early, and anticipate certain indistinct but wholly unjust claims on the score of ground rent and fuel. This he assured me was the only encumbrance. At six I passed him and his family on the road. One large bundle held their all,—bed, coffee-mill, looking-glass, hens,—all but the cat; she took to the woods and became a wild cat, and, as I learned afterward, trod in a trap set for woodchucks, and so became a dead cat at last.

I took down this dwelling the same morning, drawing the nails, and removed it to the pond-side by small cartloads, spreading the boards on the grass there to bleach and warp back again in the sun. One early thrush gave me a note or two as I drove along the woodland path. I was informed treacherously by a young Patrick that neighbor Seeley, an Irishman, in the intervals of the carting, transferred the still tolerable, straight, and drivable nails, staples, and spikes to his pocket, and then stood when I came back to pass the time of day, and look freshly up, unconcerned, with spring thoughts, at the devastation; there being a dearth of work, as he said. He was there to represent spectatordom, and help make this seemingly insignificant event one with the removal of the gods of Troy.[1]

I dug my cellar in the side of a hill sloping to the south, where a woodchuck had formerly dug his burrow, down through sumach and blackberry roots, and the lowest stain of vegetation, six feet square by seven deep, to a fine sand where potatoes would not freeze in any winter. The sides were left shelving, and not stoned;

4

5

1. Virgil's *Aeneid* begins with the hero's moving the household gods from the devastation of Troy.

but the sun having never shone on them, the sand still keeps its place. It was but two hours' work. I took particular pleasure in this breaking of ground, for in almost all latitudes men dig into the earth for an equable temperature. Under the most splendid house in the city is still to be found the cellar where they store their roots as of old, and long after the superstructure has disappeared posterity remark its dent in the earth. The house is still but a sort of porch at the entrance of a burrow.

At length, in the beginning of May, with the help of some of   6 my acquaintances, rather to improve so good an occasion for neighborliness than from any necessity, I set up the frame of my house. No man was ever more honored in the character of his raisers than I. They are destined, I trust, to assist at the raising of loftier structures one day. I began to occupy my house on the 4th of July, as soon as it was boarded and roofed, for the boards were carefully feather-edged and lapped, so that it was perfectly impervious to rain, but before boarding I laid the foundation of a chimney at one end, bringing two cartloads of stones up the hill from the pond in my arms. I built the chimney after my hoeing in the fall, before a fire became necessary for warmth, doing my cooking in the meanwhile out of doors on the ground, early in the morning: which mode I still think is in some respects more convenient and agreeable than the usual one. When it stormed before my bread was baked, I fixed a few boards over the fire, and sat under them to watch my loaf, and passed some pleasant hours in that way. In those days, when my hands were much employed, I read but little, but the least scraps of paper which lay on the ground, my holder, or tablecloth, afforded me as much entertainment, in fact answered the same purpose as the Iliad.

It would be worth the while to build still more deliberately than   7 I did, considering, for instance, what foundation a door, a window, a cellar, a garret, have in the nature of man, and perchance never raising any superstructure until we found a better reason for it than our temporal necessities even. There is some of the same fitness in a man's building his own house that there is in a bird's building its own nest. Who knows but if men constructed their dwellings with their own hands, and provided food for themselves and families simply and honestly enough, the poetic faculty would be universally developed, as birds universally sing when they are so engaged? But alas! we do like cowbirds and cuckoos, which lay their eggs in nests which other birds have built, and cheer no traveller with their chattering and unmusical notes. Shall we forever resign the pleasure of construction to the carpenter? What does architecture amount to in the experience of the mass of men? I never in all my walks came across a man engaged in so simple and natural an occupation as building his house. We belong to the community. It is not the tailor alone who is the ninth part of a man[2]; it is as much the preacher, and the merchant, and the farmer. Where is this division of labor to end? and what object does it finally serve? No doubt another *may* also think for me; but it is not therefore desirable that he should do so to the exclusion of my thinking for myself.

True, there are architects so called in this country, and I have heard of one at least possessed with the idea of making architectural ornaments have a core of truth, a necessity, and hence a beauty, as if it were a revelation to him. All very well perhaps from his point of view, but only a little better than the common dilettantism. A sentimental reformer in architecture, he began at the cornice, not at the foundation. It was only how to put a core of truth within the ornaments, that every sugarplum, in fact, might have an almond or caraway seed in it,—though I hold that almonds are most wholesome without the sugar,—and not how the inhabitant, the indweller, might build truly within and without, and let the ornaments take care of themselves. What reasonable man ever supposed that ornaments were something outward and in the skin merely,—that the tortoise got his spotted shell, or the shell-fish its mother-o'-pearl tints, by such a contract as the inhabitants of Broadway their Trinity Church? But a man has no more to do with the style of architecture of his house than a tortoise with that of its shell: nor need the soldier be so idle as to try to paint the precise *color* of his virtue on his standard. The enemy will find it out. He may turn pale when the trial comes. This man seemed to me to lean over the cornice, and timidly whisper his half truth to the rude occupants who really knew it better than he. What of architectural beauty I now see, I know has gradually grown from within outward, out of the necessities and character of the indweller, who is the only builder,—out of some unconscious truthfulness, and nobleness, without ever a thought for the appearance and whatever additional beauty of this kind is destined to be produced will be preceded by a like unconscious beauty of life. The most interesting dwellings in this country, as the painter knows, are the most unpretending, humble log huts and cottages of the poor commonly; it is the life of the inhabitants whose shells they are, and not any peculiarity in their surfaces merely, which makes them *picturesque*; and equally

2. "It takes nine tailors to make a man": a popular saying of the nineteenth century.

interesting will be the citizen's suburban box, when his life shall
be as simple and as agreeable to the imagination, and there is as
little straining after effect in the style of his dwelling. A great
proportion of architectural ornaments are literally hollow, and a
September gale would strip them off, like borrowed plumes, without
injury to the substantials. They can do without *architecture* who
have no olives nor wines in the cellar. What if an equal ado were
made about the ornaments of style in literature, and the architects
of our Bibles spent as much time about their cornices as the
architects of our churches do? So are made the *belles-lettres* and
the *beaux-arts* and their professors. Much it concerns a man, forsooth,
how a few sticks are slanted over him or under him, and what
colors are daubed upon his box. It would signify somewhat, if, in
any earnest sense, *he* slanted them and daubed it; but the spirit
having departed out of the tenant, it is of a piece with constructing
his own coffin,—the architecture of the grave,—and "carpenter"
is but another name for "coffin-maker." One man says, in his
despair or indifference to life, take up a handful of the earth at
your feet, and paint your house that color. Is he thinking of his
last and narrow house? Toss up a copper for it as well. What an
abundance of leisure he must have! Why do you take up a handful
of dirt? Better paint your house your own complexion; let it turn
pale or blush for you. An enterprise to improve the style of cottage
architecture! When you have got my ornaments ready, I will wear
them.

Before winter I built a chimney, and shingled the sides of my   9
house, which were already impervious to rain, with imperfect and
sappy shingles made of the first slice of the log, whose edges I
was obliged to straighten with a plane.

I have thus a tight shingled and plastered house, ten feet wide   10
by fifteen long, and eight-feet posts, with a garret and a closet, a
large window on each side, two trap-doors, one door at the end,
and a brick fireplace opposite. The exact cost of my house, paying
the usual price for such materials as I used, but not counting the
work, all of which was done by myself, was as follows; and I give
the details because very few are able to tell exactly what their
houses cost, and fewer still, if any, the separate cost of the various
materials which compose them:—

Boards	$8 03½, mostly shanty boards.
Refuse shingles for roof	
and sides	4 00
Laths	1 25

Two second-hand windows with glass	2 43	
One thousand old brick ...	4 00	
Two casks of lime	2 40	That was high.
Hair	0 31	More than I needed.
Mantle-tree iron	0 15	
Nails	3 90	
Hinges and screws	0 14	
Latch	0 10	
Chalk	0 01	
Transportation	1 40	I carried a good part on my back.
In all	$28 12½	

These are all the materials, excepting the timber, stones, and sand, which I claimed by squatter's right. I have also a small woodshed adjoining, made chiefly of the stuff which was left after building the house. 11

I intend to build me a house which will surpass any on the main street in Concord in grandeur and luxury, as soon as it pleases me as much and will cost me no more than my present one. 12

I thus found that the student who wishes for a shelter can obtain one for a lifetime at an expense not greater than the rent which he now pays annually. If I seem to boast more than is becoming, my excuse is that I brag for humanity rather than for myself; and my shortcomings and inconsistencies do not affect the truth of my statement. Notwithstanding much cant and hypocrisy,—chaff which I find it difficult to separate from my wheat, but for which I am as sorry as any man,—I will breathe freely and stretch myself in this respect, it is such a relief to both the moral and physical system; and I am resolved that I will not through humility become the devil's attorney. I will endeavor to speak a good word for the truth. At Cambridge College the mere rent of a student's room, which is only a little larger than my own, is thirty dollars each year, though the corporation had the advantage of building thirty-two side by side and under one roof, and the occupant suffers the inconvenience of many and noisy neighbors, and perhaps a residence in the fourth story. I cannot but think that if we had more true wisdom in these respects, not only less education would be needed, because, forsooth, more would already have been acquired, but the pecuniary expense of getting an education would in a great measure vanish. Those conveniences which the student requires at Cambridge or elsewhere cost him or somebody else ten times 13

as great a sacrifice of life as they would with proper management
on both sides. Those things for which the most money is demanded
are never the things which the student most wants. Tuition, for
instance, is an important item in the term bill, while for the far
more valuable education which he gets by associating with the
most cultivated of his contemporaries no charge is made. The mode
of founding a college is, commonly, to get up a subscription of
dollars and cents, and then, following blindly the principles of a
division of labor to its extreme,—a principle which should never
be followed but with circumspection,—to call in a contractor who
makes this a subject of speculation, and he employs Irishmen or
other operatives actually to lay the foundations, while the students
that are to be are said to be fitting themselves for it; and for these
oversights successive generations have to pay. I think that it would
be *better than this*, for the students, or those who desire to be
benefited by it, even to lay the foundation themselves. The student
who secures his coveted leisure and retirement by systematically
shirking any labor necessary to man obtains but an ignoble and
unprofitable leisure, defrauding himself of the experience which
alone can make leisure fruitful. "But," says one, "you do not
mean that the students should go to work with their hands instead
of their heads?" I do not mean that exactly, but I mean something
which he might think a good deal like that; I mean that they
should not *play* life, or *study* it merely, while the community
supports them at this expensive game, but earnestly *live* it from
beginning to end. How could youths better learn to live than by
at once trying the experiment of living? Methinks this would
exercise their minds as much as mathematics. If I wished a boy
to know something about the arts and sciences, for instance, I
would not pursue the common course, which is merely to send
him into the neighborhood of some professor, where anything is
professed and practised but the art of life;—to survey the world
through a telescope or a microscope, and never with his natural
eye; to study chemistry, and not learn how his bread is made, or
mechanics, and not learn how it is earned; to discover new satellites
to Neptune, and not detect the motes in his eyes, or to what
vagabond he is a satellite himself; or to be devoured by the monsters
that swarm all around him, while contemplating the monsters in
a drop of vinegar. Which would have advanced the most at the
end of a month,—the boy who had made his own jackknife from
the ore which he had dug and smelted, reading as much as would
be necessary for this—or the boy who had attended the lectures
on metallurgy at the Institute in the meanwhile, and had received
a Rodgers penknife from his father? Which would be most likely

to cut his fingers? ... To my astonishment I was informed on leaving college that I had studied navigation!—why, if I had taken one turn down the harbor I should have known more about it. Even the *poor* student studies and is taught only *political* economy, while that economy of living which is synonymous with philosophy is not even sincerely professed in our colleges. The consequence is, that while he is reading Adam Smith, Ricardo, and Say[3], he runs his father in debt irretrievably.

As with our colleges, so with a hundred "modern improvements"; 14 there is an illusion about them; there is not always a positive advance. The devil goes on exacting compound interest to the last for his early share and numerous succeeding investments in them. Our inventions are wont to be pretty toys, which distract our attention from serious things. They are but improved means to an unimproved end, an end which it was already but too easy to arrive at; as railroads lead to Boston or New York. We are in great haste to construct a magnetic telegraph from Maine to Texas; but Maine and Texas, it may be, have nothing important to communicate. Either is in such a predicament as the man who was earnest to be introduced to a distinguished deaf woman, but when he was presented, and one end of her ear trumpet was put into his hand, had nothing to say. As if the main object were to talk fast and not to talk sensibly. We are eager to tunnel under the Atlantic and bring the Old World some weeks nearer to the New; but perchance the first news that will leak through into the broad, flapping American ear will be that the Princess Adelaide has the whooping cough. After all, the man whose horse trots a mile a minute does not carry the most important messages; he is not an evangelist, nor does he come round eating locusts and wild honey.[4] I doubt if Flying Childers ever carried a peck of corn to mill.[5]

One says to me, "I wonder that you do not lay up money; you 15 love to travel; you might take the cars and go to Fitchburg to-day and see the country." But I am wiser than that. I have learned that the swiftest traveller is he that goes afoot. I say to my friend, Suppose we try who will get there first. The distance is thirty miles; the fare ninety cents. That is almost a day's wages. I remember when wages were sixty cents a day for laborers on this very road. Well, I start now on foot, and get there before night; I have travelled at that rate by the week together. You will in the meanwhile have earned your fare, and arrive there sometime to-morrow, or

3. Noted political economists. See the previous essay.
4. As John the Baptist did.
5. An undefeated English racehorse of the eighteenth century.

possibly this evening, if you are lucky enough to get a job in
season. Instead of going to Fitchburg, you will be working here
the greater part of the day. And so, if the railroad reached round
the world, I think that I should keep ahead of you; and as for
seeing the country and getting experience of that kind, I should
have to cut your acquaintance altogether.

Such is the universal law, which no man can ever outwit, and   16
with regard to the railroad even we may say it is as broad as it
is long. To make a railroad round the world available to all mankind
is equivalent to grading the whole surface of the planet. Men have
an indistinct notion that if they keep up this activity of joint stocks
and spades long enough all will at length ride somewhere, in next
to no time, and for nothing; but though a crowd rushes to the
depot, and the conductor shouts "All aboard!" when the smoke
is blown away and the vapor condensed, it will be perceived that
a few are riding, but the rest are run over,—and it will be called,
and will be, "A melancholy accident." No doubt they can ride at
last who shall have earned their fare, that is, if they survive so
long, but they will probably have lost their elasticity and desire
to travel by that time. This spending of the best part of one's life
earning money in order to enjoy a questionable liberty during the
least valuable part of it reminds me of the Englishman who went
to India to make a fortune first, in order that he might return to
England and live the life of a poet. He should have gone up garret
at once. "What!" exclaim a million Irishmen starting up from all
the shanties in the land, "is not this railroad which we have built
a good thing?" Yes, I answer, *comparatively* good, that is, you might
have done worse; but I wish, as you are brothers of mine, that
you could have spent your time better than digging in this dirt.

E. B. WHITE

Progress and Change

My friends in the city tell me that the Sixth Avenue El is coming   1
down, but that's a hard thing for anyone to believe who once
lived in its fleeting and audible shadow. The El was the most
distinguished and outstanding vein on the town's neck, a varicosity
tempting to the modern surgeon. One wonders whether New York

Originally published in *Harper's Magazine*, July 1939.

can survive this sort of beauty operation, performed in the name of civic splendor and rapid transit.

A resident of the city grew accustomed to the heavenly railroad which swung implausibly in air, cutting off his sun by day, wandering in and out of his bedchamber by night. The presence of the structure and the passing of the trains were by all odds the most pervasive of New York's influences. Here was a sound which, if it ever got in the conch of your ear, was ineradicable—forever singing, like the sea. It punctuated the morning with brisk tidings of repetitious adventure, and it accompanied the night with sad but reassuring sounds of life-going-on—the sort of threnody which cricket and katydid render for suburban people sitting on screened porches, the sort of lullaby which the whippoorwill sends up to the Kentucky farm wife on a summer evening.

I spent a lot of time, once, doing nothing in the vicinity of Sixth Avenue. Naturally I know something of the El's fitful charm. It was, among other things, the sort of railroad you would occasionally ride just for the hell of it, a higher existence into which you would escape unconsciously and without destination. Let's say you had just emerged from the Child's on the west side of Sixth Avenue between 14th and 15th Streets, where you had had a bowl of vegetable soup and a stack of wheat cakes. The syrup still was a cloying taste on your tongue. You intended to go back to the apartment and iron a paragraph, or wash a sock. But miraculously, at the corner of 14th, there rose suddenly in front of you a flight of stairs all wrapt in celestial light, with treads of shining steel, and risers richly carved with the names of the great, and a canopy overhead where danced the dust in the shafts of golden sunshine. As in a trance, you mounted steadily to the pavilion above, where there was an iron stove and a man's hand visible through a mousehole. And the first thing you knew you were in South Ferry, with another of life's inestimable journeys behind you—and before you the dull, throbbing necessity of getting uptown again.

For a number of years I went to work every morning on the uptown trains of the Sixth Avenue El. I had it soft, because my journey wasn't at the rush hour and I often had the platform of the car to myself. It was a good way to get where you wanted to go, looking down on life at just the right speed, and peeking in people's windows, where the sketchy pantomime of potted plant and half-buttoned undershirt and dusty loft provided a curtain raiser to the day. The railroad was tolerant and allowed its passengers to loll outdoors if they wished; and on mornings when the air was heady that was the place to be—with the sudden whiff of the candy factory telling you that your ride was half over, and

the quick eastward glance through 24th Street to check your time
with the clock in the Metropolitan Tower, visible for the tenth
part of a second.

The El always seemed to me to possess exactly the right degree   5
of substantiality: it seemed reasonably strong and able to carry its
load, and competent with that easy slovenly competence of an
old drudge; yet it was perceptibly a creature of the clouds, the
whole structure vibrating ever so slightly following the final grasping
success of the applied brake. The El had giddy spells, too—days
when a local train would shake off its patient, plodding manner
and soar away in a flight of sheer whimsy, skipping stations in a
drunken fashion and scaring the pants off everybody. To go roaring
past a scheduled stop, hell bent for 53rd Street and the plunge
into space, was an experience which befell every El rider more
than once. On this line a man didn't have to be a locomotophobe
to suffer from visions of a motorman's lifeless form slumped over
an open throttle. And if the suspense got too great and you walked
nervously to the front of the train the little window in the booth
gave only the most tantalizing view of the driver—three inert
fingers of a gloved hand, or a *Daily News* wedged in some vital
cranny.

One thing I always admired about the El was the way it tormented   6
its inexperienced customers. Veterans like myself, approaching a
station stop, knew to a fraction of an inch how close it was
advisable to stand to the little iron gates on the open type cars.
But visitors to town had no such information. When the train
halted and the guard, pulling his two levers, allowed the gates to
swing in and take the unwary full in the stomach, there was always
a dim pleasure in it for the rest of us. Life has little enough in
the way of reward; these small moments of superiority are not to
be despised.

The El turned the Avenue into an arcade. That, in a way, was   7
its chief contribution. It made Sixth Avenue as distinct from Fifth
as Fifth is from Jones Street. Its pillars, straddling the car tracks
in the long channel of the night, provided the late cruising taxicab
with the supreme challenge, and afforded the homing pedestrian,
his wine too much with him, forest sanctuary and the friendly
accommodation of a tree.

Of course I have read about the great days of the El, when it   8
was the railroad of the élite and when financial giants rode elegantly
home from Wall Street in its nicely appointed coaches. But I'm
just as glad I didn't meet the El until after it had lost its money.
Its lazy crescendos, breaking into one's dreams, will always stick
in the mind—and the soiled hands of the guards on the bellcords,

and the brusque, husky-throated bells that had long ago lost their voices, cuing each other along the whole length of the train. Yes, at this distance it's hard to realize that the Sixth Avenue El is just a problem in demolition. I can't for the life of me imagine what New York will have to offer in its place. It will have to be something a good deal racier, a good deal more open and aboveboard, than a new subway line.

I suppose a man can't ask railroads to stand still. For twenty 9 or thirty years the railroads of America stood about as still as was consistent with swift transportation. The gas mantles were removed and electric lights installed, but outside of that the cars remained pretty much the same. It's only in the past couple of years that the railroads, fretting over the competition from busses and planes, have set about transforming their interiors into cocktail lounges, ballrooms, and modern apartments.

In my isolated position here in the country, I have plenty of 10 time to study Pullman trends—which are readily accessible in full-page color ads in the popular magazines. I note that the Pullman Company, although emphasizing the high safety factor implicit in Pullman travel, is advertising a new type of accommodation called, somewhat ominously, "S.O.S." This is the Single Occupancy Section. It is for the dollar-wise and the travel-wise, the ads point out. From the illustration, the single occupancy section appears to have a dead body in it, hooded in a sheet, bound and gagged. There is also a live occupant—a girl in a pink dressing gown, apparently in the best of spirits. More careful examination of the photograph reveals that the dead body is nothing more nor less than the bed itself, which has reared up on its hind end and been lashed to the bulkhead, while the occupant (who is single, of course) stands erect and goes through the motions of dressing in comfort.

I feel that the Pullman Company, in introducing the note of 11 *comfort* into its adventurous calling, is perhaps slipping outside the particular field in which it has made such an enviable reputation. This being able to stand erect in an ordinary single berth and dress in something like ease—isn't it likely to destroy the special flavor of Pullman travel? I don't take a night journey on a railroad for the sake of duplicating the experiences and conveniences of my own home: when I travel I like to get into some new kind of difficulty, not just the same old trouble I put up with around the house.

Travelers, I will admit, differ temperamentally, differ in their 12 wants and needs; but for me the Pullman Company will never improve on its classic design of upper and lower berth. In my eyes it is a perfect thing, perfect in conception and execution, this small green hole in the dark moving night, this soft warren in a hard world. In it I have always found the peace of spirit which accompanies grotesque bodily situations, peace and a wonderful sense of participation in cosmic rhythms and designs. I have experienced these even on cold nights when I all but died from exposure, under blankets of virgin gossamer.

In a Pullman berth, a man can truly be alone with himself. (The 13 nearest approach to this condition is to be found in a hotel bedroom, but a hotel room can be mighty depressing sometimes, it stands so still.) Now if a modern Pullman proposes to provide headroom for everyone it will have to answer for whatever modification this may cause in human character. The old act of drawing one's pants on and off while in a horizontal position did much to keep Man in a mood of decent humility. It gave him a picture of himself at a moment of wild comic contortion. To tuck in the tails of a shirt while supine demanded a certain persistence, a certain virtuosity, wholly healthful and character-building.

The new single occupancy section, besides changing all this and 14 permitting a man to stand erect as though he had no ape in his family background, has another rather alarming feature. The bed not only is capable of being cocked up by the occupant, to resemble a cadaver, but it can be hoisted by a separate control from the aisle by the dark, notional hand of the porter as he glides Puckishly through the car. It does not sound conducive to calm.

In resenting progress and change, a man lays himself open to 15 censure. I suppose the explanation of anyone's defending anything as rudimentary and cramped as a Pullman berth is that such things are associated with an earlier period in one's life and that this period in retrospect seems a happy one. People who favor progress and improvements are apt to be people who have had a tough enough time without any extra inconvenience. Reactionaries who pout at innovations are apt to be well-heeled sentimentalists who had the breaks. Yet for all that, there is always a subtle danger in life's refinements, a dim degeneracy in progress. I have just been refining the room in which I sit, yet I sometimes doubt that a writer should refine or improve his workroom by so much as a dictionary: one thing leads to another and the first thing you know he has a stuffed chair and is fast asleep in it. Half a man's life is devoted to what he calls improvements, yet the original had some quality which is lost in the process. There was a fine natural spring of water on this place when I bought it. Our drinking water had to be lugged in a pail, from a wet glade of alder and tamarack.

I visited the spring often in those first years and had friends there—
a frog, a woodcock, and an eel which had churned its way all
the way up through the pasture creek to enjoy the luxury of pure
water. In the normal course of development, the spring was rocked
up, fitted with a concrete curb, a copper pipe, and an electric
pump. I have visited it only once or twice since. This year my
only gesture was the purely perfunctory one of sending a sample
to the state bureau of health for analysis. I felt cheap, as though
I were smelling an old friend's breath.

Another phase of life here which has lost something through 16
refinement is the game of croquet. We used to have an old croquet
set whose wooden balls, having been chewed by dogs, were no
rounder than eggs. Paint had faded, wickets were askew. The
course had been laid out haphazardly and eagerly by a child, and
we all used to go out there on summer nights and play good-
naturedly, with the dogs romping on the lawn in the beautiful
light, and the mosquitoes sniping at us, and everyone in good
spirits, racing after balls and making split shots for the sheer love
of battle. Last spring we decided the croquet set was beyond use,
and invested in a rather fancy new one with hoops set in small
wooden sockets, and mallets with rubber faces. The course is now
exactly seventy-two feet long and we lined the wickets up with
a string; but the little boy is less fond of it now, for we make him
keep still while we are shooting. A dog isn't even allowed to cast
his shadow across the line of play. There are frequent quarrels of
a minor nature, and it seems to me we return from the field of
honor tense and out of sorts.

ALDOUS HUXLEY

Hyperion to a Satyr

A few months before the outbreak of the Second World War I 1
took a walk with Thomas Mann on a beach some fifteen or twenty
miles southwest of Los Angeles. Between the breakers and the
highway stretched a broad belt of sand, smooth, gently sloping
and (blissful surprise!) void of all life but that of the pelicans and

From *Tomorrow and Tomorrow and Tomorrow* (1956). In Shakespeare's *Hamlet*, the
prince compares his dead father to his stepfather: "So excellent a king, that was,
to this,/Hyperion to a Satyr."

godwits. Gone was the congestion of Santa Monica and Venice. Hardly a house was to be seen; there were no children, no promenading loincloths and brassières, not a single sun-bather was practicing his strange obsessive cult. Miraculously, we were alone. Talking of Shakespeare and the musical glasses, the great man and I strolled ahead. The ladies followed. It was they, more observant than their all too literary spouses, who first remarked the truly astounding phenomenon. "Wait," they called, "wait!" And when they had come up with us, they silently pointed. At our feet, and as far as the eye could reach in all directions, the sand was covered with small whitish objects, like dead caterpillars. Recognition dawned. The dead caterpillars were made of rubber and had once been contraceptives of the kind so eloquently characterized by Mantegazza as *"una tela di ragno contro l'infezione, una corazza contro il piacere."*[1]

> *Continuous as the stars that shine*
> *And twinkle in the milky way,*
> *They stretched in never-ending line*
> *Along the margin of a bay:*
> *Ten thousand saw I at a glance . . .*[2]

Ten thousand? But we were in California, not the Lake District. The scale was American, the figures astronomical. Ten million saw I at a glance. Ten million emblems and mementoes of Modern Love.

> *O bitter barren woman! what's the name,*
> *The name, the name, the new name thou hast won?*

And the old name, the name of the bitter fertile woman—what was that? These are questions that can only be asked and talked about, never answered in any but the most broadly misleading way. Generalizing about Woman is like indicting a Nation—an amusing pastime, but very unlikely to be productive either of truth or utility.

Meanwhile, there was another, a simpler and more concrete question: How on earth had these objects got here, and why in such orgiastic profusion? Still speculating, we resumed our walk. A moment later our noses gave us the unpleasant answer. Offshore

---

1. "A cobweb against infection, a breastplate against pleasure": Paolo Mantegazza (1831–1910) was an Italian physiologist and anthropologist known for his popular works on medicine.
2. The lines are from William Wordsworth's "I Wandered Lonely as a Cloud." They describe daffodils.

from this noble beach was the outfall through which Los Angeles discharged, raw and untreated, the contents of its sewers. The emblems of modern love and the other things had come in with the spring tide. Hence that miraculous solitude. We turned and made all speed towards the parked car.

Since that memorable walk was taken, fifteen years have passed. 3
Inland from the beach, three or four large cities have leapt into existence. The bean fields and Japanese truck gardens of those ancient days are now covered with houses, drugstores, supermarkets, drive-in theaters, junior colleges, jet-plane factories, laundromats, six-lane highways. But instead of being, as one would expect, even more thickly constellated with Malthusian flotsam and unspeakable jetsam, the sands are now clean, the quarantine has been lifted. Children dig, well-basted sun-bathers slowly brown, there is splashing and shouting in the surf. A happy consummation— but one has seen this sort of thing before. The novelty lies, not in the pleasantly commonplace end—people enjoying themselves— but in the fantastically ingenious means whereby that end has been brought about.

Forty feet above the beach, in a seventy-five-acre oasis scooped 4
out of the sand dunes, stands one of the marvels of modern technology, the Hyperion Activated Sludge Plant. But before we start to discuss the merits of activated sludge, let us take a little time to consider sludge in its unactivated state, as plain, old-fashioned dirt.

Dirt, with all its concomitant odors and insects, was once accepted 5
as an unalterable element in the divinely established Order of Things. In his youth, before he went into power politics as Innocent III, Lotario de' Conti found time to write a book on the *Wretchedness of Man's Condition.* "How filthy the father," he mused, "how low the mother, how repulsive the sister!" And no wonder! For "dead, human beings give birth to flies and worms; alive, they generate worms and lice." Moreover, "consider the plants, consider the trees. They bring forth flowers and leaves and fruits. But what do *you* bring forth? Nits, lice, vermin. Trees and plants exude oil, wine, balm—and *you,* spittle, snot, urine, ordure. *They* diffuse the sweetness of all fragrance—*you,* the most abominable stink." In the Age of Faith, Homo sapiens was also Homo pediculosus, also Homo immundus—a little lower than the angels, but dirty by definition, lousy, not *per accidens*[3], but in his very essence. And as for man's helpmate—*si nec extremis digitis flegma vel stercus tangere patimur, quomodo ipsum stercoris saccum amplecti desideramus?* "We

3. "by accident"

who shrink from touching, even with the tips of our fingers, a
gob of phlegm or a lump of dung, how is it that we crave for the
embraces of this mere bag of night-soil?" But men's eyes are not,
as Odo of Cluny wished they were, "like those of the lynxes of
Boeotia"; they cannot see through the smooth and milky surfaces
into the palpitating sewage within. That is why

> *There swims no goose so grey but soon or late*
> *Some honest gander takes her for his mate.*

That is why (to translate the notion into the language of medieval
orthodoxy), every muck-bag ends by getting herself embraced—
with the result that yet another stinker-with-a-soul finds himself
embarked on a sea of misery, bound for a port which, since few
indeed can hope for salvation, is practically certain to be Hell. The
embryo of this future reprobate is composed of "foulest seed,"
combined with "blood made putrid by the heat of lust." And as
though to make it quite clear what He thinks of the whole proceeding, God has decreed that "the mother shall conceive in stink
and nastiness."

That there might be a remedy for stink and nastiness—namely   6
soap and water—was a notion almost unthinkable in the thirteenth
century. In the first place, there was hardly any soap. The substance
was known to Pliny, as an import from Gaul and Germany. But
more than a thousand years later, when Lotario de' Conti wrote
his book, the burgesses of Marseilles were only just beginning to
consider the possibility of manufacturing the stuff in bulk. In England
no soap was made commercially until halfway through the fourteenth century. Moreover, even if soap had been abundant, its
use for mitigating the "stink and nastiness," then inseparable from
love, would have seemed, to every right-thinking theologian, an
entirely illegitimate, because merely physical, solution to a problem
in ontology and morals—an escape, by means of the most vulgarly
materialistic trick, from a situation which God Himself had intended,
from all eternity, to be as squalid as it was sinful. A conception
without stink and nastiness would have the appearance—what a
blasphemy!—of being Immaculate. And finally there was the virtue
of modesty. Modesty, in that age of codes and pigeonholes, had
its Queensberry Rules—no washing below the belt. Sinful in itself,
such an offense against modesty in the present was fraught with
all kinds of perils for modesty in the future. Havelock Ellis observed,
when he was practicing obstetrics in the London slums, that modesty
was due, in large measure, to a fear of being disgusting. When
his patients realized that "I found nothing disgusting in whatever
was proper and necessary to be done under the circumstances, it

almost invariably happened that every sign of modesty at once
disappeared." Abolish "stink and nastiness," and you abolish one
of the most important sources of feminine modesty, along with
one of the most richly rewarding themes of pulpit eloquence.

A contemporary poet has urged his readers not to make love   7
to those who wash too much. There is, of course, no accounting
for tastes; but there *is* an accounting for philosophical opinions.
Among many other things, the greatly gifted Mr. Auden is a belated
representative of the school which held that sex, being metaphysically
tainted, ought also to be physically unclean.

Dirt, then, seemed natural and proper, and dirt in fact was   8
everywhere. But, strangely enough, this all-pervading squalor never
generated its own psychological antidote—the complete indifference
of habit. Everybody stank, everybody was verminous; and yet, in
each successive generation, there were many who never got used
to these familiar facts. What has changed in the course of history
is not the disgusted reaction to filth, but the moral to be drawn
from that reaction. "Filth," say the men of the twentieth century,
"is disgusting. Therefore let us quickly do something to get rid of
filth." For many of our ancestors, filth was as abhorrent as it seems
to almost all of us. But how different was the moral they chose
to draw! "Filth is disgusting," they said. "Therefore the human
beings who produce the filth are disgusting, and the world they
inhabit is a vale, not merely of tears, but of excrement. This state
of things has been divinely ordained, and all we can do is cheerfully
to bear our vermin, loathe our nauseating carcasses and hope
(without much reason, since we shall probably be damned) for
an early translation to a better place. Meanwhile it is an observable
fact that villeins are filthier even than lords. It follows, therefore,
that they should be treated as badly as they smell." This loathing
for the poor on account of the squalor in which they were condemned to live outlasted the Middle Ages and has persisted to the
present day. The politics of Shakespeare's aristocratic heroes and
heroines are the politics of disgust. "Footboys" and other members
of the lower orders are contemptible because they are lousy—not
in the metaphorical sense in which that word is now used, but
literally; for the louse, in Sir Hugh Evans' words, "is a familiar
beast to man, and signifies love." And the lousy were also the
smelly. Their clothes were old and unclean, their bodies sweaty,
their mouths horrible with decay. It made no difference that, in
the words of a great Victorian reformer, "by no prudence on their
part can the poor avoid the dreadful evil of their surroundings."
They were disgusting and that, for the aristocratic politician, was
enough. To canvass the common people's suffrages was merely

to "beg their stinking breath." Candidates for elective office were men who "stand upon the breath of garlic eaters." When the citizens of Rome voted against him, Coriolanus told them that they were creatures,[4]

> *whose breath I hate*
> *As reek o' th' rotten fens, whose loves I prize*
> *As the dead carcasses of unburied men*
> *That do corrupt my air.*

And, addressing these same citizens, "You are they," says 9 Menenius,

> *You are they*
> *That made the air unwholesome when you cast*
> *Your stinking greasy caps in hooting at*
> *Coriolanus' exile.*

Again, when Caesar was offered the crown, "the rabblement 10 shouted and clapped their chopped hands, and threw up their sweaty night-caps, and uttered such a deal of stinking breath, because Caesar had refused the crown, that it had almost choked Caesar; for he swounded and fell down at it; and for mine own part," adds Casca, "I durst not laugh for fear of opening my lips and receiving the bad air." The same "mechanic slaves, with greasy aprons" haunted Cleopatra's imagination in her last hours.

> *In their thick breaths,*
> *Rank of gross diet, shall we be enclouded,*
> *And forced to drink their vapours.*

In the course of evolution man is supposed to have sacrificed 11 the greater part of his olfactory center to his cortex, his sense of smell to his intelligence. Nevertheless, it remains a fact that in politics, no less than in love and social relations, smell judgments continue to play a major role. In the passages cited above, as in all the analogous passages penned or uttered since the days of Shakespeare, there is the implication of an argument, which can be formulated in some such terms as these. "Physical stink is a symbol, almost a symptom, of intellectual and moral inferiority. All the members of a certain group stink physically. Therefore, they are intellectually and morally vile, inferior and, as such, unfit to be treated as equals."

---

4. The indented quotations to the end of the page are from Shakespeare's plays *Coriolanus*, *Julius Caesar*, and *Antony and Cleopatra*.

Tolstoy, who was sufficiently clear-sighted to recognize the un- 12
desirable political consequences of cleanliness in high places and
dirt among the poor, was also sufficiently courageous to advocate,
as a remedy, a general retreat from the bath. Bathing, he saw,
was a badge of class distinction, a prime cause of aristocratic
exclusiveness. For those who, in Mr. Auden's words, "wash too
much," find it exceedingly distasteful to associate with those who
wash too little. In a society where, let us say, only one in five can
afford the luxury of being clean and sweet-smelling, Christian
brotherhood will be all but impossible. Therefore, Tolstoy argued,
the bathers should join the unwashed majority. Only where there
is equality in dirt can there be a genuine and unforced fraternity.

Mahatma Gandhi, who was a good deal more realistic than his 13
Russian mentor, chose a different solution to the problem of differential cleanliness. Instead of urging the bathers to stop washing,
he worked indefatigably to help the non-bathers to keep clean.
Brotherhood was to be achieved, not by universalizing dirt, vermin
and bad smells, but by building privies and scrubbing floors.

Spengler, Sorokin, Toynbee—all the philosophical historians and 14
sociologists of our time have insisted that a stable civilization
cannot be built except on the foundations of religion. But if man
cannot live by bread alone, neither can he live exclusively on
metaphysics and worship. The gulf between theory and practice,
between the ideal and the real, cannot be bridged by religion alone.
In Christendom, for example, the doctrines of God's fatherhood
and the brotherhood of man have never been self-implementing.
Monotheism has proved to be powerless against the divisive forces
first of feudalism and then of nationalistic idolatry. And within
these mutually antagonistic groups, the injunction to love one's
neighbor as oneself has proved to be as ineffective, century after
century, as the commandment to worship one God.

A century ago the prophets who formulated the theories of the 15
Manchester School were convinced that commerce, industrialization
and improved communications were destined to be the means
whereby the age-old doctrines of monotheism and human brotherhood would at last be implemented. Alas, they were mistaken.
Instead of abolishing national rivalries, industrialization greatly
intensified them. With the march of technological progress, wars
became bloodier and incomparably more ruinous. Instead of uniting
nation with nation, improved communications merely extended
the range of collective hatreds and military operations. That human
beings will, in the near future, voluntarily give up their nationalistic
idolatry, seems, in these middle years of the twentieth century,
exceedingly unlikely. Nor can one see, from this present vantage

point, any technological development capable, by the mere fact of being in existence, of serving as an instrument for realizing those religious ideals, which hitherto mankind has only talked about. Our best consolation lies in Mr. Micawber's hope that, sooner or later, "Something will Turn Up."[5]

In regard to brotherly love within the mutually antagonistic 16 groups, something *has* turned up. That something is the development, in many different fields, of techniques for keeping clean at a cost so low that practically everybody can afford the luxury of not being disgusting.

For creatures which, like most of the carnivores, make their 17 home in a den or burrow, there is a biological advantage in elementary cleanliness. To relieve nature in one's bed is apt, in the long run, to be unwholesome. Unlike the carnivores, the primates are under no evolutionary compulsion to practice the discipline of the sphincters. For these free-roaming nomads of the woods, one tree is as good as another and every moment is equally propitious. It is easy to house-train a cat or a dog, all but impossible to teach the same desirable habits to a monkey. By blood we are a good deal closer to poor Jocko than to Puss or Tray. Man's instincts were developed in the forest; but ever since the dawn of civilization, his life has been lived in the more elaborate equivalent of a rabbit warren. His notions of sanitation were not, like those of the cat, inborn, but had to be painfully acquired. In a sense the older theologians were quite right in regarding dirt as natural to man—an essential element in the divinely appointed order of his existence.

But in spite of its unnaturalness, the art of living together without 18 turning the city into a dunghill has been repeatedly discovered. Mohenjo-daro, at the beginning of the third millennium B.C., had a water-borne sewage system; so, several centuries before the siege of Troy, did Cnossos; so did many of the cities of ancient Egypt, albeit only for the rich. The poor were left to demonstrate their intrinsic inferiority by stinking, in their slums, to high heaven. A thousand years later Rome drained her swamps and conveyed her filth to the contaminated Tiber by means of the Cloaca Maxima. But these solutions to the problem of what we may politely call "unactivated sludge" were exceptional. The Hindus preferred to condemn a tithe of their population to untouchability and the daily chore of carrying slops. In China the thrifty householder tanked the family sludge and sold it, when mature, to the highest bidder. There was a smell, but it paid, and the fields recovered

5. Micawber is a luckless optimist in Charles Dickens' *David Copperfield*.

some of the phosphorus and nitrogen of which the harvesters had robbed them. In medieval Europe every alley was a public lavatory, every window a sink and garbage chute. Droves of pigs were dedicated to St. Anthony and, with bells round their necks, roamed the streets, battening on the muck. (When operating at night, burglars and assassins often wore bells. Their victims heard the reassuring tinkle, turned over in their beds and went to sleep again—it was only the blessed pigs.) And meanwhile there were cesspools (like the black hole into which that patriotic Franciscan, Brother Salimbene[6], deliberately dropped his relic of St. Dominic), there was portable plumbing, there were members of the lower orders, whose duty it was to pick up the unactivated sludge and deposit it outside the city limits. But always the sludge accumulated faster than it could be removed. The filth was chronic and, in the slummier quarters, appalling. It remained appalling until well into the nineteenth century. As late as the early years of Queen Victoria's reign sanitation in the East End of London consisted in dumping everything into the stagnant pools that still stood between the jerry-built houses. From the peak of their superior (but still very imperfect) cleanliness the middle and upper classes looked down with unmitigated horror at the Great Unwashed. "The Poor" were written and spoken about as though they were creatures of an entirely different species. And no wonder! Nineteenth-century England was loud with Non-Conformist and Tractarian piety; but in a society most of whose members stank and were unclean the practice of brotherly love was out of the question.

The first modern sewage systems, like those of Egypt before them, were reserved for the rich and had the effect of widening still further the gulf between rulers and ruled. But endemic typhus and several dangerous outbreaks of Asiatic cholera lent weight to the warnings and denunciations of the sanitary reformers. In self-defense the rich had to do something about the filth in which their less fortunate neighbors were condemned to live. Sewage systems were extended to cover entire metropolitan areas. The result was merely to transfer the sludge problem from one place to another. "The Thames," reported a Select Committee of 1836, "receives the excrementitious matter from nearly a million and a half of human beings; the washing of their foul linen; the filth

---

6. Huxley slightly misremembers a story of monastic rivalry in the *Chronicle* of the thirteenth century monk. He assumes that it was the Franciscan Salimbene who visited a Dominican monastery, begged for a relic of St. Dominic, "put it to the vilest uses, and cast it at last into the cesspool. Then he cried aloud, saying, 'Alas! help me, brothers, for I seek the relic of your saint which I have lost among the filth.'" The outline of the story iş accurate, but Huxley has confused the characters.

and refuse of many hundred manufactories; the offal and decom-
posing vegetable substances from the markets; the foul and gory
liquid from the slaughter-houses; and the purulent abominations
from hospitals and dissecting rooms, too disgusting to detail. Thus
that most noble river, which has been given us by Providence for
our health, recreation and beneficial use, is converted into the
Common sewer of London, and the sickening mixture it contains
is daily pumped up into the water for the inhabitants of the most
civilized capital of Europe."

In England the heroes of the long campaign for sanitation were   20
a strangely assorted band. There was a bishop, Blomfield of London;
there was the radical Edwin Chadwick, a disciple of Jeremy Bentham; there was a physician, Dr. Southwood Smith; there was a
low-church man of letters, Charles Kingsley; and there was the
seventh Earl of Shaftesbury, an aristocrat who had troubled to
acquaint himself with the facts of working-class life. Against them
were marshaled the confederate forces of superstition, vested interest
and brute inertia. It was a hard fight; but the cholera was a staunch
ally, and by the end of the century the worst of the mess had
been cleared up, even in the slums. Writing in 1896, Lecky[7] called
it "the greatest achievement of our age." In the historian's estimation,
the sanitary reformers had done more for general happiness and
the alleviation of human misery than all the more spectacular
figures of the long reign put together. Their labors, moreover, were
destined to bear momentous fruit. When Lecky wrote, upper-class
noses could still find plenty of occasions for passing olfactory
judgments on the majority. But not nearly so many as in the past.
The stage was already set for the drama which is being played
today—the drama whose theme is the transformation of the English
caste system into an equalitarian society. Without Chadwick and
his sewers, there might have been violent revolution, never that
leveling by democratic process, that gradual abolition of untouchability, which are in fact taking place.

Hyperion—what joy the place would have brought to those pas-   21
sionately prosaic lovers of humanity, Chadwick and Bentham! And
the association of the hallowed name with sewage, of sludge with
the great god of light and beauty—what romantic furies it would
have evoked in Keats and Blake! And Lotario de' Conti—how
thunderously, in the name of religion, he would have denounced
this presumptuous demonstration that Homo immundus can effectively modify the abjection of his predestined condition! And

7. British intellectual and social historian.

Dean Swift[8], above all—how deeply the spectacle would have disturbed him! For, if Celia could relieve nature without turning her lover's bowels, if Yahoos, footmen and even ladies of quality did not *have* to stink, then, obviously, his occupation was gone and his neurosis would be compelled to express itself in some other, some less satisfactory, because less excruciating, way.

An underground river rushes into Hyperion. Its purity of 99.7   22 per cent exceeds that of Ivory Soap. But two hundred million gallons are a lot of water; and the three thousandth part of that daily quota represents a formidable quantity of muck. But happily the ratio between muck and muckrakers remains constant. As the faecal tonnage rises, so does the population of aerobic and anaerobic bacteria. Busier than bees and infinitely more numerous, they work unceasingly on our behalf. First to attack the problem are the aerobes. The chemical revolution begins in a series of huge shallow pools, whose surface is perpetually foamy with the suds of Surf, Tide, Dreft and all the other monosyllables that have come to take the place of soap. For the sanitary engineers, these new detergents are a major problem. Soap turns very easily into something else; but the monosyllables remain intractably themselves, frothing so violently that it has become necessary to spray the surface of the aerobes' pools with overhead sprinklers. Only in this way can the suds be prevented from rising like the foam on a mug of beer and being blown about the countryside. And this is not the only price that must be paid for easier dishwashing. The detergents are greedy for oxygen. Mechanically and chemically, they prevent the aerobes from getting all the air they require. Enormous compressors must be kept working night and day to supply the needs of the suffocating bacteria. A cubic foot of compressed air to every cubic foot of sludgy liquid. What will happen when Zoom, Bang and Whiz come to replace the relatively mild monosyllables of today, nobody, in the sanitation business, cares to speculate.

When, with the assistance of the compressors, the aerobes have   23 done all they are capable of doing, the sludge, now thickly concentrated, is pumped into the Digestion System. To the superficial glance, the Digestion System looks remarkably like eighteen very large Etruscan mausoleums. In fact it consists of a battery of cylindrical tanks, each more than a hundred feet in diameter and sunk fifty feet into the ground. Within these huge cylinders steam pipes maintain a cherishing heat of ninety-five degrees—the temperature at which the anaerobes are able to do their work with

8. Jonathan Swift, represented in *The Dolphin Reader* by "A Modest Proposal."

maximum efficiency. From something hideous and pestilential the sludge is gradually transformed by these most faithful of allies into sweetness and light—light in the form of methane, which fuels nine supercharged Diesel engines, each of seventeen hundred horsepower, and sweetness in the form of an odorless solid which, when dried, pelleted and sacked, sells to farmers at ten dollars a ton. The exhaust of the Diesels raises the steam which heats the Digestion System, and their power is geared either to electric generators or centrifugal blowers. The electricity works the pumps and the machinery of the fertilizer plant, the blowers supply the aerobes with oxygen. Nothing is wasted. Even the emblems of modern love contribute their quota of hydrocarbons to the finished products, gaseous and solid. And meanwhile another torrent, this time about 99.95 per cent pure, rushes down through the submarine outfall and mingles, a mile offshore, with the Pacific. The problem of keeping a great city clean without polluting a river or fouling the beaches, and without robbing the soil of its fertility, has been triumphantly solved.

But untouchability depends on other things besides the bad 24 sanitation of slums. We live not merely in our houses, but even more continuously in our garments. And we live not exclusively in health, but very often in sickness. Where sickness rages unchecked and where people cannot afford to buy new clothes or keep their old ones clean, the occasions for being disgusting are innumerable.

Thersites, in *Troilus and Cressida*, lists a few of the commoner 25 ailments of Shakespeare's time: "the rotten diseases of the south, the guts-griping, ruptures, catarrhs, loads o' gravel i' the back, lethargies, cold palsies, raw eyes, dirt-rotten livers, wheezing lungs, bladders full of imposthume, sciaticas, lime-kilns i' the palm, incurable bone-ache, and the rivelled fee-simple of the tetter." And there were scores of others even more repulsive. Crawling, flying, hopping, the insect carriers of infection swarmed uncontrollably. Malaria was endemic, typhus never absent, bubonic plague a regular visitor, dysentery, without benefit of plumbing, a commonplace. And meanwhile, in an environment that was uniformly septic, everything that *could* suppurate *did* suppurate. The Cook, in Chaucer's "Prologue," had a "mormal," or gangrenous sore, on his shin. The Summoner's face was covered with the "whelkes" and "knobbes" of a skin disease that would not yield to any known remedy. Every cancer was inoperable, and gnawed its way, through a hideous chaos of cellular proliferation and breakdown, to its foregone conclusion. The unmitigated horror surrounding illness explains the admiration felt, throughout the Middle Ages and early modern times, for those heroes and heroines of charity who voluntarily undertook the care of the sick. It explains, too, certain actions of the saints—actions which, in the context of modern life, seem utterly incomprehensible. In their filth and wretchedness, the sick were unspeakably repulsive. This dreadful fact was a challenge to which those who took their Christianity seriously responded by such exploits as the embracing of lepers, the kissing of sores, the swallowing of pus. The modern response to this challenge is soap and water, with complete asepsis as the ultimate ideal. The great gulf of disgust which used to separate the sick and the chronically ailing from their healthier fellows, has been, not indeed completely abolished, but narrowed everywhere and, in many places, effectively bridged. Thanks to hygiene, many who, because of their afflictions, used to be beyond the pale of love or even pity, have been re-admitted into the human fellowship. An ancient religious ideal has been implemented, at least in part, by the development of merely material techniques for dealing with problems previously soluble (and then how very inadequately, so far as the sick themselves were concerned!) only by saints.

"The essential act of thought is symbolization." Our minds transform experiences into signs. If these signs adequately represent the experiences to which they refer, and if we are careful to manipulate them according to the rules of a many-valued logic, we can deepen our understanding of experience and thereby achieve some control of the world and our own destiny. But these conditions are rarely fulfilled. In all too many of the affairs of life we combine ill-chosen signs in all kinds of irrational ways, and are thus led to unrealistic conclusions and inappropriate acts. [26]

There is nothing in experience which cannot be transformed by the mind into a symbol—nothing which cannot be made to signify something else. We have seen, for example, that bad smells may be made to stand for social inferiority, dirt for a low IQ, vermin for immorality, sickness for a status beneath the human. No less important than these purely physiological symbols are the signs derived, not from the body itself, but from its coverings. A man's clothes are his most immediately perceptible attribute. Stinking rags or clean linen, liveries, uniforms, canonicals, the latest fashions— these are the symbols in terms of which men and women have thought about the relations of class with class, of person with person. In the *Institutions of Athens*, written by an anonymous author of the fifth century B.C., we read that it was illegal in Athens to assault a slave even when he refused to make way for you in the street. "The reason why this is the local custom shall [27]

be explained. If it were legal for the slave to be struck by the free
citizen, your Athenian citizen himself would always be getting
assaulted through being mistaken for a slave. Members of the free
proletariat of Athens are no better dressed than slaves or aliens
and no more respectable in appearance." But Athens—a democratic
city state with a majority of "poor whites"—was exceptional. In
almost every other society the wearing of cheap and dirty clothes
has been regarded (such is the power of symbols) as the equivalent
of a moral lapse—a lapse for which the wearers deserved to be
ostracized by all decent people. In *Les Précieuses Ridicules*[9] the high-
flown heroines take two footmen, dressed up in their masters'
clothes, for marquises. The comedy comes to its climax when the
pretenders are stripped of their symbolic finery and the girls discover
the ghastly truth. *Et eripitur persona, manet res*[10]—or, to be more*
precise, *manet altera persona*. The mask is torn off and there remains—
what? Another mask—the footman's.

In eighteenth-century England the producers of woolens were   28
able to secure legislation prohibiting the import of cotton prints
from the Orient and imposing an excise duty, not repealed until
1832, on the domestic product. But in spite of this systematic
discouragement, the new industry prospered—inevitably; for it met
a need, it supplied a vast and growing demand. Wool could not
be cleaned, cotton was washable. For the first time in the history
of Western Europe it began to be possible for all but the poorest
women to look clean. The revolution then begun is still in progress.
Garments of cotton and the new synthetic fibers have largely
abolished the ragged and greasy symbols of earlier class distinctions.
And meanwhile, for such fabrics as cannot be washed, the chemical
industry has invented a host of new detergents and solvents. In
the past, grease spots were a problem for which there was no
solution. Proletarian garments were darkly shiny with accumulated
fats and oils, and even the merchant's broadcloth, even the velvets
and satins of lords and ladies displayed the ineradicable traces
of last year's candle droppings, of yesterday's gravy. Dry cleaning is a modern art, a little younger than railway travel, a little
older than the first Atlantic cable.

In recent years, and above all in America, the revolution in   29
clothing has entered a new phase. As well as cleanliness, elegance
is being placed within the reach of practically everyone. Cheap
clothes are mass-produced from patterns created by the most expensive designers. Unfashionableness was once a stigma hardly

9. *The Affected Young Women*, a play by Molière.
10. "And snatch away the mask, the thing remains."

less damning, as a symbol of inferiority, than dirt. Fifty years ago
a girl who wore cheap clothes proclaimed herself, by their obvious
dowdiness, to be a person whom it was all but out of the question,
if one were well off, to marry. Misalliance is still deplored; but,
thanks to Sears and Ohrbach, it seems appreciably less dreadful
than it did to our fathers.

Sewage systems and dry cleaning, hygiene and washable fabrics,   30
DDT and penicillin—the catalogue represents a series of technological
victories over two great enemies: dirt and that system of untouchability, that unbrotherly contempt, to which, in the past, dirt has
given rise.

It is, alas, hardly necessary to add that these victories are in no   31
sense definitive or secure. All we can say is that, in certain highly
industrialized countries, technological advances have led to the
disappearance of some of the immemorial symbols of class distinction. But this does not guarantee us against the creation of
new symbols no less compulsive in their anti-democratic tendencies
than the old. A man may be clean; but if, in a dictatorial state,
he lacks a party card, he figuratively stinks and must be treated
as an inferior at the best and, at the worst, an untouchable.

In the nominally Christian past two irreconcilable sets of symbols   32
bedeviled the Western mind—the symbols, inside the churches,
of God's fatherhood and the brotherhood of man; and the symbols,
outside, of class distinction, mammon worship and dynastic, provincial or national idolatry. In the totalitarian future—and if we
go on fighting wars, the future of the West is bound to be totalitarian—the time-hallowed symbols of monotheism and brotherhood
will doubtless be preserved. God will be One and men will all be
His children, but in a strictly Pickwickian sense. Actually there
will be slaves and masters, and the slaves will be taught to worship
a parochial Trinity of Nation, Party and Political Boss. Samuel
Butler's Musical Banks[11] will be even more musical than they are
today, and the currency in which they deal will have even less
social and psychological purchasing power than the homilies of
the Age of Faith.

Symbols are necessary—for we could not think without them.   33
But they are also fatal—for the thinking they make possible is just
as often unrealistic as it is to the point. In this consists the essentially
tragic nature of the human situation. There is no way out, except
for those who have learned how to go beyond all symbols to a

11. In Butler's *Erewhon* (1872), English institutions are ironically reflected in an
imaginary land. Equivalent to the English churches are the Erewhonian Musical
Banks, the money in which "had no direct commercial value in the outside world."

direct experience of the basic fact of the divine immanence. *Tat tvam asi*—thou art That. When this is perceived, the rest will be added. In the meantime we must be content with such real but limited goods as Hyperion, and such essentially precarious and mutable sources of good as are provided by the more realistic of our religious symbols.

DANIEL J. BOORSTIN

Technology and Democracy

One of the most interesting and characteristic features of de- 1
mocracy is, of course, the difficulty of defining it. And this difficulty
has been compounded in the United States, where we have been
giving new meanings to almost everything. It is, therefore, especially
easy for anyone to say that democracy in America has failed.

"Democracy," according to political scientists, usually describes 2
a form of government by the people, either directly or through
their elected representatives. But I prefer to describe a democratic
society as one which is governed by a spirit of equality and dominated
by the desire to equalize, to give everything to everybody. In the
United States the characteristic wealth and skills and know-how
and optimism of our country have dominated this quest.

My first and overshadowing proposition is that our problems 3
arise not so much from our failures as from our successes. Of
course no success is complete; only death is final. But we have
probably come closer to attaining our professed objectives than
any other society of comparable size and extent, and it is from
this that our peculiarly American problems arise.

The use of technology to democratize our daily life has given 4
a quite new shape to our hopes. In this final chapter I will explore
some of the consequences of democracy, not for government but
for experience. What are the consequences for everybody every
day of this effort to democratize life in America? And especially
the consequences of our fantastic success in industry and technology
and in invention?

There have been at least four of these consequences. I begin 5
with what I call *attenuation*, which means the thinning out or the

This essay is based on a lecture delivered at the University of Michigan in 1972.

flattening of experience. We might call this the democratizing of experience. It might otherwise be described as the decline of poignancy. One of the consequences of our success in technology, of our wealth, of our energy and our imagination, has been the removal of distinctions, not just between people but between everything and everything else, between every place and every other place, between every time and every other time. For example, television removes the distinction between being here and being there. And the same kind of process, of thinning out, of removing distinctions, has appeared in one area after another of our lives.

For instance, in the seasons. One of the great unheralded 6 achievements of American civilization was the rise of transportation and refrigeration, the development of techniques of canning and preserving meat, vegetables, and fruits in such a way that it became possible to enjoy strawberries in winter, to enjoy fresh meat at seasons when the meat was not slaughtered, to thin out the difference between the diet of winter and the diet of summer. There are many unsung heroic stories in this effort.

One of them, for example, was the saga of Gustavus Swift in 7 Chicago. In order to make fresh meat available at a relatively low price to people all over the country, it was necessary to be able to transport it from the West, where the cattle were raised, to the Eastern markets and the cities where population was concentrated. Gustavus Swift found the railroad companies unwilling to manufacture refrigerator cars. They were afraid that, if refrigeration was developed, the cattle would be butchered in the West and then transported in a more concentrated form than when the cattle had to be carried live. The obvious consequence, they believed, would be to reduce the amount of freight. So they refused to develop the refrigerator car. Gustavus Swift went ahead and developed it, only to find that he had more cars than he had use for. The price of fresh meat went down in the Eastern cities, and Gustavus Swift had refrigerator cars on his hands. He then sent agents to the South and to other parts of the country, and tried to encourage people to raise produce which had to be carried in refrigerator cars. One of the consequences of this was the development of certain strains of fruit and vegetables, especially of fruit, which would travel well. And Georgia became famous for the peaches which were grown partly as a result of Swift's efforts to encourage people to raise something that he could carry in his refrigerator cars.

There were other elements in this story which we may easily 8 forget—for example, how central heating and air conditioning have affected our attitude toward the seasons, toward one time of year or another. Nowadays visitors from abroad note that wherever they are in our country, it is not unusual to find that in winter it is often too warm indoors, and in summer, often too cool.

But the development of central heating during the latter part 9 of the nineteenth century had other, less obvious consequences. For example, as people built high-rise apartments in the cities they found it impossible to have a fireplace in every room. You could not construct a high building with hundreds of apartments and have enough room for all the chimneys. So central heating was developed and this became a characteristic of city life. As central heating was developed it was necessary to have a place to put the machinery, and the machinery went in the cellar. But formerly people, even in the cities, had used their cellars to store fruit and vegetables over the winter. When the basement was heated by a furnace, of course it was no longer possible to store potatoes or other vegetables or fruit there. This increased the market for fresh fruits and vegetables that were brought in from truck farms just outside the cities or by refrigerator cars from greater distances. And this was another way of accelerating the tendency toward equalizing the seasons and equalizing the diet of people all over the country.

Also important in attenuating experience was the development 10 of what I would call homogenized space, especially the development of vertical space as a place to live in. There is a great deal less difference between living on the thirty-fifth floor and living on the fortieth floor of an apartment building than there is between living in a house in the middle of a block and living on the corner. The view is pretty much the same as you go up in the air. Vertical space is much more homogenized, and as we live in vertical space more and more, we live in places where "where we are" makes much less difference than it used to.

An important element in this which has been a product of 11 American technology is, of course, glass. We forget that the innovations in the production of glass resulting in large sheets which you could look through was an achievement largely of American technology in the nineteenth century. Of course, one by-product was the development of the technology of bottling, which is related to some of the levelings-out of the seasons which I mentioned before in relation to food. But we forget that when we admire those old leaded-glass windows which we see in medieval or early modern buildings, what we are admiring is the inability of people to produce plate glass.

When a large plate of glass became technologically possible, this 12 affected daily life in the United States. It affected merchandising, for example, because the "show window" became possible in which you could, with a relatively unobstructed view, display garments and other large objects in a way to make them appealing to people who passed by. But glass was also important in producing one of the main characteristics of modern American architecture—an architecture in which there is relatively less difference between the indoors and the outdoors than elsewhere. And that is one of the great functions of glass in modern architecture.

Along with the attenuation of places and time comes the attenuation of occasions and events. One of the more neglected aspects of modern technology is what I have called the rise of "repeatable experience." It used to be thought that one of the characteristics of life, one of the things that distinguished being alive from being dead, was the uniqueness of the individual moment. Something happened which could never happen again. If you missed it then, you were out of luck. But the growth of popular photography, which we can trace from about 1888 when Kodak #1 went on the market, began to allow everybody to make his own experience repeatable. If you had not seen this baby when he was so cute, you could still see him that way right now if you were so unlucky as to be in the living room with the parents who wanted to show you. Kodak #1 was a great achievement and was the beginning of our taking for granted that there was such a thing as a repeatable experience. 13

The phonograph, of course, beginning about 1877, created new opportunities to repeat audible experience. If you want to hear the voice of Franklin Delano Roosevelt now, you can hear him on a record. At the opening of the Woodrow Wilson Center for International Scholars at the Smithsonian Institution in 1971, part of the dedicating ceremony was the playing of a record with the voice of Woodrow Wilson. It was not a very warm voice, but it was identifiable and distinctive. The growth of the phonograph, then, has accustomed us to the fact that experience is not a one-time thing. 14

When we watch the Winter Olympics in our living room and see the ski jumper in the seventy-meter jump who makes a mistake or who performs very well, we can see the same performance just a minute later with all the failures and successes pointed out. Is instant replay the last stage in the technology of repeatable experience? 15

In the attenuating of events there is another element which I call the "pseudo-event." As more and more of the events which have public notice are planned in advance, as the accounts of them are made available before they happen, then it becomes the responsibility of the event to live up to its reputation. In this way 16

the spontaneity of experience, the unpredictableness of experience,
dissolves and disappears. The difference between the present and
the future becomes less and less.

Another aspect of this is what I have called the "neutralization   17
of risks," a result of the rise of insurance. For insurance, too, is
a way of reducing the difference between the future and the present.
You reduce risks by assuring yourself that if your house burns
down, at least you will have the money so you can rebuild it. In
this sense, insurance, and especially casualty insurance, provides
a way of thinning out the difference between present and future,
removing the suspense and the risk of experience.

What have been the everyday consequences of the democratizing   18
of property for our experience of property? In his classic defense
of property in his essay *On Civil Government* (1690), John Locke
argued that because property is the product of the mixing of a
person's labor with an object, no government has the right to take
it without his consent. This simplistic conception of property has
dominated a great deal of political and economic thinking. It was
prominent in the thinking of the authors of the Declaration of
Independence and of the Founding Fathers of the Constitution. It
was based on a simpler society where there was something poignant
and characteristic about the experience of ownership. Owning
meant the right to exclude people. You had the pleasure of
possession.

But what has happened to property in our society? Of course,   19
the most important new form of property in modern American
life is corporate property: shares of stock in a corporation. And
the diffusion of the ownership of shares is one of the most prominent
features of American life. There are companies like AT&T, for
example, which have as many as a million stockholders. What
does it mean to be a stockholder? You are a lucky person. You
own property and you have some shares. So what? One doesn't
need to be rich or even middle-class in this country to own shares
of stock. But very few of my friends who own shares of stock
know precisely what it means or what their legal powers are as
stockholders. They are solicited to send in their proxies—by somebody who has a special interest in getting them to vote for something
or other. They feel very little pleasure of control; they don't have
the sense of wreaking themselves on any object. Yet this—a share
of stock—is the characteristic and most important form of property
in modern times. This property, too, is attenuated.

Other developments in American life concerning property have   20
had a similar effect. For example, installment and credit buying.

This phenomenon first grew in connection with the wide marketing of the sewing machine and then in relation to the cash register, but its efflorescence has come with the automobile. When it became necessary to sell millions of automobiles—and necessary in order to keep the machinery of our society going to sell them to people who could not afford to lay out the full cost of an automobile—it was necessary to find ways of financing their purchases. Installment and credit buying was developed. One of the results was that people became increasingly puzzled over whether they did or did not (and if so in what sense) own their automobile. Of course, it is not uncommon for people to divest themselves of their physical control of an object like an automobile or a color television set before they have really acquired full ownership—and then to enter on another ambiguous venture of part ownership.

Another aspect of this is the rise of franchising: the development 21 of what I would call the "semi-independent businessman." In the United States today, between 35 percent and 50 percent of all retail merchandising is done through franchised outlets. Well, of course, we all know what a franchised outlet is; a typical example would be a McDonald's hamburger stand or any other outlet in which the person who is in control of the shop has been authorized to use a nationally advertised name like Midas Mufflers or Colonel Sanders' Kentucky Fried Chicken. He is then instructed in the conduct of his business. He must meet certain standards in order to be allowed to continue to advertise as a Holiday Inn or Howard Johnson or whatever. And he is in business "for himself." Now, what does that mean? If you go into a franchised outlet and you find the hamburger unsatisfactory, what can you do? Whom would you complain to? The man who runs the shop has received his instructions and his materials from the people who have franchised him. It is not his fault. And, of course, it's not the fault of the people at the center who franchised him, because the shop is probably badly run by the franchisee.

This phenomenon grew out of the needs of the automobile 22 because in order to sell Fords or any other makes, it was necessary to have an outlet which would take continuous responsibility for stocking parts. Then the purchaser could replace that part at the outlet where he had purchased the car. After automobile franchising came the franchising of filling stations. People wanted some assurance about the quality of the fuel they put in their cars; they were given this by the identification of what they purchased with some nationally advertised brand in which they had confidence.

Now, perhaps the most important example of attenuation, of 23 the decline of poignancy in our experience in relation to property, is so obvious and so universal that it has hardly been discussed. That is packaging. Until relatively recently if you went into a store to buy coffee, you would have to bring a container to the grocery store, and the grocer would ladle out the coffee to you.

Packaging began to develop in this country after the Civil War. 24 In a sense it was a by-product of the Civil War because the necessities of the war (especially the need to package flour) produced certain innovations which were important. And later there were decisive, although what seem to us rather trivial, innovations. For example, the invention of the folding box was important. Until there was a way to make boxes which could be transported and stored compactly, it was impossible or impractical to use them for industrial purposes. The folding box and certain improvements in the paper bag, such as the paper bag that had a square bottom so that it could stand up, and on the side of which you could print an advertisement—these were American inventions.

If we will risk seeming pompous or pedantic, we can say that 25 the most important consequences of packaging have been epistemological. They have had to do with the nature of knowledge and they have especially had the effect of confusing us about what knowledge is, and what's real, about what's form and what's substance. When you think about a Winston cigarette, you don't think about the tobacco inside the cigarette. You think about the package. And in one area after another of American life, the form and the content become confused, and the form becomes that which dominates our consciousness. One area perhaps in which this has ceased to be true, happily or otherwise, is the area which I have always thought of as an aspect of packaging—namely, clothing. In the United States we have developed ready-made clothing, too, in such a way as to obscure the differences of social class and even of sex.

All around us we see attenuation—as our technology has suc- 26 ceeded, as we have tried to make everything available to everybody. The very techniques we use in preparing our food, in transporting our food, in controlling the climate and temperature of the rooms we live in, the shapes of the buildings in which we do business and reside, the ways we look at past experience—in all these ways our experience becomes attenuated. As we democratize experience, the poignancy of the moment, of the season, of the control of the object, of the spontaneous event, declines.

Now to a second consequence of the success of our technology 27 for our daily experience. This is what I would call the *decline of congregation*. Or it might be called a new segregation. This is the

consequence of increasingly organized and centralized sources of anything and everything. Example: Rebecca at the well.[1] When I wrote an article for the issue of *Life* magazine which was intended to celebrate the twenty-fifth anniversary of the introduction of television in this country, I entitled the article at first "Rebecca at the TV Set." But my friends at *Life* said, "Rebecca who?" Deferring to their greater, wider knowledge of American life and of the literariness of the American people, instead we called it simply "The New Segregation."

When Rebecca lived in her village and needed to get water for the household, she went to the well. At the well she met the other women of the village; she heard the gossip; she met her fiancé there, as a matter of fact. And then what happened? With the progress of democracy and technology, running water was introduced; and Rebecca stayed in the kitchenette of her eighth-floor apartment. She turned the faucet on and got the water out of the faucet; she didn't have to go to the well any more. She had only the telephone to help her collect gossip and she would have to find other ways to meet her fiancé. This is a parable of the problem of centralizing sources of everything. 28

The growth of centralized plumbing was itself, of course, a necessary by-product of the development of the skyscraper and the concentration of population in high buildings. You had to have effective sanitary facilities. But we forget other features of this development. Even those of us who have never made much use of the old "privy" know that the privy characteristically had more than one hole in it. Why was this? The plural facility was not peculiar simply to the privy; it was also found in the sanitary arrangements of many older buildings, including some of the grandest remaining medieval structures. The development of centralized plumbing led to privatizing; "privy" was the wrong word for the old facility. The privatizing of the bodily functions made them less sociable. People engaged in them in private. 29

The most dramatic example today of the privatizing of experience by centralizing a facility is, of course, television. We could start with the newspaper, for that matter. The town crier communicated the news to people in their presence. If you wanted to hear it you had to be there, or talk to somebody else who was there when he brought the news. But as the newspaper developed, with inexpensive printing, the messages were brought to you and you could look at them privately as you sat by yourself at breakfast. Television is perhaps one of the most extreme examples of the 30

1. The wife of Isaac and mother of Jacob and Esau, Genesis 24.

decline of congregation. Until the development of television, if you wanted to see a play you had to go out to a theater; if you wanted to hear a concert you had to go to a concert hall. These performances were relatively rare. They were special events. But with the coming of television, everybody acquired his private theater. Rebecca had her theater in her kitchen. She no longer needed to go out for entertainment.

The centralized source, the centralizing of the source, then, led   31
to the isolating of the consumer. Of course, much was gained by this. But one of the prices paid was the decline of congregation— congregation being the drawing together of people where they could enjoy and react to and respond to the reactions and feelings of their fellows.

There is a third consequence of our technological success in   32
democratic America, which I would call the new determinism, or *the rising sense of momentum*. Technology has had a deep and pervasive effect on our attitude toward history, and especially on the citizen's attitude toward his control over the future. In the seventeenth century the Puritans spoke about Providence; that was their characteristic way of describing the kind of control that God exercised over futurity. In the nineteenth century, when people became more scientifically minded, they still retained some notion of divine foresight in the form of the concept of destiny or mission or purpose. But in our time in this country we have developed a different kind of approach toward futurity; and this is what I would call the sense of momentum.

Momentum in physics is the product of a body's mass and its   33
linear velocity. Increasing scale and speed of operation increase the momentum. One of the characteristics of our technology and especially of our most spectacular successes has been to increase this sense of momentum. I will mention three obvious examples. It happens that each of these developments came, too, as a result of overwhelming international pressure. When such pressures added to the forces at work inside the nation, in each case they produced a phenomenon of great mass and velocity which became very difficult to stop.

The first example is, of course, atomic research. The large-scale   34
concerted efforts in this country to build an atomic bomb began and were accelerated at the time of World War II because of rumors that the Nazis were about to succeed in nuclear fission. When this information became available, national resources were massed and organized in an unprecedented fashion; futurity was scheduled and groups were set to work in all parts of the continent exploring different possible ways of finding the right form of uranium or of

some other element. And the search for the first atomic chain reaction, which was accomplished at my University of Chicago, went on.

One of the more touching human aspects of this story is the   35
account, now well chronicled by several historians, of the frantic efforts of the atomic scientists, the people who had been most instrumental in getting this process started (Albert Einstein, Leo Szilard, and James Franck, among others), when they saw that the atomic bomb was about to become possible, to persuade the President of the United States either not to use the bomb or to use it only in a demonstration in the uninhabited mid-Pacific. Such a use, they urged, would so impress the enemy with the horrors of the bomb that he would surrender, eliminating the need for us to use the bomb against a live target. They pursued this purpose—trying to put the brakes on military use of the bomb— with a desperation that even exceeded the energy they had shown in developing the bomb. But, of course, they had no success.

They could develop the bomb, but they couldn't stop it. Why?   36
There were many reasons, including President Truman's reasonable belief that use of the bomb could in the long run save the hundreds of thousands of Japanese and American lives that would have been lost in an invasion, and also would shorten the war. But surely one reason was that there had already been too much investment in the bomb. Billions of dollars had gone into the making of it. People were organized all over the country in various ways. It was impossible to stop.

Another example of this kind of momentum is the phenomenon   37
of space exploration. I happen to be an enthusiast for space ex- ploration, so by describing this momentum I do not mean to suggest that I think the space enterprise itself has not been a good thing. Nevertheless, as a historian I am increasingly impressed by the pervasive phenomenon of momentum in our time. Billions of dollars have been spent in developing the machinery for going off to the moon or going then to Mars or elsewhere. The mass of the operation has been enormous. The velocity of it is enormous, and it becomes virtually impossible to stop. The recent problem with the SST is a good example. For when any enterprise in our society has reached a certain scale, the consequences in unemployment and in dislocation of the economy are such that it becomes every year more difficult to cease doing what we are already doing.

A third example, more in the area of institutions, is foreign aid: 38
the international pressures to give foreign aid to one country or another. We have an enormous mass of wealth being invested, a great velocity with lots of people going off all over the world and

performing this operation of giving aid, and it becomes almost impossible to stop it. The other countries resent the decline of aid and consider it a hostile act, even though they might not have felt that way if we hadn't started the aid in the first place. Foreign aid is, I think, the most characteristic innovation in foreign policy in this century.

Each of these three enterprises illustrates the attitude of the   39
American citizen in the later twentieth century toward his control over experience. Increasingly, the citizen comes to feel that events are moving, and moving so fast with such velocity and in such mass that he has very little control. The sense of momentum itself becomes possible only because of our success in achieving these large purposes which no other democratic society, no other society before us, had even imagined.

Now, what does this bring us to? Before I come to my fourth   40
and concluding point on the ways in which the successes of democracy have affected our experience, I would like briefly to recall some of the remedies that have been suggested for the ills of democracy and the problems of democracy in the past. Al Smith once said, "All the ills of democracy can be cured by more democracy." I must confess, though I admire Al Smith for some of his enterprises, the Empire State Building for example, I think he was on the wrong track here. In fact, I would take an almost contrary position. Even at the risk of seeming flip, I might sum up the democratic paradoxes that I have been describing: "Getting there is *all* the fun."

Is there a law of democratic impoverishment? Is it possible that   41
while *democratizing* enriches experience, *democracy* dilutes experience?

Example: photography. Before the invention of photography, it   42
was a remarkable experience to see an exact likeness of the Sphinx or of Notre Dame or of some exotic animal or to see a portrait of an ancestor. Then, as photography was publicized in the 1880's and thoroughly popularized in this century, it opened up a fantastic new range of experience for everybody. Suddenly people were able to see things they had never been able to see before. And then what happened? Everyone had a camera, or two or three cameras; and everywhere he went he took pictures and when he came home he had to find a victim, somebody to show the pictures to. And this became more and more difficult.

While photography was being introduced, it was life-enriching   43
and vista-opening; but once it was achieved, once everybody had a camera, the people were looking in their cameras instead of

looking at the sight they had gone to see. It had an attenuating effect. A picture came to mean less and less, simply because people saw pictures everywhere. And the experience of being there also somehow meant less because the main thing people saw everywhere was the inside of their viewfinders, and their concern over their lens cap and finding the proper exposure made it hard for them to notice what was going on around them at the moment.

Another example is, of course, the phonograph. Has the phono-   44
graph—in its universal late-twentieth-century uses—necessarily made people more appreciative of music? In the 1920's when I was raised in Tulsa, Oklahoma, I had never heard an opera, nor had I really heard any classical music properly performed by an orchestra. But in our living room we had a wind-up Victrola, and I heard Galli-Curci singing arias from *Rigoletto*, and I heard Caruso, and I heard some symphonies, and it was fantastic. And then hi-fi came and everybody had a phonograph, a hi-fi machine or a little transistor radio which you could carry with you and hear music any time.

Today when I walk into the elevator in an office building, it is   45
not impossible that I will hear Beethoven or Verdi. Sitting in the airplane I hear Mozart coming out of the public-address system. Wherever we go we hear music whether we want to hear it or not, whether we are in the mood for it or not. It becomes an everywhere, all-the-time thing. The experience is attenuated.

And one of the most serious consequences of all this, finally, is   46
the attenuation of community itself. What holds people together? What has held people together in the past? For the most part it has been their sense of humanity, their pleasure in the presence of one another, their feeling for another person's expression, the sound of a voice, the look on his or her face. But the kind of community I describe increasingly becomes attenuated. People are trying to enjoy the community all by themselves.

We are led to certain desperate quests in American life. These,   47
the by-products of our success, are clues to the vitality and energy of our country, to the quest for novelty to keep life interesting and vistas open, to the quest for community and the quest for autonomy. Can we inoculate ourselves against these perils of our technological success? Samuel Butler once said, "If I die prematurely, at any rate I shall be saved from being bored by my own success." Our problem, too, is partly that.

And now a fourth characteristic of the relation of technology   48
to democracy in our time: *the belief in solutions*. One of the most dangerous popular fallacies—nourished by American history and

by some of our most eloquent and voluble patriots—is the notion
that democracy is attainable. There is a subtle difference between
American democratic society and many earlier societies in the
extent to which their ideals could be attained. The objectives of
other societies have for the most part been definable and attainable.
Aristocracy and monarchy do present attainable ideals. Even totalitarianism presents objectives which can be attained in the sense
in which the objectives of democracy never can be.

This nation has been a place of renewal, of new beginnings for   49
nations and for man. Vagueness has been a national resource: the
vagueness of the continent, the mystery of our resources, the
vagueness of our social classes, the misty miasma of our hopes.

Our society has been most distinctively a way of reaching for   50
rather than of finding. American democracy, properly speaking,
has been a process and not a product, a quest and not a discovery.
But a great danger which has been nourished by our success in
technology has been the belief in solutions. For technological problems there *are* solutions. It is possible to set yourself the task of
developing an economic and workable internal-combustion engine,
a prefabricated house, or a way of reaching the moon. Technological
problems are capable of solutions.

We are inclined, then, using the technological problem as our   51
prototype, to believe that somehow democracy itself is a solution,
a dissolving of the human condition. But we should have learned,
and even the history of technology—especially the history of technology in our democratic society—should have taught us otherwise.

In human history in the long run there are no solutions, only   52
problems. This is what I have suggested in my description of "self-
liquidating" ideals. And the examples are all around us—in our
effort to create a pluralistic society by assimilating and Americanizing
people, in our effort to give everybody an uncrowded wilderness
vacation, in our effort to find an exciting new model each year.

Every seeming solution is a new problem. When you democratize   53
the speedy automobile and give everybody an automobile, the
result is a traffic jam; and this is the sense in which the "solution"
of technological problems presents us with obstacles to the fulfillment
of what is human in our society. When we think about American
democratic society, then, we must learn not to think about a
condition, but about a process; not about democracy, but about
the quest for democracy, which we might call "democratizing."

The most distinctive feature of our system is not a system, but   54
a quest, not a neat arrangement of men and institutions, but a

flux. What other society has ever committed itself to so tantalizing, so fulfilling, so frustrating a community enterprise?

To prepare ourselves for this view of American democracy there are two sides to our personal need. One is on the side of prudence and wisdom; the other on the side of poetry and imagination. 55

On the side of prudence, there is a need for a sense of history. Only by realizing the boundaries that we have been given can we discover how to reach beyond them. Only so can we have the wisdom not to mistake passing fads for great movements, not to mistake the fanaticisms of a few for the deep beliefs of the many, not to mistake fashion for revolution. This wisdom is necessary if we are to secure sensibly the benefits of a free society for those who have for whatever reason been deprived of its benefits. We were not born yesterday, nor was the nation. And between the day before yesterday and yesterday, crucial events have happened. We can discover these and come to terms with them only through history. As Pascal said, "It is only by knowing our condition that we can transcend it." Our technology brings us the omnipresent present. It dulls our sense of history, and if we are not careful it can destroy it. 56

We in the U.S.A. are always living in an age of transition. Yet we have tended to believe that our present is always the climax of history, even though American history shows that the climax is always in the future. By keeping suspense alive, we can prepare ourselves for the shocks of change. 57

And finally, on the side of poetry and imagination, how do we keep alive the spirit of adventure, what I would call the exploring spirit? This should be the easiest because it is the most traditional of our achievements and efforts. We must remember that we live in a new world. We must keep alive the exploring spirit. We must not sacrifice the infinite promise of the unknown, of man's unfulfilled possibilities in the universe's untouched mysteries, for the cozy satisfactions of predictable, statistical benefits. Space exploration is a symbol. 58

Recently I had the pleasure of talking with Thor Heyerdahl, the *Kon Tiki* man, whose latest venture was the Ra expedition, in which he explored the possibilities of men having come from Egypt or elsewhere in the Mediterranean to this continent long ago in boats made of reeds. He and his crew, to test their hypothesis, actually crossed the Atlantic in a reed boat. And as I talked to Thor Heyerdahl about the Ra expedition, I said that it must have 59 been a terrible feeling of risk when you suddenly left the sight of land and got out into the open sea. It seemed to me that the fear and perils of the open sea would be the greatest. Thor Heyerdahl said not at all: the great dangers, the dangers of shoals and rocks, existed along the shore. The wonderful sense of relief, he observed, came when he went out on the ocean where there was openness all around, although also high waves and strong currents. The promise of American democracy, I suggest, depends on our ability to stay at sea, to work together in community while we all reach to the open horizon.

NANCY MITFORD

A Bad Time

Apsley Cherry Garrard has said that "polar exploration is at   1
once the cleanest and most isolated way of having a bad time that has yet been devised."[1] Nobody could deny that he and the twenty-four other members of Captain Scott's expedition to the South Pole had a bad time; in fact, all other bad times, embarked on by men of their own free will, pale before it. Theirs is the last of the great classic explorations; their equipment, though they lived in our century, curiously little different from that used by Captain Cook.[2] Vitamin pills would probably have saved the lives of the Polar party, so would a wireless transmitter; an electric torch have mitigated the misery of the Winter Journey. How many things which we take completely as a matter of course had not yet been invented, such a little time ago! Scott's *Terra Nova* had the advantage over Cook's *Resolution* of steam as well as sail. Even this was a mixed blessing, as it involved much hateful shovelling, while the coal occupied space which could have been put to better account in the little wooden barque (764 tons). Three motor-sledges lashed to the deck seemed marvellously up-to-date and were the pride and joy of Captain Scott.

Mitford was at work on this essay when John Glenn made the first U.S. orbital flight in February, 1962. The British explorer Robert Falcon Scott died March 29, 1912.
1. Unless otherwise stated, the quotations in this essay are from *The Worst Journey in the World*, by Cherry-Garrard. [author's note]
2. James Cook sailed to the Antarctic on his long voyage, 1772–75.

The *Terra Nova* sailed from London 15th June 1910 and from   2
New Zealand 26th November. She was fearfully overloaded; on
deck, as well as the motor-sledges in their huge crates, there were
30 tons of coal in sacks, 2½ tons of petrol in drums, 33 dogs, and
19 ponies. She rode out a bad storm by a miracle. "Bowers and
Campbell were standing upon the bridge and the ship rolled slug-
gishly over until the lee combings of the main hatch were under
the sea . . . as a rule, if a ship goes that far over she goes down."
It took her thirty-eight days to get to McMurdo Sound, by which
time the men were in poor shape. They had slept in their clothes,
lucky if they got five hours a night, and had had no proper meals.
As soon as they dropped anchor they began to unload the ship.
This entailed dragging its cargo over ice floes which were in constant
danger of being tipped up by killer whales, a very tricky business,
specially when it came to moving ponies, motor sledges and a
pianola. Then they built the Hut which was henceforward to be
their home. Scott, tireless himself, always drove his men hard and
these things were accomplished in a fortnight. The *Terra Nova*
sailed away; she was to return the following summer, when it
was hoped that the Polar party would be back in time to be taken
off before the freezing up of the sea forced her to leave again. If
not, they would be obliged to spend a second winter on McMurdo
Sound. Winter, of course, in those latitudes, happens during our
summer months and is perpetual night, as the summer is perpetual
day. The stunning beauty of the scenery affected the men deeply.
When the sun shone the snow was never white, but brilliant
shades of pink, blue and lilac; in winter the aurora australis flamed
across the sky and the summit of Mount Erebus glowed.

The Hut, unlike so much of Scott's equipment, was a total   3
success. It was built on the shore, too near the sea, perhaps, for
absolute security in the cruel winter storms, under the active volcano
Mount Erebus, called after the ship in which Ross discovered these
regions in 1839. It was 50 feet by 25, 9 feet high. The walls had
double boarding inside and outside the frames, with layers of
quilted seaweed between the boards. The roof had six layers of
alternate wood, rubber and seaweed. Though 109 degrees of frost
was quite usual, the men never suffered from cold indoors; in
fact, with twenty-five of them living there, the cooking range at
full blast and a stove at the other end, they sometimes complained
of stuffiness.

Life during the first winter was very pleasant. Before turning in   4
for good they had done several gruelling marches, laying stores
in depots along the route of the Polar journey; they felt they needed
and had earned a rest. Their only complaint was that there were

too many lectures; Scott insisted on at least three a week and they
seem to have bored the others considerably—except for Ponting's
magic lantern slides of Japan. A gramophone and a pianola provided
background music and there was a constant flow of witticisms
which one assumes to have been unprintable until one learns that
Dr Wilson would leave the company if a coarse word were spoken.
In the Hut they chiefly lived on flesh of seals, which they killed
without difficulty, since these creatures are friendly and trustful
by nature. "A sizzling on the fire and a smell of porridge and seal
liver heralded breakfast which was at 8 a.m. in theory and a good
deal later in practice." Supper was at 7. Most were in their bunks
by 10 p.m., sometimes with a candle and a book; the acetylene
was turned off at 10.30 to economize the fuel. Cherry Garrard
tells us that the talk at meals was never dull. Most of these men
were from the Royal Navy, and sailors are often droll, entertaining
fellows possessing much out-of-the-way information. (Nobody who
heard them can have forgotten the performances of Commander
Campbell on the B.B.C.—he was one of the greatest stars they
ever had, in my view.) Heated arguments would break out on a
diversity of subjects, to be settled by recourse to an encyclopedia
or an atlas or sometimes a Latin dictionary. They wished they had
also brought a *Who's Who*. One of their discussions, which often
recurred, concerned "Why are we here? What is the force that
drives us to undergo severe, sometimes ghastly hardships of our
own free will?" The reply was The Interests of Science—it is
important that man should know the features of the world he
lives in, but this was not a complete answer. Once there was a
discussion as to whether they would continue to like Polar travel
if, by the aid of modern inventions, it became quite easy and
comfortable. They said no, with one accord. It seems as if they
really wanted to prove to themselves how much they could endure.
Their rewards were a deep spiritual satisfaction and relationships
between men who had become more than brothers.

Their loyalty to each other was fantastic—there was no jealousy,   5
bickering, bullying or unkindness. Reading between the lines of
their diaries and records it is impossible to guess whether anybody
disliked anybody else. As for The Owner, as they called Scott, they
all worshipped and blindly followed him. Cherry Garrard, the only
one who could be called an intellectual and who took a fairly
objective view of the others, gives an interesting account of Scott's
character: subtle, he says, full of light and shade. No sense of
humour—peevish by nature, highly strung, irritable, melancholy
and moody. However, such was his strength of mind that he
overcame these faults, though he could not entirely conceal long
periods of sadness. He was humane, so fond of animals that he

refused to take dogs on long journeys, hauling the sledge himself rather than see them suffer. His idealism and intense patriotism shone through all he wrote. Of course, he had the extraordinary charm without which no man can be a leader. In his diaries he appears as an affectionate person, but shyness or the necessary isolation of a sea-captain prevented him from showing this side to the others. He was poor; he worried about provision for his family when it became obvious that he would never return to them. Indeed, he was always hampered by lack of money and never had enough to finance his voyages properly. Lady Kennet, his widow, once told me that Scott only took on Cherry Garrard because he subscribed £2,000 to the expedition. He thought him too young (23), too delicate and too short-sighted, besides being quite inexperienced; he was the only amateur in the party. It is strange and disgraceful that Scott, who was already a world-famous explorer, should have had so little support from the Government for this prestigious voyage.

These men had an enemy, not with them in the Hut but ever 6 present in their minds. His shadow fell across their path before they left New Zealand, when Captain Scott received a telegram dated from Madeira, with the laconic message *Am going South Amundsen*. Now, Amundsen was known to be preparing Nansen's old ship, the *Fram*, for a journey, having announced that he intended to do some further exploring in the Arctic. Only when he was actually at sea did he tell his crew that he was on his way to try and reach the South Pole. There seemed something underhand and unfair about this. Scott's men were furious; they talked of finding the Amundsen party and having it out with them, but Scott put a good face on it and pretended not to mind at all. The two leaders could hardly have been more different. Amundsen was cleverer than Scott, "an explorer of a markedly intellectual type rather Jewish than Scandinavian." There was not much humanity or idealism about him, he was a tough, brave professional. He had a sense of humour and his description of flying over the North Pole in a dirigible with General Nobile is very funny indeed. Nobile was for ever in tears and Amundsen on the verge of striking him, the climax coming when, over the Pole, Nobile threw out armfuls of huge Italian flags which caught in the propeller and endangered their lives. All the same, Amundsen died going to the rescue of Nobile in 1928.

No doubt the knowledge that "the Norskies" were also on their 7 way to the Pole was a nagging worry to Scott all those long, dark, winter months, though he was very careful to hide his feelings and often remarked that Amundsen had a perfect right to go anywhere at any time. "The Pole is not a race," he would say. He (Scott) was going in the interests of science and not in order to "get there first." But he knew that everybody else would look on it as a race; he was only human, he longed to win it.

The chief of Scott's scientific staff and his greatest friend was 8 Dr Wilson. He was to Scott what Sir Joseph Hooker had been to Ross.[3] (Incredible as it seems, Hooker only died that very year, 1911. Scott knew him well.) Wilson was a doctor of St George's Hospital and a zoologist specializing in vertebrates. He had published a book on whales, penguins and seals and had prepared a report for the Royal Commission on grouse disease. While he was doing this Cherry Garrard met him, at a shooting lodge in Scotland, and became fired with a longing to go south. Wilson was an accomplished water-colourist. Above all, he was an adorable person: "The finest character I ever met," said Scott. Now Dr Wilson wanted to bring home the egg of an Emperor Penguin. He had studied these huge creatures when he was with Scott on his first journey to the Antarctic and thought that their embryos would be of paramount biological interest, possibly proving to be the missing link between bird and fish. The Emperors, who weigh $6\frac{1}{2}$ stone[4], look like sad little men and were often taken by early explorers for human natives of the South Polar regions, are in a low state of evolution (and of spirits). They lay their eggs in the terrible mid-winter, because only thus can their chicks, which develop with a slowness abnormal in birds, be ready to survive the next winter. They never step on shore, even to breed; they live in rookeries on sea-ice. To incubate their eggs, they balance them on their enormous feet and press them against a patch of bare skin on the abdomen protected from the cold by a lappet of skin and feathers. Paternity is the only joy known to these wretched birds and a monstrous instinct for it is implanted in their breasts; male and female hatch out the eggs and nurse the chicks, also on their feet, indiscriminately. When a penguin has to go in the sea to catch his dinner he leaves egg or chick on the ice; there is then a mad scuffle as twenty childless birds rush to adopt it, quite often breaking or killing it in the process. They will nurse a dead chick until it falls to pieces and sit for months on an addled egg or even a stone. All this happens in darkness and about a hundred degrees of frost. I often think the R.S.P.C.A.[5] ought to do something for the Emperor Penguins.

Dr Wilson had reason to suppose that there was a rookery of 9

---

3. Sir James Clark explored Antarctica 1839–43.
4. About 90 pounds.
5. Royal Society for the Prevention of Cruelty to Animals.

Emperors at Cape Crozier, about sixty miles along the coast. When the ghastly winter weather had properly set in he asked for two volunteers to go with him and collect some eggs. It was one of the rules in the Hut that everybody volunteered for everything, so Wilson really chose his own companions: "Birdie" Bowers, considered by Scott to be the hardest traveller in the world, and Cherry Garrard. The three of them left the light and warmth and good cheer of the Hut to embark upon the most appalling nightmare possible to imagine. The darkness was profound and invariable. (They steered by Jupiter.) The temperature was generally in the region of 90 degrees of frost, unless there was a blizzard, when it would rise as high as 40 degrees of frost, producing other forms of discomfort and the impossibility of moving. The human body exudes a quantity of sweat and moisture, even in the lowest temperatures, so the men's clothes were soon frozen as stiff as boards and they were condemned to remain in the bending position in which they pulled their sleigh. It was as though they were dressed in lead. The surface of the snow was so bad that they had to divide their load and bring it along by relays. They could never take off their huge gloves for fear of losing their hands by frostbite; as it was, their fingers were covered with blisters in which the liquid was always frozen, so that their hands were like bunches of marbles. The difficulty of performing the simplest action with them may be imagined; it sometimes took over an hour to light a match and as much as nine hours to pitch their tent and do the work of the camp. Everything was slow, slow. When they had a discussion it lasted a week. If Cherry Garrard had written his book in a more uninhibited age he would no doubt have told us how they managed about what the Americans call going to the bathroom.[6] As it is, this interesting point remains mysterious. Dr Wilson insisted on them spending seven hours out of the twenty-four (day and night in that total blackness were quite arbitrary) in their sleeping-bags. These were always frozen up, so that it took at least an hour to worm their way in and then they suffered the worst of all the tortures. Normally on such journeys the great comfort was sleep. Once in their warm dry sleeping-bags the men went off as if they were drugged and nothing, neither pain nor worry, could keep them awake. But now the cold was too intense for Wilson and Cherry Garrard to close an eye. They lay shivering until they thought their backs would break, enviously listening to the regular

6. "They [the savages] go to the bathroom in the street." (Report from a member of the Peace Corps in the Congo.) [author's note]

snores of Birdie. They had got a spirit lamp—the only bearable
moments they knew were when they had just swallowed a hot
drink; for a little while it was like a hot-water bottle on their
hearts; but the effect soon wore off. Their teeth froze and split to
pieces. Their toe-nails came away. Cherry Garrard began to long
for death. It never occurred to any of them to go back. The penguin's
egg assumed such importance in their minds, as they groped and
plodded their four or five miles a day, that the whole future of
the human race might have depended on their finding one.

At last, in the bleakest and most dreadful place imaginable, they   10
heard the Emperors calling. To get to the rookery entailed a long,
dangerous feat of mountaineering, since it was at the foot of an
immense cliff. Dim twilight now glowed for an hour or two at
midday, so they were able to see the birds, about a hundred of
them, mournfully huddled together, trying to shuffle away from
the intruders without losing the eggs from their feet and trumpeting
with curious metallic voices. The men took some eggs, got lost
on the cliff, were nearly killed several times by falling into crevasses
and broke all the eggs but two. That night there was a hurricane
and their tent blew away, carried out to sea, no doubt. Now that
they faced certain death, life suddenly seemed more attractive.
They lay in their sleeping-bags for two days waiting for the wind
to abate and pretending to each other that they would manage
somehow to get home without a tent, although they knew very
well that they must perish. When it was possible to move again
Bowers, by a miracle, found the tent. "We were so thankful we
said nothing." They could hardly remember the journey home—
it passed like a dreadful dream, and indeed they often slept while
pulling their sleigh. When they arrived, moribund, at the Hut,
exactly one month after setting forth, The Owner said: "Look here,
you know, this is the hardest journey that has ever been done."

I once recounted this story to a hypochondriac friend, who said,   11
horrified, "But it must have been so *bad* for them." The extraordinary
thing is that it did them no harm. They were quite recovered three
months later, in time for the Polar journey, from which, of course,
Wilson and Bowers did not return, but which they endured longer
than any except Scott himself. Cherry Garrard did most of the
Polar journey; he went through the 1914 war, in the trenches
much of the time, and lived until 1959.

As for the penguins' eggs, when Cherry Garrard got back to   12
London the first thing he did was to take them to the Natural
History Museum. Alas, nobody was very much interested in them.
The Chief Custodian, when he received Cherry Garrard after a
good long delay, simply put them down on an ink stand and went
on talking to a friend. Cherry Garrard asked if he could have a

receipt for the eggs? "It's not necessary. It's all right. You needn't wait," he was told.

The Winter Journey was so appalling that the journey to the [13] Pole, which took place in daylight and in much higher temperatures seemed almost banal by comparison; but it was terribly long (over seven hundred miles each way) and often very hard. Scott left the Hut at 11 p.m. on 1st November. He soon went back, for a book; was undecided what to take, but finally chose a volume of Browning. He was accompanied by a party of about twenty men with two motor-sledges (the third had fallen into the sea while being landed), ponies and dogs. Only four men were to go to the Pole, but they were to be accompanied until the dreaded Beardmore glacier had been climbed. The men in charge of the motors turned back first, the motors having proved a failure. They delayed the party with continual breakdowns and only covered fifty miles. The dogs and their drivers went next. The ponies were shot at the foot of the glacier. The men minded this; they had become attached to the beasts, who had done their best, often in dreadful conditions. So far the journey had taken longer than it should have. The weather was bad for travelling, too warm, the snow too soft; there were constant blizzards. Now they were twelve men, without ponies or dogs, manhauling the sledges. As they laboured up the Beardmore, Scott was choosing the men who would go to the Pole with him. Of course, the disappointment of those who were sent home at this stage was acute; they had done most of the gruelling journey and were not to share in the glory. On 20th December Cherry Garrard wrote: "This evening has been rather a shock. As I was getting my finesko on to the top of my ski Scott came up to me and said he had rather a blow for me. Of course, I knew what he was going to say, but could hardly grasp that I was going back—tomorrow night. . . . Wilson told me it was a toss-up whether Titus [Oates] or I should go on; that being so I think Titus will help him more than I can. I said all I could think of—he seemed so cut up about it, saying 'I think somehow it is specially hard on you.' I said I hoped I had not disappointed him and he caught hold of me and said 'No, no—no,' so if that is the case all is well."

There was still one more party left to be sent back after Cherry [14] Garrard's. Scott said in his diary: "I dreaded this necessity of choosing, nothing could be more heartrending." He added: "We are struggling on, considering all things against odds. The weather is a constant anxiety." The weather was against them; the winter which succeeded this disappointing summer set in early and was the worst which hardened Arctic travellers had ever experienced.

Scott had always intended to take a party of four to the Pole.   15
He now made the fatal decision to take five. Oates was the last-
minute choice; it is thought that Scott felt the Army ought to be
represented. So they were: Scott aged 43, Wilson 39, Seaman
Evans 37, Bowers 28, and Oates 32. The extra man was *de trop*[7]
in every way. There were only four pairs of skis; the tent was too
small for five, so that one man was too near the outside and
always cold; worst of all, there were now five people to eat rations
meant for four. It was an amazing mistake, but it showed that
Scott thought he was on a good wicket. The returning parties
certainly thought so; it never occurred to them that he would
have much difficulty, let alone that his life might be in danger.
But they were all more exhausted than they knew and the last
two parties only got home by the skin of their teeth, after hair-
raising experiences on the Beardmore. Scott still had 150 miles
to go.

On 16th January, only a few miles from the Pole, Bowers spied   16
something in the snow—an abandoned sledge. Then they came
upon dog tracks. Man Friday's footsteps on the sand were less
dramatic. They knew that the enemy had won. "The Norwegians
have forestalled us," wrote Scott, "and are first at the Pole. . . .
All the day dreams must go; it will be a wearisome return." And
he wrote at the Pole itself: "Great God! This is an awful place!"

Amundsen had left his base on 20th October with three other   17
men, all on skis, and sixty underfed dogs to pull his sleighs. He
went over the Axel Herberg glacier, an easier climb than the Beardmore, and reached the Pole on 16th December with no more
discomfort than on an ordinary Antarctic journey. His return only
took thirty-eight days, by which time he had eaten most of the
dogs, beginning with his own favourite. When the whole story
was known there was a good deal of feeling in England over these
animals. At the Royal Geographical Society's dinner to Amundsen
the President, Lord Curzon, infuriated his guest by ending his
speech with the words, "I think we ought to give three cheers for
the dogs."

And now for the long pull home. Evans was dying, of frostbite   18
and concussion from a fall. He never complained, just staggered
along, sometimes wandering in his mind. The relief when he died
was tremendous, as Scott had been tormented by feeling that
perhaps he ought to abandon him, for the sake of the others.
When planning the Winter Journey, Wilson had told Cherry Garrard

7. "too much"

that he was against taking seamen on the toughest ventures—he said they simply would not look after themselves. Indeed, Evans had concealed a wound on his hand which was the beginning of his troubles. A month later, the party was again delayed, by Oates's illness; he was in terrible pain from frostbitten feet. He bravely committed suicide, but too late to save the others. Scott wrote: "Oates' last thoughts were of his mother, but immediately before he took pride in thinking that his regiment would be pleased at the bold way in which he met his death. . . . He was a brave soul. He slept through the night, hoping not to wake; but he woke in the morning, yesterday. It was blowing a blizzard. He said 'I am just going outside and may be some time.' "

All, now, were ill. Their food was short and the petrol for their spirit lamp, left for them in the depots, had mostly evaporated. The horrible pemmican, with its low vitamin content, which was their staple diet was only bearable when made into a hot stew. Now they were eating it cold, keeping the little fuel they had to make hot cocoa. (This business of the petrol was very hard on the survivors. When on their way home, the returning parties had made use of it, carefully taking much less than they were told was their share. They always felt that Scott, who never realized that it had evaporated, must have blamed them in his heart for the shortage.) Now the weather changed. "They were in evil case but they would have been all right if the cold had not come down upon them; unexpected, unforetold and fatal. The cold in itself was not so tremendous until you realize that they had been out four months, that they had fought their way up the biggest glacier in the world, in feet of soft snow, that they had spent seven weeks under plateau conditions of rarified air, big winds and low temperatures." They struggled on and might just have succeeded in getting home if they had had ordinary good luck. But, eleven miles from the depot which would have saved them, a blizzard blew up so that they could not move. It blew for a week, at the end of which there was no more hope. On 29th March Scott wrote: "My dear Mrs Wilson. If this reaches you, Bill and I will have gone out together. We are very near it now and I should like you to know how splendid he was at the end—everlastingly cheerful and ready to sacrifice himself for others, never a word of blame to me for leading him into this mess. He is suffering, luckily, only minor discomforts.

His eyes have a comfortable blue look of hope and his mind is peaceful with the satisfaction of his faith, in regarding himself as part of the great scheme of the Almighty. I can do no more to comfort you than to tell you that he died, as he lived, a brave, true man—the best of comrades and staunchest of friends. My whole heart goes out to you in pity. Yours R. Scott."

And to Sir James Barrie: 21
"We are pegging out in a very comfortless spot . . . I am not at all afraid of the end but sad to miss many a humble pleasure which I had planned for the future on our long marches. . . . We have had four days of storm in our tent and nowhere's food or fuel. We did intend to finish ourselves when things proved like this but we have decided to die naturally in the track."

On 19th March Cherry Garrard and the others in the Hut, none   22
of them fit, began to be worried. The *Terra Nova* had duly come back, with longed-for mails and news of the outer world. They had to let her go again, taking those who were really ill. On 27th March Atkinson, the officer in charge, and a seaman went a little way to try and meet the Polar party, but it was a hopeless quest, and they were 100 miles from where Scott was already dead when they turned back. They now prepared for another winter in the Hut, the sadness of which can be imagined. Long, long after they knew all hope was gone they used to think they heard their friends coming in, or saw shadowy forms that seemed to be theirs. They mourned them and missed their company. Scott, Wilson and Bowers had been the most dynamic of them all, while "Titus" or "Farmer Hayseed" (Oates) was a dear, good-natured fellow whom everybody loved to tease. The weather was unimaginably awful. It seemed impossible that the Hut could stand up to the tempests which raged outside for weeks on end and the men quite expected that it might collapse at any time. When at last the sun reappeared they set forth to see if they could discover traces of their friends. They hardly expected any results, as they were firmly convinced that the men must have fallen down a crevasse on the Beardmore, a fate they had all escaped by inches at one time or another. Terribly soon, however, they came upon what looked like a cairn; it was, in fact, Scott's tent covered with snow.
"We have found them. To say it has been a ghastly day cannot   23
express it. Bowers and Wilson were sleeping in their bags. Scott had thrown the flaps of his bag open at the end. His left hand was stretched over Wilson, his lifelong friend." Everything was tidy, their papers and records in perfect order. Atkinson and Cherry Garrard read enough to find out what had happened and packed up the rest of the papers unopened. They built a cairn over the tent, which was left as they found it. Near the place where Oates disappeared they put up a cross with the inscription: "Hereabouts died a very gallant gentleman, Captain E. G. Oates of the Inniskilling

Dragoons. In March 1912, returning from the Pole, he walked willingly to his death in a blizzard to try and save his comrades, beset by hardship."

In due course Cherry Garrard and the others were taken off by 24 the *Terra Nova*. When they arrived in New Zealand Atkinson went ashore to send cables to the dead men's wives. "The Harbour Master came out in the tug with him. 'Come down here a minute,' said Atkinson to me and 'It's made a tremendous impression. I had no idea it would make so much,' he said." Indeed it had. The present writer well remembers this impression, though only seven at the time.

Amundsen had won the race, but Scott had captured his fellow 25 countrymen's imagination. It is one of our endearing qualities, perhaps unique, that we think no less of a man because he has failed—we even like him better for it. In any case, Amundsen complained that a year later a Norwegian boy at school in England was being taught that Captain Scott discovered the South Pole.

I don't quite know why I have felt the need to write down this 26 well-known story, making myself cry twice, at the inscription on Oates's cross and when Atkinson said, "It has made a tremendous impression." Perhaps the bold, bald men who get, smiling, into cupboards, as if they were playing sardines, go a little way (about as far as from London to Manchester) into the air and come out of their cupboards again, a few hours later, smiling more than ever,[8] have put me in mind of other adventurers. It is fifty years to the day, as I write this, that Scott died. Most of the wonderful books which tell of his expedition are out of print now, but they can easily be got at second hand. I should like to feel that I may have induced somebody to read them again.

Books relating to the Polar journey: *Scott's Last Expedition*; Cherry- 27 Garrard: *The Worst Journey in the World*; Priestly: *Antarctic Adventure*; E. R. Evans: *South with Scott*; Amundsen: *My Life as an Explorer*.

8. Mitford is thinking of the flights of Alan Shepard and "Gus" Grissom in 1961.

ALICE BLOOM

On a Greek Holiday

. . . Two women are walking toward us, at noon, across the 1 nearly deserted rocks. Most of the other swimmers and sunbathers

Reprinted from *The Hudson Review*, Autumn 1983.

are up in the cafe, eating lunch under the fig trees, the grapevine. These two women are not together, they walk several feet apart, and they do not look at each other. One is tall and blond, dressed in a flowered bikini and clogs, a tourist, English or American or Scandinavian or German. The other woman, a Greek, is carrying a basket, walking quickly, and gives the impression of being on a neighborhood errand. She is probably from one of the small old farms—sheep, olive trees, hens, gardens, goats—that border this stretch of sea and climb a little way into the pine and cypress woods.

Both are smoking and both walk upright. Beyond that, there is so little similarity they could belong to different planets, eras, species, sexes. The tourist looks young, the Greek looks old; actually, she looks as old as a village well and the blonde looks like a drawn-out infant, but there could be as little as five or ten years difference between them. 2

The Greek woman is short and heavy, waistless, and is wearing a black dress, a black scarf pulled low around her eyes, a black sweater, thick black stockings, black shoes. She is stupendously there, black but for the walnut of her face, in the white sun, against the white space. She looks, at once, as if she could do everything she's ever done, anything needed, and also at once, she gives off an emanation of humor, powers, secrets, determinations, acts. She is moving straight ahead, like a moving church, a black peaked roof, a hot black hat, a dark tent, like a doom, a government, a force for good and evil, an ultimatum, a determined animal. She probably can't read, or write; she may never in her life have left this island; but she is beautiful, she could crush you, love you, mend you, deliver you of child or calf or lamb or illusion, bleed a pig, spear a fish, wring a supper's neck, till a field, coax an egg into life. Her sex is like a votive lamp flickering in a black, airless room. As she comes closer, she begins to crochet—that's what's in her basket, balls of cotton string and thick white lace coming off the hook and her brown fingers. 3

The blond tourist, struggling along the hot pebbles in her clogs, is coming back to her beach mat and friends. She looks as though she couldn't dress a doll without having a fit of sulks and throwing it down in a tantrum. It may not be the case, of course. She is on holiday, on this Greek island, which fact means both money and time. She is no doubt capable, well meaning, and by the standards and expectations of most of the world's people, well educated and very rich and very comfortable. She can undoubtedly read and write, most blond people can, and has, wherever she comes from, a vote, a voice, a degree of some kind, a job, a career perhaps, money certainly, opinions, friends, health, talents, habits, 4 central heating, living relatives, personalized checks, a return ticket, a summer wardrobe, the usual bits and clamor we all, tourists, have. But presence, she has not. Nor authority, nor immediacy, nor joy for the eye, nor a look of adding to the world, not of strength nor humor nor excitement. Nearly naked, pretty, without discernible blemish, blond, tall, tan, firm, the product of red meat and whole milk, vitamins, orange juice, women's suffrage, freedom of religion, child labor laws, compulsory education, the anxious, dancing, lifelong attendance of uncounted numbers of furrow-browed adults, parents, teachers, pediatricians, orthodontists, counselors, hairdressers, diet and health and career and exercise and fashion consultants, still, she is not much to look at. She looks wonderful, but your eye, your heart, all in you that wants to look out on the substance of the people of the day, doesn't care, isn't interested long, is, in fact, diminished a little.

She could be anything—a professor of Romance languages at a 5 major university, a clerk in a Jermyn Street shop, a flight attendant, a Stockholm lawyer, but nothing shows of that life or luck or work or history, not world, not pain or freedom or sufficiency. What you think of, what her person walking toward you in the fierce noon light forces you to think of, after the momentary, automatic envy of her perfections, is that she looks as though she's never had enough—goods or rights or attention or half-decent days. Whether she is or not, she looks unutterably dissatisfied and peevish. And yet, in order to be here on this blue-white beach on this July day, unless you are chasing your own stray goat across the rocks, requires a position of luxury, mobility, and privilege common to us but beyond any imagining of the Greek woman who walks here too with a basket of string and her hot, rusty clothes but who, however, and not at all paradoxically, exudes a deep, sustained bass note of slumbering, solid contentment.

Insofar as ignorance always makes a space, romance rushes in 6 to people it. With so little fact at hand about either of these lives, fact that might make things plain and profound as only fact can do, there is little but romance, theories, guesswork, and yet, it seems, this accidental conjunction of women in the sun, considered, says it is not a matter of the one, the blonde, being discontent in spite of much and the other, the farm woman in black, being smugly, perhaps ignorantly content with little. That theory is too much the stuff of individual virtue, and of fairy tales: grateful peasant, happy with scraps and rags, and querulous, bitchy princess, untried, suffering every pea, pursued by frogs, awaiting a magic deliverance. Because in literal, daily fact, the Greek woman has more than the tourist, and the tourist, wherever she comes from

and despite her list of equipment and privileges, is also, in literal
daily fact, deprived. To see this as a possible deciphering of this
scene means to stop thinking of the good life strictly in terms of
goods, services, and various rights, and think instead, insofar as
we can, of other, almost muted because so nearly lost to us, needs
of life.

   Beyond seeing that she has two arms, two good legs, a tanned   7
skin, blond hair, and friends, I know nothing about this particular
tourist. Beyond knowing that she has two arms, two good legs,
a face that could stop or move an army, a black dress, and can
crochet lace, I know nothing about this particular peasant woman.
I don't even know, it's only a clumsy guess, that "peasant" should
be the qualifying adjective. I can only talk about these women as
they appeared, almost a mirage in the shimmer of beach heat,
almost icons, for a moment and walked past; and as they are on
an island where I, too, have spent a notch of time. Whatever the
Greek woman, and her kind, have enjoyed or missed, have suffered
or lost in war, under dictatorship, under occupation, from men,
in poverty or plenty, I don't know. The other woman, I won't
further describe, won't guess at, for she is familiar to us; she is
us.

   I don't know in what order of importance, should that order   8
exist or be articulable, the Greek woman would place what occurs
on the visible street of her life. For that is all I do see, all that we
can see, and it wrings the heart, that visible street. For one thing,
in most places, the street is not yet given over to the demands of
the motor. The Greek is still a citizen and a large part of this day
is given to whatever life goes on in public, and that life takes place
on the street. Much of what we do in private, in isolation, in small
personally chosen groups—eating, drinking, talking, staring into
space—is, in Greece, done on the impersonal, random street. This
habit of daily gathering, which is done for no particular reason,
that is, there is no special occasion, lends to every day and night
the feel of mild, but lively festival.

   Second, among the other visible things that "underdeveloped"   9
means, it means that—due either to a generous wisdom that has
survived or else to funding that is not yet available—there is not
enough money for the fit to invent shelters for the unfit. For
whatever reasons, the Greek woman still lives in a culture where
this has not yet happened. That is, not only are the streets used
by and for people, but all sorts of people are on them, still privileged
to their piece of the sun, the common bread, the work, the gossip,
the ongoing parade. Our children are pitying and amazed. After

several days on these streets they assume that in Greece there are more fat and slow and old, more crippled and maimed, more feeble of mind and body, more blind and begging, more, in general, outcast folks than we, Americans, have. They are especially amazed at how *old* people get to be in Greece. Being young and American, and not living in New York, the only city we have that approximates the fullness and variety of a village, they assume this is evidence of extreme longevity on the one hand, and evidence of extreme bad health on the other. It was as hard to explain about American nursing homes and other asylums and institutions as it was to explain about public nudity, how archeologists find hidden ruins, and other questions that came up on the trip.

A "developed" country is seldom mysterious but always mys- 10 tifying. Where do things come from and where do they go? Life can be looked at, but not often comprehended in any of its ordinary particulars: food, shelter, work, money, producing and buying and selling. The Greek woman on the beach, again for many reasons, does still live in a world that, in those particulars—food, shelter, work, product, etc.—is comprehensible. Outside the few urban, industrial areas in Greece, it is still possible to build and conduct life without the benefit of technicians, specialists, explainers, bureaucrats, middlemen, and other modern experts. This means that there is possible an understanding of, a connection with, and a lack of technological mystification to many of the elements, objects, and products commonly lived with in any day. A typical Greek house is so simple and cunning that it could be built, or destroyed, by almost anyone. This may mean less convenience, but it also means more comprehension. For the ordinary person, there is relatively little of the multiform, continual, hardly-much-thought-about incomprehensibility of daily things—where does this lamb chop come from? where does this wash water go?—that most people in developed countries live with, or manage to ignore, every day. Therefore, for this Greek woman on the beach and her kind, there is another mind possible, one that sees, and understands, and in most instances can control many details; and a mind in which, therefore, many mysteries can grow a deeper root.

Food, to take another example, is eaten in season and most of 11 it is locally grown, harvested or butchered, processed, sold, and consumed. There is no particular moral virtue in this fact, but this fact does signify the possibility of a sharper, more acute (it sees, it has to see and comprehend more details), and more satisfied intelligence. Having money means being able to buy the end product; therefore, money replaces the need for intricate knowledge of processes; therefore, money replaces knowledge. The understanding

of a glass of water or wine, a melon, an onion, or a fried fish,
from inception to end, does mean living with a different kind of
mind than the one that results from having merely bought and
consumed the wine or fish or onion at the end. In that sense,
therefore, it is possible that the unhappy peevishness and dissatisfaction on the face of the pretty tourist comes in part from a life
of being left out of knowledge of the intricate details of the complete
cycle of any single thing she is able to consume.

Including the country of Greece.   12

There is a new world everywhere now that money will buy. It   13
is a world without a nation, though it exists as an overlay of life,
something on the order of the computer, in almost any country
of the globe. It is an international accommodation, and wherever
it exists—whether in Madrid, London, Istanbul, Athens, Cleveland—
it resembles a large airport lounge. In this way, the new world
specially constructed everywhere for tourists is something like the
thousands of Greek churches, as alike as eggs, and no matter what
their size all modeled on the single great discovered design of
Constantine's Hagia Sophia.

Inside this international accommodation is allowed only so much   14
of any specific country as lends itself as background, decor, and
trinkets. In this sense, the travel posters are an accurate portrayal
of exactly how little can happen on a well-engineered trip: scenery
and "gifts." Because most of the world is still what would be
termed "poor," the more money you can spend, nearly anyplace,
the more you are removed from the rich, complex life of that
place. It is possible to buy everything that puts an average American
life—taps that mix hot and cold, flush toilets, heating and cooling
systems, menus in English—on top of any other existing world.
It is possible to pay for every familiar security and comfort and,
as the posters show, still have been *there* having it. At the end of
the trip, you can say that you were there.

However, the extent to which one buys familiarity, in most of   15
the world today, is also the extent to which one will not see,
smell, taste, feel, or in any way be subjected to, enlightened by,
or entered by that piece of the world and its people. The world's
people are not blind to this fear of the unfamiliar and uncomfortable,
nor insensitive to the dollars that will be paid to ward it off. In
the winter months, when life returns to normal, the friendly Greek
"waiters" resume their lives as masons, carpenters, builders, mechanics, schoolteachers, and so forth, a fact unknown to or overlooked by many tourists who assume, for example, that many
unfinished buildings, seen languishing in the summer season, are
due to neglect, laziness, disinterest, or what have you.

We all assume, and usually safely, that the more money you 16
have the more you can buy. In travel, however, the opposite is
true. The less money you spend, the less money you have to spend,
perhaps, the more your chances of getting a whiff, now and then,
of what another place is like. There are the ideals: walking a
country, living there, learning its language. Short of that, those
conditions which most of us cannot meet, one can try spending
as little as possible: class-D hotels, public transportation, street
meals. And then one must try to be as brave and patient and
good-humored and healthy as possible because, without a doubt,
the less money you spend the closer you come to partaking of
very annoying, confusing, exhausting, foreign, debilitating, sometimes outrageous discomfort.

For instance, the two things one would most want to avoid in 17
Greece in the summer are the intense heat and the unworldly,
unimaginable, unforeseeable amount of din. Pandemonium is, after
all, a Greek idea, but in actual life, it is hardly confined to the
hour of noon. Silence is a vacuum into which, like proverbial
nature, a single Greek will rush with a pure love of noise. Two
Greeks together produce more noise than 200 of any other Western
nation. Greeks love above all else the human voice, raised in any
emotion; next to that they love their actions with objects. One
Greek with any object—a string of beads, a two-cylinder engine,
preferably one on the eternal blink, a rug to beat, a single child
to mind, a chair to be moved—will fill all time and space with
his operation; it will be the Platonic scrape of metal chair leg on
stone street; it will be the one explanation to last for all eternity
why the child should not torture the cat in the garden. A generalization: Greeks love horns, bells, animal cries, arguments, dented
fenders, lengthy explanations, soccer games, small motors, pots
and pans, cases of empty bottles, vehicles without mufflers, cups
against saucers, fireworks, political songs, metal awnings, loudspeakers, musical instruments, grandmothers, the Orthodox liturgy,
traffic jams, the sound of breaking glass, and Mercedes taxicabs
that tootle "Mary Had a Little Lamb."

A further generalization: the above generalization is one that 18
only *not* spending money will buy. That is, you have to be in a
class-F room, in a hotel on the harbor, one flight above a taverna
frequented by fishermen, 120 degrees in the room, no screens,
mosquito coils burning in the unmoving air through the night,
and through the night—a donkey in heat tethered in the walled
garden below your shuttered, only shuttered, window. In other
words, it's quiet, and cool, at the Hilton; and there are, God and
international capitalism be thanked, no donkeys.

C. S. LEWIS

The Abolition of Man

"Man's conquest of Nature" is an expression often used to describe   1
the progress of applied science. "Man has Nature whacked" said
someone to a friend of mine not long ago. In their context the
words had a certain tragic beauty, for the speaker was dying of
tuberculosis. "No matter," he said, "I know I'm one of the casualties.
Of course there are casualties on the winning as well as on the
losing side. But that doesn't alter the fact that it is winning." I
have chosen this story as my point of departure in order to make
it clear that I do not wish to disparage all that is really beneficial
in the process described as "Man's conquest," much less all the
real devotion and self-sacrifice that has gone to make it possible.
But having done so I must proceed to analyse this conception a
little more closely. In what sense is Man the possessor of increasing
power over Nature?

Let us consider three typical examples: the aeroplane, the wireless,   2
and the contraceptive. In a civilized community, in peace-time,
anyone who can pay for them may use these things. But it cannot
strictly be said that when he does so he is exercising his own
proper or individual power over Nature. If I pay you to carry me,
I am not therefore myself a strong man. Any or all of the three
things I have mentioned can be withheld from some men by other
men—by those who sell, or those who allow the sale, or those
who own the sources of production, or those who make the goods.
What we call Man's power is, in reality, a power possessed by
some men which they may, or may not, allow other men to profit
by. Again, as regards the powers manifested in the aeroplane or
the wireless, Man is as much the patient or subject as the possessor,
since he is the target both for bombs and for propaganda. And as
regards contraceptives, there is a paradoxical, negative sense in
which all possible future generations are the patients or subjects
of a power wielded by those already alive. By contraception simply,
they are denied existence; by contraception used as a means of
selective breeding, they are, without their concurring voice, made
to be what one generation, for its own reasons, may choose to
prefer. From this point of view, what we call Man's power over

Chapter 3 of *The Abolition of Man* (1947). Originally a lecture at the University of
Durham, England.

Nature turns out to be a power exercised by some men over other men with Nature as its instrument.

It is, of course, a commonplace to complain that men have 3 hitherto used badly, and against their fellows, the powers that science has given them. But that is not the point I am trying to make. I am not speaking of particular corruptions and abuses which an increase of moral virtue would cure: I am considering what the thing called "Man's power over Nature" must always and essentially be. No doubt, the picture could be modified by public ownership of raw materials and factories and public control of scientific research. But unless we have a world state this will still mean the power of one nation over others. And even within the world state or the nation it will mean (in principle) the power of majorities over minorities, and (in the concrete) of a government over the people. And all long-term exercises of power, especially in breeding, must mean the power of earlier generations over later ones.

The latter point is not always sufficiently emphasized, because 4 those who write on social matters have not yet learned to imitate the physicists by always including Time among the dimensions. In order to understand fully what Man's power over Nature, and therefore the power of some men over other men, really means, we must picture the race extended in time from the date of its emergence to that of its extinction. Each generation exercises power over its successors: and each, in so far as it modifies the environment bequeathed to it and rebels against tradition, resists and limits the power of its predecessors. This modifies the picture which is some-times painted of a progressive emancipation from tradition and a progressive control of natural processes resulting in a continual increase of human power. In reality, of course, if any one age really attains, by eugenics and scientific education, the power to make its descendants what it pleases, all men who live after it are the patients of that power. They are weaker, not stronger: for though we may have put wonderful machines in their hands we have pre-ordained how they are to use them. And if, as is almost certain, the age which had thus attained maximum power over posterity were also the age most emancipated from tradition, it would be engaged in reducing the power of its predecessors almost as drastically as that of its successors. And we must also remember that, quite apart from this, the later a generation comes—the nearer it lives to that date at which the species becomes extinct—the less power it will have in the forward direction, because its subjects will be so few. There is therefore no question of a power vested in the race as a whole steadily growing as long as the race survives.

The last men, far from being the heirs of power, will be of all men most subject to the dead hand of the great planners and conditioners and will themselves exercise least power upon the future. The real picture is that of one dominant age—let us suppose the hundredth century A.D.—which resists all previous ages most successfully and dominates all subsequent ages most irresistibly, and thus is the real master of the human species. But even within this master generation (itself an infinitesimal minority of the species) the power will be exercised by a minority smaller still. Man's conquest of Nature, if the dreams of some scientific planners are realized, means the rule of a few hundreds of men over billions upon billions of men. There neither is nor can be any simple increase of power on Man's side. Each new power won *by* man is a power *over* man as well. Each advance leaves him weaker as well as stronger. In every victory, besides being the general who triumphs, he is also the prisoner who follows the triumphal car.

I am not yet considering whether the total result of such am-   5
bivalent victories is a good thing or a bad. I am only making clear what Man's conquest of Nature really means and especially that final stage in the conquest, which, perhaps, is not far off. The final stage is come when Man by eugenics, by pre-natal conditioning, and by an education and propaganda based on a perfect applied psychology, has obtained full control over himself. *Human* nature will be the last part of Nature to surrender to Man. The battle will then be won. We shall have "taken the thread of life out of the hand of Clotho"[1] and be henceforth free to make our species whatever we wish it to be. The battle will indeed be won. But who, precisely, will have won it?

For the power of Man to make himself what he pleases means,   6
as we have seen, the power of some men to make other men what *they* please. In all ages, no doubt, nurture and instruction have, in some sense, attempted to exercise this power. But the situation to which we must look forward will be novel in two respects. In the first place, the power will be enormously increased. Hitherto the plans of educationalists have achieved very little of what they attempted and indeed, when we read them—how Plato would have every infant "a bastard nursed in a bureau," and Elyot would have the boy see no men before the age of seven and, after

---

1. In Greek mythology, one of the Fates—female deities who supervised the destiny of humans and gods. Clotho spun the thread of destiny, Lachesis drew it, and Atropos cut it.

that, no women,[2] and how Locke wants children to have leaky shoes and no turn for poetry[3]—we may well thank the beneficent obstinacy of real mothers, real nurses, and (above all) real children for preserving the human race in such sanity as it still possesses. But the man-moulders of the new age will be armed with the powers of an omnicompetent state and an irresistible scientific technique: we shall get at last a race of conditioners who really can cut out all posterity in what shape they please. The second difference is even more important. In the older systems both the kind of man the teachers wished to produce and their motives for producing him were prescribed by the *Tao*[4]—a norm to which the teachers themselves were subject and from which they claimed no liberty to depart. They did not cut men to some pattern they had chosen. They handed on what they had received: they initiated the young neophyte into the mystery of humanity which over-arched him and them alike. It was but old birds teaching young birds to fly. This will be changed. Values are now mere natural phenomena. Judgements of value are to be produced in the pupil as part of the conditioning. Whatever *Tao* there is will be the product, not the motive, of education. The conditioners have been emancipated from all that. It is one more part of Nature which they have conquered. The ultimate springs of human action are no longer, for them, something given. They have surrendered—like electricity: it is the function of the Conditioners to control, not to obey them. They know how to *produce* conscience and decide what kind of conscience they will produce. They themselves are outside, above. For we are assuming the last stage of Man's struggle with Nature. The final victory has been won. Human

2. *The Boke Named the Governour,* I. iv: 'Al men except physitions only shulde be excluded and kepte out of the norisery.' I. vi: 'After that a childe is come to seuen yeres of age . . . the most sure counsaile is to withdrawe him from all company of women.' [author's note]

3. *Some Thoughts concerning Education,* § 7: 'I will also advise his *Feet to be wash'd* every Day in cold Water, and to have his Shoes so thin that they might leak and *let in Water,* whenever he comes near it.' § 174: 'If he have a poetick vein, 'tis to me the strangest thing in the World that the Father should desire or suffer it to be cherished or improved. Methinks the Parents should labour to have it stifled and suppressed as much as may be.' Yet Locke is one of our most sensible writers on education. [author's note]

4. Lewis uses this Chinese term, which means "the Way," to encompass the whole body of traditional wisdom that assumes ethical, moral, and aesthetic values to be "objective." He points out in an earlier chapter that these values are remarkably similar the world over.

nature has been conquered—and, of course, has conquered, in whatever sense those words may now bear.

The Conditioners, then, are to choose what kind of artificial *Tao* 7 they will, for their own good reasons, produce in the Human race. They are the motivators, the creators of motives. But how are they going to be motivated themselves? For a time, perhaps, by survivals, within their own minds, of the old "natural" *Tao*. Thus at first they may look upon themselves as servants and guardians of humanity and conceive that they have a "duty" to do it "good." But it is only by confusion that they can remain in this state. They recognize the concept of duty as the result of certain processes which they can now control. Their victory has consisted precisely in emerging from the state in which they were acted upon by those processes to the state in which they use them as tools. One of the things they now have to decide is whether they will, or will not, so condition the rest of us that we can go on having the old idea of duty and the old reactions to it. How can duty help them to decide that? Duty itself is up for trial: it cannot also be the judge. And "good" fares no better. They know quite well how to produce a dozen different conceptions of good in us. The question is which, if any, they should produce. No conception of good can help them to decide. It is absurd to fix on one of the things they are comparing and make it the standard of comparison.

To some it will appear that I am inventing a factitious difficulty 8 for my Conditioners. Other, more simple-minded, critics may ask "Why should you suppose they will be such bad men?" But I am not supposing them to be bad men. They are, rather, not men (in the old sense) at all. They are, if you like, men who have sacrificed their own share in traditional humanity in order to devote themselves to the task of deciding what "Humanity" shall henceforth mean. "Good" and "bad," applied to them, are words without content: for it is from them that the content of these words is henceforward to be derived. Nor is their difficulty factitious. We might suppose that it was possible to say "After all, most of us want more or less the same things—food and drink and sexual intercourse, amusement, art, science, and the longest possible life for individuals and for the species. Let them simply say, This is what we happen to like, and go on to condition men in the way most likely to produce it. Where's the trouble?" But this will not answer. In the first place, it is false that we all really like the same things. But even if we did, what motive is to impel the Conditioners to scorn delights and live laborious days in order that we, and posterity, may have what we like? Their duty? But that is only the *Tao*, which they may decide to impose on us, but which cannot be valid for them. If they accept it, then they are no longer the makers of conscience but still its subjects, and their final conquest over Nature has not really happened. The preservation of the species? But why should the species be preserved? One of the questions before them is whether this feeling for posterity (they know well how it is produced) shall be continued or not. However far they go back, or down, they can find no ground to stand on. Every motive they try to act on becomes at once a *petitio*.[5] It is not that they are bad men. They are not men at all. Stepping outside the *Tao*, they have stepped into the void. Nor are their subjects necessarily unhappy men. They are not men at all: they are artefacts. Man's final conquest has proved to be the abolition of Man.

Yet the Conditioners will act. When I said just now that all motives fail them, I should have said all motives except one. All motives that claim any validity other than that of their felt emotional weight at a given moment have failed them. Everything except the *sic volo, sic jubeo*[6] has been explained away. But what never claimed objectivity cannot be destroyed by subjectivism. The impulse to scratch when I itch or to pull to pieces when I am inquisitive is immune from the solvent which is fatal to my justice, or honour, or care for posterity. When all that says "it is good" has been debunked, what says "I want" remains. It cannot be exploded or "seen through" because it never had any pretensions. The Conditioners, therefore, must come to be motivated simply by their own pleasure. I am not here speaking of the corrupting influence of power nor expressing the fear that under it our Conditioners will degenerate. The very words *corrupt* and *degenerate* imply a doctrine of value and are therefore meaningless in this context. My point is that those who stand outside all judgements of value cannot have any ground for preferring one of their own impulses to another except the emotional strength of that impulse. We may legitimately hope that among the impulses which arise in minds thus emptied of all "rational" or "spiritual" motives, some will be benevolent. I am very doubtful myself whether the benevolent impulses, stripped of that preference and encouragement which the *Tao* teaches us to give them and left to their merely natural strength and frequency as psychological events, will have much influence. I am very doubtful whether history shows us one example of a man who, having stepped outside traditional morality and attained power, has used that power benevolently. I am inclined to think that the Conditioners will hate the conditioned. Though

5. *Petitio principii*: begging the question; circular argument.
6. "This I want, this I command."

regarding as an illusion the artificial conscience which they produce in us their subjects, they will yet perceive that it creates in us an illusion of meaning for our lives which compares favourably with the futility of their own: and they will envy us as eunuchs envy men. But I do not insist on this, for it is mere conjecture. What is not conjecture is that our hope even of a "conditioned" happiness rests on what is ordinarily called "chance"—the chance that benevolent impulses may on the whole predominate in our Conditioners. For without the judgement "Benevolence is good"— that is, without re-entering the *Tao*—they can have no ground for promoting or stabilizing their benevolent impulses rather than any others. By the logic of their position they must just take their impulses as they come, from chance. And Chance here means Nature. It is from heredity, digestion, the weather, and the association of ideas, that the motives of the Conditioners will spring. Their extreme rationalism, by "seeing through" all "rational" motives, leaves them creatures of wholly irrational behaviour. If you will not obey the *Tao*, or else commit suicide, obedience to impulse (and therefore, in the long run, to mere "nature") is the only course left open.

At the moment, then, of Man's victory over Nature, we find   10 the whole human race subjected to some individual men, and those individuals subjected to that in themselves which is purely "natural"—to their irrational impulses. Nature, untrammelled by values, rules the Conditioners and, through them, all humanity. Man's conquest of Nature turns out, in the moment of its consummation, to be Nature's conquest of Man. Every victory we seemed to win has led us, step by step, to this conclusion. All Nature's apparent reverses have been but tactical withdrawals. We thought we were beating her back when she was luring us on. What looked to us like hands held up in surrender was really the opening of arms to enfold us for ever. If the fully planned and conditioned world (with its *Tao* a mere product of the planning) comes into existence, Nature will be troubled no more by the restive species that rose in revolt against her so many millions of years ago, will be vexed no longer by its chatter of truth and mercy and beauty and happiness. *Ferum victorem cepit:*[7] and if the eugenics are efficient enough there will be no second revolt, but all snug beneath the Conditioners, and the Conditioners beneath her, till the moon falls or the sun grows cold.

My point may be clearer to some if it is put in a different form.   11 Nature is a word of varying meanings, which can best be understood

7. "Nature captures the victor."

if we consider its various opposites. The Natural is the opposite of the Artificial, the Civil, the Human, the Spiritual, and the Supernatural. The Artificial does not now concern us. If we take the rest of the list of opposites, however, I think we can get a rough idea of what men have meant by Nature and what it is they oppose to her. Nature seems to be the spatial and temporal, as distinct from what is less fully so or not so at all. She seems to be the world of quantity, as against the world of quality: of objects as against consciousness: of the bound, as against the wholly or partially autonomous: of that which knows no values as against that which both has and perceives value: of efficient causes (or, in some modern systems, of no causality at all) as against final causes. Now I take it that when we understand a thing analytically and then dominate and use it for our own convenience we reduce it to the level of "Nature" in the sense that we suspend our judgements of value about it, ignore its final cause (if any), and treat it in terms of quantity. This repression of elements in what would otherwise be our total reaction to it is sometimes very noticeable and even painful: something has to be overcome before we can cut up a dead man or a live animal in a dissecting room. These objects *resist* the movement of the mind whereby we thrust them into the world of mere Nature. But in other instances too, a similar price is exacted for our analytical knowledge and manipulative power, even if we have ceased to count it. We do not look at trees either as Dryads or as beautiful objects while we cut them into beams: the first man who did so may have felt the price keenly, and the bleeding trees in Virgil and Spenser may be far-off echoes of that primeval sense of impiety. The stars lost their divinity as astronomy developed, and the Dying God has no place in chemical agriculture. To many, no doubt, this process is simply the gradual discovery that the real world is different from what we expected, and the old opposition to Galileo or to "bodysnatchers" is simply obscurantism. But that is not the whole story. It is not the greatest of modern scientists who feel most sure that the object, stripped of its qualitative properties and reduced to mere quantity, is wholly real. Little scientists, and little unscientific followers of science, may think so. The great minds know very well that the object, so treated, is an artificial abstraction, that something of its reality has been lost.

From this point of view the conquest of Nature appears in a new light. We reduce things to mere Nature *in order that* we may "conquer" them. We are always conquering Nature, because "Nature" is the name for what we have, to some extent, conquered. The price of conquest is to treat a thing as mere Nature. Every conquest over Nature increases her domain. The stars do not become Nature till we can weigh and measure them: the soul does not become Nature till we can psycho-analyse her. The wresting of powers *from* Nature is also the surrendering of things *to* Nature. As long as this process stops short of the final stage we may well hold that the gain outweighs the loss. But as soon as we take the final step of reducing our own species to the level of mere Nature, the whole process is stultified, for this time the being who stood to gain and the being who has been sacrificed are one and the same. This is one of the many instances where to carry a principle to what seems its logical conclusion produces absurdity. It is like the famous Irishman who found that a certain kind of stove reduced his fuel bill by half and thence concluded that two stoves of the same kind would enable him to warm his house with no fuel at all. It is the magician's bargain: give up our soul, get power in return. But once our souls, that is, our selves, have been given up, the power thus conferred will not belong to us. We shall in fact be the slaves and puppets of that to which we have given our souls. It is in Man's power to treat himself as a mere "natural object" and his own judgements of value as raw material for scientific manipulation to alter at will. The objection to his doing so does not lie in the fact that his point of view (like one's first day in a dissecting room) is painful and shocking till we grow used to it. The pain and the shock are at most a warning and a symptom. The real objection is that if man chooses to treat himself as raw material, raw material he will be: not raw material to be manipulated, as he fondly imagined, by himself, but by mere appetite, that is, mere Nature, in the person of his dehumanized Conditioners.

We have been trying, like Lear[8], to have it both ways: to lay down our human prerogative and yet at the same time to retain it. It is impossible. Either we are rational spirit obliged for ever to obey the absolute values of the *Tao*, or else we are mere nature to be kneaded and cut into new shapes for the pleasures of masters who must, by hypothesis, have no motive but their own "natural" impulses. Only the *Tao* provides a common human law of action which can overarch rulers and ruled alike. A dogmatic belief in objective value is necessary to the very idea of a rule which is not tyranny or an obedience which is not slavery. 13

I am not here thinking solely, perhaps not even chiefly, of those who are our public enemies at the moment. The process which, 14

8. Shakespeare's King Lear surrenders his authority and then is dismayed to find that others rule him.

if not checked, will abolish Man, goes on apace among Communists
and Democrats no less than among Fascists. The methods may (at
first) differ in brutality. But many a mild-eyed scientist in pince-
nez, many a popular dramatist, many an amateur philosopher in
our midst, means in the long run just the same as the Nazi rulers
of Germany. Traditional values are to be "debunked" and mankind
to be cut out into some fresh shape at the will (which must, by
hypothesis, be an arbitrary will) of some few lucky people in one
lucky generation which has learned how to do it. The belief that
we can invent "ideologies" at pleasure, and the consequent treatment
of mankind as mere υλη, specimens, preparations, begins to affect
our very language. Once we killed bad men: now we liquidate
unsocial elements. Virtue has become *integration* and diligence
dynamism, and boys likely to be worthy of a commission are
"potential officer material." Most wonderful of all, the virtues of
thrift and temperance, and even of ordinary intelligence, are *sales-
resistance.*

The true significance of what is going on has been concealed   15
by the use of the abstraction Man. Not that the word Man is
necessarily a pure abstraction. In the *Tao* itself, as long as we
remain within it, we find the concrete reality in which to participate
is to be truly human: the real common will and common reason
of humanity, alive, and growing like a tree, and branching out,
as the situation varies, into ever new beauties and dignities of
application. While we speak from within the *Tao* we can speak
of Man having power over himself in a sense truly analogous to
an individual's self-control. But the moment we step outside and
regard the *Tao* as a mere subjective product, this possibility has
disappeared. What is now common to all men is a mere abstract
universal, an H.C.F.[9], and Man's conquest of himself means simply
the rule of the Conditioners over the conditioned human material,
the world of post-humanity which, some knowingly and some
unknowingly, nearly all men in all nations are at present labouring
to produce.

Nothing I can say will prevent some people from describing this   16
lecture as an attack on science. I deny the charge, of course: and
real Natural Philosophers (there are some now alive) will perceive
that in defending value I defend *inter alia*[10] the value of knowledge,
which must die like every other when its roots in the *Tao* are cut.
But I can go further than that. I even suggest that from Science
herself the cure might come. I have described as a "magician's

9. Highest Common Factor.
10. among other things.

bargain'' that process whereby man surrenders object after object, and finally himself, to Nature in return for power. And I meant what I said. The fact that the scientist has succeeded where the magician failed has put such a wide contrast between them in popular thought that the real story of the birth of Science is misunderstood. You will even find people who write about the sixteenth century as if Magic were a medieval survival and Science the new thing that came to sweep it away. Those who have studied the period know better. There was very little magic in the Middle Ages: the sixteenth and seventeenth centuries are the high noon of magic. The serious magical endeavour and the serious scientific endeavour are twins: one was sickly and died, the other strong and throve. But they were twins. They were born of the same impulse. I allow that some (certainly not all) of the early scientists were actuated by a pure love of knowledge. But if we consider the temper of that age as a whole we can discern the impulse of which I speak. There is something which unites magic and applied science while separating both from the "wisdom" of earlier ages. For the wise men of old the cardinal problem had been how to conform the soul to reality, and the solution had been knowledge, self-discipline, and virtue. For magic and applied science alike the problem is how to subdue reality to the wishes of men: the solution is a technique; and both, in the practice of this technique, are ready to do things hitherto regarded as disgusting and impious— such as digging up and mutilating the dead. If we compare the chief trumpeter of the new era (Bacon)[11] with Marlowe's Faustus, the similarity is striking. You will read in some critics that Faustus has a thirst for knowledge. In reality, he hardly mentions it. It is not truth he wants from his devils, but gold and guns and girls. "All things that move between the quiet poles shall be at his command" and "a sound magician is a mighty god." In the same spirit Bacon condemns those who value knowledge as an end in itself: this, for him, is to use as a mistress for pleasure what ought to be a spouse for fruit. The true object is to extend Man's power to the performance of all things possible. He rejects magic because it does not work, but his goal is that of the magician. In Paracelsus[12] the characters of magician and scientist are combined. No doubt those who really founded modern science were usually those whose love of truth exceeded their love of power; in every mixed movement the efficacy comes from the good elements not from the bad. But

---

11. Francis Bacon. See Macaulay's essay at the beginning of this section.
12. The sixteenth-century father of pharmaceutical medicine. His dictum was, "Magic is a great hidden wisdom—Reason is a great open folly."

the presence of the bad elements is not irrelevant to the direction the efficacy takes. It might be going too far to say that the modern scientific movement was tainted from its birth: but I think it would be true to say that it was born in an unhealthy neighbourhood and at an inauspicious hour. Its triumphs may have been too rapid and purchased at too high a price: reconsideration, and something like repentance, may be required.

Is it, then, possible to imagine a new Natural Philosophy, con- 17 tinually conscious that the "natural object" produced by analysis and abstraction is not reality but only a view, and always correcting the abstraction? I hardly know what I am asking for. I hear rumours that Goethe's approach to nature deserves fuller consideration— that even Dr. Steiner[13] may have seen something that orthodox researchers have missed. The regenerate science which I have in mind would not do even to minerals and vegetables what modern science threatens to do to man himself. When it explained it would not explain away. When it spoke of the parts it would remember the whole. While studying the *It* it would not lose what Martin Buber calls the *Thou*-situation. The analogy between the *Tao* of Man and the instincts of an animal species would mean for it new light cast on the unknown thing, Instinct, by the only known reality of conscience and not a reduction of conscience to the category of Instinct. Its followers would not be free with the words *only* and *merely*. In a word, it would conquer Nature without being at the same time conquered by her and buy knowledge at a lower cost than that of life.

Perhaps I am asking impossibilities. Perhaps, in the nature of 18 things, analytical understanding must always be a basilisk which kills what it sees and only sees by killing. But if the scientists themselves cannot arrest this process before it reaches the common Reason and kills that too, then someone else must arrest it. What I most fear is the reply that I am "only one more" obscurantist, that this barrier, like all previous barriers set up against the advance of science, can be safely passed. Such a reply springs from the fatal serialism of the modern imagination—the image of infinite unilinear progression which so haunts our minds. Because we have to use numbers so much we tend to think of every process as if it must be like the numeral series, where every step, to all eternity, is the same kind of step as the one before. I implore you

13. Both Goethe (German poet and dramatist, 1749–1832) and his admirer, Rudolf Steiner (Austrian social philosopher, 1861–1925) thought the analytic nature of science too restrictive. They emphasized the importance of knowledge that synthesizes human intellect and spirit with the supposedly objective world.

to remember the Irishman and his two stoves. There are progressions in which the last step is *sui generis*—incommensurable with the others—and in which to go the whole way is to undo all the labour of your previous journey. To reduce the *Tao* to a mere natural product is a step of that kind. Up to that point, the kind of explanation which explains things away may give us something, though at a heavy cost. But you cannot go on "explaining away" for ever: you will find that you have explained explanation itself away. You cannot go on "seeing through" things for ever. The whole point of seeing through something is to see something through it. It is good that the window should be transparent, because the street or garden beyond it is opaque. How if you saw through the garden too? It is no use trying to "see through" first principles. If you see through everything, then everything is transparent. But a wholly transparent world is an invisible world. To "see through" all things is the same as not to see.

NATHANIEL HAWTHORNE

The Birthmark

In the latter part of the last century there lived a man of science, ₁ an eminent proficient in every branch of natural philosophy, who not long before our story opens had made experience of a spiritual affinity more attractive than any chemical one. He had left his laboratory to the care of an assistant, cleared his fine countenance from the furnace smoke, washed the stain of acids from his fingers, and persuaded a beautiful woman to become his wife. In those days, when the comparatively recent discovery of electricity and other kindred mysteries of Nature seemed to open paths into the region of miracle, it was not unusual for the love of science to rival the love of woman in its depth and absorbing energy. The higher intellect, the imagination, the spirit, and even the heart might all find their congenial aliment in pursuits which, as some of their ardent votaries believed, would ascend from one step of powerful intelligence to another, until the philosopher should lay his hand on the secret of creative force and perhaps make new worlds for himself. We know not whether Aylmer possessed this degree of faith in man's ultimate control over Nature. He had

From *Mosses from an Old Manse* (1846).

devoted himself, however, too unreservedly to scientific studies ever to be weaned from them by any second passion. His love for his young wife might prove the stronger of the two; but it could only be by intertwining itself with his love of science and uniting the strength of the latter to his own.

Such a union accordingly took place, and was attended with truly remarkable consequences and a deeply impressive moral. One day, very soon after their marriage, Aylmer sat gazing at his wife with a trouble in his countenance that grew stronger until he spoke.

"Georgiana," said he, "has it never occurred to you that the mark upon your cheek might be removed?"

"No, indeed," said she, smiling; but, perceiving the seriousness of his manner, she blushed deeply. "To tell you the truth, it has been so often called a charm that I was simple enough to imagine it might be so."

"Ah, upon another face perhaps it might," replied her husband;   5 "but never on yours. No, dearest Georgiana, you came so nearly perfect from the hand of Nature that this slightest possible defect, which we hesitate whether to term a defect or a beauty, shocks me, as being the visible mark of earthly imperfection."

"Shocks you, my husband!" cried Georgiana, deeply hurt; at first reddening with momentary anger, but then bursting into tears. "Then why did you take me from my mother's side? You cannot love what shocks you!"

To explain this conversation, it must be mentioned that in the centre of Georgiana's left cheek there was a singular mark, deeply interwoven, as it were, with the texture and substance of her face. In the usual state of her complexion—a healthy though delicate bloom—the mark wore a tint of deeper crimson, which imperfectly defined its shape amid the surrounding rosiness. When she blushed it gradually became more indistinct, and finally vanished amid the triumphant rush of blood that bathed the whole cheek with its brilliant glow. But if any shifting motion caused her to turn pale there was the mark again, a crimson stain upon the snow, in what Aylmer sometimes deemed an almost fearful distinctness. Its shape bore not a little similarity to the human hand, though of the smallest pygmy size. Georgiana's lovers were wont to say that some fairy at her birth hour had laid her tiny hand upon the infant's cheek, and left this impress there in token of the magic endowments that were to give her such sway over all hearts. Many a desperate swain would have risked life for the privilege of pressing his lips to the mysterious hand. It must not be concealed, how-ever, that the impression wrought by this fairy sign manual varied exceedingly according to the difference of temperament in the beholders. Some fastidious persons—but they were exclusively of her own sex—affirmed that the bloody hand, as they chose to call it, quite destroyed the effect of Georgiana's beauty and rendered her countenance even hideous. But it would be as reasonable to say that one of those small blue stains which sometimes occur in the purest statuary marble would convert the Eve of Powers[1] to a monster. Masculine observers, if the birthmark did not heighten their admiration, contented themselves with wishing it away, that the world might possess one living specimen of ideal loveliness without the semblance of a flaw. After his marriage,—for he thought little or nothing of the matter before,—Aylmer discovered that this was the case with himself.

Had she been less beautiful,—if Envy's self could have found aught else to sneer at,—he might have felt his affection heightened by the prettiness of this mimic hand, now vaguely portrayed, now lost, now stealing forth again and glimmering to and fro with every pulse of emotion that throbbed within her heart; but, seeing her otherwise so perfect, he found this one defect grow more and more intolerable with every moment of their united lives. It was the fatal flaw of humanity which Nature, in one shape or another, stamps ineffaceably on all her productions, either to imply that they are temporary and finite, or that their perfection must be wrought by toil and pain. The crimson hand expressed the ineludible gripe in which mortality clutches the highest and purest of earthly mould, degrading them into kindred with the lowest, and even with the very brutes, like whom their visible frames return to dust. In this manner, selecting it as the symbol of his wife's liability to sin, sorrow, decay, and death, Aylmer's sombre imagination was not long in rendering the birthmark a frightful object, causing him more trouble and horror than ever Georgiana's beauty, whether of soul or sense, had given him delight.

At all the seasons which should have been their happiest he invariably, and without intending it, nay, in spite of a purpose to the contrary, reverted to this one disastrous topic. Trifling as it at first appeared, it so connected itself with innumerable trains of thought and modes of feeling that it became the central point of all. With the morning twilight Aylmer opened his eyes upon his wife's face and recognized the symbol of imperfection; and when they sat together at the evening hearth his eyes wandered stealthily to her cheek, and beheld, flickering with the blaze of the wood fire, the spectral hand that wrote mortality where he would fain

1. Hiram Powers was a leading American sculptor of the nineteenth century.

have worshipped. Georgiana soon learned to shudder at his gaze. It needed but a glance with the peculiar expression that his face often wore to change the roses of her cheek into a deathlike paleness, amid which the crimson hand was brought strongly out, like a bass relief of ruby on the whitest marble.

Late one night, when the lights were growing dim so as hardly to betray the stain on the poor wife's cheek, she herself, for the first time, voluntarily took up the subject.

"Do you remember, my dear Aylmer," said she, with a feeble attempt at a smile, "have you any recollection, of a dream last night about this odious hand?"

"None! none whatever!" replied Aylmer, starting; but then he added, in a dry, cold tone, affected for the sake of concealing the real depth of his emotion, "I might well dream of it; for, before I fell asleep, it had taken a pretty firm hold of my fancy."

"And you did dream of it?" continued Georgiana, hastily; for she dreaded lest a gush of tears should interrupt what she had to say. "A terrible dream! I wonder that you can forget it. Is it possible to forget this one expression?—'It is in her heart now; we must have it out!' Reflect, my husband; for by all means I would have you recall that dream."

The mind is in a sad state when Sleep, the all-involving, cannot confine her spectres within the dim region of her sway, but suffers them to break forth, affrighting this actual life with secrets that perchance belong to a deeper one. Aylmer now remembered his dream. He had fancied himself with his servant Aminadab, attempting an operation for the removal of the birthmark; but the deeper went the knife, the deeper sank the hand, until at length its tiny grasp appeared to have caught hold of Georgiana's heart; whence, however, her husband was inexorably resolved to cut or wrench it away.

When the dream had shaped itself perfectly in his memory Aylmer sat in his wife's presence with a guilty feeling. Truth often finds its way to the mind close muffled in robes of sleep, and then speaks with uncompromising directness of matters in regard to which we practise an unconscious self-deception during our waking moments. Until now he had not been aware of the tyrannizing influence acquired by one idea over his mind, and of the lengths which he might find in his heart to go for the sake of giving himself peace.

"Aylmer," resumed Georgiana, solemnly, "I know not what may be the cost to both of us to rid me of this fatal birthmark. Perhaps its removal may cause cureless deformity; or it may be the stain goes as deep as life itself. Again: do we know that there is a possibility, on any terms, of unclasping the firm gripe of this little hand which was laid upon me before I came into the world?"

"Dearest Georgiana, I have spent much thought upon the subject," hastily interrupted Aylmer. "I am convinced of the perfect practicability of its removal."

"If there be the remotest possibility of it," continued Georgiana, "let the attempt be made, at whatever risk. Danger is nothing to me; for life, while this hateful mark makes me the object of your horror and disgust,—life is a burden which I would fling down with joy. Either remove this dreadful hand, or take my wretched life! You have deep science. All the world bears witness of it. You have achieved great wonders. Cannot you remove this little, little mark, which I cover with the tips of two small fingers? Is this beyond your power, for the sake of your own peace, and to save your poor wife from madness?"

"Noblest, dearest, tenderest wife," cried Aylmer, rapturously, "doubt not my power. I have already given this matter the deepest thought—thought which might almost have enlightened me to create a being less perfect than yourself. Georgiana, you have led me deeper than ever into the heart of science. I feel myself fully competent to render this dear cheek as faultless as its fellow; and then, most beloved, what will be my triumph when I shall have corrected what Nature left imperfect in her fairest work! Even Pygmalion, when his sculptured woman assumed life, felt not greater ecstasy than mine will be."

"It is resolved, then," said Georgiana, faintly smiling. "And, Aylmer, spare me not, though you should find the birthmark take refuge in my heart at last."

Her husband tenderly kissed her cheek—her right cheek—not that which bore the impress of the crimson hand.

The next day Aylmer apprised his wife of a plan that he had formed whereby he might have opportunity for the intense thought and constant watchfulness which the proposed operation would require; while Georgiana, likewise, would enjoy the perfect repose essential to its success. They were to seclude themselves in the extensive apartments occupied by Aylmer as a laboratory, and where, during his toilsome youth, he had made discoveries in the elemental powers of Nature that had roused the admiration of all the learned societies in Europe. Seated calmly in this laboratory, the pale philosopher had investigated the secrets of the highest cloud region and of the profoundest mines; he had satisfied himself of the causes that kindled and kept alive the fires of the volcano; and had explained the mystery of the fountains, and how it is that they gush forth, some so bright and pure, and others with

such rich medicinal virtues, from the dark bosom of the earth.
Here, too, at an earlier period, he had studied the wonders of the
human frame, and attempted to fathom the very process by which
Nature assimilates all her precious influences from earth and air,
and from the spiritual world, to create and foster man, her masterpiece. The latter pursuit, however, Aylmer had long laid aside
in unwilling recognition of the truth—against which all seekers
sooner or later stumble—that our great creative Mother, while she
amuses us with apparently working in the broadest sunshine, is
yet severely careful to keep her own secrets, and, in spite of her
pretended openness, shows us nothing but results. She permits
us, indeed, to mar, but seldom to mend, and, like a jealous patentee,
on no account to make. Now, however, Aylmer resumed these
half-forgotten investigations; not, of course, with such hopes or
wishes as first suggested them; but because they involved much
physiological truth and lay in the path of his proposed scheme
for the treatment of Georgiana.

As he led her over the threshold of the laboratory, Georgiana
was cold and tremulous. Aylmer looked cheerfully into her face,
with intent to reassure her, but was so startled with the intense
glow of the birthmark upon the whiteness of her cheek that he
could not restrain a strong convulsive shudder. His wife fainted.

"Aminadab! Aminadab!" shouted Aylmer, stamping violently
on the floor.

Forthwith there issued from an inner apartment a man of low   25
stature, but bulky frame, with shaggy hair hanging about his visage,
which was grimed with the vapors of the furnace. This personage
had been Aylmer's underworker during his whole scientific career,
and was admirably fitted for that office by his great mechanical
readiness, and the skill with which, while incapable of compre-
hending a single principle, he executed all the details of his master's
experiments. With his vast strength, his shaggy hair, his smoky
aspect, and the indescribable earthiness that incrusted him, he
seemed to represent man's physical nature; while Aylmer's slender
figure, and pale, intellectual face, were no less apt a type of the
spiritual element.

"Throw open the door of the boudoir, Aminadab," said Aylmer,
"and burn a pastil."

"Yes, master," answered Aminadab, looking intently at the lifeless
form of Georgiana; and then he muttered to himself, "If she were
my wife, I'd never part with that birthmark."

When Georgiana recovered consciousness she found herself
breathing an atmosphere of penetrating fragrance, the gentle potency
of which had recalled her from her deathlike faintness. The scene
around her looked like enchantment. Aylmer had converted those

smoky, dingy, sombre rooms, where he had spent his brightest years in recondite pursuits, into a series of beautiful apartments not unfit to be the secluded abode of a lovely woman. The walls were hung with gorgeous curtains, which imparted the combination of grandeur and grace that no other species of adornment can achieve; and, as they fell from the ceiling to the floor, their rich and ponderous folds, concealing all angles and straight lines, appeared to shut in the scene from infinite space. For aught Georgiana knew, it might be a pavilion among the clouds. And Aylmer, excluding the sunshine, which would have interfered with his chemical processes, had supplied its place with perfumed lamps, emitting flames of various hue, but all uniting in a soft, impurpled radiance. He now knelt by his wife's side, watching her earnestly, but without alarm; for he was confident in his science, and felt that he could draw a magic circle round her within which no evil might intrude.

"Where am I? Ah, I remember," said Georgiana, faintly; and she placed her hand over her cheek to hide the terrible mark from her husband's eyes.

"Fear not, dearest!" exclaimed he. "Do not shrink from me! 30 Believe me, Georgiana, I even rejoice in this single imperfection, since it will be such a rapture to remove it."

"O, spare me!" sadly replied his wife. "Pray do not look at it again. I never can forget that convulsive shudder."

In order to soothe Georgiana, and, as it were, to release her mind from the burden of actual things, Aylmer now put in practice some of the light and playful secrets which science had taught him among its profounder lore. Airy figures, absolutely bodiless ideas, and forms of unsubstantial beauty came and danced before her, imprinting their momentary footsteps on beams of light. Though she had some indistinct idea of the method of these optical phenomena, still the illusion was almost perfect enough to warrant the belief that her husband possessed sway over the spiritual world. Then again, when she felt a wish to look forth from her seclusion, immediately, as if her thoughts were answered, the procession of external existence flitted across a screen. The scenery and the figures of actual life were perfectly represented, but with that bewitching yet indescribable difference which always makes a picture, an image, or a shadow so much more attractive than the original. When wearied of this, Aylmer bade her cast her eyes upon a vessel containing a quantity of earth. She did so, with little interest at first; but was soon startled to perceive the germ of a plant shooting upward from the soil. Then came the slender stalk; the leaves gradually unfolded themselves; and amid them was a perfect and lovely flower.

"It is magical!" cried Georgiana. "I dare not touch it."

"Nay, pluck it," answered Aylmer,—"pluck it, and inhale its brief perfume while you may. The flower will wither in a few moments and leave nothing save its brown seed vessels; but thence may be perpetuated a race as ephemeral as itself."

But Georgiana had no sooner touched the flower than the whole   35
plant suffered a blight, its leaves turning coal-black as if by the agency of fire.

"There was too powerful a stimulus," said Aylmer, thoughtfully.

To make up for this abortive experiment, he proposed to take her portrait by a scientific process of his own invention. It was to be effected by rays of light striking upon a polished plate of metal. Georgiana assented; but, on looking at the result, was affrighted to find the features of the portrait blurred and indefinable; while the minute figure of a hand appeared where the cheek should have been. Aylmer snatched the metallic plate and threw it into a jar of corrosive acid.

Soon, however, he forgot these mortifying failures. In the intervals of study and chemical experiment he came to her flushed and exhausted, but seemed invigorated by her presence, and spoke in glowing language of the resources of his art. He gave a history of the long dynasty of the alchemists, who spent so many ages in quest of the universal solvent by which the golden principle might be elicited from all things vile and base. Aylmer appeared to believe that, by the plainest scientific logic, it was altogether within the limits of possibility to discover this long-sought medium; "but," he added, "a philosopher who should go deep enough to acquire the power would attain too lofty a wisdom to stoop to the exercise of it." Not less singular were his opinions in regard to the elixir vitae. He more than intimated that it was at his option to concoct a liquid that should prolong life for years, perhaps interminably; but that it would produce a discord in Nature which all the world, and chiefly the quaffer of the immortal nostrum, would find cause to curse.

"Aylmer, are you in earnest?" asked Georgiana, looking at him with amazement and fear. "It is terrible to possess such power, or even to dream of possessing it."

"O, do not tremble, my love," said her husband. "I would not   40
wrong either you or myself by working such inharmonious effects upon our lives; but I would have you consider how trifling, in comparison, is the skill requisite to remove this little hand."

At the mention of the birthmark, Georgiana, as usual, shrank as if a red-hot iron had touched her cheek.

Again Aylmer applied himself to his labors. She could hear his voice in the distant furnace room giving directions to Aminadab, whose harsh, uncouth, misshapen tones were audible in response, more like the grunt or growl of a brute than human speech. After hours of absence, Aylmer reappeared and proposed that she should now examine his cabinet of chemical products and natural treasures of the earth. Among the former he showed her a small vial, in which, he remarked, was contained a gentle yet most powerful fragrance, capable of impregnating all the breezes that blow across a kingdom. They were of inestimable value, the contents of that little vial; and, as he said so, he threw some of the perfume into the air and filled the room with piercing and invigorating delight.

"And what is this?" asked Georgiana, pointing to a small crystal globe containing a gold-colored liquid. "It is so beautiful to the eye that I could imagine it the elixir of life."

"In one sense it is," replied Aylmer; "or rather, the elixir of immortality. It is the most precious poison that ever was concocted in this world. By its aid I could apportion the lifetime of any mortal at whom you might point your finger. The strength of the dose would determine whether he were to linger out years, or drop dead in the midst of a breath. No king on his guarded throne could keep his life if I, in my private station, should deem that the welfare of millions justified me in depriving him of it."

"Why do you keep such a terrific drug?" inquired Georgiana   45
in horror.

"Do not mistrust me, dearest," said her husband, smiling; "its virtuous potency is yet greater than its harmful one. But see! here is a powerful cosmetic. With a few drops of this in a vase of water, freckles may be washed away as easily as the hands are cleansed. A stronger infusion would take the blood out of the cheek, and leave the rosiest beauty a pale ghost."

"Is it with this lotion that you intend to bathe my cheek?" asked Georgiana, anxiously.

"O, no," hastily replied her husband; "this is merely superficial. Your case demands a remedy that shall go deeper."

In his interviews with Georgiana, Aylmer generally made minute inquiries as to her sensations, and whether the confinement of the rooms and the temperature of the atmosphere agreed with her. These questions had such a particular drift that Georgiana began to conjecture that she was already subjected to certain physical influences, either breathed in with the fragrant air or taken with her food. She fancied likewise, but it might be altogether fancy, that there was a stirring up of her system—a strange, indefinite sensation creeping through her veins, and tingling, half painfully, half pleasurably, at her heart. Still, whenever she dared to look into the mirror, there she beheld herself pale as a white rose and

with the crimson birthmark stamped upon her cheek. Not even
Aylmer now hated it so much as she.

To dispel the tedium of the hours which her husband found it   50
necessary to devote to the processes of combination and analysis,
Georgiana turned over the volumes of his scientific library. In many
dark old tomes she met with chapters full of romance and poetry.
They were the works of the philosophers of the middle ages, such
as Albertus Magnus, Cornelius Agrippa, Paracelsus, and the famous
friar who created the prophetic Brazen Head. All these antique
naturalists stood in advance of their centuries, yet were imbued
with some of their credulity, and therefore were believed, and
perhaps imagined themselves to have acquired from the investigation
of Nature a power above Nature, and from physics a sway over
the spiritual world. Hardly less curious and imaginative were the
early volumes of the Transactions of the Royal Society, in which
the members, knowing little of the limits of natural possibility,
were continually recording wonders or proposing methods whereby
wonders might be wrought.

But to Georgiana, the most engrossing volume was a large folio
from her husband's own hand, in which he had recorded every
experiment of his scientific career, its original aim, the methods
adopted for its development, and its final success or failure, with
the circumstances to which either event was attributable. The book,
in truth, was both the history and emblem of his ardent, ambitious,
imaginative, yet practical and laborious life. He handled physical
details as if there were nothing beyond them; yet spiritualized
them all and redeemed himself from materialism by his strong
and eager aspiration towards the infinite. In his grasp the veriest
clod of earth assumed a soul. Georgiana, as she read, reverenced
Aylmer and loved him more profoundly than ever, but with a less
entire dependence on his judgment than heretofore. Much as he
had accomplished, she could not but observe that his most splendid
successes were almost invariably failures, if compared with the
ideal at which he aimed. His brightest diamonds were the merest
pebbles, and felt to be so by himself, in comparison with the
inestimable gems which lay hidden beyond his reach. The volume,
rich with achievements that had won renown for its author, was
yet as melancholy a record as ever mortal hand had penned. It
was the sad confession and continual exemplification of the shortcomings of the composite man, the spirit burdened with clay and
working in matter, and of the despair that assails the higher nature
at finding itself so miserably thwarted by the earthly part. Perhaps
every man of genius, in whatever sphere, might recognize the
image of his own experience in Aylmer's journal.

So deeply did these reflections affect Georgiana that she laid her face upon the open volume and burst into tears. In this situation she was found by her husband.

"It is dangerous to read in a sorcerer's books," said he with a smile, though his countenance was uneasy and displeased. "Georgiana, there are pages in that volume which I can scarcely glance over and keep my senses. Take heed lest it prove detrimental to you."

"It has made me worship you more than ever," said she.

"Ah, wait for this one success," rejoined he, "then worship me 55 if you will. I shall deem myself hardly unworthy of it. But come, I have sought you for the luxury of your voice. Sing to me, dearest."

So she poured out the liquid music of her voice to quench the thirst of his spirit. He then took his leave with a boyish exuberance of gayety, assuring her that her seclusion would endure but a little longer, and that the result was already certain. Scarcely had he departed when Georgiana felt irresistibly impelled to follow him. She had forgotten to inform Aylmer of a symptom which for two or three hours past had begun to excite her attention. It was a sensation in the fatal birthmark, not painful, but which induced a restlessness throughout her system. Hastening after her husband, she intruded for the first time into the laboratory.

The first thing that struck her eye was the furnace, that hot and feverish worker, with the intense glow of its fire, which by the quantities of soot clustered above it seemed to have been burning for ages. There was a distilling apparatus in full operation. Around the room were retorts, tubes, cylinders, crucibles, and other apparatus of chemical research. An electrical machine stood ready for immediate use. The atmosphere felt oppressively close, and was tainted with gaseous odors which had been tormented forth by the processes of science. The severe and homely simplicity of the apartment, with its naked walls and brick pavement, looked strange, accustomed as Georgiana had become to the fantastic elegance of her boudoir. But what chiefly, indeed almost solely, drew her attention, was the aspect of Aylmer himself.

He was pale as death, anxious and absorbed, and hung over the furnace as if it depended upon his utmost watchfulness whether the liquid which it was distilling should be the draught of immortal happiness or misery. How different from the sanguine and joyous mien that he had assumed for Georgiana's encouragement!

"Carefully now, Aminadab; carefully, thou human machine; carefully, thou man of clay," muttered Aylmer, more to himself than his assistant. "Now, if there be a thought too much or too little, it is all over."

"Ho! ho!" mumbled Aminadab. "Look, master! look!"   60

Aylmer raised his eyes hastily, and at first reddened, then grew paler than ever, on beholding Georgiana. He rushed towards her and seized her arm with a gripe that left the print of his fingers upon it.

"Why do you come hither? Have you no trust in your husband?" cried he, impetuously. "Would you throw the blight of that fatal birthmark over my labors? It is not well done. Go, prying woman! go!"

"Nay, Aylmer," said Georgiana with the firmness of which she possessed no stinted endowment, "it is not you that have a right to complain. You mistrust your wife; you have concealed the anxiety with which you watch the development of this experiment. Think not so unworthily of me, my husband. Tell me all the risk we run, and fear not that I shall shrink; for my share in it is far less than your own."

"No, no, Georgiana!" said Aylmer, impatiently; "it must not be."

"I submit," replied she, calmly. "And, Aylmer, I shall quaff   65
whatever draught you bring me; but it will be on the same principle that would induce me to take a dose of poison if offered by your hand."

"My noble wife," said Aylmer, deeply moved, "I knew not the height and depth of your nature until now. Nothing shall be concealed. Know, then, that this crimson hand, superficial as it seems, has clutched its grasp into your being with a strength of which I had no previous conception. I have already administered agents powerful enough to do aught except to change your entire physical system. Only one thing remains to be tried. If that fail us we are ruined."

"Why did you hesitate to tell me this?" asked she.

"Because, Georgiana," said Aylmer, in a low voice, "there is danger." "Danger? There is but one danger—that this horrible stigma shall be left upon my cheek!" cried Georgiana. "Remove it, remove it, whatever be the cost, or we shall both go mad!"

"Heaven knows your words are too true," said Aylmer, sadly. "And now, dearest, return to your boudoir. In a little while all will be tested."

He conducted her back and took leave of her with a solemn   70
tenderness which spoke far more than his words how much was now at stake. After his departure Georgiana became rapt in musings. She considered the character of Aylmer and did it completer justice than at any previous moment. Her heart exulted, while it trembled, at his honorable love—so pure and lofty that it would accept nothing less than perfection nor miserably make itself contented

with an earthlier nature than he had dreamed of. She felt how much more precious was such a sentiment than that meaner kind which would have borne with the imperfection for her sake, and have been guilty of treason to holy love by degrading its perfect idea to the level of the actual; and with her whole spirit she prayed that, for a single moment, she might satisfy his highest and deepest conception. Longer than one moment she well knew it could not be; for his spirit was ever on the march, ever ascending, and each instant required something that was beyond the scope of the instant before.

The sound of her husband's footsteps aroused her. He bore a crystal goblet containing a liquor colorless as water, but bright enough to be the draught of immortality. Aylmer was pale; but it seemed rather the consequence of a highly-wrought state of mind and tension of spirit than of fear or doubt.

"The concoction of the draught has been perfect," said he, in answer to Georgiana's look. "Unless all my science have deceived me, it cannot fail."

"Save on your account, my dearest Aylmer," observed his wife, "I might wish to put off this birthmark of mortality by relinquishing mortality itself in preference to any other mode. Life is but a sad possession to those who have attained precisely the degree of moral advancement at which I stand. Were I weaker and blinder, it might be happiness. Were I stronger, it might be endured hopefully. But, being what I find myself, methinks I am of all mortals the most fit to die."

"You are fit for heaven without tasting death!" replied her husband. "But why do we speak of dying? The draught cannot fail. Behold its effect upon this plant."

On the window seat there stood a geranium diseased with yellow   75
blotches which had overspread all its leaves. Aylmer poured a small quantity of the liquid upon the soil in which it grew. In a little time, when the roots of the plant had taken up the moisture, the unsightly blotches began to be extinguished in a living verdure.

"There needed no proof," said Georgiana, quietly. "Give me the goblet. I joyfully stake all upon your word."

"Drink, then, thou lofty creature!" exclaimed Aylmer, with fervid admiration. "There is no taint of imperfection on thy spirit. Thy sensible frame, too, shall soon be all perfect."

She quaffed the liquid and returned the goblet to his hand.

"It is grateful," said she, with a placid smile. "Methinks it is like water from a heavenly fountain; for it contains I know not what of unobtrusive fragrance and deliciousness. It allays a feverish thirst that had parched me for many days. Now, dearest, let me sleep. My earthly senses are closing over my spirit like the leaves around the heart of a rose at sunset.''

She spoke the last words with a gentle reluctance, as if it required almost more energy than she could command to pronounce the faint and lingering syllables. Scarcely had they loitered through her lips ere she was lost in slumber. Aylmer sat by her side, watching her aspect with the emotions proper to a man the whole value of whose existence was involved in the process now to be tested. Mingled with this mood, however, was the philosophic investigation characteristic of the man of science. Not the minutest symptom escaped him. A heightened flush of the cheek, a slight irregularity of breath, a quiver of the eyelid, a hardly perceptible tremor through the frame,—such were the details which, as the moments passed, he wrote down in his folio volume. Intense thought had set its stamp upon every previous page of that volume; but the thoughts of years were all concentrated upon the last.

While thus employed, he failed not to gaze often at the fatal hand, and not without a shudder. Yet once, by a strange and unaccountable impulse, he pressed it with his lips. His spirit recoiled, however, in the very act; and Georgiana, out of the midst of her deep sleep, moved uneasily and murmured as if in remonstrance. Again Aylmer resumed his watch. Nor was it without avail. The crimson hand, which at first had been strongly visible upon the marble paleness of Georgiana's cheek, now grew more faintly outlined. She remained not less pale than ever; but the birthmark, with every breath that came and went lost somewhat of its former distinctness. Its presence had been awful; its departure was more awful still. Watch the stain of the rainbow fading out of the sky, and you will know how that mysterious symbol passed away.

''By Heaven! it is well nigh gone!'' said Aylmer to himself, in almost irrepressible ecstasy. ''I can scarcely trace it now. Success! success! And now it is like the faintest rose color. The lightest flush of blood across her cheek would overcome it. But she is so pale!''

He drew aside the window curtain and suffered the light of natural day to fall into the room and rest upon her cheek. At the same time he heard a gross, hoarse chuckle, which he had long known as his servant Aminadab's expression of delight.

''Ah, clod! ah, earthly mass!'' cried Aylmer, laughing in a sort of frenzy, ''you have served me well! Matter and spirit—earth and heaven—have both done their part in this! Laugh, thing of the senses! You have earned the right to laugh.''

These exclamations broke Georgiana's sleep. She slowly unclosed her eyes and gazed into the mirror which her husband had arranged for that purpose. A faint smile flitted over her lips when she recognized how barely perceptible was now that crimson hand which had once blazed forth with such disastrous brilliancy as to scare away all their happiness. But then her eyes sought Aylmer's face with a trouble and anxiety that he could by no means account for.

"My poor Aylmer!" murmured she.

"Poor? Nay, richest, happiest, most favored!" exclaimed he. "My peerless bride, it is successful! You are perfect!"

"My poor Aylmer," she repeated, with a more than human tenderness, "you have aimed loftily; you have done nobly. Do not repent that, with so high and pure a feeling, you have rejected the best the earth could offer. Aylmer, dearest Aylmer, I am dying!"

Alas! it was too true! The fatal hand had grappled with the mystery of life, and was the bond by which an angelic spirit kept itself in union with a mortal frame. As the last crimson tint of the birth-mark—that sole token of human imperfection—faded from her cheek, the parting breath of the now perfect woman passed into the atmosphere, and her soul, lingering a moment near her husband, took its heavenward flight. Then a hoarse, chuckling laugh was heard again! Thus ever does the gross fatality of earth exult in its invariable triumph over the immortal essence which, in this dim sphere of half development, demands the completeness of a higher state. Yet, had Aylmer reached a profounder wisdom, he need not thus have flung away the happiness which would have woven his mortal life of the selfsame texture with the celestial. The momentary circumstance was too strong for him; he failed to look beyond the shadowy scope of time, and, living once for all in eternity, to find the perfect future in the present.

Thinking About Progress

On June 30, 1858, three eminent statesmen burst out of a committee room in the British Houses of Parliament "in the greatest haste and confusion." Prime Minister Gladstone and Chancellor of the Exchequer Disraeli hurried along with handkerchiefs clapped to their noses; Sir James Graham, less restrained, "seemed to be attacked by a sudden fit of expectoration." The wind had shifted and was blowing off the Thames, which Disraeli described as "a stygian pool reeking with ineffable and intolerable horrors." The City of London, capital of the Industrial Revolution, had fouled its own nest. Cholera was rampant, and the smell of factory wastes and human excrement combined to make life miserable for those who couldn't escape to the less advanced countryside. Technological progress had, at any rate, been getting rather mixed reviews in the 1850s. Poets like Tennyson and Longfellow were looking resolutely backward at figures like King Arthur and Hiawatha. The great art critic John Ruskin was extolling the virtues of Gothic art and architecture. Henry David Thoreau was publishing *Walden*. The word *artificial,* which in the eighteenth century had had largely positive connotations, was now a term of condemnation.

The solution to London's "Great Stink" was not, however, to tear down the factories and send the people back to the country. Within two weeks of getting that famous noseful of London air, Disraeli had introduced legislation that would produce one of the great feats of modern engineering, Sir Joseph Bazalette's drainage system: eighty-two miles of brick sewers, tunnelled under a heavily built-up city, capable of channeling away 420 million gallons of waste daily and making London habitable again. Though some "Great Stink" seems always near—in our time, for instance, the problem of disposal of nuclear waste—modern technology has until now always managed to find a Bazalette to make life longer, safer, and more comfortable.

This long record of success, however, has not silenced those who are uneasy about technological progress. Nathaniel Hawthorne's fable of misapplied science, "The Birthmark," grows more disturbing as science grows stronger. Thoreau, though he was writing at the very beginning of engineering's golden age, didn't doubt the power of technology but rather its pertinence to the important concerns of life: "We are eager to tunnel under the Atlantic and bring the Old World some weeks nearer to the New; but perchance the first news that will leak through to the broad, flapping American ear will be that the Princess Adelaide has the whooping cough." As technology improved, it began to remove some of life's sharper edges: exploration, Nancy Mitford points out, became safer and smaller; travel, E. B. White notes, became very much like staying at home. Even staying at home may have become less satisfying than it once was: as Alice Bloom points out, affluent people in a technological society know very little about the processes that support them, where the lamb chop comes from or where the waste water goes to. The result is what Daniel Boorstin calls an "attenuation of experience": more is available to us, but less seems significant, and though society's power over the environment increases, the power of the individual may be decreased. C. S. Lewis begins his essay "The Abolition of Man" by clarifying this paradoxical situation. "If I pay you to carry me," he says, "I am not therefore myself a strong man." He then presents us with a chilling picture of a world dominated by the "Conditioners," who treat human nature as mere nature, and solve its problems with the same technical virtuosity that Bazalette applied to the Thames.

Some who read this section will feel that these are the objections (as White puts it) of "well-heeled sentimentalists who have had the breaks." Three of the section's most powerful writers agree. Adam Smith, writing at the very beginning of the Industrial Revolution, predicts quite accurately the enormous benefits it will bring to even the poorest classes. Thomas Babington Macaulay's arguments against Seneca and Plato could be turned equally effectively on Thoreau and Boorstin: "It may be worse to be angry than to be wet. But shoes have kept millions from being wet; and we doubt whether Seneca ever kept anybody from being angry." Aldous Huxley points out with glee that engineers and industrialists have done more to encourage the brotherhood of man than all the saints have done. The vigor of the argument on both sides tells us how central the theme of technological progress has become to our thinking.

QUESTIONS

1. Microbiologist Bernard Dixon, writing in *The Sciences*, once pointed out that most of us suffer these days from "the black-box blues," a feeling that we are dependent on gadgets we don't in the least understand. To what extent are you dependent on mysterious black boxes, and how does this dependence affect you?

2. Proponents of modern technology argue that rather than trapping the individual in a web of uncontrollable systems, it gives the individual new powers. What machines would you point to as particularly liberating? Do the arguments of Boorstin and Lewis make them seem less so?

3. What experiences have you had with very advanced technology? Did these experiences make you feel stronger or weaker?

4. What experiences have you had with earlier technologies: hand tools, unmechanized gardening, home canning, etc.? Did these experiences make you feel stronger or weaker? Would you want to return permanently to such a state of technology?

5. Do you feel that you are subject to the sort of psychological reshaping C. S. Lewis discusses in "The Abolition of Man"? If so, who are the shapers, and how can they be resisted? Should they be resisted?

6. As Adam Smith notes, the modern industrial world is a result of the division of labor. What experiences have you had with specialization in the workplace? Have they been positive or negative? Would you prefer undivided labor?

MASCULINITY
AND FEMININITY

VIRGINIA WOOLF

Professions for Women

When your secretary invited me to come here, she told me that   1
your Society is concerned with the employment of women and
she suggested that I might tell you something about my own
professional experiences. It is true I am a woman; it is true I am
employed; but what professional experiences have I had? It is
difficult to say. My profession is literature; and in that profession
there are fewer experiences for women than in any other, with
the exception of the stage—fewer, I mean, that are peculiar to
women. For the road was cut many years ago—by Fanny Burney,
by Aphra Behn, by Harriet Martineau, by Jane Austen, by George
Eliot—many famous women, and many more unknown and forgotten, have been before me, making the path smooth, and regulating
my steps. Thus, when I came to write, there were very few material
obstacles in my way. Writing was a reputable and harmless occupation. The family peace was not broken by the scratching of
a pen. No demand was made upon the family purse. For ten and
sixpence one can buy paper enough to write all the plays of
Shakespeare—if one has a mind that way. Pianos and models,
Paris, Vienna and Berlin, masters and mistresses, are not needed
by a writer. The cheapness of writing paper is, of course, the reason
why women have succeeded as writers before they have succeeded
in the other professions.

But to tell you my story—it is a simple one. You have only got   2
to figure to yourselves a girl in a bedroom with a pen in her hand.
She had only to move that pen from left to right—from ten o'clock
to one. Then it occurred to her to do what is simple and cheap
enough after all—to slip a few of those pages into an envelope,
fix a penny stamp in the corner, and drop the envelope into the
red box at the corner. It was thus that I became a journalist; and
my effort was rewarded on the first day of the following month—
a very glorious day it was for me—by a letter from an editor
containing a cheque for one pound ten shillings and sixpence. But
to show you how little I deserve to be called a professional woman,
how little I know of the struggles and difficulties of such lives, I
have to admit that instead of spending that sum upon bread and
butter, rent, shoes and stockings, or butcher's bills, I went out and

A paper read to the Women's Service League, circa 1930.

217

bought a cat—a beautiful cat, a Persian cat, which very soon involved me in bitter disputes with my neighbours.

What could be easier than to write articles and to buy Persian ³ cats with the profits? But wait a moment. Articles have to be about something. Mine, I seem to remember, was about a novel by a famous man. And while I was writing this review, I discovered that if I were going to review books I should need to do battle with a certain phantom. And the phantom was a woman, and when I came to know her better I called her after the heroine of a famous poem, The Angel in the House. It was she who used to come between me and my paper when I was writing reviews. It was she who bothered me and wasted my time and so tormented me that at last I killed her. You who come of a younger and happier generation may not have heard of her—you may not know what I mean by the Angel in the House. I will describe her as shortly as I can. She was intensely sympathetic. She was immensely charming. She was utterly unselfish. She excelled in the difficult arts of family life. She sacrificed herself daily. If there was chicken, she took the leg; if there was a draught she sat in it—in short she was so constituted that she never had a mind or a wish of her own, but preferred to sympathize always with the minds and wishes of others. Above all—I need not say it—she was pure. Her purity was supposed to be her chief beauty—her blushes, her great grace. In those days—the last of Queen Victoria—every house had its Angel. And when I came to write I encountered her with the very first words. The shadow of her wings fell on my page; I heard the rustling of her skirts in the room. Directly, that is to say, I took my pen in hand to review that novel by a famous man, she slipped behind me and whispered: "My dear, you are a young woman. You are writing about a book that has been written by a man. Be sympathetic; be tender; flatter; deceive; use all the arts and wiles of our sex. Never let anybody guess that you have a mind of your own. Above all, be pure." And she made as if to guide my pen. I now record the one act for which I take some credit to myself, though the credit rightly belongs to some excellent ancestors of mine who left me a certain sum of money—shall we say five hundred pounds a year?—so that it was not necessary for me to depend solely on charm for my living. I turned upon her and caught her by the throat. I did my best to kill her. My excuse, if I were to be had up in a court of law, would be that I acted in self-defence. Had I not killed her she would have killed me. She would have plucked the heart out of my writing. For, as I found, directly I put pen to paper, you cannot review even a novel without having a mind of your own, without expressing what you think to be the truth about human relations, morality, sex. And all these questions, according to the Angel in the House, cannot be dealt with freely and openly by women; they must charm, they must conciliate, they must—to put it bluntly—tell lies if they are to succeed. Thus, whenever I felt the shadow of her wing or the radiance of her halo upon my page, I took up the inkpot and flung it at her. She died hard. Her fictitious nature was of great assistance to her. It is far harder to kill a phantom than a reality. She was always creeping back when I thought I had despatched her. Though I flatter myself that I killed her in the end, the struggle was severe; it took much time that had better have been spent upon learning Greek grammar; or in roaming the world in search of adventures. But it was a real experience; it was an experience that was bound to befall all women writers at that time. Killing the Angel in the House was part of the occupation of a woman writer.

But to continue my story. The Angel was dead; what then 4 remained? You may say that what remained was a simple and common object—a young woman in a bedroom with an inkpot. In other words, now that she had rid herself of falsehood, that young woman had only to be herself. Ah, but what is "herself"? I mean, what is a woman? I assure you, I do not know. I do not believe that you know. I do not believe that anybody can know until she has expressed herself in all the arts and professions open to human skill. That indeed is one of the reasons why I have come here—out of respect for you, who are in process of showing us by your experiments what a woman is, who are in process of providing us, by your failures and successes, with that extremely important piece of information.

But to continue the story of my professional experiences. I made 5 one pound ten and six by my first review; and I bought a Persian cat with the proceeds. Then I grew ambitious. A Persian cat is all very well, I said; but a Persian cat is not enough. I must have a motor car. And it was thus that I became a novelist—for it is a very strange thing that people will give you a motor car if you will tell them a story. It is a still stranger thing that there is nothing so delightful in the world as telling stories. It is far pleasanter than writing reviews of famous novels. And yet, if I am to obey your secretary and tell you my professional experiences as a novelist, I must tell you about a very strange experience that befell me as a novelist. And to understand it you must try first to imagine a novelist's state of mind. I hope I am not giving away professional secrets if I say that a novelist's chief desire is to be as unconscious as possible. He has to induce in himself a state of perpetual lethargy. He wants life to proceed with the utmost quiet and regularity. He wants to see the same faces, to read the same books, to do the

same things day after day, month after month, while he is writing,
so that nothing may break the illusion in which he is living—so
that nothing may disturb or disquiet the mysterious nosings about,
feelings round, darts, dashes and sudden discoveries of that very
shy and illusive spirit, the imagination. I suspect that this state is
the same both for men and women. Be that as it may, I want
you to imagine me writing a novel in a state of trance. I want
you to figure to yourselves a girl sitting with a pen in her hand,
which for minutes, and indeed for hours, she never dips into the
inkpot. The image that comes to my mind when I think of this
girl is the image of a fisherman lying sunk in dreams on the verge
of a deep lake with a rod held out over the water. She was letting
her imagination sweep unchecked round every rock and cranny
of the world that lies submerged in the depths of our unconscious
being. Now came the experience, the experience that I believe to
be far commoner with women writers than with men. The line
raced through the girl's fingers. Her imagination had rushed away.
It had sought the pools, the depths, the dark places where the
largest fish slumber. And then there was a smash. There was an
explosion. There was foam and confusion. The imagination had
dashed itself against something hard. The girl was roused from
her dream. She was indeed in a state of the most acute and difficult
distress. To speak without figure she had thought of something,
something about the body, about the passions which it was unfitting
for her as a woman to say. Men, her reason told her, would be
shocked. The consciousness of what men will say of a woman
who speaks the truth about her passions had roused her from her
artist's state of unconsciousness. She could write no more. The
trance was over. Her imagination could work no longer. This I
believe to be a very common experience with women writers—
they are impeded by the extreme conventionality of the other sex.
For though men sensibly allow themselves great freedom in these
respects, I doubt that they realize or can control the extreme
severity with which they condemn such freedom in women.

These then were two very genuine experiences of my own. These   6
were two of the adventures of my professional life. The first—
killing the Angel in the House—I think I solved. She died. But
the second, telling the truth about my own experiences as a body,
I do not think I solved. I doubt that any woman has solved it yet.
The obstacles against her are still immensely powerful—and yet
they are very difficult to define. Outwardly, what is simpler than
to write books? Outwardly, what obstacles are there for a woman •
rather than for a man? Inwardly, I think, the case is very different;
she has still many ghosts to fight, many prejudices to overcome.
Indeed it will be a long time still, I think, before a woman can

sit down to write a book without finding a phantom to be slain, a rock to be dashed against. And if this is so in literature, the freest of all professions for women, how is it in the new professions which you are now for the first time entering?

Those are the questions that I should like, had I time, to ask you. And indeed, if I have laid stress upon these professional experiences of mine, it is because I believe that they are, though in different forms, yours also. Even when the path is nominally open—when there is nothing to prevent a woman from being a doctor, a lawyer, a civil servant—there are many phantoms and obstacles, as I believe, looming in her way. To discuss and define them is I think of great value and importance; for thus only can the labour be shared, the difficulties be solved. But besides this, it is necessary also to discuss the ends and the aims for which we are fighting, for which we are doing battle with these formidable obstacles. Those aims cannot be taken for granted; they must be perpetually questioned and examined. The whole position, as I see it—here in this hall surrounded by women practising for the first time in history I know not how many different professions— is one of extraordinary interest and importance. You have won rooms of your own in the house hitherto exclusively owned by men. You are able, though not without great labour and effort, to pay the rent. You are earning your five hundred pounds a year. But this freedom is only a beginning; the room is your own, but it is still bare. It has to be furnished; it has to be decorated; it has to be shared. How are you going to furnish it, how are you going to decorate it? With whom are you going to share it, and upon what terms? These, I think are questions of the utmost importance and interest. For the first time in history you are able to ask them; for the first time you are able to decide for yourselves what the answers should be. Willingly would I stay and discuss those questions and answers—but not tonight. My time is up; and I must cease.

DOROTHY SAYERS

Are Women Human?

When I was asked to come and speak to you, your Secretary made the suggestion that she thought I must be interested in the feminist movement. I replied—a little irritably, I am afraid—that

An address given to a women's society, 1938.

I was not sure I wanted to "identify myself," as the phrase goes, with feminism, and that the time for "feminism," in the old-fashioned sense of the word, had gone past. In fact, I think I went so far as to say that, under present conditions, an aggressive feminism might do more harm than good. As a result I was, perhaps not unnaturally, invited to explain myself.

I do not know that it is very easy to explain, without of-   2
fence or risk of misunderstanding, exactly what I do mean, but I will try.

The question of "sex-equality" is, like all questions affecting   3
human relationships, delicate and complicated. It cannot be settled by loud slogans or hard-and-fast assertions like "a woman is as good as a man"—or "woman's place is the home"—or "women ought not to take men's jobs." The minute one makes such assertions, one finds one has to qualify them. "A woman is as good as a man" is as meaningless as to say, "a Kaffir is as good as a Frenchman" or "a poet is as good as an engineer" or "an elephant is as good as a racehorse"—it means nothing whatever until you add: "at doing what?" In a religious sense, no doubt, the Kaffir is as valuable in the eyes of God as a Frenchman—but the average Kaffir is probably less skilled in literary criticism than the average Frenchman, and the average Frenchman less skilled than the average Kaffir in tracing the spoor of big game. There might be exceptions on either side: it is largely a matter of heredity and education. When we balance the poet against the engineer, we are faced with a fundamental difference of temperament—so that here our question is complicated by the enormous social problem whether poetry or engineering is "better" for the State, or for humanity in general. There may be people who would like a world that was all engineers or all poets—but most of us would like to have a certain number of each; though here again, we should all differ about the desirable proportion of engineering to poetry. The only proviso we should make is that people with dreaming and poetical temperaments should not entangle themselves in engines, and that mechanically-minded persons should not issue booklets of bad verse. When we come to the elephant and the racehorse, we come down to bed-rock physical differences—the elephant would make a poor showing in the Derby, and the unbeaten Eclipse himself would be speedily eclipsed by an elephant when it came to hauling logs.

That is so obvious that it hardly seems worth saying. But it is   4
the mark of all movements, however well-intentioned, that their pioneers tend, by much lashing of themselves into excitement, to lose sight of the obvious. In reaction against the age-old slogan, "woman is the weaker vessel," or the still more offensive, "woman

is a divine creature," we have, I think, allowed ourselves to drift into asserting that "a woman is as good as a man," without always pausing to think what exactly we mean by that. What, I feel, we ought to mean is something so obvious that it is apt to escape attention altogether, viz: not that every woman is, in virtue of her sex, as strong, clever, artistic, level-headed, industrious and so forth as any man that can be mentioned; but, that a woman is just as much an ordinary human being as a man, with the same individual preferences, and with just as much right to the tastes and preferences of an individual. What is repugnant to every human being is to be reckoned always as a member of a class and not as an individual person. A certain amount of classification is, of course, necessary for practical purposes: there is no harm in saying that women, as a class, have smaller bones than men, wear lighter clothing, have more hair on their heads and less on their faces, go more pertinaciously to church or the cinema, or have more patience with small and noisy babies. In the same way, we may say that stout people of both sexes are commonly better-tempered than thin ones, or that university dons of both sexes are more pedantic in their speech than agricultural labourers, or that Communists of both sexes are more ferocious than Fascists—or the other way round. What is unreasonable and irritating is to assume that *all* one's tastes and preferences have to be conditioned by the class to which one belongs. That has been the very common error into which men have frequently fallen about women—and it is the error into which feminist women are, perhaps, a little inclined to fall into about themselves.

Take, for example, the very usual reproach that women now- 5 adays always want to "copy what men do." In that reproach there is a great deal of truth and a great deal of sheer, unmitigated and indeed quite wicked nonsense. There are a number of jobs and pleasures which men have in times past cornered for themselves. At one time, for instance, men had a monopoly of classical education. When the pioneers of university training for women demanded that women should be admitted to the universities, the cry went up at once: "Why should women want to know about Aristotle?" The answer is NOT that *all* women would be the better for knowing about Aristotle—still less, as Lord Tennyson seemed to think, that they would be more companionable wives for their husbands if they did know about Aristotle—but simply: "What women want as a class is irrelevant. *I* want to know about Aristotle. It is true that most women care nothing about him, and a great many male undergraduates turn pale and faint at the thought of him—but I, eccentric individual that I am, do want to know about Aristotle, and I submit that there is nothing in my shape or bodily functions which need prevent my knowing about him."

That battle was won, and rightly won, for women. But there is a sillier side to the university education of women. I have noticed lately, and with regret, a tendency on the part of the women's colleges to "copy the men" on the side of their failings and absurdities, and this is not so good. Because the constitution of the men's colleges is autocratic, old-fashioned and in many respects inefficient, the women are rather inclined to try and cramp their own collegiate constitutions—which were mapped out on freer democratic lines—into the mediæval mould of the men's—and that is unsound. It contributes nothing to the university and it loses what might have been a very good thing. The women students, too, have a foolish trick of imitating and outdoing the absurdities of male undergraduates. To climb in drunk after hours and get gated is silly and harmless if done out of pure high spirits; if it is done "because the men do it," it is worse than silly, because it is not spontaneous and not even amusing.

Let me give one simple illustration of the difference between the right and the wrong kind of feminism. Let us take this terrible business—so distressing to the minds of bishops—of the women who go about in trousers. We are asked: "Why do you want to go about in trousers? They are extremely unbecoming to most of you. You only do it to copy the men." To this we may very properly reply: "It is true that they are unbecoming. Even on men they are remarkably unattractive. But, as you men have discovered for yourselves, they are comfortable, they do not get in the way of one's activities like skirts and they protect the wearer from draughts about the ankles. As a human being, I like comfort, and dislike draughts. If the trousers do not attract you, so much the worse; for the moment I do not want to attract you. I want to enjoy myself as a human being, and why not? As for copying you, certainly you thought of trousers first and to that extent we must copy you. But we are not such abandoned copy-cats as to attach these useful garments to our bodies with braces. There we draw the line. These machines of leather and elastic are unnecessary and unsuited to the female form. They are, moreover, hideous beyond description. And as for indecency—of which you sometimes accuse the trousers—we at least can take our coats off without becoming the half-undressed, bedroom spectacle that a man presents in his shirt and braces."

So that when we hear that women have once more laid hands upon something which was previously a man's sole privilege, I think we have to ask ourselves: is this trousers or is it braces? Is it something useful, convenient and suitable to a human being as such? Or is it merely something unnecessary to us, ugly, and adopted merely for the sake of collaring the other fellow's property? These jobs and professions, now. It is ridiculous to take on a man's job just in order to be able to say that "a woman has done it—yah!" The only decent reason for tackling any job is that it is *your* job and *you* want to do it.

At this point, somebody is likely to say: "Yes, that is all very 9 well. But it *is* the woman who is always trying to ape the man. She *is* the inferior being. You don't as a rule find the men trying to take the women's jobs away from them. They don't force their way into the household and turn women out of their rightful occupations."

Of course they do not. They have done it already. 10

Let us accept the idea that women should stick to their own 11 jobs—the jobs they did so well in the good old days before they started talking about votes and women's rights. Let us return to the Middle Ages and ask what we should get then in return for certain political and educational privileges which we should have to abandon.

It is a formidable list of jobs: the whole of the spinning industry, 12 the whole of the dyeing industry, the whole of the weaving industry. The whole catering industry and—which would not please Lady Astor,[1] perhaps—the whole of the nation's brewing and distilling. All the preserving, pickling and bottling industry, all the bacon-curing. And (since in those days a man was often absent from home for months together on war or business) a very large share in the management of landed estates. Here are the women's jobs—and what has become of them? They are all being handled by men. It is all very well to say that woman's place is the home—but modern civilisation has taken all these pleasant and profitable activities out of the home, where the women looked after them, and handed them over to big industry, to be directed and organised by men at the head of large factories. Even the dairy-maid in her simple bonnet has gone, to be replaced by a male mechanic in charge of a mechanical milking plant.

Now, it is very likely that men in big industries do these jobs 13 better than the women did them at home. The fact remains that the home contains much less of interesting activity than it used to contain. What is more, the home has so shrunk to the size of a small flat that—even if we restrict woman's job to the bearing

1. Lady Nancy Astor, first woman to sit in the British House of Commons, a champion of women's rights, public education, and temperance.

and rearing of families—there is no room for her to do even that.
It is useless to urge the modern woman to have twelve children,
like her grandmother. Where is she to put them when she has
got them? And what modern man wants to be bothered with
them? It is perfectly idiotic to take away women's traditional
occupations and then complain because she looks for new ones.
Every woman is a human being—one cannot repeat that too often—
and a human being *must* have occupation, if he or she is not to
become a nuisance to the world.

I am not complaining that the brewing and baking were taken   14
over by the men. If they can brew and bake as well as women
or better, then by all means let them do it. But they cannot have
it both ways. If they are going to adopt the very sound principle
that the job should be done by the person who does it best, then
that rule must be applied universally. If the women make better
office-workers than men, they must have the office work. If any
individual woman is able to make a first-class lawyer, doctor,
architect or engineer, then she must be allowed to try her hand
at it. Once lay down the rule that the job comes first and you
throw that job open to every individual, man or woman, fat or
thin, tall or short, ugly or beautiful, who is able to do that job
better than the rest of the world.

Now, it is frequently asserted that, with women, the job does   15
not come first. What (people cry) are women doing with this
liberty of theirs? What woman really prefers a job to a home and
family? Very few, I admit. It is unfortunate that they should so
often have to make the choice. A man does not, as a rule, have
to choose. He gets both. In fact, if he wants the home and family,
he usually has to take the job as well, if he can get it. Nevertheless,
there have been women, such as Queen Elizabeth and Florence
Nightingale, who had the choice, and chose the job and made a
success of it. And there have been and are many men who have
sacrificed their careers for women—sometimes, like Antony or
Parnell,[2] very disastrously. When it comes to a *choice*, then every
man or woman has to choose as an individual human being, and,
like a human being, take the consequences.

As human beings! I am always entertained—and also irritated—   16
by the newsmongers who inform us, with a bright air of discovery,

---

2. Marc Antony allied himself with his lover Cleopatra and—perhaps as a result—
lost to Augustus Caesar in the struggle for control of the Roman Empire. Charles
Stewart Parnell's affair with "Kitty" O'Shea, wife of a political rival, resulted in a
divorce scandal and a fall from power in 1889. Before the divorce, Parnell was a
hero in Ireland's struggle for Home Rule.

that they have questioned a number of female workers and been told by one and all that they are "sick of the office and would love to get out of it." In the name of God, what human being is *not*, from time to time, heartily sick of the office and would *not* love to get out of it? The time of female officeworkers is daily wasted in sympathising with disgruntled male colleagues who yearn to get out of the office. No human being likes work—not day in and day out. Work is notoriously a curse—and if women *liked* everlasting work they would not be human beings at all. *Being* human beings, they like work just as much and just as little as anybody else. They dislike perpetual washing and cooking just as much as perpetual typing and standing behind shop counters. Some of them prefer typing to scrubbing—but that does not mean that they are not, as human beings, entitled to damn and blast the typewriter when they feel that way. The number of men who daily damn and blast typewriters is incalculable; but that does not mean that they would he happier doing a little plain sewing. Nor would the women.

I have admitted that there are very few women who would put their job before every earthly consideration. I will go further and assert that there are very few men who would do it either. In fact, there is perhaps only one human being in a thousand who is passionately interested in his job for the job's sake. The difference is that if that one person in a thousand is a man, we say, simply, that he is passionately keen on his job; if she is a woman, we say she is a freak. It is extraordinarily entertaining to watch the historians of the past, for instance, entangling themselves in what they were pleased to call the "problem" of Queen Elizabeth. They invented the most complicated and astonishing reasons both for her success as a sovereign and for her tortuous matrimonial policy. She was the tool of Burleigh, she was the tool of Leicester, she was the fool of Essex; she was diseased, she was deformed, she was a man in disguise. She was a mystery, and must have some extraordinary solution. Only recently has it occurred to a few enlightened people that the solution might be quite simple after all. She might be one of the rare people who were born into the right job and put that job first. Whereupon a whole series of riddles cleared themselves up by magic. She was in love with Leicester—why didn't she marry him? Well, for the very same reason that numberless kings have not married their lovers—because it would have thrown a spanner into the wheels of the State machine. Why was she so blood-thirsty and unfeminine as to sign the death-warrant of Mary Queen of Scots? For much the same reasons that induced King George V to say that if the House of Lords did not pass the Parliament

Bill he would create enough new peers to force it through—
because she was, in the measure of her time, a constitutional
sovereign, and knew that there was a point beyond which a sovereign could not defy Parliament. Being a rare human being with
her eye to the job, she did what was necessary; being an ordinary
human being, she hesitated a good deal before embarking on
unsavoury measures—but as to feminine mystery, there is no such
thing about it, and nobody, had she been a man, would have
thought either her statesmanship or her humanity in any way
mysterious. Remarkable they were—but she was a very remarkable
person. Among her most remarkable achievements was that of
showing that sovereignty was one of the jobs for which the right
kind of woman was particularly well fitted.

Which brings us back to this question of what jobs, if any, are [18]
women's jobs. Few people would go so far as to say that all women
are well fitted for all men's jobs. When people do say this, it is
particularly exasperating. It is stupid to insist that there are as
many female musicians and mathematicians as male—the facts
are otherwise, and the most we can ask is that if a Dame Ethel
Smyth or a Mary Somerville[3] turns up, she shall be allowed to
do her work without having aspersions cast either on her sex or
her ability. What we ask is to be human individuals, however
peculiar and unexpected. It is no good saying: "You are a little
girl and therefore you ought to like dolls"; if the answer is, "But
I don't," there is no more to be said. Few women happen to be
natural born mechanics; but if there is one, it is useless to try and
argue her into being something different. What we must *not* do
is to argue that the occasional appearance of a female mechanical
genius proves that all women would be mechanical geniuses if
they were educated. They would not.

Where, I think, a great deal of confusion has arisen is in a failure [19]
to distinguish between special *knowledge* and special *ability*. There
are certain questions on which what is called "the woman's point
of view" is valuable, because they involve special *knowledge*. Women
should be consulted about such things as housing and domestic
architecture because, under present circumstances, they have still
to wrestle a good deal with houses and kitchen sinks and can
bring special knowledge to the problem. Similarly, some of them
(though not all) know more about children than the majority of
men, and their opinion, *as women*, is of value. In the same way,

3. Smyth (1858–1944), a prolific composer of symphonies, operas, choral works,
instrumental pieces, and songs, was also a militant suffragist. Somerville was a
nineteenth-century writer of works on celestial mechanics and physics.

the opinion of colliers is of value about coal-mining, and the opinion of doctors is valuable about disease. But there are other questions—as for example, about literature or finance—on which the "woman's point of view" has no value at all. In fact, it does not exist. No special knowledge is involved, and a woman's opinion on literature or finance is valuable only as the judgment of an individual. I am occasionally desired by congenital imbeciles and the editors of magazines to say something about the writing of detective fiction "from the woman's point of view." To such demands, one can only say, "Go away and don't be silly. You might as well ask what is the female angle on an equilateral triangle."

In the old days it used to be said that women were unsuited   20
to sit in Parliament, because they "would not be able to think imperially." That, if it meant anything, meant that their views would be cramped and domestic—in short, "the woman's point of view." Now that they *are* in Parliament, people complain that they are a disappointment: they vote like other people with their party and have contributed nothing to speak of from "the woman's point of view"—except on a few purely domestic questions, and even then they are not all agreed. It looks as though somebody was trying to have things both ways at once. Even critics must remember that women are human beings and obliged to think and behave as such. I can imagine a "woman's point of view" about town-planning, or the education of children, or divorce, or the employment of female shop-assistants, for here they have some special knowledge. But what in thunder is the "woman's point of view" about the devaluation of the franc or the abolition of the Danzig Corridor?[4] Even where women have special knowledge, they may disagree among themselves like other specialists. Do doctors never quarrel or scientists disagree? Are women really *not human*, that they should be expected to toddle along all in a flock like sheep? I think that people should be allowed to drink as much wine and beer as they can afford and is good for them; Lady Astor thinks nobody should be allowed to drink anything of the sort. Where is the "woman's point of view"? Or is one or the other of us unsexed? If the unsexed one is myself, then I am unsexed in very good company. But I prefer to think that women are human and differ in opinion like other human beings. This does not mean that their opinions, as individual opinions, are valueless; on the contrary, the more able they are the more violently their

4. At the end of World War I, the allies promised Poland a "corridor" through Danzig to the sea. Because Danzig's population was overwhelmingly German, it became a focus of Nazi expansionism.

opinions will be likely to differ. It only means that you cannot ask for "the woman's point of view," but only for the woman's special knowledge—and this, like all special knowledge, is valuable, though it is no guarantee of agreement.

"What," men have asked distractedly from the beginning of time, "what on earth do women want?" I do not know that women, *as* women, want anything in particular, but as human beings they want, my good men, exactly what you want yourselves: interesting occupation, reasonable freedom for their pleasures, and a sufficient emotional outlet. What form the occupation, the pleasures and the emotion may take, depends entirely upon the individual. You know that this is so with yourselves—why will you not believe that it is so with us. The late D. H. Lawrence, who certainly cannot be accused of underrating the importance of sex and talked a good deal of nonsense upon the subject, was yet occasionally visited with shattering glimpses of the obvious. He said in one of his *Assorted Articles*: 21

> "Man is willing to accept woman as an equal, as a man in skirts, as an angel, a devil, a baby-face, a machine, an instrument, a bosom, a womb, a pair of legs, a servant, an encyclopædia, an ideal or an obscenity; the one thing he won't accept her as is a human being, a real human being of the feminine sex."

"Accepted as a human being!"—yes; not as an inferior class and not, I beg and pray all feminists, as a superior class—not, in fact, as a class at all, except in a useful context. We are much too much inclined in these days to divide people into permanent categories, forgetting that a category only exists for its special purpose and must be forgotten as soon as that purpose is served. There is a fundamental difference between men and women, but it is not the only fundamental difference in the world. There is a sense in which my charwoman and I have more in common than either of us has with, say, Mr. Bernard Shaw; on the other hand, in a discussion about art and literature, Mr. Shaw and I should probably find we had more fundamental interests in common than either of us had with my charwoman. I grant that, even so, he and I should disagree ferociously about the eating of meat—but that is not a difference between the sexes—on that point, that late Mr. G. K. Chesterton would have sided with me against the representative of his own sex. Then there are points on which I, and many of my own generation of both sexes, should find ourselves heartily in agreement; but on which the rising generation of young men and women would find us too incomprehensibly stupid for words. A difference of age is as fundamental as a difference of sex; and 22 so is a difference of nationality. *All* categories, if they are insisted upon beyond the immediate purpose which they serve, breed class antagonism and disruption in the state, and that is why they are dangerous.

The other day, in the "Heart-to-Heart" column of one of our   23
popular newspapers, there appeared a letter from a pathetic gentleman about a little disruption threatening his married state. He wrote:

> "I have been married eleven years and think a great deal of the wedding annniversary. I remind my wife a month in advance and plan to make the evening a success. But she does not share my keenness, and, if I did not remind her, would let the day go by without a thought of its significance. I thought a wedding anniversary meant a lot to a woman. Can you explain this indifference?"

Poor little married gentleman, nourished upon generalisations—   24
and convinced that if his wife does not fit into the category of "a woman" there must be something wrong! Perhaps she resents being dumped into the same category as all the typical women of the comic stories. If so, she has my sympathy. "A" woman—not an individual person, disliking perhaps to be reminded of the remorseless flowing-by of the years and the advance of old age— but "a" woman, displaying the conventional sentimentalities attributed to her unfortunate and ridiculous sex.

A man once asked me—it is true that it was at the end of a   25
very good dinner, and the compliment conveyed may have been due to that circumstance—how I managed in my books to write such natural conversation between men when they were by themselves. Was I, by any chance, a member of a large, mixed family with a lot of male friends? I replied that, on the contrary, I was an only child and had practically never seen or spoken to any men of my own age till I was about twenty-five. "Well," said the man, "I shouldn't have expected a woman [meaning me] to have been able to make it so convincing." I replied that I had coped with this difficult problem by making my men talk, as far as possible, like ordinary human beings. This aspect of the matter seemed to surprise the other speaker; he said no more, but took it away to chew it over. One of these days it may quite likely occur to him that women, as well as men, when left to themselves, talk very much like human beings also.

Indeed, it is my experience that both men and women are   26
fundamentally human, and that there is very little mystery about either sex, except the exasperating mysteriousness of human beings in general. And though for certain purposes it may still be necessary,

as it undoubtedly was in the immediate past, for women to band themselves together, as women, to secure recognition of their requirements as a sex, I am sure that the time has now come to insist more strongly on each woman's—and indeed each man's—requirements as an individual person. It used to be said that women had no *esprit de corps*; we have proved that we have—do not let us run into the opposite error of insisting that there is an aggressively feminist "point of view" about everything. To oppose one class perpetually to another—young against old, manual labour against brain-worker, rich against poor, woman against man—is to split the foundations of the State; and if the cleavage runs too deep, there remains no remedy but force and dictatorship. If you wish to preserve a free democracy, you must base it—not on classes and categories, for this will land you in the totalitarian State, where no one may act or think except as the member of a category. You must base it upon the individual Tom, Dick and Harry, on the individual Jack and Jill—in fact, upon you and me.

JAN MORRIS

To Everest

Though I resented my body, I did not dislike it. I rather admired   1
it, as it happened. It might not be the body beautiful, but it was lean and sinewy, never ran to fat, and worked like a machine of quality, responding exuberantly to a touch of the throttle or a long haul home. Women, I think, never have quite this feeling about their bodies, and I shall never have it again. It is a male prerogative, and contributes no doubt to the male arrogance. In those days, though for that very reason I did not want it, still I recognized the merits of my physique, and had pleasure from its exercise.

I first felt its full power, as one might realize for the first time   2
the potential of a run-in car, in 1953, when I was assigned by *The Times* to join the British expedition shortly to make the first ascent of Mount Everest. This was essentially a physical undertaking.

Chapter 9 of *Conundrum* (1974). The first sentence of the book is "I was three or perhaps four years old when I realized I had been born in the wrong body, and should really be a girl." After hormone treatment and surgery, James Morris became Jan in 1972.

The paper had exclusive rights to dispatches from the mountain, and I was to be the only correspondent with the team, my job being partly to see that dispatches from the expedition's leader got safely home to London, but chiefly to write dispatches of my own. The competition would be intense and very likely violent, communications were primitive to a degree, and the only way to do the job was to climb fairly high up the mountain myself and periodically, to put a complex operation simply, run down it again with the news. It was not particularly to my credit that I was given the assignment—at an agile twenty-six I was patently better suited for it than most of my colleagues at Printing House Square. I took exercise daily (as I still do), did not smoke (and still don't), and though excessively fond of wine, seldom drank spirits, not much liking the taste of them.

I was also, being some years out of the 9th Lancers, furiously keen.[1] There is something about the newspaper life, however specious its values and ridiculous its antics, that brings out the zest in its practitioners. It may be nonsense, but it is undeniably fun. I was not especially anxious to achieve fame in the trade, for I already felt instinctively that it would not be my life's occupation, but even so I would have stooped to almost any skulduggery to achieve what was, self-consciously even then, quaintly called a scoop. The news from Everest was to be mine, and anyone who tried to steal it from me should look out for trouble. 3

In such a mood, at such an age, at the peak of a young man's physical condition, I found myself in May, 1953, high on the flank of the world's greatest mountain. 4

Let me try to describe the sensation for my readers, as it seems to me today—and especially for my women readers, who are unlikely I now see to have experienced such a conjunction of energies. 5

Imagine first the setting. This is theatrically changeable. In the morning it is like living, reduced to minuscule proportions, in a bowl of broken ice cubes in a sunny garden. Somewhere over the rim, one assumes, there are green trees, fields and flowers; within the bowl everything is a brilliant white and blue. It is silent in there. The mountain walls deaden everything and cushion the hours in a disciplinary hush. The only noise is a drip of water sometimes, the howl of a falling boulder or the rumble of a distant 6

---

1. Morris soldiered with this British regiment from 1943–47, rising to the rank of lieutenant. Among these highly professional soldiers, shows of enthusiasm, or "keenness," were considered bad form.

avalanche. The sky above is a savage blue, the sun glares mercilessly off the snow and ice, blistering one's lips, dazzling one's eyes, and filling that mountain declivity with its substance.

In the afternoon everything changes. Then the sky scowls down, high snow-clouds billow in from Tibet, a restless cruel wind blows up, and before long the snow is falling in slanted parallel across the landscape, blotting out sky, ridges, and all, and making you feel that your ice-bowl has been put back into the refrigerator. It is terribly cold. The afternoon is filled with sounds, the rush of wind, the flapping of tent-canvas, the squeak and creak of guy-ropes; and as the evening draws on the snow piles up around your tent, half burying it infinitesimally in the hulk of Everest, as though you have been prematurely incarcerated, or perhaps trapped in a sunken submarine—for you can see the line of snow slowly rising through the nylon walls of the tent, like water rising to submerge you. 7

But imagine now the young man's condition. First, he is constant against this inconstant background. His body is running not in gusts and squalls, but at a steady high speed. He actually tingles with strength and energy, as though sparks might fly from his skin in the dark. Nothing sags in him. His body has no spare weight upon it, only muscles made supple by exercise. When, in the bright Himalayan morning, he emerges from his tent to make the long trek down the mountain to the Khumbu glacier below, it is as though he could leap down there in gigantic strides, singing as he goes. And when, the same evening perhaps, he labors up again through the driving snow, it is not a misery but a challenge to him, something to be outfaced, something actually to be enjoyed, as the deep snow drags at his feet, the water trickles down the back of his neck, and his face thickens with cold, ice, and wind. 8

There is no hardship to it, for it is not imposed upon him. He is the master. He feels that anything is possible to him, and that his relative position to events will always remain the same. He does not have to wonder what his form will be tomorrow, for it will be the same as it is today. His mind, like his body, is tuned to the job, and will not splutter or falter. It is this feeling of unfluctuating control, I think, that women cannot share, and it springs of course not from the intellect or the personality, nor even so much from upbringing, but specifically from the body. The male body may be ungenerous, even uncreative in the deepest kind, but when it is working properly it is a marvelous thing to inhabit. I admit it in retrospect more than I did at the time, and I look back to those moments of supreme male fitness as one remembers champagne or a morning swim. Nothing could beat me, I knew for sure; and nothing did. 9

I think for sheer exuberance the best day of my life was my 10
last on Everest. The mountain had been climbed, and I had already
begun my race down the glacier towards Katmandu, leaving the
expedition to pack its gear behind me. By a combination of cunning
and ingenuity I had already sent a coded message through an
Indian Army radio transmitter at Namche Bazar, twenty miles
south of Everest, its operators being unaware of its meaning; but
I did not know if it had reached London safely, so I was myself
hastening back to Katmandu and the cable office with my own
final dispatch. How brilliant I felt, as with a couple of Sherpa
porters I bounded down the glacial moraine towards the green
below! I was brilliant with the success of my friends on the mountain,
I was brilliant with my knowledge of the event, brilliant with
muscular tautness, brilliant with conceit, brilliant with awareness
of the subterfuge, amounting very nearly to dishonesty, by which
I hoped to have deceived my competitors and scooped the world.
All those weeks at high altitude had suited me, too, and had given
me a kind of heightened fervor, as though my brain had been
quickened by drugs to keep pace with my body. I laughed and
sang all the way down the glacier, and when next morning I heard
from the radio that my news had reached London providentially
on the eve of Queen Elizabeth's coronation, I felt as though I had
been crowned myself.

I never mind the swagger of young men. It is their right to 11
swank, and I know the sensation!

Once more on Everest I was the outsider—formally this time, 12
as well as tacitly. None of the climbers would have guessed, I am
sure, how irrevocably distinct I felt from them; but they were
aware that I was not a climber, and had been attached to the
expedition only to watch. At first I was supposed to provide my
own victuals and equipment, but it seemed rather silly to maintain
such segregation twenty thousand feet above nowhere, so I soon
pooled my resources with theirs, and pitched my tent among them.

On Everest, nevertheless, I realized more explicitly some truths 13
about myself. Though I was as fit as most of those men, I responded
to different drives. I would have suffered almost anything to get
those dispatches safely back to London, but I did not share the
mountaineers' burning urge to see that mountain climbed. Perhaps
it was too abstract an objective for me—certainly I was not animated
by any respect for inviolate nature, which I have always disliked,
preferring like George Leigh-Mallory a blend of tame and wild. I
was pleased when they did climb Everest, but chiefly for a less
than elevated reason—patriotic pride, which I knew to be unworthy
of their efforts, but which I could not suppress.

I well understood the masochistic relish of challenge which   14
impelled them, and which stimulated me too, but the blankness
of the achievement depressed me. One of the older Everesters,
H. W. Tilman, once quoted G. K. Chesterton to illustrate the urge
of alpinism: "I think the immense act has something about it
human and excusable; and when I endeavor to analyze the reason
of this feeling I find it to lie, not in the fact that the thing was
big or bold or successful, but in the fact that the thing was perfectly
useless to everybody, including the person who did it." Leigh-
Mallory presumably meant much the same, when he talked of
climbing Everest simply "because it was there." But this elusive
prize, this snatching at air, this nothingness, left me dissatisfied,
as I think it would leave most women. Nothing had been discovered,
nothing made, nothing improved.

I have always discounted the beauty of clouds, because their   15
airy impermanence seems to me to disqualify them from the truest
beauty, just as I have never responded to kinetic art, and love the
shifting light of nature only because it reveals new shapes and
meaning in the solids down below. Nor do I like sea views, unless
there is land to be seen beyond them. A similar distrust of the
ephemeral or the un-finite weakened my response to the triumph
of Everest in 1953. It was a grand adventure, I knew, and my
part in relaying its excitements to the world was to transform my
professional life, and dog me ever after; yet even now I dislike
that emptiness at its climax, that perfect uselessness, and feel in
a slightly ashamed and ungrateful way that it was really all rather
absurd.

For it was almost like a military expedition—the colonel in   16
command, not so long from Montgomery's staff, the little army
of porters who wound their way bent-back with their loads over
the hills from Katmandu, the meticulously packed and listed stores,
the briefings, the air of ordered determination. It was a superbly
successful expedition—nobody killed, nobody disgraced—and
looking back upon it now I see its cohesion as a specifically male
accomplishment. Again constancy was the key. Men more than
women respond to the team spirit, and this is partly because, if
they are of an age, of a kind, and in a similar condition, they
work together far more like a mechanism. Elations and despon-
dencies are not so likely to distract them. Since their pace is more
regular, all can more easily keep to it. They are distinctly more
rhythm than melody.

In 1953 the rhythm was steadier than it might be now, for it   17
was conscious then as well as constitutional. Stiff upper lip and
fair play were integral to the British masculine ethos, and shame

was a powerful impulse towards achievement. Social empathy, too, strongly reinforced the sense of maleness. The functional efficiency of class I had already discovered in the Army, and it was the same on Everest. Hunt's climbers were men of the officer class, as they would then have been called, and they were bound by common tastes and values. They spoke the same language, shared the same kind of past, enjoyed the same pleasures. Three of them had been to the same school. In a social sense they formed a kind of club; in an imperial sense, and this was almost the last of the imperial adventures, they were a company of sahibs attended by their multitudinous servants.

One could not, I think, apply these categories to women of [18] equal intelligence in similar circumstances, and less and less can one now apply them to men. Class has lost its binding function; patriotism has lost its elevating force; young men are no longer ashamed of weaknesses; the stiff upper lip is no longer an ideal, only a music hall sally. The barrier between the genders is flimsier now, and no expedition will ever again go to the Himalayas so thoroughly masculine as Hunt's. It embarrasses me rather to have to admit that from that day to this, none has gone there more successfully.

I need not belabor my sense of alienation from this formidable [19] team. I liked most of its members very much, and have remained friends with some to this day, but my sense of detachment was extreme, and though I shamelessly accepted their help throughout the adventure, still I was always at pains to cherish my separateness. I hated to think of myself as one of them, and when in England we were asked to sign menus, maps, or autograph books, I used carefully to sign myself James Morris of *The Times*—until the climbers, fancying I fear altogether different motives in me, asked me not to. At the same time a wayward self-consciousness—for I was a child of the age, too—compelled me to keep up male appearances, perhaps as much for my own persuasion as for anyone else's. I even overdid it rather. I grew a beard, and when at the end of the expedition I walked into the communications room at the British Embassy in Katmandu with my tin mug jangling from the belt of my trousers, the wireless operator asked acidly if I *had* to look so jungly. He did not know how cruelly the jibe hurt, for in a few words it cut this way and that through several skins of self-protection.

Everest taught me new meanings of maleness, and emphasized [20] once more my own inner dichotomy. Yet paradoxically my most evocative memory of the experience haunts me with a truth of an altogether different kind. Often when there was a lull on the mountain I would go down the glacier and wander among the moraines. Sometimes I went south, towards the distant Buddhist temple at Thyangboehe where the deodars shaded the green turf, and the bells, gongs, and trumpets of the monks sounded from their shambled refectory. Sometimes I clambered into the snows of the north, towards the great wall of the Lho La, over whose ominous white ridge stood the peaks of Tibet. I vaguely hoped to catch a glimpse of an abominable snowman, and I was looking too for traces of the lemurs and mountain hares which sometimes, I had been told, penetrated those high deserts.

I saw no animals ever. What I found instead was a man. I saw [21] him first in the extreme distance, across an absolutely blank snow-field at about nineteen thousand feet, to which I had climbed from the glacier below for the sake of the view. At first I was frightened, for I could not make out what he was—only a small black swaying speck, indescribably alone in the desolation. As he came closer I saw that he could only be human, so I plunged through the loose snow to meet him, and presently, there near the top of the world, thousands of feet and many miles above the trees, the streams, or human habitation, we met face to face. It was the strangest encounter of my life.

He was a holy man, wandering in the mountains, I suppose, [22] for wandering's sake. His brown, crinkled, squashed-up face looked back at me expressionless from beneath a yellow hood, and found it seemed nothing strange in my presence there. He wore a long yellow cloak and hide boots, and from his waist there hung a spoon and a cloth satchel. He carried nothing else, and he wore no gloves. I greeted him as best I could, but he did not answer, only smiling at me distantly and without surprise. Perhaps he was in a trance. I offered him a piece of chocolate, but he did not take it, simply standing there before me, slightly smiling, almost as though he were made of ice himself. Presently we parted, and without a word he continued on his unfaltering journey, apparently making for Tibet without visible means of survival, and moving with a proud, gliding, and effortless motion that seemed inexorable. He did not appear to move fast, but when I looked around he had almost disappeared, and was no more than that small black speck again, inexplicably moving over the snows.

I envied him his insouciant speed, and wondered if he too felt [23] that tingling of the body, that sense of mastery, which had so deepened my sense of duality upon the slopes of Everest. But the more I thought about it, the more clearly I realized that he had no body at all.

TOM WOLFE

The Right Stuff

A young man might go into military flight training believing 1
that he was entering some sort of technical school in which he
was simply going to acquire a certain set of skills. Instead, he
found himself all at once enclosed in a fraternity. And in this
fraternity, even though it was military, men were not rated by
their outward rank as ensigns, lieutenants, commanders, or whatever. No, herein the world was divided into those who had it and
those who did not. This quality, this *it*, was never named, however,
nor was it talked about in any way.

As to just what this ineffable quality was . . . well, it obviously 2
involved bravery. But it was not bravery in the simple sense of
being willing to risk your life. The idea seemed to be that any
fool could do that, if that was all that was required, just as any
fool could throw away his life in the process. No, the idea here
(in the all-enclosing fraternity) seemed to be that a man should
have the ability to go up in a hurtling piece of machinery and
put his hide on the line and then have the moxie, the reflexes,
the experience, the coolness, to pull it back in the last yawning
moment—and then to go up again *the next day*, and the next day,
and every next day, even if the series should prove infinite—and,
ultimately, in its best expression, do so in a cause that means
something to thousands, to a people, a nation, to humanity, to
God. Nor was there *a test* to show whether or not a pilot had this
righteous quality. There was, instead, a seemingly infinite series
of tests. A career in flying was like climbing one of those ancient
Babylonian pyramids made up of a dizzy progression of steps and
ledges, a ziggurat, a pyramid extraordinarily high and steep; and
the idea was to prove at every foot of the way up that pyramid
that you were one of the elected and anointed ones who had *the
right stuff* and could move higher and higher and even—ultimately,
God willing, one day—that you might be able to join that special
few at the very top, that elite who had the capacity to bring tears
to men's eyes, the very Brotherhood of the Right Stuff itself.

None of this was to be mentioned, and yet it was acted out in 3
a way that a young man could not fail to understand. When a

Excerpted from chapter 2 of *The Right Stuff* (1980). The flight training Wolfe describes
took place in the mid-50's. Among its survivors were "Pete" Conrad and "Wally"
Schirra, astronauts in Project Mercury.

new flight (i.e., a class) of trainees arrived at Pensacola, they were brought into an auditorium for a little lecture. An officer would tell them: "Take a look at the man on either side of you." Quite a few actually swiveled their heads this way and that, in the interest of appearing diligent. Then the officer would say: "One of the three of you is not going to make it!"—meaning, not get his wings. That was the opening theme, the *motif* of primary training. We already know that one-third of you do not have the right stuff— it only remains to find out who.

Furthermore, that was the way it turned out. At every level in   4 one's progress up that staggeringly high pyramid, the world was once more divided into those men who had the right stuff to continue the climb and those who had to be *left behind* in the most obvious way. Some were eliminated in the course of the opening classroom work, as either not smart enough or not hard-working enough, and were left behind. Then came the basic flight instruction, in single-engine, propeller-driven trainers, and a few more—even though the military tried to make this stage easy— were washed out and left behind. Then came more demanding levels, one after the other, formation flying, instrument flying, jet training, all-weather flying, gunnery, and at each level more were washed out and left behind. By this point easily a third of the original candidates had been, indeed, eliminated . . . from the ranks of those who might prove to have the right stuff.

In the Navy, in addition to the stages that Air Force trainees   5 went through, the neophyte always had waiting for him, out in the ocean, a certain grim gray slab; namely, the deck of an aircraft carrier; and with it perhaps the most difficult routine in military flying, carrier landings. He was shown films about it, he heard lectures about it, and he knew that carrier landings were hazardous. He first practiced touching down on the shape of a flight deck painted on an airfield. He was instructed to touch down and gun right off. This was safe enough—the shape didn't move, at least— but it could do terrible things to, let us say, the gyroscope of the soul. *That shape!—it's so damned small!* And more candidates were washed out and left behind. Then came the day, without warning, when those who remained were sent out over the ocean for the first of many days of reckoning with the slab. The first day was always a clear day with little wind and a calm sea. The carrier was so steady that it seemed, from up there in the air, to be resting on pilings, and the candidate usually made his first carrier landing successfully, with relief and even *élan*. Many young candidates looked like terrific aviators up to that very point—and it was not until they were actually standing on the carrier deck that they first began to wonder if they had the proper stuff, after all. In the training film the flight deck was a grand piece of gray geometry, perilous, to be sure, but an amazing abstract shape as one looks down upon it on the screen. And yet once the newcomer's two feet were on it . . . *Geometry*—my God, man, this is a . . . skillet! It *heaved*, it moved up and down underneath his feet, it pitched up, it pitched down, it rolled to port (this great beast *rolled!*) and it rolled to starboard, as the ship moved into the wind and, therefore, into the waves, and the wind kept sweeping across, sixty feet up in the air out in the open sea, and there were no railings whatsoever. This was a *skillet!*—a frying pan!—a short-order grill!—not gray but black, smeared with skid marks from one end to the other and glistening with pools of hydraulic fluid and the occasional jet-fuel slick, all of it still hot, sticky, greasy, runny, virulent from God knows what traumas—still ablaze!—consumed in detonations, explosions, flames, combustion, roars, shrieks, whines, blasts, horrible shudders, fracturing impacts, as little men in screaming red and yellow and purple and green shirts with black Mickey Mouse helmets over their ears skittered about on the surface as if for their very lives (you've said it now!), hooking fighter planes onto the catapult shuttles so that they can explode their afterburners and be slung off the deck in a red-mad fury with a *kaboom!* that pounds through the entire deck—a procedure that seems absolutely controlled, orderly, sublime, however, compared to what he is about to watch as aircraft return to the ship for what is known in the engineering stoicisms of the military as "recovery and arrest." To say that an F–4 was coming back onto this heaving barbecue from out of the sky at a speed of 135 knots . . . that might have been the truth in the training lecture, but it did not begin to get across the idea of what the newcomer saw from the deck itself, because it created the notion that perhaps the plane was gliding in. On the deck one knew differently! As the aircraft came closer and the carrier heaved on into the waves and the plane's speed did not diminish and the deck did not grow steady—indeed, it pitched up and down five or ten feet per greasy heave—one experienced a neural alarm that no lecture could have prepared him for: This is not an *airplane* coming toward me, it is a brick with some poor sonofabitch riding it (*someone much like myself!*), and it is not *gliding*, it is *falling*, a thirty-thousand-pound brick, headed not for a stripe on the deck but for *me*—and with a horrible *smash!* it hits the skillet, and with a blur of momentum as big as a freight train's it hurtles toward the far end of the deck—another blinding storm!—another roar as the pilot pushes the throttle up to full military power and another smear of rubber screams out over the skillet—and this is nominal!—quite okay!—for a wire stretched across the deck has grabbed the hook on the end of the plane as it hit the deck tail down, and the smash was the rest of the fifteen-ton brute slamming onto the deck, as it tripped up, so that it is now straining against the wire at full throttle, in case it hadn't held and the plane had "boltered" off the end of the deck and had to struggle up into the air again. And already the Mickey Mouse helmets are running toward the fiery monster . . .

And the candidate, looking on, begins to *feel* that great heaving 6 sun-blazing deathboard of a deck wallowing in his own vestibular system—and suddenly he finds himself backed up against his own limits. He ends up going to the flight surgeon with so-called conversion symptoms. Overnight he develops blurred vision or numbness in his hands and feet or sinusitis so severe that he cannot tolerate changes in altitude. On one level the symptom is real. He really cannot see too well or use his fingers or stand the pain. But somewhere in his subconscious he knows it is a plea and a beg-off; he shows not the slightest concern (the flight surgeon notes) that the condition might be permanent and affect him in whatever life awaits him outside the arena of the right stuff.

Those who remained, those who qualified for carrier duty—and 7 even more so those who later on qualified for *night* carrier duty— began to feel a bit like Gideon's warriors. *So many have been left behind!* The young warriors were now treated to a deathly sweet and quite unmentionable sight. They could gaze at length upon the crushed and wilted pariahs who had washed out. They could inspect those who did not have that righteous stuff.

The military did not have very merciful instincts. Rather than 8 packing up these poor souls and sending them home, the Navy, like the Air Force and the Marines, would try to make use of them in some other role, such as flight controller. So the washout has to keep taking classes with the rest of his group, even though he can no longer touch an airplane. He sits there in the classes staring at sheets of paper with cataracts of sheer human mortification over his eyes while the rest steal looks at him . . . this man reduced to an ant, this untouchable, this poor sonofabitch. And in what test had he been found wanting? Why, it seemed to be nothing less than *manhood* itself. Naturally, this was never mentioned, either. Yet there it was. *Manliness, manhood, manly courage* . . . there was something ancient, primordial, irresistible about the challenge of this stuff, no matter what a sophisticated and rational age one might think he lived in.

Perhaps because it could not be talked about, the subject began 9 to take on superstitious and even mystical outlines. A man either had it or he didn't! There was no such thing as having *most* of it. Moreover, it could blow at any seam. One day a man would be ascending the pyramid at a terrific clip, and the next—bingo!—

he would reach his own limits in the most unexpected way. Conrad and Schirra met an Air Force pilot who had had a great pal at Tyndall Air Force Base in Florida. This man had been the budding ace of the training class; he had flown the hottest fighter-style trainer, the T–38, like a dream; and then he began the routine step of being checked out in the T–33. The T–33 was not nearly as hot an aircraft as the T–38; it was essentially the old P–80 jet fighter. It had an exceedingly small cockpit. The pilot could barely move his shoulders. It was the sort of airplane of which everybody said, "You don't get into it, you *wear* it." Once inside a T–33 cockpit this man, this budding ace, developed claustrophobia of the most paralyzing sort. He tried everything to overcome it. He even went to a psychiatrist, which was a serious mistake for a military officer if his superiors learned of it. But nothing worked. He was shifted over to flying jet transports, such as the C–135. Very demanding and necessary aircraft they were, too, and he was still spoken of as an excellent pilot. But as everyone knew—and, again, it was never explained in so many words—only those who were assigned to fighter squadrons, the "fighter jocks," as they called each other with a self-satisfied irony, remained in the true fraternity. Those assigned to transports were not humiliated like washouts—*somebody* had to fly those planes—nevertheless, they, too, had been *left behind* for lack of the right stuff.

Or a man could go for a routine physical one fine day, feeling 10 like a million dollars, and be grounded for *fallen arches*. It happened!—just like that! (And try raising them.) Or for breaking his wrist and losing only *part* of its mobility. Or for a minor deterioration of eyesight, or for any of hundreds of reasons that would make no difference to a man in an ordinary occupation. As a result all fighter jocks began looking upon doctors as their natural enemies. Going to see a flight surgeon was a no-gain proposition; a pilot could only hold his own or lose in the doctor's office. To be grounded for a medical reason was no humiliation, looked at objectively. But it was a humiliation, nonetheless!—for it meant you no longer had that indefinable, unutterable, integral stuff. (It could blow at *any* seam.)

All the hot young fighter jocks began trying to test the limits 11 themselves in a superstitious way. They were like believing Presbyterians of a century before who used to probe their own experience to see if they were truly among *the elect*. When a fighter pilot was in training, whether in the Navy or the Air Force, his superiors were continually spelling out strict rules for him, about the use of the aircraft and conduct in the sky. They repeatedly forbade so-called hot-dog stunts, such as outside loops, buzzing, flat-hatting, hedgehopping and flying under bridges. But somehow one got the

message that the man who truly *had* it could ignore those rules—
not that he should make a point of it, but that he *could*—and that
after all there was only one way to find out—and that in some
strange unofficial way, peeking through his fingers, his instructor
halfway expected him to challenge all the limits. They would give
a lecture about how a pilot should never fly without a good solid
breakfast—eggs, bacon, toast, and so forth—because if he tried to
fly with his blood-sugar level too low, it could impair his alertness.
Naturally, the next day every hot dog in the unit would get up
and have a breakfast consisting of one cup of black coffee and
take off and go up into a vertical climb until the weight of the
ship exactly canceled out the upward thrust of the engine and his
air speed was zero, and he would hang there for one thick adrenal
instant—and then fall like a rock, until one of three things happened:
he keeled over nose first and regained his aerodynamics and all
was well, he went into a spin and fought his way out of it, or he
went into a spin and had to eject or crunch it, which was always
supremely possible.

Likewise, "hassling"—mock dogfighting—was strictly forbidden, 12
and so naturally young fighter jocks could hardly wait to go up
in, say, a pair of F–100s and start the duel by making a pass at
each other at 800 miles an hour, the winner being the pilot who
could slip in behind the other one and get locked in on his tail
("wax his tail"), and it was not uncommon for some eager jock
to try too tight an outside turn and have his engine flame out,
whereupon, unable to restart it, he has to eject . . . and he shakes
his fist at the victor as he floats down by parachute and his million-
dollar aircraft goes *kaboom!* on the palmetto grass or the desert
floor, and he starts thinking about how he can get together with
the other guy back at the base in time for the two of them to get
their stories straight before the investigation: "I don't know what
happened, sir. I was pulling up after a target run, and it just flamed
out on me." Hassling was forbidden, and hassling that led to the
destruction of an aircraft was a serious court-martial offense, and
the man's superiors knew that the engine hadn't *just flamed out*,
but every unofficial impulse on the base seemed to be saying:
"Hell, we wouldn't give you a nickel for a pilot who hasn't done
some crazy rat-racing like that. It's all part of the right stuff."

The other side of this impulse showed up in the reluctance of 13
the young jocks to admit it when they had maneuvered themselves
into a bad corner they couldn't get out of. There were two reasons
why a fighter pilot hated to declare an emergency. First, it triggered
a complex and very public chain of events at the field: all other
incoming flights were held up, including many of one's comrades
who were probably low on fuel; the fire trucks came trundling

out to the runway like yellow toys (as seen from way up there), the better to illustrate one's hapless state; and the bureaucracy began to crank up the paper monster for the investigation that always followed. And second, to declare an emergency, one first had to reach that conclusion in his own mind, which to the young pilot was the same as saying: "A minute ago I still *had* it—now I need your help!" To have a bunch of young fighter pilots up in the air thinking this way used to drive flight controllers crazy. They would see a ship beginning to drift off the radar, and they couldn't rouse the pilot on the microphone for anything other than a few meaningless mumbles, and they would know he was probably out there with engine failure at a low altitude, trying to reignite by lowering his auxiliary generator rig, which had a little propeller that was supposed to spin in the slipstream like a child's pinwheel.

"Whiskey Kilo Two Eight, do you want to declare an emergency?" 14

This would rouse him!—to say: "Negative, negative, Whiskey 15 Kilo Two Eight is not declaring an emergency."

Kaboom. Believers in the right stuff would rather crash and 16 burn.

One fine day, after he had joined a fighter squadron, it would 17 dawn on the young pilot exactly how the losers in the great fraternal competition were now being left behind. Which is to say, not by instructors or other superiors or by failures at prescribed levels of competence, but by death. At this point the essence of the enterprise would begin to dawn on him. Slowly, step by step, the ante had been raised until he was now involved in what was surely the grimmest and grandest gamble of manhood. Being a fighter pilot—for that matter, simply taking off in a single-engine jet fighter of the Century series, such as an F–102, or any of the military's other marvelous bricks with fins on them—presented a man, on a perfectly sunny day, with more ways to get himself killed than his wife and children could imagine in their wildest fears. If he was barreling down the runway at two hundred miles an hour, completing the takeoff run, and the board started lighting up red, should he (a) abort the takeoff (and try to wrestle with the monster, which was gorged with jet fuel, out in the sand beyond the end of the runway) or (b) eject (and hope that the goddamned human cannonball trick works at zero altitude and he doesn't shatter an elbow or a kneecap on the way out) or (c) continue the takeoff and deal with the problem aloft (knowing full well that the ship may be on fire and therefore seconds away from exploding)? He would have one second to sort out the options and act, and this kind of little workaday decision came up all the time. Occasionally a man would look coldly at the binary problem

he was now confronting every day—Right Stuff/Death—and decide
it wasn't worth it and voluntarily shift over to transports or re-
connaissance or whatever. And his comrades would wonder, for
a day or so, what evil virus had invaded his soul . . . as they left
him behind. More often, however, the reverse would happen.
Some college graduate would enter Navy aviation through the
Reserves, simply as an alternative to the Army draft, fully intending
to return to civilian life, to some waiting profession or family
business; would become involved in the obsessive business of
ascending the ziggurat pyramid of flying; and, at the end of his
enlistment, would astound everyone back home and very likely
himself as well by signing up for another one. What on earth got
into him? He couldn't explain it. After all, the very words for it
had been amputated. A Navy study showed that two-thirds of the
fighter pilots who were rated in the top rungs of their groups—
i.e., the hottest young pilots—reenlisted when the time came, and
practically all were college graduates. By this point, a young fighter
jock was like the preacher in *Moby Dick* who climbs up into the
pulpit on a rope ladder and then pulls the ladder up behind him;
except the pilot could not use the words necessary to express the
vital lessons. Civilian life, and even home and hearth, now seemed
not only far away but far *below*, back down many levels of the
pyramid of the right stuff.

A fighter pilot soon found he wanted to associate only with   18
other fighter pilots. Who else could understand the nature of the
little proposition (right stuff/death) they were all dealing with?
And what other subject could compare with it? It was riveting!
To talk about it in so many words was forbidden, of course. The
very words *death, danger, bravery, fear* were not to be uttered except
in the occasional specific instance or for ironic effect. Nevertheless,
the subject could be adumbrated in *code* or *by example*. Hence the
endless evenings of pilots huddled together talking about flying.
On these long and drunken evenings (the bane of their family
life) certain theorems would be propounded and demonstrated—
and all by *code* and *example*. One theorem was: There are no
accidents and no fatal flaws in the machines; there are only pilots
with the wrong stuff. (I.e., blind Fate can't kill me.) When Bud
Jennings crashed and burned in the swamps at Jacksonville, the
other pilots in Pete Conrad's squadron said: *How could he have
been so stupid?* It turned out that Jennings had gone up in the SNJ
with his cockpit canopy opened in a way that was expressly forbidden in the manual, and carbon monoxide had been sucked in
from the exhaust, and he passed out and crashed. All agreed that
Bud Jennings was a good guy and a good pilot, but his epitaph
on the ziggurat was: *How could he have been so stupid?* This seemed

shocking at first, but by the time Conrad had reached the end of
that bad string at Pax River,[1] he was capable of his own corollary
to the theorem: viz., no single factor ever killed a pilot; there was
always a chain of mistakes. But what about Ted Whelan, who
fell like a rock from 8,100 feet when his parachute failed? Well,
the parachute was merely part of the chain: first, someone should
have caught the structural defect that resulted in the hydraulic
leak that triggered the emergency; second, Whelan did not check
out his seat-parachute rig, and the drogue failed to separate the
main parachute from the seat; but even after those two mistakes,
Whelan had fifteen or twenty seconds, as he fell, to disengage
himself from the seat and open the parachute manually. Why just
stare at the scenery coming up to smack you in the face! And
everyone nodded. (He failed—but I wouldn't have!) Once the
theorem and the corollary were understood, the Navy's statistics
about one in every four Navy aviators dying meant nothing. The
figures were averages, and averages applied to those with average
stuff.

A riveting subject, especially if it were one's own hide that was   19
on the line. Every evening at bases all over America, there were
military pilots huddled in officers clubs eagerly cutting the right
stuff up in coded slices so they could talk about it. What more
compelling topic of conversation was there in the world? In the
Air Force there were even pilots who would ask the tower for
priority landing clearance so that they could make the beer call
on time, at 4 p.m. sharp, at the Officers Club. They would come
right out and state the reason. The drunken rambles began at four
and sometimes went on for ten or twelve hours. Such conversations!
They diced that righteous stuff up into little bits, bowed ironically
to it, stumbled blindfolded around it, groped, lurched, belched,
staggered, bawled, sang, roared, and feinted at it with self-deprecating
humor. Nevertheless!—they never mentioned it by name. No, they
used the approved codes, such as: "Like a jerk I got myself into
a hell of a corner today." They told of how they "lucked out of
it." To get across the extreme peril of his exploit, one would use
certain oblique cues. He would say, "I looked over at Robinson"—
who would be known to the listeners as a non-com who sometimes
rode backseat to read radar—"and he wasn't talking any more,
he was just staring at the radar, like this, giving it that *zombie* look.
Then I *knew* I was in trouble!" Beautiful! Just right! For it would
also be known to the listeners that the non-coms advised one
another: "*Never* fly with a lieutenant. *Avoid* captains and majors.
Hell, man, do yourself a favor: don't fly with anybody below

1. During the "bad string," ten of Conrad's close friends had been killed in accidents.

colonel." Which in turn said: "Those young bucks shoot dice with
death!" And yet once in the air the non-com had his own standards.
He was determined to remain as outwardly cool as the pilot, so
that when the pilot did something that truly petrified him, he
would say nothing; instead, he would turn silent, catatonic, like
a zombie. Perfect! *Zombie.* There you had it, compressed into a
single word, all of the foregoing. I'm a hell of a pilot! I shoot dice
with death! And now all you fellows know it! And I haven't
spoken of that unspoken stuff even once!

The talking and drinking began at the beer call, and then the   20
boys would break for dinner and come back afterward and get
more wasted and more garrulous or else more quietly fried, drinking
good cheap PX booze until 2 a.m. The night was young! Why not
get the cars and go out for a little proficiency run? It seemed that
every fighter jock thought himself an ace driver, and he would
do anything to obtain a hot car, especially a sports car, and the
drunker he was, the more convinced he would be about his driving
skills, as if the right stuff, being indivisible, carried over into any
enterprise whatsoever, under any conditions. A little proficiency
run, boys! (There's only one way to find out!) And they would
roar off in close formation from, say, Nellis Air Force Base, down
Route 15, into Las Vegas, barreling down the highway, rat-racing,
sometimes four abreast, jockeying for position, piling into the most
listless curve in the desert flats as if they were trying to root each
other out of the groove at the Rebel 500—and then bursting into
downtown Las Vegas with a rude fraternal roar like the Hell's
Angels—and the natives chalked it up to youth and drink and the
bad element that the Air Force attracted. They knew nothing about
the right stuff, of course.

MARGARET MEAD

Sex and Achievement

There has long been a habit in western civilization of speaking   1
as if it were possible for men to have a picture of womanhood to
which women reluctantly conformed, and for women to make
demands on men to which men adjusted even more reluctantly.
This has been an accurate picture of the way in which we have

Chapter 15 of *Male and Female* (1949).

structured our society, with women as keepers of the house who insist that men wipe their feet on the door-mat, and men as keepers of women in the house who insist that their wives should stay modestly within-doors. There have been a thousand varieties of these demands, from the way a tea-cup was balanced to the prohibition on a wife's smoking or on daughter's cutting her hair. From one point of view they provided a pleasant tension on which drawing-room etiquette could be based, or by way of which a man could proclaim his natural masculine desire to be free and dirty and careless and unpunctual *if* his wife had not insisted that he be home every night promptly for dinner. The picture can be obsessively elaborated, and girls attempting to plan their own lives may stop every other moment to say, "But men don't like women who . . ." However, it is one thing to recognize these phrasings as cultural devices which maintain a working equilibrium between male and female roles, but quite another thing to take them seriously and talk about a "man-made" world, or to say, as Emily James Putnam does in the introduction to *The Lady*, "Where he put her, there she stays," and thus deny the far more fundamental fact that both men and women share the same images of what makes a marriageable or an unmarriageable woman, a good husband, a fascinating lover whom any woman would be a fool to marry, or a born old bachelor. The phrases "a man's man" or "a woman's woman" do not mean a basic disagreement between men and women about which type of man gets on better with men than with women, but a basic agreement between men and women about each kind of man or woman. When a man and a woman get into an argument about some solid, plodding, devoted young woman, and the woman says, "But she'll make some man a very good wife," and the man says "I don't believe any man will want to marry her," there is no real conflict between them. The dissenting man means the same thing as the woman speaker by the words "good wife," only he is saying, "But who wants that kind of a good wife?" In the last century, when the upper-class and middle-class worlds were so neatly protected against bad women who wore bright colours and were filled with allure, this did not mean that women thought bad women were unalluring. The man who, exhausted by the demands of a wife who had taken permanently to a sofa after the birth of her first child, sought out a glittering lady in a large plumed hat, and his wife who lay on the sofa and imagined the lady in the hat, both agreed that she was alluring, and both also agreed that it was both natural and wrong for the husband to be allured and both natural and right for his wife to resent it. So both father and mother, brother and sister, neighbour and preacher and teacher, future mother-in-law, possible mistress, local Don Juan, and the village wiseacre, as well as the comics, the radio, the films, build together the images of the different kinds of men and women who will be loved, valued, hated, and ignored by their own sex, the opposite sex, or both.

So every hesitancy in a woman and every bit of bluster in a   2
man are not to be laid to some male conspiracy to keep women in their place, any more than every bit of blundering shyness in a man or of conceited demandingness in a woman is to be laid to some female conspiracy to dominate men. Different cultures have styled the relationships between men and women differently. When they have styled the roles so that they fitted well together, so that law and custom, ideal and practical possibilities, were reasonably close together, the men and the women who lived within that society have been fortunate. But to the degree that there have been discrepancies in the two roles, to the degree that a style of beauty that was unobtainable by most people, or a style of bravery or initiative, modesty and responsiveness, was insisted upon although the culture had inadequate devices for developing such initiative or such responsiveness, then both men and women suffer. The suffering of either sex—of the male who is unable, because of the way in which he was reared, to take the strong initiating or patriarchal role that is still demanded of him, or of the female who has been given too much freedom of movement as a child to stay placidly within the house as an adult—this suffering, this discrepancy, this sense of failure in an enjoined role, is the point of leverage for social change. One has only to follow the fortunes of the demand for equal political rights for women from one country to another to note how contrasting are the responses from women in different countries, and how slight the overt relationship between low position of women and the eager demands for women's rights. Unfortunately we do not have as good comparative material on attempts to change the status of men—parallel movements such as the abolition of alimony, controversies as to whether family subsidies are to be paid to fathers or mothers, arguments over community-property laws. Attempts to free men from responsibilities and limitations that no longer appear reasonable or just are not neatly summed up under a men's-rights movement, or considered by international subcommissions on the legal status of men. Yet detailed analysis of any of these legal reforms would show quite clearly that there is a continuous movement also to free men from limitations that are out of line with the contemporary calendar. Breach-of-promise cases are a silly excrescence in a world in which women do half the proposing,

and alienation-of-affection cases between two men, which assume that the woman is a gently pliant lily, ring just as false. Alimony for a young childless woman with an education equal to that of her husband, who must postpone his next marriage to support her, is coming to seem glaringly unfair. But the historical trend that listed women among the abused minorities, and which was a natural outcome of the sorts of inspection of legal and social abuses that went with our transformation from a society of status, where rights were inherent, to a society of contract, in which rights have to be established, lingers on to obscure the issue and gives apparent point to the contention that this is a man-made world in which women have always been abused and must always fight for their rights.

It takes considerable effort on the part of both men and women 3 to reorient ourselves to thinking—when we think basically—that this is a world made not by men alone, in which women are unwilling and helpless dupes and fools or else powerful schemers hiding their power under their ruffled petticoats, but a world made by mankind for human beings of both sexes. In this world male and female roles have sometimes been styled well and sometimes badly; sometimes the men have an easier time while the women have recourse to soothsayers, day-dreams, autoerotic devices, gigolos, somatic diseases, and downright insanity. Sometimes it is the women whose role has been cast in terms so close to the realities of their fate that they present a picture of relative placidity while the men pursue phantoms. But there seems little doubt that the relative attainability of either role has its effect on both men and women. Women who seem placid while the men seem erratic and bewitched pay a price for the discrepancies in the men's role; men who appear far more favoured and more free than their women-folk have not yet reached the level of self-realization that would have been theirs had their wives and mothers also had roles that they could attain and enjoy.

Literature in the United States at present is raucous and angry 4 on this whole question of the relationship between men and women. We have had a spate of books that claim women are being masculinized, to their ill, to men's ill, to everybody's ill, and another spate, or sometimes the same spate, of books that insist that men are being feminized. When one follows the shrill insistencies of books like *Modern Woman: The Lost Sex*, which end by attacking men as well as women, one realizes that we are passing through a period of discrepancies in sex roles which are so conspicuous that efforts to disguise the price that both sexes pay are increasingly unsuccessful. Only if we perpetuate the habit of speaking about

"the position of women" in a vacuum will we fail to recognize
that where one sex suffers, the other sex suffers also. As surely
as we believe that the present troublesome problems of sex adjustment are due to the position of women alone, we commit
ourselves to a long series of false moves as we attempt to push
women out of the home, into the home, out of the home, adding
mounting confusion to the difficulties born of a changing world-
climate of opinion, a shifting technology, and an increasing rate
and violence of cultural change.

It has been fashionable in the last few years to call America a   5
matriarchy, and thus do considerable violence to a useful anthropological concept. A matriarchal society is one in which some if
not all of the legal powers relating to the ordering and governing
of the family—power over property, over inheritance, over marriage,
over the house—are lodged in women rather than in men. So
we may speak of matrilineal societies, in which a man inherits
his name, his land, and his position, or any one of these from his
mother's brother, through his mother. This may not mean a great
deal of power for women, although it is a system in which women
are sufficiently favoured so that polygamy, for instance, does not
work well within it. Or we may speak of matrilocal society, in
which house and land are owned by women and pass from mother
to daughter, and husbands move in and move out. This system
is even less compatible with polygamy, or with the exercise of
very much authority by the husband-fathers, who live under their
mother-in-law's roof. Then there are a variety of modifications,
in which a woman is returned to be buried on her own kin's land,
or in which ties through the mother play an important but different
role than do ties through the father, or where, as in Samoa, the
sister's son retains a veto in the councils of his mother's family.
There are very rare systems, such as that of the Iroquois Indians,
where political power is in women's hands, since the women
elders nominated the holders of titles who also wielded political
powers.

When contemporary American society is viewed against such
sets of arrangements, it is obvious that the word "matriarchy" not
only is not descriptive, but actually obscures the basic issues. In
the United States women take their husbands' names and the
children bear their fathers' names. Women are expected to live
where their husbands elect to live, and refusal to do so is tantamount
to desertion. Men are liable for the support of their wives and
children, and women are not liable for the support of their husbands,
nor are brothers liable for the support of their sisters. The basic
legal assumption is that a woman as a minor is dependent upon

her father, and thereafter upon her husband. In our legal forms we are a patrinominal, patrilineal, patrilocal, and legally, for the most part, a patriarchal society. The circumstance that American fathers don't conform to some folk-lore concept of a patriarch with a long beard and ten children is not relevant. Both men and women are reared within this explicit paternally oriented framework. There are laws against a man's beating his wife, but other concepts have to be invoked when his wife beats him. The female is defined by usage as helpless, in need of protection, especially of support. We are also, of course, a monogamous society in which every form of polygamy, even the most casual, is frowned upon.

This is the framework of the family we have inherited from Europe, but it was brought to this country under exceptional conditions. The power of the father over the son was sapped by the weakening of the property sanction, and the infinite possibilities in the new country for leaving home. The power of the husband over the wife was altered more subtly. In frontier days, women were few, and sheer competition made it necessary for the man to woo differently than in countries in which he had been able to pick and choose among a dozen girls, each with a dowry thrown in, or at least to relax in self-assurance as some dozen mothers threw their daughters at his head. The dowry disappeared and women were wooed for themselves. The valuation placed on female qualities shifted. Meekness, home-abidingness, timorous clinging to the saddle of a husband as he rode away for a two-mile journey, were all very well in the Old World. But an American frontier woman might have to keep a lonely farm going all by herself for weeks, disciplining the half-grown children, succouring the passing stranger, even fending off the Indians. Strong women, women with character and determination, in fact women with guts, became more and more acceptable. The stereotype of the old maid shifted from the British picture of the manlike spinster who had a tom cat and preferred her nephews to the mild little woman who kept female cats and preferred her nieces. Along with this demand for women who have strength of character and the ability to manage money and affairs, there went no parallel premium on women's looking masculine. A woman was still expected to have womanly qualities, still to be attactive, in fact she was expected to be increasingly attractive as she came to be chosen in marriage for her dowryless self alone. Marriages of choice, phrased as marriages of love, laid increasing demands on both men and women to please the opposite sex openly.

In the hurly-burly of settling a new continent, many tasks were delegated to women in addition to running the farm and disciplining the children and keeping off the Indians while their husbands were away. As rough little frontier settlements assumed the appearance of a real village, the cleaning-up process, closing down the gambling-hall or the saloon, was thought of as coinciding with the arrival of one or more good women. The finer things of life—moral and aesthetic values—were delegated to women in a new and more active form; America was not Europe, where women had been expected to do more praying than the men but not to take any responsibility outside the home. The woman crusader who flouted the dictates of feminine decorum to campaign for the right has been a familiar part of our history since the early days of Anne Hutchinson,[1] and is recognized by both men and women as a valid part of our culture. It is permitted to men to hope that their own wives may not receive the call to reform the world, but this is a hope of the same order as that permitted to a religious mother who still somehow—while she instructs her little son in his prayers—hopes he will be chosen to be a sea-captain and not a priest. An ideal arrangement of ethical behaviour in the United States would leave good works, those so-necessary good works, to widows and spinsters, thus keeping these two supernumerary classes of women happily occupied in a way that is socially useful. It has been interesting to notice the changes in attitudes towards Mrs. Roosevelt and towards her vigorous, untiring interest in social welfare. As the wife of the President, she was attacked and condemned by men who would be the first to raise their hats in tribute to the long line of noble American women who campaigned, for instance, against slavery. This resentment, however, notably decreased after President Roosevelt's death, when her continued vigorous championing of the right set a pattern for widows rather than wives.

The spinster champion of the right of education, village improvement, social legislation, freedom for oppressed minorities, has gradually been stereotyped in those occupations in which women are professionally engaged in good works, particularly education and social work. These are both fields that men enter on peril of accusations of effeminacy, unless they enter in an administrative or a financial role. "Where," asks the Englishman who is prominent in social welfare, "are your men? We see their names on the letter-heads of organizations, but when we go to international conferences, we meet almost entirely women." "Our men—oh, they are the chairmen of boards, they determine the

1. Hutchinson (c. 1591–1643), a religious leader in Puritan New England, was sentenced to banishment from Massachusetts for her religious views.

financial policy of our agencies, but they leave the practice to
women. They are too busy to go to conferences."

In such a historical development as this, it is of course impossible 10
to speak of cause and effect. We must speak rather of an endless
spiralling process, in which good women were the immediate
occasion of some reform, reform became thought of as women's
field, this attracted women into it and further styled the field as
feminine, and so kept men out. Between the two world wars there
was a marked decrease in the willingness of women to enter those
fields which had been ear-marked as fields of "service"; that is,
fields in which the bad pay and heavy work were supposed to be
ignored because they gave an opportunity to exercise womanly
qualities of caring for the young, the sick, the unfortunate, and
the helpless. This whole trend towards the professionalization of
service fields means a shift from an occupation to which one gives
oneself—as a woman still does in marriage and motherhood—to
an occupation to which one gives definite hours and specified and
limited duties. It is evident that this ideal for American women is
passing as a role both for the woman who expects to marry and
for the spinster seeking a way of life. This whole shift is part of
the assimilation of female ideal and male ideal to each other. Boys
and girls sitting at the same desks, studying the same lessons, and
absorbing the same standards alike learn that the two most respectable criteria for choosing one's life-work are that the work
should have chances for advancement and that it should be "interesting." Even social workers, every hour of whose working day
must, if they are to do their chosen tasks, be devoted to warm
helpfulness, will defend their choice of a career because it is interesting, or one in which women can do well. Only with many
apologies do they now admit to a simple desire to help human
beings.

Meanwhile, during this period of history when styles in women 11
were shifting and changing, a style in men was also being built
up. The man had to make a living, he had to deal with the harsh
realities of the competitive world, hack and slash at forests and
cut corners in a world in which any man could be President. The
average American town gave him no education in understanding
or enjoying the arts, and conventional aesthetic expressions were
closed to him, and regarded as womanish. To this day, the choice
of music or painting or poetry as a serious occupation is suspect
for an American male. Men demonstrated their maleness in the
practical world of business, of farming (where the women were
kept indoors while the men even did the milking), and of politics
(the down-to-earth, corrupt kind as compared with the milk-and-

water reform variety). As our transitional culture made more simplified values inevitable in order that immigrants from many lands
could communicate with one another, so competition increased
for these simple signs of success—money, the things that money
could buy, power over persons and over things. The harsh realities
of a competitive world where each man's pace is determined by
the pace of his rival, and the race is never ended, hit men earlier
than they hit women. The rapidly expanding economy that brought
more amenities to the lives of women made more demands on
the lives of men. Finally we arrive at the stereotypes of to-day,
the tired husband who just wants to sit at home with his shirtcollar
open and the wife who wants to be taken out, the mother who
sees too much of her children and is forever importuning the father
to see more of them, while the husband himself feels that if he
had a chance he would go fishing. To receive recognition—from
both men and women—a man in America should be, first of all,
a success in his business; he should advance, make money, go up
fast, and if possible he should also be likable, attractive, and well
groomed, a good mixer, well informed, good at the leisure-time
activities of his class, should provide well for his home, keep his
car in good condition, be attentive enough to his wife so that he
doesn't give other women an opportunity to catch his interest. A
woman to receive equal recognition should be intelligent, attractive,
know how to make the best of herself in dress and manner, be
successful in attracting and keeping first several men, finally one,
run her home and family efficiently so that her husband stays
devoted and her children all surmount the nutritional, psychological,
and ethical hazards of maturation, and are successful too; and she
should have time for "outside things," whether they be church,
grange, community activities, or Junior League. A woman who
has time only for her own home is likely to be stigmatized either
as "having too much to do," which means either that she is
incompetent, or as having a husband who doesn't make as much
as he should, or that the couple have been shiftless and had too
many children.

But success in their roles rather than the specific qualities of   12
the roles is what is emphasized. Both the successful man and the
successful woman will be liked by both sexes, rewarded for their
reaffirmation that it is possible for human beings to be what Mother
said you must be if you wanted her to love you. It is possible for
the public-opinion interviewer to ferret out a great deal of envy
among Americans. They find people who listen to programs like
"Information Please" in order to hear "college-educated people
fail." But this envy, like the detraction of the well-known personality

that fills the tabloids whenever some scandal gives opportunity, is still a small component compared with the very wide-spread pleasure Americans take in some one who is really successful, whether it be shown at the testamentary dinner to the departing executive who is taking a better job, or at the block-party for the only family that got into the new housing project. For with the carefully prepared formula that maternal care has placed in its bottle the American child drinks in the admonition to succeed, to be the right weight, to learn to walk at the right time, to go up grade by grade in school, with good marks, to make the team, to make the sorority or clique, to be the one to be chosen by others for success. For the father who disciplined a child who was conceived of as filled with Satan and in need of many beatings, and the mother who succoured and comforted the child and taught him how to avoid the beatings, we now have the mother almost alone, not curbing the child's innate wickedness, but yearningly searching for signs that he will make the grade, make good, fail to fail.

This training, which is now so similar for boys and girls, has [13] very different impacts upon them. For the boy, it has two important effects. He is trained by women to be a male, which involves no identification of the self with the mother-teacher. He is to be a boy by doing the things Mother says, but doing them in a manly way. After all, boys grow by eating the right food, they get good marks by studying—in fact by obeying Mother's admonitions— but also they must be manly, they must not be sissies, they must stand up for themselves. All fighting must be defensive, and yet it is being a sissy not to be able to fight, so situations must be arranged that will satisfy the mothers of both little males that each is fighting in self-defense, obeying the highest standards and learning how not to be a sissy at the same time. Only from older brothers and the older brothers of companions does the little boy get any straight-out tutelage in how to be a boy. It was notable how enormously juvenile delinquency increased during the last war when the older boys were withdrawn from the family. But the older brother is himself straining to meet the adult role that his mother and the world have defined for him, and the small boy who tags along imitates and follows some one whose eyes are on future things, a job, a car, a raise.

In enclaves where the newly arrived or the very unsuccessful [14] are hemmed in in slum areas this sequence of social development is distorted. The older boys are unable to take their fathers' failures as clues to a remote pattern of male success as reinterpreted by the mothers. They become gang leaders, in turn effectively short-circuiting the development of their younger brothers in the society.

This asocial gang-life of boys provides a basis for the adult criminal world in America. It high-lights the normal American development, in which a mother who understands the American world can point to a father who, while not a good enough model for the boy merely to imitate, is nevertheless on the right road—whom the boy himself will surpass. In this pattern, older boys, their faces turned not back towards an admiring juvenile audience but forward towards a welcoming, possibly applauding adult world, permit younger boys to tag along and learn—as long as they don't make any trouble. The eyes of the whole family, the whole neighbourhood, face ahead, and every male in the group is merely an indication of where and how males should advance.

No one represents a permanent place on the ladder. In peace-   15
time the small boy's heroes, whether his own father keeps a grocery store or is the president of a bank, are policemen, firemen, flyers, cow-boys, and baseball-players, men who act out in their real life roles the springing active motor impulses of the small boy's body. His mother alternates between letting him jump on the sofa because the books say children shouldn't be restricted and telling him not to break things. And in her voice, in the voice of the radio announcer who introduces his favourite radio program, in the teacher's voice at school, in the voices of every one around him, the little boy who wants to be a policeman or a baseball-player hears that he will grow up to accept some responsible money-making role. He learns that if he wants to argue for choosing the police force or professional baseball, he will have to argue not that this is what he wants to do, but that it is something in which he can make good and make money and advance. He learns that unless he has a job and a car and a wife and kids, he will never be able to respect himself—because his own self-approval, like his mother's now, will be withdrawn, leaving him lonely and unsatisfied. Life is a job at which he can succeed if he tries. All desirable qualities can be acquired if he pays attention to his looks, his skills, his relations to people. And he also learns that the reward of success is love and approval, light in his mother's eyes, bread and jam and an ice-box with no rules about raiding it, relief and pleasure in his father's eyes. Here is no mother who thrills to his war-whoop in an Indian suit—although she bought him an Indian suit because children should have some imaginative play, or because all the other children have them—but rather she thrills to his first good grades, his first earned money. Here is no father whose awareness of his own masculinity makes him feel his small masculine son as a threat and a challenge. The father has long since become a parent, and the success of his son is part of his success as a

proper husband and father. He is often, in fact, over-anxious and over-protective towards his son. So, even in wealthy middle-class suburbs, little American boys still have paper routes, and Chief Justices and presidents of companies take those paper routes when their sons are ill in bed so that the boys will not default in their business obligations. In fact, the rewards are so great for displaying to admiring and helpful parents those qualities of initiative, independence, and assertiveness in the workaday world that will ensure success later that even though there is fear of failure, the American child grows up to be exceedingly optimistic, exceedingly responsive to praise, recognition, and acclaim from others. Failure is stylized as a temporary set-back, obstacles are made to be overcome, only a sissy takes defeat as anything but a stimulus to trying harder. "The difficult we do at once, the impossible takes a little longer."

The chief trap for the boy in this pattern of maturation lies in 16 the conditional nature of the whole process. On the one hand he can always win applause by taking the next step, moving from the third team to the second team, from the position of the worst in the class to the position of the next to the worst, by gaining a pound or growing an inch; the applause is hearty and ungrudging from parents who feel they owe their children every chance to succeed and have a right to take their success as a full repayment for parental sacrifice. On the other hand, none of this acceptance and this applause is final. If the next step up is not taken, then the approval becomes only a remembered happiness, now withdrawn, which must be worked for again. Mother loves you *if* you succeed; Father is grinning and proud if you succeed, something a little ruefully comforting when you fail. But at no time in childhood, often at no time in one's whole life, is it possible to arrive, to win love and praise that are not strictly contemporary and conditional and which can never be taken away from one. This is the backgound of those American attitudes—failure to admit immigrants, ungenerous state laws about welfare settlement for indigent families— that contrast so sharply with American willingness to help others, to give freely of time and goods and services. It is not that Americans learn, as some peoples do, that the supply of goods is limited and so one man's gain is another man's loss. They rather learn that the number of prizes in the race, the number of A's in the class, are more limited than is the number of contestants. If there are more contestants, the endless race for the A's, for the prizes, becomes that much harder. It is not that the boy learns interest in defeating others, but that he fervently hopes he can beat enough others to be counted a success; the others are incidental, not so much rivals

to be worsted as entrants to be outdistanced. His upbringing permits
him no admitted glee in open battle, and later, in a competitive
world that demands harsh and sometimes savage competition, he
takes little pleasure in the game itself. He accepts the behest that
he must continue and continue and continue to succeed, to advance,
to keep his place among others. The methods he has to use are
just part of it, to be laid aside in a compensatory good-fellowship
that is often mixed right into the distasteful competitive relationship.
In those relationships between men when the competition can be
laid aside altogether, a delicious game of pretended aggression can
be played endlessly, with thrust and counter-thrust, harmless and
healing.

But the role of sisters and girls and wives is a very complex   17
one in this world in which the boy's whole springing masculinity
is diverted into the game of success. Because it is the mother's
and not the father's voice that gives the principal early approval
and disapproval, the nagging voice of conscience is feminine in
both sexes—that voice which says, "You are not being the success
you *ought* to be." The man who feels he is failing is a man who
is angry with women, and angry with those values for which
women stand—social values, social-security legislation, "sentimental
schoolmarmish goodness." And it is not only the man who is
failing who finds himself angry with women, but also the man
who is paying too high a price for his success, and so reiterates
over and over how hard he works, how self-made he is, how the
modern world is making it too soft for people. The American who
is successful without feeling he has paid too high a price will be
at ease with himself and his conscience, and give generously to
the Community Chest or the union relief fund, send food to starving
Europeans, vote for social legislation, even sit on a board to see
that his wife's pet charity gets what it needs. But at any moment
this easy good nature may shift to an angry assertiveness against
the "do-gooders," those who have set his feet on a path he cannot
bear, that path which in ruthless competitiveness seems a long
way from the task of maintaining a hospital, or raising the salaries
of school-teachers, to which he is now asked to give help. Any
great yielding to the demands of civic virtue is suspect; a man to
be a man must go out to prove he is a man, and then, and only
then, can he leave a fortune to the orphans' home. The American
ideal career is the poor boy who learned his prayers at his mother's
knee, worked his way up against fearful odds, used without womanish softness and without enjoyment the methods appropriate to
such a battle, and in the end, a millionaire, leaves his money—

not to his children to ruin their characters by denying them a gradient on which at least some sort of success is possible, but— to good works, giving to the town or to the nation schools, libraries, art galleries, and orphan asylums. These are the things his mother told him that he ought to respect while he himself puts his whole effort into being a success. Good women made him what he is, and in the end they get the proceeds for their own ends, and in between he worked hard being the man they told him he ought to want to be. So as the mother's love has become more and more conditional upon success, the mother and the school-teacher have tended to merge in the child's mind, with the teacher taking on some of the aspects of the bad mother that were once given to the stepmother in the fairy-tales of another age.

The sister in America has a very special role in the life of the 18 American boy, geared as he is to succeed on a scale in which he is measured by his age and size against others of like age and size, and rewarded by women rather than by men. The sister becomes a double rival as she grows faster than he, does her lessons more dutifully, gets into fewer scrapes, learns the woman-taught lessons more easily. Characteristically, the sister in America is the big sister, whose side the parents always take, who is so slick she always wins, who gets away with murder—that is, gets the same rewards with less effort—and the day-dream sister is the little sister, over whom one can win without effort. The habit of American mothers of egging their children on by invidious or challenging comparisons is at its most aggravated in the case of sister, girl-cousin, girl next door. The boy is taught both that he ought to be able to beat her record, as he is a boy, and that it is fair to compare their achievements on the same scale at the same age, because they both ride bicycles or sleep alone on the third floor, or are in the fast-moving section of the fourth grade. They are treated as alike whenever it suits the rest of the world, and as unlike whenever that provides a better goad. If a boy cries, he is scolded more than a girl who doesn't cry; when she outstrips him, he is told it is even worse than if he had been outstripped by a boy, and yet she may be almost twice his size and he has also been told not to hit her because she is a girl. Side by side they sit in the nursery to be compared on table-manners, side by side in school to be compared on neatness and punctuality as well as reading and writing and arithmetic. She sits and challenges him, and beats him at least half the time and often more than half, until high school provides the blessed relief of science and shop, where girls aren't encouraged to succeed any longer. And as he sits and is beaten—at least half

the time—he learns both that girls can do most of the things that
boys can do for which rewards are meted out and that it is intolerable
that they should, because it has been made humiliating.

This is expressed in later life in the relatively high accessibility   19
of most occupations to women, but also in the bitter fight that is
put up, even in those fields where women are the best trained,
as in some government services, against giving women jobs that
carry high salaries or administrative powers over people—the two
most usual ways in which men demonstrate their success. Many
societies have educated their male children on the simple device
of teaching them not to be women, but there is an inevitable loss
in such an education, for it teaches a man to fear that he will lose
what he has, and to be forever somewhat haunted by this fear.
But when in addition to learning that at all costs he must not be
a girl, he is continually forced to compete with girls at the very
age when girls mature faster than boys, and on women-set tasks
to which girls take more easily, a sharper ambivalence is established.
American men have to use at least part of their sense of masculine
self-esteem as men on beating women, in terms of money and
status. And American women agree with them and tend to despise
a man who is outdistanced by a woman. When American women
do rise to positions of power and status, they have great difficulty
in treating their male subordinates with any decent sensitivity—
for aren't they failures to be there?—and shrink with horror from
making more money than their husbands to the extent that they
wish to feel feminine, or throw their success in their husband's
faces to the extent that their own cross-sexual competitiveness has
been developed. So we end up with the contradictory picture of
a society that appears to throw its doors wide open to women,
but translates her every step towards success as having been damaging—to her own chances of marriage, and to the men whom
she passes on the road.

It is just in the middle class, and among those who aspire to   20
middle-class position, that this antagonism waxes strongest, because
the middle-class skills are those in which it is easy for women to
excel and where men find themselves most fenced in, any rampant
masculinity denied and fettered in the interest of saving and postponement of indulgence in impulse. Middle-class mothers, educated
and still at home, have a great deal of time to give to moulding
their growing children, giving and withholding love as the children
display the proper attitudes. And middle-class virtues—saving,
thrift, punctuality, foresight, hard work, control of present impulse,
respect for the opinion of others, conformity to a code of manners—
are virtues that can be learned. Those skills in which the body

plays a role and in which it is easier for men to attain superiority, such as hunting, riding, or fighting, are absent from the middle-class list. Middle-class virtues learned out of reciprocal relationships between mother and child are patterned originally in the gastro-intestinal tract, taking in, keeping, ordered giving out, in which the male child has all the complication of sorting out the control imposed on elimination from the need to keep somewhat available his impulsive masculinity. The female, although her special feminine characteristics are not evoked, has a lesser problem as she learns to observe the rules of time and place. So all through an American boy's childhood he has to compete, at home and at school, with girls who have an edge in almost all the activities for which reward is given, as one is, for example, rewarded for standing up for oneself but not for fighting. Athletics with their close relationship to bodily strength and vulnerability remains almost the only field from which female competition is barred, and they provide through life a thrilling escape, if only in the pages of a newspaper, for American boys and men. And escape is needed from a game in which all the dice are loaded and yet one must not lose—on penalty of losing love and so self-esteem.

Meanwhile, what is the position of the girl whose easy and successful competition with her brother is assured by the conditions of home and the school system? Seen through male eyes, she is big sister who has it easy, who always gets the breaks. Instead of being told that she mustn't do things because she is a girl, that she must cross her legs and lower her eyes and sit on a cushion and sew a fine seam, she is told that she must learn the same things as a boy. The boy is told that he ought to be ashamed to be beaten by a girl, and outworn symbols of sheer male physical superiority are invoked for such routine tasks as remembering to brush one's teeth or do one's lessons. The male's age-old feeling that to be sexually successful he must be strong is invoked in the interest of activities that have lost their immediate relevance. But at the same time the girl is told that she ought to be doing better than her brother, not because she will be humiliated if she fails, but because it is easier for girls to be good. This paradox of boy-girl competition was summed up in Whittier's "In School Days," one of the first poems to celebrate the pleasures and the penalties of co-education, which tells the story of the girl who worsted the boy in spelling:

> "I'm sorry that I spelt the word:
> I hate to go above you,
> Because,"—the brown eyes lower fell,—
> "Because, you see, I love you!"

And it is significant that the poet—a male—while writing so
sweetly and wistfully about her, moralizing so nicely on how her
attitude contrasts with most people's—

> *He lived to learn, in life's hard school,*
> *How few who pass above him*
> *Lament their triumph and his loss,*
> *Like her,—because they love him.—*

also very deftly and definitely kills the lady off:

> *Dear girl! the grasses on her grave*
> *Have forty years been growing!*

Just so the New Guinea native tells the story of the woman who
hands to men the symbols by which they can compensate themselves
for their inferiority to her, and then adds that they had better kill
her. Love on such terms is unbearable. So there is built into the
girl in America a conflict of another order. She too must do her
lessons and obey her mother, or she will lose her mother's love,
her teacher's approval, and the rewards that are accorded to the
successful. She too likes bread generously spread with jam and
an ice-box that is always open. These are hers, almost for the
asking. "For all little girls," reads the sign in a New York candy-
shop window, "and for *good* little boys." Hers, by natural right,
but at what a price! If she learns the rules well, if she gets good
marks, wins scholarships, gets the cub reporter's job, by so much
she has done an unforgivable thing, in her own eyes and in the
eyes of all of those around her. Each step forward in work as a
successful American regardless of sex means a step back as a
woman, and also, inferentially, a step back imposed on some male.
For maleness in America is not absolutely defined, it has to be
kept and re-earned every day, and one essential element in the
definition is beating women in every game that both sexes play,
in every activity in which both sexes engage.

To the extent that the little girl shares the attitudes of Whittier's [22]
dead heroine, she rejects the dilemma. True, she may have to spell
the word now, in the third grade, for failure is too bitter for her
small, success-oriented soul to bear. But later she will shift the
field and get out of the unfair competition, go away from the game
of loaded dice, and be a success in a different field, as a wife and
a mother. The desperate need for success remains; it is not as
strong as for the boy, because for the girl success is demanded
only as it is demanded of all human beings, and not with a threat
that if she does not succeed she will not be regarded as a true
female. Boys are unsexed by failure; girls, if they are also pretty,

may be more desirable if they need a male Galahad to help them with their lessons. But this is becoming steadily less true. Subtly the demand for the same kind of character structure for men and for women is spreading throughout the country. In a 1946 *Fortune*[2] poll, men were asked which of three girls equally good-looking a man would prefer to marry: a girl who had never held a job, a girl who had held a job and been moderately successful at it, or a girl who had held a job and been extremely successful. The preferences ran: 33.8 per cent for the moderately success-ful, 21.5 per cent for the extremely successful, and only 16.2 per cent for the girl who had never held a job. The *moderately* successful are still preferred, but with this preference goes increasing pressure on a girl to work before marriage, perhaps to work until the first child comes, and to "begin doing something," if it is only volunteer work or vigorously pursuing a hobby, as soon as her children are in school. Men want their wives both to reassure them by being less successful than they are and to gratify their competitive as-pirations, vicariously, by "being successful." It is probably safe to say that the introspective distance between the words "moderately" and "extremely" means "at some one else's expense by playing in another league" as against "beating me at my own game," with the over-all emphasis on success gradually winning out. A girl who has never held a job is becoming increasingly suspect. Maybe she couldn't get a job; maybe if she had tried she would have been a failure, and who wants a wife, however personally pliant and reassuring, who might have been a failure? It is interesting also that in the female replies, 42.2 per cent of the women thought men would prefer a moderately successful girl, only 12.1 per cent thought a man would prefer the girl who had never held a job, and only 17.4 per cent thought they would prefer the exceedingly successful. The *Fortune* commentators go on to say:

"Evidently men are not as afraid of capable girls as women [23] think they are. This is especially true of poor men, of whom 25% think that the extremely successful girl would make the most desirable wife. Poor women also give an unusually high vote for the extremely successful girl (24.7%), while women in the upper middle class give her very little backing, only 12.3%." And note that it is in the upper middle class that girls are treated most like boys in their education, compete with men most directly during childhood, and experience most directly the pressures I have been discussing.

---

2. A magazine devoted to business and finance.

So throughout her education and her development of vocational   24
expectancy, the girl is faced with the dilemma that she must display
enough of her abilities to be considered successful, but not too
successful; enough ability to get and keep a job, but without the
sort of commitment that will make her either too successful or
unwilling to give up the job entirely for marriage and motherhood.
"Two steps forward and one step back" is the dance-call she must
obey. Or take the consequences. And what are the consequences?
Failure to marry? If that were all, it might not be so serious. There
are more women than men in the world, and societies have found
it very possible to stylize vows of celibacy and poverty and still
give women dignified lives. The nun who offers her potential
wifehood and motherhood to God on behalf of all mankind, and
who substitutes prayer and care for the children of God for the
creation of particular children, can feel herself a part of God's plan,
fulfilling the duty of human beings to "cherish and protect the
lives of men and the life of the world." In the crowded bus or
cars of the subway, where men now let women stand with children
in their arms—because women make money, don't they?—seats
are still given to Sisters of Charity and Mercy.

But the woman in the United States who chooses a career   25
instead of marriage is accorded no such satisfying and accredited
place in the world. The same feeling that makes Americans, so
often generous almost without parallel in the world, vote against
the entrance of a few thousand homeless orphans, plus the feeling
that any success in a woman calls men's manliness into account,
defeats the possibility of her role's being fully rewarding. If she
succeeds in a profession like school-teaching, men either desert it
altogether, or are driven to such appalling expedients as rules that
women are incapable of teaching second-year American history,
so that the very enactment of the defensive measure further lowers
them in their own eyes. No one, neither the men themselves nor
the women with whom they compete successfully, thinks it is a
good thing for an inadequate man to get the job of principal of
a school over the heads of five better-equipped women. Neither
sex is made happy by the situation, neither the women, able,
conscientious, and hardworking, who may be 80 per cent of the
contestants, nor the men who may constitute the other 20 per
cent, a large proportion of whom suspect that the real reason for
the promotion was just because "they wanted a man."

Perhaps this situation in which able women see themselves   26
perpetually passed over in favour of a man after spending their
lives in a "service" profession, a profession in which the womanly
virtues of detailed imagination and patience with children are very

heavily called for, is one important reason why women are leaving these professions for factory work and business, where they cannot be passed over so easily. And here they can use other weapons. For where the weapons of the school-teacher and the social worker are the weapons of mother's voice and the persistent demand that men be good, the weapons of the woman in business in the United States may include those of the woman who uses her sex to attain her ambitious ends. Ilka Chase's *In Bed We Cry* is a tragedy of just this situation, of the menace that the successful business woman is to herself and to the man she loves. The little girl who hears the call of success more sharply than the call of her future wifehood and maternity hears a call to competitive action in which no holds are barred. Her brother has been better schooled than she has been for this expected behaviour in a competitive world. Fair play, no bullying, do not throw your weight around, are part of the ethics both she and he learned on the playing-fields, but here the pretence that all boys are stronger than all girls was kept up. Some of her very drive for success may come from this comparison, this statement that boys should always outdistance girls; some of her drive may come from doors barred to her because "women always leave and get married," some from a sneer from a brother or a father that "girls have no heads for figures." However this may be, she has been defined as weaker, and there are no rules in American life for the good behaviour of underdogs. To the extent that American women—most American women—follow the rules of fair play and give-and-take and no alimony, they do so because they think of themselves as strong human beings, human like the men of whom they refuse to take an advantage. But to the woman who makes a success in a man's field, good behaviour is almost impossible, because her whole society has defined it so. A woman who succeeds better than a man—and in a man's field there is no other practical alternative to beating a certain number of men— has done something hostile and destructive. To the extent that as a woman she has beauty or attractiveness of any sort, her behaviour is that much more destructive. The mannish woman, the ugly woman, may be treated as a man in disguise, and so forgiven her successes. But for the success of a feminine woman there are no alibis; the more feminine she is, the less can she be forgiven. This does not mean that every woman who enters business or fields where she is in an extreme minority is hostile and destructive. But it does mean that any woman who in the course of her childhood had an extra amount of destructiveness developed and repressed is in psychological danger when she is placed in a role that is so destructively defined. To the woman whose maternal attitudes are highly developed, the position may be wholly intolerable.

So brother and sister, boy and girl, educated together, learn   27
what each wishes from and what each can give to the other. The girl learns to discipline and mute an ambition that her society continually stimulates, as all girls working in white-collar jobs are said to have "careers," and careers are glamorous, while most men with similar skills merely have jobs. And we have the situation that looks so strange on the surface, that as more and more women work, women seem on the whole less interested in the battle that permits them to succeed professionally. A half-century ago the eyes of the specially able girl who went to college faced ahead towards a profession, towards a career. The idea of marriage was often pushed aside as a handicap. To-day, the girl of the same ability is usually willing to admit that she wants to marry, and seems more willing to sacrifice her career to marriage than to sacrifice a chance for marriage to her career. Because it is now more and more accepted that girls should work until they marry— and if one is unlucky, this means all one's life—girls work hard at acquiring skills and professions. If they have brains and ability, sheer virtuosity plus the need to succeed may lead them to become engrossed in their work, but seldom so engrossed that the desire for marriage is blocked out.

Nor will society to-day treat the woman who is not chosen with   28
the simple pity accorded the wallflower of a century ago. Less kindly verdicts—"She must be neurotic," "She doesn't pay attention," "She hasn't made the most of her chances"—come all too easily to the lips of the young unmarried woman when she speaks of the older one. Success for a woman means success in finding and keeping a husband. This is much more true than it was a generation ago, when men were still supposed to do the seeking, and some women found their new freedom outside the home so intoxicating that they could abandon themselves to their work. Nor is this surprising in a world where the unmarried man is also looked upon as a failure in human relations, a queer bird who, in spite of all of the girls there are to marry, never succeeded in finding one, some one who is just too lazy, too do-less, to make an effort. But the more successful a man is in his job, the more certain every one is that he will make a desirable husband; the more successful a woman is, the more most people are afraid she may not be a successful wife. The *Fortune* survey summarized the reasons people gave why men should prefer extremely successful girls—their greater efficiency and understanding of money and their ability to help their husbands, and it adds: "Very few look upon her intelligence as an asset, and practically none say that

she would be easier to get along with." The well-worn phrase "even the best cooks are men" should be footnoted by a recognition that American men are not reared to enjoy being the husbands of successful chefs.

NOEL PERRIN

The Androgynous Man

The summer I was 16, I took a train from New York to Steamboat Springs, Colo., where I was going to be assistant horse wrangler at a camp. The trip took three days, and since I was much too shy to talk to strangers, I had quite a lot of time for reading. I read all of "Gone With the Wind." I read all the interesting articles in a couple of magazines I had, and then I went back and read all the dull stuff. I also took all the quizzes, a thing of which magazines were even fuller then than now.

The one that held my undivided attention was called "How Masculine/Feminine Are You?" It consisted of a large number of inkblots. The reader was supposed to decide which of four objects each blot most resembled. The choices might be a cloud, a steam engine, a caterpillar and a sofa.

When I finished the test, I was shocked to find that I was barely masculine at all. On a scale of 1 to 10, I was about 1.2. Me, the horse wrangler? (And not just wrangler, either. That summer, I had to skin a couple of horses that died—the camp owner wanted the hides.)

The results of that test were so terrifying to me that for the first time in my life I did a piece of original analysis. Having unlimited time on the train, I looked at the "masculine" answers over and over, trying to find what it was that distinguished real men from people like me—and eventually I discovered two very simple patterns. It was "masculine" to think the blots looked like man-made objects, and "feminine" to think they looked like natural objects. It was masculine to think they looked like things capable of causing harm, and feminine to think of innocent things.

Even at 16, I had the sense to see that the compilers of the test were using rather limited criteria—maleness and femaleness are both more complicated than *that*—and I breathed a huge sigh of relief. I wasn't necessarily a wimp, after all.

From the "About Men" column of *The New York Times Magazine*, February 5, 1984.

That the test did reveal something other than the superficiality ₆
of its makers I realized only many years later. What it revealed
was that there is a large class of men and women both, to which
I belong, who are essentially androgynous. That doesn't mean
we're gay, or low in the appropriate hormones, or uncomfortable
performing the jobs traditionally assigned our sexes. (A few years
after that summer, I was leading troops in combat and, unfashionable
as it now is to admit this, having a very good time. War is exciting.
What a pity the 20th century went and spoiled it with high-tech
weapons.)

What it does mean to be spiritually androgynous is a kind of ₇
freedom. Men who are all-male, or he-man, or 100 percent red-
blooded Americans, have a little biological set that causes them
to be attracted to physical power, and probably also to dominance.
Maybe even to watching football. I don't say this to criticize them.
Completely masculine men are quite often wonderful people: good
husbands, good (though sometimes overwhelming) fathers, good
members of society. Furthermore, they are often so unself-con-
sciously at ease in the world that other men seek to imitate them.
They just aren't as free as us androgynes. They pretty nearly have
to be what they are; we have a range of choices open.

The sad part is that many of us never discover that. Men who ₈
are not 100 percent red-blooded Americans—say, those who are
only 75 percent red-blooded—often fail to notice their freedom.
They are too busy trying to copy the he-men ever to realize that
men, like women, come in a wide variety of acceptable types.
Why this frantic imitation? My answer is mere speculation, but
not casual. I have speculated on this for a long time.

Partly they're just envious of the he-man's unconscious ease. ₉
Mostly they're terrified of finding that there may be something
wrong with them deep down, some weakness at the heart. To
avoid discovering that, they spend their lives acting out the role
that the he-man naturally lives. Sad.

One thing that men owe to the women's movement is that this ₁₀
kind of failure is less common than it used to be. In releasing
themselves from the single ideal of the dependent woman, women
have more or less incidentally released a lot of men from the single
ideal of the dominant male. The one mistake the feminists have
made, I think, is in supposing that *all* men need this release, or
that the world would be a better place if all men achieved it. It
wouldn't. It would just be duller.

So far I have been pretty vague about just what the freedom of ₁₁
the androgynous man is. Obviously it varies with the case. In the
case I know best, my own, I can be quite specific. It has freed me
most as a parent. I am, among other things, a fairly good natural

mother. I like the nurturing role. It makes me feel good to see a child eat—and it turns me to mush to see a 4-year-old holding a glass with both small hands, in order to drink. I even enjoyed sewing patches on the knees of my daughter Amy's Dr. Dentons when she was at the crawling stage. All that pleasure I would have lost if I had made myself stick to the notion of the paternal role that I started with.

Or take a smaller and rather ridiculous example. I feel free to 12 kiss cats. Until recently it never occurred to me that I would want to, though my daughters have been doing it all their lives. But my elder daughter is now 22, and in London. Of course, I get to look after her cat while she is gone. He's a big, handsome farm cat named Petrushka, very unsentimental, though used from kittenhood to being kissed on the top of the head by Elizabeth. I've gotten very fond of him (he's the adventurous kind of cat who likes to climb hills with you), and one night I simply felt like kissing him on the top of the head, and did. Why did no one tell me sooner how silky cat fur is?

Then there's my relation to cars. I am completely unembarrassed 13 by my inability to diagnose even minor problems in whatever object I happen to be driving, and don't have to make some insider's remark to mechanics to try to establish that I, too, am a "Man With His Machine."

The same ease extends to household maintenance. I do it, of 14 course. Service people are expensive. But for the last decade my house has functioned better than it used to because I've had the aid of a volume called "Home Repairs Any Woman Can Do," which is pitched just right for people at my technical level. As a youth, I'd as soon have touched such a book as I would have become a transvestite. Even though common sense says there is really nothing sexual whatsoever about fixing sinks.

Or take public emotion. All my life I have easily been moved 15 by certain kinds of voices. The actress Siobhan McKenna's, to take a notable case. Give her an emotional scene in a play, and within 10 words my eyes are full of tears. In boyhood, my great dread was that someone might notice. I struggled manfully, you might say, to suppress this weakness. Now, of course, I don't see it as a weakness at all, but as a kind of fulfillment. I even suspect that the true he-men feel the same way, or one kind of them does, at least, and it's only the poor imitators who have to struggle to repress themselves.

Let me come back to the inkblots, with their assumption that 16 masculine equates with machinery and science, and feminine with art and nature. I have no idea whether the right pronoun for God is He, She or It. But this I'm pretty sure of. If God could somehow be induced to take that test, God would not come out macho, and not feminismo, either, but right in the middle. Fellow androgynes, it's a nice thought.

MICHAEL NORMAN

Standing His Ground

I have bruised a knuckle and bloodied another man's nose, but 1 I am not, by most measures, a fighter. The last time I broke the peace was more than a decade ago in a small restaurant on the west slope of the Rocky Mountains in Colorado. My stepfather had encountered an old nemesis. Words were exchanged and the distance between the two narrowed. I stepped in to play the peacemaker and ended up throwing the first punch. For the record, my target, a towering 230-pound horseman, easily absorbed the blow and then dispatched the gnat in front of him.

The years since have been filled with discretion—I preach it, 2 embrace it and hide behind it. I am now the careful watchman who keeps his eye on the red line and reroutes pressure before it has a chance to blow. Sometimes, I backslide and turn a domestic misdemeanor into a capital case or toss the cat out of the house without bothering to see where he lands. But I do not punch holes in the plaster or call my antagonists to the woodshed. The Furies may gather, but the storm always stays safely out to sea. And yet, lately, I have been struggling with this forced equanimity. The messenger of reason, the advocate of accord, once again has the urge to throw the first punch—in spirit at least.

All of this began rather quietly, a deep stirring that would come 3 and go and never take form, an old instinct, perhaps, trying to reassert itself. I was angry, restless, combative, but I could not say why. It was a mystery of sorts. I was what I was expected to be, the very model of a modern man, a partner instead of a husband, a proponent of peace over action, thin-skinned rather than thick, a willow instead of a stone. And yet there was something about this posture that did not fit my frame. Then, an acquaintance, a gentle man who spent his Peace Corps days among the villagers

From the "About Men" column of *The New York Times Magazine*, April 1, 1984.

of Nepal, suddenly acted out of character. He got into an argument
with a local brute in a neighborhood tavern and instead of walking
away from trouble, stood his ground. It was, he said, a senseless
confrontation, but he had no regrets, and it made me think of
Joey.

Joey, the bully of the sixth grade, used to roam the hallways   4
picking victims at random and slugging them on the arm. When
he rounded a corner, we scattered or practiced a crude form of
mysticism and tried to think ourselves invisible in the face of the
beast. Since I was slow and an inept mystic, my mother kept on
hand an adequate supply of Ben Gay to ease the bruises and
swelling.

One day, a boy named Tony told the marauder that he had had   5
enough and an epic duel was scheduled in the playground after
school. Tony had been taking boxing lessons on the sly. He had
developed a stinging left jab and when the appointed hour arrived,
he delivered it in the name of every bruised shoulder in the school.

The meek pack of which Tony was once a part took courage   6
from his example and several weeks later when a boy at my bus
stop sent me sprawling, I returned the favor.

There were only a few challenges after that. On the way up, a   7
Joey would occasionally round the corner. But in the circles I
traveled, he was the exception rather than the rule. In the Marine
Corps in Vietnam, we were consumed by a much larger kind of
warfare. In college, faculty infighting and bullying aside, violence
was considered anti-intellectual. And in the newsrooms where I
have practiced my trade, reporters generally have been satisfied
with pounding a keyboard instead of their editors.

And then came Colorado and the battle of the west slope. For   8
years, I was embarrassed by the affair. I could have walked away
and dragged my stepfather with me. As it was, we almost ended
up in jail. I had provoked a common brawl, a pointless, self-
destructive exercise. The rationalist had committed the most irrational
of acts. It was not a matter of family or honor, hollow excuses.
I had simply succumbed to instinct, and I deeply regretted it. But
not any longer. Now I see virtue in that vulgar display of macho.
It disqualifies me from the most popular male club—the brotherhood
of nurturers, fraternity sensitivus.

From analyst's couch to tavern booth, their message is the same: 9
The male animus is out of fashion. The man of the hour is supposed
to be gentle, thoughtful, endearing and compassionate, a wife to
his woman, a mother to his son, an androgynous figure with the
self-knowledge of a hermaphrodite. He takes his lumps on the
psyche, not the chin, and bleeds with emotion. Yes, in the morning,

he still puts on a three-piece suit, but his foulard, the finishing touch, is a crying towel.

He is so ridden with guilt, so pained about the sexist sins of his   10 kind, he bites at his own flanks. Not only does he say that he dislikes being a man, but broadly proclaims that the whole idea of manhood in America is pitiful.

He wants to free himself from the social conditioning of the   11 past, to cast off the yoke of traditional male roles and rise above the banality of rituals learned at boot camp or on the practice field. If science could provide it, he would swallow an antidote of testosterone, something to stop all this antediluvian thumping and bashing.

And he has gone too far. Yes, the male code needs reform. Our   12 rules and our proscriptions have trapped us in a kind of perpetual adolescence. Why else would a full-grown rationalist think he could get even with Joey by taking a poke at another bully 25 years later in a bar in Colorado? No doubt there is something pitiful about that.

But the fashion for reform, the drive to emasculate macho, has   13 produced a kind of numbing androgyny and has so blurred the lines of gender that I often find myself wanting to emulate some of the women I know—bold, aggressive, vigorous role models.

It sometimes seems that the only exclusively male trait left is   14 the impulse to throw a punch, the last male watermark, so to speak, that is clear and readable. Perhaps that is why the former Peace Corps volunteer jumped into a brawl and why I suspect that the new man—the model of sensitivity, the nurturer—goes quietly through the day with a clenched fist behind his back.

BRIGID BROPHY

Women

All right, nobody's disputing it. Women are free. At least, they   1 *look* free. They even feel free. But in reality women in the western, industrialised world today are like the animals in a modern zoo. There are no bars. It appears that cages have been abolished. Yet in practice women are still kept in their place just as firmly as the

First published in *The Saturday Evening Post*, November 1963.

animals are kept in their enclosures. The barriers which keep them in now are invisible.

It is about forty years since the pioneer feminists, several of whom were men, raised such a rumpus by rattling the cage bars— or created such a conspicuous nuisance by chaining themselves to them—that society was at last obliged to pay attention. The result was that the bars were uprooted, the cage thrown open: whereupon the majority of the women who had been held captive decided they would rather stay inside anyway.

To be more precise, they *thought* they decided; and society, which can with perfect truth point out "Look, no bars," *thought* it was giving them the choice. There are no laws and very little discrimination to prevent western, industrialised women from voting, being voted for or entering the professions. If there are still comparatively few women lawyers and engineers, let alone women presidents of the United States, what are women to conclude except that this is the result either of their own free choice or of something inherent in female nature?

Many of them do draw just this conclusion. They have come back to the old argument of the anti-feminists, many of whom were women, that women are unfit by nature for life outside the cage. And in letting this old wheel come full cycle women have fallen victim to one of the most insidious and ingenious confidence tricks ever perpetrated.

In point of fact, neither female nature nor women's individual free choice has been put to the test. As American Negroes have discovered, to be officially free is by no means the same as being actually and psychologically free. A society as adept as ours has become at propaganda—whether political or commercial—should know that "persuasion," which means the art of launching myths and artificially inducing inhibitions, is every bit as effective as force of law. No doubt the reason society eventually agreed to abolish its anti-women laws was that it had become confident of commanding a battery of hidden dissuaders which would do the job just as well. Cage bars are clumsy methods of control, which excite the more rebellious personalities inside to rattle them. Modern society, like the modern zoo, has contrived to get rid of the bars without altering the fact of imprisonment. All the zoo architect needs to do is run a zone of hot or cold air, whichever the animal concerned cannot tolerate, round the cage where the bars used to be. Human animals are not less sensitive to social climate.

The ingenious point about the new-model zoo is that it deceives both sides of the invisible barrier. Not only can the animal not see how it is imprisoned; the visitor's conscience is relieved of the unkindness of keeping animals shut up. He can say "Look, no bars round the animals," just as society can say "Look, no laws restricting women" even while it keeps women rigidly in place by zones of fierce social pressure.

There is, however, one great difference. A woman, being a   7 thinking animal, may actually be more distressed because the bars of her cage cannot be seen. What relieves society's conscience may afflict hers. Unable to perceive what is holding her back, she may accuse herself and her whole sex of craven timidity because women have not jumped at what has the appearance of an offer of freedom. Evidently quite a lot of women have succumbed to guilt of this sort, since in recent years quite an industry has arisen to assuage it. Comforting voices make the air as thick and reassuring as cotton wool while they explain that there is nothing shameful in not wanting a career, that to be intellectually unadventurous is no sin, that taking care of home and family may be personally "fulfilling" and socially valuable.

This is an argument without a flaw: except that it is addressed   8 exclusively to women. Address it to both sexes and instantly it becomes progressive and humane. As it stands, it is merely anti-woman prejudice revamped.

That many women would be happier not pursuing careers or   9 intellectual adventures is only part of the truth. The whole truth is that many *people* would be. If society had the clear sight to assure men as well as women that there is no shame in preferring to stay non-competitively and non-aggressively at home, many masculine neuroses and ulcers would be avoided, and many children would enjoy the benefit of being brought up by a father with a talent for the job instead of by a mother with no talent for it but a sense of guilt about the lack.

But society does nothing so sensible. Blindly it goes on insisting   10 on the tradition that men are the ones who go out to work and adventure—an arrangement which simply throws talent away. All the home-making talent which happens to be born inside male bodies is wasted; and our businesses and governments are staffed quite largely by people whose aptitude for the work consists solely of their being what is, by tradition, the right sex for it.

The pressures society exerts to drive men out of the house are   11 very nearly as irrational and unjust as those by which it keeps women in. The mistake of the early reformers was to assume that men were emancipated already and that therefore reform need ask only for the emancipation of women. What we ought to do now is go right back to scratch and demand the emancipation of both sexes. It is only because men are not free themselves that they have found it necessary to cheat women by the deception which makes them appear free when they are not.

The zones of hot and cold air which society uses to perpetuate its uneconomic and unreasonable state of affairs are the simplest and most effective conceivable. Society is playing on our sexual vanity. Just as the sexual regions are the most vulnerable part of the body, sexuality is the most vulnerable part of the Ego. Tell a man that he is not a real man, or a woman that she is not one hundred per cent woman, and you are threatening both with not being attractive to the opposite sex. No one can bear not to be attractive to the opposite sex. That is the climate which the human animal cannot tolerate. 12

So society has us all at its mercy. It has only to murmur to the man that staying at home is a feminine characteristic, and he will be out of the house like a bullet. It has only to suggest to the woman that logic and reason are the province of the masculine mind, whereas 'intuition' and 'feeling' are the female *forte*, and she will throw her physics textbooks out of the window, barricade herself into the house and give herself up to having wishy-washy poetical feelings while she arranges the flowers. 13

She will, incidentally, take care that her feelings *are* wishy-washy. She has been persuaded that to have cogent feelings, of the kind which really do go into great poems (most of which are by men), would make her an unfeminine woman, a woman who imitates men. In point of fact, she would not be imitating men as such, most of whom have never written a line of great poetry, but poets, most of whom so far happen to be men. But the bad logic passes muster with her because part of the mythology she has swallowed ingeniously informs her that logic is not her *forte*. 14

Should a woman's talent or intelligence be so irrepressible that she insists on producing cogent works of art or watertight meshes of argument, she will be said to have "a mind like a man's." This is simply current idiom; translated, it means "a good mind." The use of the idiom contributes to an apparently watertight proof that all good minds are masculine, since whenever they occur in women they are described as "like a man's." 15

What is more, this habit of thought actually contributes to perpetuating a state of affairs where most good minds really do belong to men. It is difficult for a woman to *want* to be intelligent when she has been told that to be so will make her like a man. She inclines to think an intelligence would be as unbecoming to her as a moustache; and many women have tried in furtive privacy to disembarrass themselves of intellect as though it were facial hair. 16

Discouraged from growing "a mind like a man's," women are   17
encouraged to have thoughts and feelings of a specifically feminine
tone. For society is cunning enough not to place its whole reliance
on threatening women with blasts of icy air. It also flatters them
with a zone of hot air. The most deceptive and cynical of its
blandishments is the notion that women have some specifically
feminine contribution to make to culture. Unfortunately, as culture
had already been shaped and largely built up by men before the
invitation was issued, this leaves women little to do. Culture consists
of reasoned thought and works of art composed of cogent feeling
and imagination. There is only one way to be reasonable, and
that is to reason correctly; and the only kind of art which is any
good is good art. If women are to eschew reason and artistic
imagination in favour of "intuition" and "feeling," it is pretty
clear what is meant. "Intuition" is just a polite name for bad
reasoning, and "feeling" for bad art.

In reality, the whole idea of a specifically feminine—or, for the   18
matter of that, masculine—contribution to culture is a contradiction
of culture. A contribution to culture is not something which could
not have been made by the other sex—it is something which could
not have been made by any other *person*. Equally, the notion that
anyone, of either sex, can create good art out of simple feeling,
untempered by discipline, is a philistine one. The arts are a sphere
where women seem to have done well; but really they have done
too well—too well for the good of the arts. Instead of women
sharing the esteem which ought to belong to artists, art is becoming
smeared with femininity. We are approaching a philistine state of
affairs where the arts are something which it is nice for women
to take up in their spare time—men having slammed out of the
house to get on with society's "serious" business, like making
money, administering the country and running the professions.

In that "serious" sphere it is still rare to encounter a woman.   19
A man sentenced to prison would probably feel his punishment
was redoubled by indignity if he were to be sentenced by a woman
judge under a law drafted by a woman legislator—and if, on
admission, he were to be examined by a woman prison doctor.
If such a thing happened every day, it would be no indignity but
the natural course of events. It has never been given the chance
to become the natural course of events and never will be so long
as women remain persuaded it would be unnatural of them to
want it.

So brilliantly has society contrived to terrorise women with this   20
threat that certain behaviour is unnatural and unwomanly that it
has left them no time to consider—or even sheerly observe—what

womanly nature really is. For centuries arrant superstitions were accepted as natural law. The physiological fact that only women can secrete milk for feeding babies was extended into the pure myth that it was women's business to cook for and wait on the entire family. The kitchen became woman's "natural" place because, for the first few months of her baby's life, the nursery really was. To this day a woman may suspect that she is unfeminine if she can discover in herself no aptitude or liking for cooking. Fright has thrown her into such a muddle that she confuses having no taste for cookery with having no breasts, and conversely assumes that nature has endowed the human female with a special handiness with frying pans.

Even psycho-analysis, which in general has been the greatest benefactor of civilisation since the wheel, has unwittingly reinforced the terrorisation campaign. The trouble was that it brought with it from its origin in medical therapy a criterion of normality instead of rationality. On sheer statistics every pioneer, genius and social reformer, including the first woman who demanded to be let out of the kitchen and into the polling booth, is abnormal, along with every lunatic and eccentric. What distinguishes the genius from the lunatic is that the genius's abnormality is justifiable by reason or aesthetics. If a woman who is irked by confinement to the kitchen merely looks round to see what other women are doing and finds they are accepting their kitchens, she may well conclude that she is abnormal and had better enlist her psycho-analyst's help towards "living with" her kitchen. What she ought to ask is whether it is rational for women to be kept to the kitchen, and whether nature really does insist on that in the way it insists women have breasts. And in a far-reaching sense to ask that question is much more normal and natural than learning to "live with" the handicap of women's inferior social status. The normal and natural thing for human beings is not to tolerate handicaps but to reform society and to circumvent or supplement nature. We don't learn to live minus a leg; we devise an artificial limb. 21

That, indeed, is the crux of the matter. Not only are the distinctions we draw between male nature and female nature largely arbitrary and often pure superstition: they are completely beside the point. They ignore the essence of *human* nature. The important question is not whether women are or are not less logical by nature than men, but whether education, effort and the abolition of our illogical social pressures can improve on nature and make them (and, incidentally, men as well) *more* logical. What distinguishes human from any other animal nature is its ability to be unnatural. Logic and art are not natural or instinctive activities; but our nature 22 includes a propensity to acquire them. It is not natural for the human body to orbit the earth; but the human mind has a natural adventurousness which enables it to invent machines whereby the body can do so. There is, in sober fact, no such creature as a natural man. Go as far back as they will, the archaeologists cannot come on a wild man in his natural habitat. At his most primitive, he has already constructed himself an artificial habitat, and decorated it not by a standardised instinctual method, as birds build nests, but by individualised—that is, abnormal—works of art or magic. And in doing so he is not limited by the fingers nature gave him; he has extended their versatility by making tools.

Civilisation consists not necessarily in defying nature but in   23
making it possible for us to do so if we judge it desirable. The higher we can lift our noses from the grindstone of nature, the wider the area we have of choice; and the more choices we have freely made, the more individualised we are. We are at our most civilised when nature does not dictate to us, as it does to animals and peasants, but when we can opt to fall in with it or better it. If modern civilisation has invented methods of education which make it possible for men to feed babies and for women to think logically, we are betraying civilisation itself if we do not set both sexes free to make a free choice.

SUSAN BROWNMILLER

Femininity

We had a game in our house called "setting the table" and I   1
was Mother's helper. Forks to the left of the plate, knives and spoons to the right. Placing the cutlery neatly, as I recall, was one of my first duties, and the event was alive with meaning. When a knife or a fork dropped on the floor, that meant a man was unexpectedly coming to dinner. A falling spoon announced the surprise arrival of a female guest. No matter that these visitors never arrived on cue, I had learned a rule of gender identification. Men were straight-edged, sharply pronged and formidable, women were softly curved and held the food in a rounded well. It made perfect sense, like the division of pink and blue that I saw in babies, an orderly way of viewing the world. Daddy, who was

Excerpted from the Prologue to *Femininity* (1984).

gone all day at work and who loved to putter at home with his pipe, tobacco and tool chest, was knife and fork. Mommy and Grandma, with their ample proportions and pots and pans, were grownup soup spoons, large and capacious. And I was a teaspoon, small and slender, easy to hold and just right for pudding, my favorite dessert.

Being good at what was expected of me was one of my earliest 2
projects, for not only was I rewarded, as most children are, for doing things right, but excellence gave pride and stability to my childhood existence. Girls were different from boys, and the expression of that difference seemed mine to make clear. Did my loving, anxious mother, who dressed me in white organdy pinafores and Mary Janes and who cried hot tears when I got them dirty, give me my first instruction? Of course. Did my doting aunts and uncles with their gifts of pretty dolls and miniature tea sets add to my education? Of course. But even without the appropriate toys and clothes, lessons in the art of being feminine lay all around me and I absorbed them all: the fairy tales that were read to me at night, the brightly colored advertisements I pored over in magazines before I learned to decipher the words, the movies I saw, the comic books I hoarded, the radio soap operas I happily followed whenever I had to stay in bed with a cold. I loved being a little girl, or rather I loved being a fairy princess, for that was who I thought I was.

As I passed through a stormy adolescence to a stormy maturity, 3
femininity increasingly became an exasperation, a brilliant, subtle esthetic that was bafflingly inconsistent at the same time that it was minutely, demandingly concrete, a rigid code of appearance and behavior defined by do's and don't-do's that went against my rebellious grain. Femininity was a challenge thrown down to the female sex, a challenge no proud, self-respecting young woman could afford to ignore, particularly one with enormous ambition that she nursed in secret, alternately feeding or starving its inchoate life in tremendous confusion.

"Don't lose your femininity" and "Isn't it remarkable how she 4
manages to retain her femininity?" had terrifying implications. They spoke of a bottom-line failure so irreversible that nothing else mattered. The pinball machine had registered "tilt," the game had been called. Disqualification was marked on the forehead of a woman whose femininity was lost. No records would be entered in her name, for she had destroyed her birthright in her wretched, ungainly effort to imitate a man. She walked in limbo, this hapless creature, and it occurred to me that one day I might see her when I looked in the mirror. If the danger was so palpable that warning

notices were freely posted, wasn't it possible that the small bundle
of resentments I carried around in secret might spill out and place
the mark on my own forehead? Whatever quarrels with femininity
I had I kept to myself; whatever handicaps femininity imposed,
they were mine to deal with alone, for there was no women's
movement to ask the tough questions, or to brazenly disregard
the rules.

Femininity, in essence, is a romantic sentiment, a nostalgic tra- 5
dition of imposed limitations. Even as it hurries forward in the
1980s, putting on lipstick and high heels to appear well dressed,
it trips on the ruffled petticoats and hoopskirts of an era gone by.
Invariably and necessarily, femininity is something that women
had more of in the past, not only in the historic past of prior
generations, but in each woman's personal past as well—in the
virginal innocence that is replaced by knowledge, in the dewy
cheek that is coarsened by age, in the "inherent nature" that a
woman seems to misplace so forgetfully whenever she steps out
of bounds. Why should this be so? The XX chromosomal message
has not been scrambled, the estrogen-dominated hormonal balance
is generally as biology intended, the reproductive organs, whatever
use one has made of them, are usually in place, the breasts of
whatever size are most often where they should be. But clearly,
biological femaleness is not enough.

Femininity always demands more. It must constantly reassure 6
its audience by a willing demonstration of difference, even when
one does not exist in nature, or it must seize and embrace a natural
variation and compose a rhapsodic symphony upon the notes.
Suppose one doesn't care to, has other things on her mind, is
clumsy or tone-deaf despite the best instruction and training? To
fail at the feminine difference is to appear not to care about men,
and to risk the loss of their attention and approval. To be insufficiently
feminine is viewed as a failure in core sexual identity, or as a
failure to care sufficiently about oneself, for a woman found wanting
will be appraised (and will appraise herself) as mannish or neutered
or simply unattractive, as men have defined these terms.

We are talking, admittedly, about an exquisite esthetic. Enormous 7
pleasure can be extracted from feminine pursuits as a creative
outlet or purely as relaxation; indeed, indulgence for the sake of
fun, or art, or attention, is among femininity's great joys. But the
chief attraction (and the central paradox, as well) is the competitive
edge that femininity seems to promise in the unending struggle
to survive, and perhaps to triumph. The world smiles favorably
on the feminine woman: it extends little courtesies and minor
privilege. Yet the nature of this competitive edge is ironic, at best,

for one works at femininity by accepting restrictions, by limiting one's sights, by choosing an indirect route, by scattering concentration and not giving one's all as a man would to his own, certifiably masculine, interests. It does not require a great leap of imagination for a woman to understand the feminine principle as a grand collection of compromises, large and small, that she simply must make in order to render herself a successful woman. If she has difficulty in satisfying femininity's demands, if its illusions go against her grain, or if she is criticized for her shortcomings and imperfections, the more she will see femininity as a desperate strategy of appeasement, a strategy she may not have the wish or the courage to abandon, for failure looms in either direction.

It is fashionable in some quarters to describe the feminine and masculine principles as polar ends of the human continuum, and to sagely profess that both polarities exist in all people. Sun and moon, yin and yang, soft and hard, active and passive, etcetera, may indeed be opposites, but a linear continuum does not illuminate the problem. (Femininity, in all its contrivances, is a very active endeavor.) What, then, is the basic distinction? The masculine principle is better understood as a driving ethos of superiority designed to inspire straightforward, confident success, while the feminine principle is composed of vulnerability, the need for protection, the formalities of compliance and the avoidance of conflict—in short, an appeal of dependence and good will that gives the masculine principle its romantic validity and its admiring applause. 8

Femininity pleases men because it makes them appear more masculine by contrast; and, in truth, conferring an extra portion of unearned gender distinction on men, an unchallenged space in which to breathe freely and feel stronger, wiser, more competent, is femininity's special gift. One could say that masculinity is often an effort to please women, but masculinity is known to please by displays of mastery and competence while femininity pleases by suggesting that these concerns, except in small matters, are beyond its intent. Whimsy, unpredictability and patterns of thinking and behavior that are dominated by emotion, such as tearful expressions of sentiment and fear, are thought to be feminine precisely because they lie outside the established route to success. 9

If in the beginnings of history the feminine woman was defined by her physical dependency, her inability for reasons of reproductive biology to triumph over the forces of nature that were the tests of masculine strength and power, today she reflects both an economic and emotional dependency that is still considered "natural," romantic and attractive. After an unsettling fifteen years in which many basic assumptions about the sexes were challenged, the 10

economic disparity did not disappear. Large numbers of women—
those with small children, those left high and dry after a mid-life
divorce—need financial support. But even those who earn their
own living share a universal need for connectedness (call it love,
if you wish). As unprecedented numbers of men abandon their
sexual interest in women, others, sensing opportunity, choose to
demonstrate their interest through variety and a change in partners.
A sociological fact of the 1980s is that female competition for two
scarce resources—men and jobs—is especially fierce.

So it is not surprising that we are currently witnessing a renewed   11
interest in femininity and an unabashed indulgence in feminine
pursuits. Femininity serves to reassure men that women need them
and care about them enormously. By incorporating the decorative
and the frivolous into its definition of style, femininity functions
as an effective antidote to the unrelieved seriousness, the pressure
of making one's way in a harsh, difficult world. In its mandate
to avoid direct confrontation and to smooth over the fissures of
conflict, femininity operates as a value system of niceness, a code
of thoughtfulness and sensitivity that in modern society is sadly
in short supply.

There is no reason to deny that indulgence in the art of feminine   12
illusion can be reassuring to a woman, if she happens to be good
at it. As sexuality undergoes some dizzying revisions, evidence
that one is a woman "at heart" (the inquisitor's question) is not
without worth. Since an answer of sorts may be furnished by
piling on additional documentation, affirmation can arise from
such identifiable but trivial feminine activities as buying a new
eyeliner, experimenting with the latest shade of nail color, or
bursting into tears at the outcome of a popular romance novel. Is
there anything destructive in this? Time and cost factors, a deflection
of energy and an absorption in fakery spring quickly to mind, and
they need to be balanced, as in a ledger book, against the affirming
advantage.

JOHN STEINBECK

The Chrysanthemums

The high grey-flannel fog of winter closed off the Salinas Valley   1
from the sky and from all the rest of the world. On every side it
sat like a lid on the mountains and made of the great valley a

From *The Long Valley*, 1965.

closed pot. On the broad, level land floor the gang plows bit deep and left the black earth shining like metal where the shares had cut. On the foothill ranches across the Salinas River, the yellow stubble fields seemed to be bathed in pale cold sunshine, but there was no sunshine in the valley now in December. The thick willow scrub along the river flamed with sharp and positive yellow leaves.

It was a time of quiet and of waiting. The air was cold and tender. A light wind blew up from the southwest so that the farmers were mildly hopeful of a good rain before long; but fog and rain do not go together.

Across the river, on Henry Allen's foothill ranch there was little work to be done, for the hay was cut and stored and the orchards were plowed up to receive the rain deeply when it should come. The cattle on the higher slopes were becoming shaggy and rough-coated.

Elisa Allen, working in her flower garden, looked down across the yard and saw Henry, her husband, talking to two men in business suits. The three of them stood by the tractor shed, each man with one foot on the side of the little Fordson. They smoked cigarettes and studied the machine as they talked.

Elisa watched them for a moment and then went back to her work. She was thirty-five. Her face was lean and strong and her eyes were as clear as water. Her figure looked blocked and heavy in her gardening costume, a man's black hat pulled low down over her eyes, clodhopper shoes, a figured print dress almost completely covered by a big corduroy apron with four big pockets to hold the snips, the trowel and scratcher, the seeds and the knife she worked with. She wore heavy leather gloves to protect her hands while she worked.

She was cutting down the old year's chrysanthemum stalks with a pair of short and powerful scissors. She looked down toward the men by the tractor shed now and then. Her face was eager and mature and handsome; even her work with the scissors was over-eager, over-powerful. The chrysanthemum stems seemed too small and easy for her energy.

She brushed a cloud of hair out of her eyes with the back of her glove, and left a smudge of earth on the cheek in doing it. Behind her stood the neat white farm house with red geraniums close-banked around it as high as the windows. It was a hard-swept looking little house, with hard-polished windows, and a clean mud-mat on the front steps.

Elisa cast another glance toward the tractor shed. The strangers were getting into their Ford coupe. She took off a glove and put her strong fingers down into the forest of new green chrysanthemum sprouts that were growing around the old roots. She spread the leaves and looked down among the close-growing stems. No aphids were there, no sowbugs or snails or cutworms. Her terrier fingers destroyed such pests before they could get started.

Elisa started at the sound of her husband's voice. He had come near quietly, and he leaned over the wire fence that protected her flower garden from cattle and dogs and chickens.

"At it again," he said. "You've got a strong new crop coming." 10

Elisa straightened her back and pulled on the gardening glove again. "Yes. They'll be strong this coming year." In her tone and on her face there was a little smugness.

"You've got a gift with things," Henry observed. "Some of those yellow chrysanthemums you had this year were ten inches across. I wish you'd work out in the orchard and raise some apples that big."

Her eyes sharpened. "Maybe I could do it, too. I've a gift with things, all right. My mother had it. She could stick anything in the ground and make it grow. She said it was having planters' hands that knew how to do it."

"Well, it sure works with flowers," he said.

"Henry, who were those men you were talking to?" 15

"Why, sure, that's what I came to tell you. They were from the Western Meat Company. I sold those thirty head of three-year-old steers. Got nearly my own price, too."

"Good," she said. "Good for you."

"And I thought," he continued, 'I thought how it's Saturday afternoon, and we might go into Salinas for dinner at a restaurant, and then to a picture show—to celebrate, you see."

"Good," she repeated. "Oh, yes. That will be good."

Henry put on his joking tone. "There's fights tonight. How'd 20 you like to go to the fights?"

"Oh, no," she said breathlessly. "No, I wouldn't like fights."

"Just fooling, Elisa. We'll go to a movie. Let's see. It's two now. I'm going to take Scotty and bring down those steers from the hill. It'll take us maybe two hours. We'll go in town about five and have dinner at the Cominos Hotel. Like that?"

"Of course I'll like it. It's good to eat away from home."

"All right, then. I'll go get up a couple of horses."

She said, "I'll have plenty of time to transplant some of these 25 sets, I guess."

She heard her husband calling Scotty down by the barn. And a little later she saw the two men ride up the pale yellow hillside in search of the steers.

There was a little square sandy bed kept for rooting the chrysanthemums. With her trowel she turned the soil over and over, and smoothed it and patted it firm. Then she dug ten parallel trenches to receive the sets. Back at the chrysanthemum bed she pulled out the little crisp shoots, trimmed off the leaves of each one with her scissors and laid it on a small orderly pile.

A squeak of wheels and plod of hoofs came from the road. Elisa looked up. The country road ran along the dense bank of willows and cottonwoods that bordered the river, and up this road came a curious vehicle, curiously drawn. It was an old spring-wagon, with a round canvas top on it like the cover of a prairie schooner. It was drawn by an old bay horse and a little grey-and-white burro. A big stubble-bearded man sat between the cover flaps and drove the crawling team. Underneath the wagon, between the hind wheels, a lean and rangy mongrel dog walked sedately. Words were painted on the canvas in clumsy, crooked letters. "Pots, pans, knives, sisors, lawn mores. Fixed." Two rows of articles and the triumphantly definitive "Fixed" below. The black paint had run down in little sharp points beneath each letter.

Elisa, squatting on the ground, watched to see the crazy, loose-jointed wagon pass by. But it didn't pass. It turned into the farm road in front of her house, crooked old wheels skirling and squeaking. The rangy dog darted from between the wheels and ran ahead. Instantly the two ranch shepherds flew out at him. Then all three stopped, and with stiff and quivering tails, with taut straight legs, with ambassadorial dignity, they slowly circled, sniffing daintily. The caravan pulled up to Elisa's wire fence and stopped. Now the newcomer dog, feeling out-numbered, lowered his tail and retired under the wagon with raised hackles and bared teeth.

The man on the wagon seat called out. "That's a bad dog in a fight when he gets started." 30

Elisa laughed. "I see he is. How soon does he generally get started?"

The man caught up her laughter and echoed it heartily. "Sometimes not for weeks and weeks," he said. He climbed stiffly down, over the wheel. The horse and the donkey drooped like unwatered flowers.

Elisa saw that he was a very big man. Although his hair and beard were greying, he did not look old. His worn black suit was wrinkled and spotted with grease. The laughter had disappeared from his face and eyes the moment his laughing voice ceased. His eyes were dark, and they were full of the brooding that gets in the eyes of teamsters and of sailors. The calloused hands he rested on the wire fence were cracked, and every crack was a black line. He took off his battered hat.

"I'm off my general road, ma'am," he said. "Does this dirt road cut over across the river to the Los Angeles highway?"

Elisa stood up and shoved the thick scissors in her apron pocket. 35

"Well, yes, it does, but it winds around and then fords the river. I don't think your team could pull through the sand."

He replied with some asperity. "It might surprise you what them beasts can pull through."

"When they get started?" she asked.

He smiled for a second. "Yes. When they get started."

"Well," said Elisa, "I think you'll save time if you go back to the Salinas road and pick up the highway there."

He drew a big finger down the chicken wire and made it sing. 40 "I ain't in any hurry, ma'am. I go from Seattle to San Diego and back every year. Takes all my time. About six months each way. I aim to follow nice weather."

Elisa took off her gloves and stuffed them in the apron pocket with the scissors. She touched the under edge of her man's hat, searching for fugitive hairs. "That sounds like a nice kind of a way to live," she said.

He leaned confidentially over the fence. "Maybe you noticed the writing on my wagon. I mend pots and sharpen knives and scissors. You got any of them things to do?"

"Oh, no," she said quickly. "Nothing like that." Her eyes hardened with resistance.

"Scissors is the worst thing," he explained. "Most people just ruin scissors trying to sharpen 'em but I know how. I got a special tool. It's a little bobbit kind of thing, and patented. But it sure does the trick."

"No. My scissors are all sharp." 45

"All right, then. Take a pot," he continued earnestly, "a bent pot, or a pot with a hole. I can make it like new so you don't have to buy no new ones. That's a saving for you."

"No," she said shortly. "I tell you I have nothing like that for you to do."

His face fell to an exaggerated sadness. His voice took on a whining undertone. "I ain't had a thing to do today. Maybe I won't have no supper tonight. You see I'm off my regular road. I know folks on the highway clear from Seattle to San Diego. They save their things for me to sharpen up because they know I do it so good and save them money."

"I'm sorry," Elisa said irritably. "I haven't anything for you to do."

His eyes left her face and fell to searching the ground. They 50 roamed about until they came to the chrysanthemum bed where she had been working. "What's them plants, ma'am?"

The irritation and resistance melted from Elisa's face. "Oh, those are chrysanthemums, giant whites and yellows. I raise them every year, bigger than anybody around here."

"Kind of a long-stemmed flower? Looks like a quick puff of colored smoke?" he asked.

"That's it. What a nice way to describe them."

"They smell kind of nasty till you get used to them," he said.

"It's a good bitter smell," she retorted, "not nasty at all."   55

He changed his tone quickly. "I like the smell myself."

"I had ten-inch blooms this year," she said.

The man leaned farther over the fence. "Look. I know a lady down the road a piece, has got the nicest garden you ever seen. Got nearly every kind of flower but no chrysanthemums. Last time I was mending a copper-bottom washtub for her (that's a hard job but I do it good), she said to me, 'If you ever run acrost some nice chrysanthemums I wish you'd try to get me a few seeds.' That's what she told me."

Elisa's eyes grew alert and eager. "She couldn't have known much about chrysanthemums. You can raise them from seed, but it's much easier to root the little sprouts you see there."

"Oh," he said. "I s'pose I can't take none to her, then."   60

"Why yes you can," Elisa cried. "I can put some in damp sand, and you can carry them right along with you. They'll take root in the pot if you keep them damp. And then she can transplant them."

"She'd sure like to have some, ma'am. You say they're nice ones?"

"Beautiful," she said. "Oh, beautiful." Her eyes shone. She tore off the battered hat and shook out her dark pretty hair. "I'll put them in a flower pot, and you can take them right with you. Come into the yard."

While the man came through the picket gate Elisa ran excitedly along the geranium-bordered path to the back of the house. And she returned carrying a big red flower pot. The gloves were forgotten now. She kneeled on the ground by the starting bed and dug up the sandy soil with her fingers and scooped it into the bright new flower pot. Then she picked up the little pile of shoots she had prepared. With her strong fingers she pressed them into the sand and tamped around them with her knuckles. The man stood over her. "I'll tell you what to do," she said. "You remember so you can tell the lady."

"Yes, I'll try to remember."   65

"Well, look. These will take root in about a month. Then she must set them out, about a foot apart in good rich earth like this, see?" She lifted a handful of dark soil for him to look at. "They'll grow fast and tall. Now remember this. In July tell her to cut them down, about eight inches from the ground."

"Before they bloom?" he asked.

"Yes, before they bloom." Her face was tight with eagerness. "They'll come right up again. About the last of September the buds will start."

She stopped and seemed perplexed. "It's the budding that takes the most care," she said hesitantly. "I don't know how to tell you." She looked deep into his eyes, searchingly. Her mouth opened a little, and she seemed to be listening. "I'll try to tell you," she said. "Did you ever hear of planting hands?"

"Can't say I have, ma'am."   70

"Well, I can only tell you what it feels like. It's when you're picking off the buds you don't want. Everything goes right down into your fingertips. You watch your fingers work. They do it themselves. You can feel how it is. They pick and pick the buds. They never make a mistake. They're with the plant. Do you see? Your fingers and the plant. You can feel that, right up your arm. They know. They never make a mistake. You can feel it. When you're like that you can't do anything wrong. Do you see that? Can you understand that?"

She was kneeling on the ground looking up at him. Her breast swelled passionately.

The man's eyes narrowed. He looked away, self-consciously. "Maybe I know," he said. "Sometimes in the night in the wagon there—"

Elisa's voice grew husky. She broke in on him. "I've never lived as you do, but I know what you mean. When the night is dark— why, the stars are sharp-pointed, and there's quiet. Why, you rise up and up! Every pointed star gets driven into your body. It's like that. Hot and sharp and—lovely."

Kneeling there, her hand went out toward his legs in the greasy   75
black trousers. Her hesitant fingers almost touched the cloth. Then her hand dropped to the ground. She crouched low like a fawning dog.

He said, "It's nice, just like you say. Only when you don't have no dinner, it ain't."

She stood up then, very straight, and her face was ashamed. She held the flower pot out to him and placed it gently in his arms. "Here. Put it in your wagon, on the seat, where you can watch it. Maybe I can find something for you to do."

At the back of the house she dug in the can pile and found two old and battered aluminum saucepans. She carried them back and gave them to him. "Here, maybe you can fix these."

His manner changed. He became professional. "Good as new I can fix them." At the back of his wagon he set a little anvil, and out of an oily tool box dug a small machine hammer. Elisa came through the gate to watch him while he pounded out the dents in the kettles. His mouth grew sure and knowing. At a difficult part of the work he sucked his under-lip.

"You sleep right in the wagon?" Elisa asked. 80

"Right in the wagon, ma'am. Rain or shine I'm dry as a cow in there."

"It must be nice," she said. "It must be very nice. I wish women could do such things."

"It ain't the right kind of a life for a woman."

Her upper lip raised a little, showing her teeth. "How do you know? How can you tell?" she said.

"I don't know ma'am," he protested. "Of course I don't know. 85 Now here's your kettles, done. You don't have to buy no new ones."

"How much?"

"Oh, fifty cents'll do. I keep my prices down and my work good. That's why I have all them satisfied customers up and down the highway."

Elisa brought him a fifty-cent piece from the house and dropped it in his hand. "You might be surprised to have a rival some time. I can sharpen scissors, too. And I can beat the dents out of little pots. I could show you what a woman might do."

He put his hammer back in the oily box and shoved the little anvil out of sight. "It would be a lonely life for a woman, ma'am, and a scarey life, too, with animals creeping under the wagon all night." He climbed over the singletree, steadying himself with a hand on the burro's white rump. He settled himself in the seat, picked up the lines. "Thank you kindly, ma'am," he said. "I'll do like you told me; I'll go back and catch the Salinas road."

"Mind," she called, "if you're long in getting there, keep the 90 sand damp."

"Sand, ma'am? . . . Sand? Oh, sure. You mean round the chrysanthemums. Sure I will." He clucked his tongue. The beasts leaned luxuriously into their collars. The mongrel dog took his place between the back wheels. The wagon turned and crawled out the entrance road and back the way it had come, along the river.

Elisa stood in front of her wire fence watching the slow progress of the caravan. Her shoulders were straight, her head thrown back, her eyes half-closed, so that the scene came vaguely into them. Her lips moved silently, forming the words "Good-bye—good-bye." Then she whispered. "That's a bright direction. There's a glowing there." The sound of her whisper startled her. She shook herself free and looked about to see whether anyone had been listening. Only the dogs had heard. They lifted their heads toward her from their sleeping in the dust, and then stretched out their chins and settled asleep again. Elisa turned and ran hurriedly into the house.

In the kitchen she reached behind the stove and felt the water tank. It was full of hot water from the noonday cooking. In the bathroom she tore off her soiled clothes and flung them into the corner. And then she scrubbed herself with a little block of pumice, legs and thighs, loins and chest and arms, until her skin was scratched and red. When she had dried herself she stood in front of a mirror in her bedroom and looked at her body. She tightened her stomach and threw out her chest. She turned and looked over her shoulder at her back.

After a while she began to dress, slowly. She put on her newest underclothing and her nicest stockings and the dress which was the symbol of her prettiness. She worked carefully on her hair, pencilled her eyebrows and rouged her lips.

Before she was finished she heard the little thunder of hoofs   95
and the shouts of Henry and his helper as they drove the red steers into the corral. She heard the gate bang shut and set herself for Henry's arrival.

His step sounded on the porch. He entered the house calling "Elisa, where are you?"

"In my room, dressing. I'm not ready. There's hot water for your bath. Hurry up. It's getting late."

When she heard him splashing in the tub, Elisa laid his dark suit on the bed, and shirt and socks and tie beside it. She stood his polished shoes on the floor beside the bed. Then she went to the porch and sat primly and stiffly down. She looked toward the river road where the willow-line was still yellow with frosted leaves so that under the high grey fog they seemed a thin band of sunshine. This was the only color in the grey afternoon. She sat unmoving for a long time. Her eyes blinked rarely.

Henry came banging out of the door, shoving his tie inside his vest as he came. Elisa stiffened and her face grew tight. Henry stopped short and looked at her. "Why—why, Elisa. You look so nice!"

"Nice? You think I look nice? What do you mean by 'nice'?"   100

Henry blundered on. "I don't know. I mean you look different, strong and happy."

"I am strong? Yes, strong. What do you mean 'strong'?"

He looked bewildered. "You're playing some kind of a game," he said helplessly. "It's a kind of a play. You look strong enough to break a calf over your knee, happy enough to eat it like a watermelon."

For a second she lost her rigidity. "Henry! Don't talk like that. You didn't know what you said." She grew complete again. "I'm strong," she boasted. "I never knew before how strong."

Henry looked down toward the tractor shed, and when he brought 105 his eyes back to her, they were his own again. "I'll get out the car. You can put on your coat while I'm starting."

Elisa went into the house. She heard him drive to the gate and idle down his motor, and then she took a long time to put on her hat. She pulled it here and pressed it there. When Henry turned the motor off she slipped into her coat and went out.

The little roadster bounced along on the dirt road by the river, raising the birds and driving the rabbits into the brush. Two cranes flapped heavily over the willow-line and dropped into the river-bed.

Far ahead on the road Elisa saw a dark speck. She knew.

She tried not to look as they passed it, but her eyes would not obey. She whispered to herself sadly. "He might have thrown them off the road. That wouldn't have been much trouble, not very much. But he kept the pot," she explained. "He had to keep the pot. That's why he couldn't get them off the road."

The roadster turned a bend and she saw the caravan ahead. 110 She swung full around toward her husband so she could not see the little covered wagon and the mismatched team as the car passed them.

In a moment they had left behind them the man who had not known or needed to know what she said, the bargainer. She did not look back.

To Henry, she said loudly, to be heard above the motor, "It will be good, to-night, a good dinner."

"Now you're changed again," Henry complained. He took one hand from the wheel and patted her knee. "I ought to take you in to dinner oftener. It would be good for both of us. We get so heavy out on the ranch."

"Henry," she asked, "could we have wine at dinner?"

"Sure. Say! That will be fine." 115

She was silent for a while; then she said, "Henry, at those prize fights do the men hurt each other very much?"

"Sometimes a little, not often. Why?"

"Well, I've read how they break noses, and blood runs down their chests. I've read how the fighting gloves get heavy and soggy with blood."

He looked round at her. "What's the matter, Elisa? I didn't know you read things like that." He brought the car to a stop, then turned to the right over the Salinas River bridge.

"Do any women ever go to the fights?" she asked.   120

"Oh, sure, some. What's the matter, Elisa? Do you want to go? I don't think you'd like it, but I'll take you if you really want to go."

She relaxed limply in the seat. "Oh, no. I don't want to go. I'm sure I don't." Her face was turned away from him. "It will be enough if we can have wine. It will be plenty." She turned up her coat collar so he could not see that she was crying weakly— like an old woman.

Thinking About Masculinity and Femininity

In the early 1930s Margaret Mead, like almost all Americans, assumed that there was a masculine temperament and a feminine one, separate and constant. There were, to be sure, some manly women and some womanly men, but the exception somehow proved the rule. Masculinity and femininity seemed as immutable as species had before Darwin. Then Mead did anthropological field work in New Guinea, where she found within a hundred-mile area three isolated tribes: in one both men and women had the mild disposition attributed to American women; in one both men and women were fiercely aggressive; in the third the men wore curls, went shopping, and said catty things about each other, while the plainly dressed women were energetic and managerial. New Guinea was for Mead what the Galapagos had been for Darwin a century earlier. The immutable masculine and feminine types suddenly seemed richly varied. Gender became just one of several threads nature provided; humans were free to choose how they would weave it into "the beautiful imaginative social fabric we call civilization."

Varied as the gender roles were in Mead's three societies, each was itself quite clear. Each created a standard from which few individuals deviated. Until fairly recently, the prescribed gender roles in European and American cultures were also quite clear. Shakespeare's Lady Macbeth, when she decides to indulge in the hearty masculine pastimes of ambition and murder, calls on the spirits to "unsex" her. Coventry Patmore, when he wrote "The Angel in the House" in 1854, separated his genders as neatly as Shakespeare had: Woman was a sweet civilizing influence that makes "brutes men and men divine!" The clarity of the division between masculine and feminine attributes had not changed much when Virginia Woolf developed ambitions as a writer; she called on no spirits to unsex her, but she did struggle quite consciously against the Angel in the House. It was not a struggle many women had the resources to win. By 1938, when Dorothy Sayers delivered her address "Are Women Human?", the climate had changed considerably and Sayers argued that the time for "feminism, in the old-fashioned sense of the word, has gone past." Women, she believed, were now free to choose the role suited to them as individuals. Sayers's announcement of women's emancipation may have been premature, but the pressures to conform to traditional feminine roles had at least become more subtle when Brigid Brophy discussed them in 1964. Today, as Susan Brownmiller points out, women face newer problems created by increasing freedom to choose. Traditional and contemporary definitions of femininity must be balanced "as in a ledger book," advantages set off against disadvantages.

And what about men? A redefinition of femininity implies a redefinition of masculinity that is in some ways even more difficult. Many women are glad to give up their role as the Angel in the House or the Clinging Vine, but men are generally more reluctant to give up their role as the Heroic Adventurer or the Sturdy Oak. Two of the essays included in the section are almost case studies of the traditional masculine role: Jan Morris's "To Everest" and Tom Wolfe's "The Right Stuff." Margaret Mead's "Sex and Achievement" shows how child-rearing practices in post-war America began to erode that role, and essays by Noel Perrin and Michael Norman take opposite views of society's newer ideal of the androgynous male.

The short story in the section, John Steinbeck's "Chrysanthemums" will be read somewhat differently by those who see great differences in the temperaments of the sexes and those who see men and women as very much alike. Is it a story about the frustration of a human being who happens to be a woman, or is it a story about a specifically feminine struggle with biology and society?

QUESTIONS

1. To what extent are the lives of men and women psychologically different?

2. How dramatically have the relations between the sexes changed in the last 60 years? The last 40 years? The last 20 years?

3. If we weigh the traditional roles of women against their contemporary roles, what are the advantages and disadvantages of each? Can we say that there has been progress?

4. If we weigh the traditional roles of men against their contemporary roles, what are the advantages and disadvantages of each? Can we say that there has been progress?

5. What ideals of femininity or masculinity exist in our society that are not well discussed in this section?

6. Where in contemporary society do you find pressure exerted on men or women to conform to a prescribed sex role?

7. The distinction between male and female is only one of many that our society makes. How does it compare in importance to the distinction between old and young, white and non-white, rich and poor, or any other distinction you can name?

STATUS

C. S. LEWIS

The Inner Ring

May I read you a few lines from Tolstoi's *War and Peace*?   1

> When Boris entered the room, Prince Andrey was listening to an old general, wearing his decorations, who was reporting something to Prince Andrey, with an expression of soldierly servility on his purple face. "Alright. Please wait!" he said to the general, speaking in Russian with the French accent which he used when he spoke with contempt. The moment he noticed Boris he stopped listening to the general who trotted imploringly after him and begged to be heard, while Prince Andrey turned to Boris with a cheerful smile and a nod of the head. Boris now clearly understood—what he had already guessed—that side by side with the system of discipline and subordination which were laid down in the Army Regulations, there existed a different and a more real system—the system which compelled a tightly laced general with a purple face to wait respectfully for his turn while a mere captain like Prince Andrey chatted with a mere second lieutenant like Boris. Boris decided at once that he would be guided not by the official system but by this other unwritten system.[1]

When you invite a middle-aged moralist to address you, I suppose   2
I must conclude, however unlikely the conclusion seems, that you have a taste for middle-aged moralising. I shall do my best to gratify it. I shall in fact give you advice about the world in which you are going to live. I do not mean by this that I am going to attempt to talk on what are called current affairs. You probably know quite as much about them as I do. I am not going to tell you—except in a form so general that you will hardly recognise it—what part you ought to play in post-war reconstruction. It is not, in fact, very likely that any of you will be able, in the next ten years, to make any direct contribution to the peace or prosperity of Europe. You will be busy finding jobs, getting married, acquiring facts. I am going to do something more old-fashioned than you perhaps expected. I am going to give advice. I am going to issue warnings. Advice and warnings about things which are so perennial that no one calls them "current affairs."

And of course everyone knows what a middle-aged moralist of   3
my type warns his juniors against. He warns them against the World, the Flesh, and the Devil. But one of this trio will be enough

The Memorial Oration at King's College, University of London, 1944.
1. Part III, chapter 9. [author's note]

to deal with today. The Devil, I shall leave strictly alone. The association between him and me in the public mind has already gone quite as deep as I wish: in some quarters it has already reached the level of confusion, if not of identification. I begin to realise the truth of the old proverb that he who sups with that formidable host needs a long spoon. As for the Flesh, you must be very abnormal young people if you do not know quite as much about it as I do. But on the World I think I have something to say.

In the passage I have just read from Tolstoi, the young second ⁴ lieutenant Boris Dubretskoi discovers that there exist in the army two different systems or hierarchies. The one is printed in some little red book and anyone can easily read it up. It also remains constant. A general is always superior to a colonel and a colonel to a captain. The other is not printed anywhere. Nor is it even a formally organised secret society with officers and rules which you would be told after you had been admitted. You are never formally and explicitly admitted by anyone. You discover gradually, in almost indefinable ways, that it exists and that you are outside it; and then later, perhaps, that you are inside it. There are what correspond to passwords, but they too are spontaneous and informal. A particular slang, the use of particular nicknames, an allusive manner of conversation, are the marks. But it is not constant. It is not easy, even at a given moment, to say who is inside and who is outside. Some people are obviously in and some are obviously out, but there are always several on the border-line. And if you come back to the same Divisional Headquarters, or Brigade Headquarters, or the same regiment or even the same company, after six weeks' absence, you may find this second hierarchy quite altered. There are no formal admissions or expulsions. People think they are in it after they have in fact been pushed out of it, or before they have been allowed in: this provides great amusement for those who are really inside. It has no fixed name. The only certain rule is that the insiders and outsiders call it by different names. From inside it may be designated, in simple cases, by mere enumeration: it may be called "You and Tony and me." When is very secure and comparatively stable in membership it calls itself "we." When it has to be suddenly expanded to meet a particular emergency it calls itself "All the sensible people at this place." From outside, if you have despaired of getting into it, you call it "That gang" or "They" or "So-and-so and his set" or "the Caucus" or "the Inner Ring." If you are a candidate for admission you probably don't call it anything. To discuss it with the other outsiders would make you feel outside yourself. And to mention it in talking to the man who is inside, and who may help you if this present conversation goes well, would be madness.

Badly as I may have described it, I hope you will all have recognised the thing I am describing. Not, of course, that you have been in the Russian Army or perhaps in any army. But you have met the phenomenon of an Inner Ring. You discovered one in your house at school before the end of the first term. And when you had climbed up to somewhere near it by the end of your second year, perhaps you discovered that within the Ring there was a Ring yet more inner, which in its turn was the fringe of the great school Ring to which the house Rings were only satellites. It is even possible that the School Ring was almost in touch with a Masters' Ring. You were beginning, in fact, to pierce through the skins of the onion. And here, too, at your university—shall I be wrong in assuming that at this very moment, invisible to me, there are several rings—independent systems or concentric rings—present in this room? And I can assure you that in whatever hospital, inn of court, diocese, school, business, or college you arrive after going down, you will find the Rings—what Tolstoi calls the second or unwritten systems.

All this is rather obvious. I wonder whether you will say the same of my next step, which is this. I believe that in all men's lives at certain periods, and in many men's lives at all periods between infancy and extreme old age, one of the most dominant elements is the desire to be inside the local Ring and the terror of being left outside. This desire, in one of its forms, has indeed had ample justice done to it in literature. I mean, in the form of snobbery. Victorian fiction is full of characters who are hag-ridden by the desire to get inside that particular Ring which is, or was, called Society. But it must be clearly understood that "Society," in that sense of the word, is merely one of a hundred Rings and snobbery therefore only one form of the longing to be inside. People who believe themselves to be free, and indeed are free, from snobbery, and who read satires on snobbery with tranquil superiority, may be devoured by the desire in another form. It may be the very intensity of their desire to enter some quite different Ring which renders them immune from the allurements of high life. An invitation from a duchess would be very cold comfort to a man smarting under the sense of exclusion from some artistic or communist côterie. Poor man—it is not large, lighted rooms, or champagne, or even scandals about peers and Cabinet Ministers that he wants: it is the sacred little attic or studio, the heads bent together, the fog of tobacco smoke, and the delicious knowledge that we—we four or five all huddled beside this stove—

are the people who *know*. Often the desire conceals itself so well that we hardly recognize the pleasures of fruition. Men tell not only their wives but themselves that it is a hardship to stay late at the office or the school on some bit of important extra work which they have been let in for because they and So-and-so and the two others are the only people left in the place who really know how things are run. But it is not quite true. It is a terrible bore, of course, when old Fatty Smithson draws you aside and whispers "Look here, we've got to get you in on this examination somehow" or "Charles and I saw at once that you've got to be on this committee." A terrible bore . . . ah, but how much more terrible if you were left out! It is tiring and unhealthy to lose your Saturday afternoons: but to have them free because you don't matter, that is much worse.

Freud would say, no doubt, that the whole thing is a subterfuge 7 of the sexual impulse. I wonder whether the shoe is not sometimes on the other foot, I wonder whether, in ages of promiscuity, many a virginity has not been lost less in obedience to Venus than in obedience to the lure of the caucus. For of course, when promiscuity is the fashion, the chaste are outsiders. They are ignorant of something that other people know. They are uninitiated. And as for lighter matters, the number who first smoked or first got drunk for a similar reason is probably very large.

I must now make a distinction. I am not going to say that the 8 existence of Inner Rings is an evil. It is certainly unavoidable. There must be confidential discussions: and it is not only not a bad thing, it is (in itself) a good thing, that personal friendship should grow up between those who work together. And it is perhaps impossible that the official hierarchy of any organisation should quite coincide with its actual workings. If the wisest and most energetic people invariably held the highest posts, it might coincide; since they often do not, there must be people in high positions who are really deadweights and people in lower positions who are more important than their rank and seniority would lead you to suppose. In that way the second, unwritten system is bound to grow up. It is necessary; and perhaps it is not a necessary evil. But the desire which draws us into Inner Rings is another matter. A thing may be morally neutral and yet the desire for that thing may be dangerous. As Byron has said:

> *Sweet is a legacy, and passing sweet*
> *The unexpected death of some old lady.*

The painless death of a pious relative at an advanced age is not an evil. But an earnest desire for her death on the part of her heirs is not reckoned a proper feeling, and the law frowns on even the gentlest attempt to expedite her departure. Let Inner Rings be an unavoidable and even an innocent feature of life, though certainly not a beautiful one: but what of our longing to enter them, our anguish when we are excluded, and the kind of pleasure we feel when we get in?

I have no right to make assumptions about the degree to which 9 any of you may already be compromised. I must not assume that you have ever first neglected, and finally shaken off, friends whom you really loved and who might have lasted you a lifetime, in order to court the friendship of those who appeared to you more important, more esoteric. I must not ask whether you have ever derived actual pleasure from the loneliness and humiliation of the outsiders after you yourself were in: whether you have talked to fellow members of the Ring in the presence of outsiders simply in order that the outsiders might envy; whether the means whereby, in your days of probation, you propitiated the Inner Ring, were always wholly admirable. I will ask only one question—and it is, of course, a rhetorical question which expects no answer. In the whole of your life as you now remember it, has the desire to be on the right side of that invisible line ever prompted you to any act or word on which, in the cold small hours of a wakeful night, you can look back with satisfaction? If so, your case is more fortunate than most.

But I said I was going to give advice, and advice should deal 10 with the future, not the past. I have hinted at the past only to awake you to what I believe to be the real nature of human life. I don't believe that the economic motive and the erotic motive account for everything that goes on in what we moralists call the World. Even if you add Ambition I think the picture is still incomplete. The lust for the esoteric, the longing to be inside, take many forms which are not easily recognisable as Ambition. We hope, no doubt, for tangible profits from every Inner Ring we penetrate: power, money, liberty to break rules, avoidance of routine duties, evasion of discipline. But all these would not satisfy us if we did not get in addition the delicious sense of secret intimacy. It is no doubt a great convenience to know that we need fear no official reprimands from our official senior because he is old Percy, a fellow-member of our Ring. But we don't value the intimacy only for the sake of convenience; quite equally we value the convenience as a proof of the intimacy.

My main purpose in this address is simply to convince you that 11 this desire is one of the great permanent mainsprings of human action. It is one of the factors which go to make up the world as we know it—this whole pell-mell of struggle, competition, confusion, graft, disappointment and advertisement, and if it is one of the permanent mainsprings then you may be quite sure of this. Unless you take measures to prevent it, this desire is going to be one of the chief motives of your life, from the first day on which you enter your profession until the day when you are too old to care. That will be the natural thing—the life that will come to you of its own accord. Any other kind of life, if you lead it, will be the result of conscious and continuous effort. If you do nothing about it, if you drift with the stream, you will in fact be an "inner ringer." I don't say you'll be a successful one; that's as may be. But whether by pining and moping outside Rings that you can never enter, or by passing triumphantly further and further in—one way or the other you will be that kind of man.

I have already made it fairly clear that I think it better for you 12
not to be that kind of man. But you may have an open mind on the question. I will therefore suggest two reasons for thinking as I do.

It would be polite and charitable, and in view of your age 13
reasonable too, to suppose that none of you is yet a scoundrel. On the other hand, by the mere law of averages (I am saying nothing against free will) it is almost certain that at least two or three of you before you die will have become something very like scoundrels. There must be in this room the makings of at least that number of unscrupulous, treacherous, ruthless egotists. The ·
choice is still before you: and I hope you will not take my hard words about your possible future characters as a token of disrespect to your present characters. And the prophecy I make is this. To nine out of ten of you the choice which could lead to scoundrelism will come, when it does come, in no very dramatic colours. Obviously bad men, obviously threatening or bribing, will almost certainly not appear. Over a drink or a cup of coffee, disguised as a triviality and sandwiched between two jokes, from the lips of a man, or woman, whom you have recently been getting to know rather better and whom you hope to know better still—just at the moment when you are most anxious not to appear crude, or naïf or a prig—the hint will come. It will be the hint of something which is not quite in accordance with the technical rules of fair play: something which the public, the ignorant, romantic public, would never understand: something which even the outsiders in your own profession are apt to make a fuss about: but something, says your new friend, which "we"—and at the word "we" you try not to blush for mere pleasure—something "we always do." And you will be drawn in, if you are drawn in, not by desire for gain or ease, but simply because at that moment, when the cup was so

near your lips, you cannot bear to be thrust back again into the cold outer world. It would be so terrible to see the other man's face—that genial, confidential, delightfully sophisticated face—turn suddenly cold and contemptuous, to know that you had been tried for the Inner Ring and rejected. And then, if you are drawn in, next week it will be something a little further from the rules, and next year something further still, but all in the jolliest, friendliest spirit. It may end in a crash, a scandal, and penal servitude: it may end in millions, a peerage and giving the prizes at your old school. But you will be a scoundrel.

That is my first reason. Of all the passions the passion for the 14 Inner Ring is most skilful in making a man who is not yet a very bad man do very bad things.

My second reason is this. The torture allotted to the Danaids in 15 the classical underworld, that of attempting to fill sieves with water, is the symbol not of one vice but of all vices. It is the very mark of a perverse desire that it seeks what is not to be had. The desire to be inside the invisible line illustrates this rule. As long as you are governed by that desire you will never get what you want. You are trying to peel an onion: if you succeed there will be nothing left. Until you conquer the fear of being an outsider, an outsider you will remain.

This is surely very clear when you come to think of it. If you 16 want to be made free of a certain circle for some wholesome reason—if, say, you want to join a musical society because you really like music—then there is a possibility of satisfaction. You may find yourself playing in a quartet and you may enjoy it. But if all you want is to be in the know, your pleasure will be short-lived. The circle cannot have from within the charm it had from outside. By the very act of admitting you it has lost its magic. Once the first novelty is worn off the members of this circle will be no more interesting than your old friends. Why should they be? You were not looking for virtue or kindness or loyalty or humour or learning or wit or any of the things that can be really enjoyed. You merely wanted to be "in." And that is a pleasure that cannot last. As soon as your new associates have been staled to you by custom, you will be looking for another Ring. The rainbow's end will still be ahead of you. The old Ring will now be only the drab background for your endeavour to enter the new one.

And you will always find them hard to enter, for a reason you 17 very well know. You yourself, once you are in, want to make it hard for the next entrant, just as those who are already in made it hard for you. Naturally. In any wholesome group of people which holds together for a good purpose, the exclusions are in a sense accidental. Three or four people who are together for the sake of some piece of work exclude others because there is work only for so many or because the others can't in fact do it. Your little musical group limits its numbers because the rooms they meet in are only so big. But your genuine Inner Ring exists for exclusion. There'd be no fun if there were no outsiders. The invisible line would have no meaning unless most people were on the wrong side of it. Exclusion is no accident: it is the essence.

The quest of the Inner Ring will break your hearts unless you   18
break it. But if you break it, a surprising result will follow. If in your working hours you make the work your end, you will presently find yourself all unawares inside the only circle in your profession that really matters. You will be one of the sound craftsmen, and other sound craftsmen will know it. This group of craftsmen will by no means coincide with the Inner Ring or the Important People or the People in the Know. It will not shape that professional policy or work up that professional influence which fights for the profession as a whole against the public: nor will it lead to those periodic scandals and crises which the Inner Ring produces. But it will do those things which that profession exists to do and will in the long run be responsible for all the respect which that profession in fact enjoys and which the speeches and advertisements cannot maintain. And if in your spare time you consort simply with the people you like, you will again find that you have come unawares to a real inside: that you are indeed snug and safe at the centre of something which, seen from without, would look exactly like an Inner Ring. But the difference is that its secrecy is accidental, and its exclusiveness a by-product, and no one was led thither by the lure of the esoteric: for it is only four or five people who like one another meeting to do things that they like. This is friendship. Aristotle placed it among the virtues. It cause perhaps half of all the happiness in the world, and no Inner Ring can ever have it.

We are told in Scripture that those who ask get. That is true,   19
in senses I can't now explore. But in another sense there is much truth in the schoolboy's principle "them as asks shan't have." To a young person, just entering on adult life, the world seems full of "insides," full of delightful intimacies and confidentialities, and he desires to enter them. But if he follows that desire he will reach no "inside" that is worth reaching. The true road lies in quite another direction. It is like the house in *Alice Through the Looking Glass*.[2]

2. Lewis Carroll's Alice imagines that the mirror over her mantel is actually a window through which she sees another room in another house.

SAMUEL JOHNSON

Affectation

The hatred, which dissimulation always draws upon itself, is so 1
great, that if I did not know how much cunning differs from
wisdom, I should wonder that any men have so little knowledge
of their own interest, as to aspire to wear a mask for life, to try
to impose upon the world a character, to which they feel themselves
void of any just claim; and to hazard their quiet, their fame, and
even their profit, by exposing themselves to the danger of that
reproach, malevolence, and neglect, which such a discovery as
they have always to fear will certainly bring upon them.

It might be imagined, that the pleasure of reputation should 2
consist in the satisfaction of having our opinion of our own merit
confirmed by the suffrage of the publick; and that, to be extolled
for a quality, which a man knows himself to want, should give
him no other happiness than to be mistaken for the owner of an
estate, over which he chances to be travelling. But he, who subsists
upon affectation, knows nothing of this delicacy; like a desperate
adventurer in commerce, he takes up reputation upon trust, mortgages possessions which he never had, and enjoys, to the fatal
hour of bankruptcy, though with a thousand terrors and anxieties,
the unnecessary splendour of borrowed riches.

Affectation is to be always distinguished from hypocrisy, as being
the art of counterfeiting those qualities which we might, with
innocence and safety, be known to want. Thus the man, who, to
carry on any fraud, or, to conceal any crime, pretends to rigours
of devotion, and exactness of life, is guilty of hypocrisy; and his
guilt is greater, as the end, for which he puts on the false appearance,
is more pernicious. But he that, with an awkward address, and
unpleasing countenance, boasts of the conquests made by him
among the ladies, and counts over the thousands, which he might
have possessed, if he would have submitted to the yoke of matrimony
is chargeable only with affectation. Hypocrisy is the necessary
burthen of villainy, affectation part of the chosen trappings of folly;
the one completes a villain, the other only finishes a fop. Contempt
is the proper punishment of affectation, and detestation the just
consequence of hypocrisy.

From *The Rambler*, a "newspaper" published twice weekly and containing a single
essay written by Johnson. "Affectation" is the twentieth essay, published in 1750.
Capitalization has been modernized.

With the hypocrite, it is not at present my intention to expostulate,   4
though even he might be taught the excellency of virtue, by the
necessity of seeming to be virtuous; but the man of affectation
may, perhaps, be reclaimed, by finding how little he is likely to
gain by perpetual constraint, and incessant vigilance, and how
much more securely he might make his way to esteem, by cultivating
real, than displaying counterfeit qualities.

Every thing future is to be estimated by a wise man, with regard   5
to the probability of attaining it, and its value, when attained; and
neither of these considerations will much contribute to the encouragement of affectation. For, if the pinnacles of fame be, at
best, slippery, how unsteady must his footing be, who stands upon
pinnacles without foundation! If praise be made, by the inconstancy
and malice of those who must confer it, a blessing which no man
can promise himself from the most conspicuous merit, and vigorous
industry, how faint must be the hope of gaining it, when the
uncertainty is multiplied by the weakness of the pretensions! He
that pursues fame with just claims, trusts his happiness to the
winds; but he that endeavours after it, by false merit, has to fear,
not only the violence of the storm, but the leaks of his vessel.
Though he should happen to keep above water for a time, by the
help of a soft breeze, and a calm sea, at the first gust he must
inevitably founder, with this melancholy reflexion, that, if he would
have been content with his natural station, he might have escaped
his calamity. Affectation may possibly succeed for a time, and a
man may, by great attention, persuade others, that he really has
the qualities, which he presumes to boast; but the hour will come,
when he must exert them, and then whatever he enjoyed in praise,
he must suffer in reproach.

Applause and admiration are by no means to be counted among   6
the necessaries of life, and therefore any indirect arts to obtain
them have very little claim to pardon or compassion. There is
scarcely any man without some valuable or improveable qualities,
by which he might always secure himself from contempt; and
perhaps exemption from ignominy is the most eligible reputation,
as freedom from pain is, among some philosophers, the definition
of happiness.

If we therefore compare the value of the praise obtained by   7
fictitious excellence, even while the cheat is yet undiscovered, with
that kindness, which every man may win by his virtue, and that
esteem, which most men may gain by common understanding,
steadily and honestly applied, we shall find that when from the
adscititious happiness all the deductions are made, by fear and

accident there will remain nothing equiponderant to the security of truth. The state of the possessor of humble virtues, to the affecter of great excellencies, is that of a small well built cottage of stone, to the palace raised with ice by the Empress of *Russia*; it was for a time splendid and luminous, but the first sunshine melted it to nothing.

MARK TWAIN

Old Times on the Mississippi

When I was a boy, there was but one permanent ambition among my comrades in our village on the west bank of the Mississippi River. That was, to be a steamboatman. We had transient ambitions of other sorts, but they were only transient. When a circus came and went, it left us all burning to become clowns; now and then we had a hope that if we lived and were good, God would permit us to be pirates. These ambitions faded out, each in its turn; but the ambition to be a steamboatman always remained.

Once a day a cheap, gaudy packet arrived upward from St. Louis, and another downward from Keokuk. Before these events had transpired, the day was glorious with expectancy; after they had transpired, the day was a dead and empty thing. Not only the boys, but the whole village, felt this. After all these years I can picture that old time to myself now, just as it was then: the white town drowsing in the sunshine of a summer's morning; the streets empty, or pretty nearly so; one or two clerks sitting in front of the Water Street stores, with their splint-bottomed chairs tilted back against the wall, chins on breasts, hats slouched over their faces, asleep—with shingle shavings enough around to show what broke them down; a sow and a litter of pigs loafing along the sidewalk, doing a good business in water-melon rinds and seeds; two or three lonely little freight piles scattered about the levee; a pile of skids on the slope of the stone-paved wharf, and the fragrant town drunkard asleep in the shadow of them; two or three wood flats at the head of the wharf, but nobody to listen to the peaceful lapping of the wavelets against them; the great Mississippi, the

Originally published in *The Atlantic Monthly*, 1875.

majestic, the magnificent Mississippi, rolling its mile-wide tide along, shining in the sun; the dense forest away on the other side; the point above the town, and the point below, bounding the river glimpse and turning it into a sort of sea, and withal a very still and brilliant and lonely one. Presently a film of dark smoke appears above one of those remote points; instantly a negro drayman, famous for his quick eye and prodigious voice, lifts up the cry, "S-t-e-a-m-boat a-comin'!" and the scene changes! The town drunkard stirs, the clerks wake up, a furious clatter of drays follows, every house and store pours out a human contribution, and all in a twinkling the dead town is alive and moving. Drays, carts, men, boys, all go hurrying from many quarters to a common centre, the wharf.

Assembled there, the people fasten their eyes upon the coming 3 boat as upon a wonder they are seeing for the first time. And the boat *is* rather a handsome sight, too. She is long and sharp and trim and pretty; she has two tall, fancy-topped chimneys, with a gilded device of some kind swung between them; a fanciful pilot-house, all glass and gingerbread, perched on top of the texas deck behind them; the paddle-boxes are gorgeous with a picture or with gilded rays above the boat's name; the boiler deck, the hurricane deck, and the texas deck are fenced and ornamented with clean white railings; there is a flag gallantly flying from the jack-staff; the furnace doors are open and the fires glaring bravely; the upper decks are black with passengers; the captain stands by the big bell, calm, imposing, the envy of all; great volumes of the blackest smoke are rolling and tumbling out of the chimneys—a husbanded grandeur created with a bit of pitch pine just before arriving at a town; the crew are grouped on the forecastle; the broad stage is run far out over the port bow, and an envied deck-hand stands picturesquely on the end of it with a coil of rope in his hand; the pent steam is screaming through the gauge-cocks; the captain lifts his hand, a bell rings, the wheels stop; then they turn back, churning the water to foam, and the steamer is at rest. Then such a scramble as there is to get aboard, and to get ashore, and to take in freight and to discharge freight, all at one and the same time; and such a yelling and cursing as the mates facilitate it all with! Ten minutes later the steamer is under way again, with no flag on the jack-staff and no black smoke issuing from the chimneys. After ten more minutes the town is dead again, and the town drunkard asleep by the skids once more.

My father was a justice of the peace, and I suppose he possessed 4 the power of life and death over all men and could hang anybody that offended him. This was distinction enough for me as a general thing; but the desire to be a steamboatman kept intruding, nevertheless. I first wanted to be a cabin-boy, so that I could come out with a white apron on and shake a table-cloth over the side, where all my old comrades could see me; later I thought I would rather be the deck-hand who stood on the end of the stage-plank with the coil of rope in his hand, because he was particularly conspicuous. But these were only daydreams—they were too heavenly to be contemplated as real possibilities.

By and by one of our boys went away. He was not heard of 5 for a long time. At last he turned up as apprentice engineer or "striker" on a steamboat. This thing shook the bottom out of all my Sunday-school teachings. That boy had been notoriously worldly, and I just the reverse; yet he was exalted to this eminence, and I left in obscurity and misery. There was nothing generous about this fellow in his greatness. He would always manage to have a rusty bolt to scrub while his boat tarried at our town, and he would sit on the inside guard and scrub it, where we could all see him and envy him and loathe him. And whenever his boat was laid up he would come home and swell around the town in his blackest and greasiest clothes, so that nobody could help remembering that he was a steamboatman; and he used all sorts of steamboat technicalities in his talk, as if he were so used to them that he forgot common people could not understand them. He would speak of the "labboard" side of a horse in an easy, natural way that would make one wish he was dead. And he was always talking about "St. Looy" like an old citizen; he would refer casually to occasions when he "was coming down Fourth Street," or when he was "passing by the Planter's House," or when there was a fire and he took a turn on the brakes of "the old Big Missouri"; and then he would go on and lie about how many towns the size of ours were burned down there that day.

This fellow had money, too, and hair oil. Also an ignorant silver 6 watch and a showy brass watch chain. He wore a leather belt and used no suspenders. If ever a youth was cordially admired and hated by his comrades, this one was. No girl could withstand his charms. He cut out every boy in the village. When his boat blew up at last, it diffused a tranquil contentment among us such as we had not known for months. But when he came home the next week, alive, renowned, and appeared in church all battered up and bandaged, a shining hero, stared at and wondered over by everybody, it seemed to us that the partiality of Providence for an undeserving reptile had reached a point where it was open to criticism.

This creature's career could produce but one result, and it speedily followed. Boy after boy managed to get on the river. The minister's son became an engineer The doctor's and the postmaster's sons became "mud clerks"; the wholesale liquor dealer's son became a barkeeper on a boat; four sons of the chief merchant, and two sons of the county judge, became pilots. Pilot was the grandest position of all. The pilot, even in those days of trivial wages, had a princely salary—from a hundred and fifty to two hundred and fifty dollars a month, and no board to pay. Two months of his wages would pay a preacher's salary for a year. Now some of us were left disconsolate. We could not get on the river—at least our parents would not let us.   7

So by and by I ran away. I said I never would come home again till I was a pilot and could come in glory. But somehow I could not manage it. I went meekly aboard a few of the boats that lay packed together like sardines at the long St. Louis wharf, and very humbly inquired for the pilots, but got only a cold shoulder and short words from mates and clerks. I had to make the best of this sort of treatment for the time being, but I had comforting daydreams of a future when I should be a great and honored pilot, with plenty of money, and could kill some of these mates and clerks and pay for them.   8

Months afterward the hope within me struggled to a reluctant death, and I found myself without an ambition. But I was ashamed to go home. I was in Cincinnati, and I set to work to map out a new career. I packed my valise, and took passage on an ancient tub called the *Paul Jones*, for New Orleans. For the sum of sixteen dollars I had the scarred and tarnished splendors of her main saloon principally to myself, for she was not a creature to attract the eye of wiser travelers.   9

When we presently got under way and went poking down the broad Ohio, I became a new being, and the subject of my own admiration. I was a traveler! A word never had tasted so good in my mouth before. I had an exultant sense of being bound for mysterious lands and distant climes which I never have felt in so uplifting a degree since.   10

We reached Louisville in time—at least the neighborhood of it. We stuck hard and fast on the rocks in the middle of the river and lay there four days. I was now beginning to feel a strong sense of being a part of the boat's family, a sort of infant son to   11 the captain and younger brother to the officers. There is no estimating the pride I took in this grandeur, or the affection that began to swell and grow in me for those people. I could not know how the lordly steamboatman scorns that sort of presumption in a mere landsman. I particularly longed to acquire the least trifle of notice from the big stormy mate, and I was on the alert for an opportunity to do him a service to that end. It came at last. The riotous powwow of setting a spar was going on down on the forecastle, and I went down there and stood around in the way—or mostly skipping out of it—till the mate suddenly roared a general order for somebody to bring him a capstan bar. I sprang to his side and said: "Tell me where it is—I'll fetch it!"

If a rag-picker had offered to do a diplomatic service for the Emperor of Russia, the monarch could not have been more astounded than the mate was. He even stopped swearing. He stood and stared down at me. It took him ten seconds to scrape his disjointed remains together again. Then he said impressively: "Well, if this don't beat hell!" and turned to his work with the air of a man who had been confronted with a problem too abstruse for solution. 12

I crept away, and courted solitude for the rest of the day. I did not go to dinner; I stayed away from supper until everybody else had finished. I did not feel so much like a member of the boat's family now as before. However, my spirits returned, in installments, as we pursued our way down the river. I was sorry I hated the mate so, because it was not in (young) human nature not to admire him. He was huge and muscular, his face was bearded and whiskered all over; he had a red woman and a blue woman tatooed on his right arm,—one on each side of a blue anchor with a red rope to it; and in the matter of profanity he was perfect. When he was getting out cargo at a landing, I was always where I could see and hear. He felt all the sublimity of his great position, and made the world feel it, too. When he gave even the simplest order, he discharged it like a blast of lightning, and sent a long, reverberating peal of profanity thundering after it. I could not help contrasting the way in which the average landsman would give an order, with the mate's way of doing it. If the landsman should wish the gang-plank moved a foot farther forward, he would probably say: "James, or William, one of you push that plank forward, please"; but put the mate in his place, and he would roar out: "Here, now, start that gang-plank for'ard! Lively, now! *What*'re you about! Snatch it! *snatch* it! There! there! Aft again! aft again! Don't you hear me? Dash to it dash! are you going to *sleep* over it! 'Vast 13 heaving. 'Vast heaving, I tell you! Going to heave it clear astern? WHERE're you going with that barrel! *for'ard* with it 'fore I make you swallow it, you dash-dash-dash-*dashed* split between a tired mud-turtle and a crippled hearse-horse!"

I wished I could talk like that.   14

When the soreness of my adventure with the mate had somewhat   15
worn off, I began timidly to make up to the humblest official connected with the boat—the night watchman. He snubbed my advances at first, but I presently ventured to offer him a new chalk pipe, and that softened him. So he allowed me to sit with him by the big bell on the hurricane deck, and in time he melted into conversation. He could not well have helped it, I hung with such homage on his words and so plainly showed that I felt honored by his notice. He told me the names of dim capes and shadowy islands as we glided by them in the solemnity of the night, under the winking stars, and by and by got to talking about himself.

He seemed over-sentimental for a man whose salary was six   16
dollars a week—or rather he might have seemed so to an older person than I. But I drank in his words hungrily, and with a faith that might have moved mountains if it had been applied judiciously. What was it to me that he was soiled and seedy and fragrant with gin? What was it to me that his grammar was bad, his construction worse, and his profanity so void of art that it was an element of weakness rather than strength in his conversation? He was a wronged man, a man who had seen trouble, and that was enough for me.

As he mellowed into his plaintive history his tears dripped upon   17
the lantern in his lap, and I cried, too, from sympathy. He said he was the son of an English nobleman—either an earl or an alderman, he could not remember which, but believed he was both; his father, the nobleman, loved him, but his mother hated him from the cradle; and so while he was still a little boy he was sent to "one of them old, ancient colleges"—he couldn't remember which; and by and by his father died and his mother seized the property and "shook" him, as he phrased it. After his mother shook him, members of the nobility with whom he was acquainted used their influence to get him the position of "lob-lolly-boy in a ship"; and from that point my watchman threw off all trammels of date and locality and branched out into a narrative that bristled all along with incredible adventures; a narrative that was so reeking with bloodshed and so crammed with hair-breadth escapes and the most engaging and unconscious personal villainies, that I sat speechless, enjoying, shuddering, wondering, worshiping.

It was a sore blight to find out afterwards that he was a low, 18
vulgar, ignorant, sentimental, half-witted humbug, an untraveled
native of the wilds of Illinois, who had absorbed wildcat literature
and appropriated its marvels, until in time he had woven odds
and ends of the mess into this yarn, and then gone on telling it
to fledgelings like me, until he had come to believe it himself.

RUSSELL LYNES

The New Snobbism

There was a time not long ago when a snob was a snob and 1
as easy to recognize as a cock pheasant. In the days when Ward
McAllister was the arbiter of Newport society and when there
were precisely four hundred souls in New York worth knowing[1]
and only "nobodies" lived west of the Alleghenies, snobbishness
was a nice cleancut business that made careers for otherwise un-
occupied women and gave purpose to otherwise barren lives. In
those days the social order was stratified as tidily as the terracing
of an Italian garden, and a man could take his snobs or leave
them. But now the social snob, while not extinct, has gone underground (except for professionals such as head waiters and met-
ropolitan-hotel room clerks), and snobbery has emerged in a whole
new set of guises, for it is as indigenous to man's nature as ambition
and a great deal easier to exercise.

Snobbery has assumed so many guises, in fact, that it is, I believe, 2
time that someone attempt to impose order on what is at best a
confused situation. There are a few basic categories of snobs that
seem to include most of the more common species that one is
likely to encounter, or, indeed, to be. None of these categories is
new; there have always been, I presume, snobs of every sort,[2] but
now that the pre-eminence of the social variety has been submerged
in a wave of political and economic egalitarianism, and now that

From *Harper's Magazine*, November 1950.
1. McAllister retired from his legal practice in 1852 to devote himself to organizing
New York social life. He drew up a list of the city's top four hundred socialites for
Mrs. William Astor, who was hosting a small ball.
2. It is 102 years since William Makepeace Thackeray published his *Book of Snobs*,
a series of facetious essays that originally appeared in *Punch*. Mr. Thackeray's snobs
are largely of the social sort. [author's note]

we find ourselves in an era in which the social scientists believe that it is somehow good for us to be ticketed and classified, let us sort out the most common practitioners of the sneer.

The Intellectual Snob is of such distinguished lineage and comes   3
from such established precedent that he is dignified by a mention in Webster's ("one who repels the advances of those whom he regards as his inferiors; as, an intellectual snob"). The other categories are less well known and less well documented. For convenience, let us call them the Regional Snobs, the Moral Snobs, the Sensual Snobs, the Emotional Snobs, the Physical Snobs, the Occupational Snobs, and finally, the Reverse Snobs or Anti-snob Snobs. Before we examine these, we should be aware that economic and social boundaries, while they may occasionally serve as guide ropes, are on the whole unimportant in considering the various forms of condescension and the various attitudes of superiority that distinguish the true snob from the merely vain man, woman, or child.

Snobbishness, as we will use the word, implies both an upward   4
and a downward movement—a scramble upward to emulate or outdo those whose position excels one's own, and a look downward on (or sometimes straight through) those less happily endowed than one's self. The true snob never rests; there is always a higher goal to attain, and there are, by the same token, always more and more people to look down upon. The snob is almost by definition insecure in his social (in the larger sense) relationships, and he resorts to snobbishness as a means of massaging his ego. Since scarcely anyone is so secure that his ego does not sometimes need a certain amount of external manipulation, there is scarcely anyone who isn't a snob of some sort. As a matter of fact the gods of the Greeks and the Romans were frightful snobs, morally, physically, and emotionally, and it is not uncommon for civilized peoples to worship snobbery. It is the Christian religion that promoted the virtue of humility for us, and of all the virtues it is the most difficult to come by. Let us not, then, be snobbish about snobs—at least not yet.

It is not my intention to apply the scientific method to the   5
definition of the categories which we shall examine, though each species will be seen to have its sub-species and each sub-species to have many variants. I mean this to be suggestive, merely a sketch that will enable the reader to glimpse the vast possibilities that a methodical study of snobs by a diligent social scientist might uncover.

II

Our first category is the Regional Snobs, commonly known in   6
the south as Virginians, in the West as Californians, and in the

East as Bostonians. This, however, should be recognized for what it is, a mere colloquialism. The Regional Snob can come from anywhere, and is readily distinguished by his patronizing attitude toward anywhere else. He lets it be known that there is no place to match the seat of his origin; indeed, he seems surprised or amused that people in other places are so much like people. The Asturians who live in the north of Spain, for example, look with special distaste on the citizens of the neighboring province, Galicia, and they have a saying that "a Galician is the animal that most closely resembles a human being." In Texas it is said that you should never ask a man where he comes from. "If he's a Texan," they say, "he'll tell you. If he's not don't embarrass him." These are not as extreme cases as they might seem. It was recorded a decade ago that a boy who lived on Martha's Vineyard, an island off the Massachusetts coast, was assigned the problem in school of writing a composition about the then Duce of Italy. His paper started with the sentence: "Mussolini is an off-islander."

But let us consider more common types of Regional Snobs. In Vermont, for example, the Regional Snob is generally called a "native" to distinguish him from the group known as "summer people." The aloofness of the Vermont native, a man proud of his thrift, of the bleakness of his winters, and especially of the fact that he has managed to squeeze a living out of rocky hillsides and out of "summer people,"[3] has a special laconic quality that is guaranteed to freeze the marrow of, say, a Texan. This kind of Regional snobbism is of the *We've had it tougher than anybody* variety, and is the opposite of the California type which is of the *We know how to live better than you do* kind, or of the Gracious Living types found in the South, notably in Virginia, in South Carolina, and in the New Orleans vicinity.

These types are, more or less, Area Snobs and should be distinguished from the local or home-town varieties which demonstrate certain cultural patterns quite different from those found in general geographical areas. The local snob does not even in many cases recognize his home town as anything very special; his vision may be myopic to the extent of permitting everything beyond the end of his particular street to go out of focus. "The other side of the tracks" is a phrase less frequently heard than it was a generation or so ago. We live in an age of "developments"—real estate developments, housing developments, community developments—

---

3. And more recently, with the advent of the Ski Snobs, out of "winter people" as well. [author's note]

of "projects" and of subdivisions, and the railroad tracks have lost
some of their social significance in this age of busses and automobiles.
So we have subdivision dwellers looking down upon development
dwellers, and development dwellers turning their heads away from
project dwellers, and project dwellers scornful of tenement dwellers.
But the genuine home-town snob is rather more special than any
of these.

Boston is too well known for its special brand of provincial   9
hauteur to need discussion here, but the New York brand is less
well documented and will serve to demonstrate one of the extreme
forms of local snobbism. This is the Cultural Capital variety, or
Anything or anybody of any interest comes here kind, that makes the
New Yorker when visiting in any other city assume an air of
condescension that has both an overhead spin and a reverse twist.
"You know," the New Yorker[4] will say when visiting a city in the
Middle West, "I think it's really terribly interesting *out here.*" It
is a wonder that so few New Yorkers get their throats cut in what
they think of as (but do not call) "the provinces." In its most
advanced forms Cultural Capital Snobbism will bend all the way
over backward and touch its heels with its hair with some such
observation as: "I think New Yorkers are the most provincial
people in the world, don't you?" The born and bred New Yorker
is rare (or at least thinks of himself as rare), and in general the
New Yorker by adoption is the more virulent of the species.

At the other end of the scale we find Small Town Snobbism: 10
the *I have lived here longer than anyone* type vies with the type who
makes much of the fact that only people who rub elbows with
the members of a small community really understand the meaning
of life. This latter type, like the Cultural Capital Snob, is usually
a member of the community by adoption, having fled from the
city in order to discover what he calls "real values." Sometimes
the members of this group are summer people gone native who
retain certain characteristic attributes of their type such as station
wagons, and dress themselves in more elaborately rural costumes
(blue jeans, checked wool shirts, even straw hats) than any genuinely
rural inhabitant would consider proper or necessary. Another variant
of this species is the ex-urbanite who buys a farm in order to "get
next to the soil." These might be called the Eternal Verities Snobs,
Back to the Land Division, and are very likely to be authors.[5]

4. Not to be confused with the magazine of the same name. It is not within the
scope of this essay to discuss institutional snobbism. [author's note]
5. Indeed, Connecticut and Bucks County have been so overrun by authors that
a real farmer can hardly afford to buy land there. [author's note]

Before we proceed to our next category, there is one offshoot 11
of the Regional Snobs which bears brief mention: The World Is
My Home species,[6] made up of people who pride themselves on
the fact that they are as much as home in Shepheard's Hotel in
Cairo as in the Casino at Monte Carlo or in the Ritz Bar in Paris
or in the Pump Room in Chicago or in less expensive saloons in
any of these places. The members of this category like to think of
themselves as "the international set" and are frequently remittance
men, decayed nobility, career diplomats, overseas respresentatives
(and their wives) of American industries, wealthy divorcees, or
rich refugees. They regard every international problem or crisis
chiefly as a personal inconvenience, and every visa in their passports
as a mark of sophistication. The natives of any place they visit
have no other function but to serve them, and their technique for
insulting waiters is unsurpassed. Although the world is their home,
they are in one sense the most provincial snobs of all, for their
real world consists of a few thousand wanderers, and their horizons
are limited to the chips on the table, the bottles on the bar, and
the crystals in the chandeliers of hotel dining rooms, and when
out of doors, they darken their little world with sun glasses.[7] They
have an unmitigated scorn for all tourists and are ashamed and
embarrassed by their compatriots who travel abroad.

It is probable that as the world grows smaller, Regional Snobbism 12
will increase. It is a logical antidote to political efforts to make
man love his neighbor.

III

Like the Regional Snobs, the number of Moral Snobs is legion 13
and they love their neighbors no more dearly. Oscar Wilde, a
really accomplished snob, said that "Morality is simply the attitude
we adopt toward people we personally dislike." But the Moral
Snob carries it further than that; his snobbishness extends to people
he doesn't even know. Morality is both a public and a private
matter, to be sure, and it is characteristic of the Moral Snob to
put a good deal of ornamental fretwork on his public façade and
let the private places of his personality be slovenly. To call him a
hypocrite would be to attribute vices to his virtues; he is not so
positive a character as that. He does not necessarily want to get

6. Not to be confused with the One World Snobs. [author's note]
7. There are two important variants of this species: (1) the Language Snob, who
pretends to five or six languages and sprinkles his conversation with French, Spanish,
and German phrases, and (2) the Reverse Language Snob, who prides himself on
getting along everywhere with his native tongue on the assumption that anyone
who doesn't know it is a fool or worse. [author's note]

away with anything, but he is always quite sure that everyone
else does, or would if he didn't keep a sharp eye on them.

In our day there are two main categories of Moral Snobs—the   14
Religious Snobs and the Tolerance Snobs. In mentioning the former,
I am aware that I am on delicate ground, but the Religious Snobs
are identified with no particular sect or creed, and the true believer
is rarely, if ever, snobbish about it. The only thing that they seem
to have in common is the conviction that those who disapprove
of their faith or the methods by which they try to spread it are
"bigots."[8]

Sometimes opposed to the Religious Snob and sometimes allied   15
with him is the Tolerance Snob, a species of comparatively recent
origin. It should be noted that he turns the tables on the Religious
Snob for lack of tolerance toward disbelievers and backsliders, and
in such cases he often calls the Religious Snob a "bigot." The
bigot is a most useful foil to the Tolerance Snob. But whether he
is at loggerheads with the Religious Snob or not, the *I am more
tolerant than anybody* Snob has a special predilection for getting
his name printed on the letterheads of societies for the prevention
and furthering of things.

In contrast with the Moral Snobs are the Sensual Snobs who   16
take special pride in being able to wrest more pleasure per cell
from the flesh than anyone else. In this general category which
is even more elastic than I mean to make it we find the Food and
Drink, the Sex, the Indolence, and the Health and Hygiene Snobs.

The Food and Drink species is almost too common to require   17
more than a passing word. The Food and Herb Snobs while somewhat old-fashioned still persist; but this species, I believe, is less
in the ascendancy now than the Pot Luck Snobs, Casserole Division,
or the *This is something I just threw together at the last minute* species.
The mussels-snails-brains-and-garlic group continues to operate,
especially in areas where mussels, snails, brains, and garlic are
still considered somewhat outrageous, and the Plain American
Food Group ("If you want a good cup of coffee and a decent
hamburger, eat in a diner.") flourishes in metropolitan areas where
good foreign cooking is commonplace.

The Foreign Food Snob often can be identified by his attitude   18
of frustration. The "little place" that he discovered and which used

8. The most extreme example of this type of snobbism I have heard of is credited
to the family of the Duc de Levis-Mirepoix, one of the oldest important French
titles, that dates back to the ninth century. The family is purported to be descended
from the sister of the Virgin Mary, and when the members of the Levis-Mirepoix
family pray, they are said to say: *"Ave Maria, ma cousine . . . ."* [author's note]

to be so good has always just recently gone to pot. "You know how it is," he says. "The frog legs Provençal used to be superb, but now the place has got popular, and the food isn't fit to eat any more."

The Drink Snobs are, of all categories, the easiest to identify 19 since the rules are so well established. They insist that their whiskey be bonded; they know what proof it is; and they drink it neat or "on the rocks"; their Scotch is "V.O." or "V.V.O."; their martinis are as dry as almost no vermouth can make them (in restaurants where they suspect the martinis may be somewhat amber in hue they order Gibsons and remove the onions); and they always nod at the waiter after looking at the date on a bottle of wine. Only the genuine connoisseur has the self-assurance to send back a bottle of wine. Some Drink Snobs take special pride in the amount they can consume and not show it; others take special pride in having a worse hangover than anybody ever had before.

The Sex Snobs have been adequately documented by the Phys- 20 iology Department of Indiana University. It may, however, be interesting to note that the publication of Dr. Kinsey's first volume, *Sexual Behavior in the Human Male*, produced two new manifestations of the Sex Snob: first, those of the *I could tell Kinsey a thing or two* variety; and second, the species that insisted that the excitement about the book was all nonsense—"Why I've known that for years." The attitude of the British towards the Kinsey Report reveals an interesting provincialism. I was told by Dr. Kinsey that in general the reaction of the British professional and, if I may be permitted the phrase, the lay press, was: "No doubt this is all very true about Americans, but we are not interested. The British don't behave like that."

The Indolence Snobs, on the other hand, have been epitomized 21 by an Englishman, Cyril Connolly, in his book, *The Unquiet Grave*. "Others merely live," he wrote; "I vegetate." An interesting counterpart to Mr. Connolly's form of snobbism is to be found in those who make a great show of doing nothing, of sleeping late, of lying in the sun, of always having time to amuse themselves and their friends, and who at the same time produce a great deal of work. These are the people who express their superiority by saying, "I just tossed off this novel in my spare time," or, "I just thought of this new international trade combine over a game of canasta in Miami one evening."

The Health and Hygiene Snobs may more properly belong with 22 the Moral Snobs than with the Sensual Snobs. There is no denying, however, that there is sensual pleasure in the subjugation of the flesh, and that this is part of the routine behavior of the Health and Hygiene Snob. It is a far stronger motive than mere laziness that keeps a man or woman horizontal in the hot sun for a few hours in order to turn first red and then brown; it is certainly not morality that sends men and women to gymnasiums to reduce one portion of the anatomy and exaggerate another; nor is it laziness that makes them diet, abstain from (or at least be ostentatiously moderate about) liquor, and get to bed at what they call "a reasonable hour." It is the delight of being able to look down upon those who, to use their phrase, "don't take proper care of themselves." Sex, of course, enters strongly into this, but then so does a feeling of moral superiority. I have no doubt that the social scientists will in time be able to isolate the Health and Hygiene Snob from the Moral Snob.

While we are on the subject of the body, let us not overlook   23
the Physical Prowess Snobs, more common among males than among females, but by no means limited to one sex. The Physical Prowess Snob is not necessarily an expert athlete; indeed he is likely not to be. It is the mediocre tennis player, for example, hitting everything hard if inaccurately, who is lofty about the player who may be able to beat him merely by getting the ball back.

No matter what you may think of the Sensual Snobs, it cannot   24
be denied that, unlike the Moral Snobs, they are a great pleasure to themselves.

                                              •

                                   IV

Since the emotions carry us rapidly in dangerous directions and   25
soon lead us to the darkest corners of man's nature, we must proceed to the dissection of the Emotional Snobs with caution. This is the *I feel things more deeply than anybody* variety, and there is likely to be at least one in every family.

Probably the largest single subdivision of this category is the   26
Love Snob, a type which finds its roots among adolescents, who since they are having their first encounter with sexual love, believe that no one has ever been so in love before. Their intolerance of their juniors is matched only by their scorn for their elders, and this can set a pattern for adult love that is difficult to break. The so-called "great lovers" do not, I believe, belong in the Love Snob category but rather in that of the Sex Snob. It was surely not about the intensity of his emotions that Don Giovanni, with his list of 1,100 ladies, was vain.

The Mother Love Snob, or *I give my all for my children* type, is   27
not uncommon among women who are not Sex Snobs, and it is probable that the second volume of the Kinsey Report may shed

some light on this. The Filial Love Snob, or Mom Snob, is not in my experience nearly so common as English authors, such as Geoffrey Gorer, or Americans, such as Philip Wylie, contend that it is. That is not to say that the exploitation of Mom Snobbery by the florists once a year has not given it at least a seasonal boost.

The Marital and/or Soul Mate Snobs are not rare, though they are particularly tiresome because they are, by the very nature of their snobbery, raised to a higher power. Since it takes two to make Soul Mates, they are twice as tiresome as other snobs. 28

The Popularity Snobs also belong in the Emotional group; in a sense they are everybody's Soul Mate. To use their own vernacular, they have a "way with people" and can "get along with anybody." Theirs is the hauteur of affable condescension, and traditionally the species is common among traveling salesmen, Rotarians, public relations counselors, and politicians, though it would be a mistake not to recognize the far wider ramifications of this type wherever we meet them. Mass demonstrations of Popularity Snobbism are known as conventions.[9] The typical member of this species rarely uses the form "mister" in addressing anyone, no matter how brief or perfunctory the acquaintance. He is strictly a first-name man, and has little respect for anyone's dignity or privacy. He assumes that everybody loves him, and he reasons there is no privacy in a public love affair. 29

By contrast the Unpopularity Snob, or *Nobody can get along with me* type, takes two principal forms.[10] The first is an imperious and often petulant species who by dint of the loftiness of his position or intellect makes much of the fact that he can't be bothered with boors and idiots. He works with his door closed; he throws all second-class mail into the wastebasket without opening it; and he never seems to be able to remember anyone's name, or if he does, he mispronounces it. When you meet him, he says "hello," but looks past you, as though you were obstructing his view. The second is the sensitive, or *I'm too special,* type who is "misunderstood" by crass and materialistic people. This species is likely to gravitate in the general direction of the arts and crafts and sooner or later to metropolitan areas. 30

9. College Reunions also figure in this category. They provide opportunities for the temporary renewal of Popularity Snobbism in those who were popular in college but have been slipping ever since. [author's note]

10. The persistence of one type of Unpopularity Snob is demonstrated by the number of adults who take special care to make the point that anybody who amounts to anything was "unhappy in school." It is likely to express itself in some such direct statement as "I was the most unpopular boy (girl) in my class." [author's note]

V

Somewhere between the Emotional Snobs and the Intellectual   31
Snobs[11] are the Sensitivity or Taste Snobs—those who are scornful
of any whose aesthetic antennae they consider less receptive than
their own. It is customary, I believe, to classify the Art Snobs, the
Literary Snobs, and the Musical Snobs with the Intellectual Snobs,
but it seems to me that they belong in a limbo between the
Emotional and the Intellectual categories, with plenty of latitude
to permit them to jump either way.[12] Furthermore the matter of
taste comprehends more than just the arts (and, as we shall see,
includes certain other vagaries of man's predilection for lording it
over man). But let us take the arts first.

To categorize the Art Snobs into all of their many subdivisions   32
would be an intricate and, I am afraid, tiresome business. We
would, for example, have to consider the various shadings that
range all the way from the Traditionalist or Permanent Value Snobs
to the Modern or *I always keep an open mind* group. There are,
however, a few basic behavior patterns that betray the Art Snob
at any level. In a gallery he can be observed to stand back from
a picture at some distance, his head cocked slightly to one side,
and then after a rather long period of gazing (during which he
may occasionally squint his eyes) he will approach to within a
few inches of the picture and examine the brush-work; he will
then return to his former distant position, give the picture another
glance, and walk away. The Art Snob can be recognized in the
home (*i.e.* your home) by the quick look he gives the pictures on
your walls, quick but penetrating, as though he were undressing
them. This is followed either by complete and obviously pained
silence or by a comment such as, "That's really a very pleasant
little water color you have there." In his own house his manner
is also slightly deprecating. If you admire a print on his wall, he
is likely to say, "I'm glad you like it. It's really not bad considering
it is such a late impression." Or if he is in the uppermost reaches
of Art Snobs and owns an "old master" which you admire, he
will say, "Of course Berenson lists it as a Barna da Sienna, but

---

11. So commonly known and, as we have noted, so well established as to need
no discussion in this brief survey. [author's note]
12. It is interesting to note in connection with the publication of a new (1950)
typographically eccentric magazine devoted to taste, that as an undergraduate Thackeray at Cambridge in 1829 contributed to a magazine called the *Snob.* An advertisement
described it as follows: "Each number contained only six pages . . . printed on tinted
paper of different colors, green, pink, and yellow." The *Snob* lasted for eleven
numbers. [author's note]

I've never satisfied myself that it isn't from the hand of one of his pupils."

The Literary Snob has not only read the book you are reading, 33 but takes pleasure in telling you the names of all the earlier and more obscure books by the same author, and why each one was superior to the better known one that has come to your attention.

Musical Snobs are in general of two sorts—Classical Snobs and 34 Jazz Snobs. The former can sometimes be identified at concerts because they keep their eyes closed. This can for obvious reasons be misleading, but if closed eyes are accompanied by a regular movement of the hands in time with the music, it is clear that the listener is beating time to himself. This is characteristic of the lower orders of Classical Snobs. If he has a score of the music which he follows while it is being played, he may be a professional musician looking for subtleties of interpretation; he may, on the other hand, merely be a higher order of Classical Snob. The surest way to identify the Classical Snob is to see whether he comes back after the intermission or not; if he stays only for the more difficult or abstruse part of the program and ignores the more popular portion, he is either a snob or a professional critic, or possibly both.

Musical Snobs, Jazz Division, beat time not with their hands 35 but with their feet. They do not talk about records or recordings but about specific choruses, solo passages, or "breaks." They know the dates and numbers of original pressings and occasionally they collect never-played records much the way some book collectors prefer rare copies with uncut pages. They are well grounded in the brand of jazz they refer to as "authentic" (New Orleans, Memphis, Chicago) and they are extremely partisan about what they consider to be "advanced" (Progressive Jazz, Bebop, or even Dixieland). There are some overtones of social and racial snobbery in the way Jazz Snobs identify themselves with jazz musicians.

Also among the Taste Snobs are to be found the Clothes Snobs, 36 both male and female. In this instance the female is a good deal more interesting and varied than the male, for while the male "sharp dressers" are snobs of a sort, there is only one male Dress Snob who needs to arrest our attention: the Conservative Dress Snob. The buttons on the sleeves of his jacket actually unbutton. There is no padding on his shoulders. The collar of his shirt is a little too high for him, so that it bulges and wrinkles slightly, and it buttons down. He cares deeply about good leather and good tweed, but most of all he cares about being conspicuously inconspicuous.

The female Dress Snobs offer a far more complicated range of   37
types and it requires some temerity on the part of a man to broach
this subject at all. In general, however, women seem to fall into
the following categories of sartorial superiority:

1. The Under-dressed Snob, who wouldn't be caught dead at a
cocktail party in a cocktail dress, and a similar type, the next on
our list. . . .

2. The Basic Dress Snob, who believes that she has so much
personality that she can get away anywhere in a simple black
("basic") dress and one piece of "heirloom" jewelry.

3. The Good Quality Snob, or wearer of muted tweeds, cut almost
exactly the same from year to year, often with a hat of the same
material. This type is native to the Boston North Shore, the Chicago
North Shore, the North Shore of Long Island, to Westchester County,
the Philadelphia Main Line, the Peninsula Area of San Francisco,
etc. It rides horses and is rare in Southern California, except for
Pasadena.

4. The Band Box Snob—common among professional fashion
models and among other young women trying to make their way
in the big city. They look as though they had just stepped out of
Vogue or *Mademoiselle*. They are never ahead of the fashion, but
they are screamingly up-to-date.

5. The Dowdy, or *Who the hell cares about fashion,* Snob.

6. The Personal Style, or *I know more about my type than the experts,*
Snob. This final type considers her taste to be above the whims
of mere fashion. She is so chic that she believes that it is un-chic
to be merely fashionable.[13]

Good taste is everyone's prerogative (no one willingly confesses   38
to bad taste), and so nearly everyone is a Taste Snob of one sort
or another, and often of many sorts at the same time.

VI

Our next category, the Occupational or Job Snobs, are of two   39
sorts: those who are snobbish about the kind of occupation by
which they live, and those who are snobbish about how they
perform in their occupation. Few women, for example, are snobbish
about being housekeepers; many are snobbish about the way they
keep house. Many men, on the other hand, are snobbish about
the positions they hold and less snobbish about how they perform

---

13. The outstanding example of this in our time is the Queen Mother of England.
[author's note]

in them. But first let's take the women. The woman whose dearest ambition is an absolutely well ordered and efficiently run house looks down upon the woman who firmly believes that it is nonsense to spend so much time over the household that there is not time for what she calls "life." She in turn looks down upon the whole-souled housekeeper. It boils down to a conflict between two aphorisms—"cleanliness is next to godliness" and "a little dirt never hurt anybody"—which, if we weren't careful, would lead us back to our discussion of Moral Snobs. Of course both of these types are looked upon with scorn by the female Career Snob who manages with overbearing aplomb both a job and a household.

The hierarchy within which men work is quite different, and makes quite different demands. The professional man feels somewhat lordly toward the business man or "money grubber" and considers him lacking in sensibility and intellectual curiosity and nearsighted to the point of seeing nothing beyond the sales chart but the golf course or the bridge table. He is likely to blame the world's ills on the business man's greed and lack of cultural understanding. The business man, on the other hand, thinks of many professional men as "dreamers" and "idealists" or even as "panty-waists." This applies especially to artists, writers, actors, musicians, scholars, and editors. The business man is less likely to be snobbish about physicians, lawyers, and engineers because he considers them, like himself, to be "practical" men. His most unlimited scorn is for bureaucrats who "have never met a payroll."

Performance on the job is less likely to matter than position, as I have said, but there is the Efficiency Snob whose pose is primarily one of crispness. He answers the phone by barking just his last name; he is inclined to have rows of buttons on his telephone or desk and almost no papers. His memoranda are brief to the point of being curt, he considers the word "please" something that has no place among desks and typewriters, and he wants things done "soonest." He thinks of himself as a "trouble shooter" and makes lists of possible troubles to shoot. As each one is shot, it is crossed off the list with a firm black line. Accomplishment is measured by the number of black lines, and everyone who doesn't measure up to his particular standards of efficiency is "hopeless." The reverse of this type, also common, is the man who lives behind a mess of papers, pencils, and paper clips and "can never find anything" and yet manages to get out the work.

The results produced by the Efficiency Snob and the Inefficiency Snob are just about the same.

Performance off the job often reveals the Manual Dexterity Snob who can do complicated mechanical things with his hands and who considers all who can't to be fumbling idiots, and the opposite of this, the All-Thumbs Snob, commonly found among women. Men who are all thumbs are sometimes reticient about it; women rarely are.

VII

We have noted as we went along that almost every kind of snobbism has its opposite; the Moral Snob contrasts with the Sensual Snob, the Manual Dexterity Snob with the All-Thumbs Snob, the Efficiency Snob with the Inefficiency Snob, and so on. But these contrasting sources of the sneer should not be confused with our final category, the Reverse Snob or Anti-snob Snob. This is the snob who finds snobbery so distasteful that he (or she) is extremely snobbish about nearly everybody since nearly everybody is a snob about something. This is the man who tries so hard to be "natural," so hard to be "just folks," so hard to avoid having anyone else think he is a snob, that he plays a game which (if I may be forgiven for being a Language Snob for a moment) is *faux naif* He would not, for example, ever be caught using a foreign phrase, as I have, lest it be thought pretentious even when it serves better than any other he can think of to covey its meaning. Or if he is forced to use it (or even a foreign name, let's say) he Americanizes its pronunciation lest anyone think him up-stage.[14] He makes much of the fact that simple, uneducated people are wiser and nicer than sophisticated and educated people, even wise and nice educated people. He plays down his own education and accomplishments with an elaborate display of modesty and is likely to introduce a very erudite and perceptive observation with the phrase, "Of course I know so little about this I have no right to an opinion," or, "I know this is probably stupid of me, but. . . ." Of all the snobs the Reverse Snob is probably the most snobbish; he is so sure of himself that he intentionally puts other people in a position where they have to play his game or feel like snobs themselves. The false simplicity of the Reverse Snob stands in direct and glaring contrast to the genuinely modest man.

By and large it is only the very great who are not snobbish at all. They are the ones who are modest about their accomplishments because they have devoted their lives to achieving some kind of understanding and so have developed a deep tolerance for ignorance. By the same token the serious professionals in any field are not likely to be snobbish about other serious professionals, whether they are doctors or actors or writers or mechanics or business men

44

45

14. "They spell it Vinci and pronounce it Vinchy; foreigners always spell better than they pronounce."—Mark Twain, *The Innocents Abroad.* [author's note]

or masons or even, let it be said, housekeepers. As we noted at the outset, it is those who are unsure of themselves and are seeking security in their social relationships who have provided us with this incomplete list of Snobs.

It will not have escaped the reader (and so I might as well admit 46 it) that this cursory attempt to classify and define snobs is an example not only of Intellectual Snobbism but of Moral, Sensual, Occupational, Political, Emotional, and above all of Reverse or Anti-snob Snobbism. I am sure there is no greater snob than a snob who thinks he can define a snob.

TOM WOLFE

Hugh Hefner

Now, about Hefner. I was heading for California from New York 1 and I happened to stop off in Chicago. I was walking down North Michigan Avenue when I ran into a man from the Playboy organization, Lee Gottlieb. Something he said made me assume that Hefner was out of town.

"Out of town?" said Gottlieb. "Hef never leaves his house." 2

"Never?" 3

Never, said Gottlieb. At least not for months at a time, and even 4 then only long enough to get in a limousine and go to the airport and fly to New York for a TV show or to some place or other for the opening of a new Playboy Club. This fascinated me, the idea that Hefner, the Main Playboy himself, was now a recluse. The next afternoon I went to the Playboy offices on East Ohio Street to see about getting in to see him. In the office they kept track of Hefner's physical posture in his Mansion, which was over on North State Parkway, as if by play-by-play Telex. He was flat out in bed asleep, they told me, and wouldn't be awake until around midnight. That night I was killing time in a dive in downtown Chicago when a courier materialized and told me Hefner was now on his feet and could see me.

Hefner's Playboy Mansion had a TV eye at the front portals and 5 huge black guards or major-domos inside. *Nubian slaves,* I kept saying to myself. One of the blacks led me up a grand staircase covered in red wall-to-wall, to a massive carved-wood doorway

Excerpted from the introduction to *The Pump House Gang* (1969).

bearing the inscription, *Si Non Oscillas, Noli Tintinnare,* "If you don't swing, don't ring." Inside were Hefner's private chambers. Hefner came charging out of a pair of glass doors within. He was wound up and ready to go. "Look at this!" he said. "Isn't this fantastic!" It was an issue of *Ramparts* magazine that had just come. It had a glossy foldout, like the one in *Playboy.* Only this one had a picture of Hefner. In the picture he was wearing a suit and smoking a pipe. "Isn't this fantastic!" Hefner kept saying. Right now he was wearing silk pajamas, a bathrobe, and a pair of slippers with what looked like embroidered wolf heads on them. This was not, however, because he had just gotten up. It was his standard wear for the day, this day, every day, the uniform of the contemporary recluse.

There were several people in attendance at the midnight hour.   6
The *dame d'honneur* of the palace, who was named Michele; Gottlieb; a couple of other Playboy personnel; the blacks: they were all dressed, however. Hefner showed me through his chambers. The place was kept completely draped and shuttered. The only light, day or night, was electric. It would be impossible to keep track of the days in there. And presently Hefner jumped onto . . . the center of his world, the bed in his bedroom. Aimed at the bed was a TV camera he was very proud of. Later on *Playboy* ran a cartoon showing a nude man and woman in a huge bed with a TV set facing them, and the man is saying, "And now, darling, how about an instant replay." Hefner hit a dial and the bed started revolving . . .

All I could think of at that moment was Jay Gatsby in the   7
Fitzgerald novel. Both were scramblers who came up from out of nowhere to make their fortunes and build their palaces and ended up in regal isolation. But there was a major difference between Hefner and Gatsby. Hefner no longer dreamed, if he ever did, of making the big social leap to East Egg. It was at least plausible for Gatsby to hope to make it into Society. But Hefner? He has made a fortune, created an empire, and the Playboy Beacon shines out over the city and the Great Lakes. But socially Hefner is still a man who runs a tit magazine and a string of clubs that recall the parlor floor; not the upper floors but the parlor floor—of a red-flock whorehouse. There is no Society in Chicago for Hugh Hefner.

So he has gone them one better. He has started his own league.   8
He has created his own world, in his own palace. He has created his own statusphere. The outside world comes to him, including the talented and the celebrated. Jules Feiffer stays awhile in his scarlet guest suite. Norman Mailer skinnydips in his Playboy swimming pool. He has his courtiers, his girls, and his Nubian slaves.

Not even God's own diurnal light rhythm intrudes upon the order that Hefner has founded inside.

What a marvelous idea! After all, the community has never 9 been one great happy family for all men. In fact, I would say the opposite has been true. Community status systems have been games with few winners and many who feel like losers. What an intriguing thought—for a man to take his new riches and free time and his machines and *split* from *communitas* and start his own league. He will still have status competition—but he invents the rules.

Why has no one ever done it before? Well, of course, people 10 have. Robin Hood did it. Spades, homosexuals, artists, and street gangs have done it. All sorts of outlaws, and outcasts, by necessity or choice. The intriguing thing today, I was to find, is that so many Americans and Englishmen of middle and lower incomes are now doing the same thing. Not out of "rebellion" or "alienation"—they just want to be happy winners for a change.

What is a California electronics worker making $18,000 a year 11 supposed to do with his new riches? Set about getting his son into Culver Military and himself and the wife into the Doral Beach Country Club? Socially, he is a glorified mechanic. Why not, à la Hefner, put it all into turning his home into a palace of technological glories—and extend that abroad in the land with a Buick Estate Wagon and a Pontiac GTO—and upon the seas with an Evinrude cruiser and even into the air with a Cessna 172? Why not surround the palace with my favorite piece of landscaping of the happy worker suburbs of the American West, the Home Moat. It is about three feet wide and a foot and a half deep. Instructions for placing rocks, flowers, and shrubs are available. The Home Moat is a psychological safeguard against the intrusion of the outside world. The Home Moat guards against the fear that *It* is going to creep up in the night and press its nose against your picture window.

PAUL FUSSELL

The Middle Class

The middle class is distinguishable more by its earnestness and 1 psychic insecurity than by its middle income. I have known some very rich people who remain stubbornly middle-class, which is to say they remain terrified at what others think of them, and to

Excerpted from *Class: A Guide through the American Status System* (1984).

avoid criticism are obsessed with doing everything right. The middle class is the place where table manners assume an awful importance and where net curtains flourish to conceal activities like hiding the salam' (a phrase no middle-class person would indulge in, surely: the fatuous *making love* is the middle-class equivalent). The middle class, always anxious about offending, is the main market for "mouthwashes," and if it disappeared the whole "deodorant" business would fall to the ground. If physicians tend to be upper-middle-class, dentists are gloomily aware that they're middle, and are said to experience frightful status anxieties when introduced socially to "physicians"—as dentists like to call them. (Physicians call themselves *doctors,* and enjoy doing this in front of dentists, as well as college professors, chiropractors, and divines.)

"Status panic": that's the affliction of the middle class, according to C. Wright Mills, author of *White Collar* (1951) and *The Power Elite* (1956). Hence the middles' need to accumulate credit cards and take in *The New Yorker,* which it imagines registers upper-middle taste. Its devotion to that magazine, or its ads, is a good example of Mills's description of the middle class as the one that tends "to borrow status from higher elements." *New Yorker* advertisers have always known this about their audience, and some of their pseudo-upper-middle gestures in front of the middles are hilarious, like one recently flogging expensive stationery, here, a printed invitation card. The pretentious Anglophile spelling of the second word strikes the right opening note:

> In honour of
> Dr and Mrs Leonard Adam Westman,
> Dr and Mrs Jeffrey Logan Brandon
> request the pleasure of your company for

[at this point the higher classes might say *cocktails,* or, if thoroughly secure, *drinks.* But here, "Dr." and Mrs. Brandon are inviting you to consume specifically—]

> Champagne and Caviar
> on Friday, etc., etc.
> Valley Hunt Club,
> Stamford, Conn., etc.

The only thing missing is the brand names of the refreshments.

If the audience for that sort of thing used to seem the most deeply rooted in time and place, today it seems the class that's the most rootless. Members of the middle class are not only the sort of people who buy their own heirlooms, silver, etc. They're also the people who do most of the moving long-distance (generally to very unstylish places), commanded every few years to pull up stakes by the corporations they're in bondage to. They are the geologist employed by the oil company, the computer programmer, the aeronautical engineer, the salesman assigned a new territory, and the "marketing" (formerly *sales*) manager deputed to keep an eye on him. These people and their families occupy the suburbs and developments. Their "Army and Navy," as William H. Whyte, Jr., says, is their corporate employer. IBM and DuPont hire these people from second-rate colleges and teach them that they are nothing if not members of the team. Virtually no latitude is permitted to individuality or the milder forms of eccentricity, and these employees soon learn to avoid all ideological statements, notably, as we'll see, in the furnishing of their living rooms. Terrified of losing their jobs, these people grow passive, their humanity diminished as they perceive themselves mere parts of an infinitely larger structure. And interchangeable parts, too. "The training makes our men interchangeable," and IBM executive was once heard to say.

It's little wonder that, treated like slaves most of the time, the 4 middle class lusts for the illusion of weight and consequence. One sign is their quest for heraldic validation ("This beautiful embossed certificate will show your family tree"). Another is their custom of issuing annual family newsletters announcing the most recent triumphs in the race to become "professional":

> John, who is now 22, is in his first year at the Dental School of Wayne State University.
> Caroline has a fine position as an executive secretary for a prestigious firm in Boise, Idaho.

Sometimes these letters really wring the heart, with their proud lists of new "affiliations" achieved during the past year: "This year Bob became a member of the Junior Chamber of Commerce, the Beer Can Collectors League of North America, the Alumni Council of the University of Evansville, and the Young Republicans of Vanderburgh County." (Cf. Veblen:[1] "Since conservatism is a characteristic of the wealthier and therefore more reputable portion of the community, it has acquired a certain honorific or decorative value.") Nervous lest she be considered nobody, the middle-class wife is careful to dress way up when she goes shopping. She knows by instinct what one middle-class woman told an inquiring sociologist: "You know there's class when you're in a department store and a well-dressed lady gets treated better."

"One who makes birth or wealth the sole criterion of worth": 5 that's a conventional dictionary definition of a *snob*, and the place

---

1. Thorstein Veblen's *The Theory of the Leisure Class* (1899) was one of the earliest books to recognize the economic importance of the struggle for status.

to look for the snob is in the middle class. Worried a lot about their own taste and about whether it's working for or against them, members of the middle class try to arrest their natural tendency to sink downward by associating themselves, if ever so tenuously, with the imagined possessors of money, power, and taste. "Correctness" and doing the right thing become obsessions, prompting middle-class people to write thank-you notes after the most ordinary dinner parties, give excessively expensive or correct presents, and never allude to any place—Fort Smith, Arkansas, for example—that lacks known class. It will not surprise readers who have traveled extensively to hear that Neil Mackwood, a British authority on snobbery, finds the greatest snobs worldwide emanating from Belgium, which can also be considered world headquarters of the middle class.

The desire to belong, and to belong by some mechanical act   6
like purchasing something, is another sign of the middle class. Words like *club* and *guild* (as in Book-of-the-Month Club and Literary Guild) extend a powerful invitation. The middle class is thus the natural target for developers' ads like this:

> You Belong
>   in Park Forest!
> The moment you come to our town you know:
> You're Welcome.
> You're part of a big group. . . .

Oddity, introversion, and the love of privacy are the big enemies, a total reversal of the values of the secure upper orders. Among the middles there's a convention that erecting a fence or even a tall hedge is an affront. And there's also a convention that you may drop in on neighbors or friends without a telephone inquiry first. Being naturally innocent and well disposed and aboveboard, a member of the middle class finds it hard to believe that all are not. Being timid and conventional, no member of the middle class would expect that anyone is copulating in the afternoon instead of the evening, clearly, for busy and well-behaved corporate personnel, the correct time for it. When William H. Whyte, Jr., was poking around one suburb studying the residents, he was told by one quintessentially middle-class woman: "The street behind us is nowhere near as friendly. They knock on doors over there."

If the women treasure "friendliness," the men treasure having   7
a genteel occupation (usually more important than money), with emphasis on the word (if seldom the thing) *executive*. (As a matter of fact, an important class divide falls between those who feel veneration before the term *executive* and those who feel they want

to throw up.) Having a telephone-answering machine at home is an easy way of simulating (at relatively low cost) high professional desirability, but here you wouldn't think of a facetious or eccentric text (delivered in French, for example, or in the voice of Donald Duck or Richard Nixon) asking the caller to speak his bit after the beeping sound. For the middle-class man is scared. As C. Wright Mills notes, "He is always somebody's man, the corporation's, the government's, the army's. . . ." One can't be too careful. One "management adviser" told Studs Terkel: "Your wife, your children have to behave properly. You've got to fit in the mold. You've got to be on guard." In *Coming Up for Air* (1939) George Orwell, speaking for his middle-class hero, gets it right:

> There's a lot of rot talked about the sufferings of the working class. I'm not so sorry for the proles myself. . . . The prole suffers physically, but he's a free man when he isn't working. But in every one of those little stucco boxes there's some poor bastard who's *never* free except when he's fast asleep.

Because he is essentially a salesman, the middle-class man de-   8
velops a salesman's style. Hence his optimism and his belief in the likelihood of self-improvement if you'll just hurl yourself into it. One reason musicals like *Annie* and *Man of La Mancha* make so much money is that they offer him and his wife songs, like "Tomorrow" and "The Impossible Dream," that seem to promise that all sorts of good things are on the way. A final stigma of the middle class, an emanation of its social insecurity, is its habit of laughing at its own jests. Not entirely certain what social effect he's transmitting, and yet obliged, by his role as "salesman," to promote goodwill and optimism, your middle-class man serves as his own enraptured audience. Sometimes, after uttering some would-be clever formulation in public, he will look all around to gauge the response of the audience. Favorable, he desperately hopes.

The young men of the middle class are chips off the old block.   9
If you want to know who reads John T. Molloy's books, hoping to break into the upper-middle class by formulas and mechanisms, they are your answer. You can see them on airplanes especially, being forwarded from one corporate training program to another. Their shirts are implausibly white, their suits are excessively dark, their neckties resemble those worn by undertakers, and their hair is cut in the style of the 1950s. Their talk is of *the bottom line,* and for *no* they are likely to say *no way.* Often their necks don't seem long enough, and their eyes tend to be too much in motion, flicking back and forth rather than up and down. They will enter adult life as corporate trainees and, after forty-five faithful years, leave it as corporate personnel, wondering whether this is all.

JAMES FALLOWS

Why Paul Fussell Thinks
He's Better Than You

The jokes in *Hustler* magazine are usually at the expense of black 1
people. Black men are lured into traps with watermelon as bait.
They resemble apes in the zoo. They give white women the business
with their stupendous sexual tools. And so on.

Larry Flynt has tried to laugh it all away by saying that, contrary 2
to appearances, he is actually making fun of racial stereotypes and
building goodwill. He says that the jokes are in the same affectionate
spirit as two blacks calling each other "nigger." I doubt that even
Flynt can believe this. What his magazine in fact dishes out is
brutal, racist hatred, a hundred times more offensive than anything
that Earl Butz or James Watt ever said in public and considerably
worse than what *Hustler* does to its female models, who presumably
participate voluntarily.

Paul Fussell, who has more in common with Flynt than was 3
previously apparent, would probably also say that he is making
fun of class stereotypes by writing a book about them that is,
according to his publisher, "deeply ironic," rich with "iconoclastic
wit . . . sometimes acid, sometimes affectionate." You can hear
him telling his academic colleagues that only earthbound morons
could possibly take the book for what it seems to be: one long,
mean-spirited sneer.

Far from being "fun" or "ironic," *Class* is in fact a contemptible 4
piece of work, reeking of the very attitudes it means to mock, a
shameful misuse of Fussell's great talents. My animus against this
book does not arise from the source Fussell suggests in his intro-
ductory section: the discomfort many Americans feel with the very
notion of "class." Indeed, I have invested much of my time in
the last few years trying to understand the same subject. Nor, as
that might indicate, are my views twisted by professional jealousy.
Fussell has been, until now, one of the handful of writers I most
admire. His finest book, *The Great War and Modern Memory*, which
won the National Book Award in 1976, will endure. I began *Class*
with high hopes.

It is precisely Fussell's stature that makes the book such a shock. 5
From the creators of the *Official Preppy Handbook* or the assorted

From *The Washington Monthly*, December 1983.

"dress (eat/buy/pray) for success" tomes, lectures about the ugliness of Montgomery Ward clothing and of mobile homes are just what we'd expect. But not from Paul Fussell—not from the man who, in *The Great War* and in his *New Republic* article about dropping the bomb on Hiroshima (he was for it, because of the infantrymen's lives it saved) explored the soul of the men who, when out of uniform, would be wearing those inelegant suits and living in those tacky trailers. This is not quite the same collapse as William Faulkner's writing drivel for the "Lux Video Theater," but it's in the ballpark. The Lux stage in Faulkner's career tells us something about the distortions imposed on artists' lives by the need to make a living. The *Class* stage of Fussell's may tell us more about class than the text of his book.

Taken at face value, Fussell's book is a taxonomy of the nine   6
different classes of American society, defined mainly by their tastes. He makes the "deeply ironic" suggestion that the "Top out of sight" and the "Bottom out of sight" classes display a "curious similarity, if not actual brotherhood." You don't think so? Well, consider this: "Just as the tops are hidden away on their islands or behind the peek-a-boo walls of their estates, the bottoms are equally invisible, when not put away in institutions or claustrated in monasteries, lamaseries, or communes, then hiding from creditors, deceived bail bondsmen, and gulled merchants intent on repossessing cars and furniture. . . . And a further similarity: members of both classes carry very little cash on their persons." This is a fair specimen of the book's "iconoclastic wit."

But Fussell pays only cursory attention to the extremes; his real   7
quarry is the vast "middle" and "working" classes, the difficult-to-define swath that excludes only the chronically unemployed at one end and those with inherited wealth at the other. Each gradation within this range suffers its own fallibility, in Fussell's view: the upper-middles are driven and lack the self-confident freedom of the true uppers; the middle live in meek terror of putting a foot wrong; and as for everyone else, whom Fussell consistently refers to as proles, they are fat, ugly, unlearned, uninteresting, and usually dressed in poor taste.

For example: "The prole either has his jaw set in bitterness and   8
defiance or his mouth open in doltish wonder." (This is accompanied by a nice pair of drawings, one showing the over-bred, slightly equine profile of an "upper middle," the other the swinish features of a "prole.") "It's the three prole classes that get fat; fast food and beer are two of the causes, but anxiety about slipping down a rung, resulting in nervous overeating, plays its part too, especially among high proles." (This one has a drawing of a prole couple,

she with hair in curlers and thighs bursting out of checkered polyester pants, he with no neck, a gaping mouth, and an untucked shirt in an American flag motif.) "Proles take to visor caps instinctively, which accounts for the vast popularity among them of what we must simply call the prole cap. . . . Regardless of the precise style of the prole cap, it seems crucial that it be ugly." "If the upper orders have yachts, what do the proles have? Bowling. . . . It's one sport you don't have to strip down to play; you can be good at it and still keep your prole fatty tissue decently covered."

What's even funnier about the lower and middle ranks is that *they don't know how pathetic they are.* They try to overreach by using big words, but their blunders reveal their ignorance: "Proles signal their identity partly by pronunciation, like the Texan on the [William F.] Buckley show who said *pro-mis-kitty* and 'I am a prole' at the same time. . . . Another prole problem is difficulty with the complex sentence, resulting in structures displaying elaborate pseudo-correct participles like 'being that it was a cold day, the furnace was on.' " 9

The high proles and the middles may try to dignify their "mean little houses" with brass eagles and other classy ornamentation, but they only trumpet their insecurity in making the attempt. Try as they might, they can't conceal their vulgar tastes and habits— even their pretensions to culture give them away. ("Are you sent to an extraordinary degree by the cuckoo in Beethoven's *Pastoral Symphony*? Then you're middle class.") The striving middle orders think they are dignifying themselves by acquiring collections of functionless items—beer mugs, porcelain thimbles. Fussell asks the reader to imagine himself face-to-face with the results of such pitiable behavior: "You realize with a start that this country must be swarming with middle-class novelty-thimble collectors. And this sweet lady who's showing you her collection thinks not merely that it's interesting; she thinks it's valuable, and that's the awful thing. 10

"I feel very sorry for this woman." 11

Why did he do it? What could have made a serious author write 200 pages of this sort of thing? 12

One possibility is that Fussell just made a big but innocent mistake. He may have thought it was all in good fun and not have realized that he sounds like a complacent jerk sneering at proles and reading them out of consideration as fully-human beings. 13

This hypothesis is supported by the overall shoddiness of the book, considered simply as a work of literary craftsmanship. Most of Fussell's "evidence" consists of quotes from the standard class-in-America reading list, which runs from Thorstein Veblen and C. 14

Wright Mills to Andrew Levinson and Paul Blumberg. The rest comes from TV shows he's watched, items he's clipped from the *National Enquirer* (the easiest way to do cross-class reporting), or things that caught his eye while he was making his round in town. There is no "research," in the normal sense of the term, in the book, nor any indication that Fussell interviewed a single person to develop or check his views. When the upper class speaks in his book, it is through quotes from Cornelius Vanderbilt Whitney's memoirs. When the proles speak, it is from—who knows where, since the book contains not one citation or reference note.

Having put so little effort into gathering material, Fussell naturally   15
makes sloppy, easily avoidable mistakes. Trying to conjure up a vision of proledom, and to suggest how little a college degree means when even the proles can get one, Fussell hypothesizes a pickup truck with a three-rifle rack in the rear window and a Southern Methodist University sticker on the bumper. But SMU, of course, is Texas's answer to Princeton, and the sticker would be more natural on a Dallas stockbroker's Cadillac or big Buick in Highland Park. Similarly, to support his theme that the Sunbelt as a whole is unacceptable to the upper class, Fussell says: "It's not considered good form to live in New Jersey, except in Bernardsville and perhaps Princeton, but any place in New Jersey beats Sunnyvale, Cypress, and Compton, California." What's wrong here? The three towns in California, which Fussell apparently finds indistinguishable, could hardly be more different. Compton is a hard-bitten, mainly black, industrial portion of Los Angeles, while Sunnyvale is the high-rent heart of the Silicon Valley, and Cypress is a standard suburb in Orange County.

I know, even to argue about his classifications is to play Fussell's   16
own game. My point is not to debate Fussell about where SMU or Sunnyvale should be ranked but to illustrate how little he cares about getting things right. Daily life has apparently taught him about Bernardsville, so he drops in that accurate allusion; for the list of California cities, he seems to have been content to work from a map.

A still stronger piece of evidence for the hypothesis that *Class*   17
is just a gigantic miscalculation is Fussell's final chapter, on the people in "Category X."

Happily enough for such people, they alone are free of the pains   18
of class. They do what they like, without fear of being thought either uncouth or stuck-up. Their sublimely refined taste guides them to the truly fine things in life. They dress to please themselves; indeed, that is how they live. They are not fat. But why should I try to paraphrase? Fussell makes it so much more vivid himself:

"When an X person, male or female, meets a member of an   19
identifiable class, the costume, no matter what it is, conveys the
message 'I am freer and less terrified than you are,' or—in extreme
circumstances—'I am more intelligent and interesting than you
are; please do not bore me.' . . .

"The places where X people choose to live usually have a decent   20
delicatessen or good wine store. . . . Regardless of the style of the
cuisine, X food is always 1) good, and 2) unpraised by the company,
its excellence taken for granted. . . .

"Instinctively unprovincial, X people tend to be unostentatiously   21
familiar with the street layouts and landmarks of London, Paris,
and Rome—and sometimes Istanbul and Karachi. This is in accord
with their habit of knowing a lot for the pleasure of it. . . . The
X reader reads everything, his curiosity being without limit. On
occasion he will even read best-sellers, but largely to see if their
cliche content is as high as usual. . . .

"They're good at languages. . . . Instead of the occasional dress-   22
up foreign word of the middle and upper-middle classes (gourmet,
arrivederci, kaput) Xs can deliver whole paragraphs in French,
Italian, German, or Spanish, and sometimes Russian or Chinese
as well."

There is much, much more, all in the same vein. Mr. Fussell,   23
when not writing, teaches English at the University of Pennsylvania,
and his vision of the X people bears great resemblance to the
vision many college professors have always had of themselves and
their class. The professors' yearning for a meritocracy of taste is
entirely natural: They do not make as much money as others with
comparable education, such as doctors or lawyers, and they do
not have political power. What they have is a command of refined
distinctions—how they do it in Karachi, how they say it in Madrid.
(Journalists used to display a milder version of the same trait,
before their status revolution of the last generation left them with
bigger salaries.)

Fussell's vision of the X people also bears great resemblance to   24
the way Fussell apparently thinks of himself. He takes no critical
distance from the wondrous X-style he is describing. Here his
fabled irony is nowhere to be found. He ends the X chapter—and
the book—with a hint that others might someday share the freedom
he and other Xs enjoy: "The society of Xs is not large at the
moment. It could be larger, for many can join who've not yet
understood that they have received an invitation."

This conclusion has all the graciousness and dignity of a Mensa[1]   25

1. An organization for people with IQ's above 140.

official's encouraging his friends to apply because—who knows?—they just might be able to qualify. Perhaps I am not doing Fussell justice; he may have thought that Category X was such a broad and obvious joke no one would take it seriously. But if his last chapter is not a parody—if it is as totally lacking in self-awareness as it seems—then its very clumsiness is the strongest evidence that Fussell's book is merely misconceived, rather than cynical. If Fussell truly thought himself part of the aristocracy of taste, free of the status anxieties that hamper everyone else, then why not share his blunt, "ironic" views about the proles? After all, he has told us that one sign of the Xs' freedom is their eagerness to "eschew euphemism" and tell it straight.

The other possibility is that Paul Fussell understood exactly how 26 this book would look and sound, and went ahead anyway. The evidence, I fear, points to this conclusion.

One indication is Fussell's determination to omit any mention 27 of race—more precisely, to speak only of class division among white Americans. Perhaps the most important contemporary class difference is that within black America. Many blacks are doing better than ever before, but many others—a growing proportion—are doing worse. The overall rate of illegitimate births and teenage pregnancies is rising among blacks—even as those black families that stay intact enjoy dramatically higher incomes than ten years ago. Some of the opposition to school busing plans arose from simple racism, but more of it concerns class: class tensions between the judges who lived in Wellesley and the students who lived in South Boston, as well as fears about the underclass black culture of violence and disruption.

How could Fussell have left out race altogether? His explanation 28 is that he has stuck to those class traits "that reflect choice." More fatuous words have rarely been written. Except when describing the sainted Xs, Fussell mainly talks about traits that reflect "choice" less than circumstance: accent, level of schooling, family connections, physiognomy.

Perhaps Fussell omitted the blacks because it would have meant 29 actual research, of the sort he has otherwise avoided. But I suspect the real reason is that he understood he would get into trouble. Following the logic of his "prole" portrayals, he would have to start talking about thick-lipped, kinky-haired "niggers" and randy "bucks." Fussell was shrewd enough to realize he could not get away with this when talking about blacks—but could safely use vicious stereotypes about working-class whites.

A second indication of Fussell's cynicism is his whole history 30 as a writer. His most powerful and eloquent writing has been about warfare and the military, and some of his most affecting passages concern the class identities and anxieties that soldiers bring with them to battle. The gulf between the gentlemen-officers and the working-class Tommies of the British army was the subtext of *The Great War*. In his article about Hiroshima, he said that infantry soldiers—of which he was one—cheered when they heard that the bomb had been dropped. The bomb killed 100,000 people, mainly civilians; it probably saved the one million lives, Japanese and American alike, that would have been lost in a D-Day style invasion of Japan. The moral agonizing, he said, came from genteel civilian strategists, thousands of miles from the war zone, who ran no risk of being killed in an invasion of Japan. Could the man who described those feelings now know how repugnant it would be to write about fat, ugly proles?

Significantly, the one book from the class-in-America canon 31 from which Fussell does not quote or cite is Richard Sennett's and Jonathan Cobb's brilliant *The Hidden Injuries of Class*. That book, published nearly ten years ago, drew on a painstaking, subtle effort to understand how people really felt about their class position in life. In contrast to Fussell's impervious proles, too obtuse to notice what they're missing, Sennett and Cobb portrayed a never-ending struggle in which "proles" attempt to measure up to the wider world's standards of success and mercilessly hold themselves accountable when they fail.

The clinching evidence against Fussell occupies a mere eight 32 lines near the beginning of the book, lines entirely out of character with everything that follows. They are:

"Probably the most awful class division in America, one that 33 cuts deeply across the center of society and that will poison life here for generations, is the one separating those whose young people were killed or savaged in the Vietnam war and those who, thanks largely to the infamous S-2 deferment for college students, escaped. Anyone uncertain about class consciousness in this country should listen to a working-class father whose son was killed."

Fussell is right, of course; but the true importance of this passage 34 is what it reveals about the author. It proves that *he knows*. He knows that class differences are not simply a matter of having a tractor-tire planter in your front yard versus having a curved driveway. They affect the way we make our public choices, do our business, fight our wars. They affect the adaptability of our economy, our ability to pay our way. They can make one business more resilient than another. Their bitter intensity contributed to the downfall of Detroit and Youngstown, and their comparative absence is part of the explanation for the economic boom in the Southwest.

Fussell also knows something more important, something worse.   35
He knows that the very attitudes he will go on to promulgate in
the rest of the book helped create the tragedy he describes. *If those
proles are so dumb and ugly, why not let them go get shot?*

Paul Fussell knew these things, and still he produced this book.   36
Is the explantation merely economic—the hope of big sales? Who
can say? In any case, he presumably could have still earned money
with a respectable book, even one on this very theme, which he
has been writing around for at least the last ten years. He could
have explored our obsession with social gradations, instead of
pandering to it.

He did not do those things, and that is the final evil of his book.   37
Differences of taste and style exist, as they always have. As Richard
Sennett and Jonathan Cobb demonstrated, they deserve the most
careful study. While their book differs from Fussell's in its higher
craftsmanship, the more fundamental difference is the authors'
intention. Sennett and Cobb immersed themselves in a study of
class and status differences in order to understand how to blunt
their destructive psychological and economic effects. Paul Fussell
could have done the same thing—he has done versions of it in
his previous works. But this time, he used his intellect and erudition
not for understanding, but for aggression. *Class* is a cruel book,
meant to inflict new wounds and open old ones. Above all, it is
designed to place its author at the top of the heap.

This last comment may seem like a disingenuous sermonette: 38
why would anyone write except to display his talents to their best
advantage? (I, for example, hope your reaction on finishing this
piece is not, "This guy is a dope.") And in calling Fussell a snob,
I realize that I run the risk of seeming like a bigger one.

But remember Sennett and Cobb. They are every bit as smart   39
as Fussell. But to compare the two books is to see two fundamentally
different uses to which intelligence can be put. Sennett and Cobb
employed their profound understanding, not to sneer at other
people's inadequacies as Fussell has done, but to point readers
toward an understanding that less insightful people might not have
found.

I am not suggesting that every word published between every   40
set of covers need have a redeeming social purpose. But when a
formidable mind wrestles with a crucially important topic, the
reader expects more than a sleazy tag-team match. Paul Fussell
could have helped us understand how our sense of class limits
us, as individuals and as a society. Such are his powers that he
might even have been able to suggest alternate ways to conceive
of "success" and "class." He could have helped still that tense

inner voice, whispering within a million brains, *How am I looking? Have I slipped up yet? How can I make the other guy slip more?* That he has instead aroused those fears is our loss, and his shame.

In Defense of Snobs

I discovered my snobbery the way most people learn grave truths   1
about themselves these days, from an expert. I was discussing
prison conditions with a sociologist, who agreed with me that they
were bad and then went on to suggest extraordinary remedies.
The first step, he said, was to change nomenclature; instead of
penitentiaries, guards, and *convicts,* we must speak of *penal hospitals, psychiatric aides,* and *social patients.*

"Then we can establish outpatient clinics," he continued, "and   2
give these sick people treatment. Remember, we're dealing with
the emotionally underprivileged. Basically they're no worse than
the rest of us."

I spent several years covering police courts for newspapers, and,   3
remembering a certain ax murderer in Baltimore, I said, "They're
worse than I am."

A sharp exchange followed. The sociologist looked more and   4
more upset. He had always known me as a liberal; a supporter
of foreign aid, birth control and equality at the lunch counter.
Now, clearly, I was sick. What was worse, I had a social disease.

"I'm afraid you're a snob," he said diagnostically.   5

I knew the word "snob" had evolved much during the past   6
generation, but this was the first time I had heard it used in what
is becoming its ultimate sense: to describe someone who regards
himself better than anyone—literally *any*one—else. I hope no one
will confuse me with a Ku Kluxer when I say that I'll have to get
off here and walk back. I've passed my stop. I'm willing to grant
that men often preen themselves for absurd reasons, but they're
not *my* kind of snob. I don't see why the fact that some standards
are idiotic means there oughtn't to be any standards at all, and I
refuse to slink away because I didn't hear Caryl Chessman's bell
tolling for me.[1]

Originally published in *Esquire,* December 1962
1. Caryl Chessman, convicted of murder in 1948, repeatedly asserted his innocence
and published articulate denunciations of capital punishment. His liberal supporters
forced thirteen stays of execution. He was electrocuted in May, 1960.

I refuse, in a word, to become an egalitarian. I am aware that 7
I'm being unfashionable. In his classic work on snobs and snob
worship, Thomas Carlyle observes that every age reverences its
"gilt Popinjays" and "soot-smeared Mumbojumbos." The current
totem is this curious theory of equality. Of course, scarcely anyone
calls it egalitarianism. Most egalitarians prefer to think of themselves
as lower case democrats. "We're terribly democratic," they say,
and they are, they're terribly democratic, though, of course, they
don't mean it that way. One of the conveniences of egalitaria is
that is you denounce all precepts, you yourself needn't conform
to any. You needn't, for example, use words properly. Someday
I'm going to shove an egalitarian nose in *The Oxford English Dictionary*,
whispering all the while in an egalitarian ear that democracy is a
political concept, a form of government; that only in the last
generation has it acquired its present significance. I doubt, however,
that I shall be as successful as the managing editor of a large
metropolitan newspaper, who appointed an assistant city editor
and then found himself confronted by an office petition requesting
him to change the appointment. "We've voted," the chairman of
the petition committee explained brightly. "We're against Smith.
We want Jones." The editor, a Democrat at the polls but a snob
elsewhere, turned on his heel. "I believe in democracy," he snapped,
"but this newspaper is not one."

If popular usage is undoing the concept of democracy, that of 8
snobbery is already undone. William Makepeace Thackeray would
be appalled to see the ruin of it. It was he who popularized the
word, in whose changing definitions one can read a lot of social
history, some of it spendid, some dismaying. In 1830, when Thackeray was a Cambridge undergraduate, a snob was a member of
the community who wasn't connected with the university—in
short, a townie. Nobs were better than snobs, and that was that.
Then Thackeray observed that certain members of the lower classes
were getting uppity. Writing in *Punch*, he broadened the term to
include them, giving it an interpretation almost precisely opposite
its meaning today.

Thackeray didn't live to see his word and his world turned 9
upside down. After his death, contempt for the dirty shirt was
succeeded by contempt for the stuffed shirt. In England nobs were
transformed into tax fugitives, in the United States *Town and Country*
chronicled the blurring of class lines, and in Webster a snob became
a man with an extravagant notion of his own worth. A dart once
aimed *down* was now fired *up*. It was, in fact, becoming bad form
to have any notion of worth at all. If you acquired a light, you
cast about quickly for a bushel. As early as 1916 Yale athletes
were observed wearing their letter sweaters inside out; today letter

sweaters are rarely seen anywhere. Nor are Legion of Honor ribbons seen, nor Pi Beta Kappa keys, nor any of the bijoux of distinction in which people once took pride. In their place is a strange, false humility, sometimes ludicrous, sometimes moving. The most striking example of it I have ever seen occurred in the Summer of 1945, when a group of veterans of Iwo Jima and Okinawa were decorated by the U.S. Marine Corps, an organization of insufferable snobs devoted to democracy. As the ceremony broke up, men unpinned their medals and thrust them in their pockets and shuffled off, as though in shame.

Preposterous? Of course. Yet it made a hideous kind of sense. 10
Today a great war, a Depression, another great war, Vietnam, and Watergate have destroyed respect for the image of authority. It has become awkward to admit that you have the conn—awkward even to acknowledge achievements, since superiority of any kind is suspect. Thus everyone tries to look as much as possible like everyone else, and thus all distinctions which once separated man from man have become unsavory. Instead of football captains we have co-captains, or revolving captaincies which change with each game; instead of judges we have referees; instead of a chief executive we have a team; instead of a general-in-chief we have a chairman of the joint chiefs; and in lieu of graceful manners we have the cult of informality, which, in a way that eludes me, is regarded as a democratic virtue—as though Mirabeau and Tom Paine would have smiled benignly on jeans and come-as-you-are barbecues and, most frightful of all, the aggressive use of nicknames.

The decline of formal address deserves special mention. It becomes 11
increasingly difficult to find out to whom you're talking. Everyone you meet is plain Pete, or Al, or Jane, or Jill. A President of the United States is Ike or Gerry. The Secretary of State is simply Henry the K. We know these men from their pictures, but what happens when you drop down a ledge or two? Confusion happens, that's what. A dazzling Washington hostess I know holds parties around her swimming pool at which guests, clad in bathing suits, are introduced to strangers by coy diminutives. Once she led me to two elderly Englishmen dozing in the sun. "Billy," she said, "This is Denny and Bobby." Exit the hostess, into water. After a reticent, fumbling conversation I discovered that Denny was an eminent political scientist from Thackeray's university, and Bobby had been an Air Vice-Marshal of the R.A.F. during the Battle of Britain. ("You *have* heard of the Battle of Britain, haven't you?" he asked wistfully.)

After such an affair men mutter to their wives—or, in this de- 12
liciously casual age, to the wives they happen to have in tow—

"Who was that bearded Cuban? You don't suppose. . . ." No real harm done, though in public this custom, or absence of custom, can be highly embarrassing. When my first book was published I appeared in an hour-long radio program at the invitation of Mary Margaret McBride. There was another writer present, a gray, shaggily handsome man to whom she presented me moments before the broadcast. "Here's Bob," she told me. I was about to inquire further when I found we were on the air. I hadn't his other name, so I called him by that one for the first ten minutes; then the mistress of ceremonies informed the audience and me that this Bob had been awarded *four* Pulitzer prizes. He was Robert Sherwood. I writhed for the rest of the hour. I had no way to greet him. I could hardly start using his surname, yet Bob now stuck in my throat; at the age of twenty-eight I wasn't his equal, and if Miss McBride did not realize that, Billy keenly did.

Nominal equality has become a fetish in modern offices. Once an employee was expected to sir his boss. Now he's not even allowed to mister him. Here and there a thin red line[2] of snobs fights a gallant rearguard action (when Roy Howard ordered New York *World-Telegram* reporters to call him Roy, A. J. Liebling cited his record on the paper and concluded, "Now may I please call you Mr. Howard?"), but they are hopelessly outnumbered by dense squares of jovial executives who, during coffee breaks and at company parties, stridently insist that nobody rise, let's not stand on ceremony, feel free, and remember, we're all Joes here. One Joe may have absolute power over the other Joe's career. One may be the pile-driving force behind the firm; the other may be a forelock-tugging serf. Still they speak as brothers, and if Big Joe has an order to deliver he prefaces it with some such groveling remark as, "Just let me give you my thinking on this," or, "This is off the top of my head," or, "Probably I don't know what I'm talking about." Is this democracy? I think it's hypocrisy. 13

In any event, snobbery is dead. 14

Or is it? 15

Twenty-five years ago Russell Lynes picked up Thackeray's fallen pen and pricked what he called The New Snobbism. Like his predecessor, he recognized that the essence of snobbery is ego manipulation. Every honest snob will cheerfully acknowledge that. Lynes went on to say that since nearly every ego needs some titillation, we are all snobs of one sort or another. He listed some of the chief categories he had found: social snobs, intellectual 16

2. The Duke of Wellington's phrase for the British infantrymen who repelled the attacks of Napoleon's troops.

snobs, regional snobs, moral snobs, sensual snobs, physical snobs and occupational snobs. We've all encountered varieties of these. In any group there are people who are proud of the schools they attended, or the clubs which have admitted them, or the books they have read, or the fact that they go to Florida every winter, or stay physically fit (or don't), or can replace a faucet washer (or can't), or have a taste for fine wines (or can't tell one from another). Frequently the reason for a man's vanity is as fatuous as that of Aesop's fly, who sat on the axle of a chariot and marveled at the dust he raised, but often it is entirely justified: Omar Bradley *is* a famous soldier, Mayor Daley *is* a gifted politician. Anyhow, pride is here to stay; no vigorous society can do without it. The Russians tried to abolish distinctions in the twenties; by the thirties they had brought back fashion shows, hand-kissing, saluting, and full-dress clothes—for banquets on the anniversary of the Revolution.

Today's American effort is more determined, which brings us   17 to Lynes' final category—the reverse snob, or anti-snob snob. I have already introduced him as the egalitarian. He is the pious worshiper of the Divine Average, the man who adopts what Robert Frost described as a "tenderer-than-thou" attitude toward social problems. Sometimes he is as transparently bogus as the late Diego Rivera, who used to dress carefully in a khaki shirt and greasy corduroys before being driven in a limousine to rallies of Mexican workers. Other times he is pitifully sincere, like the president of the teachers' federation who warned his colleagues several years ago that they were "in danger of considering themselves as just a little bit better" than the rank and file of laborers. At all times, however, he is bent on downstaging the rest of us, carrying himself with an air of craven modesty and reproaching with cow eyes everyone who holds himself erect. He is, as Lynes suggested, the worst sort of snob, and he behaves in execrable taste.

No well-bred snob, for example, would dream of sneering openly   18 at those who lack what he prizes. It would violate his sense of decency to imply that there's something wrong about a house furnished with Grand Rapids imitations, say, or to let on that it's a bit shaming to have been born outside Virginia (or Boston, or Charleston). I may give low marks to the man who prefers C. S. Forester to E. M. Forster, thinks Jackie Gleason funnier than Alec Guinness, enjoys Atlantic City more than Watch Hill, and orders a Scarlett O'Hara when martinis are available. I shouldn't tell him that to his face, though; that would be shabby of me. The egalitarian has fewer scruples. He attacks religious snobs in the religious press, cultural snobs in parent-teacher journals ("What Can We Do About Snobbery?" "Don't Raise a Snob!"), and intellectual snobs on the floor of the Senate. Evidence cannot stand against him: if genetic research turns up new evidence of inherited characteristics, then the geneticists are anti-democratic impostors. No national priority deflects him: on the eve of Hitler's invasion of Poland, the superegalitarian J. B. Priestley actually charged in the London *News Chronicle* that the greatest threat to Great Britain was snobbery. And to simplify his argument, the enemy of standards has completely corrupted Thackeray's meaning. Margaret Kennedy tells the story of a Welsh woman who learned that a neighbor's daughter was about to be married, although not pregnant. She exclaimed, "There's snob for you!"

Against such tumidity the proper snob, a courteous chap, is 19 almost helpless. "Snobbery," wrote Dixon Wecter, "may be regarded as a form of self protection against the social consequences of democracy." Its critics notwithstanding, it is essentially defensive, and it seems to me that it grows more defensive each year. In the last generation a George Bernard Shaw could assert that England's snobs were actually her greatest strength; a Virginia Woolf could defiantly proclaim her artistic superiority; a José Ortega y Gasset could observe that the average citizen is "incapable of receiving the sacrament of art, blind and deaf to pure beauty." Today, either because of the bitterness of the assault or because the other-directed virus has infected even us, we snobs are more diffident, more anxious not to appear gross. And so the virtue of our time has become what Bertrand Russell ironically called "the superior virtue of the oppressed." And so the gray tide of mediocrity rises higher and higher. Of mediocrity—and of worse.

The greatest egalitarian gains were made in the years immediately 20 after World War II. It was in 1946 that the Army's Doolittle Board, goaded by wartime egalitarians like William Mauldin, stripped rank of its privileges. Indeed, it was a novel about the Army, James Jones' *From Here to Eternity*, which most clearly expressed the reverse values of the new egalitaria. The measure of a man's worth was in inverse proportion to his pay grade, education and civility. Anyone with a commission was an outcast. Women were similarly graded. The essense of purity was the prostitute. The faithful wife was a fallen sister.

A subtler specimen of egalitarian literature is *The Man in the* 21 *Gray Flannel Suit*. Sloan Wilson's seraphim aren't dope fiends and hookers, but like Jones, Nelson Algren, and Tennessee Williams he stands on his hands to look at the world. His protagonist is a man who wants to make more money. He leaves an easy berth for a job with a higher salary and discovers his new employer expects him to work. His reaction is moral outrage. He concedes that the employer is dedicated, but cannot admire him, because the old man is industrious and diligent—in approved cant, he is a driven neurotic. The employer is apologetic, as villains are in all sophisticated melodramas; he can only plead for understanding. "Atlas," wrote Carlyle, "the hero of old has had to cramp himself into strange places: the world knows not well at any time what to do with him, so foreign is his aspect in the world!"

In supporting this twaddle, the passionate egalitarian tirelessly   22
generalizes from the specific. He had this second john,[3] see, and the creep couldn't even read a map. (Leaders are incompetent.) Talk about swinging from both sides of the plate—Charles Dickens kept a mistress. (Moralists are phonies.) A junior exec in the front office just fired a man for wearing Bermudas. (Bosses are black-guards.) But this is cheating. The issue is not whether rules are broken. It is whether we ought to have any rules at all. Snobbery's quarrel with the anti-snob isn't that he's affronted by snobs who blot their copybooks, for he's not; he exults in them; they support his argument. This argument, and the real issue, is that every homo Sap is like every other homo Sap—that the differences between us are infinitesimal, and may be put down to external influence. If evil is done, society is to blame. If evil is redressed, society is triumphant. It naturally follows that anyone who believes this, and is honestly convinced that we are all children of the same gravid earth bitch, must regard any pretension as a bugbear and any authority as a fee-faw-fum.

As illogical as a superstition, this notion also has a superstition's   23
power. It would be hard to find an American citadel free of its spell. Certainly the home isn't. The dictatorial father of Freud's time is virtually extinct. Once he roamed the land in vast herds, snorting virile snorts and refreshing himself in austere men's clubs walled with fumed oak, before thundering home to preside over his cave. In the 1970's he exists as a flaccid parody of his grandfather, a comic figure on television programs whose cretin blunders are deftly corrected by his amused family. The teen-ager who wants to get married while in high school does so, because, as a mother explained to me, "Kids are people and have a right to make up their own minds." Her husband was unreconciled, but he recognized that he was a low, atavistic creature, and he merely looked un-comfortable when she added airily, "We believe in democracy at home."

"Democracy at home." Is this the last slogan of egalitaria? It is   24
more than a slogan. It is a course of study in grade schools. Snobs

---

3. Second lieutenant.

suffered one of their first routs in public education; they have no
friends among the jitney messiahs of bread-and-circuses curricula.
The number of classrooms which vote on what they are to be
taught is small, but pupils are polled on nearly everything else,
including the personality of the teacher, the value of her instruction,
and the real-life meaning of a course: "How many think Lincoln
was well-adjusted? Hands, please." Popular sovereignty extends
to the intellectual coin of the realm, the language which, according
to egalitarian dialectic, should be determined by a kind of continuing
voice vote. If sufficient people say, "I feel badly," or "It is me,"
then grammatical snobs are confounded; the error is accepted.
"That's what we mean by usage," an Ed. D. blandly explained to
me, though he twitched when I asked whether he would endorse
the usage of the Massachusetts legislator who said, "Teachers is
cheap."

Democracy at home: teachers is cheap. There is a rough justice   25
in this equation, in which, please note, there is no allowance for
the variable factor of ability. Young intellectual snobs must be
suckled on the thin broth of the insipid mean; to give them a
richer diet would, in the glib cliché, be undemocratic. It is not
undemocratic, of course, to provide special schools for retarded
children; they are below the general level and must be brought
up to it. Thus we see again the topsy-turvy dogma—the same
twisted thinking which corrupted Franklin D. Roosevelt's "The
poorest are no longer necessarily the most ignorant part of society"
to mean "The commoner the man, the wiser he." Gifted children
("double-domes") are distrusted. The dull and delinquent ("underprivileged," "sick," "victims of society") belong to a privileged
caste. We must look down on those above us, up to those beneath
us. So sacred is this doublethink that we rarely challenge it, though
sometimes it is carried to a Tartuffian extreme and we see a glimmer
in the night. The last time I visited the Barnum and Bailey sideshow,
the barker interrupted his spiel to deliver a brief sermon. He just
wanted us to know that these fine tatooed, misshapen and deformed
people on the stage were folks, same as you and me. Why, you'd
be glad to have any of them in your home, he said. Sure, they
were interesting. But—and his voice dropped to a tactful whisper—
they weren't *freaks.*

Meanwhile, what of the snob? Prayer seems to be all that he   26
has left. Every institution in the republic, from the Army to the
pulpit, is at his throat. Here and there a country club holds out
like a Beau Geste fort in the Sahara, but to the thoroughbred snob
these odious allies are worse than none at all. Apparently he is a
doomed species, destined to die without heirs. Yet we are left with

a paradox. Why do the anti-snobs persist in railing against snobbism's tattered remnant? Why can't they leave us with our illusions of superiority, which they are so sure are spurious? There are two excellent reasons. The first is that they aren't at all sure. Deep in every egalitarian breast there is a gnawing suspicion that he is inferior and, since the suspicion is fully justified, it won't be still. The second reason is that they desperately need us. They are what they are because we are what we are. They, like all snobs, must look down on someone. To satisfy this human craving they have created their own inverted pecking order, with us at the bottom of the pyramid. Neglect us, and they would lose their illusions; forget us entirely, and each of them would be obliged to recognize the clod in his shaving mirror.

Shall we then scorch the earth, recant, disperse? No, that's not   27
our way. Like that grand old snob Homer, who urged warriors into battle by reminding them of their heroic lineages, we must hold fast and trust that victory may yet ride at our stirrups. It won't be easy. Belonging to an élite has never been easy, and we may as well face it; these are the times that try snobs' souls. There are endless snubs ahead from Joes who think they are better than we are because their manners are worse, their pasts shadier, their brainpans smaller. Decorated veterans will be insulted by soldiers with unimpeachable records of cowardice. Hi fi women will be cut dead by the arrogantly unchaste. Offspring will deride us because they are dependent upon us, and unlettered graduates of Teachers College, Columbia, will leer when we don't talk like they think we should. Still we must keep our noses high, even when the press traduces us:

"The real triumph of democracy will not be recorded until every   28
man jack American practices equality in his daily rubs against the coat sleeves of his fellows."

Every man jack?   29

And: "Call no man democratic who forgets that his barber, cook   30
and errand boy are made of the same human clay as himself."

My barber? *My* cook? *My* errand boy?   31

And, from a wartime patriot: "Many an elevator's boy's life is   32
made intolerable by the little Hitler who is his elevator starter; he wonders how much good will be accomplished by getting rid of the big Hitler if the little Schicklgrubers still [sic] persist."

It is dark in the Führenbunker tonight. Outside, the egalitarian   33
legions press harder and harder, led by AWOL privates and nursed by Florence Nightingales on leave from call-girl clienteles. We can no longer see properly. An athletic snob is doing push ups, a travel snob fingers lovingly the thick visa inserts in his passport, a music

snob rewinds his gramophone and replaces a Bach with a Bartók, but the rest of us are at loose ends. Directly across from me an F.F.V.[4] representative has put aside her stars-and-bars embroidery. Beside her a Harvard man (Porcellian Club) has abandoned his translation of *Ajax*. Others were reading Rilke; were reading Wilbur; were hanging Braque canvases; were rearranging Biedermeier furniture. Now they are sitting idle on the bunker floor in an arc— rather a cramped arc, since no one wants to be on the left. Yet none of us is bored. We are carrying on bravely in the spirit of Tommy Carlyle, Billy Thackeray, Bobby Frost, Bert Russell, Georgie Shaw, Ginger Woolf, Evvy Waugh and Josy Gasset. Russ Lynes started the conversation, and now everyone has joined it.

We're bragging.   34

4. A member of the First Families of Virginia, a supposedly elite organization.

FLANNERY O'CONNOR

Revelation

The doctor's waiting room, which was very small, was almost   1
full when the Turpins entered and Mrs. Turpin, who was very large, made it look even smaller by her presence. She stood looming at the head of the magazine table set in the center of it, a living demonstration that the room was inadequate and ridiculous. Her little bright black eyes took in all the patients as she sized up the seating situation. There was one vacant chair and a place on the sofa occupied by a blond child in a dirty blue romper who should have been told to move over and make room for the lady. He was five or six, but Mrs. Turpin saw at once that no one was going to tell him to move over. He was slumped down in the seat, his arms idle at his sides and his eyes idle in his head; his nose ran unchecked.

Mrs. Turpin put a firm hand on Claud's shoulder and said in a voice that included everyone that wanted to listen, "Claud, you sit in that chair there," and gave him a push down into the vacant one. Claud was florid and bald and sturdy, somewhat shorter than Mrs. Turpin, but he sat down as if he were accustomed to doing what she told him to.

First published in *The Sewanee Review*, Spring 1964.

Mrs. Turpin remained standing. The only man in the room besides Claud was a lean stringy old fellow with a rusty hand spread out on each knee, whose eyes were closed as if he were asleep or dead or pretending to be so as not to get up and offer her his seat. Her gaze settled agreeably on a well-dressed grey-haired lady whose eyes met hers and whose expression said: if that child belonged to me, he would have some manners and move over—there's plenty of room there for you and him too.

Claud looked up with a sigh and made as if to rise.

"Sit down," Mrs. Turpin said. "You know you're not supposed   5
to stand on that leg. He has an ulcer on his leg," she explained.

Claud lifted his foot onto the magazine table and rolled his trouser leg up to reveal a purple swelling on a plump marble-white calf.

"My!" the pleasant lady said. "How did you do that?"

"A cow kicked him," Mrs. Turpin said.

"Goodness!" said the lady.

Claud rolled his trouser leg down.   10

"Maybe the little boy would move over," the lady suggested, but the child did not stir.

"Somebody will be leaving in a minute," Mrs. Turpin said. She could not understand why a doctor—with as much money as they made charging five dollars a day just to stick their head in the hospital door and look at you—couldn't afford a decent-sized waiting room. This one was hardly bigger than a garage. The table was cluttered with limp-looking magazines and at one end of it there was a big green glass ash tray full of cigaret butts and cotton wads with little blood spots on them. If she had had anything to do with the running of the place, that would have been emptied every so often. There were no chairs against the wall at the head of the room. It had a rectangular-shaped panel in it that permitted a view of the office where the nurse came and went and the secretary listened to the radio. A plastic fern in a gold pot sat in the opening and trailed its fronds down almost to the floor. The radio was softly playing gospel music.

Just then the inner door opened and a nurse with the highest stack of yellow hair Mrs. Turpin had ever seen put her face in the crack and called for the next patient. The woman sitting beside Claud grasped the two arms of her chair and hoisted herself up; she pulled her dress free from her legs and lumbered through the door where the nurse had disappeared.

Mrs. Turpin eased into the vacant chair, which held her tight as a corset. "I wish I could reduce," she said, and rolled her eyes and gave a comic sigh.

"Oh, *you* aren't fat," the stylish lady said.   15

"Ooooo I am too," Mrs. Turpin said. "Claud he eats all he
wants to and never weighs over one hundred and seventy-five
pounds, but me I just look at something good to eat and I gain
some weight," and her stomach and shoulders shook with laughter.
"You can eat all you want to, can't you, Claud?" she asked turning
to him.

Claud only grinned.

"Well, as long as you have such a good disposition," the stylish
lady said, "I don't think it makes a bit of difference what size you
are. You just can't beat a good disposition."

Next to her was a fat girl of eighteen or nineteen, scowling into
a thick blue book which Mrs. Turpin saw was entitled *Human
Development*. The girl raised her head and directed her scowl at
Mrs. Turpin as if she did not like her looks. She appeared annoyed
that anyone should speak while she tried to read. The poor girl's
face was blue with acne and Mrs. Turpin thought how pitiful it
was to have a face like that at that age. She gave the girl a friendly
smile but the girl only scowled the harder. Mrs. Turpin herself
was fat but she had always had good skin, and, though she was
forty-seven years old, there was not a wrinkle in her face except
around her eyes from laughing too much.

Next to the ugly girl was the child, still in exactly the same   20
position, and next to him was a thin leathery old woman in a
cotton print dress. She and Claud had three sacks of chicken feed
in their pump house that was in the same print. She had seen
from the first that the child belonged with the old woman. She
could tell by the way they sat—kind of vacant and white-trashy,
as if they would sit there until Doomsday if nobody called and
told them to get up. And at right angles but next to the well-
dressed pleasant lady was a lank-faced woman who was certainly
the child's mother. She had on a yellow sweat shirt and wine-
colored slacks, both gritty-looking, and the rims of her lips were
stained with snuff. Her dirty yellow hair was tied behind with a
piece of red paper ribbon. Worse than niggers any day, Mrs. Turpin
thought.

The gospel hymn playing was, "When I looked up and He
looked down," and Mrs. Turpin, who knew it, supplied the last
line mentally, "And wona these days I know I'll we-eara crown."

Without appearing to, Mrs. Turpin always noticed people's feet.
The well-dressed lady had on red and grey suede shoes to match
her dress. Mrs. Turpin had on her good black patent leather pumps.
The ugly girl had on Girl Scout shoes and heavy socks. The old
woman had on tennis shoes and the white-trashy mother had on

what appeared to be bedroom slippers, black straw with gold braid threaded through them—exactly what you would have expected her to have on.

Sometimes at night when she couldn't go to sleep, Mrs. Turpin would occupy herself with the question of who she would have chosen to be if she couldn't have been herself. If Jesus had said to her before he made her, "There's only two places available for you. You can either be a nigger or white-trash," what would she have said? "Please, Jesus, please," she would have said, "just let me wait until there's another place available," and he would have said, "No, you have to go right now and I have only those two places so make up your mind." She would have wiggled and squirmed and begged and pleaded but it would have been no use and finally she would have said, "All right, make me a nigger then—but that don't mean a trashy one." And he would have made her a neat clean respectable Negro woman, herself but black.

Next to the child's mother was a red-headed youngish woman, reading one of the magazines and working a piece of chewing gum, hell for leather, as Claud would say. Mrs. Turpin could not see the woman's feet. She was not white-trash, just common. Sometimes Mrs. Turpin occupied herself at night naming the classes of people. On the bottom of the heap were most colored people, not the kind she would have been if she had been one, but most of them; then next to them—not above, just away from—were the white-trash; then above them were the home-owners, and above them the home-and-land owners, to which she and Claud belonged. Above she and Claud were people with a lot of money and much bigger houses and much more land. But here the complexity of it would begin to bear in on her, for some of the people with a lot of money were common and ought to be below she and Claud and some of the people who had good blood had lost their money and had to rent and then there were colored people who owned their homes and land as well. There was a colored dentist in town who had two red Lincolns and a swimming pool and a farm with registered white-face cattle on it. Usually by the time she had fallen asleep all the classes of people were moiling and roiling around in her head, and she would dream they were all crammed in together in a box car, being ridden off to be put in a gas oven.

"That's a beautiful clock," she said and nodded to her right. It was a big wall clock, the face encased in a brass sunburst.

"Yes, it's very pretty," the stylish lady said agreeably. "And right on the dot too," she added, glancing at her watch.

The ugly girl beside her cast an eye upward at the clock, smirked, then looked directly at Mrs. Turpin and smirked again. Then she returned her eyes to her book. She was obviously the lady's daughter because, although they didn't look anything alike as to disposition, they both had the same shape of face and same blue eyes. On the lady they sparkled pleasantly but in the girl's seared face they appeared alternately to smolder and to blaze.

What if Jesus had said, "All right, you can be white-trash or a nigger or ugly!"

Mrs. Turpin felt an awful pity for the girl, though she thought it was one thing to be ugly and another to act ugly.

The woman with the snuff-stained lips turned around in her 30 chair and looked up at the clock. Then she turned back and appeared to look a little to the side of Mrs. Turpin. There was a cast in one of her eyes. "You want to know wher you can get one of themther clocks?" she asked in a loud voice.

"No, I already have a nice clock," Mrs. Turpin said. Once somebody like her got a leg in the conversation, she would be all over it.

"You can get you one with green stamps," the woman said. "That's most likely wher he got hisn. Save you up enough, you can get you most anythang. I got me some joo'ry."

Ought to have got you a wash rag and some soap, Mrs. Turpin thought.

"I get contour sheets with mine," the pleasant lady said.

The daughter slammed her book shut. She looked straight in 35 front of her, directly through Mrs. Turpin and on through the yellow curtain and the plate glass window which made the wall behind her. The girl's eyes seemed lit all of a sudden with a peculiar light, an unnatural light like night road signs give. Mrs. Turpin turned her head to see if there was anything going on outside that she should see, but she could not see anything. Figures passing cast only a pale shadow through the curtain. There was no reason the girl should single her out for her ugly looks.

"Miss Finley," the nurse said, cracking the door. The gum-chewing woman got up and passed in front of her and Claud and went into the office. She had on red high-heeled shoes.

Directly across the table, the ugly girl's eyes were fixed on Mrs. Turpin as if she had some very special reason for disliking her.

"This is wonderful weather, isn't it?" the girl's mother said.

"It's good weather for cotton if you can get the niggers to pick it," Mrs. Turpin said, "but niggers don't want to pick cotton any more. You can't get the white folks to pick it and now you can't get the niggers—because they got to be right up there with the white folks."

"They gonna *try* anyways," the white-trash woman said, leaning 40 forward.

"Do you have one of those cotton-picking machines?" the pleasant lady asked.

"No," Mrs. Turpin said, "they leave half the cotton in the field. We don't have much cotton anyway. If you want to make it farming now, you have to have a little of everything. We got a couple of acres of cotton and a few hogs and chickens and just enough white-face that Claud can look after them himself."

"One thang I don't want," the white-trash woman said, wiping her mouth with the back of her hand. "Hogs. Nasty stinking things, a-gruntin and a-rootin all over the place."

Mrs. Turpin gave her the merest edge of her attention. "Our hogs are not dirty and they don't stink," she said. "They're cleaner than some children I've seen. Their feet never touch the ground. We have a pig-parlor—that's where you raise them on concrete," she explained to the pleasant lady, "and Claud scoots them down with the hose every afternoon and washes off the floor." Cleaner by far than that child right there, she thought. Poor nasty little thing. He had not moved except to put the thumb of his dirty hand into his mouth.

The woman turned her face away from Mrs. Turpin. "I know   45
I wouldn't scoot down no hog with no hose," she said to the wall.

You wouldn't have no hog to scoot down, Mrs. Turpin said to herself.

"A-gruntin and a-rootin and a-groanin," the woman muttered.

"We got a little of everything," Mrs. Turpin said to the pleasant lady. "It's no use in having more than you can handle yourself with help like it is. We found enough niggers to pick our cotton this year but Claud he has to go after them and take them home again in the evening. They can't walk that half a mile. No they can't. I tell you," she said and laughed merrily, "I sure am tired of buttering up niggers, but you got to love em if you want em to work for you. When they come in the morning, I run out and I say, 'Hi yawl this morning?' and when Claud drives them off to the field I just wave to beat the band and they just wave back." And she waved her hand rapidly to illustrate.

"Like you read out of the same book," the lady said, showing she understood perfectly.

"Child, yes," Mrs. Turpin said. "And when they come in from   50
the field, I run out with a bucket of icewater. That's the way it's going to be from now on," she said. "You may as well face it."

"One thang I know," the white-trash woman said. "Two thangs I ain't going to do: love no niggers or scoot down no hog with no hose." And she let out a bark of contempt.

The look that Mrs. Turpin and the pleasant lady exchanged indicated they both understood that you had to *have* certain things before you could *know* certain things. But every time Mrs. Turpin exchanged a look with the lady, she was aware that the ugly girl's peculiar eyes were still on her, and she had trouble bringing her attention back to the conversation.

"When you got something," she said, "you got to look after it." And when you ain't got a thing but breath and britches, she added to herself, you can afford to come to town every morning and just sit on the Court House coping and spit.

A grotesque revolving shadow passed across the curtain behind her and was thrown palely on the opposite wall. Then a bicycle clattered down against the outside of the building. The door opened and a colored boy glided in with a tray from the drug store. It had two large red and white paper cups on it with tops on them. He was a tall, very black boy in discolored white pants and a green nylon shirt. He was chewing gum slowly, as if to music. He set the tray down in the office opening next to the fern and stuck his head through to look for the secretary. She was not in there. He rested his arms on the ledge and waited, his narrow bottom stuck out, swaying slowly to the left and right. He raised a hand over his head and scratched the base of his skull.

"You see that button there, boy?" Mrs. Turpin said. "You can punch that and she'll come. She's probably in the back somewhere." 55

"Is thas right?" the boy said agreeably, as if he had never seen the button before. He leaned to the right and put his finger on it. "She sometime out," he said and twisted around to face his audience, his elbows behind him on the counter. The nurse appeared and he twisted back again. She handed him a dollar and he rooted in his pocket and made the change and counted it out to her. She gave him fifteen cents for a tip and he went out with the empty tray. The heavy door swung to slowly and closed at length with the sound of suction. For a moment no one spoke.

"They ought to send all them niggers back to Africa," the white-trash woman said. "That's wher they come from in the first place."

"Oh, I couldn't do without my good colored friends," the pleasant lady said.

"There's a heap of things worse than a nigger," Mrs. Turpin agreed. "It's all kinds of them just like it's all kinds of us."

"Yes, and it takes all kinds to make the world go round," the 60 lady said in her musical voice.

As she said it, the raw-complexioned girl snapped her teeth together. Her lower lip turned downwards and inside out, revealing the pale pink inside her mouth. After a second it rolled back up.

It was the ugliest face Mrs. Turpin had ever seen anyone make and for a moment she was certain that the girl had made it at her. She was looking at her as if she had known and disliked her all her life—all of Mrs. Turpin's life, it seemed too, not just all the girl's life. Why, girl, I don't even know you, Mrs. Turpin said silently.

She forced her attention back to the discussion. "It wouldn't be practical to send them back to Africa," she said. "They wouldn't want to go. They got it too good here."

"Wouldn't be what they wanted—if I had anythang to do with it," the woman said.

"It wouldn't be a way in the world you could get all the niggers back over there," Mrs. Turpin said. "They'd be hiding out and lying down and turning sick on you and wailing and hollering and raring and pitching. It wouldn't be a way in the world to get them over there."

"They got over here," the trashy woman said. "Get back like 65
they got over."

"It wasn't so many of them then," Mrs. Turpin explained.

The woman looked at Mrs. Turpin as if here was an idiot indeed but Mrs. Turpin was not bothered by the look, considering where it came from.

"Nooo," she said, "they're going to stay here where they can go to New York and marry white folks and improve their color. That's what they all want to do, every one of them, improve their color."

"You know what comes of that, don't you?" Claud asked.

"No, Claud, what?" Mrs. Turpin said.   70

Claud's eyes twinkled. "White-faced niggers," he said with never a smile.

Everybody in the office laughed except the white-trash and the ugly girl. The girl gripped the book in her lap with white fingers. The trashy woman looked around her from face to face as if she thought they were all idiots. The old woman in the feed sack dress continued to gaze expressionless across the floor at the high-top shoes of the man opposite her, the one who had been pretending to be asleep when the Turpins came in. He was laughing heartily, his hands still spread out on his knees. The child had fallen to the side and was lying now almost face down in the old woman's lap.

While they recovered from their laughter, the nasal chorus on the radio kept the room from silence.

> *You go to blank blank*
> *And I'll go to mine*

But we'll all blank along
To-geth-ther,
And all along the blank
We'll hep eachother out
Smile-ling in any kind of
Weath-ther!

Mrs. Turpin didn't catch every word but she caught enough to agree with the spirit of the song and it turned her thoughts sober. To help anybody out that needed it was her philosophy of life. She never spared herself when she found somebody in need, whether they were white or black, trash or decent. And of all she had to be thankful for, she was most thankful that this was so. If Jesus had said, "You can be high society and have all the money you want and be thin and svelte-like, but you can't be a good woman with it," she would have had to say, "Well don't make me that then. Make me a good woman and it don't matter what else, how fat or how ugly or how poor!" Her heart rose. He had not made her a nigger or white-trash or ugly! He had made her herself and given her a little of everything. Jesus, thank you! she said. Thank you thank you thank you! Whenever she counted her blessings she felt as buoyant as if she weighed one hundred and twenty-five pounds instead of one hundred and eighty.

"What's wrong with your little boy?" the pleasant lady asked the white-trashy woman.

"He has a ulcer," the woman said proudly. "He ain't give me a minute's peace since he was born. Him and her are just alike," she said, nodding at the old woman, who was running her leathery fingers through the child's pale hair. "Look like I can't get nothing down them two but Co' Cola and candy."

That's all you try to get down em, Mrs. Turpin said to herself. Too lazy to light the fire. There was nothing you could tell her about people like them that she didn't know already. And it was not just that they didn't have anything. Because if you gave them everything, in two weeks it would all be broken or filthy or they would have chopped it up for lightwood. She knew all this from her own experience. Help them you must, but help them you couldn't.

All at once the ugly girl turned her lips inside out again. Her eyes were fixed like two drills on Mrs. Turpin. This time there was no mistaking that there was something urgent behind them.

Girl, Mrs. Turpin exclaimed silently, I haven't done a thing to you! The girl might be confusing her with somebody else. There was no need to sit by and let herself be intimidated. "You must be in college," she said boldly, looking directly at the girl. "I see you reading a book there."

The girl continued to stare and pointedly did not answer.

Her mother blushed at this rudeness. "The lady asked you a   80
question, Mary Grace," she said under her breath.

"I have ears," Mary Grace said.

The poor mother blushed again. "Mary Grace goes to Wellesley College," she explained. She twisted one of the buttons on her dress. "In Massachusetts," she added with a grimace. "And in the summer she just keeps right on studying. Just reads all the time, a real book worm. She's done real well at Wellesley; she's taking English and Math and History and Psychology and Social Studies," she rattled on, "and I think it's too much. I think she ought to get out and have fun."

The girl looked as if she would like to hurl them all through the plate glass window.

"Way up north," Mrs. Turpin murmured and thought, well, it hasn't done much for her manners.

"I'd almost rather to have him sick," the white-trash woman   85
said, wrenching the attention back to herself. "He's so mean when he ain't. Look like some children just take natural to meanness. It's some gets bad when they get sick but he was the opposite. Took sick and turned good. He don't give me no trouble now. It's me waitin to see the doctor," she said.

If I was going to send anybody back to Africa, Mrs. Turpin thought, it would be your kind, woman. "Yes, indeed," she said aloud, but looking up at the ceiling, "it's a heap of things worse than a nigger." And dirtier than a hog, she added to herself.

"I think people with bad dispositions are more to be pitied than anyone on earth," the pleasant lady said in a voice that was decidedly thin.

"I thank the Lord he has blessed me with a good one," Mrs. Turpin said. "The day has never dawned that I couldn't find something to laugh at."

"Not since she married me anyways," Claud said with a comical straight face.

Everybody laughed except the girl and the white-trash.   90

Mrs. Turpin's stomach shook. "He's such a caution," she said, "that I can't help but laugh at him."

The girl made a loud ugly noise through her teeth.

Her mother's mouth grew thin and tight. "I think the worst thing in the world," she said, "is an ungrateful person. To have everything and not appreciate it. I know a girl," she said, "who has parents who would give her anything, a little brother who loves her dearly, who is getting a good education, who wears the

best clothes, but who can never say a kind word to anyone, who
never smiles, who just criticizes and complains all day long."

"Is she too old to paddle?" Claud asked.

The girl's face was almost purple.   95

"Yes," the lady said, "I'm afraid there's nothing to do but leave
her to her folly. Some day she'll wake up and it'll be too late."

"It never hurt anyone to smile," Mrs. Turpin said. "It just makes
you feel better all over."

"Of course," the lady said sadly, "but there are just some people
you can't tell anything to. They can't take criticism."

"If it's one thing I am," Mrs. Turpin said with feeling, "it's
grateful. When I think who all I could have been besides myself
and what all I got, a little of everything, and a good disposition
besides, I just feel like shouting, 'Thank you, Jesus, for making
everything the way it is!' It could have been different!" For one
thing, somebody else could have got Claud. At the thought of this,
she was flooded with gratitude and a terrible pang of joy ran
through her. "Oh thank you, Jesus, Jesus, thank you!" she cried
aloud.

The book struck her directly over her left eye. It struck almost   100
at the same instant that she realized the girl was about to hurl it.
Before she could utter a sound, the raw face came crashing across
the table toward her, howling. The girl's fingers sank like clamps
into the soft flesh of her neck. She heard the mother cry out and
Claud shout, "Whoa!" There was an instant when she was certain
that she was about to be in an earthquake.

All at once her vision narrowed and she saw everything as if
it were happening in a small room far away, or as if she were
looking at it through the wrong end of a telescope. Claud's face
crumpled and fell out of sight. The nurse ran in, then out, then
in again. Then the gangling figure of the doctor rushed out of the
inner door. Magazines flew this way and that as the table turned
over. The girl fell with a thud and Mrs. Turpin's vision suddenly
reversed itself and she saw everything large instead of small. The
eyes of the white-trashy woman were staring hugely at the floor.
There the girl, held down on one side by the nurse and on the
other by her mother, was wrenching and turning in their grasp.
The doctor was kneeling astride her, trying to hold her arm down.
He managed after a second to sink a long needle into it.

Mrs. Turpin felt entirely hollow except for her heart which
swung from side to side as if it were agitated in a great empty
drum of flesh.

"Somebody that's not busy call for the ambulance," the doctor
said in the off-hand voice young doctors adopt for terrible occasions.

Mrs. Turpin could not have moved a finger. The old man who

had been sitting next to her skipped nimbly into the office and
made the call, for the secretary still seemed to be gone.

"Claud!" Mrs. Turpin called.   105

He was not in his chair. She knew she must jump up and find
him but she felt like some one trying to catch a train in a dream,
when everything moves in slow motion and the faster you try to
run the slower you go.

"Here I am," a suffocated voice, very unlike Claud's, said.

He was doubled up in the corner on the floor, pale as paper,
holding his leg. She wanted to get up and go to him but she could
not move. Instead, her gaze was drawn slowly downward to the
churning face on the floor, which she could see over the doctor's
shoulder.

The girl's eyes stopped rolling and focused on her. They seemed
a much lighter blue than before, as if a door that had been tightly
closed behind them was now open to admit light and air.

Mrs. Turpin's head cleared and her power of motion returned.   110
She leaned forward until she was looking directly into the fierce
brilliant eyes. There was no doubt in her mind that the girl did
know her, knew her in some intense and personal way, beyond
time and place and condition. "What you got to say to me?" she
asked hoarsely and held her breath, waiting, as for a revelation.

The girl raised her head. Her gaze locked with Mrs. Turpin's.
"Go back to hell where you came from, you old wart hog," she
whispered. Her voice was low but clear. Her eyes burned for a
moment as if she saw with pleasure that her message had struck
its target.

Mrs. Turpin sank back in her chair.

After a moment the girl's eyes closed and she turned her head
wearily to the side.

The doctor rose and handed the nurse the empty syringe. He
leaned over and put both hands for a moment on the mother's
shoulders, which were shaking. She was sitting on the floor, her
lips pressed together, holding Mary Grace's hand in her lap. The
girl's fingers were gripped like a baby's around her thumb. "Go
on to the hospital," he said. "I'll call and make the arrangements."

"Now let's see that neck," he said in a jovial voice to Mrs.   115
Turpin. He began to inspect her neck with his two fingers. Two
little moon-shaped lines like pink fish bones were indented over
her windpipe. There was the beginning of an angry red swelling
above her eye. His fingers passed over this also.

"Let me be," she said thickly and shook him off. "See about
Claud. She kicked him."

"I'll see about him in a minute," he said and felt her pulse. He was a thin grey-haired man, given to pleasantries. "Go home and have yourself a vacation the rest of the day," he said and patted her on the shoulder.

Quit your pattin me, Mrs. Turpin growled to herself.

"And put an ice pack over that eye," he said. Then he went and squatted down beside Claud and looked at his leg. After a moment he pulled him up and Claud limped after him into the office.

Until the ambulance came, the only sounds in the room were the tremulous moans of the girl's mother, who continued to sit on the floor. The white-trash woman did not take her eyes off the girl. Mrs. Turpin looked straight ahead at nothing. Presently the ambulance drew up, a long dark shadow, behind the curtain. The attendants came in and set the stretcher down beside the girl and lifted her expertly onto it and carried her out. The nurse helped the mother gather up her things. The shadow of the ambulance moved silently away and the nurse came back in the office.

"That ther girl is going to be a lunatic, ain't she?" the white-trash woman asked the nurse, but the nurse kept on to the back and never answered her.

"Yes, she's going to be a lunatic," the white-trash woman said to the rest of them.

"Po' critter," the old woman murmured. The child's face was still in her lap. His eyes looked idly out over her knees. He had not moved during the disturbance except to draw one leg up under him.

"I thank Gawd," the white-trash woman said fervently, "I ain't a lunatic."

Claud came limping out and the Turpins went home.

As their pick-up truck turned into their own dirt road and made the crest of the hill, Mrs. Turpin gripped the window ledge and looked out suspiciously. The land sloped gracefully down through a field dotted with lavender weeds and at the start of the rise their small yellow frame house, with its little flower beds spread out around it like a fancy apron, sat primly in its accustomed place between two giant hickory trees. She would not have been startled to see a burnt wound between two blackened chimneys.

Neither of them felt like eating so they put on their house clothes and lowered the shade in the bedroom and lay down, Claud with his leg on a pillow and herself with a damp washcloth over her eye. The instant she was flat on her back, the image of a razor-backed hog with warts on its face and horns coming out behind its ears snorted into her head. She moaned, a low quiet moan.

"I am not," she said tearfully, "a wart hog. From hell." But the denial had no force. The girl's eyes and her words, even the tone of her voice, low but clear, directed only to her, brooked no repudiation. She had been singled out for the message, though there was trash in the room to whom it might justly have been applied. The full force of this fact struck her only now. There was a woman there who was neglecting her own child but she had been overlooked. The message had been given to Ruby Turpin, a respectable, hard-working, church-going woman. The tears dried. Her eyes began to burn instead with wrath.

She rose on her elbow and the washcloth fell into her hand. Claud was lying on his back, snoring. She wanted to tell him what the girl had said. At the same time, she did not wish to put the image of herself as a wart hog from hell into his mind.

"Hey, Claud," she muttered and pushed his shoulder.   130

Claud opened one pale baby blue eye.

She looked into it warily. He did not think about anything. He just went his way.

"Wha, whasit?" he said and closed the eye again.

"Nothing," she said. "Does your leg pain you?"

"Hurts like hell," Claud said.   135

"It'll quit terreckly," she said and lay back down. In a moment Claud was snoring again. For the rest of the afternoon they lay there. Claud slept. She scowled at the ceiling. Occasionally she raised her fist and made a small stabbing motion over her chest as if she was defending her innocence to invisible guests who were like the comforters of Job, reasonable-seeming but wrong.

About five-thirty Claud stirred. "Got to go after those niggers," he sighed, not moving.

She was looking straight up as if there were unintelligible hand-writing on the ceiling. The proturberance over her eye had turned a greenish-blue. "Listen here," she said.

"What?"

"Kiss me."   140

Claud leaned over and kissed her loudly on the mouth. He pinched her side and their hands interlocked. Her expression of ferocious concentration did not change. Claud got up, groaning and growling, and limped off. She continued to study the ceiling.

She did not get up until she heard the pick-up truck coming back with the Negroes. Then she rose and thrust her feet in her brown oxfords, which she did not bother to lace, and stumped out onto the back porch and got her red plastic bucket. She emptied a tray of ice cubes into it and filled it half full of water and went out into the back yard. Every afternoon after Claud brought the hands in, one of the boys helped him put out hay and the rest waited in the back of the truck until he was ready to take them home. The truck was parked in the shade under one of the hickory trees.

"Hi yawl this evening?" Mrs. Turpin asked grimly, appearing with the bucket and the dipper. There were three women and a boy in the truck.

"Us doin nicely," the oldest woman said. "Hi you doin?" and her gaze struck immediately on the dark lump on Mrs. Turpin's forehead. "You done fell down, ain't you?" she asked in a solicitous voice. The old woman was dark and almost toothless. She had on an old felt hat of Claud's set back on her head. The other two women were younger and lighter and they both had new bright green sun hats. One of them had hers on her head; the other had taken hers off and the boy was grinning beneath it.

Mrs. Turpin set the bucket down on the floor of the truck.   145
"Yawl hep yourselves," she said. She looked around to make sure Claud had gone. "No. I didn't fall down," she said, folding her arms. "It was something worse than that."

"Ain't nothing bad happen to you!" the old woman said. She said it as if they all knew that Mrs. Turpin was protected in some special way by Divine Providence. "You just had you a little fall."

"We were in town at the doctor's office for where the cow kicked Mr. Turpin," Mrs. Turpin said in a flat tone that indicated they could leave off their foolishness. "And there was this girl there. A big fat girl with her face all broke out. I could look at that girl and tell she was peculiar but I couldn't tell how. And me and her mama were just talking and going along and all of a sudden WHAM! She throws this big book she was reading at me and . . ."

"Naw!" the old woman cried out.

"And then she jumps over the table and commences to choke me."

"Naw!" they all exclaimed, "naw!"   150

"Hi come she do that?" the old woman asked. "What ail her?"

Mrs. Turpin only glared in front of her.

"Somethin ail her," the old woman said.

"They carried her off in an ambulance," Mrs. Turpin continued, "but before she went she was rolling on the floor and they were trying to hold her down to give her a shot and she said something to me." She paused. "You know what she said to me?"

"What she say?" they asked.   155

"She said," Mrs. Turpin began, and stopped, her face very dark and heavy. The sun was getting whiter and whiter, blanching the

sky overhead so that the leaves of the hickory tree were black in
the face of it. She could not bring forth the words. "Something
real ugly," she muttered.

"She sho shouldn't said nothin ugly to you," the old woman
said. "You so sweet. You the sweetest lady I know."

"She pretty too," the one with the hat on said.

"And stout," the other one said. "I never knowed no sweeter
white lady."

"That's the truth befo' Jesus," the old woman said. "Amen!   160
You jes as sweet and pretty as you can be."

Mrs. Turpin knew just exactly how much Negro flattery was
worth and it added to her rage. "She said," she began again and
finished this time with a fierce rush of breath, "that I was an old
wart hog from hell."

There was an astounded silence.

"Where she at?" the youngest woman cried in a piercing voice.
"Lemme see her. I'll kill her!"

"I'll kill her with you!" the other one cried.   165

"She b'long in the sylum," the old woman said emphatically.
"You the sweetest white lady I know."

"She pretty too," the other two said. "Stout as she can be and
sweet. Jesus satisfied with her!"

"Deed he is," the old woman declared.

Idiots! Mrs. Turpin growled to herself. You could never say
anything intelligent to a nigger. You could talk at them but not
with them. "Yawl ain't drunk your water," she said shortly. "Leave
the bucket in the truck when you're finished with it. I got more
to do than just stand around and pass the time of day," and she
moved off and into the house.

She stood for a moment in the middle of the kitchen. The dark   170
protuberance over her eye looked like a miniature tornado cloud
which might any moment sweep across the horizon of her brow.
Her lower lip protruded dangerously. She squared her massive
shoulders. Then she marched into the front of the house and out
the side door and started down the road to the pig parlor. She
had the look of a woman going single-handed, weaponless, into
battle.

The sun was a deep yellow now like a harvest moon and was
rising westward very fast over the far tree line as if it meant to
reach the hogs before she did. The road was rutted and she kicked
several good-sized stones out of her path as she strode along. The
pig parlor was on a little knoll at the end of a lane that ran off
from the side of the barn. It was a square of concrete as large as
a small room, with a board fence about four feet high around it.

The concrete floor sloped slightly so that the hog wash could drain off into a trench where it was carried to the field for fertilizer. Claud was standing on the outside, on the edge of the concrete, hanging onto the top board, hosing down the floor inside. The hose was connected to the faucet of a water trough nearby.

Mrs. Turpin climbed up beside him and glowered down at the hogs inside. There were seven long-snouted bristly shoats in it— tan with liver-colored spots—and an old sow a few weeks off from farrowing. She was lying on her side grunting. The shoats were running about shaking themselves like idiot children, their little slit pig eyes searching the floor for anything left. She had read that pigs were the most intelligent animal. She doubted it. They were supposed to be smarter than dogs. There had even been a pig astronaut. He had performed his assignment perfectly but died of a heart attack afterwards because they left him in his electric suit, sitting upright throughout his examination when naturally a hog should be on all fours.

A-gruntin and a-rootin and a-groanin.

"Gimme that hose," she said, yanking it away from Claud. "Go on and carry them niggers home and then get off that leg."

"You look like you might have swallowed a mad dog," Claud observed, but he got down and limped off. He paid no attention to her humors.

Until he was out of earshot, Mrs. Turpin stood on the side of the pen, holding the hose and pointing the stream of water at the hind quarters of any shoat that looked as if it might try to lie down. When he had had time to get over the hill, she turned her head slightly and her wrathful eyes scanned the path. He was nowhere in sight. She turned back again and seemed to gather herself up. Her shoulders rose and she drew in her breath.

"What do you send me a message like that for?" she said in a low fierce voice, barely above a whisper but with the force of a shout in its concentrated fury. "How am I a hog and me both? How am I saved and from hell too?" Her free fist was knotted and with the other she gripped the hose, blindly pointing the stream of water in and out of the eye of the old sow whose outraged squeal she did not hear.

The pig parlor commanded a view of the back pasture where their twenty beef cows were gathered around the hay-bales Claud and the boy had put out. The freshly cut pasture sloped down to the highway. Across it was their cotton field and beyond that a dark green dusty wood which they owned as well. The sun was behind the wood, very red, looking over the paling of trees like a farmer inspecting his own hogs.

"Why me?" she rumbled. "It's no trash around here, black or white, that I haven't given to. And break my back to the bone every day working. And do for the church."

She appeared to be the right size woman to command the arena   180
before her. "How am I a hog?" she demanded. "Exactly how am I like them?" and she jabbed the stream of water at the shoats. "There was plenty of trash there. It didn't have to be me.

"If you like trash better, go get yourself some trash then," she railed. "You could have made me trash. Or a nigger. If trash is what you wanted why didn't you make me trash?" She shook her fist with the hose in it and a watery snake appeared momentarily in the air. "I could quit working and take it easy and be filthy," she growled. "Lounge about the sidewalks all day drinking root beer. Dip snuff and spit in every puddle and have it all over my face. I could be nasty.

"Or you could have made me a nigger. It's too late for me to be a nigger," she said with deep sarcasm, "but I could act like one. Lay down in the middle of the road and stop traffic. Roll on the ground."

In the deepening light everything was taking on a mysterious hue. The pasture was growing a peculiar glassy green and the streak of highway had turned lavender. She braced herself for a final assault and this time her voice rolled out over the pasture. "Go on," she yelled, "call me a hog! Call me a hog again. From hell. Call me a wart hog from hell. Put that bottom rail on top. There'll still be a top and bottom!"

A garbled echo returned to her.

A final surge of fury shook her and she roared, "Who do you   185
think you are?"

The color of everything, field and crimson sky, burned for a moment with a transparent intensity. The question carried over the pasture and across the highway and the cotton field and returned to her clearly like an answer from beyond the wood.

She opened her mouth but no sound came out of it.

A tiny truck, Claud's, appeared on the highway, heading rapidly out of sight. Its gears scraped thinly. It looked like a child's toy. At any moment a bigger truck might smash into it and scatter Claud's and the niggers' brains all over the road.

Mrs. Turpin stood there, her gaze fixed on the highway, all her muscles rigid, until in five or six minutes the truck reappeared, returning. She waited until it had had time to turn into their own road. Then like a monumental statue coming to life, she bent her head slowly and gazed, as if through the very heart of mystery, down into the pig parlor at the hogs. They had settled all in one corner around the old sow who was grunting softly. A red glow suffused them. They appeared to pant with a secret life.

Until the sun slipped finally behind the tree line, Mrs. Turpin remained there with her gaze bent to them as if she were absorbing some abysmal life-giving knowledge. At last she lifted her head. There was only a purple streak in the sky, cutting through a field of crimson and leading, like an extension of the highway, into the descending dusk. She raised her hands from the side of the pen in a gesture hieratic and profound. A visionary light settled in her eyes. She saw the streak as a vast swinging bridge extending upward from the earth through a field of living fire. Upon it a vast horde of souls were rumbling toward heaven. There were whole companies of white-trash, clean for the first time in their lives, and bands of black niggers in white robes, and battalions of freaks and lunatics shouting and clapping and leaping like frogs. And bringing up the end of the procession was a tribe of people whom she recognized at once as those who, like herself and Claud, had always had a little of everything and the God-given wit to use it right. She leaned forward to observe them closer. They were marching behind the others with great dignity, accountable as they had always been for good order and common sense and respectable behavior. They alone were on key. Yet she could see by their shocked and altered faces that even their virtues were being burned away. She lowered her hands and gripped the rail of the hog pen, her eyes small but fixed unblinkingly on what lay ahead. In a moment the vision faded but she remained where she was, immobile.

At length she got down and turned off the faucet and made her slow way on the darkening path to the house. In the woods around her the invisible cricket choruses had struck up, but what she heard were the voices of the souls climbing upward into the starry field and shouting hallelujah.

Thinking About Status

Perhaps the most astonishing battles for status ever waged on this continent were the potlatches of certain Indians of the Pacific Northwest. The potlatch began as a ceremonial feast, given by a man who had advanced to a higher social position: the higher the position, the more elaborate the feast and the gifts for the guests. But, of course, no guest of comparable social status could hold up his head unless he reciprocated with a still larger potlatch with more elaborate gifts. Inevitably, the potlatches grew more frequent and more ostentatious—sometimes with valuable gifts being thrown into the fire for dramatic effect—until they became ruinously expensive. The tribes invented a system of interest-bearing loans, and potlatchers mortgaged their children's futures to buy gifts. Some enlivened their potlatches by burning their houses. The *Encyclopaedia Britannica* laconically notes that "economic factors were more responsible" for the demise of this custom than were "interests working for Indian assimilation."

The madness of the potlatch certainly seems far from our daily experience, but this section contains examples of status seeking that are much more familiar and almost as unlikely. Mark Twain, for instance, remembers that among the boys who grew up in his town, the pinnacle of social status was occupied by a boy whose chief accomplishments were cursing, misapplying nautical jargon, and keeping himself constantly dirty. Tom Wolfe shows us Hugh Hefner, who displays his superiority by wearing pajamas day and night. Flannery O'Connor sets at least four equally peculiar status systems into collision in her short story "Revelation," and Russell Lynes catalogues his modern American snobberies as thoroughly as an anthropologist might catalogue the magical practices of a New Guinea tribe.

What makes us so adept at status games in the first place? What determines the particular form our status seeking will take? Beyond the amusement it provides for observers like Lynes, is the desire for status a good thing or a bad thing? Questions like these underlie the whole status section, and are dealt with very directly in essays by Samuel Johnson, C. S. Lewis, and William Manchester. Lewis's essay is important for those who want to think clearly about the role of status as one of the "great permanent mainsprings of human action." Manchester's is provocative because his position runs contrary to the "democratic" instincts most of us share.

The section also contains an excerpt from Paul Fussell's *Class*, a book that made readers squirm for a variety of reasons: some because it was accurate, some because it was distorted, many because it seemed unkind. Immediately following the Fussell selection is a thoughtful review of the book by James Fallows, the sort of review that must keep a writer awake at night. This sharp controversy over *Class* is in many ways a miniature of our complex involvement with class itself. We smile at snobbery and status seeking, but it is an uneasy smile. We are too self-conscious to laugh out loud.

QUESTIONS

1. The writers in this section disagree considerably about the motive that underlies the drive for status. Identify the motives they offer and comment on them. Which motives seem most likely, which least?

2. You will find in this section several unusual and even comic forms of status seeking—forms that would never be recommended in a self-help book like *How to Win Friends and Influence People* or *Dress for Success*. What specimen can you add to this exotic collection?

3. Some of the writers in the section treat the desire for status as essentially harmless; others warn that it can turn a person into a contemptible (Johnson), mean-spirited (Fallows) scoundrel (Lewis). Which writers seem to you to be nearest the mark?

4. Is it possible to distinguish between a beneficial and a harmful desire for status? Is there such a thing as a good snobbery?

5. Issues of status, snobbery, and reverse snobbery affect the style of these essays as well as their content. The author's tone (the attitude he or she takes toward the audience and the subject) can range from the extremely "democratic" and chummy to the extremely distant and formal. What sorts of word choices and sentence structures make a style "democratic" or "elitist"? Is it possible to have a style that is status-free? Is it desirable?

6. It may be that generations define themselves by the snobberies they embrace. College students of the sixties, for instance, were often reverse (or anti-snob) snobs and non-conformity snobs. Those in the seventies were often snobbish about their pragmatism and level-headedness. Is there a characteristic snobbery among college students of the eighties?

7. Three pillars of status that are mentioned repeatedly in this section are wealth, power, and taste. Does your own observation

tell you which of these is most important in contemporary society? What additional pillar would you add to these three?

8. Lewis argues that the longing to be inside some circle of higher prestige is "one of the great permanent mainsprings of human action," comparable in power and importance to the desire for power, money, or sex. Does this seem to you to be an overstatement?

OUTSIDERS

DOROTHY PARKER

Good Souls

All about us, living in our very families, it may be, there exists 1
a race of curious creatures. Outwardly, they possess no marked
peculiarities; in fact, at a hasty glance, they may be readily mistaken
for regular human beings. They are built after the popular design;
they have the usual number of features, arranged in the conventional
manner; they offer no variations on the general run of things in
their habits of dressing, eating, and carrying on their business.

Yet, between them and the rest of the civilized world, there 2
stretches an impassable barrier. Though they live in the very thick
of the human race, they are forever isolated from it. They are
fated to go through life, congenital pariahs. They live out their
little lives, mingling with the world, yet never a part of it.

They are, in short, Good Souls. 3

And the piteous thing about them is that they are wholly un- 4
conscious of their condition. A Good Soul thinks he is just like
anyone else. Nothing could convince him otherwise. It is heartrending to see him, going cheerfully about, even whistling or
humming as he goes, all unconscious of his terrible plight. The
utmost he can receive from the world is an attitude of good-
humored patience, a perfunctory word of approbation, a praising
with faint damns, so to speak—yet he firmly believes that everything
is all right with him.

There is no accounting for Good Souls. 5

They spring up anywhere. They will suddenly appear in families 6
which, for generations, have had no slightest stigma attached to
them. Possibly they are throw-backs. There is scarcely a family
without at least one Good Soul somewhere in it at the present
moment—maybe in the form of an elderly aunt, an unmarried
sister, an unsuccessful brother, an indigent cousin. No household
is complete without one.

The Good Soul begins early; he will show signs of his condition 7
in extreme youth. Go now to the nearest window, and look out
on the little children playing so happily below. Any group of
youngsters that you may happen to see will do perfectly. Do you
observe the child whom all the other little dears make "it" in their
merry games? Do you follow the child from whom the other little
ones snatch the cherished candy, to consume it before his streaming

First published in *Vanity Fair* in June 1919.

eyes? Can you get a good look at the child whose precious toys
are borrowed for indefinite periods by the other playful youngsters,
and are returned to him in fragments? Do you see the child upon
whom all the other kiddies play their complete repertory of childhood's winsome pranks—throwing bags of water on him, running
away and hiding from him, shouting his name in quaint rhymes,
chalking coarse legends on his unsuspecting back?

Mark that child well. He is going to be a Good Soul when he   8
grows up.

Thus does the doomed child go through early youth and ado-   9
lescence. So does he progress towards the fulfillment of his destiny.
And then, some day, when he is under discussion, someone will
say of him, "Well, he means well, anyway." That settles it. For
him, that is the end. Those words have branded him with the
indelible mark of his pariahdom. He has come into his majority;
he is a full-fledged Good Soul.

The activities of the adult of the species are familiar to us all.   10
When you are ill, who is it that hastens to your bedside bearing
molds of blanc-mange, which, from infancy, you have hated with
unspeakable loathing? As usual, you are way ahead of me, gentle
reader—it is indeed the Good Soul. It is the Good Souls who
efficiently smooth out your pillow when you have just worked it
into the comfortable shape, who creak about the room on noisy
tiptoe, who tenderly lay on your fevered brow damp cloths which
drip ceaselessly down your neck. It is they who ask, every other
minute, if there isn't something that they can do for you. It is
they who, at great personal sacrifice, spend long hours sitting
beside your bed, reading aloud the continued stories in the *Woman's
Home Companion,* or chatting cozily on the increase in the city's
death rate.

In health, as in illness, they are always right there, ready to   11
befriend you. No sooner do you sit down, than they exclaim that
they can see you aren't comfortable in that chair, and insist on
your changing places with them. It is the Good Souls who just
know that you don't like your tea that way, and who bear it
masterfully away from you to alter it with cream and sugar until
it is a complete stranger to you. At the table, it is they who always
feel that their grapefruit is better than yours and who have to be
restrained almost forcibly from exchanging with you. In a restaurant
the waiter invariably makes a mistake and brings them something
which they did not order—and which they refuse to have changed,
choking it down with a wistful smile. It is they who cause traffic
blocks, by standing in subway entrances arguing altruistically as
to who is to pay the fare.

At the theater, should they be members of a box-party, it is the 12
Good Souls who insist on occupying the rear chairs; if the seats
are in the orchestra, they worry audibly, all through the performance,
about their being able to see better than you, until finally in
desperation you grant their plea and change seats with them. If,
by so doing, they can bring a little discomfort on themselves—sit
in a draught, say, or behind a pillar—then their happiness is complete. To feel the genial glow of martyrdom—that is all they ask
of life. . . .

The lives of Good Souls are crowded with Occasions, each with 13
its own ritual which must be solemnly followed. On Mother's Day,
Good Souls conscientiously wear carnations; on St. Patrick's Day,
they faithfully don boutonnieres of shamrocks; on Columbus Day,
they carefully pin on miniature Italian flags. Every feast must be
celebrated by the sending out of cards—Valentine's Day, Arbor,
Groundhog Day, and all the other important festivals, each is duly
observed. They have a perfect genius for discovering appropriate
cards of greeting for the event. It must take hours of research.

If it's too long a time between holidays, then the Good Soul 14
will send little cards or little mementoes, just by way of surprises.
He is strong on surprises, anyway. It delights him to drop in
unexpectedly on his friends. Who has not known the joy of those
evenings when some Good Soul just runs in, as a surprise? It is
particularly effective when a chosen company of other guests happens to be present—enough for two tables of bridge, say. This
means that the Good Soul must sit wistfully by, patiently watching
the progress of the rubber,[1] or else must cut in at intervals, volubly
voicing his desolation at causing so much inconvenience, and
apologizing constantly during the evening.

His conversation, admirable though it is, never receives its just 15
due of attention and appreciation. He is one of those who believe
and frequently quote the exemplary precept that there is good in
everybody; hanging in his bedchamber is the whimsically phrased,
yet vital, statement, done in burned leather—"There is so much
good in the worst of us and so much bad in the best of us that
it hardly behooves any of us to talk about the rest of us." This,
too, he archly quotes on appropriate occasions. Two or three may
be gathered together, intimately discussing some mutual acquaintance. It is just getting really absorbing, when comes the Good
Soul, to utter his dutiful, "We mustn't judge harshly—after all,
we must always remember that many times our own actions may

---

1. In bridge, a rubber is a series of games, of which two out of three or three out
of five must be won.

be misconstrued." Somehow, after several of these little reminders, there seems to be a general waning of interest; the little gathering breaks up, inventing quaint excuses to get away and discuss the thing more fully, adding a few really good details, some place where the Good Soul will not follow. While the Good Soul, pitifully ignorant of their evil purpose, glows with the warmth of conscious virtue, and settles himself to read the Contributors' Club, in the *Atlantic Monthly*, with a sense of duty well done. . . .

Good Souls are no mean humorists. They have a time-honored   16
formula of fun-making, which must be faithfully followed. Certain words or phrases must be whimsically distorted every time they are used. "Over the river," they dutifully say, whenever they take their leave. "Don't you cast any asparagus on me," they warn, archly; and they never fail to speak of "three times in concussion." According to their ritual, these screaming phrases must be repeated several times, for the most telling effect, and are invariably followed by hearty laughter from the speaker, to whom they seem eternally new.

Perhaps the most congenial role of the Good Soul is that of   17
advice-giver. He loves to take people aside and have serious little personal talks, all for their own good. He thinks it only right to point out faults or bad habits which are, perhaps unconsciously, growing on them. He goes home and laboriously writes long, intricate letters, invariably beginning, "Although you may feel that this is no affair of mine, I think that you really ought to know," and so on, indefinitely. In his desire to help, he reminds one irresistibly of Marcelline, who used to try so pathetically and so fruitlessly to be of some assistance in arranging the circus arena, and who brought such misfortunes on his own innocent person thereby.

The Good Souls will, doubtless, gain their reward in Heaven;   18
on this earth, certainly, theirs is what is technically known as a rough deal. The most hideous outrages are perpetrated on them. "Oh, he won't mind," people say. "He's a Good Soul." And then they proceed to heap the rankest impositions upon him. When Good Souls give a party, people who have accepted weeks in advance call up at the last second and refuse, without the shadow of an excuse save that of a subsequent engagement. Other people are invited to all sorts of entertaining affairs; the Good Soul, unasked, waves them a cheery good-bye and hopes wistfully that they will have a good time. His is the uncomfortable seat in the motor car; he is the one to ride backwards in the train; he is the one who is always chosen to solicit subscriptions and make up deficits. People borrow his money, steal his servants, lose his golf balls, use him as a sort of errand boy, leave him flat whenever something

more attractive offers—and carry it all off with their cheerful slogan, "Oh, he won't mind—he's a Good Soul."

And that's just it—Good Souls never do mind. After each fresh [19] atrocity they are more cheerful, forgiving and virtuous, if possible, than they were before. There is simply no keeping them down— back they come, with their little gifts, and their little words of advice, and their little endeavors to be of service, always anxious for more.

Yes, there can be no doubt about it—their reward will come to [20] them in the next world.

Would that they were even now enjoying it! [21]

E. M. FORSTER

Jew-Consciousness

Long, long ago, while Queen Victoria[1] reigned, I attended two [1] preparatory schools. At the first of these, it was held to be a disgrace to have a sister. Any little boy who possessed one was liable to get teased. The word would go round: "Oh, you men, have you seen the Picktoes' sister?" The men would then reel about with sideway motions, uttering cries of "sucks" and pretending to faint with horror, while the Picktoes, who had hitherto held their own socially in spite of their name, found themselves banished into the wilderness, where they mourned, Major with Minor, in common shame. Naturally anyone who had a sister hid her as far as possible, and forbade her to sit with him at a Prizegiving or to speak to him except in passing and in a very formal manner. Public opinion was not bitter on the point, but it was quite definite. Sisters were disgraceful. I got through all right myself, because my conscience was clear, and though charges were brought against me from time to time they always fell through.

It was a very different story at my second school. Here, sisters [2] were negligible, but it was a disgrace to have a mother. Crabbe's mother, Gob's mother, eeugh! No words were too strong, no sounds too shrill. And since mothers at that time of life are commoner than sisters, and also less biddable, the atmosphere of this school

Originally published in *New Statesman and Nation*, January 7, 1939.
1. Queen of England from 1837 to 1901. Forster was at preparatory school during the last years of her reign.

was less pleasant, and the sense of guilt stronger. Nearly every little boy had a mother in a cupboard, and dreadful revelations occurred. A boy would fall ill and a mother would swoop and drive him away in a cab. A parcel would arrive with "From Mummy for her darling" branded upon it. Many tried to divert suspicion by being aggressive and fastening female parents upon the weak. One or two, who were good at games and had a large popularity-surplus, took up a really heroic line, acknowledged their mother brazenly, and would even be seen walking with her across the playing-field, like King Carol with Madame Lupescu.[2] We admired such boys and envied them, but durst not imitate them. The margin of safety was too narrow. The convention was established that a mother spelt disgrace, and no individual triumph could reverse this.

Those preparatory schools prepared me for life better than I realised, for having passed through two imbecile societies, a sister-conscious and a mother-conscious, I am now invited to enter a third. I am asked to consider whether the people I meet and talk about are or are not Jews, and to form an opinion on them until this fundamental point has been settled. What revolting tosh! Neither science nor religion nor common sense has one word to say in its favour. All the same, Jew-consciousness is in the air, and it remains to be seen how far it will succeed in poisoning it. I don't think we shall ever reintroduce ghettos into England; I wouldn't say for certain, since no one knows what wickedness may not develop in his country or in himself if circumstances change. I don't think we shall go savage. But I do think we shall go silly. Many people have gone so already. Today, the average man suspects the people he dislikes of being Jews, and is surprised when the people he likes are Jews. Having been a Gentile at my first preparatory school and a Jew at my second, I know what I am talking about. I know how the poison works, and I know that if the average man is anyone in particular he is a preparatory school boy. On the surface, things do not look too bad. Labour and Liberalism behave with their expected decency and denounce persecution, and respectability generally follows suit. But beneath the surface things are not so good and anyone who keeps his ears open in railway carriages or pubs or country lanes can hear a very different story. A nasty side of our nation's character has been scratched up—the sniggering side. People who would not ill-treat

2. Carol II (1893–1953) King of Rumania, and his mistress, with whom he lived after being forced to renounce his right of succession to the throne in 1925.

Jews themselves, or even be rude to them, enjoy tittering over their misfortunes; they giggle when pogroms[3] are instituted by someone else and synagogues defiled vicariously. "Serve them right really, Jews." This makes unpleasant reading, but anyone who cares to move out of his own enlightened little corner will discover that it is true. The grand Nordic argument, "He's a bloody capitalist so he must be a Jew, and as he's a Jew he must be a Red," has already taken root in our filling-stations and farms. Men employ it more frequently than women, and young men more frequently than old ones. The best way of confuting it is to say sneeringly, "That's propaganda." When "That's propaganda" has been repeated several times, the sniggering stops, for no goose likes to think that he has been got at. There is another reply which is more intellectual but which requires more courage. It is to say, "Are you sure you're not a Jew yourself? Do you know who your eight great-grandparents were? Can you swear that all the eight are Aryan?" Cool reasonableness would be best of all, of course, but it does not work in the world of today any better than in my preparatory schools. The only effective check to silliness is silliness of a cleverer type.

Jew-mania was the one evil which no one foretold at the close 4 of the last war. All sorts of troubles were discerned and discernible— nationalism, class-warfare, the split between the haves and the have-nots, the general lowering of cultural values. But no prophet, so far as I know, had foreseen this anti-Jew horror, whereas today no one can see the end of it. There had been warnings, of course, but they seemed no more ominous than a poem by Hilaire Belloc.[4] Back in India, in 1921, a Colonel lent me the Protocols of the Elders of Zion,[5] and it was such an obvious fake that I did not worry. I had forgotten my preparatory schools, and did not see that they were about to come into their own. To me, anti-Semitism is now the most shocking of all things. It is destroying much more than the Jews; it is assailing the human mind at its source, and inviting it to create false categories before exercising judgment. I am sure we shall win through. But it will take a long time. Perhaps a hundred years must pass before men can think back to the

---

3. Organized massacres, particularly of Jews.
4. English writer, 1870–1953, noted for the loveliness of much of his work.
5. A fake document purporting to give the proceedings of a conference of Jews in the late nineteenth century, at which they proposed to overthrow Christianity and control the world.

mentality of 1918, or can say with the Prophet Malachi, "Have we not all one father? Hath not one God created us?"[6] For the moment, all that we can do is to dig in our heels, and prevent silliness from sliding into insanity.

6. Malachi 2:10.

ROGER WILKINS

Confessions of a Blue-Chip Black

Early in the spring of 1932—six months after Earl's brother, 1 Roy, left Kansas City to go to New York to join the national staff of the National Association for the Advancement of Colored People, and eight months before Franklin Roosevelt was elected president for the first time—Earl and Helen Wilkins had the first and only child to be born of their union. I was born in a little segregated hospital in Kansas City called Phillis Wheatley.[1] The first time my mother saw me, she cried. My head was too long and my color, she thought, was blue.

My parents never talked about slavery or my ancestors. Images 2 of Africa were images of backwardness and savagery. Once, when I was a little boy, I said to my mother after a friend of my parents left the house: "Mr. Bledsoe is black, isn't he, mama."

"Oh," she exclaimed. "Never say anybody is black. That's a 3 terrible thing to say."

Next time Mr. Bledsoe came to the house, I commented, "Mama, 4 Mr. Bledsoe is navy blue."

When I was two years old and my father was in the tuberculosis 5 sanitarium, he wrote me a letter, which I obviously couldn't read, but which tells a lot about how he planned to raise his Negro son.

Friday, March 22, 1934

Dear Roger—
    Let me congratulate you upon having reached your second birthday. Your infancy is now past and it is now that you should begin to turn your thoughts upon those achievements which are expected of a brilliant young gentleman well on his way to manhood.

Originally published in *Harper's*, April 1982.
1. Black American poet, 1753?–1784.

During the next year, you should learn the alphabet; you should learn certain French and English idioms which are a part of every cultivated person's vocabulary: you should gain complete control of those natural functions which, uncontrolled, are a source of worry and embarrassment to even the best of grandmothers: you should learn how to handle table silver so that you will be able to eat gracefully and conventionally: and you should learn the fundamental rules of social living—politeness, courtesy, consideration for others, and the rest.

This should not be difficult for you. You have the best and most patient of mothers in your sterling grandmother and your excellent mother. Great things are expected of you. Never, never forget that.

Love,
Your Father

We lived in a neat little stucco house on a hill in a small Negro   6
section called Roundtop. I had no sense of being poor or of any anxiety about money. At our house, not only was there food and furniture and all the rest, there was even a baby grand piano that my mother would play sometimes. And there was a cleaning lady, Mrs. Turner, who came every week.

When it was time for me to go to school, the board of education   7
provided us with a big yellow bus, which carried us past four or five perfectly fine schools down to the middle of the large Negro community, to a very old school called Crispus Attucks.[2] I have no memories of those bus rides except for my resentment of the selfishness of the whites who wouldn't let us share those newer-looking schools near to home.

My father came home when I was four and died when I was   8
almost nine. He exuded authority. He thought the women hadn't been sufficiently firm with me, so he instituted a spanking program with that same hard hairbrush that my grandmother had used so much to try to insure that I didn't have "nigger-looking" hair.

After my father's death, the family moved to New York. Our   9
apartment was in that legendary uptown area called Sugar Hill, where blacks who had it made were said to live the sweet life. I lived with my mother, my grandmother, and my mother's younger sister, Zelma. My Uncle Roy and his wife, Minnie, a New York social worker, lived on the same floor. My Aunt Marvel and her husband, Cecil, lived one floor down.

---

2. American mulatto, 1723?–1770; led mob in "Boston Massacre" and was killed by British troops.

As life in New York settled into a routine, my life came to be   10
dominated by four women: my mother, her sisters, and her mother.
Nobody else had any children, so everybody concentrated on me.

Sometime early in 1943 my mother's work with the YMCA took   11
her to Grand Rapids, Michigan, where she made a speech and
met a forty-four-year-old bachelor doctor who looked like a white
man. He had light skin, green eyes, and "good hair"—that is, hair
that was as straight and as flat as white people's hair. He looked
so like a white person that he could have passed for white. There
was much talk about people who had passed. They were generally
deemed to be bad people, for they were not simply selfish, but
also cruel to those whom they left behind. On the other hand,
people who could pass, but did not, were respected.

My mother remarried in October 1943, and soon I was once   12
more on a train with my grandmother, heading toward Grand
Rapids and my new home. This train also took me, at the age of
twelve, beyond the last point in my life when I would feel totally
at peace with my blackness.

My new home was in the north end of Grand Rapids, a completely   13
white neighborhood. This would be the place I would henceforth
think of as home. And it would be the place where I would become
more Midwestern than Harlemite, more American than black, and
more complex than was comfortable or necessary for the middle-
class conformity that my mother had in mind for me.

Grand Rapids was pretty single-family houses and green spaces.   14
The houses looked like those in *Look* magazine or in *Life*. You
could believe, and I did, that there was happiness inside. To me,
back then, the people seemed to belong to the houses as the houses
belonged to the land, and all of it had to do with being white.
They moved and walked and talked as if the place, the country,
and the houses were theirs, and I envied them.

I spent the first few weeks exploring Grand Rapids on a new   15
bike my stepfather had bought for me. The people I passed would
look back at me with intense and sometimes puzzled looks on
their faces as I pedaled by. Nobody waved or even smiled. They
just stopped what they were doing to stand and look. As soon as
I saw them looking, I would look forward and keep on riding.

One day I rode for miles, down and up and down again. I was   16
past Grand Rapids' squatty little downtown, and farther south
until I began to see some Negro people. There were black men
and women and some girls, but it was the boys I was looking for.
Then I saw a group: four of them. They were about my age, and

they were dark. Though their clothes were not as sharp as the boys' in the Harlem Valley, they were old, and I took the look of poverty and the deep darkness of their faces to mean that they were like the hard boys of Harlem.

One of them spotted me riding toward them and pointed. "Hey, lookit that bigole skinny bike," he said. Then they all looked at my bike and at me. I couldn't see expressions on their faces; only the blackness and the coarseness of their clothes. Before any of the rest of them had a chance to say anything, I stood up on the pedals and wheeled the bike in a U-turn and headed back on up toward the north end of town. It took miles for the terror to finally subside. 17

Farther on toward home, there was a large athletic field. As I neared the field, I could see some large boys in shorts moving determinedly around a football. When I got to the top of the hill that overlooked the field, I stopped and stood, one foot on the ground and one leg hanging over the crossbar, staring down at them. All the boys were white and big and old—sixteen to eighteen. I had never seen a football workout before, and I was fascinated. I completely forgot everything about color, theirs or mine. 18

Then one of them saw me. He pointed and said, "Look, there's the little coon watchin us." 19

I wanted to be invisible. I was horrified. My heart pounded, and my arms and legs shook, but I managed to get back on my bike and ride home. 20

The first white friend I made was named Jerry Schild. On the second day of our acquaintance, he took me to his house, above a store run by his parents. I met his three younger siblings, including a very little one toddling around in bare feet and a soiled diaper. 21

While Jerry changed the baby, I looked around the place. It was cheap, all chintz and linoleum. The two soft pieces of furniture, a couch and an overstuffed chair, had gaping holes and were hemorrhaging their fillings. And there were an awful lot of empty brown beer bottles sitting around, both in the kitchen and out on the back porch. While the place was not dirty, it made me very sad. Jerry and his family were poor in a way I had never seen people be poor before, in Kansas City or even in Harlem. 22

Jerry's father wasn't there that day and Jerry didn't mention him. But later in the week, when I went to call for Jerry, I saw him. I yelled for Jerry from downstairs in the back and his father came to the railing of the porch on the second floor. He was a skinny man in overalls with the bib hanging down crookedly because it was fastened only on the shoulder. His face was narrow 23

and wrinkled and his eyes were set deep in dark hollows. He had
a beer bottle in his hand and he looked down at me. "Jerry ain't
here," he said. He turned away and went back inside.

One day our front doorbell rang and I could hear my mother's   24
troubled exclamation. "Jerry! What's wrong?" Jerry was crying
so hard he could hardly talk. "My father says I can't play with
you anymore because you're not good enough for us."

Creston High School, which served all the children from the   25
north end of Grand Rapids, was all white and middle-class. Nobody
talked to me that first day, but I was noticed. When I left school
at the end of the day I found my bike leaning up against the fence
where I had left it, with a huge glob of slimy spit on my shaggy
saddle cover. People passed by on their way home and looked at
me and spit. I felt a hollowness behind my eyes, but I didn't cry.
I just got on the bike, stood up on the pedals, and rode it home
without sitting down. And it went that way for about the first
two weeks. After the third day, I got rid of the saddle cover because
the plain leather was a lot easier to clean.

But the glacier began to thaw. One day in class, the freckle-   26
faced kid with the crewcut sitting next to me was asking everybody
for a pencil. And then he looked at me and said, "Maybe you
can lend me one." Those were the best words I had heard since
I first met Jerry. This kid had included me in the human race in
front of everybody. His name was Jack Waltz.

And after a while when the spitters had subsided and I could   27
ride home sitting down, I began to notice that little kids my size
were playing pickup games in the end zones of the football field.
It looked interesting, but I didn't know anybody and didn't know
how they would respond to me. So I just rode on by for a couple
for weeks, slowing down each day, trying to screw up my courage
to go in.

But then one day, I saw Jack Waltz there. I stood around the   28
edges of the group watching. It seemed that they played forever
without even noticing me, but finally someone had to go home
and the sides were unbalanced. Somebody said, "Let's ask him."

As we lined up for our first huddle, I heard somebody on the   29
other side say, "I hope he doesn't have a knife." One of the guys
on my side asked me, "Can you run the ball?" I said yes, so they
gave me the ball and I ran three quarters of the length of the field
for a touchdown. And I made other touchdowns and other long
runs before the game was over. When I thought about it later that
night, I became certain that part of my success was due to the

imaginary knife that was running interference for me. But no matter. By the end of the game, I had a group of friends. Boys named Andy and Don and Bill and Gene and Rich. We left the field together and some of them waved and yelled, "See ya tomorra, Rog."

And Don De Young, a pleasant round-faced boy, even lived 30 quite near me. So, after parting from everybody else, he and I went on together down to the corner of Coit and Knapp. As we parted, he suggested that we meet to go to school together the next day. I had longed for that but I hadn't suggested it for fear of a rebuff for overstepping the limits of my race. I had already learned one of the great tenets of Negro survival in America: to live the reactive life. It was like the old Negro comedian who once said, "When the man asks how the weather is, I know nuff to look keerful at his face 'fore even I look out the window." So, I waited for him to suggest it, and my patience was rewarded. I was overjoyed and grateful.

I didn't spend all my time in the north end. Soon after I moved 31 to Grand Rapids, Pop introduced me to some patients he had with a son my age. The boy's name was Lloyd Brown, and his father was a bellman downtown at the Pantlind Hotel. Lloyd and I often rode bikes and played basketball in his backyard. After a while, my mother asked me why I never had Lloyd come out to visit me. It was a question I dreaded, but she pressed on. "After all," she said, "you've had a lot of meals at his house and it's rude not to invite him back." I knew she was right and I also hated the whole idea of it.

With my friends in the north, race was never mentioned. Ever. 32 I carried my race around with me like an open basket of rotten eggs. I knew I could drop one at any moment and it would explode with a stench over everything. This was in the days when the movies either had no blacks at all or featured rank stereotypes like Stepin Fetchit,[3] and the popular magazines like *Life, Look,* the *Saturday Evening Post,* and *Colliers* carried no stories about Negroes, had no ads depicting Negroes, and generally gave the impression that we did not exist in this society. I knew that my white friends, being well brought up, were just too polite to mention this disability that I had. And I was grateful to them, but terrified, just the same, that maybe someday one of them would have the bad taste to notice what I was.

3. A lazy black character in the film *Hearts in Dixie* (1929).

It seemed to me that my tenuous purchase in this larger white   33
world depended on the maintenance between me and my friends
in the north end of our unspoken bargain to ignore my difference,
my shame, and their embarrassment. If none of us had to deal
with it, I thought, we could all handle it. My white friends behaved
as if they perceived the bargain exactly as I did. It was a delicate
equation, and I was terrified that Lloyd's presence in the North
End would rip apart the balance.

I am so ashamed of that shame now that I cringe when I write   34
it. But I understand that boy now as he could not understand
himself then. I was an American boy, though I did not fully
comprehend that either. I was fully shaped and formed by America,
where white people had all the power in sight, and they owned
everything in sight except our house. Their beauty was the real
beauty; there wasn't any other beauty. A real human being had
straight hair, a white face, and thin lips. Other people, who looked
different, were lesser beings.

No wonder, then, that most black men desired the forbidden   35
fruit of white loins. No wonder, too, that we thought that the
most beautiful and worthy Negro people were those who looked
most white. We blacks used to have a saying: "If you're white,
you're all right. If you're brown, stick around. If you're black,
stand back." I was brown.

It was not that we in my family were direct victims of racism.   36
On the contrary, my stepfather clearly had a higher income than
the parents of most students in my high school. Unlike those of
most of my contemporaries, black and white, my parents had
college degrees. Within Grand Rapids' tiny Negro community, they
were among the elite. The others were the lawyer, the dentist,
the undertaker, and the other doctor.

But that is what made race such exquisite agony. I did have a   37
sense that it was unfair for poor Negroes to be relegated to bad
jobs—if they had jobs at all—and to bad or miserable housing,
but I didn't feel any great sense of identity with them. After all,
the poor blacks in New York had also been the hard ones: the
ones who tried to take my money, to beat me up, and to keep
me perpetually intimidated. Besides, I had heard it intimated around
my house that their behavior, sexual or otherwise, left a good deal
to be desired.

So I thought that maybe they just weren't ready for this society,   38
but that I was. And it was dreadfully unfair for white people to
just look at my face and lips and hair and decide that I was inferior.

By being a model student and leader, I thought I was demonstrating how well Negroes could perform if only the handicaps were removed and they were given a chance. But deep down I guess I was also trying to demonstrate that I was not like those other people; that I was different. My message was quite clear: I was *not nigger.* But the world didn't seem quite ready to make such fine distinctions, and it was precisely that fact—though at the time I could scarcely even have admitted it to myself—that was the nub of the race issue for me.

I would sometimes lie on my back and stare up at passing clouds 39 and wonder why God had played a dirty trick by making me a Negro. It all seemed so random. So unfair to me. To *me!* But in school I was gaining more friends, and the teachers respected me. It got so that I could go for days not thinking very much about being Negro, until something made the problem unavoidable.

One day in history class, for instance, the teacher asked each 40 of us to stand and tell in turn where our families had originated. Many of the kids in the class were Dutch with names like Vander Jagt, De Young, and Ripstra. My pal Andy was Scots-Irish. When it came my turn, I stood up and burned with shame and when I would speak, I lied. And then I was even more ashamed because I exposed a deeper shame. "Some of my family was English," I said—Wilkins is an English name—"and the rest of it came from . . . Egypt." Egypt!

One Saturday evening after one of our sandlot games, I went 41 over to Lloyd's. Hearing my stories, Lloyd said mildly that he'd like to come up and play some Saturday. I kept on talking, but all the time my mind was repeating: "Lloyd wants to play. He wants to come up to the North End on Saturday. Next Saturday. Next Saturday." I was trapped.

So, after the final story about the final lunge, when I couldn't 42 put it off any longer, I said. "Sure. Why not?" But, later in the evening, after I had had some time to think, I got Lloyd alone. "Say, look," I said. "Those teams are kinda close, ya know. I mean, we don't switch around. From team to team. Or new guys, ya know?"

Lloyd nodded, but he was getting a funny look on his face . . . 43 part unbelieving and part hurt. So I quickly interjected before he could say anything, "Naw, man. Naw. Not like you shouldn't come and play. Just that we gotta have some good reason for you to play on our team, you dig?"

"Yeah," Lloyd said, his face still puzzled, but no longer hurt. 44

"Hey, I know," I said. "I got it. We'll say you're my cousin. If 45
you're my cousin, see, then you gotta play. Nobody can say you
can't be on my team, because you're family, right?"

"Oh, right. Okay," Lloyd said, his face brightening. "Sure, we'll 46
say we're cousins. Solid."

I felt relieved as well. I could have a Negro cousin. It wasn't 47
voluntary. It wouldn't be as if I had gone out and made a Negro
friend deliberately. A person couldn't help who his cousins were.

There began to be a cultural difference between me and other 48
blacks my age too. Black street language had evolved since my
Harlem days, and I had not kept pace. Customs, attitudes, and
the other common social currencies of everyday black life had
evolved away from me. I didn't know how to talk, to banter, to
move my body. If I was tentative and responsive in the North
End, where I lived, I was tense, stiff, and awkward when I was
with my black contemporaries. One day I was standing outside
the church trying, probably at my mother's urging, to make contact.
Conversational sallies flew around me while I stood there stiff and
mute, unable to participate. Because the language was so foreign
to me, I understood little of what was being said, but I did know
that the word used for a white was *paddy*. Then a boy named
Nickerson, the one whom my mother particularly wanted me to
be friends with, inclined his head slightly toward me and said, to
whoops of laughter, "technicolor paddy." My feet felt rooted in
stone, and my head was aflame. I never forgot that phrase.

I have rarely felt so alone as I did that day riding home from 49
church. Already partly excluded by my white friends, I was now
almost completely alienated from my own people as well. But I
felt less uncomfortable and less vulnerable in the white part of
town. It was familiar enough to enable me to ward off most
unpleasantness.

And then there was the problem of girls. They were everywhere, 50
the girls. They all had budding bosoms, they all smelled pink, they
all brushed against the boys in the hall, they were all white, and,
in 1947–49, they were all inaccessible.

There were some things you knew without ever knowing how 51
you knew them. You knew that Mississippi was evil and dangerous,
that New York was east, and the Pacific ocean was west. And in
the same way you knew that white women were the most desirable
and dangerous objects in the world. Blacks were lynched in Mississippi and such places sometimes just for looking with the wrong
expression at white women. Blacks of a very young age knew

that white women of any quality went with the power and style that went with the governance of America—though, God knows, we had so much self-hate that when a white woman went with a Negro man, we promptly decided she was trash, and we also figured that if she would go with him she would go with any Negro.

Nevertheless, as my groin throbbed at fifteen and sixteen and seventeen, *they* were often the only ones there. One of them would be in the hallway opening her locker next to mine. Her blue sweater sleeve would be pushed up to just below the elbow, and as she would reach high on a shelf to stash away a book, I would see the tender dark hair against the white skin of her forearm. And I would ache and want to touch that arm and follow that body hair to its source.

Some of my friends, of course, did touch some of those girls. My friends and I would talk about athletics and school and their loves. But they wouldn't say a word about the dances and the hayrides they went to.

I perceived they liked me and accepted me as long as I moved aside when life's currents took them to where I wasn't supposed to be. I fit into their ways when they talked about girls, even their personal girls. And, indeed, I fit into the girls' lives when they were talking about boys, most particularly their own personal boys. Because I was a boy, I had insight. But I was also Negro, and therefore a neuter. So a girl who was alive and sensuous night after night in my fantasies would come to me earnestly in the day and talk about Rich or Gene or Andy. She would ask what he thought about her, whether he liked to dance, whether, if she invited him to her house for a party, he would come. She would tell me her fears and her yearnings, never dreaming for an instant that I had yearnings too and that she was their object.

There may be few more powerful obsessions than a teenage boy's fixation on a love object. In my case it came down to a thin brunette named Marge McDowell. She was half a grade behind me, and she lived in a small house on a hill. I found excuses to drive by it all the time. I knew her schedule at school, so I could manage to be in most of the hallways she had to use going from class to class. We knew each other, and she had once confided a strong but fleeting yearning for my friend Rich Kippen. I thought about her constantly.

Finally, late one afternoon after school, I came upon her alone in a hallway. "Marge," I blurted, "can I ask you something?"

She stopped and smiled and said, "Sure, Roger, what?"   57
"Well I was wondering," I said. "I mean. Well, would you go   58
to the hayride next week with me."

Her jaw dropped and her eyes got huge. Then she uttered a   59
small shriek and turned, hugging her books to her bosom the way
girls do, and fled. I writhed with mortification in my bed that
night and for many nights after.

In my senior year, I was elected president of the Creston High   60
School student council. It was a breakthrough of sorts.

RICHARD RODRIGUEZ

Going Home Again:
The New American Scholarship Boy

At each step, with every graduation from one level of education   1
to the next, the refrain from bystanders was strangely the same:
"Your parents must be so proud of you." I suppose that my parents
were proud, although I suspect, too, that they felt more than pride
alone as they watched me advance through my education. They
seemed to know that my education was separating us from one
another, making it difficult to resume familiar intimacies. Mixed
with the instincts of parental pride, a certain hurt also communicated
itself—too private ever to be adequately expressed in words, but
real nonetheless.

The autobiographical facts pertinent to this essay are simply   2
stated in two sentences, though they exist in somewhat awkward
juxtaposition to each other. I am the son of Mexican-American
parents, who speak a blend of Spanish and English, but who read
neither language easily. I am about to receive a Ph.D. in English
Renaissance literature. What sort of life—what tensions, feelings,
conflicts—connects these two sentences? I look back and remember
my life from the time I was seven or eight years old as one of
constant movement away from a Spanish-speaking folk culture
toward the world of the English-language classroom. As the years
passed, I felt myself becoming less like my parents and less comfortable with the assumption of visiting relatives that I was still

Originally published in *The American Scholar,* Winter 1974.

the Spanish-speaking child they remembered. By the time I began college, visits home became suffused with silent embarrassment: there seemed so little to share, however strong the ties of our affection. My parents would tell me what happened in their lives or in the lives of relatives; I would respond with news of my own. Polite questions would follow. Our conversations came to seem more like interviews.

A few months ago, my dissertation nearly complete, I came 3 upon my father looking through my bookcase. He quietly fingered the volumes of Milton's tracts and Augustine's theology with that combination of reverence and distrust those who are not literate sometimes show for the written word. Silently, I watched him from the door of the room. However much he would have insisted that he was "proud" of his son for being able to master the texts, I knew, if pressed further, he would have admitted to complicated feelings about my success. When he looked across the room and suddenly saw me, his body tightened slightly with surprise, then we both smiled.

For many years I kept my uneasiness about becoming a success 4 in education to myself. I did so in part because I wanted to avoid vague feelings that, if considered carefully, I would have no way of dealing with; and in part because I felt that no one else shared my reaction to the opportunity provided by education. When I began to rehearse my story of cultural dislocation publicly, however, I found many listeners willing to admit to similar feelings from their own pasts. Equally impressive was the fact that many among those I spoke with were *not* from nonwhite racial groups, which made me realize that one can grow up to enter the culture of the academy and find it a "foreign" culture for a variety of reasons, ranging from economic status to religious heritage. But why, I next wondered, was it that, though there were so many of us who came from childhood cultures alien to the academy's, we voiced our uneasiness to one another and to ourselves so infrequently? Why did it take *me* so long to acknowledge publicly the cultural costs I had paid to earn a Ph.D. in Renaissance English literature? Why, more precisely, am I writing these words only now when my connection to my past barely survives except as nostalgic memory?

Looking back, a person risks losing hold of the present while 5 being confounded by the past. For the child who moves to an academic culture from a culture that dramatically lacks academic traditions, looking back can jeopardize the certainty he has about the desirability of this new academic culture. Richard Hoggart's description, in *The Uses of Literacy,* of the cultural pressures on such a student, whom Hoggart calls the "scholarship boy," helps make the point. The scholarship boy must give nearly unquestioning allegiance to academic culture, Hoggart argues, if he is to succeed at all, so different is the milieu of the classroom from the culture he leaves behind. For a time, the scholarship boy may try to balance his loyalty between his concretely experienced family life and the more abstract mental life of the classroom. In the end, though, he must choose between the two worlds: if he intends to succeed as a student, he must, literally and figuratively, separate himself from his family, with its gregarious life, and find a quiet place to be alone with his thoughts.

After a while, the kind of allegiance the young student might 6 once have given his parents is transferred to the teacher, the new parent. Now without the support of the old ties and certainties of the family, he almost mechanically acquires the assumptions, practices, and style of the classroom milieu. For the loss he might otherwise feel, the scholarship boy substitutes an enormous enthusiasm for nearly everything having to do with school.

How readily I read my own past into the portrait of Hoggart's 7 scholarship boy. Coming from a home in which mostly Spanish was spoken, for example, I had to decide to forget Spanish when I began my education. To succeed in the classroom, I needed psychologically to sever my ties with Spanish. Spanish represented an alternate culture as well as another language—and the basis of my deepest sense of relationship to my family. Although I recently taught myself to read Spanish, the language that I see on the printed page is not quite the language I heard in my youth. That other Spanish, the spoken Spanish of my family, I remember with nostalgia and guilt: guilt because I cannnot explain to aunts and uncles why I do not answer their questions any longer in their own idiomatic language. Nor was I able to explain to teachers in graduate school, who regularly expected me to read and speak Spanish with ease, why my very ability to reach graduate school as a student of English literature in the first place required me to loosen my attachments to a language I spoke years earlier. Yet, having lost the ability to speak Spanish, I never forgot it so totally that I could not understand it. Hearing Spanish spoken on the street reminded me of the community I once felt a part of, and still cared deeply about. I never forgot Spanish so thoroughly, in other words, as to move outside the range of its nostalgic pull.

Such moments of guilt and nostalgia were, however, just that— 8 momentary. They punctuated the history of my otherwise successful progress from *barrio*[1] to classroom. Perhaps they even encouraged it. Whenever I felt my determination to succeed wavering, I tightened my hold on the conventions of academic life.

Spanish was one aspect of the problem, my parents another. They could raise deeper, more persistent doubts. They offered encouragement to my brothers and me in our work, but they also spoke, only half jokingly, about the way education was putting "big ideas" into our heads. When we would come home, for example, and challenge assumptions we earlier believed, they would be forced to defend their beliefs (which, given our new verbal skills, they did increasingly less well) or, more frequently, to submit to our logic with the disclaimer, "It's what we were taught in our time to believe. . . ." More important, after we began to leave home for college, they voiced regret about how "changed" we had become, how much further away from one another we had grown. They partly yearned for a return to the time before education assumed their children's primary loyalty. This yearning was renewed each time they saw their nieces and nephews (none of whom continued their education beyond high school, all of whom continued to speak fluent Spanish) living according to the conventions and assumptions of their parents' culture. If I was already troubled by the time I graduated from high school by that refrain of congratulations ("Your parents must be so proud. . . ."), I realize now how much more difficult and complicated was my progress into academic life for my parents, as they saw the cultural foundation of their family erode, than it was for me.

Yet my parents were willing to pay the price of alienation and continued to encourage me to become a scholarship boy because they perceived, as others of the lower classes had before them, the relation between education and social mobility. Lacking the former themselves made them acutely aware of its necessity as prerequisite for the latter. They sent their children off to school in the hopes of their acquiring something "better" beyond education. Notice the assumption here that education is something of a tool or license—a means to an end, which has been the traditional way the lower or working classes have viewed the value of education in the past. That education might alter children in more basic ways than providing them with skills, certificates of proficiency, and even upward mobility, may come as a surprise for some, but the financial cost is usually tolerated.

1. The Hispanic neighborhood within a city.

Complicating my own status as a scholarship boy in the last 11
ten years was the rise, in the mid-1960s, of what was then called
"the Third World Student Movement." Racial minority groups,
led chiefly by black intellectuals, began to press for greater access
to higher education. The assumption behind their criticism, like
the assumption of white working-class families, was that educational
opportunity was useful for economic and social advancement. The
racial minority leaders went one step further, however, and it was
this step that was probably most revolutionary. Minority students
came to the campus feeling that they were representative of larger
groups of people—that, indeed, they were advancing the condition
of entire societies by their matriculation. Actually, this assumption
was not altogether new to me. Years before, educational success
was something my parents urged me to strive for precisely because
it would reflect favorably on *all* Mexican-Americans—specifically,
my intellectual achievement would help deflate the stereotype of
the "dumb Pancho." This early goal was only given greater currency
by the rhetoric of the Third World spokesmen. But it was the fact
that I felt myself suddenly much more a "public" Mexican-American,
a representative of sorts, that was to prove so crucial for me during
these years.

One college admissions officer assured me one day that he rec- 12
ognized my importance to his school precisely as deriving from
the fact that, after graduation, I would surely be "going back to
[my] community." More recently, teachers have urged me not to
trouble over the fact that I am not "representative" of my culture,
assuring me that I can serve as a "model" for those still in the
barrio working toward academic careers. This is the line that I
hear, too, when being interviewed for a faculty position. The interviewer almost invariably assumes that, because I am racially a
Mexican-American, I can serve as a special counselor to minority
students. The expectation is that I still retain the capacity for
intimacy with "my people."

This new way of thinking about the possible uses of education 13
is what has made the entrance of minority students into higher
education so dramatic. When the minority group student was
accepted into the academy, he came—in everyone's mind—as part
of a "group." When I began college, I barely attracted attention
except perhaps as a slightly exotic ("Are you from India?") brown-
skinned student; by the time I graduated, my presence was annually
noted by, among others, the college public relations office as "one
of the fifty-two students with Spanish surnames enrolled this year."
By having his presence announced to the campus in this way, the
minority group student was unlike any other scholarship boy the

campus had seen before. The minority group student now dramatized more publicly, if also in new ways, the issues of cultural dislocation that education forces, issues that are not solely racial in origin. When Richard Rodriguez *became* a Chicano,[2] the dilemmas he earlier had as a scholarship boy were complicated but not decisively altered by the fact that he had assumed a group identity.

The assurance I heard that, somehow, I was being useful to my community by being a student was gratefully believed, because it gave me a way of dealing with the guilt and cynicism that each year came my way along with the scholarships, grants, and, lately, job offers from schools which a few years earlier would have refused me admission as a student. Each year, in fact, it became harder to believe that my success had anything to do with my intellectual performance, and harder to resist the conclusion that it was due to my minority group status. When I drove to the airport, on my way to London as a Fulbright Fellow[3] last year, leaving behind cousins of my age who were already hopelessly burdened by financial insecurity and dead-end jobs, momentary guilt could be relieved by the thought that somehow my trip was beneficial to persons other than myself. But, of course, if the thought was a way of dealing with the guilt, it was also the reason for the guilt. Sitting in a university library, I would notice a janitor of my own race and grow uneasy; I was, I knew, in a rough way a beneficiary of his condition. Guilt was accompanied by cynicism. The most dazzlingly talented minority students I know today refuse to believe that their success is wholly based on their own talent, or even that when they speak in a classroom anyone hears them as anything but *the* voice of their minority group. It is scarcely surprising, then, though initially it probably seemed puzzling, that so many of the angriest voices on the campus against the injustices of racism came from those not visibly its primary victims.

It became necessary to believe the rhetoric about the value of one's presence on campus simply as a way of living with one's "success." Among ourselves, however, minority group students often admitted to a shattering sense of loss—the feeling that, somehow, something was happening to us. Especially from students who had not yet become accustomed, as by that time I had, to the campus, I remember hearing confessions of extreme discomfort and isolation. Our close associations, the separate dining-room

14

15

2. An American of Mexican descent.
3. The Fulbright Act (1946) provides an exchange program for American students and teachers and those of many other countries.

tables, and the special dormitories helped to relieve some of the pain, but only some of it.

Significant here was the development of the ethnic studies concept—black studies, Chicano studies, et cetera—and the related assumption held by minority group students in a number of departments that they could keep in touch with their old cultures by making these cultures the subject of their study. Here again one notices how different the minority student was from other comparable students: other scholarship boys—poor Jews and the sons of various immigrant cultures—came to the academy singly, much more inclined to accept the courses and material they found. The ethnic studies concept was an indication that, for a multitude of reasons, the new racial minority group students were not willing to give up so easily their ties with their old cultures.

The importance of these new ethnic studies was that they introduced the academy to subject matter that generally deserved to be studied, and at the same time offered a staggering critique of the academy's tendency toward parochialism. Most minority group intellectuals never noted this tendency toward academic parochialism. They more often saw the reason for, say, the absence of a course on black literature in an English department as a case of simple racism. That it might instead be an instance of the fact that academic culture can lose track of human societies and whole areas of human experience was rarely raised. Never asking such a question, the minority group students never seemed to wonder either if as teachers their own courses might suffer the same cultural limitations other seminars and classes suffered. Consequently, in a peculiar way the new minority group critics of higher education came to justify the academy's assumptions. The possibility that academic culture could encourage one to grow out of touch with cultures beyond its conceptual horizon was never seriously considered.

Too often in the last ten years one heard minority group students repeat the joke, never very funny in the first place, about the racial minority academic who ended up sounding more "white" than white academics. Behind the scorn for such a figure was the belief that the new generation of minority group students would be able to avoid having to make similar kinds of cultural concessions. The pressures that might have led to such conformity went unexamined.

For the last few years my annoyance at hearing such jokes was doubtless related to the fact that I was increasingly beginning to sense that I was the "bleached" academic the minority group students found so laughable. I suppose I had always sensed that my cultural allegiance was undergoing subtle alterations as I was being educated. Only when I finished my course work in graduate school and went off to England for my dissertation year did I grasp how far I had traveled from my cultural origins. My year in England was actually my first opportunity to write and reflect upon the kind of material that I would spend my life producing. It was my first chance, too, to be free simultaneously of the distractions of course-work and of the insecurities of trying to find my niche in academic life. Sitting in the reading room of the British Museum, I no longer doubted that I had joined academic society. Ironically, this feeling of having finally arrived allowed me to look back to the community whence I came. That I was geographically farther away from my home than I had ever been lent a metaphorical resonance to the cultural distance I suddenly felt.

But that feeling was not pleasing. The reward of feeling a part   20
of the world of the British Museum was an odd one. Each morning I would arrive at the reading room and grow increasingly depressed by the silence and what the silence implied—that my life as a scholar would require self-absorption. Who, I wondered, would find my work helpful enough to want to read it? Was not my dissertation—whose title alone would puzzle my relatives—only my grandest exercise thus far in self-enclosure? The sight of the heads around me bent over their texts and papers, many so thoroughly engrossed that they wouldn't look up at the silent clock overhead for hours at a stretch, made me recall the remarkable noises of life in my family home. The tedious prose I was writing, a prose constantly qualified by footnotes, reminded me of the capacity for passionate statement those of the culture I was born into commanded—and which, could it be, I had now lost.

As I remembered it during those gray English afternoons, the   21
past rushed forward to define more precisely my present condition. Remembering my youth, a time when I was not restricted to a chair but ran barefoot under a summer sun that tightened my skin with its white heat, made the fact that it was only my mind that "moved" each hour in the library painfully obvious.

I did need to figure out where I had lost touch with my past.   22
I started to become alien to my family culture the day I became a scholarship boy. In the British Museum the realization seemed obvious. But later, returning to America, I returned to minority group students who were still speaking of their cultural ties to their past. How was I to tell them what I had learned about myself in England?

A short while ago, a group of enthusiastic Chicano undergraduates   23
came to my office to ask me to teach a course to high school students in the *barrio* on the Chicano novel. This new literature,

they assured me, has an important role to play in helping to shape the consciousness of a people currently without adequate representation in literature. Listening to them I was struck immediately with the cultural problems raised by their assumption. I told them that the novel is not capable of dealing with Chicano experience adequately, simply because most Chicanos are not literate, or are at least not yet comfortably so. This is not something Chicanos need to apologize for (though, I suppose, remembering my own childhood ambition to combat stereotypes of the Chicano as mental menial, it is not something easily admitted). Rather the genius and value of those Chicanos who do not read seem to me to be largely that their reliance on voice, the spoken word, has given them the capacity for intimate conversation that I, as someone who now relies heavily on the written word, can only envy. The second problem, I went on, is more in the nature of a technical one: the novel, in my opinion, is not a form capable of being true to the basic sense of communal life that typifies Chicano culture. What the novel as a literary form is best capable of representing is solitary existence set against a large social background. Chicano novelists, not coincidentally, nearly always fail to capture the breathtakingly rich family life of most Chicanos, and instead often describe only the individual Chicano in transit between Mexican and American cultures.

I said all of this to the Chicano students in my office, and could see that little of it made an impression. They seemed only frustrated by what they probably took to be a slick, academic justification for evading social responsibility. After a time, they left me, sitting alone. . . . 24

There is a danger of being misunderstood here. I am not suggesting that an academic cannot reestablish ties of any kind with his old culture. Indeed, he can have an impact on the culture of his childhood. But as an academic, one exists by definition in a culture separate from one's nonacademic roots and, therefore, any future ties one has with those who remain "behind" are complicated by one's new cultural perspective. 25

Paradoxically, the distance separating the academic from his nonacademic past can make his past seem, if not closer, then clearer. It is possible for the academic to understand the culture from which he came "better" than those who still live within it. In my own experience, it has only been as I have come to appraise my past through categories and notions derived from the social sciences that I have been able to think of Chicano life in cultural terms at all. Characteristics I took for granted or noticed only in passing—the spontaneity, the passionate speech, the trust in concrete 26 experience, the willingness to think communally rather than in-dividually—these are all significant phenomena to me now as aspects of a total culture. (My parents have neither the time nor the inclination to think about their culture as a culture.) Able to conceptualize a sense of Chicano culture, I am now also more attracted to that culture than I was before. The temptation now is to try to preserve those traits of my old culture that have not yet, in effect, atrophied.

The racial self-consciousness of minority group students during   27
the last few years evident in the ethnic costumes, the stylized gestures, and the idiomatic though often evasive devices for insisting on one's continuing membership in the community of the past, are also indications that the minority group student has gained a new appreciation of the culture of his origin precisely because of his earlier alienation from it. As a result, Chicano students sometimes become more Chicano than most Chicanos. I remember, for example, my father's surprise when, walking across my college campus one afternoon, we came upon two Chicano academics wearing serapes. He and my mother were also surprised—indeed offended—when they earlier heard student activists use the word "Chicano." For them the term was a private one, primarily descriptive of persons they knew. It suggested intimacy. Hearing the word shouted into a microphone by a stranger left them bewildered. What they could not understand was that the student activist finds it easier than they to use "Chicano" in a more public way, for his distance from their culture and his membership in academic culture permits a wider and more abstract view.

The Mexican-Americans who begin to call themselves Chicanos   28
in this new way are actually forming a new version of what it means to be a Chicano. The culture that didn't see itself as a culture is suddenly prized and identified for being one. The price one pays for this new self-consciousness is the knowledge of just that—it is *new*—and this knowledge is not available to those who remain at home. So it is knowledge that separates as well as unites people. Wanting more desperately than ever to assert his ties with the newly visible culture, the minority group student is tempted to exploit those characteristics of that culture that might yet survive in him. But the self-consciousness never allows one to feel completely at ease with the old culture. Worse, the knowledge of the culture of the past often leaves one feeling strangely solitary. At home, I hear relatives speak and find myself analyzing too much of what they say. It is embarrassing being a cultural anthropologist in one's own family kitchen. I keep feeling myself little more than a cultural voyeur. I often come away from family gatherings suspecting, in fact, that what conceptions of my culture I carry with me are no

more than illusions. Because they were never there before, because no one back home shares them, I grow less and less to trust their reliability: too often they seem no more than mental bubbles floating before an academic's eye.

Many who have taught minority group students in the last 29 decade testify to sensing characteristics of a childhood culture still very much alive in these students. Should the teacher make these students aware of these characteristics? Initially, most of us would probably answer negatively. Better to trust the unconscious survival of the past than the always problematical, sometimes even clownish, re-creations of it. But the cultural past cannot be assured of survival; perhaps many of its characteristics are lost simply because the student is never encouraged to look for them. Even those that do survive do so tenuously. As a teacher, one can only hope that the best qualities in his minority group students' cultural legacy aren't altogether snuffed out by academic education.

More easy to live with and distinguishable from self-conscious 30 awareness of the past are the ways the past unconsciously survives— perhaps even yet survives in me. As it turns out, the issue becomes less acute with time. With each year, the chance that the student is unaware of his cultural legacy is diminished as the habit of academic reflectiveness grows stronger. Although the culture of the academy makes innocence about one's cultural past less likely, this same culture, and the conceptual tools it provides, increases the desire to want to write and speak about the past. The paradox persists.

Awaiting the scholarship boy who finally acknowledges the fact 31 that his perceptions of reality have changed is the dilemma of action. The sentimental reaction to this knowledge entails merely a refusal to renew contact with one's nonacademic culture lest one contaminate it. The problem, however, with this sentimental solution is that it overlooks the way academic culture renders one capable of dealing with the transactions of mass society. Academic culture, with its habits of conceptualization and abstraction, allows those of us from other cultures to deal with each other in a mass society. In this sense academic culture does have a profound political impact. Although people intent upon social mobility think of ed- ucation as a means to an end, education does become an end: its culture allows one to exist more easily in a society increasingly anonymous and impersonal. The truth is, the academic's distance from his own experience brings the capacity for communicating with bureaucracies and understanding one's position in society— a prerequisite for political action.

If the sentimental reaction to nonacademic culture is to fear 32 changing it, the political response, typical especially of working-class and lately minority group leaders, is to see higher education solely in terms of its political and social possibilities. Its cultural consequences, in this view, are disregarded. At this time when we are so keenly aware of social and economic inequality, it might seem beside the point to warn those who are working to bring about equality that education alters culture as well as economic status. And yet, if there is one main criticism that I, as a minority group student, must make of minority group leaders in their past attacks on the "racism" of the academy, it is that they never distinguished between my right to higher education and the desirability of my actually entering the academy—which is another way of saying again that they never recognized that there were things I could lose by becoming a scholarship boy.

Certainly, the academy changes those from alien cultures more [33] than it is changed by them. While minority groups had an impact on higher education, largely because of their advantage in coming as a group, within the last few years students such as myself, who finally ended up certified as academics, also ended up sounding very much like the academics we found when we came to the campus. I do not enjoy making such admissions. But perhaps now the time has come when questions about the cultural costs of education ought to be delayed no longer. Those of us who have been scholarship boys know in our bones that our education has exacted a large price in exchange for the large benefits it has conferred upon us. And what is sadder to consider, after we have paid that price, we go home and casually change the cultures that nurtured us. My parents today understand how they are "Chicanos" in a large and impersonal sense. The gains from such knowledge are clear. But so, too, are the reasons for regret.

JOAN DIDION

On Going Home

I am home for my daughter's first birthday. By "home" I do [1] not mean the house in Los Angeles where my husband and I and the baby live, but the place where my family is, in the Central Valley of California. It is a vital although troublesome distinction. My husband likes my family but is uneasy in their house, because

First published in *The Saturday Evening Post* in 1967.

once there I fall into their ways, which are difficult, oblique, deliberately inarticulate, not my husband's ways. We live in dusty houses ("D-U-S-T," he once wrote with his finger on surfaces all over the house, but no one noticed it) filled with mementos quite without value to him (what could the Canton dessert plates[1] mean to him? how could he have known about the assay scales,[2] why should he care if he did know?), and we appear to talk exclusively about people we know who have been committed to mental hospitals, about people we know who have been booked on drunk-driving charges, and about property, particularly about property, land, price per acre and C-2 zoning and assessments and freeway access. My brother does not understand my husband's inability to perceive the advantage in the rather common real-estate transaction known as "sale-leaseback," and my husband in turn does not understand why so many of the people he hears about in my father's house have recently been committed to mental hospitals or booked on drunk-driving charges. Nor does he understand that when we talk about sale-leasebacks and right-of-way condemnations we are talking in code about the things we like best, the yellow fields and the cottonwoods and the rivers rising and falling and the mountain roads closing when the heavy snow comes in. We miss each other's points, have another drink and regard the fire. My brother refers to my husband, in his presence, as "Joan's husband." Marriage is the classic betrayal.

Or perhaps it is not any more. Sometimes I think that those of   2
us who are now in our thirties were born into the last generation to carry the burden of "home," to find in family life the source of all tension and drama. I had by all objective accounts a "normal" and a "happy" family situation, and yet I was almost thirty years old before I could talk to my family on the telephone without crying after I had hung up. We did not fight. Nothing was wrong. And yet some nameless anxiety colored the emotional charges between me and the place that I came from. The question of whether or not you could go home again was a very real part of the sentimental and largely literary baggage with which we left home in the fifties; I suspect that it is irrelevant to the children born of the fragmentation after World War II. A few weeks ago in a San Francisco bar I saw a pretty young girl on crystal take off her clothes and dance for the cash prize in an "amateur-topless" contest. There was no particular sense of moment about this, none

---

1. Fine Chinese porcelain.
2. Scales used in the process of assaying—determining the proportion of metal in ore and metallurgical products.

of the effect of romantic degradation, of "dark journey," for which my generation strived so assiduously. What sense could that girl possibly make of, say *Long Day's Journey into Night*?[3] Who is beside the point?

That I am trapped in this particular irrelevancy is never more apparent to me than when I am home. Paralyzed by the neurotic lassitude engendered by meeting one's past at every turn, around every corner, inside every cupboard, I go aimlessly from room to room. I decide to meet it head-on and clean out a drawer, and I spread the contents on the bed. A bathing suit I wore the summer I was seventeen. A letter of rejection from *The Nation*,[4] an aerial photograph of the site for a shopping center my father did not build in 1954. Three teacups hand-painted with cabbage roses and signed "E.M.," my grandmother's initials. There is no final solution for letters of rejection from *The Nation* and teacups hand-painted in 1900. Nor is there any answer to snapshots of one's grandfather as a young man on skis, surveying around Donner Pass in the year 1910. I smooth out the snapshot and look into his face, and do and do not see my own. I close the drawer, and have another cup of coffee with my mother. We get along very well, veterans of a guerrilla war we never understood.

Days pass. I see no one. I come to dread my husband's evening call, not only because he is full of news of what by now seems to me our remote life in Los Angeles, people he has seen, letters which require attention, but because he asks what I have been doing, suggests uneasily that I get out, drive to San Francisco or Berkeley. Instead I drive across the river to a family graveyard. It has been vandalized since my last visit and the monuments are broken, overturned in the dry grass. Because I once saw a rattlesnake in the grass I stay in the car and listen to a country-and-Western station. Later I drive with my father to a ranch he has in the foothills. The man who runs his cattle on it asks us to the roundup, a week from Sunday, and although I know that I will be in Los Angeles I say, in the oblique way my family talks, that I will come. Once home I mention the broken monuments in the graveyard. My mother shrugs.

I go to visit my great-aunts. A few of them think now that I am my cousin, or their daughter who died young. We recall an anecdote about a relative last seen in 1948, and they ask if I still

---

3. Play by American dramatist Eugene O'Neill (1888–1953); his tragic autobiographical masterpiece.
4. Journal devoted to covering political and social problems, as well as literature and the arts.

like living in New York City. I have lived in Los Angeles for three years, but I say that I do. The baby is offered a horehound drop, and I am slipped a dollar bill "to buy a treat." Questions trail off, answers are abandoned, the baby plays with the dust motes in a shaft of afternoon sun.

It is time for the baby's birthday party: a white cake, strawberry-   6
marshmallow ice cream, a bottle of champagne saved from another party. In the evening, after she has gone to sleep, I kneel beside the crib and touch her face, where it pressed against the slats, with mine. She is an open and trusting child, unprepared for and unaccustomed to the ambushes of family life, and perhaps it is just as well that I can offer her little of that life. I would like to give her more. I would like to promise her that she will grow up with a sense of her cousins and of rivers and of her great-grand-mother's teacups, would like to pledge her a picnic on a river with fried chicken and her hair uncombed, would like to give her *home* for her birthday, but we live differently now and I can promise her nothing like that. I give her a xylophone and a sundress from Madeira, and promise to tell her a funny story.

CYNTHIA OZICK

We Are the Crazy Lady
and Other Feisty Feminist Fables

I. THE CRAZY LADY DOUBLE

A long, long time ago, in another century—1951, in fact—when   1
you, dear younger readers, were most likely still in your nuclear-family playpen (where, if female, you cuddled a rag-baby to your potential titties, or, if male, let down virile drool over your plastic bulldozer), The Famous Critic[1] told me never, never to use a parenthesis in the very first sentence. This was in a graduate English seminar at Columbia University. To get into this seminar, you had to submit to a grilling wherein you renounced all former allegiance to the then-current literary religion, New Criticism, which considered that only the text existed, not the world. I passed the interview

First published in *Ms. Magazine*, Spring 1973.
1. Lionel Trilling, influential literary critic and writer (1905–1975).

by lying—cunningly, and against my real convictions. I said that probably the world *did* exist—and walked triumphantly into the seminar room.

There were four big tables arranged in a square, with everyone's feet sticking out into the open middle of the square. You could tell who was nervous, and how much, by watching the pairs of feet twist around each other. The Great Man presided awesomely from the high bar of the square. His head was a majestic granite-gray, like a centurion in command; he *looked* famous. His clean shoes twitched only slightly, and only when he was angry.

It turned out he was angry at me a lot of the time. He was angry because he thought me a disrupter, a rioter, a provocateur, and a fool; also crazy. And this was twenty years ago, before these things were *de rigueur*[2] in the universities. Everything was very quiet in those days: there were only the Cold War and Korea and Joe McCarthy and the Old Old Nixon, and the only revolutionaries around were in Henry James's *The Princess Casamassima*.

Habit governed the seminar. Where you sat the first day was where you settled forever. So, to avoid the stigmatization of the ghetto, I was careful not to sit next to the other woman in the class: the Crazy Lady.

At first the Crazy Lady appeared to be remarkably intelligent. She was older than the rest of us, somewhere in her thirties (which was why we thought of her as a Lady), with wild tan hair, a noticeably breathing bosom, eccentric gold-rimmed old-pensioner glasses, and a tooth-crowded wild mouth that seemed to get wilder the more she talked. She talked like a motorcycle, fast and urgent. Everything she said was almost brilliant, only not actually on point, and frenetic with hostility. She was tough and negative. She volunteered a lot and she stood up and wobbled with rage, pulling at her hair and mouth. She fought the Great Man point for point, piecemeal and wholesale, mixing up queerly-angled literary insights with all sorts of private and public fury. After the first meetings he was fed up with her. The rest of us accepted that she probably wasn't all there, but in a room where everyone was on the make for recognition—you talked to save your life, and the only way to save your life was to be the smartest one that day—she was a nuisance, a distraction, a pain in the ass. The class became a bunch of Good Germans, determinedly indifferent onlookers to a vindictive

2. "Indispensable," required; in this instance Ozick means "a matter of course, usual."

match between the Critic and the Crazy Lady, until finally he subdued her by shutting his eyes, and, when that didn't always work, by cutting her dead and lecturing right across the sound of her strong, strange voice.

All this was before R. D. Laing[3] had invented the superiority of   6
madness, of course, and, cowards all, no one liked the thought of being tarred with the Crazy Lady's brush. Ignored by the boss, in the middle of everything she would suddenly begin to mutter to herself. She mentioned certain institutions she'd been in, and said we all belonged there. The people who sat on either side of her shifted chairs. If the Great Man ostracized the Crazy Lady, we had to do it too. But one day the Crazy Lady came in late and sat down in the seat next to mine, and stayed there the rest of the semester.

Then an odd thing happened. There, right next to me, was the   7
noisy Crazy Lady, tall, with that sticking-out sighing chest of hers, orangey curls dripping over her nose, snuffling furiously for attention. And there was I, a brownish runt, a dozen years younger and flatter and shyer than the Crazy Lady, in no way her twin, physically or psychologically. In those days I was bone-skinny, small, sallow and myopic, and so scared I could trigger diarrhea at one glance from the Great Man. All this stress on looks is important: the Crazy Lady and I had our separate bodies, our separate brains. We handed in our separate papers.

But the Great Man never turned toward me, never at all, and   8
if ambition broke feverishly through shyness so that I dared to push an idea audibly out of me, he shut his eyes when I put up my hand. This went on for a long time. I never got to speak, and I began to have the depressing feeling that he hated me. It was no small thing to be hated by the man who had written the most impressive criticism of the century. What in hell was going on? I was in trouble; like everyone else in that demented contest, I wanted to excel. Then, one slow afternoon, wearily, the Great Man let his eyes fall on me. He called me by name, but it was not my name—it was the Crazy Lady's. The next week the papers came back—and there, right at the top of mine, in the Great Man's own handwriting, was a rebuke to the Crazy Lady for starting an essay with a parenthesis in the first sentence, a habit he took to be a continuing sign of that unruly and unfocused mentality so often exhibited in class. And then a Singular Revelation crept

3. Scottish psychiatrist (b. 1927) whose lifework has been devoted to the study of insanity, especially schizophrenia.

coldly through me: because the Crazy Lady and I sat side by side, because we were a connected blur of Woman, the Famous Critic, master of ultimate distinctions, couldn't tell us apart. The Crazy Lady and I! He couldn't tell us apart! It didn't matter that the Crazy Lady was crazy! *He couldn't tell us apart!*

Moral 1: All cats are gray at night,   9
             all darkies look alike.

Moral 2: Even among intellectual humanists, every woman has   10
a *Doppelgänger*[4]—every other woman.

II. THE LECTURE, 1

I was invited by a women's group to be guest speaker at a Book-   11
Author Luncheon. The women themselves had not really chosen me: the speaker had been selected by a male leader and imposed on them. The plan was that I would autograph copies of my book, eat a good meal and then lecture. The woman in charge of the programming telephoned to ask me what my topic would be. This was a matter of some concern, since they had never had a woman author before, and no one knew how the idea would be received. I offered as my subject "The Contemporary Poem."

When the day came, everything went as scheduled—the au-   12
tographing, the food, the welcoming addresses. Then it was time to go to the lectern. I aimed at the microphone and began to speak of poetry. A peculiar rustling sound flew up from the audience. All the women were lifting their programs to the light, like hundreds of wings. Confused murmurs ran along the walls. Something was awry; I began to feel very uncomfortable. Then I too took up the program. It read: "Topic: The Contemporary Home."

Moral: Even our ears practice the caste system.   13

III. THE LECTURE, 2

I was in another country, the only woman at a philosophical   14
seminar lasting three days. On the third day, I was to read a paper. I had accepted the invitation with a certain foreknowledge. I knew, for instance, that I could not dare to be the equal of any other speaker. To be an equal would be to be less. I understood that mine had to be the most original and powerful paper of all. I had no choice; I had to toil beyond my most extreme possibilities. This was not ambition, but only fear of disgrace.

---

4. German for "double-goer": a ghostly double.

For the first two days, I was invisible. When I spoke, people   15
tapped impatiently, waiting for the interruption to end. No one
took either my presence or my words seriously. At meals, I sat
with my colleagues' wives.

The third day arrived, and I read my paper. It was successful   16
beyond my remotest imaginings. I was interviewed, and my remarks
appeared in newspapers in a language I could not understand.
The Foreign Minister invited me to his home. I hobnobbed with
famous poets.

Now my colleagues noticed me. But they did not notice me as   17
a colleague. They teased and kissed me. I had become their mascot.

Moral: There is no route out of caste which does not instantly   18
lead back into it.

IV. PROPAGANDA

For many years I had noticed that no book of poetry by a woman   19
was ever reviewed without reference to the poet's sex. The curious
thing was that, in the two decades of my scrutiny, there were *no*
exceptions whatever. It did not matter whether the reviewer was
a man or woman: in every case the question of the "feminine
sensibility" of the poet was at the center of the reviewer's response.
The maleness of the male poets, on the other hand, hardly ever
seemed to matter.

Determined to ridicule this convention, I wrote a tract, a piece   20
of purely tendentious mockery, in the form of a short story. I
called it "Virility."

The plot was, briefly, as follows: A very bad poet, lustful for   21
fame, is despised for his pitiful lucubrations and remains unpublished.
But luckily, he comes into possession of a cache of letters written
by his elderly spinster aunt, who lives an obscure and secluded
working-class life in a remote corner of England. The letters contain
a large number of remarkable poems; the aunt, it turns out, is a
genius. The bad poet publishes his find under his own name, and
instantly attains world-wide adulation. Under the title *Virility,* the
poems become immediate classics. They are translated into dozens
of languages and are praised and revered for their unmistakably
masculine qualities: their strength, passion, wisdom, energy, boldness, brutality, worldliness, robustness, authenticity, sensuality,
compassion. A big, handsome, sweating man, the poet swaggers
from country to country, courted everywhere, pursued by admirers,
yet respected by the most demanding critics.

Meanwhile, the old aunt dies. The supply of genius runs out.   22
Bravely and contritely the poor poet confesses his ruse, and, in a

burst of honesty, publishes the last batch under the real poet's name; the book is entitled *Flowers from Liverpool*. But the poems are at once found negligible and dismissed: "Thin feminine art," say the reviews, "a lovely girlish voice." And: "Limited one-dimensional vision." "Choked with female inwardness." "The fine womanly intuition of a competent poetess." The poems are utterly forgotten.

I included this fable in a collection of short stories. In every   23
review the salvo went unnoticed. Not one reviewer recognized that the story was a sly tract. Not one reviewer saw the smirk or the point. There was one delicious comment, though. "I have some reservations," a man in Washington, D.C., wrote, "about the credibility of some of her male characters when they are chosen as narrators."

Moral: In saying what is obvious, never choose cunning. Yelling   24
works better.

V. HORMONES

During a certain period of my life, I was reading all the time,   25
and fairly obsessively. Sometimes, though, sunk in a book of criticism or philosophy, I would be brought up short. Consider: here is a paragraph that excites the intellect; inwardly, one assents passionately to its premises; the writer's idea is an exact diagram of one's own deepest psychology or conviction; one feels oneself seized as for a portrait. Then the disclaimer, the excluding shove: "It is, however, otherwise with the female sex. . . ." A rebuke from the World of Thinking: *I didn't mean you, lady.* In the instant one is in possession of one's humanity most intensely, it is ripped away.

These moments I discounted. What is wrong—intrinsically, psy-   26
chologically, culturally, morally—can be dismissed.

But to dismiss in this manner is to falsify one's most genuine   27
actuality. A Jew reading of the aesthetic glories of European civilization without taking notice of his victimization during, say, the era of the building of the great cathedrals, is self-forgetful in the most dangerous way. So would be a black who read of King Cotton[5] with an economist's objectivity.

I am not offering any strict analogy between the situation of   28
women and the history of Jews or colonialized blacks, as many

---

5. The reference is to the importance of cotton in the economy of the American South in the first half of the nineteenth century—a condition heavily dependent on the labor of black slaves.

politically radical women do (though the analogy with blacks is
much the more frequent one). It seems to me to be abusive of
language in the extreme when some women speak, in the generation
after Auschwitz, of the "oppression" of women. Language makes
culture, and we make a rotten culture when we abuse words. We
raise up rotten heroines. I use "rotten" with particular attention
to its precise meaning: foul, putrid, tainted, stinking. I am thinking
now especially of a radical women's publication, *Off Our Backs,*
which not long ago presented Leila Khaled, terrorist and foiled
murderer, as a model for the political conduct of women.

But if I would not support the extreme analogy (and am never   29
surprised when black women, who have a more historical comprehension of actual, not figurative, oppression, refuse to support
the analogy), it is anyhow curious to see what happens to the
general culture when any enforced class in any historical or social
condition is compelled to doubt its own self-understanding—when
identity is externally defined, when individual humanity is called
into question as being different from "standard" humanity. What
happens is that the general culture, along with the object of its
debasement, is also debased. If you laugh at women, you play
Beethoven in vain.

If you laugh at women, your laboratory will lie.   30

We can read in Charlotte Perkins Gilman's[6] 1912 essay, "Are   31
Women Human Beings?", an account of an opinion current sixty
years ago. Women, said one scientist, are not only "not the human
race—they are not even half the human race, but a sub-species
set apart for purposes of reproduction merely."

A physician said: "No doctor can ever lose sight of the fact that   32
the mind of woman is always threatened with danger from the
reverberations of her physiological emergencies." He concluded
this entirely on the basis of his invalid patients.

Though we are accustomed to the idea of "progress" in science   33
and medicine, if not in civilization generally, the fact is that more
information has led to somehing very like regression.

I talked with an intelligent physician, the Commissioner of Health   34
of a middle-sized city in Connecticut, a man who sees medicine
not discretely but as part of the social complex—was treated to a
long list of all the objective differences between men and women,
including particularly an account of current endocrinal studies
relating to female hormones. Aren't all of these facts? he asked.

---

6. An American feminist writer (1860–1935).

How can you distrust facts? Very good, I said, I'm willing to take your medically-educated word for it. I'm not afraid of facts, I welcome facts—*but a congeries of facts is not equivalent to an idea.* This is the essential fallacy of the so-called "scientific" mind. People who mistake facts for ideas are incomplete thinkers; they are gossips.

You tell me, I said, that my sense of my own humanity as being 35 "standard" humanity—which is, after all, a subjective idea—is refuted by hormonal research. My psychology, you tell me, which in your view is the source of my ideas, is the result of my physiology: it is not I who express myself, it is my hormones which express me. A part is equal to the whole, you say. Worse yet, the whole is simply the issue of the part: my "I" is a flash of chemicals. You are willing to define all my humanity by hormonal investigation under a microscope: this you call "objective irrefutable fact," as if tissue-culture were equivalent to culture. But each scientist can assemble his own (subjective) constellation of "objective irrefutable fact," just as each social thinker can assemble his own (subjective) selection of traits to define "humanity" by. Who can prove what is "standard" humanity, and which sex, class, or race is to be exempted from whole participation in it? On what basis do you regard female hormones as causing a modification from normative humanity? And what better right do you have to define normative humanity by what males have traditionally apperceived than by what females have traditionally apperceived—assuming (as I, lacking presumptuousness, do not) that their apperceptions have not been the same? Only Tiresias—that mythological character who was both man and woman[7]—is in a position to make the comparison and present the proof. And then not even Tiresias, because to be a hermaphrodite is to be a monster, and not human.

"Why are you so emotional about all this?" said the Commissioner 36 of Health. "You see how it is? Those are your female hormones working on you right now."

Moral: Defamation is only applied research.   37

VI. AMBITION

After thirteen years, I at last finished a novel. The first seven 38 years were spent in a kind of apprenticeship—the book that came

---

7. In Greek mythology, Tiresias the seer, after being transformed for a time into a woman, was asked by the gods to settle an argument as to whether men or women enjoyed love more. Having seen it from both sides, he voted in favor of women.

out of that time was abandoned without much regret. A second one was finished in six weeks and buried. It took six years to write the third novel, and this one was finally published.

How I lived through those years is impossible to recount in a   39
short space. I was a recluse, a priest of Art. I read seas of books.
I believed in the idea of masterpieces. I was scornful of the world
of journalism, jobs, everydayness. I did not live like any woman
I knew, although it never occurred to me to reflect on this of my
own volition. I lived like some men I had read about—Flaubert,
or Proust, or James: the subjects of those literary biographies I
endlessly drank in. I did not think of them as men but as writers.
I read the diaries of Virginia Woolf, and biographies of George
Eliot, but I did not think of them as women. I thought of them
as writers. I thought of myself as a writer. I went on reading and
writing.

It goes without saying that all this time my relatives regarded   40
me as abnormal. I accepted this. It seemed to me, from what I
had read, that most writers were abnormal. Yet on the surface I
could easily have passed for normal. The husband goes to work,
the wife stays home—that is what is normal. Well, I was married.
My husband went to his job every day. His job paid the rent and
bought the groceries. I stayed home, reading and writing, and felt
myself to be an economic parasite. To cover guilt, I joked that I
had been given a grant from a very private, very poor, foundation;
I meant my husband.

But my relatives never thought of me as a parasite. The very   41
thing I was doubtful about—my economic dependence—they considered my due as a woman. They saw me not as a failed writer
without an income, but as a childless housewife, a failed woman.
They did not think me abnormal because I was a writer, but
because I was not properly living my life as a woman. In one
respect we were in agreement utterly—my life was failing terribly,
terribly. For me it was because, already deep into my thirties, I
had not yet published a book. For them, it was because I had not
yet borne a child.

I was a pariah,[8] not only because I was a deviant, but because   42
I was not recognized as the kind of deviant I meant to be. A failed
woman is not the same as a failed writer. Even as a pariah I was
the wrong kind of pariah.

Still, relations are only relations, and what I aspired to, what I   43
was in thrall to, was Art; was Literature; not familial contentment.
I knew how to distinguish the trivial from the sublime. In Literature

---

8. A social outcast.

and in Art, I saw, my notions were not pariah notions: *there*, I inhabited the mainstream. So I went on reading and writing; I went on believing in Art, and my intention was to write a masterpiece. Not a saucer of well-polished craft (the sort of thing "women writers" are always accused of being accomplished at), but something huge, contemplative, Tolstoyan. My ambition was a craw.

I called the book *Trust*. I began it in the summer of 1957 and finished it in November of 1963, on the day President John Kennedy was assassinated. In manuscript it was 801 pages divided into four parts: "America," "Europe," "Birth," "Death." The title was meant to be ironic. In reality, it was about distrust. It seemed to me I had touched on distrust in every order or form of civilization. It seemed to me I had left nothing out. It was (though I did not know this then) a very hating book. What it hated above all was the whole—the whole!—of Western Civilization. It told how America had withered into another Europe; it dreamed dark and murderous pagan dreams, and hated what it dreamed.

In style, the book was what has come to be called "mandarin": a difficult, aristocratic, unrelenting virtuoso prose. It was, in short, unreadable. I think I knew this; I was sardonic enough to say, echoing Joyce about *Finnegans Wake*,[9] "I expect you to spend your life at this." In any case, I had spent a decade-and-a-half of my own life at it, and though I did not imagine the world would fall asunder at its appearance, I thought—at the very least—the ambition, the all-swallowingness, the wild insatiability of the writer would be plain to everyone who read it. I had, after all, taken History for my subject: not merely History as an aggregate of events, but History as a judgment on events. No one could say my theme was flighty. Of all the novelists I read—and in those days I read them all, broiling in the envy of the unpublished, which is like no envy on earth—who else had dared so vastly?

During that period, Françoise Sagan's[10] first novel was published. I held the thin little thing and laughed. Women's pulp!

My own novel, I believed, contained everything—the whole world.

But there was one element I had consciously left out, though on principle I did not like to characterize it or think about it much. The truth is I was thinking about it all the time. It was only a fiction-technicality, but I was considerably afraid of it. It was the

9. Notoriously difficult novel by Irish novelist James Joyce (1882–1941).
10. French novelist (b. 1935). Her first work, *Bonjour Tristesse* ("Hello, Sadness"), is the story of an adolescent's tragic attempt to prevent her father's remarriage.

question of the narrator's "sensibility." The narrator, as it happened, was a young woman; I had chosen her to be the eye—and the "I"—of the novel because all the other characters in some way focused on her, and she was the one most useful to my scheme. Nevertheless, I wanted her not to live. Everything I was reading in reviews of other people's books made me fearful: I would have to be very, very cautious, I would have to drain my narrator of emotive value of any kind. I was afraid to be pegged as having written a "women's" novel, and nothing was more certain to lead to that than a point-of-view seemingly lodged in a woman; no one takes a woman's novel seriously. I was in terror, above all, of sentiment and feeling, those telltale taints. I kept the fury and the passion for other, safer, characters.

So what I left out of my narrator entirely, sweepingly, with   49
exquisite consciousness of what exactly I *was* leaving out, was any shred of "sensibility." I stripped her of everything, even a name. I crafted and carpentered her; she was for me a bloodless device, fulcrum or pivot, a recording voice, a language-machine. She confronted moment or event, took it in, gave it out. And what to me was all the more wonderful about this nameless fiction-machine I had invented was that the machine itself, though never alive, was a character in the story, without ever influencing the story. My machine-narrator was there for efficiency only, for flexibility, for craftiness, for sublety, but never, never, as a "woman." I wiped the "woman" out of her. And I did it out of fear, out of vicarious vindictive critical imagination, out of the terror of my ambition, out of, maybe, paranoia. I meant my novel to be taken for what it really was. I meant to make it impossible for it to be mistaken for something else.

Publication.   50

Review in *The New York Times* Sunday Book Review.   51

Review is accompanied by a picture of a naked woman seen   52
from the back. Her bottom is covered by some sort of drapery.

Title of review: "Daughter's Reprieve."   53

Excerpts from review: "These events, interesting in themselves,   54
exist to reveal the sensibility of the narrator." "She longs to play some easy feminine role." "She has been unable to define herself as a woman." "Thus the daughter, at the age of twenty-two, is eager for the prerequisites that should have been hers as a woman, but is floundering badly in their pursuit." "Her protagonist insists on coming to terms with the recalcitrant sexual elements in her life." "The main body of the novel, then, is a revelation of the narrator's inner, turbulent, psychic dream."

O rabid rotten Western Civilization, where are you? O judging   55
History, O foul Trust and fouler Distrust, where?

O Soap Opera, where did you come from?   56
(Meanwhile the review in *Time* was calling me a "housewife.")   57
Pause.   58
All right, let us take up the rebuttals one by one.   59
Q. Maybe you *did* write a soap opera without knowing it. Maybe   60
you only *thought* you were writing about Western Civilization
when you were really only rewriting Stella Dallas.[11]
A. A writer may be unsure of everything—trust the tale not the   61
teller is a good rule—but not of his obsessions; of these he is
certain. If I were rewriting Stella Dallas, I would turn her into the
Second Crusade and demobilize her.
Q. Maybe you're like the blind Jew who wants to be a pilot,   62
and when they won't give him the job he says they're anti-Semitic.
Look, the book was lousy, you deserved a lousy review.
A. You mistake me, I never said it was a bad review. It was in   63
fact an extremely favorable review, full of gratifying adjectives.
Q. But your novel languished anyhow?   64
A. Perished, is dead and buried. I sometimes see it exhumed   65
on the shelf in the public library. It's always there. No one ever
borrows it.
Q. Dummy! You should've written a soap opera. Women are   66
good at that.
A. Thank you. You almost remind me of another Moral: In   67
conceptual life, junk prevails. Even if you do not produce junk,
it will be taken for junk.
Q. What does that have to do with women?   68
A. The products of women are frequently taken for junk.   69
Q. And if a woman *does* produce junk . . . ?   70
A. Glory—they will treat her almost like a man who produces   71
junk. They will say her name on television.
Q. Bitter, bitter!   72
A. Not at all. Again you misunderstand. You see, I have come   73
round to thinking (I learned it from television commercials, as a
matter of fact) that there *is* a Women's Culture—a sort of tribal,
separatist, ghettoized thing. And I propose that we cultivate it.
Q. You mean *really* writing Women's Novels? On purpose?   74
A. Nothing like that. The novel was invented by men. It isn't   75
ours, you see, and to us it is to *assimilate*. I see now where I went

---

11. *Stella Dallas* (1923) was originally a magazine serial by Olive Higgins Prouty.
The story was taken up by almost every conceivable genre (novel, film, play) and
finally became a long-running soap opera, which is what its name connotes today.

wrong! So I propose that we return to our pristine cultural origins,
earn the respect of the male race, and regain our self-esteem.
Q. All that? Really? How?   76
A. *We will revive the Quilting Bee!*   77
Q. Oh, splendid, splendid! What a genius you are!   78
A. I always knew it.   79

RANDALL JARRELL

A Sad Heart at the Supermarket

The Emperor Augustus[1] would sometimes say to his Senate: 1
"Words fail me, my Lords; nothing I can say could possibly indicate
the depth of my feelings in this matter." But in this matter of
mass culture, the mass media, I am speaking not as an emperor
but as a fool, a suffering, complaining, helplessly non-conforming
poet-or-artist-of-a-sort, far off at the obsolescent rear of things;
what I say will indicate the depth of my feelings and the shallowness
and one-sidedness of my thoughts. If those English lyric poets who
went mad during the eighteenth century had told you why the
Age of Enlightenment was driving them crazy, it would have had
a kind of documentary interest: what I say may have a kind of
documentary interest. *The toad beneath the harrow knows/ Exactly
where each tooth-point goes:*[2] if you tell me that the field is being
harrowed to grow grain for bread, and to create a world in which
there will be no more famines, or toads either, I will say: "I know";
but let me tell you where the tooth-points go, and what the harrow
looks like from below.

Advertising men, businessmen speak continually of *media* or *the*   2
media or *the mass media*. One of their trade journals is named,
simply, *Media*. It is an impressive word: one imagines Mephistopheles
offering Faust[3] *media that no man has ever known;* one feels, while

---

The title essay in *A Sad Heart at the Supermarket* (1962).
1. First Roman emperor (63 B.C.–A.D. 14).
2. From English writer Rudyard Kipling's (1865–1936) *Departmental Ditties*.
3. According to legend, Mephistopheles (the personification of the devil) offered
the learned doctor Faust youth, knowledge, and magic—in exchange for his soul.
In the German dramatist Goethe's (1749–1832) *Faust*, Mephistopheles tells Faust,
"I am giving you things that no man has ever known."

the word is in one's ear, that abstract, overmastering powers, of a scale and intensity unimagined yesterday, are being offered one by the technicians who discovered and control them—offered, and at a price. The word has the clear fatal ring of that new world whose space we occupy so luxuriously and precariously; the world that produces mink stoles, rockabilly records, and tactical nuclear weapons by the million; the world that Attila, Galileo, Hansel and Gretel never knew.

And yet, it's only the plural of *medium*. "*Medium*," says the   3
dictionary, "that which lies in the middle; hence, middle condition or degree . . . A substance through which a force acts or an effect is transmitted . . . That through or by which anything is accomplished; as, an advertising *medium* . . . *Biol.* A nutritive mixture or substance, as broth, gelatin, agar, for cultivating bacteria, fungi, etc."

Let us name *our* trade journal *The Medium*. For all these media—   4
television, radio, movies, newspapers, magazines, and the rest—
are a single medium, in whose depths we are all being cultivated.
This Medium is of middle condition or degree, mediocre; it lies in the middle of everything, between a man and his neighbor, his wife, his child, his self; it, more than anything else, is the substance through which the forces of our society act upon us, and make us into what our society needs.

And what does it need? For us to need.   5

Oh, it needs for us to do or be many things: workers, technicians,   6
executives, soldiers, housewives. But first of all, last of all, it needs for us to be buyers; consumers; beings who want much and will want more—who want consistently and insatiably. Find some spell to make us turn away from the stoles, the records, and the weapons, and our world will change into something to us unimaginable.
Find some spell to make us see that the product or service that yesterday was an unthinkable luxury today is an inexorable necessity, and our world will go on. It is the Medium which casts this spell—which is this spell. As we look at the television set, listen to the radio, read the magazines, the frontier of necessity is always being pushed forward. The Medium shows us what our new needs are—how often, without it, we should not have known!—and it shows us how they can be satisfied by buying something. The act of buying something is at the root of our world; if anyone wishes to paint the genesis of things in our society, he will paint a picture of God holding out to Adam a check-book or credit card or Charge-A-Plate.

But how quickly our poor naked Adam is turned into a consumer,   7
is linked to others by the great chain of buying!

No outcast he, bewildered and depressed:
Along his infant veins are interfused
The gravitation and the filial bond
Of nature that connect him with the world.[4]

Children of three or four can ask for a brand of cereal, sing some
soap's commercial; by the time that they are twelve or thirteen
they are not children but teen-age consumers, interviewed, graphed,
analyzed. They are well on their way to becoming that ideal figure
of our culture, the knowledgeable consumer. Let me define him:
the knowledgeable consumer is someone who, when he comes
to Weimar, knows how to buy a Weimaraner.[5]

Daisy's voice sounded like money; everything about the knowl-   8
edgeable consumer looks like or sounds like or feels like money,
and informed money at that. To live is to consume, to understand
life is to know what to consume: he has learned to understand
this, so that his life is a series of choices—correct ones—among
the products and services of the world. He is able to choose to
consume something, of course, only because sometime, somewhere,
he or someone else produced something—but just when or where
or what no longer seems to us of as much interest. We may still
go to Methodist or Baptist or Presbyterian churches on Sunday,
but the Protestant ethic of frugal industry, of production for its
own sake, is gone.

Production has come to seem to our society not much more   9
than a condition prior to consumption. "The challenge of today,"
an advertising agency writes, "is to make the consumer raise his
level of demand." This challenge has been met: the Medium has
found it easy to make its people feel the continually increasing
lacks, the many specialized dissatisfactions (merging into one great
dissatisfaction, temporarily assuaged by new purchases) that it
needs for them to feel. When in some magazine we see the Medium
at its most nearly perfect, we hardly know which half is entertaining
and distracting us, which half making us buy: some advertisement
may be more ingeniously entertaining than the text beside it, but
it is the text which has made us long for a product more passionately.
When one finishes *Holiday* or *Harper's Bazaar* or *House and Garden*
or *The New Yorker* or *High Fidelity* or *Road and Track* or—but make
your own list—buying something, going somewhere seems a necessary completion to the act of reading the magazine.

Reader, isn't buying or fantasy-buying an important part of your   10
and my emotional life? (If you reply, *No,* I'll think of you with

---

4. Wordsworth, *The Prelude*, 2: 241–44.
5. Breed of dog developed in Germany.

bitter envy as more than merely human; as deeply un-American.) It is a standard joke that when a woman is bored or sad she buys something, to cheer herself up; but in this respect we are all women together, and can hear complacently the reminder of how feminine this consumer-world of ours has become. One imagines as a characteristic dialogue of our time an interview in which someone is asking of a vague gracious figure, a kind of Mrs. America: "But while you waited for the intercontinental ballistic missiles what did you *do?*" She answers: "I bought things."

She reminds one of the sentinel at Pompeii[6]—a space among ashes, now, but at his post: she too did what she was supposed to do. Our society has delivered us—most of us—from the bonds of necessity, so that we no longer struggle to find food to keep from starving, clothing and shelter to keep from freezing; yet if the ends for which we work and of which we dream are only clothes and restaurants and houses, possessions, consumption, how have we escaped?—we have exchanged man's old bondage for a new voluntary one. It is more than a figure of speech to say that the consumer is trained for his job of consuming as the factory-worker is trained for his job of producing; and the first can be a longer, more complicated training, since it is easier to teach a man to handle a tool, to read a dial, than it is to teach him to ask, always, for a name-brand aspirin—to want, someday, a stand-by generator.

What is that? You don't know? I used not to know, but the readers of *House Beautiful* all know, so that now I know. It is the electrical generator that stands in the basement of the suburban houseowner, shining, silent, till at last one night the lights go out, the furnace stops, the freezer's food begins to—

Ah, but it's frozen for good, the lights are on forever; the owner has switched on the stand-by generator.

But you don't see that he really needs the generator, you'd rather have seen him buy a second car? He has two. A second bathroom? He has four. When the People of the Medium doubled everything, he doubled everything; and now that he's gone twice round he will have to wait three years, or four, till both are obsolescent—but while he waits there are so many new needs that he can satisfy, so many things a man can buy. "Man wants but little here below/ Nor wants that little long," said the poet;[7]

---

6. The ancient Italian city of Pompeii was buried by an eruption of Mt. Vesuvius in A.D. 79: the cinders and ashes remarkably preserved the city's ruins, including human beings who died on the spot.
7. English poet Oliver Goldsmith (1728–1744).

what a lie! Man wants almost unlimited quantities of almost everything, and he wants it till the day he dies.

Sometimes in *Life* or *Look* we see a double-page photograph of   15
some family standing on the lawn among its possessions: station-
wagon, swimming-pool, power-cruiser, sports-car, tape-recorder,
television sets, radios, cameras, power lawn-mower, garden tractor,
lathe, barbecue-set, sporting equipment, domestic appliances—all
the gleaming, grotesquely imaginative paraphernalia of its existence.
It was hard to get everything on two pages, soon it will need four.
It is like a dream, a child's dream before Christmas; yet if the
members of the family doubt that they are awake, they have only
to reach out and pinch something. The family seems pale and
small, a negligible appendage, beside its possessions; only a human
being would need to ask: "Which owns which?" We are fond of
saying that something is not just something but "a way of life";
this too is a way of life—our way, the way.

Emerson, in his spare stony New England, a few miles from   16
Walden, could write: "Things are in the saddle/ And ride mankind."[8]
He could say more now: that they are in the theater and studio,
and entertain mankind; are in the pulpit and preach to mankind.
The values of business, in a business society like our own, are
reflected in every sphere: values which agree with them are reinforced, values which disagree are cancelled out or have lip service
paid to them. In business what sells is good, and that's the end
of it—that is what *good* means; if the world doesn't beat a path
to your door, your mouse-trap wasn't better. The values of the
Medium—which is both a popular business itself and the cause
of popularity in other businesses—are business values: money,
success, celebrity. If we are representative members of our society,
the Medium's values are ours; and even if we are unrepresesntative,
non-conforming, our hands are—too often—subdued to the element
they work in, and our unconscious expectations are all that we
consciously reject. Darwin said that he always immediately wrote
down evidence against a theory because otherwise, he'd noticed,
he would forget it; in the same way, we keep forgetting the existence
of those poor and unknown failures whom we might rebelliously
love and admire.

If you're so smart why aren't you rich? is the ground-bass of our   17
society, a grumbling and quite unanswerable criticism, since the
society's non-monetary values *are* directly convertible into money.

8. American poet and philosopher Ralph Waldo Emerson (1803–1882), a friend
of Henry David Thoreau (see excerpt from Thoreau's *Walden*, p. 123 in *The Dolphin
Reader*).

Celebrity turns into testimonials, lectures, directorships, presidencies, the capital gains of an autobiography *Told To* some professional ghost who photographs the man's life as Bachrach[9] photographs his body. I read in the newspapers a lyric and perhaps exaggerated instance of this direct conversion of celebrity into money: his son accompanied Adlai Stevenson[10] on a trip to Russia, took snapshots of his father, and sold them (to accompany his father's account of the trip) to *Look* for $20,000. When Liberace[11] said that his critics' unfavorable reviews hurt him so much that he cried all the way to the bank, one had to admire the correctness and penetration of his press-agent's wit—in another age, what might not such a man have become!

Our culture is essentially periodical: we believe that all that is 18 deserves to perish and to have something else put in its place. We speak of planned obsolescence, but it is more than planned, it is felt; is an assumption about the nature of the world. We feel that the present is better and more interesting, more real, than the past, and that the future will be better and more interesting, more real, than the present; but, consciously, we do not hold against the present its prospective obsolescence. Our standards have become to an astonishing degree the standards of what is called the world of fashion, where mere timeliness—being orange in orange's year, violet in violet's—is the value to which all other values are reducible. In our society the word *old-fashioned* is so final a condemnation that someone like Norman Vincent Peale[12] can say about atheism or agnosticism simply that it is old-fashioned; the homely recommendation of the phrase *Give me that good old-time religion* has become, after a few decades, the conclusive rejection of the phrase *old-fashioned atheism.*

All this is, at bottom, the opposite of the world of the arts, where 19 commercial and scientific progress do not exist; where the bone of Homer and Mozart and Donatello is there, always, under the mere blush of fashion; where the past—the remote past, even— is responsible for the way that we understand, value, and act in, the present. (When one reads an abstract expressionist's remark that Washington studios are "eighteen months behind" those of his colleagues in New York, one realizes something of the terrible power of business and fashion over those most overtly hostile to

9. Well-known photography studios.
10. American statesman (1900–1965).
11. American popular pianist, famous—and rich—because of his so-called tastelessness.
12. American writer (b. 1898) whose primary message is that one can help oneself through positive thinking and prayer.

them.) An artist's work and life presuppose continuing standards, values extended over centuries or millenia, a future that is the continuation and modification of the past, not its contradiction of irrelevant replacement. He is working for the time that wants the best that he can do: the present, he hopes—but if not that, the future. If he sees that fewer and fewer people are any real audience for the serious artists of the past, he will feel that still fewer are going to be an audience for the serious artists of the present: for those who, willingly or unwillingly, sacrifice extrinsic values to intrinsic ones, immediate effectiveness to that steady attraction which, the artist hopes, true excellence will always exert.

The past's relation to the artist or man of culture is almost the   20
opposite of its relation to the rest of our society. To him the present is no more than the last ring on the trunk, understandable and valuable only in terms of all the earlier rings. The rest of our society sees only that great last ring, the enveloping surface of the trunk; what's underneath is a disregarded, almost mythical foundation. When Northrop Frye[13] writes that "the preoccupation of the humanities with the past is sometimes made a reproach against them by those who forget that we face the past: it may be shadowy, but it is all that is there," he is saying what for the artist or man of culture is self-evidently true. Yet for the Medium and the People of the Medium it is as self-evidently false: for them the present— or a past so recent, so quick-changing, so soon-disappearing, that it might be called the specious present—is all that is there.

In the past our culture's body of common knowledge—its frame   21
of reference, its possibility of comprehensible allusion—changed slowly and superficially; the amount added to it or taken away from it, in any ten years, was surprisingly small. Now in any ten years a surprisingly large proportion of the whole is replaced. Most of the information people have in common is something that four or five years from now they will not even remember having known. A newspaper story remarks in astonishment that television quiz-programs "have proved that ordinary citizens can be conversant with such esoterica as jazz, opera, the Bible, Shakespeare, poetry, and fisticuffs." You may exclaim: "Esoterica! If the Bible and Shakespeare are esoterica, what is there that's common knowledge?" The answer, I suppose, is that Elfrida von Nordroff and Teddy Nadler—the ordinary citizens on the quiz-programs—are common knowledge; though not for long. Songs disappear in two or three months, celebrities in two or three years; most of the Medium is little felt and soon forgotten. Nothing is as dead as day-before-

13. Canadian literary critic (b. 1912).

yesterday's newspaper, the next-to-the-last number on the roulette wheel; but most of the knowledge people have in common and lose in common is knowledge of such newspapers, such numbers. Yet the novelist or poet or dramatist, when he moves a great audience, depends upon the deep feelings, the living knowledge, that the people of that audience share; if so much has become contingent, superficial, ephemeral, it is disastrous for him.

New products and fashions replace the old, and the fact that they replace them is proof enough of their superiority. Similarly, the Medium does not need to show that the subjects which fill it are interesting or timely or important; the fact that they are its subjects makes them so. If *Time, Life,* and the television shows are full of Tom Fool this month, he's no fool. And when he has been gone from them a while, we do not think him a fool—we do not think of him at all. He no longer exists, in the fullest sense of the word *exist:* to be is to be perceived, to be a part of the Medium of our perception. Our celebrities are not kings, romantic in exile, but Representatives who, defeated, are forgotten; they had, always, only the qualities that we delegated to them.

After driving for four or five minutes along the road outside my door, I come to a row of one-room shacks about the size of kitchens, made out of used boards, metal signs, old tin roofs. To the people who live in them an electric dishwasher of one's own is as much a fantasy as an ocean liner of one's own. But since the Medium (and those whose thought is molded by it) does not perceive them, these people are themselves a fantasy. No matter how many millions of such exceptions to the general rule there are, they do not really exist, but have a kind of anomalous, statistical subsistence; our moral and imaginative view of the world is no more affected by them than by the occupants of some home for the mentally deficient a little farther along the road. If some night one of these out-moded, economically deficient ghosts should scratch at my window, I could say only: "Come back twenty or thirty years ago." And if I myself, as an old-fashioned, one-room poet, a friend of "quiet culture," a "meek lover of the good," should go out some night to scratch at another window, shouldn't I hear someone's indifferent or regretful: "Come back a century or two ago"?

When those whose existence the Medium recognizes ring the chimes of the writer's doorbell, fall through his letter-slot, float out onto his televison-screen, what is he to say to them? A man's unsuccessful struggle to get his family food is material for a work of art—for tragedy, almost; his unsuccessful struggle to get his family a stand-by generator is material for what? Comedy? Farce?

Comedy on such a scale, at such a level, that our society and its standards seem, almost, farce? And yet it is the People of the Medium—those who struggle for and get, or struggle for and don't get, the generator—whom our society finds representative: they are there, there primarily, there to be treated first of all. How shall the artist treat them? And the Medium itself—an end of life and a means of life, something essential to people's understanding and valuing of their existence, something many of their waking hours are spent listening to or looking at—how is *it* to be treated as subject-matter for art? The artist cannot merely reproduce it; should he satirize or parody it? But by the time the artist's work reaches its audience, the portion of the Medium which it satirized will already have been forgotten; and parody is impossible, often, when so much of the Medium is already an unintentional parody. (Our age might be defined as the age in which real parody became impossible, since any parody had already been duplicated, or parodied, in earnest.) Yet the Medium, by now, is an essential part of its watchers. How can you explain those whom Mohammedans call the People of the Book[14] in any terms that omit the Book? We are people of the television-set, the magazine, the radio, and are inexplicable in any terms that omit them.

Oscar Wilde said that Nature imitates Art, that before Whistler   25
painted them there were no fogs along the Thames.[15] If his statement were not false, it would not be witty. But to say that Nature imitates Art, when the Nature is human nature and the Art that of television, radio, motion-pictures, magazines, is literally true. The Medium shows its People what life is, what people are, and its People believe it: expect people to be that, try themselves to be that. Seeing is believing; and if what you see in *Life* is different from what you see in life, which of the two are you to believe? For many people it is what you see in *Life* (and in the movies, over television, on the radio) that is real life; and everyday existence, mere local or personal variation, is not real in the same sense.

The Medium mediates between us and raw reality, and the   26
mediation more and more replaces reality for us. Many radio-

14. The term that Islam gives to Jews, Christians, and Zoroastrians because all possess divine books: the Torah, the Gospel, the Avesta. This term is to distinguish them from "heathens," whose religions are not founded on divine revelation.
15. Wilde, an Irish writer and wit (1854–1900), was turning the conventional wisdom—that Art imitates Nature—on its head. James A.M. Whistler (1834–1903) was an American painter noted for his sense of color and design (evident in many of his paintings of London scenes)—and, on occasion, for trading barbed retorts with Oscar Wilde.

stations have a news-broadcast every hour, and many people like and need to hear it. In many houses either the television set or the radio is turned on during most of the hours the family is awake. It is as if they longed to be established in reality, to be reminded continually of the "real," "objective" world—the created world of the Medium—rather than to be left at the mercy of actuality, of the helpless contingency of the world in which the radio-receiver or television set is sitting. And surely we can sympathize: which of us hasn't found a similar refuge in the "real," created world of Cézanne or Goethe or Verdi? Yet Dostoievsky's world is too different from Wordsworth's, Piero della Francesca's from Goya's, Bach's from Wolf's, for us to be able to substitute one homogeneous mediated reality for everyday reality in the belief that it *is* everyday reality. For many watchers, listeners, readers, the world of events and celebrities and performers—the Great World—has become the world of primary reality: how many times they have sighed at the colorless unreality of their own lives and families, and sighed for the bright reality of, say, Elizabeth Taylor's. The watchers call the celebrities by their first names, approve or disapprove of "who they're dating," handle them with a mixture of love, identification, envy, and contempt. But however they handle them, they *handle* them: the Medium has given everyone so terrible a familiarity with everyone that it takes great magnanimity of spirit not to be affected by it. These celebrities are not heroes to us, their valets.

Better to have these real ones play themselves, and not sacrifice too much of their reality to art; better to have the watcher play himself, and not lose too much of himself in art. Usually the watcher is halfway between two worlds, paying full attention to neither: half distracted from, half distracted by, this distraction; and able for the moment not to be too greatly affected, have too great demands made upon him, by either world. For in the Medium, which we escape to from work, nothing is ever *work*, makes intellectual or emotional or imaginative demands which we might find it difficult to satisfy. Here in the half-world everything is homogeneous—is, as much as possible, the same as everything else: each familiar novelty, novel familiarity has the same treatment on top and the same attitude and conclusion at bottom; only the middle, the particular subject of the particular program or article, is different. If it *is* different: everyone is given the same automatic "human interest" treatment, so that it is hard for us to remember, unnecessary for us to remember, which particular celebrity we're reading about this time—often it's the same one, we've just moved on to a different magazine.

Francesco Caraccioli[16] said that the English have a hundred   28
religions and one sauce; so do we; and we are so accustomed to
this sauce or dye or style of presentation, the aesthetic equivalent
of Standard Brands, that a very simple thing can seem obscure or
perverse without it. And, too, we find it hard to have to shift from
one genre to another, to vary our attitudes and expectations, to
use our unexercised imaginations. Poetry disappeared long ago,
even for most intellectuals; each year fiction is a little less important.
Our age is the age of articles: we buy articles in stores, read articles
in magazines, exist among the interstices of articles: of columns,
interviews, photographic essays, documentaries; of facts condensed
into headlines or expanded into non-fiction best-sellers; of real
facts about real people.

Art lies to us to tell us the (sometimes disquieting) truth. The   29
Medium tells us truths, facts, in order to make us believe some
reassuring or entertaining lie or half-truth. These actually existing
celebrities, of universally admitted importance, about whom we
are told directly authoritative facts—how can fictional characters
compete with these? These *are* our fictional characters, our Lears
and Clytemnestras. (This is ironically appropriate, since many of
their doings and sayings are fictional, made up by public relations
officers, columnists, agents, or other affable familiar ghosts.) And
the Medium gives us such facts, such tape-recordings, such clinical
reports not only about the great but also about (representative
samples of) the small. When we have been shown so much about
so many—*can* be shown, we feel, anything about anybody—does
fiction seem so essential as it once seemed? Shakespeare or Tolstoy
can show us all about someone, but so can *Life;* and when *Life*
does, it's someone real.

The Medium is half life and half art, and competes with both   30
life and art. It spoils its audience for both; spoils both for its
audience. For the People of the Medium life isn't sufficiently a
matter of success and glamor and celebrity, isn't entertaining enough,
distracting enough, *mediated* enough; and art is too difficult or
individual or novel, too much a matter of tradition and the past,
too much a matter of special attitudes and aptitudes—its mediation
sometimes is queer or excessive, and sometimes is not even recognizable as mediation. The Medium's mixture of rhetoric and
reality, in which people are given what they know they want to
be given in the form in which they know they want to be given
it, is something more efficient and irresistible than any real art. If
a man has all his life been fed a combination of marzipan and

16. Neopolitan naval commander (1752–1799), executed by British admiral Horatio
Nelson for desertion to the French during the Napoleonic wars.

ethyl alcohol—if eating, to him, is a matter of being knocked unconscious by an ice cream soda—can he, by taking thought, come to prefer a diet of bread and wine, apples and well-water? Will a man who has spent his life watching gladiatorial games come to prefer listening to chamber music? And those who produce the bread and the wine and the quartets for him—won't they be tempted either to give up producing them, or else to produce a bread that's half sugar and half alcohol, a quartet that ends with the cellist at the violist's bleeding throat?

Any outsider who has worked for the Medium will have observed 31 that the one thing which seems to its managers most unnatural is for someone to do something naturally, to speak or write as an individual speaking or writing to other individuals, and not as a sub-contractor supplying a standardized product to the Medium. It is as if producers and editors and supervisors—middle men— were particles forming a screen between maker and public, one which will let through only particles of their own size and weight (or as they say, the public's). As you look into their strained puréed faces, their big horn-rimmed eyes, you despair of Creation itself, which seems for the instant made in their own owl-eyed image. There are so many extrinsic considerations involved in the presentation of his work, the maker finds, that by the time it is presented almost any intrinsic consideration has come to seem secondary. No wonder that the professional who writes the ordinary commercial success—the ordinary script, scenario, or best seller—resembles imaginative writers less than he resembles editors, producers, executives. The supplier has come to resemble those he supplies, and what he supplies them resembles both. With an artist you never know what you will get; with him you know what you will get. He is a reliable source for a standard product. He is almost exactly the opposite of the imaginative artist: instead of stubbornly or helplessly sticking to what he sees and feels—to what is right for him, true to his reality, regardless of what the others think and want—he gives the others what they think and want, regardless of what he himself sees and feels.

The Medium represents, to the artist, all that he has learned not 32 to do: its sure-fire stereotypes seem to him what any true art, true spirit, has had to struggle past on its way to the truth. The artist sees the values and textures of this art-substitute replacing those of his art, so far as most of society is concerned; conditioning the expectations of what audience his art has kept. Mass culture either corrupts or isolates the writer. His old feeling of oneness—of speaking naturally to an audience with essentially similar standards—is gone; and writers no longer have much of the consolatory feeling that took its place, the feeling of writing for the happy few, the kindred

spirits whose standards are those of the future. (Today they feel:
the future, should there be one, will be worse.) True works of art
are more and more produced away from or in opposition to society.
And yet the artist needs society as much as society needs him: as
our cultural enclaves get smaller and drier, more hysterical or
academic, one mourns for the artists inside and the public outside.
An incomparable historian of mass culture, Ernest van den Haag,
has expressed this with laconic force: "The artist who, by refusing
to work for the mass market, becomes marginal, cannot create
what he might have created had there been no mass market. One
may prefer a monologue to addressing a mass meeting. But it is
still not a conversation."

Even if the rebellious artist's rebellion is whole-hearted, it can   33
never be whole-stomach'd, whole-unconscious'd. Part of him wants
to be like his kind, is like his kind; longs to be loved and admired
and successful. Our society—and the artist, in so far as he is truly
a part of it—has no place set aside for the different and poor and
obscure, the fools for Christ's sake: they all go willy-nilly into
Limbo. The artist is tempted, consciously, to give his society what
it wants—or if he won't or can't, to give it nothing at all; is
tempted, unconsciously, to give it superficially independent or
contradictory works which are at heart works of the Medium. But
it is hard for him to go on serving both God and Mammon when
God is so really ill-, Mammon so really well-organized.

"Shakespeare wrote for the Medium of his day; if Shakespeare   34
were alive now he'd be writing *My Fair Lady*; isn't *My Fair Lady*,
then, our *Hamlet*? shouldn't you be writing *Hamlet* instead of sitting
there worrying about your superego? I need my *Hamlet*!" So society
speaks to the artist, reasons with the artist; and after he has written
it its *Hamlet* it is satisfied, and tries to make sure that he will never
do it again. There are many more urgent needs that it wants him
to satisfy: to lecture to it; to be interviewed; to appear on television
programs; to give testimonials; to attend book luncheons; to make
trips abroad for the State Department; to judge books for Book
Clubs; to read for publishers, judge for publishers, to be a publisher
for publishers; to edit magazines; to teach writing at colleges or
conferences; to write scenarios or scripts or articles—articles about
his home town for *Holiday*, about cats or clothes or Christmas for
Vogue, about "How I Wrote *Hamlet*" for anything; to—

But why go on? I once heard a composer, lecturing, say to a   35
poet, lecturing: "They'll pay us to do *anything*, so long as it isn't
writing music or writing poems." I knew the reply that as a member
of my society I should have made: "As long as they pay you,
what do you care?" But I didn't make it: it was plain that they
cared . . . But how many more learn not to care, to love what

they once endured! It is a whole so comprehensive that any alternative seems impossible, any opposition irrelevant; in the end a man says in a small voice: "I accept the Medium." The Enemy of the People winds up as the People—but where there is no enemy, the people perish.

The climate of our culture is changing. Under these new rains, 36 new suns, small things grow great, and what was great grows small; whole species disappear and are replaced. The American present is very different from the American past: so different that our awareness of the extent of the changes has been repressed, and we regard as ordinary what is extraordinary—ominous perhaps—both for us and for the rest of the world. The American present is many other peoples' future: our cultural and economic example is to much of the world mesmeric, and it is only its weakness and poverty that prevent it from hurrying with us into the Roman future. But at this moment of our power and success, our thought and art are full of a troubled sadness, of the conviction of our own decline. When the President of Yale University writes that "the ideal of the good life has faded from the educational process, leaving only miscellaneous prospects of jobs and joyless hedonism," are we likely to find it unfaded among our entertainers and executives? Is the influence of what I have called the Medium likely to lead us to any good life? to make us love and try to attain any real excellence, beauty, magnanimity? or to make us understand these as obligatory but transparent rationalizations behind which the realities of money and power are waiting?

The tourist Matthew Arnold[17] once spoke about our green culture 37 in terms that have an altered relevance—but are not yet irrelevant—to our ripe one. He said: "What really dissatisfies in American civilization is the want of the *interesting*, a want due chiefly to the want of those two great elements of the interesting, which are elevation and beauty." This use of *interesting*—and, perhaps, this tone of a curator pointing out what is plain and culpable—shows how far along in the decline of the West Arnold came: it is only in the latter days that we ask to be interested. He had found the word, he tells us, in Carlyle.[18] Carlyle is writing to a friend to persuade him not to emigrate to the United States; he asks: "Could you banish yourself from all that is interesting to your mind, forget the history, the glorious institutions, the noble principles of old Scotland—that you might eat a better dinner, perhaps?" We smile, and feel like reminding Carlyle of the history, the glorious insti-

17. English poet and critic Matthew Arnold (1822–1888) traveled in the United States in the 1880s.
18. Thomas Carlyle (1795–1881) was an English writer and social critic who had considerable influence on Arnold.

tutions, the noble principles of new America—of that New World which is, after all, the heir of the Old.

And yet . . . Can we smile as comfortably, today, as we could 38 have smiled yesterday? Nor could we listen as unconcernedly, if on taking leave of us some other tourist should conclude, with the penetration and obtuseness of his kind:

"I remember reading somewhere: that which you inherit from 39 your fathers you must earn in order to possess. I have been so much impressed with your power and your possessions that I have neglected, perhaps, your principles. The elevation or beauty of your spirit did not equal, always, that of your mountains and skyscrapers: it seems to me that your society provides you with 'all that is interesting to the mind' only exceptionally, at odd hours, in little reservations like those of your Indians. But as for your dinners, I've never seen anything like them: your daily bread comes *flambé.*[19] And yet—wouldn't you say—the more dinners a man eats, the more comforts he possesses, the hungrier and more uncomfortable some part of him becomes: inside every fat man there is a man who is starving. Part of you is being starved to death, and the rest of you is being stuffed to death. But this will change: no one goes on being stuffed to death or starved to death forever.

"This is a gloomy, an equivocal conclusion? Oh yes, I come 40 from an older culture, where things are accustomed to coming to such conclusions; where there is no last-paragraph fairy to bring one, always, a happy ending—or that happiest of all endings, no ending at all. And have I no advice to give you as I go? None. You are too successful to need advice, or to be able to take it if it were offered; but if ever you should fail, it is there waiting for you, the advice or consolation of all the other failures."

19. A dish served with flaming rum or brandy. (Generally considered very fancy.)

RALPH ELLISON

Prologue to "The Invisible Man"

I am an invisible man. No, I am not a spook like those who 1 haunted Edgar Allan Poe; nor am I one of your Hollywood-movie ectoplasms. I am a man of substance, of flesh and bone, fiber and

First edition published 1952.

liquids—and I might even be said to possess a mind. I am invisible, understand, simply because people refuse to see me. Like the bodiless heads you see sometimes in circus sideshows, it is as though I have been surrounded by mirrors of hard, distorting glass. When they approach me they see only my surroundings, themselves, or figments of their imagination—indeed, everything and anything except me.

Nor is my invisibility exactly a matter of a bio-chemical accident to my epidermis. That invisibility to which I refer occurs because of a peculiar disposition of the eyes of those with whom I come in contact. A matter of the construction of their *inner* eyes, those eyes with which they look through their physical eyes upon reality. I am not complaining, nor am I protesting either. It is sometimes advantageous to be unseen, although it is most often rather wearing on the nerves. Then too, you're constantly being bumped against by those of poor vision. Or again, you often doubt if you really exist. You wonder whether you aren't simply a phantom in other people's minds. Say, a figure in a nightmare which the sleeper tries with all his strength to destroy. It's when you feel like this that, out of resentment, you begin to bump people back. And, let me confess, you feel that way most of the time. You ache with the need to convince yourself that you do exist in the real world, that you're a part of all the sound and anguish, and you strike out with your fists, you curse and you swear to make them recognize you. And, alas, it's seldom successful.

One night I accidentally bumped into a man, and perhaps because of the near darkness he saw me and called me an insulting name. I sprang at him, seized his coat lapels and demanded that he apologize. He was a tall blond man, and as my face came close to his he looked insolently out of his blue eyes and cursed me, his breath hot in my face as he struggled. I pulled his chin down sharp upon the crown of my head, butting him as I had seen the West Indians do, and I felt his flesh tear and the blood gush out, and I yelled, "Apologize! Apologize!" But he continued to curse and struggle, and I butted him again and again until he went down heavily, on his knees, profusely bleeding. I kicked him repeatedly, in a frenzy because he still uttered insults though his lips were frothy with blood. Oh yes, I kicked him! And in my outrage I got out my knife and prepared to slit his throat, right there beneath the lamplight in the deserted street, holding him by the collar with one hand, and opening the knife with my teeth— when it occurred to me that the man had not *seen* me, actually; that he, as far as he knew, was in the midst of a walking nightmare! And I stopped the blade, slicing the air as I pushed him away, letting him fall back to the street. I stared at him hard as the lights of a car stabbed through the darkness. He lay there, moaning on the asphalt; a man almost killed by a phantom. It unnerved me. I was both disgusted and ashamed. I was like a drunken man myself, wavering about on weakened legs. Then I was amused. Something in this man's thick head had sprung out and beaten him within an inch of his life. I began to laugh at this crazy discovery. Would he have awakened at the point of death? Would Death himself have freed him for wakeful living? But I didn't linger. I ran away into the dark, laughing so hard I feared I might rupture myself. The next day I saw his picture in the *Daily News,* beneath a caption stating that he had been "mugged." Poor fool, poor blind fool, I thought with sincere compassion, mugged by an invisible man!

Most of the time (although I do not choose as I once did to deny the violence of my days by ignoring it) I am not so overtly violent. I remember that I am invisible and walk softly so as not to awaken the sleeping ones. Sometimes it is best not to awaken them; there are few things in the world as dangerous as sleepwalkers. I learned in time though that it is possible to carry on a fight against them without their realizing it. For instance, I have been carrying on a fight with Monopolated Light & Power for some time now. I use their service and pay them nothing at all, and they don't know it. Oh, they suspect that power is being drained off, but they don't know where. All they know is that according to the master meter back there in their power station a hell of a lot of free current is disappearing somewhere into the jungle of Harlem. The joke, of course, is that I don't live in Harlem but in a border area. Several years ago (before I discovered the advantage of being invisible) I went through the routine process of buying service and paying their outrageous rates. But no more. I gave up all that, along with my apartment, and my old way of life: That way based upon the fallacious assumption that I, like other men, was visible. Now, aware of my invisibility, I live rent-free in a building rented strictly to whites, in a section of the basement that was shut off and forgotten during the nineteenth century, which I discovered when I was trying to escape in the night from Ras the Destroyer. But that's getting too far ahead of the story, almost to the end, although the end is in the beginning and lies far ahead.

The point now is that I found a home—or a hole in the ground, ₅ as you will. Now don't jump to the conclusion that because I call my home a "hole" it is damp and cold like a grave; there are cold holes and warm holes. Mine is a warm hole. And remember, a bear retires to his hole for the winter and lives until spring; then he comes strolling out like the Easter chick breaking from its shell.

I say all this to assure you that it is incorrect to assume that, because I'm invisible and live in a hole, I am dead. I am neither dead nor in a state of suspended animation. Call me Jack-the-Bear, for I am in a state of hibernation.

My hole is warm and full of light. Yes, *full* of light. I doubt if there is a brighter spot in all New York than this hole of mine, and I do not exclude Broadway. Or the Empire State Building on a photographer's dream night. But that is taking advantage of you. Those two spots are among the darkest of our whole civilization— pardon me, our whole *culture* (an important distinction, I've heard)— which might sound like a hoax, or a contradiction, but that (by contradiction, I mean) is how the world moves: Not like an arrow, but a boomerang. (Beware of those who speak of the *spiral* of history; they are preparing a boomerang. Keep a steel helmet handy.) I know; I have been boomeranged across my head so much that I now can see the darkess of lightness. And I love light. Perhaps you'll think it strange that an invisible man should need light, desire light, love light. But maybe it is exactly because I *am* invisible. Light confirms my reality, gives birth to my form. A beautiful girl once told me of a recurring nightmare in which she lay in the center of a large dark room and felt her face expand until it filled the whole room, becoming a formless mass while her eyes ran in bilious jelly up the chimney. And so it is with me. Without light I am not only invisible, but formless as well; and to be unaware of one's form is to live a death. I myself, after existing some twenty years, did not become alive until I discovered my invisibility.

That is why I fight my battle with Monopolated Light & Power. The deeper reason, I mean: It allows me to feel my vital aliveness. I also fight them for taking so much of my money before I learned to protect myself. In my hole in the basement there are exactly 1,369 lights. I've wired the entire ceiling, every inch of it. And not with fluorescent bulbs, but with the older, more-expensive-to-operate kind, the filament type. An act of sabotage, you know. I've already begun to wire the wall. A junk man I know, a man of vision, has supplied me with wire and sockets. Nothing, storm or flood, must get in the way of our need for light and ever more and brighter light. The truth is the light and light is the truth. When I finish all four walls, then I'll start on the floor. Just how that will go, I don't know. Yet when you have lived invisible as long as I have you develop a certain ingenuity. I'll solve the problem. And maybe I'll invent a gadget to place my coffeepot on the fire while I lie in bed, and even invent a gadget to warm my bed—like the fellow I saw in one of the picture magazines who made himself a gadget to warm his shoes! Though invisible, I am in the great American tradition of tinkers. That makes me kin to Ford, Edison and Franklin. Call me, since I have a theory and a concept, a "thinker-tinker." Yes, I'll warm my shoes; they need it, they're usually full of holes. I'll do that and more.

Now I have one radio-phonograph; I plan to have five. There is a certain acoustical deadness in my hole, and when I have music I want to *feel* its vibration, not only with my ear but with my whole body. I'd like to hear five recordings of Louis Armstrong playing and singing "What Did I Do to Be so Black and Blue"— all at the same time. Sometimes now I listen to Louis while I have my favorite dessert of vanilla ice cream and sloe gin. I pour the red liquid over the white mound, watching it glisten and the vapor rising as Louis bends that military instrument into a beam of lyrical sound. Perhaps I like Louis Armstrong because he's made poetry out of being invisible. I think it must be because he's unaware that he *is* invisible. And my own grasp of invisibility aids me to understand his music. Once when I asked for a cigarette, some jokers gave me a reefer, which I lighted when I got home and sat listening to my phonograph. It was a strange evening. Invisibility, let me explain, gives one a slightly different sense of time, you're never quite on the beat. Sometimes you're ahead and sometimes behind. Instead of the swift and imperceptible flowing of time, you are aware of its nodes, those points where time stands still or from which it leaps ahead. And you slip into the breaks and look around. That's what you hear vaguely in Louis' music.

Once I saw a prizefighter boxing a yokel. The fighter was swift and amazingly scientific. His body was one violent flow of rapid rhythmic action. He hit the yokel a hundred times while the yokel held up his arms in stunned surprise. But suddenly the yokel, rolling about in the gale of boxing gloves, struck one blow and knocked science, speed and footwork as cold as a well-digger's posterior. The smart money hit the canvas. The long shot got the nod. The yokel had simply stepped inside of his opponent's sense of time. So under the spell of the reefer I discovered a new analytical way of listening to music. The unheard sounds came through, and each melodic line existed of itself, stood out clearly from all the rest, said its piece, and waited patiently for the other voices to speak. That night I found myself hearing not only in time, but in space as well. I not only entered the music but descended, like Dante, into its depths. And *beneath the swiftness of the hot tempo there was a slower tempo and a cave and I entered it and looked around and heard an old woman singing a spiritual as full of Weltschmerz as flamenco, and beneath that lay a still lower level on which I saw a beautiful girl the color of ivory pleading in a voice like my mother's as*

*she stood before a group of slave owners who bid for her naked body,
and below that I found a lower level and a more rapid tempo and I
heard someone shout:*

"Brothers and sisters, my text this morning is the 'Blackness of
Blackness.' "   10

*And a congregation of voices answered: "That blackness is most black,
brother, most black . . ."*

"In the beginning . . ."

"At the very start," *they cried.*

". . . there was blackness . . ."

"Preach it . . ."   15

". . . and the sun . . ."

"The sun, Lawd . . ."

". . . was bloody red . . ."

"Red . . ."

"Now black is . . ." *the preacher shouted.*   20

"Bloody . . ."

"I said black is . . ."

"Preach it, brother . . ."

". . . an' black ain't . . ."

"Red, Lawd, red: He said it's red!"   25

"Amen, brother . . ."

"Black will git you . . ."

"Yes, it will . . ."

". . . an' black won't . . ."

"Naw, it won't!"   30

"It do . . ."

"It do, Lawd . . ."

". . . an' it don't."

"Halleluiah . . ."

". . . It'll put you, glory, glory, Oh my Lawd, in the WHALE'S   35
BELLY."

"Preach it, dear brother . . ."

". . . an' make you tempt . . ."

"Good God a-mighty!"

"Old Aunt Nelly!"

"Black will make you . . ."   40

"Black . . ."

". . . or black will un-make you."

"Ain't it the truth, Lawd?"

*And at that point a voice of trombone timbre screamed at me, "Git
out of here, your fool! Is you ready to commit treason?"*

And I tore myself away, hearing the old singer of spirituals moaning,   45
"Go curse your God, boy, and die."

I stopped and questioned her, asked her what was wrong.

"I dearly loved my master, son," she said.

"You should have hated him," I said.

"He gave me several sons," she said, "and because I loved my sons I learned to love their father though I hated him too."

"I too have become acquainted with ambivalence," I said. "That's   50 why I'm here."

"What's that?"

"Nothing, a word that doesn't explain it. Why do you moan?"

"I moan this way 'cause he's dead," she said.

"Then tell me, who is that laughing upstairs?"

"Them's my sons. They glad."   55

"Yes, I can understand that too," I said.

"I laughs too, but I moans too. He promised to set us free but he never could bring hisself to do it. Still I loved him . . ."

"Loved him? You mean . . ."

"Oh yes, but I loved something else even more."

"What more?"   60

"Freedom."

"Freedom," I said. "Maybe freedom lies in hating."

"Naw, son, it's in loving. I loved him and give him the poison and he withered away like a frost-bit apple. Them boys woulda tore him to pieces with they homemake knives."

"A mistake was made somewhere," I said, "I'm confused." And I wished to say other things, but the laughter upstairs became too loud and moan-like for me and I tried to break out of it, but I couldn't. Just as I was leaving I felt an urgent desire to ask her what freedom was and went back. She sat with her head in her hands, moaning softly; her leather-brown face was filled with sadness.

"Old woman, what is this freedom you love so well?" I asked around   65 a corner of my mind.

She looked surprised, then thoughtful, then baffled. "I done forgot, son. It's all mixed up. First I think it's one thing, then I think it's another. It gits my head to spinning. I guess now it ain't nothing but knowing how to say what I got up in my head. But it's a hard job, son. Too much is done happen to me in too short a time. Hit's like I have a fever. Ever' time I starts to walk my head gits to swirling and I falls down. Or if it ain't that, it's the boys; they gits to laughing and wants to kill up the white folks. They's bitter, that's what they is . . ."

"But what about freedom?"

"Leave me 'lone, boy; my head aches!"

I left her, feeling dizzy myself. I didn't get far.

Suddenly one of the sons, a big fellow six feet tall, appeared out of   70 nowhere and struck me with his fist.

"What's the matter, man?" I cried.

"You made Ma cry!"

"But how?" I said, dodging a blow.

"Askin' her them questions, that's how. Git outa here and stay, and next time you got questions like that, ask yourself!"

He held me in a grip like cold stone, his fingers fastening upon my windpipe until I thought I would suffocate before he finally allowed me to go. I stumbled about dazed, the music beating hysterically in my ears. It was dark. My head cleared and I wandered down a dark narrow passage, thinking I heard his footsteps hurrying behind me. I was sore, and into my being had come a profound craving for tranquillity, for peace and quiet, a state I felt I could never achieve. For one thing, the trumpet was blaring and the rhythm was too hectic. A tom-tom beating like heart-thuds began drowning out the trumpet, filling my ears. I longed for water and I heard it rushing through the cold mains my fingers touched as I felt my way, but I couldn't stop to search because of the footsteps behind me.

"Hey, Ras," I called. "Is it you, Destroyer? Rinehart?"

No answer, only the rhythmic footsteps behind me. Once I tried crossing the road, but a speeding machine struck me, scraping the skin from my leg as it roared past.

Then somehow I came out of it, ascending hastily from this underworld of sound to hear Louis Armstrong innocently asking,

> *What did I do*
> *To be so black*
> *And blue?*

At first I was afraid; this familiar music had demanded action, the kind of which I was incapable, and yet had I lingered there beneath the surface I might have attempted to act. Nevertheless, I know now that few really listen to this music. I sat on the chair's edge in a soaking sweat, as though each of my 1,369 bulbs had everyone become a klieg light in an individual setting for a third degree with Ras and Rinehart in charge. It was exhausting—as though I had held my breath continuously for an hour under the terrifying serenity that comes from days of intense hunger. And yet, it was a strangely satisfying experience for an invisible man to hear the silence of sound. I had discovered unrecognized compulsions of my being—even though I could not answer "yes" to their promptings. I haven't smoked a reefer since, however; not because they're illegal, but because to *see* around corners is enough (that is not unusual when you are invisible). But to hear around them is too much; it inhibits action. And despite Brother Jack and all that sad, lost period of the Brotherhood, I believe in nothing if not in action.

Please, a definition: A hibernation is a covert preparation for a more overt action.

Besides, the drug destroys one's sense of time completely. If that happened, I might forget to dodge some bright morning and some cluck would run me down with an orange and yellow steet car, or a bilious bus! Or I might forget to leave my hole when the moment for action presents itself.

Meanwhile I enjoy my life with the compliments of Monopolated Light & Power. Since you never recognize me even when in closest contact with me, and since, no doubt, you'll hardly believe that I exist, it won't matter if you know that I tapped a power line leading into the building and ran it into my hole in the ground. Before that I lived in the darkness into which I was chased, but now I see. I've illuminated the blackness of my invisibility—and vice versa. And so I play the invisible music of my isolation. The last statement doesn't seem just right, does it? But it is; you hear this music simply because music is heard and seldom seen, except by musicians. Could this compulsion to put invisibility down in black and white be thus an urge to make music of invisibility? But I am an orator, a rabble rouser—Am I? I *was,* and perhaps shall be again. Who knows? All sickness is not unto death, neither is invisibility.

I can hear you say, "What a horrible, irresponsible bastard!" And you're right. I leap to agree with you. I am one of the most irresponsible beings that ever lived. Irresponsibility is part of my invisibility; any way you face it, it is a denial. But to whom can I be responsible, and why should I be, when you refuse to see me? And wait until I reveal how truly irresponsible I am. Responsibility rests upon recognition, and recognition is a form of agreement. Take a man whom I almost killed: Who was responsible for that near murder—I? I don't think so, and I refuse it. I won't buy it. You can't give it to me. *He* bumped *me, he* insulted *me.* Shouldn't he, for his own personal safety, have recognized my hysteria, my "danger potential"? He, let us say, was lost in a dream world. But didn't *he* control that dream world—which, alas, is only too real!—and didn't *he* rule me out of it? And if he had yelled for a policeman, wouldn't *I* have been taken for the offending one? Yes, yes, yes! Let me agree with you, I was the irresponsible one; for I should have used my knife to protect the higher interests of society. Some day that kind of foolishness will cause us tragic trouble. All dreamers and sleepwalkers must pay the price, and even the invisible victim is responsible for the fate of all. But I shirked that reponsibility; I became too snarled in the incompatible notions that buzzed within my brain. I was a coward . . .

But what did *I* do to be so blue? Bear with me.

ALICE MUNRO

Day of the Butterfly

I do not remember when Myra Sayla came to town, though she must have been in our class at school for two or three years. I start remembering her in the last year, when her little brother Jimmy Sayla was in Grade One. Jimmy Sayla was not used to going to the bathroom by himself and he would have to come to the Grade Six door and ask for Myra and she would take him downstairs. Quite often he would not get to Myra in time and there would be a big dark stain on his little button-on cotton pants. Then Myra had to come and ask the teacher, "Please may I take my brother home, he has wet himself?"

That was what she said the first time and everybody in the front seats heard her—though Myra's voice was the lightest singsong—and there was a muted giggling which alerted the rest of the class. Our teacher, a cold gentle girl who wore glasses with thin gold rims and in the stiff solicitude of certain poses resembled a giraffe, wrote something on a piece of paper and showed it to Myra. And Myra recited uncertainly: "My brother has had an accident, please, teacher."

Everybody knew of Jimmy Sayla's shame and at recess (if he was not being kept in, as he often was, for doing something he shouldn't in school) he did not dare go out on the school grounds, where the other little boys, and some bigger ones, were waiting to chase him and corner him against the back fence and thrash him with tree branches. He had to stay with Myra. But at our school there were the two sides, the Boys' Side and the Girls' Side, and it was believed that if you so much as stepped on the side that was not your own you might easily get the strap. Jimmy could not go out on the Girls' Side and Myra could not go out on the Boys' Side, and no one was allowed to stay in the school unless it was raining or snowing. So Myra and Jimmy spent every recess standing in the little back porch between the two sides. Perhaps they watched the baseball games, the tag and skipping and building of leaf houses in the fall and snow forts in the winter; perhaps they did not watch at all. Whenever you happened to look at them their heads were slightly bent, their narrow bodies hunched in, quite still. They had long smooth oval faces, melancholy

First published in Munro's first collection of short stories, *Dance of the Happy Shades* (1968).

and discreet—dark, oily, shining hair. The little boy's was long, clipped at home, and Myra's was worn in heavy braids coiled on top of her head so that she looked, from a distance, as if she was wearing a turban too big for her. Over their dark eyes the lids were never fully raised; they had a weary look. But it was more than that. They were like children in a medieval painting, they were like small figures carved of wood, for worship or magic, with faces smooth and aged, and meekly, cryptically uncommunicative.

Most of the teachers at our school had been teaching for a long time and at recess they would disappear into the teachers' room and not bother us. But our own teacher, the young woman of the fragile gold-rimmed glasses, was apt to watch us from a window and sometimes come out, looking brisk and uncomfortable, to stop a fight among the little girls or start a running game among the big ones, who had been huddled together playing Truth or Secrets. One day she came out and called, "Girls in Grade Six, I want to talk to you!" She smiled persuasively, earnestly, and with dreadful unease, showing fine gold rims around her teeth. She said, "There is a girl in Grade Six called Myra Sayla. She *is* in your grade, isn't she?"

We mumbled. But there was a coo from Gladys Healey. "Yes,   5
Miss Darling!"

"Well, why is she never playing with the rest of you? Every day I see her standing in the back porch, never playing. Do you think she looks very happy standing back there? Do you think you would be very happy, if *you* were left back there?"

Nobody answered; we faced Miss Darling, all respectful, self-possessed, and bored with the unreality of her question. Then Gladys said, "Myra can't come out with us, Miss Darling. Myra has to look after her little brother!"

"Oh," said Miss Darling dubiously. "Well you ought to try to be nicer to her anyway. Don't you think so? Don't you? You will try to be nicer, won't you? I *know* you will." Poor Miss Darling! Her campaigns were soon confused, her persuasions turned to bleating and uncertain pleas.

When she had gone Gladys Healey said softly, "You will try to be nicer, won't you? I *know* you will!" and then drawing her lip back over her big teeth she yelled exuberantly, "I don't care if it rains or freezes." She went through the whole verse and ended it with a spectacular twirl of her Royal Stuart tartan skirt. Mr. Healey ran a Dry Goods and Ladies' Wear, and his daughter's leadership in our class was partly due to her flashing plaid skirts and organdie blouses and velvet jackets with brass buttons, but also to her early-maturing bust and the fine brutal force of her personality. Now we all began to imitate Miss Darling.

We had not paid much attention to Myra before this. But now a game was developed; it started with saying, "Let's be nice to Myra!" Then we would walk up to her in formal groups of three or four and at a signal, say together, "Hel-lo Myra, Hello *My*-ra!" and follow up with something like, "What do you wash your hair in, Myra, it's so nice and shiny, *My*-ra." "Oh she washes it in cod-liver oil, don't you, Myra, she washes it in cod-liver oil, can't you smell it?"

And to tell the truth there was a smell about Myra, but it was a rotten-sweetish smell as of bad fruit. That was what the Saylas did, kept a little fruit store. Her father sat all day on a stool by the window, with his shirt open over his swelling stomach and tufts of black hair showing around his belly button; he chewed garlic. But if you went into the store it was Mrs. Sayla who came to wait on you, appearing silently between the limp print curtains hung across the back of the store. Her hair was crimped in black waves and she smiled with her full lips held together, stretched as far as they would go; she told you the price in a little rapping voice, daring you to challenge her and, when you did not, handed you the bag of fruit with open mockery in her eyes.

One morning in the winter I was walking up the school hill very early; a neighbour had given me a ride into town. I lived about half a mile out of town, on a farm, and I should not have been going to the town school at all, but to a country school nearby where there were half a dozen pupils and a teacher a little demented since her change of life. But my mother, who was an ambitious woman, had prevailed on the town trustees to accept me and my father to pay the extra tuition, and I went to school in town. I was the only one in the class who carried a lunch pail and ate peanut-butter sandwiches in the high, bare, mustard-coloured cloakroom, the only one who had to wear rubber boots in the spring, when the roads were heavy with mud. I felt little danger, on account of this; but I could not tell exactly what it was.

I saw Myra and Jimmy ahead of me on the hill; they always went to school very early—sometimes so early that they had to stand outside waiting for the janitor to open the door. They were walking slowly, and now and then Myra half turned around. I had often loitered in that way, wanting to walk with some important girl who was behind me, and not quite daring to stop and wait.

Now it occurred to me that Myra might be doing this with me.
I did not know what to do. I could not afford to be seen walking
with her, and I did not even want to—but, on the other hand,
the flattery of those humble, hopeful turnings was not lost on me.
A role was shaping for me that I could not resist playing. I felt a
great pleasurable rush of self-conscious benevolence; before I thought
what I was doing I called, "Myra! Hey, Myra, wait up, I got some
Cracker Jack!" and I quickened my pace as she stopped.

Myra waited, but she did not look at me; she waited in the
withdrawn and rigid attitude with which she always met us. Perhaps
she thought I was playing a trick on her, perhaps she expected
me to run past and throw an empty Cracker Jack box in her face.
And I opened the box and held it out to her. She took a little.
Jimmy ducked behind her coat and would not take any when I
offered the box to him.

"He's shy," I said reassuringly. "A lot of little kids are shy like   15
that. He'll probably grow out of it."

"Yes," said Myra.

"I have a brother four," I said. "He's awfully shy." He wasn't.
"Have some more Cracker Jack," I said. "I used to eat Cracker
Jack all the time but I don't any more. I think it's bad for your
complexion."

There was a silence.

"Do you like Art?" said Myra faintly.

"No. I like Social Studies and Spelling and Health."   20

"I like Art and Arithmetic." Myra could add and multiply in
her head faster than anyone else in the class.

"I wish I was as good as you. In Arithmetic," I said, and felt
magnanimous.

"But I am no good at Spelling," said Myra. "I make the most
mistakes, I'll fail maybe." She did not sound unhappy about this,
but pleased to have such a thing to say. She kept her head turned
away from me staring at the dirty snowbanks along Victoria Street,
and as she talked she made a sound as if she was wetting her lips
with her tongue.

"You won't fail," I said. "You are too good in Arithmetic. What
are you going to be when you grow up?"

She looked bewildered. "I will help my mother," she said. "And   25
work in the store."

"Well I am going to be an airplane hostess," I said. "But don't
mention it to anybody. I haven't told many people."

"No, I won't," said Myra. "Do you read Steve Canyon in the
paper?"

"Yes." It was queer to think that Myra, too, read the comics, or that she did anything at all, apart from her role at the school. "Do you read Rip Kirby?"

"Do you read Orphan Annie?"

"Do you read Betsy and the Boys?"   30

"You haven't had hardly any Cracker Jack," I said. "Have some. Take a whole handful."

Myra looked into the box. "There's a prize in there," she said. She pulled it out. It was a brooch, a little tin butterfly, painted gold with bits of coloured glass stuck onto it to look like jewels. She held it in her brown hand, smiling slightly.

I said, "Do you like that?"

Myra said, "I like them blue stones. Blue stones are sapphires."

"I know. My birthstone is sapphire. What is your birthstone?"   35

"I don't know."

"When is your birthday?"

"July."

"Then yours is ruby."

"I like sapphire better," said Myra. "I like yours." She handed   40
me the brooch.

"You keep it," I said. "Finders keepers."

Myra kept holding it out, as if she did not know what I meant. "Finders keepers," I said.

"It was your Cracker Jack," said Myra, scared and solemn. "You bought it."

"Well, you found it."

"No—" said Myra.   45

"Go on!" I said. "Here, I'll *give* it to you." I took the brooch from her and pushed it back into her hand.

We were both surprised. We looked at each other; I flushed but Myra did not. I realized the pledge as our fingers touched; I was panicky, but *all right.* I thought, I can come early and walk with her other mornings. I can go and talk to her at recess. Why not? *Why not?*

Myra put the brooch in her pocket. She said, "I can wear it on my good dress. My good dress is blue."

I knew it would be. Myra wore out her good dresses at school. Even in midwinter among the plaid wool skirts and serge tunics, she glimmered sadly in sky-blue taffeta, in dusty turquoise crepe, a grown woman's dress made over, weighted by a big bow at the v of the neck and folding empty over Myra's narrow chest.

And I was glad she had not put it on. If someone asked her   50
where she got it, and she told them, what would I say?

It was the day after this, or the week after, that Myra did not come to school. Often she was kept at home to help. But this time she did not come back. For a week, then two weeks, her desk was empty. Then we had a moving day at school and Myra's books were taken out of her desk and put on a shelf in the closet. Miss Darling said, "We'll find a seat when she comes back." And she stopped calling Myra's name when she took attendance.

Jimmy Sayla did not come to school either, having no one to take him to the bathroom.

In the fourth week or the fifth, that Myra had been away, Gladys Healey came to school and said, "Do you know what—Myra Sayla is sick in the hospital."

It was true. Gladys Healey had an aunt who was a nurse. Gladys put up her hand in the middle of Spelling and told Miss Darling. "I thought you might like to know," she said. "Oh yes," said Miss Darling. "I do know."

"What has she got?" we said to Gladys.   55

And Gladys said, "Akemia,[1] or something. And she has blood transfusions." She said to Miss Darling, "My aunt is a nurse."

So Miss Darling had the whole class write Myra a letter, in which everybody said, Dear Myra, We are all writing you a letter. We hope you will soon be better and be back to school, Yours truly . . ." And Miss Darling said, "I've thought of something. Who would like to go up to the hospital and visit Myra on the twentieth of March, for a birthday party?"

I said, "Her birthday's in July."

"I know," said Miss Darling. "It's the twentieth of July. So this year she could have it on the twentieth of March, because she's sick."

"But her *birthday* is in July."   60

"Because she's sick," said Miss Darling, with a warning shrillness. "The cook at the hospital could make a cake and you could all give a little present, twenty-five cents or so. It would have to be between two and four, because that's visiting hours. And we couldn't all go, it'd be too many. So who wants to go and who wants to stay here and do supplementary reading?"

We all put up our hands. Miss Darling got out the spelling records and picked out the first fifteen, twelve girls and three boys. Then the three boys did not want to go so she picked out the next three girls. And I do not know when it was, but I think it

---

1. That is, leukemia, a usually fatal disease of the blood.

was probably at this moment that the birthday party of Myra Sayla became fashionable.

Perhaps it was because Gladys Healey had an aunt who was a nurse, perhaps it was the excitement of sickness and hospitals, or simply the fact that Myra was so entirely, impressively set free of all the rules and conditions of our lives. We began to talk of her as if she were something we owned, and her party became a cause; with womanly heaviness we discussed it at recess, and decided that twenty-five cents was too low.

We all went up to the hospital on a sunny afternoon when the snow was melting, carrying our presents, and a nurse led us upstairs, single file, and down a hall past half-closed doors and dim conversations. She and Miss Darling kept saying, "Sh-sh," but we were going on tiptoe anyway; our hospital demeanor was perfect.

At this small country hospital there was no children's ward, and Myra was not really a child; they had put her in with two grey old women. A nurse was putting screens around them as we came in.

Myra was sitting up in bed, in a bulky stiff hospital gown. Her hair was down, the long braids falling over her shoulders and down the coverlet. But her face was the same, always the same.

She had been told something about the party, Miss Darling said, so the surprise would not upset her; but it seemed she had not believed, or had not understood what it was. She watched us as she used to watch in the school grounds when we played.

"Well, here we are!" said Miss Darling. "Here we are!"

And we said, "Happy birthday, Myra! Hello, Myra, happy birthday!" Myra said, "My birthday is in July." Her voice was lighter than ever, drifting, expressionless.

"Never mind when it is, really," said Miss Darling. "Pretend it's now! How old are you, Myra?"

"Eleven," Myra said. "In July."

Then we all took off our coats and emerged in our party dresses, and laid our presents, in their pale flowery wrappings on Myra's bed. Some of our mothers had made immense, complicated bows of fine satin ribbon, some of them had even taped on little bouquets of imitation roses and lilies of the valley. "Here Myra," we said, "here Myra, happy birthday." Myra did not look at us, but at the ribbons, pink and blue and speckled with silver, and the miniature bouquets; they pleased her, as the butterfly had done. An innocent look came into her face, a partial, private smile.

"Open them, Myra," said Miss Darling. "They're for you!"

Myra gathered the presents around her, fingering them, with this smile, and a cautious realization, an unexpected pride. She said, "Saturday I'm going to London to St. Joseph's Hospital."

"That's where my mother was at," somebody said. "We went   75
and saw her. They've got all nuns there."

"My father's sister is a nun," said Myra calmly.

She began to unwrap the presents, with an air that not even Gladys could have bettered, folded the tissue paper and the ribbons, and drawing out books and puzzles and cutouts as if they were all prizes she had won. Miss Darling said that maybe she should say thank you, and the person's name with every gift she opened, to make sure she knew whom it was from, and so Myra said, "Thank you, Mary Louise, thank you, Carol," and when she came to mine she said, "Thank you, Helen." Everyone explained their presents to her and there was talking and excitement and a little gaiety, which Myra presided over, though she was not gay. A cake was brought in with *Happy Birthday Myra* written on it, pink on white, and eleven candles. Miss Darling lit the candles and we all sang Happy Birthday to You, and cried, "Make a wish, Myra, make a wish—" and Myra blew them out. Then we all had cake and strawberry ice cream.

At four o'clock a buzzer sounded and the nurse took out what was left of the cake, and the dirty dishes, and we put on our coats to go home. Everybody said, "Goodbye, Myra," and Myra sat in the bed watching us go, her back straight, not supported by any pillow, her hands resting on the gifts. But at the door I heard her call; she called "Helen!" Only a couple of the others heard; Miss Darling did not hear, she had gone out ahead. I went back to the bed.

Myra said, "I got too many things. You take something."

"What?" I said. "It's for your birthday. You always get a lot at   80
a birthday."

"Well you take something," Myra said. She picked up a leatherette case with a mirror in it, a comb and a nail file and a natural lipstick and a small handkerchief edged with gold thread. I had noticed it before. "You take that," she said.

"Don't you want it?"

"You take it." She put it into my hand. Our fingers touched again.

"When I come back from London," Myra said, "you can come and play at my place after school."

"Okay," I said. Outside the hospital window there was a clear   85
carrying sound of somebody playing in the street, maybe chasing

with the last snowballs of the year. This sound made Myra, her triumph and her bounty, and most of her future in which she had found this place for me, turn shadowy, turn dark. All the presents on the bed, the folded paper and ribbons, those guilt-tinged offerings, had passed into this shadow, they were no longer innocent objects to be touched, exchanged, accepted without danger. I didn't want to take the case now but I could not think how to get out of it, what lie to tell. I'll give it away, I thought, I won't ever play with it. I would let my little brother pull it apart.

The nurse came back, carrying a glass of chocolate milk.

"What's the matter, didn't you hear the buzzer?"

So I was released, set free by the barriers which now closed about Myra, her unknown, exalted, ether-smelling hospital world, and by the treachery of my own heart. "Well, thank you," I said. "Thank you for the thing. Goodbye."

Did Myra ever say goodbye? Not likely. She sat in her high bed, her delicate brown neck, rising out of a hospital gown too big for her, her brown carved face immune to treachery, her offering perhaps already forgotten, prepared to be set apart for legendary uses, as she was even in the back porch at school.

Thinking About Outsiders

Among the Greek heroes who set out for Troy was Philoctetes, commander of 350 archers and inheritor of the bow of Hercules— a miraculous weapon that never missed its mark. Unfortunately, when the Greek fleet stopped on a small island, Philoctetes was bitten by a snake. As his foot swelled and stiffened, the pain became overwhelming, and his cries began to dishearten the whole army. His friends tried at first to distract and amuse him, but soon began to avoid him because they couldn't tolerate either his moans or the horrid stench of his oozing and incurable wound. He had become a liability, and at Odysseus' suggestion the Greeks marooned him on the island, setting sail while Philoctetes slept. Ten years later, the Greeks realized that Troy would never fall without the bow of Philoctetes, and they dispatched Odysseus to the island once more, this time to convince the wretched man—who had lived for ten years in a cave nursing his still fetid wound—that it had all been a simple misunderstanding among friends. Odysseus' mission succeeded, though poets have been hard pressed to explain why, and the bowman rejoined the Greeks for the final assault on Troy.

In some ways, Philoctetes is the archetype of the outsider. For reasons that he cannot control, he is disliked by his fellow men. He knows that any attention he receives from them is forced, calculated, motivated by self-interest or (worse yet) a shallow pity. He knows that just out of earshot they whisper, weighing the malodorous wound against the miraculous bow. What happens to a person who is cast out of society and views it with an alien's eye? What sort of person does he become? According to the Greek playwright Sophocles, he turns misanthrope:

> *I understand these men.*
> *Once their wickedness is hatched, their minds*
> *Breed nothing but wickedness, nothing but crime.*

The Frenchman André Gide, however, has a different view. In his *Philoctète*, ten years of isolation broaden the bowman's mind, raising him to a wisdom far above the wiliness of Odysseus. He stops groaning when he realizes there is no one to hear and begins to notice the suffering of the creatures around him. He forgets his bitterness toward his old comrades, but also his hatred of the Trojans: "On this island, you know, I have become every day less Greek, every day more human."

Two broad themes unite this section. E. M. Forster's "Jew Consciousness," Dorothy Parker's "Good Souls," and Alice Munro's "The Day of the Butterfly" all are concerned with the wound: the flaw, imagined or real, that isolates a person from society. Other selections reflect the special understanding the wound produces in its victim. Roger Wilkins and Richard Rodriguez write with great insight because they are doubly marooned, separated by race from complete acceptance in the white world and by acculturation from complete fellowship with other blacks or Hispanics. Cynthia Ozick gives us an outsider's perspective on the academic and intellectual circles where she, as a woman, has been resented or patronized. Joan Didion writes about the more subtle isolation that comes when marriage makes a person an outsider in her own family. Randall Jarrell speaks as a poet abandoned or betrayed by the society of "the Medium." And Ralph Ellison's Invisible Man is a twentieth-century Philoctetes, a bitter black man living "rent free in a building rented strictly to whites, in a section of basement that was shut off and forgotten during the nineteenth century."

QUESTIONS

1. The line between the outsider and the insider is often very finely drawn, as both E. M. Forster and Alice Munro show us. Setting major distinctions like sex, race, and religion aside for the time, examine the more subtle signs that exclude someone from a group to which you belong. What is it that makes someone a nerd, a loser, a pariah?

2. What role do mass media (or "the Medium" of Jarrell's essay) have in determining who will end up an outsider to society at large? Is this influence evil or benign? How is it exerted?

3. Gide suggests that outsiders may achieve a special wisdom or insight. Does this strike you as likely? Do you know of any examples from personal experience?

4. Where in your community do you encounter people most alienated from society? What is the effect of their alienation? Do you think they will ever return from their isolation?

5. When have you encountered the sort of situation Rodriguez and Wilkins discuss—a false assumption by group X that you must identify yourself with group Y? How has this affected your relations with each group?

6. In the essays collected here, do you find any in which the outsider's bitterness overwhelms his or her wisdom? Are any of our authors busy feeling sorry for themselves?

ART AND SPORT

JOHAN HUIZINGA

The Nature and Significance of Play

In tackling the problem of play as a function of culture proper 1
and not as it appears in the life of the animal or the child, we
begin where biology and psychology leave off. In culture we find
play as a given magnitude existing before culture itself existed,
accompanying it and pervading it from the earliest beginnings right
up to the phase of civilization we are now living in. We find play
present everywhere as a well-defined quality of action which is
different from "ordinary" life. We can disregard the question of
how far science has succeeded in reducing this quality to quantitative
factors. In our opinion it has not. At all events it is precisely this
quality, itself so characteristic of the form of life we call "play",
which matters. Play as a special form of activity, as a "significant
form", as a social function—that is our subject. We shall not look
for the natural impulses and habits conditioning play in general,
but shall consider play in its manifold concrete forms as itself a
social construction. We shall try to take play as the player himself
takes it: in its primary significance. If we find that play is based
on the manipulation of certain images, on a certain "imagination"
of reality (i.e. its conversion into images), then our main concern
will be to grasp the value and significance of these images and
their "imagination". We shall observe their action in play itself
and thus try to understand play as a cultural factor in life.

The great archetypal activities of human society are all permeated 2
with play from the start. Take language, for instance—that first
and supreme instrument which man shapes in order to communicate, to teach, to command. Language allows him to distinguish,
to establish, to state things; in short, to name them and by naming
them to raise them into the domain of the spirit. In the making
of speech and language the spirit is continually "sparking" between
matter and mind, as it were, playing with this wondrous nominative
faculty. Behind every abstract expression there lie the boldest of
metaphors, and every metaphor is a play upon words. Thus in
giving expression to life man creates a second, poetic world alongside
the world of nature.

Or take myth. This, too, is a transformation or an "imagination" 3
of the outer world, only here the process is more elaborate and
ornate than is the case with individual words. In myth, primitive

Excerpt from Chapter 1 of *Homo Ludens* (1955).

man seeks to account for the world of phenomena by grounding it in the Divine. In all the wild imaginings of mythology a fanciful spirit is playing on the border-line between jest and earnest. Or finally, let us take ritual. Primitive society performs its sacred rites, its sacrifices, consecrations and mysteries, all of which serve to guarantee the well-being of the world, in a spirit of pure play truly understood.

Now in myth and ritual the great instinctive forces of civilized   4
life have their origin: law and order, commerce and profit, craft and art, poetry, wisdom and science. All are rooted in the primaeval soil of play.

The object of the present essay is to demonstrate that it is more   5
than a rhetorical comparison to view culture *sub specie ludi.*[1] The thought is not at all new. There was a time when it was generally accepted, though in a limited sense quite different from the one intended here: in the 17th century, the age of world theatre. Drama, in a glittering succession of figures ranging from Shakespeare and Calderon to Racine, then dominated the literature of the West. It was the fashion to liken the world to a stage on which every man plays his part. Does this mean that the play-element in civilization was openly acknowledged? Not at all. On closer examination this fashionable comparison of life to a stage proves to be little more than an echo of the Neo-platonism that was then in vogue, with a markedly moralistic accent. It was a variation on the ancient theme of the vanity of all things. The fact that play and culture are actually interwoven with one another was neither observed nor expressed, whereas for us the whole point is to show that genuine, pure play is one of the main bases of civilisation.

To our way of thinking, play is the direct opposite of seriousness.   6
At first sight this opposition seems as irreducible to other categories as the play-concept itself. Examined more closely, however, the contrast between play and seriousness proves to be neither conclusive nor fixed. We can say: play is non-seriousness. But apart from the fact that this proposition tells us nothing about the positive qualities of play, it is extraordinarily easy to refute. As soon as we proceed from "play is non-seriousness" to "play is not serious", the contrast leaves us in the lurch—for some play can be very serious indeed. Moreover we can immediately name several other fundamental categories that likewise come under the heading "non-seriousness" yet have no correspondence whatever with "play". Laughter, for instance, is in a sense the opposite of seriousness

1. "in the aspect of play"

without being absolutely bound up with play. Children's games, football, and chess are played in profound seriousness; the players have not the slightest inclination to laugh. It is worth noting that the purely physiological act of laughing is exclusive to man, whilst the significant function of play is common to both men and animals. The Aristotelian *animal ridens* characterizes man as distinct from the animal almost more absolutely than *homo sapiens*.[2]

What is true of laughter is true also of the comic. The comic [7] comes under the category of non-seriousness and has certain affinities with laughter—it provokes to laughter. But its relation to play is subsidiary. In itself play is not comical either for player or public. The play of young animals or small children may sometimes be ludicrous, but the sight of grown dogs chasing one another hardly moves us to laughter. When we call a farce or a comedy "comic", it is not so much on account of the play-acting as such as on account of the situation or the thoughts expressed. The mimic and laughter-provoking art of the clown is comic as well as ludicrous, but it can scarcely be termed genuine play.

The category of the comic is closely connected with *folly* in the [8] highest and lowest sense of that word. Play, however, is not foolish. It lies outside the antithesis of wisdom and folly. The later Middle Ages tended to express the two cardinal moods of life—play and seriousness—somewhat imperfectly by opposing *folie* to *sense*, until Erasmus in his *Laus Stultitiae*[3] showed the inadequacy of the contrast.

All the terms in this loosely connected group of ideas—play, [9] laughter, folly, wit, jest, joke, the comic, etc.—share the characteristic which we had to attribute to play, namely, that of resisting any attempt to reduce it to other terms. Their rationale and their mutual relationships must lie in a very deep layer of our mental being.

The more we try to mark off the form we call "play" from other [10] forms apparently related to it, the more the absolute independence of the play-concept stands out. And the segregation of play from the domain of the great categorical antitheses does not stop there. Play lies outside the antithesis of wisdom and folly, and equally outside those of truth and falsehood, good and evil. Although it is a non-material activity it has no moral function. The valuations of vice and virtue do not apply here.

If, therefore, play cannot be directly referred to the categories [11] of truth or goodness, can it be included perhaps in the realm of

2. "laughing being"; "thinking man"
3. *In Praise of Folly*, a satirical work by the Dutch humanist Desiderius Erasmus (1466–1536). In it, Folly, personified, tells how important her rule is to human beings.

the aesthetic? Here our judgement wavers. For although the attribute
of beauty does not attach to play as such, play nevertheless tends
to assume marked elements of beauty. Mirth and grace adhere at
the outset to the more primitive forms of play. In play the beauty
of the human body in motion reaches its zenith. In its more
developed forms it is saturated with rhythm and harmony, the
noblest gifts of aesthetic perception known to man. Many and
close are the links that connect play with beauty. All the same,
we cannot say that beauty is inherent in play as such; so we must
leave it at that: play is a function of the living, but is not susceptible
of exact definition either logically, biologically, or aesthetically.
The play-concept must always remain distinct from all the other
forms of thought in which we express the structure of mental and
social life. Hence we shall have to confine ourselves to describing
the main characteristics of play.

Since our theme is the relation of play to culture we need not   12
enter into all the possible forms of play but can restrict ourselves
to its social manifestations. These we might call the higher forms
of play. They are generally much easier to describe than the more
primitive play of infants and young animals, because they are
more distinct and articulate in form and their features more various
and conspicuous, whereas in interpreting primitive play we immediately come up against that irreducible quality of pure playfulness
which is not, in our opinion, amenable to further analysis. We
shall have to speak of contests and races, of performances and
exhibitions, of dancing and music, pageants, masquerades and
tournaments. Some of the characteristics we shall enumerate are
proper to play in general, others to social play in particular.

First and foremost, then, all play is a voluntary activity. Play to   13
order is no longer play: it could at best be but a forcible imitation
of it. By this quality of freedom alone, play marks itself off from
the course of the natural process. It is something added thereto
and spread out over it like a flowering, an ornament, a garment.
Obviously, freedom must be understood here in the wider sense
that leaves untouched the philosophical problem of determinism.
It may be objected that this freedom does not exist for the animal
and the child; they *must* play because their instinct drives them
to it and because it serves to develop their bodily faculties and
their powers of selection. The term "instinct", however, introduces
an unknown quantity, and to presuppose the utility of play from
the start is to be guilty of a *petitio principii*.[4] Child and animal play
because they enjoy playing, and therein precisely lies their freedom.

---

4. begging the question

Be that as it may, for the adult and responsible human being   14
play is a function which he could equally well leave alone. Play
is superfluous. The need for it is only urgent to the extent that
the enjoyment of it makes it a need. Play can be deferred or
suspended at any time. It is never imposed by physical necessity
or moral duty. It is never a task. It is done at leisure, during "free
time". Only when play is a recognized cultural function—a rite,
a ceremony—is it bound up with notions of obligation and duty.

Here, then, we have the first main characteristic of play: that   15
it is free, is in fact freedom. A second characteristic is closely
connected with this, namely, that play is not "ordinary" or "real"
life. It is rather a stepping out of "real" life into a temporary sphere
of activity with a disposition all of its own. Every child knows
perfectly well that he is "only pretending", or that it was "only
for fun". How deep-seated this awareness is in the child's soul is
strikingly illustrated by the following story, told to me by the father
of the boy in question. He found his four-year-old son sitting at
the front of a row of chairs, playing "trains". As he hugged him
the boy said: "Don't kiss the engine, Daddy, or the carriages won't
think it's real". This "only pretending" quality of play betrays a
consciousness of the inferiority of play compared with "seriousness",
a feeling that seems to be something as primary as play itself.
Nevertheless, as we have already pointed out, the consciousness
of play being "only a pretend" does not by any means prevent it
from proceeding with the utmost seriousness, with an absorption,
a devotion that passes into rapture and, temporarily at least, completely abolishes that troublesome "only" feeling. Any game can
at any time wholly run away with the players. The contrast between
play and seriousness is always fluid. The inferiority of play is
continually being offset by the corresponding superiority of its
seriousness. Play turns to seriousness and seriousness to play. Play
may rise to heights of beauty and sublimity that leave seriousness
far beneath. Tricky questions such as these will come up for discussion when we start examining the relationship between play
and ritual.

As regards its formal characteristics, all students lay stress on   16
the *disinterestedness* of play. Not being "ordinary" life it stands
outside the immediate satisfaction of wants and appetites, indeed
it interrupts the appetitive process. It interpolates itself as a temporary
activity satisfying in itself and ending there. Such at least is the
way in which play presents itself to us in the first instance: as an
intermezzo, and *interlude* in our daily lives. As a regularly recurring
relaxation, however, it becomes the accompaniment, the comple-
ment, in fact an integral part of life in general. It adorns life,
amplifies it and is to that extent a necessity both for the individual—

as a life function—and for society by reason of the meaning it contains, its significance, its expressive value, its spiritual and social associations, in short, as a culture function. The expression of it satisfies all kinds of communal ideals. It thus has its place in a sphere superior to the strictly biological processes of nutrition, reproduction and self-preservation. This assertion is apparently contradicted by the fact that play, or rather sexual display, is predominant in animal life precisely at the mating-season. But would it be too absurd to assign a place *outside* the purely physiological, to the singing, cooing and strutting of birds just as we do to human play? In all its higher forms the latter at any rate always belongs to the sphere of festival and ritual—the sacred sphere.

Now, does the fact that play is a necessity, that it subserves   17
culture, or indeed that it actually becomes culture, detract from its disinterested character? No, for the purposes it serves are external to immediate material interests or the individual satisfaction of biological needs. As a sacred activity play naturally contributes to the well-being of the group, but in quite another way and by other means than the acquisition of the necessities of life.

Play is distinct from "ordinary" life both as to locality and   18
duration. This is the third main characteristic of play: its secludedness, its limitedness. It is "played out" within certain limits of time and place. It contains its own course and meaning.

Play begins, and then at a certain moment it is "over." It plays   19
itself to an end. While it is in progress all is movement, change, alternation, succession, association, separation. But immediately connected with its limitation as to time there is a further curious feature of play: it at once assumes fixed form as a cultural phenomenon. Once played, it endures as a new-found creation of the mind, a treasure to be retained by the memory. It is transmitted, it becomes tradition. It can be repeated at any time, whether it be "child's play" or a game of chess, or at fixed intervals like a mystery. In this faculty of repetition lies one of the most essential qualities of play. It holds good not only of play as a whole but also of its inner structure. In nearly all the higher forms of play the elements of repetition and alternation (as in the *refrain*), are like the warp and woof of a fabric.

More striking even than the limitation as to time is the limitation   20
as to space. All play moves and has its being within a play-ground marked off beforehand either materially or ideally, deliberately or as a matter of course. Just as there is no formal difference between play and ritual, so the "consecrated spot" cannot be formally distinguished from the play-ground. The arena, the card-table, the

magic circle, the temple, the stage, the screen, the tennis court, the court of justice, etc., are all in form and function play-grounds, i.e. forbidden spots, isolated, hedged round, hallowed, within which special rules obtain. All are temporary worlds within the ordinary world, dedicated to the performance of an act apart.

Inside the play-ground an absolute and peculiar order reigns. 21 Here we come across another, very positive feature of play: it creates order, *is* order. Into an imperfect world and into the confusion of life it brings a temporary, a limited perfection. Play demands order absolute and supreme. The least deviation from it "spoils the game", robs it of its character and makes it worthless. The profound affinity between play and order is perhaps the reason why play, as we noted in passing, seems to lie to such a large extent in the field of aesthetics. Play has a tendency to be beautiful. It may be that this aesthetic factor is identical with the impulse to create orderly form, which animates play in all its aspects. The words we use to denote the elements of play belong for the most part to aesthetics, terms with which we try to describe the effects of beauty: tension, poise, balance, contrast, variation, solution, resolution, etc. Play casts a spell over us; it is "enchanting", "captivating". It is invested with the noblest qualities we are capable of perceiving in things: rhythm and harmony.

The element of tension in play to which we have just referred 22 plays a particularly important part. Tension means uncertainty, chanciness; a striving to decide the issue and so end it. The player wants something to "go", to "come off"; he wants to "succeed" by his own exertions. Baby reaching for a toy, pussy patting a bobbin, a little girl playing ball—all want to achieve something difficult, to succeed, to end a tension. Play is "tense", as we say. It is this element of tension and solution that governs all solitary games of skill and application such as puzzles, jig-saws, mosaic-making, patience, target-shooting, and the more play bears the character of competition the more fervent it will be. In gambling and athletics it is at its height. Though play as such is outside the range of good and bad, the element of tension imparts to it a certain ethical value in so far as it means a testing of the player's prowess: his courage, tenacity, resources and, last but not least, his spiritual powers—his "fairness"; because, despite his ardent desire to win, he must still stick to the rules of the game.

These rules in their turn are a very important factor in the play- 23 concept. All play has its rules. They determine what "holds" in the temporary world circumscribed by play. The rules of a game are absolutely binding and allow no doubt. Paul Valéry once in passing gave expression to a very cogent thought when he said:

"No scepticism is possible where the rules of a game are concerned, for the principle underlying them is an unshakable truth. . . ." Indeed, as soon as the rules are transgressed the whole play-world collapses. The game is over. The umpire's whistle breaks the spell and sets "real" life going again.

The player who trespasses against the rules or ignores them is   24 a "spoil-sport". The spoil-sport is not the same as the false player, the cheat; for the latter pretends to be playing the game and, on the face of it, still acknowledges the magic circle. It is curious to note how much more lenient society is to the cheat than to the spoil-sport. This is because the spoil-sport shatters the play-world itself. By withdrawing from the game he reveals the relativity and fragility of the play-world in which he had temporarily shut himself with others. He robs play of its *illusion*—a pregnant word which means literally "in-play" (from *inlusio, illudere* or *inludere*). Therefore he must be cast out, for he threatens the existence of the play-community. The figure of the spoil-sport is most apparent in boys' games. The little community does not enquire whether the spoil-sport is guilty of defection because he dares not enter into the game or because he is not allowed to. Rather, it does not recognize "not being allowed" and calls it "not daring". For it, the problem of obedience and conscience is no more than fear of punishment. The spoil-sport breaks the magic world, therefore he is a coward and must be ejected. In the world of high seriousness, too, the cheat and the hypocrite have always had an easier time of it than the spoil-sports, here called apostates, heretics, innovators, prophets, conscientious objectors, etc. It sometimes happens, however, that the spoil-sports in their turn make a new community with rules of its own. The outlaw, the revolutionary, the cabbalist or member of a secret society, indeed heretics of all kinds are of a highly associative if not sociable disposition, and a certain element of play is prominent in all their doings.

A play-community generally tends to become permanent even   25 after the game is over. Of course, not every game of marbles or every bridge-party leads to the founding of a club. But the feeling of being "apart together" in an exceptional situation, of sharing something important, of mutually withdrawing from the rest of the world and rejecting the usual norms, retains its magic beyond the duration of the individual game. The club pertains to play as the hat to the head. It would be rash to explain all the associations which the anthropologist calls "phratria"—e.g. clans, brotherhoods, etc.—simply as play-communities; nevertheless it has been shown again and again how difficult it is to draw the line between, on the one hand, permanent social groupings—particularly in archaic cultures with their extremely important, solemn, indeed sacred customs—and the sphere of play on the other.

The exceptional and special position of play is most tellingly illustrated by the fact that it loves to surround itself with an air of secrecy. Even in early childhood the charm of play is enhanced by making a "secret" out of it. This is for *us*, not for the "others". What the "others" do "outside" is no concern of ours at the moment. Inside the circle of the game the laws and customs of ordinary life no longer count. We are different and do things differently. This temporary abolition of the ordinary world is fully acknowledged in child-life, but it is no less evident in the great ceremonial games of savage societies. During the great feast of initiation when the youths are accepted into the male community, it is not the neophytes only that are exempt from the ordinary laws and regulations: there is a truce to all feuds in the tribe. All retaliatory acts and vendettas are suspended. This temporary suspension of normal social life on account of the sacred play-season has numerous traces in the more advanced civilizations as well. Everything that pertains to saturnalia and carnival customs belongs to it. Even with us a bygone age of robuster private habits than ours, more marked class-privileges and a more complaisant police recognized the orgies of young men of rank under the name of a "rag". The saturnalian licence of young men still survives, in fact, in the ragging at English universities, which the *Oxford English Dictionary* defines as "an extensive display of noisy and disorderly conduct carried out in defiance of authority and discipline".

The "differentness" and secrecy of play are most vividly expressed in "dressing up". Here the "extra-ordinary" nature of play reaches perfection. The disguised or masked individual "plays" another part, another being. He *is* another being. The terrors of childhood, open-hearted gaiety, mystic fantasy and sacred awe are all inextricably entangled in this strange business of masks and disguises.

Summing up the formal characteristics of play we might call it a free activity standing quite consciously outside "ordinary" life as being "not serious", but at the same time absorbing the player intensely and utterly. It is an activity connected with no material interest, and no profit can be gained by it. It proceeds within its own proper boundaries of time and space according to fixed rules and in an orderly manner. It promotes the formation of social groupings which tend to surround themselves with secrecy and to stress their difference from the common world by disguise or other means.

JOAN DIDION

Georgia O'Keeffe

"Where I was born and where and how I have lived is un-   1
important," Georgia O'Keeffe[1] told us in the book of paintings
and words published in her ninetieth year on earth. She seemed
to be advising us to forget the beautiful face in the Stieglitz photographs.[2] She appeared to be dismissing the rather condescending
romance that had attached to her by then, the romance of extreme
good looks and advanced age and deliberate isolation. "It is what
I have done with where I have been that should be of interest."
I recall an August afternoon in Chicago in 1973 when I took my
daughter, then seven, to see what Georgia O'Keeffe had done with
where she had been. One of the vast O'Keeffe "Sky Above Clouds"
canvases floated over the back stairs in the Chicago Art Institute
that day, dominating what seemed to be several stories of empty
light, and my daughter looked at it once, ran to the landing, and
kept on looking. "Who drew it," she whispered after a while. I
told her. "I need to talk to her," she said finally.

My daughter was making, that day in Chicago, an entirely un-   2
conscious but quite basic assumption about people and the work
they do. She was assuming that the glory she saw in the work
reflected a glory in its maker, that the painting was the painter
as the poem is the poet, that every choice one made alone—every
word chosen or rejected, every brush stroke laid or not laid down—
betrayed one's character. *Style is character.* It seemed to me that
afternoon that I had rarely seen so instinctive an application of
this familiar principle, and I recall being pleased not only that my
daughter responded to style as character but that it was Georgia
O'Keeffe's particular style to which she responded: this was a hard
woman who had imposed her 192 square feet of clouds on Chicago.

"Hardness" has not been in our century a quality much admired   3
in women, nor in the past twenty years has it even been in official
favor for men. When hardness surfaces in the very old we tend
to transform it into "crustiness" or eccentricity, some tonic pep-

First published in *The Saturday Evening Post* 1976.
1. American painter (1887–1986).
2. Alfred Stieglitz (1864–1946), one of the most famous American photographers,
was married to O'Keeffe in 1924. Among his major works is a series of striking
photographs of her.

466

periness to be indulged at a distance. On the evidence of her work and what she has said about it, Georgia O'Keeffe is neither "crusty" nor eccentric. She is simply hard, a straight shooter, a woman clean of received wisdom and open to what she sees. This is a woman who could early on dismiss most of her contemporaries as "dreamy," and would later single out one she liked as "a very poor painter." (And then add, apparently by way of softening the judgment: "I guess he wasn't a painter at all. He had no courage and I believe that to create one's own world in any of the arts takes courage.") This is a woman who in 1939 could advise her admirers that they were missing her point, that their appreciation of her famous flowers was merely sentimental. "When I paint a red hill," she observed coolly in the catalogue for an exhibition that year, "you say it is too bad that I don't always paint flowers. A flower touches almost everyone's heart. A red hill doesn't touch everyone's heart." This is a woman who could describe the genesis of one of her most well-known paintings—the "Cow's Skull: Red, White and Blue" owned by the Metropolitan—as an act of quite deliberate and derisive orneriness. "I thought of the city men I had been seeing in the East," she wrote. "They talked so often of writing the Great American Novel—the Great American Play—the Great American Poetry. . . . So as I was painting my cow's head on blue I thought to myself, 'I'll make it an American painting. They will not think it great with the red stripes down the sides— Red, White and Blue—but they will notice it.' "

The city men. The men. They. The words crop up again and again   4 as this astonishingly aggressive woman tells us what was on her mind when she was making her astonishingly aggressive paintings. It was those city men who stood accused of sentimentalizing her flowers: "I made you take time to look at what I saw and when you took time to really notice my flower you hung all your associations with flowers on my flower and you write about my flower as if I think and see what you think and see—and I don't." *And I don't.* Imagine those words spoken, and the sound you hear is *don't tread on me.* "The men" believed it impossible to paint New York, so Georgia O'Keeffe painted New York. "The men" didn't think much of her bright color, so she made it brighter. The men yearned toward Europe so she went to Texas, and then New Mexico. The men talked about Cézanne,[3] "long involved remarks about the 'plastic quality' of his form and color," and took one another's long involved remarks, in the view of this angelic rattlesnake in their midst, altogether too seriously. "I can

3. French post-Impressionist painter (1839–1906).

paint one of those dismal-colored paintings like the men," the woman who regarded herself always as an outsider remembers thinking one day in 1922, and she did: a painting of a shed "all low-toned and dreary with the tree beside the door." She called this act of rancor "The Shanty" and hung it in her next show. "The men seemed to approve of it," she reported fifty-four years later, her contempt undimmed. "They seemed to think that maybe I was beginning to paint. That was my only low-toned dismal-colored painting."

Some women fight and others do not. Like so many successful 5 guerrillas in the war between the sexes, Georgia O'Keeffe seems to have been equipped early with an immutable sense of who she was and a fairly clear understanding that she would be required to prove it. On the surface her upbringing was conventional. She was a child on the Wisconsin prairie who played with china dolls and painted watercolors with cloudy skies because sunlight was too hard to paint and, with her brother and sisters, listened every night to her mother read stories of the Wild West, of Texas, of Kit Carson and Billy the Kid. She told adults that she wanted to be an artist and was embarrassed when they asked what kind of artist she wanted to be: she had no idea "what kind." She had no idea what artists did. She had never seen a picture that interested her, other than a pen-and-ink Maid of Athens in one of her mother's books, some Mother Goose illustrations printed on cloth, a tablet cover that showed a little girl with pink roses, and the painting of Arabs on horseback that hung in her grandmother's parlor. At thirteen, in a Dominican convent, she was mortified when the sister corrected her drawing. At Chatham Episcopal Institute in Virginia she painted lilacs and sneaked time alone to walk out to where she could see the line of the Blue Ridge Mountains on the horizon. At the Art Institute in Chicago she was shocked by the presence of live models and wanted to abandon anatomy lessons. At the Art Students League in New York one of her fellow students advised her that, since he would be a great painter and she would end up teaching painting in a girls' school, any work of hers was less important than modeling for him. Another painted over her work to show her how the Impressionists did trees. She had not before heard how the Impressionists did trees and she did not much care.

At twenty-four she left all those opinions behind and went for 6 the first time to live in Texas, where there were no trees to paint and no one to tell her how not to paint them. In Texas there was only the horizon she craved. In Texas she had her sister Claudia with her for a while, and in the late afternoons they would walk away from town and toward the horizon and watch the evening star come out. "That evening star fascinated me," she wrote. "It was in some way very exciting to me. My sister had a gun, and as we walked she would throw bottles into the air and shoot as many as she could before they hit the ground. I had nothing but to walk into nowhere and the wide sunset space with the star. Ten watercolors were made from that star." In a way one's interest is compelled as much by the sister Claudia with the gun as by the painter Georgia with the star, but only the painter left us this shining record. Ten watercolors were made from that star.

ERNEST HEMINGWAY

Bullfighting

The bullfight is not a sport in the Anglo-Saxon sense of the word, that is, it is not an equal contest or an attempt at an equal contest between a bull and a man. Rather it is a tragedy; the death of the bull, which is played, more or less well, by the bull and the man involved and in which there is danger for the man but certain death for the animal. This danger to the man can be increased by the bullfighter at will in the measure in which he works close to the bull's horns. Keeping within the rules for bullfighting on foot in a closed ring formulated by years of experience, which, if known and followed, permit a man to perform certain actions with a bull without being caught by the bull's horns, the bullfighter may, by decreasing his distance from the bull's horns, depend more and more on his own reflexes and judgment of that distance to protect him from the points. This danger of goring, which the man creates voluntarily, can be changed to certainty of being caught and tossed by the bull if the man, through ignorance, slowness, torpidness, blind folly or momentary grogginess breaks any of these fundamental rules for the execution of the different suertes. Everything that is done by the man in the ring is called a "suerte." It is the easiest term to use as it is short. It means act, but the word act has, in English, a connotation of the theatre that makes its use confusing. 1

Chapter 2 of Hemingway's famous book on bullfighting in Spain, *Death in the Afternoon* (1960).

People seeing their first bullfight say, "But the bulls are so stupid.   2
They always go for the cape and not for the man."

The bull only goes for the percale of the cape or for the scarlet   3
serge of the muleta[1] if the man makes him and so handles the
cloth that the bull sees it rather than the man. Therefore to really
start to see bullfights a spectator should go to the novilladas or
apprentice fights. There the bulls do not always go for the cloth
because the bullfighters are learning before your eyes the rules of
bullfighting and they do not always remember or know the proper
terrain to take and how to keep the bull after the lure and away
from the man. It is one thing to know the rules in principle and
another to remember them as they are needed when facing an
animal that is seeking to kill you, and the spectator who wants
to see men tossed and gored rather than judge the manner in
which the bulls are dominated should go to a novillada before he
sees a corrida de toros or complete bullfight. It should be a good
thing for him to see a novillada first anyway if he wants to learn
about technique, since the employment of knowledge that we call
by that bastard name is always most visible in its imperfection.
At a novillada the spectator may see the mistakes of the bullfighters,
and the penalties that these mistakes carry. He will learn something
too about the state of training or lack of training of the men and
the effect this has on their courage.

One time in Madrid I remember we went to a novillada in the   4
middle of the summer on a very hot Sunday when every one who
could afford it had left the city for the beaches of the north or
the mountains and the bullfight was not advertised to start until
six o'clock in the evening, to see six Tovar bulls killed by three
aspirant matadors[2] who have all since failed in their profession.
We sat in the first row behind the wooden barrier and when the
first bull came out it was clear that Domingo Hernandorena, a
short, thick-ankled, graceless Basque with a pale face who looked
nervous and incompletely fed in a cheap rented suit, if he was to
kill this bull would either make a fool of himself or be gored.
Hernandorena could not control the nervousness of his feet. He
wanted to stand quietly and play the bull with the cape with a
slow movement of his arms, but when he tried to stand still as
the bull charged his feet jumped away in short, nervous jerks. His
feet were obviously not under his personal control and his effort

---

1. The small red cloth cape with which the bullfighter makes passes at the bull.
2. A *matador* is the principal performer—along with the bull—in bullfighting; he
is the one who works the muletas and kills the bull with a sword thrust between
the shoulder blades.

to be statuesque while his feet jittered him away out of danger was very funny to the crowd. It was funny to them because many of them knew that was how their own feet would behave if they saw the horns coming toward them, and as always, they resented any one else being in there in the ring, making money, who had the same physical defects which barred them, the spectators, from that supposedly highly paid way of making a living. In their turn the other two matadors were very fancy with the cape and Hernandorena's nervous jerking was even worse after their performance. He had not been in the ring with a bull for over a year and he was altogether unable to control his nervousness. When the banderillas[3] were in and it was time for him to go out with the red cloth and the sword to prepare the bull for killing and to kill, the crowd which had applauded ironically at every nervous move he had made knew something very funny would happen. Below us, as he took the muleta and the sword and rinsed his mouth out with water I could see the muscles of his cheeks twitching. The bull stood against the barrier watching him. Hernandorena could not trust his legs to carry him slowly toward the bull. He knew there was only one way he could stay in one place in the ring. He ran out toward the bull, and ten yards in front of him dropped to both knees on the sand. In that position he was safe from ridicule. He spread the red cloth with his sword and jerked himself forward on his knees toward the bull. The bull was watching the man and the triangle of red cloth, his ears pointed, his eyes fixed, and Hernandorena knee-ed himself a yard closer and shook the cloth. The bull's tail rose, his head lowered and he charged and, as he reached the man, Hernandorena rose solidly from his knees into the air, swung over like a bundle, his legs in all directions now, and then dropped to the ground. The bull looked for him, found a wide-spread moving cape held by another bullfighter instead, charged it, and Hernandorena stood up with sand on his white face and looked for his sword and the cloth. As he stood up I saw the heavy, soiled gray silk of his rented trousers open cleanly and deeply to show the thigh bone from the hip almost to the knee. He saw it too and looked very surprised and put his hand on it while people jumped over the barrier and ran toward him to carry him to the infirmary. The technical error that he had committed was in not keeping the red cloth of the muleta between himself and the bull until the charge; then at the moment of jurisdiction as it is called, when the bull's lowered head reaches

3. Short, barbed sticks planted in the bull's sides by the *banderilleros*, men on foot who assist the matador.

the cloth, swaying back while he held the cloth, spread by the stick and the sword, far enough forward so that the bull following it would be clear of his body. It was a simple technical error.

That night at the café I heard no word of sympathy for him. He was ignorant, he was torpid, and he was out of training. Why did he insist on being a bullfighter? Why did he go down on both knees? Because he was a coward, they said. The knees are for cowards. If he was a coward why did he insist on being a bullfighter? There was no natural sympathy for uncontrollable nervousness because he was a paid public performer. It was preferable that he be gored rather than run from the bull. To be gored was honorable; they would have sympathized with him had he been caught in one of his nervous uncontrollable jerky retreats, which, although they mocked, they knew were from lack of training, rather than for him to have gone down on his knees. Because the hardest thing when frightened by the bull is to control the feet and let the bull come, and any attempt to control the feet was honorable even though they jeered at it because it looked ridiculous. But when he went on both knees, without the technique to fight from that position; the technique that Marcial Lalanda, the most scientific of living bullfighters, has, and which alone makes that position honorable; then Hernandorena admitted his nervousness. To show his nervousness was not shameful; only to admit it. When, lacking the technique and thereby admitting his inability to control his feet, the matador went down on both knees before the bull the crowd had no more sympathy with him than with a suicide.

For myself, not being a bullfighter, and being much interested in suicides, the problem was one of depiction and waking in the night I tried to remember what it was that seemed just out of my remembering and that was the thing that I had really seen and, finally, remembering all around it, I got it. When he stood up, his face white and dirty and the silk of his breeches opened from waist to knee, it was the dirtiness of the rented breeches, the dirtiness of his slit underwear and the clean, clean, unbearably clean whiteness of the thigh bone that I had seen, and it was that which was important.

At the novilladas, too, besides the study of technique, and the consequences of its lack you have a chance to learn about the manner of dealing with defective bulls since bulls which cannot be used in a formal bullfight because of some obvious defect are killed in the apprentice fights. Nearly all bulls develop defects in the course of any fight which must be corrected by the bullfighter, but in the novillada these defects, those of vision for instance, are many times obvious at the start and so the manner of their correcting, or the result of their not being corrected, is apparent.

The formal bullfight is a tragedy, not a sport, and the bull is 8 certain to be killed. If the matador cannot kill him and, at the end of the allotted fifteen minutes for the preparation and killing, the bull is led and herded out of the ring alive by steers to dishonor the killer, he must, by law, be killed in the corrals. It is one hundred to one against the matador de toros or formally invested bullfighter being killed unless he is inexperienced, ignorant, out of training or too old and heavy on his feet. But the matador, if he knows his profession, can increase the amount of the danger of death that he runs exactly as much as he wishes. He should, however, increase this danger, *within the rules provided for his protection.* In other words it is to his credit if he does something that he knows how to do in a highly dangerous but still geometrically possible manner. It is to his discredit if he runs danger through ignorance, through disregard of the fundamental rules, through physical or mental slowness, or through blind folly.

The matador must dominate the bulls by knowledge and science. 9 In the measure in which this domination is accomplished with grace will it be beautiful to watch. Strength is of little use to him except at the actual moment of killing. Once some one asked Rafael Gomez, "El Gallo," nearing fifty years old, a gypsy, brother of Jose Gomez, "Gallito," and the last living member of the great family of gypsy bullfighters of that name, what physical exercise he, Gallo, took to keep his strength up for bullfighting.

"Strength," Gallo said. "What do I want with strength, man? 10 The bull weighs half a ton. Should I take exercises for strength to match him? Let the bull have the strength."

If the bulls were allowed to increase their knowledge as the 11 bullfighter does and if those bulls which are not killed in the allotted fifteen minutes in the ring were not afterwards killed in the corrals but were allowed to be fought again they would kill all the bullfighters, if the bullfighters fought them according to the rules. Bullfighting is based on the fact that it is the first meeting between the wild animal and a dismounted man. This is the fundamental premise of modern bullfighting; that the bull has never been in the ring before. In the early days of bullfighting bulls were allowed to be fought which had been in the ring before and so many men were killed in the bull ring that on November 20, 1567, Pope Pius the Fifth issued a Papal edict excommunicating all Christian princes who should permit bullfights in their countries and denying Christian burial to any person killed in the bull ring.

The Church only agreed to tolerate bullfighting, which continued steadily in Spain in spite of the edict, when it was agreed that the bulls should only appear once in the ring.

You would think then that it would make of bullfighting a true 12
sport, rather than merely a tragic spectacle, if bulls that had been in the ring were allowed to reappear. I have seen such bulls fought, in violation of the law, in provincial towns in improvised arenas made by blocking the entrances to the public square with piled-up carts in the illegal capeas, or town-square bullfights with used bulls. The aspirant bullfighters, who have no financial backing, get their first experience in capeas. It is a sport, a very savage and primitive sport, and for the most part a truly amateur one. I am afraid however due to the danger of death it involves it would never have much success among the amateur sportsmen of America and England who play games. We, in games, are not fascinated by death, its nearness and its avoidance. We are fascinated by victory and we replace the avoidance of death by the avoidance of defeat. It is a very nice symbolism but it takes more cojones[4] to be a sportsman when death is a closer party to the game. The bull in the capeas is rarely killed. This should appeal to sportsmen who are lovers of animals. The town is usually too poor to afford to pay for the killing of the bull and none of the aspirant bullfighters has enough money to buy a sword or he would not have chosen to serve his apprenticeship in the capeas. This would afford an opportunity for the man who is a wealthy sportsman, for he could afford to pay for the bull and buy himself a sword as well.

However, due to the mechanics of a bull's mental development 13
the used bull does not make a brilliant spectacle. After his first charge or so he will stand quite still and will only charge if he is certain of getting the man or boy who is tempting him with a cape. When there is a crowd and the bull charges into it he will pick one man out and follow him, no matter how he may dodge, run and twist until he gets him and tosses him. If the tips of the bull's horns have been blunted this chasing and tossing is good fun to see for a little while. No one has to go in with the bull who does not want to, although of course many who want to very little go in to show their courage. It is very exciting for those who are down in the square, that is one test of a true amateur sport, whether it is more enjoyable to player than to spectator (as soon as it becomes enjoyable enough to the spectator for the charging of admission to be profitable the sport contains the germ of professionalism), and the smallest evidence of coolness or com-

---

4. Testicles—but Hemingway means the more earthy sense, "balls."

posure brings immediate applause. But when the bull's horns are sharp-pointed it is a disturbing spectacle. The men and boys try cape work with sacks, blouses and old capes on the bull just as they do when his horns have been blunted; the only difference is that when the bull catches them and tosses them they are liable to come off the horn with wounds no local surgeon can cope with. One bull which was a great favorite in the capeas of the province of Valencia killed sixteen men and boys and badly wounded over sixty in a career of five years. The people who go into these capeas do so sometimes as aspirant professionals to get free experience with bulls but most often as amateurs, purely for sport, for the immediate excitement, and it is very great excitement; and for the retrospective pleasure, of having shown their contempt for death on a hot day in their own town square. Many go in from pride, hoping that they will be brave. Many find they are not brave at all; but at least they went in. There is absolutely nothing for them to gain except the inner satisfaction of having been in the ring with a bull; itself a thing that any one who has done it will always remember. It is a strange feeling to have an animal come toward you consciously seeking to kill you, his eyes open looking at you, and see the oncoming of the lowered horn that he intends to kill you with. It gives enough of a sensation so that there are always men willing to go into the capeas for the pride of having experienced it and the pleasure of having tried some bullfighting manœuvre with a real bull although the actual pleasure at the time may not be great. Sometimes the bull is killed if the town has the money to afford it, or if the populace gets out of control; every one swarming on him at once with knives, daggers, butcher knives and rocks; a man perhaps between his horns, being swung up and down, another flying through the air, surely several holding his tail, a swarm of choppers, thrusters and stabbers pushing into him, laying on him or cutting up at him until he sways and goes down. All amateur or group killing is a very barbarous, messy, though exciting business and is a long way from the ritual of the formal bullfight.

The bull which killed the sixteen and wounded the sixty was killed in a very odd way. One of those he had killed was a gypsy boy of about fourteen. Afterwards the boy's brother and sister followed the bull around hoping perhaps to have a chance to assassinate him when he was loaded in his cage after a capea. That was difficult since, being a very highly valued performer, the bull was carefully taken care of. They followed him around for two years, not attempting anything, simply turning up wherever the bull was used. When the capeas were again abolished, they are always being abolished and re-abolished, by government order, the bull's owner decided to send him to the slaughter-house in Valencia, for the bull was getting on in years anyway. The two gypsies were at the slaughter-house and the young man asked permission, since the bull had killed his brother, to kill the bull. This was granted and he started in by digging out both the bull's eyes while the bull was in his cage, and spitting carefully into the sockets, then after killing him by severing the spinal marrow between the neck vertebræ with a dagger, he experienced some difficulty in this, he asked permission to cut off the bull's testicles, which being granted, he and his sister built a small fire at the edge of the dusty street outside the slaughter-house and roasted the two glands on sticks and when they were done, ate them. They then turned their backs on the slaughter-house and went away along the road and out of town.

E. M. FORSTER

Art for Art's Sake

I believe in art for art's sake. It is an unfashionable belief, and 1
some of my statements must be of the nature of an apology. Sixty years ago I should have faced you with more confidence. A writer or a speaker who chose "Art for Art's Sake" for his theme sixty years ago could be sure of being in the swim, and could feel so confident of success that he sometimes dressed himself in aesthetic costumes suitable to the occasion—in an embroidered dressing-gown, perhaps, or a blue velvet suit with a Lord Fauntleroy collar; or a toga, or a kimono, and carried a poppy or a lily or a long peacock's feather in his mediaeval hand. Times have changed. Not thus can I present either myself or my theme to-day. My aim rather is to ask you quietly to reconsider for a few minutes a phrase which has been much misused and much abused, but which has, I believe, great importance for us—has, indeed, eternal importance.

Now we can easily dismiss those peacock's feathers and other 2
affectations—they are but trifles—but I want also to dismiss a more dangerous heresy, namely the silly idea that only art matters, an idea which has somehow got mixed up with the idea of art for

First published in *Harper's Magazine*, August 1949.

art's sake, and has helped to discredit it. Many things besides art, matter. It is merely one of the things that matter, and high though the claims are that I make for it, I want to keep them in proportion. No one can spend his or her life entirely in the creation or the appreciation of masterpieces. Man lives, and ought to live, in a complex world, full of conflicting claims, and if we simplified them down into the aesthetic he would be sterilised. Art for art's sake does not mean that only art matters and I would also like to rule out such phrases as, "The Life of Art," "Living for Art," and "Art's High Mission." They confuse and mislead.

What does the phrase mean? Instead of generalising, let us take ₃ a specific instance—Shakespeare's *Macbeth*, for example, and pronounce the words, *"Macbeth for Macbeth's sake."* What does that mean? Well, the play has several aspects—it is educational, it teaches us something about legendary Scotland, something about Jacobean England,[1] and a good deal about human nature and its perils. We can study its origins, and study and enjoy its dramatic technique and the music of its diction. All that is true. But *Macbeth* is furthermore a world of its own, created by Shakespeare and existing in virtue of its own poetry. It is in this aspect *Macbeth for Macbeth's* sake, and that is what I intend by the phrase "art for art's sake." A work of art—whatever else it may be—is a self-contained entity, with a life of its own imposed on it by its creator. It has internal order. It may have external form. That is how we recognise it.

Take for another example that picture of Seurat's which I saw ₄ two years ago in Chicago—*"Le Grande Jatte."*[2] Here again there is much to study and to enjoy: the pointillism, the charming face of the seated girl, the nineteenth-century Parisian Sunday sunlight, the sense of motion in immobility. But here again there is something more; *"La Grande Jatte"* forms a world of its own, created by Seurat and existing by virtue of its own poetry: *"La Grande Jatte" pour "La Grande Jatte": l'art pour l'art*. Like *Macbeth* it has internal order and internal life.

It is to the conception of order that I would now turn. This is ₅ important to my argument, and I want to make a digression, and glance at order in daily life, before I come to order in art.

In the world of daily life, the world which we perforce inhabit, ₆ there is much talk about order, particularly from statesmen and politicians. They tend, however, to confuse order with orders, just

---

1. England in the reign of King James I (1603–1625).
2. Georges Seurat, French neo-Impressionist painter (1859–1891); this painting is often considered his masterpiece.

as they confuse creation with regulations. Order, I suggest, is something evolved from within, not something imposed from without; it is an internal stability, a vital harmony, and in the social and political category it has never existed except for the convenience of historians. Viewed realistically, the past is really a series of *dis*orders, succeeding one another by discoverable laws, no doubt, and certainly marked by an increasing growth of human interference, but disorders all the same. So that, speaking as a writer, what I hope for to-day is a disorder which will be more favourable to artists than is the present one, and which will provide them with fuller inspirations and better material conditions. It will not last—nothing lasts—but there have been some advantageous disorders in the past—for instance, in ancient Athens, in Renaissance Italy, eighteenth-century France, periods in China and Persia—and we may do something to accelerate the next one. But let us not again fix our hearts where true joys are not to be found. We were promised a new order after the first world war through the League of Nations. It did not come, nor have I faith in present promises, by whomsoever endorsed. The implacable offensive of Science forbids. We cannot reach social and political stability for the reason that we continue to make scientific discoveries and to apply them, and thus to destroy the arrangements which were based on more elementary discoveries. If Science would discover rather than apply—if, in other words, men were more interested in knowledge than in power—mankind would be in a far safer position, the stability statesmen talk about would be a possibility, there could be a new order based on vital harmony, and the earthly millennium might approach. But Science shows no signs of doing this: she gave us the internal combustion engine, and before we had digested and assimilated it with terrible pains into our social system, she harnessed the atom, and destroyed any new order that seemed to be evolving. How can man get into harmony with his surroundings when he is constantly altering them? The future of our race is, in this direction, more unpleasant than we care to admit, and it has sometimes seemed to me that its best chance lies through apathy, uninventiveness, and inertia. Universal exhaustion might promote that Change of Heart which is at present so briskly recommended from a thousand pulpits. Universal exhaustion would certainly be a new experience. The human race has never undergone it, and is still too perky to admit that it may be coming and might result in a sprouting of new growth through the decay.

I must not pursue these speculations any further—they lead me too far from my terms of reference and maybe from yours. But I do want to emphasize that order in daily life and in history, order   7 in the social and political category, is unattainable under our present psychology.

Where is it attainable? Not in the astronomical category, where 8 it was for many years enthroned. The heavens and the earth have become terribly alike since Einstein. No longer can we find a reassuring contrast to chaos in the night sky and look up with George Meredith to the stars, the army of unalterable law, or listen for the music of the spheres. Order is not there. In the entire universe there seem to be only two possibilities for it. The first of them—which again lies outside my terms of reference—is the divine order, the mystic harmony, which according to all religions is available for those who can contemplate it. We much admit its possibility, on the evidence of the adepts, and we must believe them when they say that it is attained, if attainable, by prayer. "O thou who changest not, abide with me," said one of its poets. *"Ordina questo amor, o tu che m'ami,"* said another: "Set love in order thou who lovest me." The existence of a divine order, though it cannot be tested, has never been disproved.

The second possibility for order lies in the aesthetic category, 9 which is my subject here: the order which an artist can create in his own work, and to that we must now return. A work of art, we are all agreed, is a unique product. But why? It is unique not because it is clever or noble or beautiful or enlightened or original or sincere or idealistic or useful or educational—it may embody any of those qualities—but because it is the only material object in the universe which may possess internal harmony. All the others have been pressed into shape from outside, and when their mould is removed they collapse. The work of art stands up by itself, and nothing else does. It achieves something which has often been promised by society, but always delusively. Ancient Athens made a mess—but the *Antigone* stands up. Renaissance Rome made a mess—but the ceiling of the Sistine got painted. James I made a mess—but there was *Macbeth*. Louis XIV—but there was *Phedre*.[3] Art for art's sake? I should just think so, and more so than ever at the present time. It is the one orderly product which our muddling race has produced. It is the cry of a thousand sentinels, the echo from a thousand labyrinths; it is the lighthouse which cannot be hidden: *c'est le meilleur temoignage que nous puissions donner de notre*

---

3. *Antigone*: a tragedy by Greek dramatist Sophocles; *Ceiling of the Sistine . . .* : the reference is to Michelangelo's masterful decoration of the ceiling of the Sistine Chapel in the Vatican; *Phèdre*, a tragedy by the French dramatist Racine, based on *Hippolytus*, a tragedy by Euripides.

dignite.[4] *Antigone for Antigone's* sake, *Macbeth* for *Macbeth's,* *"La Grande Jatte"* pour *"La Grande Jatte."*

If this line of argument is correct, it follows that the artist will   10
tend to be an outsider in the society to which he has been born,
and that the nineteenth century conception of him as a Bohemian[5]
was not inaccurate. The conception erred in three particulars: it
postulated an economic system where art could be a full-time job,
it introduced the fallacy that only art matters, and it overstressed
idiosyncrasy and waywardness—the peacock-feather aspect—rather
than order. But it is a truer conception than the one which prevails
in official circles on my side of the Atlantic—I don't know about
yours: the conception which treats the artist as if he were a particularly bright government advertiser and encourages him to be
friendly and matey with his fellow citizens, and not to give himself
airs.

Estimable is mateyness, and the man who achieves it gives many   11
a pleasant little drink to himself and to others. But it has no
traceable connection with the creative impulse, and probably acts
as an inhibition on it. The artist who is seduced by mateyness
may stop himself from doing the one thing which he, and he
alone, can do—the making of something out of words or sounds
or paint or clay or marble or steel or film which has internal
harmony and presents order to a permanently disarranged planet.
This seems worth doing, even at the risk of being called uppish
by journalists. I have in mind an article which was published some
years ago in the London *Times,* an article called "The Eclipse of
the Highbrow," in which the "Average Man" was exalted, and
all contemporary literature was censured if it did not toe the line,
the precise position of the line being naturally known to the writer
of the article. Sir Kenneth Clark, who was at that time director
of our National Gallery, commented on this pernicious doctrine
in a letter which cannot be too often quoted. "The poet and the
artist," wrote Clark, "are important precisely because they are not
average men; because in sensibility, intelligence, and power of
invention they far exceed the average." These memorable words,
and particularly the words "power of invention," are the Bohemian's
passport. Furnished with it, he slinks about society, saluted now
by a brickbat and now by a penny, and accepting either of them
with equanimity. He does not consider too anxiously what his

4. "it is the best proof we can offer of our dignity."
5. Term applied to writers and artists, generally because of their unconventional
habits. The name was originally given to gypsies in the supposition that they had
come to western Europe from Bohemia (western Czechoslovakia).

relations with society may be, for he is aware of something more important than that—namely the invitation to invent, to create order, and he believes he will be better placed for doing this if he attempts detachment. So round and round he slouches, with his hat pulled over his eyes, and maybe with a louse in his beard, and—if he really wants one—with a peacock's feather in his hand.

If our present society should disintegrate—and who dare prophesy   12
that it won't?—this old-fashioned and demode figure will become clearer:[6] the Bohemian, the outsider, the parasite, the rat—one of those figures which have at present no function either in a warring or a peaceful world. It may not be dignified to be a rat, but many of the ships are sinking, which is not dignified either—the officials did not build them properly. Myself, I would sooner be a swimming rat than a sinking ship—at all events I can look around me for a little longer—and I remember how one of us, a rat with particularly bright eyes called Shelley, squeaked out, "Poets are the unacknowledged legislators of the world," before he vanished into the waters of the Mediterranean.[7]

What laws did Shelley propose to pass? None. The legislation   13
of the artist is never formulated at the time, though it is sometimes discerned by future generations. He legislates through creating. And he creates through his sensitiveness and power to impose form. Without form the sensitiveness vanishes. And form is as important to-day, when the human race is trying to ride the whirlwind, as it ever was in those less agitating days of the past, when the earth seemed solid and the stars fixed, and the discoveries of science were made slowly, slowly. Form is not tradition. It alters from generation to generation. Artists always seek a new technique, and will continue to do so as long as their work excites them. But form of some kind is imperative. It is the surface crust of the internal harmony, it is the outward evidence of order.

My remarks about society may have seemed too pessimistic, but   14
I believe that society can only represent a fragment of the human spirit, and that another fragment can only get expressed through art. And I wanted to take this opportunity, this vantage ground, to assert not only the existence of art, but its pertinacity. Looking back into the past, it seems to me that that is all there has ever been: vantage grounds for discussion and creation, little vantage

6. See Randall Jarrell's "A Sad Heart at the Supermarket," especially p. 427, in *The Dolphin Reader*.
7. Percy Bysshe Shelley (1792–1822), one of the greatest English poets, drowned along with his friend Edward Williams while sailing in the Bay of Lerici in northwest Italy. Their bodies were washed ashore at Viareggio, where they were burned in the presence of their friends and fellow poets Byron and Leigh Hunt.

grounds in the changing chaos, where bubbles have been blown and webs spun, and the desire to create order has found temporary gratification, and the sentinels have managed to utter their challenges, and the huntsmen, though lost individually, have heard each other's calls through the impenetrable wood, and the lighthouses have never ceased sweeping the thankless seas. In this pertinacity there seems to me, as I grow older, something more and more profound, something which does in fact concern people who do not care about art at all.

In conclusion, let me summarise the various categories that have   15
laid claim to the possession of Order.

1. The social and political category. Claim disallowed on the evidence of history and of our own experience. If man altered psychologically, order here might be attainable: not otherwise.

2. The astronomical category. Claim allowed up to the present century, but now disallowed on the evidence of the physicists.

3. The religious category. Claim allowed on the evidence of the mystics.

4. The aesthetic category. Claim allowed on the evidence of various works of art, and on the evidence of our own creative impulses, however weak these may be or however imperfectly they may function. Works of art, in my opinion, are the only objects in the material universe to possess internal order, and that is why, though I don't believe that only art matters, I do believe in Art for Art's Sake.

GEORGE ORWELL

Benefit of Clergy:
Some Notes on Salvador Dali

Autobiography is only to be trusted when it reveals something   1
disgraceful. A man who gives a good account of himself is probably lying, since any life when viewed from the inside is simply a series of defeats. However, even the most flagrantly dishonest book (Frank Harris's autobiographical writings are an example)[1] can without

First published in *Dickens, Dali and Others* (1946).
1. Harris, a British-American author (1856–1931), is said to have "deliberately falsified" the facts of his life. His three-volume autobiography is generally regarded to be as unreliable as it is unabashedly erotic.

intending it give a true picture of its author. Dali's recently published *Life*[2] comes under this heading. Some of the incidents in it are flatly incredible, others have been rearranged and romanticised, and not merely the humiliation but the persistent *ordinariness* of everyday life has been cut out. Dali is even by his own diagnosis narcissistic, and his autobiography is simply a strip-tease act conducted in pink limelight. But as a record of fantasy, of the perversion of instinct that has been made possible by the machine age, it has great value.

Here, then, are some of the episodes in Dali's life, from his earliest years onward. Which of them are true and which are imaginary hardly matters: the point is that this is the kind of thing that Dali would have *liked* to do.

When he is six years old there is some excitement over the appearance of Halley's comet:

> "Suddenly one of my father's office clerks appeared in the drawing-room doorway and announced that the comet could be seen from the terrace. . . . While crossing the hall I caught sight of my little three-year-old sister crawling unobtrusively through a doorway. I stopped, hesitated a second, then gave her a terrible kick in the head as though it had been a ball, and continued running, carried away with a 'delirious joy' induced by this savage act. But my father, who was behind me, caught me and led me down into his office, where I remained as a punishment till dinner-time."

A year earlier than this Dali had "suddenly, as most of my ideas occur," flung another little boy off a suspension bridge. Several other incidents of the same kind are recorded, including (this was when he was twenty-nine years old) knocking down and trampling on a girl "until they had to tear her, bleeding, out of my reach."

When he is about five he gets hold of a wounded bat which he puts into a tin pail. Next morning he finds that the bat is almost dead and is covered with ants which are devouring it. He puts it in his mouth, ants and all, and bites it almost in half.

When he is adolescent a girl falls desperately in love with him. He kisses and caresses her so as to excite her as much as possible, but refuses to go further. He resolves to keep this up for five years (he calls it his "five-year plan"), enjoying her humiliation and the sense of power it gives him. He frequently tells her that at the end of five years he will desert her, and when the time comes he does so.

2. *The Secret Life of Salvador Dali* (The Dial Press 1942) [author's note]. Dali (b. 1904) is a Spanish surrealist painter.

Till well into adult life he keeps up the practice of masturbation,   7
and likes to do this, apparently, in front of a looking-glass. For
ordinary purposes he is impotent, it appears, till the age of thirty
or so. When he first meets his future wife, Gala, he is greatly
tempted to push her off a precipice. He is aware that there is
something that she wants him to do to her, and after their first
kiss the confession is made:

> "I threw back Gala's head, pulling it by the hair, and trembling
> with complete hysteria, I commanded:
> " 'Now tell me what you want me to do with you! But tell me
> slowly, looking me in the eye, with the crudest, the most ferociously
> erotic words that can make both of us feel the greatest shame'!
> ". . . Then Gala, transforming the last glimmer of her expression
> of pleasure into the hard light of her own tyranny, answered:
> " 'I want you to kill me!' "

He is somewhat disappointed by this demand, since it is merely   8
what he wanted to do already. He contemplates throwing her
off the bell-tower of the Cathedral of Toledo, but refrains from
doing so.

During the Spanish Civil War[3] he astutely avoids taking sides,   9
and makes a trip to Italy. He feels himself more and more drawn
towards the aristocracy, frequents smart *salons*, finds himself wealthy
patrons, and is photographed with the plump Vicomte de Noailles,
whom he describes as his "Maecenas." When the European War[4]
approaches he has one preoccupation only: how to find a place
which has good cookery and from which he can make a quick
bolt if danger comes too near. He fixes on Bordeaux, and duly
flees to Spain during the Battle of France. He stays in Spain long
enough to pick up a few anti-red atrocity stories, then makes for
America. The story ends in a blaze of respectability. Dali, at thirty-
seven, has become a devoted husband, is cured of his aberrations,
or some of them, and is completely reconciled to the Catholic
Church. He is also, one gathers, making a good deal of money.

However, he has by no means ceased to take pride in the pictures   10
of his Surrealist[5] period, with titles like "The Great Masturbator,"
"Sodomy of a Skull with a Grand Piano," etc. There are reproductions of these all the way through the book. Many of Dali's

---

3. 1936–1939 war in which traditionalist and conservative forces overthrew the
moderate government of the Second Republic and set up a dictatorship under
Generalissimo Francisco Franco.
4. World War II.
5. Early twentieth-century movement in art and literature characterized by the
expression of dreamlike imagination ungoverned by convention or control.

drawings are simply representational and have a characteristic to be noted later. But from his Surrealist paintings and photographs the two things that stand out are sexual perversity and necrophilia. Sexual objects and symbols—some of them well known, like our old friend the high-heeled slipper, others, like the crutch and the cup of warm milk, patented by Dali himself—recur over and over again, and there is a fairly well-marked excretory motif as well. In his painting, *Le Jeu Lugubre,* he says, "the drawers bespattered with excrement were painted with such minute and realistic complacency that the whole little Surrealist group was anguished by the question: Is he coprophagic or not?"[6] Dali adds firmly that he is *not,* and that he regards this aberration as "repulsive," but it seems to be only at that point that his interest in excrement stops. Even when he recounts the experience of watching a woman urinate standing up, he has to add the detail that she misses her aim and dirties her shoes. It is not given to any one person to have all the vices, and Dali also boasts that he is not homosexual, but otherwise he seems to have as good an outfit of perversions as anyone could wish for.

However, his most notable characteristic is his necrophilia. He himself freely admits to this, and claims to have been cured of it. Dead faces, skulls, corpses of animals occur fairly frequently in his pictures, and the ants which devoured the dying bat make countless reappearances. One photograph shows an exhumed corpse, far gone in decomposition. Another shows the dead donkeys putrefying on top of grand pianos which formed part of the Surrealist film, *Le Chien Andalou.* Dali still looks back on these donkeys with great enthusiasm.

> "I 'made up' the putrefaction of the donkeys with great pots of sticky glue which I poured over them. Also I emptied their eye-sockets and made them larger by hacking them out with scissors. In the same way I furiously cut their mouths open to make the rows of their teeth show to better advantage, and I added several jaws to each mouth, so that it would appear that although the donkeys were already rotting they were vomiting up a little more of their own death, above those other rows of teeth formed by the keys of the black pianos."

And finally there is the picture—apparently some kind of faked photograph—of "Mannequin rotting in a taxicab." Over the already somewhat bloated face and breast of the apparently dead girl, huge snails were crawling. In the caption below the picture Dali notes that these are Burgundy snails—that is, the edible kind.

---

6. Relating to the eating of excrement.

Of course, in this long book of 400 quarto pages there is more than I have indicated, but I do not think that I have given an unfair account of his moral atmosphere and mental scenery. It is a book that stinks. If it were possible for a book to give a physical stink off its pages, this one would—a thought that might please Dali, who before wooing his future wife for the first time rubbed himself all over with an ointment made of goat's dung boiled up in fish glue. But against this has to be set the fact that Dali is a draughtsman of very exceptional gifts. He is also, to judge by the minuteness and the sureness of his drawings, a very hard worker. He is an exhibitionist and a careerist, but he is not a fraud. He has fifty times more talent than most of the people who would denounce his morals and jeer at his paintings. And these two sets of facts, taken together, raise a question which for lack of any basis of agreement seldom gets a real discussion.

The point is that you have here a direct, unmistakable assault   13
on sanity and decency; and even—since some of Dali's pictures would tend to poison the imagination like a pornographic postcard— on life itself. What Dali has done and what he has imagined is debatable, but in his outlook, his character, the bedrock decency of a human being does not exist. He is as anti-social as a flea. Clearly, such people are undesirable, and a society in which they can flourish has something wrong with it.

Now, if you showed this book, with its illustrations, to Lord   14
Elton, to Mr. Alfred Noyes, to *The Times* leader-writers who exult over the "eclipse of the highbrow"—in fact, to any "sensible" art-hating English person—it is easy to imagine what kind of response you would get. They would flatly refuse to see any merit in Dali whatever. Such people are not only unable to admit that what is morally degraded can be æsthetically right, but their real demand of every artist is that he shall pat them on the back and tell them that thought is unnecessary. And they can be especially dangerous at a time like the present, when the Ministry of Information and the British Council put power into their hands. For their impulse is not only to crush every new talent as it appears, but to castrate the past as well. Witness the renewed highbrow-baiting that is now going on in this country and America, with its outcry not only against Joyce, Proust and Lawrence, but even against T. S. Eliot.

But if you talk to the kind of person who *can* see Dali's merits,   15
the response that you get is not as a rule very much better. If you say that Dali, though a brilliant draughtsman, is a dirty little scoundrel, you are looked upon as a savage. If you say that you don't like rotting corpses, and that people who do like rotting corpses

are mentally diseased, it is assumed that you lack the æsthetic sense. Since "Mannequin rotting in a taxicab" is a good composition (as it undoubtedly is), it cannot be a disgusting, degrading picture; whereas Noyes, Elton, etc., would tell you that because it is disgusting it cannot be a good composition. And between these two fallacies there is no middle position; or, rather, there is a middle position, but we seldom hear much about it. On the one side *Kulturbol-schewismus:*[7] on the other (though the phrase itself is out of fashion) "Art for Art's sake." Obscenity is a very difficult question to discuss honestly. People are too frightened either of seeming to be shocked or of seeming not to be shocked, to be able to define the relationship between art and morals.

It will be seen that what the defenders of Dali are claiming is a kind of *benefit of clergy*. The artist is to be exempt from the moral laws that are binding on ordinary people. Just pronounce the magic word "Art," and everything is O.K. Rotting corpses with snails crawling over them are O.K.; kicking little girls in the head is O.K.; even a film like *L'Age d'Or* is O.K.[8] It is also O.K. that Dali should batten on France for years and then scuttle off like a rat as soon as France is in danger. So long as you can paint well enough to pass the test, all shall be forgiven you.

One can see how false this is if one extends it to cover ordinary crime. In an age like our own, when the artist is an altogether exceptional person, he must be allowed a certain amount of irresponsibility, just as a pregnant woman is. Still, no one would say that a pregnant woman should be allowed to commit murder, nor would anyone make such a claim for the artist, however gifted. If Shakespeare returned to the earth to-morrow, and if it were found that his favourite recreation was raping little girls in railway carriages, we should not tell him to go ahead with it on the ground that he might write another *King Lear*. And, after all, the worst crimes are not always the punishable ones. By encouraging necrophilic reveries one probably does quite as much harm as by, say, picking pockets at the races. One ought to be able to hold in one's head simultaneously the two facts that Dali is a good draughtsman and a disgusting human being. The one does not invalidate or, in a sense, affect the other. The first thing that we

7. "Cultural bolshevism." After the Russian Revolution, the Bolshevicks turned their attention to cultural affairs, attempting to make art available to the masses and simultaneously to use it to teach uplifting ideals.
8. Dali mentions *L'Age d'Or* and adds that its first public showing was broken up by hooligans, but he does not say in detail what it was about. According to Henry Miller's account of it, it showed among other things some fairly detailed shots of a woman defecating. [author's note]

demand of a wall is that it shall stand up. If it stands up, it is a good wall, and the question of what purpose it serves is separable from that. And yet even the best wall in the world deserves to be pulled down if it surrounds a concentration camp. In the same way it should be possible to say, "This is a good book or a good picture, and it ought to be burned by the public hangman." Unless one can say that, at least in imagination, one is shirking the implications of the fact that an artist is also a citizen and a human being.

Not, of course, that Dali's autobiography, or his pictures, ought 18 to be suppressed. Short of the dirty post cards that used to be sold in Mediterranean seaport towns, it is doubtful policy to suppress anything, and Dali's fantasies probably cast useful light on the decay of capitalist civilisation. But what he clearly needs is diagnosis. The question is not so much *what* he is as *why* he is like that. It ought not to be in doubt that he is a diseased intelligence, probably not much altered by his alleged conversion, since genuine penitents, or people who have returned to sanity, do not flaunt their past vices in that complacent way. He is a symptom of the world's illness. The important thing is not to denounce him as a cad who ought to be horsewhipped, or to defend him as a genius who ought not to be questioned, but to find out *why* he exhibits that particular set of aberrations.

The answer is probably discoverable in his pictures, and those 19 I myself am not competent to examine. But I can point to one clue which perhaps takes one part of the distance. This is the old-fashioned, over-ornate, Edwardian style of drawing to which Dali tends to revert when he is not being Surrealist. Some of Dali's drawings are reminiscent of Dürer, one (p. 113) seems to show the influence of Beardsley, another (p. 269) seems to borrow something from Blake. But the most persistent strain is the Edwardian one. When I opened the book for the first time and looked at its innumerable marginal illustrations, I was haunted by a resemblance which I could not immediately pin down. I fetched up at the ornamental candlestick at the beginning of Part I (p. 7). What did this remind me of? Finally I tracked it down. It reminded me of a large, vulgar, expensively got-up edition of Anatole France (in translation) which must have been published about 1914. That had ornamental chapter headings and tailpieces after this style. Dali's candlestick displays at one end a curly fish-like creature that looks curiously familiar (it seems to be based on the conventional dolphin), and at the other is the burning candle. This candle, which recurs in one picture after another, is a very old friend. You will find it, with the same picturesque gouts of wax arranged on its sides, in those phoney electric lights done up as candlesticks which are popular in sham-Tudor country hotels. This candle, and the design beneath it, convey at once an intense feeling of sentimentality. As though to counteract this, Dali has spattered a quill-ful of ink all over the page, but without avail. The same impression keeps popping up on page after page. The design at the bottom of page 62, for instance, would nearly go into *Peter Pan*. The figure on page 224, in spite of having her cranium elongated into an immense sausage-like shape, is the witch of the fairy-tale books. The horse on page 234 and the unicorn on page 218 might be illustrations to James Branch Cabell. The rather pansified drawings of youths on pages 97, 100 and elsewhere convey the same impression. Picturesqueness keeps breaking in. Take away the skulls, ants, lobsters, telephones and other paraphernalia, and every now and again you are back in the world of Barrie, Rackham, Dunsany and *Where the Rainbow Ends*.

Curiously enough, some of the naughty-naughty touches in Dali's autobiography tie up with the same period. When I read the passage I quoted at the beginning, about the kicking of the little sister's head, I was aware of another phantom resemblance. What was it? Of course! *Ruthless Rhymes for Heartless Homes*, by Harry Graham. Such rhymes were very popular round about 1912, and one that ran:

> ''Poor little Willy is crying so sore,
> A sad little boy is he,
> For he's broken his little sister's neck
> And he'll have no jam for tea,''

might almost have been founded on Dali's anecdote. Dali, of course, is aware of his Edwardian leanings, and makes capital out of them, more or less in a spirit of pastiche. He professes an especial affection for the year 1900, and claims that every ornamental object of 1900 is full of mystery, poetry, eroticism, madness, perversity, etc. Pastiche, however, usually implies a real affection for the thing parodied. It seems to be, if not the rule, at any rate distinctly common for an intellectual bent to be accompanied by a non-rational, even childish urge in the same direction. A sculptor, for instance, is interested in planes and curves, but he is also a person who enjoys the physical act of mucking about with clay or stone. An engineer is a person who enjoys the feel of tools, the noise of dynamos and the smell of oil. A psychiatrist usually has a leaning towards some sexual aberration himself. Darwin became a biologist partly because he was a country gentleman and fond of animals. It may be, therefore, that Dali's seemingly perverse cult of Edwardian things (for example, his "discovery" of the 1900 subway entrances) is merely the symptom of a much deeper, less conscious affection. The innumerable, beautifully executed copies of textbook illustrations, solemnly labelled *le rossignol, une montre*[9] and so on, which he scatters all over his margins, may be meant partly as a joke. The little boy in knickerbockers playing with a diabolo on page 103 is a perfect period piece. But perhaps these things are also there because Dali can't help drawing that kind of thing because it is to that period and that style of drawing that he really belongs.

If so, his aberrations are partly explicable. Perhaps they are a 21 way of assuring himself that he is not commonplace. The two qualities that Dali unquestionably possesses are a gift for drawing and an atrocious egoism. "At seven," he says in the first paragraph of his book, "I wanted to be Napoleon. And my ambition has been growing steadily ever since." This is worded in a deliberately startling way, but no doubt it is substantially true. Such feelings are common enough. "I knew I was a genius," somebody once said to me, "long before I knew what I was going to be a genius *about.*" And suppose that you have nothing in you except your egoism and a dexterity that goes no higher than the elbow; suppose that your real gift is for a detailed, academic, representational style of drawing, your real *métier*[10] to be an illustrator of scientific textbooks. How then do you become Napoleon?

There is always one escape: *into wickedness.* Always do the thing 22 that will shock and wound people. At five, throw a little boy off a bridge, strike an old doctor across the face with a whip and break his spectacles—or, at any rate, dream about doing such things. Twenty years later, gouge the eyes out of dead donkeys with a pair of scissors. Along those lines you can always feel yourself original. And after all, it pays! It is much less dangerous than crime. Making all allowance for the probable suppressions in Dali's autobiography, it is clear that he has not had to suffer for his eccentricities as he would have done in an earlier age. He grew up into the corrupt world of the nineteen-twenties, when sophistication was immensely widespread and every European capital swarmed with aristocrats and *rentiers*[11] who had given up sport and politics and taken to patronising the arts. If you threw dead donkeys at people, they threw money back. A phobia for grasshoppers—which a few decades back would merely have provoked a snigger—was now an interesting "complex" which could

9. "the nightingale, a watch"
10. Work for which one is especially well suited.
11. Persons of independent wealth.

be profitably exploited. And when that particular world collapsed before the German Army, America was waiting. You could even top it all up with religious conversion, moving at one hop and without a shadow of repentance from the fashionable *salons* of Paris to Abraham's bosom.

That, perhaps, is the essential outline of Dali's history. But why his aberrations should be the particular ones they were, and why it should be so easy to "sell" such horrors as rotting corpses to a sophisticated public—those are questions for the psychologist and the sociological critic. Marxist criticism has a short way with such phenomena as Surrealism. They are "bourgeois decadence" (much play is made with the phrases "corpse poisons" and "decaying *rentier* class"), and that is that. But though this probably states a fact, it does not establish a connection. One would still like to know *why* Dali's leaning was towards necrophilia (and not, say, homosexuality), and *why* the *rentiers* and the aristocrats should buy his pictures instead of hunting and making love like their grandfathers. Mere moral disapproval does not get one any further. But neither ought one to pretend, in the name of "detachment," that such pictures as "Mannequin rotting in a taxicab" are morally neutral. They are diseased and disgusting, and any investigation ought to start out from that fact.

23

KENNETH CLARK

Las Meninas

Our first feeling is of being there.[1] We are standing just to the right of the King and Queen, whose reflections we can see in the distant mirror, looking down an austere room in the Alcazar (hung with del Mazo's copies of Rubens) and watching a familiar situation. The Infanta Doña Margarita doesn't want to pose. She has been painted by Velasquez[2] ever since she could stand. She is now five years old, and she has had enough. But this is to be something different; an enormous picture, so big that it stands on the floor, in which she is going to appear with her parents; and somehow the Infanta must be persuaded. Her ladies-in-waiting, known by

1

From *Looking at Pictures* (1960).
1. See the reproduction of *Las Meninas* on page 492.
2. Spanish painter, 1599–1660; he was the court painter to King Philip IV.

Las Meninas (The Ladies-in-Waiting) by Diego de Silva y Velasquez (1599-1660). Oils on canvas; 123¼ × 108½''. Velasquez painted it in 1656 for King Philip IV of Spain, whose daughter, the Infanta Margarita, stands at the center of the scene. The kneeling menina, offering the Infanta a pot of chocolate, is Doña María Augustina Sarmiento; the other menina is Doña Isabel de Velasco. The dwarfs (at right) are named Maribárbola and Nicolasito. The figure behind Doña Isabel is Doña Marcella de Ulloa, the *guardadamas*. The man in the doorway is Don José Nieto Velasquez, thought to be a relative of Velasquez, who stands at the left of the scene.

the Portuguese name of *meninas*, are doing their best to cajole her, and have brought her dwarfs, Maribárbola and Nicolasito, to amuse her. But in fact they alarm her almost as much as they alarm us, and it will be some time before the sitting can take place. So far as we know, the huge official portrait was never painted.

After all that has been written about the nature of art, it seems   2 rather absurd to begin by considering a great picture as a record of something that really happened. I can't help it. That is my first impression, and I should be slightly sceptical of anyone who said that they felt anything else.

Of course, we do not have to look for long before recognising   3 that the world of appearances has been politely put in its place. The canvas has been divided into quarters horizontally and sevenths vertically. The *meninas* and the dwarfs form a triangle of which the base is one-seventh of the way up, and the apex is four-sevenths; and within the large triangle are three subsidiary ones, of which the little Infanta is the centre. But these and other devices were commonplaces of workshop tradition. Any Italian hack of the seventeenth century could have done the same, and the result would not have interested us. The extraordinary thing is that these calculations are subordinate to an absolute sense of truth. Nothing is emphasised, nothing forced. Instead of showing us with a whoop of joy how clever, how perceptive or how resourceful he is, Velasquez leaves us to make all these discoveries for ourselves. He does not beckon to the spectator any more than he flatters the sitter. Spanish pride? Well, we have only to imagine the *Meninas* painted by Goya,[3] who, heaven knows, was Spanish enough, to realise that Velasquez' reserve transcends nationality. His attitude of mind, scrupulous and detached, respecting our feelings and scorning our opinions, might have been encountered in the Greece of Sophocles or the China of Wang Wei.

It seems almost vulgar to ask what he was like, he so carefully   4 effaced himself behind his works; and in fact it is chiefly from them that we must deduce his character. Like Titian,[4] he shows no signs of impulsiveness or non-conformity, and like Titian, his life was apparently one of unbroken success. But there the likeness ends. He lives at a different temperature. We read of no passions, no appetites, no human failings; and equally there are no sensuous images burning in the back of his mind. When he was quite a young man he achieved once or twice a poetic intensity of vision, as in his *Immaculate Conception*, but this passed, as it so often does;

3. Spanish painter, 1746–1828.
4. Italian painter, 1490–1576.

or perhaps I should say that it was absorbed into his pursuit of
the whole.

He was born in 1599, and commended himself to the King as   5
early as 1623. Thenceforward he rose steadily in the Court service.
His all-powerful patron, the Count-Duke of Olivares, was dismissed
in 1643, and in the same year Velasquez was promoted to be a
Gentleman of the Bedchamber, an Assistant Superintendent of
Works and, in 1658, to the horror of the official classes, he was
invested with the Order of Santiago. Two years later he died. There
is evidence that the royal family regarded him as a friend, yet we
read of none of the cabals and jealousies which distorted the lives
of Italian painters of the same date. Modesty and sweetness of
character would not have been enough to protect him. He must
have been a man of remarkable judgement. His mind was occupied
almost entirely with problems of painting, and in this, too, he was
fortunate, for he had formed a clear idea of what he wanted to
do. It was extremely difficult, it took him thirty years of steady
work, and in the end he achieved it.

His aim was simply to tell the whole truth about a complete   6
visual impression. Italian theorists, following antiquity, had claimed
that this was the end of art as early as the fifteenth century; but
they had never really believed it; in fact, they had always qualified
it by talking about grace, grandeur, correct proportions and other
abstract concepts. Consciously or unconsciously they all believed
in the Ideal, and thought that art must bring to perfection what
nature had left in the raw. This is one of the most defensible
theories of aesthetics ever proposed, but it had no appeal to the
Spanish mind. "History," said Cervantes,[5] "is something sacred
because it is true, and where truth is, God is, truth being an aspect
of divinity." Velasquez recognised the value of ideal art. He bought
antiquities for the royal collection, he copied Titian, he was the
friend of Rubens.[6] But none of this deflected him from his aim,
to tell the whole truth about what he saw.

To some extent this was a technical problem. It is not very   7
difficult to paint a small inanimate object so that it seems real.
But when one begins to paint a figure in its setting "Oh alors!"
as Degas said. And to paint a whole group on a large scale in
such a way that no one seems too prominent, each is easily related
to the other, and all breathe the same air: that requires a most
unusual gift.

5. Miguel de Cervantes, 1547–1616, Spanish novelist, author of *Don Quixote*, a
brilliant reflection of the character of the Spanish people.
6. Peter Paul Rubens, Flemish painter, 1577–1640.

As we look about us, our eyes proceed from point to point, and 8
whenever they come to rest they are focussed in the centre of an
oval pool of colour which grows vaguer and more distorted towards
the perimeter. Each focal point involves us in a new set of relations;
and to paint a complex group like the *Meninas*, the painter must
carry in his head a single consistent scale of relations which he
can apply throughout. He may use all kinds of devices to help
him do this—perspective is one of them—but ultimately the truth
about a complete visual impression depends on one thing, truth
of tone. Drawing may be summary, colour drab, but if the relations
of tone are true, the picture will hold. For some reason truth of
tone cannot be achieved by trial and error, but seems to be an
intuitive—almost a physical—endowment, like absolute pitch in
music; and gives, when we perceive it, a pure and timeless pleasure.

Velasquez had this endowment in the highest degree. Every day 9
I look at *Las Meninas* I find myself exclaiming with delight as I
recognise the absolute rightness of some passage of tone, the grey
skirt of the standing *menina*, the green skirt of her kneeling companion, the window recess on the right, which is exactly like a
Vermeer[7] of the same date, and above all, the painter himself, in
his modest, yet confident, penumbra.[8] Only one figure makes me
uneasy, the humble-looking attendant (known as a *guardadamas*)
behind Maribárbola, who looks transparent; but I think he has
suffered from some early restoration; and so has the head of the
standing *menina*, Doña Isabel de Velasco, where the shadows are
a little too black. Otherwise everything falls into place like a theorem
in Euclid, and wherever we look the whole complex of relations
is maintained.

One should be content to accept it without question, but one 10
cannot look for long at *Las Meninas* without wanting to find out
how it is done. I remember that when it hung in Geneva in 1939
I used to go very early in the morning, before the gallery was
open, and try to stalk it, as if it really were alive. (This is impossible
in the Prado,[9] where the hushed and darkened room in which it
hangs is never empty.) I would start from as far away as I could,
when the illusion was complete, and come gradually nearer, until
suddenly what had been a hand, and a ribbon, and a piece of
velvet, dissolved into a salad of beautiful brush strokes. I thought
I might learn something if I could catch the moment at which

---

7. Jan Vermeer, Dutch painter, 1632–75.
8. Velasquez has painted himself into the painting; he stands aside, in a shadow.
9. National Spanish museum of painting and sculpture in Madrid. It houses a
number of Velasquez's masterpieces.

this transformation took place, but it proved to be as elusive as the moment between waking and sleeping.

Prosaically minded people, from Palomino[10] onwards, have as- 11
serted that Velasquez must have used exceptionally long brushes, but the brushes he holds in the *Meninas* are of normal length, and he also carries a mahlstick,[11] which implies that he put on the last delicate touches from very close to. The fact is that, like all transformations in art, it was not achieved by a technical trick, which can be found out and described, but by a flash of imaginative perception. At the moment when Velasquez' brush turned appearances into paint, he was performing an act of faith which involved his whole being.

Velasquez himself would have repudiated such a high-flown 12
interpretation. At most he would have said that it was his duty to satisfy his royal master with a correct record. He might have gone on to say that in his youth he had been able to paint single heads accurately enough in the Roman manner, but that they seemed to him lacking in life. Later he had learnt from the Venetians how to give to his figures the appearance of flesh and blood, but they did not seem to be surrounded by air. Finally, he had found a means of doing this too, by broader strokes of the brush, but how precisely this came about he could not tell.

This is usually the way in which good painters speak about their 13
work. But after two centuries of aesthetic philosophy we cannot leave it at that. No reasonable person can still believe that imitation is the end of art. To do so is like saying that the writing of history consists in recording all the known facts. Every creative activity of the human race depends on selection, and selection implies both a power to perceive relationships and the existence of a pre-established pattern in the mind. Nor is this activity peculiar to the artist, scientist or historian. We measure, we match colours, we tell stories. All through the day we are committed to low-grade aesthetic activities. We are being abstract artists when we arrange our hair brushes, impressionists when we are suddenly charmed by a lilac shadow, and portrait-painters when we see a revelation of character in the shape of a jaw. All these responses are wholly inexplicable and remain unrelated until a great artist unites and perpetuates them, and makes them convey his own sense of order.

With these speculations in mind I return to the *Meninas* and it 14
occurs to me what an extraordinarily personal selection of the

10. Spanish painter and writer on art, 1655–1726.
11. Wooden stick with a pad at one end, held by painters to steady the wrist of the hand holding the brush.

facts Velasquez has made. That he has chosen to present this
selection as a normal optical impression may have misled his
contemporaries, but should not mislead us. There is, to begin with,
the arrangement of the forms in space, that most revealing and
personal expression of our sense of order; and then there is the
interplay of their glances, which creates a different network of
relationships. Finally there are the characters themselves. Their
disposition, which seems so natural, is really very peculiar. It is
true that the Infanta dominates the scene, both by her dignity—
for she has already the air of one who is habitually obeyed—and
by the exquisite beauty of her pale gold hair. But after looking at
her, one's eye passes immediately to the square, sullen countenance
of her dwarf, Maribárbola, and to her dog, brooding and detached,
like some saturnine philosopher. These are in the first plane of
reality. And who are in the last? The King and Queen, reduced
to reflections in a shadowy mirror. To his royal master this may
have seemed no more than the record of a scene which had taken
his fancy. But must we suppose that Velasquez was unconscious
of what he was doing when he so drastically reversed the accepted
scale of values?

As I stand in the big Velasquez room of the Prado I am almost   15
oppressed by his uncanny awareness of human character. It makes
me feel like those spiritualistic mediums who complain that they
are being disturbed by 'presences'. Maribárbola is such a disturbing
element. While the other protagonists in the *Meninas*, out of sheer
good manners, take their parts in a sort of *tableau vivant*,[12] she
affronts the spectator like a blow from a muffled fist; and I remember
the strange and poignant relationship which Velasquez had with
all the dwarfs and buffoons whom he painted. No doubt it was
part of his duties to record the likenesses of these Court favourites,
but in the main Velasquez room of the Prado there are as many
portraits of buffoons as there are of the royal family (nine of each).
Surely that goes beyond official instructions and expresses a strong
personal preference. Some of his reasons may have been purely
pictorial. Buffoons could be made to sit still longer than royal
persons, and he could look more intensely at their heads. But was
there not also the feeling that their physical humiliations gave
them a reality which his royal sitters lacked? Take away the carapace
of their great position, and how pink and featureless the King and
Queen become, like prawns without their shells. They cannot look
at us with the deep questioning gaze of Sebastián de Morra or
the fierce sullen independence of Maribárbola. And I begin to

12. "living picture"

reflect on what would happen to *Las Meninas* if Maribárbola had
been removed and a graceful young lady of the Court put in her
place. We should still feel that we were there; the colour would
be as subtle, the tone as scrupulously correct. But the temperature
would have dropped: we should have lost a whole dimension of
truth.

ROBERT FROST

The Poetry of
Edwin Arlington Robinson

It may come to the notice of posterity (and then again it may   1
not) that this, our age, ran wild in the quest of new ways to be
new. The one old way to be new no longer served. Science put
it into our heads that there must be new ways to be new. Those
tried were largely by subtraction—elimination. Poetry, for example,
was tried without punctuation. It was tried without capital letters.
It was tried without metric frame on which to measure the rhythm.
It was tried without any images but those to the eye; and a loud
general intoning had to be kept up to cover the total loss of specific
images to the ear, those dramatic tones of voice which had hitherto
constituted the better half of poetry. It was tried without content
under the trade name of poesie pure. It was tried without phrase,
epigram, coherence, logic and consistency. It was tried without
ability. I took the confession of one who had had deliberately to
unlearn what he knew. He made a back-pedalling movement of
his hands to illustrate the process. It was tried premature like the
delicacy of unborn calf in Asia. It was tried without feeling or
sentiment like murder for small pay in the underworld. These
many things was it tried without, and what had we left? Still
something. The limits of poetry had been sorely strained, but the
hope was that the idea had been somewhat brought out.

Robinson[1] stayed content with the old-fashioned way to be new.   2
I remember bringing the subject up with him. How does a man
come on his difference, and how does he feel about it when he
first finds it out? At first it may well frighten him, as his difference

First published as the introduction to Robinson's poem *King Jasper* (1935).
1. Edwin Arlington Robinson, American poet, 1869–1935.

with the Church frightened Martin Luther.[2] There is such a thing as being too willing to be different. And what shall we say to people who are not only willing but anxious? What assurance have they that their difference is not insane, eccentric, abortive, unintelligible? Two fears should follow us through life. There is the fear that we shan't prove worthy in the eyes of someone who knows us at least as well as we know ourselves. That is the fear of God. And there is the fear of Man—the fear that men won't understand us and we shall be cut off from them.

We began in infancy by establishing correspondence of eyes with eyes. We recognized that they were the same feature and we could do the same things with them. We went on to the visible motion of the lips—smile answered smile; then cautiously, by trial and error, to compare the invisible muscles of the mouth and throat. They were the same and could make the same sounds. We were still together. So far, so good. From here on the wonder grows. It has been said that recognition in art is all. Better say correspondence is all. Mind must convince mind that it can uncurl and wave the same filaments of subtlety, soul convince soul that it can give off the same shimmers of eternity. At no point would anyone but a brute fool want to break off this correspondence. It is all there is to satisfaction; and it is salutary to live in the fear of its being broken off.

The latest proposed experiment of the experimentalists is to use poetry as a vehicle of grievances against the un-Utopian state. As I say, most of their experiments have been by subtraction. This would be by addition of an ingredient that latter-day poetry has lacked. A distinction must be made between griefs and grievances. Grievances are probably more useful than griefs. I read in a sort of Sunday-school leaflet from Moscow, that the grievances of Chekhov[3] against the sordidness and dullness of his home-town society have done away with the sordidness and dullness of home-town society all over Russia. They were celebrating the event. The grievances of the great Russians of the last century have given Russia a revolution. The grievances of their great followers in America may well give us, if not a revolution, at least some palliative pensions. We must suffer them to put life at its ugliest and forbid them not, as we value our reputation for liberality.

I had it from one of the youngest lately: "Whereas we once thought literature should be without content, we now know it should be charged full of propaganda." Wrong twice, I told him.

---

2. German religious reformer (1483–1546) whose criticism of the Catholic Church gave rise to the Protestant Reformation.
3. Russian short story writer and dramatist, 1860–1904.

Wrong twice and of theory prepense. But he returned to his position after a moment out for reassembly: "Surely art can be considered good only as it prompts to action." How soon, I asked him. But there is danger of undue levity in teasing the young. The experiment is evidently started. Grievances are certainly a power and are going to be turned on. We must be very tender of our dreamers. They may seem like picketers or members of the committee on rules for the moment. We shan't mind what they seem, if only they produce real poems.

But for me, I don't like grievances. I find I gently let them alone   6
wherever published. What I like is griefs and I like them Robinsonianly profound. I suppose there is no use in asking, but I should think we might be indulged to the extent of having grievances restricted to prose if prose will accept the imposition, and leaving poetry free to go its way in tears.

Robinson was a prince of heartachers amid countless achers of   7
another part. The sincerity he wrought in was all sad. He asserted the sacred right of poetry to lean its breast to a thorn and sing its dolefullest. Let weasels suck eggs. I know better where to look for melancholy. A few superficial irritable grievances, perhaps, as was only human, but these are forgotten in the depth of griefs to which he plunged us.

Grievances are a form of impatience. Griefs are a form of patience.   8
We may be required by law to throw away patience as we have been required to surrender gold; since by throwing away patience and joining the impatient in one last rush on the citadel of evil, the hope is we may end the need of patience. There will be nothing left to be patient about. The day of perfection waits on unanimous social action. Two or three more good national elections should do the business. It has been similarly urged on us to give up courage, make cowardice a virtue, and see if that won't end war, and the need of courage. Desert religion for science, clean out the holes and corners of the residual unknown, and there will be no more need of religion. (Religion is merely consolation for what we don't know.) But suppose there was some mistake, and the evil stood siege, the war didn't end, and something remained unknowable. Our having disarmed would make our case worse than it had ever been before. Nothing in the latest advices from Wall Street, the League of Nations, or the Vatican incline me to give up my holdings in patient grief.

There were Robinson and I, it was years ago, and the place   9
(near Boston Common) was the Place, as we liked afterward to call it, of Bitters, because it was with bitters, though without bitterness, we could sit there and look out on the welter of dis-

satisfaction and experiment in the world around us. It was too long ago to remember who said what, but the sense of the meeting was, we didn't care how arrant a reformer or experimentalist a man was if he gave us real poems. For ourselves, we should hate to be read for any theory upon which we might be supposed to write. We doubted any poem could persist for any theory upon which it might have been written. Take the theory that poetry in our language could be treated as quantitative, for example. Poems had been written in spite of it. And poems are all that matter. The utmost of ambition is to lodge a few poems where they will be hard to get rid of, to lodge a few irreducible bits where Robinson lodged more than his share.

For forty years it was phrase on phrase on phrase with Robinson, and every one the closest delineation of something that *is* something. Any poet, to resemble him in the least, would have to resemble him in that grazing closeness to the spiritual realities. If books of verse were to be indexed by lines first in importance instead of lines first in position, many of Robinson's poems would be represented several times over. This should be seen to. The only possible objection is that it could not be done by any mere hireling of the moment, but would have to be the work of someone who had taken his impressions freely before he had any notion of their use. A particular poem's being represented several times would only increase the chance of its being located.

The first poet I ever sat down with to talk about poetry was Ezra Pound.[4] It was in London in 1913. The first poet we talked about, to the best of my recollection, was Edwin Arlington Robinson. I was fresh from America and from having read *The Town Down the River*. Beginning at that book, I have slowly spread my reading of Robinson twenty years backward and forward, about equally in both directions.

I remember the pleasure with which Pound and I laughed over the fourth "thought" in

> Miniver thought, and thought, and thought,
> And thought about it.

Three "thoughts" would have been "adequate" as the critical praise-word then was. There would have been nothing to complain of, if it had been left at three. The fourth made the intolerable touch of poetry. With the fourth, the fun began. I was taken out on the strength of our community of opinion here, to be rewarded with an introduction to Miss May Sinclair, who had qualified as

4. American poet and critic, 1885–1972.

the patron authority on young and new poets by the sympathy she had shown them in *The Divine Fire.*[5]

There is more to it than the number of "thoughts." There is the   14
way the last one turns up by surprise round the corner, the way
the shape of the stanza is played with, the easy way the obstacle
of verse is turned to advantage. The mischief is in it.

> *One pauses half afraid*
> *To say for certain that he played—*

a man as sorrowful as Robinson. His death was sad to those who
knew him, but nowhere near as sad as the lifetime of poetry to
which he attuned our ears. Nevertheless, I say his much-admired
restraint lies wholly in his never having let grief go further than
it could in play. So far shall grief go, so far shall philosophy go,
so far shall confidences go, and no further. Taste may set the limit.
Humor is a surer dependence.

> *And once a man was there all night*
> *Expecting something every minute.*

I know what the man wanted of Old King Cole.[6] He wanted   15
the heart out of his mystery. He was the friend who stands at the
end of a poem ready in waiting to catch you by both hands with
enthusiasm and drag you off your balance over the last punctuation
mark into more than you meant to say. "I understand the poem
all right, but please tell me what is behind it?" Such presumption
needs to be twinkled at and baffled. The answer must be, "If I
had wanted you to know, I should have told you in the poem."

We early have Robinson's word for it: 16

> *The games we play*
> *To fill the frittered minutes of a day*
> *Good glasses are to read the spirit through.*

He speaks somewhere of Crabbe's stubborn skill.[7] His own was   17
a happy skill. His theme was unhappiness itself, but his skill was
as happy as it was playful. There is that comforting thought for
those who suffered to see him suffer. Let it be said at the risk of

---

5. Sinclair's most famous novel (1904), supposedly based on the life of poet Ernest Dowson.
6. The reference is to Robinson's poem "Old King Cole," in which a man who sits up with the king all night gets only a "dim reward": he falls asleep without understanding the king's philosophy—that he would "rather live than weep."
7. George Crabbe, 1754–1852, English poet known for unsentimental, realistic descriptions of life.

offending the humorless in poetry's train (for there are a few such): his art was more than playful; it was humorous.

The style is the man. Rather say the style is the way the man   18
takes himself; and to be at all charming or even bearable, the way is almost rigidly prescribed. If it is with outer seriousness, it must be with inner humor. If it is with outer humor, it must be with inner seriousness. Neither one alone without the other under it will do. Robinson was thinking as much in his sonnet on Tom Hood. One ordeal of Mark Twain was the constant fear that his occluded seriousness would be overlooked. That betrayed him into his two or three books of out-and-out seriousness.

Miniver Cheevy was long ago. The glint I mean has kept coming   19
to the surface of the fabric all down the years. Yesterday in conversation, I was using "The Mill." Robinson could make lyric talk like drama. What imagination for speech in "John Gorham"! He is at his height between quotation marks.

> The miller's wife had waited long,
>   The tea was cold, the fire was dead;
> And there might yet be nothing wrong
>   In how he went and what he said:
> "There are no millers any more,"
>   Was all that she had heard him say.

"There are no millers any more." It might be an edict of some   20
power against industrialism. But no, it is of wider application. It is a sinister jest at the expense of all investors of life or capital. The market shifts and leaves them with a car-barn full of dead trolley cars. At twenty I commit myself to a life of religion. Now, if religion should go out of fashion in twenty-five years, there would I be, forty-five years old, unfitted for anything else and too old to learn anything else. It seems immoral to have to bet on such high things as lives of art, business, or the church. But in effect, we have no alternative. None but an all-wise and all-powerful government could take the responsibility of keeping us out of the gamble or of insuring us against loss once we were in.

The guarded pathos of "Mr. Flood's Party" is what makes it   21
merciless. We are to bear in mind the number of moons listening. Two, as on the planet Mars. No less. No more ("No more, sir; that will do"). One moon (albeit a moon, no sun) would have laid grief too bare. More than two would have dissipated grief entirely and would have amounted to dissipation. The emotion had to be held at a point.

> He set the jug down slowly at his feet
> With trembling care, knowing that most things break;

> *And only when assured that on firm earth*
> *It stood, as the uncertain lives of men*
> *Assuredly did not . . .*

There twice it gleams. Nor is it lost even where it is perhaps   22
lost sight of in the dazzle of all those golden girls at the end of
"The Sheaves." Granted a few fair days in a world where not all
days are fair.

> *"Well, Mr. Flood, we have the harvest moon*
> *Again, and we may not have many more;*
> *The bird is on the wing, the poet says,*
> *And you and I have said it here before.*
> *Drink to the bird."*

Poetry transcends itself in the playfulness of the toast.   23
Robinson has gone to his place in American literature and left   24
his human place among us vacant. We mourn, but with the qualification that, after all, his life was a revel in the felicities of language.
And not just to no purpose. None has deplored.

> *The inscrutable profusion of the Lord*
> *Who shaped as one of us a thing*

so sad and at the same time so happy in achievement. Not for me
to search his sadness to its source. He knew how to forbid encroachment. And there is solid satisfaction in a sadness that is not
just a fishing for ministration and consolation. Give us immedicable
woes—woes that nothing can be done for—woes flat and final.
And then to play. The play's the thing. Play's the thing. All virtue
in "as if."

> *As if the last of days*
> *Were fading and all wars were done.*

As if they were. As if, as if!   25

GARRISON KEILLOR

Attitude

Long ago I passed the point in life when major-league ballplayers   1
begin to be younger than yourself. Now all of them are, except
for a few aging trigenarians and a couple of quadros who don't

First published in *The New Yorker*, August 27, 1979.

get around on the fastball as well as they used to and who sit out the second games of doubleheaders. However, despite my age (thirty-nine), I am still active and have a lot of interests. One of them is slow-pitch softball,[1] a game that lets me go through the motions of baseball without getting beaned or having to run too hard. I play on a pretty casual team, one that drinks beer on the bench and substitutes freely. If a player's wife or girlfriend wants to play, we give her a glove and send her out to right field, no questions asked, and if she lets a pop fly drop six feet in front of her, nobody agonizes over it.

Except me. This year. For the first time in my life, just as I am   2
entering the dark twilight of my slow-pitch career, I find myself taking the game seriously. It isn't the bonehead play that bothers me especially—the pop fly that drops untouched, the slow roller juggled and the ball then heaved ten feet over the first baseman's head and into the next diamond, the routine singles that go through outfielders' legs for doubles and triples with gloves flung after them. No, it isn't our stone-glove fielding or pussyfoot base-running or limp-wristed hitting that gives me fits, though these have put us on the short end of some mighty ridiculous scores this summer. It's our attitude.

Bottom of the ninth, down 18–3, two outs, a man on first and   3
a woman on third, and our third baseman strikes out. *Strikes out!* In slow-pitch, not even your grandmother strikes out, but this guy does, and after his third strike—a wild swing at a ball that bounces on the plate—he topples over in the dirt and lies flat on his back, laughing. *Laughing!*

Same game, earlier. They have the bases loaded. A weak grounder   4
is hit toward our second baseperson. The runners are running. She picks up the ball, and she looks at them. She looks at first, at second, at home. We yell, "Throw it! Throw it!" and she throws it, underhand, at the pitcher, who has turned and run to back up the catcher. The ball rolls across the third-base line and under the bench. Three runs score. The batter, a fatso, chugs into second. The other team hoots and hollers, and what does she do? She shrugs and smiles ("Oh, silly me"); after all, it's only a game. Like the aforementioned strikeout artist, she treats her error as a joke. They have forgiven themselves instantly, which is unforgivable. It is *we* who should forgive them, who can say, "It's all right, it's only a game." They are supposed to throw up their hands and kick the dirt and hang their heads, as if this boner, even if it is

1. A variant of softball with slower action, somewhat different rules, and 10, not 9, players to a team.

their sixteenth of the afternoon—*this* is the one that really and
truly breaks their hearts.

That attitude sweetens the game for everyone. The sinner feels   5
sweet remorse. The fatso feels some sense of accomplishment; this
is no bunch of rumdums he forced into an error but a team with
some class. We, the sinner's teammates, feel momentary anger at
her—dumb! dumb play!—but then, seeing her grief, we sympathize
with her in our hearts (any one of us might have made that mistake
or one worse), and we yell encouragement, including the shortstop,
who, moments before, dropped an easy throw for a force at second.
"That's all right! Come on! We got 'em!" we yell. "Shake it off!
These turkeys can't hit!" This makes us all feel good, even though
the turkeys now lead us by ten runs. We're getting clobbered, but
we have a winning attitude.

Let me say this about attitude: Each player is responsible for   6
his or her own attitude, and to a considerable degree you can
create a good attitude by doing certain little things on the field.
These are certain little things that ballplayers do in the Bigs, and
we ought to be doing them in the Slows.

1. When going up to bat, don't step right into the batter's box as
if it were an elevator. The box is your turf, your stage. Take
possession of it slowly and deliberately, starting with a lot of back-
bending, knee-stretching, and torso-revolving in the on-deck circle.
Then, approaching the box, stop outside it and tap the dirt off
your spikes with your bat. You don't have spikes, you have sneakers,
of course, but the significance of the tapping is the same. Then,
upon entering the box, spit on the ground. It's a way of saying,
"This here is mine. This is where I get my hits."

2. Spit frequently. Spit at all crucial moments. Spit correctly. Spit
should be *blown*, not ptuied weakly with the lips, which often
results in dribble. Spitting should convey forcefulness of purpose,
concentration, pride. Spit down, not in the direction of others.
Spit in the glove and on the fingers, especially after making a real
knucklehead play; it's a way of saying, "I dropped the ball because
my glove was dry."

3. At bat and in the field, pick up dirt. Rub dirt in the fingers
(especially after spitting on them). Toss dirt, as if testing the wind
for velocity and direction. Smooth the dirt. Be involved with dirt.
If no dirt is available (e.g., in the outfield), pluck tufts of grass.
Fielders should be grooming their areas constantly between plays,
flicking away tiny sticks and bits of gravel.

4. Take your time. Tie your laces. Confer with your teammates
about possible situations that may arise and conceivable options

in dealing with them. Extend the game. Three errors on three consecutive plays can be humiliating if the plays occur within the space of a couple of minutes, but if each error is separated from the next by extensive conferences on the mound, lace-tying, glove adjustments, and arguing close calls (if any), the effect on morale is minimized.

5. Talk. Not just an occasional "Let's get a hit now" but continuous rhythmic chatter, a flow of syllables: "Hey babe hey babe c'mon babe good stick now hey babe long tater take him downtown babe . . . hey good eye good eye."

Infield chatter is harder to maintain. Since the slow-pitch pitch is required to be a soft underhand lob, infielders hesitate to say, "Smoke him babe hey low heat hey throw it on the black babe chuck it in there back him up babe no hit no hit." Say it anyway.

6. One final rule, perhaps the most important of all: When your team is up and has made the third out, the batter and the players who were left on base do not come back to the bench for their gloves. *They remain on the field, and their teammates bring their gloves out to them.* This requires some organization and discipline, but it pays off big in morale. It says, "Although we're getting our pants knocked off, still we must conserve our energy."

Imagine that you have bobbled two fly balls in this rout and now you have just tried to stretch a single into a double and have been easily thrown out sliding into second base, where the base runner ahead of you had stopped. It was the third out and a dumb play, and your opponents smirk at you as they run off the field. You are the goat, a lonely and tragic figure sitting in the dirt. You curse yourself, jerking your head sharply forward. You stand up and kick the base. How miserable! How degrading! Your utter shame, though brief, bears silent testimony to the worthiness of your teammates, whom you have let down, and they appreciate it. They call out to you now as they take the field, and as the second baseman runs to his position he says, "Let's get 'em now," and tosses you your glove. Lowering your head, you trot slowly out to right. There you do some deep knee bends. You pick grass. You find a pebble and fling it into foul territory. As the first batter comes to the plate, you check the sun. You get set in your stance, poised to fly. Feet spread, hands on hips, you bend slightly at the waist and spit the expert spit of a veteran ballplayer—a player who has known the agony of defeat but who always bounces back, a player who has lost a stride on the base paths but can still make the big play.

This is *ball*, ladies and gentlemen. This is what it's all about.

7

8

A Sense of Where You Are

Bradley[1] is one of the few basketball players who have ever   1
been appreciatively cheered by a disinterested away-from-home
crowd while warming up. This curious event occurred last March,
just before Princeton eliminated the Virginia Military Institute, the
year's Southern Conference champion, from the N.C.A.A. championships. The game was played in Philadelphia and was the last
of a tripleheader. The people there were worn out because most
of them were emotionally committed to either Villanova or Temple—
two local teams that had just been involved in enervating battles
with Providence and Connecticut, respectively, scrambling for a
chance at the rest of the country. A group of Princeton boys
shooting basketballs miscellaneously in preparation for still another
game hardly promised to be a high point of the evening, but
Bradley, whose routine in the warmup time is a gradual crescendo
of activity, is more interesting to watch before a game than most
players are in play. In Philadelphia that night, what he did was,
for him, anything but unusual. As he does before all games, he
began by shooting set shots close to the basket, gradually moving
back until he was shooting long sets from twenty feet out, and
nearly all of them dropped into the net with an almost mechanical
rhythm of accuracy. Then he began a series of expandingly difficult
jump shots, and one jumper after another went cleanly through
the basket with so few exceptions that the crowd began to murmur.
Then he started to perform whirling reverse moves before another
cadence of almost steadily accurate jump shots, and the murmur
increased. Then he began to sweep hook shots into the air. He
moved in a semicircle around the court. First with his right hand,
then with his left, he tried seven of these long, graceful shots—
the most difficult ones in the orthodoxy of basketball—and
ambidextrously made them all. The game had not even begun,
but the presumably unimpressible Philadelphians were applauding
like an audience at an opera.

Bradley has a few unorthodox shots, too. He dislikes flamboyance,   2
and, unlike some of basketball's greatest stars, has apparently never

---

First published in *The New Yorker*, January 23, 1965.
1. Bill Bradley (b. 1943) played collegiate basketball at Princeton University from
1961 to 1965 and professional basketball with the New York Knickerbockers from
1967 to 1977.

made a move merely to attract attention. While some players are eccentric in their shooting, his shots, with only occasional exceptions, are straightforward and unexaggerated. Nonetheless, he does make something of a spectacle of himself when he moves in rapidly parallel to the baseline, glides through the air with his back to the basket, looks for a teammate he can pass to, and, finding none, tosses the ball into the basket over one shoulder, like a pinch of salt. Only when the ball is actually dropping through the net does he look around to see what has happened, on the chance that something might have gone wrong, in which case he would have to go for the rebound. That shot has the essential characteristics of a wild accident, which is what many people stubbornly think they have witnessed until they see him do it for the third time in a row. All shots in basketball are supposed to have names—the set, the hook, the lay-up, the jump shot, and so on—and one weekend last July, while Bradley was in Princeton working on his senior thesis and putting in some time in the Princeton gymnasium to keep himself in form for the Olympics, I asked him what he called his over-the-shoulder shot. He said that he had never heard a name for it, but that he had seen Oscar Robertson, of the Cincinnati Royals, and Jerry West, of the Los Angeles Lakers, do it, and had worked it out for himself. He went on to say that it is a much simpler shot than it appears to be, and, to illustrate, he tossed a ball over his shoulder and into the basket while he was talking and looking me in the eye. I retrieved the ball and handed it back to him. "When you have played basketball for a while, you don't need to look at the basket when you are in close like this," he said, throwing it over his shoulder again and right through the hoop. "You develop a sense of where you are."

Bradley is not an innovator. Actually, basketball has had only a few innovators in its history—players like Hank Luisetti, of Stanford, whose introduction in 1936 of the running one-hander did as much to open up the game for scoring as the forward pass did for football; and Joe Fulks, of the old Philadelphia Warriors, whose twisting two-handed heaves, made while he was leaping like a salmon, were the beginnings of the jump shot, which seems to be basketball's ultimate weapon. Most basketball players appropriate fragments of other players' styles, and thus develop their own. This is what Bradley has done, but one of the things that set him apart from nearly everyone else is that the process has been conscious rather than osmotic. His jump shot, for example, has had two principal influences. One is Jerry West, who has one of the best jumpers in basketball. At a summer basketball camp in Missouri some years ago, West told Bradley that he always gives an extra

hard bound to the last dribble before a jump shot, since this seems
to catapult him to added height. Bradley has been doing that ever
since. Terry Dischinger, of the Detroit Pistons, has told Bradley
that he always slams his foot to the floor on the last step before
a jump shot, because this stops his momentum and thus prevents
drift. Drifting while aloft is the mark of a sloppy jump shot.

Bradley's graceful hook shot is a masterpiece of eclecticism. It   4
consists of the high-lifted knee of the Los Angeles Lakers' Darrall
Imhoff, the arms of Bill Russell, of the Boston Celtics, who extends
his idle hand far under his shooting arm and thus magically stabilizes
the shot, and the general corporeal form of Kentucky's Cotton
Nash, a rookie this year with the Lakers. Bradley carries his analyses
of shots further than merely identifying them with pieces of other
people. "There are five parts to the hook shot," he explains to
anyone who asks. As he continues, he picks up a ball and stands
about eighteen feet from a basket. "Crouch," he says, crouching,
and goes on to demonstrate the other moves. "Turn your head
to look for the basket, step, kick, follow through with your arms."
Once, as he was explaining this to me, the ball curled around the
rim and failed to go in.

"What happened then?" I asked him.   5
"I didn't kick high enough," he said.   6
"Do you always know exactly why you've missed a shot?"   7
"Yes," he said, missing another one.   8
"What happened that time?"   9
"I was talking to you. I didn't concentrate. The secret of shooting 10
is concentration."

His set shot is borrowed from Ed Macauley, who was a St. Louis   11
University All-American in the late forties and was later a star
member of the Boston Celtics and the St. Louis Hawks. Macauley
runs the basketball camp Bradley first went to when he was fifteen.
In describing the set shot, Bradley is probably quoting a Macauley
lecture. "Crouch like Groucho Marx," he says. "Go off your feet
a few inches. You shoot with your legs. Your arms merely guide
the ball." Bradley says that he has more confidence in his set shot
than in any other. However, he seldom uses it, because he seldom
has to. A set shot is a long shot, usually a twenty-footer, and
Bradley, with his speed and footwork, can almost always take
some other kind of shot, closer to the basket. He will take set
shots when they are given to him, though. Two seasons ago,
Davidson lost to Princeton, using a compact zone defense that
ignored the remoter areas of the court. In one brief sequence,
Bradley sent up seven set shots, missing only one. The missed one
happened to rebound in Bradley's direction, and he leaped up,
caught it with one hand, and scored.

Even his lay-up shot has an ancestral form; he is full of admiration 12 for "the way Cliff Hagan pops up anywhere within six feet of the basket," and he tries to do the same. Hagan is a former Kentucky star who now plays for the St. Louis Hawks. Because opposing teams always do everything they can to stop Bradley, he gets an unusual number of foul shots. When he was in high school, he used to imitate Bob Pettit, of the St. Louis Hawks, and Bill Sharman, of the Boston Celtics, but now his free throw is more or less his own. With his left foot back about eighteen inches—"wherever it feels comfortable," he says—he shoots with a deep-bending rhythm of knees and arms, one-handed, his left hand acting as a kind of gantry for the ball until the moment of release. What is most interesting, though, is that he concentrates his attention on one of the tiny steel eyelets that are welded under the rim of the basket to hold the net to the hoop—on the center eyelet, of course— before he lets fly. One night, he scored over twenty points on free throws alone; Cornell hacked at him so heavily that he was given twenty-one free throws, and he made all twenty-one, finishing the game with a total of thirty-seven points.

When Bradley, working out alone, practices his set shots, hook 13 shots, and jump shots, he moves systematically from one place to another around the basket, his distance from it being appropriate to the shot, and he does not permit himself to move on until he has made at least ten shots out of thirteen from each location. He applies this standard to every kind of shot, with either hand, from any distance. Many basketball players, including reasonably good ones, could spend five years in a gym and not make ten out of thirteen left-handed hook shots, but that is part of Bradley's daily routine. He talks to himself while he is shooting, usually reminding himself to concentrate but sometimes talking to himself the way every high-school j.v. basketball player has done since the dim twenties—more or less imitating a radio announcer, and saying, as he gathers himself up for a shot, "It's pandemonium in Dillon Gymnasium. The clock is running out. He's up with a jumper. Swish!"

Last summer, the floor of the Princeton gym was being resurfaced, 14 so Bradley had to put in several practice sessions at the Lawrenceville School. His first afternoon at Lawrenceville, he began by shooting fourteen-foot jump shots from the right side. He got off to a bad start, and he kept missing them. Six in a row hit the back rim of the basket and bounced out. He stopped, looking discomfited, and seemed to be making an adjustment in his mind. Then he went up for another jump shot from the same spot and hit it cleanly. Four more shots went in without a miss, and then he paused and said, "You want to know something? That basket is about an inch and a half low." Some weeks later, I went back to Lawrenceville with a steel tape, borrowed a stepladder, and measured the height of the basket. It was nine feet ten and seven-eighths inches above the floor, or one and one-eighth inches too low.

Being a deadly shot with either hand and knowing how to   15
make the moves and fakes that clear away the defense are the
primary skills of a basketball player, and any player who can do
these things half as well as Bradley can has all the equipment he
needs to make a college team. Many high-scoring basketball players,
being able to make so obvious and glamorous a contribution to
their team in the form of point totals, don't bother to develop the
other skills of the game, and leave subordinate matters like defense
and playmaking largely to their teammates. Hence, it is usually
quite easy to parse a basketball team. Bringing the ball up the
floor are playmaking backcourt men—selfless fellows who can
usually dribble so adeptly that they can just about freeze the ball
by themselves, and who can also throw passes through the eye
of a needle and can always be counted on to feed the ball to a
star at the right moment. A star is often a point-hungry gunner,
whose first instinct when he gets the ball is to fire away, and
whose playing creed might be condensed to "When in doubt,
shoot." Another, with legs like automobile springs, is part of the
group because of an unusual ability to go high for rebounds. Still
another may not be especially brilliant on offense but has defensive
equipment that could not be better if he were carrying a trident
and a net.

The point-hungry gunner aside, Bradley is all these. He is a   16
truly complete basketball player. He can play in any terrain; in
the heavy infighting near the basket, he is master of all the gestures
of the big men, and toward the edge of play he shows that he
has all the fast-moving skills of the little men, too. With remarkable
speed for six feet five, he can steal the ball and break into the
clear with it on his own; as a dribbler, he can control the ball
better with his left hand than most players can with their right;
he can go down court in the middle of a fast break and fire passes
to left and right, closing in on the basket, the timing of his passes
too quick for the spectator's eye. He plays any position—up front,
in the post, in the backcourt. And his playmaking is a basic characteristic of his style. His high-scoring totals are the result of his
high percentage of accuracy, not of an impulse to shoot every
time he gets the ball.

He passes as generously and as deftly as any player in the game.   17
When he is dribbling, he can pass accurately without first catching

the ball. He can also manage almost any pass without appearing to cock his arm, or even bring his hand back. He just seems to flick his fingers and the ball is gone. Other Princeton players aren't always quite expecting Bradley's passes when they arrive, for Bradley is usually thinking a little bit ahead of everyone else on the floor. When he was a freshman, he was forever hitting his teammates on the mouth, the temple, or the back of the head with passes as accurate as they were surprising. His teammates have since sharpened their own faculties, and these accidents seldom happen now. "It's rewarding to play with him," one of them says. "If you get open, you'll get the ball." And, with all the defenders in between, it sometimes seems as if the ball has passed like a ray through several walls.

Bradley's play has just one somewhat unsound aspect, and it is the result of his mania for throwing the ball to his teammates. He can't seem to resist throwing a certain number of passes that are based on nothing but theory and hope; in fact, they are referred to by the Princeton coaching staff as Bradley's hope passes. They happen, usually, when something has gone just a bit wrong. Bradley is recovering a loose ball, say, with his back turned to the other Princeton players. Before he turned it, he happened to notice a screen, or pick-off, being set by two of his teammates, its purpose being to cause one defensive man to collide with another player and thus free an offensive man to receive a pass and score. Computations whir in Bradley's head. He hasn't time to look, but the screen, as he saw it developing, seemed to be working, so a Princeton man should now be in the clear, running toward the basket with one arm up. He whips the ball over his shoulder to the spot where the man ought to be. Sometimes a hope pass goes flying into the crowd, but most of the time they hit the receiver right in the hand, and a gasp comes from several thousand people. Bradley is sensitive about such dazzling passes, because they look flashy, and an edge comes into his voice as he defends them. "When I was halfway down the court, I saw a man out of the corner of my eye who had on the same color shirt I did," he said recently, explaining how he happened to fire a scoring pass while he was falling out of bounds. "A little later, when I threw the pass, I threw it to the spot where that man should have been if he had kept going and done his job. He was there. Two points."

Since it appears that by nature Bradley is a passer first and a scorer second, he would probably have scored less at a school where he was surrounded by other outstanding players. When he went to Princeton, many coaches mourned his loss not just to themselves but to basketball, but as things have worked out, much

of his national prominence has been precipitated by his playing
for Princeton, where he has had to come through with points in
order to keep his team from losing. He starts slowly, as a rule.
During much of the game, if he has a clear shot, fourteen feet
from the basket, say, and he sees a teammate with an equally
clear shot ten feet from the basket, he sends the ball to the teammate.
Bradley apparently does not stop to consider that even though
the other fellow is closer to the basket he may be far more likely
to miss the shot. This habit exasperates his coaches until they
clutch their heads in despair. But Bradley is doing what few people
ever have done—he is playing basketball according to the foundation
pattern of the game. Therefore, the shot goes to the closer man.
Nothing on earth can make him change until Princeton starts to
lose. Then he will concentrate a little more on the basket.

Something like this happened in Tokyo last October, when the   20
United States Olympic basketball team came close to being beaten
by Yugoslavia. The Yugoslavian team was reasonably good—better
than the Soviet team, which lost to the United States in the final—
and it heated up during the second half. With two minutes to go,
Yugoslavia cut the United States' lead to two points. Bradley was
on the bench at the time, and Henry Iba, the Oklahoma State
coach, who was coach of the Olympic team, sent him in. During
much of the game, he had been threading passes to others, but
at that point, he says, he felt that he had to try to do something
about the score. Bang, bang, bang—he hit a running one-hander,
a seventeen-foot jumper, and a lay-up on a fast break, and the
United States won by eight points.

Actually, the United States basketball squad encountered no real   21
competition at the Olympics, despite all sorts of rumbling cumulus
beforehand to the effect that some of the other teams, notably
Russia's, were made up of men who had been playing together
for years and were now possibly good enough to defeat an American
Olympic basketball team for the first time. But if the teams that
the Americans faced were weaker than advertised, there were
nonetheless individual performers of good calibre, and it is a further
index to Bradley's completeness as a basketball player that Henry
Iba, a defensive specialist as a coach, regularly assigned him to
guard the stars of the other nations. "He didn't show too much
tact at defense when he started, but he's a coach's basketball
player, and he came along," Iba said after he had returned to
Oklahoma. "And I gave him the toughest man in every game."

Yugoslavia's best man was a big forward who liked to play in   22
the low post, under the basket. Bradley went into the middle with

him, crashing shoulders under the basket, and held him to thirteen points while scoring eighteen himself. Russia's best man was Yuri Korneyev, whose specialty was driving; that is, he liked to get the ball somewhere out on the edge of the action and start for the basket with it like a fullback, blasting everything out of the way until he got close enough to ram in a point-blank shot. With six feet five inches and two hundred and forty pounds to drive, Korneyev was what Iba called "a real good driver." Bradley had lost ten pounds because of all the Olympics excitement, and Korneyev outweighed him by forty-five pounds. Korneyev kicked, pushed, shoved, bit, and scratched Bradley. "He was tough to stop," Bradley says. "After all, he was playing for his life." Korneyev got eight points.

Bradley was one of three players who had been picked unan-   23
imously for the twelve-man Olympic team. He was the youngest member of the squad and the only undergraduate. Since his trip to Tokyo kept him away from Princeton for the first six weeks of the fall term, he had to spend part of his time reading, and the course he worked on most was Russian History 323. Perhaps because of the perspective this gave him, his attitude toward the Russian basketball team was not what he had expected it to be. With the help of three Australian players who spoke Russian, Bradley got to know several members of the Russian team fairly well, and soon he was feeling terribly sorry for them. They had a leaden attitude almost from the beginning. "All we do is play basketball," one of them told him forlornly. "After we go home, we play in the Soviet championships. Then we play in the Satellite championships. Then we play in the European championships. I would give anything for five days off." Bradley says that the Russian players also told him they were paid eighty-five dollars a month, plus housing. Given the depressed approach of the Russians, Bradley recalls, it was hard to get excited before the Russian-American final. "It was tough to get chills," he says. "I had to imagine we were about to play Yale." The Russians lost, 73–59.

Bradley calls practically all men "Mister" whose age exceeds   24
his own by more than a couple of years. This includes N.B.A. players he happens to meet, Princeton trainers, and Mr. Willem Hendrik van Breda Kolff, his coach. Van Breda Kolff was a Princeton basketball star himself, some twenty years ago, and went on to play for the New York Knickerbockers. Before returning to Princeton in 1962, he coached at Lafayette and Hofstra. His teams at the three colleges have won two hundred and fifty-one games and

lost ninety-six. Naturally, it was a virtually unparalleled stroke of good fortune for van Breda Kolff to walk into his current coaching job in the very year that Bradley became eligible to play for the varsity team, but if the coach was lucky to have the player, the player was also lucky to have the coach. Van Breda Kolff, a cheerful and uncomplicated man, has a sportman's appreciation of the nuances of the game, and appears to feel that mere winning is far less important than winning with style. He is an Abstract Expressionist[2] of basketball. Other coaches have difficulty scouting his teams, because he does not believe in a set offense. He likes his offense free-form.

Van Breda Kolff simply tells his boys to spread out and keep the ball moving. "Just go fast, stay out of one another's way, pass, move, come off guys, look for one-on-ones, two-on-ones, two-on-twos, three-on-threes. That's about the extent," he says. That is, in fact, about the substance of basketball, which is almost never played as a five-man game anymore but is, rather, a constant search, conducted semi-independently by five players, for smaller combinations that will produce a score. One-on-one is the basic situation of the game—one man, with the ball, trying to score against one defensive player, who is trying to stop him, with nobody else involved. Van Breda Kolff does not think that Bradley is a great one-on-one player. "A one-on-one player is a hungry player," he explains. "Bill is not hungry. At least ninety percent of the time, when he gets the ball, he is looking for a pass." Van Breda Kolff has often tried to force Bradley into being more of a one-on-one player, through gentle persuasion in practice, through restrained pleas during timeouts, and even through open clamor. During one game last year, when Princeton was losing and Bradley was still flicking passes, van Breda Kolff stood up and shouted, *"Will . . . you . . . shoot . . . that . . . ball?"* Bradley, obeying at once, drew his man into the vortex of a reverse pivot, and left him standing six feet behind as he made a soft, short jumper from about ten feet out.

If Bradley were more interested in his own statistics, he could score sixty or seventy-five points, or maybe even a hundred, in some of his games. But this would merely be personal aggrandizement, done at the expense of the relative balance of his own team and causing unnecessary embarrassment to the opposition, for it would only happen against an opponent that was heavily

2. The allusion is to a movement of abstract painting dating from the mid-1940s and revealing great stylistic diversity and originality.

outmatched anyway. Bradley's highest point totals are almost always made when the other team is strong and the situation demands his scoring ability. He has, in fact, all the mechanical faculties a great one-on-one player needs. As van Breda Kolff will point out, for example, Bradley has "a great reverse pivot," and this is an essential characteristic of a one-on-one specialist. A way of getting rid of a defensive man who is playing close, it is a spin of the body, vaguely similar to what a football halfback does when he spins away from a would-be tackler, and almost exactly what a lacrosse player does when he "turns his man." Say that Bradley is dribbling hard toward the basket and the defensive man is all over him. Bradley turns, in order to put his body between his opponent and the ball; he continues his dribbling but shifts the ball from one hand to the other; if his man is still crowding in on him, he keeps on turning until he has made one full revolution and is once more headed toward the basket. This is a reverse pivot. Bradley can execute one in less than a second. The odds are that when he has completed the spin the defensive player will be behind him, for it is the nature of basketball that the odds favor the man with the ball—if he knows how to play them.

Bradley doesn't need to complete the full revolution every time. 27
If his man steps away from him in anticipation of a reverse pivot, Bradley can stop dead and make a jump shot. If the man stays close to him but not close enough to be turned, Bradley can send up a hook shot. If the man moves over so that he will be directly in Bradley's path when Bradley comes out of the turn, Bradley can scrap the reverse pivot before he begins it, merely suggesting it with his shoulders and then continuing his original dribble to the basket, making his man look like a pedestrian who has leaped to get out of the way of a speeding car.

The metaphor of basketball is to be found in these compounding 28
alternatives. Every time a basketball player takes a step, an entire new geometry of action is created around him. In ten seconds, with or without the ball, a good player may see perhaps a hundred alternatives and, from them, make half a dozen choices as he goes along. A great player will see even more alternatives and will make more choices, and this multiradial way of looking at things can carry over into his life. At least, it carries over into Bradley's life. The very word "alternatives" bobs in and out of his speech with noticeable frequency. Before his Rhodes Scholarship[3] came

3. Scholarships to Oxford University in England; established by British businessman Cecil Rhodes.

along and eased things, he appeared to be worrying about dozens
of alternatives for next year. And he still fills his days with alternatives. He apparently always needs to have eight ways to jump,
not because he is excessively prudent but because that is what
makes the game interesting.

The reverse pivot, of course, is just one of numerous one-on-   29
one moves that produce a complexity of possibilities. A rocker
step, for example, in which a player puts one foot forward and
rocks his shoulders forward and backward, can yield a set shot if
the defensive man steps back, a successful drive to the basket if
the defensive man comes in too close, a jump shot if he tries to
compromise. A simple cross-over—shifting a dribble from one hand
to the other and changing direction—can force the defensive man
to overcommit himself, as anyone knows who has ever watched
Oscar Robertson use it to break free and score. Van Breda Kolff
says that Bradley is "a great mover," and points out that the basis
of all these maneuvers is footwork. Bradley has spent hundreds
of hours merely rehearsing the choreography of the game—shifting
his feet in the same patterns again and again, until they have worn
into his motor subconscious. "The average basketball player only
likes to play basketball," van Breda Kolff says. "When he's left
to himself, all he wants to do is get a two-on-two or a three-on-
three going. Bradley practices techniques, making himself learn
and improve instead of merely having fun."

Because of Bradley's super-serious approach to basketball, his   30
relationship to van Breda Kolff is in some respects a reversal of
the usual relationship between a player and a coach. Writing to
van Breda Kolff from Tokyo in his capacity as captain-elect, Bradley
advised his coach that they should prepare themselves for "the
stern challenge ahead." Van Breda Kolff doesn't vibrate to that
sort of tune. "Basketball is a game," he says. "It is not an ordeal.
I think Bradley's happiest whenever he can deny himself pleasure."
Van Breda Kolff's handling of Bradley has been, in a way, a
remarkable feat of coaching. One man cannot beat five men—at
least not consistently—and Princeton loses basketball games. Until
this season, moreover, the other material that van Breda Kolff has
had at his disposal has been for the most part below even the
usual Princeton standard, so the fact that his teams have won two
consecutive championships is about as much to his credit as to
his star's.

Van Breda Kolff says, "I try to play it just as if he were a normal   31
player. I don't want to overlook him, but I don't want to overlook for him, either, if you see what I'm trying to say." Bradley's
teammates sometimes depend on him too much, the coach explains,

or, in a kind of psychological upheaval, get self-conscious about being on the court with a superstar and, perhaps to prove their independence, bring the ball up the court five or six times without passing it to him. When this happens, van Breda Kolff calls time out. "Hey, boys," he says. "What have we got an All-American for?" He refers to Bradley's stardom only when he has to, however. In the main, he takes Bradley with a calculated grain of salt. He is interested in Bradley's relative weaknesses rather than in his storied feats, and has helped him gain poise on the court, learn patience, improve his rebounding, and be more aggressive. He refuses on principle to say that Bradley is the best basketball player he has ever coached, and he is also careful not to echo the general feeling that Bradley is the most exemplary youth since Lochinvar, but he will go out of his way to tell about the reaction of referees to Bradley. "The refs watch Bradley like a hawk, but, because he never complains, they feel terrible if they make an error against him," he says. "They just love him because he is such a gentleman. They get upset if they call a bad one on him." I asked van Breda Kolff what he thought Bradley would be doing when he was forty. "I don't know," he said. "I guess he'll be the governor of Missouri."[4]

Many coaches, on the reasonable supposition that Bradley cannot   32
beat their teams alone, concentrate on choking off the four other Princeton players, but Bradley is good enough to rise to such occasions, as he did when he scored forty-six against Texas, making every known shot, including an eighteen-foot running hook. Some coaches, trying a standard method of restricting a star, set up four of their players in either a box-shaped or a diamond-shaped zone defensive formation and put their fifth player on Bradley, man-to-man. Wherever Bradley goes under these circumstances, he has at least two men guarding him, the man-to-man player and the fellow whose zone he happens to be passing through. This is a dangerous defense, however, because it concedes an imbalance of forces, and also because Bradley is so experienced at being guarded by two men at once that he can generally fake them both out with a single move; also, such overguarding often provides Bradley with enough free throws to give his team the margin of victory.

Most coaches have played Princeton straight, assigning their best   33
defensive man to Bradley and letting it go at that. This is what St. Joseph's College did in the opening round of the N.C.A.A. Tournament in 1963. St. Joseph's had a strong, well-balanced

4. Bradley was elected United States Senator from New Jersey in 1978 (at the age of 35), an office he still holds.

team, which had lost only four games of a twenty-five-game schedule and was heavily favored to rout Princeton. The St. Joseph's player who was to guard Bradley promised his teammates that he would hold Bradley below twenty points. Bradley made twenty points in the first half.

He made another twenty points in the first sixteen minutes of   34 the second half. In the group battles for rebounds, he won time after time. He made nearly sixty per cent of his shots, and he made sixteen out of sixteen from the foul line. The experienced St. Joseph's man could not handle him, and the whole team began to go after him in frenzied clusters. He would dribble through them, disappearing in the ruck and emerging a moment later, still dribbling, to float up toward the basket and score. If St. Joseph's forced him over toward the sideline, he would crouch, turn his head to look for the distant basket, step, kick his leg, and follow through with his arms, sending a long, high hook shot—all five parts intact—into the net. When he went up for a jump shot, St. Joseph's players would knock him off balance, but he would make the shot anyway, crash to the floor, get up, and sink the dividend foul shot, scoring three points instead of two on the play.

On defense, he guarded St. Joseph's highest-scoring player, Tom   35 Wynne, and held him to nine points. The defense was expensive, though. An aggressive defensive player has to take the risk of committing five personal fouls, after which a player is obliged by the rules to leave the game. With just under four minutes to go, and Princeton comfortably ahead by five points, Bradley committed his fifth foul and left the court. For several minutes, the game was interrupted as the crowd stood and applauded him; the game was being played in Philadelphia, where hostility toward Princeton is ordinarily great but where the people know a folk hero when they see one. After the cheering ended, the blood drained slowly out of Princeton, whose other players could not hold the lead. Princeton lost by one point. Dr. Jack Ramsay, the St. Joseph's coach, says that Bradley's effort that night was the best game of basketball he has ever seen a college boy play.

Some people, hearing all the stories of Bradley's great moments,   36 go to see him play and are disappointed when he does not do something memorable at least once a minute. Actually, basketball is a hunting game. It lasts for forty minutes, and there are ten men on the court, so the likelihood is that any one player, even a superstar, will actually have the ball in his hands for only four of those minutes, or perhaps a little more. The rest of the time, a player on offense either is standing around recovering his breath or is on the move, foxlike, looking for openings, sizing up chances, attempting to screen off a defensive man—by "coming off guys," as van Breda Kolff puts it—and thus upset the balance of power.

The depth of Bradley's game is most discernible when he doesn't 37
have the ball. He goes in and swims around in the vicinity of the basket, back and forth, moving for motion's sake, making plans and abandoning them, and always watching the distant movement of the ball out of the corner of his eye. He stops and studies his man, who is full of alertness because of the sudden break in the rhythm. The man is trying to watch both Bradley and the ball. Bradley watches the man's head. If it turns too much to the right, he moves quickly to the left. If it turns too much to the left, he goes to the right. If, ignoring the ball, the man focusses his full attention on Bradley, Bradley stands still and looks at the floor. A high-lobbed pass floats in, and just before it arrives Bradley jumps high, takes the ball, turns, and scores.

If Princeton has an out-of-bounds play under the basket, Bradley 38
takes a position just inside the baseline, almost touching the team-mate who is going to throw the ball into play. The defensive man crowds in to try to stop whatever Bradley is planning. Bradley whirls around the defensive man, blocking him out with one leg, and takes a bounce pass and lays up the score. This works only against naïve opposition, but when it does work it is a marvel to watch.

To receive a pass from a backcourt man, Bradley moves away 39
from the basket and toward one side of the court. He gets the ball, gives it up, goes into the center, and hovers there awhile. Nothing happens. He goes back to the corner. He starts toward the backcourt again to receive a pass like the first one. His man, who is eager and has been through this before, moves out toward the backcourt a step ahead of Bradley. This is a defensive error. Bradley isn't going that way; he was only faking. He heads straight for the basket, takes a bounce pass, and scores. This maneuver is known in basketball as going back door. Bradley is able to go back door successfully and often, because of his practiced footwork. Many players, once their man has made himself vulnerable, rely on surprise alone to complete a back-door play, and that isn't always enough. Bradley's fake looks for all the world like the beginning of a trip to the outside; then, when he goes for the basket, he has all the freedom he needs. When he gets the ball after breaking free, other defensive players naturally leave their own men and try to stop him. In these three-on-two or two-on-one situations, the obvious move is to pass to a teammate who has moved into a position to score. Sometimes, however, no team-mate has moved, and Bradley sees neither a pass nor a shot, so

he veers around and goes back and picks up his own man. "I take him on into the corner for a one-on-one," he says, imagining what he might do. "I move toward the free-throw line on a dribble. If the man is overplaying me to my right, I reverse pivot and go in for a left-handed lay-up. If the man is playing even with me, but off me a few feet, I take a jump shot. If the man is playing me good defense—honest—and he's on me tight, I keep going. I give him a head-and-shoulder fake, keep going all the time, and drive to the basket, or I give him a head-and-shoulder fake and take a jump shot. Those are all the things you need—the fundamentals."

Bradley develops a relationship with his man that is something   40
like the relationship between a yoyoist and his yoyo. "I'm on the side of the floor," he postulates, "and I want to play with my man a little bit, always knowing where the ball is but not immediately concerned with getting it. Basketball is a game of two or three men, and you have to know how to stay out of a play and not clutter it up. I cut to the baseline. My man will follow me. I'll cut up to the high-post position. He'll follow me. I'll cut to the low-post position. He'll follow me. I'll go back out to my side position. He'll follow. I'll fake to the center of the floor and go hard to the baseline, running my man into a pick set at the low-post position. I'm not running him into a pick in order to get free for a shot— I'm doing it simply to irritate him. I come up on the other side of the basket, looking to see if a teammate feels that I'm open. They can't get the ball to me at that instant. Now my man is back with me. I go out to the side. I set a screen for the guard. He sees the situation. He comes toward me. He dribbles hard past me, running his man into my back. I feel the contact. My man switches off me, leaving the pass lane open for a split second. I go hard to the basket and take a bounce pass for a shot. Two points."

Because Bradley's inclination to analyze every gesture in basketball   41
is fairly uncommon, other players look at him as if they think him a little odd when he seeks them out after a game and asks them to show him what they did in making a move that he particularly admired. They tell him that they're not sure what he is talking about, and that even if they could remember, they couldn't possibly explain, so the best offer they can make is to go back to the court, try to set up the situation again, and see what it was that provoked his appreciation. Bradley told me about this almost apologetically, explaining that he had no choice but to be analytical in order to be in the game at all. "I don't have that much natural ability," he said, and went on to tell a doleful tale about how his legs lacked spring, how he was judged among the worst of the

Olympic candidates in ability to get high off the floor, and so on, until he had nearly convinced me that he was a motor moron. In actuality, Bradley does have certain natural advantages. He has been six feet five since he was fifteen years old, so he had most of his high-school years in which to develop his coördination, and it is now exceptional for a tall man. His hand span, measuring only nine and a half inches, does not give him the wraparound control that basketball players like to have, but, despite relatively unimpressive shoulders and biceps, he is unusually strong, and he can successfully mix with almost anyone in the Greco-Roman battles under the backboards.

His most remarkable natural gift, however, is his vision. During a game, Bradley's eyes are always a glaze of panoptic attention, for a basketball player needs to look at everything, focussing on nothing, until the last moment of commitment. Beyond this, it is obviously helpful to a basketball player to be able to see a little more than the next man, and the remark is frequently made about basketball superstars that they have unusual peripheral vision. People used to say that Bob Cousy, the immortal backcourt man of the Boston Celtics, could look due east and enjoy a sunset. Ed Macauley once took a long auto trip with Cousy when they were teammates, and in the course of it Cousy happened to go to sleep sitting up. Macauley swears that Cousy's eyelids, lowered as far as they would go, failed to cover his coleopteran eyes.

Bradley's eyes close normally enough, but his astounding passes to teammates have given him, too, a reputation for being able to see out of the back of his head. To discover whether there was anything to all the claims for basketball players' peripheral vision, I asked Bradley to go with me to the office of Dr. Henry Abrams, a Princeton ophthalmologist, who had agreed to measure Bradley's total field. Bradley rested his chin in the middle of a device called a perimeter, and Dr. Abrams began asking when he could see a small white dot as it was slowly brought around from behind him, from above, from below, and from either side. To make sure that Bradley wasn't, in effect, throwing hope passes, Dr. Abrams checked each point three times before plotting it on a chart. There was a chart for each eye, and both charts had irregular circles printed on them, representing the field of vision that a typical perfect eye could be expected to have. Dr. Abrams explained as he worked that these printed circles were logical rather than experimentally established extremes, and that in his experience the circles he had plotted to represent the actual vision fields of his patients had without exception fallen inside the circles printed on the charts. When he finished plotting Bradley's circles, the one for each eye

was larger than the printed model and, in fact, ran completely
outside it.

With both eyes open and looking straight ahead, Bradley sees   44
a hundred and ninety-five degrees on the horizontal and about
seventy degrees straight down, or about fifteen and five degrees
more, respectively, than what is officially considered perfection.
Most surprising, however, is what he can see above him. Focussed
horizontally, the typical perfect eye, according to the chart, can
see about forty-seven degrees upward. Bradley can see seventy
degrees upward. This no doubt explains why he can stare at the
floor while he is waiting for lobbed passes to arrive from above.
Dr. Abrams said that he doubted whether a person who tried to
expand his peripheral vision through exercises could succeed, but
he was fascinated to learn that when Bradley was a young boy
he tried to do just that. As he walked down the main street of
Crystal City, for example, he would keep his eyes focussed straight
ahead and try to identify objects in the windows of stores he was
passing. For all this, however, Bradley cannot see behind himself.
Much of the court and, thus, a good deal of the action are often
invisible to a basketball player, so he needs more than good eyesight.
He needs to know how to function in the manner of a blind man
as well. When, say, four players are massed in the middle of things
behind Bradley, and it is inconvenient for him to look around,
his hands reach back and his fingers move rapidly from shirt to
shirt or hip to hip. He can read the defense as if he were reading
Braille.

Bradley's optical endowments notwithstanding, Coach van Breda   45
Kolff agrees with him that he is "not a great physical player," and
goes on to say, "Others can run faster and jump higher. The
difference between Bill and other basketball players is self-discipline."
The two words that Bradley repeats most often when he talks
about basketball are "discipline" and "concentration," and through
the exercise of both he has made himself an infectious example
to younger players. "Concentrate!" he keeps shouting to himself
when he is practicing on his own. His capacity for self-discipline
is so large that it is almost funny. For example, he was a bit
shocked when the Olympic basketball staff advised the Olympic
basketball players to put in one hour of practice a day during the
summer, because he was already putting in two hours a day—
often in ninety-five-degree temperatures, with his feet squishing
in sneakers that had become so wet that he sometimes skidded
and crashed to the floor. His creed, which he picked up from Ed
Macauley, is "When you are not practicing, remember, someone
somewhere is practicing, and when you meet him he will win."

He also believes that the conquest of pain is essential to any 46
seriously sustained athletic endeavor. In 1963, he dressed for a
game against Harvard although he had a painful foot injury. Then,
during the pregame warmup, it bothered him so much that he
decided to give up, and he started for the bench. He changed his
mind on the way, recalling that a doctor had told him that his
foot, hurt the night before at Dartmouth, was badly bruised but
was not in danger of further damage. If he sat down, he says, he
would have lowered his standards, for he believes that "there has
never been a great athlete who did not know what pain is." So
he played the game. His heavily taped foot went numb during the
first ten minutes, but his other faculties seemed to sharpen in
response to the handicap. His faking quickened to make up for
his reduced speed, and he scored thirty-two points, missing only
five shots during the entire evening.

ROGER ANGELL

In the Country

Baseball is a family for those who care about it, and members 1
of close families like to exchange letters. Three years ago, I received
a letter from a woman named Linda Kittell, who was living in
Clinton, Montana.

"I was born in 1952," she wrote. "I remember listening to the 2
Yankees—with Mel Allen, it must have been—on a little yellow
transistor radio on an island in Lake Champlain, where we spent
our summers. Not listening but sort of doing the everyday things
of an eight- or ten-year-old—drinking chocolate milk and eating
animal crackers—while my sister, two years older, flirted with her
boyfriend, who *listened* to the Yankee games on the yellow radio.
I only paid attention when I heard Mickey Mantle's name or Roger
Maris's name. And I was in love with Whitey Ford. Maris was
hitting home runs as often as we went uptown that summer—
every day. . . .

"I forgot about baseball later, except in September, when I paid 3
attention if the Yankees were close to getting into the Series. I
went to college, and then to graduate school in Montana. One
night in a bar in Missoula, I met a man who just about fell flat

First published in *The New Yorker*, August 17, 1981.

when I complained about the games on the TV set there because
they didn't put on the Yankees enough. He looked at me as if
he'd been struck. You're a *Yankee* fan? I told him I had a perfect
right, because I was from upstate New York and because I'd been
in love with Whitey Ford all my life, practically. Ron was a Mantle
fan (his name is Ron Goble; he's a lanky six foot five), and I
tended more toward Maris, but we both loved Whitey Ford. We
talked and drank beer. He'd played Legion ball for five years in
his home town of Boise, Idaho, and he'd won a baseball scholarship
to Linfield College, in Oregon. He'd been scouted in school by the
Yankees, the Angels, and the Pirates. He's a left-handed pitcher.
His fastball was clocked at more than ninety m.p.h., and he told
me he'd held back on it, at that, because he was afraid of hurting
his arm. He said how he'd recognized the scouts in the stands
because they were all tan in May and June in southern Idaho.
He talked about how he'd come to think a college education was
more important than athletics, and how the student riots in the
late nineteen-sixties had turned him against sports, so he'd stopped
playing. He talked about Vietnam and drugs and what it was like
then, and what a waste it had been for him to forget about ball.

   "We started living together about three years ago. Christmases,   4
birthdays, surprises from me—all those special days had to do with
baseball. A baseball book, a baseball picture, a pack of new baseball
cards—anything. Then last year Seattle got the Mariners. Our vacation from Montana was a twelve-hour train ride and three days'
worth of games—*Yankee* games: the Yankees at the Kingdome. I
cried when I saw them out there. Ron said I was being silly. But,
God, there was Mickey Rivers. I mean, Mickey Rivers! . . .

   "The third day, I found a sympathetic usher who let me stand   5
down close to the field with about ten little kids trying to get
autographs. I lied through my teeth and said one of them was my
little brother. Sparky Lyle and Catfish and Chambliss were playing
pepper, and then a player out beyond them called, 'Hey, you girl!'
I looked up. 'Yeah, you,' and he threw me a ball. Paul Blair threw
me a baseball. All the little boys waist-high around me looked
disgusted. 'Why'd he throw *her* a ball?' . . . 'Mom, Dad, that one
threw that *girl* a ball.' It was an Official American League ball. I
read it over and rushed up to my seat, where Ron was waiting
for the game to start. 'It's a real ball,' I told him. '*Look* at it.' There
I was, a perfectly sensible, sensitive twenty-four-year-old woman
getting goose bumps over a baseball. I asked Ron if I should go
down for more autographs, but something had changed. He rubbed
the ball and kept looking at it. He was years away, and sad about
it. . . . I went back down, and the autograph I got in the end was

Elston Howard's. Memory and imagination make you think about anything you want. I'd picked Ellie Howard—and not Mickey Rivers or Catfish Hunter or Thurman Munson—because I thought it would make him happy, and because his name reminded me of my little yellow radio back in Vermont on August afternoons. Because I'm sentimental.

"We drove back to Montana with a friend, and Ron and I sat   6
in the back seat. 'Can I see the ball again?' he said. I handed it to him and watched Ron hold it for a fastball, a slider, a curve. He looked far-off still. . . .

"This spring, there was an article in *The Sporting News* about a   7
Class A team being formed in Boise, called the Buckskins. Tryouts were in June, and you needed three thousand dollars from a sponsor if you made the team. Something different, all right, but it was a chance to play ball. They'd signed the Sundown Kid— Danny Thomas—and a twenty-seven-year-old catcher from southern Idaho. I wanted Ron to go down and try out. He said he wasn't in shape. He said he was happy playing on the Clinton Clowns, our town's fast-pitch softball team. It was obvious that he *wasn't* happy playing softball, and especially obvious in the fall, when he'd pitch by himself—pitch baseball by throwing rotten apples from our tree against a telephone pole, and call balls and strikes, hits and outs. . . ."

Linda persuaded Ron to try out for the Buckskins, but he didn't   8
get around to it until a few days before their season was about to begin. A letter from the Buckskin manager, Gerry Craft, said they were looking for a left-handed pitcher, and that did the trick.

"Our truck broke down," Linda's letter went on. "Planes were   9
on strike. Finally, Ron's brother George drove him down. Ron was signed on the first day he threw—a good rotation on his curveball, they said. I didn't even know what Ron meant by that when he told me about it by long-distance. Gerry Craft had said he could go far in baseball, but what Gerry didn't know was that Ron had thrown his arm out—just about ruined it, it turned out— with the second curve he'd thrown. So Ron waited, in ice packs. Three days later, he came home with a swollen arm and a professional baseball player's contract. Five hundred dollars a month. We started packing up his stuff and spent long hours looking for a sponsor. We ended up putting up our own money. Three thousand dollars may not sound like much to some people, but it was everything we had. I served Ron a steak dinner and kissed him goodbye.

"I don't think it really sank in until I made the trip down to   10
Boise to see the Buckskins play in their first home stand. Ron was

standing there in his tan-and-black uniform, with a satin warmup jacket and real cleats, and I was just as excited about that as I'd been when I saw Mickey Rivers on the field in Seattle. I was goofy. . . .

"Now, anyone will tell you that this Buckskins team is different. 11 The general manager, Lanny Moss [Lanny Moss is a woman], is very religious, and so is Gerry Craft. In right field at their park there's a huge billboard with 'JESUS' written on it in twelve-foot letters. In left field there's a strange picture of Christ Himself. Craft says he had a vision that told him to look around Spokane for a cabin in the woods, and that's where he found Danny Thomas, the Sundown Kid. Danny left major-league ball [Thomas, an out-fielder, had played for two seasons with the Brewers] because his religion required him to read the Bible from sundown Friday to sundown Saturday, which meant he mostly couldn't play on those days. And Craft has game strategy confirmed to him by the Bible, and stuff. Some of his ballplayers have been baptized on their road trips—I picture a clean white sink at the Salem Inn as the font, with the neat sample Ivory soap tablets resting at the side. But these ballplayers are the nicest people I've ever met.

"I'm not the typical wife/girlfriend of a baseball player—those 12 women you see on TV with their hair done up and their Rose Bowl Parade wave to the crowds. I like to watch baseball. I love the game, and I'm one of the loudest fans in the stands. And when Ron's pitching I find myself almost praying for a win. But the Buckskins don't win many games. The newspapers around the league have put too much stress on the religious aspect of the team. The players aren't all Jesus people. Most of them drink beer and swear. Gerry Craft rhubarbs with the umps with his hands in his jacket pockets. Danny Thomas hits a grand-slammer half an hour before sunset and trots around the bases on his way to his Bible. It's all wonderful. The beer, the hot dogs with everything on them, and seeing old Ron Goble out on the mound working on his curveball and about to turn twenty-seven. What a good way to turn twenty-seven—finally doing something you've tried to ignore for eight years. I love it. It's a hit in the bottom of the ninth, with the score tied and the ball sailing over the rightfield wall.''

I answered this letter, needless to say, and in time Linda wrote 13 back. We became baseball correspondents and baseball friends. She wrote in October that year and told me about the rest of the Buckskins' season. The team had gone bad, at one point losing eleven straight games. Money was short, and the team's religious fervor made for difficulties. After the Buckskins suffered a 25–3 loss to the Salem Senators, Gerry Craft released the losing pitcher, saying that God had made it clear to him that He didn't want that pitcher on the team. In Eugene, Oregon, Craft announced that God had told him they were going to lose a game to the Emeralds, and, sure enough, they did, blowing a 6–4 lead in the ninth. Some of the benchwarmers on the club began to wonder if they were being kept on the roster because of their three-thousand-dollar sponsor deposits—an inevitable development, perhaps. The Buckskins finished last in the Northwest League, fourteen games behind their divisional winner, Eugene, and twenty-five games worse than the eventual champions, the Gray's Harbor (Washington) Loggers. Danny Thomas led the league with a .359 batting average, but the Buckskins had the worst pitching in the league—a club earned-run average of 6.42. Ron Goble wound up with a 2–3 record and an earned-run average of 8.18—his lifetime figures in professional baseball.

There were some good moments, even in a season like that.   14

"I went down to Boise in August," Linda wrote in that next   15
letter. "Ron met me at the airport, and we went straight to the field. There was talk that Charlie Finley had sent for the Sundowner, to help his Oakland A's, and talk that two new pitchers were coming from Milwaukee. It was hot—a hundred degrees, easy. I sat in the only shade in the ballpark and watched batting practice. Danny Thomas was running around with a coonskin cap on, and Bo McConnaughy, one of my favorites on the team, came out in a bright-yellow hard hat. Bo was the Buckskins' shortstop—a ballplayers' ballplayer. He had been in the minor leagues for years, in the Orioles organization—the wrong place at the wrong time, because the Orioles had a shortstop named Mark Belanger. Then Bo had gotten too old to be of any interest to them. Bo loves baseball, and you don't notice his gray hair until he's back in street clothes.

"Raymie Odermott started the game against Bend that night,   16
and went six and two-thirds innings, until Gerry brought in Ron with the score 4–3, Boise. Two outs, men on first and second. Ron went in, and this left-hand batter was waiting for him and got a hit that tied the score. Boise scored two runs in the seventh and one in the eighth, and Ron held Bend scoreless the rest of the game, striking out their last two batters. Just fine.

"He was off in the ozone the rest of the night. He sat over a   17
beer with friends, quietly reviewing the game. His curveball had been right for the first time since the June tryout. We both thought—or hoped, I suppose—that the days of Tenderyl and the threat of

cortisone were over. It's hard to explain how happy he was that night. It's as if he believed for a moment that he wasn't eight years too late. . . .

"Still, there were rumblings on the team. Pitchers went to Gerry   18
and complained that they didn't get to pitch. Mark Garland was one, and he got to start. He got blown away. The next night, it was Dennis Love, who'd also complained. He looked real bad, too, and Gerry brought in Ron. Ron let up a home run—to the first batter. It was a bad time. The next day, at batting practice, Dennis Love said he'd been released, along with Mark Garland. Ron went in to talk to Gerry about *his* future, and I drove down to the Circle K to get some pop. Mark Garland was crying beside a bridge over an irrigation canal. And I hoped I wouldn't end up comforting Ron some day, squeezing his hand and talking softly to him, the way Mark's wife stood comforting him.

"The last two weeks of the season, the team played without   19
pay, until Lanny Moss could borrow the money to pay their checks. Danny Thomas left, saying he wasn't going to play ball for free. There was no money for hotels or food. Once, the bus broke down, and the team had to sleep on the floor of a church. They left on a last road trip to Victoria and Bellingham. I went up to visit friends in Seattle and to catch some of the Bellingham games. The Kingdome didn't wow me so much this time. The Yankees were there again, but I knew more about people on the field than I used to. I got Ron Guidry's autograph, and I still loved Mickey Rivers, but it was different. People, not heroes. In Bellingham, I spent a rainy evening watching 'Monday Night Baseball' with Ron and Bo. Then I danced with all the team, at Bellingham's imitation disco.

"Season's over. Ron's been back a month. Two weeks ago, he   20
went grouse hunting with the dogs and a friend, and came home tipsy drunk. He'd remembered his doctor's appointment the next day, and had spent his time trying to forget about it. He made a mock pitch for me, and his elbow *clicked* at the end of the motion. He said, 'At least, Gerry Craft told me I could have been in the bigs. I know that much. It's enough.'

"A shot of cortisone and rest. Ron doesn't lie to the scouts about   21
his age, you know. He and Bo are honest about that. We have tons of fallen apples, if Ron's arm starts to come around. Bo's in Boise, studying to be a mechanic. Gerry's been released. Everybody's waiting through the winter."

There were more letters back and forth. It meant a lot to me   22
to hear from someone—from two people, really—who could tell

me what baseball was like far from the crowds and the noise and the fame and the big money that I had been writing about for many summers. And by this time, of course, I cared about Ron and Linda, and worried about what would happen to them. Linda wrote me that Ron and his brother George and a friend named Ray were spending a great deal of their time that winter playing an extremely complicated baseball-by-dice game called Extra Innings. From time to time, Ron would get out his mitt and persuade someone to catch him, but when he threw, in gingerly fashion, he found that his elbow was still horribly painful. He couldn't get over how foolish he had been to throw that hard curve during his Buckskins tryout. He read a book by Jim Bouton, in which Bouton said that his sore arm felt as if it had been bitten by alligators; Ron's felt exactly the same way. The Buckskins, in any case, had folded. The Phillies had expressed some interest in picking them up as a farm team, but the city of Boise would not refurbish its ancient ballpark, so the Phillies went elsewhere. Then the Northwest League adopted a rule favoring younger players and making it harder for older players to find a place on its team rosters—the last blow for Ron. That winter, he sent letters to all the major-league clubs asking for some kind of employment in their organizations, but the answers were a long time coming back. He told Linda he had really been collecting major-league letterheads. Linda described an evening of theirs on the town, and its ending: "We walked through the streets of Missoula in the 4 A.M. drizzle, Ron in his Buckskin jacket and me feeling very maudlin, remembering the walk from the field to the Buckskins' dressing room. What fun it was being a Baseball Annie, arm in arm with some semblance of a professional ballplayer, rain drizzling on my arm and on the satin warm-up jacket. How romantic and far away it seems now."

At about this time, I wrote an article about the difficulties that women sports reporters had experienced in gaining access to the clubhouses of major-league ball teams on their beat, and Linda commented on that, too: "Oh, as to women in the clubhouse, I think they're a necessity. Why, this summer when the Buckskins got locked out of their locker room, I was the only one who could fit through the window and over the top row of the lockers, to unlock the door. And for that one quiet moment between lockers and door I imagined myself in uniform, imagined the feel of oiled leather and dust, the long trip from this town to the next." 23

There was a long trip just ahead for Ron and Linda—from Montana to northwestern Vermont, where they moved into a farmhouse about forty miles from Burlington: "It took us six days 24 to drive across the country in a calico Chevy truck, with the two dogs in back and a U-Haul in back of that. I think the only thing that got Ron across the plains was the radio reception. We kept tuning in game after game, from all the big-league cities along the way, including a French-Canadian station, near the end, with the Expos on it. French baseball cracked me up. We're close to Montreal here, and we went to an Expos-Cardinals doubleheader last weekend. Saw Cash's grand slam and drank Canadian beer. Ron was frustrated by the French and English announcements— a whole bunch of French with 'Ellis Valentine' in the middle of it. Whenever the Expos did anything, the French-Canadians sitting around us would slap each other on the back and pull on their pints of vodka."

Linda had come East to be closer to her family for a while. (She was born in Troy, New York, and Burlington is on Lake Champlain, where she passed those early summers listening to the Yankees.) She went to work as a feature writer and sports editor for a Vermont newspaper, the *Lamoille County Weekly*. The main object, she wrote me, was to get as many players' names as possible into her stories, so that their mothers would buy the paper. "I have a funny press pass that the publisher made up," she added. "It's an attempt to make me seem very professional, but the publisher, who's an old friend of mine, can't spell very well. 'This card,' it says, 'entitles the barer . . .' It didn't get me into the press room in Montreal."

Ron was working as a carpenter and a substitute high-school teacher, and he and Linda were excited by the discovery that Burlington had a team (more than one team, it turned out) in a local semi-pro league. Ron hoped to play there—hoped to pitch, in fact, if he got any help from a local orthopedist who was said to specialize in sports medicine. "We'll see," Linda concluded. "I'd rather see Ron pitching and playing than substituting Great Civilization." She urged me to come and visit them, and watch Ron pitch.

I put it in my mind to keep that date—it would be the coming summer, the summer of 1980—but the next letter changed my plans. Ron had cancer. They had found a lump in his abdomen, which was removed by surgery. Subsequently, he underwent another operation and lost one testicle. It was seminoma—a highly curable form of the disease, the doctors said. Ron was going into the Burlington hospital every day for radiation treatments. "I can't stand to see him hooked up to all those tubes in the hospital, and worried about how he's going to look in the locker room," Linda wrote. "I'm not sure I understand why it is that good people and athletes can be struck this way. It's pretty weird, is all. But Ron is unflappable. He's out pitching snowballs at trees and making plans to play on the Burlington team somehow. But I have a feeling it's going to take a lot to get the boy in shape this spring. Street & Smith's are out [the early-season baseball yearbook]. Ron and his buddies are ranking the teams and giving them their finishing places this year. Winner gets a six-pack from each loser."

Ron Goble had a good summer, though—much better than he 28 or anyone else had expected. In May and June, he coached a team of thirteen-to-fifteen-year-olds in the local Babe Ruth League, and at the same time he tried out for the Burlington A's, in the semi-pro Northern League, and made the club. For a time, he was so weak from the effects of his illness and the radiation that he could pitch no more than two or three innings at a stretch, but he learned how to conserve his energy by warming up only briefly and by trying to throw ground-ball outs. By the end of the brief season, he was able to pitch a full game, and he wound up with a respectable 4–1 record. He never told anyone on the club, last year or this year, that he had had cancer. Last winter, he worked as a teacher's aide at the Bellows Free Academy, in St. Albans, Vermont, and as a custodian at the local rink, but most of his energy went into an attempt to organize a new Northern League club in St. Albans. It fell through—not enough local money, not enough local commercial enthusiasm—but by springtime Ron had been signed on as a regional commission scout by the Milwaukee Brewers (Gerry Craft, his old manager, was a Brewers district scout, and had recommended Ron), and he was umpiring high-school games. He would pitch again for the A's this summer. Linda was teaching humanities courses at the local community college. Things were looking good; they wanted me to drive up and see them.

The bad news, Linda wrote, had come earlier and from far away: 29 Danny Thomas had hanged himself in a jail cell in Alabama, where he had been facing trial on a rape charge. "It came as a real shock," Linda wrote. "What bothers me is that baseball has been a savior for Ron. Last spring, it brought back his confidence in himself and in his body. And here's someone like Danny Thomas who saw baseball as his pain. Danny had a strange look in his eyes when he talked about religion, and reporters were always after him to talk about his beliefs. Everyone knew he was slightly wacko, but the man had principles. His wife, Judy, was really afraid he'd take Charlie Finley up on that offer to come back to major-league ball. She said she couldn't stand that stuff again.

Ron says Danny could hit a baseball farther than anyone he's ever seen. I saw him hit a home run out of every ballpark where I saw the Buckskins play. The last day I saw him play was in Bellingham. It was raining, and Danny's little daughter, Renee, was sitting up in the bleachers with Gerry Craft's daughter, Maizee, and singing 'Take me out to the ballgame, take me out to the ballgame,' slapping their hands on their thighs. The girls didn't know any of the other words, so they sang that over and over again.''

On a cool, windy-bright Saturday at the end of last June, I drove straight north through Connecticut, through Massachusetts, and into Vermont, crossing and recrossing the narrowing Connecticut River along the way, and at last, over the river one more time, I found the Burlington A's at play against the Walpole (New Hampshire) Blue Jays on the Walpole home field—a neat little American Legion diamond just beneath a steep, thickly wooded hillside, hard by the Hubbard Farms fertilizer plant. At play and then *not* at play, since the A's had knocked off the Jays, 4–1, at the moment of my arrival, in the first game of a doubleheader. I met Linda Kittell at the field—a dark-haired young woman in faded bluejeans, with pale eyes, an open, alert expression, and an enormous smile. Then I shook hands with the A's manager, Paul Farrar; with Paul's wife, Sue; and, at last, with Ron Goble—a pitcher, all right: long arms, long hands, long body, very long legs, a sun-burnished nose, a surprising blondish Fu Manchu mustache, a shy smile, and one bulging cheek (not tobacco, it turned out, but sunflower seeds). Ron and Paul said what a shame it was I'd missed the opener, and then quickly ducked back out onto the field and into their little concrete dugout to get ready for the next one—Ron to chart pitches and keep score (he would pitch the next day, down in Brattleboro), and his skipper, of course, to worry. Linda and I sat down in an upper row of a tiny rack of bleachers in short right field. We had no trouble finding seats. My quick count of the house, after the nightcap had begun, came to thirty-three, including babies in strollers. Several young women—players' wives or players' girlfriends, probably—were lying on blankets spread out behind the backstop, where they took turns slathering each other's backs with suntan goop. Near the Walpole dugout, a ten- or twelve-year-old girl on an aluminum camp chair watched the game in company with a big chocolate-brown Labrador, holding him out of the action (and breaking his heart) with a yellow leash. Whenever a foul ball flew past us, someone in the audience would get up and amble after it, while we in the bleachers called out directions

30

("More right, more right—*now* another step!") until it had been tracked down in the thick meadow weeds around the field. There was a lot of clapping and cries of encouragement ("Good eye, batter! Good eye!") from the little crowd, and between batters and innings you could hear the cool, gusty northwest wind working through the green treetop canopies of ash and oak and maple on the hillside out beyond right field.

In the first inning, the Walpole batters whacked some long drives against the visitors' starting pitcher, and some short ones, too, and pretty soon Burlington's designated hitter, Darcy Spear, came out of the dugout and began warming up with a catcher—not a good turn of events, Linda told me, because the team had been able to scrape up only four pitchers for its two-day, four-game weekend road trip here to the southern end of the league. The players had driven down in their own cars and pickups, but the team, she said, would pay for their motel accommodations in Brattleboro that night. There were no programs, and I was lucky to have Linda there to identify some of the A's whose style afield or at the plate I was beginning to pick up—a diminutive second baseman, Greg Wells, who had a nice way of looking the ball into his glove on grounders; a strong-armed shortstop named Rob DelBianco; and Tinker Jarvis, at third, who had driven in a pair of runs in the top of the first inning with a line-drive double and then singled sharply in the third. The A's wore the same combination of garish buttercup-yellow shirts, white pants, and white shoes first made famous by the Oakland A's, while the Walpole nine sported a variation of Toronto Blue Jays home whites, but there was no connection between these local teams and their big-league name-sakes, Linda explained; rather, the manufacturer supplying the Northern League had offered bargain rates on these pre-styled uniforms—sort of like a Seventh Avenue dress house knocking off mass copies of Diors and Balmains. A distinguishing feature of this particular summer line was the names of various home-town commercial sponsors that the players wore on their backs, and before long I realized that I had begun to identify the different A's players by these billboards rather than by the names that Linda had murmured to me. Thus Darcy Spear became Uncle Sam's Dairy Bar, and it was Coca-Cola, the left-handed first baseman, who kept up a patter of encouraging talk to Red Barn on the mound (Red Barn had settled down after that first inning), while Slayton's Roofing (Manager Farrar) paced up and down in front of his dugout and waited for a chance to send the large and menacing-looking Cake World up to pinch-hit and get something started out there. Linda said it was all right for me to think of the players this way, because they often called each other by the sponsors' names anyway, for fun—except for Ron (Community Bingo), who was called Pigeon, because of his sunflower seeds. The A's players had been expected to hunt up their own sponsors at the beginning of the season, but not all of them, I noticed, had been successful. Each sponsor had put up a hundred dollars for his walking (or running and throwing, and sometimes popping-up-in-the-clutch) advertisement, and each sponsored player had sewn on his own commercial or had prevailed upon someone else—his mother, perhaps—to sew it on for him.

The Northern League, which encompasses six teams—the Bur-   32
lington A's, the Burlington Expos, the South Burlington Queen City Royals, the Walpole Blue Jays, the Brattleboro Maples, and the Saxtons River Pirates—and also plays against the Glens Falls (New York) Glensox, is a semi-professional circuit, with the stronger emphasis, I had begun to understand, falling on the "semi." In the distant past, semi-pro ball teams were often composed of skilled local amateurs plus a handful of ringers—a couple of hard-hitting rookie outfielders just starting on their professional careers, perhaps, or a wily, shopworn pro pitcher at the very end of his—who played for modest salaries, or even for a flat per-game fee. This system fell into difficulties when increasing numbers of young athletes began to go off to college, where they found that they were not permitted to play varsity ball, because their semi-pro experience had compromised their status as amateurs. An earlier, extremely popular Northern League, with teams at Burlington, Montpelier, Rutland, St. Johnsbury, and other northwestern New England towns, came apart in 1952, partly because its Big Ten college stars were withdrawn by their schools to prevent the loss of their amateur status, and thus never appeared in games with professionals of the likes of Johnny Antonelli, Robin Roberts, Ray Scarborough, Snuffy Stirnweiss, Johnny Podres, and Boo Ferriss, who had all played on its diamonds at one time or another before moving on up through the minors and then to fame and success as major-leaguers. Nowadays, many semi-pro teams simply find summer jobs for their players—a lumber company, let's say, putting a college fastball pitcher to work in the drying sheds by day so that he may advertise the concern out on the mound at the town field by night or on weekend afternoons—but only the Burlington Expos, who are looked upon as the Yankees of the Northern League, had managed to arrange this kind of tie-in this summer, and then only for a few of their players.

The Northern League is an independent body, with its own   33
commissioner, its own set of rules (the d.h., aluminum bats for

those who want to use them), and its own ways (including a ritual handshake between the players on rival clubs at the conclusion of every game—a pleasing custom probably lifted from the National Hockey League, whose teams line up and shake hands at the conclusion of each Stanley Cup elimination series). The six clubs play an official two-month schedule, from late May to late July, with playoffs and a championship series thereafter—about twenty-five or twenty-seven games each, with a good number of additional, informal, outside-the-standings games thrown in whenever they can be arranged. A minimum team budget, I learned, runs about three thousand dollars, and, beyond the obvious expenditures for equipment, goes for umpires (two umps, at twenty-five dollars each, for every game), a league fee of two hundred dollars (to keep statistics, handle publicity, and stage the league's All-Star Game), a modest insurance policy covering minor player injuries, and so forth. Income, beyond sponsorships, comes from ticket sales—a dollar for adults, fifty cents for children, babies and dogs free. The Burlington A's' entire season's operation probably costs less than a major-league team's bill for adhesive tape and foul balls during a week's play, but the Northern League, now in its third year, is doing well and expects to add at least two more clubs next summer.

All semi-pro leagues, it should be understood, are self-sustaining, and have no farm affiliation or other connection with the twenty-six major-league clubs, or with the seventeen leagues and hundred and fifty-two teams (ranging from Rookie League at the lowest level, to Class A and Summer Class A, up to the AAA designation at the highest) that make up the National Association—the minors, that is. There is no central body of semi-pro teams, and semi-pro players are not included among the six hundred and fifty major-leaguers, the twenty-five hundred-odd minor-leaguers, plus all the managers, coaches, presidents, commissioners, front-office people, and scouts, who, taken together, constitute the great tent called organized ball. (A much diminished tent, at that; back in 1949, the minors included fifty-nine leagues, about four hundred and forty-eight teams, and perhaps ten thousand players.) Also outside the tent, but perhaps within its shade, are five college leagues, ranging across the country from Cape Cod to Alaska, where the most promising freshman, sophomore, and junior-college ballplayers may compete against each other in the summertime without losing their amateur status; the leagues are administered by the National Collegiate Athletic Association and receive indirect support—bats, balls, uniforms, and the like—from the major leagues, whose scouts keep a careful eye on their young stars. If the college leagues are semi-pro, the accent there probably should fall on the second word, for a considerable number of their best batters and pitchers are snapped up in the major-league amateur draft toward the end of their college careers. Scouts cover the Northern League as well— two pitchers with the Burlington Expos were signed to professional contracts this June, and they moved along at once to join their assigned minor-league clubs—but the level of play is not up to that of the college leagues. Most of the A's players, I learned in time, are undergraduates or recent graduates of local or eastern colleges (five of them from the University of Vermont, one from the University of New Hampshire, one from Amherst, one from the University of New Haven, and so on) who play for the fun of the game and the heat of the competition, and perhaps with half an eye turned toward the stands between pitches, in search of a major-league scout sitting there one afternoon who might just possibly be writing notes about this one good-looking outfielder or batter out there, whom he had somehow passed over the first time around. Ron Goble, at twenty-nine, was the oldest regular with the Burlington A's, and one of the few players in the league with any experience in professional ball.

How well did the A's play baseball? I found the question a 35 difficult one at first, for the over-all quality of play in any one game tends to blur one's baseball judgment, but it did seem plain that most of the young players here on the Walpole ball field were far too slow afoot to merit comparison with professionals. Some threw well, as I have said, and others attacked the ball at the plate with consistency and power, but these two gifts did not seem to coexist in any one player. Most of all, the A's seemed young. They were all extremely cheerful, and, as I now found out, they loved to win. Down a run in their last at-bats (the seventh inning, in this doubleheader), the A's put their lead-off man aboard on a walk and instantly moved him up with a dazzling bunt by second baseman Greg Wells, who also knocked the catcher's peg out of the first baseman's mitt as he crossed the bag, and was safe. A moment later, with the bases loaded, Uncle Sam's Dairy Bar (Darcy Spear) whacked a single, good for two runs, and then the commercially anonymous catcher (Bob Boucher) tripled to deep center. Walpole, whose handful of wives and parents had gone speechless with dismay, changed pitchers, but Churchill's (Tinker Jarvis) singled, too, and before it was over the visiting A's had scored six runs and won the game, 9–4, sweeping the doubleheader. Ron Goble, ambling over to join us, hugged Linda and grinned at me and asked if I couldn't take the rest of the summer off to watch the A's and thus bring them through the rest of their season undefeated.

Steve Gallacher pitched the opener against the Brattleboro Maples   36
the next afternoon—a strong twenty-two-year-old right-hander
with a good, live fastball. The A's took up their hitting where they
had left off the previous evening and moved smartly to a three-
run lead in the top of the first. Linda and I sat in the last row of
the grandstand, behind the decaying foul screen; it was a high-
school field, a bit seedy but with a nice view to the south of some
distant farms and silos and long fields of young corn sloping down
toward the Connecticut River.

Linda told me that Steve Gallacher was said to have been the   37
last man cut at a Pirates' tryout camp a year or two ago, and later
had a Dodger scout on his trail, although nothing had come of
it. I asked her how many people in the league still hoped to make
a career in professional ball someday.

"If you have a chance, you have to see it through," she said   38
at once. "It doesn't mean anything if you don't do something
about it—really find out. So many of these players are unrealistic
to think they could ever play minor-league ball. They go out and
buy these expensive A's warmup jackets, which they can't really
afford. I can see them all seventy-five years from now, saying,
'Well, I used to play semi-pro ball. And Ron will probably be
saying, 'I pitched this one great game for the Boise Buckskins.'
I'd like to see something better than that for him in the end. Ron
is always looking backward, and I think I like to look ahead.
When he goes out scouting for the Brewers, he watches pitchers
a lot, and maybe left-handed pitchers most of all. I think he still
thinks he's better than most of the young pitchers he scouts."

She had been talking in an edged, hard tone I had not heard   39
before, but now she stopped and shook her head and then laughed
at herself a little—a habit of hers, I had begun to notice. "I guess
Ron is even more of a hero to me than Whitey Ford was," she
said more softly. "I like heroes. I have a lot of trouble with reality,
too. I hate it when he plays softball, because all the other players
on his team take it so seriously. Softball is—well, it's like badminton,
or something. It's nothing, compared to baseball. I've told Ron
he'll have to give up baseball when he looks better in his street
clothes than he does in his uniform." She laughed again—almost
a giggle. "He's still a long way from *that!*" she said.

We watched the game for a while, but Linda seemed tense and   40
distracted, and it came to me at last that she was worrying about

how well Ron would pitch in the second game. Suddenly she said, "With all the people I've known in baseball, I can't think of one happy ending. Danny Thomas, Gerry Craft, Ron—none of it came out happily. You know, it isn't like Chris Chambliss coming up in the ninth inning of that playoff game and unbuttoning the top button of his shirt and then hitting that home run. You just don't see that happen. Ron hurt his arm before he got started. Gerry Craft got up as far as Lodi, in the Orioles system, and he was on his way—a good outfielder. Then he got hurt and it was all finished, overnight. Danny Thomas is dead. What's the reality? I ask myself that all the time."

The Brattleboro hitters kept after Steve Gallacher, and then caught   41
up with him and went ahead by 5–4 in the bottom of the fifth, with three solid blows. They were looking for his fastball by this time, and I wondered what would happen if he could show them a breaking pitch now and then in a tough spot. Young pitchers love the heater, but so do good young hitters. The A's put their lead-off man aboard in the top of the seventh, but the Maples' pitcher, a young redhead named Parmenter, threw some impressive-looking sliders and shut off the rally. It was a quick, well-played game, and the local fans—a much better turnout today—gave their boys a good hand at the end.

Ron Goble started the second game, and I found that I was a   42
bit nervous, too. I needn't have worried. He set down the side in order in the first, and even though the Maples touched him up for a pair of runs in the second, on a walk and a couple of singles, he looked unstressed and in control out there, never attempting to force a delivery or to work beyond his capacities. He ended up the inning by fanning the side—a good sign. He is a graceful-looking pitcher. My game notes about him read:

> Tall, v. long legs. Minimal rock & motion. Drops glove behind leg-crook (southpaw). Long upper-bod. and uses good upper-bod. with fastball. Fastball just fair. Good curve. Goes sidearm at times for strikeout. About ¾ otherwise. Good pitcher's build. Control fair. Long stride but doesn't drop down. Curve/slider break down. Changes speed w/o effort. Sense of flow. Pitches patterned. Intell. Knows how to pitch.

On this particular day, Ron also had the A's hitters going for   43
him, for they came up with six runs in the third and six more in the sixth, the latter outburst including two singles, a nifty squeeze bunt, a double, a pinch-hit triple by Cake World, and a home run by Coca-Cola. The last batter of the inning was Manager Paul Farrar, who sent himself up as a pinch-hitter now that matters were in hand. He is a friendly, medium-sized man with curly hair

and metal-rimmed glasses—he is also a backup catcher for the club—and his players razzed him happily when he stepped up to the plate, calling him Satch and asking if he didn't want the Maples' pitcher to throw from farther back out there. He fanned, to raucous cheers. The A's won it by 16–4—a laugher, but Ron had pitched well, surrendering only four hits. Near the end, Linda began to relax a little in her seat. At one point, she saw me watching her, and she laughed and shrugged. "Ron's mother used to tell me what to do when he was pitching," she said. "She always said, 'Watch the ball, not the pitcher. Never look at the pitcher.' I wish I could remember that."

Ron and Linda live in a worn brown farmhouse next to a 44
collapsing gray shingle barn, at the very end of a twisting, climbing two-mile-long dirt road. On a map, they are in the upper northwest corner of the state. St. Albans, the nearest real town, is fifteen miles to the west, on the shore of Lake Champlain, and the Canadian border is about the same distance due north. The house, which they rent, is on the side of a hill (*everything* in Vermont is on the side of a hill) and is set about with maples, an elderly lilac bush, and a high stand of burdock. Ron's vegetable garden is up the hill, behind the house. There is a small unpainted front porch with missing steps, which makes it look a little like the front stoop of a sharecropper's place. No matter: the view from here is across many miles of hazy-green rolling farmland toward some distant blue mountains. There isn't much furniture inside—a few castoff schoolroom chairs, with iron pedestal bases, that stand around the dining table, and one overflowing easy chair. The most prominent object is a modern cast-iron heating stove, right in the middle of the room, with a long outlet pipe snaking up through the ceiling. Upstairs, the bathroom has been recently panelled and fitted out with a shower. The best room in the house is a sun-filled upstairs bedroom, five windows wide. A cluster of sports pennants is pinned to one wall there, with their points all streaming to starboard, as if in a stiff breeze: the Mariners, the Yankees, Idaho U., the Clinton Clowns (Ron's old softball team), and one banner with a misshapen felt baseball and the words "I'm a Backer" (a Buckskin backer, that is) on it. On the opposite wall, there is a framed Idaho potato bag depicting (as best one can depict on burlap) a full-rigged ship and inscribed "Tradewind Brand." Linda's desk and Selectric are under one window, next to an overflowing bookshelf: contemporary poets (she writes poetry), classics, English Lit. textbooks—everything. On one windowsill, a philodendron is growing in a small white pot in the shape of a baseball shoe; on another rests a narrow

cardboard box containing the complete 1981 Topps bubble-gum baseball-card collection. At the other end of the room, another bookcase offers a considerable paperback collection of contemporary Latin-American fiction, in translation: Borges, García Márquez, Jorge Amado, Machado de Assis, and others. These, I learned, are Ron's. "When I finished my season with the Buckskins, I was told my arm might heal if I could rest it long enough," he told me, "and I began to fantasize that it *would* heal. It was an excuse not to work, so I just sat and read. I was reading García Márquez's 'Leaf Storm' just then, and when I finished that I read 'One Hundred Years of Solitude' and then 'The Autumn of the Patriarch.' I drank a lot of Colombian coffee while I read, and it was like I'd gone off to another country."

When Ron Goble graduated from Capital High School in Boise 45 in the spring of 1969, he accepted a fifteen-hundred-dollar baseball scholarship at Linfield, a small (one thousand students) college in McMinnville, Oregon. He had been an outstanding player in his local American Legion baseball program for several summers (young ballplayers who start in the Little Leagues at the age of eight may graduate to the Babe Ruth League at the age of thirteen and then move along to American Legion teams at sixteen), and he had been named to the all-state team in his senior year at school, as a first baseman. His pitching arm began to mature at about the same time, and when his fastball was clocked at better than ninety miles an hour the scouts began to take notice of him. When he went to Linfield, his real hope was not just to pitch for the varsity team there but to find a more relaxed and varied social and political atmosphere. At Capital High, sports and unquestioning patriotism had seemed to go hand in hand. Capital's teams were known as the Eagles, and varsity athletes were told to keep their hair cut in the "Eagle-pride" style—so short that it couldn't be parted— and there was constant pressure on the larger and quicker boys to make their major school commitment to the football team. Ron played tight end and safety and sometimes quarterback for the Eagles, but he didn't much like football; he was also made uncomfortable by the fact that his own sport, baseball, was considered effete—"sort of a pansy game," as he put it. But things weren't much different at Linfield, he discovered. The jocks there were expected to keep their hair cut short, too, and to think more about winning seasons than about Vietnam and Cambodia and the other political and social crises that were convulsing the nation at the time. Ron was not an activist, but his parents—his father is a state fire-insurance inspector—had always encouraged their three sons to think for themselves. Ron's older brother, Dale, had been an undergraduate at Columbia during the student riots there in 1968, and had brought home tapes he had recorded of the impassioned speeches and the crowd roars during those tumultuous days, and Ron had played these over many times. He was an athlete but he was also a reader and a student, and he felt isolated at Linfield. Early in May of his freshman year, he heard the news of the appalling events at Kent State University, and he and five or six friends went to the Linfield student-union building and lowered the flags there, in honor of the demonstrating students who had been shot by National Guardsmen in Ohio. Only two or three people of the hundreds who walked by stopped to ask what the lowered flags meant, and the next day one of Ron's coaches told him that he had "the wrong orientation" about politics. The next fall, Ron transferred to the University of Idaho and gave up varsity sports.

Ron told me all this in a quiet, almost apologetic manner. His voice is modulated and unforced, and somehow suggests his pitching motion. Like some other young men and women of his generation, or quarter-generation, he takes pains never to sound assured, never to strike an attitude. "I wasn't a real political dissident, you understand," he said. "I cared—I still care—but I didn't know what I was doing. At Idaho, I went down to the R.O.T.C. Building one night and stole Richard Nixon's picture out of its frame there. Big piddly-assed deal." 46

He laughed, and Linda joined in the laughter. We were sitting out on their porch, drinking beer, and their two English setters, Boone and Hannah, were running and sniffing through an overgrown meadow before us, with their feathery white tails marking their progress through the long grass. Once, Boone got on the trail of something and took off downhill, but Ron turned him with a piercing, two-fingered whistle. 47

"Tell about the time you decided to go back and play ball," Linda said. 48

"Oh, geezum," Ron said, smiling. "Well, after a while there at Moscow"—Moscow, Idaho, is the university seat—"I began to reconcile sports and politics a little, and I saw that I wasn't quite the great political radical I'd thought I was. For a while, I'd even stopped collecting baseball cards, but I sure missed playing ball, especially in the spring, and so one day I went down to see the baseball coach. I was going to offer to come out, if he wanted me, but when I got there his office was closed, and I took that as a sign. I decided it wasn't my karma to play ball yet." 49

"It wasn't your *karma!*" Linda said, doubled over with laughter. "Can you *believe* that now!" They cracked up, thinking about it. 50

In his last two years at Idaho, Ron lived with two friends on a   51
farm twenty-six miles away from the campus, where they raised
chickens and helped the farmer with his planting and other chores.
Ron was a pre-law student, majoring in political science, and he
had looked forward to going to law school, but now something
had changed for him, and he found himself more interested in
the farm and in outdoor life. "I just got tired of school," he said.
He had let his hair grow long, and he realized that most of his
classmates probably thought of him as a hippie. After he graduated,
he moved to Missoula because he loved its setting—the high country
and the cold streams of the Bitterroot Range and the Garnet Mountains—and found work as a janitor at the University of Montana.

"I just wanted something to do so I could keep on fishing and   52
backpacking," he said. "There were a lot of people with the same
idea there at that time. It was what was happening. That's great
country, out along the Clark Fork and the Big Blackfoot, if you
like fishing. You could walk across the Milwaukee Road railroad
tracks behind our house and cross the floodplain and you'd be
fishing in just five minutes."

Our house: He had met Linda, and they had moved into a log   53
cabin in Clinton, which is twenty miles southeast of Missoula.
She was in graduate school at Montana, majoring in creative
writing. She also tutored undergraduates in English and Greek,
and after she had picked up her master's degree she worked in a
Poetry in the Schools program in the state school system and then
became poet-in-residence and a teacher at a private school in
Missoula. She and Ron talked baseball and followed the Yankees
from a distance, as she wrote me in her first letter, but softball
was the only game in town.

Ron said, "Every spring, I'd think, Geezum, I've made it through   54
the winter again—and they were long, long winters there, you
know—and I'd get that little urge. I'd go off fishing, and when I
got my arm working back and forth with the fishing pole [he said
"pole," not "rod"] it was sort of like throwing a curveball. I was
spring-strong, and I'd get to wondering what I could have done
if I'd gone on in baseball. Each spring was like that. Then when
I read that notice in *The Sporting News* about the Buckskins' tryout
camp, I realized that it had been eight years since I'd pitched in
a ballgame. I couldn't believe it."

This must have sounded self-pitying to Ron when he said it to   55
me, there on the porch, and he corrected himself at once. "It was
my own fault," he said. "There was fear, I guess, and then I began
to rationalize it all and remind myself that I'd have to go to a

tryout camp if I wanted to come back, and maybe I'd fail. What I'd had was a marginal talent—a pretty good high-school fastball—and if I was ever going to do something with it, I would have had to pay the price. I didn't want to have to work at it, I think, or else I just didn't want to work that hard. So I let it go by."

Late one afternoon that week, I watched another team of country ballplayers wearing sponsors' names on the backs of their uniform shirts—Waterville Garage, Tobin Construction, Gerald W. Tatro—in a game played on still another hillside diamond. The field was unfenced, and the woods and brush along the rightfield foul line crowded in so close that there wouldn't have been room for bleachers or any other kind of seats there. It was a *field:* the shaggy grass around second base was white with clover blossoms. We were in Belvidere, Vermont—a Green Mountain village a bit to the north and east of Mt. Mansfield—and the game pitted the home team of Belvidere-Waterville against the visiting Morrisville nine. These were Babe Ruth League teams, whose players range in age from thirteen to fifteen years, but the Belvidere-Watervilles seemed to be outweighed by a couple of dozen pounds and outsized by a couple of inches at almost every position. Outmanned, too: only eight home-team players had turned up for the game, and their coach, Curt Koonz, was filling in at shortstop. The disparity was most noticeable on the mound, for the Belvidere-Waterville pitcher, Earl Domina, was so short that the white pants of his uniform were within an inch or two of swallowing his shoes. He worked hard out there, toeing the rubber in good style and hiding the ball behind his hip while he stared in at his catcher for the sign, but he wasn't big enough to get much stuff on his pitches, and it sometimes looked as if he were throwing uphill against the tall, half-grinning Morrisville boys. Earl was being hit hard—the bases were repeatedly loaded and then unloaded against him in the two or three innings I saw him play—and he also had to put up with a few throwing-uphill jokes from his own teammates, but he kept his concentration and his seriousness, jutting his jaw on the mound and staring the base runners into place before each pitch, and in time the smiles and the jokes died away. He was a battler.

I had heard a good deal about the problems and triumphs of the Belvidere-Waterville Babe Ruth League team from its previous coach, Ron Goble, who had been greeted with hand slaps and jokes and cheerful body blocks by his former troops when we turned up at the game that afternoon. (He and Linda lived in Waterville when they first came to Vermont, but their present house is some thirty miles to the northwest—too far for him to keep up with his Babe Ruth League coaching while he also continues to pitch for the A's.) Now he pointed out some of his stalwarts from the previous year's squad—Peanut Coburn, the team's best shortstop, best outfielder, best first baseman, best everything, who had graduated to assistant coach; the Eldred brothers, Keith and Mike; some others. He said that a few of his players last year had come up through a Little League program, but others had never played an inning of baseball before their season got under way. There weren't many players in either category, to tell the truth, so everybody got a chance to play, including Kim Wescom and Angie Tourangeau, who are girls. Kim, a second baseperson, always wore blue eyeshadow with her game uniform—a complicated announcement, Linda thought. All the teams that Belvidere-Waterville faced were larger and more experienced than they were, and the enemy players razzed them unmercifully for playing girls and for looking like hicks.

"Well, we *were* hicks," Ron said to me. "We were a country   58 team, and most of our players came from poor families, so after a while we took that as our team name. We became the Hicks." The razzing never got entirely out of hand, in any case, because after a couple of innings of it, Frank Machia, the Belvidere-Waterville first baseman, would take a few steps over toward the other team bench and invite the critics there to step forward. Frank was fifteen, but he has a Boog Powell-style chest and belly, topped off by a full beard, and so things usually quieted down in a hurry. The continuing trouble—the real trouble—was that the team wasn't good enough to win. One very bad day came at Stowe, a wealthy ski-resort town at the foot of Mt. Mansfield (its Babe Ruth League team even has different uniforms for home and away games), where the game was called, by mutual consent, when Belvidere-Waterville had fallen behind by 35–3, or 36–5, or something like that.

Ron told me that one of the team's handicaps had been the   59 lack of a decent home field to practice and play on, and after the Stowe disaster he and Linda and a few other devout team backers—Larry and Shirley Brown, Olive McClain, and Emmett Eldred—went over to the abandoned Smithville diamond, in Belvidere, which had long ago turned into a meadow, and attacked it with hand mowers. After three long, hot days' work—a horrendous job, everyone agreed—the hay was cut and raked, and a new backstop had been erected, just in time for the return game against

Stowe, which turned up with a considerable entourage to watch the continuation of the slaughter.

"Well, we didn't beat them," Ron said. "It was 9–6, Stowe, in   60
the end, but we *almost* beat them, and they sure knew they'd been in a game. We showed them we could play, and that made the whole season worthwhile."

I asked how the team had fared after that.   61

"The truth is, we lost all fourteen games on our schedule," he   62
said. "No, that's not right—we took one on a forfeit, when the other team didn't turn up. But it meant a lot to these kids, learning how to play ball, learning to enjoy it. By the end of the season, they were backing up plays and sometimes hitting the cutoff man on their throws, even though that was mostly because they couldn't throw the ball all the way home anyway. They're all good kids. There isn't much else to do around here in the summers, you know, and that kept them at it."

The game we had been watching ended at 11–4, Morrisville,   63
and the young players began to drift away, some in their parents' cars and pickups, some on bikes, and some on foot. The Belvidere-Waterville bats and batting helmets were stuffed into a gunnysack and toted away. It was evening, or almost evening, by now, but the field was at once repopulated by softball players—a pickup, slow-pitch game, arranged by telephone earlier that day. Ron played and so did Earl Domina—a long pitcher and a very short one, both playing in the same outfield now—and more cars pulled up by the field as the news of the game got around, and soon there were twelve or thirteen players on a side out there in the warm, mosquitoey half-light. Linda didn't play, and I sat it out, too, keeping her company. We were at a worn, teetery old picnic table, where we gnawed on some cold roast chicken she had brought along, and in time we were joined there by Larry Brown, a shy, slightly built, soft-spoken man, who often looks at the ground when he speaks. Larry Brown is the Branch Rickey of Belvidere baseball. He is an asbestos miner—a laborer—with a modest seasonal sideline in maple syrup made from his own hillside sugar bush. Still in his forties, he has six children and two grandchildren.

He told me that he had been a catcher for the Belvidere town   64
team when he was a younger man. "It was all town teams around here then," he said. "I'd like to see those days come back again. Maybe they will. Back when I was a boy, all I had was a bat and one old taped-up ball. It wasn't all organized, the way it is now.

Now I don't think there's a single town team in Lamoille County,
but there are eight hundred boys playing Little League and Babe
Ruth ball."

His doing—in part, at least. Larry Brown got the Belvidere Little   65
League started, about five years ago. (In fact, a Little League game
had been in progress off at the other end of the same field that
the Babe Ruth teams were using that afternoon, and I had been
struck by the fact that all the players on both teams had full
uniforms. Seeing so many players in action at the same time almost
reminded me of spring training.) Larry Brown found sponsors, got
the parents involved, raised the money for uniforms and bats and
balls. Last year, when Ron and Linda turned up in Waterville, he
sought out Ron and persuaded him to take on the town's very
first Babe Ruth team. Larry didn't know that Ron was still recovering
from his cancer surgery and from the debilitating radiation treatments
that had ensued, but Larry had been wonderfully persuasive, and
the job, Ron must have realized almost at once, was a perfect one
for him at that moment: cheerful and funny and full of hope.
When the season ended, with most of those hopes still unrewarded,
Larry Brown and his wife threw a big potluck dinner for the team.
Ron gave a speech, summarizing the summer's high points—the
time Mike Eldred lost both sneakers while trying to steal second
base (and turned back at once to get them), Angie Tourangeau's
single that didn't count because the ump said he wasn't ready,
the two games against Stowe. . . . Everyone had such a good time
at the dinner that they all decided to chip in and arrange a team
trip up to Montreal for an Expos game. Later in the summer, they
did it again. Baseball has caught on in Belvidere.

I asked Larry Brown if anyone from Lamoille County had ever   66
made it to the big leagues.

"No, I don't think so," he said, still smiling and still looking at   67
the ground. "Though there was so many that played ball and
watched ball around here in the old days you'd think it'd happen,
wouldn't you? Why, I can remember going over to St. Albans
when they had a team in the old Northern League here—the
Giants, they were—and they'd have a thousand people there at
Coote Field. A thousand, easy. But we had some mighty good
players around here. Don McCuin played for our team—the Belvidere team, I mean—right after the war. He was a left-handed
pitcher. He was signed by the Cardinals organization, but when
he got down there he found he couldn't play ball in the heat,
there in the South. And there was another good left-hander, named

Sonny Davis, just about that time. Funny you'd have two so good, who was both the same kind. He played for Stowe. He signed up with the Braves, back in the nineteen-forties. Sonny told me once that he'd played in a game with young Henry Aaron, who was just a beginner, too, at the time, and when Sonny saw Aaron hit some drives in batting practice he suddenly understood that he was never going to make it in major-league baseball."

All three of us laughed. It was almost dark now, and whenever 68 somebody on the ball field made contact (with that heavy, smacking sound that a softball makes against the bat), the arching ball looked like some strange gray night bird suddenly rising out of the treetops.

"Leonard McCuin was as good as Don was, from all I hear," 69 Larry went on. "He was Don's father. Leonard once played on a team over to Saranac Lake, where Christy Mathewson was his coach. Mathewson was there because he had tuberculosis, you know. I guess he was about dead of it by then. Funny, I always thought Don McCuin had the head for major-league baseball. It was his arm that was at fault. But I liked the way he pitched. I always compared Don to Warren Spahn—a classic left-hander with that high kick. I don't think there was ever a smarter pitcher than Spahn. But I'm not one of those who goes around always saying that the old players were the best. I've been up to Montreal for some games, now that the teams are so close—I almost went *broke* the first summer the Expos was playing!—and I think there's been no better players than some we've seen in our time. You only have to go back a few years to when Aaron and Mays and Clemente were still playing, you know, and you just couldn't come up with a better outfield than that. They say Roberto Clemente was the least appreciated ballplayer of his time. Well, *I* appreciated him."

It was dark now, and the softball game had ended at last. Ron 70 joined us at the picnic table, and some of his friends sat down with us, too, drinking beer and swatting mosquitoes. Little Earl Domina had gone home, waving shyly to us as he walked away into the shadows, and I told Larry how much I'd admired him in the Babe Ruth League game we'd seen.

"He's about half size for his age, but he always puts out," Larry 71 said. "There are others I wished cared as much about it as he does. Size don't have much to do with it in this game."

Roberto Clemente and Leonard McCuin, Don McCuin and Warren 72 Spahn, Sonny Davis and Hank Aaron, Christy Mathewson and Earl Domina—they were all together in baseball for Larry Brown. For him, the game had no fences.

I was pleased but in fact not much surprised to find someone   73
like Larry Brown here in a corner of Vermont, for I had already
met other friends of Ron's and Linda's who seemed sustained and
nourished by a similar passion for baseball. One of them was Paul
Farrar, the A's' manager, who normally gives six or seven hours
of his day to the team during the season, beginning at four in the
afternoon on weekdays, when he gets off work at the I.B.M. plant
in Burlington. If there is a home game (there are also practices
on some off days) at the University of Vermont's Centennial Field,
where the A's play, Farrar is usually the first man to arrive. He
carries in the field rakes from his car and then unlocks the concession
stand and carries out the dusty bases that have been stored there
since the last game. The players begin to drift onto the field while
he is raking the base paths or carefully laying down the foul lines
and the batter's boxes with a lime cart, and he kids them cheerfully
and asks about their bruises. Long before this, while he paused
at home to put on his uniform, he has picked up the day's team
telephone messages from his wife, Sue. Tinker Jarvis will have to
work until past seven tonight, she told him, which means not
only that he won't be there in time to play but that his girlfriend,
Helen Rigby, probably won't be around to work in the hotdog
stand. Southpaw Joe Gay's arm is coming along, his father called
to say, but the doctor still thinks it'll be another week before he'll
be ready to pitch. One of the troubles is that Joe has this summer
job as a housepainter, which makes it hard for him to give his
arm the kind of rest it should have. (Why can't Joe paint *right*-
handed for a while, Paul wonders for an instant.) The other team
tonight will be perfectly willing to play nine innings, instead of
seven, if the A's want to, but which of them will pay the seventy-
five bucks that U.V.M. wants as a fee for using the lights? Then,
there are the automobile arrangements to be made for the weekend
doubleheader over at Saxtons River. . . . Paul thinks about some
of this while he pitches batting practice, but then he tries to put
it all out of his head when he makes out his lineup in the dugout
and begins to concentrate on the game at hand. Who's got to play
if we're going to win? Who ought to play because he hasn't got
into enough games lately? . . .

Paul grew up in the Bronx and, of course, dreamed of playing   74
in Yankee Stadium someday, as a big-leaguer. Then his family
moved to South Burlington, and in time Paul went off to Rensselaer
Polytechnic, in Troy, New York, where he played catcher for four
years on the varsity team. Then he coached at R.P.I. for two years,
as an assistant with the varsity, while he got his graduate degree.

He is a senior associate engineer with I.B.M. He is twenty-six years old.

"Ron and I and Tinker Jarvis are the old men on the team,"   75
he said to me, "but I think it may be more fun for us than for
the others. And managing is—well, it's *involving*. These games
don't mean anything, but I play them again in my mind when
they're over. The bunt signal we missed. The pitcher I maybe took
out one batter too late. I lie in bed and play baseball in my head
in the middle of the night."

Herbie Pearo lives in East Alburg, Vermont, on a peninsula   76
jutting into Lake Champlain. He is the manager of the East Alburg
Beavers, an amateur slow-pitch softball team that Ron plays for
whenever the A's' schedule permits it. Upstairs in his house there,
one walks into a narrow room and a narrow loft above it—a
baseball museum—stuffed to bursting with baseball uniforms, autographed baseball bats, autographed baseballs, caps, pairs of spikes,
old baseball photographs, albums of baseball tickets, baseball programs, bubble-gum baseball cards, everything. Some of the uniform
shirts are framed, showing names and numbers on their backs,
and these include the shirts of many present and recently past
Expos—Andre Dawson, Ellis Valentine, Steve Rogers, Rusty Staub,
Warren Cromartie—for Herbie is a terrific Expos fan. He is also a
former terrific Mets fan. The centerpiece of his present collection
is Tom Seaver's 1967 Mets uniform (1967 was Seaver's first year
in the majors), which Herbie values at one thousand dollars. "Not
that I'd automatically sell it," he adds. Selling items like these is
Herbie Pearo's business—a baseball-souvenir-and-tradables line
known as Centerfield Eight Sales. The business is advertised in
most standard baseball publications, and the turnover is brisk.
Brisk but often painful, because Herbie, one senses quickly, would
much rather hold on to his best stuff. He is still writhing over the
recent loss of a genuine Rogers Hornsby St. Louis Browns uniform.
"I *had* to do it," he says apologetically. "The man made me an
offer I couldn't refuse—seven guaranteed All-Stars' uniforms, plus
a lot of other things, but still . . ." His voice trails off, and in his
face you can almost see the Hornsby uniform still hanging in its
old place on the long wall.

Centerfield Eight is one of the hardest stores to walk out of I   77
have ever walked into. I was there for an hour or more, and each
time I edged closer to the staircase my eye would fasten on some
new wonder or Herbie would draw me back to look at something
else. He wasn't trying to sell me anything; he simply wanted to

share it all. He was a great curator, and we were at the Louvre.
. . . Here is a ball signed by Sadaharu Oh, and a bat signed by
the Babe. Here is Pete Rose's very first Reds' shirt—with a rookie's
number, 33, on the back. Here is a Reggie Jackson Oakland A's
shirt; here is a Roberto Clemente shirt (in the old, sleeveless Pirates'
style); and over here is an orange Charlie Finley baseball (Finley
once lobbied to have the major leagues shift to orange baseballs);
and—oh, yes—upstairs, there in the corner, is a player's battered
old locker from Connie Mack Stadium, now long gone, alas. And
look *here* (here in a desk drawer): A pair of genuine Phillies World
Series tickets from 1962—the year the Phillies folded so horribly
and didn't make the Series after all. Here is a genuine scout's
contract, signed by Connie Mack himself. This is a photograph of
the 1908 Portland Mohawks ("Maine's Premier Amateur Baseball
Team"), and here are some 1975 White Sox World Series ducats
(another blasted hope), and that's an usher's cap from Anaheim
Stadium—a bargain at twenty-five bucks. But oh, *wait!* And he
holds up a pair of snowy, still pressed Washington Senator home-
uniform shirts on wire hangers, with a "1" on one of them and
a "2" on the other—commemorative shirts made for presentation
to President Nixon and Vice-President Agnew at the Senators'
opening game in 1970. I stare at these particular relics in slow
surprise, astounded by the possibility that I have at last come upon
an object—*two* objects—in this world that may truly be said to
have no meaning whatsoever.

Stunned with memorabilia, I descend the stairs at last (the balusters   78
are bats, each with its own history), and Herbie Pearo's voice
follows me down. "I wish you'd seen my Carl Furillo shirt, from
the 1957 season," he says. "The real thing. I wish I hadn't sold
that. I've been *kicking* myself ever since . . ."

As I have explained, my trip to visit Linda Kittell and Ron Goble   79
was something I had looked forward to for years. It came while
the midsummer major-league baseball strike was about two weeks
along, but there was no connection between the two events. I
was not visiting a semi-pro player because I would have preferred
to call on a big-leaguer. I was not out to prove some connection
or lack of connection between the expensive upper flowerings of
the game and its humble underbrush. Everyone in Vermont talked
about the strike, but not for long; we wanted it over, because we
missed the games and the standings and the news of the sport,
but I heard no bitter talk about money and free agency, "spoiled"
ballplayers or selfish owners. At the same time, it occurred to me
again and again while I was there (it would have been impossible

to ignore the comparison or not to think about its ironies) to wonder how many big-league owners and famous players and baseball businessmen (the league presidents, and so forth, and perhaps even some of the writers) had an involvement in the game—a connection that was simply part of life itself—like Ron Goble's and Larry Brown's and Linda Kittell's. Not many, I would think, and yet at the same time it seemed quite likely to me— almost a certainty, in fact—that if I had stopped and visited friends in almost any other county or state corner in the United States I would have found their counterparts there, their friends in baseball.

Late one afternoon, Linda and Ron and I drove into Burlington 80 for an A's game against the Queen City Royals. We were in their wheezy, ancient red Vega, and Ron kept cocking his head and listening to the engine in a nervous sort of way; a couple of weeks earlier, the car had conked out altogether on the same trip, and he had missed the game and his turn on the mound. He was in uniform tonight, but he wasn't going to play; his next start would be the following night, against the hated Burlington Expos. We were all eating ice-cream cones.

I asked Ron if he could tell me a little more about his summer 81 with the Boise Buckskins, when he had pitched in organized ball for the first time, and everything had gone so badly for him and his teammates.

"In some ways, it wasn't exactly what you'd call a rewarding 82 experience," he said after a moment or two. "Our pitching was downright terrible. We won on opening day, and that was sort of the highlight. Gerry Craft said opening day was God's greatest blessing but the rest of it was our trial. We had those ugly uniforms, and the fans got on us because of the religion thing, and we were always jumping off buses and going right into some park to play. It was good we had a few things going for us, like Danny Thomas. The real battle for me was not to let any of that bother me too much. I was there to prove myself. That summer answered a lot of questions for me that I would have gone on asking myself all my life. I got that albatross off my neck at last. What I discovered was that I'd had a talent at one time for throwing the ball—maybe not a major-league talent, at that. But I found out that although I couldn't throw by then—not really—I was at least a pitcher." He paused and then added his little disclaimer: "Although that may be too much of a complimentary term."

What was it about Danny Thomas, I asked. What had made 83 him so special to them and to the whole team?

"Well, he was tall and he had those good long muscles," Ron   84
said. "You know—he looked like a ballplayer."

"And that fantastic smile," Linda said from the back seat.   85

"Yes, there was never a better-looking ballplayer, anywhere," 86
Ron said. "And his hitting! I remember once when we were playing
against the Emeralds on a road trip, and the whole park was down
on us for some reason—everyone yelling and booing and laughing.
Because we'd been looking so bad, I guess. And then he hit one.
I mean, he *hit* it—it went out over the lights and out of the ballpark,
and even before he got to first base there was this absolute hush
in the place. It was beautiful. He'd shut them up."

"Plus he wore No. 7," Linda said.   87

"That's right," Ron said at once. "The same number."   88

It was a minute before I understood. Mickey Mantle's old number 89
had been 7.

At this moment, the Vega gave a couple of despairing wheezes   90
and slowly glided to halt. We came to rest at meadowside on a
singularly unpopulated and unpromising stretch of macadam.

"Damn *carburetor,*" Ron said. He popped the hood. "Hammer,"   91
he said, swinging his long legs out, and Linda, reaching down
between her feet, found a hammer and wordlessly handed it to
him, exactly like a good instrument nurse working with a surgeon.
This operation entailed some thunderous banging noises from up
forward—not a promising prognosis at all, I thought—but when
Ron reappeared, red-faced, and restarted the engine, it spluttered
and groaned but then caught. A miracle. "Remind me to park
facing downhill when we get there," he muttered as we resumed
our course.

And so I asked him about his pitching now—pitching for the   92
Burlington A's.

"Well, it's still enjoyable," he said. "The thing about pitching 93
is—it's that it requires your concentration. It requires your entire
thought. There aren't many things in life that can bring that to
you. And every situation, every day and every inning, is different.
You have to work on so many little details. Finding the fluidity
of your body. Adjusting for different mounds. Bringing the leg up
higher, bringing it over more. You kind of expect standards of
yourself, and when they're not there you have to find out what's
going wrong, and why. Maybe you're not opening up quickly
enough. Maybe you're not following through enough, or maybe
you're throwing too much across your body. Some days, you're
not snapping your wrist so much. Some days, the seams on the
ball aren't so nice. It's always different."

He shook his head, and laughed at himself again. "Actually,"   94 he went on, "at some level I'm always pitching in the hope that the curveball—the real old curveball—might come back someday. Geezum, wouldn't that be nice, I think to myself. It doesn't happen, though. It's gone. Now it's different, being a pitcher, and sometimes I think it's almost more fun, because you can't just throw it by them now. You've got to trick 'em, because you've got nothing much to get them out with. So you try to set them up—get them looking away and then throw them inside. Get them backing off, and go down and away. I don't play often enough to have that happen too much—just to be able to think about location like that—but that's what it's all about."

He was right: this is what pitching is all about. I have heard a good many big-league pitchers talk about their craft—hundreds of them, I suppose, including a few of the best of our time—and when they got into it, really got talking pitching, they all sounded almost exactly like Ron Goble. He probably would have denied it if I'd said it, but he was one of them, too—a pitcher.

"I know baseball is important to me," he said after another moment or two. "Playing now is like getting a present, and you don't expect presents."

In Burlington, Ron swung into a gravelly downhill road leading to Centennial Field, and then stopped the Vega unexpectedly and walked over to a small shed on the left-hand side of the road and took from it a large, triangular wooden sign, hinged at the top like a kitchen stepladder. He and Linda carried it up to East Avenue, which we had just left, and set it up on the sidewalk there. "BASEBALL TODAY," it read. "6:00." We parked facing downhill and went down to the park—an ancient dark-green beauty, with the outfield terminating in a grove of handsome old trees. The roofed stands were steeply tilted, and the cast-iron arm at the end of each row of seats bore a "UVM" stamped into the metal. Swallows dipped in and out of the shadows under the grandstand roof. Linda and Ron pointed out the football stadium that rose beyond the left-field fence, and then drew my attention to the back of the football press box perched on its topmost rim—a good hundred feet up there, I suppose. This was history: history made about two weeks earlier, when Darcy Spear had whacked a home run against the Expos that cleared the top of the press box—a Kingman shot, an all-timer.

Ron went off to batting practice, and Linda told me she would be selling tickets up at the main automobile gate. It was still a good hour before the game with the Queen City Royals would begin, and I went along. Linda was carrying a big roll of blue

tickets and a small envelope of loose change. "Shall we abscond?"
I said. She looked into the envelope. "Better wait until a few
customers turn up," she said. We leaned on the chain-link fence
beside the open gate, listening to the distant crack of bats from
the field below, and passed a bottle of warmish beer back and
forth. It was a heavy, quiet summer evening.

Linda said she had hardly ever heard Ron talk about his pitching   99
the way he had talked in the car that night. "Basically, I realize
I know absolutely nothing about baseball compared to Ron," she
said. "But I get tired of the other women around players, who
say 'Don't you get tired of him talking about nothing but baseball?'
I *hate* that. I think I like the part of Ron that I don't understand.
I feel I could get all the knowledge of baseball that he has, and
still not understand, because I never played baseball. It's a mystery
between us, and I like that. If you know everything about a person,
it's sort of a letdown. I just have no idea what he goes through
out there on the mound. I get glimpses sometimes, but that's all.

"Ron is truly modest about his talent—you've seen that. I believe   100
all the things about him that he doesn't think or say himself. I
believe he could have been a major-league pitcher. I wanted everyone to know about it when he was pitching and was still sick,
but he wouldn't let me tell anyone. He didn't want to bother them
with it. I think that's sort of heroic. He still doesn't have his fastball
back, you know."

The first two or three cars rolled up and stopped for their tickets. 101
"Looks like a nice evening," one man said.

"Yes, it does," Linda said. "Have a nice time, now."   102

She came back and leaned against the fence again. "I get scared   103
about the day when he can't play ball anymore," she said. "I get
teary thinking about it sometimes. He couldn't have planned his
life any differently, but sometimes I wish he wouldn't give up on
himself so much. There are a lot of other things he could have
done. But if he'd planned his life differently I wouldn't be around.
There's no one here he can ask, but I get the idea that he knows
as much about the technical side of pitching as anyone else. He
just learned it himself, I think."

I said I had exactly the same impression.   104

"Sometimes he asks me to watch a particular thing when he's   105
pitching—whether he's opening his hips, say. But if he asks me
about something else afterward—where his foot is coming down,
or something like that—then I've totally missed it. I keep wishing
his brother George was here, so he could talk baseball with him.
There's so much *to* it. To me, baseball is like learning a foreign
language. You never learn all the vocabulary, all the endings and
idioms. It's what I love about languages."

It came back to me—it was stupid of me not to have remembered   106
it, all this time—that Linda had gone to college right here. The
main college buildings were just behind us, over the top of the
hill. This was her campus. I asked her what languages she had
taken, here at U.V.M.

"The Classics Department got upset with me, because I always   107
wanted to take up more languages, all at the same time," she
said, smiling. "I was studying classical Greek, modern Greek, Latin,
Russian, and Japanese. I switched majors over and over. I'd do
more than anyone expected of me in one thing—like creative
writing—and let everything else slide. If I had to do a Milton
paper, or something, I'd do it in twenty minutes and hand it in—
I didn't care. But if I was studying something like rondo alliteration
or chiastic alliteration, I'd get so excited I'd forget everything else."
She shook her head. "Not *organized*."

I asked about her own poetry. She had declined to show me   108
her poems.

"I'll never catch up in baseball, but I have my own world," she   109
said. "Ron can read something I've written and he'll say 'That
has a nice sound,' or something, but he doesn't see that for once
I've got a good slant rhyme in there. And he'll never see things
I suddenly notice when I'm reading—that 'chrysanthemum' is such
a perfect iambic word, for instance—that so excite me. When we
went out to some friends who were having Hayden Carruth for
dinner—Ron has read maybe one poem of Carruth's, I'd say—I
said to him, 'Remember, you're having dinner with Mickey Mantle.'
But maybe I should have said Catfish Hunter, because Ron respects
Catfish Hunter in such a special way." She giggled.

More cars were coming in now. A man in one car said, "I'm   110
one of the umpires," and Linda waved him in. He waved back
and drove in. His license plate said "UMP."

"I feel a little disappointed in my own career," Linda went on   111
during the next pause. "But it isn't as if you're ever too old to
write a good poem. But I don't know many ninety-year-old pitchers—do you? Maybe Ron and I are both wrong to make baseball
so important to us. But what the hell, writing a poem isn't so
important, either."

I asked what would happen to Ron in the next couple of years.   112

"If he isn't going to go on playing ball—and he can't for much   113
longer—and if he can't find something that will take up as much
of his attention as baseball, I don't know what's going to happen
to him," she said. "Maybe he'll get into teaching, or some kind
of coaching. He's supposed to teach in a kids' baseball camp later
this summer, and then maybe . . ." She shrugged. "He lets things
happen. He's that kind of a person. At least he found out he's a

professional-level pitcher, but I think he'd feel better if it had got him to the major leagues. And he'll never feel he knows everything about baseball. Sometimes I'll watch him in the store when we're shopping together, and he'll have a cantaloupe in his hands and he'll be practicing his motion, right there in the store. It's true! And sometimes I'll see him sitting at home in the evening and shaking his head, and I'll ask him why, and he'll say, 'I can't *believe* I threw that pitch.' "

Some cars were rolling up to the gate, and Linda went over to   114
meet them. "I know one thing," she said. "You can't rewrite a pitch."

The A's had another easy time of it that night. Charlie Corbally   115
pitched and went the distance, and Darcy Spear had three hits and four runs batted in, and the team rolled to a 12–3 win over the Royals. I'd had a hard time finding out the A's place in the standings, because Ron said he couldn't always remember which games counted in the league and which were the informal ones, but he asked Paul, who said the club was now four and four in the league, and something like eight and five for the season over all. None of it mattered much. The next night was what mattered— the game against the Expos.

A lot of people turned out for that one—more than three hundred   116
fans, including Larry Brown, who had brought his wife, Shirley, and one of his daughters, Laureen, and one of his sons, Stephen, and Earl Domina. We all sat together, behind first base. Even before the game began, I could see that the Expos—they wore the same parti-colored red-and-blue-and-white caps that the Montreal players do—were quicker and much more confident than most of the other Northern League players I had seen. They all looked like ballplayers. It was a wonderful game, it turned out, stuffed with close plays and heads-up, opportunistic baseball, and the A's won it, 3–2. Darcy Spear got the big hit once again—a two-run, two-out single in the third. Ron Goble started, but Paul Farrar had said beforehand he wouldn't let him pitch more than four innings; then he would bring in Steve Gallacher to mop up. Both pitchers were tired, and the staff was a little thin just now. Ron retired the first two Expos batters in the first and then gave up a bunt single. He walked the next man. He was falling behind on the count, and I noticed that he didn't seem to have his full, free motion out there. The next batter hit a sure third-out grounder to Greg Wells, but the ball took a bad hop at the last instant and jumped over Wells' glove for a single and an Expos run. Ron walked the next batter, and Paul came out to the mound to settle him down. Ron fell behind on the following batter, too, and

eventually walked him, forcing in another run. Linda stared out at the field without expression. The next Expo rammed a hard shot toward third, but Tinker Jarvis made a good play on the ball and threw to second for the force, ending the inning.

In the next inning, Ron gave up two trifling singles through the middle. With two out, the Expos tried a fancy delayed double steal, with the base runner heading toward second intentionally getting himself hung up in the hope that his man from third could score before the out, but Greg Wells made the play perfectly, stopping and wheeling and firing to the plate in time to nail the runner there. Ron also got through the third unscathed, although he surrendered a single and hit a batter with one of his pitches. From time to time, Ron came off the mound between pitches and stared at the ground, his hands on his hips. In the top of the fourth, now defending a 3—2 lead, he walked the lead-off Expos hitter. The next Expos batter, a right-handed hitter, stood in and Ron hit him on the knee with his first pitch, and Paul Farrar came onto the field slowly and took him out of the game. It hadn't been a disastrous outing—with a couple of small breaks, Ron probably could have gone his four innings without giving up a run—but his struggles on the mound in search of his control had been painful to watch, especially for those of us who remembered his easy, elegant dominance over the batters in his previous game, down in Brattleboro. This kind of turnabout is a frightful commonplace for pitchers, as Ron had said himself, the day before in the car: It's always different.

Steve Gallacher came in and got the next Expos man to rap into an instant double play, and then retired the next man on a fly-ball, ending the threat. Then Gallacher set down the remaining nine men in succession, fanning four of them—an outstanding pitching performance that nailed down the win. He got a terrific hand when he came off the field, and he deserved it.

After the game, Ron spotted Larry Brown's car just as it was about to leave the parking lot and ran over to say hello. He squatted down beside the driver's side of the car for a good five minutes, talking to Larry about the game. All around the parking lot, you could see the young Expo and A's players standing in their uniforms beside their cars, tossing their spikes and gloves into the back seats, lifting a beer here and there, and laughing with little groups of friends and with their young wives or girlfriends. I was sorry to be leaving. I was staying in Burlington that night, at a motel, so that I could make an early start back to New York the next morning.

Ron and Linda and I went to a bar-restaurant she knew, up a flight of stairs in Burlington. Linda and I ordered drinks and sand-

wiches. Ron asked for three large glasses of water, and drank them
off, one after the other. Then he had a gin rickey and a sandwich,
too. He was still in uniform.

"I learned how to drink in here, I think," Linda said, looking   121
around. "A long time ago."

Ron said, "The last time I pitched, I started from the middle of   122
the plate and began to work it out toward the corners. Tonight,
it was the other way around. I started on the outside and I never
did get it together." He shook his head. "I can't think how long
it's been since I hit two batters."

"Well, at least we won," Linda said.   123

"Yes, at least we won," I said. "You guys ought to keep me   124
around some more."

Ron had stopped listening. He was staring across the room, with   125
a quiet, faraway look on his face. Linda put her hand on his
crossed left leg, just above the white part of his cutouts, and
watched him with an expression of immense care and affection.
He was still in the game.

GABRIEL GARCÍA MÁRQUEZ

Balthazar's Marvelous Afternoon

The cage was finished. Balthazar hung it under the eave, from   1
force of habit, and when he finished lunch everyone was already
saying that it was the most beautiful cage in the world. So many
people came to see it that a crowd formed in front of the house,
and Balthazar had to take it down and close the shop.

"You have to shave," Ursula, his wife, told him. "You look like
a Capuchin."[1]

"It's bad to shave after lunch," said Balthazar.

He had two weeks' growth, short, hard, and bristly hair like
the mane of a mule, and the general expression of a frightened
boy. But it was a false expression. In February he was thirty; he
had been living with Ursula for four years, without marrying her
and without having children, and life had given him many reasons
to be on guard but none to be frightened. He did not even know
that for some people the cage he had just made was the most

First published in *No One Writes to the Colonel, and Other Stories* (1968).
1. A Roman Catholic order of friars. "Capuchin" means "hooded one" in Italian.

beautiful one in the world. For him, accustomed to making cages since childhood, it had been hardly any more difficult than the others.

"Then rest for a while," said the woman. "With that beard you ⁵ can't show yourself anywhere."

While he was resting, he had to get out of his hammock several times to show the cage to the neighbors. Ursula had paid little attention to it until then. She was annoyed because her husband had neglected the work of his carpenter's shop to devote himself entirely to the cage, and for two weeks had slept poorly, turning over and muttering incoherencies, and he hadn't thought of shaving. But her annoyance dissolved in the face of the finished cage. When Balthazar woke up from his nap, she had ironed his pants and a shirt; she had put them on a chair near the hammock and had carried the cage to the dining table. She regarded it in silence.

"How much will you charge?" she asked.

"I don't know," Balthazar answered. "I'm going to ask for thirty pesos to see if they'll give me twenty."

"Ask for fifty," said Ursula. "You've lost a lot of sleep in these two weeks. Furthermore, it's rather large. I think it's the biggest cage I've ever seen in my life."

Balthazar began to shave. ¹⁰

"Do you think they'll give me fifty pesos?"

"That's nothing for Mr. Chepe Montiel, and the cage is worth it," said Ursula. "You should ask for sixty."

The house lay in the stifling shadow. It was the first week of April and the heat seemed less bearable because of the chirping of the cicadas. When he finished dressing, Balthazar opened the door to the patio to cool off the house, and a group of children entered the dining room.

The news had spread. Dr. Octavio Giraldo, an old physician, happy with life but tired of his profession, thought about Balthazar's cage while he was eating lunch with his invalid wife. On the inside terrace, where they put the table on hot days, there were many flowerpots and two cages with canaries. His wife liked birds, and she liked them so much that she hated cats because they could eat them up. Thinking about her, Dr. Giraldo went to see a patient that afternoon, and when he returned he went by Balthazar's house to inspect the cage.

There were a lot of people in the dining room. The cage was ¹⁵ on display on the table: with its enormous dome of wire, three stories inside, with passageways and compartments especially for eating and sleeping and swings in the space set aside for the birds' recreation, it seemed like a small-scale model of a gigantic ice factory. The doctor inspected it carefully, without touching it, thinking that in effect the cage was better than its reputation, and much more beautiful than any he had ever dreamed of for his wife.

"This is a flight of the imagination," he said. He sought out Balthazar among the group of people and, fixing his maternal eyes on him, added, "You would have been an extraordinary architect."

Balthazar blushed.

"Thank you," he said.

"It's true," said the doctor. He was smoothly and delicately fat, like a woman who had been beautiful in her youth, and he had delicate hands. His voice seemed like that of a priest speaking Latin. "You wouldn't even need to put birds in it," he said, making the cage turn in front of the audience's eyes as if he were auctioning it off. "It would be enough to hang it in the trees so it could sing by itself." He put it back on the table, thought a moment, looking at the cage, and said:

"Fine, then I'll take it."   20

"It's sold," said Ursula.

"It belongs to the son of Mr. Chepe Montiel," said Balthazar. "He ordered it specially."

The doctor adopted a respectful attitude.

"Did he give you the design?"

"No," said Balthazar. "He said he wanted a large cage, like this   25
one, for a pair of troupials."

The doctor looked at the cage.

"But this isn't for troupials."

"Of course it is, Doctor," said Balthazar, approaching the table. The children surrounded him. "The measurements are carefully calculated," he said, pointing to the different compartments with his forefinger. Then he struck the dome with his knuckles, and the cage filled with resonant chords.

"It's the strongest wire you can find, and each joint is soldered outside and in," he said.

"It's even big enough for a parrot," interrupted one of the   30
children.

"That it is," said Balthazar.

The doctor turned his head.

"Fine, but he didn't give you the design," he said. "He gave you no exact specifications, aside from making it a cage big enough for troupials. Isn't that right?"

"That's right," said Balthazar.

"Then there's no problem," said the doctor. "One thing is a   35 cage big enough for troupials, and another is this cage. There's no proof that this one is the one you were asked to make."

"It's this very one," said Balthazar, confused. "That's why I made it."

The doctor made an impatient gesture.

"You could make another one," said Ursula, looking at her husband. And then, to the doctor: "You're not in any hurry."

"I promised it to my wife for this afternoon," said the doctor.

"I'm very sorry, Doctor," said Balthazar, "but I can't sell you something that's sold already." 40

The doctor shrugged his shoulders. Drying the sweat from his neck with a handkerchief, he contemplated the cage silently with the fixed, unfocused gaze of one who looks at a ship which is sailing away.

"How much did they pay you for it?"

Balthazar sought out Ursula's eyes without replying.

"Sixty pesos," she said.

The doctor kept looking at the cage. "It's very pretty." He sighed. 45 "Extremely pretty." Then, moving toward the door, he began to fan himself energetically, smiling, and the trace of that episode disappeared forever from his memory.

"Montiel is very rich," he said.

In truth, José Montiel was not as rich as he seemed, but he would have been capable of doing anything to become so. A few blocks from there, in a house crammed with equipment, where no one had ever smelled a smell that couldn't be sold, he remained indifferent to the news of the cage. His wife, tortured by an obsession with death, closed the doors and windows after lunch and lay for two hours with her eyes opened to the shadow of the room, while José Montiel took his siesta. The clamor of many voices surprised her there. Then she opened the door to the living room and found a crowd in front of the house, and Balthazar with the cage in the middle of the crowd, dressed in white, freshly shaved, with that expression of decorous candor with which the poor approach the houses of the wealthy.

"What a marvelous thing!" José Montiel's wife exclaimed, with a radiant expression, leading Balthazar inside. "I've never seen anything like it in my life," she said, and added, annoyed by the crowd which piled up at the door:

"But bring it inside before they turn the living room into a grandstand."

Balthazar was no stranger to José Montiel's house. On different 50 occasions, because of his skill and forthright way of dealing, he had been called in to do minor carpentry jobs. But he never felt at ease among the rich. He used to think about them, about their ugly and argumentative wives, about their tremendous surgical operations, and he always experienced a feeling of pity. When he entered their houses, he couldn't move without dragging his feet.

"Is Pepe home?" he asked.

He had put the cage on the dining-room table.

"He's at school," said José Montiel's wife. "But he shouldn't be long," and she added, "Montiel is taking a bath."

In reality, José Montiel had not had time to bathe. He was giving himself an urgent alcohol rub, in order to come out and see what was going on. He was such a cautious man that he slept without an electric fan so he could watch over the noises of the house while he slept.

"Adelaide!" he shouted. "What's going on?"   55

"Come and see what a marvelous thing!" his wife shouted.

José Montiel, obese and hairy, his towel draped around his neck, appeared at the bedroom window.

"What is that?"

"Pepe's cage," said Balthazar.

His wife looked at him perplexedly.   60

"Whose?"

"Pepe's," replied Balthazar. And then, turning toward José Montiel, "Pepe ordered it."

Nothing happened at that instant, but Balthazar felt as if someone had just opened the bathroom door on him. José Montiel came out of the bedroom in his underwear.

"Pepe!" he shouted.

"He's not back," whispered his wife, motionless.   65

Pepe appeared in the doorway. He was about twelve, and had the same curved eyelashes and was as quietly pathetic as his mother.

"Come here," José Montiel said to him. "Did you order this?"

The child lowered his head. Grabbing him by the hair, José Montiel forced Pepe to look him in the eye.

"Answer me."

The child bit his lip without replying.   70

"Montiel," whispered his wife.

José Montiel let the child go and turned toward Balthazar in a fury. "I'm very sorry, Balthazar," he said. "But you should have consulted me before going on. Only to you would it occur to contract with a minor." As he spoke, his face recovered its serenity. He lifted the cage without looking at it and gave it to Balthazar.

"Take it away at once, and try to sell it to whomever you can,"
he said. "Above all, I beg you not to argue with me." He patted
him on the back and explained, "The doctor has forbidden me to
get angry."

The child had remained motionless, without blinking, until Balthazar looked at him uncertainly with the cage in his hand. Then
he emitted a guttural sound, like a dog's growl, and threw himself
on the floor screaming.

José Montiel looked at him, unmoved, while the mother tried   75
to pacify him. "Don't even pick him up," he said. "Let him break
his head on the floor, and then put salt and lemon on it so he
can rage to his heart's content." The child was shrieking tearlessly
while his mother held him by the wrists.

"Leave him alone," José Montiel insisted.

Balthazar observed the child as he would have observed the
death throes of a rabid animal. It was almost four o'clock. At that
hour, at his house, Ursula was singing a very old song and cutting
slices of onion.

"Pepe," said Balthazar.

He approached the child, smiling, and held the cage out to him.
The child jumped up, embraced the cage which was almost as big
as he was, and stood looking at Balthazar through the wirework
without knowing what to say. He hadn't shed one tear.

"Balthazar," said José Montiel softly. "I told you already to take   80
it away."

"Give it back," the woman ordered the child.

"Keep it," said Balthazar. And then, to José Montiel: "After all,
that's what I made it for."

José Montiel followed him into the living room.

"Don't be foolish, Balthazar," he was saying, blocking his path.
"Take your piece of furniture home and don't be silly. I have no
intention of paying you a cent."

"It doesn't matter," said Balthazar. "I made it expressly as a   85
gift for Pepe. I didn't expect to charge anything for it."

As Balthazar made his way through the spectators who were
blocking the door, José Montiel was shouting in the middle of
the living room. He was very pale and his eyes were beginning
to get red.

"Idiot!" he was shouting. "Take your trinket out of here. The
last thing we need is for some nobody to give orders in my house.
Son of a bitch!"

In the pool hall, Balthazar was received with an ovation. Until
that moment, he thought that he had made a better cage than

ever before, that he'd had to give it to the son of José Montiel so
he wouldn't keep crying, and that none of these things was particularly important. But then he realized that all of this had a
certain importance for many people, and he felt a little excited.

"So they gave you fifty pesos for the cage."

"Sixty," said Balthazar.   90

"Score one for you," someone said. "You're the only one who
has managed to get such a pile of money out of Mr. Chepe Montiel.
We have to celebrate."

They bought him a beer, and Balthazar responded with a round
for everybody. Since it was the first time he had ever been out
drinking, by dusk he was completely drunk, and he was talking
about a fabulous project of a thousand cages, at sixty pesos each,
and then of a million cages, till he had sixty million pesos. "We
have to make a lot of things to sell to the rich before they die,"
he was saying, blind drunk. "All of them are sick, and they're
going to die. They're so screwed up they can't even get angry any
more." For two hours he was paying for the jukebox, which played
without interruption. Everybody toasted Balthazar's health, good
luck, and fortune, and the death of the rich, but at mealtime they
left him alone in the pool hall.

Ursula had waited for him until eight, with a dish of fried meat
covered with slices of onion. Someone told her that her husband
was in the pool hall, delirious with happiness, buying beers for
everyone, but she didn't believe it, because Balthazar had never
got drunk. When she went to bed, almost at midnight, Balthazar
was in a lighted room where there were little tables, each with
four chairs, and an outdoor dance floor, where the plovers were
walking around. His face was smeared with rouge, and since he
couldn't take one more step, he thought he wanted to lie down
with two women in the same bed. He had spent so much that he
had had to leave his watch in pawn, with the promise to pay the
next day. A moment later, spread-eagled in the street, he realized
that his shoes were being taken off, but he didn't want to abandon
the happiest dream of his life. The women who passed on their
way to five-o'clock Mass didn't dare look at him, thinking he was
dead.

Translated by J. S. Bernstein

Thinking About Art and Sport

Some readers will look at the table of contents for this section and think that it contains very strange bedfellows. But the relation between art and sport is stronger than it first appears. In their purest forms, as Johan Huizinga points out, both are separate from "real" life, contributing nothing to our practical well-being; both play themselves out in very limited times and spaces; both impose an order on life's disorder; both deliberately create and resolve tension; both demand an absolute surrender to the rules (or, as Samuel Taylor Coleridge put it, a "willing suspension of disbelief"). Even professional sports—which some will argue have ceased to be games at all—occasionally give us a glimpse of the kinship of games and art: the moment in a Wimbledon match, for instance, when Chris Evert Lloyd overruled the umpire's favorable call, pointing out that the lob she had put over her opponent's racquet had been made as the ball touched the court a second time. "One bounce," as someone said, "and we have tennis; one and a half, and we have the naked opportunism of the world at large."

Artists often talk in a similar way about the voluntary restraints of their work. Robert Frost went so far as to say (to the irritation of many contemporary poets and critics) that writing poetry unrestrained by meter is like "playing tennis with the net down." But it wasn't merely metrical restraint he admired. In an essay reprinted in this section, he calls Edwin Arlington Robinson "the prince of heartachers" whose "theme was unhappiness itself," but he also tells us that Robinson's "much admired restraint lies wholly in his never having let grief go further than it could in play." We can see Frost's point if we look at Robinson's "Miniver Cheevy":

> Miniver Cheevy, child of scorn,
> > Grew lean while he assailed the seasons;
> He wept that he was ever born,
> > And he had reasons.
>
> Miniver loved the days of old
> > When swords were bright and steeds were prancing;
> The vision of a warrior bold
> > Would set him dancing.
>
> Miniver sighed for what was not,
> > And dreamed, and rested from his labors;

He dreamed of Thebes and Camelot,
  And Priam's neighbors.

Miniver mourned the ripe renown
  That made so many a name so fragrant;
He mourned Romance, now on the town,
  And Art, a vagrant.

Miniver loved the Medici,
  Albeit he had never seen one;
He would have sinned incessantly
  Could he have been one.

Miniver cursed the commonplace
  And eyed a khaki suit with loathing;
He missed the medieval grace
  Of iron clothing.

Miniver scorned the gold he sought,
  But sore annoyed was he without it;
Miniver thought, and thought, and thought,
  And thought about it.

Miniver Cheevy, born too late,
  Scratched his head and kept on thinking;
Miniver coughed, and called it fate,
  And kept on drinking.

Robinson gets each stroke off cleanly, playfully, never letting the heartache trail off into bathos.

We so commonly think of art as a serious endeavor and sport as mere recreation that we forget how gravely athletes may play and how playfully artists may work. Each selection in this section makes us re-examine our preconceptions. Roger Angell's "In the Country" shows us that for its devotees baseball is a separate world, almost a religion, with its own mysteries, saints, and relics: those who are skeptical about the analogy between art and sport should read this essay beside E. M. Forster's "Art for Art's Sake" and Gabriel García Márquez's "Balthazar's Marvelous Afternoon." In an essay that will offend some readers, Ernest Hemingway insists that the bullfight is a tragedy, too serious to be confused with mere recreation, and too lofty to be criticized as cruel. This is just the sort of argument for artistic "Benefit of Clergy" that George Orwell refuses to accept. It is something like the wonderfully eccentric argument in "Attitude," Garrison Keillor's attempt to raise the tone of slow-pitch softball. The essays by Joan Didion,

Kenneth Clark, and John McPhee all show the way the great artist or sportsperson manages to find self-expression within the tight confines of the game.

QUESTIONS

1. Huizinga's description of play is highly abstract and theoretical. Is it a philosophical mirage? Where do you find art or sport conforming to it? failing to conform?

2. Several of the essays in this section emphasize the work of art as "a self-contained entity" (Forster) insulated by form from the outside world. Where do you find art (high or low) that fails because it is not sufficiently self-contained? Where do you find art that is *too* self-contained, too gamelike?

3. Angell and García Márquez (and perhaps Clark and Frost) write about people who seem unremarkable outside the confines of their sport or art, as though the game itself calls something unexpected from them. Where have you seen examples of the same phenomenon? What unexpected qualities did the game bring out?

4. Hemingway, Orwell, Didion, and McPhee all write about people whose art is a reflection in a different medium of the qualities they exhibit in daily life. Where have you found examples of this phenomenon? How exact is the reflection?

5. Does the association of art and sport with what Huizinga calls the play instinct make it difficult to distinguish between high and low art, high and low sport? How might such a distinction be made?

6. If we use the presence of the play instinct as our test for art and sport, what unexpected activities or works show up under one class or the other? What activities or works are unexpectedly excluded?

POWER AND
POWERLESSNESS

Jacob and Esau

I remember very vividly the Sunday-school room where I spent   1
the Sabbaths of my early years. It had been newly built after a
disastrous fire; the room was large and full of sunlight; nice new
chairs were grouped around where the classes met. My class was
in the center, so that I could look out upon the elms of Main
Street and see the passersby. But I was interested usually in the
lessons and in my fellow students and the frail rather nervous
teacher, who tried to make the Bible and its ethics clear to us.
We were a trial to her, full of mischief, restless and even noisy;
but perhaps more especially when we asked questions. And on
the story of Jacob and Esau we did ask questions. My judgment
then and my judgment now is very unfavorable to Jacob. I thought
that he was a cad and a liar and I did not see how possibly he
could be made the hero of a Sunday-school lesson.

Many days have passed since then and the world has gone   2
through astonishing changes. But basically, my judgment of Jacob
has not greatly changed and I have often promised myself the
pleasure of talking about him publicly, and especially to young
people. This is the first time that I have had the opportunity.

My subject then is "Jacob and Esau," and I want to examine   3
these two men and the ideas which they represent; and the way
in which those ideas have come to our day. Of course, our whole
interpretation of this age-old story of Jewish mythology has greatly
changed. We look upon these Old Testament stories today not as
untrue and yet not as literally true. They are simple, they have
their truths, and yet they are not by any means the expression of
eternal verity. Here were brought forward for the education of
Jewish children and for the interpretation of Jewish life to the
world, two men: one small, lithe and quick-witted; the other tall,
clumsy and impetuous; a hungry, hard-bitten man.

Historically, we know how these two types came to be set forth   4
by the Bards of Israel. When the Jews marched north after escaping
from slavery in Egypt, they penetrated and passed through the
land of Edom; the land that lay between the Dead Sea and Egypt.
It was an old center of hunters and nomads and the Israelites,
while they admired the strength and organization of the Edomites,

Commencement address delivered at Talladega College, Talladega, Tennessee, June
5, 1944. For the story of Jacob and Esau, see Genesis 25–28.

looked down upon them as lesser men; as men who did not have the Great Plan. Now the Great Plan of the Israelites was the building of a strong, concentered state under its own God, Jehovah, devoted to agriculture and household manufacture and trade. It raised its own food by careful planning. It did not wander and depend upon chance wild beasts. It depended upon organization, strict ethics, absolute devotion to the nation through strongly integrated planned life. It looked upon all its neighbors, not simply with suspicion, but with the exclusiveness of a chosen people, who were going to be the leaders of earth.

This called for sacrifice, for obedience, for continued planning. The man whom we call Esau was from the land of Edom, or intermarried with it, for the legend has it that he was twin of Jacob the Jew but the chief fact is that, no matter what his blood relations were, his cultural allegiance lay among the Edomites. He was trained in the free out-of-doors; he chased and faced the wild beasts; he knew vast and imperative appetite after long self-denial, and even pain and suffering; he gloried in food, he traveled afar; he gathered wives and concubines and he represented continuous primitive strife.

The legacy of Esau has come down the ages to us. It has not been dominant, but it has always and continually expressed and re-expressed itself; the joy of human appetites, the quick resentment that leads to fighting, the belief in force, which is war.

As I look back upon my own conception of Esau, he is not nearly as clear and definite a personality as Jacob. There is something rather shadowy about him; and yet he is curiously human and easily conceived. One understands his contemptuous surrender of his birthright; he was hungry after long days of hunting; he wanted rest and food, the stew of meat and vegetables which Jacob had in his possession, and determined to keep unless Esau bargained. "And Esau said, Behold, I am at the point to die: and what profit shall this birthright be to me? And Jacob said, Swear to me this day; and he swore unto him: and he sold his birthright unto Jacob."

On the other hand, the legacy of Jacob which has come down through the years, not simply as a Jewish idea, but more especially as typical of modern Europe, is more complicated and expresses itself something like this: life must be planned for the Other Self, for that personification of the group, the nation, the empire, which has eternal life as contrasted with the ephemeral life of individuals. For this we must plan, and for this there must be timeless and unceasing work. Out of this, the Jews as chosen children of Jehovah would triumph over themselves, over all Edom and in time over the world.

Now it happens that so far as actual history is concerned, this 9
dream and plan failed. The poor little Jewish nation was dispersed
to the ends of the earth by the overwhelming power of the great
nations that arose East, North, and South and eventually became
united in the vast empire of Rome. This was the diaspora, the
dispersion of the Jews. But the idea of the Plan with a personality
of its own took hold of Europe with relentless grasp and this was
the real legacy of Jacob, and of other men of other peoples, whom
Jacob represents.

There came the attempt to weld the world into a great unity, 10
first under the Roman Empire, then under the Catholic Church.
When this attempt failed, the empire fell apart, there arose the
individual states of Europe and of some other parts of the world;
and these states adapted the idea of individual effort to make each
of them dominant. The state was *all,* the individual subordinate,
but right here came the poison of the Jacobean idea. How could
the state get this power? Who was to wield the power within the
state? So long as power was achieved, what difference did it make
how it was gotten? Here then was war—but not Esau's war of
passion, hunger and revenge, but Jacob's war of cold acquisition
and power.

Granting to Jacob, as we must, the great idea of the family, the 11
clan, and the state as dominant and superior in its claims, nevertheless, there is the bitter danger in trying to seek these ends
without reference to the great standards of right and wrong. When
men begin to lie and steal, in order to make the nation to which
they belong great, then comes not only disaster, but rational contradiction which in many respects is worse than disaster, because
it ruins the leadership of the divine machine, the human reason,
by which we chart and guide our actions.

It was thus in the middle age and increasingly in the seventeenth 12
and eighteenth and more especially in the nineteenth century,
there arose the astonishing contradiction: that is, the action of
men like Jacob who were perfectly willing and eager to lie and
steal so long as their action brought profit to themselves and power
to their state. And soon identifying themselves and their class with
the state they identified their own wealth and power as that of
the state. They did not listen to any arguments of right or wrong;
might was right; they came to despise and deplore the natural
appetites of human beings and their very lives, so long as by their
suppression, they themselves got rich and powerful. There arose
a great, rich Italy; a fabulously wealthy Spain; a strong and cultured
France and, eventually, a British Empire which came near to
dominating the world. The Esaus of those centuries were curiously
represented by various groups of people: by the slum-dwellers and

the criminals who, giving up all hope of profiting by the organized state, sold their birthrights for miserable messes of pottage. But more than that, the great majority of mankind, the peoples who lived in Asia, Africa and America and the islands of the sea, became subordinate tools for the profit-making of the crafty planners of great things, who worked regardless of religion or ethics.

It is almost unbelievable to think what happened in those cen- 13 turies, when it is put in cold narrative; from whole volumes of tales, let me select only a few examples. The peoples of whole islands and countries were murdered in cold blood for their gold and jewels. The mass of the laboring people of the world were put to work for wages which led them into starvation, ignorance and disease. The right of the majority of mankind to speak and to act; to play and to dance was denied, if it interfered with profit-making work for others, or was ridiculed if it could not be capitalized. Karl Marx writes of Scotland: "As an example of the method of obtaining wealth and power in nineteenth century; the story of the Duchess of Sutherland will suffice here. This Scottish noblewoman resolved, on entering upon the government of her clan of white Scottish people, to turn the whole country, whose population had already been, by earlier processes, reduced to 15,000, into a sheep pasture. From 1814 to 1820 these 15,000 inhabitants were systematically hunted and rooted out. All their villages were destroyed and burnt, all their fields turned into pasture. Thus this lady appropriated 794,000 acres of land that had from time immemorial been the property of the people. She assigned to the expelled inhabitants about 6,000 acres on the seashore. The 6,000 acres had until this time lain waste, and brought in no income to their owners. The Duchess, in the nobility of her heart, actually went so far as to let these at an average rent of 50 cents per acre to clansmen, who for centuries had shed their blood for her family. The whole of the stolen clan-land she divided into 29 great sheep farms, each inhabited by a single imported English family. In the year 1835 the 15,000 Scotsmen were already replaced by 131,000 sheep."

The discovery of gold and silver in America, the extirpation, 14 enslavement and entombment in mines of the Indian population, the beginning of the conquest and looting of the East Indies, the turning of Africa into a warren for the commercial hunting of black-skins, signalized the rosy dawn of power of those spiritual children of Jacob, who owned the birthright of the masses by fraud and murder. These idyllic proceedings are the chief momenta of primary accumulation of capital in private hands. On their heels tread the commercial wars of the European nations, with the globe

for a theater. It begins with the revolt of the Netherlands from Spain, assumes giant dimensions in England's anti-jacobin war, and continues in the opium wars against China. . . .

Of the Christian colonial system, Howitt says: "The barbarities and desperate outrages of the so-called Christians, throughout every region of the world, and upon people they have been able to subdue, are not to be paralleled by those of any other race, in any age of the earth." This history of the colonial administration of Holland—and Holland was the head capitalistic nation of the seventeenth century—is one of the most extraordinary relations of treachery, bribery, massacre, and meanness. 15

Nothing was more characteristic than the Dutch system of stealing men, to get slaves for Java. The men-stealers were trained for this purpose. The thief, the interpreter, and the seller were the chief agents in this trade; the native princes, the chief sellers. The young people stolen, were thrown in the secret dungeons of Celebes, until they were ready for sending to the slave ships. . . . 16

The English East India Company, in the seventeenth and eighteenth centuries, obtained, besides the political rule in India, the exclusive monopoly of the tea trade, as well as of the Chinese trade in general, and of the transport of goods to and from Europe. But the coasting trade of India was the monopoly of the higher employees of the company. The monopolies of salt, opium, betel nuts and other commodities, were inexhaustible mines of wealth. The employees themselves fixed the price and plundered at will the unhappy Hindus. The Governor General took part in this private traffic. His favorites received contracts under conditions whereby they, cleverer than the alchemists, made gold out of nothing. Great English fortunes sprang up like mushrooms in a day; investment profits went on without the advance of a shilling. The trial of Warren Hastings swarms with such cases. Here is an instance: a contract for opium was given to a certain Sullivan at the moment of his departure on an official mission. Sullivan sold his contract to one Binn for $200,000; Binn sold it the same day for $300,000 and the ultimate purchaser who carried out the contract declared that after all he realized an enormous gain. According to one of the lists laid before Parliament, the East India Company and its employees from 1757 to 1766 got $30,000,000 from Indians as gifts alone. . . . 17

The treatment of the aborigines was, naturally, more frightful in plantation colonies destined for export trade only, such as the West Indies, and in rich and well-populated countries, such as Mexico and India, that were given over to plunder. But even in the colonies properly so called, the followers of Jacob outdid him. 18

These sober Protestants, the Puritans of New England, in 1703, by decrees of their assembly set a premium of $200 on every Indian scalp and every captured redskin: in 1720 a premium of $500 on every scalp; in 1744, after Massachusetts Bay had proclaimed a certain tribe as rebels, the following prices prevailed: for a male scalp of 12 years upward, $500 (new currency); for a male prisoner, $525; for women and children prisoners, $250; for scalps of women and children, $250. Some decades later, the colonial system took its revenge on the descendants of the pious pilgrim fathers, who had grown seditious in the meantime. At English instigation and for English pay they were tomahawked by redskins. The British Parliament proclaimed bloodhounds and scalping as "means that God and Nature had given into its hands."

With the development of national industry during the eighteenth [19] century, the public opinion of Europe had lost the last remnant of shame and conscience. The nations bragged cynically of every infamy that served them as a means to accumulating private wealth. Read, e.g., the naive *Annals of Commerce* of Anderson. Here it is trumpeted forth as a triumph of English statecraft that at the Peace of Utrecht, England extorted from the Spaniards by the Asiento Treaty the privilege of being allowed to ply the slave trade, between Africa and Spanish America. England thereby acquired the right of supplying Spanish America until 1743 with 4,800 Negroes yearly. This threw, at the same time, an official cloak over British smuggling, Liverpool waxed fat on the slave trade. . . . Aikin (1795) quotes that spirit of bold adventure which has characterized the trade of Liverpool and rapidly carried it to its present state of prosperity; has occasioned vast employment for shipping and sailors, and greatly augmented the demand for the manufactures of the country; Liverpool employed in the slave trade, in 1730, 15 ships; in 1760, 74; in 1770, 96; and in 1792, 132.

Henry George wrote of *Progress and Poverty* in the 1890s. He [20] says: "At the beginning of this marvelous era it was natural to expect, and it was expected, that labor-saving inventions would lighten the toil and improve the condition of the laborer; that the enormous increase in the power of producing wealth would make real poverty a thing of the past. Could a man of the last century [the eighteenth]—a Franklin or a Priestley—have seen, in a vision of the future, the steamship taking the place of the sailing vessel; the railroad train, of the wagon; the reaping machine, of the scythe; the threshing machine, of the flail; could he have heard the throb of the engines that in obedience to human will, and for the satisfaction of the human desire, exert a power greater than that of all the men and all the beasts of burden of the earth combined; could he have seen the forest tree transformed into finished lumber—into doors, sashes, blinds, boxes or barrels, with hardly the touch of a human hand; the great workshops where boots and shoes are turned out by the case with less labor than the old-fashioned cobbler could have put on a sole; the factories where, under the eye of one girl, cotton becomes cloth faster than hundreds of stalwart weavers could have turned it out with their hand-looms; could he have seen steam hammers shaping mammoth shafts and mighty anchors, and delicate machinery making tiny watches; the diamond drill cutting through the heart of the rocks, and coal oil sparing the whale; could he have realized the enormous saving of labor resulting from improved facilities of exchange and communication—sheep killed in Australia eaten fresh in England, and the order given by the London banker in the afternoon executed in San Francisco in the morning of the same day; could he have conceived of the hundred thousand improvements which these only suggest, what would he have inferred as to the social condition of mankind?

"It would not have seemed like an'inference; further than the 21 vision went it would have seemed as though he saw; and his heart would have leaped and his nerves would have thrilled, as one who from a height beholds just ahead of the thirst-stricken caravan the living gleam of rustling woods and the glint of laughing waters. Plainly, in the sight of the imagination, he would have beheld these new forces elevating society from its very foundations, lifting the very poorest above the possibility of want, exempting the very lowest from anxiety for the material needs of life; he would have seen these slaves of the lamp of knowledge taking on themselves the traditional curse, these muscles of iron and sinews of steel making the poorest laborer's life a holiday, in which every high quality and noble impulse could have scope to grow."

This was the promise of Jacob's life. This would establish the 22 birthright which Esau despised. But, says George, "Now, however, we are coming into collision with facts which there can be no mistaking. From all parts of the civilized world," he says speaking fifty years ago, "come complaints of industrial depression; of labor condemned to involuntary idleness; of capital massed and wasting; of pecuniary distress among businessmen; of want and suffering and anxiety among the working classes. All the full, deadening pain, all the keen, maddening anguish, that to great masses of men are involved in the words 'hard times,' afflict the world today." What would Henry George have said in 1933 after airplane and radio and mass production, turbine and electricity had come?

Science and art grew and expanded despite all this, but it was 23 warped by the poverty of the artist and the continuous attempt to make science subservient to industry. The latter effort finally succeeded so widely that modern civilization became typified as industrial technique. Education became learning a trade. Men thought of civilization as primarily mechanical and the mechanical means by which they reduced wool and cotton to their purposes, also reduced and bent humankind to their will. Individual initiative remained but it was cramped and distorted and there spread the idea of patriotism to one's country as the highest virtue, by which it became established, that just as in the case of Jacob, a man not only could lie, steal, cheat and murder for his native land, but by doing so he became a hero whether his cause was just or unjust.

One remembers that old scene between Esau who had thought- 24
lessly surrendered his birthright and the father who had blessed his lying son; "Jacob came unto his father, and said, My Father: and he said, Here am I; who art thou? And Jacob said unto his father, I am Esau thy firstborn; I have done according as thou badest me: arise, I pray thee, sit and eat of my venison, that thy soul may bless me." In vain did clumsy, careless Esau beg for a blessing—some little blessing. It was denied and Esau hated Jacob because of the blessing: and Esau said in his heart, "The days of mourning for my father are at hand; then I will slay my brother Jacob." So revolution entered—so revolt darkened a dark world.

The same motif was repeated in modern Europe and America 25
in the nineteenth and twentieth centuries, when there grew the superstate called the Empire. The Plan had now regimented the organization of men covering vast territories, dominating immense force and immeasurable wealth and determined to reduce to subserviency as large a part as possible, not only of Europe's own internal world, but of the world at large. Colonial imperialism swept over the earth and initated the First World War, in envious scramble for division of power and profit.

Hardly a moment of time passed after that war, a moment in 26
the eyes of the eternal forces looking down upon us when again the world, using all of that planning and all of that technical superiority for which its civilization was noted; and all of the accumulated and accumulating wealth which was available, proceeded to commit suicide on so vast a scale that it is almost impossible for us to realize the meaning of the catastrophe. Of course, this sweeps us far beyond anything that the peasant lad Jacob, with his petty lying and thievery had in mind. Whatever was begun there of ethical wrong among the Jews was surpassed in every particular by the white world of Europe and America and carried to such length of universal cheating, lying and killing that no comparisons remain.

We come therefore to the vast impasse of today: to the great 27
question, what was the initial right and wrong of the original

Jacobs and Esaus and of their spiritual descendants the world over? We stand convinced today, at least those who remain sane, that lying and cheating and killing will build no world organization worth the building. We have got to stop making income by unholy methods; out of stealing the pittances of the poor and calling it insurance; out of seizing and monopolizing the natural resources of the world and then making the world's poor pay exorbitant prices for aluminum, copper and oil, iron and coal. Not only have we got to stop these practices, but we have got to stop lying about them and seeking to convince human beings that a civilization based upon the enslavement of the majority of men for the income of the smart minority is the highest aim of man.

But as is so usual in these cases, these transgressions of Jacob 28 do not mean that the attitude of Esau was flawless. The conscienceless greed of capital does not excuse the careless sloth of labor. Life cannot be all aimless wandering and indulgence if we are going to constrain human beings to take advantage of their brain and make successive generations stronger and wiser than the previous. There must be reverence for the *birthright* of inherited *culture* and that birthright cannot be sold for a dinner course, a dress suit or a winter in Florida. It must be valued and conserved.

The method of conservation is work, endless and tireless and 29 planned work and this is the legacy which the Esaus of today who condemn the Jacobs of yesterday have got to substitute as their path of life, not vengeful revolution, but building and rebuilding. Curiously enough, it will not be difficult to do this, because the great majority of men, the poverty-stricken and diseased are the *real workers* of the world. They are the ones who have made and are making the *wealth* of this universe, and their future path is clear. It is to accumulate such knowledge and balance of judgment that they can reform the world, so that the workers of the world receive just share of the wealth which they make and that all human beings who are capable of work shall work. Not national glory and empire for the few, but food, shelter and happiness for the many. With the disappearance of systematic lying and killing, we may come into the birthright which so long we have called Freedom: that is, the right to act in a manner that seems to be beautiful; which makes life worth living and joy the only possible end of life. This is the experience which is Art and planning for this is the highest satisfaction of civilized needs. So that looking back upon the allegory and the history, tragedy and promise, we may change our subject and speak in closing of Esau and Jacob, realizing that neither was perfect, but that of the two, Esau had the elements which lead more naturally and directly to the salvation of man; while Jacob with all his crafty planning and cold sacrifice, held in his soul the things that are about to ruin mankind: exaggerated national patriotism, individual profit, the despising of men who are not the darlings of our particular God and the consequent lying and stealing and killing to monopolize power.

May we not hope that in the world after this catastrophe of blood, sweat and fire, we may have a new Esau and Jacob; a new allegory of men who enjoy life for life's sake; who have the Freedom of Art and wish for all men of all sorts the same freedom and enjoyment that they seek themselves and who work for all this and work hard. [30]

Gentlemen and ladies of the class of 1944: in the days of the years of my pilgrimage, I have greeted many thousands of young men and women at the commencement of their careers as citizens of the select commonwealth of culture. In no case have I welcomed them to such a world of darkness and distractions as that into which I usher you. I take joy only in the thought that if work to be done is measure of man's opportunity you inherit a mighty fortune. You have only to remember that the birthright which is today in symbol draped over your shoulders is a heritage which has been preserved all too often by the lying, stealing and murdering of the Jacobs of the world, and if these are the only means by which this birthright can be preserved in the future, it is not worth the price. I do not believe this, and I lay it upon your hearts to prove that this not only need not be true, but is eternally and forever false. [31]

N. SCOTT MOMADAY

The Way to Rainy Mountain

A single knoll rises out of the plain in Oklahoma, north and west of the Wichita Range. For my people, the Kiowas, it is an old landmark, and they gave it the name Rainy Mountain. The hardest weather in the world is there. Winter brings blizzards, hot tornadic winds arise in the spring, and in summer the prairie is an anvil's edge. The grass turns brittle and brown, and it cracks beneath your feet. There are green belts along the rivers and creeks, linear groves of hickory and pecan, willow and witch hazel. At a distance in July or August the steaming foliage seems almost to [1]

Originally published as *The Journey of Tai-me*, 1968.

writhe in fire. Great green-and-yellow grasshoppers are everywhere in the tall grass, popping up like corn to sting the flesh, and tortoises crawl about on the red earth, going nowhere in the plenty of time. Loneliness is an aspect of the land. All things in the plain are isolate; there is no confusion of objects in the eye, but *one* hill or *one* tree or *one* man. To look upon that landscape in the early morning, with the sun at your back, is to lose the sense of proportion. Your imagination comes to life, and this, you think, is where Creation was begun.

I returned to Rainy Mountain in July. My grandmother had died in the spring, and I wanted to be at her grave. She had lived to be very old and at last infirm. Her only living daughter was with her when she died, and I was told that in death her face was that of a child.

I like to think of her as a child. When she was born, the Kiowas were living that last great moment of their history. For more than a hundred years they had controlled the open range from the Smoky Hill River to the Red, from the headwaters of the Canadian to the fork of the Arkansas and Cimarron. In alliance with the Comanches, they had ruled the whole of the southern Plains. War was their sacred business, and they were among the finest horsemen the world has every known. But warfare for the Kiowas was preeminently a matter of disposition rather than of survival, and they never understood the grim, unrelenting advance of the U.S. Cavalry. When at last, divided and ill-provisioned, they were driven onto the Staked Plains in the cold rains of autumn, they fell into panic. In Palo Duro Canyon they abandoned their crucial stores to pillage and had nothing then but their lives. In order to save themselves, they surrendered to the soldiers at Fort Sill and were imprisoned in the old stone corral that now stands as a military museum. My grandmother was spared the humiliation of those high gray walls by eight or ten years, but she must have known from birth the affliction of defeat, the dark brooding of old warriors.

Her name was Aho, and she belonged to the last culture to evolve in North America. Her forebears came down from the high country in western Montana nearly three centuries ago. They were a mountain people, a mysterious tribe of hunters whose language has never been positively classified in any major group. In the late seventeenth century they began a long migration to the south and east. It was a long journey toward the dawn, and it led to a golden age. Along the way the Kiowas were befriended by the Crows, who gave them the culture and religion of the Plains. They acquired horses, and their ancient nomadic spirit was suddenly free of the ground. They acquired Tai-me, the sacred Sun Dance doll, from that moment the object and symbol of their worship, and so shared in the divinity of the sun. Not least, they acquired the sense of destiny, therefore courage and pride. When they entered upon the southern Plains, they had been transformed. No longer were they slaves to the simple necessity of survival; they were a lordly and dangerous society of fighters and thieves, hunters and priests of the sun. According to their origin myth, they entered the world through a hollow log. From one point of view, their migration was the fruit of an old prophecy, for indeed they emerged from a sunless world.

Although my grandmother lived out her long life in the shadow   5
of Rainy Mountain, the immense landscape of the continental interior lay like memory in her blood. She could tell of the Crows, whom she had never seen, and of the Black Hills, where she had never been. I wanted to see in reality what she had seen more perfectly in the mind's eye, and traveled fifteen hundred miles to begin my pilgrimage.

Yellowstone, it seemed to me, was the top of the world, a region   6
of deep lakes and dark timber, canyons and waterfalls. But, beautiful as it is, one might have the sense of confinement there. The skyline in all directions is close at hand, the high wall of the woods and deep cleavages of shade. There is a perfect freedom in the mountains, but it belongs to the eagle and the elk, the badger and the bear. The Kiowas reckoned their stature by the distance they could see, and they were bent and blind in the wilderness.

Descending eastward, the highland meadows are a stairway to   7
the plain. In July the inland slope of the Rockies is luxuriant with flax and buckwheat, stonecrop and larkspur. The earth unfolds and the limit of the land recedes. Clusters of trees and animals grazing far in the distance cause the vision to reach away and wonder to build upon the mind. The sun follows a longer course in the day, and the sky is immense beyond all comparison. The great billowing clouds that sail upon it are shadows that move upon the grain like water, dividing light. Farther down, in the land of the Crows and Blackfeet, the plain is yellow. Sweet clover takes hold of the hills and bends upon itself to cover and seal the soil. There the Kiowas paused on their way; they had come to the place where they must change their lives. The sun is at home on the plains. Precisely there does it have the certain character of a god. When the Kiowas came to the land of the Crows, they could see the dark lees of the hill at dawn across the Bighorn River, the profusion of light on the grain shelves, the oldest deity ranging after the solstices. Not yet would they veer southward to the caldron of the land that lay below; they must wean their blood

from the northern winter and hold the mountains a while longer in their view. They bore Tai-me in procession to the east.

A dark mist lay over the Black Hills, and the land was like iron. 8 At the top of a ridge I caught sight of Devil's Tower upthrust against the gray sky as if in the birth of time the core of the earth had broken through its crust and the motion of the world was begun. There are things in nature that engender an awful quiet in the heart of man; Devil's Tower is one of them. Two centuries ago, because they could not do otherwise, the Kiowas made a legend at the base of the rock. My grandmother said:

> "Eight children were there at play, seven sisters and their brother. Suddenly the boy was struck dumb; he trembled and began to run upon his hands and feet. His fingers became claws, and his body was covered with fur. Directly there was a bear where the boy had been. The sisters were terrified; they ran, and the bear after them. They came to the stump of a great tree, and the tree spoke to them. It bade them climb upon it and as they did so, it began to rise into the air. The bear came to kill them, but they were just beyond its reach. It reared against the tree and scored the bark all around with its claws. The seven sisters were borne into the sky, and they became the stars of the Big Dipper."

From that moment, and so long as the legend lives, the Kiowas have kinsmen in the night sky. Whatever they were in the mountains, they could be no more. However tenuous their well-being, however much they had suffered and would suffer again, they had found a way out of the wilderness.

My grandmother had a reverence for the sun, a holy regard that 9 now is all but gone out of mankind. There was a wariness in her and an ancient awe. She was a Christian in her later years, but she had come a long way about, and she never forgot her birthright. As a child she had been to the Sun Dances; she had taken part in those annual rites, and by them she had learned the restoration of her people in the presence of Tai-me. She was about seven when the last Kiowa Sun Dance was held in 1887 on the Washita River above Rainy Mountain Creek. The buffalo were gone. In order to consummate the ancient sacrifice—to impale the head of a buffalo bull upon the medicine tree—a delegation of old men journeyed into Texas, there to beg and barter for an animal from the Goodnight herd. She was ten when the Kiowas came together for the last time as a living Sun Dance culture. They could find no buffalo; they had to hang an old hide from the sacred tree. Before the dance could begin, a company of soldiers rode out from Fort Sill under orders to disperse the tribe. Forbidden without cause the essential act of their faith, having seen the wild herds slaughtered and left to rot upon the ground, the Kiowas backed away forever from the medicine tree. That was July 20, 1890, at the great bend of the Washita. My grandmother was there. Without bitterness, and for as long as she lived, she bore a vision of deicide.

Now that I can have her only in memory, I see my grandmother 10 in the several postures that were peculiar to her: standing at the wood stove on a winter morning and turning meat in a great iron skillet; sitting at the south window, bent above her beadwork, and afterwards, when her vision had failed, looking down for a long time into the fold of her hands; going out upon a cane, very slowly as she did when the weight of age came upon her; praying. I remember her most often at prayer. She made long, rambling prayers out of suffering and hope, having seen many things. I was never sure that I had the right to hear, so exclusive were they of all mere custom and company. The last time I saw her she prayed standing by the side of her bed at night, naked to the waist, the light of a kerosene lamp moving upon her dark skin. Her long, black hair, always drawn and braided in the day, lay upon her shoulders and against her breasts like a shawl. I do not speak Kiowa, and I never understood her prayers, but there was something inherently sad in the sound, some merest hesitation upon the syllables of sorrow. She began in a high and descending pitch, exhausting her breath to silence; then again and again—and always the same intensity of effort, of something that is, and is not, like urgency in the human voice. Transported so in the dancing light among the shadows of her room, she seemed beyond the reach of time. But that was illusion; I think I knew then that I should not see her again.

Houses are like sentinels in the plain, old keepers of the weather 11 watch. There, in a very little while, wood takes on the appearance of great age. All colors wear soon away in the wind and rain, and then the wood is burned gray and the grain appears and the nails turn red with rust. The windowpanes are black and opaque; you imagine there is nothing within, and indeed there are many ghosts, bones given up to the land. They stand here and there against the sky, and you approach them for a longer time than you expect. They belong in the distance; it is their domain.

Once there was a lot of sound in my grandmother's house, a 12 lot of coming and going, feasting and talk. The summers there were full of excitement and reunion. The Kiowas are a summer people; they abide the cold and keep to themselves; but when the season turns and the land becomes warm and vital, they cannot hold still; an old love of going returns upon them. The aged visitors who came to my grandmother's house when I was a child were made of lean and leather, and they bore themselves upright. They wore great black hats and bright ample shirts that shook in the wind. They rubbed fat upon their hair and wound their braids with strips of colored cloth. Some of them painted their faces and carried the scars of old and cherished enmities. They were an old council of warlords, come to remind and be reminded of who they were. Their wives and daughters served them well. The women might indulge themselves; gossip was at once the mark and compensation of their servitude. They made loud and elaborate talk among themselves, full of jest and gesture, fright and false alarm. They went abroad in fringed and flowered shawls, bright beadwork and German silver. They were at home in the kitchen, and they prepared meals that were banquets.

There were frequent prayer meetings, and great nocturnal feasts. 13 When I was a child, I played with my cousins outside, where the lamplight fell upon the ground and the singing of the old people rose up around us and carried away into the darkness. There were a lot of good things to eat, a lot of laughter and surprise. And afterwards, when the quiet returned, I lay down with my grandmother and could hear the frogs away by the river and feel the motion of the air.

Now there is a funeral silence in the rooms, the endless wake 14 of some final word. The walls have closed in upon my grandmother's house. When I returned to it in mourning, I saw for the first time in my life how small it was. It was late at night, and there was a white moon, nearly full. I sat for a long time on the stone steps by the kitchen door. From there I could see out across the land; I could see the long row of trees by the creek, the low light upon the rolling plains, and the stars of the Big Dipper. Once I looked at the moon and caught sight of a strange thing. A cricket had perched upon the handrail, only a few inches away from me. My line of vision was such that the creature filled the moon like a fossil. It had gone there, I thought, to live and die, for there of all places, was its small definition made whole and eternal. A warm wind rose up and purled like the longing within me.

The next morning I awoke at dawn and went out on the dirt 15 road to Rainy Mountain. It was already hot, and the grasshoppers began to fill the air. Still, it was early in the morning, and the birds sang out of the shadows. The long yellow grass on the mountain shone in the bright light, and a scissortail hied above the land. There, where it ought to be, at the end of a long and legendary way, was my grandmother's grave. Here and there on the dark stones were ancestral names. Looking back once, I saw the mountain and came away.

GEORGE ORWELL

Shooting an Elephant

In Moulmein, in Lower Burma, I was hated by large numbers   1
of people—the only time in my life that I have been important
enough for this to happen to me. I was sub-divisional police officer
of the town, and in an aimless, petty kind of way anti-European
feeling was very bitter. No one had the guts to raise a riot, but if
a European woman went through the bazaars alone somebody
would probably spit betel juice over her dress. As a police officer
I was an obvious target and was baited whenever it seemed safe
to do so. When a nimble Burman tripped me up on the football
field and the referee (another Burman) looked the other way, the
crowd yelled with hideous laughter. This happened more than
once. In the end the sneering yellow faces of young men that met
me everywhere, the insults hooted after me when I was at a safe
distance, got badly on my nerves. The young Buddhist priests were
the worst of all. There were several thousands of them in the town
and none of them seemed to have anything to do except stand
on street corners and jeer at Europeans.

All this was perplexing and upsetting. For at that time I had   2
already made up my mind that imperialism was an evil thing and
the sooner I chucked up my job and got out of it the better.
Theoretically—and secretly, of course—I was all for the Burmese
and all against their oppressors, the British. As for the job I was
doing, I hated it more bitterly than I can perhaps make clear. In
a job like that you see the dirty work of Empire at close quarters.
The wretched prisoners huddling in the stinking cages of the lock-
ups, the grey, cowed faces of the long-term convicts, the scarred
buttocks of the men who had been flogged with bamboos—all
these oppressed me with an intolerable sense of guilt. But I could
get nothing into perspective. I was young and ill-educated and I
had to think out my problems in the utter silence that is imposed
on every Englishman in the East. I did not even know that the
British Empire is dying, still less did I know that it is a great deal
better than the younger empires that are going to supplant it. All
I knew was that I was stuck between my hatred of the empire I
served and my rage against the evil-spirited little beasts who tried
to make my job impossible. With one part of my mind I thought
of the British Raj as an unbreakable tyranny, as something clamped

Orwell served in the Indian Imperial Police in Burma from 1922 to 1927. This essay
was written in 1936.

down, in *saecula saeculorum,* upon the will of prostrate peoples; with another part I thought that the greatest joy in the world would be to drive a bayonet into a Buddhist priest's guts. Feelings like these are the normal by-products of imperialism; ask any Anglo-Indian official, if you can catch him off duty.

One day something happened which in a roundabout way was   3 enlightening. It was a tiny incident in itself, but it gave me a better glimpse than I had had before of the real nature of imperialism— the real motives for which despotic governments act. Early one morning the sub-inspector at a police station the other end of the town rang me up on the 'phone and said than an elephant was ravaging the bazaar. Would I please come and do something about it? I did not know what I could do, but I wanted to see what was happening and I got on to a pony and started out. I took my rifle, an old .44 Winchester and much too small to kill an elephant, but I thought the noise might be useful *in terrorem.* Various Burmans stopped me on the way and told me about the elephant's doings. It was not, of course, a wild elephant, but a tame one which had gone "must." It had been chained up, as tame elephants always are when their attack of "must" is due, but on the previous night it had broken its chain and escaped. Its mahout, the only person who could manage it when it was in that state, had set out in pursuit, but had taken the wrong direction and was now twelve hours' journey away, and in the morning the elephant had suddenly reappeared in the town. The Burmese population had no weapons and were quite helpless against it. It had already destroyed some-body's bamboo hut, killed a cow and raided some fruit-stalls and devoured the stock; also it had met the municipal rubbish van and, when the driver jumped out and took to his heels, had turned the van over and inflicted violences upon it.

The Burmese sub-inspector and some Indian constables were   4 waiting for me in the quarter where the elephant had been seen. It was a very poor quarter, a labyrinth of squalid bamboo huts, thatched with palm-leaf, winding all over a steep hillside. I remember that it was a cloudy, stuffy morning at the beginning of the rains. We began questioning the people as to where the elephant had gone and, as usual, failed to get any definite information. That is invariably the case in the East; a story always sounds clear enough at a distance, but the nearer you get to the scene of events the vaguer it becomes. Some of the people said that the elephant had gone in one direction, some said that he had gone in another, some professed not even to have heared of any elephant. I had almost made up my mind that the whole story was a pack of lies, when we heard yells a little distance away. There was a loud, scandalized cry of "Go away, child! Go away this instant!" and an old woman with a switch in her hand came round the corner of a hut, violently shooing away a crowd of naked children. Some more women followed, clicking their tongues and exclaiming; evidently there was something that the children ought not to have seen. I rounded the hut and saw a man's dead body sprawling in the mud. He was an Indian, a black Dravidian coolie, almost naked, and he could not have been dead many minutes. The people said that the elephant had come suddenly upon him round the corner of the hut, caught him with its trunk, put its foot on his back and ground him into the earth. This was the rainy season and the ground was soft, and his face had scored a trench a foot deep and a couple of yards long. He was lying on his belly with arms crucified and head sharply twisted to one side. His face was coated with mud, the eyes wide open, the teeth bared and grinning with an expression of unendurable agony. (Never tell me, by the way, that the dead look peaceful. Most of the corpses I have seen look devilish.) The friction of the great beast's foot had stripped the skin from his back as neatly as one skins a rabbit. As soon as I saw the dead man I sent an orderly to a friend's house nearby to borrow an elephant rifle. I had already sent back the pony, not wanting it to go mad with fright and throw me if it smelt the elephant.

The orderly came back in a few minutes with a rifle and five   5 cartridges, and meanwhile some Burmans had arrived and told us that the elephant was in the paddy fields below, only a few hundred yards away. As I started forward practically the whole population of the quarter flocked out of the houses and followed me. They had seen the rifle and were all shouting excitedly that I was going to shoot the elephant. They had not shown much interest in the elephant when he was merely ravaging their homes, but it was different now that he was going to be shot. It was a bit of fun to them, as it would be to an English crowd; besides they wanted the meat. It made me vaguely uneasy. I had no intention of shooting the elephant—I had merely sent for the rifle to defend myself if necessary—and it is always unnerving to have a crowd following you. I marched down the hill, looking and feeling a fool, with the rifle over my shoulder and an ever-growing army of people jostling at my heels. At the bottom, when you got away from the huts, there was a metalled road and beyond that a miry waste of paddy fields a thousand yards across, not yet ploughed but soggy from the first rains and dotted with coarse grass. The elephant was standing eight yards from the road, his left side towards us. He took not the slightest notice of the crowd's approach. He was tearing up bunches of grass, beating them against his knees to clean them and stuffing them into his mouth.

I had halted on the road. As soon as I saw the elephant I knew with perfect certainty that I ought not to shoot him. It is a serious matter to shoot a working elephant—it is comparable to destroying a huge and costly piece of machinery—and obviously one ought not to do it if it can possibly be avoided. And at that distance, peacefully eating, the elephant looked no more dangerous than a cow. I thought then and I think now that his attack of "must" was already passing off; in which case he would merely wander harmlessly about until the mahout came back and caught him. Moreover, I did not in the least want to shoot him. I decided that I would watch him for a little while to make sure that he did not turn savage again, and then go home.

But at that moment I glanced round at the crowd that had followed me. It was an immense crowd, two thousand at the least and growing every minute. It blocked the road for a long distance on either side. I looked at the sea of yellow faces above the garish clothes—faces all happy and excited over this bit of fun, all certain that the elephant was going to be shot. They were watching me as they would watch a conjurer about to perform a trick. They did not like me, but with the magical rifle in my hands I was momentarily worth watching. And suddenly I realized that I should have to shoot the elephant after all. The people expected it of me and I had got to do it; I could feel their two thousand wills pressing me forward, irresistibly. And it was at this moment, as I stood there with the rifle in my hands, that I first grasped the hollowness, the futility of the white man's dominion in the East. Here was I, the white man with his gun, standing in front of the unarmed native crowd—seemingly the leading actor of the piece; but in reality I was only an absurd puppet pushed to and fro by the will of those yellow faces behind. I perceived in this moment that when the white man turns tyrant it is his own freedom that he destroys. He becomes a sort of hollow, posing dummy, the conventionalized figure of a sahib. For it is the condition of his rule that he shall spend his life in trying to impress the "natives," and so in every crisis he has got to do what the "natives" expect of him. He wears a mask, and his face grows to fit it. I had got to shoot the elephant. I had committed myself to doing it when I sent for the rifle. A sahib has got to act like a sahib; he has got to appear resolute, to know his own mind and do definite things. To come all that way, rifle in hand, with two thousand people marching at my heels, and then to trail feebly away, having done nothing—no, that was impossible. The crowd would laugh at me. And my whole life, every white man's life in the East, was one long struggle not to be laughed at.

But I did not want to shoot the elephant. I watched him beating   8
his bunch of grass against his knees, with that preoccupied grand-motherly air that elephants have. It seemed to me that it would be murder to shoot him. At that age I was not squeamish about killing animals, but I had never shot an elephant and never wanted to. (Somehow it always seems worse to kill a *large* animal.) Besides, there was the beast's owner to be considered. Alive, the elephant was worth at least a hundred pounds; dead, he would only be worth the value of his tusks, five pounds, possibly. But I had got to act quickly. I turned to some experienced-looking Burmans who had been there when we arrived, and asked them how the elephant had been behaving. They all said the same thing; he took no notice of you if you left him alone, but he might charge if you went too close to him.

It was perfectly clear to me what I ought to do. I ought to walk   9
up to within, say, twenty-five yards of the elephant and test his behavior. If he charged, I could shoot; if he took no notice of me, it would be safe to leave him until the mahout came back. But also I knew that I was going to do no such thing. I was a poor shot with a rifle and the ground was soft mud into which one would sink at every step. If the elephant charged and I missed him, I should have about as much chance as a toad under a steam-roller. But even then I was not thinking particularly of my own skin, only of the watchful yellow faces behind. For at that moment, with the crowd watching me, I was not afraid in the ordinary sense, as I would have been if I had been alone. A white man mustn't be frightened in front of "natives"; and so, in general, he isn't frightened. The sole thought in my mind was that if anything went wrong those two thousand Burmans would see me pursued, caught, trampled on and reduced to a grinning corpse like that Indian up the hill. And if that happened it was quite probable that some of them would laugh. That would never do. There was only one alternative. I shoved the cartridges into the magazine and lay down on the road to get a better aim.

The crowd grew very still, and a deep, low, happy sigh, as of   10
people who see the theatre curtain go up at last, breathed from innumerable throats. They were going to have their bit of fun after all. The rifle was a beautiful German thing with cross-hair sights. I did not then know that in shooting an elephant one would shoot

to cut an imaginary bar running from ear-hole to ear-hole. I ought, therefore, as the elephant was sideways on, to have aimed straight at his ear-hole; actually I aimed several inches in front of this, thinking the brain would be further forward.

When I pulled the trigger I did not hear the bang or feel the 11 kick—one never does when a shot goes home—but I heard the devilish roar of glee that went up from the crowd. In that instant, in too short a time, one would have thought, even for the bullet to get there, a mysterious, terrible change had come over the elephant. He neither stirred nor fell, but every line of his body had altered. He looked suddenly stricken, shrunken, immensely old, as though the frightful impact of the bullet had paralysed him without knocking him down. At last, after what seemed a long time—it might have been five seconds, I dare say—he sagged flabbily to his knees. His mouth slobbered. An enormous senility seemed to have settled upon him. One could have imagined him thousands of years old. I fired again into the same spot. At the second shot he did not collapse but climbed with desperate slowness to his feet and stood weakly upright, with legs sagging and head drooping. I fired a third time. That was the shot that did for him. You could see the agony of it jolt his whole body and knock the last remnant of strength from his legs. But in falling he seemed for a moment to rise, for as his hind legs collapsed beneath him he seemed to tower upward like a huge rock toppling, his trunk reaching skywards like a tree. He trumpeted, for the first and only time. And then down he came, his belly towards me, with a crash that seemed to shake the ground even where I lay.

I got up. The Burmans were already racing past me across the 12 mud. It was obvious that the elephant would never rise again, but he was not dead. He was breathing very rhythmically with long rattling gasps, his great mound of a side painfully rising and falling. His mouth was wide open—I could see far down into caverns of pale pink throat. I waited a long time for him to die, but his breathing did not weaken. Finally I fired my two remaining shots into the spot where I thought his heart must be. The thick blood welled out of him like red velvet, but still he did not die. His body did not even jerk when the shots hit him, the tortured breathing continued without a pause. He was dying, very slowly and in great agony, but in some world remote from me where not even a bullet could damage him further. I felt that I had got to put an end to that dreadful noise. It seemed dreadful to see the great beast lying there, powerless to move and yet powerless to die, and not even to be able to finish him. I sent back for my small rifle and poured shot after shot into his heart and down his throat. They seemed to make no impression. The tortured gasps continued as steadily as the ticking of a clock.

In the end I could not stand it any longer and went away. I   13 heard later that it took him half an hour to die. Burmans were bringing dahs and baskets even before I left, and I was told they had stripped his body almost to the bones by the afternoon.

Afterwards, of course, there were endless discussions about the   14 shooting of the elephant. The owner was furious, but he was only an Indian and could do nothing. Besides, legally I had done the right thing, for a mad elephant has to be killed, like a mad dog, if its owner fails to control it. Among the Europeans opinion was divided. The older men said I was right, the younger men said it was a damn shame to shoot an elephant for killing a coolie, because an elephant was worth more than any damn Coringhee coolie. And afterwards I was very glad that the coolie had been killed; it put me legally in the right and it gave me a sufficient pretext for shooting the elephant. I often wondered whether any of the others grasped that I had done it solely to avoid looking a fool.

JAMES BALDWIN

Fifth Avenue, Uptown: A Letter from Harlem

There is a housing project standing now where the house in   1 which we grew up once stood, and one of those stunted city trees is snarling where our doorway used to be. This is on the rehabilitated side of the avenue. The other side of the avenue—for progress takes time—has not been rehabilitated yet and it looks exactly as it looked in the days when we sat with our noses pressed against the windowpane, longing to be allowed to go "across the street." The grocery store which gave us credit is still there, and there can be no doubt that it is still giving credit. The people in the project certainly need it—far more, indeed, than they ever needed the project. The last time I passed by, the Jewish proprietor was still standing among his shelves, looking sadder and heavier but scarcely

First published in *Esquire*, July 1960.

any older. Farther down the block stands the shoe-repair store in which our shoes were repaired until reparation became impossible and in which, then, we bought all our "new" ones. The Negro proprietor is still in the window, head down, working at the leather.

These two, I imagine, could tell a long tale if they would (perhaps   2 they would be glad to if they could), having watched so many, for so long, struggling in the fishhooks, the barbed wire, of this avenue.

The avenue is elsewhere the renowned and elegant Fifth. The   3 area I am describing, which, in today's gang parlance, would be called "the turf," is bounded by Lenox Avenue on the west, the Harlem River on the east, 135th Street on the north, and 130th Street on the south. We never lived beyond these boundaries; this is where we grew up. Walking along 145th Street—for example— familiar as it is, and similar, does not have the same impact because I did not know any of the people on the block. But when I turn east on 131st Street and Lenox Avenue, there is first a soda-pop joint, then a shoeshine "parlor," then a grocery store, then a dry cleaners', then the houses. All along the street there are people who watched me grow up, people who grew up with me, people I watched grow up along with my brothers and sisters; and, some- times in my arms, sometimes underfoot, sometimes at my shoulder— or on it—their children, a riot, a forest of children, who include my nieces and nephews.

When we reach the end of this long block, we find ourselves   4 on wide, filthy, hostile Fifth Avenue, facing that project which hangs over the avenue like a monument to the folly, and the cowardice, of good intentions. All along the block, for anyone who knows it, are immense human gaps, like craters. These gaps are not created merely by those who have moved away, inevitably into some other ghetto; or by those who have risen, almost always into a greater capacity for self-loathing and self-delusion; or yet by those who, by whatever means—War II, the Korean war, a policeman's gun or billy, a gang war, a brawl, madness, an overdose of heroin, or, simply, unnatural exhaustion—are dead. I am talking about those who are left, and I am talking principally about the young. What are they doing? Well, some, a minority, are fanatical churchgoers, members of the more extreme of the Holy Roller sects. Many, many more are "moslems," by affiliation or sympathy, that is to say that they are united by nothing more—and nothing less—than a hatred of the white world and all its works. They are present, for example, at every Buy Black street-corner meeting— meetings in which the speaker urges his hearers to cease trading with white men and establish a separate economy. Neither the speaker nor his hearers can possibly do this, of course, since Negroes do not own General Motors or RCA or the A & P, nor, indeed, do they own more than a wholly insufficient fraction of anything else in Harlem (those who *do* own anything are more interested in their profits than in their fellows). But these meetings nevertheless keep alive in the participators a certain pride of bitterness without which, however futile this bitterness may be, they could scarcely remain alive at all. Many have given up. They stay home and watch the TV screen, living on the earnings of their parents, cousins, brothers, or uncles, and only leave the house to go to the movies or to the nearest bar. "How're you making it?" one may ask, running into them along the block, or in the bar. "Oh, I'm TV-ing it"; with the saddest, sweetest, most shame-faced of smiles, and from a great distance. This distance one is compelled to respect; anyone who has traveled so far will not easily be dragged again into the world. There are further retreats, of course, than the TV screen or the bar. There are those who are simply sitting on their stoops, "stoned," animated for a moment only, and hideously, by the approach of someone who may lend them the money for a "fix." Or by the approach of someone from whom they can purchase it, one of the shrewd ones, on the way to prison or just coming out.

And the others, who have avoided all of these deaths, get up   5
in the morning and go downtown to meet "the man." They work in the white man's world all day and come home in the evening to this fetid block. They struggle to instill in their children some private sense of honor or dignity which will help the child survive. This means, of course, that they must struggle, stolidly, incessantly, to keep this sense alive in themselves, in spite of the insults, the indifference, and the cruelty they are certain to encounter in their working day. They patiently browbeat the landlord into fixing the heat, the plaster, the plumbing; this demands prodigious patience; nor is patience usually enough. In trying to make their hovels habitable, they are perpetually throwing good money after bad. Such frustration, so long endured, is driving many strong, admirable men and women whose only crime is color to the very gates of paranoia.

One remembers them from another time—playing handball in   6
the playground, going to church, wondering if they were going to be promoted at school. One remembers them going off to war— gladly, to escape this block. One remembers their return. Perhaps one remembers their wedding day. And one sees where the girl is now—vainly looking for salvation from some other embittered,

trussed, and struggling boy—and sees the all-but-abandoned children in the streets.

Now I am perfectly aware that there are other slums in which white men are fighting for their lives, and mainly losing. I know that blood is also flowing through those streets and that the human damage there is incalculable. People are continually pointing out to me the wretchedness of white people in order to console me for the wretchedness of blacks. But an itemized account of the American failure does not console me and it should not console anyone else. That hundreds of thousands of white people are living, in effect, no better than the "niggers" is not a fact to be regarded with complacency. The social and moral bankruptcy suggested by this fact is of the bitterest, most terrifying kind. 7

The people, however, who believe that this democratic anguish has some consoling value are always pointing out that So-and-So, white, and So-and-So, black, rose from the slums into the big time. The existence—the public existence—of, say, Frank Sinatra and Sammy Davis, Jr. proves to them that America is still the land of opportunity and that inequalities vanish before the determined will. It proves nothing of the sort. The determined will is rare—at the moment, in this country, it is unspeakably rare—and the inequalities suffered by the many are in no way justified by the rise of a few. A few have always risen—in every country, every era, and in the teeth of regimes which can by no stretch of the imagination be thought of as free. Not all of these people, it is worth remembering, left the world better than they found it. The determined will is rare, but it is not invariably benevolent. Furthermore, the American equation of success with the big times reveals an awful disrespect for human life and human achievement. This equation has placed our cities among the most dangerous in the world and has placed our youth among the most empty and most bewildered. The situation of our youth is not mysterious. Children have never been very good at listening to their elders, but they have never failed to imitate them. They must, they have no other models. That is exactly what our children are doing. They are imitating our immorality, our disrespect for the pain of others. 8

All other slum dwellers, when the bank account permits it, can move out of the slum and vanish altogether from the eye of persecution. No Negro in this country has ever made that much money and it will be a long time before any Negro does. The Negroes in Harlem, who have no money, spend what they have on such gimcracks as they are sold. These include "wider" TV screens, more "faithful" hi-fi sets, more "powerful" cars, all of which, of course, are obsolete long before they are paid for. Anyone 9

who has ever struggled with poverty knows how extremely expensive it is to be poor; and if one is a member of a captive
population, economically speaking, one's feet have simply been
placed on the treadmill forever. One is victimized, economically,
in a thousand ways—rent, for example, or car insurance. Go shopping one day in Harlem—for anything—and compare Harlem prices
and quality with those downtown.

The people who have managed to get off this block have only   10
got as far as a more respectable ghetto. This respectable ghetto
does not even have the advantages of the disreputable one—friends,
neighbors, a familiar church, and friendly tradesmen; and it is not,
moreover, in the nature of any ghetto to remain respectable long.
Every Sunday, people who have left the block take the lonely ride
back, dragging their increasingly discontented children with them.
They spend the day talking, not always with words, about the
trouble they've seen and the trouble—one must watch their eyes
as they watch their children—they are only too likely to see. For
children do not like ghettos. It takes them nearly no time to
discover exactly why they are there.

The projects in Harlem are hated. They are hated almost as   11
much as policemen, and this is saying a great deal. And they are
hated for the same reason: both reveal, unbearably, the real attitude
of the white world, no matter how many liberal speeches are
made, no matter how many lofty editorials are written, no matter
how many civil-rights commissions are set up.

The projects are hideous, of course, there being a law, apparently   12
respected throughout the world, that popular housing shall be as
cheerless as a prison. They are lumped all over Harlem, colorless,
bleak, high, and revolting. The wide windows look out on Harlem's
invincible and indescribable squalor: the Park Avenue railroad
tracks, around which, about forty years ago, the present dark
community began; the unrehabilitated houses, bowed down, it
would seem, under the great weight of frustration and bitterness
they contain; the dark, the ominous schoolhouses from which the
child may emerge maimed, blinded, hooked, or enraged for life;
and the churches, churches, block upon block of churches, niched
in the walls like cannon in the walls of a fortress. Even if the
administration of the projects were not so insanely humiliating
(for example: one must report raises in salary to the management,
which will then eat up the profit by raising one's rent; the management has the right to know who is staying in your apartment;
the managment can ask you to leave, at their discretion), the

projects would still be hated because they are an insult to the meanest intelligence.

Harlem got its first private project, Riverton[1]—which is now, naturally, a slum—about twelve years ago because at that time Negroes were not allowed to live in Stuyvesant Town. Harlem watched Riverton go up, therefore, in the most violent bitterness of spirit, and hated it long before the builders arrived. They began hating it at about the time people began moving out of their condemned houses to make room for this additional proof of how thoroughly the white world despised them. And they had scarcely moved in, naturally, before they began smashing windows, defacing walls, urinating in the elevators, and fornicating in the playgrounds. Liberals, both white and black, were appalled at the spectacle. I was appalled by the liberal innocence—or cynicism, which comes out in practice as much the same thing. Other people were delighted to be able to point to proof positive that nothing could be done to better the lot of the colored people. They were, and are, right in one respect: that nothing can be done as long as they are treated like colored people. The people in Harlem know they are living there because white people do not think they are good enough to live anywhere else. No amount of "improvement" can sweeten this fact. Whatever money is now being earmarked to improve this, or any other ghetto, might as well be burnt. A ghetto can be improved in one way only: out of existence.

Similarly, the only way to police a ghetto is to be oppressive. None of the Police Commissioner's men, even with the best will in the world, have any way of understanding the lives led by the people they swagger about in twos and threes controlling. Their very presence is an insult, and it would be, even if they spent their entire day feeding gumdrops to children. They represent the force of the white world, and the world's real intentions are, simply, for the world's criminal profit and ease, to keep the black man corraled up here, in his place. The badge, the gun in the

1. The inhabitants of Riverton were much embittered by this description; they have, apparently, forgotten how their project came into being; and have repeatedly informed me that I cannot possibly be referring to Riverton, but to another housing project which is directly across the street. It is quite clear, I think, that I have no interest in accusing any individuals or families of the depredations herein described: but neither can I deny the evidence of my own eyes. Nor do I blame anyone in Harlem for making the best of a dreadful bargain. But anyone who lives in Harlem and imagines that he has *not* struck this bargain, or that what he takes to be his status (in whose eyes?) protects him against the common pain, demoralization, and danger, is simply self deluded. [author's note]

holster, and the swinging club make vivid what will happen should
his rebellion become overt. Rare, indeed, is the Harlem citizen,
from the most circumspect church member to the most shiftless
adolescent, who does not have a long tale to tell of police incompetence, injustice, or brutality. I myself have witnessed and endured
it more than once. The businessmen and racketeers also have a
story. And so do the prostitutes. (And this is not, perhaps, the
place to discuss Harlem's very complex attitude toward black policemen, nor the reasons, according to Harlem, that they are nearly
all downtown.)

It is hard, on the other hand, to blame the policeman, blank,   15
good-natured, thoughtless, and insuperably innocent, for being
such a perfect representative of the people he serves. He, too,
believes in good intentions and is astounded and offended when
they are not taken for the deed. He has never, himself, done
anything for which to be hated—which of us has?—and yet he
is facing, daily and nightly, people who would gladly see him
dead, and he knows it. There is no way for him not to know it:
there are few things under heaven more unnerving than the silent,
accumulating contempt and hatred of a people. He moves through
Harlem, therefore, like an occupying soldier in a bitterly hostile
country; which is precisely what, and where, he is, and is the
reason he walks in twos and threes. And he is not the only one
who knows why he is always in company: the people who are
watching him know why, too. Any street meeting, sacred or secular,
which he and his colleagues uneasily cover has as its explicit or
implicit burden the cruelty and injustice of the white domination.
And these days, of course, in terms increasingly vivid and jubilant,
it speaks of the end of that domination. The white policeman
standing on a Harlem street corner finds himself at the very center
of the revolution now occurring in the world. He is not prepared
for it—naturally, nobody is—and, what is possibly much more to
the point, he is exposed, as few white people are, to the anguish
of the black people around him. Even if he is gifted with the
merest mustard grain of imagination, something must seep in. He
cannot avoid observing that some of the children, in spite of their
color, remind him of children he has known and loved, perhaps
even of his own children. He knows that he certainly does not
want *his* children living this way. He can retreat from his uneasiness
in only one direction: into a callousness which very shortly becomes
second nature. He becomes more callous, the population becomes
more hostile, the situation grows more tense, and the police force
is increased. One day, to everyone's astonishment, someone drops
a match in the powder keg and everything blows up. Before the

dust has settled or the blood congealed, editorials, speeches, and civil-rights commissions are loud in the land, demanding to know what happened. What happened is that Negroes want to be treated like men.

Negroes want to be treated like men: a perfectly straightforward 16 statement, containing only seven words. People who have mastered Kant, Hegel, Shakespeare, Marx, Freud, and the Bible find this statement utterly impenetrable. The idea seems to threaten profound, barely conscious assumptions. A kind of panic paralyzes their features, as though they found themselves trapped on the edge of a steep place. I once tried to describe to a very well-known American intellectual the conditions among Negroes in the South. My recital disturbed him and made him indignant; and he asked me in perfect innocence, "Why don't all the Negroes in the South move North?" I tried to explain what *has* happened, unfailingly, whenever a significant body of Negroes move North. They do not escape Jim Crow: they merely encounter another, not-less-deadly variety. They do not move to Chicago, they move to the South Side; they do not move to New York, they move to Harlem. The pressure within the ghetto causes the ghetto walls to expand, and this expansion is always violent. White people hold the line as long as they can, and in as many ways as they can, from verbal intimidation to physical violence. But inevitably the border which has divided the ghetto from the rest of the world falls into the hands of the ghetto. The white people fall back bitterly before the back horde; the landlords make a tidy profit by raising the rent, chopping up the rooms, and all but dispensing with the upkeep; and what has once been a neighborhood turns into a "turf." This is precisely what happened when the Puerto Ricans arrived in their thousands— and the bitterness thus caused is, as I write, being fought out all up and down those streets.

Northerners indulge in an extremely dangerous luxury. They 17 seem to feel that because they fought on the right side during the Civil War, and won, they have earned the right merely to deplore what is going on in the South, without taking any responsibility for it; and that they can ignore what is happening in Northern cities because what is happening in Little Rock or Birmingham is worse. Well, in the first place, it is not possible for anyone who has not endured both to know which is "worse." I know Negroes who prefer the South and white Southerners, because "At least there, you haven't got to play any guessing games!" The guessing games referred to have driven more than one Negro into the narcotics ward, the madhouse, or the river. I know another Negro, a man very dear to me, who says with conviction and with truth,

"The spirit of the South is the spirit of America." He was born in the North and did his military training in the South. He did not, as far as I can gather, find the South "worse"; he found it, if anything, all too familiar. In the second place, though, even if Birmingham *is* worse, no doubt Johannesburg, South Africa, beats it by several miles, and Buchenwald was one of the worst things that ever happened in the entire history of the world. The world has never lacked for horrifying examples; but I do not believe that these examples are meant to be used as justification for our own crimes. This perpetual justification empties the heart of all human feeling. The emptier our hearts become, the greater will be our crimes. Thirdly, the South is not merely an embarrassingly backward region, but a part of this country, and what happens there concerns every one of us.

As far as the color problem is concerned, there is but one difference   18
between the Southern white and the Northerner: the Southerner remembers, historically and in his own psyche, a kind of Eden in which he loved black people and they loved him. Historically, the flaming sword laid across this Eden is the Civil War. Personally, it is the Southerner's sexual coming of age, when, without any warning, unbreakable taboos are set up between himself and his past. Everything, thereafter, is permitted him except the love he remembers and has never ceased to need. The resulting, indescribable torment affects every Southern mind and is the basis of the Southern hysteria.

None of this is true for the Northerner. Negroes represent nothing   19
to him personally, except, perhaps, the dangers of carnality. He never sees Negroes. Southerns see them all the time. Northerners never think about them whereas Southerners are never really thinking of anything else. Negroes are, therefore, ignored in the North and are under surveillance in the South, and suffer hideously in both places. Neither the Southerner nor the Northerner is able to look on the Negro simply as a man. It seems to be indispensable to the national self-esteem that the Negro be considered either as a kind of ward (in which case we are told how many Negroes, comparatively, bought Cadillacs last year and how few, comparatively, were lynched), or as a victim (in which case we are promised that he will never vote in our assemblies or go to school with our kids). They are two sides of the same coin and the South will not change—*cannot* change—until the North changes. The country will not change until it re-examines itself and discovers what it really means by freedom. In the meantime, generations keep being born, bitterness is increased by incompetence, pride, and folly, and the world shrinks around us.

It is a terrible, an inexorable, law that one cannot deny the   20
humanity of another without diminishing one's own: in the face
of one's victim, one sees oneself. Walk through the streets of
Harlem and see what we, this nation, have become.

CLARENCE DARROW

Address to the Prisoners
in the Cook County Jail

If I looked at jails and crimes and prisoners in the way the   1
ordinary person does, I should not speak on this subject to you.
The reason I talk to you on the question of crime, its cause and
cure, is that I really do not in the least believe in crime. There is
no such thing as a crime as the word is generally understood. I
do not believe there is any sort of distinction between the real
moral conditions of the people in and out of jail. One is just as
good as the other. The people here can no more help being here
than the people outside can avoid being outside. I do not believe
that people are in jail because they deserve to be. They are in jail
simply because they cannot avoid it on account of circumstances
which are entirely beyond their control and for which they are
in no way responsible.

I suppose a great many people on the outside would say I was   2
doing you harm if they should hear what I say to you this afternoon,
but you cannot be hurt a great deal anyway, so it will not matter.
Good people outside would say that I was really teaching you
things that were calculated to injure society, but it's worth while
now and then to hear something different from what you ordinarily
get from preachers and the like. These will tell you that you should
be good and then you will get rich and be happy. Of course we
know that people do not get rich by being good, and that is the
reason why so many of you people try to get rich some other
way, only you do not understand how to do it quite as well as
the fellow outside.

There are people who think that everything in this world is an   3
accident. But really there is no such thing as an accident. A great
many folks admit that many of the people in jail ought to be there,

Delivered in the Cook County, Illinois, penitentiary in 1902.

and many who are outside ought to be in. I think none of them ought to be here. There ought to be no jails; and if it were not for the fact that people on the outside are so grasping and heartless in their dealings with the people on the inside, there would be no such institution as jails.

I do not want you to believe that I think all you people here   4
are angels. I do not think that. You are people of all kinds, all of you doing the best you can—and that is evidently not very well. You are people of all kinds and conditions and under all circumstances. In one sense everybody is equally good and equally bad. We all do the best we can under the circumstances. But as to the exact things for which you are sent here, some of you are guilty and did the particular act because you needed the money. Some of you did it because you are in the habit of doing it, and some of you because you are born to it, and it comes to be as natural as it does, for instance, for me to be good.

Most of you probably have nothing against me, and most of   5
you would treat me the same way as any other person would, probably better than some of the people on the outside would treat me, because you think I believe in you and they know I do not believe in them. While you would not have the least thing against me in the world, you might pick my pockets. I do not think all of you would, but I think some of you would. You would not have anything against me, but that's your profession, a few of you. Some of the rest of you, if my doors were unlocked, might come in if you saw anything you wanted—not out of any malice to me, but because that is your trade. There is no doubt there are quite a number of people in this jail who would pick my pockets. And still I know this—that when I get outside pretty nearly everybody picks my pocket. There may be some of you who would hold up a man on the street, if you did not happen to have something else to do, and needed the money; but when I want to light my house or my office the gas company holds me up. They charge me one dollar for something that is worth twenty-five cents. Still all these people are good people; they are pillars of society and support the churches, and they are respectable.

When I ride on the streetcars I am held up—I pay five cents   6
for a ride that is worth two and a half cents, simply because a body of men have bribed the city council and the legislature, so that all the rest of us have to pay tribute to them.

If I do not want to fall into the clutches of the gas trust and   7
choose to burn oil instead of gas, then good Mr. Rockefeller holds me up, and he uses a certain portion of his money to build uni-

versities and support churches which are engaged in telling us
how to be good.

Some of you are here for obtaining property under false pre- 8
tenses—yet I pick up a great Sunday paper and read the advertisements of a merchant prince—"Shirtwaists for 39 cents, marked
down from $3.00."

When I read the advertisements in the paper I see they are all 9
lies. When I want to get out and find a place to stand anywhere
on the face of the earth, I find that it has all been taken up long
ago before I came here, and before you came here, and somebody
says, "Get off, swim into the lake, fly into the air; go anywhere,
but get off." That is because these people have the police and they
have the jails and the judges and the lawyers and the soldiers and
all the rest of them to take care of the earth and drive everybody
off that comes in their way.

A great many people will tell you that all this is true, but that 10
it does not excuse you. These facts do not excuse some fellow
who reaches into my pocket and takes out a five-dollar bill. The
fact that the gas company bribes the members of the legislature
from year to year, and fixes the law, so that all you people are
compelled to be "fleeced" whenever you deal with them; the fact
that the streetcar companies and the gas companies have control
of the streets; and the fact that the landlords own all the earth—
this, they say, has nothing to do with you.

Let us see whether there is any connection between the crimes 11
of the respectable classes and your presence in the jail. Many of
you people are in jail because you have really committed burglary;
many of you, because you have stolen something. In the meaning
of the law, you have taken some other person's property. Some
of you have entered a store and carried off a pair of shoes because
you did not have the price. Possibly some of you have committed
murder. I cannot tell what all of you did. There are a great many
people here who have done some of these things who really do
not know themselves why they did them. I think I know why
you did them—every one of you; you did these things because
you were bound to do them. It looked to you at the time as if
you had a chance to do them or not, as you saw fit; but still, after
all, you had no choice. There may be people here who had some
money in their pockets and who still went out and got some more
money in a way society forbids. Now, you may not yourselves
see exactly why it was you did this thing, but if you look at the
question deeply enough and carefully enough you will see that
there were circumstances that drove you to do exactly the thing

which you did. You could not help it any more than we outside can help taking the positions that we take. The reformers who tell you to be good and you will be happy, and the people on the outside who have property to protect—they think that the only way to do it is by building jails and locking you up in cells on weekdays and praying for you Sundays.

I think that all of this has nothing whatever to do with right 12 conduct. I think it is very easily seen what has to do with right conduct. Some so-called criminals—and I will use this word because it is handy, it means nothing to me—I speak of the criminals who get caught as distinguished from the criminals who catch them— some of these so-called criminals are in jail for their first offenses, but nine tenths of you are in jail because you did not have a good lawyer and, of course, you did not have a good lawyer because you did not have enough money to pay a good lawyer. There is no very great danger of a rich man going to jail.

Some of you may be here for the first time. If we would open 13 the doors and let you out, and leave the laws as they are today, some of you would be back tomorrow. This is about as good a place as you can get anyway. There are many people here who are so in the habit of coming that they would not know where else to go. There are people who are born with the tendency to break into jail every chance they get, and they cannot avoid it. You cannot figure out your life and see why it was, but still there is a reason for it; and if we were all wise and knew all the facts, we could figure it out.

In the first place, there are a good many more people who go 14 to jail in the wintertime than in the summer. Why is this? Is it because people are more wicked in winter? No, it is because the coal trust begins to get in its grip in the winter. A few gentlemen take possession of the coal, and unless the people will pay seven or eight dollars a ton for something that is worth three dollars, they will have to freeze. Then there is nothing to do but to break into jail, and so there are many more in jail in the winter than in summer. It costs more for gas in the winter because the nights are longer, and people go to jail to save gas bills. The jails are electric-lighted. You may not know it, but these economic laws are working all the time, whether we know it or do not know it.

There are more people who go to jail in hard times than in 15 good times—few people, comparatively, go to jail except when they are hard up. They go to jail because they have no other place to go. They may not know why, but it is true all the same. People are not more wicked in hard times. That is not the reason. The fact is true all over the world that in hard times more people go to jail than in good times, and in winter more people go to jail than in summer. Of course it is pretty hard times for people who go to jail at any time. The people who go to jail are almost always poor people—people who have no other place to live, first and last. When times are hard, then you find large numbers of people who go to jail who would not otherwise be in jail.

Long ago, Mr. Buckle, who was a great philosopher and historian, collected facts, and he showed that the number of people who are arrested increased just as the price of food increased. When they put up the price of gas ten cents a thousand, I do not know who will go to jail, but I do know that a certain number of people will go. When the meat combine raises the price of beef, I do not know who is going to jail, but I know that a large number of people are bound to go. Whenever the Standard Oil Company raises the price of oil, I know that a certain number of girls who are seamstresses, and who work night after night long hours for somebody else, will be compelled to go out on the streets and ply another trade, and I know that Mr. Rockefeller and his associates are responsible and not the poor girls in the jails. 16

First and last, people are sent to jail because they are poor. Sometimes, as I say, you may not need money at the particular time, but you wish to have thrifty forehanded habits, and do not always wait until you are in absolute want. Some of you people are perhaps plying the trade, the profession, which is called burglary. No man in his right senses will go into a strange house in the dead of night and prowl around with a dark lantern through unfamiliar rooms and take chances of his life, if he has plenty of the good things of the world in his own home. You would not take any such chances as that. If a man had clothes in his clothes-press and beefsteak in his pantry and money in the bank, he would not navigate around nights in houses where he knows nothing about the premises whatever. It always requires experience and education for this profession, and people who fit themselves for it are no more to blame than I am for being a lawyer. A man would not hold up another man on the street if he had plenty of money in his own pocket. He might do it if he had one dollar or two dollars, but he wouldn't if he had as much money as Mr. Rockefeller has. Mr. Rockefeller has a great deal better hold-up game than that. 17

The more that is taken from the poor by the rich, who have the chance to take it, the more poor people there are who are compelled to resort to these means for a livelihood. They may not understand it, they may not think so at once, but after all they are driven into that line of employment. 18

There is a bill before the legislature of this state to punish kidnaping   19
children with death. We have wise members of the legislature.
They know the gas trust when they see it and they always see
it—they can furnish light enough to be seen; and this legislature
thinks it is going to stop kidnaping children by making a law
punishing kidnapers of children with death. I don't believe in
kidnaping children, but the legislature is all wrong. Kidnaping
children is not a crime, it is a profession. It has been developed
with the times. It has been developed with our modern industrial
conditions. There are many ways of making money—many new
ways that our ancestors knew nothing about. Our ancestors knew
nothing about a billion-dollar trust; and here comes some poor
fellow who has no other trade and he discovers the profession of
kidnaping children.

This crime is born, not because people are bad; people don't   20
kidnap other people's children because they want the children or
because they are devilish, but because they see a chance to get
some money out of it. You cannot cure this crime by passing a
law punishing by death kidnapers of children. There is one way
to cure it. There is one way to cure all these offenses, and that is
to give the people a chance to live. There is no other way, and
there never was any other way since the world began; and the
world is so blind and stupid that it will not see. If every man and
woman and child in the world had a chance to make a decent,
fair, honest living, there would be no jails and no lawyers and
no courts. There might be some persons here or there with some
peculiar formation of their brain, like Rockefeller, who would do
these things simply to be doing them; but they would be very,
very few, and those should be sent to a hospital and treated, and
not sent to jail; and they would entirely disappear in the second
generation, or at least in the third generation.

I am not talking pure theory. I will just give you two or three   21
illustrations.

The English people once punished criminals by sending them   22
away. They would load them on a ship and export them to Australia.
England was owned by lords and nobles and rich people. They
owned the whole earth over there, and the other people had to
stay in the streets. They could not get a decent living. They used
to take their criminals and send them to Australia—I mean the
class of criminals who got caught. When these criminals got over
there, and nobody else had come, they had the whole continent
to run over, and so they could raise sheep and furnish their own
meat, which is easier than stealing it. These criminals then became
decent, respectable people because they had a chance to live. They

did not commit any crimes. They were just like the English people who sent them there, only better. And in the second generation the descendants of those criminals were as good and respectable a class of people as there were on the face of the earth, and then they began building churches and jails themselves.

A portion of this country was settled in the same way, landing ₂₃ prisoners down on the southern coast; but when they got here and had a whole continent to run over and plenty of chances to make a living, they became respectable citizens, making their own living just like any other citizen in the world. But finally the descendants of the English aristocracy who sent the people over to Australia found out they were getting rich, and so they went over to get possession of the earth as they always do, and they organized land syndicates and got control of the land and ores, and then they had just as many criminals in Australia as they did in England. It was not because the world had grown bad; it was because the earth had been taken away from the people.

Some of you people have lived in the country. It's prettier than ₂₄ it is here. And if you have ever lived on a farm you understand that if you put a lot of cattle in a field, when the pasture is short they will jump over the fence; but put them in a good field where there is plenty of pasture, and they will be law-abiding cattle to the end of time. The human animal is just like the rest of the animals, only a little more so. The same thing that governs in the one governs in the other.

Everybody makes his living along the lines of least resistance. ₂₅ A wise man who comes into a country early sees a great undeveloped land. For instance, our rich men twenty-five years ago saw that Chicago was small and knew a lot of people would come here and settle, and they readily saw that if they had all the land around here it would be worth a good deal, so they grabbed the land. You cannot be a landlord because somebody has got it all. You must find some other calling. In England and Ireland and Scotland less than five per cent own all the land there is, and the people are bound to stay there on any kind of terms the landlords give. They must live the best they can, so they develop all these various professions—burglary, picking pockets, and the like.

Again, people find all sorts of ways of getting rich. These are ₂₆ diseases like everything else. You look at people getting rich, or- ganizing trusts and making a million dollars, and somebody gets the disease and he starts out. He catches it just as a man catches the mumps or the measles; he is not to blame, it is in the air. You will find men speculating beyond their means, because the mania of money-getting is taking possession of them. It is simply a disease—nothing more, nothing less. You cannot avoid catching it; but the fellows who have control of the earth have the advantage of you. See what the law is: when these men get control of things, they make the laws. They do not make the laws to protect anybody; courts are not instruments of justice. When your case gets into court it will make little difference whether you are guilty or innocent, but it's better if you have a smart lawyer. And you cannot have a smart lawyer unless you have money. First and last it's a question of money. Those men who own the earth make the laws to protect what they have. They fix up a sort of fence or pen around what they have, and they fix the law so the fellow on the outside cannot get in. The laws are really organized for the protection of the men who rule the world. They were never organized or enforced to do justice. We have no system for doing justice, not the slightest in the world.

Let me illustrate: Take the poorest person in this room. If the 27 community had provided a system of doing justice, the poorest person in this room would have as good a lawyer as the richest, would he not? When you went into court you would have just as long a trial and just as fair a trial as the richest person in Chicago. Your case would not be tried in fifteen or twenty minutes, whereas it would take fifteen days to get through with a rich man's case.

Then if you were rich and were beaten, your case would be 28 taken to the Appellate Court. A poor man cannot take his case to the Appellate Court; he has not the price. And then to the Supreme Court. And if he were beaten there he might perhaps go to the United States Supreme Court. And he might die of old age before he got into jail. If you are poor, it's a quick job. You are almost known to be guilty, else you would not be there. Why should anyone be in the criminal court if he were not guilty? He would not be there if he could be anywhere else. The officials have no time to look after all these cases. The people who are on the outside, who are running banks and building churches and making jails, they have no time to examine 600 or 700 prisoners each year to see whether they are guilty or innocent. If the courts were organized to promote justice the people would elect somebody to defend all these ciminals, somebody as smart as the prosecutor— and give him as many detectives and as many assistants to help, and pay as much money to defend you as to prosecute you. We have a very able man for state's attorney, and he has many assistants, detectives, and policemen without end, and judges to hear the cases—everything handy.

Most all of our criminal code consists in offenses against property. People are sent to jail because they have committed a crime against property. It is of very little consequence whether one hundred people more or less go to jail who ought not to go—you must protect property, because in this world property is of more importance than anything else.

How is it done? These people who have property fix it so they can protect what they have. When somebody commits a crime it does not follow that he has done something that is morally wrong. The man on the outside who has committed no crime may have done something. For instance: to take all the coal in the United States and raise the price two dollars or three dollars when there is no need of it, and thus kill thousands of babies and send thousands of people to the poorhouse and tens of thousands to jail, as is done every year in the United States—this is a greater crime than all the people in our jails ever committed; but the law does not punish it. Why? Because the fellows who control the earth make the laws. If you and I had the making of the laws, the first thing we would do would be to punish the fellow who gets control of the earth. Nature put this coal in the ground for me as well as for them and nature made the prairies up here to raise wheat for me as well as for them, and then the great railroad companies came along and fenced it up.

Most all of the crimes for which we are punished are property crimes. There are a few personal crimes, like murder—but they are very few. The crimes committed are mostly those against property. If this punishment is right the criminals must have a lot of property. How much money is there in this crowd? And yet you are all here for crimes against property. The people up and down the Lake Shore have not committed crime; still they have so much property they don't know what to do with it. It is perfectly plain why these people have not committed crimes against property; they make the laws and therefore do not need to break them. And in order for you to get some property you are obliged to break the rules of the game. I don't know but what some of you may have had a very nice chance to get rich by carrying a hod for one dollar a day, twelve hours. Instead of taking that nice, easy profession, you are a burglar. If you had been given a chance to be a banker you would rather follow that. Some of you may have had a chance to work as a switchman on a railroad where you know, according to statistics, that you cannot live and keep all your limbs more than seven years, and you can get fifty dollars or seventy-five dollars a month for taking your lives in your hands;

and instead of taking that lucrative position you chose to be a
sneak thief, or something like that. Some of you made that sort
of choice. I don't know which I would take if I was reduced to
this choice. I have an easier choice.

I will guarantee to take from this jail, or any jail in the world,   32
five hundred men who have been the worst criminals and law-
breakers who ever got into jail, and I will go down to our lowest
streets and take five hundred of the most abandoned prostitutes,
and go out somewhere where there is plenty of land, and will
give them a chance to make a living, and they will be as good
people as the average in the community.

There is one remedy for the sort of condition we see here. The   33
world never finds it out, or when it does find it out it does not
enforce it. You may pass a law punishing every person with death
for burglary, and it will make no difference. Men will commit it
just the same. In England there was a time when one hundred
different offenses were punishable with death, and it made no
difference. The English people strangely found out that so fast as
they repealed the severe penalties and so fast as they did away
with punishing men by death, crime decreased instead of increased;
that the smaller the penalty the fewer the crimes.

Hanging men in our county jails does not prevent murder. It   34
makes murderers.

And this has been the history of the world. It's easy to see how   35
to do away with what we call crime. It is not so easy to do it. I
will tell you how to do it. It can be done by giving the people a
chance to live—by destroying special privileges. So long as big
criminals can get the coal fields, so long as the big criminals have
control of the city council and get the public streets for streetcars
and gas rights—this is bound to send thousands of poor people
to jail. So long as men are allowed to monopolize all the earth,
and compel others to live on such terms as these men see fit to
make, then you are bound to get into jail.

The only way in the world to abolish crime and criminals is to   36
abolish the big ones and the little ones together. Make fair conditions
of life. Give men a chance to live. Abolish the right of private
ownership of land, abolish monopoly, make the world partners
in production, partners in the good things of life. Nobody would
steal if he could get something of his own some easier way. Nobody
will commit burglary when he has a house full. No girl will go
out on the streets when she has a comfortable place at home. The
man who owns a sweatshop or a department store may not be
to blame himself for the condition of his girls, but when he pays
them five dollars, three dollars, and two dollars a week, I wonder

where he thinks they will get the rest of their money to live. The only way to cure these conditions is by equality. There should be no jails. They do not accomplish what they pretend to accomplish. If you would wipe them out there would be no more criminals than now. They terrorize nobody. They are a blot upon any civilization, and a jail is an evidence of the lack of charity of the people on the outside who make the jails and fill them with the victims of their greed.

VIRGINIA WOOLF

The Patriarchy

The scene, if I may ask you to follow me, was now changed. The leaves were still falling, but in London now, not Oxbridge;[1] and I must ask you to imagine a room, like many thousands, with a window looking across people's hats and vans and motor-cars to other windows, and on the table inside the room a blank sheet of paper on which was written in large letters WOMEN AND FICTION, but no more. The inevitable sequel to lunching and dining at Oxbridge seemed, unfortunately, to be a visit to the British Museum. One must strain off what was personal and accidental in all these impressions and so reach the pure fluid, the essential oil of truth. For that visit to Oxbridge and the luncheon and the dinner had started a swarm of questions. Why did men drink wine and women water? Why was one sex so prosperous and the other so poor? What effect has poverty on fiction? What conditions are necessary for the creation of works of art?—a thousand questions at once suggested themselves. But one needed answers, not questions; and an answer was only to be had by consulting the learned and the unprejudiced, who have removed themselves above the strife of tongue and the confusion of body and issued the result of their reasoning and research in books which are to be found in the British Museum. If truth is not to be found on the shelves of the

Editor's title for Chapter 2 of *A Room of One's Own,* a book based on addresses given to women's societies in 1928. In the book Woolf recreates her thinking as she attempts to prepare a talk on Women in Fiction.
1. A portmanteau word for the universities of Oxford and Cambridge, the scene of the first chapter.

British Museum, where I asked myself, picking up a notebook
and a pencil, is truth?

Thus provided, thus confident and enquiring, I set out in the   2
pursuit of truth. The day, though not actually wet, was dismal,
and the streets in the neighborhood of the Museum were full of
open coal-holes, down which sacks were showering; four-wheeled
cabs were drawing up and depositing on the pavement corded
boxes containing, presumably, the entire wardrobe of some Swiss
or Italian family seeking fortune or refuge or some other desirable
commodity which is to be found in the boarding-houses of
Bloomsbury in the winter. The usual hoarse-voiced men paraded
the streets with plants on barrows. Some shouted; others sang.
London was like a workshop. London was like a machine. We
were all being shot backwards and forwards on this plain foundation
to make some pattern. The British Museum was another department
of the factory. The swing-doors swung open; and there one stood
under the vast dome, as if one were a thought in the huge bald
forehead which is so splendidly encircled by a band of famous
names. One went to the counter; one took a slip of paper; one
opened a volume of the catalogue, and . . . . . the five dots here
indicate five separate minutes of stupefaction, wonder and bewilderment. Have you any notion how many books are written
about women in the course of one year? Have you any notion
how many are written by men? Are you aware that you are,
perhaps, the most discussed animal in the universe? Here had I
come with a notebook and a pencil proposing to spend a morning
reading, supposing that at the end of the morning I should have
transferred the truth to my notebook. But I should need to be a
herd of elephants, I thought, and a wilderness of spiders, desperately
referring to the animals that are reputed longest lived and most
multitudinously eyed, to cope with all this. I should need claws
of steel and beak of brass even to penetrate the husk. How shall
I ever find the grains of truth embedded in all this mass of paper,
I asked myself, and in despair began running my eye up and down
the long list of titles. Even the names of the books gave me food
for thought. Sex and its nature might well attract doctors and
biologists; but what was surprising and difficult of explanation
was the fact that sex—woman, that is to say—also attracts agreeable
essayists, light-fingered novelists, young men who have taken the
M.A. degree; men who have taken no degree; men who have no
apparent qualification save that they are not women. Some of
these books were, on the face of it, frivolous and facetious; but
many, on the other hand, were serious and prophetic, moral and

hortatory. Merely to read the titles suggested innumerable school-masters, innumerable clergymen mounting their platforms and pulpits and holding forth with a loquacity which far exceeded the hour usually allotted to such discourse on this one subject. It was a most strange phenomenon; and apparently—here I consulted the letter M—one confined to male sex. Women do not write books about men—a fact that I could not help welcoming with relief, for if I had first to read all that men have written about women, then all that women have written about men, the aloe that flowers once in a hundred years would flower twice before I could set pen to paper. So, making a perfectly arbitrary choice of a dozen volumes or so, I sent my slips of paper to lie in the wire tray, and waited in my stall, among the other seekers for the essential oil of truth.

What could be the reason, then, of this curious disparity, I wondered, drawing cart-wheels on the slips of paper provided by the British taxpayer for other purposes. Why are women, judging from this catalogue, so much more interesting to men than men to women? A very curious fact it seemed, and my mind wandered to picture the lives of men who spend their time writing books about women; whether they were old or young, married or un-married, red-nosed or hump-backed—anyhow, it was flattering, vaguely, to feel oneself the object of such attention, provided that it was not entirely bestowed by the crippled and the infirm—so I pondered until all such frivolous thoughts were ended by an avalanche of books sliding down on to the desk in front of me. Now the trouble began. The student who has been trained in research at Oxbridge has no doubt some method of shepherding his question past all distractions till it runs into its answer as a sheep runs into its pen. The student by my side, for instance, who was copying assiduously from a scientific manual was, I felt sure, extracting pure nuggets of the essential ore every ten minutes or so. His little grunts of satisfaction indicated so much. But if, un-fortunately, one has had no training in a university, the question far from being shepherded to its pen flies like a frightened flock hither and thither, helter-skelter, pursued by a whole pack of hounds. Professors, schoolmasters, sociologists, clergymen, novelists, essayists, journalists, men who had no qualification save that they were not women, chased my simple and single question—Why are women poor?—until it became fifty questions; until the fifty questions leapt frantically into mid-stream and were carried away. Every page in my notebook was scribbled over with notes. To show the state of mind I was in, I will read you a few of them,

³

explaining that the page was headed quite simply, WOMEN AND POVERTY, in block letters; but what followed was something like this:

> Condition in Middle Ages of,
> Habits in the Fiji Islands of,
> Worshipped as goddesses by,
> Weaker in moral sense than,
> Idealism of,
> Greater conscientiousness of,
> South Sea Islanders, age of puberty among,
> Attractiveness of,
> Offered as sacrifice to,
> Small size of brain of,
> Profounder sub-consciousness of,
> Less hair on the body of,
> Mental, moral and physical inferiority of,
> Love of children of,
> Greater length of life of,
> Weaker muscles of,
> Strength of affections of,
> Vanity of,
> Higher education of,
> Shakespeare's opinion of,
> Lord Birkenhead's opinion of,
> Dean Inge's opinion of,
> La Bruyère's opinion of,
> Dr. Johnson's opinion of,
> Mr. Oscar Browning's opinion of, . . .

Here I drew breath and added, indeed, in the margin, Why does Samuel Butler say, "Wise men never say what they think of women"? Wise men never say anything else apparently. But, I continued, leaning back in my chair and looking at the vast dome in which I was a single but by now somewhat harassed thought, what is so unfortunate is that wise men never think the same thing about women. Here is Pope:

> Most women have no character at all.

And here is La Bruyère:

> Les femmes sont extrêmes; elles sont meilleures ou pires que les hommes—[2]

---

2. "Women are extreme; they are better or worse than men."

a direct contradiction by keen observers who were contemporary. Are they capable of education or incapable? Napoleon thought them incapable. Dr. Johnson thought the opposite. Have they souls or have they not souls? Some savages say they have none. Others, on the contrary, maintain that women are half divine and worship them on that account. Some sages hold that they are shallower in the brain; others that they are deeper in the consciousness. Goethe honoured them; Mussolini despises them. Wherever one looked men thought about women and thought differently. It was impossible to make head or tail of it all, I decided, glancing with envy at the reader next door who was making the neatest abstracts, headed often with an A or a B or a C, while my own notebook rioted with the wildest scribble of contradictory jottings. It was distressing, it was bewildering, it was humiliating. Truth had run through my fingers. Every drop had escaped.

I could not possibly go home, I reflected, and add as a serious 4 contribution to the study of women and fiction that women have less hair on their bodies than men, or that the age of puberty among the South Sea Islanders is nine—or is it ninety?—even the handwriting had become in its distraction indecipherable. It was disgraceful to have nothing more weighty or respectable to show after a whole morning's work. And if I could not grasp the truth about W. (as for brevity's sake I had come to call her) in the past, why bother about W. in the future? It seemed pure waste of time to consult all those gentlemen who specialise in women and her effect on whatever it may be—politics, children, wages, morality— numerous and learned as they are. One might as well leave their books unopened.

But while I pondered I had unconsciously, in my listlessness, 5 in my desperation, been drawing a picture where I should, like my neighbour, have been writing a conclusion. I had been drawing a face, a figure. It was the face and figure of Professor von X. engaged in writing his monumental work entitled *The Mental, Moral, and Physical Inferiority of the Female Sex*. He was not in my picture a man attractive to women. He was heavily built; he had a great jowl; to balance that he had very small eyes; he was very red in the face. His expression suggested that he was labouring under some emotion that made him jab his pen on the paper as if he were killing some noxious insect as he wrote, but even when he had killed it that did not satisfy him; he must go on killing it; and even so, some cause for anger and irritation remained. Could it be his wife, I asked, looking at my picture. Was she in love with a cavalry officer? Was the cavalry officer slim and elegant and dressed in astrachan? Had he been laughed at, to adopt the

Freudian theory, in his cradle by a pretty girl? For even in his cradle the professor, I thought, could not have been an attractive child. Whatever the reason, the professor was made to look very angry and very ugly in my sketch, as he wrote his great book upon the mental, moral and physical inferiority of women. Drawing pictures was an idle way of finishing an unprofitable morning's work. Yet it is in our idleness, in our dreams, that the submerged truth sometimes comes to the top. A very elementary exercise in psychology, not to be dignified by the name of psycho-analysis, showed me, on looking at my notebook, that the sketch of the angry professor had been made in anger. Anger had snatched my pencil while I dreamt. But what was anger doing there? Interest, confusion, amusement, boredom—all these emotions I could trace and name as they succeeded each other throughout the morning. Had anger, the black snake, been lurking among them? Yes, said the sketch, anger had. It referred me unmistakably to the one book, to the one phrase, which had roused the demon; it was the professor's statement about the mental, moral and physical inferiority of women. My heart had leapt. My cheeks had burnt. I had flushed with anger. There was nothing specially remarkable, however foolish, in that. One does not like to be told that one is naturally the inferior of a little man—I looked at the student next me—who breathes hard, wears a ready-made tie, and has not shaved this fortnight. One has certain foolish vanities. It is only human nature, I reflected, and began drawing cartwheels and circles over the angry professor's face till he looked like a burning bush or a flaming comet—anyhow, an apparition without human semblance or significance. The professor was nothing now but a faggot burning on the top of Hampstead Heath. Soon my own anger was explained and done with; but curiosity remained. How explain the anger of the professors? Why were they angry? For when it came to analysing the impression left by these books there was always an element of heat. This heat took many forms; it showed itself in satire, in sentiment, in curiosity, in reprobation. But there was another element which was often present and could not immediately be identified. Anger, I called it. But it was anger that had gone underground and mixed itself with all kinds of other emotions. To judge from its odd effects, it was anger disguised and complex, not anger simple and open.

Whatever the reason, all these books, I thought, surveying the 6
pile on the desk, are worthless for my purposes. They were worthless scientifically, that is to say, though humanly they were full of instruction, interest, boredom, and very queer facts about the habits of the Fiji Islanders. They had been written in the red light of

emotion and not in the white light of truth. Therefore they must be returned to the central desk and restored each to his own cell in the enormous honeycomb. All that I had retrieved from that morning's work had been the one fact of anger. The professors— I lumped them together thus—were angry. But why, I asked myself, having returned the books, why, I repeated, standing under the colonnade among the pigeons and the prehistoric canoes. why are they angry? And, asking myself this question, I strolled off to find a place for luncheon. What is the real nature of what I call for the moment their anger? I asked. Here was a puzzle that would last all the time that it takes to be served with food in a small restaurant somewhere near the British Museum. Some previous luncher had left the lunch edition of the evening paper on a chair, and, waiting to be served, I began idly reading the headlines. A ribbon of very large letters ran across the page. Somebody had made a big score in South Africa. Lesser ribbons announced that Sir Austen Chamberlain was at Geneva. A meat axe with human hair on it had been found in a cellar, Mr. Justice —— commented in the Divorce Courts upon the Shamelessness of Women. Sprinkled about the paper were other pieces of news. A film actress had been lowered from a peak in California and hung suspended in mid-air. The weather was going to be foggy. The most transient visitor to this planet, I thought, who picked up this paper could not fail to be aware, even from this scattered testimony, that England is under the rule of a patriarchy. Nobody in their senses could fail to detect the dominance of the professor. His was the power and the money and the influence. He was the proprietor of the paper and its editor and sub-editor. He was the Foreign Secretary and the Judge. He was the cricketer; he owned the racehorses and the yachts. He was the director of the company that pays two hundred per cent to its shareholders. He left millions to charities and colleges that were ruled by himself. He suspended the film actress in mid-air. He will decide if the hair on the meat axe is human; he it is who will acquit or convict the murderer, and hang him, or let him go free. With the exception of the fog he seemed to control everything. Yet he was angry. I knew that he was angry by this token. When I read what he wrote about women I thought, not of what he was saying, but of himself. When an arguer argues dispassionately he thinks only of the argument; and the reader cannot help thinking of the argument too. If he had written dispassionately about women, had used indisputable proofs to establish his argument and had shown no trace of wishing that the result should be one thing rather than another, one would not have been angry either. One would have accepted the fact, as one accepts the fact that a pea is green or a canary yellow. So be it, I should have said. But I had been angry because he was angry. Yet it seemed absurd, I thought, turning over the evening paper, that a man with all this power should be angry. Or is anger, I wondered, somehow, the familiar, the attendant sprite on power? Rich people, for example, are often angry because they suspect that the poor want to seize their wealth. The professors, or patriarchs, as it might be more accurate to call them, might be angry for that reason partly, but partly for one that lies a little less obviously on the surface. Possibly they were not "angry" at all; often, indeed, they were admiring, devoted, exemplary in the relations of private life. Possibly when the professor insisted a little too emphatically upon the inferiority of women, he was concerned not with their inferiority, but with his own superiority. That was what he was protecting rather hot-headedly and with too much emphasis, because it was a jewel to him of the rarest price. Life for both sexes—and I looked at them, shouldering their way along the pavement—is arduous, difficult, a perpetual struggle. It calls for gigantic courage and strength. More than anything, perhaps, creatures of illusion as we are, it calls for confidence in oneself. Without self-confidence we are as babes in the cradle. And how can we generate this imponderable quality, which is yet so invaluable, most quickly? By thinking that other people are inferior to oneself. By feeling that one has some innate superiority—it may be wealth, or rank, a straight nose, or the portrait of a grandfather by Romney—for there is no end to the pathetic devices of the human imagination—over other people. Hence the enormous importance to a patriach who has to conquer, who has to rule, of feeling that great numbers of people, half the human race indeed, are by nature inferior to himself. It must indeed be one of the chief sources of his power. But let me turn the light of this observation on to real life, I thought. Does it help to explain some of those psychological puzzles that one notes in the margin of daily life? Does it explain my astonishment the other day when Z, most humane, most modest of men, taking up some book by Rebecca West and reading a passage in it, exclaimed, "The arrant feminist! She says that men are snobs!" The exclamation, to me so surprising—for why was Miss West an arrant feminist for making a possibly true if uncomplimentary statement about the other sex?—was not merely the cry of wounded vanity; it was a protest against some infringement of his power to believe in himself. Women have served all these centuries as looking-glasses possessing the magic and delicious power of reflecting the figure of man at twice its natural size. Without that power probably the earth would still be swamp and jungle. The glories of all our wars would be unknown. We should still be scratching the outlines of deer on the remains of mutton bones and bartering flints for sheepskins or whatever simple ornament took our unsophisticated taste. Supermen and Fingers of Destiny would never have existed. The Czar and the Kaiser would never have worn their crowns or lost them. Whatever may be their use in civilised societies, mirrors are essential to all violent and heroic action. That is why Napoleon and Mussolini both insist so emphatically upon the inferiority of women, for if they were not inferior, they would cease to enlarge. That serves to explain in part the necessity that women so often are to men. And it serves to explain how restless they are under her criticism; how impossible it is for her to say to them this book is bad, this picture is feeble, or whatever it may be, without giving far more pain and rousing far more anger than a man would do who gave the same criticism. For if she begins to tell the truth, the figure in the looking-glass shrinks; his fitness for life is diminished. How is he to go on giving judgement, civilising natives, making laws, writing books, dressing up and speechifying at banquets, unless he can see himself at breakfast and at dinner at least twice the size he really is? So I reflected, crumbling my bread and stirring my coffee and now and again looking at the people in the street. The looking-glass vision is of supreme importance because it charges the vitality; it stimulates the nervous system. Take it away and man may die, like the drug fiend deprived of his cocaine. Under the spell of that illusion, I thought, looking out of the window, half the people on the pavement are striding to work. They put on their hats and coats in the morning under its agreeable rays. They start the day confident, braced, believing themselves desired at Miss Smith's tea party; they say to themselves as they go into the room, I am the superior of half the people here, and it is thus that they speak with that self-confidence, that self-assurance, which have had such profound consequences in public life and lead to such curious notes in the margin of the private mind.

But these contributions to the dangerous and fascinating subject [7] of the psychology of the other sex—it is one, I hope, that you will investigate when you have five hundred a year of your own— were interrupted by the necessity of paying the bill. It came to five shillings and ninepence. I gave the waiter a ten-shilling note and he went to bring me change. There was another ten-shilling note in my purse; I noticed it, because it is a fact that still takes my breath away—the power of my purse to breed ten-shilling notes automatically. I open it and there they are. Society gives me chicken and coffee, bed and lodging, in return for a certain number of pieces of paper which were left me by an aunt, for no other reason than that I share her name.

My aunt, Mary Beton, I must tell you, died by a fall from her   8
horse when she was riding out to take the air in Bombay. The news of my legacy reached me one night about the same time that the act was passed that gave votes to women. A solicitor's letter fell into the post-box and when I opened it I found that she had left me five hundred pounds a year for ever. Of the two— the vote and the money—the money, I own, seemed infinitely the more important. Before that I had made my living by cadging odd jobs from newspapers, by reporting a donkey show here or a wedding there; I had earned a few pounds by addressing envelopes, reading to old ladies, making artificial flowers, teaching the alphabet to small children in a kindergarten. Such were the chief occupations that were open to women before 1918. I need not, I am afraid, describe in any detail the hardness of the work, for you know perhaps women who have done it; nor the difficulty of living on the money when it was earned, for you may have tried. But what still remains with me as a worse infliction than either was the poison of fear and bitterness which those days bred in me. To begin with, always to be doing work that one did not wish to do, and to do it like a slave, flattering and fawning, not always necessarily perhaps, but it seemed necessary and the stakes were too great to run risks; and then the thought of that one gift which it was death to hide—a small one but dear to the possessor—perishing and with it myself, my soul—all this became like a rust eating away the bloom of the spring, destroying the tree at its heart. However, as I say, my aunt died; and whenever I change a ten-shilling note a little of that rust and corrosion is rubbed off; fear and bitterness go. Indeed, I thought, slipping the silver into my purse, it is re-markable, remembering the bitterness of those days, what a change of temper a fixed income will bring about. No force in the world can take from me my five hundred pounds. Food, house and clothing are mine for ever. Therefore not merely do effort and labour cease, but also hatred and bitterness. I need not hate any man; he cannot hurt me. I need not flatter any man; he has nothing to give me. So imperceptibly I found myself adopting a new attitude towards the other half of the human race. It was absurd to blame any class or any sex, as a whole. Great bodies of people are never responsible for what they do. They are driven by instincts which are not within their control. They too, the patriarchs, the professors, had endless difficulties, terrible drawbacks

to contend with. Their education had been in some ways as faulty
as my own. It had bred in them defects as great. True, they had
money and power, but only at the cost of harbouring in their
breasts an eagle, a vulture, for ever tearing the liver out and
plucking at the lungs—the instinct for possession, the rage for
acquisition which drives them to desire other people's fields and
goods perpetually; to make frontiers and flags; battleships and
poison gas; to offer up their own lives and their children's lives.
Walk through the Admiralty Arch (I had reached that monument),
or any other avenue given up to trophies and cannon, and reflect
upon the kind of glory celebrated there. Or watch in the spring
sunshine the stockbroker and the great barrister going indoors to
make money and more money and more money when it is a fact
that five hundred pounds a year will keep one alive in the sunshine.
These are unpleasant instincts to harbour, I reflected. They are
bred of the conditions of life; of the lack of civilisation, I thought,
looking at the statue of the Duke of Cambridge, and in particular
at the feathers in his cocked hat, with a fixity that they have
scarcely ever received before. And, as I realised these drawbacks,
by degrees fear and bitterness modified themselves into pity and
toleration; and then in a year or two, pity and toleration went,
and the greatest release of all came, which is freedom to think of
things in themselves. That building, for example, do I like it or
not? Is that picture beautiful or not? Is that in my opinion a good
book or a bad? Indeed my aunt's legacy unveiled the sky to me,
and substituted for the large and imposing figure of a gentleman,
which Milton recommended for my perpetual adoration, a view
of the open sky.

So thinking, so speculating, I found my way back to my house ⁹
by the river. Lamps were being lit and an indescribable change
had come over London since the morning hour. It was as if the
great machine after labouring all day had made with our help a
few yards of something very exciting and beautiful—a fiery fabric
flashing with red eyes, a tawny monster roaring with hot breath.
Even the wind seemed flung like a flag as it lashed the houses
and rattled the hoardings.

In my little street, however, domesticity prevailed. The house ₁₀
painter was descending his ladder; the nursemaid was wheeling
the perambulator carefully in and out back to nursery tea; the
coal-heaver was folding his empty sacks on top of each other; the
woman who keeps the green-grocer's shop was adding up the
day's takings with her hands in red mittens. But so engrossed was
I with the problem you have laid upon my shoulders that I could
not see even these usual sights without referring them to one

centre. I thought how much harder it is now than it must have
been even a century ago to say which of these employments is
the higher, the more necessary. Is it better to be a coal-heaver or
a nursemaid; is the charwoman who has brought up eight children
of less value to the world than the barrister who has made a
hundred thousand pounds? It is useless to ask such questions; for
nobody can answer them. Not only do the comparative values of
the charwomen and lawyers rise and fall from decade to decade,
but we have no rods with which to measure them even as they
are at the moment. I had been foolish to ask my professor to
furnish me with "indisputable proofs" of this or that in his argument
about women. Even if one could state the value of any one gift
at the moment, those values will change; in a century's time very
possibly they will have changed completely. Moreover, in a hundred
years, I thought, reaching my own doorstep, women will have
ceased to be the protected sex. Logically they will take part in all
the activities and exertions that were once denied them. The nursemaid will heave coal. The shop-woman will drive an engine. All
assumptions founded on the facts observed when women were
the protected sex will have disappeared—as, for example (here a
squad of soldiers marched down the street), that women and
clergymen and gardeners live longer than other people. Remove
that protection expose them to the same exertions and activities,
make them solders and sailors and engine-drivers and dock labourers, and will not women die off so much younger, so much
quicker, than men that one will say, "I saw a woman today," as
one used to say, "I saw an aeroplane." Anything may happen
when womanhood has ceased to be a protected occupation, I
thought, opening the door. But what bearing has all this upon
the subject of my paper, Women and Fiction? I asked, going
indoors.

PEARL S. BUCK

America's Medieval Women

I

    I am an American woman but I had no opportunity until a few   1
years ago to know women in America. Living as I did in China,
it is true that I saw a few American women; but that is not the

From *Harper's Magazine*, August 1938.

same thing. One was still not able to draw many conclusions from them about American women. I gathered, however, that they felt that girls in China had a hard time of it, because here every family liked sons better than daughters, and, in the average family, did not give them the same education or treatment. In America, however, they said people welcomed sons and daughters equally and treated them the same. This, after years in a country which defines a woman's limitations very clearly, seemed nothing short of heaven— if true.

When I came to America to live therefore I was interested particularly in her women. And during these immediate past years I have come to know a good many of them—women in business, artists, housewives in city and country, women young and old. I have taken pains to know them. More than that, I have made my own place as a woman in America. And I find that what I anticipated before I came here is quite wrong. It seems to me that women are very badly treated in America. A few of them know it, more of them dimly suspect it, and most of them, though they know they ought to be glad they live in a Christian country where women are given an education, do not feel as happy in their lonely hearts as they wish they did. The reason for this unhappiness is a secret sense of failure, and this sense of failure comes from a feeling of inferiority, and the feeling of inferiority comes from a realization that actually women are not much respected in America. 2

I know quite well that any American man hearing this will laugh his usual tolerant laughter, though tolerant laughter is the cruelest form of contempt. He always laughs tolerantly when the subject of women is broached, for that is the attitude in which he has been bred. And immaturely, he judges the whole world of women by the only woman he knows at all—his wife. Nor does he want the sort of wife at whom he cannot laugh tolerantly. I was once amazed to see a certain American man, intelligent, learned, and cultivated, prepare to marry for his second wife a woman as silly and unfit for him as the first one had been, whom he had just divorced. I had to exclaim before it was too late, "Why do you do the same thing over again? She's merely younger and prettier than the other one—that's all. And even those differences are only temporary." To which he growled, "I do not want a damned intelligent woman in the house when I come home at night. I want my mind to rest." 3

What he did not see of course—though he found it out later— was that there could be no rest for him of any kind. He was irritated by a thousand stupidities and follies and beaten in the end by his own cowardice. He died a score of years too soon, 4

exhausted not by work but by nervous worry. His two wives go
hardily on, headed for a hundred, since he left them what is called
"well provided for." Neither of them has ever done an honest
day's work in her life, and he literally sacrificed his valuable life
to keep them alive.

And yet, going home that day from his funeral and wondering   5
how it could have been helped, I knew it could not have been
helped. He was doomed to the unhappiness, or at least to the
mediocre happiness, with which many if not most American men
must be satisfied in their relationships with their women. For if
he had been married to an intelligent superior woman he would
have been yet more unhappy, since, with all his brilliance as a
scientist, he belonged to that vast majority of American men who
still repeat to-day the cry of traditional male pride, "I don't want
my wife to work."

That is, he wanted a woman who would contain herself dociley   6
within four walls. And he could not have seen that an intelligent,
energetic, educated woman cannot be kept in four walls—even
satin-lined, diamond-studded walls—without discovering sooner
or later that they are still a prison cell. No home offers scope
enough to-day for the trained energies of an intelligent modern
woman. Even children are not enough. She may want them, need
them and have them, love them and enjoy them, but they are not
enough for her, even during the short time they preoccupy her.
Nor is her husband, however dear and congenial, enough for her.
He may supply all her needs for human companionship, but there
is still more to life than that. There is the individual life. She must
feel herself growing and becoming more and more complete as
an individual, as well as a wife and mother, before she can even
be a good wife and mother. I heard a smug little gray-haired
woman say last week, "No, I don't know anything about politics.
It takes all my time to be a good wife and mother. I haven't time
to keep up with other things." Unfortunately, her husband, successful
doctor that he is, has time to keep up not only with his business
and with being what she calls a "wonderful husband and father,"
but with another woman as well. But that too is one of the things
she knows nothing about. . . . Yet who can blame him? He is
clever and full of interest in many things, and his wife is dulled
with years of living in the four walls he put round her. It is a
little unfair that he so encouraged her to stay in the walls that
she came to believe in them competely as her place.

But tradition is very strong in this backward country of ours.   7
We Americans are a backward nation in everything except in the

making and using of machines. And we are nowhere more backward than we are in our attitude toward our women. We still, morally, shut the door of her home on a woman. We say to her, "Your home ought to be enough for you if you are a nice woman. Your husband ought to be enough—and your children." If she says, "But they aren't enough—what shall I do?", we say, "Go and have a good time, that's a nice girl. Get yourself a new hat or something, or go to the matinée or join a bridge club. Don't worry your pretty head about what is not your business."

If she persists in being interested in things beyond her home 8 we insist that she must be neglecting her home. If she still persists and makes a success through incredible dogged persistence we laugh at her. We even sneer at her and sometimes we treat her with unbelievable rudeness. I do not know the Secretary of Labor in our government but I have seen her. She looks a quiet, serious, unassuming woman. I have taken pains to inquire of people who know, and it seems her home is not neglected. She has done at least as good a job in Washington as a number of men there in leading positions. But the slurs that have been cast upon her, the rudenesses of private and public talk, the injustices that have been done her merely because she is a woman in a place heretofore occupied by a man, have been amazing to a person unaccustomed to the American attitude toward women. It seems nothing short of barbarous.

And yet, vicious circle that it is, I cannot blame Americans for 9 distrusting the ability of their women. For if the intelligent woman obeys the voice of tradition and limits herself to the traditional four walls she joins the vast ranks of the nervous, restless, average American women whose whimsies torture their families, who spoil the good name of all women because they are often flighty, unreliable, without good judgment in affairs, and given to self-pity. In short, she becomes a neurotic, if not all the time, a good deal of the time. Without knowing it or meaning it she falls too often to being a petty dictator in the home, a nag to her husband and children, and a gossip among her women friends. Too often too she takes no interest in any matters of social importance and refuses all responsibility in the community which she can avoid. She may be either a gadabout and extravagant or she may turn into a recluse and pride herself on being a "home woman." Neither of these escapes deceives the discerning. When will American men learn that they cannot expect happiness with a wife who is not her whole self? A restless unfulfilled woman is not going to be a satisfied wife or satisfactory lover. It is not that "women are like that." Anyone would be "like that" if he were put into such circumstances—that is, trained and developed for opportunity later denied.

"Plenty of men like that too nowadays," someone may murmur.   10

Yes, but the times have done it, and not tradition. There is a   11
difference. And one man has as good a chance as another to win or lose, even in hard times. But no woman has a man's chance in hard times, or in any times.

II

I am not so naïve, however, as to believe that one sex is responsible   12
for this unfortunate plight of the American woman. I am not a feminist, but I am an individualist. I do not believe there is any important difference between men and women—certainly not as much as there may be between one woman and another or one man and another. There are plenty of women—and men, for that matter—who would be completely fulfilled in being allowed to be as lazy as possible. If someone will ensconce them in a pleasant home and pay their bills they ask no more of life. It is quite all right for these men and women to live thus so long as fools can be found who will pay so much for nothing much in return. Gigolos, male and female, are found in every class and in the best of homes. But when a man does not want to be a gigolo he has the freedom to go out and work and create as well as he can. But a woman has not. Even if her individual husband lets her, tradition in society is against her.

For another thing we Americans cannot seem to believe or   13
understand is that women—some women, any woman, or as I believe, most women—are able to be good wives, ardent lovers, excellent mothers, and yet be themselves too. This seems strange, for as a nation we have fitted woman to be an individual as well as a woman by giving her a physical and mental education and a training superior to that of women in any other nation. But when she comes eagerly to life, ready to contribute her share, not only to home, but to government, sciences, and arts, we raise the old sickening cry of tradition, "This isn't your business! Woman's place is in the home—" and we shut the door in her face.

I am aware that at this point American men will be swearing   14
and shouting, "You don't know what you're talking about! Why, we give our women more than any women on earth have!" With that I perfectly agree. American women are the most privileged in the world. They have all the privileges—far too many. They have so many privileges that a good many of them are utterly spoiled. They have privileges but they have no equality. "Nobody

keeps them back," the American man declares. Ah, nobody, but everybody! For they are kept back by tradition expressed through the prejudices not only of men but of stupid, unthinking, tradition-bound women. Here is what I heard a few days ago.

A young woman wanted a new book to read and her father 15 offered to send it to her. "What do you want?" he asked.

"Anything, only not one by a woman," she said carelessly. "I 16 have a prejudice against books written by women."

Ignoring the rudeness, I asked, "Why?" 17

"Oh, I dislike women," she said. What she really meant was 18 she despised women so much that she actually disliked women who did anything beyond the traditional jobs that the average women do. There are thousands of women who uphold medieval tradition in America more heartily than do men—just as in China it is the ignorant tradition-bound women who have clung to foot binding for themselves and their daughters. . . . No, women have many enemies among women. It goes back of course to the old jealous sense of general female inferiority. Tradition, if it binds one, should bind all, they feel.

Sometimes, I confess, I do not see how American men can 19 endure some of their women—their imperiousness, their peevishness, their headstrongness, their utter selfishness, their smallness of mind and outlook, their lack of any sense of responsibility toward society, even to be pleasant. And their laziness—look at the motion-picture houses, the theaters, the lecture halls—crowded all day with women! The average house, even with no servant, can be no full-time job or they wouldn't be there in such hordes—they couldn't be there. But children go to school as soon as they stop being babies, and electricity cleans and washes the house and clothing, and husbands are away all day. So what is there for the restless woman to do? She goes to the show—and comes home, if she has any sense, to wonder what life is for, and to think that marriage isn't so much after all, though if she hadn't been married she would have been ashamed of herself. For tradition is there too, and it would have made her seem, if unmarried, unsuccessful as a female.

"But what are we going to do?" the harassed American man 20 cries. "There aren't enough jobs now to go round. And women are getting into industries more and more."

This is nonsense and a masculine bugaboo, though merely getting 21 a job is not what I mean. The truth is the number of women in industries is increasing at so slow a rate that it is shocking when one considers how long they have had an equal chance with men for education and training. In the past fifty years—that is, half a century, during which education for women has enormously increased—the percentage of women in industry and the professions has increased from fourteen per cent only to twenty-two per cent. That means millions of women have been made ready for work they either had no chance to do or never wanted to do.

As to what men are going to do with women, I do not pretend to know. But I know I have never seen in any country—and I have seen most of the countries of the world—such unsatisfactory personal relationships between men and women as are in America—no, not even in Japan, where women as a class are depressed. For the Japanese are wiser in their treatment of women that we Americans are. They keep them down from the beginning so that they never hope for or expect more than life is to give them. They are not restless or neurotic or despotic, nor are they spoiled children. They have not been trained for equality and they do not expect it. They know they are upper servants, and they fulfill their duties gracefully and ably, and are happier on the whole than women in America. To know what one can have and to do with it, being prepared for no more, is the basis of equilibrium. 22

III

No, what is wrong in America is this matter of educating women. Life for the American woman is still controlled by old traditions. Men think of women, if at all, in the old simple traditional ways. Then women ought to be prepared for this sort of life and shaped through childhood and girlhood for what is to come. The root of the discontent in American women is that they are too well educated. What is the use of it? They do not need college educations nor even high school educations. What they ought to have is a simple course in reading, writing, and arithmetic—and advanced courses in cosmetics, bridge, sports, how to conduct a club meeting gracefully, how to be an attractive hostess, with or without servants, and how to deal with very young children in the home. This last course, obviously, should be purely optional. 23

But all this higher present education is unfortunate. It has led American women into having ideas which they can never realize when they come to maturity. A college education may, for instance, persuade a girl to become interested in biology, which may lead her into wanting to become a doctor. And yet she will never have the chance to become a first-rate doctor, however gifted she is by birth. People will not allow it—not only men, but women will not allow it. They will look at her tentative little shingle and shrug their shoulders and say, "I don't feel I'd *trust* a woman doctor as I would a man." So after a while, since she has to earn something, 24 she takes her shingle down and accepts a secondary position in a hospital or a school or goes into baby-clinic work, supplemented by magazine articles on child care—or she just marries a doctor. But inside herself she knows she still wants to *be* a doctor, only she cannot. Tradition does not allow it.

Or a college education may lead a girl into wanting to be a banker. It is natural for women to be interested in finance since they own about seventy per cent of America's money. But it is unfortunate if a woman thinks she can be a real banker. I have talked with a good many women who work in our American banking system. Not one is a where she hoped to be when she began, and a fair percentage are not where they should be with their high executive ability, or where they would be if they were men. As one of the most brilliant of them said to me bitterly, "I know if I were a man I should now, at the age of fifty, and after thirty years of experience, be a bank president. But I'll never be anything but an assistant to a vice-president. I reached the top— for a woman—years ago. I'll never be allowed to go on."

"Why can't you?" I inquired, being then too innocent.

"They say no one would want to put money in a bank run by a woman," she said.

I pondered this. I had then just come from Shanghai, where one of the best modern banks was run and controlled entirely by modern Chinese women. It was a prosperous bank because most people there thought women were probably more honest than men and more practical in the handling of money. So the Chinese women bankers did very well.

A good deal is said too about the profession of teaching for women. There are a great many women teachers in America— many more in proportion to men than in other countries. Men here, it seems, allow women to teach in lower schools because they themselves do not want to teach in anything less than a college. And even the best men do not like to teach in women's colleges nor in co-educational colleges. The finest teaching in America, I am told, is done by men for men.

As for the arts, I know very well that the odds are strongly against the woman. Granted an equally good product, the man is given the favor always. Women artists in any field are not often taken seriously, however serious their work. It is true that they often achieve high popular success. But this counts against them as artists. American men critics may show respect to a foreign woman artist, feeling that perhaps the foreign women are better than their own. But they cannot believe that the fools they see in department stores, in the subways and buses, or running to the movies and lectures, or even in their own homes, can amount to anything in the arts. Indeed they cannot think of a woman at all, about only of "women." And the pathetic efforts of American women to improve their minds by reading and clubs have only heightened the ridicule and contempt in which their men hold them. To educate women, therefore, to think, so that they need the personal fulfillment of activity and participation in all parts of life is acute cruelty, for they are not allowed this fulfillment. They should be educated not to think beyond the demands of simple household affairs or beyond the small arts and graces of pleasing men who seem always to want mental rest. The present method is not only cruel; it is extremely wasteful. Good money is spent teaching women to do things for which there will be no need. Men strain themselves to furnish educations for their daughters which they would be happier without, and not only happier but better women because they would be more contented women.

It is not only wasteful but dangerous. To educate women as we 31 do for our present state of traditionalism is to put new wine into old bottles. A good deal of ferment is going on. And if we keep this up more will come of it. No one knows the effect upon children, for instance, of so many discontented women as mothers. Amiable, ignorant, bovine women make much better mothers than neurotic college graduates. And a woman does not need to complain aloud to let her children know she is unhappy. The atmosphere about her is gray with her secret discontent and children live deprived of that essential gayety in which they thrive as in sunshine. So few American women are really gay. This must have an effect.

IV

So, though I am impressed with the fact that American women 32 do not, as a group, seem happy, privileged as they are, I am not surprised. I know that happiness comes to an individual only as a result of personal fulfillment through complete functioning of all the energies and capabilities with which one is born. I do not for a moment mean that all women must go out and find jobs and "do something" outside the home. That would be as silly and general a mistake as our present general clinging to tradition. I simply mean let us be realistic. Let us face the fact that as a nation we are in a medieval state of mind about the place of women in society. Let each man ask himself—he need not answer aloud— where he really wants his woman. The majority, if they are honest, must acknowledge that they would like contented adoring women who want no more than their homes. I do not quarrel with that. What is, is. All I say is, let us realize facts. Tradition rules the relation of the sexes in America. Women are not welcome outside the home except in subsidiary positions, doing, on the whole, things men do not want to do. The great injustice to women is in not recognizing this frankly and in not preparing them for it.

Of course there is the chimeralike possibility that we might change tradition. But I do not see anyone capable of changing it. Men certainly will not. They do not even want to talk about it. They do not want the woman question stirred up, having as they say, "enough on their hands already." To them, of course, women "stirred up" simply means nervous, illogical, clamoring children who must be placated in one way or another. They cannot conceive of woman as a rational being, equal to themselves and not always fundamentally connected with sex. Emotionally, as it has been truly said, many American men are adolescents—kind, delightful, charming adolescents. "He's just like a boy" seems to be considered a compliment to a man in America. It ought to be an insult. This horrible boyishness lingering in persons who should be adult is as dismaying as mental retardation. It is responsible for our childish tendencies to "jazz things up," to make "whoopee," to think of being drunk, of removing "inhibitions," of playing the clown, as the only way to have a good time, to the complete destruction of adult conversation and real wit and subtler humor. It certainly is responsible for wanting women to be nothing but wives, mothers, or leggy relaxations for tired business men. Even a pretty college girl said despairingly not long ago in my presence, "You can't get anywhere with men if you show any brains. I have to make myself a nit-wit if I want dates. Oh, well, that's the way they are!" There are too many nice and rather sad American women who patiently accept even their middle-aged and old men as perennial "boys." "Men are like that," they say, at least as often as men say, "women are like that."

Nothing could show a greater misunderstanding between the sexes than this frequent fatalistic remark. Neither men nor women are like that if "that" means what they now seem to each other. It is a strange fact that in new America, as in old India or China, the real life of each sex is not with each other but away from each other. Men and women in America meet stiffly for social functions, drink together in an earnest effort to feel less inhibited, play the fool guardedly and feel queer about it afterward. Or they meet for physical sex, in the home or out. And they jog along in family life. Of the delight of exploring each other's differing but equally important personalities and points of view, of the pleasure of real mutual comprehension and appreciation and companionship, there is almost none, inside the home or out. Tradition decrees that after marriage real companionship between persons of opposite sex must cease except between husband and wife. Tradition decrees that all companionship indeed between men and women is tinged with sex. Such an idea as interest in each other as persons, aside from sex, is almost unknown. Women, talking of this among themselves, say, "Men don't want anything else." I am inclined to think they are right. The average American man demands amazingly little from his women—nothing much except to look as pretty as possible on as little money as possible, to run the home economically with as little trouble as possible to the man when he comes home tired. What educated, intelligent, clever, gifted woman is going to be satisfied with that? What average woman would be satisfied even? Ask the average man if he would change places with a woman—any woman. The idea horrifies him. Yet women are far more like him than he knows or wants to know, and modern times have done everything to make her more so.

No, our men, perennial boys, most of them, will not do anything   35
about changing tradition. They do not know how, absorbed as they are in the game of business, abashed as they are in the presence of sex as anything except simply physical, and afraid as they are of women. They are, naturally, afraid of women or they would not cling so to tradition. They were afraid of their mothers when they were children, their imperious, discontented mothers, and that fear carries over into fear of their wives and fear of all women, in industry as well as at home. It leads to the attitude of petty deception which so many perennially boyish men maintain toward their women.

So, naturally enough, men do not want women "getting too   36
smart." I heard a carpenter working in my home say pontifically to his assistant about to be married, "And why would you want a woman eddicated? Says I, if I want eddication I can go to the public library. A woman should know just so much as when it rains she stands on the sheltered side of the street. It's enough." And after a moment he added solemnly, "You don't want a woman what can talk smart. You want one what can keep quiet smart."

The voice of America's perennial boys, I thought—speaking out   37
in a carpenter, but heard as clearly in the embarrassed reserves of an after-dinner circle in a drawing-room. And yet, I do not blame them. There are so many women who chatter without thought, who stop all attempts at conversation with continual commonplaces uttered with all the petty authority of ignorance. And the fetters of another tradition—that of chivalry—still hang upon American men. Foolish, haughty women, standing in crowded buses, staring at a tired man in a seat, accepting favors as their

right; peevish, idle women, wasting their husbands' money; dogmatic women talking ignorantly about practical important matters—men must try to be polite to them all alike. I do not blame American men, except for not seeing that not all women are the same.

We are so clever with machines, we Americans. But we have done a silly thing with our women. We have put modern high-powered engines into old antiquated vehicles. It is no wonder the thing is not working. And there are only two courses to follow if we do want it to work. We must go back to the old simple one-horse-power engine or else we must change the body to suit the engine—one or the other. If the first, then tradition must be held to from the moment a woman is born, not, as it now is, clamped upon her when, after a free and extraordinarily equal childhood and girlhood with boys, she attempts to enter into a free and equal adult life with men and finds it denied her, to discover then that her education has had nothing to do with her life. 38

Or else we must be willing to let her go on as she began. This means that American men must cease being "sweet boys" and grow up emotionally as well as physically and face women as adult men. But they, poor things, have not been fitted for that either! Besides of course they are afraid of what women might do. And women, inexperienced and eager, will probably do as many foolish things as men have until they have had as much practice. 39

Of one thing I am sure, however. There will be no real content among American women unless they are made and kept more ignorant or unless they are given equal opportunity with men to use what they have been taught. And American men will not be really happy until their women are. 40

HARRY GOLDEN

The Vertical Negro Plan

Those who love North Carolina will jump at the chance to share in the great responsibility confronting our Governor and the State Legislature. A special session of the Legislature (July 25–28, 1956) passed a series of amendments to the State Constitution. These 1

First published in 1956 in *The Carolina Israelite,* Golden's one-man newspaper.

proposals submitted by the Governor and his Advisory Education
Committee included the following:

> (A) The elimination of the compulsory attendance law, "to prevent
> any child from being forced to attend a school with a child of another
> race."
> (B) The establishment of "Education Expense Grants" for education
> in a private school, "in the case of a child assigned to a public school
> attended by a child of another race."
> (C) A "uniform system of local option" whereby a majority of the
> folks in a school district may suspend or close a school if the situation
> becomes "intolerable."

But suppose a Negro child applies for this "Education Expense   2
Grant" and says he wants to go to a private school too? There
are fourteen Supreme Court decisions involving the use of public
funds; there are only two "decisions" involving the elimination
of racial discrimination in the public schools.

The Governor has said that critics of these proposals have not   3
offered any constructive advice or alternatives. Permit me, therefore,
to offer an idea for the consideration of the members of the regular
sessions. A careful study of my plan, I believe, will show that it
will save millions of dollars in tax funds and eliminate forever the
danger to our public education system. Before I outline my plan,
I would like to give you a little background.

One of the factors involved in our tremendous industrial growth   4
and economic prosperity is the fact that the South, voluntarily,
has all but eliminated VERTICAL SEGREGATION. The tremendous buying
power of the twelve million Negroes in the South has been based
wholly on the absence of racial segregation. The white and Negro
stand at the same grocery and supermarket counters; deposit money
at the same bank teller's window; pay phone and light bills to
the same clerk; walk through the same dime and department
stores, and stand at the same drugstore counters.

It is only when the Negro "sets" that the fur begins to fly.   5

Now, since we are not even thinking about restoring VERTICAL   6
SEGREGATION, I think my plan would not only comply with the
Supreme Court decisions, but would maintain "sitting-down" segregation. Now here is the GOLDEN VERTICAL NEGRO PLAN. Instead of
all those complicated proposals, all the next session needs to do
is pass one small amendment which would provide only desks in
all the public schools of our state—no seats.

The desks should be those standing-up jobs, like the old-fashioned   7
bookkeeping desk. Since no one in the South pays the slightest
attention to a VERTICAL NEGRO, this will completely solve our problem.

And it is not such a terrible inconvenience for young people to stand up during their classroom studies. In fact, this may be a blessing in disguise. They are not learning to read sitting down, anyway; maybe standing up will help. This will save more millions of dollars in the cost of our remedial English course when the kids enter college. In whatever direction you look with the GOLDEN VERTICAL NEGRO PLAN, you save millions of dollars, to say nothing of eliminating forever any danger to our public education system upon which rests the destiny, hopes, and happiness of this society.

My WHITE BABY PLAN offers another possible solution to the seg- 8
regation problem—this time in a field other than education.

Here is an actual case history of the "White Baby Plan to End 9
Racial Segregation":

Some months ago there was a revival of the Laurence Olivier 10
movie, *Hamlet*, and several Negro schoolteachers were eager to see it. One Saturday afternoon they asked some white friends to lend them two of their little children, a three-year-old girl and a six-year-old boy, and, holding these white children by the hands, they obtained tickets from the movie-house cashier without a moment's hesitation. They were in like Flynn.

This would also solve the baby-sitting problem for thousands 11
and thousands of white working mothers. There can be a mutual exchange of references, then the people can sort of pool their children at a central point in each neighborhood, and every time a Negro wants to go to the movies all she need to do is pick up a white child—and go.

Eventually the Negro community can set up a factory and man- 12
ufacture white babies made of plastic, and when they want to go to the opera or to a concert, all they need do is carry that plastic doll in their arms. The dolls, of course, should all have blond curls and blue eyes, which would go even further; it would give the Negro woman and her husband priority over the whites for the very best seats in the house.

While I still have faith in the WHITE BABY PLAN, my final proposal 13
may prove to be the most practical of all.

Only after a successful test was I ready to announce formally 14
the GOLDEN "OUT-OF-ORDER" PLAN.

I tried my plan in a city of North Carolina, where the Negroes 15
represent 39 per cent of the population.

I prevailed upon the manager of a department store to shut the 16
water off in his "white" water fountain and put up a sign, "Out-of-Order." For the first day or two the whites were hesitant, but little by little they began to drink out of the water fountain belonging

to the "coloreds"—and by the end of the third week everybody was drinking the "segregated" water; with not a single solitary complaint to date.

I believe the test is of such sociological significance that the   17
Governor should appoint a special committee of two members of the House and two Senators to investigate the GOLDEN "OUT-OF-ORDER" PLAN. We kept daily reports on the use of the unsegregated water fountain which should be of great value to this committee. This may be the answer to the necessary uplifting of the white morale. It is possible that the whites may accept desegregation if they are assured that the facilities are still "separate," albeit "Out-of-Order."

As I see it now, the key to my Plan is to keep the "Out-of-   18
Order" sign up for at least two years. We must do this thing gradually.

JONATHAN SWIFT

A Modest Proposal

FOR PREVENTING THE CHILDREN OF IRELAND
FROM
BEING A BURDEN TO THEIR PARENTS
OR
COUNTRY;
AND
FOR MAKING THEM BENEFICIAL TO THE
PUBLICK

It is a melancholly Object to those, who walk through this great   1
Town or travel in the Country; when they see the Streets, the Roads, and Cabbin-doors crowded with Beggars of the Female Sex, followed by three, four, or six Children, all in Rags, and importuning every Passenger for an Alms. These Mothers, instead of being able to work for their honest Livelyhood, are forced to employ all their Time in stroling to beg Sustenance for their helpless Infants; who, as they grow up, either turn Thieves for want of

Published in Dublin in 1729 as a pamphlet. The flyleaf gave the author as "Doctor Swift" rather than "Dean Swift," the title he used as dean of St. Patrick's Cathedral, London.

Work; or leave their dear Native Country, to fight for the Pretender in Spain, or sell themselves to the Barbadoes.

I think it is agreed by all Parties, that this prodigious number 2 of Children in the Arms, or on the Backs, or at the Heels of their Mothers, and frequently of their Fathers, is in the present deplorable state of the Kingdom, a very great additional Grievance; and therefore, whoever could find out a fair, cheap, and easy Method of making these Children sound and useful Members of the Commonwealth, would deserve so well of the Publick, as to have his Statue set up for a Preserver of the Nation.

But my Intention is very far from being confined to provide 3 only for the Children of professed Beggars: It is of a much greater Extent, and shall take in the whole Number of Infants at a certain Age, who are born of Parents in effect as little able to support them, as those who demand our Charity in the Streets.

As to my own Part, having turned my Thoughts, for many Years, 4 upon this important Subject, and maturely weighed the several Schemes of other Projectors, I have always found them grossly mistaken in their Computation. It is true, a Child, just dropt from its Dam, may be supported by her Milk, for a Solar Year with little other Nourishment; at most not above the Value of two Shillings; which the Mother may certainly get, or the Value in Scraps, by her lawful Occupation of Begging: and it is exactly at one Year old that I propose to provide for them in such a manner, as, instead of being a Charge upon their Parents or the Parish, or wanting Food and Raiment for the rest of their Lives; they shall, on the contrary, contribute to the Feeding and partly to the Cloathing, of many Thousands.

There is likewise another great Advantage in my Scheme, that 5 it will prevent those voluntary Abortions, and that horrid practice of Women murdering their Bastard Children, alas! too frequent among us; Sacrificing the poor innocent Babes, I doubt, more to avoid the Expence than the Shame; which would move Tears and Pity in the most Savage and inhuman breast.

The number of Souls in Ireland being usually reckoned one 6 Million and a half; of these I calculate there may be about Two hundred Thousand Couple whose Wives are Breeders; from which number I subtract thirty Thousand Couples, who are able to maintain their own Children, although I apprehend there cannot be so many under the present Distresses of the Kingdom; but this being granted, there will remain an Hundred and Seventy Thousand Breeders. I again Subtract Fifty Thousand, for those Women who miscarry, or whose Children die by Accident, or Disease, within the Year. There only remain an Hundred and Twenty Thousand Children of poor Parents, annually born: The Question therefore is, How this Number shall be reared, and provided for? Which, as I have already said, under the present Situation of Affairs, is utterly impossible, by all the Methods hitherto proposed: For we can neither employ them in Handicraft or Agriculture; we neither build Houses, (I mean in the Country) nor cultivate Land: They can very seldom pick up a Livelyhood by Stealing until they arrive at six Years old; except where they are of towardly Parts; although, I confess, they learn the Rudiments much earlier; during which Time, they can, however be properly looked upon only as Probationers; as I have been informed by a principal Gentleman in the County of Cavan, who protested to me, that he never knew above one or two Instances under the Age of six, even in a part of the Kingdom so renowned for the quickest Proficiency in that Art.

I am assured by our Merchants, that a Boy or a Girl before 7 twelve Years old, is no saleable Commodity; and even when they come to this Age, they will not yield above Three Pounds, or Three Pounds and half a Crown at most, on the Exchange; which cannot turn to Account either to the Parents or the Kingdom; the Charge of Nutriment and Rags, having been at least four Times that Value.

I shall now therefore humbly propose my own Thoughts; which 8 I hope will not be liable to the least Objection.

I have been assured by a very knowing American of my Ac- 9 quaintance in London, that a young healthy Child, well nursed is, at a Year old, a most delicious, nourishing and wholesome Food, whether Stewed, Roasted, Baked, or Boiled; and I make no doubt that it will equally serve in a Fricasie, or Ragoust.

I do therefore humbly offer it to publick Consideration, that of 10 the Hundred and Twenty Thousand Children, already computed, Twenty thousand may be reserved for Breed; whereof only one Fourth Part to be Males; which is more than we allow to Sheep, black Cattle, or Swine; and my Reason is, that these Children are seldom the Fruits of Marriage, a Circumstance not much regarded by our Savages; therefore, one Male will be sufficient to serve four Females. That the remaining Hundred thousand, may, at a Year old be offered in Sale to the Persons of Quality and Fortune, through the Kingdom; always advising the Mother to let them suck plentifully in the last Month, so as to render them plump, and fat for a good Table. A Child will make two Dishes at an Entertainment for Friends; and when the Family dines alone, the fore or hind Quarter will make a reasonable Dish; and seasoned with a little Pepper or Salt, will be very good Boiled on the fourth Day, especially in Winter.

I have reckoned upon a Medium, that a Child just born will 11
weight Twelve Pounds; and in a Solar Year, if tolerably nursed,
increaseth to 28 Pounds.

I grant this Food will be somewhat dear, and therefore very 12
proper for Landlords; who, as they have already devoured most
of the Parents, seem to have the best Title to the Children.

Infant's Flesh will be in Season throughout the Year; but more 13
plentiful in March, and a little before and after; for we are told
by a grave Author an eminent French Physician, that Fish being
a prolifick Dyet, there are more Children born in Roman Catholick
Countries about Nine Months after Lent, than at any other Season:
Therefore reckoning a Year after Lent, the Markets will be more
glutted than usual; because the Number of Popish Infants, is, at
least, three to one in this Kingdom; and therefore it will have one
other Collateral advantage; by lessening the Number of Papists
among us.

I have already computed the Charge of nursing a Beggar's Child 14
(in which List I reckon all Cottagers, Labourers, and Four fifths
of the Farmers) to be about two Shillings per Annum, Rags included;
and I believe no Gentleman would repine to give Ten Shillings
for the Carcase of a good fat Child; which, as I have said, will
make four Dishes of excellent nutritive meat, when he hath only
some particular Friend, or his own Family, to dine with him. Thus
the Squire will learn to be a good Landlord, and grow popular
among his Tenants; the Mother will have Eight Shillings net Profit,
and be fit for Work till she produceth another Child.

Those who are more thrifty (as I must confess the Times require) 15
may flay the Carcase; the Skin of which artifically dressed, will
make admirable Gloves for Ladies, and Summer Boots for fine
Gentlemen.

As to our City of Dublin; Shambles[1] may be appointed for this 16
Purpose, in the most convenient Parts of it, and Butchers we may
be assured will not be wanting; although I rather recommend
buying the Children alive, and dressing them hot from the Knife,
as we do roasting Pigs.

A very worthy Person, a true Lover of his Country, and whose 17
Virtues I highly esteem, was lately pleased, in discoursing on this
Matter, to offer a Refinement upon my Scheme. He said, that
many Gentlemen of this Kingdom, having of late destroyed their
Deer; he conceived that the Want of Venison might be well supplied
by the Bodies of young Lads and Maidens, not exceeding fourteen

1. Slaughterhouses

Years of Age, nor under twelve; so great a Number of both Sexes in every County being ready to Starve, for want of Work and Service: And these to be disposed of by their Parents, if alive, or otherwise by their nearest Relations. But with due Deference to so excellent a Friend, and so deserving a Patriot, I cannot be altogether in his Sentiments. For as to the Males, my American Acquaintance assured me from frequent Experience, that their Flesh was generally tough and lean, like that of our School-boys, by continual Exercise, and their Taste disagreeable; and to fatten them would not answer the Charge. Then, as to the Females, it would, I think, with humble Submission, be a Loss to the Publick, because they soon would become Breeders themselves: And besides it is not improbable, that some scrupulous[2] People might be apt to censure such a Practice, (although indeed very unjustly) as a little bordering upon Cruelty; which, I confess, hath always been with me the strongest Objection against any Project, how well soever intended.

But in order to justify my Friend; he confessed, that this Expedient 18 was put into his Head by the famous Salmanaazor, a Native of the Island Formosa, who came from thence to London, above twenty Years ago, and in Conversation told my Friend, that in his Country, when any young Person happened to be put to Death, the executioner sold the Carcase to Persons of Quality, as a prime Dainty, and that, in his Time, the Body of a plump Girl of fifteen, who was crucified for an Attempt to poison the Emperor, was sold to his Imperial Majesty's prime Minister of State, and other great Mandarins of the Court, in Joints from the Gibbet, at Four hundred Crowns. Neither indeed can I deny, that if the same Use were made of several plump young girls in this Town, who, without one single Groat to their Fortunes, cannot stir Abroad without a Chair, and appear at the Play-house, and Assemblies in foreign fineries, which they never will pay for; the Kingdom would not be the worse.

Some Persons of a desponding Spirit are in great Concern about 19 the vast Number of poor People, who are Aged, Diseased, or Maimed; and I have been desired to imploy my Thoughts what Course may be taken, to ease the Nation of so grievous an In-cumbrance. But I am not in the least Pain upon that Matter; because it is very well known, that they are every Day dying, and rotting, by Cold and Famine, and Filth, and Vermin, as fast as can be reasonably expected. And as to the younger Labourers, they are now in almost as hopeful a Condition: They cannot get

---

2. "Over-nice or meticulous in matters of right and wrong" (*Oxford English Dictionary*).

Work, and consequently pine away for Want of Nourishment, to a Degree, that if at any Time they are accidentally hired to common Labour, they have not Strength to perform it; and thus the Country, and themselves, are in a fair Way of being delivered from the Evils to come.

I have too long digressed; and therefore shall return to my Subject. I think the Advantages by the Proposal which I have made are obvious, and many, as well as of the highest Importance. 20

For First, as I have already observed, it would greatly lessen the Number of Papists, with whom we are Yearly overrun; being the principal Breeders of the Nation, as well as our most dangerous Enemies; and who stay at home on Purpose, with a Design to deliver the Kingdom to the Pretender;[3] hoping to take their Advantage by the Absence of so many good Protestants, who have chosen rather to leave their Country, than stay at home, and pay Tithes against their Conscience, to an idolatrous Episcopal Curate.[4] 21

Secondly, The poorer Tenants will have something valuable of their own, which, by Law, may be made liable to Distress,[5] and help to pay their Landlord's Rent; their Corn and Cattle being already seized, and Money a Thing unknown. 22

Thirdly, Whereas the Maintenance of an Hundred Thousand Children, from two Years old, and upwards, cannot be computed at less than ten Shillings a Piece per Annum, the Nation's Stock will be thereby encreased Fifty Thousand Pounds per Annum; besides the Profit of a new Dish, introduced to the Tables of all Gentlemen of Fortune in the Kingdom, who have any Refinement in Taste; and the Money will circulate among ourselves, the Goods being entirely of our own Growth and Manufacture. 23

Fourthly, The constant Breeders, besides the Gain of Eight Shillings Sterling per Annum, by the Sale of their Children, will be rid of the Charge of maintaining them after the first Year. 24

Fifthly, This Food would likewise bring great Custom[6] to Taverns, where the Vintners will certainly be so prudent, as to procure the best Receipts[7] for dressing it to Perfection; and consequently, have their Houses frequented by all the fine Gentlemen, who justly value themselves upon their Knowledge in good Eating; and a 25

3. James Francis Edward Stuart claimed ("pretended to") the British throne by right of succession from his father, James II. He attempted to win it by force of arms in 1715.
4. To a minister of the Church of England.
5. Impoundment for debt.
6. Business.
7. Recipes.

skilful Cook, who understands how to oblige his Guests, will contrive to make it as expensive as they please.

Sixthly, This would be a great Inducement to Marriage, which 26 all wise Nations have either encouraged by Rewards, or enforced by Laws and Penalties. It would encrease the Care and Tenderness of Mothers towards their Children, when they were sure of a Settlement for Life, to the poor Babes, provided in some Sort by the Publick, to their annual Profit instead of Expence. We should soon see an honest Emulation among the married Women, which of them could bring the fattest Child to the Market. Men would become as fond of their Wives, during the Time of their Pregnancy, as they are now of their Mares in Foal, their Cows in Calf, or Sows when they are ready to farrow; nor offer to beat or kick them, (as is too frequent a Practice) for fear of a Miscarriage.

Many other Advantages might be enumerated. For instance, the 27 Addition of some Thousand Carcases in our Exportation of barrel'd Beef: The Propagation of Swine's Flesh, and Improvement in the Art of making good Bacon; so much wanted among us by the great Destruction of Pigs, too frequent at our Tables, and are no way comparable in Taste, or Magnificence, to a well-grown, fat yearling Child; which, roasted whole, will make a considerable Figure at a Lord Mayor's Feast, or any other publick Entertainment. But this, and many others, I omit; being studious of Brevity.

Supposing that one Thousand Families in this City, would be 28 constant Customers for Infants Flesh, besides others who might have it at merry Meetings, particularly Weddings and Christenings; I compute that Dublin would take off, annually, about Twenty Thousand Carcasses; and the rest of the Kingdom (where probably they will be sold somewhat cheaper) the remaining Eighty Thousand.

I can think of no one Objection, that will possibly be raised 29 against this Proposal; unless it should be urged, that the Number of People will be thereby much lessened in the Kingdom. This I freely own; and it was indeed one principal Design in offering it to the World. I desire the Reader will observe, that I calculate my Remedy for this one individual Kingdom of Ireland, and for no other that ever was, is, or, I think, ever can be upon Earth. Therefore, let no man talk to me of other Expedients: Of taxing our Absentees[8] at five Shillings a Pound: Of using neither Cloaths, nor Household Furniture, except what is of our own Growth and Manufacture: Of utterly rejecting the Materials and Instruments that promote foreign Luxury: Of curing the Expensiveness of Pride, Vanity, Idle-

8. Absentee landlords; that is, those who owned estates in Ireland but lived in England.

ness, and Gaming in our Women: Of introducing a Vein of Parsimony, Prudence and Temperance: Of learning to love our Country, wherein we differ even from Laplanders, and the Inhabitants of Topinamboo: Of quitting our Animosities, and Factions; nor act any longer like the Jews, who were murdering one another at the very Moment their City was taken: Of being a little cautious not to sell our Country and Consciences for nothing: Of teaching Landlords to have, at least, one Degree of Mercy towards their Tenants. Lastly, of Putting a Spirit of Honesty, Industry, and Skill into our Shopkeepers; who, if a Resolution could now be taken to buy only our native Goods, would immediately unite to cheat and exact upon us in the Price, the Measure, and the Goodness; nor could ever yet be brought to make one fair Proposal of just Dealing, though often and earnestly invited to it.

Therefore I repeat, let no Man talk to me of these and the like 30 Expedients; till he hath, a least, a Glimpse of Hope, that there will ever be some hearty and sincere Attempt to put them in Practice.

But, as to my self; having been wearied out for many Years 31 with offering vain, idle, visionary Thoughts; and at length utterly despairing of Success, I fortunately fell upon this Proposal; which, as it is wholly new, so it hath something solid and real, of no Expence and little Trouble, full in our own Power; and whereby we can incur no Danger in disobliging England: For this Kind of Commodity will not bear Exportation; the Flesh being of too tender a Consistence, to admit a long Continuance in Salt; although, perhaps, I could name a Country, which would be glad to eat up our whole Nation without it.

After all, I am not so violently bent upon my own Opinion, as 32 to reject any Offer, proposed by wise Men, which shall be found equally innocent, cheap, easy, and effectual. But before something of that Kind shall be advanced in Contradiction to my Scheme, and offering a better; I desire the Author, or Authors, will be pleased maturely to consider two Points. First, As Things now stand, how they will be able to find Food and Raiment, for a Hundred Thousand useless Mouths and Backs? And Secondly, There being a round Million of Creatures in human Figure, throughout this Kingdom; whose whole Subsistence, put into a common Stock, would leave them in Debt two Million Pounds Sterling; adding those, who are Beggars by Profession, to the Bulk of Farmers, Cottagers and Labourers, with their Wives and Children, who are Beggars in Effect; I desire those Politicians, who dislike my Overture, and may perhaps be so bold to attempt an Answer, that they will first ask the Parents of these Mortals, Whether they would not at this Day think it a great Happiness to have been

sold for Food at a Year old, in the Manner I prescribe; and thereby
have avoided such a perpetual Scene of Misfortunes, as they have
since gone though; by the Oppression of Landlords; the Impossibility
of paying Rent, without Money or Trade; the Want of common
Sustenance, with neither House nor Cloaths, to cover them from
the Inclemencies of the Weather; and the most inevitable Prospect
of intailing the like, or greater Miseries upon their Breed for ever.

I profess, in the Sincerity of my Heart, that I have not the least   33
personal Interest, in endeavouring to promote this necessary Work,
having no other Motive than the publick Good of my Country,
by advancing our Trade, providing for Infants, relieving the Poor,
and giving some Pleasure to the Rich. I have no Children, by
which I can propose to get a single Penny; the youngest being
nine Years Old and my Wife past Child-bearing.

NADINE GORDIMER

Which New Era Would That Be?

Jake Alexander, a big, fat coloured[1] man, half Scottish, half   1
African, was shaking a large pan of frying bacon on the gas stove
in the back room of his Johannesburg printing shop when he
became aware that someone was knocking on the door at the
front of the shop. The sizzling fat and the voices of the five men
in the back room with him almost blocked sounds from without,
and the knocking was of the steady kind that might have been
going on for quite a few minutes. He lifted the pan off the flame
with one hand and with the other made an impatient silencing
gesture, directed at the bacon as well as the voices. Interpreting
the movement as one of caution, the men hurriedly picked up
the tumblers and cups in which they had been taking their end-
of-the-day brandy at their ease, and tossed the last of it down.
Little yellow Klaas, whose hair was like ginger-coloured wire wool,
stacked the cups and glasses swiftly and hid them behind the dirty
curtain that covered a row of shelves.

"Who's that?" yelled Jake, wiping his greasy hands down his
pants.

From *Six Feet of the Country* (1956). The story is set in South Africa, where Gordimer
lives.
1. In South Africa, *coloured* means of mixed white and black ancestry.

There was a sharp and playful tattoo, followed by an English voice: "Me—Alister. For heaven's sake, Jake!"

The fat man put the pan back on the flame and tramped through the dark shop, past the idle presses, to the door, and flung it open. "Mr Halford!" he said. "Well, good to see you. Come in, man. In the back there, you can't hear a thing." A young Englishman with gentle eyes, a stern mouth, and flat, colourless hair which grew in an untidy, confused spiral from a double crown, stepped back to allow a young woman to enter ahead of him. Before he could introduce her, she held out her hand to Jake, smiling, and shook his firmly. "Good evening. Jennifer Tetzel," she said.

"Jennifer, this is Jake Alexander," the young man managed to get in, over her shoulder.

The two had entered the building from the street through an archway lettered NEW ERA BUILDING. "Which new era would that be?" the young woman had wondered aloud, brightly, while they were waiting in the dim hallway for the door to be opened, and Alister Halford had not known whether the reference was to the discovery of deep-level gold mining that had saved Johannesburg from the ephemeral fate of a mining camp in the 'nineties, or to the optimism after the settlement of labour troubles in the 'twenties, or to the recovery after the world went off the gold standard in the 'thirties—really, one had no idea of the age of these buildings in this run-down end of the town. Now, coming in out of the deserted hallway gloom, which smelled of dust and rotting wood— the smell of waiting—they were met by the live, cold tang of ink and the homely, lazy odour of bacon fat—the smell of acceptance. There was not much light in the deserted workshop. The host blundered to the wall and switched on a bright naked bulb, up in the ceiling. The three stood blinking at one another for a moment: a coloured man with the fat of the man-of-the-world upon him, grossly dressed—not out of poverty but obviously because he liked it that way—in a rayon sports shirt that gaped and showed two hairy stomach rolls hiding his naval in a lipless grin, the pants of a good suit misbuttoned and held up round the waist by a tie instead of a belt, and a pair of expensive sports shoes, worn without socks; a young Englishman in a worn greenish tweed suit with a neo-Edwardian cut to the waistcoat that labelled it a leftover from undergraduate days; a handsome white woman who, as the light fell upon her, was immediately recognizable to Jake Alexander.

He had never met her before but he knew the type well—had seen it over and over again at meetings of the Congress of Democrats, and other organizations where progressive whites met progressive blacks. These were the white women who, Jake knew, persisted in regarding themselves as your equal. That was even worse, he thought, than the parsons who persisted in regarding *you* as *their* equal. The parsons had had ten years at school and seven years at a university and theological school; you had carried sacks of vegetables from the market to white people's cars from the time you were eight years old until you were apprenticed to a printer, and your first woman, like your mother, had been a servant, whom you had visited in a backyard room, and your first gulp of whisky, like many of your other pleasures, had been stolen while a white man was not looking. Yet the good parson insisted that your picture of life was exactly the same as his own: *you* felt as *he* did. But these women—oh, Christ!—these women felt as *you* did. They were sure of it. They thought they understood the humiliation of the black man walking the streets only by the permission of a pass written out by a white person, and the guilt and swagger of the coloured man light-faced enough to slink, fugitive from his own skin, into the preserves—the cinemas, bars, libraries—marked "EUROPEANS ONLY." Yes, breathless with stout sensitivity, they insisted on walking the whole teeter-totter of the colour line. There was no escaping their understanding. They even insisted on feeling the resentment *you* must feel at their identifying themselves with your feelings . . .

Here was the black hair of a determined woman (last year they wore it pulled tightly back into an oddly perched knot; this year it was cropped and curly as a lap dog's), the round, bony brow unpowdered in order to show off the tan, the red mouth, the unrouged cheeks, the big, lively, handsome eyes, dramatically painted, that would look into yours with such intelligent, eager honesty—eager to mirror what Jake Alexander, a big, fat coloured man interested in women, money, brandy, and boxing, was feeling. Who the hell wants a woman to look at you honestly, anyway? What has all this to do with a *woman*—with what men and women have for each other in their eyes? She was wearing a wide black skirt, a white cotton blouse baring a good deal of her breasts, and ear-rings that seemed to have been made by a blacksmith out of bits of scrap iron. On her feet she had sandals whose narrow thongs wound between her toes, and the nails of the toes were painted plum colour. By contrast, her hands were neglected-looking—sallow, unmanicured—and on one thin finger there swivelled a huge gold seal-ring. She was good-looking, he supposed with disgust.

He stood there, fat, greasy, and grinning at the two visitors so lingeringly that his grin looked insolent. Finally he asked, "What brings you this end of town, Mr Halford? Sight-seeing with the lady?"

The young Englishman gave Jake's arm a squeeze, where the short sleeve of the rayon shirt ended. "Just thought I'd look you up, Jake," he said, jolly.

"Come on in, come on in," said Jake on a rising note, shambling ahead of them into the company of the back room. "Here, what about a chair for the lady?" He swept a pile of handbills from the seat of a kitchen chair onto the dusty concrete floor, picked up the chair, and planked it down again in the middle of the group of men who had risen awkwardly at the visitors' entrance. "You know Maxie Ndube? And Temba?" Jake said, nodding at two of the men who surrounded him.

Alister Halford murmured with polite warmth his recognition of Maxie, a small, dainty-faced African in neat, businessman's dress, then said inquiringly and hesitantly to Temba, "Have we? When?"

Temba was a coloured man—a mixture of the bloods of black slaves and white masters, blended long ago, in the days when the Cape of Good Hope was a port of refreshment for the Dutch East India Company. He was tall and pale, with a large Adam's apple, enormous black eyes, and the look of a musician in a jazz band; you could picture a trumpet lifted to the ceiling in those long yellow hands, that curved spine hunched forward to shield a low note. "In Durban last year, Mr Halford, you remember?" he said eagerly. "I'm sure we met—or perhaps I only saw you there."

"Oh, at the Congress? Of course I remember you!" Halford apologized. "You were in a delegation from the Cape?"

"Miss—?" Jake Alexander waved a hand between the young woman, Maxie, and Temba.

"Jennifer. Jennifer Tetzel," she said again clearly, thrusting out her hand. There was a confused moment when both men reached for it at once and then hesitated, each giving way to the other. Finally the handshaking was accomplished, and the young woman seated herself confidently on the chair.

Jake continued, offhand, "Oh, and of course Billy Boy—" Alister signalled briefly to a black man with sad, blood-shot eyes, who stood awkwardly, back a few steps, against some rolls of paper—"and Klaas and Albert." Klaas and Albert had in their mixed blood some strain of the Bushman, which gave them a batrachian yellowness and toughness, like one of those toads that (prehistoric as the Bushman is) are mythically believed to have survived into modern times (hardly more fantastically than the Bushman himself has survived) by spending centuries shut up in an air bubble in a rock. Like Billy Boy, Klaas and Albert had backed away, and, as if abasement against the rolls of paper, the wall, or the window were a greeting in itself, the two little coloured men and the big African only stared back at the masculine nods of Alister and the bright smile of the young woman.

"You up from the Cape for anything special now?" Alister said to Temba as he made a place for himself on a corner of a table that was littered with photographic blocks, bits of type, poster proofs, a bottle of souring milk, a bow-tie, a pair of red braces, and a number of empty Coca-Cola bottles.

"I've been living in Durban for a year. Just got the chance of a lift to Jo'burg," said the gangling Temba.

Jake had set himself up easily, leaning against the front of the   20
stove and facing Miss Jennifer Tetzel on her chair. He jerked his head towards Temba and said, "Real banana boy." Young white men brought up in the strong Anglo-Saxon tradition of the province of Natal are often referred to, and refer to themselves, as "banana boys," even though fewer and fewer of them have any connection with the dwindling number of vast banana estates that once made their owners rich. Jake's broad face, where the bright-pink cheeks of a Highland complexion—inherited, along with his name, from his Scottish father—showed oddly through his coarse, beige skin, creased up in appreciation of his own joke. And Temba threw back his head and laughed, his Adam's apple bobbing, at the idea of himself as a cricket-playing white public-school boy.

"There's nothing like Cape Town, is there?" said the young woman to him, her head charmingly on one side, as if this conviction were something she and he shared.

"Miss Tetzel's up here to look us over. She's from Cape Town," Alister explained.

She turned to Temba with her beauty, her strong provocativeness, full on, as it were. "So we're neighbours?"

Jake rolled one foot comfortably over the other and a spluttering laugh pursed out the pink inner membrane of his lips.

"Where did you live?" she went on, to Temba.   25

"Cape Flats," he said. Cape Flats is a desolate coloured slum in the bush outside Cape Town.

"Me, too," said the girl, casually.

Temba said politely, "You're kidding," and then looked down uncomfortably at his hands, as if they had been guilty of some clumsy movement. He had not meant to sound so familiar; the words were not the right ones.

"I've been there nearly ten months," she said.

"Well, some people've got queer tastes," Jake remarked, laughing, to no one in particular, as if she were not there.

"How's that?" Temba was asking her shyly, respectfully.

She mentioned the name of a social rehabilitation scheme that was in operation in the slum. "I'm assistant director of the thing at the moment. It's connected with the sort of work I do at the university, you see, so they've given me fifteen months' leave from my usual job."

Maxie noticed with amusement the way she used the word "job," as if she were a plumber's mate; he and his educated African friends—journalists and schoolteachers—were careful to talk only of their "professions." "Good works," he said, smiling quietly.

She planted her feet comfortably before her, wriggling on the hard chair, and said to Temba with mannish frankness, "It's a ghastly place. How in God's name did you survive living there? I don't think I can last out more than another few months, and I've always got my flat in Cape Town to escape to on Sundays, and so on."

While Temba smiled, turning his protruding eyes aside slowly, Jake looked straight at her and said, "Then why do you, lady, why *do* you?"

"Oh, I don't know. Because I don't see why anyone else—any one of the people who live there—should have to, I suppose." She laughed before anyone else could at the feebleness, the phil-anthropic uselessness of what she was saying, "Guilt, what-have-you . . ."

Maxie shrugged, as if at the mention of some expensive illness he had never been able to afford and whose symptoms he could not imagine.

There was a moment of silence; the two coloured men and the big black man standing back against the wall watched anxiously, as if some sort of signal might be expected, possibly from Jake Alexander, their boss, the man who, like themselves, was not white, yet who owned his own business and had a car and money and strange friends—sometimes even white people, such as these. The three of them were dressed in the ill-matched cast-off clothing that all humble workpeople who are not white wear in Johan-nesburg, and they had not lost the ability of rural people to stare, unembarrassed and unembarrassing.

Jake winked at Alister; it was one of his mannerisms—a bookie's wink, a stage comedian's wink. "Well, how's it going, boy, how's it going?" he said. His turn of phrase was bar-room bonhomie; with luck, he *could* get into a bar, too. With a hat to cover his hair and his coat collar well up, and only a bit of greasy pink

cheek showing, he had slipped into the bars of the shabbier Johannesburg hotels with Alister many times and got away with it.
Alister, on the other hand, had got away with the same sort of
thing narrowly several times, too, when he had accompanied Jake
to a shebeen[2] in a coloured location, where it was illegal for a
white man to be, as well as illegal for anyone at all to have a
drink; twice Alister had escaped a raid by jumping out of a window.
Alister had been in South Africa only eighteen months, as correspondent for a newspaper in England, and because he was only
two or three years away from undergraduate escapades such incidents seemed to give him a kind of nostalgic pleasure; he found
them funny. Jake, for his part, had decided long ago (with the
great help of the money he had made) that he would take the
whole business of the colour bar as humorous. The combination
of these two attitudes, stemming from such immeasurably different
circumstances, had the effect of making their friendship less self-
conscious than is usual between a white man and a coloured one.

"They tell me it's going to be a good thing on Saturday night?"   40
said Alister, in the tone of questioning someone in the know. He
was referring to a boxing match between two coloured heavyweights,
one of whom was a protégé of Jake.

Jake grinned deprecatingly, like a fond mother. "Well, Pikkie's
a good boy," he said. "I tell you, it'll be something to see." He
danced about a little on his clumsy toes in pantomine of the way
a boxer nimbles himself, and collapsed against the stove, his belly
shaking with laughter at his breathlessness.

"Too much smoking, too many brandies, Jake," said Alister.

"With me, it's too many women, boy."

"We were just congratulating Jake," said Maxie in his soft,
precise voice, the indulgent, tongue-in-cheek tone of the protégé
who is superior to his patron, for Maxie was one of Jake's boys,
too—of a different kind. Though Jake had decided that for him
being on the wrong side of a colour bar was ludicrous, he was
as indulgent to those who took it seriously and politically, the
way Maxie did, as he was to any up-and-coming youngster who,
say, showed talent in the ring or wanted to go to America and
become a singer. They could all make themselves free of Jake's
pocket, and his printing shop, and his room in the lower end of
the town, where the building had fallen below the standard of
white people but was far superior to the kind of thing most coloureds
and blacks were accustomed to.

"Congratulations on what?" the young white woman asked.   45

2. Unlicensed bar.

She had a way of looking up around her, questioningly, from face to face, that came of long familiarity with being the centre of attention at parties.

"Yes, you can shake my hand, boy," said Jake to Alister. "I didn't see it, but these fellows tell me that my divorce went through. It's in the papers today."

"Is that so? But from what I hear, you won't be a free man long," Alister said teasingly.

Jake giggled, and pressed at one gold-filled tooth with a strong fingernail. "You heard about the little parcel I'm expecting from Zululand?" he asked.

"Zululand?" said Alister. "I thought your Lila came from Stellenbosch."

Maxie and Temba laughed.

"Lila? *What* Lila?" said Jake with exaggerated innocence.

"You're behind the times," said Maxie to Alister.

"You know I like them—well, sort of round," said Jake. "Don't care for the thin kind, in the long run."

"But Lila had red hair!" Alister goaded him. He remembered the incongruously dyed, straightened hair on a fine coloured girl whose nostrils dilated in the manner of certain fleshy water-plants seeking prey.

Jennifer Tetzel got up and turned the gas off on the stove, behind Jake. "That bacon'll be like charred string," she said.

Jake did not move—merely looked at her lazily. "This is not the way to talk with a lady around." He grinned, unapologetic.

She smiled at him and sat down, shaking her ear-rings. "Oh, I'm divorced myself. Are we keeping you people from your supper? Do go ahead and eat. Don't bother about us."

Jake turned around, gave the shrunken rashers a mild shake, and put the pan aside. "Hell, no," he said. "Any time. But—" turning to Alister—"won't you have something to eat?" He looked about, helpless and unconcerned, as if to indicate an absence of plates and a general careless lack of equipment such as white women would be accustomed to use when they ate. Alister said quickly, no, he had promised to take Jennifer to Moorjee's.

Of course, Jake should have known; a woman like that would *want* to be taken to eat at an Indian place in Vrededorp, even though she was white, and free to eat at the best hotel in town. He felt suddenly, after all, the old gulf opening between himself and Alister: what did *they* see in such women—bristling, sharp, all-seeing, knowing women, who talked like men, who wanted to show all the time that, apart from sex, they were exactly the same as men? He looked at Jennifer and her clothes, and thought

of the way a white woman could look: one of those big, soft,
European women with curly yellow hair, with very high-heeled
shoes that made them shake softly when they walked, with a
strong scent, like hot flowers, coming up, it seemed, from their
jutting breasts under the lace and pink and blue and all the other
pretty things they wore—women with nothing resistant about
them except, buried in white, boneless fingers, those red, pointed
nails that scratched faintly at your palms.

"You should have been along with me at lunch today," said   60
Maxie to no one in particular. Or perhaps the soft voice, a vocal
tiptoe, was aimed at Alister, who was familiar with Maxie's work
as an organizer of African trade unions. The group in the room
gave him their attention (Temba with the little encouraging grunt
of one who has already heard the story), but Maxie paused a
moment, smiling ruefully at what he was about to tell. Then he
said, "You know George Elson?" Alister nodded. The man was a
white lawyer who had been arrested twice for his participation in
anti-colour-bar movements.

"Oh, George? I've worked with George often in Cape Town,"
put in Jennifer.

"Well," continued Maxie," George Elson and I went out to one
of the industrial towns on the East Rand. We were interviewing
the bosses, you see, not the men, and at the beginning it was
all right, though, once or twice the girls in the offices thought I
was George's driver—'Your boy can wait outside.' " He laughed,
showing small, perfect teeth; everything about him was finely
made—his straight-fingered dark hands, the curved African nostrils
of his small nose, his little ears, which grew close to the sides of
his delicate head. The others were silent, but the young woman
laughed, too.

"We even got tea in one place," Maxie went on. "One of the
girls came in with two cups and a tin mug. But old George took
the mug."

Jennifer Tetzel laughed again, knowingly.

"Then, just about lunch time, we came to this place I wanted   65
to tell you about. Nice chap, the manager. Never blinked an eye
at me, called me Mister. And after we'd talked, he said to George,
'Why not come home with me for lunch?' So of course George
said, 'Thanks, but I'm with my friend here.' 'Oh, that's O.K.,' said
the chap. 'Bring him along.' 'Well, we go along to this house, and
the chap disappears into the kitchen, and then he comes back and
we sit in the lounge and have a beer, and then the servant comes
along and says lunch is ready. Just as we're walking into the
dining room, the chap takes me by the arm and says, 'I've had

your lunch laid on a table on the stoep. You'll find it's all perfectly clean and nice, just what we're having ourselves.' "

"Fantastic," murmured Alister.

Maxie smiled and shrugged, looking around at them all. "It's true."

"After he'd asked you, and he'd sat having a drink with you?" Jennifer said closely, biting in her lower lip, as if this were a problem to be solved psychologically.

"Of course," said Maxie.

Jake was shaking with laughter, like some obscene Silenus. There was no sound out of him, but saliva gleamed on his lips, and his belly, at the level of Jennifer Tetzel's eyes, was convulsed.

Temba said soberly, in the tone of one whose good will makes it difficult for him to believe in the unease of his situation, "I certainly find it worse here than at the Cape. I can't remember, y'know, about buses. I keep getting put off European buses."

Maxie pointed to Jake's heaving belly. "Oh, I'll tell you a better one than that," he said. "Something that happened in the office one day. Now, the trouble with me is, apparently, I don't talk like a native." This time everyone laughed, except Maxie himself, who, with the instinct of a good raconteur, kept a polite, modest, straight face.

"You know that's true," interrupted the young white woman. "You have none of the usual softening of the vowels of most Africans. And you haven't got an Afrikaans[3] accent, as some Africans have, even if they get rid of the African thing."

"Anyway, I'd had to phone a certain firm several times," Maxie went on, "and I'd got to know the voice of the girl at the other end, and she'd got to know mine. As a matter of fact, she must have liked the sound of me, because she was getting very friendly. We fooled about a bit, exchanged first names, like a couple of kids—hers was Peggy—and she said, eventually, 'Aren't you ever going to come to the office yourself?' " Maxie paused a moment, and his tongue flicked at the side of his mouth in a brief, nervous gesture. When he spoke again, his voice was flat, like the voice of a man who is telling a joke and suddenly thinks that perhaps it is not such a good one after all. "So I told her I'd be in next day, about four. I walked in, sure enough, just as I said I would. She was a pretty girl, blonde, you know, with very tidy hair—I guessed she'd just combed it to be ready for me. She looked up and said 'Yes?' holding out her hand for the messenger's book or

3. One of the languages of South Africa, developed from Dutch settlement in that country in the seventeeth century.

70

parcel she thought I'd brought. I took her hand and shook it and
said, 'Well, here I am, on time—I'm Maxie—Maxie Ndube.' "

"What'd she do?" asked Temba eagerly.   75

The interruption seemed to restore Maxie's confidence in his
story. He shrugged gaily. "She almost dropped my hand, and then
she pumped it like a mad thing, and her neck and ears went so
red I thought she'd burn up. Honestly, her ears were absolutely
shining. She tried to pretend she'd known all along, but I could
see she was terrified someone would come from the inner office
and see her shaking hands with a native. So I took pity on her
and went away. Didn't even stay for my appointment with her
boss. When I went back to keep the postponed appointment the
next week, we pretended we'd never met."

Temba was slapping his knee. "God, I'd have loved to see her
face!" he said.

Jake wiped away a tear from his fat cheek—his eyes were light
blue, and produced tears easily when he laughed—and said, "That'll
teach you not to talk swanky, man. Why can't you talk like the
rest of us?"

"Oh, I'll watch out on the 'Missus' and 'Baas' stuff in future,"
said Maxie.

Jennifer Tetzel cut into their laughter with her cool, practical   80
voice. "Poor little girl, she probably liked you awfully, Maxie, and
was really disappointed. You mustn't be too harsh on her. It's
hard to be punished for not being black."

The moment was one of astonishment rather than irritation.
Even Jake, who had been sure that there could be no possible
situation between white and black he could not find amusing,
only looked quickly from the young woman to Maxie, in a hiatus
between anger, which he had given up long ago, and laughter,
which suddenly failed him. On this face was admiration more
than anything else—sheer, grudging admiration. This one was the
best one yet. This one was the coolest ever.

"Is it?" said Maxie to Jennifer, pulling in the corners of his
mouth and regarding her from under slightly raised eyebrows.
Jake watched. Oh, she'd have a hard time with Maxie. Maxie
wouldn't give up his suffering-tempered blackness so easily. You
hadn't much hope of knowing what Maxie was feeling at any
given moment, because Maxie not only never let you know but
made you guess wrong. But this one was the best yet.

She looked back at Maxie, opening her eyes very wide, twisting
her sandalled foot on the swivel of its ankle, smiling, "Really, I
assure you it is."

Maxie bowed to her politely, giving way with a falling gesture of his hand.

Alister had slid from his perch on the crowded table, and now, prodding Jake playfully in the paunch, he said, "We have to get along."

Jake scratched his ear and said again, "Sure you won't have something to eat?"

Alister shook his head. "We had hoped you'd offer us a drink, but—"

Jake wheezed with laughter, but this time was sincerely concerned. "Well, to tell you the truth, when we heard the knocking, we just swallowed the last of the bottle off, in case it was someone it shouldn't be. I haven't a drop in the place till tomorrow. Sorry, chappie. Must apologize to you, lady, but we black men've go to drink in secret. If we'd've known it was you two . . ."

Maxie and Temba had risen. The two wizened coloured men, Klaas and Albert, and the sombre black Billy Boy shuffled helplessly, hanging about.

Alister said, "Next time, Jake, next time. We'll give you fair warning and you can lay it on."

Jennifer shook hands with Temba and Maxie, called "Goodbye! Goodbye!" to the others, as if they were somehow out of earshot in that small room. From the door, she suddenly said to Maxie, "I feel I must tell you. About that other story—your first one, about the lunch. I don't believe it. I'm sorry, but I honestly don't. It's too illogical to hold water."

It was the final self-immolation by honest understanding. There was absolutely no limit to which that understanding would not go. Even if she could not believe Maxie, she must keep her determined good faith with him by confessing her disbelief. She would go to the length of calling him a liar to show by frankness how much she respected him—to insinuate, perhaps, that she was *with him*, even in the need to invent something about a white man that she, because she herself was white, could not believe. It was her last bid for Maxie.

The small, perfectly-made man crossed his arms and smiled, watching her go. Maxie had no price.

Jake saw his guests out of the shop, and switched off the light after he had closed the door behind them. As he walked back through the dark, where his presses smelled metallic and cool, he heard, for a few moments, the clear voice of the white woman and the low, noncommittal English murmur of Alister, his friend, as they went out through the archway into the street.

He blinked a little as he came back to the light and the faces 95
that confronted him in the back room. Klaas had taken the dirty
glasses from behind the curtain and was holding them one by one
under the tap in the sink. Billy Boy and Albert had come closer
out of the shadows and were leaning their elbows on a roll of
paper. Temba was sitting on the table, swinging his foot. Maxie
had not moved, and stood just as he had, with his arms folded.
No one spoke.

Jake began to whistle softly through the spaces between his
front teeth, and he picked up the pan of bacon, looked at the
twisted curls of meat, jellied now in cold white fat, and put it
down again absently. He stood a moment, heavily, regarding them
all, but no one responded. His eye encountered the chair that he
had cleared for Jennifer Tetzel to sit on. Suddenly he kicked it,
hard, so that it went flying on to its side. Then, rubbing his big
hands together and bursting into loud whistling to accompany an
impromptu series of dance steps, he said "Now, boys!" and as
they stirred, he planked the pan down on the ring and turned the
gas up till it roared beneath it.

Thinking About Power and Powerlessness

Read today, Thomas Jefferson's famous sentence from the Declaration of Independence seems perfectly clear.

> We hold these truths to be self-evident: that all men are created equal; that they are endowed by their Creator with certain inalienable rights; that among them is life, liberty, and the pursuit of happiness; that to secure these rights, governments are instituted, deriving their just powers from the consent of the governed.

When, in 1857, Chief Justice Roger B. Taney wrote the majority opinion of the United States Supreme Court in *Dred Scott vs. Sandford*, he also thought that Jefferson's meaning was very clear. After all, he argued, the framers of the Declaration were highly literate men:

> They perfectly understood the meaning of the language they used and how it would be understood by others; and they knew that it would not in any part of the civilized world be supposed to embrace the Negro race, which, by common consent, had been excluded from civilized governments and the family of nations and doomed to slavery. They spoke and acted according to the then established doctrines and principles and the ordinary language of the day, and no one misunderstood them. The unhappy black race were separated from the white by indelible marks, and laws long before established, and were never thought of or spoken of except as property and when the claims of the owner or the profit of the trader were supposed to need protection.

Only after the Civil War was the meaning of "all men" extended to include black males. American Indians and women were not considered equal "according to the . . . established doctrines and principles" until the twentieth century.

The essays in Power and Powerlessness are concerned with the exclusion of some groups from the political community of "all men." As W. E. B. Du Bois points out, this exclusion has often been based on race because European colonists and adventurers in the last four centuries have used "the great majority of mankind, the peoples who lived in Asia, Africa, America, and the islands of the sea" as "subordinate tools" for making money. On this continent, the result is most clearly seen in the exploitation of blacks (a situation that is difficult to reverse by simple good will, as James Baldwin shows in "Fifth Avenue, Uptown") and in the destruction of native cultures like the Kiowas' (see Momaday's

"The Way to Rainy Mountain"). But this section gives us far-flung glimpses of oppressors and oppressed: we see George Orwell, hapless representative of a colonial system he despises, being forced to "act like a sahib" in Burma; and we see the tension between blacks and white liberals in contemporary South Africa in Nadine Gordimer's "Which New Era Would That Be?"

Not all political colonization involves what Rudyard Kipling called (at least half-ironically) "the white man's burden" of ruling "new-caught sullen peoples" with darker skins. The exploitation of Catholic Ireland by Protestant England is the provocation for Jonathan Swift's "A Modest Proposal." Clarence Darrow argues that jails are internal colonies, populated by the victims of our greed: "There ought to be no jails; and if it were not for the fact that the people on the outside are so grasping and heartless in their dealings with the people on the inside, there would be no such institution as jails." Feminists have argued that women, too, have formed an internal colony, ruled by a patriarchy that Virginia Woolf distills into the formidable Professor von X, and that Pearl Buck dismisses as "perpetual boys" unaware of the price they pay for their dominion.

QUESTIONS

1. Several groups that have suffered political repression are represented in this section—women, blacks, American Indians, the Burmese, the Irish, the poor. To what extent are these groups really comparable? Contrast two that you think should not be thought of in the same terms, or compare two that you feel are more similar than some people would suspect.

2. Some of the essays in this section suggest that there is a personality type that rises to power in Western societies. Describe the "power personality" as you see it. How does your version compare to the versions given in the essays?

3. The essays by Pearl Buck, Harry Golden, and Jonathan Swift all contain elements of irony, mild or bitter. Since irony involves saying one thing and meaning another it often only confuses the reader. Is the irony in these essays successful? What are the conditions that make successful irony possible?

4. Groups are sometimes oppressed because their oppression is unrecognized by the general public. What groups not represented in the essays collected here should be represented? Consider in some detail the plight of one such group.

5. Some groups (or factions within groups), on the other hand, seem to exploit their exploitation. They use their apparent

powerlessness to achieve inordinate power. Describe such a group, or defend a group that has been charged with this sort of exploitation.

6. Most of the writers in this section concentrate their attention on a group to which they belong, either as a typical or an atypical member. Orwell, for instance, explores the ways in which he is and is not a representative British imperialist. Woolf notes that while she shares many of the problems that beset women, the inheritance of a substantial income saves her from others. Describe your relation to a group recognizable for its power or powerlessness, or both.

COMMUNITY

H. D. F. KITTO

The Polis

"Polis" is the Greek word which we translate "city-state." It is 1
a bad translation, because the normal polis was not much like a
city, and was very much more than a state. But translation, like
politics, is the art of the possible; since we have not got the thing
which the Greeks called "the polis," we do not possess an equivalent
word. From now on, we will avoid the misleading term "city-
state", and use the Greek word instead. In this chapter we will
first inquire how this political system arose, then we will try to
reconstitute the word "polis" and recover its real meaning by
watching it in action. It may be a long task, but all the time we
shall be improving our acquaintance with the Greeks. Without a
clear conception what the polis was, and what it meant to the
Greeks, it is quite impossible to understand properly Greek history,
the Greek mind, or the Greek achievement.

First then, what was the polis? In the *Iliad* we discern a political 2
structure that seems not unfamiliar—a structure that can be called
an advanced or a degenerate form of tribalism, according to taste.
There are kings, like Achilles, who rule their people, and there is
the great king, Agamemnon, King of Men, who is something like
a feudal overlord. He is under obligation, whether of right or of
custom to consult the other kings or chieftains in matters of common
interest. They form a regular council, and in its debates the sceptre,
symbol of authority, is held by the speaker for the time being.
This is recognizably European, not Oriental; Agamemnon is no
despot, ruling with the unquestioned authority of a god. There
are also signs of a shadowy Assembly of the People, to be consulted
on important occasions: though Homer, a courtly poet, and in any
case not a constitutional historian, says little about it.

Such, in outline, is the tradition about pre-conquest Greece. 3
When the curtain goes up again after the Dark Age we see a very
different picture. No longer is there a "wide-ruling Agamemnon"
lording it in Mycenae. In Crete, where Idomeneus had been ruling
as sole king, we find over fifty quite independent poleis, fifty small
"states" in the place of one. It is a small matter that the kings
have disappeared; the important thing is that the kingdoms have
gone too. What is true of Crete is true of Greece in general, or at
least of those parts which play any considerable part in Greek

From *The Greeks* (1951).

history—Ionia, the islands, the Peloponnesus except Arcadia, Central Greece except the western parts, and South Italy and Sicily when they became Greek. All these were divided into an enormous number of quite independent and autonomous political units.

It is important to realize their size. The modern reader picks up   4
a translation of Plato's *Republic* or Aristotle's *Politics*; he finds Plato ordaining that his ideal city shall have 5,000 citizens, and Aristotle that each citizen should be able to know all the others by sight; and he smiles, perhaps, at such philosophic fantasies. But Plato and Aristotle are not fantasts. Plato is imagining a polis on the normal Hellenic scale; indeed he implies that many existing Greek poleis are too small—for many had less than 5,000 citizens. Aristotle says, in his amusing way—Aristotle sometimes sounds very like a don[1]—that a polis of ten citizens would be impossible, because it could not be self-sufficient, and that a polis of a hundred thousand would be absurd, because it could not govern itself properly. And we are not to think of these "citizens" as a "master-class" owning and dominating thousands of slaves. The ordinary Greek in these early centuries was a farmer, and if he owned a slave he was doing pretty well. Aristotle speaks of a hundred thousand citizens; if we allow each to have a wife and four children, and then add a liberal number of slaves and resident aliens, we shall arrive at something like a million—the population of Birmingham; and to Aristotle an independent "state" as populous as Birmingham is a lecture-room joke. Or we may turn from the philosophers to a practical man, Hippodamas, who laid out the Piraeus in the most up-to-date American style; he said that the ideal number of citizens was ten thousand, which would imply a total population of about 100,000.

In fact, only three poleis had more than 20,000 citizens—Syracuse   5
and Acragas (Girgenti) in Sicily, and Athens. At the outbreak of the Peloponnesian War the population of Attica was probably about 350,000, half Athenian (men, women and children), about a tenth resident aliens, and the rest slaves. Sparta, or Lacedaemon, had a much smaller citizen-body, though it was larger in area. The Spartans had conquered and annexed Messenia, and possessed 3,200 square miles of territory. By Greek standards this was an enormous area: it would take a good walker two days to cross it. The important commercial city of Corinth had a territory of 330 square miles—about the size of Huntingdonshire. The island of Ceos, which is about as big as Bute, was divided into four poleis. It had therefore four armies, four governments, possibly four different

1. A tutor or fellow of one of the colleges at Oxford or Cambridge. That is, Aristotle sounds professorial.

calendars, and, it may be, four different currencies and systems of measures—though this is less likely. Mycenae was in historical times a shrunken relic of Agamemnon's capital, but still independent. She sent an army to help the Greek cause against Persia at the battle of Plataea; the army consisted of eighty men. Even by Greek standards this was small, but we do not hear that any jokes were made about an army sharing a cab.

To think on this scale is difficult for us, who regard a state of ten million as small, and are accustomed to states which, like the U.S.A. and the U.S.S.R., are so big that they have to be referred to by their initials; but when the adjustable reader has become accustomed to the scale, he will not commit the vulgar error of confusing size with significance. The modern writer is sometimes heard to speak with splendid scorn of "those petty Greek states, with their interminable quarrels." Quite so; Plataea, Sicyon, Aegina and the rest are petty, compared with modern states. The Earth itself is petty, compared with Jupiter—but then, the atmosphere of Jupiter is mainly ammonia, and that makes a difference. We do not like breathing ammonia—and the Greeks would not much have liked breathing the atmosphere of the vast modern State. They knew of one such, the Persian Empire—and thought it very suitable, for barbarians. Difference of scale, when it is great enough, amounts to difference of kind. 6

But before we deal with the nature of the polis, the reader might like to know how it happened that the relatively spacious pattern of pre-Dorian Greece became such a mosaic of small fragments. The Classical scholar too would like to know; there are no records, so that all we can do is to suggest plausible reasons. There are historical, geographical and economic reasons; and when these have been duly set forth, we may conclude perhaps that the most important reason of all is simply that this is the way in which the Greeks preferred to live. 7

The coming of the Dorians was not an attack made by one organized nation upon another. The invaded indeed had their organization, loose though it was; some of the invaders—the main body that conquered Lacedaemon—must have been a coherent force; but others must have been small groups of raiders, profiting from the general turmoil and seizing good land where they could find it. A sign of this is that we find members of the same clan in different states. Pindar for example, was a citizen of Thebes and a member of the ancient family of the Aegidae. But there were Aegidae too in Aegina and Sparta, quite independent poleis, and Pindar addresses them as kinsmen. This particular clan therefore was split up in the invasions. In a country like Greece this would be very natural. 8

In a period so unsettled the inhabitants of any valley or island   9
might at a moment's notice be compelled to fight for their fields.
Therefore a local strong-point was necessary, normally a defensible
hill-top somewhere in the plain. This, the "acropolis" ("high-
town"), would be fortified, and here would be the residence of
the king. It would also be the natural place of assembly, and the
religious centre.

This is the beginning of the town. What we have to do is to   10
give reasons why the town grew, and why such a small pocket
of people remained an independent political unit. The former task
is simple. To begin with, natural economic growth made a central
market necessary. We saw that the economic system implied by
Hesiod and Homer was "close household economy"; the estate,
large or small, produced nearly everything that it needed, and
what it could not produce it did without. As things became more
stable a rather more specialized economy became possible: more
goods were produced for sale. Hence the growth of a market.

At this point we may invoke the very sociable habits of the   11
Greeks, ancient or modern. The English farmer likes to build his
house on his land, and to come into town when he has to. What
little leisure he has he likes to spend on the very satisfying occupation
of looking over a gate. The Greek prefers to live in the town or
village, to walk out to his work, and to spend his rather ampler
leisure talking in the town or village square. Therefore the market
becomes a market-town, naturally beneath the Acropolis. This
became the centre of the communal life of the people—and we
shall see presently how important that was.

But why did not such towns form larger units? This is the   12
important question.

There is an economic point. The physical barriers which Greece   13
has so abundantly made the transport of goods difficult, except
by sea, and the sea was not yet used with any confidence. Moreover,
the variety of which we spoke earlier enabled quite a small area
to be reasonably self-sufficient for a people who made such small
material demands on life as the Greek. Both of these facts tend
in the same direction; there was in Greece no great economic
interdependence, no reciprocal pull between the different parts of
the country, strong enough to counteract the desire of the Greek
to live in small communities.

There is a geographical point. It is sometimes asserted that this   14
system of independent poleis was imposed on Greece by the physical
character of the country. The theory is attractive, especially to
those who like to have one majestic explanation of any phenomenon,
but it does not seem to be true. It is of course obvious that the

physical subdivision of the country helped; the system could not have existed, for example, in Egypt, a country which depends entirely on the proper management of the Nile flood, and therefore must have a central government. But there are countries cut up quite as much as Greece—Scotland, for instance—which have never developed the polis-system; and conversely there were in Greece many neighbouring poleis, such as Corinth and Sicyon, which remained independent of each other although between them there was no physical barrier that would seriously incommode a modern cyclist. Moreover, it was precisely the most mountainous parts of Greece that never developed poleis, or not until later days—Arcadia and Aetolia, for example, which had something like a canton-system. The polis flourished in those parts where communications were relatively easy. So that we are still looking for our explanation.

Economics and geography helped, but the real explanation is the character of the Greeks—which those determinists may explain who have the necessary faith in their omniscience. As it will take some time to deal with this, we may first clear out of the way an important historical point. How did it come about that so preposterous a system was able to last for more than twenty minutes?

The ironies of history are many and bitter, but at least this must be put to the credit of the gods, that they arranged for the Greeks to have the Eastern Mediterranean almost to themselves long enough to work out what was almost a laboratory-experiment to test how far, and in what conditions, human nature is capable of creating and sustaining a civilization. In Asia, the Hittite Empire had collapsed, the Lydian kingdom was not aggressive, and the Persian power, which eventually overthrew Lydia, was still embryonic in the mountainous recesses of the continent; Egypt was in decay; Macedon, destined to make nonsense of the polis-system, was and long remained in a state of ineffective semi-barbarism; Rome had not yet been heard of, nor any other power in Italy. There were indeed the Phoenicians, and their western colony, Carthage, but these were traders first and last. Therefore this lively and intelligent Greek people was for some centuries allowed to live under the apparently absurd system which suited and developed its genius instead of becoming absorbed in the dull mass of a large empire, which would have smothered its spiritual growth, and made it what it afterwards became, a race of brilliant individuals and opportunists. Obviously some day somebody would create a strong centralized power in the Eastern Mediterranean—a successor to the ancient sea-power of King Minos. Would it be Greek, Oriental, or something else? This question must be the theme of a later chapter, but no history of Greece can be intelligible until one has understood what the polis meant to the Greek; and when we have understood that, we shall also understand why the Greeks developed it, and so obstinately tried to maintain it. Let us then examine the word in action.

It meant at first that which was later called the Acropolis, the [17] stronghold of the whole community and the centre of its public life. The town which nearly always grew up around this was designated by another word, "asty." But "polis" very soon meant either the citadel or the whole people which, as it were, "used" this citadel. So we read in Thucydides, "Epidamnus is a polis on the right as you sail into the Ionian gulf." This is not like saying "Bristol is a city on the right as you sail up the Bristol Channel," for Bristol is not an independent state which might be at war with Gloucester, but only an urban area with a purely local administration. Thucydides' words imply that there is a town—though possibly a very small one—called Epidamnus, which is the political centre of the Epidamnians, who live in the territory of which the town is the centre—not the "capital"—and are Epidamnians whether they live in the town or in one of the villages in this territory.

Sometimes the territory and the town have different names. [18] Thus, Attica is the territory occupied by the Athenian people; it comprised Athens—the "polis" in the narrower sense—the Piraeus, and many villages; but the people collectively were Athenians, not Attics, and a citizen was an Athenian in whatever part of Attica he might live.

In this sense "polis" is our "state." In Sophocles' *Antigone* Creon [19] comes forward to make his first proclamation as king. He begins, "Gentlemen, as for the polis, the gods have brought it safely through the storm, on even keel." It is the familiar image of the Ship of State, and we think we know where we are. But later in the play he says what we should naturally translate, "Public proclamation has been made . . ." He says in fact, "It has been proclaimed to the polis . . ."—not to the "state," but to the "people." Later in the play he quarrels violently with his son; "What?" he cries, "is anyone but me to rule in this land?" Haemon answers, "It is no polis that is ruled by one man only." The answer brings out another important part of the whole conception of a polis, namely that it is a community, and that its affairs are the affairs of all. The actual business of governing might be entrusted to a monarch, acting in the name of all according to traditional usages, or to the heads of certain noble families, or to a council of citizens owning so much property, or to all the citizens. All these, and many modifications of them, were natural forms of "polity"; all were sharply distinguished by the Greek from Oriental monarchy, in which the monarch is irresponsible, not holding his powers in trust by the grace of god, but being himself a god. If there was irresponsible government there was no polis. Haemon is accusing his father of talking like a "tyrannos"[2] and thereby destroying the polis—but not "the State."

To continue our exposition of the word. The chorus in Aristophanes' *Acharnians*, admiring the conduct of the hero, turns to the audience with an appeal which I render literally, "Dost thou see, O whole polis?" The last words are sometimes translated "thou thronging city," which sounds better, but obscures an essential point, namely that the size of the polis made it possible for a member to appeal to all his fellow-citizens in person, and this he naturally did if he thought that another member of the polis had injured him. It was the common assumption of the Greeks that the polis took its origin in the desire for Justice. Individuals are lawless, but the polis will see to it that wrongs are redressed. But not by an elaborate machinery of state-justice, for such a machine could not be operated except by individuals, who may be as unjust as the original wrongdoer. The injured party will be sure of obtaining justice only if he can declare his wrongs to the whole polis. The word therefore now means "people" in actual distinction from "state."

Iocasta, the tragic Queen in the *Oedipus*, will show us a little more of the range of the word. It becomes a question if Oedipus her husband is not after all the accursed man who had killed the previous king Laius. "No, no," cries Iocasta, "it cannot be! The slave said it was 'brigands' who had attacked them, not 'a brigand.' He cannot go back on his word now. The polis heard him, not I alone." Here the word is used without any "political" association at all; it is, as it were, off duty, and signifies "the whole people." This is a shade of meaning which is not always so prominent, but is never entirely absent.

Then Demosthenes the orator talks of a man who, literally, "avoids the city"—a translation which might lead the unwary to suppose that he lived in something corresponding to the Lake District, or Purley. But the phrase "avoids the polis" tells us nothing about his domicile; it means that he took no part in public life—and was therefore something of an oddity. The affairs of the community did not interest him.

2. I prefer to use the Greek form of this (apparently) Oriental word. It is the Greek equivalent of "dictator," but it does not necessarily have the colour of our word "tyrant." [author's note]

We have now learned enough about the word polis to realize   23
that there is no possible English rendering of such a common
phrase as, "It is everyone's duty to help the polis." We cannot
say "help the state," for that arouses no enthusiasm; it is "the
state" that takes half our incomes from us. Not "the community,"
for with us "the community" is too big and too various to be
grasped except theoretically. One's village, one's trade union, one's
class, are entities that mean something to us at once, but "work
for the community," though an admirable sentiment, is to most
of us vague and flabby. In the years before the war, what did
most parts of Great Britain know about the depressed areas? How
much do bankers, miners and farmworkers understand each other?
But the "polis" every Greek knew; there it was, complete, before
his eyes. He could see the fields which gave it its sustenance—or
did not, if the crops failed; he could see how agriculture, trade
and industry dove-tailed into one another; he knew the frontiers,
where they were strong and where weak; if any malcontents were
planning a *coup*, it was difficult for them to conceal the fact. The
entire life of the polis, and the relation between its parts, were
much easier to grasp, because of the small scale of things. Therefore
to say "It is everyone's duty to help the polis" was not to express
a fine sentiment but to speak the plainest and most urgent common
sense.[3] Public affairs had an immediacy and a concreteness which
they cannot possibly have for us.

One specific example will help. The Athenian democracy taxed   24
the rich with as much disinterested enthusiasm as the British, but
this could be done in a much more gracious way, simply because
the State was so small and intimate. Among us, the payer of super-
tax (presumably) pays much as the income-tax payer does: he
writes his cheque and thinks, "There! *That's* gone down the drain!"
In Athens, the man whose wealth exceeded a certain sum had,
in a yearly rota, to perform certain "liturgies"—literally, "folk-
works." He had to keep a warship in commission for one year
(with the privilege of commanding it, if he chose), or finance the
production of plays at the Festival, or equip a religious procession.
It was a heavy burden, and no doubt unwelcome, but at least
some fun could be got out of it and some pride taken in it. There
was satisfaction and honour to be gained from producing a trilogy
worthily before one's fellow-citizens. So, in countless other ways,
the size of the polis made vivid and immediate, things which to
us are only abstractions or wearisome duties. Naturally this cut
both ways. For example, an incompetent or unlucky commander

3. It did not, of course, follow that the Greek obeyed common sense any oftener
than we do. [author's note]

was the object not of a diffused and harmless popular indignation, but of direct accusation; he might be tried for his life before an Assembly, many of whose past members he had led to death.

Pericles' Funeral Speech, recorded or recreated by Thucydides, will illustrate this immediacy, and will also take our conception of the polis a little further. Each year, Thucydides tells us, if citizens had died in war—and they had, more often than not—a funeral oration was delivered by "a man chosen by the polis." Today, that would be someone nominated by the Prime Minister, or the British Academy, or the B.B.C. In Athens it meant that someone was chosen by the Assembly who had often spoken to that Assembly; and on this occasion Pericles spoke from a specially high platform, that his voice might reach as many as possible. Let us consider two phrases that Pericles used in that speech.

He is comparing the Athenian polis with the Spartan, and makes the point that the Spartans admit foreign visitors only grudgingly, and from time to time expel all strangers, "while we make our polis common to all." "Polis" here is not the political unit; there is no question of naturalizing foreigners—which the Greeks did rarely, simply because the polis was so intimate a union. Pericles means here: "We throw open to all our common cultural life," as is shown by the words that follow, difficult though they are to translate: "nor do we deny them any instruction or spectacle" —words that are almost meaningless until we realize that the drama, tragic and comic, the performance of choral hymns, public recitals of Homer, games, were all necessary and normal parts of "political" life. This is the sort of thing Pericles has in mind when he speaks of "instruction and spectacle," and of "making the polis open to all."

But we must go further than this. A perusal of the speech will show that in praising the Athenian polis Pericles is praising more than a state, a nation, or a people: he is praising a way of life; he means no less when, a little later, he calls Athens the "school of Hellas."—And what of that? Do not we praise "the English way of life"? The difference is this; we expect our State to be quite indifferent to "the English way of life"—indeed, the idea that the State should actively try to promote it would fill most of us with alarm. The Greeks thought of the polis as an active, formative thing, training the minds and characters of the citizens; we think of it as a piece of machinery for the production of safety and convenience. The training in virtue, which the medieval state left to the Church, and the polis made its own concern, the modern state leaves to God knows what.

"Polis," then, originally "citadel," may mean as much as "the whole communal life of the people, political, cultural, moral"—

25

26

27

28

even "economic," for how else are we to understand another phrase in this same speech, "the produce of the whole world comes to us, because of the magnitude of our polis"? This must mean "our national wealth."

Religion too was bound up with the polis—though not every   29
form of religion. The Olympian gods were indeed worshipped by Greeks everywhere, but each polis had, if not its own gods, at least its own particular cults of these gods. Thus, Athena of the Brazen House was worshipped at Sparta, but to the Spartans Athena was never what she was to the Athenians, "Athena Polias," Athena guardian of the City. So Hera, in Athens, was a goddess worshipped particularly by women, as the goddess of hearth and home, but in Argos "Argive Hera" was the supreme deity of the people. We have in these gods tribal deities, like Jehovah, who exist as it were on two levels at once, as gods of the individual polis, and gods of the whole Greek race. But beyond these Olympians, each polis had its minor local deities, "heroes" and nymphs, each worshipped with his immemorial rite, and scarcely imagined to exist outside the particular locality where the rite was performed. So that in spite of the panhellenic Olympian system, and in spite of the philosophic spirit which made merely tribal gods impossible for the Greek, there is a sense in which it is true to say that the polis is an independent religious, as well as political, unit. The tragic poets at least could make use of the old belief that the gods desert a city which is about to be captured. The gods are the unseen partners in the city's welfare.

How intimately religious and "political" thinking were connected   30
we can best see from the *Oresteia* of Aeschylus. This trilogy is built around the idea of Justice. It moves from chaos to order, from conflict to reconciliation; and it moves on two planes at once, the human and the divine. In the *Agamemnon* we see one of the moral Laws of the universe, that punishment must follow crime, fulfilled in the crudest possible way; one crime evokes another crime to avenge it, in apparently endless succession—but always with the sanction of Zeus. In the *Choephori* this series of crimes reaches its climax when Orestes avenges his father by killing his mother. He does this with repugnance, but he is commanded to do it by Apollo, the son and the mouthpiece of Zeus—Why? Because in murdering Agamemnon the King and her husband, Clytemnestra has committed a crime which, unpunished, would shatter the very fabric of society. It is the concern of the Olympian gods to defend Order; they are particularly the gods of the Polis. But Orestes' matricide outrages the deepest human instincts; he is therefore implacably pursued by other deities, the Furies. The Furies have no interest in social

order, but they cannot permit this outrage on the sacredness of the blood-tie, which it is their office to protect. In the *Eumenides* there is a terrific conflict between the ancient Furies and the younger Olympians over the unhappy Orestes. The solution is that Athena comes with a new dispensation from Zeus. A jury of Athenian citizens is empanelled to try Orestes on the Acropolis where he has fled for protection—this being the first meeting of the Council of the Areopagus. The votes on either side are equal; therefore, as an act of mercy, Orestes is acquitted. The Furies, cheated of their legitimate prey, threaten Attica with destruction, but Athena persuades them to make their home in Athens, with their ancient office not abrogated (as at first they think) but enhanced, since henceforth they will punish violence within the polis, not only within the family.

So, to Aeschylus, the mature polis becomes the means by which   31
the Law is satisfied without producing chaos, since public justice supersedes private vengeance; and the claims of authority are reconciled with the instincts of humanity. The trilogy ends with an impressive piece of pageantry. The awful Furies exchange their black robes for red ones, no longer Furies, but "Kindly Ones" (Eumenides); no longer enemies of Zeus, but his willing and honoured agents, defenders of his now perfected social order against intestine violence. Before the eyes of the Athenian citizens assembled in the theatre just under the Acropolis—and indeed guided by citizen-marshals—they pass out of the theatre to their new home on the other side of the Acropolis. Some of the most acute of man's moral and social problems have been solved, and the means of the reconciliation is the Polis.

A few minutes later, on that early spring day of 458 B.C., the   32
citizens too would leave the theatre, and by the same exits as the Eumenides. In what mood? Surely no audience has had such an experience since. At the time, the Athenian polis was confidently riding the crest of the wave. In this trilogy there was exaltation, for they had seen their polis emerge as the pattern of Justice, of Order, of what the Greeks called Cosmos; the polis, they saw, was—or could be—the very crown and summit of things. They had seen their goddess herself acting as President of the first judicial tribunal—a steadying and sobering thought. But there was more than this. The rising democracy had recently curtailed the powers of the ancient Court of the Areopagus, and the reforming statesman had been assassinated by his political enemies. What of the Eumenides, the awful inhabitants of the land, the transformed Furies, whose function it was to avenge the shedding of a kinsman's blood? There was warning here, as well as exaltation, in the

thought that the polis had its divine as well as its human members. There was Athena, one of those Olympians who had presided over the formation of ordered society, and there were the more primitive deities who had been persuaded by Athena to accept this pattern of civilized life, and were swift to punish any who, by violence from within, threatened its stability.

To such an extent was the religious thought of Aeschylus in-   33
tertwined with the idea of the polis; and not of Aeschylus alone, but of many other Greek thinkers too—notably of Socrates, Plato, and Aristotle. Aristotle made a remark which we most inadequately translate "Man is a political animal." What Aristotle really said is "Man is a creature who lives in a polis"; and what he goes on to demonstrate, in his *Politics*, is that the polis is the only framework within which man can fully realize his spiritual, moral and intellectual capacities.

Such are some of the implications of this word: we shall meet   34
more later, for I have deliberately said little about its purely "political" side—to emphasize the fact that it is so much more than a form of political organization. The polis was a living community, based on kinship, real or assumed—a kind of extended family, turning as much as possible of life into family life, and of course having its family quarrels, which were the more bitter because they were family quarrels.

This it is that explains not only the polis but also much of what   35
the Greek made and thought, that he was essentially social. In the winning of his livelihood he was essentially individualist: in the filling of his life he was essentially "communist." Religion, art, games, the discussion of things—all these were needs of life that could be fully satisfied only through the polis—not, as with us, through voluntary associations of like-minded people, or through *entrepreneurs* appealing to individuals. (This partly explains the difference between Greek drama and the modern cinema.) Moreover, he wanted to play his own part in running the affairs of the community. When we realize how many of the necessary, interesting and exciting activities of life the Greek enjoyed through the polis, all of them in the open air, within sight of the same acropolis, with the same ring of mountains or of sea visibly enclosing the life of every member of the state—then it becomes possible to understand Greek history, to understand that in spite of the promptings of common sense the Greek could not bring himself to sacrifice the polis, with its vivid and comprehensive life, to a wider but less interesting unity. We may perhaps record an Imaginary Conversation between an Ancient Greek and a member of the Athenaeum. The member regrets the lack of political sense shown

by the Greeks. The Greek replies, "How many clubs are there in London?" The member, at a guess, says about five hundred. The Greek then says, "Now, if all these combined, what splendid premises they could build. They could have a club-house as big as Hyde Park." "But," says the member, "that would no longer be a club." "Precisely," says the Greek, "and a polis as big as yours is no longer a polis."

After all, modern Europe, in spite of its common culture, common   36
interests, and ease of communication, finds it difficult to accept the idea of limiting national sovereignty, though this would increase the security of life without notably adding to its dullness; the Greek had possibly more to gain by watering down the polis—but how much more to lose. It was not common sense that made Achilles great, but certain other qualities.

PLATO

Crito

Socrates.[1]   Why have you come at this hour, Crito? it must be   1
quite early?

Crito.   Yes, certainly.

Soc.   What is the exact time?

Cr.   The dawn is breaking.

Soc.   I wonder that the keeper of the prison would let you in.   5

Cr.   He knows me, because I often come, Socrates; moreover, I have done him a kindness.

Soc.   And are you only just arrived?

Cr.   No, I came some time ago.

Soc.   Then why did you sit and say nothing, instead of at once awakening me?

Cr.   I should not have liked myself, Socrates, to be in such great   10
trouble and unrest as you are—indeed I should not: I have been

One of the dialogues of the Greek philosopher Plato, (427–347 B.C.), written c. 400 B.C.
1. Socrates (469–399 B.C.), a Greek teacher and philosopher, is known to posterity through the writings of Plato. Accused of corrupting the youth of Athens by his questioning manner of teaching, he was brought to trial and sentenced to death; subsequently, he was given poison hemlock to drink. Crito, a friend and follower of Socrates, here tries to persuade him to escape from prison, but Socrates refuses to break the laws of Athens.

watching with amazement your peaceful slumbers; and for that reason I did not awake you, because I wished to minimize the pain. I have always thought you to be of a happy disposition; but never did I see anything like the easy, tranquil manner in which you bear this calamity.

Soc.   Why, Crito, when a man has reached my age he ought not to be repining at the approach of death.

Cr.   And yet other old men find themselves in similar misfortunes, and age does not prevent them from repining.

Soc.   That is true. But you have not told me why you come at this early hour.

Cr.   I come to bring you a message which is sad and painful; not, as I believe, to yourself, but to all of us who are your friends, and saddest of all to me.

Soc.   What? Has the ship come from Delos, on the arrival of 15 which I am to die?

Cr.   No, the ship has not actually arrived, but she will probably be here to-day, as persons who have come from Sunium tell me that they left her there; and therefore tomorrow, Socrates, will be the last day of your life.

Soc.   Very well, Crito; if such is the will of God, I am willing; but my belief is that there will be a delay of a day.

Cr.   Why do you think so?

Soc.   I will tell you. I am to die on the day after the arrival of the ship.

Cr.   Yes; that is what the authorities say.   20

Soc.   But I do not think that the ship will be here until to-morrow; this I infer from a vision which I had last night, or rather only just now, when you fortunately allowed me to sleep.

Cr.   And what was the nature of the vision?

Soc.   There appeared to me the likeness of a woman, fair and comely, clothed in bright raiment, who called to me and said: O Socrates,

> *"The third day hence to fertile Phthia shalt thou go."*

Cr.   What a singular dream, Socrates!

Soc.   There can be no doubt about the meaning, Crito, I think.   25

Cr.   Yes; the meaning is only too clear. But, oh! my beloved Socrates, let me entreat you once more to take my advice and escape. For if you die I shall not only lose a friend who can never be replaced, but there is another evil: people who do not know you and me will believe that I might have saved you if I had been willing to give money, but that I did not care. Now, can there be a worse disgrace than this—that I should be thought to value money more than the life of a friend? For the many will not be persuaded that I wanted you to escape, and that you refused.

Soc.   But why, my dear Crito, should we care about the opinion of the many? Good men, and they are the only persons who are worth considering, will think of these things truly as they occurred.

Cr.   But you see, Socrates, that the opinion of the many must be regarded, for what is now happening shows that they can do the greatest evil to any one who has lost their good opinion.

Soc.   I only wish it were so, Crito; and that the many could do the greatest evil; for then they would also be able to do the greatest good—and what a fine thing this would be! But in reality they can do neither; for they cannot make a man either wise or foolish; and whatever they do is the result of chance.

Cr.   Well, I will not dispute with you; but please to tell me,   30 Socrates, whether you are not acting out of regard to me and your other friends: are you not afraid that if you escape from prison we may get into trouble with the informers for having stolen you away, and lose either the whole or a great part of our property; or that even a worse evil may happen to us? Now, if you fear on our account, be at ease; for in order to save you, we ought surely to run this, or even a greater risk; be persuaded, then, and do as I say.

Soc.   Yes, Crito, that is one fear which you mention, but by no means the only one.

Cr.   Fear not—there are persons who are willing to get you out of prison at no great cost; and as for the informers, they are far from being exorbitant in their demands—a little money will satisfy them. My means, which are certainly ample, are at your service, and if you have a scruple about spending all mine, here are strangers who will give you the use of theirs; and one of them, Simmias the Theban, has brought a large sum of money for this very purpose; and Cebes and many others are prepared to spend their money in helping you to escape. I say, therefore, do not hesitate on our account, and do not say, as you did in the court, that you will have a difficulty in knowing what to do with yourself anywhere else. For men will love you in other places to which you may go, and not in Athens only; there are friends of mine in Thessaly, if you like to go to them, who will value and protect you, and no Thessalian will give you any trouble. Nor can I think that you are at all justified, Socrates, in betraying your own life when you might be saved; in acting thus you are playing into the hands of your enemies, who are hurrying on your destruction. And further I should say that you are deserting your own children; for you might bring them up and educate them; instead of which you go away and leave them, and they will have to take their chance; and if they do not meet with the usual fate of orphans, there will be small thanks to you. No man should bring children into the world who is unwilling to persevere to the end in their nurture and education. But you appear to be choosing the easier part, not the better and manlier, which would have been more becoming in one who professes to care for virtue in all his actions, like yourself. And, indeed, I am ashamed not only of you, but of us who are your friends, when I reflect that the whole business will be attributed entirely to our want of courage. The trial need never have come on, or might have been managed differently; and this last act, or crowning folly, will seem to have occurred through our negligence and cowardice, who might have saved you, if we had been good for anything; and you might have saved yourself, for there was no difficulty at all. See now, Socrates, how sad and discreditable are the consequences, both to us and you. Make up your mind, then, or rather have your mind already made up, for the time of deliberation is over, and there is only one thing to be done, which must be done this very night, and if we delay at all will be no longer practicable or possible; I beseech you therefore, Socrates, be persuaded by me, and do as I say.

Soc.   Dear Crito, your zeal is invaluable, if a right one; but if wrong, the greater the zeal the greater the danger; and therefore we ought to consider whether I shall or shall not do as you say. For I am and always have been one of those natures who must be guided by reason, whatever the reason may be which upon reflection appears to me to be the best; and now that this chance has befallen me, I cannot repudiate my own words: the principles which I have hitherto honoured and revered I still honour, and unless we can at once find other and better principles, I am certain not to agree with you; no, not even if the power of the multitude could inflict many more imprisonments, confiscations, deaths, frightening us like children with hobgoblin terrors. What will be the fairest way of considering the question? Shall I return to our old argument about the opinions of men?—we were saying that some of them are to be regarded, and others, not. Now, were we right in maintaining this before I was condemned? And has the argument which was once good now proved to be talk for the sake of talking—mere childish nonsense? That is what I want to consider with your help, Crito:—whether, under my present circumstances, the argument appears to be in any way different or not; and is to be allowed by me or disallowed. That argument, which, as I believe, is maintained by many persons of authority, was to the effect, as I was saying, that the opinions of some men are to be regarded, and of other men not to be regarded. Now you, Crito, are not going to die tomorrow—at least, there is no human probability of this—and therefore you are disinterested and not liable to be deceived by the circumstances in which you are placed. Tell me, then, whether I am right in saying that some opinions, and the opinions of some men only, are to be valued, and that other opinions, and the opinions of other men, are not to be valued. I ask you whether I was right in maintaining this?

Cr. Certainly.

Soc. The good are to be regarded, and not the bad? 35

Cr. Yes.

Soc. And the opinions of the wise are good, and the opinions of the unwise are evil?

Cr. Certainly.

Soc. And what was said about another matter? Is the pupil who devotes himself to the practice of gymnastic supposed to attend to the praise and blame and opinion of every man, or of one man only—his physician or trainer, whoever he may be?

Cr. Of one man only. 40

Soc. And he ought to fear the censure and welcome the praise of that one only, and not of the many?

Cr. Clearly so.

Soc. And he ought to act and train, and eat and drink in the way which seems good to his single master who has understanding, rather than according to the opinion of all other men put together?

Cr. True.

Soc. And if he disobeys and disregards the opinion and approval 45 of the one, and regards the opinion of the many who have no understanding, will he not suffer evil?

Cr. Certainly he will.

Soc. And what will the evil be, whither tending and what affecting, in the disobedient person?

Cr. Clearly, affecting the body; that is what is destroyed by the evil.

Soc. Very good; and is not this true, Crito, of other things which we need not separately enumerate? In questions of just and unjust, fair and foul, good and evil, which are the subjects of our present consultation, ought we to follow the opinion of the many and to fear them; or the opinion of the one man who has understanding? ought we not to fear and reverence him more than all the rest of the world: and if we desert him shall we not destroy and injure that principle in us which may be assumed to be improved by justice and deteriorated by injustice;—there is such a principle?

Cr. Certainly there is, Socrates. 50

Soc. Take a parallel instance:—if, acting under the advice of those who have no understanding, we destroy that which is improved by health and is deteriorated by disease, would life be worth having? And that which has been destroyed is—the body?

Cr. Yes.

Soc. Could we live, having an evil and corrupted body?

Cr. Certainly not.

Soc. And will life be worth having, if that higher part of man   55
be destroyed, which is improved by justice and depraved by injustice? Do we suppose that principle, whatever it may be in man, which has to do with justice and injustice, to be inferior to the body?

Cr. Certainly not.

Soc. More honourable than the body?

Cr. Far more.

Soc. Then, my friend, we must not regard what the many say of us: but what he, the one man who has understanding of just and unjust, will say, and what the truth will say. And therefore you begin in error when you advise that we should regard the opinion of the many about just and unjust, good and evil, honourable and dishonourable.—"Well," some one will say, "But the many can kill us."

Cr. Yes, Socrates; that will clearly be the answer.   60

Soc. And it is true: but still I find with surprise that the old argument is unshaken as ever. And I should like to know whether I may say the same of another proposition—that not life, but a good life, is to be chiefly valued?

Cr. Yes, that also remains unshaken.

Soc. And a good life is equivalent to a just and honourable one—that holds also?

Cr. Yes, it does.

Soc. From these premises I proceed to argue the question whether   65
I ought or ought not to try to escape without the consent of the Athenians: and if I am clearly right in escaping, then I will make the attempt; but if not, I will abstain. The other considerations which you mention, of money and loss of character and the duty of educating one's children, are, I fear, only the doctrines of the multitude, who would be as ready to restore people to life, if they were able, as they are to put them to death—and with as little reason. But now, since the argument has thus far prevailed, the only question which remains to be considered is, whether we shall do rightly either in escaping or in suffering others to aid in our escape and paying them in money and thanks, or whether in reality we shall not do rightly; and if the latter, then death or any other calamity which may ensue on my remaining here must not be allowed to enter into the calculation.

Cr. I think that you are right, Socrates; how then shall we proceed?

Soc. Let us consider the matter together, and do you either refute me if you can, and I will be convinced; or else cease, my dear friend, from repeating to me that I ought to escape against the wishes of the Athenians: for I highly value your attempts to persuade me to do so, but I may not be persuaded against my own better judgment. And now please to consider my first position, and try how you can best answer me.

Cr. I will.

Soc. Are we to say that we are never intentionally to do wrong, or that in one way we ought and in another way we ought not to do wrong, or is doing wrong always evil and dishonourable, as I was just now saying, and as has been already acknowledged by us? Are all our former admissions which were made within a few days to be thrown away? And have we, at our age, been earnestly discoursing with one another all our life long only to discover that we are no better than children? Or, in spite of the opinion of the many, and in spite of consequences whether better or worse, shall we insist on the truth of what was then said, that injustice is always an evil and dishonour to him who acts unjustly? Shall we say so or not?

Cr. Yes.   70

Soc. Then we must do no wrong?

Cr. Certainly not.

Soc. Nor when injured injure in return, as the many imagine; for we must injure no one at all?

Cr. Clearly not.

Soc. Again, Crito, may we do evil?   75

Cr. Surely not, Socrates.

Soc. And what of doing evil in return for evil, which is the morality of the many—is that just or not?

Cr. Not just.

Soc. For doing evil to another is the same as injuring him?

Cr. Very true.   80

Soc. Then we ought not to retaliate or render evil for evil to any one, whatever evil we may have suffered from him. But I would have you consider, Crito, whether you really mean what you are saying. For this opinion has never been held, and never will be held, by any considerable number of persons; and those who are agreed and those who are not agreed upon this point have no common ground, and can only despise one another when they see how widely they differ. Tell me, then, whether you agree with and assent to my first principle, that neither injury nor retaliation nor warding off evil by evil is ever right. And shall that be the premise of our argument? Or do you decline and dissent from this? For so I have ever thought, and continue to think; but, if you are of another opinion, let me hear what you have to say. If, however, you remain of the same mind as formerly, I will proceed to the next step.

Cr. You may proceed, for I have not changed my mind.

Soc. Then I will go on to the next point, which may be put in the form of a question:—Ought a man to do what he admits to be right, or ought he to betray the right?

Cr. He ought to do what he thinks right.

Soc. But if this is true, what is the application? In leaving the prison against the will of the Athenians, do I wrong any? or rather do I not wrong those whom I ought least to wrong? Do I not desert the principles which were acknowledged by us to be just— what do you say?   85

Cr. I cannot tell, Socrates; for I do not know.

Soc. Then consider the matter in this way:—Imagine that I am about to play truant (you may call the proceeding by any name which you like), and the laws and the government come and interrogate me: "Tell us, Socrates," they say; "what are you about? are you not going by an act of yours to overturn us—the laws, and the whole state, as far as in you lies? Do you imagine that a state can subsist and not be overthrown, in which the decisions of law have no power, but are set aside and trampled upon by individuals?" What will be our answer, Crito, to these and the like words? Any one, and especially a rhetorician, will have a good deal to say on behalf of the law which requires a sentence to be carried out. He will argue that this law should not be set aside; and shall we reply, "Yes; but the state has injured us and given an unjust sentence." Suppose I say that?

Cr. Very good, Socrates.

Soc. "And was that our agreement with you?" the laws would answer; "or were you to abide by the sentence of the state?" And if I were to express my astonishment at their words, the laws would probably add: "Answer, Socrates, instead of opening your eyes—you are in the habit of asking and answering questions. Tell us,—What complaint have you to make against us which justifies you in attempting to destroy us and the state? In the first place did we not bring you into existence? Your father married your mother by our aid and begat you. Say whether you have any objection to urge against those of us who regulate marriage?" None, I should reply. "Or against those of us who after birth regulate the nurture and education of children, in which you also were trained? Were not the laws, which have the charge of education, right in commanding your father to train you in music and gymnastic?'' Right, I should reply. ''Well, then, since you were brought into the world and nurtured and educated by us, can you deny in the first place that you are our child and slave, as your fathers were before you? And if this is true, you are not on equal terms with us; nor can you think that you have a right to do to us what we are doing to you. Would you have any right to strike or revile or do any other evil to your father or your master, if you had one, because you have been struck or reviled by him, or received some other evil at his hands?—you would not say this? And because we think right to destroy you, do you think that you have any right to destroy us in return, and your country as far as in you lies? Will you, O professor of true virtue, pretend that you are justified in this? Has a philosopher like you failed to discover that our country is more to be valued and higher and holier far than mother or father or any ancestor, and more to be regarded in the eyes of the gods and of men of understanding? also to be soothed, and gently and reverently entreated when angry, even more than a father, and either to be persuaded, or if not persuaded, to be obeyed? And when we are punished by her, whether with imprisonment or stripes, the punishment is to be endured in silence; and if she lead us to wounds or death in battle, thither we follow as is right; neither may any one yield or retreat or leave his rank, but whether in battle or in a court of law, or in any other place, he must do what his city and his country order him; or he must change their view of what is just: and if he may do no violence to his father or mother, much less may he do violence to his country.'' What answer shall we make to this, Crito? Do the laws speak truly, or do they not?

Cr. I think that they do. 90

Soc. Then the laws will say: ''Consider, Socrates, if we are speaking truly that in your present attempt you are going to do us an injury. For, having brought you into the world, and nurtured and educated you, and given you and every other citizen a share in every good which we had to give, we further proclaim to any Athenian by the liberty which we allow him, that if he does not like us when he has become of age and has seen the ways of the city, and made our acquaintance, he may go where he pleases and take his goods with him. None of us laws will forbid him or interfere with him. Any one who does not like us and the city, and who wants to emigrate to a colony or to any other city, may go where he likes, retaining his property. But he who has experience of the manner in which we order justice and administer the State, and still remains, has entered into an implied contract that he will do as we command him. And he who disobeys us is, as we maintain, thrice wrong; first, because in disobeying us he is disobeying his parents; secondly, because we are the authors of his education; thirdly, because he has made an agreement with us that he will duly obey our commands; and he neither obeys them nor convinces us that our commands are unjust; and we do not rudely impose them, but give him the alternative of obeying or convincing us;—that is what we offer, and he does neither.

"These are the sort of accusations to which, as we were saying, you, Socrates, will be exposed if you accomplish your intentions; you, above all other Athenians." Suppose now I ask, why I rather than anybody else? they will justly retort upon me that I above all other men have acknowledged the agreement. "There is clear proof," they will say, "Socrates, that we and the city were not displeasing to you. Of all Athenians you have been the most constant resident in the city, which, as you never leave, you may be supposed to love. For you never went out of the city either to see the games, except once when you went to the Isthmus, or to any other place unless when you were on military service; nor did you travel as other men do. Nor had you any curiosity to know other States or their laws: your affections did not go beyond us and our State; we were your special favourites, and you acquiesced in our government of you; and here in this city you begat your children, which is a proof of your satisfaction. Moreover, you might in the course of the trial, if you had liked, have fixed the penalty at banishment; the State which refuses to let you go now would have let you go then. But you pretended that you preferred death to exile, and that you were not unwilling to die. And now you have forgotten these fine sentiments, and pay no respect to us, the laws, of whom you are the destroyer; and are doing what only a miserable slave would do, running away and turning your back upon the compacts and agreements which you made as a citizen. And, first of all, answer this very question: Are we right in saying that you agreed to be governed according to us in deed, and not in word only? Is that true or not?" How shall we answer, Crito? Must we not assent?

Cr. We cannot help it, Socrates.

Soc. Then will they not say: "You, Socrates, are breaking the covenants and agreements which you made with us at your leisure, not in any haste or under any compulsion or deception, but after you have had seventy years to think of them, during which time you were at liberty to leave the city, if we were not to your mind, or if our covenants appeared to you to be unfair. You had your choice, and might have gone either to Lacedaemon or Crete, both

which States are often praised by you for their good government,
or to some other Hellenic or foreign State. Whereas you, above
all other Athenians, seemed to be so fond of the State, or, in other
words, of us, her laws (and who would care about a State which
has no laws?), that you never stirred out of her; the halt, the
blind, the maimed were not more stationary in her than you were.
And now you run away and forsake your agreements. Not so,
Socrates, if you will take our advice; do not make yourself ridiculous
by escaping out of the city.

"For just consider, if you trangress and err in this sort of way,   95
what good will you do either to yourself or to your friends? That
your friends will be driven into exile and deprived of citizenship,
or will lose their property, is tolerably certain; and you yourself,
if you fly to one of the neighbouring cities, as, for example, Thebes
or Megara, both of which are well governed, will come to them
as an enemy, Socrates, and their government will be against you,
and all patriotic citizens will cast an evil eye upon you as a subverter
of the laws, and you will confirm in the minds of the judges the
justice of their own condemnation of you. For he I say, is humming
in my ears, and prevents me from hearing any other. And I know
that anything more which you may say will be vain. Yet speak,
if you have anything to say.

Cr. I have nothing to say, Socrates.

Soc. Leave me then, Crito, to fulfil the will of God, and to
follow whither he leads.

HENRY DAVID THOREAU

Civil Disobedience

I heartily accept the motto,—"That government is best which   1
governs least;" and I should like to see it acted up to more rapidly
and systematically. Carried out, it finally amounts to this, which
also I believe,—"That government is best which governs not at
all;" and when men are prepared for it, that will be the kind of
government which they will have. Government is at best but an
expedient; but most governments are usually, and all governments
are sometimes, inexpedient. The objections which have been brought
against a standing army, and they are many and weighty, and

Written in 1849 and first published in *Aesthetic Papers.*

deserve to prevail, may also at last be brought against a standing government. The standing army is only an arm of the standing government. The government itself, which is only the mode which the people have chosen to execute their will, is equally liable to be abused and perverted before the people can act through it. Witness the present Mexican war,[1] the work of comparatively a few individuals using the standing government as their tool; for, in the outset, the people would not have consented to this measure.

This American government,—what is it but a tradition, though   2
a recent one, endeavoring to transmit itself unimpaired to posterity, but each instant losing some of its integrity? It has not the vitality and force of a single living man; for a single man can bend it to his will. It is a sort of wooden gun to the people themselves. But it is not the less necessary for this; for the people must have some complicated machinery or other, and hear its din, to satisfy that idea of government which they have. Governments show thus how successfully men can be imposed on, even impose on themselves, for their own advantage. It is excellent, we must all allow. Yet this government never of itself furthered any enterprise, but by the alacrity with which it got out of its way. *It* does not keep the country free. *It* does not settle the West. *It* does not educate. The character inherent in the American people has done all that has been accomplished; and it would have done somewhat more, if the government had not sometimes got in its way. For government is an expedient by which men would fain succeed in letting one another alone; and, as has been said, when it is most expedient, the governed are most let alone by it. Trade and commerce, if they were not made of India-rubber, would never manage to bounce over the obstacles which legislators are continually putting in their way; and, if one were to judge these men wholly by the effects of their actions and not partly by their intentions, they would deserve to be classed and punished with those mischievous persons who put obstructions on the railroads.

But, to speak practically and as a citizen, unlike those who call   3
themselves no-government men, I ask for, not at once no government, but *at once* a better government. Let every man make known what kind of government would command his respect, and that will be one step toward obtaining it.

After all, the practical reason why, when the power is once in   4
the hands of people, a majority are permitted, and for a long period continue, to rule is not because they are most likely to be

1. 1846–48 conflict between Mexico and the United States, brought about by boundary disputes and the U.S. annexation of Texas.

in the right, nor because this seems fairest to the minority, but because they are physically the strongest. But a government in which the majority rule in all cases cannot be based on justice, even as far as men understand it. Can there not be a government in which majorities do not virtually decide right and wrong, but conscience?—in which majorities decide only those questions to which the rule of expediency is applicable? Must the citizen ever for a moment, or in the least degree, resign his conscience to the legislator? Why has every man a conscience, then? I think that we should be men first, and subjects afterward. It is not desirable to cultivate a respect for the law, so much as for the right. The only obligation which I have a right to assume is to do at any time what I think right. It is truly enough said, that a corporation has no conscience; but a corporation of conscientious men is a corporation *with* a conscience. Law never made men a whit more just; and, by means of their respect for it, even the well-disposed are daily made the agents of injustice. A common and natural result of an undue respect for law is, that you may see a file of soldiers, colonel, captain, corporal, privates, powder-monkeys, and all, marching in admirable order over hill and dale to the wars, against their wills, ay, against their common sense and consciences, which makes it very steep marching indeed, and produces a palpitation of the heart. They have no doubt that it is a damnable business in which they are concerned; they are all peaceably inclined. Now, what are they? Men at all? or small movable forts and magazines, at the service of some unscrupulous man in power? Visit the Navy-Yard, and behold a marine, such a man as an American government can make, or such as it can make a man with its black arts,—a mere shadow and reminiscence of humanity, a man laid out alive and standing, and already, as one may say, buried under arms with funeral accompaniments, though it may be,—

> "*Not a drum was heard, not a funeral note,*
>   *As his corse to the rampart we hurried;*
> *Not a soldier discharged his farewell shot*
>   *O'er the grave where our hero we buried.*"[2]

The mass of men serve the state thus, not as men mainly, but ⁵ as machines, with their bodies. They are the standing army, and the militia, jailers, constables, posse comitatus, etc. In most cases

2. From "Burial of Sir John Moore at Corunna" by Charles Wolfe (1817).

there is no free exercise whatever of the judgment or of the moral sense; but they put themselves on a level with wood and earth and stones; and wooden men can perhaps be manufactured that will serve the purpose as well. Such command no more respect than men of straw or a lump of dirt. They have the same sort of worth only as horses and dogs. Yet such as these even are commonly esteemed good citizens. Others—as most legislators, politicians, lawyers, ministers, and office-holders—serve the state chiefly with their heads; and, as they rarely make any moral distinctions, they are as likely to serve the Devil, without *intending* it, as God. A very few, as heroes, patriots, martyrs, reformers in the great sense, and *men,* serve the state with their consciences also, and so necessarily resist it for the most part; and they are commonly treated as enemies by it. A wise man will only be useful as a man, and will not submit to be "clay," and "stop a hole to keep the wind away," but leave that office to his dust at least:—

> *"I am too high-born to be propertied,*
> *To be a secondary at control,*
> *Or useful serving-man and instrument*
> *To any sovereign state throughout the world."*[3]

He who gives himself entirely to his fellow-men appears to them   6
useless and selfish; but he who gives himself partially to them is pronounced a benefactor and philanthropist.

How does it become a man to behave toward this American   7
government to-day? I answer, that he cannot without disgrace be associated with it. I cannot for an instant recognize that political organization as *my* government which is the *slave's* government also.

All men recognize the right of revolution; that is, the right to   8
refuse allegiance to, and to resist, the government, when its tyranny or its inefficiency are great and unendurable. But almost all say that such is not the case now. But such was the case, they think, in the Revolution of '75.[4] If one were to tell me that this was a bad government because it taxed certain foreign commodities brought to its ports, it is most probable that I should not make an ado about it, for I can do without them. All machines have their friction; and possibly this does enough good to counterbalance the evil. At any rate, it is a great evil to make a stir about it. But when the friction comes to have its machine, and oppression and

---

3. The line before the indented quotation is from *Hamlet* V. i. 236–37; the indented quotation is *King John* V. ii. 79–82.
4. That is, the war for independence from Great Britain, 1775–83.

robbery are organized, I say, let us not have such a machine any longer. In other words, when a sixth of the population of a nation which has undertaken to be the refuge of liberty are slaves, and a whole country is unjustly overrun and conquered by a foreign army, and subjected to military law, I think that it is not too soon for honest men to rebel and revolutionize. What makes this duty the more urgent is the fact that the country so overrun is not our own, but ours is the invading army.

Paley,[5] a common authority with many on moral questions, in his chapter on the "Duty of Submission to Civil Government," resolves all civil obligation into expediency; and he proceeds to say, "that so long as the interest of the whole society requires it, that is, so long as the established government cannot be resisted or changed without public inconveniency, it is the will of God that the established government be obeyed, and no longer. . . . This principle being admitted, the justice of every particular case of resistance is reduced to a computation of the quantity of the danger and grievance on the one side, and of the probability and expense of redressing it on the other." Of this, he says, every man shall judge for himself. But Paley appears never to have contemplated those cases to which the rule of expediency does not apply, in which a people, as well as an individual, must do justice, cost what it may. If I have unjustly wrested a plank from a drowning man, I must restore it to him though I drown myself. This, according to Paley, would be inconvenient. But he that would save his life, in such a case, shall lose it. This people must cease to hold slaves, and to make war on Mexico, though it cost them their existence as a people.

9

In their practice, nations agree with Paley; but does any one think that Massachusetts does exactly what is right at the present crisis?

10

"A drab of state, a cloth-o'-silver slut,
To have her train borne up, and her soul trail in the dirt."

Practically speaking, the opponents to a reform in Massachusetts are not a hundred thousand politicians at the South, but a hundred thousand merchants and farmers here, who are more interested in commerce and agriculture than they are in humanity, and are not prepared to do justice to the slave and to Mexico, *cost what it may*. I quarrel not with far-off foes, but with those who, near

5. William Paley (1743–1805), English theologian.

at home, coöperate with, and do the bidding of, those far away, and without whom the latter would be harmless. We are accustomed to say, that the mass of men are unprepared; but improvement is slow, because the few are not materially wiser or better than the many. It is not so important that many should be as good as you, as that there be some absolute goodness somewhere; for that will leaven the whole lump. There are thousands who are *in opinion* opposed to slavery and to the war, who yet in effect do nothing to put an end to them; who, esteeming themselves children of Washington and Franklin, sit down with their hands in their pockets, and say that they know not what to do, and do nothing; who even postpone the question of freedom to the question of free-trade, and quietly read the prices-current along with the latest advices from Mexico, after dinner, and, it may be, fall asleep over them both. What is the price-current of an honest man and patriot to-day? They hesitate, and they regret, and sometimes they petition; but they do nothing in earnest and with effect. They will wait, well disposed, for others to remedy the evil, that they may no longer have it to regret. At most, they give only a cheap vote, and a feeble countenance and Godspeed, to the right, as it goes by them. There are nine hundred and ninety-nine patrons of virtue to one virtuous man. But it is easier to deal with the real possessor of a thing than with the temporary guardian of it.

All voting is a sort of gaming, like checkers or backgammon,   11
with a slight moral tinge to it, a playing with right and wrong, with moral questions; and betting naturally accompanies it. The character of the voters is not staked. I cast my vote, perchance, as I think right; but I am not vitally concerned that that right should prevail. I am willing to leave it to the majority. Its obligation, therefore, never exceeds that of expediency. Even voting *for the right* is *doing* nothing for it. It is only expressing to men feebly your desire that it should prevail. A wise man will not leave the right to the mercy of chance, nor wish it to prevail through the power of the majority. There is but little virtue in the action of masses of men. When the majority shall at length vote for the abolition of slavery, it will be because they are indifferent to slavery, or because there is but little slavery left to be abolished by their vote. *They* will then be the only slaves. Only *his* vote can hasten the abolition of slavery who asserts his own freedom by his vote.

I hear of a convention to be held at Baltimore, or elsewhere,   12
for the selection of a candidate for the Presidency, made up chiefly of editors, and men who are politicians by profession; but I think, what is it to any independent, intelligent, and respectable man what decision they may come to? Shall we not have the advantage

of his wisdom and honesty, nevertheless? Can we not count upon some independent votes? Are there not many individuals in the country who do not attend conventions? But no: I find that the respectable man, so called, has immediately drifted from his position, and despairs of his country, when his country has more reason to despair of him. He forthwith adopts one of the candidates thus selected as the only *available* one, thus proving that he is himself *available* for any purposes of the demagogue. His vote is of no more worth than that of any unprincipled foreigner or hireling native, who may have been bought. O for a man who is a *man,* and, as my neighbor says, has a bone in his back which you cannot pass your hand through! Our statistics are at fault: the population has been returned too large. How many *men* are there to a square thousand miles in this country? Hardly one. Does not America offer any inducement for men to settle here? The American has dwindled into an Odd Fellow,—one who may be known by the development of his organ of gregariousness, and a manifest lack of intellect and cheerful self-reliance; whose first and chief concern, on coming into the world, is to see that the Almshouses are in good repair; and, before yet he has lawfully donned the virile garb, to collect a fund for the support of the widows and orphans that may be; who, in short, ventures to live only by the aid of the Mutual Insurance company, which has promised to bury him decently.

It is not a man's duty, as a matter of course, to devote himself   13
to the eradication of any, even the most enormous wrong; he may still properly have other concerns to engage him; but it his duty, at least, to wash his hands of it, and, if he gives it no thought longer, not to give it practically his support. If I devote myself to other pursuits and contemplations, I must first see, at least, that I do not pursue them sitting upon another man's shoulders. I must get off him first, that he may pursue his contemplations too. See what gross inconsistency is tolerated. I have heard some of my townsmen say, "I should like to have them order me out to help put down an insurrection of the slaves, or to march to Mexico;— see if I would go;" and yet these very men have each, directly by their allegiance, and so indirectly, at least, by their money, furnished a substitute. The soldier is applauded who refuses to serve in an unjust war by those who do not refuse to sustain the unjust government which makes the war; is applauded by those whose own act and authority he disregards and sets at naught; as if the state were penitent to that degree that it hired one to scourge it while it sinned, but not to that degree that it left off sinning for a moment. Thus, under the name of Order and Civil Government,

we are all made at last to pay homage to and support our own meanness. After the first blush of sin comes its indifference; and from immoral it becomes, as it were, *un*moral, and not quite unnecessary to that life which we have made.

The broadest and most prevalent error requires the most dis-   14 interested virtue to sustain it. The slight reproach to which the virtue of patriotism is commonly liable, the noble are most likely to incur. Those who, while they disapprove of the character and measures of a government, yield to it their allegiance and support are undoubtedly its most conscientious supporters, and so frequently the most serious obstacles to reform. Some are petitioning the state to dissolve the Union, to disregard the requisitions of the President. Why do they not dissolve it themselves,—the union between themselves and the state,—and refuse to pay their quota into its treasury? Do not they stand in the same relation to the state that the state does to the Union? And have not the same reasons prevented the state from resisting the Union which have prevented them from resisting the state?

How can a man be satisfied to entertain an opinion merely, and   15 enjoy *it?* Is there any enjoyment in it, if his opinion is that he is aggrieved? If you are cheated out of a single dollar by your neighbor, you do not rest satisfied with knowing that you are cheated, or with saying that you are cheated, or even with petitioning him to pay you your due; but you take effectual steps at once to obtain the full amount, and see that you are never cheated again. Action from principle, the perception and the performance of right, changes things and relations; it is essentially revolutionary, and does not consist wholly with anything which was. It not only divides states and churches, it divides families; ay, it divides the *individual,* separating the diabolical in him from the divine.

Unjust laws exist: shall we be content to obey them, or shall   16 we endeavor to amend them, and obey them until we have succeeded, or shall we transgress them at once? Men generally, under such a government as this, think that they ought to wait until they have persuaded the majority to alter them. They think that, if they should resist, the remedy would be worse than the evil. But it is the fault of the government itself that the remedy *is* worse than the evil. *It* makes it worse. Why is it not more apt to anticipate and provide for reform? Why does it not cherish its wise minority? Why does it cry and resist before it is hurt? Why does it not encourage its citizens to be on the alert to point out its faults, and *do* better than it would have them? Why does it always crucify Christ, and excommunicate Copernicus and Luther, and pronounce Washington and Franklin rebels?

One would think, that a deliberate and practical denial of its authority was the only offense never contemplated by government; else, why has it not assigned its definite, its suitable and proportionate penalty? If a man who has no property refuses but once to earn nine shillings for the state, he is put in prison for a period unlimited by any law that I know, and determined only by the discretion of those who placed him there; but if he should steal ninety times nine shillings from the state, he is soon permitted to go at large again.

If the injustice is part of the necessary friction of the machine of government, let it go, let it go: perchance it will wear smooth,— certainly the machine will wear out. If the injustice has a spring, or a pulley, or a rope, or a crank, exclusively for itself, then perhaps you may consider whether the remedy will not be worse than the evil; but if it is of such a nature that it requires you to be the agent of injustice to another, then, I say, break the law. Let your life be a counter friction to stop the machine. What I have to do is to see, at any rate, that I do not lend myself to the wrong which I condemn.

As for adopting the ways which the state has provided for remedying the evil, I know not of such ways. They take too much time, and a man's life will be gone. I have other affairs to attend to. I came into this world, not chiefly to make this a good place to live in, but to live in it, be it good or bad. A man has not everything to do, but something; and because he cannot do *every-thing*, it is not necessary that he should do *something* wrong. It is not my business to be petitioning the Governor or the Legislature any more than it is theirs to petition me; and if they should not hear my petition, what should I do then? But in this case the state has provided no way: its very Constitution is the evil. This may seem to be harsh and stubborn and unconciliatory; but it is to treat with the utmost kindness and consideration the only spirit that can appreciate or deserves it. So is all change for the better, like birth and death, which convulse the body.

I do not hesitate to say, that those who call themselves Abolitionists should at once effectually withdraw their support, both in person and property, from the government of Massachusetts, and not wait till they constitute a majority of one, before they suffer the right to prevail through them. I think that it is enough if they have God on their side, without waiting for that other one. Moreover, any man more right than his neighbors constitutes a majority of one already.

I meet this American government, or its representative, the state government, directly, and face to face, once a year—no more—

in the person of its tax-gatherer; this is the only mode in which
a man situated as I am necessarily meets it; and it then says
distinctly, Recognize me; and the simplest, the most effectual, and,
in the present posture of affairs, the indispensablest mode of treating
with it on this head, of expressing your little satisfaction with and
love for it, is to deny it then. My civil neighbor, the tax-gatherer,
is the very man I have to deal with,—for it is, after all, with men
and not with parchment that I quarrel,—and he has voluntarily
chosen to be an agent of the government. How shall he ever know
well what he is and does as an officer of the government, or as
a man, until he is obliged to consider whether he shall treat me,
his neighbor, for whom he has respect, as a neighbor and well-
disposed man, or as a maniac and disturber of the peace, and see
if he can get over this obstruction to his neighborliness without
a ruder and more impetuous thought or speech corresponding
with his action. I know this well, that if one thousand, if one
hundred, if ten men whom I could name,—if ten *honest* men
only,—ay, if *one* HONEST man, in this State of Massachusetts, *ceasing
to hold slaves,* were actually to withdraw from this copartnership,
and be locked up in the county jail therefor, it would be the
abolition of slavery in America. For it matters not how small the
beginning may seem to be: what is once well done is done forever.
But we love better to talk about it: that we say is our mission.
Reform keeps many scores of newspapers in its service, but not
one man. If my esteemed neighbor, the State's ambassador, who
will devote his days to the settlement of the question of human
rights in the Council Chamber, instead of being threatened with
the prisons of Carolina, were to sit down the prisoner of Massachusetts, that State which is so anxious to foist the sin of slavery
upon her sister,—though at present she can discover only an act
of inhospitality to be the ground of a quarrel with her,—the Legislature would not wholly waive the subject the following winter.

Under a government which imprisons any unjustly, the true   22
place for a just man is also a prison. The proper place to-day, the
only place which Massachusetts has provided for her freer and
less desponding spirits, is in her prisons, to be put out and locked
out of the State by her own act, as they have already put themselves
out by their principles. It is there that the fugitive slave, and the
Mexican prisoner on parole, and the Indian come to plead the
wrongs of his race should find them; on that separate, but more
free and honorable ground, where the State places those who are
not *with* her, but *against* her,—the only house in a slave State in
which a free man can abide with honor. If any think that their
influence would be lost there, and their voices no longer afflict

the ear of the State, that they would not be as an enemy within its walls, they do not know by how much truth is stronger than error, nor how much more eloquently and effectively he can combat injustice who has experienced a little in his own person. Cast your whole vote, not a strip of paper merely, but your whole influence. A minority is powerless while it conforms to the majority; it is not even a minority then; but it is irresistible when it clogs by its whole weight. If the alternative is to keep all just men in prison, or give up war and slavery, the State will not hesitate which to choose. If a thousand men were not to pay their tax-bills this year, that would not be a violent and bloody measure, as it would be to pay them, and enable the State to commit violence and shed innocent blood. This is, in fact, the definition of a peaceable revolution, if any such is possible. If the tax-gatherer, or any other public officer, asks me, as one has done, "But what shall I do?" my answer is, "If you really wish to do anything, resign your office." When the subject has refused allegiance, and the officer has resigned his office, then the revolution is accomplished. But even suppose blood should flow. Is there not a sort of blood shed when the conscience is wounded? Through this wound a man's real manhood and immortality flow out, and he bleeds to an everlasting death. I see this blood flowing now.

I have contemplated the imprisonment of the offender, rather than the seizure of his goods,—though both will serve the same purpose,—because they who assert the purest right, and consequently are most dangerous to a corrupt State, commonly have not spent much time in accumulating property. To such the State renders comparatively small service, and a slight tax is wont to appear exorbitant, particularly if they are obliged to earn it by special labor with their hands. If there were one who lived wholly without the use of money, the State itself would hesitate to demand it of him. But the rich man—not to make any invidious comparison— is always sold to the institution which makes him rich. Absolutely speaking, the more money, the less virtue; for money comes between a man and his objects, and obtains them for him; and it was certainly no great virtue to obtain it. It puts to rest many questions which he would otherwise be taxed to answer; while the only new question which it puts is the hard but superfluous one, how to spend it. Thus his moral ground is taken from under his feet. The opportunities of living are diminished in proportion as what are called the "means" are increased. The best thing a man can do for his culture when he is rich is to endeavor to carry out those schemes which he entertained when he was poor. Christ answered the Herodians according to their condition. "Show me the tribute- 23 money," said he;—and one took a penny out of his pocket;—if you use money which has the image of Cæsar on it, and which he has made current and valuable, that is, *if you are men of the State*, and gladly enjoy the advantages of Cæsar's government, then pay him back some of his own when he demands it. "Render therefore to Cæsar that which is Cæsar's, and to God those things which are God's,"—leaving them no wiser than before as to which was which; for they did not wish to know.

When I converse with the freest of my neighbors, I perceive   24
that, whatever they may say about the magnitude and seriousness of the question, and their regard for the public tranquillity, the long and the short of the matter is, that they cannot spare the protection of the existing government, and they dread the consequences to their property and families of disobedience to it. For my own part, I should not like to think that I ever rely on the protection of the State. But, if I deny the authority of the State when it presents its tax-bill, it will soon take and waste all my property, and so harass me and my children without end. This is hard. This makes it impossible for a man to live honestly, and at the same time comfortably, in outward respects. It will not be worth the while to accumulate property; that would be sure to go again. You must hire or squat somewhere, and raise but a small crop, and eat that soon. You must live within yourself, and depend upon yourself always tucked up and ready for a start, and not have many affairs. A man may grow rich in Turkey even, if he will be in all respects a good subject of the Turkish government. Confucius said: "If a state is governed by the principles of reason, poverty and misery are subjects of shame; if a state is not governed by the principles of reason, riches and honors are the subjects of shame." No: until I want the protection of Massachusetts to be extended to me in some distant Southern port, where my liberty is endangered, or until I am bent solely on building up an estate at home by peaceful enterprise, I can afford to refuse allegiance to Massachusetts, and her right to my property and life. It costs me less in every sense to incur the penalty of disobedience to the State than it would to obey. I should feel as if I were worth less in that case.

Some years ago, the State met me in behalf of the Church, and   25
commanded me to pay a certain sum toward the support of a clergyman whose preaching my father attended, but never I myself. "Pay," it said, "or be locked up in the jail." I declined to pay. But, unfortunately, another man saw fit to pay it. I did not see why the schoolmaster should be taxed to support the priest, and not the priest the schoolmaster; for I was not the State's schoolmaster,

but I supported myself by voluntary subscription. I did not see why the lyceum should not present its tax-bill, and have the State to back its demand, as well as the Church. However, at the request of the selectmen, I condescended to make some such statement as this in writing:—"Know all men by these presents, that I, Henry Thoreau, do not wish to be regarded as a member of any incorporated society which I have not joined." This I gave to the town clerk; and he has it. The State, having thus learned that I did not wish to be regarded as a member of that church, has never made a like demand on me since; though it said that it must adhere to its original presumption that time. If I had known how to name them, I should then have signed off in detail from all the societies which I never signed on to; but I did not know where to find a complete list.

I have paid no poll-tax[6] for six years. I was put into a jail once on this account, for one night; and, as I stood considering the walls of solid stone, two or three feet thick, the door of wood and iron, a foot thick, and the iron grating which strained the light, I could not help being struck with the foolishness of that institution which treated me as if I were mere flesh and blood and bones, to be locked up. I wondered that it should have concluded at length that this was the best use it could put me to, and had never thought to avail itself of my services in some way. I saw that, if there was a wall of stone between me and my townsmen, there was a still more difficult one to climb or break through before they could get to be as free as I was. I did not for a moment feel confined, and the walls seemed a great waste of stone and mortar. I felt as if I alone of all my townsmen had paid my tax. They plainly did not know how to treat me, but behaved like persons who are underbred. In every threat and in every compliment there was a blunder; for they thought that my chief desire was to stand the other side of that stone wall. I could not but smile to see how industriously they locked the door on my meditations, which followed them out again without let or hindrance, and *they* were really all that was dangerous. As they could not reach me, they had resolved to punish my body; just as boys, if they cannot come at some person against whom they have a spite, will abuse his dog. I saw that the State was half-witted, that it was timid as a lone woman with her silver spoons, and that it did not know its friends from its foes, and I lost all my remaining respect for it, and pitied it.

6. Tax assessed against a person (not property); payment was frequently prerequisite for voting.

Thus the State never intentionally confronts a man's sense, in-   27
tellectual or moral, but only his body, his senses. It is not armed
with superior wit or honesty, but with superior physical strength.
I was not born to be forced. I will breathe after my own fashion.
Let us see who is the strongest. What force has a multitude? They
only can force me who obey a higher law than I. They force me
to become like themselves. I do not hear of *men* being *forced* to
live this way or that by masses of men. What sort of life were
that to live? When I meet a government which says to me, "Your
money or your life," why should I be in haste to give it my money?
It may be in a great strait, and not know what to do: I cannot
help that. It must help itself; do as I do. It is not worth the while
to snivel about it. I am not responsible for the successful working
of the machinery of society. I am not the son of the engineer. I
perceive that, when an acorn and a chestnut fall side by side, the
one does not remain inert to make way for the other, but both
obey their own laws, and spring and grow and flourish as best
they can, till one, perchance, overshadows and destroys the other.
If a plant cannot live according to its nature, it dies; and so
a man.

The night in prison was novel and interesting enough. The   28
prisoners in their shirt-sleeves were enjoying a chat and the evening
air in the doorway, when I entered. But the jailer said, "Come,
boys, it is time to lock up;" and so they dispersed, and I heard
the sound of their steps returning into the hollow apartments. My
room-mate was introduced to me by the jailer as "a first-rate fellow
and a clever man." When the door was locked, he showed me
where to hang my hat, and how he managed matters there. The
rooms were whitewashed once a month; and this one, at least,
was the whitest, most simply furnished, and probably the neatest
apartment in the town. He naturally wanted to know where I
came from, and what brought me there; and, when I had told
him, I asked him in my turn how he came there, presuming him
to be an honest man, of course; and, as the world goes, I believe
he was. "Why," said he, "they accuse me of burning a barn; but
I never did it." As near as I could discover, he had probably gone
to bed in a barn when drunk, and smoked his pipe there; and so
a barn was burnt. He had the reputation of being a clever man,
had been there some three months waiting for his trial to come
on, and would have to wait as much longer; but he was quite
domesticated and contented, since he got his board for nothing,
and thought that he was well treated.

He occupied one window, and I the other; and I saw that if   29
one stayed there long, his principal business would be to look out

the window. I had soon read all the tracts that were left there, and examined where former prisoners had broken out, and where a grate had been sawed off, and heard the history of the various occupants of that room; for I found that even here there was a history and a gossip which never circulated beyond the walls of the jail. Probably this is the only house in the town where verses are composed, which are afterward printed in a circular form, but not published. I was shown quite a long list of verses which were composed by some young men who had been detected in an attempt to escape, who avenged themselves by singing them.

I pumped my fellow-prisoner as dry as I could, for fear I should   30
never see him again; but at length he showed me which was my bed, and left me to blow out the lamp.

It was like traveling into a far country, such as I had never   31
expected to behold, to lie there for one night. It seemed to me that I never had heard the town-clock strike before, nor the evening sounds of the village; for we slept with the windows open, which were inside the grating. It was to see my native village in the light of the Middle Ages, and our Concord was turned into a Rhine stream, and visions of knights and castles passed before me. They were the voices of old burghers that I heard in the streets. I was an involuntary spectator and auditor of whatever was done and said in the kitchen of the adjacent village-inn,—a wholly new and rare experience to me. It was a closer view of my native town. I was fairly inside of it. I never had seen its institutions before. This is one of its peculiar institutions; for it is a shire town. I began to comprehend what its inhabitants were about.

In the morning, our breakfasts were put through the hole in   32
the door, in small oblong-square tin pans, made to fit, and holding a pint of chocolate, with brown bread, and an iron spoon. When they called for the vessels again, I was green enough to return what bread I had left; but my comrade seized it, and said that I should lay that up for lunch or dinner. Soon after he was let out to work at haying in a neighboring field, whither he went every day, and would not be back till noon; so he bade me good-day, saying that he doubted if he should see me again.

When I came out of prison,—for some one interfered, and paid   33
that tax,—I did not perceive that great changes had taken place on the common, such as he observed who went in a youth and emerged a tottering and gray-headed man; and yet a change had to my eyes come over the scene,—the town, and State, and coun-try,—greater than any that mere time could effect. I saw yet more distinctly the State in which I lived. I saw to what extent the people among whom I lived could be trusted as good neighbors

and friends; that their friendship was for summer weather only; that they did not greatly propose to do right; that they were a distinct race from me by their prejudices and superstitions, as the Chinamen and Malays are; that in their sacrifices to humanity they ran no risks, not even to their property; that after all they were not so noble but they treated the thief as he had treated them, and hoped, by a certain outward observance and a few prayers, and by walking in a particular straight though useless path from time to time, to save their souls. This may be to judge my neighbors harshly; for I believe that many of them are not aware that they have such an institution as the jail in their village.

It was formerly the custom in our village, when a poor debtor   34
came out of jail, for his acquaintances to salute him, looking through their fingers, which were crossed to represent the grating of a jail window, "How do ye do?" My neighbors did not thus salute me, but first looked at me, and then at one another, as if I had returned from a long journey. I was put into jail as I was going to the shoemaker's to get a shoe which was mended. When I was let out the next morning, I proceeded to finish my errand, and, having put on my mended shoe, joined a huckleberry party, who were impatient to put themselves under my conduct; and in half an hour,—for the horse was soon tackled,—was in the midst of a huckleberry field, on one of our highest hills, two miles off, and then the State was nowhere to be seen.

This is the whole history of "My Prisons."   35

I have never declined paying the highway tax, because I am as   36
desirous of being a good neighbor as I am of being a bad subject; and as for supporting schools, I am doing my part to educate my fellow-countrymen now. It is for no particular item in the tax-bill that I refuse to pay it. I simply wish to refuse allegiance to the State, to withdraw and stand aloof from it effectually. I do not care to trace the course of my dollar, if I could, till it buys a man or a musket to shoot one with,—the dollar is innocent,—but I am concerned to trace the effects of my allegiance. In fact, I quietly declare war with the State, after my fashion, though I will still make what use and get what advantage of her I can, as is usual in such cases.

If others pay the tax which is demanded of me, from a sympathy   37
with the State, they do but what they have already done in their own case, or rather they abet injustice to a greater extent than the State requires. If they pay the tax from a mistaken interest in the individual taxed, to save his property, or prevent his going to

jail, it is because they have not considered wisely how far they let their private feelings interfere with the public good.

This, then, is my position at present. But one cannot be too 38 much on his guard in such a case, lest his action be biased by obstinacy or an undue regard for the opinions of men. Let him see that he does only what belongs to himself and to the hour.

I think sometimes, Why, this people mean well, they are only 39 ignorant; they would do better if they knew how: why give your neighbors this pain to treat you as they are not inclined to? But I think again, This is no reason why I should do as they do, or permit others to suffer much greater pain of a different kind. Again, I sometimes say to myself, When many millions of men, without heat, without ill will, without personal feeling of any kind, demand of you a few shillings only, without the possibility, such is their constitution, of retracting or altering their present demand, and without the possibility, on your side, of appeal to any other millions, why expose yourself to this overwhelming brute force? You do not resist cold and hunger, the winds and the waves, thus obstinately; you quietly submit to a thousand similar necessities. You do not put your head into the fire. But just in proportion as I regard this as not wholly a brute force, but partly a human force, and consider that I have relations to those millions as to so many millions of men, and not of mere brute or inanimate things, I see that appeal is possible, first and instantaneously, from them to the Maker of them, and, secondly, from them to themselves. But if I put my head deliberately into the fire, there is no appeal to fire or to the Maker of fire, and I have only myself to blame. If I could convince myself that I have any right to be satisfied with men as they are, and to treat them accordingly, and not according, in some respects, to my requisitions and expectations of what they and I ought to be, then, like a good Mussulman and fatalist, I should endeavor to be satisfied with things as they are, and say it is the will of God. And, above all, there is this difference between resisting this and a purely brute or natural force, that I can resist this with some effect; but I cannot expect, like Orpheus, to change the nature of the rocks and trees and beasts.

I do not wish to quarrel with any man or nation. I do not wish 40 to split hairs, to make fine distinctions, or set myself up as better than my neighbors. I seek rather, I may say, even an excuse for conforming to the laws of the land. I am but too ready to conform to them. Indeed, I have reason to suspect myself on this head; and each year, as the tax-gatherer comes round, I find myself disposed to review the acts and position of the general and State governments, and the spirit of the people, to discover a pretext for conformity.

> "We must affect our country as our parents,
> And if at any time we alienate
> Our love or industry from doing it honor,
> We must respect effects and teach the soul
> Matter of conscience and religion,
> And not desire of rule or benefit."

I believe that the State will soon be able to take all my work of this sort out of my hands, and then I shall be no better a patriot than my fellow-countrymen. Seen from a lower point of view, the Constitution, with all its faults, is very good; the law and the courts are very respectable; even this State and this American government are, in many respects, very admirable, and rare things, to be thankful for, such as a great many have described them; but seen from a point of view a little higher, they are what I have described them; seen from a higher still, and the highest, who shall say what they are, or that they are worth looking at or thinking of at all?

However, the government does not concern me much, and I 41 shall bestow the fewest possible thoughts on it. It is not many moments that I live under a government, even in this world. If a man is thought-free, fancy-free, imagination-free, that which *is not* never for a long time appearing *to be* to him, unwise rulers or reformers cannot fatally interrupt him.

I know that most men think differently from myself; but those 42 whose lives are by profession devoted to the study of these or kindred subjects content me as little as any. Statesmen and legislators, standing so completely within the institution, never distinctly and nakedly behold it. They speak of moving society, but have no resting-place without it. They may be men of a certain experience and discrimination, and have no doubt invented ingenious and even useful systems, for which we sincerely thank them; but all their wit and usefulness lie within certain not very wide limits. They are wont to forget that the world is not governed by policy and expediency. Webster[7] never goes behind government, and so cannot speak with authority about it. His words are wisdom to those legislators who contemplate no essential reform in the existing government; but for thinkers, and those who legislate for all time,

---

7. Daniel Webster (1782–1852), American political leader.

he never once glances at the subject. I know of those whose serene and wise speculations on this theme would soon reveal the limits of his mind's range and hospitality. Yet, compared with the cheap professions of most reformers, and the still cheaper wisdom and eloquence of politicians in general, his are almost the only sensible and valuable words, and we thank Heaven for him. Comparatively, he is always strong, original, and, above all, practical. Still, his quality is not wisdom, but prudence. The lawyer's truth is not Truth, but consistency or a consistent expediency. Truth is always in harmony with herself, and is not concerned chiefly to reveal the justice that may consist with wrong-doing. He well deserves to be called, as he has been called, the Defender of the Constitution. There are really no blows to be given by him but defensive ones. He is not a leader, but a follower. His leaders are the men of '87.[8] "I have never made an effort," he says, "and never propose to make an effort; I have never countenanced an effort, and never mean to countenance an effort, to disturb the arrangement as originally made, by which the various States came into the Union." Still thinking of the sanction which the Constitution gives to slavery, he says, "Because it was a part of the original compact,—let it stand." Notwithstanding his special acuteness and ability, he is unable to take a fact out of its merely political relations, and behold it as it lies absolutely to be disposed of by the intellect,—what, for instance, it behooves a man to do here in America to-day with regard to slavery,—but ventures, or is driven, to make some such desperate answer as the following, while professing to speak absolutely, and as a private man,—from which what new and singular code of social duties might be inferred? "The manner," says he, "in which the governments of those States where slavery exists are to regulate it is for their own consideration, under their responsibility to their constituents, to the general laws of propriety, humanity, and justice, and to God. Associations formed elsewhere, springing from a feeling of humanity, or any other cause, have nothing whatever to do with it. They have never received any encouragement from me, and they never will."

They who know of no purer sources of truth, who have traced 43
up its stream no higher, stand, and wisely stand, by the Bible and the Constitution, and drink at it there with reverence and humility; but they who behold where it comes trickling into this lake or that pool, gird up their loins once more, and continue their pilgrimage toward its fountain-head.

---

8. That is, the delegates who created and signed the Constitution of the United States in 1787.

No man with a genius for legislation has appeared in America. 44
They are rare in the history of the world. There are orators, politicians, and eloquent men, by the thousand; but the speaker has
not yet opened his mouth to speak who is capable of settling the
much-vexed questions of the day. We love eloquence for its own
sake, and not for any truth which it may utter, or any heroism
it may inspire. Our legislators have not yet learned the comparative
value of free-trade and of freedom, of union, and of rectitude, to
a nation. They have no genius or talent for comparatively humble
questions of taxation and finance, commerce and manufactures
and agriculture. If we were left solely to the wordy wit of legislators
in Congress for our guidance, uncorrected by the seasonable experience and the effectual complaints of the people, America would
not long retain her rank among the nations. For eighteen hundred
years, though perchance I have no right to say it, the New Testament
has been written; yet where is the legislator who has wisdom and
practical talent enough to avail himself of the light which it sheds
on the science of legislation?

The authority of government, even such as I am willing to submit 45
to,—for I will cheerfully obey those who know and can do better
than I, and in many things even those who neither know nor can
do so well,—is still an impure one: to be strictly just, it must have
the sanction and consent of the governed. It can have no pure
right over my person and property but what I concede to it. The
progress from an absolute to a limited monarchy, from a limited
monarchy to a democracy, is a progress toward a true respect for
the individual. Even the Chinese philosopher was wise enough to
regard the individual as the basis of the empire. Is a democracy,
such as we know it, the last improvement possible in government?
Is it not possible to take a step further towards recognizing and
organizing the rights of man? There will never be a really free
and enlightened State until the State comes to recognize the individual as a higher and independent power, from which all its
own power and authority are derived, and treats him accordingly.
I please myself with imagining a State at last which can afford to
be just to all men, and to treat the individual with respect as a
neighbor; which even would not think it inconsistent with its own
repose if a few were to live aloof from it, not meddling with it,
nor embraced by it, who fulfilled all the duties of neighbors and
fellow-men. A State which bore this kind of fruit, and suffered it
to drop off as fast as it ripened, would prepare the way for a still
more perfect and glorious State, which also I have imagined, but
not yet anywhere seen.

Letter From Birmingham Jail

MARTIN LUTHER KING, JR.
Birmingham City Jail
April 16, 1963

Bishop C. C. J. CARPENTER
Bishop JOSEPH A. DURICK
Rabbi MILTON L. GRAFMAN
Bishop PAUL HARDIN
Bishop NOLAN B. HARMON
The Rev. GEORGE M. MURRAY
The Rev. EDWARD V. RAMAGE
The Rev. EARL STALLINGS

My dear Fellow Clergymen,

While confined here in the Birmingham City Jail, I came across 1
your recent statement calling our present activities "unwise and
untimely." Seldom, if ever, do I pause to answer criticism of my
work and ideas. If I sought to answer all of the criticisms that
cross my desk, my secretaries would be engaged in little else in
the course of the day and I would have no time for constructive
work. But since I feel that you are men of genuine good will and
your criticisms are sincerely set forth, I would like to answer your
statement in what I hope will be patient and reasonable terms.

I think I should give the reason for my being in Birmingham, 2
since you have been influenced by the argument of "outsiders
coming in." I have the honor of serving as president of the Southern
Christian Leadership Conference, an organization operating in every
Southern state with headquarters in Atlanta, Georgia. We have
some eighty-five affiliate organizations all across the South—one
being the Alabama Christian Movement for Human Rights. Whenever necessary and possible we share staff, educational, and financial
resources with our affiliates. Several months ago our local affiliate
here in Birmingham invited us to be on call to engage in a nonviolent
direct action program if such were deemed necessary. We readily

Written in the Birmingham, Alabama, jail in 1963, to the eight clergymen named
at the beginning of the letter. King had been jailed, along with his supporters, for
demonstrating against the segregation of the city's lunch counters.

consented and when the hour came we lived up to our promises. So I am here, along with several members of my staff, because we were invited here. I am here because I have basic organizational ties here. Beyond this, I am in Birmingham because injustice is here. Just as the eighth century prophets left their little villages and carried their "thus saith the Lord" far beyond the boundaries of their home town, and just as the Apostle Paul left his little village of Tarsus and carried the gospel of Jesus Christ to practically every hamlet and city of the Graeco-Roman world, I too am compelled to carry the gospel of freedom beyond my particular home town. Like Paul, I must constantly respond to the Macedonian call for aid.

Moreover, I am cognizant of the interrelatedness of all communities and states. I cannot sit idly by in Atlanta and not be concerned about what happens in Birmingham. Injustice anywhere is a threat to justice everywhere. We are caught in an inescapable network of mutuality tied in a single garment of destiny. Whatever affects one directly affects all indirectly. Never again can we afford to live with the narrow, provincial "outside agitator" idea. Anyone who lives inside the United States can never be considered an outsider anywhere in this country.

You deplore the demonstrations that are presently taking place in Birmingham. But I am sorry that your statement did not express a similar concern for the conditions that brought the demonstrations into being. I am sure that each of you would want to go beyond the superficial social analyst who looks merely at effects, and does not grapple with underlying causes. I would not hesitate to say that it is unfortunate that so-called demonstrations are taking place in Birmingham at this time, but I would say in more emphatic terms that it is even more unfortunate that the white power structure of this city left the Negro community with no other alternative.

In any nonviolent campaign there are four basic steps: (1) collection of the facts to determine whether injustices are alive; (2) negotiation; (3) self-purification; and (4) direct action. We have gone through all of these steps in Birmingham. There can be no gainsaying of the fact that racial injustice engulfs this community. Birmingham is probably the most thoroughly segregated city in the United States. Its ugly record of police brutality is known in every section of this country. Its unjust treatment of Negroes in the courts is a notorious reality. There have been more unsolved bombings of Negro homes and churches in Birmingham than any city in this nation. These are the hard, brutal, and unbelievable facts. On the basis of these conditions Negro leaders sought to negotiate with the city fathers. But the political leaders consistently refused to engage in good faith negotiation.

Then came the opportunity last September to talk with some 6 of the leaders of the economic community. In these negotiating sessions certain promises were made by the merchants—such as the promise to remove the humiliating racial signs from the stores. On the basis of these promises Rev. Shuttlesworth and the leaders of the Alabama Christian Movement for Human Rights agreed to call a moratorium on any type of demonstrations. As the weeks and months unfolded we realized that we were the victims of a broken promise. The signs remained. As in so many experiences of the past we were confronted with blasted hopes, and the dark shadow of a deep disappointment settled upon us. So we had no alternative except that of preparing for direct action, whereby we would present our very bodies as a means of laying our case before the conscience of the local and national community. We were not unmindful of the difficulties involved. So we decided to go through a process of self-purification. We started having workshops on nonviolence and repeatedly asked ourselves the questions, "Are you able to accept blows without retaliating?" "Are you able to endure the ordeals of jail?"

We decided to set our direct action program around the Easter 7 season, realizing that with the exception of Christmas, this was the largest shopping period of the year. Knowing that a strong economic withdrawal program would be the by-product of direct action, we felt that this was the best time to bring pressure on the merchants for the needed changes. Then it occurred to us that the March election was ahead, and so we speedily decided to postpone action until after election day. When we discovered that Mr. Connor was in the run-off, we decided again to postpone action so that the demonstrations could not be used to cloud the issues. At this time we agreed to begin our nonviolent witness the day after the run-off.

This reveals that we did not move irresponsibly into direct action. 8 We too wanted to see Mr. Connor defeated; so we went through postponement after postponement to aid in this community need. After this we felt that direct action could be delayed no longer.

You may well ask, "Why direct action? Why sit-ins, marches, 9 etc.? Isn't negotiation a better path?" You are exactly right in your call for negotiation. Indeed, this is the purpose of direct action. Nonviolent direct action seeks to create such a crisis and establish such creative tension that a community that has constantly refused to negotiate is forced to confront the issue. It seeks so to dramatize the issue that it can no longer be ignored. I just referred to the creation of tension as a part of the work of the nonviolent resister. This may sound rather shocking. But I must confess that I am not afraid of the word tension. I have earnestly worked and preached against violent tension, but there is a type of constructive nonviolent tension that is necessary for growth. Just as Socrates felt that it was necessary to create a tension in the mind so that individuals could rise from the bondage of myths and half-truths to the unfettered realm of creative analysis and objective appraisal, we must see the need of having nonviolent gadflies to create the kind of tension in society that will help men rise from the dark depths of prejudice and racism to the majestic heights of understanding and brotherhood. So the purpose of the direct action is to create a situation so crisis-packed that it will inevitably open the door to negotiation. We, therefore, concur with you in your call for negotiation. Too long has our beloved Southland been bogged down in the tragic attempt to live in monologue rather than dialogue.

One of the basic points in your statement is that our acts are   10
untimely. Some have asked, "Why didn't you give the new administration time to act?" The only answer that I can give to this inquiry is that the new administration must be prodded about as much as the outgoing one before it acts. We will be sadly mistaken if we feel that the election of Mr. Boutwell will bring the millennium to Birmingham. While Mr. Boutwell is much more articulate and gentle than Mr. Connor, they are both segregationists dedicated to the task of maintaining the status quo. The hope I see in Mr. Boutwell is that he will be reasonable enough to see the futility of massive resistance to desegregation. But he will not see this without pressure from the devotees of civil rights. My friends, I must say to you that we have not made a single gain in civil rights without determined legal and nonviolent pressure. History is the long and tragic story of the fact that privileged groups seldom give up their privileges voluntarily. Individuals may see the moral light and voluntarily give up their unjust posture; but as Reinhold Niebuhr has reminded us, groups are more immoral than individuals.

We know through painful experience that freedom is never   11
voluntarily given by the oppressor; it must be demanded by the oppressed. Frankly I have never yet engaged in a direct action movement that was "well timed," according to the timetable of those who have not suffered unduly from the disease of segregation. For years now I have heard the word "Wait!" It rings in the ear of every Negro with a piercing familiarity. This "wait" has almost always meant "never." It has been a tranquilizing thalidomide, relieving the emotional stress for a moment, only to give birth to

an ill-formed infant of frustration. We must come to see with the distinguished jurist of yesterday that "justice too long delayed is justice denied." We have waited for more than three hundred and forty years for our constitutional and God-given rights. The nations of Asia and Africa are moving with jet-like speed toward the goal of political independence, and we still creep at horse and buggy pace toward the gaining of a cup of coffee at a lunch counter.

I guess it is easy for those who have never felt the stinging darts 12 of segregation to say wait. But when you have seen vicious mobs lynch your mothers and fathers at will and drown your sisters and brothers at whim; when you have seen hate filled policemen curse, kick, brutalize, and even kill your black brothers and sisters with impunity; when you see the vast majority of your twenty million Negro brothers smothering in an air-tight cage of poverty in the midst of an affluent society; when you suddenly find your tongue twisted and your speech stammering as you seek to explain to your six-year-old daughter why she can't go to the public amusement park that has just been advertised on television, and see tears welling up in her little eyes when she is told that Funtown is closed to colored children, and see the depressing clouds of inferiority begin to form in her little mental sky, and see her begin to distort her little personality by unconsciously developing a bitterness toward white people; when you have to concoct an answer for a five-year-old son asking in agonizing pathos: "Daddy, why do white people treat colored people so mean?"; when you take a cross country drive and find it necessary to sleep night after night in the uncomfortable corners of your automobile because no motel will accept you; when you are humiliated day in and day out by nagging signs reading "white" men and "colored"; when your first name becomes "nigger" and your middle name becomes "boy" (however old you are) and your last name becomes "John," and when your wife and mother are never given the respected title "Mrs."; when you are harried by day and haunted by night by the fact that you are a Negro, living constantly at tip-toe stance never quite knowing what to expect next, and plagued with inner fears and outer resentments; when you are forever fighting a degenerating sense of "nobodiness";—then you will understand why we find it difficult to wait. There comes a time when the cup of endurance runs over, and men are no longer willing to be plunged into an abyss of injustice where they experience the bleakness of corroding despair. I hope, sirs, you can understand our legitimate and unavoidable impatience.

You express a great deal of anxiety over our willingness to break 13 laws. This is certainly a legitimate concern. Since we so diligently urge people to obey the Supreme Court's decision of 1954 outlawing segregation in the public schools, it is rather strange and paradoxical to find us consciously breaking laws. One may well ask, "How can you advocate breaking some laws and obeying others?" The answer is found in the fact that there are two types of laws. There are *just* laws and there are *unjust* laws. I would be the first to advocate obeying just laws. One has not only a legal but moral responsibility to obey just laws. Conversely, one has a moral responsibility to disobey unjust laws. I would agree with Saint Augustine that "An unjust law is no law at all."

Now what is the difference between the two? How does one   14
determine when a law is just or unjust? A just law is a man-made code that squares with the moral law or the law of God. An unjust law is a code that is out of harmony with the moral law. To put it in the terms of Saint Thomas Aquinas, an unjust law is a human law that is not rooted in eternal and natural law. Any law that uplifts human personality is just. Any law that degrades human personality is unjust. All segregation statutes are unjust because segregation distorts the soul and damages the personality. It gives the segregator a false sense of superiority and the segregated a false sense of inferiority. To use the words of Martin Buber, the great Jewish philosopher, segregation substitutes an "I-it" relationship for the "I-thou" relationship, and ends up relegating persons to the status of things. So segregation is not only politically, economically, and sociologically unsound, but it is morally wrong and sinful. Paul Tillich has said that sin is separation. Isn't segregation an existential expression of man's tragic separation, an expression of his awful estrangement, his terrible sinfulness? So I can urge men to obey the 1954 decision of the Supreme Court because it is morally right, and I can urge them to disobey segregation ordinances because they are morally wrong.

Let us turn to a more concrete example of just and unjust laws.   15
An unjust law is a code that a majority inflicts on a minority that is not binding on itself. This is *difference* made legal. On the other hand a just law is a code that a majority compels a minority to follow that it is willing to follow itself. This is *sameness* made legal.

Let me give another explanation. An unjust law is a code inflicted   16
upon a minority which that minority had no part in enacting or creating because they did not have the unhampered right to vote. Who can say the legislature of Alabama which set up the segregation laws was democratically elected? Throughout the state of Alabama all types of conniving methods are used to prevent Negroes from becoming registered voters and there are some counties without a single Negro registered to vote despite the fact that the Negro

constitutes a majority of the population. Can any law set up in such a state be considered democratically structured?

These are just a few examples of unjust and just laws. There are some instances when a law is just on its face but unjust in its application. For instance, I was arrested Friday on a charge of parading without a permit. Now there is nothing wrong with an ordinance which requires a permit for a parade, but when the ordinance is used to preserve segregation and to deny citizens the First Amendment privilege of peaceful assembly and peaceful protest, then it becomes unjust. 17

I hope you can see the distinction I am trying to point out. In no sense do I advocate evading or defying the law as the rabid segregationist would do. This would lead to anarchy. One who breaks an unjust law must do it *openly, lovingly* (not hatefully as the white mothers did in New Orleans when they were seen on television screaming "nigger, nigger, nigger") and with a willingness to accept the penalty. I submit that an individual who breaks a law that conscience tells him is unjust, and willingly accepts the penalty by staying in jail to arouse the conscience of the community over its injustice, is in reality expressing the very highest respect for law. 18

Of course there is nothing new about this kind of civil disobedience. It was seen sublimely in the refusal of Shadrach, Meshach, and Abednego to obey the laws of Nebuchadnezzar because a higher moral law was involved. It was practiced superbly by the early Christians who were willing to face hungry lions and the excruciating pain of chopping blocks, before submitting to certain unjust laws of the Roman Empire. To a degree academic freedom is a reality today because Socrates practiced civil disobedience. 19

We can never forget that everything Hitler did in Germany was "legal" and everything the Hungarian freedom fighters did in Hungary was "illegal." It was "illegal" to aid and comfort a Jew in Hitler's Germany. But I am sure that, if I had lived in Germany during that time, I would have aided and comforted my Jewish brothers even though it was illegal. If I lived in a communist country today where certain principles dear to the Christian faith are suppressed, I believe I would openly advocate disobeying these antireligious laws. 20

I must make two honest confessions to you, my Christian and Jewish brothers. First I must confess that over the last few years I have been gravely disappointed with the white moderate. I have almost reached the regrettable conclusion that the Negroes' great stumbling block in the stride toward freedom is not the White Citizens' "Counciler" or the Ku Klux Klanner, but the white mod- 21

erate who is more devoted to "order" than to justice; who prefers
a negative peace which is the absence of tension to a positive
peace which is the presence of justice; who constantly says "I
agree with you in the goal you seek, but I can't agree with your
methods of direct action"; who paternalistically feels that he can
set the time-table for another man's freedom; who lives by the
myth of time and who constantly advises the Negro to wait until
a "more convenient season." Shallow understanding from people
of good will is more frustrating than absolute misunderstanding
from people of ill will. Lukewarm acceptance is much more bewildering than outright rejection.

I had hoped that the white moderate would understand that   22
law and order exist for the purpose of establishing justice, and
that when they fail to do this they become the dangerously structured
dams that block the flow of social progress. I had hoped that the
white moderate would understand that the present tension in the
South is merely a necessary phase of the transition from an ob-
noxious negative peace, where the Negro passively accepted his
unjust plight, to a substance-filled positive peace, where all men
will respect the dignity and worth of human personality. Actually,
we who engage in nonviolent direct action are not the creators
of tension. We merely bring to the surface the hidden tension that
is already alive. We bring it out in the open where it can be seen
and dealt with. Like a boil that can never be cured as long as it
is covered up but must be opened with all its pus-flowing ugliness
to the natural medicines of air and light, injustice must likewise
be exposed, with all of the tension its exposing creates, to the light
of human conscience and the air of national opinion before it can
be cured.

In your statement you asserted that our actions, even though   23
peaceful, must be condemned because they precipitate violence.
But can this assertion be logically made? Isn't this like condemning
the robbed man because his possession of money precipitated the
evil act of robbery? Isn't this like condemning Socrates because
his unswerving commitment to truth and his philosophical delvings
precipitated the misguided popular mind to make him drink the
hemlock? Isn't this like condemning Jesus because His unique
God consciousness and never-ceasing devotion to His will precipitated the evil act of crucifixion? We must come to see, as federal
courts have consistently affirmed, that it is immoral to urge an
individual to withdraw his efforts to gain his basic constitutional
rights because the quest precipitates violence. Society must protect
the robbed and punish the robber.

I had also hoped that the white moderate would reject the myth 24
of time. I received a letter this morning from a white brother in
Texas which said: "All Christians know that the colored people
will receive equal rights eventually, but is it possible that you are
in too great of a religious hurry? It has taken Christianity almost
2000 years to accomplish what it has. The teachings of Christ take
time to come to earth." All that is said here grows out of a tragic
misconception of time. It is the strangely irrational notion that
there is something in the very flow of time that will inevitably
cure all ills. Actually time is neutral. It can be used either destructively
or constructively. I am coming to feel that the people of ill will
have used time much more effectively than the people of good
will. We will have to repent in this generation not merely for the
vitriolic words and actions of the bad people, but for the appalling
silence of the good people. We must come to see that human
progress never rolls in on wheels of inevitability. It comes through
the tireless efforts and persistent work of men willing to be coworkers with God, and without this hard work time itself becomes
an ally of the forces of social stagnation.

We must use time creatively, and forever realize that the time 25
is always ripe to do right. Now is the time to make real the promise
of democracy, and transform our pending national elegy into a
creative psalm of brotherhood. Now is the time to lift our national
policy from the quicksand of racial injustice to the solid rock of
human dignity.

You spoke of our activity in Birmingham as extreme. At first I 26
was rather disappointed that fellow clergymen would see my nonviolent efforts as those of the extremist. I started thinking about
the fact that I stand in the middle of two opposing forces in the
Negro community. One is a force of complacency made up of
Negroes who, as a result of long years of oppression, have been
so completely drained of self-respect and a sense of "somebodiness"
that they have adjusted to segregation, and of a few Negroes in
the middle class who, because of a degree of academic and economic
security, and because at points they profit by segregation, have
unconsciously become insensitive to the problems of the masses.
The other force is one of bitterness and hatred and comes perilously
close to advocating violence. It is expressed in the various black
nationalist groups that are springing up over the nation, the largest
and best known being Elijah Muhammad's Muslim movement.
This movement is nourished by the contemporary frustration over
the continued existence of racial discrimination. It is made up of
people who have lost faith in America, who have absolutely re-

pudiated Christianity, and who have concluded that the white man is an incurable "devil." I have tried to stand between these two forces saying that we need not follow the "do-nothingism" of the complacent or the hatred and despair of the black nationalist. There is the more excellent way of love and nonviolent protest. I'm grateful to God that, through the Negro church, the dimension of nonviolence entered our struggle. If this philosophy had not emerged I am convinced that by now many streets of the South would be flowing with floods of blood. And I am further convinced that if our white brothers dismiss us as "rabble rousers" and "outside agitators"—those of us who are working through the channels of nonviolent direct action—and refuse to support our nonviolent efforts, millions of Negroes, out of frustration and despair, will seek solace and security in black nationalist ideologies, a development that will lead inevitably to a frightening racial nightmare.

Oppressed people cannot remain oppressed forever. The urge   27
for freedom will eventually come. This is what has happened to the American Negro. Something within has reminded him of his birthright of freedom; something without has reminded him that he can gain it. Consciously and unconsciously, he has been swept in by what the Germans call the *Zeitgeist*,[1] and with his black brothers of Africa, and his brown and yellow brothers of Asia, South America, and the Caribbean, he is moving with a sense of cosmic urgency toward the promised land of racial justice. Recognizing this vital urge that has engulfed the Negro community, one should readily understand public demonstrations. The Negro has many pent-up resentments and latent frustrations. He has to get them out. So let him march sometime; let him have his prayer pilgrimages to the city hall; understand why he must have sit-ins and freedom rides. If his repressed emotions do not come out in these nonviolent ways, they will come out in ominous expressions of violence. This is not a threat; it is a fact of history. So I have not said to my people, "Get rid of your discontent." But I have tried to say that this normal and healthy discontent can be channeled through the creative outlet of nonviolent direct action. Now this approach is being dismissed as extremist. I must admit that I was initially disappointed in being so categorized.

But as I continued to think about the matter I gradually gained   28
a bit of satisfaction from being considered an extremist. Was not Jesus an extremist in love? "Love your enemies, bless them that curse you, pray for them that despitefully use you." Was not Amos

---

1. The predominant outlook or spirit of a time or a generation.

an extremist for justice—"Let justice roll down like waters and righteousness like a mighty stream." Was not Paul an extremist for the gospel of Jesus Christ—"I bear in my body the marks of the Lord Jesus." Was not Martin Luther an extremist—"Here I stand; I can do none other so help me God." Was not John Bunyan an extremist—"I will stay in jail to the end of my days before I make a butchery of my conscience." Was not Abraham Lincoln an extremist—"This nation cannot survive half slave and half free." Was not Thomas Jefferson an extremist—"We hold these truths to be self evident that all men are created equal." So the question is not whether we will be extremist but what kind of extremist will we be. Will we be extremists for hate or will we be extremists for love? Will we be extremists for the preservation of injustice— or will we be extremists for the cause of justice? In that dramatic scene on Calvary's hill three men were crucified. We must never forget that all three were crucified for the same crime—the crime of extremism. Two were extremists for immorality, and thus fell below their environment. The other, Jesus Christ, was an extremist for love, truth, and goodness, and thereby rose above His environment. So, after all, maybe the South, the nation, and the world are in dire need of creative extremists.

29 I had hoped that the white moderate would see this. Maybe I was too optimistic. Maybe I expected too much. I guess I should have realized that few members of a race that has oppressed another race can understand or appreciate the deep groans and passionate yearnings of those that have been oppressed, and still fewer have the vision to see that injustice must be rooted out by strong, persistent, and determined action. I am thankful, however, that some of our white brothers have grasped the meaning of this social revolution and committed themselves to it. They are still all too small in quantity, but they are big in quality. Some like Ralph McGill, Lillian Smith, Harry Golden, and James Dabbs have written about our struggle in eloquent, prophetic, and understanding terms. Others have marched with us down nameless streets of the South. They have languished in filthy, roach-infested jails, suffering the abuse and brutality of angry policemen who see them as "dirty nigger lovers." They, unlike so many of their moderate brothers and sisters, have recognized the urgency of the moment and sensed the need for powerful "action" antidotes to combat the disease of segregation.

30 Let me rush on to mention my other disappointment. I have been so greatly disappointed with the white Church and its leadership. Of course there are some notable exceptions. I am not unmindful of the fact that each of you has taken some significant

stands on this issue. I commend you, Rev. Stallings, for your
Christian stand on this past Sunday, in welcoming Negroes to
your worship service on a nonsegregated basis. I commend the
Catholic leaders of this state for integrating Springhill College several
years ago.

But despite these notable exceptions I must honestly reiterate   31
that I have been disappointed with the Church. I do not say that
as one of those negative critics who can always find something
wrong with the Church. I say it as a minister of the gospel, who
loves the Church; who was nurtured in its bosom; who has been
sustained by its spiritual blessings and who will remain true to it
as long as the cord of life shall lengthen.

I had the strange feeling when I was suddenly catapulted into   32
the leadership of the bus protest in Montgomery[2] several years
ago that we would have the support of the white Church. I felt
that the white ministers, priests, and rabbis of the South would
be some of our strongest allies. Instead, some have been outright
opponents, refusing to understand the freedom movement and
misrepresenting its leaders; all too many others have been more
cautious than courageous and have remained silent behind the
anesthetizing security of stained glass windows.

In spite of my shattered dreams of the past, I came to Birmingham   33
with the hope that the white religious leadership of the community
would see the justice of our cause and, with deep moral concern,
serve as the channel through which our just grievances could get
to the power structure. I had hoped that each of you would
understand. But again I have been disappointed.

I have heard numerous religious leaders of the South call upon   34
their worshippers to comply with a desegregation decision because
it is the law, but I have longed to hear white ministers say follow
this decree because integration is morally right and the Negro is
your brother. In the midst of blatant injustices inflicted upon the
Negro, I have watched white churches stand on the sideline and
merely mouth pious irrelevancies and sanctimonious trivialities.
In the midst of a mighty struggle to rid our nation of racial and
economic injustice, I have heard so many ministers say, "Those
are social issues with which the Gospel has no real concern," and
I have watched so many churches commit themselves to a completely

2. In 1955–56 King led a boycott by Montgomery, Alabama, blacks against the
city's segregated buses, advocating a policy of passive resistance to segregation. The
desegregation of Montgomery buses in 1956 was a major victory for the civil rights
movement.

other-worldly religion which made a strange distinction between body and soul, the sacred and the secular.

So here we are moving toward the exit of the twentieth century 35
with a religious community largely adjusted to the status quo, standing as a tail light behind other community agencies rather than a headlight leading men to higher levels of justice.

I have travelled the length and breadth of Alabama, Mississippi, 36
and all the other Southern states. On sweltering summer days and crisp autumn mornings I have looked at her beautiful churches with their spires pointing heavenward. I have beheld the impressive outlay of her massive religious education buildings. Over and over again I have found myself asking: "Who worships here? Who is their God? Where were their voices when the lips of Governor Barnett[3] dripped with words of interposition and nullification? Where were they when Governor Wallace[4] gave the clarion call for defiance and hatred? Where were their voices of support when tired, bruised, and weary Negro men and women decided to rise from the dark dungeons of complacency to the bright hills of creative protest?"

Yes, these questions are still in my mind. In deep disappointment, 37
I have wept over the laxity of the Church. But be assured that my tears have been tears of love. There can be no deep disappointment where there is not deep love. Yes, I love the Church; I love her sacred walls. How could I do otherwise? I am in the rather unique position of being the son, the grandson, and the great grandson of preachers. Yes, I see the Church as the body of Christ. But, oh! How we have blemished and scarred that body through social neglect and fear of being nonconformist.

There was a time when the Church was very powerful. It was 38
during that period when the early Christians rejoiced when they were deemed worthy to suffer for what they believed. In those days the Church was not merely a thermometer that recorded the ideas and principles of popular opinion; it was a thermostat that transformed the mores of society. Wherever the early Christians entered a town the power structure got disturbed and immediately sought to convict them for being "disturbers of the peace" and "outside agitators." But they went on with the conviction that they were a "colony of heaven" and had to obey God rather than

3. Ross Barnett, governor of Mississippi, in 1962 ordered resistance to the registration of a black student, James Meredith, at the University of Mississippi.
4. George Wallace, governor of Alabama, stood in a doorway of the University of Alabama in a symbolic effort to block the registration of two black students in 1963.

man. They were small in number but big in commitment. They were too God-intoxicated to be "astronomically intimidated." They brought an end to such ancient evils as infanticide and gladiatorial contest.

Things are different now. The contemporary Church is so often   39
a weak, ineffectual voice with an uncertain sound. It is so often the arch-supporter of the status quo. Far from being disturbed by the presence of the Church, the power structure of the average community is consoled by the Church's silent and often vocal sanction of things as they are.

But the judgment of God is upon the Church as never before.   40
If the Church of today does not recapture the sacrificial spirit of the early Church, it will lose its authentic ring, forfeit the loyalty of millions, and be dismissed as an irrelevant social club with no meaning for the twentieth century. I am meeting young people every day whose disappointment with the Church has risen to outright disgust.

Maybe again I have been too optimistic. Is organized religion   41
too inextricably bound to the status quo to save our nation and the world? Maybe I must turn my faith to the inner spiritual Church, the church within the Church, as the true *ecclesia*[5] and the hope of the world. But again I am thankful to God that some noble souls from the ranks of organized religion have broken loose from the paralyzing chains of conformity and joined us as active partners in the struggle for freedom. They have left their secure congregations and walked the streets of Albany, Georgia, with us. They have gone through the highways of the South on torturous rides for freedom. Yes, they have gone to jail with us. Some have been kicked out of their churches and lost the support of their bishops and fellow ministers. But they have gone with the faith that right defeated is stronger than evil triumphant. These men have been the leaven in the lump of the race. Their witness has been the spiritual salt that has preserved the true meaning of the Gospel in these troubled times. They have carved a tunnel of hope through the dark mountain of disappointment.

I hope the Church as a whole will meet the challenge of this   42
decisive hour. But even if the Church does not come to the aid of justice, I have no despair about the future. I have no fear about the outcome of our struggle in Birmingham, even if our motives are presently misunderstood. We will reach the goal of freedom in Birmingham and all over the nation, because the goal of America is freedom. Abused and scorned though we may be, our destiny is tied up with the destiny of America. Before the pilgrims landed

5. "assembly of the people"

at Plymouth, we were here. Before the pen of Jefferson etched across the pages of history the majestic words of the Declaration of Independence, we were here. For more than two centuries our foreparents labored in this country without wages; they made cotton "king"; and they built the homes of their masters in the midst of brutal injustice and shameful humiliation—and yet out of a bottomless vitality they continued to thrive and develop. If the inexpressible cruelties of slavery could not stop us, the opposition we now face will surely fail. We will win our freedom because the sacred heritage of our nation and the eternal will of God are embodied in our echoing demands.

43   I must close now. But before closing I am impelled to mention one other point in your statement that troubled me profoundly. You warmly commended the Birmingham police force for keeping "order" and "preventing violence." I don't believe you would have so warmly commended the police force if you had seen its angry violent dogs literally biting six unarmed, nonviolent Negroes. I don't believe you would so quickly commend the policemen if you would observe their ugly and inhuman treatment of Negroes here in the city jail; if you would watch them push and curse old Negro women and young Negro girls; if you would see them slap and kick old Negro men and young Negro boys; if you will observe them, as they did on two occasions, refuse to give us food because we wanted to sing our grace together. I'm sorry that I can't join you in your praise for the police department.

44   It is true that they have been rather disciplined in their public handling of the demonstrators. In this sense they have been rather publicly "nonviolent." But for what purpose? To preserve the evil system of segregation. Over the last few years I have consistently preached that nonviolence demands that the means we use must be as pure as the ends we seek. So I have tried to make it clear that it is wrong to use immoral means to attain moral ends. But now I must affirm that it is just as wrong, or even more so, to use moral means to preserve immoral ends. Maybe Mr. Connor and his policemen have been rather publicly nonviolent, as Chief Prichett was in Albany, Georgia, but they have used the moral means of nonviolence to maintain the immoral end of flagrant racial injustice. T. S. Eliot has said that there is no greater treason than to do the right deed for the wrong reason.

45   I wish you had commended the Negro sit-inners and demonstrators of Birmingham for their sublime courage, their willingness to suffer, and their amazing discipline in the midst of the most inhuman provocation. One day the South will recognize its real heroes. They will be the James Merediths, courageously and with a majestic sense of purpose, facing jeering and hostile mobs and

the agonizing loneliness that characterizes the life of the pioneer. They will be old, oppressed, battered Negro women, symbolized in a seventy-two year old woman of Montgomery, Alabama, who rose up with a sense of dignity and with her people decided not to ride the segregated buses, and responded to one who inquired about her tiredness with ungrammatical profundity: "My feets is tired, but my soul is rested." They will be young high school and college students, young ministers of the gospel and a host of the elders, courageously and nonviolently sitting in at lunch counters and willingly going to jail for conscience sake. One day the South will know that when these disinherited children of God sat down at lunch counters they were in reality standing up for the best in the American dream and the most sacred values in our Judeo-Christian heritage, and thus carrying our whole nation back to great wells of democracy which were dug deep by the founding fathers in the formulation of the Constitution and the Declaration of Independence.

Never before have I written a letter this long (or should I say   46
a book?). I'm afraid that it is much too long to take your precious time. I can assure you that it would have been much shorter if I had been writing from a comfortable desk, but what else is there to do when you are alone for days in the dull monotony of a narrow jail cell other than write long letters, think strange thoughts, and pray long prayers?

If I have said anything in this letter that is an overstatement of   47
the truth and is indicative of an unreasonable impatience, I beg you to forgive me. If I have said anything in this letter that is an understatement of the truth and is indicative of my having a patience that makes me patient with anything less than brotherhood, I beg God to forgive me.

I hope this letter finds you strong in the faith. I also hope that   48
circumstances will soon make it possible for me to meet each of you, not as an integrationist or a civil rights leader, but as a fellow clergyman and a Christian brother. Let us all hope that the dark clouds of racial prejudice will soon pass away and the deep fog of misunderstanding will be lifted from our fear-drenched communities and in some not too distant tomorrow the radiant stars of love and brotherhood will shine over our great nation with all of their scintillating beauty.

Yours for the cause of
Peace and Brotherhood

MARTIN LUTHER KING, JR.

H. L. MENCKEN

The Nature of Liberty

Every time an officer of the constabulary, in the execution of 1
his just and awful powers under American law, produces a compound fracture of the occiput of some citizen in his custody, with
hemorrhage, shock, coma and death, there comes a feeble, falsetto
protest from specialists in human liberty. Is it a fact without significance that this protest is never supported by the great body of
American freemen, setting aside the actual heirs and creditors of
the victim? I think not. Here, as usual, public opinion is very
realistic. It does not rise against the policeman for the plain and
simple reason that it does not question his right to do what he
has done. Policemen are not given nightsticks for ornament. They
are given them for the purpose of cracking the skulls of the recalcitrant plain people, Democrats and Republicans alike. When
they execute that high duty they are palpably within their rights.

The specialists aforesaid are the same fanatics who shake the 2
air with sobs every time the Postmaster-General of the United
States bars a periodical from the mails because its ideas do not
please him, and every time some poor Russian is deported for
reading Karl Marx, and every time a Prohibition enforcement
officer murders a bootlegger who resists his levies, and every time
agents of the Department of Justice throw an Italian out of the
window, and every time the Ku Klux Klan or the American Legion
tars and feathers a Socialist evangelist. In brief, they are Radicals,
and to scratch one with a pitchfork is to expose a Bolshevik. They
are men standing in contempt of American institutions and in
enmity to American idealism. And their evil principles are no less
offensive to right-thinking and red-blooded Americans when they
are United States Senators or editors of wealthy newspapers than
when they are degraded I. W. W.'s[1] throwing dead cats and infernal
machines into meetings of the Rotary Club.

What ails them primarily is the ignorant and uncritical monomania 3
that afflicts every sort of fanatic, at all times and everywhere.
Having mastered with their limited faculties the theoretical principles
set forth in the Bill of Rights, they work themselves into a passionate
conviction that those principles are identical with the rules of law
and justice, and ought to be enforced literally, and without the

From *Prejudices* (1919–27).
1. Industrial Workers of the World.

slightest regard for circumstance and expediency. It is precisely as if a High Church rector, accidentally looking into the Book of Chronicles, and especially Chapter II, should suddenly issue a mandate from his pulpit ordering his parishioners, on penalty of excommunication and the fires of hell, to follow exactly the example set forth, to wit: "And Jesse begat his first born Eliab, and Abinadab the second, and Shimma the third, Netheneel the fourth, Raddai the fifth, Ozen the sixth, David the seventh," and so on. It might be very sound theoretical theology, but it would surely be out of harmony with modern ideas, and the rev. gentleman would be extremely lucky if the bishop did not give him 10 days in the diocesan hoosegow.

So with the Bill of Rights. As adopted by the Fathers of the   4 Republic, it was gross, crude, inelastic, a bit fanciful and transcendental. It specified the rights of a citizen, but it said nothing whatever about his duties. Since then, by the orderly processes of legislative science and by the even more subtle and beautiful devices of juridic art, it has been kneaded and mellowed into a far greater pliability and reasonableness. On the one hand, the citizen still retains the great privilege of membership in the most superb free nation ever witnessed on this earth. On the other hand, as a result of countless shrewd enactments and sagacious decisions, his natural lusts and appetites are held in laudable check, and he is thus kept in order and decorum. No artificial impediment stands in the way of his highest aspiration. He may become anything, including even a policeman. But once a policeman, he is protected by the legislative and judicial arms in the peculiar rights and prerogatives that go with his high office, including especially the right to jug the laity at his will, to sweat and mug them, to subject them to the third degree, and to subdue their resistance by beating out their brains. Those who are unaware of this are simply ignorant of the basic principles of American jurisprudence, as they have been exposed times without number by the courts of first instance and ratified in lofty terms by the Supreme Court of the United States. The one aim of the controlling decisions, magnificently attained, is to safeguard public order and the public security, and to substitute a judicial process for the inchoate and dangerous interaction of discordant egos.

Let us imagine an example. You are, say, a peaceable citizen   5 on your way home from your place of employment. A police sergeant, detecting you in the crowd, approaches you, lays his hand on your collar, and informs you that you are under arrest for killing a trolley conductor in Altoona, Pa., in 1917. Amazed by the accusation, you decide hastily that the officer has lost his wits, and take to your heels. He pursues you. You continue to run. He draws his revolver and fires at you. He misses you. He fires again and fetches you in the leg. You fall and he is upon you. You prepare to resist his apparently maniacal assault. He beats you into insensibility with his espantoon, and drags you to the patrol box.

Arrived at the watch house you are locked in a room with five   6
detectives, and for six hours they question you with subtle art. You grow angry—perhaps robbed of your customary politeness by the throbbing in your head and leg—and answer tartly. They knock you down. Having failed to wring a confession from you, they lock you in a cell, and leave you there all night. The next day you are taken to police headquarters, your photograph is made for the Rogues' Gallery, and a print is duly deposited in the section labeled "Murderers." You are then carted to jail and locked up again. There you remain until the trolley conductor's wife comes down from Altoona to identify you. She astonishes the police by saying that you are not the man. The actual murderer, it appears, was an Italian. After holding you a day or two longer, to search your house for stills, audit your income tax returns, and investigate the premarital chastity of your wife, they let you go.

You are naturally somewhat irritated by your experience and   7
perhaps your wife urges you to seek redress. Well, what are your remedies? If you are a firebrand, you reach out absurdly for those of a preposterous nature: the instant jailing of the sergeant, the dismissal of the Police Commissioner, the release of Mooney, a fair trial for Sacco and Vanzetti,[2] free trade with Russia, One Big Union. But if you are a 100 per cent American and respect the laws and institutions of your country, you send for your solicitor— and at once he shows you just how far your rights go, and where they end. You cannot cause the arrest of the sergeant, for you resisted him when he attempted to arrest you, and when you resisted him he acquired an instant right to take you by force. You cannot proceed against him for accusing you falsely, for he has a right to make summary arrests for felony, and the courts have many times decided that a public officer, so long as he cannot be charged with corruption or malice, is not liable for errors of judgment made in the execution of his sworn duty. You cannot

---

2. *Thomas Mooney,* American labor leader, was convicted of exploding a bomb at a parade in San Francisco in 1916. Sentenced to die, he received a commutation to life imprisonment and was subsequently pardoned. The case drew worldwide attention. *Niccola Sacco and Bartolomeo Vanzetti* were Italian aliens convicted of murdering two men in Massachusetts in 1920. They were sentenced to die, but their cause was taken up vigorously by the liberal community, which believed them to be the victims of prejudice and an unfair trial. After a series of delays, however, they were executed in 1927.

get the detectives on the mat, for when they questioned you you were a prisoner accused of murder, and it was their duty and their right to do so. You cannot sue the turnkey at the watch house or the warden at the jail for locking you up, for they received your body, as the law says, in a lawful and regular manner, and would have been liable to penalty if they had turned you loose.

But have you no redress whatever, no rights at all? Certainly 8 you have a right, and the courts have jealously guarded it. You have a clear right, guaranteed to you under the Constitution, to go into a court of equity and apply for a mandamus[3] requiring the *Polizei*[4] to cease forthwith to expose your portrait in the Rogues' Gallery among the murderers. This is your inalienable right, and no man or men on earth can take it away from you. You cannot prevent them cherishing your portrait in their secret files, but you can get an order commanding them to refrain forever from exposing it to the gaze of idle visitors, and if you can introduce yourself unseen into their studio and prove that they disregard that order, you can have them haled into court for contempt and fined by the learned judge.

Thus the law, statute, common and case, protects the free Amer- 9 ican against injustice. It is ignorance of that subtle and perfect process and not any special love of liberty *per se* that causes radicals of anti-American kidney to rage every time an officer of the *gendarmerie*,[5] in the simple execution of his duty, knocks a citizen in the head. The *gendarme* plainly has an inherent and inalienable right to knock him in the head: it is an essential part of his general prerogative as a sworn officer of the public peace and a representative of the sovereign power of the state. He may, true enough, exercise that prerogative in a manner liable to challenge on the ground that it is imprudent and lacking in sound judgment. On such questions reasonable men may differ. But it must be obvious that the sane and decorous way to settle differences of opinion of that sort is not by public outcry and florid appeals to sentimentality, not by ill-disguised playing to class consciousness and antisocial prejudice, but by an orderly resort to the checks and remedies superimposed upon the Bill of Rights by the calm deliberation and austere logic of the courts of equity.

The law protects the citizen. But to get its protection he must 10 show due respect for its wise and delicate processes.

---

3. A writ, from a court, directing that a person or body enforce the enactment of a public duty.
4. Italian for "police."
5. French national police force; used here to mean simply any policeman.

E. M. FORSTER

What I Believe

I do not believe in Belief. But this is an age of faith, and there   1
are so many militant creeds that, in self-defence, one has to formulate
a creed of one's own. Tolerance, good temper and sympathy are
no longer enough in a world which is rent by religious and racial
persecution, in a world where ignorance rules, and science, who
ought to have ruled, plays the subservient pimp. Tolerance, good
temper and sympathy—they are what matter really, and if the
human race is not to collapse they must come to the front before
long. But for the moment they are not enough, their action is no
stronger than a flower, battered beneath a military jackboot. They
want stiffening, even if the process coarsens them. Faith, to my
mind, is a stiffening process, a sort of mental starch, which ought
to be applied as sparingly as possible. I dislike the stuff. I do not
believe in it, for its own sake, at all. Herein I probably differ from
most people, who believe in Belief, and are only sorry they cannot
swallow even more than they do. My law-givers are Erasmus and
Montaigne, not Moses and St. Paul. My temple stands not upon
Mount Moriah but in that Elysian Field where even the immoral
are admitted. My motto is: "Lord, I disbelieve—help thou my
unbelief."[1]

I have, however, to live in an Age of Faith—the sort of epoch   2
I used to hear praised when I was a boy. It is extremely unpleasant
really. It is bloody in every sense of the word. And I have to keep
my end up in it. Where do I start?

With personal relationships. Here is something comparatively   3
solid in a world full of violence and cruelty. Not absolutely solid,
for Psychology has split and shattered the idea of a "Person," and
has shown that there is something incalculable in each of us, which
may at any moment rise to the surface and destroy our normal
balance. We don't know what we are like. We can't know what
other people are like. How, then, can we put any trust in personal
relationships, or cling to them in the gathering political storm? In

Written in 1939.
1. *Erasmus/Montaigne*: humanists, not religious figures, as were *Moses* and *Paul*; *Mt.
Moriah*: Biblical site where Abraham was to sacrifice his son Isaac; *Elysian Fields*:
in Greek mythology, Paradise, a happy land; *Lord, I disbelieve*: Forster's adaptation
of the words of a man witnessing Jesus' performance of a miracle in healing his
son—"Lord, I believe . . ." (Mark 9:24).

theory we cannot. But in practice we can and do. Though A is not unchangeably A or B unchangeably B, there can still be love and loyalty between the two. For the purpose of living one has to assume that the personality is solid, and the "self" is an entity, and to ignore all contrary evidence. And since to ignore evidence is one of the characteristics of faith, I certainly can proclaim that I believe in personal relationships.

Starting from them, I get a little order into the contemporary 4 chaos. One must be fond of people and trust them if one is not to make a mess of life, and it is therefore essential that they should not let one down. They often do. The moral of which is that I must, myself, be as reliable as possible, and this I try to be. But reliability is not a matter of contract—that is the main difference between the world of personal relationships and the world of business relationships. It is a matter for the heart, which signs no documents. In other words, reliability is impossible unless there is a natural warmth. Most men possess this warmth, though they often have bad luck and get chilled. Most of them, even when they are politicians, *want* to keep faith. And one can, at all events, show one's own little light here, one's own poor little trembling flame, with the knowledge that it is not the only light that is shining in the darkness, and not the only one which the darkness does not comprehend. Personal relations are despised today. They are regarded as bourgeois luxuries, as products of a time of fair weather which is now past, and we are urged to get rid of them, and to dedicate ourselves to some movement or cause instead. I hate the idea of causes, and if I had to choose between betraying my country and betraying my friend, I hope I should have the guts to betray my country. Such a choice may scandalise the modern reader, and he may stretch out his patriotic hand to the telephone at once and ring up the police. It would not have shocked Dante, though. Dante places Brutus and Cassius in the lowest circle of Hell[2] because they had chosen to betray their friend Julius Caesar rather than their country Rome. Probably one will not be asked to make such an agonising choice. Still, there lies at the back of every creed something terrible and hard for which the worshipper may one day be required to suffer, and there is even a terror and a hardness in this creed of personal relationships, urbane and mild though it sounds. Love and loyalty to an individual can run counter to the claims of the State. When they

---

2. In *The Divine Comedy*, masterpiece of Italian poet Dante Alighieri (1265–1321).

do—down with the State, say I, which means that the State would down me.

This brings me along to Democracy, "even Love, the Beloved Republic, which feeds upon Freedom and lives." Democracy is not a Beloved Republic really, and never will be. But it is less hateful than other contemporary forms of government, and to that extent it deserves our support. It does start from the assumption that the individual is important, and that all types are needed to make a civilisation. It does not divide its citizens into the bossers and the bossed—as an efficiency-regime tends to do. The people I admire most are those who are sensitive and want to create something or discover something, and do not see life in terms of power, and such people get more of a chance under a democracy than elsewhere. They found religions, great or small, or they produce literature and art, or they do disinterested scientific research, or they may be what is called "ordinary people," who are creative in their private lives, bring up their children decently, for instance, or help their neighbours. All these people need to express themselves; they cannot do so unless society allows them liberty to do so, and the society which allows them most liberty is a democracy.

Democracy has another merit. It allows criticism, and if there is not public criticism there are bound to be hushed-up scandals. That is why I believe in the Press, despite all its lies and vulgarity, and why I believe in Parliament. Parliament is often sneered at because it is a Talking Shop. I believe in it *because* it is a talking shop. I believe in the Private Member who makes himself a nuisance. He gets snubbed and is told that he is cranky or ill-informed, but he does expose abuses which would otherwise never have been mentioned, and very often an abuse gets put right just by being mentioned. Occasionally, too, a well-meaning public official starts losing his head in the cause of efficiency, and thinks himself God Almighty. Such officials are particularly frequent in the Home Office. Well, there will be questions about them in Parliament sooner or later, and then they will have to mind their steps. Whether Parliament is either a representative body or an efficient one is questionable, but I value it because it criticises and talks, and because its chatter gets widely reported.

So Two Cheers for Democracy: one because it admits variety and two because it permits criticism. Two cheers are quite enough: there is no occasion to give three. Only Love the Beloved Republic deserves that.

What about Force, though? While we are trying to be sensitive and advanced and affectionate and tolerant, an unpleasant question pops up: does not all society rest upon force? If a government cannot count upon the police and the army, how can it hope to rule? And if an individual gets knocked on the head or sent to a labour camp, of what significance are his opinions?

This dilemma does not worry me as much as it does some. I realise that all society rests upon force. But all the great creative actions, all the decent human relations, occur during the intervals when force has not managed to come to the front. These intervals are what matter. I want them to be as frequent and as lengthy as possible, and I call them "civilisation." Some people idealise force and pull it into the foreground and worship it, instead of keeping it in the background as long as possible. I think they make a mistake, and I think that their opposites, the mystics, err even more when they declare that force does not exist. I believe that it exists, and that one of our jobs is to prevent it from getting out of its box. It gets out sooner or later, and then it destroys us and all the lovely things which we have made. But it is not out all the time, for the fortunate reason that the strong are so stupid. Consider their conduct for a moment in the Niebelung's Ring.[3] The giants there have the guns, or in other words the gold; but they do nothing with it, they do not realise that they are all-powerful, with the result that the catastrophe is delayed and the castle of Walhalla, insecure but glorious, fronts the storms. Fafnir, coiled round his hoard, grumbles and grunts; we can hear him under Europe today; the leaves of the wood already tremble, and the Bird calls its warnings uselessly. Fafnir will destroy us, but by a blessed dispensation he is stupid and slow, and creation goes on just outside the poisonous blast of his breath. The Nietzschean would hurry the monster up, the mystic would say he did not exist, but Wotan, wiser than either, hastens to create warriors before doom declares itself. The Valkyries are symbols not only of courage but of intelligence; they represent the human spirit snatching its opportunity while the going is good, and one of them even finds time to love. Brünnhilde's last song hymns the recurrence of love, and since it is the privilege of art to exaggerate, she goes even further, and proclaims the love which is eternally triumphant and feeds upon freedom, and lives.

So that is what I feel about force and violence. It is, alas! the ultimate reality on this earth, but it does not always get to the front. Some people call its absences "decadence"; I call them

3. *Der Ring des Nibelungen* (1876), opera in four parts by German composer Richard Wagner, based on medieval Scandinavian legends. Forster, writing on the eve of World War II, sees in the story certain lessons for his contemporaries.

"civilisation" and find in such interludes the chief justification for the human experiment. I look the other way until fate strikes me. Whether this is due to courage or to cowardice in my own case I cannot be sure. But I know that if men had not looked the other way in the past, nothing of any value would survive. The people I respect most behave as if they were immortal and as if society was eternal. Both assumptions are false: both of them must be accepted as true if we are to go on eating and working and loving, and are to keep open a few breathing holes for the human spirit. No millennium seems likely to descend upon humanity; no better and stronger League of Nations will be instituted; no form of Christianity and no alternative to Christianity will bring peace to the world or integrity to the individual; no "change of heart" will occur. And yet we need not despair, indeed, we cannot despair; the evidence of history shows us that men have always insisted on behaving creatively under the shadow of the sword; that they have done their artistic and scientific and domestic stuff for the sake of doing it, and that we had better follow their example under the shadow of the aeroplanes. Others, with more vision or courage than myself, see the salvation of humanity ahead, and will dismiss my conception of civilisation as paltry, a sort of tip-and-run game. Certainly it is presumptuous to say that we *cannot* improve, and that Man, who has only been in power for a few thousand years, will never learn to make use of his power. All I mean is that, if people continue to kill one another as they do, the world cannot get better than it is, and that since there are more people than formerly, and their means for destroying one another superior, the world may well get worse. What is good in people—and consequently in the world—is their insistence on creation, their belief in friendship and loyalty for their own sakes; and though Violence remains and is, indeed, the major partner in this muddled establishment, I believe that creativeness remains too, and will always assume direction when violence sleeps. So, though I am not an optimist, I cannot agree with Sophocles that it were better never to have been born. And although, like Horace, I see no evidence that each batch of births is superior to the last, I leave the field open for the more complacent view. This is such a difficult moment to live in, one cannot help getting gloomy and also a bit rattled, and perhaps short-sighted.

In search of a refuge, we may perhaps turn to hero-worship. But here we shall get no help, in my opinion. Hero-worship is a dangerous vice, and one of the minor merits of a democracy is that it does not encourage it, or produce that unmanageable type of citizen known as the Great Man. It produces instead different kinds of small men—a much finer achievement. But people who cannot get interested in the variety of life, and cannot make up their own minds, get discontented over this, and they long for a hero to bow down before and to follow blindly. It is significant that a hero is an integral part of the authoritarian stock-in-trade today. An efficiency-regime cannot be run without a few heroes stuck about it to carry off the dullness—much as plums have to be put into a bad pudding to make it palatable. One hero at the top and a smaller one each side of him is a favourite arrangement, and the timid and the bored are comforted by the trinity, and, bowing down, feel exalted and strengthened.

No, I distrust Great Men. They produce a desert of uniformity   12
around them and often a pool of blood too, and I always feel a little man's pleasure when they come a cropper. Every now and then one reads in the newspapers some such statement as: "The coup d'état appears to have failed, and Admiral Toma's whereabouts is at present unknown." Admiral Toma had probably every qualification for being a Great Man—an iron will, personal magnetism, dash, flair, sexlessness—but fate was against him, so he retires to unknown whereabouts instead of parading history with his peers. He fails with a completeness which no artist and no lover can experience, because with them the process of creation is itself an achievement, whereas with him the only possible achievement is success.

I believe in aristocracy, though—if that is the right word, and   13
if a democrat may use it. Not an aristocracy of power, based upon rank and influence, but an aristocracy of the sensitive, the considerate and the plucky. Its members are to be found in all nations and classes, and all through the ages, and there is a secret understanding between them when they meet. They represent the true human tradition, the one permanent victory of our queer race over cruelty and chaos. Thousands of them perish in obscurity, a few are great names. They are sensitive for others as well as for themselves, they are considerate without being fussy, their pluck is not swankiness but the power to endure, and they can take a joke. I give no examples—it is risky to do that—but the reader may as well consider whether this is the type of person he would like to meet and to be, and whether (going farther with me) he would prefer that this type should *not* be an ascetic one. I am against asceticism myself. I am with the old Scotsman who wanted less chastity and more delicacy. I do not feel that my aristocrats are a real aristocracy if they thwart their bodies, since bodies are the instruments through which we register and enjoy the world. Still, I do not insist. This is not a major point. It is clearly possible to be sensitive, considerate

and plucky and yet be an ascetic too, if anyone possesses the first three qualities, I will let him in! On they go—an invincible army, yet not a victorious one. The aristocrats, the elect, the chosen, the Best People—all the words that describe them are false, and all attempts to organise them fail. Again and again Authority, seeing their value, has tried to net them and to utilise them as the Egyptian Priesthood or the Christian Church or the Chinese Civil Service or the Group Movement, or some other worthy stunt. But they slip through the net and are gone; when the door is shut, they are no longer in the room; their temple, as one of them remarked, is the Holiness of the Heart's Affection,[4] and their kingdom, though they never possess it, is the wide-open world.

With this type of person knocking about, and constantly crossing one's path if one has eyes to see or hands to feel, the experiment of earthly life cannot be dismissed as a failure. But it may well be hailed as a tragedy, the tragedy being that no device has been found by which these private decencies can be transmitted to public affairs. As soon as people have power they go crooked and sometimes dotty as well, because the possession of power lifts them into a region where normal honesty never pays. For instance, the man who is selling newspapers outside the Houses of Parliament can safely leave his papers to go for a drink and his cap beside them: anyone who takes a paper is sure to drop a copper into the cap. But the men who are inside the Houses of Parliament— they cannot trust one another like that, still less can the Government they compose trust other governments. No caps upon the pavement here, but suspicion, treachery and armaments. The more highly public life is organised the lower does its morality sink; the nations of today behave to each other worse than they ever did in the past, they cheat, rob, bully and bluff, make war without notice, and kill as many women and children as possible; whereas primitive tribes were at all events restrained by taboos. It is a humiliating outlook—though the greater the darkness, the brighter shine the little lights, reassuring one another, signalling: "Well, at all events, I'm still here. I don't like it very much, but how are you?" Unquenchable lights of my aristocracy! Signals of the invincible army! "Come along—anyway, let's have a good time while we can." I think they signal that too.

The Saviour of the future—if ever he comes—will not preach a new Gospel. He will merely utilise my aristocracy, he will make effective the good will and the good temper which are already

---

4. English poet John Keats (1795–1823) wrote "I am certain of nothing but the holiness of the Heart's affection and the truth of Imagination."

existing. In other words, he will introduce a new technique. In economics, we are told that if there was a new technique of distribution, there need be no poverty, and people would not starve in one place while crops were being ploughed under in another. A similar change is needed in the sphere of morals and politics. The desire for it is by no means new; it was expressed, for example, in theological terms by Jacopone da Todi over six hundred years ago. "Ordina questo amore, O tu che m'ami," he said; "O thou who lovest me—set this love in order." His prayer was not granted, and I do not myself believe that it ever will be, but here, and not through a change of heart, is our probable route. Not by becoming better, but by ordering and distributing his native goodness, will Man shut up Force into its box, and so gain time to explore the universe and to set his mark upon it worthily. At present he only explores it at odd moments, when Force is looking the other way, and his divine creativeness appears as a trivial byproduct, to be scrapped as soon as the drums beat and the bombers hum.

Such a change, claim the orthodox, can only be made by Christianity, and will be made by it in God's good time: man always has failed and always will fail to organise his own goodness, and it is presumptuous of him to try. This claim—solemn as it is— leaves me cold. I cannot believe that Christianity will ever cope with the present world-wide mess, and I think that such influence as it retains in modern society is due to the money behind it, rather than to its spiritual appeal. It was a spiritual force once, but the indwelling spirit will have to be restated if it is to calm the waters again, and probably restated in a non-Christian form. Naturally a lot of people, and people who are not only good but able and intelligent, will disagree here; they will vehemently deny that Christianity has failed, or they will argue that its failure proceeds from the wickedness of men, and really proves its ultimate success. They have Faith, with a large F. My faith has a very small one, and I only intrude it because these are strenuous and serious days, and one likes to say what one thinks while speech is comparatively free: it may not be free much longer. 16

The above are the reflections of an individualist and a liberal who has found liberalism crumbling beneath him and at first felt ashamed. Then, looking around, he decided there was no special reason for shame, since other people, whatever they felt, were equally insecure. And as for individualism—there seems no way of getting off this, even if one wanted to. The dictator-hero can grind down his citizens till they are all alike, but he cannot melt them into a single man. That is beyond his power. He can order them to merge, he can incite them to mass-antics, but they are 17

obliged to be born separately, and to die separately, and, owing
to these unavoidable termini, will always be running off the totalitarian rails. The memory of birth and the expectation of death
always lurk within the human being, making him separate from
his fellows and consequently capable of intercourse with them.
Naked I came into the world, naked I shall go out of it! And a
very good thing too, for it reminds me that I am naked under my
shirt, whatever its colour.

JANE JACOBS

The Uses of Sidewalks

Streets in cities serve many purposes besides carrying vehicles,   1
and city sidewalks—the pedestrian parts of the streets—serve many
purposes besides carrying pedestrians. These uses are bound up
with circulation but are not identical with it and in their own
right they are at least as basic as circulation to the proper workings
of cities.

A city sidewalk by itself is nothing. It is an abstraction. It means   2
something only in conjunction with the buildings and other uses
that border it, or border other sidewalks very near it. The same
might be said of streets, in the sense that they serve other purposes
besides carrying wheeled traffic in their middles. Streets and their
sidewalks, the main public places of a city, are its most vital organs.
Think of a city and what comes to mind? Its streets. If a city's
streets look interesting, the city looks interesting; if they look dull,
the city looks dull.

More than that, and here we get down to the first problem, if   3
a city's streets are safe from barbarism and fear, the city is thereby
tolerably safe from barbarism and fear. When people say that a
city, or a part of it, is dangerous or is a jungle what they mean
primarily is that they do not feel safe on the sidewalks.

But sidewalks and those who use them are not passive beneficiaries   4
of safety or helpless victims of danger. Sidewalks, their bordering
uses, and their users, are active participants in the drama of civilization versus barbarism in cities. To keep the city safe is a fundamental task of a city's streets and its sidewalks.

An excerpt from Chapter 2 of *The Life and Death of Great American Cities* (1969).

This task is totally unlike any service that sidewalks and streets   5
in little towns or true suburbs are called upon to do. Great cities
are not like towns, only larger. They are not like suburbs, only
denser. They differ from towns and suburbs in basic ways, and
one of these is that cities are, by definition, full of strangers. To
any one person, strangers are far more common in big cities than
acquaintances. More common not just in places of public assembly,
but more common at a man's own doorstep. Even residents who
live near each other are strangers, and must be, because of the
sheer number of people in small geographical compass.

The bedrock attribute of a successful city district is that a person   6
must feel personally safe and secure on the street among all these
strangers. He must not feel automatically menaced by them. A
city district that fails in this respect also does badly in other ways
and lays up for itself, and for its city at large, mountain on mountain
of trouble.

Today barbarism has taken over many city streets, or people   7
fear it has, which comes to much the same thing in the end. "I
live in a lovely, quiet residential area," says a friend of mine who
is hunting another place to live. "The only disturbing sound at
night is the occasional scream of someone being mugged." It does
not take many incidents of violence on a city street, or in a city
district, to make people fear the streets. And as they fear them,
they use them less, which makes the streets still more unsafe.

To be sure, there are people with hobgoblins in their heads,   8
and such people will never feel safe no matter what the objective
circumstances are. But this is a different matter from the fear that
besets normally prudent, tolerant and cheerful people who show
nothing more than common sense in refusing to venture after
dark—or in a few places, by day—into streets where they may
well be assaulted, unseen or unrescued until too late.

The barbarism and the real, not imagined, insecurity that gives   9
rise to such fears cannot be tagged a problem of the slums. The
problem is most serious, in fact, in genteel-looking "quiet residential
areas" like that my friend was leaving.

It cannot be tagged as a problem of older parts of cities. The   10
problem reaches its most baffling dimensions in some examples
of rebuilt parts of cities, including supposedly the best examples
of rebuilding, such as middle-income projects. The police precinct
captain of a nationally admired project of this kind (admired by
planners and lenders) has recently admonished residents not only
about hanging around outdoors after dark but has urged them
never to answer their doors without knowing the caller. Life here
has much in common with life for the three little pigs or the seven

little kids of the nursery thrillers. The problem of sidewalk and doorstep insecurity is as serious in cities which have made conscientious efforts at rebuilding as it is in those cities that have lagged. Nor is it illuminating to tag minority groups, or the poor, or the outcast with responsibility for city danger. There are immense variations in the degree of civilization and safety found among such groups and among the city areas where they live. Some of the safest sidewalks in New York City, for example, at any time of day or night, are those along which poor people or minority groups live. And some of the most dangerous are in streets occupied by the same kinds of people. All this can also be said of other cities.

Deep and complicated social ills must lie behind delinquency 11 and crime, in suburbs and towns as well as in great cities. This book will not go into speculation on the deeper reasons. It is sufficient, at this point, to say that if we are to maintain a city society that can diagnose and keep abreast of deeper social problems, the starting point must be, in any case, to strengthen whatever workable forces for maintaining safety and civilization do exist— in the cities we do have. To build city districts that are custom made for easy crime is idiotic. Yet that is what we do.

The first thing to understand is that the public peace—the sidewalk 12 and street peace—of cities is not kept primarily by the police, necessary as police are. It is kept primarily by an intricate, almost unconscious, network of voluntary controls and standards among the people themselves, and enforced by the people themselves. In some city areas—older public housing projects and streets with very high population turnover are often conspicuous examples— the keeping of public sidewalk law and order is left almost entirely to the police and special guards. Such places are jungles. No amount of police can enforce civilization where the normal, casual enforcement of it has broken down.

The second thing to understand is that the problem of insecurity 13 cannot be solved by spreading people out more thinly, trading the characteristics of cities for the characteristics of suburbs. If this could solve danger on the city streets, then Los Angeles should be a safe city because superficially Los Angeles is almost all suburban. It has virtually no districts compact enough to qualify as dense city areas. Yet Los Angeles cannot, any more than any other great city, evade the truth that, being a city, it *is* composed of strangers not all of whom are nice. Los Angeles' crime figures are flabbergasting. Among the seventeen standard metropolitan areas with populations over a million, Los Angeles stands so pre-eminent in crime that it is in a category by itself. And this is markedly true of crimes associated with personal attack, the crimes that make people fear the streets.

Los Angeles, for example, has a forcible rape rate (1958 figures) [14] of 31.9 per 100,000 population, more than twice as high as either of the next two cities, which happen to be St. Louis and Philadelphia; three times as high as the rate of 10.1 for Chicago, and more than four times as high as the rate of 7.4 for New York.

In aggravated assault, Los Angeles has a rate of 185, compared [15] with 149.5 for Baltimore and 139.2 for St. Louis (the two next highest), and with 90.9 for New York and 79 for Chicago.

The overall Los Angeles rate for major crimes is 2,507.6 per 100,000 people, far ahead of St. Louis and Houston, which come next with 1,634.5 and 1,541.1, and of New York and Chicago, which have rates of 1,145.3 and 943.5.

The reasons for Los Angeles' high crime rates are undoubtedly [16] complex, and at least in part obscure. But of this we can be sure: thinning out a city does not insure safety from crime and fear of crime. This is one of the conclusions that can be drawn within individual cities too, where pseudosuburbs or superannuated suburbs are ideally suited to rape, muggings, beatings, hold-ups and the like.

Here we come up against an all-important question about any [17] city street: How much easy opportunity does it offer to crime? It may be that there is some absolute amount of crime in a given city, which will find an outlet somehow (I do not believe this). Whether this is so or not, different kinds of city streets garner radically different shares of barbarism and fear of barbarism.

Some city streets afford no opportunity to street barbarism. The [18] streets of the North End of Boston are outstanding examples. They are probably as safe as any place on earth in this respect. Although most of the North End's residents are Italian or of Italian descent, the district's streets are also heavily and constantly used by people of every race and background. Some of the strangers from outside work in or close to the district; some come to shop and stroll; many, including members of minority groups who have inherited dangerous districts previously abandoned by others, make a point of cashing their paychecks in North End stores and immediately making their big weekly purchases in streets where they know they will not be parted from their money between the getting and the spending.

Frank Havey, director of the North End Union, the local settlement [19] house, says, "I have been here in the North End twenty-eight years, and in all that time I have never heard of a single case of rape, mugging, molestation of a child or other street crime of that sort in the district. And if there had been any, I would have heard of it even if it did not reach the papers." Half a dozen times or so in the past three decades, says Havey, would-be molesters have made an attempt at luring a child or, late at night, attacking a woman. In every such case the try was thwarted by passers-by, by kibitzers from windows, or shopkeepers.

Meantime, in the Elm Hill Avenue section of Roxbury, a part   20
of inner Boston that is suburban in superficial character, street assaults and the ever present possibility of more street assaults with no kibitzers to protect the victims, induce prudent people to stay off the sidewalks at night. Not surprisingly, for this and other reasons that are related (dispiritedness and dullness), most of Roxbury has run down. It has become a place to leave.

I do not wish to single out Roxbury or its once fine Elm Hill   21
Avenue section especially as a vulnerable area; its disabilities, and especially its Great Blight of Dullness, are all too common in other cities too. But differences like these in public safety within the same city are worth noting. The Elm Hill Avenue section's basic troubles are not owing to a criminal or a discriminated against or a poverty-stricken population. Its troubles stem from the fact that it is physically quite unable to function safely and with related vitality as a city district.

Even within supposedly similar parts of supposedly similar places,   22
drastic differences in public safety exist. An incident at Washington Houses, a public housing project in New York, illustrates this point. A tenants' group at this project, struggling to establish itself, held some outdoor ceremonies in mid-December 1958, and put up three Christmas trees. The chief tree, so cumbersome it was a problem to transport, erect, and trim, went into the project's inner "street," a landscaped central mall and promenade. The other two trees, each less than six feet tall and easy to carry, went on two small fringe plots at the outer corners of the project where it abuts a busy avenue and lively cross streets of the old city. The first night, the large tree and all its trimmings were stolen. The two smaller trees remained intact, lights, ornaments and all, until they were taken down at New Year's. "The place where the tree was stolen, which is *theoretically* the most safe and sheltered place in the project, is the same place that is unsafe for people too, especially children," says a social worker who had been helping the tenants' group. "People are no safer in that mall than the Christmas tree. On the other hand, the place where the other trees were safe, where the project is just one corner out of four, happens to be safe for people."

This is something everyone already knows: A well-used city   23
street is apt to be a safe street. A deserted city street is apt to be

unsafe. But how does this work, really? And what makes a city
street well used or shunned? Why is the sidewalk mall in Washington
Houses, which is supposed to be an attraction, shunned? Why are
the sidewalks of the old city just to its west not shunned? What
about streets that are busy part of the time and then empty abruptly?

A city street equipped to handle strangers, and to make a safety   24
asset, in itself, out of the presence of strangers, as the streets of
successful city neighborhoods always do, must have three main
qualities:

First, there must be a clear demarcation between what is public   25
space and what is private space. Public and private spaces cannot
ooze into each other as they do typically in suburban settings or
in projects.

Second, there must be eyes upon the street, eyes belonging to   26
those we might call the natural proprietors of the street. The
buildings on a street equipped to handle strangers and to insure
the safety of both residents and strangers, must be oriented to the
street. They cannot turn their backs or blank sides on it and leave
it blind.

And third, the sidewalk must have users on it fairly continuously,   27
both to add to the number of effective eyes on the street and to
induce the people in buildings along the street to watch the sidewalks
in sufficient numbers. Nobody enjoys sitting on a stoop or looking
out a window at an empty street. Almost nobody does such a
thing. Large numbers of people entertain themselves, off and on,
by watching street activity.

In settlements that are smaller and simpler than big cities, controls 28
on acceptable public behavior, if not on crime, seem to operate
with greater or lesser success through a web of reputation, gossip,
approval, disapproval and sanctions, all of which are powerful if
people know each other and word travels. But a city's streets,
which must control not only the behavior of the people of the
city but also of visitors from suburbs and towns who want to have
a big time away from the gossip and sanctions at home, have to
operate by more direct, straightforward methods. It is a wonder
cities have solved such an inherently difficult problem at all. And
yet in many streets they do it magnificently.

It is futile to try to evade the issue of unsafe city streets by   29
attempting to make some other features of a locality, say interior
courtyards, or sheltered play spaces, safe instead. By definition
again, the streets of a city must do most of the job of handling
strangers for this is where strangers come and go. The streets must
not only defend the city against predatory strangers, they must
protect the many, many peaceable and well-meaning strangers

who use them, insuring their safety too as they pass through. Moreover, no normal person can spend his life in some artificial haven, and this includes children. Everyone must use the streets.

On the surface, we seem to have here some simple aims: To try to secure streets where the public space is unequivocally public, physically unmixed with private or with nothing-at-all space, so that the area needing surveillance has clear and practicable limits; and to see that these public street spaces have eyes on them as continuously as possible.

But it is not so simple to achieve these objects, especially the latter. You can't make people use streets they have no reason to use. You can't make people watch streets they do not want to watch. Safety on the streets by surveillance and mutual policing of one another sounds grim, but in real life it is not grim. The safety of the street works best, most casually, and with least frequent taint of hostility or suspicion precisely where people are using and most enjoying the city streets voluntarily and are least conscious, normally, that they are policing.

The basic requisite for such surveillance is a substantial quantity of stores and other public places sprinkled along the sidewalks of a district; enterprises and public places that are used by evening and night must be among them especially. Stores, bars and restaurants, as the chief examples, work in several different and complex ways to abet sidewalk safety.

First, they give people—both residents and strangers—concrete reasons for using the sidewalks on which these enterprises face.

Second, they draw people along the sidewalks past places which have no attractions to public use in themselves but which become traveled and peopled as routes to somewhere else; this influence does not carry very far geographically, so enterprises must be frequent in a city district if they are to populate with walkers those other stretches of street that lack public places along the sidewalk. Moreover, there should be many different kinds of enterprises, to give people reasons for crisscrossing paths.

Third, storekeepers and other small businessmen are typically strong proponents of peace and order themselves; they hate broken windows and holdups; they hate having customers made nervous about safety. They are great street watchers and sidewalk guardians if present in sufficient numbers.

Fourth, the activity generated by people on errands, or people aiming for food or drink, is itself an attraction to still other people.

This last point, that the sight of people attracts still other people, is something that city planners and city architectural designers seem to find incomprehensible. They operate on the premise that city people seek the sight of emptiness, obvious order and quiet. Nothing could be less true. People's love of watching activity and other people is constantly evident in cities everywhere. This trait reaches an almost ludicrous extreme on upper Broadway in New York, where the street is divided by a narrow central mall, right in the middle of traffic. At the cross-street intersections of this long north-south mall, benches have been placed behind big concrete buffers and on any day when the weather is even barely tolerable these benches are filled with people at block after block after block, watching the pedestrians who cross the mall in front of them, watching the traffic, watching the people on the busy sidewalks, watching each other. Eventually Broadway reaches Columbia University and Barnard College, one to the right, the other to the left. Here all is obvious order and quiet. No more stores, no more activity generated by the stores, almost no more pedestrians cross-ing—and no more watchers. The benches are there but they go empty in even the finest weather. I have tried them and can see why. No place could be more boring. Even the students of these institutions shun the solitude. They are doing their outdoor loitering, outdoor homework and general street watching on the steps over-looking the busiest campus crossing.

It is just so on city streets elsewhere. A lively street always has 38 both its users and pure watchers. Last year I was on such a street in the Lower East Side of Manhattan, waiting for a bus. I had not been there longer than a minute, barely long enough to begin taking in the street's activity of errand goers, children playing, and loiterers on the stoops, when my attention was attracted by a woman who opened a window on the third floor of a tenement across the street and vigorously yoo-hooed at me. When I caught on that she wanted my attention and responded, she shouted down, "The bus doesn't run here on Saturdays!" Then by a com-bination of shouts and pantomime she directed me around the corner. This woman was one of thousands upon thousands of people in New York who casually take care of the streets. They notice strangers. They observe everything going on. If they need to take action, whether to direct a stranger waiting in the wrong place or to call the police, they do so. Action usually requires, to be sure, a certain self-assurance about the actor's proprietorship of the street and the support he will get if necessary, matters which will be gone into later in this book. But even more fundamental than the action and necessary to the action, is the watching itself.

Not everyone in cities helps to take care of the streets, and many 39 a city resident or city worker is unaware of why his neighborhood is safe. The other day an incident occurred on the street where I live, and it interested me because of this point.

My block of the street, I must explain, is a small one, but it contains a remarkable range of buildings, varying from several vintages of tenements to three- and four-story houses that have been converted into low-rent flats with stores on the ground floor, or returned to single-family use like ours. Across the street there used to be mostly four-story brick tenements with stores below. But twelve years ago several buildings, from the corner to the middle of the block, were converted into one building with elevator apartments of small size and high rents. 40

The incident that attracted my attention was a suppressed struggle going on between a man and a little girl of eight or nine years old. The man seemed to be trying to get the girl to go with him. By turns he was directing a cajoling attention to her, and then assuming an air of nonchalance. The girl was making herself rigid, as children do when they resist, against the wall of one of the tenements across the street. 41

As I watched from our second-floor window, making up my mind how to intervene if it seemed advisable, I saw it was not going to be necessary. From the butcher shop beneath the tenement had emerged the woman who, with her husband, runs the shop; she was standing within earshot of the man, her arms folded and a look of determination on her face. Joe Cornacchia, who with his sons-in-law keeps the delicatessen, emerged about the same moment and stood solidly to the other side. Several heads poked out of the tenement windows above, one was withdrawn quickly and its owner reappeared a moment later in the doorway behind the man. Two men from the bar next to the butcher shop came to the doorway and waited. On my side of the street, I saw that the locksmith, the fruit man and the laundry proprietor had all come out of their shops and that the scene was also being surveyed from a number of windows besides ours. That man did not know it, but he was surrounded. Nobody was going to allow a little girl to be dragged off, even if nobody knew who she was. 42

I am sorry—sorry purely for dramatic purposes—to have to report that the little girl turned out to be the man's daughter. 43

Throughout the duration of the little drama, perhaps five minutes in all, no eyes appeared in the windows of the high-rent, small-apartment building. It was the only building of which this was true. When we first moved to our block, I used to anticipate happily that perhaps soon all the buildings would be rehabilitated like that one. I know better now, and can only anticipate with 44

gloom and foreboding the recent news that exactly this transformation is scheduled for the rest of the block frontage adjoining
the high-rent building. The high-rent tenants, most of whom are
so transient we cannot even keep track of their faces,[1] have not
the remotest idea of who takes care of their street, or how. A city
neighborhood can absorb and protect a substantial number of these
birds of passage, as our neighborhood does. But if and when the
neighborhood finally *becomes* them, they will gradually find the
streets less secure, they will be vaguely mystified about it, and if
things get bad enough they will drift away to another neighborhood
which is mysteriously safer.

In some rich city neighborhoods, where there is little do-it-   45
yourself surveillance, such as residential Park Avenue or upper
Fifth Avenue in New York, street watchers are hired. The monotonous sidewalks of residential Park Avenue, for example, are
surprisingly little used; their putative users are populating, instead,
the interesting store-, bar- and restaurant-filled sidewalks of Lex-
ington Avenue and Madison Avenue to east and west, and the
cross streets leading to these. A network of doormen and super-
intendents, of delivery boys and nursemaids, a form of hired neighborhood, keeps residential Park Avenue supplied with eyes. At
night, with the security of the doormen as a bulwark, dog walkers
safely venture forth and supplement the doormen. But this street
is so blank of built-in eyes, so devoid of concrete reasons for using
or watching it instead of turning the first corner off of it, that if
its rents were to slip below the point where they could support
a plentiful hired neighborhood of doormen and elevator men, it
would undoubtedly become a woefully dangerous street.

Once a street is well equipped to handle strangers, once it has   46
both a good, effective demarcation between private and public
spaces and has a basic supply of activity and eyes, the more strangers
the merrier.

Strangers become an enormous asset on the street on which I   47
live, and the spurs off it, particularly at night when safety assets
are most needed. We are fortunate enough, on the street, to be
gifted not only with a locally supported bar and another around
the corner, but also with a famous bar that draws continuous
troops of strangers from adjoining neighborhoods and even from
out of town. It is famous because the poet Dylan Thomas used to
go there, and mentioned it in his writing. This bar, indeed, works

---

1. Some, according to the storekeepers, live on beans and bread and spend their
sojourn looking for a place to live where all their money will not go for rent.
[author's note]

two distinct shifts. In the morning and early afternoon it is a social gathering place for the old community of Irish longshoremen and other craftsmen in the area, as it always was. But beginning in midafternoon it takes on a different life, more like a college bull session with beer, combined with a literary cocktail party, and this continues until the early hours of the morning. On a cold winter's night, as you pass the White Horse, and the doors open, a solid wave of conversation and animation surges out and hits you; very warming. The comings and goings from this bar do much to keep our street reasonably populated until three in the morning, and it is a street always safe to come home to. The only instance I know of a beating in our street occurred in the dead hours between the closing of the bar and dawn. The beating was halted by one of our neighbors who saw it from his window and, unconsciously certain that even at night he was part of a web of strong street law and order, intervened.

A friend of mine lives on a street uptown where a church youth **48** and community center, with many night dances and other activities, performs the same service for his street that the White Horse bar does for ours. Orthodox planning is much imbued with puritanical and Utopian conceptions of how people should spend their free time, and in planning, these moralisms on people's private lives are deeply confused with concepts about the workings of cities. In maintaining city street civilization, the White Horse bar and the church-sponsored youth center, different as they undoubtedly are, perform much the same public street civilizing service. There is not only room in cities for such differences and many more in taste, purpose and interest of occupation; cities also have a need for people with all these differences in taste and proclivity. The preferences of Utopians, and of other compulsive managers of other people's leisure, for one kind of legal enterprise over others is worse than irrelevant for cities. It is harmful. The greater and more plentiful the range of all legitimate interests (in the strictly legal sense) that city streets and their enterprises can satisfy, the better for the streets and for the safety and civilization of the city.

Bars, and indeed all commerce, have a bad name in many city **49** districts precisely because they do draw strangers, and the strangers do not work out as an asset at all.

This sad circumstance is especially true in the dispirited gray **50** belts of great cities and in once fashionable or at least once solid inner residential areas gone into decline. Because these neighborhoods are so dangerous, and the streets typically so dark, it is commonly believed that their trouble may be insufficient street lighting. Good lighting is important, but darkness alone does not account for the gray areas' deep, functional sickness, the Great Blight of Dullness.

The value of bright street lights for dispirited gray areas rises   51
from the reassurance they offer to some people who need to go out on the sidewalk, or would like to, but lacking the good light would not do so. Thus the lights induce these people to contribute their own eyes to the upkeep of the street. Moreover, as is obvious, good lighting augments every pair of eyes, makes the eyes count for more because their range is greater. Each additional pair of eyes, and every increase in their range, is that much to the good for dull gray areas. But unless eyes are there, and unless in the brains behind those eyes is the almost unconscious reassurance of general street support in upholding civilization, lights can do no good. Horrifying public crimes can, and do, occur in well-lighted subway stations when no effective eyes are present. They virtually never occur in darkened theaters where many people and eyes are present. Street lights can be like that famous stone that falls in the desert where there are no ears to hear. Does it make a noise? Without effective eyes to see, does a light cast light? Not for practical purposes.

Suppose we continue with building, and with deliberate re-   52
building, of unsafe cities. How do we live with this insecurity? From the evidence thus far, there seem to be three modes of living with it; maybe in time others will be invented but I suspect these three will simply be further developed, if that is the word for it.

The first mode is to let danger hold sway, and let those unfortunate   53
enough to be stuck with it take the consequences. This is the policy now followed with respect to low-income housing projects, and to many middle-income housing projects.

The second mode is to take refuge in vehicles. This is a technique   54
practiced in the big wild-animal reservations of Africa, where tourists are warned to leave their cars under no circumstances until they reach a lodge. It is also the technique practiced in Los Angeles. Surprised visitors to that city are forever recounting how the police of Beverly Hills stopped them, made them prove their reasons for being afoot, and warned them of the danger. This technique of public safety does not seem to work too effectively yet in Los Angeles, as the crime rate shows, but in time it may. And think what the crime figures might be if more people without metal shells were helpless upon the vast, blind-eyed reservation of Los Angeles.

People in dangerous parts of other cities often use automobiles   55
as protection too, of course, or try to. A letter to the editor in the

New York Post, reads, "I live on a dark street off Utica Avenue in Brooklyn and therefore decided to take a cab home even though it was not late. The cab driver asked that I get off at the corner of Utica, saying he did not want to go down the dark street. If I had wanted to walk down the dark street, who needed him?"

The third mode . . . was developed by hoodlum gangs and has 56 been adopted widely by developers of the rebuilt city. This mode is to cultivate the institution of Turf.

Under the Turf system in its historical form, a gang appropriates 57 as its territory certain streets or housing projects or parks—often a combination of the three. Members of other gangs cannot enter this Turf without permission from the Turf-owning gang, or if they do so it is at peril of being beaten or run off. In 1956, the New York City Youth Board, fairly desperate because of gang warfare, arranged through its gang youth workers a series of truces among fighting gangs. The truces were reported to stipulate, among other provisions, a mutual understanding of Turf boundaries among the gangs concerned and agreement not to trespass.

The city's police commissioner, Stephen P. Kennedy, thereupon 58 expressed outrage at agreements respecting Turf. The police, he said, aimed to protect the right of every person to walk any part of the city in safety and with impunity as a basic right. Pacts about Turf, he indicated, were intolerably subversive both of public rights and public safety.

I think Commissioner Kennedy was profoundly right. However, 59 we must reflect upon the problem facing the Youth Board workers. It was a real one, and they were trying as well as they could to meet it with whatever empirical means they could. The safety of the city, on which public right and freedom of movement ultimately depend, was missing from the unsuccessful streets, parks and projects dominated by these gangs. Freedom of the city, under these circumstances, was a rather academic ideal.

Now consider the redevelopment projects of cities: the mid- 60 dle- and upper-income housing occupying many acres of city, many former blocks, with their own grounds and their own streets to serve these "islands within the city," "cities within the city," and "new concepts in city living," as the advertisements for them say. The technique here is also to designate the Turf and fence the other gangs out. At first the fences were never visible. Patrolling guards were sufficient to enforce the line. But in the past few years the fences have become literal.

Perhaps the first was the high cyclone fence around a Radiant 61 Garden City project adjoining Johns Hopkins Hospital in Baltimore (great educational institutions seem to be deplorably inventive with Turf devices). In case anyone mistakes what the fence means,

the signs on the project street also say "Keep Out. No Trespassing."
It is uncanny to see a city neighborhood, in a civilian city, walled
off like this. It looks not only ugly, in a deep sense, but surrealistic.
You can imagine how it sits with the neighbors, in spite of the
antidote message on the project church's bulletin board: "Christ's
Love Is The Best Tonic Of All."

New York has been quick to copy the lesson of Baltimore, in   62
its own fashion. Indeed, at the back of Amalgamated Houses on
the Lower East Side, New York has gone further. At the northern
end of the project's parklike central promenade, an iron-bar gate
has been permanently padlocked and is crowned not with mere
metal netting but with a tangle of barbed wire. And does this
defended promenade give out on depraved old megalopolis? Not
at all. Its neighbor is a public playground and beyond this more
project housing for a different income class.

In the rebuilt city it takes a heap of fences to make a balanced   63
neighborhood. The "juncture" between two differently price-tagged
populations, again in the rebuilt Lower East Side, that between
middle-income cooperative Corlears Hook and low-income Vladeck
Houses, is especially elaborate. Corlears Hook buffers its Turf against
its next-door neighbors with a wide parking lot running the full
width of the super-block juncture, next a spindly hedge and a six-
foot-high cyclone fence, next a completely fenced-in no man's
land some thirty feet wide consisting mainly of dirty blowing
papers and deliberately inaccessible to anything else. Then begins
the Vladeck Turf.

Similarly, on the Upper West Side, the rental agent of Park West   64
Village, "Your Own World in the Heart of New York," on whom
I have foisted myself as a prospective tenant, tells me reassuringly,
"Madam, as soon as the shopping center is completed, the entire
grounds will be fenced in."

"Cyclone fences?"   65

"That is correct, madam. And eventually"—waving his hand at   66
the city surrounding his domain—"all that will go. Those people
will go. We are the pioneers here."

I suppose it is rather like pioneer life in a stockaded village,   67
except that the pioneers were working toward greater security for
their civilization, not less.

Some members of the gangs on the new Turfs find this way of   68
life hard to take. Such was one who wrote a letter to the *New
York Post* in 1959: "The other day for the first time my pride at
being a resident of Stuyvesant Town and of New York City was
replaced by indignation and shame. I noticed two boys about 12
years old sitting on a Stuyvesant Town bench. They were deep in

conversation, quiet, well-behaved—and Puerto Rican. Suddenly two Stuyvesant Town guards were approaching—one from the north and one from the south. The one signaled the other by pointing to the two boys. One went up to the boys and after several words, quietly spoken on both sides, the boys rose and left. They tried to look unconcerned . . . How can we expect people to have any dignity and self-respect if we rip it from them even before they reach adulthood? How really poor are we of Stuyvesant Town and of New York City, too, that we can't share a bench with two boys."

The Letters Editor gave this communication the headline, "Stay in Your Own Turf." [69]

But on the whole, people seem to get used very quickly to living in a Turf with either a figurative or a literal fence, and to wonder how they got on without it formerly. This phenomenon was described, before the Turf fences came into the city, by the *New Yorker*, with reference not to fenced city but to fenced town. It seems that when Oak Ridge, Tennessee, was de-militarized after the war, the prospect of losing the fence that went with the militarization drew frightened and impassioned protests from many residents and occasioned town meetings of high excitement. Everyone in Oak Ridge had come, not many years before, from unfenced towns or cities, yet stockade life had become normal and they feared for their safety without the fence. [70]

Just so, my ten-year-old nephew David, born and brought up in Stuyvesant Town, "A City Within a City," comments in wonder that anyone at all can walk on the street outside our door. "Doesn't anybody keep track whether they pay rent on this street?" he asks. "Who puts them out if they don't belong here?" [71]

The technique of dividing the city into Turfs is not simply a New York solution. It is a Rebuilt American City solution. At the Harvard Design Conference of 1959, one of the topics pondered by city architectural designers turned out to be the puzzle of Turf, although they did not use that designation. The examples discussed happened to be the Lake Meadows middle-income project of Chicago and the Lafayette Park high-income project of Detroit. Do you keep the rest of the city out of these blind-eyed purlieus? How difficult and how unpalatable. Do you invite the rest of the city in? How difficult and how impossible. [72]

Like the Youth Board workers, the developers and residents of Radiant City and Radiant Garden City and Radiant Garden City Beautiful have a genuine difficulty and they have to do the best they can with it by the empirical means at their disposal. They have little choice. Wherever the rebuilt city rises the barbaric concept [73] of Turf must follow, because the rebuilt city has junked a basic function of the city street and with it, necessarily, the freedom of the city.

Under the seeming disorder of the old city, wherever the old 74 city is working successfully, is a marvelous order for maintaining the safety of the streets and the freedom of the city. It is a complex order. Its essence is intricacy of sidewalk use, bringing with it a constant succession of eyes. This order is all composed of movement and change, and although it is life, not art, we may fancifully call it the art form of the city and liken it to the dance—not to a simple-minded precision dance with everyone kicking up at the same time, twirling in unison and bowing off en masse, but to an intricate ballet in which the individual dancers and ensembles all have distinctive parts which miraculously reinforce each other and compose an orderly whole. The ballet of the good city sidewalk never repeats itself from place to place, and in any one place is always replete with new improvisations.

The stretch of Hudson Street where I live is each day the scene 75 of an intricate sidewalk ballet. I make my own first entrance into it a little after eight when I put out the garbage can, surely a prosaic occupation, but I enjoy my part, my little clang, as the droves of junior high school students walk by the center of the stage dropping candy wrappers. (How do they eat so much candy so early in the morning?)

While I sweep up the wrappers I watch the other rituals of 76 morning: Mr. Halpert unlocking the laundry's handcart from its mooring to a cellar door, Joe Cornacchia's son-in-law stacking out the empty crates from the delicatessen, the barber bringing out his sidewalk folding chair. Mr. Goldstein arranging the coils of wire which proclaim the hardware store is open, the wife of the tenement's superintendent depositing her chunky three-year-old with a toy mandolin on the stoop, the vantage point from which he is learning the English his mother cannot speak. Now the primary children, heading for St. Luke's, dribble through to the south; the children for St. Veronica's cross, heading to the west, and the children for P.S. 41, heading toward the east. Two new entrances are being made from the wings: well-dressed and even elegant women and men with brief cases emerge from doorways and side streets. Most of these are heading for the bus and subways, but some hover on the curbs, stopping taxis which have miraculously appeared at the right moment, for the taxis are part of a wider morning ritual: having dropped passengers from midtown in the downtown financial district, they are now bringing down-towners up to midtown. Simultaneously, numbers of women in housedresses have emerged and as they crisscross with one another they pause for quick conversations that sound with either laughter or joint indignation, never, it seems, anything between. It is time for me to hurry to work too, and I exchange my ritual farewell with Mr. Lofaro, the short, thick-bodied, white-aproned fruit man who stands outside his doorway a little up the street, his arms folded, his feet planted, looking solid as earth itself. We nod; we each glance quickly up and down the street, then look back to each other and smile. We have done this many a morning for more than ten years, and we both know what it means: All is well.

The heart-of-the-day ballet I seldom see, because part of the 77 nature of it is that working people who live there, like me, are mostly gone, filling the roles of strangers on other sidewalks. But from days off, I know enough of it to know that it becomes more and more intricate. Longshoremen who are not working that day gather at the White Horse or the Ideal or the International for beer and conversation. The executives and business lunchers from the industries just to the west throng the Dorgene restaurant and the Lion's Head coffee house; meat-market workers and communications scientists fill the bakery lunchroom. Character dancers come on, a strange old man with strings of old shoes over his shoulders, motor-scooter riders with big beards and girl friends who bounce on the back of the scooters and wear their hair long in front of their faces as well as behind, drunks who follow the advice of the Hat Council and are always turned out in hats, but not hats the Council would approve. Mr. Lacey, the locksmith, shuts up his shop for a while and goes to exchange the time of day with Mr. Slube at the cigar store. Mr. Koochagian, the tailor, waters the luxuriant jungle of plants in his window, gives them a critical look from the outside, accepts a compliment on them from two passers-by, fingers the leaves on the plane tree in front of our house with a thoughtful gardener's appraisal, and crosses the street for a bite at the Ideal where he can keep an eye on customers and wigwag across the message that he is coming. The baby carriages come out, and clusters of everyone from toddlers with dolls to teen-agers with homework gather at the stoops.

When I get home after work, the ballet is reaching its crescendo. 78 This is the time of roller skates and stilts and tricycles, and games in the lee of the stoop with bottletops and plastic cowboys; this is the time of bundles and packages, zigzagging from the drug

store to the fruit stand and back over to the butcher's; this is the
time when teen-agers, all dressed up, are pausing to ask if their
slips show or their collars look right; this is the time when beautiful
girls get out of MG's; this is the time when the fire engines go
through; this is the time when anybody you know around Hudson
Street will go by.

As darkness thickens and Mr. Halpert moors the laundry cart   79
to the cellar door again, the ballet goes on under lights, eddying
back and forth but intensifying at the bright spotlight pools of
Joe's sidewalk pizza dispensary, the bars, the delicatessen, the
restaurant and the drug store. The night workers stop now at the
delicatessen, to pick up salami and a container of milk. Things
have settled down for the evening but the street and its ballet
have not come to a stop.

I know the deep night ballet and its seasons best from waking   80
long after midnight to tend a baby and, sitting in the dark, seeing
the shadows and hearing the sounds of the sidewalk. Mostly it is
a sound like infinitely pattering snatches of party conversation
and, about three in the morning, singing, very good singing. Sometimes there is sharpness and anger or sad, sad weeping, or a flurry
of search for a string of beads broken. One night a young man
came roaring along, bellowing terrible language at two girls whom
he had apparently picked up and who were disappointing him.
Doors opened, a wary semicircle formed around him, not too close,
until the police came. Out came the heads, too, along Hudson
Street, offering opinion, "Drunk . . . Crazy . . . A wild kid from
the surburbs."[2]

Deep in the night, I am almost unaware how many people are   81
on the street unless something calls them together, like the bagpipe.
Who the piper was and why he favored our street I have no idea.
The bagpipe just skirled out in the February night, and as if it
were a signal the random, dwindled movements of the sidewalk
took on direction. Swiftly, quietly, almost magically a little crowd
was there, a crowd that evolved into a circle with a Highland fling
inside it. The crowd could be seen on the shadowy sidewalk, the
dancers could be seen, but the bagpiper himself was almost invisible
because his bravura was all in his music. He was a very little man
in a plain brown overcoat. When he finished and vanished, the

---

2. He turned out to be a wild kid from the suburbs. Sometimes, on Hudson Street,
we are tempted to believe the suburbs must be a difficult place to bring up children.
[author's note]

dancers and watchers applauded, and applause came from the galleries too, half a dozen of the hundred windows on Hudson Street. Then the windows closed, and the little crowd dissolved into the random movements of the night street.

The strangers on Hudson Street, the allies whose eyes help us natives keep the peace of the street, are so many that they always seem to be different people from one day to the next. That does not matter. Whether they are so many always-different people as they seem to be, I do not know. Likely they are. When Jimmy Rogan fell through a plate-glass window (he was separating some scuffling friends) and almost lost his arm, a stranger in an old T shirt emerged from the Ideal bar, swiftly applied an expert tourniquet and, according to the hospital's emergency staff, saved Jimmy's life. Nobody remembered seeing the man before and no one has seen him since. The hospital was called in this way: a woman sitting on the steps next to the accident ran over to the bus stop, wordlessly snatched the dime from the hand of a stranger who was waiting with his fifteen-cent fare ready, and raced into the Ideal's phone booth. The stranger raced after her to offer the nickel too. Nobody remembered seeing him before, and no one has seen him since. When you see the same stranger three or four times on Hudson Street, you begin to nod. This is almost getting to be an acquaintance, a public acquaintance, of course.

I have made the daily ballet of Hudson Street sound more frenetic than it is, because writing it telescopes it. In real life, it is not that way. In real life, to be sure, something is always going on, the ballet is never at a halt, but the general effect is peaceful and the general tenor even leisurely. People who know well such animated city streets will know how it is. I am afraid people who do not will always have it a little wrong in their heads—like the old prints of rhinoceroses made from travelers' descriptions of rhinoceroses.

On Hudson Street, the same as in the North End of Boston or in any other animated neighborhoods of great cities, we are not innately more competent at keeping the sidewalks safe than are the people who try to live off the hostile truce of Turf in a blind-eyed city. We are the lucky possessors of a city order that makes it relatively simple to keep the peace because there are plenty of eyes on the street. But there is nothing simple about that order itself, or the bewildering number of components that go into it. Most of those components are specialized in one way or another. They unite in their joint effect upon the sidewalk, which is not specialized in the least. That is its strength.

82

83

84

GRETEL EHRLICH

Wyoming: The Solace of Open Spaces

It's May, and I've just awakened from a nap, curled against   1
sagebrush the way my dog taught me to sleep—sheltered from
wind. A front is pulling the huge sky over me, and from the dark
a hailstone has hit me on the head. I'm trailing a band of 2000
sheep across a stretch of Wyoming badland, a fifty-mile trip that
takes five days because sheep shade up in hot sun and won't
budge until it cools. Bunched together now, and excited into a
run by the storm, they drift across dry land, tumbling into draws
like water and surging out again onto the rugged, choppy plateaus
that are the building blocks of this state.

The name Wyoming comes from an Indian word meaning "at   2
the great plains," but the plains are really valleys, great arid valleys,
1600 square miles, with the horizon bending up on all sides into
mountain ranges. This gives the vastness a sheltering look.

Winter lasts six months here. Prevailing winds spill snowdrifts   3
to the east, and new storms from the northwest replenish them.
This white bulk is sometimes dizzying, even nauseating, to look
at. At twenty, thirty, and forty degrees below zero, not only does
your car not work but neither do your mind and body. The landscape
hardens into a dungeon of space. During the winter, while I was
riding to find a new calf, my legs froze to the saddle, and in the
silence that such cold creates I felt like the first person on earth,
or the last.

Today the sun is out—only a few clouds billowing. In the east,   4
where the sheep have started off without me, the benchland tilts
up in a series of red-earthed, eroded mesas, planed flat on top by
a million years of water; behind them, a bold line of muscular
scarps rears up 10,000 feet to become the Big Horn Mountains.
A tidal pattern is engraved into the ground, as if left by the sea
that once covered this state. Canyons curve down like galaxies to
meet the oncoming rush of flat land.

To live and work in this kind of open country, with its hundred-   5
mile views, is to lose the distinction between background and
foreground. When I asked an older ranch hand to describe Wyoming's openness, he said, "It's all a bunch of nothing—wind and

First published in *The Atlantic*, 1981.

rattlesnakes—and so much of it you can't tell where you're going or where you've been and it don't make much difference." John, a sheepman I know, is tall and handsome and has an explosive temperament. He has a perfect intuition about people and sheep. They call him "Highpockets," because he's so long-legged; his graceful stride matches the distances he has to cover. He says, "Open space hasn't affected me at all. It's all the people moving in on it." The huge ranch he was born on takes up much of one county and spreads into another state; to put 100,000 miles on his pickup in three years and never leave home is not unusual. A friend of mine has an aunt who ranched on Powder River and didn't go off her place for eleven years. When her husband died, she quickly moved to town, bought a car, and drove around the States to see what she'd been missing.

Most people tell me they've simply driven through Wyoming, 6
as if there were nothing to stop for. Or else they've skied in Jackson Hole, a place Wyomingites acknowledge uncomfortably, because its green beauty and chic affluence are mismatched with the rest of the state. Most of Wyoming has a "lean-to" look. Instead of big, roomy barns and Victorian houses, there are dugouts, low sheds, log cabins, sheep camps, and fence lines that look like driftwood blown haphazardly into place. People here still feel pride because they live in such a harsh place, part of the glamorous cowboy past, and they are determined not to be the victims of a mining-dominated future.

Most characteristic of the state's landscape is what a developer 7
euphemistically describes as "indigenous growth right up to your front door"—a reference to waterless stands of salt sage, snakes, jackrabbits, deerflies, red dust, a brief respite of wildflowers, dry washes, and no trees. In the Great Plains, the vistas look like music, like kyries of grass, but Wyoming seems to be the doing of a mad architect—tumbled and twisted, ribboned with faded, deathbed colors, thrust up and pulled down as if the place had been startled out of a deep sleep and thrown into a pure light.

I came here four years ago. I had not planned to stay, but I 8
couldn't make myself leave. John, the sheepman, put me to work immediately. It was spring, and shearing time. For fourteen days of fourteen hours each, we moved thousands of sheep through sorting corrals to be sheared, branded, and deloused. I suspect that my original motive for coming here was to "lose myself" in new and unpopulated territory. Instead of producing the numbness I thought I wanted, life on the sheep ranch woke me up. The

vitality of the people I was working with flushed out what had become a hallucinatory rawness inside me. I threw away my clothes and bought new ones; I cut my hair. The arid country was a clean slate. Its absolute indifference steadied me.

Sagebrush covers 58,000 square miles of Wyoming. The biggest   9
city has a population of 50,000, and there are only five settlements that could be called cities in the whole state. The rest are towns, scattered across the expanse with as much as sixty miles between them, their populations 2000, fifty, or ten. They are fugitive-looking, perched on a barren, windblown bench, or tagged onto a river or a railroad, or laid out straight in a farming valley with implement stores and a block-long Mormon church. In the eastern part of the state, which slides down into the Great Plains, the new mining settlements are boomtowns, trailer cities, metal knots on flat land.

Despite the desolate look, there's a coziness to living in this   10
state. There are so few people (only 470,000) that ranchers who buy and sell cattle know each other statewide; the kids who choose to go to college usually go to the state's one university, in Laramie; hired hands work their way around Wyoming in a lifetime of hirings and firings. And, despite the physical separation, people stay in touch, often driving two or three hours to another ranch for dinner.

Seventy-five years ago, when travel was by buckboard or horse-   11
back, cowboys who were temporarily out of work rode the grub line—drifting from ranch to ranch, mending fences or milking cows, and receiving in exchange a bed and meals. Gossip and messages traveled this slow circuit with them, creating an intimacy between ranchers who were three and four weeks' ride apart. One old-time couple I know, whose turn-of-the-century homestead was used by an outlaw gang as a relay station for stolen horses, recall that if you were traveling, desperado or not, any lighted ranch house was a welcome sign. Even now, for someone who lives in a remote spot, arriving at a ranch or coming to town for supplies is cause for celebration. To emerge from isolation can be disorienting. Everything looks bright, new, vivid. After I had been herding sheep for only three days, the sound of the camp-tender's pickup flustered me. Longing for human company, I felt a foolish grin take over my face, yet I had to resist an urgent temptation to run and hide.

Things happen suddenly in Wyoming: the change of seasons   12
and weather; for people, the violent swings in and out of isolation. But goodnaturedness is concomitant with severity. Friendliness is a tradition. Strangers passing on the road wave hello. A common sight is two pickups stopped side by side far out on a range, on

a dirt track winding through the sage. The drivers will share a cigarette, uncap their thermos bottles, and pass a battered cup, steaming with coffee, between windows. These meetings summon up the details of several generations, because in Wyoming, private histories are largely public knowledge.

Because ranch work is a physical and, these days, economic 13 strain, being "at home on the range" is a matter of vigor, self-reliance, and common sense. A person's life is not a series of dramatic events for which he or she is applauded or exiled but a slow accumulation of days, seasons, years, fleshed out by the generational weight of one's family and anchored by a land-bound sense of place.

In most parts of Wyoming, the human population is visibly 14 outnumbered by the animal. Not far from my town of fifty, I rode into a narrow valley and startled a herd of 200 elk. Eagles look like small people as they eat car-killed deer by the road. Antelope, moving in small, graceful bands, travel at 60 miles an hour, their mouths open as if drinking in the space.

The solitude in which westerners live makes them quiet. They 15 telegraph thoughts and feelings by the way they tilt their heads and listen; pulling their Stetsons into a steep dive over their eyes, or pigeon-toeing one boot over the other, they lean against a fence with a fat wedge of snoose beneath their lower lips and take the whole scene in. These detached looks of quiet amusement are sometimes cynical, but they can also come from a dry-eyed humility as lucid as the air is clear.

Conversation goes on in what sounds like a private code; a few 16 phrases imply a complex of meanings. Asking directions, you get a curious list of details. While trailing sheep, I was told to "ride up to that kinda upturned rock, follow the pink wash, turn left at the dump, and then you'll see the waterhole." One friend told his wife on roundup to "turn at the salt lick and the dead cow," which turned out to be a scattering of bones and no salt lick at all.

Sentence structure is shortened to the skin and bones of a thought. 17 Descriptive words are dropped, even verbs; a cowboy looking over a corral full of horses will say to a wrangler, "Which one needs rode?" People hold back their thoughts in what seems to be a dumbfounded silence, then erupt with an excoriating, perceptive remark. Language, so compressed, becomes metaphorical. A rancher ended a relationship with one remark: "You're a bad check," meaning bouncing in and out was intolerable, and even coming back would be no good.

What's behind this laconic style is shyness. There is no vocabulary   18
for the subject of feelings. It's not a hangdog shyness, or anything
coy—always there's a robust spirit in evidence behind the restraint,
as if the earth-dredging wind that pulls across Wyoming had carried
its people's voices away but everything else in them had shouldered
confidently into the breeze.

I've spent hours riding to sheep camp at dawn in a pickup when   19
nothing was said; eaten meals in the cookhouse when the only
words spoken were a mumbled "Thank you, ma'am" at the end
of dinner. The silence is profound. Instead of talking, we seem to
share one eye. Keenly observed, the world is transformed. The
landscape is engorged with detail, every movement on it chillingly
sharp. The air between people is charged. Days unfold, bathed in
their own music. Nights become hallucinatory; dreams, prescient.

Spring weather is capricious and mean. It snows, then blisters   20
with heat. There have been tornadoes. They lay their elephant
trunks out in the sage until they find houses, then slurp everything
up and leave. I've noticed that melting snowbanks hiss and rot,
viperous, then drip into calm pools where ducklings hatch and
livestock, being trailed to summer range, drink. With the ice cover
gone, rivers churn a milkshake brown, taking culverts and small
bridges with them. Water in such an arid place (the average annual
rainfall where I live is less than eight inches) is like blood. It
festoons drab land with green veins: a line of cottonwoods following
a stream; a strip of alfalfa; and on ditchbanks, wild asparagus
growing.

I've moved to a small cattle ranch owned by friends. It's at the   21
foot of the Big Horn Mountains. A few weeks ago, I helped them
deliver a calf who was stuck halfway out of his mother's body.
By the time he was freed, we could see a heartbeat, but he was
straining against a swollen tongue for air. Mary and I held him
upside down by his back feet, while Stan, on his hands and knees
in the blood, gave the calf mouth-to-mouth resuscitation. I have
a vague memory of being pneumonia-choked as a child, my mother
giving me her air, which may account for my romance with this
windswept state.

If anything is endemic to Wyoming, it is wind. This big room   22
of space is swept out daily, leaving a boneyard of fossils, agates,
and carcasses in every stage of decay. Though it was water that
initially shaped the state, wind is the meticulous gardener, raising
dust and pruning the sage.

I try to imagine a world of uncharted land, in which one could   23
look over an uncompleted map and ride a horse past where all

the lines have stopped. There is no wilderness left; wilderness, yes, but true wilderness has been gone on this continent since the time of Lewis and Clark's overland journey.

Two hundred years ago, the Crow, Shoshone, Arapaho, Cheyenne, 24 and Sioux roamed the intermountain West, orchestrating their movements according to hunger, season, and warfare. Once they acquired horses, they traversed the spines of all the big Wyoming ranges—the Absarokas, the Wind Rivers, the Tetons, the Big Horns—and wintered on the unprotected plains that fan out from them. Space was life. The world was their home.

What was life-giving to native Americans was often nightmarish 25 to sodbusters who arrived encumbered with families and ethnic pasts to be transplanted in nearly uninhabitable land. The great distances, the shortage of water and trees, and the loneliness created unexpected hardships for them. In her book *O Pioneers!*, Willa Cather gives a settler's version of the bleak landscape:

> The little town behind them had vanished as if it had never been, had fallen behind the swell of the prairie, and the stern frozen country received them into its bosom. The homesteads were few and far apart; here and there a windmill gaunt against the sky, a sod house crouching in a hollow.

The emptiness of the West was for others a geography of possibility. 26 Men and women who amassed great chunks of land and struggled to preserve unfenced empires were, despite their self-serving motives, unwitting geographers. They understood the lay of the land. But by the 1850s, the Oregon and Mormon trails sported bumper-to-bumper traffic. Wealthy landowners, many of them aristocratic absentee landlords, known as remittance men because they were paid to come West and get out of their families' hair, overstocked the range with more than a million head of cattle. By 1885, the feed and water were desperately short, and the winter of 1886 laid out the gaunt bodies of dead animals so closely together that when the thaw came, one rancher from Kaycee claimed to have walked on cowhide all the way to Crazy Woman Creek, twenty miles away.

Territorial Wyoming was a boy's world. The land was generous 27 with everything but water. At first there was room enough, food enough, for everyone. And, as with all beginnings, an expansive mood set in. The young cowboys, drifters, shopkeepers, school-teachers, were heroic, lawless, generous, rowdy, and tenacious. The individualism and optimism generated during those times have endured.

John Tisdale rode north with the trail herds from Texas. He was 28 a college-educated man with enough money to buy a small outfit

near the Powder River. While driving home from the town of
Buffalo with a buckboard full of Christmas toys for his family and
a winter's supply of food, he was shot in the back by an agent
of the cattle barons who resented the encroachment of small-time
stockmen like him. The wealthy cattlemen tried to control all the
public grazing land by restricting membership in the Wyoming
Stock Growers Association, as if it were a country club. They
ostracized from roundups and brandings cowboys and ranchers
who were not members, then denounced them as rustlers. Tisdale's
death, the second such cold-blooded murder, kicked off the Johnson
County cattle war, which was no simple good-guy-bad-guy shoot-
out but a complicated class struggle between landed gentry and
less affluent settlers—a shocking reminder that the West was not
an egalitarian sanctuary after all.

Fencing ultimately enforced boundaries, but barbed wire abrogated   29
space. It was stretched across the beautiful valleys, into the mountains, over desert badlands, through buffalo grass. The "anything
is possible" fever—the lure of any new place—was constricted.
The integrity of the land as a geographical body, and the freedom
to ride anywhere on it, was lost.

I punched cows with a young man named Martin, who is the   30
great-grandson of John Tisdale. His inheritance is not the open
land that Tisdale knew and prematurely lost but a rage against
restraint.

Wyoming tips down as you head northeast; the highest ground—   31
the Laramie Plains—is on the Colorado border. Up where I live,
the Big Horn River leaks into difficult, arid terrain. In the basin
where it's dammed, sandhill cranes gather and, with delicate leg-
work, slice through the stilled water. I was driving by with a
rancher one morning when he commented that cranes are "old-
fashioned." When I asked why, he said, "Because they mate for
life." Then he looked at me with a twinkle in his eyes, as if to
say he really did believe in such things but also understood why
we break our own rules.

In all this open space, values crystallize quickly. People are   32
strong on scruples but tenderhearted about quirky behavior. A
friend and I found one ranch hand, who's "not quite right in the
head," sitting in front of the badly decayed carcass of a cow,
shaking his finger and saying, "Now, I don't want you to do this
ever again!" When I asked what was wrong with him, I was told,
"He's goofier than hell, just like the rest of us." Perhaps because
the West is historically new, conventional morality is still felt to
be less important than rock-bottom truths. Though there's always

a lot of teasing and sparring around, people are blunt with each other, sometimes even cruel, believing honesty is stronger medicine than sympathy, which may console but often conceals.

The formality that goes hand in hand with the rowdiness is   33
known as "the Western Code." It's a list of practical dos and don'ts, faithfully observed. A friend, Cliff, who runs a trapline in the winter, cut off half his foot while axing a hole in the ice. Alone, he dragged himself to his pickup and headed for town, stopping to open the ranch gate as he left, and getting out to close it again, thus losing, in his observance of rules, precious time and blood. Later, he commented, "How would it look, them having to come to the hospital to tell me their cows had gotten out?"

Accustomed to emergencies, my friends doctor each other from   34
the vet's bag with relish. When one old-timer suffered a heart attack in hunting camp, his partner quickly stirred up a brew of red horse liniment and hot water and made the half-conscious victim drink it, then tied him onto a horse and led him twenty miles to town. He regained consciousness and lived.

The roominess of the state has affected political attitudes as well.   35
Ranchers keep up with world politics and the convulsions of the economy but are basically isolationists. Being used to running their own small empires of land and livestock, they're suspicious of big government. It's a "don't fence me in" holdover from a century ago. They still want the elbow room their grandfathers had, so they're strongly conservative, but with a populist twist.

Summer is the season when we get our "cowboy tans"—on   36
the lower parts of our faces and on three fourths of our arms. Excessive heat, in the nineties and higher, sends us outside with the mosquitoes. In winter, we're tucked inside our houses, and the white wasteland outside appears to be expanding, but in summer, all the greenery abridges space. Summer is a go-ahead season. Every living thing is off the block and in the race: battalions of bugs in flight and biting; bats swinging around my log cabin as if the bases were loaded and someone had hit a home run. Some of summer's high-speed growth is ominous: larkspur, death camas, and green greasewood can kill sheep—an ironic idea, dying in this desert from eating what is too verdant. With sixteen hours of daylight, farmers and ranchers irrigate feverishly. There are first, second, and third cuttings of hay, some crews averaging only four hours of sleep a night for weeks. And, like the cowboys who in summer ride the night rodeo circuit, nighthawks make daredevil dives at dusk with an eerie whirring that sounds like a plane going down on the shimmering horizon.

In the town where I live, they've had to board up the dance-   37
hall windows because there have been so many fights. There's so
little to do except work that people wind up in a state of idle
agitation that becomes fatalistic, as if there were nothing to be
done about all this untapped energy. So the dark side to the
grandeur of these spaces is the small-mindedness that seals people
in. Men become hermits; women go mad. Cabin fever explodes
into suicides, or into grudges and lifelong family feuds. Two sisters
in my area inherited a ranch but found they couldn't get along.
They fenced the place in half. When one's cows got out and mixed
with the other's, the women went at each other with shovels.
They ended up in the same hospital room, but never spoke a word
to each other for the rest of their lives.

Eccentricity ritualizes behavior. It's a shortcut through unman-   38
ageable emotions and strict social conventions. I knew a sheepherder
named Fred who, at seventy-eight, still had a handsome face,
which he kept smooth by plastering it each day with bag balm
and Vaseline. He was curious, well-read, and had a fact-keeping
mind to go along with his penchant for hoarding. His reliquary
of gunnysacks, fence wire, wood, canned food, unopened Christmas
presents, and magazines matched his odd collages of meals: sardines
with maple syrup; vegetable soup garnished with Fig Newtons.
His wagon was so overloaded that he had to sleep sitting up
because there was no room on the bed. Despite his love of up-
to-date information, Fred died from gangrene when an old-timer's
remedy of fresh sheep manure, applied as a poultice to a bad cut,
failed to save him.

After the brief lushness of summer, the sun moves south. The   39
range grass is brown. Livestock has been trailed back down from
the mountains. Waterholes begin to frost over at night. Last fall
Martin asked me to accompany him on a pack trip. With five
horses, we followed a river into the mountains behind the tiny
Wyoming town of Meeteetse. Groves of aspen, red and orange,
gave off a light that made us look toasted. Our hunting camp was
so high that clouds skidded across our foreheads, then slowed to
sail out across the warm valleys. Except for a bull moose who
wandered into our camp and mistook our black gelding for a rival,
we shot at nothing.

One of our evening entertainments was to watch the night sky.   40
My dog, who also came on the trip, a dingo bred to herd sheep,
is so used to the silence and empty skies that when an airplane
flies over he always looks up and eyes the distant intruder quizzically.

The sky, lately, seems to be much more crowded than it used to be. Satellites make their silent passes in the dark with great regularity. We counted eighteen in one hour's viewing. How odd to think that while they circumnavigated the planet, Martin and I had moved only six miles into our local wilderness, and had seen no other human for the two weeks we stayed there.

At night, by moonlight, the land is whittled to slivers—a ridge, 41 a river, a strip of grassland stretching to the mountains, then the huge sky. One morning a full moon was setting in the west just as the sun was rising. I felt precariously balanced between the two as I loped across a meadow. For a moment, I could believe that the stars, which were still visible, work like cooper's bands, holding everything above Wyoming together.

Space has a spiritual equivalent, and can heal what is divided 42 and burdensome in us. My grandchildren will probably use space shuttles for a honeymoon trip or to recover from heart attacks, but closer to home we might also learn how to carry space inside ourselves in the effortless way we carry our skins. Space represents sanity, not a life purified, dull, or "spaced out" but one that might accommodate intelligently any idea or situation.

From the clayey soil of northern Wyoming is mined bentonite, 43 which is used as a filler in candy, gum, and lipstick. We Americans are great on fillers, as if what we have, what we are, is not enough. We have a cultural tendency toward denial, but, being affluent, we strangle ourselves with what we can buy. We have only to look at the houses we build to see how we build *against* space, the way we drink against pain and loneliness. We fill up space as if it were a pie shell, with things whose opacity further obstructs our ability to see what is already there.

PHYLLIS McGINLEY

Suburbia: of Thee I Sing

Twenty miles east of New York City as the New Haven Railroad 1 flies sits a village I shall call Spruce Manor. The Boston Post Road, there, for the length of two blocks, becomes Main Street, and on

From *Province of the Heart* (1949).

one side of that thundering thoroughfare are the grocery stores and the drug stores and the Village Spa where teen-agers gather of an afternoon to drink their cokes and speak their curious confidences. There one finds the shoe repairers and the dry cleaners and the second-hand stores which sell "antiques" and the stationery stores which dispense comic books to ten-year-olds and greeting cards and lending library masterpieces to their mothers. On the opposite side stand the bank, the fire house, the public library. The rest of this town of perhaps four or five thousand people lies to the south and is bounded largely by Long Island Sound, curving protectively on three borders. The movie theater (dedicated to the showing of second-run, single-feature pictures) and the grade schools lie north, beyond the Post Road, and that is a source of worry to Spruce Manorites. They are always a little uneasy about the children, crossing, perhaps, before the lights are safely green. However, two excellent policemen—Mr. Crowley and Mr. Lang—station themselves at the intersections four times a day, and so far there have been no accidents.

Spruce Manor in the spring and summer and fall is a pretty 2 town, full of gardens and old elms. (There are few spruces, but the village Council is considering planting a few on the station plaza, out of sheer patriotism.) In the winter, the houses reveal themselves as comfortable, well-kept, architecturally insignificant. Then one can see the town for what it is and has been since it left off being farm and woodland some sixty years ago—the epitome of Suburbia, not the country and certainly not the city. It is a commuter's town, the living center of a web which unrolls each morning as the men swing aboard the locals, and contracts again in the evening when they return. By day, with even the children pent in schools, it is a village of women. They trundle mobile baskets at the A&P, they sit under driers at the hairdressers, they sweep their porches and set out bulbs and stitch up slip covers. Only on weekends does it become heterogeneous and lively, the parking places difficult to find.

Spruce Manor has no country club of its own, though devoted 3 golfers have their choice of two or three not far away. It does have a small yacht club and a beach which can be used by anyone who rents or owns a house here. The village supports a little park with playground equipment and a counselor, where children, unattended by parents, can spend summer days if they have no more pressing engagements.

It is a town not wholly without traditions. Residents will point 4 out the two-hundred-year-old manor house, now a minor museum; and in the autumn they line the streets on a scheduled evening to watch the Volunteer Firemen parade. That is a fine occasion, with so many heads of households marching in their red blouses and white gloves, some with flaming helmets, some swinging lanterns, most of them genially out of step. There is a bigger parade on Memorial Day with more marchers than watchers and with the Catholic priest, the rabbi, and the Protestant ministers each delivering a short prayer when the paraders gather near the War Memorial. On the whole, however, outside of contributing generously to the Community Chest, Manorites are not addicted to municipal get-togethers.

No one is very poor here and not many families rich enough   5
to be awesome. In fact, there is not much to distinguish Spruce Manor from any other of a thousand suburbs outside of New York City or San Francisco or Detroit or Chicago or even Stockholm, for that matter. Except for one thing. For some reason, Spruce Manor has become a sort of symbol to writers and reporters familiar only with its name or trivial aspects. It has become a symbol of all that is middle-class in the worst sense, of settled-downness or rootlessness, according to what the writer is trying to prove; of smug and prosperous mediocrity—or even, in more lurid novels, of lechery at the country club and Sunday morning hangovers.

To condemn Suburbia has long been a literary cliché, anyhow.   6
I have yet to read a book in which the suburban life was pictured as the good life or the commuter as a sympathetic figure. He is nearly as much a stock character as the old stage Irishman: the man who "spends his life riding to and from his wife," the eternal Babbitt[1] who knows all about Buicks and nothing about Picasso, whose sanctuary is the club locker room, whose ideas spring ready-made from the illiberal newspapers. His wife plays politics at the P.T.A. and keeps up with the Joneses. Or—if the scene is more gilded and less respectable—the commuter is the high-powered advertising executive with a station wagon and an eye for the ladies, his wife a restless baggage given to too many cocktails in the afternoon.

These clichés I challenge. I have lived in the country, I have   7
lived in the city. I have lived in an average Middle Western small town. But for the best eleven years of my life I have lived in Suburbia and I like it.

"Compromise!" cried our friends when we came here from an   8
expensive, inconvenient, moderately fashionable tenement in Manhattan. It was the period in our lives when everyone was

---

1. Title character in Sinclair Lewis's novel *Babbitt* (1922); the word has come to mean a smug, unimaginative, middle-class person.

moving somewhere. Farther uptown, farther downtown, across town to Sutton Place, to a half-dozen rural acres in Connecticut or New Jersey or even Vermont. But no one in our rather rarefied little group was thinking of moving to the suburbs except us. They were aghast that we could find anything appealing in the thought of a middle-class house on a middle-class street in a middle-class village full of middle-class people. That we were tired of town and hoped for children, that we couldn't afford both a city apartment and a farm, they put down as feeble excuses. To this day they cannot understand us. You see, they read the books. They even write them.

Compromise? Of course we compromise. But compromise, if   9 not the spice of life, is its solidity. It is what makes nations great and marriages happy and Spruce Manor the pleasant place it is. As for its being middle-class, what is wrong with acknowledging one's roots? And how free we are! Free of the city's noise, of its ubiquitous doormen, of the soot on the windowsill and the radio in the next apartment. We have released ourselves from the seasonal hegira to the mountains or the seashore. We have only one address, one house to keep supplied with paring knives and blankets. We are free from the snows that block the countryman's roads in winter and his electricity which always goes off in a thunderstorm. I do not insist that we are typical. There is nothing really typical about any of our friends and neighbors here, and therein lies my point. The true suburbanite needs to conform less than anyone else; much less than the gentleman farmer with his remodeled salt-box or than the determined cliff dweller with his necessity for living at the right address. In Spruce Manor all addresses are right. And since we are fairly numerous here, we need not fall back on the people nearest us for total companionship. There is not here, as in a small city away from truly urban centers, some particular family whose codes must be ours. And we could not keep up with the Joneses even if we wanted to, for we know many Joneses and they are all quite different people leading the most various lives.

The Albert Joneses spend their weekends sailing, the Bertram   10 Joneses cultivate their delphinium, the Clarence Joneses—Clarence being a handy man with a cello—are enthusiastic about amateur chamber music. The David Joneses dote on bridge, but neither of the Ernest Joneses understands it, and they prefer staying home of an evening so that Ernest Jones can carve his witty caricatures out of pieces of old fruit wood. We admire each other's gardens, applaud each other's sailing records; we are too busy to compete. So long as our clapboards are painted and our hedges decently trimmed, we have fulfilled our community obligations. We can live as anonymously as in a city or we can call half the village by their first names.

On our half-acre or three-quarters, we can raise enough tomatoes 11 for our salads and assassinate enough beetles to satisfy the gardening urge. Or we can buy our vegetables at the store and put the whole place to lawn without feeling that we are neglecting our property. We can have privacy and shade and the changing of the seasons and also the Joneses next door from whom to borrow a cup of sugar or a stepladder. Despite the novelists, the shadow of the country club rests lightly on us. Half of us wouldn't be found dead with a golf stick in our hands, and loathe Saturday dances. Few of us expect to be deliriously wealthy or world-famous or divorced. What we do expect is to pay off the mortgage and send our healthy children to good colleges.

For when I refer to life here, I think, of course, of living with 12 children. Spruce Manor without children would be a paradox. The summer waters are full of them, gamboling like dolphins. The lanes are alive with them, the yards overflow with them, they possess the tennis courts and the skating pond and the vacant lots. Their roller skates wear down the asphalt, and their bicycles make necessary the twenty-five-mile speed limit. They converse interminably on the telephones and make rich the dentist and the pediatrician. Who claims that a child and a half is the American middle-class average? A nice medium Spruce Manor family runs to four or five, and we count proudly, but not with amazement, the many solid households running to six, seven, eight, even up to twelve. Our houses here are big and not new, most of them, and there is a temptation to fill them up, let the décor fall where it may.

Besides, Spruce Manor seems designed by providence and town 13 planning for the happiness of children. Better designed than the city; better, I say defiantly, than the country. Country mothers must be constantly arranging and contriving for their children's leisure time. There is no neighbor child next door for playmate, no school within walking distance. The ponds are dangerous to young swimmers, the woods full of poison ivy, the romantic dirt roads unsuitable for bicycles. An extra acre or two gives a fine sense of possession to an adult; it does not compensate children for the give-and-take of our village, where there is always a contemporary to help swing the skipping rope or put on the catcher's mitt. Where in the country is the Friday evening dancing class or the Saturday morning movie (approved by the P.T.A.)? It is the greatest fallacy of all time that children love the country as a year-around plan. Children would take a dusty corner of Washington Square or a city sidewalk, even, in preference to the lonely sermons in stones and books in running brooks which their contemporaries cannot share.

As for the horrors of bringing up progeny in the city, for all its   14
museums and other cultural advantages (so perfectly within reach of suburban families if they feel strongly about it), they were summed up for me one day last winter. The harried mother of one, speaking to me on the telephone just after Christmas, sighed and said, "It's been a really wonderful time for me, as vacations go. Barbara has had an engagement with a child in our apartment house every afternoon this week. I have had to take her almost nowhere." Barbara is eleven. For six of those eleven years, I realized, her mother must have dreaded Christmas vacation, not to mention spring, as a time when Barbara had to be entertained. I thought thankfully of my own daughters whom I had scarcely seen since school closed, out with their skis and their sleds and their friends, sliding down the roped-off hill half a block away, coming in hungrily for lunch and disappearing again, hearty, amused, and safe—at least as safe as any sled-borne child can be.

Spruce Manor is not Eden, of course. Our taxes are higher than   15
we like, and there is always that eight-eleven in the morning to be caught, and we sometimes resent the necessity of rushing from a theater to a train on a weekday evening. But the taxes pay for our really excellent schools and for our garbage collections (so that the pails of orange peels need not stand in the halls overnight as ours did in the city) and for our water supply which does not give out every dry summer as it frequently does in the country. As for the theaters—they are twenty miles away and we don't get to them more than twice a month. But neither, I think, do many of our friends in town. The eight-eleven is rather a pleasant train, too, say the husbands; it gets them to work in thirty-four minutes and they read the papers restfully on the way.

"But the suburban mind!" cry our die-hard friends in Manhattan   16
and Connecticut. "The suburban conversation! The monotony!" They imply that they and I must scintillate or we perish. Let me anatomize Spruce Manor, for them and for the others who envision Suburbia as a congregation of mindless housewives and amoral go-getters.

From my window, now, on a June morning, I have a view. It   17
contains neither solitary hills nor dramatic skyscrapers. But I can see my roses in bloom, and my foxglove, and an arch of trees over the lane. I think comfortably of my friends whose houses line this and other streets rather like it. Not one of them is, so far

as I know, doing any of the things that suburban ladies are popularly supposed to be doing. One of them, I happen to know, has gone bowling for her health and figure, but she had already tidied up her house and arranged to be home before the boys return from school. Some, undoubtedly, are ferociously busy in the garden. One lady is on her way to Ellis Island, bearing comfort and gifts to a Polish boy—a seventeen-year-old stowaway who did slave labor in Germany and was liberated by a cousin of hers during the war—who is being held for attempting to attain the land of which her cousin told him. The boy has been on the Island for three months. Twice a week she takes this tedious journey, meanwhile besieging courts and immigration authorities on his behalf. This lady has a large house, a part-time maid, and five children.

My friend around the corner is finishing her third novel. She [18] writes daily from nine-thirty until two. After that her son comes back from school and she plunges into maternity; at six, she combs her pretty hair, refreshes her lipstick, and is charming to her doctor husband. The village dancing school is run by another neighbor, as it has been for twenty years. She has sent a number of ballerinas on to the theatrical world as well as having shepherded for many a successful season the white-gloved little boys and full-skirted little girls through their first social tasks.

Some of the ladies are no doubt painting their kitchens or a [19] nursery; one of them is painting the portrait, on assignment, of a very distinguished personage. Some of them are nurses' aides and Red Cross workers and supporters of good causes. But all find time to be friends with their families and to meet the 5:32 five nights a week. They read something besides the newest historical novel, Braque is not unidentifiable to most of them, and their conversation is for the most part as agreeable as the tables they set. The tireless bridge players, the gossips, the women bored by their husbands live perhaps in our suburb, too. Let them. Our orbits need not cross.

And what of the husbands, industriously selling bonds or practicing [20] law or editing magazines or looking through microscopes or managing offices in the city? Do they spend their evenings and their weekends in the gaudy bars of Fifty-second Street? Or are they the perennial householders, their lives a dreary round of taking down screens and mending drains? Well, screens they have always with them, and a man who is good around the house can spend happy hours with the plumbing even on a South Sea island. Some of them cut their own lawns and some of them try to break par and some of them sail their little boats all summer with their families for crew. Some of them are village trustees for nothing a year and some listen to symphonies and some think Milton Berle ought to be President. There is a scientist who plays wonderful bebop, and an insurance salesman who has bought a big old house nearby and with his own hands is gradually tearing it apart and reshaping it nearer to his heart's desire. Some of them are passionate hedge-clippers and some read Plutarch for fun. But I do not know many—though there may be such—who either kiss their neighbor's wives behind doors or whose idea of sprightly talk is to tell you the plot of an old movie.

It is June, now, as I have said. This afternoon my daughters 21 will come home from school with a crowd of their peers at their heels. They will eat up the cookies and drink up the ginger ale and go down for a swim at the beach if the water is warm enough, that beach which is only three blocks away and open to all Spruce Manor. They will go unattended by me, since they have been swimming since they were four, and besides there are lifeguards and no big waves. (Even our piece of ocean is a compromise.) Presently it will be time for us to climb into our very old Studebaker— we are not car-proud in Spruce Manor—and meet the 5:32. That evening expedition is not vitally necessary, for a bus runs straight down our principal avenue from the station to the shore, and it meets all trains. But it is an event we enjoy. There is something delightfully ritualistic about the moment when the train pulls in and the men swing off, with the less sophisticated children running squealing to meet them. The women move over from the driver's seat, surrender the keys, and receive an absent-minded kiss. It is the sort of picture that wakes John Marquand screaming from his sleep. But, deluded people that we are, we do not realize how mediocre it all seems. We will eat our undistinguished meal, probably without even a cocktail to enliven it. We will drink our coffee at the table, not carry it into the living room; if a husband changes for dinner here it is into old and spotty trousers and more comfortable shoes. The children will then go through the regular childhood routine—complain about their homework, grumble about going to bed, and finally accomplish both ordeals. Perhaps later the Gerard Joneses will drop in. We will talk a great deal of unimportant chatter and compare notes on food prices; we will also discuss the headlines and disagree. (Some of us in the Manor are Republicans, some are Democrats, a few lean plainly leftward. There are probably anti-Semites and anti-Catholics and even anti-Americans. Most of us are merely anti-antis.) We will all have one highball, and the Joneses will leave early. Tomorrow and tomorrow and tomorrow the pattern will be repeated. This is Suburbia.

But I think that some day people will look back on our little   22
interval here, on our Spruce Manor way of life, as we now look
back on the Currier and Ives kind of living, with nostalgia and
respect. In a world of terrible extremes, it will stand out as the
safe, important medium.

Suburbia, of thee I sing!   23

GARRETT HARDIN

The Tragedy of the Commons

At the end of a thoughtful article on the future of nuclear war,   1
Wiesner and York concluded that: "Both sides in the arms race
are . . . confronted by the dilemma of steadily increasing military
power and steadily decreasing national security. *It is our considered
professional judgment that this dilemma has no technical solution.* If
the great powers continue to look for solutions in the area of
science and technology only, the result will be to worsen the
situation."

I would like to focus your attention not on the subject of the   2
article (national security in a nuclear world) but on the kind of
conclusion they reached, namely that there is no technical solution
to the problem. An implicit and almost universal assumption of
discussions published in professional and semipopular scientific
journals is that the problem under discussion has a technical solution.
A technical solution may be defined as one that requires a change
only in the techniques of the natural sciences, demanding little or
nothing in the way of change in human values or ideas of morality.

In our day (though not in earlier times) technical solutions are   3
always welcome. Because of previous failures in prophecy, it takes
courage to assert that a desired technical solution is not possible.
Wiesner and York exhibited this courage; publishing in a science
journal, they insisted that the solution to the problem was not to
be found in the natural sciences. They cautiously qualified their
statement with the phrase, "It is our considered professional judgment. . . ." Whether they were right or not is not the concern of
the present article. Rather, the concern here is with the important
concept of a class of human problems which can be called "no

First published in *Science,* December 13, 1968.

technical solution problems," and, more specifically, with the identification and discussion of one of these.

It is easy to show that the class is not a null class. Recall the   4
game of tick-tack-toe. Consider the problem, "How can I win the
game of tick-tack-toe?" It is well known that I cannot, if I assume
(in keeping with the conventions of game theory) that my opponent
understands the game perfectly. Put another way, there is no
"technical solution" to the problem. I can win only by giving a
radical meaning to the word "win." I can hit my opponent over
the head; or I can drug him; or I can falsify the records. Every
way in which I "win" involves, in some sense, an abandonment
of the game, as we intuitively understand it. (I can also, of course,
openly abandon the game—refuse to play it. This is what most
adults do.)

The class of "No technical solution problems" has members.   5
My thesis is that the "population problem," as conventionally
conceived, is a member of this class. How it is conventionally
conceived needs some comment. It is fair to say that most people
who anguish over the population problem are trying to find a way
to avoid the evils of overpopulation without relinquishing any of
the privileges they now enjoy. They think that farming the seas
or developing new strains of wheat will solve the problem—technologically. I try to show here that the solution they seek cannot
be found. The population problem cannot be solved in a technical
way, any more than can the problem of winning the game of tick-
tack-toe.

WHAT SHALL WE MAXIMIZE?

Population, as Malthus[1] said, naturally tends to grow "geo-   6
metrically," or, as we would now say, exponentially. In a finite
world this means that the per capita share of the world's goods
must steadily decrease. Is ours a finite world?

A fair defense can be put forward for the view that the world   7
is infinite; or that we do not know that it is not. But, in terms of
the practical problems that we must face in the next few generations
with the foreseeable technology, it is clear that we will greatly
increase human misery if we do not, during the immediate future,
assume that the world available to the terrestrial human population
is finite. "Space" is no escape.

A finite world can support only a finite population; therefore,   8
population growth must eventually equal zero. (The case of perpetual
wide fluctuations above and below zero is a trivial variant that

---

1. English economist Thomas Malthus (1766–1834).

need not be discussed.) When this condition is met, what will be the situation of mankind? Specifically, can Bentham's[2] goal of "the greatest good for the greatest number" be realized?

No—for two reasons, each sufficient by itself. The first is a theoretical one. It is not mathematically possible to maximize for two (or more) variables at the same time. This was clearly stated by von Neumann and Morgenstern, but the principle is implicit in the theory of partial differential equations, dating back at least to D'Alembert (1717–1783). 9

The second reason springs directly from biological facts. To live, any organism must have a source of energy (for example, food). This energy is utilized for two purposes: mere maintenance and work. For man, maintenance of life requires about 1600 kilocalories a day ("maintenance calories"). Anything that he does over and above merely staying alive will be defined as work, and is supported by "work calories" which he takes in. Work calories are used not only for what we call work in common speech; they are also required for all forms of enjoyment, from swimming and automobile racing to playing music and writing poetry. If our goal is to maximize population it is obvious what we must do: We must make the work calories per person approach as close to zero as possible. No gourmet meals, no vacations, no sports, no music, no literature, no art. . . . I think that everyone will grant, without argument or proof, that maximizing population does not maximize goods. Bentham's goal is impossible. 10

In reaching this conclusion I have made the usual assumption that it is the acquisition of energy that is the problem. The appearance of atomic energy has led some to question this assumption. However, given an infinite source of energy, population growth still produces an inescapable problem. The problem of the acquisition of energy is replaced by the problem of its dissipation, as J. H. Fremlin has so wittily shown. The arithmetic signs in the analysis are, as it were, reversed; but Bentham's goal is still unobtainable. 11

The optimum population is, then, less than the maximum. The difficulty of defining the optimum is enormous; so far as I know, no one has seriously tackled this problem. Reaching an acceptable and stable solution will surely require more than one generation of hard analytical work—and much persuasion. 12

We want the maximum good per person; but what is good? To one person it is wilderness, to another it is ski lodges for thousands. To one it is estuaries to nourish ducks for hunters to shoot; to another it is factory land. Comparing one good with another is, 13

2. English philosopher Jeremy Bentham (1748–1832).

we usually say, impossible because goods are incommensurable. Incommensurables cannot be compared.

Theoretically this may be true; but in real life incommensurables 14 *are* commensurable. Only a criterion of judgment and a system of weighting are needed. In nature the criterion is survival. Is it better for a species to be small and hideable, or large and powerful? Natural selection commensurates the incommensurables. The compromise achieved depends on a natural weighting of the values of the variables.

Man must imitate this process. There is no doubt that in fact 15 he already does, but unconsciously. It is when the hidden decisions are made explicit that the arguments begin. The problem for the years ahead is to work out an acceptable theory of weighting. Synergistic effects, nonlinear variation, and difficulties in discounting the future make the intellectual problem difficult, but not (in principle) insoluble.

Has any cultural group solved this practical problem at the present 16 time, even on an intuitive level? One simple fact proves that none has: there is no prosperous population in the world today that has, and has had for some time, a growth rate of zero. Any people that has intuitively identified its optimum point will soon reach it, after which its growth rate becomes and remains zero.

Of course, a positive growth rate might be taken as evidence 17 that a population is below its optimum. However, by any reasonable standards, the most rapidly growing populations on earth today are (in general) the most miserable. This association (which need not be invariable) casts doubt on the optimistic assumption that the positive growth rate of a population is evidence that it has yet to reach its optimum.

We can make little progress in working toward optimum population size until we explicitly exorcize the spirit of Adam Smith 18 in the field of practical demography. In economic affairs, *The Wealth of Nations* (1776) popularized the "invisible hand," the idea that an individual who "intends only his own gain," is, as it were, "led by an invisible hand to promote . . . the public interest." Adam Smith did not assert that this was invariably true, and perhaps neither did any of his followers. But he contributed to a dominant tendency of thought that has ever since interfered with positive action based on rational analysis, namely, the tendency to assume that decisions reached individually will, in fact, be the best decisions for an entire society. If this assumption is correct it justifies the continuance of our present policy of laissez-faire in reproduction. If it is correct we can assume that men will control their individual fecundity so as to produce the optimum population.

If the assumption is not correct, we need to reexamine our individual freedoms to see which ones are defensible.

TRAGEDY OF FREEDOM IN A COMMONS

The rebuttal to the invisible hand in population control is to be ^{19} found in a scenario first sketched in a little-known pamphlet in 1833 by a mathematical amateur named William Forster Lloyd (1794–1852). We may well call it "the tragedy of the commons," using the word "tragedy" as the philosopher Whitehead used it: "The essence of dramatic tragedy is not unhappiness. It resides in the solemnity of the remorseless working of things." He then goes on to say, "This inevitableness of destiny can only be illustrated in terms of human life by incidents which in fact involve unhappiness. For it is only by them that the futility of escape can be made evident in the drama."

The tragedy of the commons develops in this way. Picture a ^{20} pasture open to all. It is to be expected that each herdsman will try to keep as many cattle as possible on the commons. Such an arrangement may work reasonably satisfactorily for centuries because tribal wars, poaching, and disease keep the numbers of both man and beast well below the carrying capacity of the land. Finally, however, comes the day of reckoning, that is, the day when the long-desired goal of social stability becomes a reality. At this point, the inherent logic of the commons remorselessly generates tragedy.

As a rational being, each herdsman seeks to maximize his gain. ^{21} Explicitly or implicitly, more or less consciously, he asks, "What is the utility *to me* of adding one more animal to my herd?" This utility has one negative and one positive component.

1. The positive component is a function of the increment of one ^{22} animal. Since the herdsman receives all the proceeds from the sale of the additional animal, the positive utility is nearly $+1$.

2. The negative component is a function of the additional over- ^{23} grazing created by one more animal. Since, however, the effects of overgrazing are shared by all the herdsmen, the negative utility for any particular decision-making herdsman is only a fraction of -1.

Adding together the component partial utilities, the rational ^{24} herdsman concludes that the only sensible course for him to pursue is to add another animal to his herd. And another; and another. . . . But this is the conclusion reached by each and every rational herdsman sharing a commons. Therein is the tragedy. Each man is locked into a system that compels him to increase his herd without limit—in a world that is limited. Ruin is the destination toward which all men rush, each pursuing his own best interest in a society that believes in the freedom of the commons. Freedom in a commons brings ruin to all.

Some would say that this is a platitude. Would that it were! In 25 a sense, it was learned thousands of years ago, but natural selection favors the forces of psychological denial. The individual benefits as an individual from his ability to deny the truth even though society as a whole, of which he is a part, suffers. Education can counteract the natural tendency to do the wrong thing, but the inexorable succession of generations requires that the basis for this knowledge be constantly refreshed.

A simple incident that occurred a few years ago in Leominster, 26 Massachusetts, shows how perishable the knowledge is. During the Christmas shopping season the parking meters downtown were covered with plastic bags that bore tags reading: "Do not open until after Christmas. Free parking courtesy of the mayor and city council." In other words, facing the prospect of an increased demand for already scarce space, the city fathers reinstituted the system of the commons. (Cynically, we suspect that they gained more votes than they lost by this retrogressive act.)

In an approximate way, the logic of the commons has been 27 understood for a long time, perhaps since the discovery of agriculture or the invention of private property in real estate. But it is understood mostly only in special cases which are not sufficiently generalized. Even at this late date, cattlemen leasing national land on the western ranges demonstrate no more than an ambivalent under-standing, in constantly pressuring federal authorities to increase the head count to the point where overgrazing produces erosion and weed-dominance. Likewise, the oceans of the world continue to suffer from the survival of the philosophy of the commons. Maritime nations still respond automatically to the shibboleth of the "freedom of the seas." Professing to believe in the "inexhaustible resources of the oceans," they bring species after species of fish and whales closer to extinction.

The national parks present another instance of the working out 28 of the tragedy of the commons. At present, they are open to all, without limit. The parks themselves are limited in extent—there is only one Yosemite Valley—whereas population seems to grow without limit. The values that visitors seek in the parks are steadily eroded. Plainly, we must soon cease to treat the parks as commons or they will be of no value to anyone.

What shall we do? We have several options. We might sell them 29 off as private property. We might keep them as public property, but allocate the right to enter them. The allocation might be on the basis of wealth, by the use of an auction system. It might be on the basis of merit, as defined by some agreed-upon standards. It might be by lottery. Or it might be on a first-come, first-served basis, administered to long queues. These, I think, are all the reasonable possibilities. They are all objectionable. But we must choose—or acquiesce in the destruction of the commons that we call our national parks.

POLLUTION

In a reverse way, the tragedy of the commons reappears in problems of pollution. Here it is not a question of taking something out of the commons, but of putting something in—sewage, or chemical, radioactive, and heat wastes into water; noxious and dangerous fumes into the air; and distracting and unpleasant advertising signs into the line of sight. The calculations of utility are much the same as before. The rational man finds that his share of the cost of the wastes he discharges into the commons is less than the cost of purifying his wastes before releasing them. Since this is true for everyone, we are locked into a system of "fouling our own nest," so long as we behave only as independent, rational, free-enterprisers. {30}

The tragedy of the commons as a food basket is averted by private property, or something formally like it. But the air and waters surrounding us cannot readily be fenced, and so the tragedy of the commons as a cesspool must be prevented by different means, by coercive laws or taxing devices that make it cheaper for the polluter to treat his pollutants than to discharge them untreated. We have not progressed as far with the solution of this problem as we have with the first. Indeed, our particular concept of private property, which deters us from exhausting the positive resources of the earth, favors pollution. The owner of a factory on the bank of a stream—whose property extends to the middle of the stream—often has difficulty seeing why it is not his natural right to muddy the waters flowing past his door. The law, always behind the times, requires elaborate stitching and fitting to adapt it to this newly perceived aspect of the commons. {31}

The pollution problem is a consequence of population. It did not much matter how a lonely American frontiersman disposed of his waste. "Flowing water purifies itself every ten miles," my grandfather used to say, and the myth was near enough to the truth when he was a boy, for there were not too many people. But as population became denser, the natural chemical and biological recycling processes became overloaded, calling for a redefinition of property rights. {32}

HOW TO LEGISLATE TEMPERANCE?

Analysis of the pollution problem as a function of population   33
density uncovers a not generally recognized principle of morality,
namely: *the morality of an act is a function of the state of the system
at the time it is performed.* Using the commons as a cesspool does
not harm the general public under frontier conditions, because
there is no public; the same behavior in a metropolis is unbearable.
A hundred and fifty years ago a plainsman could kill an American
bison, cut out only the tongue for his dinner, and discard the rest
of the animal. He was not in any important sense being wasteful.
Today, with only a few thousand bison left, we would be appalled
at such behavior.

In passing, it is worth noting that the morality of an act cannot   34
be determined from a photograph. One does not know whether
a man killing an elephant or setting fire to the grassland is harming
others until one knows the total system in which his act appears.
"One picture is worth a thousand words," said an ancient Chinese;
but it may take 10,000 words to validate it. It is as tempting to
ecologists as it is to reformers in general to try to persuade others
by way of the photographic shortcut. But the essence of an argument
cannot be photographed: it must be presented rationally—in words.

That morality is system-sensitive escaped the attention of most   35
codifiers of ethics in the past. "Thou shalt not . . ." is the form of
traditional ethical directives which make no allowance for particular
circumstances. The laws of our society follow the pattern of ancient
ethics, and therefore are poorly suited to governing a complex,
crowded, changeable world. Our epicyclic solution is to augment
statutory law with administrative law. Since it is practically impossible to spell out all the conditions under which it is safe to
burn trash in the back yard or to run an automobile without
smog-control, by law we delegate the details to bureaus. The result
is administrative law, which is rightly feared for an ancient reason—
Quis custodiet ipsos custodes?—"Who shall watch the watchers themselves?" John Adams said that we must have "a government of
laws and not men." Bureau administrators, trying to evaluate the
morality of acts in the total system, are singularly liable to corruption,
producing a government by men, not laws.

Prohibition is easy to legislate (though not necessarily to enforce);   36
but how do we legislate temperance? Experience indicates that it
can be accomplished best through the mediation of administrative
law. We limit possibilities unnecessarily if we suppose that the
sentiment of *Quis custodiet* denies us the use of administrative law.
We should rather retain the phrase as a perpetual reminder of
fearful dangers we cannot avoid. The great challenge facing us

now is to invent the corrective feedbacks that are needed to keep custodians honest. We must find ways to legitimate the needed authority of both the custodians and the corrective feedbacks.

FREEDOM TO BREED IS INTOLERABLE

The tragedy of the commons is involved in population problems 37 in another way. In a world governed solely by the principal of "dog eat dog"—if indeed there ever was such a world—how many children a family had would not be a matter of public concern. Parents who bred too exuberantly would leave fewer descendants, not more, because they would be unable to care adequately for their children. David Lack and others have found that such a negative feedback demonstrably controls the fecundity of birds. But men are not birds, and have not acted like them for millenniums, at least.

If each human family were dependent only on its own resources; 38 *if* the children of improvident parents starved to death; *if*, thus, overbreeding brought its own "punishment" to the germ line— *then* there would be no public interest in controlling the breeding of families. But our society is deeply committed to the welfare state, and hence is confronted with another aspect of the tragedy of the commons.

In a welfare state, how shall we deal with the family, the religion, 39 the race, or the class (or indeed any distinguishable and cohesive group) that adopts overbreeding as a policy to secure its own aggrandizement? To couple the concept of freedom to breed with the belief that everyone born has an equal right to the commons is to lock the world into a tragic course of action.

Unfortunately this is just the course of action that is being pursued 40 by the United Nations. In late 1967, some thirty nations agreed to the following:

> The Universal Declaration of Human Rights describes the family as the natural and fundamental unit of society. It follows that any choice and decision with regard to the size of the family must irrevocably rest with the family itself, and cannot be made by anyone else.

It is painful to have to deny categorically the validity of this 41 right; denying it, one feels as uncomfortable as a resident of Salem, Massachusetts, who denied the reality of witches in the seventeenth century. At the present time, in liberal quarters, something like a taboo acts to inhibit criticism of the United Nations. There is a feeling that the United Nations is "our last and best hope," that we shouldn't find fault with it; we shouldn't play into the hands of the archconservatives. However, let us not forget what Robert

Louis Stevenson said: "The truth that is suppressed by friends is the readiest weapon of the enemy." If we love the truth we must openly deny the validity of the Universal Declaration of Human Rights, even though it is promoted by the United Nations. We should also join with Kingsley Davis in attempting to get Planned Parenthood-World Population to see the error of its ways in embracing the same tragic ideal.

CONSCIENCE IS SELF-ELIMINATING

It is a mistake to think that we can control the breeding of 42 mankind in the long run by an appeal to conscience. Charles Galton Darwin made this point when he spoke on the centennial of the publication of his grandfather's great book. The argument is straight-forward and Darwinian.

People vary. Confronted with appeals to limit breeding, some 43 people will undoubtedly respond to the plea more than others. Those who have more children will produce a larger fraction of the next generation than those with more susceptible consciences. The difference will be accentuated, generation by generation.

In C. G. Darwin's words: "It may well be that it would take 44 hundreds of generations for the progenitive instinct to develop in this way, but if it should do so, nature would have taken her revenge, and the variety *Homo contracipiens* would become extinct and would be replaced by the variety *Homo progenitivus*."[3]

The argument assumes that conscience or the desire for children 45 (no matter which) is hereditary—but hereditary only in the most general formal sense. The result will be the same whether the attitude is transmitted through germ cells, or exosomatically, to use A. J. Lotka's term. (If one denies the latter possibility as well as the former, then what's the point of education?) The argument has here been stated in the context of the population problem, but it applies equally well to any instance in which society appeals to an individual exploiting a commons to restrain himself for the general good—by means of his conscience. To make such an appeal is to set up a selective system that works toward the elimination of conscience from the race.

PATHOGENIC EFFECTS OF CONSCIENCE

The long-term disadvantage of an appeal to conscience should 46 be enough to condemn it; but has serious short-term disadvantages as well. If we ask a man who is exploiting a commons to desist

3. Roughly, man the contraceptionist (preventer of birth) . . . man the founder (of a family).

"in the name of conscience," what are we saying to him? What does he hear?—not only at the moment but also in the wee small hours of the night when, half asleep, he remembers not merely the words we used but also the nonverbal communication cues we gave him unawares? Sooner or later, consciously or subconsciously, he senses that he has received two communications, and that they are contradictory: (i) (intended communication) "If you don't do as we ask, we will openly condemn you for not acting like a responsible citizen"; (ii) (the unintended communication) "If you *do* behave as we ask, we will secretly condemn you for a simpleton who can be shamed into standing aside while the rest of us exploit the commons."

Every man then is caught in what Bateson has called a "double 47 bind." Bateson and his coworkers have made a plausible case for viewing the double bind as an important causative factor in the genesis of schizophrenia. The double bind may not always be so damaging, but it always endangers the mental health of anyone to whom it is applied. "A bad conscience," said Nietzsche, "is a kind of illness."

To conjure up a conscience in others is tempting to anyone who 48 wishes to extend his control beyond the legal limits. Leaders at the highest level succumb to this temptation. Has any president during the past generation failed to call on labor unions to moderate voluntarily their demands for higher wages, or to steel companies to honor voluntary guidelines on prices? I can recall none. The rhetoric used on such occasions is designed to produce feelings of guilt in noncooperators.

For centuries it was assumed without proof that guilt was a 49 valuable, perhaps even an indispensable, ingredient of the civilized life. Now, in this post-Freudian world, we doubt it.

Paul Goodman speaks from the modern point of view when he 50 says: "No good has ever come from feeling guilty, neither intelligence, policy, nor compassion. The guilty do not pay attention to the object but only to themselves, and not even to their own interests, which might make sense, but to their anxieties."

One does not have to be a professional psychiatrist to see the 51 consequences of anxiety. We in the Western world are just emerging from a dreadful two-centuries-long Dark Ages of Eros that was sustained partly by prohibition laws, but perhaps more effectively by the anxiety-generating mechanism of education. Alex Comfort has told the story well in *The Anxiety Makers*; it is not a pretty one.

Since proof is difficult, we may even concede that the results 52 of anxiety may sometimes, from certain points of view, be desirable.

The larger question we should ask is whether, as a matter of policy, we should ever encourage the use of a technique the tendency (if not the intention) of which is psychologically pathogenic. We hear much talk these days of responsible parenthood; the coupled words are incorporated into the titles of some organizations devoted to birth control. Some people have proposed massive propaganda campaigns to instill responsibility into the nation's (or the world's) breeders. But what is the meaning of the word responsibility in this context? Is it not merely a synonym for the word conscience? When we use the word responsibility in the absence of substantial sanctions are we not trying to browbeat a free man in a commons into acting against his own interest? Responsibility is a verbal counterfeit for a substantial *quid pro quo.*[4] It is an attempt to get something for nothing.

If the word responsibility is to be used at all, I suggest that it   53
be in the sense Charles Frankel uses it. "Responsibility," says this philosopher, "is the product of definite social arrangements." Notice that Frankel calls for social arrangements—not propaganda.

MUTUAL COERCION MUTUALLY AGREED UPON

The social arrangements that produce responsibility are arrange-   54
ments that create coercion, of some sort. Consider bank-robbing. The man who takes money from a bank acts as if the bank were a commons. How do we prevent such action? Certainly not by trying to control his behavior solely by a verbal appeal to his sense of responsibility. Rather than rely on propaganda we follow Frankel's lead and insist that a bank is not a commons; we seek the definite social arrangements that will keep it from becoming a commons. That we thereby infringe on the freedom of would-be robbers we neither deny nor regret.

The morality of bank-robbing is particularly easy to understand   55
because we accept complete prohibition of this activity. We are willing to say "Thou shalt not rob banks," without providing for exceptions. But temperance also can be created by coercion. Taxing is a good coercive device. To keep downtown shoppers temperate in their use of parking space we introduce parking meters for short periods, and traffic fines for longer ones. We need not actually forbid a citizen to park as long as he wants to; we need merely make it increasingly expensive for him to do so. Not prohibition, but carefully biased options are what we offer him. A Madison Avenue man might call this persuasion; I prefer the greater candor of the word coercion.

Coercion is a dirty word to most liberals now, but it need not   56

4. An equal exchange.

forever be so. As with the four-letter words, its dirtiness can be cleansed away by exposure to the light, by saying it over and over without apology or embarrassment. To many, the word coercion implies arbitrary decisions of distant and irresponsible bureaucrats; but this is not a necessary part of its meaning. The only kind of coercion I recommend is mutual coercion, mutually agreed upon by the majority of the people affected.

To say that we mutually agree to coercion is not to say that we 57 are required to enjoy it, or even to pretend we enjoy it. Who enjoys taxes? We all grumble about them. But we accept compulsory taxes because we recognize that voluntary taxes would favor the conscienceless. We institute and (grumblingly) support taxes and other coercive devices to escape the horror of the commons.

An alternative to the commons need not be perfectly just to be 58 preferable. With real estate and other material goods, the alternative we have chosen is the institution of private property coupled with legal inheritance. Is this system perfectly just? As a genetically trained biologist I deny that it is. It seems to me that, if there are to be differences in individual inheritance, legal possession should be perfectly correlated with biological inheritance—that those who are biologically more fit to be the custodians of property and power should legally inherit more. But genetic recombination continually makes a mockery of the doctrine of "like father, like son" implicit in our laws of legal inheritance. An idiot can inherit millions, and a trust fund can keep his estate intact. We must admit that our legal system of private property plus inheritance is unjust—but we put up with it because we are not convinced, at the moment, that anyone has invented a better system. The alternative of the commons is too horrifying to contemplate. Injustice is preferable to total ruin.

It is one of the peculiarities of the warfare between reform and 59 the status quo that it is thoughtlessly governed by a double standard. Whenever a reform measure is proposed it is often defeated when its opponents triumphantly discover a flaw in it. As Kingsley Davis has pointed out, worshippers of the status quo sometimes imply that no reform is possible without unanimous agreement, an implication contrary to historical fact. As nearly as I can make out, automatic rejection of proposed reforms is based on one of two unconscious assumptions: (i) that the status quo is perfect; or (ii) that the choice we face is between reform and no action; if the proposed reform is imperfect, we presumably should take no action at all, while we wait for a perfect proposal.

But we can never do nothing. That which we have done for 60 thousands of years is also action. It also produces evils. Once we are aware that the status quo is action, we can then compare its discoverable advantages and disadvantages with the predicted advantages and disadvantages of the proposed reform, discounting as best we can for our lack of experience. On the basis of such a comparison, we can make a rational decision which will not involve the unworkable assumption that only perfect systems are tolerable.

RECOGNITION OF NECESSITY

Perhaps the simplest summary of this analysis of man's population problems is this: the commons, if justifiable at all, is justifiable only under conditions of low-population density. As the human population has increased, the commons has had to be abandoned in one aspect after another. 61

First we abandoned the commons in food gathering, enclosing farm land and restricting pastures and hunting and fishing areas. These restrictions are still not complete throughout the world. 62

Somewhat later we saw that the commons as a place for waste disposal would also have to be abandoned. Restrictions on the disposal of domestic sewage are widely accepted in the Western world; we are still struggling to close the commons to pollution by automobiles, factories, insecticide sprayers, fertilizing operations, and atomic energy installations. 63

In a still more embryonic state is our recognition of the evils of the commons in matters of pleasure. There is almost no restriction on the propagation of sound waves in the public medium. The shopping public is assaulted with mindless music, without its consent. Our government is paying out billions of dollars to create supersonic transport which will disturb 50,000 people for every one person who is whisked from coast to coast three hours faster. Advertisers muddy the airwaves of radio and television and pollute the view of travelers. We are a long way from outlawing the commons in matters of pleasure. Is this because our Puritan inheritance makes us view pleasure as something of a sin, and pain (that is, the pollution of advertising) as the sign of virtue? 64

Every new enclosure of the commons involves the infringement of somebody's personal liberty. Infringements made in the distant past are accepted because no contemporary complains of a loss. It is the newly proposed infringements that we vigorously oppose; cries of "rights" and "freedom" fill the air. But what does "freedom" mean? When men mutually agreed to pass laws against robbing, mankind became more free, not less so. Individuals locked into the logic of the commons are free only to bring on universal ruin; once they see the necessity of mutual coercion, they become free to pursue other goals. I believe it was Hegel who said, "Freedom is the recognition of necessity." 65

The most important aspect of necessity that we must now rec- 66
ognize, is the necessity of abandoning the commons in breeding.
No technical solution can rescue us from the misery of overpopulation. Freedom to breed will bring ruin to all. At the moment,
to avoid hard decisions many of us are tempted to propagandize
for conscience and responsible parenthood. The temptation must
be resisted, because an appeal to independently acting consciences
selects for the disappearance of all conscience in the long run, and
an increase in anxiety in the short.

The only way we can preserve and nurture other and more 67
precious freedoms is by relinquishing the freedom to breed, and
that very soon. "Freedom is the recognition of necessity"—and it
is the role of education to reveal to all the necessity of abandoning
the freedom to breed. Only so, can we put an end to this aspect
of the tragedy of the commons.

JOHN BERGER

An Independent Woman

Catherine seized each man to embrace him. Her long arms pulled 1
him towards her tall body. First Nicolas her brother, then Jean-
François the neighbour. She kissed them on both cheeks, near the
mouth. At seventy-four, she was just the eldest of the three.

"It's buried one metre deep," said Catherine, "I can hear Mathieu
telling me that. One metre deep."

"Where does it cross the field?" shouted Nicolas.

She shrugged her shoulders. "Fifty years is a long time, but I
remember him saying it was one metre deep."

Two months ago, when she was helping her brother bring in 5
his second hay, she had told him that the water to the *bassin*[1]
beside her house was no longer flowing. After that, she had refused
to mention the subject again. She was going to be dependent on
nobody. Yet now the expression in her eyes was excited as though
she had willed the two men to come.

"The spring must be at the top," said Jean-François and he
began to climb the field, disappearing into the fog.

From *Pig Earth* (1979).
1. Basin, reservoir.

"Jean-François," she cried out, "come back before I lose sight of you."

Born into another house Catherine would surely have married, but each year of her life more men had left the valley, and she herself had inherited too little to propose to any of them that they remain.

She seized hold of Jean-François by the arm. "You shouldn't have come to give up a whole day."

"We dig one metre deep, at right angles to the line. Begin at   10 the top and come down to the bottom. That way we're bound to arrive at the pipe."

"And the pipe will lead us to the spring! Jésus, Marie and Joseph! We'll have it by midday."

They began digging. Underneath the snow, the ground was still unfrozen.

When Catherine came from the house, carrying in a canvas bag glasses, a jug of hot wine and some bread and cheese, she heard the men before she could see them. At a distance of twenty metres the white fog merged into the white snow on the ground. Each time Jean-François bent his back to strike the pick into the earth, he grunted. And she heard Nicolas scraping his spade so the earth should not stick to it.

She had worked once as a waitress in a café near the Gare de Lyon in Paris. She and her brother Mathieu, the one who had laid the pipe and the one who was killed by the Germans during the Occupation, were the first members of the family ever to earn wages. And to do this they both went to Paris. He was a porter. She was a waitress. Her lasting impression of the capital was one of money continually changing hands. There, without money, you could literally do nothing. Not even drink water. With money you could do anything. He who could buy courage was brave, even if he was a coward.

The two men had dug the trench exactly one metre deep. From   15 time to time they had measured it. It was straight and impeccably cut and cleaned out. On one side was stacked the turf; on the other, the earth. All the stones lifted out were piled in a heap together.

Nicolas scrambled out of the trench and Jean-François plunged his spade into the loose soil, as if in the hope that it would disappear into the centre of the earth. Living by himself in the corner under the mountain, he had the habit of making violent movements; in his solitude such violence was a kind of company. Catherine poured out the hot wine. The men kept the glasses up to their faces between sips, their noses in the steam which smelt of cloves and cinnamon.

"In God's name it must be here," Nicolas grumbled.

"I tell you if it's not in this field, there's no fire in hell."

During the second half of the day Nicolas continued the long trench already begun. Jean-François dug another higher up. And Catherine started digging a third near the pair of apple trees. When she had cut the turf, she kicked the snow off before lifting the pieces up. She disliked having cold hands or feet. At night she took three hot bricks to bed with her, one for each foot and one for the small of her back. As she swung the pick the breath came out of her with a whistle, quite unlike Jean-François' grunt.

After working in the restaurant by the Gare de Lyon she became   20
a maid in a doctor's house. The doctor worked at the hospital of St Antonine and lived a few streets away in the rue Charles V. Her principal jobs were cleaning grates, washing floors and laundering. The first time she laundered, she had asked the cook where the wood ash was kept. "Wood ash!" repeated the cook, incredulous. "To clean the sheets," explained Catherine. The cook told her to go back to her goat shit. It was the first time Catherine heard the word *peasant* used as an insult.

They dug until the fog absorbed the dusk.

Jean-François looked down at his trench which was now a good fifteen metres long.

"Not quite wide enough for a coffin."

"We are all of us thin," said Catherine.   25

"Three graves, one for each of us."

"A grave for each of us!" roared Nicolas.

When she returned from Paris, Catherine had found her sister-in-law dying of puerperal fever. During the next fifteen years she brought up her two nieces like daughters.

Jean-François abruptly picked up a stone and threw it up the field into the dark.

Catherine began hustling the two men towards the house. Outside the kitchen door she placed a bowl of heated water for them to wash in. She took hold of Jean-François' wrists and placed his hands in the water. Then she draped a towel round his neck.

The last time the three of them had sat round the table in the   30
kitchen was when she believed she might die. The doctor said it was pleurisy. She refused to go to hospital. If she was going to die, she wanted death to pass by the things she knew. Her two rooms were bare, there was neither armchair nor carpets nor curtains. But there were certain objects which were intimate to

her: her yellow coffee-pot, the stove which she kept as shiny as a groomed black horse, her high bed, the picture of the Madonna above it, her work-basket. Death must run the gauntlet of these. Each night she laid out her linen and stockings before climbing into the bed, so that Nicolas should know exactly how to dress her for the coffin.

One night when he came to the house, Nicolas noticed the linen laid out.

"What's that for?"

"To dress me in the morning if I shut my umbrella in the night." She spoke in a hoarse whisper.

At that moment there was a scuffling noise against the door and a voice had intoned, like a lament:

"Four wild boar! I've seen them with my own eyes, charging down the hill!"

Jean-François had stumbled in, clutching a rifle. Drunk, he came   35
up to the bed.

"Catherine, what will we do without you? They tell me you are very sick."

"Is the gun loaded?" she whispered.

He handed it to her and she took out the cartridges.

When she was working at the doctor's house, she had received   40
the letter from Mathieu saying that his wife was ill and that she must return immediately. By leaving so abruptly she lost two months' wages. She protested to the doctor's wife that nobody could foresee illness. For illness there are hospitals, was the reply. Catherine picked up one of the pokers she had polished every morning. The doctor's wife screamed for help. The cook came running to the rescue. She found the mistress of the house clutching the curtains as if she had been surprised naked. And the mad Savoyard maid was standing with a poker in her hand looking at the fire.

"Tomorrow," Jean-François said, "we'll come and cup you. Eh, Nicolas?"

"I might be better off on the other side," she said.

"Seigneur!" screamed her brother. "Stop talking like that. We're coming tomorrow."

When they came, the two men stuffed the stove with wood. She stripped naked to the waist and sat on a chair. "It's not the first time you've seen a woman," she said to Jean-François.

"What difference does that make?" demanded Nicolas. "We're   45
going to cure you."

On the table was a set of glasses with a candle. Jean-François lit the candle, wiped a glass, tore a shred of newspaper, put it in the candle flame and when it was burning, placed it in the glass. Nicolas pressed the rim of the glass hard against his sister's back. Almost immediately the flame went out. The skin beneath her shoulder-blade was white and soft, not very different from when she was a young woman. Tentatively, Nicolas' large hand abandoned the glass to see whether the vacuum would hold it against the flesh. Glass and flesh stayed firm.

Jean-François prepared the fire in a second glass.

"Put it," he said, "where there's plenty of meat."

"Never on the vertebral column," proclaimed Nicolas.

"I said where there's meat!"   50

They applied five glasses. Her skin rose up inside them like pies in an oven. She held the table with her arms to steady herself against the hurt.

"I don't want you to hear me cry out."

"I'll sing," offered Nicolas.

He sang:

> La vie est une rose
> La rose piquera . . .[2]

When it came to removing the glasses, Jean-François did it   55
because Nicolas' nails were too broken. He ran his finger-nail round the rim of the glass, making a tiny trench in the flesh, to let the air in.

"Ah," she sighed, as each glass came off. "Thank you, my friend!" Two days later she was cured.

Now together in the same kitchen the three of them were dispirited by the day's work which had yielded nothing.

"They have a machine," mused Jean-François, "for detecting water underground, like a water diviner's stick, only it's electronic. And it finds where water is to twenty centimetres."

"Where?" asked Catherine, on the edge of her chair.

"It costs seventy thousand francs to hire."   60

"Merde de merde!" said Catherine.

Next morning the three of them surveyed the three trenches. During the night, as if encouraged by their digging, moles had thrown up their own earthworks over most of the field. This made all the digging look less systematic.

"In this earth," roared Nicolas—and between each phrase he struck with his pick—"in this damned earth of this damned field in this damned fog I have a rendez-vous with the Devil!"

---

2. "Life is a rose/The rose will prick."

By the afternoon they had still not found any sign of any pipe. Occasionally in the kitchen Catherine heard one of their raised voices. She could not distinguish the words but the tone of the shouting was enough to tell her how discouraged they must be. "If they don't find it today, they won't come back tomorrow."

She put more wood on the stove, took her slippers out of the oven and shut the oven door. "I have wasted two of their days," she muttered. She set about preparing some pastry. When it was rolled out, she made small pastry purses, each large enough to hold a five-franc piece. Into the purses she put purée of apples. She made twenty-five.

She packed the pastries with the coffee-pot, *gnôle* and cups into her canvas bag, and strode across the orchard. Before the men became visible through the fog she stopped and adjusted the scarf tied round her head. She held out the bowl of sugar so that each man could sugar his coffee to his taste. She herself poured the *eau-de-vie*[3] plentifully into their cups. The men held them with both hands and gazed around them into the fog.

"Mathieu!" muttered Nicolas. "Mathieu was cunning. He could have laid this pipe at a depth of eighty centimetres and it would still have been safe from the hardest frost. But no! Not Mathieu. He had to lay it at a metre!"

"The moles have eaten the pipe."

"The pipe has gone to La Roche, I tell you!"

Corner by corner, she unfolded the napkin wrapped round the pastries. Baked a light brown, they steamed in the air. The smell made the two men glance at each other and smile with complicity.

"We used to eat them after midnight mass at Christmas," said Nicolas quietly.

"The blood's coming back," said Jean-François.

Between mouthfuls of coffee, they ate them one by one.

When they were finished, Catherine issued her command: "No more work today."

The two men put on their coats and, by an accord of common tact, nobody mentioned tomorrow.

She woke up when it was still dark. She did not expect the men to return for a third day's work. After she had fed the goats and cleaned the stable, the sky was as blue and large as it only is over the mountains. In the valley, through the transparent early-morning mist were church, dairy, cemetery, two cafés, post office: the village. The worst about real fog is that it hangs square like

3. Referring to the *gnôle* above: brandy.

a curtain. Vertical and horizontal. The best about it lifting is that all the slopes are revealed and everything is precipitous.

She went to fetch her water, downhill, across two fields. She had done this ever since the water had dried up. All her father's life and grandfather's life the sound of water had marked the place below where it was easy to fill buckets.

What she feared was the ice. The ice would soon be back. The pine trees, only one hundred metres higher up towards La Roche, were white with hoar-frost, not a needle, not a spider's web had escaped its white load. She feared that when the slope was frozen with ice, she might slip as she carried the buckets, and break a leg, and lie there all day without being found.

"On the other side I'd have no goats to look after, no potatoes to lift, no chickens to feed. I would have all the time in the world, and I could make all the visits I don't make now. Yet I don't want to die out of the house. I want to see death come past the things I've lived with. Then I can concentrate and not be distracted."

In the clear air which no longer muffled sounds, she heard   80
Jean-François' voice, high up, in the field by the orchard.

"I tell you where it is! Here! Here is where I am betting it is! You'll see. I thought about it in the night. This is where it is. Within half a metre of here!"

Leaving the two buckets, she clambered up, shouting, "I don't believe it!"

They did not begin digging where Jean-François had driven in his spade to mark his bet. They systematically extended the long trench which would eventually come to the point he had indicated.

After two hours, Nicolas said: "The earth has been worked here. Fifty years ago maybe, but the earth has been worked here."

The only sign of his impatience was that he wielded the pick   85
with shorter pauses.

"I told you so!"

He pointed, at the bottom of the trench, to a reddish mark in the earth, the size of a small flower.

"Rust!"

"Rust!"

"Catherine!"

The three of them looked down at the pipe at the bottom of   90
the trench.

"It's in perfect condition."

"It's a well-turned pipe."

Jean-François jumped down and scratched at it with his knife.

"The metal is shiny underneath."   95

"I knew it when we saw the rust."

"It was there all the time," shouted Nicolas.

"The pipe under the field was there all the time."

"Exactly one metre down. Measure it."

Jean-François measured it.   100

"Exactly one metre."

"All we do now is to follow it."

"The spring should be here."

They stood looking down at the coarse grass.

"We'd have found it yesterday if we'd gone on," Nicolas shouted.   105
He surveyed everything: the snow peaks, the rock-faces, the white
forest, the ledges of land, the valley. "You'd have found it, Catherine,
if you'd dug another two metres by the apple trees." He gazed
up at the spaceless blue sky. "I'd have found it if I'd dug upwards
instead of downwards! And Jean-François found it where he said
he would!"

Impatiently Catherine started cutting the turf. The two men
ambled away, opened their trousers and pissed.

They unearthed the reservoir after half an hour's further digging.

"It's a huge stone," announced Jean-François, "it must be two
metres wide, the lid."

Nicolas peered at the flat stone being uncovered. "Where could
he have found a stone like that. From La Roche!"

"We'll need crowbars to prise it off."   110

"Is it all one stone?"

"He placed it well, he knew how to place it, did Mathieu. I
told you he was cunning."

"It's going to weigh a ton!"

"How did he get it here?"

"It's huge."   115

"As huge as a tomb."

"It's Jésus' tomb!"

"Jésus' tomb," repeated Catherine.

Jean-François scraped at the stone, his unshaven face almost
touching it.

"We've got to roll it away."   120

Catherine went to fetch what bars she could find in the stable.
They forced in two to steady it, and they used one to prise with.
The flat stone did not shift. All three strained to use all their weight.

"Jésus' . . . tomb!"

"We're opening it."

"Op—en—ing!"

"Up!"   125

"Up!"

"What's inside?"

Jean-François peered through the narrow space under the prised-up flat stone.

"Shit!"

"He says Jésus' tomb is full of shit!"   130

"Fifty years of shit!" said Catherine.

"Slide it now."

"Gently."

"There!"

In the great current of their triple laughter, words they had   135
already used surfaced, turned and eddied, disappeared, reappeared
and were carried on, submerged by the laughter.

—Jésus, Marie and Joseph!—

—Mathieu knew what he was doing!—

—It was easy for him.—

—It's big enough to dip a sheep in.—

—The tomb of Jésus, that's what it is.—   140

They plunged in their arms up to their armpits, to find where
the outlet pipe was. Their arms came out black. With a bucket
they began emptying out the sediment, until the water no longer
overspilled.

"Run to the *bassin,* Catherine, and see if it's coming."

"It's coming," she screamed. "It's coming out brown like coffee."

The sun had set before they stopped dredging.

The men carried the tools to the house. Close against the wall,   145
in the shelter of the eaves, water gushed out of the mouth of the
pipe. As it fell, it became tangled and silver.

Inside the kitchen it was warm. Catherine strode around the
room, particularly between stove and table, serving.

"Sit down, woman!"

"I never expected you to come today," she said.

"Tonight it's going to freeze."

"The water from the spring will never freeze," she said.   150

"Today is the last day we could have dug."

"This morning I never said you'd both come."

"Catherine, you have always expected too little," Jean-François
announced.

"Listen a moment!" roared Nicolas.

The three of them placed their knives on the table and through   155
the window they listened to the frivolous sound of the running
water.

Thinking About Community

There is no such thing as an independent ant. The caste distinctions in the colony are so strict that the specialists in reproduction—the blimp-like queens and feeble males—would perish without the aid of the female workers and soldiers. But there is more to it than caste. Take a worker out of the nest and put her in a separate jar with food and water and dirt to dig in. Sheer loneliness will make her disorganized and lazy. Her productivity (measured in volume of dirt moved) will drop to a fraction of what it had been. Whether kept alone or with half a dozen others, she will pine for the bustle of the colony and will die prematurely. The absolute dependence of its citizens has made ant society notoriously totalitarian. When T. H. White devised a slogan for the ant colony in *The Once and Future King,* it was, "Everything not forbidden is compulsory." Actually, this translation is far too sophisticated: the only adjectives in his ant language are "done" and "not-done."

It is surprising how like an anthill human society seems when it is described by the ancient Greek political theorists. Plato divides citizens into three castes—statesmen, soldiers, and citizens—and gives the statesmen control of the other two. Citizens of every caste exist to serve the state. They march down the narrow path of duty, looking neither right nor left for private pleasure. Aristotle is, by comparison, a libertarian. He believes that the state exists for the individual, to give each person a place to find happiness and to exercise the intellectual and moral virtues. Still, the anthill reasserts itself. There is, in Aristotle's view, no such thing as an independent human. "Man," he says, "is a political animal"; that is, a creature designed to live in the *polis,* the city-state. "The person who by nature, not accident, does not belong to a polis is either a wild animal or a god."

Aristotle's views may have sounded like truisms to his students, prosperous young men living in Athens at the height of its civilization. They fall differently on American or Canadian ears. We are inheritors of a frontier culture that values rugged individualism. Our picture of human virtue includes the isolated homesteader, quite self-sufficient and largely self-educated, capable of becoming, if necessary, the soldier, worker, and statesman all at once. One wonders what Aristotle or Plato would have said about Abraham Lincoln.

We know, in effect, what Lincoln had to say about them. They were comfortable with the fact that some people were destined "from birth onward" to rule others, and specifically that some people were born to be slaves, "living tools." Lincoln, who was accustomed to use his own hands in menial chores as well as affairs of state, would accept no such arrangement: "No man is good enough to govern another man without that other's consent." Plato habitually turned an ethical question outward, examining how it will affect the polis. Lincoln habitually turned even public policy inward: "I desire so to conduct the affairs of this administration that if at the end, when I come to lay down the reins of power, I have lost every other friend on earth, I shall have at least one friend left, and that friend shall be down inside me."

There are in this section several essays that reject the ant heap and encourage the self-sufficient individual. Henry David Thoreau's "Civil Disobedience" may be the most influential of these; it traveled to India to help shape Gandhi's nonviolent resistance movement and returned to America to inspire the Civil Rights movement so closely associated with another of our writers, Martin Luther King, Jr. Another admirer of Thoreau, E.M. Forster, writing at a time when fascism was rising in Europe, gives democracy two cheers because it allows the development of private virtues and keeps open "a few breathing holes for the human spirit." But the section is not a soapbox for individualism. Kitto's essay on the polis presents the Greek ideal of a public life as something richer than modern individualism can produce. Plato's "Crito" shows how heroic the individual's dedication to his society can be. H.L. Mencken, in an essay convoluted by irony, upbraids "specialists in human liberty" who keep the police from doing their work of making society safe, and Garrett Hardin argues that unchecked individualism is pushing the community inexorably toward ruin.

How one perceives the balance between individual liberty and community responsibility depends, in large measure, on the sort of community one knows. Our four remaining selections examine four remarkably different places. A French peasant community is the setting for John Berger's story, the wide-open spaces for Gretel Ehrlich's tribute to Wyoming, the comfortable suburbs for Phyllis McGinley's defense of middle-class living. In Jane Jacobs's essay we find ourselves in streets where strangers throng like ants, or like dancers in the city's "intricate ballet."

QUESTIONS

1. According to H.D.F. Kitto, the Greeks thought the ideal population for a polis was 50,000 to 200,000 (including noncitizens). What seems to you to be an ideal size for a modern community? What

differences in the conditions of our social life might make our ideal community larger or smaller than the Greeks'?

2. What factors other than size are important to your conception of an ideal community? How are these factors related to the balance of individual happiness and civic responsibility?

3. Most of us have had experiences that changed our views of the balance between the interests of the community and the individual. Describe such an experience and the corresponding change. Did the change bring your thinking into sympathy with any of the writers presented here?

4. Discuss a situation in which you have faced a fairly clear choice between personal and social values. How did you resolve the conflict? Was your choice more like Plato's or Forster's? Was it right?

5. The family, as political philosophers seem always to be pointing out, is a little state. What sort of state is your family? Is it totalitarian or democratic? How do you think the politics of family life have shaped your thinking about politics in the larger community?

6. H.D.F. Kitto argues that modern nations are too large to inspire the sort of patriotism that the Greeks felt for their *poleis*. Does this seem to you to be true? Is there a political unit today larger than the family but smaller than the nation that inspires loyalty as the Greek polis did?

7. Martin Luther King, Jr., says that it is right to obey just laws and wrong to obey unjust laws. What objections would Plato, H.L. Mencken, and Garrett Hardin have to this philosophy? Do you object to it?

MORTALITY

JEREMY TAYLOR

Holy Dying

A man is a bubble, said the Greek proverb; which Lucian rep- 1
resents with advantages and its proper circumstances, to this purpose;
saying, that all the world is a storm, and men rise up in their
several generations like bubbles descending *à Jove pluvio*, from
God and the dew of heaven, from a tear and drop of man, from
nature and Providence: and some of these instantly sink into the
deluge of their first parent and are hidden in a sheet of water,
having had no other business in the world but to be born that
they might be able to die; others float up and down two or three
turns and suddenly disappear and give their place to others; and
they that live longest upon the face of the waters are in perpetual
motion, restless and uneasy, and being crushed with the great
drop of a cloud sink into flatness and a froth; the change not
being great, it being hardly possible it should be more a nothing
than it was before. So is every man: he is born in vanity and sin;
he comes into the world like morning mushrooms, soon thrusting
up their heads into the air and conversing with their kindred of
the same production, and as soon they turn into dust and forgetfulness; some of them without any other interest in the affairs
of the world but that they made their parents a little glad, and
very sorrowful; others ride longer in the storm; it may be until
seven years of vanity be expired, and then peradventure the sun
shines hot upon their heads and they fall into the shades below,
into the cover of death and darkness of the grave to hide them.
But if the bubble stands the shock of a bigger drop, and outlives
the chances of a child, of a careless nurse, of drowning in a pail
of water, of being overlaid by a sleepy servant, or such little
accidents, then the young man dances like a bubble, empty and
gay, and shines like a dove's neck, or the image of a rainbow,
which hath no substance, and whose very imagery and colors are
fantastical; and so he dances out the gaiety of his youth, and is
all the while in a storm, and endures only because he is not
knocked on the head by a drop of bigger rain, or crushed by the
pressure of a load of indigested meat, or quenched by the disorder

From *The Rule and Exercises of Holy Dying*, 1651.

of an ill-placed humor:[1] and to preserve a man alive in the midst of so many chances and hostilities is as great a miracle as to create him; to preserve him from rushing into nothing, and at first to draw him up from nothing were equally the issues of an Almighty power. And therefore the wise men of the world have contended who shall best fit man's condition with words signifying his vanity and short abode. Homer calls a man "a leaf," the smallest, the weakest piece of a short-lived, unsteady plant: Pindar calls him "the dream of a shadow": another, "the dream of the shadow of smoke": but St. James spake by a more excellent spirit, saying, "our life is but a vapor," viz., drawn from the earth by a celestial influence; made of smoke, or the lighter parts of water, tossed with every wind, moved by the motion of a superior body, without virtue in itself, lifted up on high or left below, according as it pleases the sun its foster-father. But it is lighter yet. It is but "appearing"; a fantastic vapor, an apparition, nothing real; it is not so much as a mist, not the matter of a shower, nor substantial enough to make a cloud; but it is like Cassiopeia's chair, or Pelops' shoulder, or the circles of heaven, φαινόμενα,[2] than which you cannot have a word that can signify a verier nothing. And yet the expression is one degree more made diminutive: a "vapor," and "fantastical," or a "mere appearance," and this but for a little while neither; the very dream, the phantasm disappears in a small time, "like the shadow that departeth"; or "like a tale that is told"; or "as a dream when one awaketh." A man is so vain, so unfixed, so perishing a creature, that he cannot long last in the scene of fancy: a man goes off, and is forgotten, like the dream of a distracted person. The sum of all is this: that thou art a man, than whom there is not in the world any greater instance of heights and declensions, of lights and shadows, of misery and folly, of laughter and tears, of groans and death.

And because this consideration is of great usefulness and great necessity to many purposes of wisdom and the spirit; all the succession of time, all the changes in nature, all the varieties of light and darkness, the thousand thousands of accidents in the world, and every contingency to every man, and to every creature, does preach our funeral sermon, and calls us to look, and see how the

2

1. In seventeenth-century medical theory, health depended on the proper balance and distribution of the four humors, or fluids, of the body: black bile, blood, phlegm, and yellow bile.
2. "Apparent." The reference is to the celestial spheres supposed, in the discredited Ptolemaic system, to hold the stars and planets in their orbits around the earth.

old sexton Time throws up the earth, and digs a grave where we must lay our sins or our sorrows, and sow our bodies till they rise again in a fair, or in an intolerable eternity. Every revolution which the sun makes about the world divides between life and death; and death possesses both those portions by the next morrow; and we are dead to all those months which we have already lived, and we shall never live them over again: and still God makes little periods of our age. First, we change our world, when we come from the womb to feel the warmth of the sun. Then we sleep and enter into the image of death, in which state we are unconcerned in all the changes of the world: and if our mothers or our nurses die, or a wild boar destroy our vineyards, or our king be sick, we regard it not, but during that state are as disinterested as if our eyes were closed with the clay that weeps in the bowels of the earth. At the end of seven years our teeth fall and die before us, representing a formal prologue to the tragedy; and still every seven years it is odds but we shall finish the last scene: and when nature, or chance, or vice, takes our body in pieces, weakening some parts and loosing others, we taste the grave and the solemnities of our own funerals, first, in those parts that ministered to vice, and next in them that served for ornament, and in a short time even they that served for necessity become useless, and entangled like the wheels of a broken clock. Baldness is but a dressing to our funerals, the proper ornament of mourning, and of a person entered very far into the regions and possession of death: and we have many more of the same signification: gray hairs, rotten teeth, dim eyes, trembling joints, short breath, stiff limbs, wrinkled skin, short memory, decayed appetite. Every day's necessity calls for a reparation of that portion which death fed on all night, when we lay in his lap and slept in his outer chambers. The very spirits of a man prey upon the daily portion of bread and flesh, and every meal is a rescue from one death and lays up for another; and while we think a thought, we die; and the clock strikes, and reckons on our portion of eternity: we form our words with the breath of our nostrils, we have the less to live upon for every word we speak.

Thus nature calls us to meditate of death by those things which are the instruments of acting it; and God by all the variety of his providence makes us see death everywhere, in all variety of circumstances, and dressed up for all the fancies and the expectation of every single person. Nature hath given us one harvest every year, but death hath two: and the spring and the autumn send throngs of men and women to charnel-houses; and all the summer long men are recovering from their evils of the spring, till the dog-days come, and then the Sirian star makes the summer deadly;[3] and the fruits of autumn are laid up for all the year's provision, and the man that gathers them eats and surfeits, and dies and needs them not, and himself is laid up for eternity; and he that escapes till winter only stays for another opportunity, which the distempers of that quarter minister to him with great variety. Thus death reigns in all the portions of our time. The autumn with its fruits provides disorders for us, and the winter's cold turns them into sharp diseases, and the spring brings flowers to strew our hearse, and the summer gives green turf and brambles to bind upon our graves. Calentures[4] and surfeit, cold and agues, are the four quarters of the year, and all minister to death; and you can go no whither but you tread upon a dead man's bones.

The wild fellow in Petronius that escaped upon a broken table [4] from the furies of a shipwreck, as he was sunning himself upon the rocky shore, espied a man rolled upon his floating bed of waves, ballasted with sand in the folds of his garment and carried by his civil enemy, the sea, towards the shore to find a grave, and it cast him into some sad thoughts: that peradventure this man's wife in some part of the Continent, safe and warm, looks next month for the good man's return; or, it may be, his son knows nothing of the tempest; or his father thinks of that affectionate kiss, which still is warm upon the good old man's cheek ever since he took a kind farewell; and he weeps with joy to think how blessed he shall be when his beloved boy returns into the circle of his father's arms. These are the thoughts of mortals, this is the end and the sum of all their designs: a dark night and an ill guide, a boisterous sea and a broken cable, a hard rock and a rough wind, dashed in pieces the fortune of a whole family, and they that shall weep loudest for the accident are not yet entered into the storm, and yet have suffered shipwreck. Then looking upon the carcass, he knew it, and found it to be the master of the ship, who the day before cast up the accounts of his patrimony and his trade, and named the day when he thought to be at home: see how the man swims who was so angry two days since; his passions are becalmed with the storm, his accounts cast up, his cares at an end, his voyage done, and his gains are the strange events of death, which whether they be good or evil, the men

---

3. The rise of Sirius, the Dog Star, has been popularly associated since Roman times with the famine and disease of the Dog Days of summer.
4. Fevers brought on by heat.

that are alive seldom trouble themselves concerning the interest of the dead.

But seas alone do not break our vessel in pieces: everywhere we may be shipwrecked. A valiant general, when he is to reap the harvest of his crowns and triumphs, fights unprosperously, or falls into a fever with joy and wine, and changes his laurel into cypress, his triumphal chariot to a hearse; dying the night before he was appointed to perish in the drunkenness of his festival joys. It was a sad arrest of the loosenesses and wilder feasts of the French court, when their king Henry the Second was killed really by the sportive image of a fight.[5] And many brides have died under the hands of paranymphs[6] and maidens, dressing them for uneasy joy, the new and undiscerned chains of marriage: according to the sayings of Bensirah, the wise Jew, "The bride went into her chamber, and knew not what should befall her there." Some have been paying their vows, and giving thanks for a prosperous return to their own house, and the roof hath descended upon their heads and turned their loud religion into the deeper silence of a grave. And how many teeming mothers have rejoiced over their swelling wombs, and pleased themselves in becoming the channels of blessing to a family; and the mid-wife hath quickly bound their heads and feet, and carried them forth to burial! Or else the birthday of an heir hath seen the coffin of the father brought into the house, and the divided mother hath been forced to travail twice, with a painful birth, and a sadder death.

There is no state, no accident, no circumstance of our life, but it hath been soured by some sad instance of a dying friend: a friendly meeting often ends in some sad mischance and makes an eternal parting: and when the poet Æschylus was sitting under the walls of his house, an eagle hovering over his bald head mistook it for a stone, and let fall his oyster, hoping there to break the shell, but pierced the poor man's skull.

Death meets us everywhere, and is procured by every instrument and in all chances, and enters in at many doors: by violence and secret influence, by the aspect of a star and the stink of a mist, by the emissions of a cloud and the meeting of a vapor, by the fall of a chariot and the stumbling at a stone, by a full meal or an empty stomach, by watching at the wine or by watching at prayers, by the sun or the moon, by a heat or a cold, by sleepless nights or sleeping days, by water frozen into the hardness and sharpness of a dagger, or water thawed into the floods of a river,

---

5. He was killed in a jousting match.
6. Bridesmaids.

by a hair or a raisin, by violent motion or sitting still, by severity or dissolution, by God's mercy or God's anger; by everything in providence and everything in manners, by everything in nature and everything in chance; we take pains to heap up things useful to our life, and get our death in the purchase; and the person is snatched away, and the goods remain. And all this is the law and constitution of nature; it is a punishment to our sins, the unalterable event of providence and the decree of heaven. The chains that confine us to this condition are strong as destiny, and immutable as the eternal laws of God.

I have conversed with some men who rejoiced in the death or   8 calamity upon others, and accounted it as a judgment upon them for being on the other side, and against them in the contention; but within the revolution of a few months, the same man met with a more uneasy and unhandsome death: which when I saw, I wept, and was afraid; for I knew that it must be so with all men; for we also shall die, and end our quarrels and contentions by passing to a final sentence.

ROBERT LOUIS STEVENSON

Aes Triplex

The changes wrought by death are in themselves so sharp and   1 final, and so terrible and melancholy in their consequences, that the thing stands alone in man's experience, and has no parallel upon earth. It outdoes all other accidents because it is the last of them. Sometimes it leaps suddenly upon its victims like a Thug;[1] sometimes it lays a regular siege and creeps upon their citadel during a score of years. And when the business is done, there is sore havoc made in other people's lives, and a pin knocked out by which many subsidiary friendships hung together. There are empty chairs, solitary walks, and single beds at night. Again, in taking away our friends, death does not take them away utterly,

---

From *Virginibus Pueresque* (1881). The title refers to Horace's ode depicting the dangers of a sea voyage. The first sailor, says the poet, must have wrapped himself in armor of oak and triple bronze (aes triplex) before entrusting his life to a frail vessel on the open sea.
1. The reference is not to a gangster but to a religious sect in India that devoted itself to professional murder.

but leaves behind a mocking, tragical, and soon intolerable residue, which must be hurriedly concealed. Hence a whole chapter of sights and customs striking to the mind, from the pyramids of Egypt to the gibbets and dule trees of mediæval Europe. The poorest persons have a bit of pageant going toward the tomb; memorial stones are set up over the least memorable; and, in order to preserve some show of respect for what remains of our old loves and friendships, we must accompany it with much grimly ludicrous ceremonial, and the hired undertaker parades before the door. All this, and much more of the same sort, accompanied by the eloquence of poets, has gone a great way to put humanity in error; nay, in many philosophies the error has been embodied and laid down with every circumstance of logic; although in real life the bustle and swiftness, in leaving people little time to think, have not left them time enough to go dangerously wrong in practice.

As a matter of fact, although few things are spoken of with 2 more fearful whisperings than this prospect of death, few have less influence on conduct under healthy circumstances. We have all heard of cities in South America built upon the side of fiery mountains, and how, even in this tremendous neighborhood, the inhabitants are not a jot more impressed by the solemnity of mortal conditions than if they were delving gardens in the greenest corner of England. There are serenades and suppers and much gallantry among the myrtles overhead; and meanwhile the foundation shudders underfoot, the bowels of the mountain growl, and at any moment living ruin may leap sky-high into the moonlight, and tumble man and his merry-making in the dust. In the eyes of very young people, and very dull old ones, there is something indescribably reckless and desperate in such a picture. It seems not credible that respectable married people, with umbrellas, should find appetite for a bit of supper within quite a long distance of a fiery mountain; ordinary life begins to smell of high-handed debauch when it is carried on so close to a catastrophe; and even cheese and salad, it seems, could hardly be relished in such circumstances without something like a defiance of the Creator. It should be a place for nobody but hermits dwelling in prayer and maceration, or mere born-devils drowning care in a perpetual carouse.

And yet, when one comes to think upon it calmly, the situation 3 of these South American citizens forms only a very pale figure for the state of ordinary mankind. This world itself, travelling blindly and swiftly in overcrowded space, among a million other worlds travelling blindly and swiftly in contrary directions, may very well come by a knock that would set it into explosion like a penny squib. And what, pathologically looked at, is the human body with all its organs, but a mere bagful of petards?[2] The least of these is as dangerous to the whole economy as the ship's powder-magazine to the ship; and with every breath we breathe, and every meal we eat, we are putting one or more of them in peril. If we clung as devotedly as some philosophers pretend we do to the abstract idea of life, or were half as frightened as they make out we are, for the subversive accident that ends it all, the trumpets might sound by the hour and no one would follow them into battle—the blue peter might fly at the truck,[3] but who would climb into a sea-going ship? Think (if these philosophers were right) with what a preparation of spirit we should affront the daily peril of the dinner-table: a deadlier spot than any battle-field in history, where the far greater proportion of our ancestors have miserably left their bones! What woman would ever be lured into marriage, so much more dangerous than the wildest sea? And what would it be to grow old? For, after a certain distance, every step we take in life we find the ice growing thinner below our feet, and all around us and behind us we see our contemporaries going through. By the time a man gets well into the seventies, his continued existence is a mere miracle; and when he lays his old bones in bed for the night, there is an overwhelming probability that he will never see the day. Do the old men mind it, as a matter of fact? Why, no. They were never merrier; they have their grog at night, and tell the raciest stories; they hear of the death of people about their own age, or even younger, not as if it was a grisly warning, but with a simple childlike pleasure at having outlived some one else; and when a draught might puff them out like a guttering candle, or a bit of a stumble shatter them like so much glass, their old hearts keep sound and unaffrighted, and they go on, bubbling with laughter, through years of man's age compared to which the valley of Balaclava[4] was as safe and peaceful as a village cricket-green on Sunday. It may fairly be questioned (if we look to the peril only) whether it was a much more daring feat for Curtius[5] to plunge into the gulf, than for any old gentleman of ninety to doff his clothes and clamber into bed.

2. Grenades.
3. British merchant vessels displayed a blue signal flag on the masthead ("truck") to signal that they were about to sail.
4. The Valley of Death through which The Light Brigade charged during the Crimean War.
5. According to legend, an earthquake opened a chasm in the heart of Rome in 362 B.C. Soothsayers announced that it could be closed only by the sacrifice of Rome's greatest treasure. Gold and gems were dropped into the chasm with no effect. But when Marcus Curtius threw himself in, fully armed, the chasm closed after him.

Indeed, it is a memorable subject for consideration, with what 4
unconcern and gaiety mankind pricks on along the Valley of the
Shadow of Death. The whole way is one wilderness of snares,
and the end of it, for those who fear the last pinch, is irrevocable
ruin. And yet we go spinning through it all, like a party for the
Derby. Perhaps the reader remembers one of the humorous devices
of the deified Caligula: how he encouraged a vast concourse of
holiday-makers on to his bridge over Baiæ bay; and when they
were in the height of their enjoyment, turned loose the Prætorian
guards among the company, and had them tossed into the sea.
This is no bad miniature of the dealings of nature with the transitory
race of man. Only, what a checkered picnic we have of it, even
while it lasts! and into what great waters, not to be crossed by
any swimmer, God's pale Prætorian throws us over in the end!

We live the time that a match flickers; we pop the cork of a 5
ginger-beer bottle, and the earthquake swallows us on the instant.
Is it not odd, is it not incongruous, is it not, in the highest sense
of human speech, incredible, that we should think so highly of
the ginger-beer, and regard so little the devouring earthquake?
The love of Life and the fear of Death are two famous phrases
that grow harder to understand the more we think about them.
It is a well-known fact that an immense proportion of boat accidents
would never happen if people held the sheet in their hands instead
of making it fast; and yet, unless it be some martinet of a professional
mariner or some landsman with shattered nerves, every one of
God's creatures makes it fast. A strange instance of man's unconcern
and brazen boldness in the face of death!

We confound ourselves with metaphysical phrases, which we 6
import into daily talk with noble inappropriateness. We have no
idea of what death is, apart from its circumstances and some of
its consequences to others; and although we have some experience
of living, there is not a man on earth who has flown so high into
abstraction as to have any practical guess at the meaning of the
word *life*. All literature, from Job and Omar Khayyam to Thomas
Carlyle or Walt Whitman, is but an attempt to look upon the
human state with such largeness of view as shall enable us to rise
from the consideration of living to the Definition of Life. And our
sages give us about the best satisfaction in their power when they
say that it is a vapor, or a show, or made of the same stuff with
dreams. Philosophy, in its more rigid sense, has been at the same
work for ages; and after a myriad bald heads have wagged over
the problem, and piles of words have been heaped one upon
another into dry and cloudy volumes without end, philosophy
has the honor of laying before us, with modest pride, her contribution
toward the subject: that life is a Permanent Possibility of Sensation.

Truly a fine result! A man may very well love beef, or hunting, or a woman; but surely, surely, not a Permanent Possibility of Sensation! He may be afraid of a precipice, or a dentist, or a large enemy with a club, or even an undertaker's man; but not certainly of abstract death. We may trick with the word life in its dozen senses until we are weary of tricking; we may argue in terms of all the philosophies on earth, but one fact remains true throughout— that we do not love life, in the sense that we are greatly preoccupied about its conservation—that we do not, properly speaking, love life at all, but living. Into the views of the least careful there will enter some degree of providence; no man's eyes are fixed entirely on the passing hour; but although we have some anticipation of good health, good weather, wine, active employment, love, and self-approval, the sum of these anticipations does not amount to anything like a general view of life's possibilities and issues; nor are those who cherish them most vividly, at all the most scrupulous of their personal safety. To be deeply interested in the accidents of our existence, to enjoy keenly the mixed texture of human experience, rather leads a man to disregard precautions, and risk his neck against a straw. For surely the love of living is stronger in an Alpine climber roping over a peril, or a hunter riding merrily at a stiff fence, than in a creature who lives upon a diet and walks a measured distance in the interest of his constitution.

There is a great deal of very vile nonsense talked upon both sides of the matter: tearing divines reducing life to the dimensions of a mere funeral procession, so short as to be hardly decent; and melancholy unbelievers yearning for the tomb as if it were a world too far away. Both sides must feel a little ashamed of their performances now and again when they draw in their chairs to dinner. Indeed, a good meal and a bottle of wine is an answer to most standard works upon the question. When a man's heart warms to his viands, he forgets a great deal of sophistry, and soars into a rosy zone of contemplation. Death may be knocking at the door, like the Commander's statue;[6] we have something else in hand, thank God, and let him knock. Passing bells are ringing all the world over. All the world over, and every hour, some one is parting company with all his aches and ecstasies. For us also the trap is laid. But we are so fond of life that we have no leisure to entertain

7

---

6. At the height of his licentious career, the fictional Don Juan seduces a young noblewoman and then kills her father, the Commander, when he comes to avenge the seduction. Later Don Juan visits the Commander's tomb and invites the commemorative statue to dinner. The statue appears at Don Juan's door, foreshadowing his death.

the terror of death. It is a honeymoon with us all through, and none of the longest. Small blame to us if we give our whole hearts to this glowing bride of ours, to the appetites, to honor, to the hungry curiosity of the mind, to the pleasure of the eyes in nature, and the pride of our own nimble bodies.

We all of us appreciate the sensations; but as for caring about the Permanence of the Possibility, a man's head is generally very bald, and his senses very dull, before he comes to that. Whether we regard life as a lane leading to a dead wall—a mere bag's end, as the French say—or whether we think of it as a vestibule or gymnasium, where we wait our turn and prepare our faculties for some more noble destiny; whether we thunder in a pulpit, or pule in little atheistic poetry-books, about its vanity and brevity; whether we look justly for years of health and vigor, or are about to mount into a Bath chair, as a step toward the hearse; in each and all of these views and situations there is but one conclusion possible: that a man should stop his ears against paralyzing terror, and run the race that is set before him with a single mind. No one surely could have recoiled with more heartache and terror from the thought of death than our respected lexicographer;[7] and yet we know how little it affected his conduct, how wisely and boldly he walked, and in what a fresh and lively vein he spoke of life. Already an old man, he ventured on his Highland tour; and his heart, bound with triple brass, did not recoil before twenty-seven individual cups of tea. As courage and intelligence are the two qualities best worth a good man's cultivation, so it is the first part of intelligence to recognize our precarious estate in life, and the first part of courage to be not at all abashed before the fact. A frank and somewhat headlong carriage, not looking too anxiously before, not dallying in maudlin regret over the past, stamps the man who is well armored for this world.

And not only well armored for himself, but a good friend and a good citizen to boot. We do not go to cowards for tender dealing; there is nothing so cruel as panic; the man who has least fear for his own carcass, has most time to consider others. That eminent chemist who took his walks abroad in tin shoes, and subsisted wholly upon tepid milk, had all his work cut out for him in considerate dealings with his own digestion. So soon as prudence has begun to grow up in the brain, like a dismal fungus, it finds its first expression in a paralysis of generous acts. The victim begins to shrink spiritually; he develops a fancy for parlors with a regulated temperature, and takes his morality on the principle of tin shoes

7. Samuel Johnson.

and tepid milk. The care of one important body or soul becomes so engrossing, that all the noises of the outer world begin to come thin and faint into the parlor with the regulated temperature; and the tin shoes go equably forward over blood and rain. To be overwise is to ossify; and the scruple-monger ends by standing stock-still. Now the man who has his heart on his sleeve, and a good whirling weathercock of a brain, who reckons his life as a thing to be dashingly used and cheerfully hazarded, makes a very different acquaintance of the world, keeps all his pulses going true and fast, and gathers impetus as he runs, until, if he be running toward anything better than wildfire, he may shoot up and become a constellation in the end. Lord, look after his health; Lord, have a care of his soul, says he; and he has at the key of the position, and swashes through incongruity and peril toward his aim. Death is on all sides of him with pointed batteries, as he is on all sides of all of us; unfortunate surprises gird him round; mim-mouthed[8] friends and relations hold up their hands in quite a little elegiacal synod about his path: and what cares he for all this? Being a true lover of living, a fellow with something pushing and spontaneous in his inside, he must, like any other soldier, in any other stirring, deadly warfare, push on at his best pace until he touch the goal. "A peerage or Westminster Abbey!" cried Nelson in his bright, boyish, heroic manner. These are great incentives; not for any of these, but for the plain satisfaction of living, of being about their business in some sort or other, do the brave, serviceable men of every nation tread down the nettle danger, and pass flyingly over all the stumbling-blocks of prudence. Think of the heroism of Johnson, think of that superb indifference to mortal limitation that set him upon his dictionary, and carried him through triumphantly until the end! Who, if he were wisely considerate of things at large, would ever embark upon any work much more considerable than a half penny post card? Who would project a serial novel, after Thackeray and Dickens had each fallen in mid-course? Who would find heart enough to begin to live, if he dallied with the consideration of death?

And, after all, what sorry and pitiful quibbling all this is! To 10 forego all the issues of living in a parlor with the regulated temperature—as if that were not to die a hundred times over, and for ten years at a stretch! As if it were not to die in one's own lifetime, and without even the sad immunities of death! As if it were not to die, and yet be the patient spectators of our own pitiable change! The Permanent Possibility is preserved, but the

8. Close-mouthed.

sensations carefully held at arm's length, as if one kept a photographic plate in a dark chamber. It is better to lose health like
a spendthrift than to waste it like a miser. It is better to live and
be done with it, than to die daily in the sickroom. By all means
begin your folio; even if the doctor does not give you a year, even
if he hesitates about a month, make one brave push and see what
can be accomplished in a week. It is not only in finished undertakings
that we ought to honor useful labor. A spirit goes out of the man
who means excecution, which outlives the most untimely ending.
All who have meant good work with their whole hearts, have
done good work, although they may die before they have the
time to sign it. Every heart that has beat strong and cheerfully
has left a hopeful impulse behind it in the world, and bettered
the tradition of mankind. And even if death catch people, like an
open pitfall, and in mid-career, laying out vast projects, and planning
monstrous foundations, flushed with hope, and their mouths full
of boastful language, they should be at once tripped up and silenced:
is there not something brave and spirited in such a termination?
and does not life go down with a better grace, foaming in full
body over a precipice, than miserably straggling to an end in sandy
deltas? When the Greeks made their fine saying that those whom
the gods love die young, I cannot help believing they had this
sort of death also in their eye. For surely, at whatever age it
overtake the man, this is to die young. Death has not been suffered
to take so much as an illusion from his heart. In the hot-fit of
life, a-tiptoe on the highest point of being, he passes at a bound
on to the other side. The noise of the mallet and chisel is scarcely
quenched, the trumpets are hardly done blowing, when, trailing
with him clouds of glory, this happy-starred, full-blooded spirit
shoots into the spiritual land.

RICHARD SELZER

The Discus Thrower

I spy on my patients. Ought not a doctor to observe his patients   1
by any means and from any stance, that he might the more fully
assemble evidence? So I stand in the doorways of hospital rooms

Originally published in *Harper's Magazine*, November 1977.

and gaze. Oh, it is not all that furtive an act. Those in bed need
only look up to discover me. But they never do.

From the doorway of Room 542 the man in the bed seems   2
deeply tanned. Blue eyes and close-cropped white hair give him
the appearance of vigor and good health. But I know that his skin
is not brown from the sun. It is rusted, rather, in the last stage
of containing the vile repose within. And the blue eyes are frosted,
looking inward like the windows of a snowbound cottage. This
man is blind. This man is also legless—the right leg missing from
midthigh down, the left from just below the knee. It gives him
the look of a bonsai, roots and branches pruned into the dwarfed
facsimile of a great tree.

Propped on pillows, he cups his right thigh in both hands. Now   3
and then he shakes his head as though acknowledging the intensity
of his suffering. In all of this he makes no sound. Is he mute as
well as blind?

The room in which he dwells is empty of all possessions—no   4
get-well cards, small, private caches of food, day-old flowers, slippers,
all the usual kickshaws of the sickroom. There is only the bed, a
chair, a nightstand, and a tray on wheels that can be swung across
his lap for meals.

What time is it?" he asks.   5
"Three o'clock."
"Morning or afternoon?"
"Afternoon."
He is silent. There is nothing else he wants to know.
"How are you?" I say.   10
"Who is it?" he asks.
"It's the doctor. How do you feel?"
He does not answer right away.
"Feel?" he says.
"I hope you feel better," I say.   15
I press the button at the side of the bed.
"Down you go," I say.
"Yes, down," he says.
He falls back upon the bed awkwardly. His stumps, unweighted
by legs and feet, rise in the air, presenting themselves. I unwrap
the bandages from the stumps, and begin to cut away the black
scabs and the dead, glazed fat with scissors and forceps. A shard
of white bone comes loose. I pick it away. I wash the wounds
with disinfectant and redress the stumps. All this while, he does
not speak. What is he thinking behind those lids that do not blink?
Is he remembering a time when he was whole? Does he dream
of feet? Of when his body was not a rotting log?

He lies solid and inert. In spite of everything, he remains im-   20
pressive, as though he were a sailor standing athwart a slanting
deck.

"Anything more I can do for you?" I ask.

For a long moment he is silent.

"Yes," he says at last and without the least irony. "You can
bring me a pair of shoes."

In the corridor, the head nurse is waiting for me.

"We have to do something about him." she says. "Every morning   25
he orders scrambled eggs for breakfast, and, instead of eating them,
he picks up the plate and throws it against the wall."

"Throws his plate?"

"Nasty. That's what he is. No wonder his family doesn't come
to visit. They probably can't stand him any more than we can."

She is waiting for me to do something.

"Well?"

"We'll see," I say.   30

The next morning I am waiting in the corridor when the kitchen
delivers his breakfast. I watch the aide place the tray on the stand
and swing it across his lap. She presses the button to raise the
head of the bed. Then she leaves.

In time the man reaches to find the rim of the tray, then on to
find the dome of the covered dish. He lifts off the cover and places
it on the stand. He fingers across the plate until he probes the
eggs. He lifts the plate in both hands, sets it on the palm of his
right hand, centers it, balances it. He hefts it up and down slightly,
getting the feel of it. Abruptly, he draws back his right arm as far
as he can.

There is the crack of the plate breaking against the wall at the
foot of his bed and the small wet sound of the scrambled eggs
dropping to the floor.

And then he laughs. It is a sound you have never heard. It is
something new under the sun. It could cure cancer.

Out in the corridor, the eyes of the head nurse narrow.   35

"Laughed, did he?"

She writes something down on her clipboard.

A second aide arrives, brings a second breakfast tray, puts it on
the nightstand, out of his reach. She looks over at me shaking
her head and making her mouth go. I see that we are to be
accomplices.

"I've got to feed you," she says to the man.

"Oh, no you don't," the man says.   40

"Oh, yes I do," the aide says, "after the way you just did. Nurse
says so."

"Get me my shoes," the man says.

"Here's oatmeal," the aide says. "Open." And she touches the spoon to his lower lip.

"I ordered scrambled eggs," says the man.

"That's right," the aide says.   45

I step forward.

"Is there anything I can do?" I say.

"Who are you?" the man asks.

In the evening I go once more to that ward to make my rounds. The head nurse reports to me that Room 542 is deceased. She has discovered this quite by accident, she says. No, there had been no sound. Nothing. It's a blessing, she says.

I go into his room, a spy looking for secrets. He is still there in   50
his bed. His face is relaxed, grave, dignified. After a while, I turn to leave. My gaze sweeps the wall at the foot of the bed, and I see the place where it has been repeatedly washed, where the wall looks very clean and very white.

ANNIE DILLARD

The Deer at Providencia

There were four of us North Americans in the jungle, in the   1
Ecuadorian jungle on the banks of the Napo River in the Amazon watershed. The other three North Americans were metropolitan men. We stayed in tents in one riverside village, and visited others. At the village called Providencia we saw a sight which moved us, and which shocked the men.

The first thing we saw when we climbed the riverbank to the   2
village of Providencia was the deer. It was roped to a tree on the grass clearing near the thatch shelter where we would eat lunch.

The deer was small, about the size of a whitetail fawn, but   3
apparently full-grown. It had a rope around its neck and three feet caught in the rope. Someone said that the dogs had caught it that morning and the villagers were going to cook and eat it that night.

From *Teaching a Stone to Talk* (1982).

This clearing lay at the edge of the little thatched-hut village.   4
We could see the villagers going about their business, scattering
feed corn for hens about their houses, and wandering down paths
to the river to bathe. The village headman was our host; he stood
beside us as we watched the deer struggle. Several village boys
were interested in the deer; they formed part of the circle we made
around it in the clearing. So also did four businessmen from Quito
who were attempting to guide us around the jungle. Few of the
very different people standing in this circle had a common language.
We watched the deer, and no one said much.

The deer lay on its side at the rope's very end, so the rope   5
lacked slack to let it rest its head in the dust. It was "pretty,"
delicate of bone like all deer, and thin-skinned for the tropics. Its
skin looked virtually hairless, in fact, and almost translucent, like
a membrane. Its neck was no thicker than my wrist; it was rubbed
open on the rope, and gashed. Trying to paw itself free of the
rope, the deer had scratched its own neck with its hooves. The
raw underside of its neck showed red stripes and some bruises
bleeding inside the muscles. Now three of its feet were hooked in
the rope under its jaw. It could not stand, of course, on one leg,
so it could not move to slacken the rope and ease the pull on its
throat and enable it to rest its head.

Repeatedly the deer paused, motionless, its eyes veiled, with   6
only its rib cage in motion, and its breaths the only sound. Then,
after I would think, "It has given up; now it will die," it would
heave. The rope twanged; the tree leaves clattered; the deer's free
foot beat the ground. We stepped back and held our breaths. It
thrashed, kicking, but only one leg moved; the other three legs
tightened inside the rope's loop. Its hip jerked; its spine shook.
Its eyes rolled; its tongue, thick with spittle, pushed in and out.
Then it would rest again. We watched this for fifteen minutes.

Once three young native boys charged in, released its trapped   7
legs, and jumped back to the circle of people. But instantly the
deer scratched up its neck with its hooves and snared its forelegs
in the rope again. It was easy to imagine a third and then a fourth
leg soon stuck, like Brer Rabbit and the Tar Baby.

We watched the deer from the circle, and then we drifted on   8
to lunch. Our palm-roofed shelter stood on a grassy promontory
from which we could see the deer tied to the tree, pigs and hens
walking under village houses, and black-and-white cattle standing
in the river. There was even a breeze.

Lunch, which was the second and better lunch we had that   9
day, was hot and fried. There was a big fish called *doncella*, a kind

of catfish, dipped whole in corn flour and beaten egg, then deep
fried. With our fingers we pulled soft fragments of it from its sides
to our plates, and ate; it was delicate fish-flesh, fresh and mild.
Someone found the roe, and I ate of that too—it was fat and
stronger, like egg yolk, naturally enough, and warm.

There was also a stew of meat in shreds with rice and pale   10
brown gravy. I had asked what kind of deer it was tied to the
tree; Pepe had answered in Spanish, "*Gama.*" Now they told us
this was *gama* too, stewed. I suspect the word means merely game
or venison. At any rate, I heard that the village dogs had cornered
another deer just yesterday, and it was this deer which we were
now eating in full sight of the whole article. It was good. I was
surprised at its tenderness. But it is a fact that high levels of lactic
acid, which builds up in muscle tissues during exertion, tenderizes.

After the fish and meat we ate bananas fried in chunks and   11
served on a tray; they were sweet and full of flavor. I felt terrific.
My shirt was wet and cool from swimming; I had had a night's
sleep, two decent walks, three meals, and a swim—everything
tasted good. From time to time each one of us, separately, would
look beyond our shaded roof to the sunny spot where the deer
was still convulsing in the dust. Our meal completed, we walked
around the deer and back to the boats.

That night I learned that while we were watching the deer, the   12
others were watching me.

We four North Americans grew close in the jungle in a way   13
that was not the usual artificial intimacy of travelers. We liked
each other. We stayed up all that night talking, murmuring, as
though we rocked on hammocks slung above time. The others
were from big cities: New York, Washington, Boston. They all
said that I had no expression on my face when I was watching
the deer—or at any rate, not the expression they expected.

They had looked to see how I, the only woman, and the youngest,   14
was taking the sight of the deer's struggles. I looked detached,
apparently, or hard, or calm, or focused, still. I don't know. I was
thinking. I remember feeling very old and energetic. I could say
like Thoreau that I have traveled widely in Roanoke, Virginia. I
have thought a great deal about carnivorousness; I eat meat. These
things are not issues; they are mysteries.

Gentlemen of the city, what surprises you? That there is suffering   15
here, or that I know it?

We lay in the tent and talked. "If it had been my wife," one   16
man said with special vigor, amazed, "she wouldn't have cared

what was going on; she would have dropped *everything* right at that moment and gone in the village from here to there to there, she would not have *stopped* until that animal was out of its suffering one way or another. She couldn't *bear* to see a creature in agony like that."

I nodded.   17

Now I am home. When I wake I comb my hair before the mirror   18
above my dresser. Every morning for the past two years I have seen in that mirror, beside my sleep-softened face, the blackened face of a burnt man. It is a wire-service photograph clipped from a newspaper and taped to my mirror. The caption reads: "Alan McDonald in Miami hospital bed." All you can see in the photograph is a smudged triangle of face from his eyelids to his lower lip; the rest is bandages. You cannot see the expression in his eyes; the bandages shade them.

The story, headed MAN BURNED FOR SECOND TIME, begins: 19

> "Why does God hate me?" Alan McDonald asked from his hospital bed.
> "When the gunpowder went off, I couldn't believe it," he said. "I just couldn't believe it. I said, 'No, God couldn't do this to me again.' "

He was in a burn ward in Miami, in serious condition. I do not even know if he lived. I wrote him a letter at the time, cringing.

He had been burned before, thirteen years previously, by flaming   20
gasoline. For years he had been having his body restored and his face remade in dozens of operations. He had been a boy, and then a burnt boy. He had already been stunned by what could happen, by how life could veer.

Once I read that people who survive bad burns tend to go crazy;   21
they have a very high suicide rate. Medicine cannot ease their pain; drugs just leak away, soaking the sheets, because there is no skin to hold them in. The people just lie there and weep. Later they kill themselves. They had not known, before they were burned, that the world included such suffering, that life could permit them personally such pain.

This time a bowl of gunpowder had exploded on McDonald.   22

> "I didn't realize what had happened at first," he recounted. "And then I heard that sound from 13 years ago. I was burning. I rolled to put the fire out and I thought, 'Oh God, not again.'
> "If my friend hadn't been there, I would have jumped into a canal with a rock around my neck."

His wife concludes the piece, "Man, it just isn't fair."

I read the whole clipping again every morning. This is the Big 23
Time here, every minute of it. Will someone please explain to
Alan McDonald in his dignity, to the deer at Providencia in his
dignity, what is going on? And mail me the carbon.

When we walked by the deer at Providencia for the last time, 24
I said to Pepe, with a pitying glance at the deer, *"Pobrecito"*—
"poor little thing." But I was trying out Spanish. I knew at the
time it was a ridiculous thing to say.

PATRICIA HAMPL

Teresa

And my grandmother, the elderly art nouveau figure, finally 1
disappeared. She ended up in a nursing home, in the modern
way. We all hated it. My father cried and made a fist in his pocket.
My mother, who got her household back after years of the ignorant
lowness ruining her roses, ruining her role as chatelaine, was not
happy and wanted her back, and did not root up the chive plant
in the back yard but allowed it to take over so that even today
there are chives everywhere, even in the chinks of the sidewalk.
My aunts said, "What else can we do?" And what else could we.

I wasn't living at home anymore, but I got letters from my 2
mother. The card parties and Czech lodge meetings with other old
ladies who spoke some nineteenth-century version of Czech known
only to themselves had come to an end. There weren't even any
wakes or funerals for my grandmother to go to anymore; apparently
everyone was dead, except for her. She had kept up her relentless
cooking and the deep concern for her looks, a discipline held so
long it had become a kind of honor. But slowly, steadily, as if
they followed a plot, my mother's letters led to the nursing home:
Grandma had burned herself one day when she didn't notice she'd
left the gas flame on the stove. Her housedresses, cotton flower-
print dresses with rickrack trim (her uniform at home), were often
not clean: unbelievable.

Then an account of how Grandma had gotten into the bathtub 3
and couldn't hoist herself out; she had sat there, her skin puckering
in the water for three hours until my mother heard strange heave-
ho noises in the apartment and came in to pull her out. Later,

Chapter 6 of Part II of *A Romantic Education* (1981).

another report that Aunt Sylvia had decided to come every week to clean the apartment ("the kitchen is filthy"). Then Aunt Sylvia suggested that my grandmother should take a bath only when someone was with her. There was a follow-up report that Aunt Sylvia, cleaning the apartment, had been unable to pull Grandma out of the tub and had started to cry. My grandmother began to laugh. It was a stand-off, one of them too weak from crying, the other from laughing. Finally, my aunt called in my mother from next door, and the hoist was accomplished, their big elderly baby laughing because there was nothing else to do.

Then a letter came saying Grandma had fallen down the basement 4 stairs. It might be a stroke. She would have to go to a nursing home: for a while, maybe for longer. She couldn't take care of herself. My mother and father both worked; no one was at home during the day.

A few days later I got a brief note from my mother saying my 5 grandmother was in the nursing home (address included, suggestion that I send a card) and was confined to a wheelchair. She of the endless avidity and the boundless faith that work was life. My grandmother *sitting*—it was a contradiction in terms. Maybe it was an effect of the stroke, no one seemed sure. But she said she couldn't walk and sank into the wheelchair with no apparent intention of walking again.

For several months she was taken to physical therapy, but finally 6 the head nurse told my father he might as well buy a wheelchair; the rented one was not economical for long-term cases. Then the therapy ended and she had a catheter as a permanent appendage, and showed it to her visitors, unasked, with a kind of wonder at its obvious functionalism. There was no more talk of her walking.

I think she went through some kind of nervous breakdown. It's 7 strange to think of a dark night of the soul coming to someone eighty-seven or eighty-eight. By then it would seem that the husk of the personality has rigidified so that if it splits apart at all, it is only into the splinters of senility. I would not have thought of a very old person cracking the personality open and hurling out its pain and experience in sorrow and then, as if there were a future, turning upward in a huge cleansing wave, leaving the soul spent but free and wise at the last shore of its life. But something like that happened to my grandmother.

It took about two years. There are several indications that she 8 went through the spiritual cleansing that saints and mystics describe. I was most struck when my father told me that she had said, apropos of nothing (not even of pain: there wasn't a lot of pain at the end), "Well, I think it's time to die tonight." And she did. Her body and soul were that finely meshed by the end. As my aunt said, she knew *what she was*. She knew she was about to be dead.

At first, in the nursing home, she fought like a tiger. She did   9
not fight the good fight the physical therapy people wanted her to fight. She must have sensed that there was no future in being a goody-goody. She was out to break the joint. She fought her roommates who, each in turn, asked to be moved out. She fought the medication. She fought being put in bed and then snarled when she was taken out again and put in her wheelchair. She hated the food, but complained that she didn't get enough. She cried and demanded to go home; she sulked and then said casually that when she got home she intended to buy herself a new bed like the one she had in the nursing home—the best bed of her life, she said. She spoke authoritatively, as if acquisition implied mobility. And when no one, out of kindness, reminded her that she wouldn't be going back to her apartment, she reported to her next visitor that she was soon going home.

Her children or grandchildren and their children came every   10
day to visit. Everyone talked to her, to each other, about what a nice place the nursing home was, how friendly the staff was, how clean the rooms were, how there were lots of people around to play cards with, and that the best part was that they could take her home anytime for dinners, picnics, holidays. And then they left, and hardly got out the front door before they burst into tears and cried aloud: why did their mother have to be there, in that nice, clean, friendly place?

This was not one of the miserable holes for the aged, gigantic   11
and crowded, with loudspeakers blatting endless messages, not one of the sleazy places that is marginally in the news because of some legislative inquiry about mishandling of public funds. It was what we told her, told each other: a nice, clean, friendly place, modern and light with lots of windows, a yard too small and too near busy traffic perhaps, but the staff was competent, not cruelly overworked, often affectionate. The rooms were not large but were bigger than hospital rooms, and there were only two beds in each one, with a certain commitment to privacy. Large windows, a bath for each room, bright and tiled. I never saw or tasted the food, but my aunts said it was all right. My grandmother was diagnosed as a diabetic soon after arriving so her diet was restricted, probably bland. My family, always clannish, liked to visit her, liked to be with her, and it was generally agreed that even though the place was *very nice*, it didn't do any harm to make it clear that Mrs. Hampl in 106 had four children, innumerable other relatives, and that they came, one or another of them, every day to visit her. *If*

the staff merely put on an act for visitors, our endless parade
would keep them busily at it. This was the watchful thought.

In an effort to get her interested in the world around her, away   12
from the apartment she kept refurnishing in her mind and conversation, her children and the staff tried to introduce her to other
people. They got her to play cards, always her favorite pastime.
But years of playing five hundred with indulgent children who
let her cheat without much comment had blunted her technique,
of playing and of cheating. She was hurt and angry, as chronic
cheaters always are, when her new companions bluntly told her
to cut it out. Besides, she said, some of them didn't talk right.
This was the beginning of her acquaintance with those who,
as she put it, were touched. Eventually, if she saw one of her
visitors foolishly attempting conversation with someone woefully
touched, she discreetly tapped her finger on her own forehead
and shook her head, more savvy than her children about the signs
around her.

Her wild-tiger time, when she fought the place, lasted less than   13
a year, but it continued in occasional energetic jags for two years.
It was a denial of the place and its purpose. She never talked
about death or dying. Nor about illness or infirmity. She wanted
to go home.

One of the last times I visited her, while I was home for a   14
vacation, I noticed a change. It frightened me; I thought she was
going to become one of the touched. She was sitting in her wheelchair moaning when I came in. This was something I hadn't seen
her do before. She didn't stop or try to cover her tears. I thought
she might be in physical pain, might need a nurse. But that wasn't
it. She kept moaning and crying, rocking herself back and forth,
not oblivious to my presence, but somewhere out of reach of the
conventions of etiquette, the charm that had been one of her
enduring principles, deep in her own anguish, not about to abandon
her intimacy with it. She took my hand (any hand), stroked her
own cheek with it, cried that she was lonely, lonely, looonely,
hanging on to the *o* sound. She wanted to die. She made me
promise I would come to her funeral. But mostly she did not talk.
She moaned and rocked back and forth, like one of the anonymous
touched. She wouldn't talk and acknowledged my inept affection
(I held her hand, stroked her hair) only from a great distance.
That is when she said, more greenhorn than grandmother, "You're
good, you're kind."

When I left she didn't have me wheel her down to the big   15
lounge picture window, as she had every other time, so that she
could wave to me as I drove off—a procedure that always made

me feel like a culprit and, really a culprit, made me glad to get away fast. This time she stayed where she was and continued to moan. I felt guilty, I still feel wrong, but I left her moaning there. Anything to get away from that mantra of sorrow, that awful moaning, toneless, impersonal, not *her*. It—if not she—seemed prepared to go on moaning endlessly. That was the worst part: the eternity in that moan.

When I got home one of my aunts was visiting my mother;   16
everybody was glad to see me: coffee, Christmas cookies, kisses around. I didn't want to tell them about the moaning. In some odd, callous way, I was already seeing it as less important than it had seemed at the time. And then my aunt said—mostly to my mother, for my mother—how good I was to take time during my vacation to visit my grandmother, and I began to focus, by degrees, on that aspect of the visit: my kindness. It had been my grandmother's comment too.

I thought this was the beginning of her descent into senility   17
and mindlessness. And that the next time I went to visit her she would be babbling and incoherent, her mind woolly with bent memories. I thought her sadness had no bottom, or that there was no trap door to that moan, no escape but death. It occurred to me that she might arrive, in senility, back in Bohemia, the life and country she had had so little memory of, and that she would live there alone in her antiquated, mashed form of the language, mumbling, back in the embrace of the peasantry, lumpen. I didn't want to visit her again. I only saw her once or twice more.

But she wasn't senile and she didn't, ever again, moan that   18
way. The curtain in her heart that split in half from top to bottom that day had mended—or hadn't been rent? I almost wondered if I had imagined it. She had become calm and humorous, patient, not the same as before—she had always been feisty—but not senile. After her death, my father wrote me about the end. There was a tone of wonder in his letter. The last six months of her life, he wrote, something strange had happened. He didn't know what to call it, he wrote. She just became, after her tiger period, very *kind*. It was she who talked sensibly and naturally to those who were touched in the worst, most unreachable ways; she who held a hand, wheeled herself over to someone sitting vacant and weird in a corner. She cheered the nurses (the nurses said; it was beyond a polite remark, my father wrote). She seemed to understand everybody's troubles, asked for nothing, gave amazing light. Everyone wanted to be around her. Teresa, they called her: her name, of course, but unusual to be called by one's most personal, authentic name in these end-of-the-line places where false affection makes

everyone Grandma or, more courteously, more coolly, Mrs. this or that. She died Teresa, a person.

I didn't see any of this. I wasn't around during those last months. I know it from my father who was amazed, bemused by this turn of events. She had gone down and down, and, then, when everyone had every reason to expect her to go even more desperately down— into senility, into woeful bitterness—she made that strange, luminous turn. She glittered at the end not with charm, but with pure spirit, more than a brave salute. Our immigrant became a noble.

I did not go home for her funeral. I was living in a tiny river town in Illinois, right on the river in fact, so close to the bank that in spring the channel flooded the narrow frontage road and almost reached the strand of houses facing the water. There was no getting away from St. Paul; we were still connected, in a direct line, by the river. In St. Paul the Mississippi is not the Father of Waters; it is narrow and threads its unromantic way past industrial plants. But in Illinois where it begins to become the river of Mark Twain and billows out in a wider, plainlike channel, it becomes aloof and serious.

After my mother called with the news of my grandmother's death—it hadn't been expected—I went outside by the river. I felt a satisfying finality, what I took to be acceptance. The river glided by, still, grand, metaphoric. I didn't go home for the funeral because a friend of mine had just had twin babies and I felt, solemnly and sincerely, that I was choosing life over death, staying near my friend who wanted me there. My grandmother, who had had twins herself, would have approved, I thought.

She would not have approved. But I was impervious to the last to her personality. I considered, philosophically, the misty middle ground between life and death that old people inhabit at the end. It was almost pleasant, this idea of fading. I thought I had probably already said my good-bye to her years before when she first began to get really old, or when she went to the nursing home. Or maybe the day in her room when she had moaned and moaned, as if she were no one in particular, just that grievous sound. She died a long time ago, I thought, as I stood by the wide river, and this recent death is just the expression of it. She had just made it into her tenth decade: she had been ninety on Columbus Day and she died in November. A long life, such a long life as hers, cannot end all of a sudden, I felt. She is at peace, I thought. And so am I.

Several weeks later I woke, jolted out of deep sleep in the middle of the night by nothing at all. I was drenched in sweat. I hadn't

been dreaming, or hadn't remembered that I was. I was sobbing—
I had no idea why at first. Then I focused: I had made a *terrible
mistake* and should have gone to her funeral. This was the knowledge—not a dream—that had awakened me. And not having gone,
there was no way to undo it.

I cried at sudden, unpredictable moments for two weeks after   24
that, sobbing as I drove home, hunched over the steering wheel,
unable to see through the tears, as if I were beating my way
through a Minnesota blizzard. I moaned aloud in the public library
stacks one day, again to my utter surprise. There was an elderly
man on the other side of the stacks who peered through a chink
in the wall of books to see what the matter was. He was wearing
rimless glasses. Those are the cleanest glasses I've ever seen, I
thought, and stared at them, fascinated, as if he were the apparition
and not I.

I must have looked more astonished than miserable; my attacks   25
(as I thought of them) were the advance guard of my emotions.
I sobbed, I moaned stupidly, and only after the sound did I think,
"Oh, it's Grandma. Because she's dead." The sobbing and moaning
were acts dissociated from feeling. It was a weird sensation: to
moan aloud in a supermarket check-out line, and then to look
sheepishly at the bemused, unsobbing people around me. Yet I
didn't miss her. And after a while the sobbing and my sudden
public moans diminished and finally, left me entirely.

The picture of the luscious art nouveau girl[1] with her lute went   26
to my Aunt Therese. There was no will, nothing that self-conscious.
Things just went, of their own accord, to the family members who
wanted or needed them. My cousin ended up with the purple
satin eiderdown, perhaps the most Bohemian of my grandmother's
possessions: the great goose-down quilt of middle Europe. My
father wrote in his letter that it seemed as if Grandma had everything
beautifully timed: her savings left exactly enough for her burial
and for checks of $500 to each of her four children and to Frank's
daughter: she had left heirs. If she had lived a few more months,
her money would have run out. Nothing would have changed,
but welfare—or some version of it—would have paid her way.
Ever the housekeeper, she had arranged to the end, tidily. She
stopped on a dime.

I asked for the album of Prague views. My aunt wrote back   27
that nobody could find it; somehow or other it was lost. She sent

---

1. This picture had hung over Hampl's grandmother's sofa for decades and symbolized
for Hampl the ideal of beauty to which women of her grandmother's generation
aspired.

me instead my grandmother's ring, a Bohemian garnet set in white
gold with an art nouveau design. I felt someone else should have
had it, Frank's daughter perhaps, but this was the object that came
to me, apparently it was what I was meant to have. I put it on
my finger, the one on which the other women in the family wear
their wedding rings; I was the only unmarried one among them.

Then, our personal Europe dead and buried, I decided I must   28
go there.[2]

2. See "Prague," *Dolphin Reader*, pp. 895–900.

WILLIAM MANCHESTER

My Old Man:
The Last Years of H. L. Mencken

"The cooks here do a swell job with soft-shell crabs," Mencken   1
said in a gravelly voice, peering at me over his spectacles. Beneath
the old-fashioned center part of his white hair his pot-blue eyes
gleamed like twin gas jets. "They fry them in the altogether," he
rasped. "Then they add a small jockstrap of bacon."

It was June 2, 1947. We were in the dining room of the Maryland   2
Club. The meeting was our first—I had just flown in from a Midwestern graduate school, where I was writing my dissertation on
his early literary criticism—and it was the beginning of a seven-
year friendship, an April–December relationship which I cherished,
and cherish still, despite the dirty tricks fate began to play on him
eighteen months after it began.

"This is a very high-toned club," he said over the crabs. "Nothing 3
but men. Any member who suffers a heart attack must be carried
outside to the front steps before a nurse can attend him."

He was in fine form that Monday noon. The thought that he   4
himself might fall the victim of a seizure and wind up in the hands
of nurses was very far away. At sixty-six he was still at the height
of his remarkable powers and had, in fact, just completed the most
productive period in his career. Since 1940 he had been feuding
with his paper, the Baltimore *Sun*, as a result of the *Sun*'s support

From *Controversy and other Essays in Journalism* (1976). Mencken's essay "The Nature
of Liberty" appears on pages 723–26 of *The Dolphin Reader*.

of what he had called "Roosevelt's War." Holed up in his study
at 1524 Hollins Street, he had written *Happy Days, Newspaper Days,*
Heathen Days, A Christmas Story, A New Dictionary of Quotations, and
two massive supplements to *The American Language* and was, when
we met, at work on *A Mencken Chrestomathy.* His machete was still
long and sharp and heavy, and he had never swung it with greater
gusto.

Face-to-face with the man himself, I was enormously impressed. 5
Alistair Cooke once observed that Mencken had "the longest torso
on the shortest legs in the entire history of legmen," and Mencken
himself said there would be no point in erecting a statue to him,
because it would just look like a monument to a defeated alderman,
but actually he was a man of great physical presence. To be sure,
his torso was ovoid, his ruddy face homely, and his legs not only
stubby but also thin and bowed. Nevertheless there was a sense
of dignity and purpose about all his movements, and when you
were with him it was impossible to forget that you were watching
a great original. Nobody else could stuff Uncle Willie stogies into
a seersucker jacket with the flourish of Mencken, or wipe a blue
bandanna across his brow so dramatically. His friends treasured
everything about him, because the whole of the man was manifest
in each of his aspects—the tilt of his head, his close-fitting clothes,
his high-crowned felt hat creased in the distinct fashion of the
1920's, his strutting walk, his abrupt gestures, his habit of holding
a cigar between his thumb and forefinger like a baton, the roupy
inflection of his voice, and, most of all, those extraordinary eyes:
so large, and intense, and merry. He was sui generis in all ways,
and the instant I saw him I wanted to write his biography.

After reading my thesis the following summer, he agreed. ("I 6
marvel at the hard work you put into it," he wrote me. "It tells
me many things about my own self that I didn't know myself.
. . . You will be rewarded in Heaven throughout eternity.") He
did more. Swallowing his pride, he asked the *Sun* to give me a
job, so that I could support myself while working on the book.
My journalistic career was launched that September, and while I
was unlikely to match the trajectory of his soaring star—at my
age, twenty-five, he had been a managing editor—it did give us
something else to talk about.

Beginning that autumn, we talked a great deal, sometimes at 7
the *Sun,* which he now began visiting with growing frequency;
other times in his club, his home, the Enoch Pratt Free Library,
Miller Brothers' restaurant, and on long walks through downtown
Baltimore. There was, of course, no pretense to conversation between
equals; I regarded him with the special deference of the fledgling

writer for the master. The high-ceilinged Hollins Street sitting room, with its cheery fireplace, dark rosewood furniture, and Victorian bric-a-brac became a kind of shrine to me. I treasured his letters to me, which were even more frequent than our talks, for he loved correspondence, always preferring the written word to the telephone. And I kept elaborate notes on all our contacts, which, he being Mencken, really were notable.

One warm day I covered a fire in his neighborhood. He appeared friskily at the height of it, carrying a pencil and perspiring happily. "I'm like the hippopotamus," he said in greeting, "an essentially tropical animal." Like the hippo, he was also a creature of exaggeration. He never asked me just to join him for a beer; I was invited to "hoist a schooner of malt." He couldn't order sweetbreads at Miller's without explaining that they were taken from "the pancreases of horned cattle, the smaller intestines of swine, and the vermiform appendix of the cow"—thereby causing me to choose something else. Anthony Comstock hadn't merely been a censor; he had been "a great smeller." Mencken was forever stuffing letters to me with advertisements for chemical water closets, quack-remedy broadsides, and religious pamphlets. Once, while showing me his manuscript collection in the Pratt Library, he said he was worried about its security; the stack containing it was locked, but he wanted a sign, too. "Saying 'KEEP OUT'?" I asked. "No," he said. "Saying: 'WARNING: TAMPERING WITH THIS GATE WILL RELEASE CHLORINE GAS UNDER 250 POUNDS PRESSURE.'"

By the spring of 1948 he was a daily visitor to the *Sun*. In the paper's morgue he advised a man updating the Mencken obituary to "Leave it as it is. Just add one line: 'As he grew older, he grew worse.'" One afternoon on Charles Street we encountered two sedate women from the *Sun*'s library coming the other way, and Mencken cried out heartily, "Hello, girls! How's the profession?" Later one of them said to me, "Of course, he didn't mean it the way it sounded." I knew that was exactly how he had meant it. By then, though, it was clear that he was yearning for a consummation of his rapprochement with the paper. The feud formally ended the following summer, when he arrived in Philadelphia to join the *Sun* men covering that year's presidential nominations and write happily of "the traditional weather of a national convention . . . a rising temperature, very high humidity, and lazy puffs of gummy wind from the mangrove swamps surrounding the city." Of the three political parties then taking the field, he preferred the Progressives, because they were the most preposterous. After Wallace had been nominated, he received a delegation of young Progressives in the hotel suite housing the *Sun* delegation and proposed that they join him in singing "The Star-Spangled Banner." He deliberately picked the impossible key of F Major. After crooning a few bars in his rasping tenor, he dropped out, waiting to hear his guests crack up, as was inevitable, on the impossible high E. When it happened, they looked appealingly to him for help. He just stuck his cigar in his mouth and beamed back at them.

My best recollection of the campaign which followed is of a   10
Wallace rally in Baltimore's Fifth Regiment Armory which I covered with Mencken. By then everyone in the audience had read the old man's *Sun* articles taunting their hero, and they knew the old man would be there that night. After the speeches, a mob of them crowded around the press bench, where, incredibly, he had un-sheathed his portable typewriter and set to work. He had decided to knock out his piece with them watching. I know of no other writer who could have performed under the circumstances. There were perhaps a score of hostile, humorless men and women in an arc behind him, peering over his shoulder, and behind them were others who were calling out, "What's he saying about us?" The outrageous phrases were called back, the crowd growled— and the old man hunted and pecked on, enjoying himself hugely. He even hummed that catchy little ditty, "Friendly Henry Wallace."

Mencken was immensely amused, as the *Sun* hierarchy was not,   11
by Truman's unexpected victory. He felt that it justified his assessment of democracy as a comic spectacle. He returned to Hollins Street, refreshed, to tackle a new book. Meantime I had written the opening sections of my biography, and he had read them. On September 27 he had written me, "It seems to me that, as they stand, the first two chapters are excellent. Some of your gener-alizations surprise me, and even horrify me, but they are yours, not mine. Don't let anyone tell you how to write it. Do it in your own way. You are obviously far ahead of most young writers, and I have every confidence in you." Thus we were both busy with thickening manuscripts as winter approached. On Wednesday, November 24, we were to take a break. A luncheon reservation had been made at the Maryland Club for four—Mencken, Evelyn Waugh, a Jesuit priest, and me. Waugh and Mencken had never met; the priest and I had arranged everything, like seconds before a duel. The encounter never took place, however, because disaster struck the old man the evening before.

Mencken was fascinated by the frailties of the human body, his   12
own and everybody else's. He was constantly studying medical journals, reading up on diseases of the bronchial tubes, gall bladder, etc., and he was the most considerate visitor of the sick in Baltimore.

Acquaintances who, in health, would not see him for weeks, found him at their hospital doors each evening, as long as they remained bedridden, fascinated by their progress, or, even more, by their lack of it. His letters to me and to others reflected his preoccupation with illness and anatomy. "Imagine," he wrote typically, "hanging the stones of a man *outside*, where they are forever getting themselves knocked, pinched and bruised. Any decent mechanic would have put them in the exact center of the body, protected by a body envelope twice as thick as even a Presbyterian's skull. Moreover, consider certain parts of the female—always too large or too small. The elemental notion of standardization seems to have never presented itself to the celestial Edison."

He ended another note: "As for me, I am enjoying my usual 13 decrepitude. A new disease has developed, hitherto unknown to the faculty: a dermatitis caused by the plates I wear for my arches. No one knows how to cure it. I shall thus go limping to the crematory." He was always having a tumor dug out of his foot, or entering St. Agnes Hospital to have a folded membrane in his rectum investigated, or, depressed, shipping out samples of his body wastes to all the Baltimore pathologists he knew, which meant all the pathologists in the city. (A note of desperation here: "I begin to believe that in the end, as the hearse approaches the cemetery, I shall rise up and give three cheers.") Some weeks not a screed would go into the mailbox without some complaint, such as, "I have a sore mouth, can't smoke, it is 90 degrees, and at least twenty pests are in town," or, "My liver is swelled to a thickness of seven inches, and there are spiders in my urine." Other times he would audit his agonies—"an onslaught of pimples, aches, razor cuts, arch pains, and asthma," or, "asthma, piles, tongue trouble, hay fever, alcoholic liver, weak heels, dandruff, etc." Once he wrote George Jean Nathan:

> My ailments this morning come to the following:
> a. A burn on the tongue (healing)
> b. A pimple inside the jaw
> c. A sour stomach
> d. Pain in the prostate
> e. Burning in the gospel pipe (always a preliminary of the hay fever season)
> f. A cut finger
> g. A small pimple inside the nose (going away)
> h. A razor cut, smarting
> i. Tired eyes

Nathan, feeling that this was too much, sent him a set of false 14 teeth, a hairpiece, a cork leg, six bottles of liniment, and a copy of *What Every Boy Should Know*. In the return mail he received a querulous note asking why a bottle of asthma medicine had been omitted. "I am hacking and wheezing like Polonius."

It seemed to me that his hay fever sufferings were no greater   15
than those of other victims, though they may have been exacerbated by his willingness to try every nostrum on the market. ("My carcass is a battleground, and I am somewhat rocky. Hay fever pollen is pouring into my nose by the quart, but in my arteries it encounters the violent opposition of hay fever vaccine, and as a result there is a considerable boiling and bubbling.") This tendency had increased with the years and the advent of other complaints. In his preface to *Supplement Two*,[1] published in the spring of 1948, he wrote that his readers must not expect a third supplement, because "at my age a man encounters frequent reminders, some of them disconcerting, that his body is no more than a highly unstable congeries of the compounds of carbon."

By that autumn he was convinced that the end was near—with   16
some reason. His friends had long ago written him off as a hypochondriac, for he had been crying "Wolf!" as long as they could remember, but a real wolf had been quietly stalking him for ten years. On April 12, 1938, he had suffered a slight stroke. Two years later his doctor had found evidence that his cerebral circulation had been impaired. Mencken immediately started a journal to document the stages in his disintegration. By the evening of November 23, 1948, when he called at the apartment of his secretary, Rosalind C. Lohrfinck, preparatory to taking her to dinner, his deathwatch on himself amounted to a thick sheaf of typescript, some fifty pages in all. There were to be no entries after that, for that was the night his preoccupation with afflictions stopped being funny.

He was having a cocktail with Mrs. Lohrfinck when, in the   17
middle of a lucid sentence, he began to babble incoherently. Alarmed, she called his physician. When the doctor arrived, Mencken was pacing back and forth, ranting. At Johns Hopkins Hospital it was found that he had again been stricken by a cerebral thrombosis affecting his speech center and paralyzing his entire right side. He hovered for days at the threshold of death; then, slowly, he began to improve. The disability in his right side eased gradually and, after a month and a half of extensive treatment, left his arm and leg completely. But his speech center remained affected, and he could neither write nor read. Since boyhood his life had been built around the reading of the written word and the expression of his

1. Of *The American Language.*

reflections. Now everything which had given meaning to his existence was gone.

The burden of caring for him—and it was to be a heavy one—   18
fell on his unmarried younger brother August, a retired engineer who looked and sounded uncannily like him and with whom he shared the Hollins Street house. After Mencken's fifth week of hospitalization August brought the old man home. His condition was appalling. In conversation he tried again and again to summon the right word, and failed. Sometimes he would resort to pantomime, raising an imaginary cup to his lips when he could not recall the word for drinking. Other times he would try circumlocutions, saying "the thing you cut with," for example, when he meant "scissors." And occasionally nonsense words came forth: "yarb" for "yard," "ray" for "rain," "scoot" for "coat," etc.

It was a bitter blow for the author of *The American Language*,   19
and the worst of it was that he was fully aware of what was happening, understood the extent of the brain damage, and knew that his aphasia was incurable. In the Hopkins he had threatened to kill himself, but for all his thundering prose he had never been, and was not now, capable of violence. What actually happened was that he sank into a dreadful depression. He would stand in his study window, looking across at Union Square, on the opposite side of Hollins Street, saying almost inaudibly, "I wish this hideous existence would stop," saying, "How can anyone so stupid live," saying, "That a man like me, able to produce something, with the drive I had. . . . It's comic; it's just comic." In that first year of his disability he refused to allow anyone to read to him, refused to look at magazines with enlarged print, and wouldn't even listen to phonograph records. In one of his few remaining flashes of humor he hoarsely told me, "When I get to heaven, I'm going to speak to God very sharply."

Each time I called at his home I thought it was the last time,   20
but he lingered and lingered. The 1940's became the 1950's; my biography, *Disturber of the Peace* was published—in an act of conspicuous gallantry, he had managed to initial his approval of every quotation from his correspondence—and still his agony continued undiminished. Late in 1951 he suffered a massive heart attack. Again the Hopkins put him on the critical list, but after five months in the hospital he was released once more. August asked me to lend a hand, and together we brought his brother back to Hollins Street.

During the next two years I rarely saw the Menckens, for I was   21
moving up at the *Sun*, which meant assignments farther and farther from home. The ultimate outpost, for me, was New Delhi. After

the better part of a year as the paper's Indian correspondent, I
returned to Baltimore, and I had just finished covering the Army-
McCarthy hearings when August told me that his brother's mood
had changed slightly. He was now willing to be read to. Did I
know anyone who could spend mornings as his companion? I
hesitated for a moment. By then love had died between me and
the *Sun*, and there was no hope of a reconciliation. So I answered
August: "Yes. Me."

In those twilight years Mencken's day began at 8 A.M., when   22
Renshaw, a hospital orderly, arrived at the house after an all-night
shift in the Johns Hopkins accident room. "Rancho," as the old
man always called him, gave him a rubdown in his third-floor
bedroom, helped him wash and dress, and entertained him with
vivid stories of colorful cases he had seen during the night. Meanwhile August was preparing his brother's breakfast downstairs—
fruit juice, two soft-boiled eggs, and a slice of bread. Mencken ate
this in his second-floor study, swiveling his chair around to the
window so he could watch elementary school pupils trooping to
school while he drank his coffee.

Children had become dear to him; unlike their parents they   23
were natural in his presence, unembarrassed by his condition. He
enjoyed trips to the barber because he could admire a kindergarten
class playing across the street while his hair was cut, and two
small boys who saw him almost every day were five-year-old
Butch, who lived in the house next to his, and Alvin, a six-year-
old Negro from down the street. He would stroke Butch's rather
emaciated little dog—all pets look starved on Hollins Street; since
Mencken's own childhood the neighborhood had gone downhill
and was, his own home apart, virtually a slum—and congratulated
Alvin on the racing speed of his pet turtle. Emma, the Mencken
cook, nearly always had cookies for the boys. And each Christmas
the old man distributed huge sacks of candy to all the children
who lived around Union Square.

After breakfast Mrs. Lohrfinck came in. Together the two of   24
them went through the morning mail; painful though all communication had become for him, he insisted that everyone who
wrote him receive some sort of answer. Then she would riffle
through miscellaneous notes in his files, reading them to him, and
he would make a simple editorial judgment over the suitability of
each. (The resulting collection was published four months after
his death as *Minority Report*.) At ten o'clock she left. Her employer
accompanied her downstairs to the front door. Then, unless the
weather was impossible for him, he turned, trudged through the

house, took his cap from a peg in the dining room, and went outside.

For Mencken admirers, the geography of the backyard at 1524 25
Hollins Street is often clearer than scenes from their own childhood. To the left, as you came out the kitchen door, stood a high brick wall which he had begun building after the First World War. In it were set various tiles, with a concrete replica of Beethoven's life mask and the first five bars of his Fifth Symphony at the far end. To the right of the back gate was a green-and-white shed which had sheltered Mencken's pony when he was a boy, and which now housed August's tools. In warm seasons morning glories blossomed over the shed, raising their lovely green fingers against the West Baltimore sky. Beside the shed, sloping toward the house, was a workbench and a woodpile splashed with outrageously bright colors. Nearby stood a child's wagon; an unsuccessful thief had left it behind one night, and it, too, was splotched with purples, yellows, greens, and reds. Between these giddy hues and the kitchen was a brick terrace over which, on sunny mornings, the devoted August would hoist an awning. He would work at the bench, puffing a pipe and glancing up at the sky from time to time while his brother sat on a canvas chair, his hands lying in his lap like weapons put to rest.

When the noon whistle blew, they reentered the house and 26
Emma prepared lunch. Afterward they sat in the yard again until the children returned from school. Mencken then napped, and after an early supper they drank two ·martinis and retired. Often friends joined them for the evening cocktails. August controlled the social calendar. He excluded those who he thought might upset the old man and everyone he regarded as trivial—which, August being a misogynist, included all women except Blanche Knopf. The most frequent visitors were Louis Cheslock, Dr. Arnold Rich, Hamilton Owens of the *Sun*, and me.

There were variations in this routine. On sultry mornings, for 27
example, Mencken went through an elaborate stage business with the backyard thermometer, inspecting it and denouncing it. The brothers had no use for dry cleaning, and once I found them in the yard washing their suits and coats with a garden hose. Saturday afternoons Mencken listened to the Metropolitan broadcasts. Saturday evenings the brothers called on the Cheslocks. And at least once a week they went to a movie. This was a new medium for Mencken. Had he retained his ability to read, he would have finished life without having seen more than a half-dozen films, but now his disability left him with little choice. Depite his disability he retained his scorn for artistic dishonesty; he enjoyed Walt Disney

full-length cartoon features, Alec Guinness comedies, *Show Boat*, and *Lili*, but he despised melodrama or mawkishness in any form, and positively loathed anything about sports.

Starting in June of 1954 I arrived each morning as Mrs. Lohrfinck   28
was leaving. Usually Mencken was ready for me. If he wasn't, and the sun was shining, I would wait in the yard. Balmy weather was a good sign; he would greet me cheerily, saying, "Well, it's very nice out today; that should make us feel good," or "It's not too bad, we might be able to do a little work today." Even if rain was falling, we could sit in the shed, provided the day wasn't actually raw. When the weather was impossible—when it was sleeting, say—I would approach Hollins Street with dread, knowing that his mood would be grim. "Did you ever see anything like this? Isn't it ghastly?" he would groan, or "I feel very wobbly this morning; I'm going to pieces." At such times August would intervene, raising a hand like a traffic policeman and growling back at him, "Look, you don't feel any worse than I do." And his brother, instantly concerned, would say, "Is that right? Don't you feel well, August?"

Our sessions always began with the *Sun*. If it was the hay fever   29
season we always started with the report of the pollen count. Otherwise, as I leafed through the paper, he would ask, "Well, what's been happening? Any good stuff there, anything rich? Any murders or rapes? Any robberies?" Complex events—Germany's entry into NATO; McCarthyism—were beyond him now. He tried to grasp the tumultuous changes in China, but he couldn't, so we settled for small calamities. Sometimes there were none, and I would tell him so. He would stare at me, his eyes wide with amazement. "What?" he would say. "It's hard to believe. I don't know what's wrong with people nowadays. They're not killing one another any more. August, did you hear that?" And his brother, usually in the midst of painting some object a ghastly orange, or repairing a model boat for Alvin, would lay down his brush to echo his astonishment.

One day the *Sun* carried a story about a husband who had killed   30
his wife, her lover and himself. "You know," Mencken said, "it's probably the only decent thing he did in his life." Another high point was Dr. Samuel Shepard's trial for the murder of his wife. For Mencken it had everything: high theater, the physician who wasn't really a physician, the pillar of the community exposed as a hypocrite. Of Mrs. Shepard, Mencken said with a deep sigh, "Well, she's a goner now. She's up there with the angels." We sat for a moment in meditation, contemplating the sublime fate

of the doctor's victim. Then Mencken gestured impatiently at the paper. "Come on," he rasped. "How the hell did he croak her?"

On less favored days we turned to serious reading, and in retrospect I marvel on how much we got through that year: all of Twain and most of Conrad. I was struck by his observation that *Huckleberry Finn* breaks down at the point where Huck is reunited with Tom; Hemingway had said the same thing. Apart from that, both felt, it was a perfect novel. The most moving book we read, however, was Conrad's *Youth*. Conrad never mastered our idiom, Mencken said; he was translating Polish into English. Yet he admired the Pole more than any other writer of his time. The rich prose of *Youth* evoked memories of his own youth. I too was deeply affected. I had first read the book in college and hadn't understood it at all. Now in my early thirties the torrent of energy with which I had written my first two books was beginning to slacken. I glimpsed what lay ahead—literally glimpsed it, for there was Mencken beside me—and deeply felt a profound sense of sadness for the irretrievable stamina of the receding past.

One morning I stumbled over a hi-fi set in the front vestibule. It had arrived the previous afternoon, a present from Alfred Knopf, and the thoughtful dealer had included the latest Liberace record. Both brothers were exasperated. They didn't know how the thing worked. My own mechanical IQ is very low, but I can remove an appliance from a carton, stick a plug into the wall, lay a plastic disc on a turntable, and flip a switch—which was all that was necessary. We played perhaps thirty seconds of Liberace; then Mencken muttered something obscene and I switched it off. That evening I loaned him my Gilbert and Sullivan collection, however, and he was pathetically pleased by a new source of pleasure. Later, because *The Mikado* was his favorite, I bought him the album. I also introduced him to FM music. He had begun listening to AM stations before retiring and had been complaining sourly about their programing. August and I found the best FM stations for him, and that helped.

Apart from the reading, there was no fixed schedule for our mornings, but certain patterns recurred. Twice a week, after we had left the kitchen to Emma and settled in the yard beneath the gaudy awning, we would hear the distant clatter of garbage can lids. "Ah!" Mencken would breathe, brightening visibly; "here come the professors!" Watching the trash men empty his own cans—each of which was gaily painted "1524 Hollins Street" in red and yellow—he would remark, "You know, they do that very

well. The professors are really very elegant men." Now and then
visitors came to the front door. They rarely saw him. He ordered
William Randolph Hearst, Jr., turned away, and shook his head
when I suggested that I ask John Dos Passos to come in from the
York Road and visit him. He still had his pride; he didn't want
strangers or slight acquaintances to see him in this condition.

Often he was even uncomfortable with August and me. His   34
aphasia came and went. When it was bad, he couldn't remember
simple words or terms. He always recalled his brother's name, but
there were times when he couldn't think of Mrs. Lohrfinck's,
Emma's, Rancho's, Butch's, Alvin's, or mine; and he despaired.
Those sessions were grim for all of us, most of all for him. At his
best, however, he was very like his old self. He described with
gusto his vasectomy at Johns Hopkins when he was younger, and
the fecund woman in New York who had voluntarily tested the
success of the operation from time to time over the next year. He
also told me that he knew twenty men, none of them braggarts,
who had told him in confidence that they had bedded a famous
Baltimore beauty during what she herself had called her "fast"
youth. To him all women were either ladies, to be treated with
elaborate chivalry, or sex objects. There was no third category. He
was particularly hard on female journalists. He would dismiss them
with a snort or a few corrosive phrases. ("God, what an elephant,"
he said of one. "She makes you want to burn every bed in the
world.")

Occasionally he would talk of two books he had planned to   35
write, which would now remain unwritten; the first on the human
condition, for which he had completed two chapters, and the
second on American politics. And sometimes he spoke of other
writers: of James T. Farrell, who was a good friend to the end;
of Scott Fitzgerald, whose alcoholism had disgusted him; of Nathan,
whose late marriage he regarded as highly comic; and of Sinclair
Lewis's dermatological problems—"The only thing to do with Red,"
he reflected one morning, "was to skin him."

After reading and talking we would sit a while watching August   36
wield his bright paint brush, dabbing it dry from time to time on
the outside of the woodpile. "Isn't that gorgeous work my brother's
doing?" the old man would say from time to time. But he rarely
sat idle through an entire session. He had to be doing something;
even make-work was preferable to no work at all. Heaving up
from his canvas chair, he would drop to his knees among the
shrubs, stripping leaves from fallen branches for his compost heap
and binding the twigs into fagots for the fireplace. On hot days
he would periodically mutter, "Here, I'd better quit this or I'll fall

to pieces, this is knocking me out." But after an interval he would start groping among the bushes again.

Our most strenuous activity—I shared in it—was adding to the woodpile. On bitter days his fireplace was his chief solace. Cutting wood for it, and burning the wood, gave him extraordinary pleasure; it appealed, he said, to the boyhood love of vandalism which lingered in every man. The gathering of the fuel was as important to him as feeding it to the flames. His friends ordered seasoned cords over the telephone. In his view it was far nobler to scavenge neighborhood alleys and then saw up the loot.

Rising from his chair he would say to me, "Let's see what we can find outside. You can't tell—we might turn up something really superb." Strolling down the narrow lanes with the child's wagon and poking among the trash cans, we would uncover a variety of burnable junk—piano stools, fence posts, broom handles, discarded chairs, hatracks, broken coffee tables, ancient lounge chairs. If I spotted a particularly hideous specimen of Grand Rapids golden oak, he would gape and say, "Wow! *Look* at that, will you!" As we returned from patrol, he would call ahead, "August, I found something really rich. Isn't that beautiful? It's simply exquisite." Then a shade of comic doubt would cross his ruddy face. He would ask us gravely, "But don't you think it's a shame to burn a lovely piece like that?" After deliberation his brother would say, "It's a shame, all right, Harry, but we've got a long winter ahead." "It seems hard," the old man would say worriedly, and August would make a great show of winning him over by promising to save it for a very special occasion. This was the quintessential Mencken, clothing the preposterous in the robes of high seriousness. A passing stranger would have taken him literally, and he would have been in good company; Mencken had misled humorless critics thus for a half-century.

He himself wasn't well enough to do much sawing, so he sat by the end of the workbench, making outrageous comments while August and I took turns sinking the blade deep. We had a ritual; the length of each piece cut was determined by a measuring stick which was the exact width of the fireplace within. A certain percentage of our output had to be backlogs, and if our alley loot didn't include lengths of the proper thickness, we would nail odds and ends together—two mop handles, say, affixed to a broken crucifix, the base of a peach basket, and the wooden remains of a dilapidated plumber's helper. The more absurd the result, the uneasier Mencken grew over the propriety of feeding it to the flames. When its turn came at the hearth, he would wrestle audibly with his conscience before flinging it on the grate.

Eventually everything combustible went up in smoke, with one   40
memorable exception. One morning we were prowling in an alley,
furtively lifting galvanized lids and looking, I'm sure, like refugees
in postwar Europe searching for a scrap of meat, when he saw,
standing against a fence, a shabby chest of drawers. The rats had
been at it; we were far from Mencken's back gate; whether it was
worth dragging all that way was questionable. As we were debating,
a third figure joined us—a short, swart man in seedy khaki. He
asked us whether we wanted the dresser. We told him we didn't
know. He explained: his little daughter needed a place to store
her clothes. If we weren't going to take it, he would.

Disconcerted, and beset this time by genuine pangs, Mencken   41
stammered that we were merely hunting for firewood; by all means
the child should have it. The young man brightened with gratitude.
He would be back shortly, he said. His car was parked across the
street; he would fetch it and whisk the dresser home. As he dashed
off we reexamined the rat holes. They were really enormous. It
was a marvel that the thing stood. It had seemed worthless; it
still did.

"Poor fellow," Mencken said.   42

In the long silence that followed we contemplated the plight of   43
a father reduced to scrounging among castoffs for his children's
furniture.

Then the hush was broken by the deep-throated roar of a finely   44
tuned engine, and into the lane backed the longest, fattest, shiniest
pink Cadillac I had ever seen. The man leaped out, the chest of
drawers disappeared into its cavernous trunk, and then the Cadillac
vanished, too, gone in a cloud of exhaust.

Mencken's mouth fell open in amazement. "*Jesus Christ!*" he   45
gasped. "Did you see *that*?" I told him I could hardly have missed
it. "Think of it," he mused. "Imagine that man raising a family,
sending his children off to learn the principles of Americanism,
keeping his mother off the poor farm, raising money to cure his
wife of gallstones—and driving around in a rose-colored hearse!
August!" he hoarsed as we neared home. "We just saw the god-
damndest animal in Baltimore!"

As the noon whistle sounded he would methodically measure   46
the wood sawed. "Say, we got a lot of work done today," he
would say, standing back and admiring the stack. "Look how high
that pile is now." As winter deepened it shrank again, for unless
there was a thaw the brothers laid a fire every night. Evenings
when I dropped in to listen to their growing collection of LP

classics, the three of us would stare into the vivid coals. Like everything else about Mencken, his fires were unique. Their colors ranged all over the spectrum, for he cherished a hoard of chemically treated wood which, when ignited, matched the rainbow. I never learned to share his taste for after-dinner martinis, but I was tremendously impressed by those spectacular flames, and I said so.

When warm weather returned in the spring of 1955, Gertrude [47] Mencken arrived from her farm and joined us for two nerve-wracking hours. I had never met the brothers' sister before, and I think I came to understand something of their attitude toward women that evening. She was pleasant enough, but she couldn't seem to stop talking. The monologue went on and on, while August stared gloomily into the purple and orange fire and Mencken swelled with frustration. When she had departed the old man turned to his brother. In a slurred, gritty voice he demanded, "Where's the thing that makes music?" August replied, "You mean the gramaphone, Harry?" Mencken nodded grimly. He said, "I want the ghastly one. Lib—Lib—" "Liberace," I supplied, and August brought it from across the room. Mencken ordered, "Throw it on the fire." For once August hesitated. "It will make a terrible stink," he said. "Baloney," said Mencken. "It will be elegant. We need it to finish off this classy occasion." Into the flames it went. The stench was dreadful; after a while the old man stalked wordlessly off to bed and August removed the record with tongs. Even so, the odor was evident the next morning, and Emma had to air the house all day.

When summer arrived I said my last good-bye at Hollins Street. [48] I was leaving Baltimore for New England and had found a Hopkins graduate student who would come in mornings and read the paper to Mencken. It was a wrench for me; he obviously didn't want me to go, and at first he said so vehemently. That evening August reminded him that I had my own writing to do, and the next morning the old man had swung around completely; he offered his congratulations and said he expected me to write some swell books. His generosity, and his pretense that he had changed his mind, were typical of him. I have never known a public figure who was so different from his reputation. His readers thought of him as bigoted, cantankerous, wrathful, and rude, and he was none of those things. He was the elderly friend of Butch and Alvin. He was the cripple who was always solicitous about his brother's health. He was the stricken man who forced himself to initial the pages of my first manuscript, who always asked me in the shed whether I was properly clad; who, when he was in the depth of

his worst depressions, would excuse himself and retire to his bedroom because he didn't want to burden me with his troubles.

We both knew we would never meet again, for all our talk of   49
reunions. He was failing rapidly now. Yet he rallied gallantly that
last afternoon, and as I turned to leave through the vestibule he
struck a pose, one foot in front of the other, one hand on the
banister and the other, fisted, on his hip. "You know, I had a
superb time while it lasted," he said in that inimitable voice. "Very
soon it will stop, and I will go straight to heaven. Won't that be
exquisite? It will be very high-toned."

We shook hands; he trudged up the stairs into shadow, and I   50
departed carrying two farewell gifts, an Uncle Willie stogie and a
piece of the treated firewood. Seven months later an Associated
Press reporter called me in Connecticut to tell me that Mencken
had died in his sleep. His ashes were deposited in Baltimore's
Loudon Park Cemetery. Long afterward I read of his brother's
death, and later word reached me that the Hollins Street house—
"as much a part of me as my two hands," Mencken had once
said of it—was now occupied by the University of Maryland's
School of Social Work. That evening I carefully laid the piece of
treated firewood in my own fireplace. I didn't expect much; after
all that time, I thought, the chemicals would have lost their potency.
But I was wrong. Instantly a bright blue flame sprang up. Blue
changed to crimson, and after a few minutes there was another
change. It was eerie. From end to end the wood blazed up in a
deep green which would have been familiar to anyone who had
ever held a copy of *The American Mercury*.

Fleetingly I thought: *If only the Mercury were still being published!*   51
And: *If only he were still alive!* I remembered him lamenting the
fact that there was no decent memorial service for nonbelievers.
This little fire, I realized, was the closest I would ever come to
one for him. Now his home had become a headquarters for a
profession he had ridiculed. Miller Brothers' eating house, where
we had drained steins of pilsener, was being torn down; the name
of the restaurant lived on ignominiously in a sterile new Hilton
Hotel. The Baltimore which delighted Mencken as a young reporter,
when, he wrote, "the days chased one another like kittens chasing
their tails," was swiftly vanishing, as the flames on my andirons
were vanishing; soon the Baltimore I had known would disappear,
too. Briefly I was near tears. And then I checked myself. I realized
what Mencken's reaction to the maudlin fireside scene would have
been. He would have split it into sentimental flinders with one
vast gravelly chuckle.

E. B. WHITE

Once More to the Lake

One summer, along about 1904, my father rented a camp on   1
a lake in Maine and took us all there for the month of August.
We all got ringworm from some kittens and had to rub Pond's
Extract on our arms and legs night and morning, and my father
rolled over in a canoe with all his clothes on; but outside of that
the vacation was a success and from then on none of us ever
thought there was any place in the world like that lake in Maine.
We returned summer after summer—always on August 1st for
one month. I have since become a salt-water man, but sometimes
in summer there are days when the restlessness of the tides and
the fearful cold of the sea water and the incessant wind which
blows across the afternoon and into the evening make me wish
for the placidity of a lake in the woods. A few weeks ago this
feeling got so strong I bought myself a couple of bass hooks and
a spinner and returned to the lake where we used to go, for a
week's fishing and to revisit old haunts.

I took along my son, who had never had any fresh water up   2
his nose and who had seen lily pads only from train windows.
On the journey over to the lake I began to wonder what it would
be like. I wondered how time would have marred this unique,
this holy spot—the coves and streams, the hills that the sun set
behind, the camps and the paths behind the camps. I was sure
the tarred road would have found it out and I wondered in what
other ways it would be desolated. It is strange how much you
can remember about places like that once you allow your mind
to return into the grooves which lead back. You remember one
thing, and that suddenly reminds you of another thing. I guess I
remembered clearest of all the early mornings, when the lake was
cool and motionless, remembered how the bedroom smelled of
the lumber it was made of and of the wet woods whose scent
entered through the screen. The partitions in the camp were thin
and did not extend clear to the top of the rooms, and as I was
always the first up I would dress softly so as not to wake the
others, and sneak out into the sweet outdoors and start out in the
canoe, keeping close along the shore in the long shadows of the

First published in *Harper's Magazine*, August 1941.

pines. I remembered being very careful never to rub my paddle against the gunwale for fear of disturbing the stillness of the cathedral.

The lake had never been what you would call a wild lake. There were cottages sprinkled around the shores, and it was in farming country although the shores of the lake were quite heavily wooded. Some of the cottages were owned by nearby farmers, and you would live at the shore and eat your meals at the farmhouse. That's what our family did. But although it wasn't wild, it was a fairly large and undisturbed lake and there were places in it which, to a child at least, seemed infinitely remote and primeval. 3

I was right about the tar: it led to within half a mile of the shore. But when I got back there, with my boy, and we settled into a camp near a farmhouse and into the kind of summertime I had known, I could tell that it was going to be pretty much the same as it had been before—I knew it, lying in bed the first morning, smelling the bedroom, and hearing the boy sneak quietly out and go off along the shore in a boat. I began to sustain the illusion that he was I, and therefore, by simple transposition, that I was my father. This sensation persisted, kept cropping up all the time we were there. It was not an entirely new feeling, but in this setting it grew much stronger. I seemed to be living a dual existence. I would be in the middle of some simple act, I would be picking up a bait box or laying down a table fork, or I would be saying something, and suddenly it would be not I but my father who was saying the words or making the gesture. It gave me a creepy sensation. 4

We went fishing the first morning. I felt the same damp moss covering the worms in the bait can, and saw the dragonfly alight on the tip of my rod as it hovered a few inches from the surface of the water. It was the arrival of this fly that convinced me beyond any doubt that everything was as it always had been, that the years were a mirage and there had been no years. The small waves were the same, chucking the rowboat under the chin as we fished at anchor, and the boat was the same boat, the same color green and the ribs broken in the same places, and under the floor-boards the same fresh-water leavings and débris—the dead helgramite,[1] the wisps of moss, the rusty discarded fishhook, the dried blood from yesterday's catch. We stared silently at the tips of our rods, at the dragonflies that came and went. I lowered the tip of mine into the water, tentatively, pensively dislodging the fly, which darted two feet away, poised, darted two feet back, and came to rest again a little farther up the rod. There had been no years 5

1. An insect larva used for bait.

between the ducking of this dragonfly and the other one—the one that was part of memory. I looked at the boy, who was silently watching his fly, and it was my hands that held his rod, my eyes watching. I felt dizzy and didn't know which rod I was at the end of.

We caught two bass, hauling them in briskly as though they 6 were mackerel, pulling them over the side of the boat in a businesslike manner without any landing net, and stunning them with a blow on the back of the head. When we got back for a swim before lunch, the lake was exactly where we had left it, the same number of inches from the dock, and there was only the merest suggestion of a breeze. This seemed an utterly enchanted sea, this lake you could leave to its own devices for a few hours and come back to, and find that it had not stirred, this constant and trustworthy body of water. In the shallows, the dark, water-soaked sticks and twigs, smooth and old, were undulating in clusters on the bottom against the clean ribbed sand, and the track of the mussel was plain. A school of minnows swam by, each minnow with its small individual shadow, doubling the attendance, so clear and sharp in the sunlight. Some of the other campers were in swimming, along the shore, one of them with a cake of soap, and the water felt thin and clear and unsubstantial. Over the years there had been this person with the cake of soap, this cultist, and here he was. There had been no years.

Up to the farmhouse to dinner through the teeming, dusty field, 7 the road under our sneakers was only a two-track road. The middle track was missing, the one with the marks of the hooves and the splotches of dried, flaky manure. There had always been three tracks to choose from in choosing which track to walk in; now the choice was narrowed down to two. For a moment I missed terribly the middle alternative. But the way led past the tennis court, and something about the way it lay there in the sun reassured me; the tape had loosened along the backline, the alleys were green with plantains and other weeds, and the net (installed in June and removed in September) sagged in the dry noon, and the whole place steamed with midday heat and hunger and emptiness. There was a choice of pie for dessert, and one was blueberry and one was apple, and the waitresses were the same country girls, there having been no passage of time, only the illusion of it as in a dropped curtain—the waitresses were still fifteen; their hair had been washed, that was the only difference—they had been to the movies and seen the pretty girls with the clean hair.

Summertime, oh summertime, pattern of life indelible, the fade- 8 proof lake, the woods unshatterable, the pasture with the sweetfern

and the juniper forever and ever, summer without end; this was
the background, and the life along the shore was the design, the
cottages with their innocent and tranquil design, their tiny docks
with the flagpole and the American flag floating against the white
clouds in the blue sky, the little paths over the roots of the trees
leading from camp to camp and the paths leading back to the
outhouses and the can of lime for sprinkling, and at the souvenir
counters at the store the miniature birch-bark canoes and the post
cards that showed things looking a little better than they looked.
This was the American family at play, escaping the city heat,
wondering whether the newcomers in the camp at the head of
the cove were "common" or "nice," wondering whether it was
true that the people who drove up for Sunday dinner at the
farmhouse were turned away because there wasn't enough chicken.

It seemed to me, as I kept remembering all this, that those times   9
and those summers had been infinitely precious and worth saving.
There had been jollity and peace and goodness. The arriving (at
the beginning of August) had been so big a business in itself, at
the railway station the farm wagon drawn up, the first smell of
the pine-laden air, the first glimpse of the smiling farmer, and the
great importance of the trunks and your father's enormous authority
in such matters, and the feel of the wagon under you for the long
ten-mile haul, and at the top of the last long hill catching the first
view of the lake after eleven months of not seeing this cherished
body of water. The shouts and cries of the other campers when
they saw you, and the trunks to be unpacked, to give up their
rich burden. (Arriving was less exciting nowadays, when you
sneaked up in your car and parked it under a tree near the camp
and took out the bags and in five minutes it was all over, no fuss,
no loud wonderful fuss about trunks.)

Peace and goodness and jollity. The only thing that was wrong   10
now, really, was the sound of the place, an unfamiliar nervous
sound of the outboard motors. This was the note that jarred, the
one thing that would sometimes break the illusion and set the
years moving. In those other summertimes all motors were inboard;
and when they were at a little distance, the noise they made was
a sedative, an ingredient of summer sleep. They were one-cylinder
and two-cylinder engines, and some were make-and-break and
some were jump-spark, but they all made a sleepy sound across
the lake. The one-lungers throbbed and fluttered, and the twin-
cylinder ones purred and purred, and that was a quiet sound too.
But now the campers all had outboards. In the daytime, in the
hot mornings, these motors made a petulant, irritable sound; at
night, in the still evening when the afterglow lit the water, they
whined about one's ears like mosquitoes. My boy loved our rented

outboard, and his great desire was to achieve singlehanded mastery over it, and authority, and he soon learned the trick of choking it a little (but not too much), and the adjustment of the needle valve. Watching him I would remember the things you could do with the old one-cylinder engine with the heavy flywheel, how you could have it eating out of your hand if you got really close to it spiritually. Motor boats in those day didn't have clutches, and you would make a landing by shutting off the motor at the proper time and coasting in with a dead rudder. But there was a way of reversing them, if you learned the trick, by cutting the switch and putting it on again exactly on the final dying revolution of the flywheel, so that it would kick back against compression and begin reversing. Approaching a dock in a strong following breeze, it was difficult to slow up sufficiently by the ordinary coasting method, and if a boy felt he had complete mastery over his motor, he was tempted to keep it running beyond its time and then reverse it a few feet from the dock. It took a cool nerve, because if you threw the switch a twentieth of a second too soon you would catch the flywheel when it still had speed enough to go up past center, and the boat would leap ahead, charging bull-fashion at the dock.

We had a good week at the camp. The bass were biting well and the sun shone endlessly, day after day. We would be tired at night and lie down in the accumulated heat of the little bedrooms after the long hot day and the breeze would stir almost imperceptibly outside and the smell of the swamp drift in through the rusty screens. Sleep would come easily and in the morning the red squirrel would be on the roof, tapping out his gay routine. I kept remembering everything, lying in bed in the mornings—the small steamboat that had a long rounded stern like the lip of a Ubangi, and how quietly she ran on the moonlight sails, when the older boys played their mandolins and the girls sang and we ate doughnuts dipped in sugar, and how sweet the music was on the water in the shining night, and what it had felt like to think about girls then. After breakfast we would go up to the store and the things were in the same place—the minnows in a bottle, the plugs and spinners disarranged and pawed over by the youngsters from the boys' camp, the fig newtons and the Beeman's gum. Outside, the road was tarred and cars stood in front of the store. Inside, all was just as it had always been, except there was more Coca-Cola and not so much Moxie and root beer and birch beer and sarsaparilla. We would walk out with a bottle of pop apiece and sometimes the pop would backfire up our noses and hurt. We explored the streams, quietly, where the turtles slid off the sunny logs and dug their way into the soft bottom; and we lay on the town wharf and fed worms to the tame bass. Everywhere we went I had trouble making out which was I, the one walking at my side, the one walking in my pants.

One afternoon while we were there at that lake a thunderstorm came up. It was like the revival of an old melodrama that I had seen long ago with childish awe. The second-act climax of the drama of the electrical disturbance over a lake in America had not changed in any important respect. This was the big scene, still the big scene. The whole thing was so familiar, the first feeling of oppression and heat and a general air around camp of not wanting to go very far away. In midafternoon (it was all the same) a curious darkening of the sky, and a lull in everything that had made life tick; and then the way the boats suddenly swung the other way at their moorings with the coming of a breeze out of the new quarter, and the premonitory rumble. Then the kettle drum, then the snare, then the bass drum and cymbals, then crackling light against the dark, and the gods grinning and licking their chops in the hills. Afterward the calm, the rain steadily rustling in the calm lake, the return of light and hope and spirits, and the campers running out in joy and relief to go swimming in the rain, their bright cries perpetuating the deathless joke about how they were getting simply drenched, and the children screaming with delight at the new sensation of bathing in the rain, and the joke about getting drenched linking the generations in a strong indestructible chain. And the comedian who waded in carrying an umbrella. 12

When the others went swimming my son said he was going in too. He pulled his dripping trunks from the line where they had hung all through the shower, and wrung them out. Languidly, and with no thought of going in, I watched him, his hard little body, skinny and bare, saw him wince slightly as he pulled up around his vitals the small, soggy, icy garment. As he buckled the swollen belt suddenly my groin felt the chill of death. 13

ALICE WALKER

To Hell with Dying

"To hell with dying," my father would say. "These children want Mr. Sweet!" 1

From *In Love and Trouble* (1967).

Mr. Sweet was a diabetic and an alcoholic and a guitar player 2
and lived down the road from us on a neglected cotton farm. My
older brothers and sisters got the most benefit from Mr. Sweet,
for when they were growing up he had quite a few years ahead
of him and so was capable of being called back from the brink of
death any number of times—whenever the voice of my father
reached him as he lay expiring. "To hell with dying, man," my
father would say, pushing the wife away from the bedside (in
tears although she knew the death was not necessarily the last
one unless Mr. Sweet really wanted it to be). "These children
want Mr. Sweet!" And they did want him, for at a signal from
Father they would come crowding around the bed and throw
themselves on the covers, and whoever was the smallest at the
time would kiss him all over his wrinkled brown face and tickle
him so that he would laugh all down in his stomach, and his
mustache, which was long and sort or straggly, would shake like
Spanish moss and was also that color.

Mr. Sweet had been ambitious as a boy, wanted to be a doctor 3
or lawyer or sailor, only to find that black men fare better if they
are not. Since he could become none of these things he turned
to fishing as his only earnest career and playing the guitar as his
only claim to doing anything extraordinarily well. His son, the
only one that he and his wife, Miss Mary, had, was shiftless as
the day is long and spent money as if he were trying to see the
bottom of the mint, which Mr. Sweet would tell him was the
clean brown palm of his hand. Miss Mary loved her "baby,"
however, and worked hard to get him the "li'l necessaries" of
life, which turned out mostly to be women.

Mr. Sweet was a tall, thinnish man with thick kinky hair going 4
dead white. He was dark brown, his eyes were squinty and sort
of bluish, and he chewed Brown Mule tobacco. He was constantly
on the verge of being blind drunk, for he brewed his own liquor
and was not in the least a stingy sort of man, and was always
very melancholy and sad, though frequently when he was "feelin'
good" he'd dance around the yard with us, usually keeling over
just as my mother came to see what the commotion was.

Toward all of us children he was very kind, and had the grace 5
to be shy with us, which is unusual in grown-ups. He had great
respect for my mother for she never held his drunkenness against
him and would let us play with him even when he was about to
fall in the fireplace from drink. Although Mr. Sweet would sometimes
lose complete or nearly complete control of his head and neck so
that he would loll in his chair, his mind remained strangely acute
and his speech not too affected. His ability to be drunk and sober
at the same time made him an ideal playmate, for he was as weak

as we were and we could usually best him in wrestling, all the while keeping a fairly coherent conversation going.

We never felt anything of Mr. Sweet's age when we played 6 with him. We loved his wrinkles and would draw some on our brows to be like him, and his white hair was my special treasure and he knew it and would never come to visit us just after he had had his hair cut off at the barbershop. Once he came to our house for something, probably to see my father about fertilizer for his crops because, although he never paid the slightest attention to his crops, he liked to know what things would be best to use on them if he ever did. Anyhow, he had not come with his hair since he had just had it shaved off at the barbershop. He wore a huge straw hat to keep off the sun and also to keep his head away from me. But as soon as I saw him I ran up and demanded that he take me up and kiss me with his funny beard which smelled so strongly of tobacco. Looking forward to burying my small fingers into his woolly hair I threw away his hat only to find he had done something to his hair, that it was no longer there! I let out a squall which made my mother think that Mr. Sweet had finally dropped me in the well or something and from that day I've been wary of men in hats. However, not long after, Mr. Sweet showed up with his hair grown out and just as white and kinky and impenetrable as it ever was.

Mr. Sweet used to call me his princess, and I believed it. He 7 made me feel pretty at five and six, and simply outrageously devastating at the blazing age of eight and a half. When he came to our house with his guitar the whole family would stop whatever they were doing to sit around him and listen to him play. He liked to play "Sweet Georgia Brown," that was what he called me sometimes, and also he liked to play "Caldonia" and all sorts of sweet, sad, wonderful songs which he sometimes made up. It was from one of these songs that I heard that he had had to marry Miss Mary when he had in fact loved somebody else (now living in Chi-ca-go, or De-stroy, Michigan). He was not sure that Joe Lee, her "baby," was also his baby. Sometimes he would cry and that was an indication that he was about to die again. And so we would all get prepared, for we were sure to be called upon.

I was seven the first time I remember actually participating in 8 one of Mr. Sweet's "revivals"—my parents told me I had participated before, I had been the one chosen to kiss him and tickle him long before I knew the rite of Mr. Sweet's rehabilitation. He had come to our house, it was a few years after his wife's death, and was very sad, and also, typically, very drunk. He sat on the floor next to me and my older brother, the rest of the children were grown up and lived elsewhere, and began to play his guitar and cry. I held his woolly head in my arms and wished I could have been old enough to have been the woman he loved so much and that I had not been lost years and years ago.

When he was leaving, my mother said to us that we'd better sleep light that night for we'd probably have to go over to Mr. Sweet's before daylight. And we did. For soon after we had gone to bed one of the neighbors knocked on our door and called my father and said that Mr. Sweet was sinking fast and if he wanted to get in a word before the crossover he'd better shake a leg and get over to Mr. Sweet's house. All the neighbors knew to come to our house if something was wrong with Mr. Sweet, but they did not know how we always managed to make him well, or at least stop him from dying, when he was so often near death. As soon as we heard the cry we got up, my brother and I and my mother and father, and put on our clothes. We hurried out of the house and down the road for we were always afraid that we might someday be too late and Mr. Sweet would get tired of dallying.

When we got to the house, a very poor shack really, we found the front room full of neighbors and relatives and someone met us at the door and said it was all very sad that old Mr. Sweet Little (for Little was his family name, although we mostly ignored it) was about to kick the bucket. My parents were advised not to take my brother and me into the "death room," seeing we were so young and all, but we were so much more accustomed to the death room than he that we ignored him and dashed in without giving his warning a second thought. I was almost in tears, for these deaths upset me fearfully, and the thought of how much depended on me and my brother (who was such a ham most of the time) made me very nervous.

The doctor was bending over the bed and turned back to tell us for at least the tenth time in the history of my family that, alas, old Mr. Sweet Little was dying and that the children had best not see the face of implacable death (I didn't know what "implacable" was, but whatever it was, Mr. Sweet was not!). My father pushed him rather abruptly out of the way saying, as he always did and very loudly for he was saying it to Mr. Sweet, "To hell with dying, man, these children want Mr. Sweet"—which was my cue to throw myself upon the bed and kiss Mr. Sweet all around the whiskers and under the eyes and around the collar of his nightshirt where he smelled so strongly of all sorts of things, mostly liniment.

I was very good at bringing him around, for as soon as I saw that he was struggling to open his eyes I knew he was going to be all right, and so could finish my revival sure of success. As

soon as his eyes were open he would begin to smile and that way
I knew that I had surely won. Once, though, I got a tremendous
scare, for he could not open his eyes and later I learned that he
had had a stroke and that one side of his face was stiff and hard
to get into motion. When he began to smile I could tickle him in
earnest because I was sure that nothing would get in the way of
his laughter, although once he began to cough so hard that he
almost threw me off his stomach, but that was when I was very
small, little more than a baby, and my bushy hair had gotten in
his nose.

When we were sure he would listen to us we would ask him   13
why he was in bed and when he was coming to see us again and
could we play his guitar, which more than likely would be leaning
against the bed. His eyes would get all misty and he would sometimes
cry out loud, but we never let it embarrass us, for he knew that
we loved him and that we sometimes cried too for no reason. My
parents would leave the room to just the three of us; Mr. Sweet,
by that time, would be propped up in bed with a number of
pillows behind his head and with me sitting and lying on his
shoulder and along his chest. Even when he had trouble breathing
he would not ask me to get down. Looking into my eyes he would
shake his white head and run a scratchy old finger all around my
hairline, which was rather low down, nearly to my eyebrows, and
made some people say I looked like a baby monkey.

My brother was very generous in all this, he let me do all the   14
revivaling—he had done it for years before I was born and so was
glad to be able to pass it on to someone new. What he would do
while I talked to Mr. Sweet was pretend to play the guitar, in fact
pretend that he was a young version of Mr. Sweet, and it always
made Mr. Sweet glad to think that someone wanted to be like
him—of course, we did not know this then, we played the thing
by ear, and whatever he seemed to like, we did. We were desperately
afraid that he was just going to take off one day and leave us.

It did not occur to us that we were doing anything special; we   15
had not learned that death was final when it did come. We thought
nothing of triumphing over it so many times, and in fact became
a trifle contemptuous of people who let themselves be carried
away. It did not occur to us that if our father had been dying we
could not have stopped it, that Mr. Sweet was the only person
over whom we had power.

When Mr. Sweet was in his eighties I was studying in the   16
university many miles from home. I saw him whenever I went
home, but he was never on the verge of dying that I could tell
and I began to feel that my anxiety for his health and psychological

well-being was unnecessary. By this time he not only had a mustache but a long flowing snow-white beard, which I loved and combed and braided for hours. He was very peaceful, fragile, gentle, and the only jarring note about him was his old steel guitar, which he still played in the old sad, sweet, down-home blues way.

On Mr. Sweet's ninetieth birthday I was finishing my doctorate 17 in Massachusetts and had been making arrangements to go home for several weeks' rest. That morning I got a telegram telling me that Mr. Sweet was dying again and could I please drop everything and come home. Of course I could. My dissertation could wait and my teachers would understand when I explained to them when I got back. I ran to the phone, called the airport, and within four hours I was speeding along the dusty road to Mr. Sweet's.

The house was more dilapidated than when I was last there, 18 barely a shack, but it was overgrown with yellow roses which my family had planted many years ago. The air was heavy and sweet and very peaceful. I felt strange walking through the gate and up the old rickety steps. But the strangeness left me as I caught sight of the long white beard I loved so well flowing down the thin body over the familiar quilt coverlet. Mr. Sweet!

His eyes were closed tight and his hands, crossed over his stomach, 19 were thin and delicate, no longer scratchy. I remembered how always before I had run and jumped up on him just anywhere; now I knew he would not be able to support my weight. I looked around at my parents, and was surprised to see that my father and mother also looked old and frail. My father, his own hair very gray, leaned over the quietly sleeping old man, who, incidentally, smelled still of wine and tobacco, and said, as he'd done so many times, "To hell with dying, man! My daughter is home to see Mr. Sweet!" My brother had not been able to come as he was in the war in Asia. I bent down and gently stroked the closed eyes and gradually they began to open. The closed, wine-stained lips twitched a little, then parted in a warm, slightly embarrassed smile. Mr. Sweet could see me and he recognized me and his eyes looked very spry and twinkly for a moment. I put my head down on the pillow next to his and we just looked at each other for a long time. Then he began to trace my peculiar hairline with a thin, smooth finger. I closed my eyes when his finger halted above my ear (he used to rejoice at the dirt in my ears when I was little), his hand stayed cupped around my cheek. When I opened my eyes, sure that I had reached him in time, his were closed.

Even at twenty-four how could I believe that I had failed? that 20 Mr. Sweet was really gone? He had never gone before. But when I looked at my parents I saw that they were holding back tears.

They had loved him dearly. He was like a piece of rare and delicate china which was always being saved from breaking and which finally fell. I looked long at the old face, the wrinkled forehead, the red lips, the hands that still reached out to me. Soon I felt my father pushing something cool into my hands. It was Mr. Sweet's guitar. He had asked them months before to give it to me; he had known that even if I came next time he would not be able to respond in the old way. He did not want me to feel that my trip had been for nothing.

The old guitar! I plucked the strings, hummed "Sweet Georgia   21
Brown." The magic of Mr. Sweet lingered still in the cool steel box. Through the window I could catch the fragrant delicate scent of tender yellow roses. The man on the high old-fashioned bed with the quilt coverlet and the flowing white beard had been my first love.

ERNEST HEMINGWAY

Indian Camp

At the lake shore there was another rowboat drawn up. The   1
two Indians stood waiting.

Nick and his father got in the stern of the boat and the Indians shoved it off and one of them got in to row. Uncle George sat in the stern of the camp rowboat. The young Indian shoved the camp boat off and got in to row Uncle George.

The two boats started off in the dark. Nick heard the oarlocks of the other boat quite a way ahead of them in the mist. The Indians rowed with quick choppy strokes. Nick lay back with his father's arm around him. It was cold on the water. The Indian who was rowing them was working very hard, but the other boat moved further ahead in the mist all the time.

"Where are we going, Dad?" Nick asked.

"Over to the Indian camp. There is an Indian lady very sick."   5

"Oh," said Nick.

Across the bay they found the other boat beached. Uncle George was smoking a cigar in the dark. The young Indian pulled the boat way up on the beach. Uncle George gave both the Indians cigars.

They walked up from the beach through a meadow that was

From *In Our Time* (1925).

soaking wet with dew, following the young Indian who carried a lantern. Then they went into the woods and followed a trail that led to the logging road that ran back into the hills. It was much lighter on the logging road as the timber was cut away on both sides. The young Indian stopped and blew out his lantern and they all walked on along the road.

They came around a bend and a dog came out barking. Ahead were the lights of the shanties where the Indian bark-peelers lived. More dogs rushed out at them. The two Indians sent them back to the shanties. In the shanty nearest the road there was a light in the window. An old woman stood in the doorway holding a lamp.

Inside on a wooden bunk lay a young Indian woman. She had been trying to have her baby for two days. All the old women in the camp had been helping her. The men had moved off up the road to sit in the dark and smoke out of range of the noise she made. She screamed just as Nick and the two Indians followed his father and Uncle George into the shanty. She lay in the lower bunk, very big under a quilt. Her head was turned to one side. In the upper bunk was her husband. He had cut his foot very badly with an ax three days before. He was smoking a pipe. The room smelled very bad.

Nick's father ordered some water to be put on the stove, and while it was heating he spoke to Nick.

"This lady is going to have a baby, Nick," he said.

"I know," said Nick.

"You don't know," said his father. "Listen to me. What she is going through is called being in labor. The baby wants to be born and she wants it to be born. All her muscles are trying to get the baby born. That is what is happening when she screams."

"I see," Nick said.

Just then the woman cried out.

"Oh, Daddy, can't you give her something to make her stop screaming?" asked Nick.

"No. I haven't any anæsthetic," his father said. "But her screams are not important. I don't hear them because they are not important."

The husband in the upper bunk rolled over against the wall.

The woman in the kitchen motioned to the doctor that the water was hot. Nick's father went into the kitchen and poured about half of the water out of the big kettle into a basin. Into the water left in the kettle he put several things he unwrapped from a handkerchief.

"Those must boil," he said, and began to scrub his hands in the basin of hot water with a cake of soap he had brought from the camp. Nick watched his father's hands scrubbing each other with the soap. While his father washed his hands very carefully and thoroughly, he talked.

"You see, Nick, babies are supposed to be born head first but sometimes they're not. When they're not they make a lot of trouble for everybody. Maybe I'll have to operate on this lady. We'll know in a little while."

When he was satisfied with his hands he went in and went to work.

"Pull back that quilt, will you, George?" he said. "I'd rather not touch it."

Later when he started to operate Uncle George and three Indian   25 men held the woman still. She bit Uncle George on the arm and Uncle George said, "Damn squaw bitch!" and the young Indian who had rowed Uncle George over laughed at him. Nick held the basin for his father. It all took a long time.

His father picked the baby up and slapped it to make it breathe and handed it to the old woman.

"See, it's a boy, Nick," he said. "How do you like being an interne?"

Nick said, "All right." He was looking away so as not to see what his father was doing.

"There. That gets it," said his father and put something into the basin.

Nick didn't look at it.   30

"Now," his father said, "there's some stitches to put in. You can watch this or not, Nick, just as you like. I'm going to sew up the incision I made."

Nick did not watch. His curiosity had been gone for a long time.

His father finished and stood up. Uncle George and the three Indian men stood up. Nick put the basin out in the kitchen.

Uncle George looked at his arm. The young Indian smiled reminiscently.

"I'll put some peroxide on that, George," the doctor said.   35

He bent over the Indian woman. She was quiet now and her eyes were closed. She looked very pale. She did not know what had become of the baby or anything.

"I'll be back in the morning," the doctor said, standing up. "The nurse should be here from St. Ignace by noon and she'll bring everything we need."

He was feeling exalted and talkative as football players are in the dressing room after a game.

"That's one for the medical journal, George," he said. "Doing a Cæsarian with a jack-knife and sewing it up with nine-foot, tapered gut leaders."

Uncle George was standing against the wall, looking at his arm.   40
"Oh, you're a great man, all right," he said.

"Ought to have a look at the proud father. They're usually the worst sufferers in these little affairs," the doctor said. "I must say he took it all pretty quietly."

He pulled back the blanket from the Indian's head. His hand came away wet. He mounted on the edge of the lower bunk with the lamp in one hand and looked in. The Indian lay with his face toward the wall. His throat had been cut from ear to ear. The blood had flowed down into a pool where his body sagged the bunk. His head rested on his left arm. The open razor lay, edge up, in the blankets.

"Take Nick out of the shanty, George," the doctor said.

There was no need of that. Nick, standing in the door of the   45
kitchen, had a good view of the upper bunk when his father, the lamp in one hand, tipped the Indian's head back.

It was just beginning to be daylight when they walked along the logging road back toward the lake.

"I'm terribly sorry I brought you along, Nickie," said his father, all his post-operative exhilaration gone. "It was an awful mess to put you through."

"Do ladies always have such a hard time having babies?" Nick asked.

"No, that was very, very exceptional."

"Why did he kill himself, Daddy?"   50

"I don't know, Nick. He couldn't stand things, I guess."

"Do many men kill themselves, Daddy?"

"Not very many, Nick."

"Do many women?"

"Hardly ever."   55

"Don't they ever?"

"Oh, yes. They do sometimes."

"Daddy?"

"Yes."

"Where did Uncle George go?"   60

"He'll turn up all right."

"Is dying hard, Daddy?"

"No, I think it's pretty easy, Nick. It all depends."

They were seated in the boat, Nick in the stern, his father rowing. The sun was coming up over the hills. A bass jumped, making a circle in the water. Nick trailed his hand in the water. It felt warm in the sharp chill of the morning.

In the early morning on the lake sitting in the stern of the boat   65
with his father rowing, he felt quite sure that he would never die.

Thinking About Mortality

The summer I turned twenty-three I spent two weeks doing practically nothing except reading the poetry and sermons of John Donne, one of Shakespeare's most famous contemporaries. It was an alarming experience. The poetry is so filled with plagues, funeral shrouds, cemeteries, and worm-riddled carcasses that I once found myself reading with my hand on my throat, subconsciously checking my carotid pulse. The last straw was Isaak Walton's description of Donne's final days, including the painting of his funeral portrait. From his sickbed, Donne had ordered a carver to make a wooden pedestal in the shape of a burial urn. When it was finished, he had several fires lit to keep the chill out of his study, then

> . . . he brought with him into that place his winding-sheet in his hand, and having put off all his clothes, had this sheet put on him, and so tied with knots at his head and feet, and his hands so placed as dead bodies are usually fitted, to be shrowded and put into their coffin, or grave. Upon this Urn he thus stood, with his eyes shut, and with so much of the sheet turned aside as might shew his lean, pale, and death-like face, which was purposely turned toward the East, from whence he expected the second coming of his and our Saviour Jesus. In this posture he was drawn at this just height; and when the picture was fully finished, he caused it to be set by his bedside, where it continued and became his hourly object till his death. . . .

All this was too much for me, and I wrote an essay that was supposed to be about Donne the poet but was really about Donne the morbid neurotic.

My teacher quietly dismantled my thesis at our next meeting. He reminded me that as a baby-boom American I was part of the first generation on earth to concern itself seriously with tooth decay. He guessed (quite rightly) that my health was robust, that all my siblings were alive, that my father was still capable of beating me at tennis, that my mother could nearly pass for a college student, and that my grandparents were aging quietly in some distant city and would die under professional supervision in a hospital. Donne, on the other hand, experienced life and death the old-fashioned way. Two of his siblings died in infancy, and three others in childhood. His father died when he was four. Of Donne's own twelve children, three died in childhood and two were stillborn. His wife died in childbirth. When Donne was in his fifties, the plague, which had killed his brother thirty years earlier, returned. Donne buried hundreds of his parishioners and reported that in the summer of 1625 a thousand people were dying per day in London and that "the Citizens fled away, as out of a house on fire," many of them dying of exposure on the highways or in the fields. A young person of my generation, my teacher said, might try to avoid death by looking the other way: for most of human history there has been no other way to look.

Looking the other way, he added, would only serve so long. He smiled and turned around to show me the bald spot on his head: his *memento mori*, the equivalent of the skull that scholars of Donne's time kept on their writing tables.

My teacher's rebuttal didn't quite make me comfortable with the beautiful and almost affectionate dwelling on death one finds in Donne's poetry or in Jeremy Taylor's "Holy Dying." There is something "brave and spirited," as Robert Louis Stevenson says, in acting immortal; we are moved by people who resist disease and death as violently as Richard Selzer's patient in "The Discus Thrower." But our culture has gone well beyond keeping a stiff upper lip: the sociologist Geoffrey Gorer once pointed out that "the natural processes of corruption and decay have become disgusting, as disgusting as the natural processes of birth and copulation were a century ago." We have abandoned the public forms of mourning and are increasingly abandoning the mourners as well, not knowing how to deal with their grief. We avoid the elderly, the suffering, the mortally ill. Several of the selections in this section—those by Patricia Hampl, William Manchester, Annie Dillard, and Alice Walker, especially—are remarkably clear-sighted looks at the things we now turn our eyes from. E.B. White's "Once More to the Lake" and Ernest Hemingway's "Indian Camp" are less direct: in them the theme of mortality appears suddenly, like an animal emerging from a thicket.

QUESTIONS

1. Two generations ago, almost every high school student had to memorize the peroration of William Cullen Bryant's "Thanatopsis":

> *So live, that when thy summons comes to join*
> *The innumerable caravan, that moves*
> *To that mysterious realm, where each shall take*
> *His chamber in the silent halls of death,*
> *Thou go not like a quarry-slave at night,*
> *Scourged to his dungeon, but, sustained and soothed*
> *By an unfaltering trust, approach thy grave*
> *Like one who wraps the drapery of his couch*
> *About him, and lies down to pleasant dreams.*

Do you know people who share Bryant's attitude toward life and death? Is such an attitude common today? What might be changing our attitudes?

2. Hampl, Manchester, Walker, and Selzer all notice the way that a person's last days bring out his or her character traits, expected or unexpected, serious or comic. Have you had an experience comparable to any of theirs?

3. What memory do you have of your earliest experiences with the death of a friend or relative? Can you relate your experience to Walker's or Hampl's or Nick's in "Indian Camp"?

4. Have you had experiences with death or suffering that troubled you as deeply as Annie Dillard was troubled by the events she describes in "The Deer at Providencia"?

5. How accurate is Gorer's statement that we now find death pornographic in the same way Victorians found sex pornographic? What evidence for your answer can you find in the media and in the attitudes and customs of your family and community?

6. Whom do you know, personally or through the media, whose attitudes toward life and death strike you as particularly admirable? What are these attitudes?

JOURNEYS

ANNA LEONOWENS

The English Governess at the
Siamese Court

In 1825 a royal prince of Siam[1] (his birthright wrested from   1
him by an elder half-brother and his life imperilled) took refuge
in a Buddhist monastery and assumed the yellow garb of a priest.

Finally in 1851, at the age of 45, he emerged from his cloister,   2
and was crowned, with the title of Somedtch-Phra Paramendr
Maha Mongkut (duke, and royal bearer of the great crown).

For twenty-five years had the true heir to the throne of the   3
Phra-batts (the Golden-footed), patiently biding his time, lain perdu
in his monastery, diligently devoting himself to the study of Sanskrit,
Bali, theology, history, geology, chemistry, and especially astronomy.

In the Oriental tongues this progressive king was eminently   4
proficient; and toward priests, preachers, and teachers, of all creeds,
sects, and sciences, an enlightened exemplar of tolerance. It was
likewise his peculiar vanity to pass for an accomplished English
scholar, and to this end he maintained in his palace at Bangkok
a private printing establishment, with fonts of English type, which
he was at no loss to keep in "copy." Perhaps it was the printing-
office which suggested, quite naturally, an English governess for
the *élite* of his wives and concubines, and their offspring,—in
number amply adequate to the constitution of a royal school, and
in material most attractively fresh and romantic. Happy thought!
Wherefore, behold me, just after sunset on a pleasant day in April,
1862, on the threshhold of the outer court of the Grand Palace,
accompanied by my own brave little boy, and escorted by a
compatriot.

A flood of light sweeping through the spacious Hall of Audience   5
displayed a throng of noblemen in waiting. None turned a glance,
or seemingly a thought, on us, and, my child being tired and
hungry, I urged Captain B—— to present us without delay. At
once we mounted the marble steps, and entered the brilliant hall
unannounced. Ranged on the carpet were many prostrate, mute,
and motionless forms, over whose heads to step was a temptation

From *The English Governess at the Siamese Court,* serialized in *The Atlantic* in 1870.
These memoirs were the basis of the novel *Anna and the King of Siam* (1944) by
Margaret London, which was in turn the basis of the musical *The King and I.*
1. Now Thailand.

as drolly natural as it was dangerous. His Majesty spied us quickly, and advanced abruptly, petulantly screaming, "Who? who? who?"

Captain B—— (who, by the by, is a titled nobleman of Siam)   6
introduced me as the English governess, engaged for the royal family. The king shook hands with us, and immediately proceeded to march up and down in quick step, putting one foot before the other with mathematical precision, as if under drill. "Forewarned, forearmed," my friend whispered that I should prepare myself for a sharp cross-questioning as to my age, my husband, children, and other strictly personal concerns. Suddenly his Majesty, having cogitated sufficiently in his peculiar manner, with one long final stride halted in front of us, and pointing straight at me with his forefinger, asked, "How old shall you be?"

Scarcely able to repress a smile at a proceeding so absurd, and   7
with my sex's distaste for so serious a question, I demurely replied, "One hundred and fifty years old."

Had I made myself much younger, he might have ridiculed or   8
assailed me; but now he stood surprised and embarrassed for a few moments, then resumed his quick march, and at last, beginning to perceive the jest, coughed, laughed, coughed again, and then in a high, sharp key asked, "In what year were you borned?"

Instantly I "struck" a mental balance, and answered, as gravely   9
as I could, "In 1788."

At this point the expression of his Majesty's face was indescribably   10
comical. Captain B—— slipped behind a pillar to laugh; but the king only coughed, with a significant emphasis that startled me, and addressed a few words to his prostrate courtiers, who smiled at the carpet,—all except the prime minister, who turned to look at me. But his Majesty was not to be baffled so: again he marched with vigor, and then returned to the attack with *élan*.

"How many years shall you be married?"   11

"For several years, your Majesty."   12

He fell into a brown study; then suddenly rushed at me, and   13
demanded triumphantly:—

"Ha! How many grandchildren shall you now have? Ha! ha!   14
How many? How many? Ha! ha! ha!"

Of course we all laughed with him; but the general hilarity   15
admitted of a variety of constructions.

Then suddenly he seized my hand, and dragged me, *nolens*   16
volens,[2] my little Louis holding fast by my skirt, through several sombre passages along which crouched duennas, shrivelled and

---

2. Willy-nilly, having no alternative.

grotesque, and many youthful women, covering their faces, as if blinded by the splendor of the passing Majesty. At length he stopped before one of the many-curtained recesses, and, drawing aside the hangings, disclosed a lovely, childlike form. He stooped and took her hand (she naïvely hiding her face), and placing it in mine, said: "This is my wife, the Lady T. She desires to be educated in English. She is as renowned for her talents as for her beauty, and it is our pleasure to make her a good English scholar. You shall educate her for me."

I replied that the office would give me much pleasure; for nothing   17
could be more eloquently winning than the modest, timid bearing of that tender young creature in the presence of her lord. She laughed low and pleasantly as he translated my sympathetic words to her, and seemed so enraptured with the graciousness of his act that I took my leave of her with a sentiment of profound pity.

He led me back by the way we had come; and now we met   18
many children, who put my patient boy to much childish torture for the gratification of their startled curiosity.

"I have sixty-seven children," said his Majesty, when we had   19
returned to the Audience Hall. "You shall educate them; and as many of my wives, likewise, as may wish to learn English. And I have much correspondence in which you must assist me. And, moreover, I have much difficulty for reading and translating French letters; for French are fond of using gloomily deceiving terms. You must undertake; and you shall make all their murky sentences and gloomily deceiving propositions clear to me. And, furthermore, I have by every mail many foreign letters whose writing is not easily read by me. You shall copy on round hand, for my readily perusal thereof."

Nil desperandum;[3] but I began by despairing of my ability to   20
accomplish tasks so multifarious. I simply bowed, however, and so dismissed myself for that evening.

When next I "interviewed" the king, I was accompanied by the   21
premier's sister, a fair and pleasant woman, whose whole stock of English was, "Good morning, sir"; and with this somewhat irrelevant greeting, a dozen times in an hour, though the hour were night, she relieved her pent-up feelings and gave expression to her sympathy and regard for me. We found his Majesty in a less genial mood than at my first reception. He approached us coughing loudly and repeatedly, a sufficiently ominous fashion of announcing himself. He then approached me, and said, in a loud and domineering tone,—

3. "Never despair."

"It is our pleasure that you shall reside within this palace with   22
our family."

I replied that it would be quite impossible for me to do so; that,   23
being as yet unable to speak the language, and the gates being
shut every evening, I should feel like an unhappy prisoner in the
palace.

"Where do you go every evening?" he demanded.   24

"Not anywhere, your Majesty. I am a stranger here."   25

"Then why you shall object to the gates being shut?"   26

"I do not clearly know," I replied, with a secret shudder at the   27
idea of sleeping within those walls; "but I am afraid I could not
do it. I beg your Majesty will remember that in your gracious
letter you promised me 'a residence adjoining the royal palace,'
not within it."

He turned and looked at me, his face growing almost purple   28
with rage. "I do not know I have promised. I do not know former
condition. I do not know anything but you are our servant; and
it is our pleasure that you must live in this palace, and *you shall
obey.*" Those last three words he fairly screamed.

I trembled in every limb, and for some time I knew not how   29
to reply. At length I ventured to say: "I am prepared to obey all
your Majesty's commands, within the obligation of my duty to
your family; but beyond that I can promise no obedience."

"You *shall* live in palace," he roared,—"you shall live in palace.   30
I will give woman slaves to wait on you. You shall commence
royal school in this pavilion on Thursday next. That is the best
day for such undertaking, in the estimation of our astrologers."

With that, he addressed, in a frantic manner, commands, un-   31
intelligible to me, to some of the old women about the pavilion.
I turned and saw the king beckoning and calling to me. I bowed
to him profoundly, but passed on through the brass door.

But kings who are not mad have their sober second thoughts   32
like other rational people. His Golden-footed Majesty presently
repented him of his arbitrary "cantankerousness," and in due time,
my ultimatum was accepted. . . .

His Majesty was the most capricious of kings as to his working   33
moods,—busy when the average man should be sleeping, sleeping
while letters, papers, despatches, messengers, mailboats waited.
More than once had we been aroused at dead of night by noisy
female slaves, and dragged in hot haste and consternation to the
Hall of Audience, only to find that his Majesty was, not at his last
gasp, as we had feared, but simply bothered to find in Webster's

Dictionary some word that was to be found nowhere but in his own fertile brain.

Before my arrival in Bangkok it had been his not uncommon practice to send for a missionary at midnight, have him beguiled or abducted from his bed, and conveyed by boat to the palace, some miles up the river, to inquire if it would not be more elegant to write *murky* instead of *obscure*, or *gloomily dark* rather than *not clearly apparent*. And if the wretched man should venture to declare his honest preference for the ordinary over the extraordinary form of expression, he was forthwith dismissed with irony, arrogance, or even insult, and without a word of apology for the rude invasion of his rest.

His Majesty usually passed his mornings in study or dictating or writing English letters and despatches. His breakfast, though a repast sufficiently frugal for Oriental royalty, was served with awesome forms. In an antechamber adjoining a noble hall, rich in grotesque carvings and gildings, a throng of females waited, while his Majesty sat at a long table, near which knelt twelve women before great silver trays laden with twelve varieties of viands,— soups, meats, game, poultry, fish, vegetables, cakes, jellies, preserves, sauces, fruits, and teas. Each tray, in its order, was passed by three ladies to the head wife or concubine, who removed the silver covers, and at least seemed to taste the contents of each dish; and then, advancing on her knees, she set them on the long table before the king.

But his Majesty was notably temperate in his diet, and by no means a gastronome. In his long seclusion in a Buddhist cloister he had acquired habits of severe simplicity and frugality, as a preparation for the exercise of those powers of mental concentration for which he was remarkable. At these morning repasts it was his custom to detain me in conversation, relating to some topic of interest derived from his studies, or in reading or translating. He was more systematically educated, and a more capacious devourer of books and news, than perhaps any man of equal rank in our day. But much learning had made him morally mad; his extensive reading had engendered in his mind an extreme scepticism concerning all existing religious systems. In inborn integrity and steadfast principle he had no faith whatever, and he honestly pitied the delusion that pinned its faith on human truth and virtue.

Ah! if this man could but have cast off the cramping yoke of his intellectual egotism, and been loyal to the free government of his own true heart, what a demigod might he not have been, among the lower animals of Asiatic royalty!

When the sweet, bright little princess, Somdetch Chowfa Chan-   38
drmondol (who was so dear to me by her pet name of Fâ-ying),
was seized with cholera on the night of the 13th of May, 1863,
his Majesty wrote to me:—

MY DEAR MAM:

"Our well-beloved daughter, your favorite pupil, is attacked with
cholera, and has earnest desire to see you, and is heard much to
make frequent repetition of your name. I beg that you will favor her
wish. I fear her illness is mortal, as there has been three deaths since
morning. She is best beloved of my children.
"I am your afflicted friend,

"S. P. P. MAHA MONGKUT."

In a moment I was in my boat. I entreated, I flattered, I scolded,   39
the rowers. How slow they were! how strong the opposing current!
And when at last I stood panting at the door of my Fâ-ying's
chamber—too late! even Dr. Campbell (the surgeon of the British
consulate) had come too late.

An attendant hurried me to the king, who, reading the heavy   40
tidings in my silence, covered his face with his hands and wept
passionately. Strange and terrible were the tears of such a man.
What could I say? What could I do but weep with him; and then
steal quietly away, and leave the king to the father?

WALKER PERCY

Sightseer

Every explorer names his island Formosa, beautiful. To him it   1
is beautiful because, being first, he has access to it and can see it
for what it is. But to no one else is it ever as beautiful—except
the rare man who manages to recover it, who knows that it has
to be recovered.

Garcia López de Cárdenas discovered the Grand Canyon and   2
was amazed at the sight. It can be imagined: One crosses miles
of desert, breaks through the mesquite, and there it is at one's
feet. Later the government set the place aside as a national park,
hoping to pass along to millions the experience of Cárdenas. Does

Excerpted from "The Loss of the Creature," first published in 1954.

not one see the same sight from the Bright Angel Lodge that Cárdenas saw?

The assumption is that the Grand Canyon is a remarkably interesting and beautiful place and that if it had a certain value P for Cárdenas, the same value P may be transmitted to any number of sightseers—just as Banting's discovery of insulin can be transmitted to any number of diabetics. A counterinfluence is at work, however, and it would be nearer the truth to say that if the place is seen by a million sightseers, a single sightseer does not receive value P but a millionth part of value P.

It is assumed that since the Grand Canyon has the fixed interest value P, tours can be organized for any number of people. A man in Boston decides to spend his vacation at the Grand Canyon. He visits his travel bureau, looks at the folder, signs up for a two-week tour. He and his family take the tour, see the Grand Canyon, and return to Boston. May we say that this man has seen the Grand Canyon? Possibly he has. But it is more likely that what he has done is the one sure way not to see the canyon.

Why is it almost impossible to gaze directly at the Grand Canyon under these circumstances and see it for what it is—as one picks up a strange object from one's back yard and gazes directly at it? It is almost impossible because the Grand Canyon, the thing as it is, has been appropriated by the symbolic complex which has already been formed in the sightseer's mind. Seeing the canyon under approved circumstances is seeing the symbolic complex head on. The thing is no longer the thing as it confronted the Spaniard; it is rather that which has already been formulated—by picture postcard, geography book, tourist folders, and the words *Grand Canyon*. As a result of this preformulation, the source of the sightseer's pleasure undergoes a shift. Where the wonder and delight of the Spaniard arose from his penetration of the thing itself, from a progressive discovery of depths, patterns, colors, shadows, etc., now the sightseer measures his satisfaction *by the degree to which the canyon conforms to the preformed complex*. If it does so, if it looks just like the postcard, he is pleased; he might even say, "Why it is every bit as beautiful as a picture postcard!" He feels he has not been cheated. But if it does not conform, if the colors are somber, he will not be able to see it directly; he will only be conscious of the disparity between what it is and what it is supposed to be. He will say later that he was unlucky in not being there at the right time. The highest point, the term of the sightseer's satisfaction, is not the sovereign discovery of the thing before him; it is rather the measuring up of the thing to the criterion of the preformed symbolic complex.

Seeing the canyon is made even more difficult by what the   6
sightseer does when the moment arrives, when sovereign knower
confronts the thing to be known. Instead of looking at it, he
photographs it. There is not confrontation at all. At the end of
forty years of preformulation and with the Grand Canyon yawning
at his feet, what does he do? He waives his right of seeing and
knowing and records symbols for the next forty years. For him
there is no present; there is only the past of what has been formulated
and seen and the future of what has been formulated and not
seen. The present is surrendered to the past and the future.

The sightseer may be aware that something is wrong. He may   7
simply be bored; or he may be conscious of the difficulty: that
the great thing yawning at his feet somehow eludes him. The
harder he looks at it, the less he can see. It eludes everybody. The
tourist cannot see it; the bellboy at the Angel Lodge cannot see
it: for him it is only one side of the space he lives in, like one
wall of a room; to the ranger it is a tissue of everyday signs relevant
to his own prospects—the blue haze down there means that he
will probably get rained on during the donkey ride.

How can the sightseer recover the Grand Canyon? He can recover   8
it in any number of ways, all sharing in common the strategem
of avoiding the approved confrontation of the tour and the Park
Service.

It may be recovered by leaving the beaten track. The tourist   9
leaves the tour, camps in the back country. He arises before dawn
and approaches the South Rim through a wild terrain where there
are no trails and no railed-in lookout points. In other words, he
sees the canyon by avoiding all the facilities for seeing the canyon.
If the benevolent Park Service hears about this fellow and thinks
he has a good idea and places the following notice in the Bright
Angel Lodge: *Consult ranger for information on getting off the beaten
track*—the end result will only be the closing of another access to
the canyon.

It may be recovered by a dialectical movement which brings   10
one back to the beaten track but at a level above it. For example,
after a lifetime of avoiding the beaten track and guided tours, a
man may deliberately seek out the most beaten track of all, the
most commonplace tour imaginable: he may visit the canyon by
a Greyhound tour in the company of a party from Terre Haute—
just as a man who has lived in New York all his life may visit
the Statue of Liberty. (Such dialectical savorings of the familiar as
the familiar are, of course, a favorite strategem of *The New Yorker*
magazine.) The thing is recovered from familiarity by means of
an exercise in familiarity. Our complex friend stands behind the
fellow tourists at the Bright Angel Lodge and sees the canyon

through them and their predicament, their picture taking and busy disregard. In a sense, he exploits his fellow tourists; he stands on their shoulders to see the canyon.

Such a man is far more advanced in the dialectic than the 11 sightseer who is trying to get off the beaten track—getting up at dawn and approaching the canyon through the mesquite. This stratagem is, in fact, for our complex man the weariest, most beaten track of all.

It may be recovered as a consequence of a breakdown of the 12 symbolic machinery by which the experts present the experience to the consumer. A family visits the canyon in the usual way. But shortly after their arrival, the park is closed by an outbreak of typhus in the south. They have the canyon to themselves. What do they mean when they tell the home folks of their good luck: "We had the whole place to ourselves"? How does one see the thing better when the others are absent? Is looking like sucking: the more lookers, the less there is to see? They could hardly answer, but by saying this they testify to a state of affairs which is considerably more complex than the simple statement of the schoolbook about the Spaniard and the millions who followed him. It is a state in which there is a complex distribution of sovereignty, of zoning.

It may be recovered in a time of national disaster. The Bright 13 Angel Lodge is converted into a rest home, a function that has nothing to do with the canyon a few yards away. A wounded man is brought in. He regains consciousness; there outside his window is the canyon.

The most extreme case of access by privilege conferred by disaster 14 is the Huxleyan[1] novel of the adventures of the surviving remnant after the great wars of the twentieth century. An expedition from Australia lands in Southern California and heads east. They stumble across the Bright Angel Lodge, now fallen into ruins. The trails are grown over, the guard rails fallen away, the dime telescope at Battleship Point rusted. But there is the canyon, exposed at last. Exposed by what? By the decay of those facilities which were designed to help the sightseer.

This dialectic of sightseeing cannot be taken into account by 15 planners, for the object of the dialectic is nothing other than the subversion of the efforts of the planners.

The dialectic is not known to objective theorists, psychologists, 16 and the like. Yet it is quite well known in the fantasy-consciousness

---

1. English writer Aldous Huxley (1894–1963) wrote a number of novels—*Brave New World* chief among them—that depict the decline of modern society.

of the popular arts. The devices by which the museum exhibit, the Grand Canyon, the ordinary thing, is recovered have long since been stumbled upon. A movie shows a man visiting the Grand Canyon. But the moviemaker knows something the planner does not know. He knows that one cannot take the sight frontally. The canyon must be approached by the stratagems we have mentioned: the Inside Track, the Familiar Revisited, the Accidental Encounter. Who is the stranger at the Bright Angel Lodge? Is he the ordinary tourist from Terre Haute that he makes himself out to be? He is not. He has another objective in mind, to revenge his wronged brother, counterespionage, etc. By virtue of the fact that he has other fish to fry, he may take a stroll along the rim after supper and then we can see the canyon through him. The movie accomplishes its purpose by concealing it. Overtly the characters (the American family marooned by typhus) and we the onlookers experience pity for the sufferers, and the family experience anxiety for themselves; covertly and in truth they are the happiest of people and we are happy through them, for we have the canyon to ourselves. The movie cashes in on the recovery of sovereignty through disaster. Not only is the canyon now accessible to the remnant: the members of the remnant are now accessible to each other; a whole new ensemble of relations becomes possible—friendship, love, hatred, clandestine sexual adventures. In a movie when a man sits next to a woman on a bus, it is necessary either that the bus break down or that the woman lose her memory. (The question occurs to one: Do you imagine there are sightseers who see sights just as they are supposed to? a family who live in Terre Haute, who decide to take the canyon tour, who go there, see it, enjoy it immensely, and go home content? a family who are entirely innocent of all the barriers, zones, losses of sovereignty I have been talking about? Wouldn't most people be sorry if Battleship Point fell into the canyon, carrying all one's fellow passengers to their death, leaving one alone on the South Rim? I cannot answer this. Perhaps there are such people. Certainly a great many American families would swear they had no such problems, that they came, saw, and went away happy. Yet it is just these families who would be happiest if they had gotten the Inside Track and been among the surviving remnant.)

It is now apparent that as between the many measures which   17
may be taken to overcome the opacity, the boredom, of the direct confrontation of the thing or creature in its citadel of symbolic investiture, some are less authentic than others. That is to say, some stratagems obviously serve other purposes than that of providing access to being—for example, various unconscious motivations which it is not necessary to go into here.

Let us take an example in which the recovery of being is am- 18
biguous, where it may under the same circumstances contain both
authentic and unauthentic components. An American couple, we
will say, drives down into Mexico. They see the usual sights and
have a fair time of it. Yet they are never without the sense of
missing something. Although Taxco and Cuernavaca are interesting
and picturesque as advertised, they fall short of "it." What do the
couple have in mind by "it"? What do they really hope for. What
sort of experience could they have in Mexico so that upon their
return, they would feel that "it" had happened? We have a clue:
Their hope has something to do with their own role as tourists
in a foreign country and the way in which they conceive this role.
It has something to do with other American tourists. Certainly
they feel that they are very far from "it" when, after traveling five
thousand miles, they arrive at the plaza in Guanajuato only to
find themselves surrounded by a dozen other couples from the
Midwest.

Already we may distinguish authentic and unauthentic elements. 19
First, we see the problem the couple faces and we understand
their efforts to surmount it. The problem is to find an "unspoiled"
place. "Unspoiled" does not mean only that a place is left physically
intact; it means also that it is not encrusted by renown and by
the familiar (as in Taxco), that it has not been discovered by others.
We understand that the couple really want to get at the place and
enjoy it. Yet at the same time we wonder if there is not something
wrong in their dislike of their compatriots. Does access to the place
require the exclusion of others?

Let us see what happens.   20

The couple decide to drive from Guanajuato to Mexico City.   21
On the way they get lost. After hours on a rocky mountain road,
they find themselves in a tiny valley not even marked on the map.
There they discover an Indian village. Some sort of religious festival
is going on. It is apparently a corn dance in supplication of the
rain god.

The couple know at once that this is "it." They are entranced. 22
They spend several days in the village, observing the Indians and
being themselves observed with friendly curiosity.

Now may we not say that the sightseers have at last come face 23
to face with an authentic sight, a sight which is charming, quaint,
picturesque, unspoiled, and that they see the sight and come away
rewarded? Possibly this may occur. Yet it is more likely that what
happens is a far cry indeed from an immediate encounter with
being, that the experience, while masquerading as such, is in truth
a rather desperate impersonation. I use the word *desperate* advisedly
to signify an actual loss of hope.

The clue to the spuriousness of their enjoyment of the village 24 and the festival is a certain restiveness in the sightseers themselves. It is given expression by their repeated exclamations that "this is too good to be true," and by their anxiety that it may not prove to be so perfect, and finally by their downright relief at leaving the valley and having the experience in the bag, so to speak— that is, safely embalmed in memory and movie film.

What is the source of their anxiety during the visit? Does it not 25 mean that the couple are looking at the place with a certain standard of performance in mind? Are they like Fabre,[2] who gazed at the world about him with wonder, letting it be what it is; or are they not like the overanxious mother who sees her child as one performing, now doing badly, now doing well? The village is their child and their love for it is an anxious love because they are afraid that at any moment it might fail them.

We have another clue in their subsequent remark to an ethnologist 26 friend. "How we wished you had been there with us! What a perfect goldmine of folkways! Every minute we would say to each other, if only you were here! You must return with us." This surely testifies to a generosity of spirit, a willingness to share their experience with others, not at all like their feelings toward their fellow Iowans on the plaza at Guanajuato!

I am afraid this is not the case at all. It is true that they longed 27 for their ethnologist friend, but it was for an entirely different reason. They wanted him, not to share their experience, but to certify their experience as genuine.

"This is it" and "Now we are really living" do not necessarily 28 refer to the sovereign encounter of the person with the sight that enlivens the mind and gladdens the heart. It means that now at last we have the acceptable experience. The present experience is always measured by a prototype, the "it" of their dreams. "Now I am really living" means that now I am filling the role of sightseer and the sight is living up to the prototype of sights. This quaint and picturesque village is measured by a Platonic ideal of the Quaint and the Picturesque.

Hence their anxiety during the encounter. For at any minute 29 something could go wrong. A fellow Iowan might emerge from a 'dobe hut; the chief might show them his Sears catalogue. (If the failures are "wrong" enough, as these are, they might still be turned to account as rueful conversation pieces: "There we were expecting the chief to bring us a churinga and he shows up with

2. Henri Fabre (1823–1915), French scientist who studied the behavior of insects.

a Sears catalogue!") They have snatched victory from disaster, but their experience always runs the danger of failure.

They need the ethnologist to certify their experience as genuine. This is borne out by their behavior when the three of them return for the next corn dance. During the dance, the couple do not watch the goings-on; instead they watch the ethnologist! Their highest hope is that their friend should find the dance interesting. And if he should show signs of true absorption, an interest in the goings-on so powerful that he becomes oblivious of his friends— then their cup is full. "Didn't we tell you?" they say at last. What they want from him is not ethnological explanations; all they want is his approval.

What has taken place is a radical loss of sovereignty over that which is as much theirs as it is the ethnologist's. The fault does not lie with the ethnologist. He has no wish to stake a claim to the village; in fact, he desires the opposite: he will bore his friends to death by telling them about the village and the meaning of the folkways. A degree of sovereignty has been surrendered by the couple. It is the nature of the loss, moreover, that they are not aware of the loss, beyond a certain uneasiness. (Even if they read this and admitted it, it would be very difficult for them to bridge the gap in their confrontation of the world. Their consciousness of the corn dance cannot escape their consciousness of their consciousness, so that with the onset of the first direct enjoyment, their higher consciousness pounces and certifies: "Now you are doing it! Now you are really living!" and, in certifying the experience, sets it at nought.)

Their basic placement in the world is such that they recognize a priority of title of the expert over his particular department of being. The whole horizon of being is staked out by "them," the experts. The highest satisfaction of the sightseer (not merely the tourist but any layman seer of sights) is that his sight should be certified as genuine. The worst of this impoverishment is that there is no sense of impoverishment. The surrender of title is so complete that it never even occurs to one to reassert title. A poor man may envy the rich man, but the sightseer does not envy the expert. When a caste system becomes absolute, envy disappears. Yet the caste of layman-expert is not the fault of the expert. It is due altogether to the eager surrender of sovereignty by the layman so that he may take up the role not of the person but of the consumer.

I do not refer only to the special relation of layman to theorist. I refer to the general situation in which sovereignty is surrendered to a class of privileged knowers, whether these be theorists or artists. A reader may surrender sovereignty over that which has been written about, just as a consumer may surrender sovereignty over a thing which has been theorized about. The consumer is content to receive an experience just as it has been presented to him by theorists and planners. The reader may also be content to judge life by whether it has or has not been formulated by those who know and write about life. A young man goes to France. He too has a fair time of it, sees the sights, enjoys the food. On his last day, in fact as he sits in a restaurant in Le Havre waiting for his boat, something happens. A group of French students in the restaurant get into an impassioned argument over a recent play. A riot takes place. Madame la concierge joins in, swinging her mop at the rioters. Our young American is transported. This is "it." And he had almost left France without seeing "it"!

But the young man's delight is ambiguous. On the one hand, 34 it is a pleasure for him to encounter the same Gallic temperament he had heard about from Puccini[3] and Rolland.[4] But on the other hand, the source of his pleasure testifies to a certain alienation. For the young man is actually barred from a direct encounter with anything French excepting only that which has been set forth, authenticated by Puccini and Rolland—those who know. If he had encountered the restaurant scene without reading Hemingway, without knowing that the performance was so typically, charmingly French, he would not have been delighted. He would only have been anxious at seeing things get so out of hand. The source of his delight is the sanction of those who know.

This loss of sovereignty is not a marginal process, as might 35 appear from my example of estranged sightseers. It is a generalized surrender of the horizon to those experts within whose competence a particular segment of the horizon is thought to lie. Kwakiutls are surrendered to Franz Boas[5]; decaying Southern mansions are surrendered to Faulkner and Tennessee Williams. So that, although it is by no means the intention of the expert to expropriate sovereignty—in fact he would not even know what sovereignty meant in this context—the danger of theory and consumption is a seduction and deprivation of the consumer.

---

3. Giacomo Puccini (1853–1924), Italian composer, one of whose most beloved operas is *La Bohème,* a story of the artistic life in Paris in the nineteenth century.
4. Romaine Rolland (1866–1944), French writer whose works reflect French civilization.
5. Franz Boas, influential American anthropologist (1858–1942). Kwakiutls are Native Americans of the Pacific Northwest.

LAWRENCE DURRELL

Landscape and Character

"You write", says a friendly critic in Ohio, "as if the landscape   1
were more important than the characters." If not exactly true, this
is near enough the mark, for I have evolved a private notion about
the importance of landscape, and I willingly admit to seeing "characters" almost as functions of a landscape. This has only come
about in recent years after a good deal of travel—though here
again I doubt if this is quite the word, for I am not really a "travel-
writer" so much as a "residence-writer." My books are always
about living in places, not just rushing through them. But as you
get to know Europe slowly, tasting the wines, cheeses and characters
of the different countries you begin to realize that the important
determinant of any culture is after all—the spirit of place. Just as
one particular vineyard will always give you a special wine with
discernible characteristics so a Spain, an Italy, a Greece will always
give you the same type of culture—will express itself through the
human being just as it does through its wild flowers. We tend to
see "culture" as a sort of historic pattern dictated by the human
will, but for me this is no longer absolutely true. I don't believe
the British character, for example, or the German has changed a
jot since Tacitus first described it; and so long as people keep
getting born Greek or French or Italian their culture-productions
will bear the unmistakable signature of the place.

And this, of course, is the target of the travel-writer; his task is   2
to isolate the germ in the people which is expressed by their
landscape. Strangely enough one does not necessarily need special
knowledge for the job, though of course a knowledge of language
is a help. But how few they are those writers! How many can
write a *Sea and Sardinia* or a *Twilight in Italy* to match these two
gems of D. H. Lawrence? When he wrote them his Italian was
rudimentary. The same applies to Norman Douglas' *Fountains in
the Sand*—one of the best portraits of North Africa.

We travel really to try and get to grips with this mysterious   3
quality of "Greekness" or "Spanishness"; and it is extraordinary
how unvaryingly it remains true to the recorded picture of it in
the native literature: true to the point of platitude. Greece, for
example, cannot have a single real Greek left (in the racial sense)

First published in *The New York Times Magazine* June 12, 1960.

after so many hundreds of years of war and resettlement; the present racial stocks are the fruit of countless invasions. Yet if you want a bit of real live Aristophanes you only have to listen to the chaffering of the barrow-men and peddlers in the Athens Plaka. It takes less than two years for even a reserved British resident to begin using his fingers in conversation without being aware of the fact. But if there are no original Greeks left what is the curious constant factor that we discern behind the word "Greekness"? It is surely the enduring faculty of self-expression inhering in landscape. At least I would think so as I recall two books by very different writers which provide an incomparable nature-study of the place. One is *Mani* by Patrick Leigh Fermor, and the other Miller's *Colossus of Maroussi*.

I believe you could exterminate the French at a blow and resettle 4
the country with Tartars, and within two generations discover, to your astonishment, that the national characteristics were back at norm—the restless metaphysical curiosity, the tenderness for good living and the passionate individualism: even though their noses were now flat. This is the invisible constant in a place with which the ordinary tourist can get in touch just by sitting quite quietly over a glass of wine in a Paris *bistrot*. He may not be able to formulate it very clearly to himself in literary terms, but he will taste the unmistakable keen knife-edge of happiness in the air of Paris: the pristine brilliance of a national psyche which knows that art is as important as love or food. He will not be blind either to the hard metallic rational sense, the irritating *coeur raisonnable*[1] of the men and women. When the French want to be *malins*,[2] as they call it, they can be just as we can be when we stick our toes in over some national absurdity.

Yes, human beings are expressions of their landscape, but in 5
order to touch the secret springs of a national essence you need a few moments of quiet with yourself. Truly the intimate knowledge of landscape, if developed scientifically, could give us a political science—for half the political decisions taken in the world are based on what we call national character. We unconsciously acknowledge this fact when we exclaim, "How typically Irish" or "It would take a Welshman to think up something like that." And indeed we all of us jealously guard the sense of minority individuality in our own nations—the family differences. The great big nations like say the Chinese or the Americans present a superficially homo-

---

1. reasonable heart
2. malicious, mischievous

geneous appearance; but I've noticed that while we Europeans can hardly tell one American from another, my own American friends will tease each other to death at the lunch-table about the intolerable misfortune of being born in Ohio or Tennessee—a recognition of the validity of place which we ourselves accord to the Welshman, Irishman and Scotsman at home. It is a pity indeed to travel and not get this essential sense of landscape values. You do not need a sixth sense for it. It is there if you just close your eyes and breathe softly through your nose; you will hear the whispered message, for all landscapes ask the same question in the same whisper. "I am watching you—are you watching yourself in me?" Most travellers hurry too much. But try just for a moment sitting on the great stone omphalos, the navel of the ancient Greek world, at Delphi. Don't ask mental questions, but just relax and empty your mind. It lies, this strange amphora-shaped object, in an overgrown field above the temple. Everything is blue and smells of sage. The marbles dazzle down below you. There are two eagles moving softly softly on the sky, like distant boats rowing across an immense violet lake.

Ten minutes of this sort of quiet inner identification will give   6 you the notion of the Greek landscape which you could not get in twenty years of studying ancient Greek texts. But having got it, you will at once get all the rest; the key is there, so to speak, for you to turn. After that you will not be able to go on a shopping expedition in Athens without running into Agamemnon or Clytemnestra—and often under the same names. And if you happen to go to Eleusis in springtime you will come upon more than one blind Homer walking the dusty roads. The secret is identification. If you sit on the top of the Mena House pyramid at sunset and try the same thing (forgetting the noise of the donkey-boys, and all the filthy litter of other travellers—old cartons and Coca-Cola bottles): if you sit quite still in the landscape-diviner's pose—why, the whole rhythm of ancient Egypt rises up from the damp cold sand. You can hear its very pulse tick. Nothing is strange to you at such moments—the old temples with their death-cults, the hieroglyphs, the long slow whirl of the brown Nile among the palm-fringed islets, the crocodiles and snakes. It is palpably just as it was (its essence) when the High Priest of Ammon initiated Alexander into the Mysteries. Indeed the Mysteries themselves are still there for those who might seek initiation—the shreds and shards of the Trismegistic lore still being studied and handed on by small secret sects. Of course you cannot arrange to be initiated through a travel agency! You would have to reside and work your way in through the ancient crust—a tough one—of daily life.

And how different is the rhythm of Egypt to that of Greece! One isn't surprised by the story that the High Priest at Thebes said contemptuously: "You Greeks are mere children." He could not bear the tireless curiosity and sensuality of the Greek character— the passionate desire to conceptualize things metaphysically. They didn't seem to be able to relax, the blasted Greeks! Incidentally it is a remark which the French often repeat today about the Americans, and it is always uttered in the same commiserating tone of voice as once the High Priest used. Yet the culture of Greece (so different from that of Egypt) springs directly from the Nile Valley— I could name a dozen top Greek thinkers or philosophers who were trained by Egyptians, like Plato, Pythagoras, Anaxagoras, Democritos. And the "tiresome children" certainly didn't waste their time, for when they got back home to their own bare islands the pure flower of Greek culture spread its magnificent wings in flights of pure magic to astonish and impregnate the Mediterranean. But just to hand the eternal compliment along they invented the word "barbarians" for all those unfortunate savages who lived outside the magic circle of Greece, deprived of its culture. The barbarians of course were one day to produce Dante, Goethe, Bach, Shakespeare.

As I say the clue, then, is identification; for underneath the purely superficial aspects of apparent change the old tide-lines remain. The dullest travel poster hints at it. The fascinating thing is that Dickens characters still walk the London streets; that any game of village cricket will provide us with clues to the strange ritualistic mystery of the habits of the British. While if you really want to intuit the inner mystery of the island try watching the sun come up over Stonehenge. It may seem a dull and "touristic" thing to do, but if you do it in the right spirit you find yourself walking those woollen secretive hills arm in arm with the Druids. [7]

Taken in this way travel becomes a sort of science of intuitions which is of the greatest importance to everyone—but most of all to the artist who is always looking for nourishing soils in which to put down roots and create. Everyone finds his own "correspondences" in this way—landscapes where you suddenly feel bounding with ideas, and others where half your soul falls asleep and the thought of pen and paper brings on nausea. It is here that the travel-writer stakes his claim, for writers each seem to have a personal landscape of the heart which beckons them. The whole Arabian world, for example, has never been better painted and framed than in the works of Freya Stark, whose delicate eye and insinuating slow-moving orchestrations of place and evocations [8] of history have placed her in the front rank of travellers. Could one do better than *Valley of the Assassins*?

These ideas, which may seem a bit far-fetched to the modern ⁹ reader, would not have troubled the men and women of the ancient world, for their notion of culture was one of psychic education, the education of the sensibility; ours is built upon a notion of mentation, the cramming of the skull with facts and pragmatic data which positively stifle the growth of the soul. Travel wouldn't have been necessary in the time (I am sure such a time really existed some time after the Stone Age) when there really was a world religion which made full allowance for the different dialects of the different races practising it: and which realized that the factor of variation is always inevitably the landscape and not the people. Nowadays such a psychic uniformity sounds like a dream; but already comparative anthropology and archaelogy are establishing the truth of it. When we think about such formulations as "World-Government" we always think of the matter politically, as groups of different people working upon an agreed agenda of sorts; a ten-point programme, or some such set of working propositions. The landscape always fools us, and I imagine always will. Simply because the same propositions don't mean the same in Greek, Chinese and French.

Another pointer worth thinking about is institutions; have you ¹⁰ ever wondered why Catholicism, for example, can be such a different religion in different places? Ireland, Italy, Spain, Argentina—it is theologically the same, working on the same premises, but in each case it is subtly modified to suit the spirit of place. People have little to do with the matter except inasmuch as they themselves are reflections of their landscape. Of course there are places where you feel that the inhabitants are not really attending to and interpreting their landscape; whole peoples or nations sometimes get mixed up and start living at right angles to the land, so to speak, which gives the traveller a weird sense of alienation. I think some of the troubles which American artists talk about are not due to "industrialization" or "technocracy" but something rather simpler—people not attending to what the land is saying, not conforming to the hidden magnetic fields which the landscape is trying to communicate to the personality. It was not all nonsense what D. H. Lawrence had to say in his communion with the "ghosts" in the New World. He was within an ace, I think, of making real contact with the old Indian cultures. Genius that he was, he carried too much intellectual baggage about him on his travels, too many preconceptions; and while the mirror he holds up to Mexico, Italy, England is a marvellous triumph of art, the image is often a bit out of focus. He couldn't hold or perhaps wouldn't hold the camera steady enough—he refused to use the tripod (first invented by the oracles in Greece!).

The traveller, too, has his own limitations, and it is doubtful if [11] he is to be blamed. The flesh is frail. I have known sensitive and inquisitive men so disheartened by the sight of a Greek lavatory as to lose all sense of orientation and fly right back to High Street Clapham without waiting for the subtler intimations of the place to dawn on them. I have known people educated up to Ph.D. standard who were so completely unhinged by French plumbing that they could speak of nothing else. We are all of us unfair in this way. I know myself to be a rash, hasty and inconsiderate man, and while I am sitting here laying down the law about travel I feel I must confess that I also have some blind spots. I have never been fair to the Scots. In fact I have always been extremely unfair to them—and all because I arrived on my first visit to Scotland late on a Saturday evening. I do not know whether it is generally known that you can simply die of exposure and starvation in relatively civilized places like Inverness simply because the inhabitants are too religious to cut a sandwich or pour coffee? It sounds fantastic I know. Nevertheless it is true. The form of Sabbatarianism which the Scots have developed passes all understanding. Nay, it cries out for the strait-jacket. And sitting on a bench at Inverness Station in a borrowed deerstalker and plaid you rack your brains to remember the least pronouncement in the Old or New Testaments which might account for it. There is none—or else I have never spotted the reference. They appear to have made a sort of Moloch[3] of Our Lord, and are too scared even to brush their teeth on the Sabbath. How can I be anything but unfair to them? And yet Scotland herself—the poetry, and the poverty and naked joyous insouciance of mountain life, you will find on every page of Burns's autobiographical papers. Clearly she is a queenly country and a wild mountainous mate for poets. Why have the Scots not caught on? What ails them in their craggy fastnesses? (But I expect I shall receive a hundred indignant letters from Americans who have adopted Scotland, have pierced her hard heart and discovered the landscape-mystery of her true soul. Nevertheless, I stand by what I say; and one day when I am rich I shall have a memorial plaque placed over that bench on Inverness Station platform—a plaque reading "Kilroy was here—but oh so

---

3. An ancient Phoenician god to whom children were sacrificed; anything considered to demand a horrible sacrifice.

briefly"!) But I must not fail to add that I have always admired the magnificent evocations of Scots landscape in the books of Stevenson; they are only adventure tales, but the landscape comes shining through.

So that I imagine the traveller in each of us has a few blind 12 spots due to some traumatic experience with an empty tea-urn or the room-on-the-landing. This cannot be helped. The great thing is to try and travel with the eyes of the spirit wide open, and not too much factual information. To tune in, without reverence, idly—but with real inward attention. It is to be had for the feeling, that mysterious sense of *rapport,* of identity with the ground. You can extract the essence of a place once you know how. If you just get as still as a needle you'll be there.

I remember seeing a photo-reportage in *Life* magazine once 13 which dealt with the extraordinary changes in physique which emigrants to the U.S.A. underwent over such relatively short periods as two or three generations. Some of the smaller races like Chinese and Filipinos appeared to have gained almost eight inches in height, over the statutory period investigated, while their physical weight had also increased in the most extraordinary way. The report was based on the idea that diet and environment were the real answers, and while obviously such factors are worth considering I found myself wondering if the reporters were right; surely the control experiment would fail if one fed a group of Chinese *in China* exclusively on an American diet? I don't see them growing a speck larger myself. They might get fat and rosy on the diet, but I believe the landscape, in pursuit of its own mysterious purposes, would simply cut them down to the required size suitable to homegrown Chinese.

One last word about the sense of place; I think that not enough 14 attention is paid to it as a purely literary criterion. What makes "big" books is surely as much to do with their site as their characters and incidents. I don't mean the books which are devoted entirely to an elucidation of a given landscape like Thoreau's *Walden* is. I mean ordinary novels. When they are well and truly anchored in nature they usually become classics. One can detect this quality of "bigness" in most books which are so sited from *Huckleberry Finn* to *The Grapes of Wrath.* They are tuned in to the sense of place. You could not transplant them without totally damaging their ambience and mood; any more than you could transplant *Typee.* This has nothing I think to do with the manners and habits of the human beings who populate them; for they exist in nature, as a function of place.

GEORGE ORWELL

Marrakech

As the corpse went past the flies left the restaurant table in a   1
cloud and rushed after it, but they came back a few minutes later.

The little crowd of mourners—all men and boys, no women—   2
threaded their way across the market-place between the piles of
pomegranates and the taxis and the camels, wailing a short chant
over and over again. What really appeals to the flies is that the
corpses here are never put into coffins, they are merely wrapped
in a piece of rag and carried on a rough wooden bier on the
shoulders of four friends. When the friends get to the burying-
ground they hack an oblong hole a foot or two deep, dump the
body in it and fling over it a little of the dried-up, lumpy earth,
which is like broken brick. No gravestone, no name, no identifying
mark of any kind. The burying-ground is merely a huge waste of
hummocky earth, like a derelict building-lot. After a month or
two no one can even be certain where his own relatives are buried.

When you walk through a town like this[1]—two hundred thousand   3
inhabitants, of whom at least twenty thousand own literally nothing
except the rags they stand up in—when you see how the people
live, and still more how easily they die, it is always difficult to
believe that you are walking among human beings. All colonial
empires are in reality founded upon that fact. The people have
brown faces—besides, there are so many of them! Are they really
the same flesh as yourself? Do they even have names? Or are they
merely a kind of undifferentiated brown stuff, about as individual
as bees or coral insects? They rise out of the earth, they sweat
and starve for a few years, and then they sink back into the
nameless mounds of the graveyard and nobody notices that they
are gone. And even the graves themselves soon fade back into the
soil. Sometimes, out for a walk, as you break your way through
the prickly pear, you notice that it is rather bumpy underfoot, and
only a certain regularity in the bumps tells you that you are
walking over skeletons.

I was feeding one of the gazelles in the public gardens.   4

Gazelles are almost the only animals that look good to eat when   5
they are still alive, in fact, one can hardly look at their hindquarters
without thinking of mint sauce. The gazelle I was feeding seemed

From *Such, Such Were the Joys* (1953).
1. Marrakech is a city in the northern African country Morocco.

to know that this thought was in my mind, for though it took the piece of bread I was holding out it obviously did not like me. It nibbled rapidly at the bread, then lowered its head and tried to butt me, then took another nibble and then butted again. Probably its idea was that if it could drive me away the bread would somehow remain hanging in mid-air.

An Arab navvy working on the path nearby lowered his heavy hoe and sidled slowly towards us. He looked from the gazelle to the bread and from the bread to the gazelle, with a sort of quiet amazement, as though he had never seen anything quite like this before. Finally he said shyly in French:

"*I* could eat some of that bread."

I tore off a piece and he stowed it gratefully in some secret place under his rags. This man is an employee of the Municipality.

When you go through the Jewish quarters you gather some idea of what the medieval ghettoes were probably like. Under their Moorish rulers the Jews were only allowed to own land in certain restricted areas, and after centuries of this kind of treatment they have ceased to bother about overcrowding. Many of the streets are a good deal less than six feet wide, the houses are completely windowless, and sore-eyed children cluster everywhere in unbelievable numbers, like clouds of flies. Down the centre of the street there is generally running a little river of urine.

In the bazaar huge families of Jews, all dressed in the long black robe and little black skull-cap, are working in dark fly-infested booths that look like caves. A carpenter sits crosslegged at a prehistoric lathe, turning chair-legs at lightning speed. He works the lathe with a bow in his right hand and guides the chisel with his left foot, and thanks to a lifetime of sitting in this position his left leg is warped out of shape. At his side his grandson, aged six, is already starting on the simpler parts of the job.

I was just passing the coppersmiths' booths when somebody noticed that I was lighting a cigarette. Instantly, from the dark holes all round, there was a frenzied rush of Jews, many of them old grandfathers with flowing grey beards, all clamouring for a cigarette. Even a blind man somewhere at the back of one of the booths heard a rumour of cigarettes and came crawling out, groping in the air with his hand. In about a minute I had used up the whole packet. None of these people, I suppose, works less than twelve hours a day, and every one of them looks on a cigarette as a more or less impossible luxury.

As the Jews live in self-contained communities they follow the same trades as the Arabs, except for agriculture. Fruit-sellers, potters, silversmiths, blacksmiths, butchers, leatherworkers, tailors, water-

carriers, beggars, porters—whichever way you look you see nothing
but Jews. As a matter of fact there are thirteen thousand of them,
all living in the space of a few acres. A good job Hitler wasn't
here. Perhaps he was on his way, however. You hear the usual
dark rumours about the Jews, not only from the Arabs but from
the poorer Europeans.

"Yes, mon vieux, they took my job away from me and gave it   13
to a Jew. The Jews! They're the real rulers of this country, you
know. They've got all the money. They control the banks, finance—
everything."

"But," I said, "isn't it a fact that the average Jew is a labourer   14
working for about a penny an hour?"

"Ah, that's only for show! They're all moneylenders really. They're   15
cunning, the Jews."

In just the same way, a couple of hundred years ago, poor old   16
women used to be burned for witchcraft when they could not
even work enough magic to get themselves a square meal.

All people who work with their hands are partly invisible, and   17
the more important the work they do, the less visible they are.
Still, a white skin is always fairly conspicuous. In northern Europe,
when you see a labourer ploughing a field, you probably give him
a second glance. In a hot country, anywhere south of Gibraltar
or east of Suez, the chances are that you don't even see him. I
have noticed this again and again. In a tropical landscape one's
eye takes in everything except the human beings. It takes in the
dried-up soil, the prickly pear, the palm tree and the distant mountain, but it always misses the peasant hoeing at his patch. He is
the same colour as the earth, and a great deal less interesting to
look at.

It is only because of this that the starved countries of Asia and   18
Africa are accepted as tourist resorts. No one would think of running
cheap trips to the Distressed Areas. But where the human beings
have brown skins their poverty is simply not noticed. What does
Morocco mean to a Frenchman? An orange-grove or a job in
Government service. Or to an Englishman? Camels, castles, palm
trees, Foreign Legionnaires, brass trays, and bandits. One could
probably live there for years without noticing that for nine-tenths
of the people the reality of life is an endless, back-breaking struggle
to wring a little food out of an eroded soil.

Most of Morocco is so desolate that no wild animal bigger than   19
a hare can live on it. Huge areas which were once covered with
forest have turned into a treeless waste where the soil is exactly
like broken-up brick. Nevertheless a good deal of it is cultivated,

with frightful labour. Everything is done by hand. Long lines of women, bent double like inverted capital L's, work their way slowly across the fields, tearing up the prickly weeds with their hands, and the peasant gathering lucerne for fodder pulls it up stalk by stalk instead of reaping it, thus saving an inch or two on each stalk. The plough is a wretched wooden thing, so frail that one can easily carry it on one's shoulder, and fitted underneath with a rough iron spike which stirs the soil to a depth of about four inches. This is as much as the strength of the animals is equal to. It is usual to plough with a cow and a donkey yoked together. Two donkeys would not be quite strong enough, but on the other hand two cows would cost a little more to feed. The peasants possess no harrows, they merely plough the soil several times over in different directions, finally leaving it in rough furrows, after which the whole field has to be shaped with hoes into small oblong patches to conserve water. Except for a day or two after the rare rainstorms there is never enough water. Along the edges of the fields channels are hacked out to a depth of thirty or forty feet to get at the tiny trickles which run through the subsoil.

Every afternoon a file of very old women passes down the road 20 outside my house, each carrying a load of firewood. All of them are mummified with age and the sun, and all of them are tiny. It seems to be generally the case in primitive communities that the women, when they get beyond a certain age, shrink to the size of children. One day a poor old creature who could not have been more than four feet tall crept past me under a vast load of wood. I stopped her and put a five-sou piece (a little more than a farthing) into her hand. She answered with a shrill wail, almost a scream, which was partly gratitude but mainly surprise. I suppose that from her point of view, by taking any notice of her, I seemed almost to be violating a law of nature. She accepted her status as an old woman, that is to say as a beast of burden. When a family is travelling it is quite usual to see a father and a grown-up son riding ahead on donkeys, and an old woman following on foot, carrying the baggage.

But what is strange about these people is their invisibility. For 21 several weeks, always at about the same time of day, the file of old women had hobbled past the house with their firewood, and though they had registered themselves on my eyeballs I cannot truly say that I had seen them. Firewood was passing—that was how I saw it. It was only that one day I happened to be walking behind them, and the curious up-and-down motion of a load of wood drew my attention to the human being beneath it. Then for the first time I noticed the poor old earth-coloured bodies, bodies reduced to bones and leathery skin, bent double under the crushing weight. Yet I suppose I had not been five minutes on Moroccan soil before I noticed the overloading of the donkeys and was infuriated by it. There is no question that the donkeys are damnably treated. The Moroccan donkey is hardly bigger than a St. Bernard dog, it carries a load which in the British Army would be considered too much for a fifteen-hands mule, and very often its pack-saddle is not taken off its back for weeks together. But what is peculiarly pitiful is that it is the most willing creature on earth, it follows its master like a dog and does not need either bridle or halter. After a dozen years of devoted work it suddenly drops dead, whereupon its master tips it into the ditch and the village dogs have torn its guts out before it is cold.

This kind of thing makes one's blood boil, whereas—on the   22
whole—the plight of the human beings does not. I am not commenting, merely pointing to a fact. People with brown skins are
next door to invisible. Anyone can be sorry for the donkey with
its galled back, but it is generally owing to some kind of accident
if one even notices the old woman under her load of sticks.

JOAN DIDION

Salvador

The three-year-old El Salvador International Airport is glassy   1
and white and splendidly isolated, conceived during the waning
of the Molina "National Transformation" as convenient less to the
capital (San Salvador is forty miles away, until recently a drive of
several hours) than to a central hallucination of the Molina and
Romero regimes, the projected beach resorts, the Hyatt, the Pacific
Paradise, tennis, golf, water-skiing, condos, *Costa del Sol;* the visionary
invention of a tourist industry in yet another republic where the
leading natural cause of death is gastrointestinal infection. In the
general absence of tourists these hotels have since been abandoned,
ghost resorts on the empty Pacific beaches, and to land at this
airport built to service them is to plunge directly into a state in
which no ground is solid, no depth of field reliable, no perception
so definite that it might not dissolve into its reverse.

The only logic is that of acquiescence. Immigration is negotiated   2

Excerpted from *Salvador* (1983).

in a thicket of automatic weapons, but by whose authority the
weapons are brandished (Army or National Guard or National
Police or Customs Police or Treasury Police or one of a continuing
proliferation of other shadowy and overlapping forces) is a blurred
point. Eye contact is avoided. Documents are scrutinized upside
down. Once clear of the airport, on the new highway that slices
through green hills rendered phosphorescent by the cloud cover
of the tropical rainy season, one sees mainly underfed cattle and
mongrel dogs and armored vehicles, vans and trucks and Cherokee
Chiefs fitted with reinforced steel and bulletproof Plexiglas an inch
thick. Such vehicles are a fixed feature of local life, and are popularly
associated with disappearance and death. There was the Cherokee
Chief seen following the Dutch television crew killed in Chalatenango
province in March of 1982. There was the red Toyota three-quarter-
ton pickup sighted near the van driven by the four American-
Catholic workers on the night they were killed in 1980. There
were, in the late spring and summer of 1982, the three Toyota
panel trucks, one yellow, one blue, and one green, none bearing
plates, reported present at each of the mass detentions (a "detention"
is another fixed feature of local life, and often precedes a "disappearance") in the Amatepec district of San Salvador. These are
the details—the models and the colors of armored vehicles, the
makes and calibers of weapons, the particular methods of dis-
memberment and decapitation used in particular instances—on
which the visitor to Salvador learns immediately to concentrate,
to the exclusion of past or future concerns, as in a prolonged
amnesiac fugue.

Terror is the given of the place. Black-and-white police cars   3
cruise in pairs, each with the barrel of a rifle extruding from an
open window. Roadblocks materialize at random, soldiers fanning
out from trucks and taking positions, fingers always on triggers,
safeties clicking on and off. Aim is taken as if to pass the time.
Every morning *El Diario de Hoy* and *La Prensa Gráfica* carry cautionary
stories. *"Una madre y sus dos hijos fueron asesinados con arma cortante
(corvo) por ocho sujetos desconocidos el lunes en la noche"*: A mother
and her two sons hacked to death in their beds by eight *desconocidos,*
unknown men. The same morning's paper: the unidentified body
of a young man, strangled, found on the shoulder of a road. Same
morning, different story: the unidentified bodies of three young
men, found on another road, their faces partially destroyed by
bayonets, one faced carved to represent a cross.

It is largely from these reports in the newspapers that the United   4
States embassy compiles its body counts, which are transmitted
to Washington in a weekly dispatch referred to by embassy people

as "the grim-gram." These counts are presented in a kind of tortured code that fails to obscure what is taken for granted in El Salvador, that government forces do most of the killing. In a January 15 1982 memo to Washington, for example, the embassy issued a "guarded" breakdown on its count of 6,909 "reported" political murders between September 16 1980 and September 15 1981. Of these 6,909, according to the memo, 922 were "believed committed by security forces," 952 "believed committed by leftist terrorists," 136 "believed committed by rightist terrorists," and 4,889 "committed by unknown assailants," the famous *desconocidos* favored by those San Salvador newspapers still publishing. (The figures actually add up not to 6,909 but to 6,899, leaving ten in a kind of official limbo.) The memo continued:

> "The uncertainty involved here can be seen in the fact that responsibility cannot be fixed in the majority of cases. We note, however, that it is generally believed in El Salvador that a large number of the unexplained killings are carried out by the security forces, officially or unofficially. The Embassy is aware of dramatic claims that have been made by one interest group or another in which the security forces figure as the primary agents of murder here. El Salvador's tangled web of attack and vengeance, traditional criminal violence and political mayhem make this an impossible charge to sustain. In saying this, however, we make no attempt to lighten the responsibility for the deaths of many hundreds, and perhaps thousands, which can be attributed to the security forces. . . ."

The body count kept by what is generally referred to in San Salvador as "the Human Rights Commission" is higher than the embassy's, and documented periodically by a photographer who goes out looking for bodies. These bodies he photographs are often broken into unnatural positions, and the faces to which the bodies are attached (when they are attached) are equally unnatural, sometimes unrecognizable as human faces, obliterated by acid or beaten to a mash of misplaced ears and teeth or slashed ear to ear and invaded by insects. "*Encontrado en Antiguo Cuscatlán el día 25 de Marzo 1982: camison de dormir celeste,*" the typed caption reads on one photograph: found in Antiguo Cuscatlán March 25 1982 wearing a sky-blue nightshirt. The captions are laconic. Found in Soyapango May 21 1982. Found in Mejicanos June 11 1982. Found at El Playón May 30, 1982, white shirt, purple pants, black shoes.

The photograph accompanying that last caption shows a body with no eyes, because the vultures got to it before the photographer did. There is a special kind of practical information that the visitor to El Salvador acquires immediately, the way visitors to other places acquire information about the currency rates, the hours for the museums. In El Salvador one learns that vultures go first for the soft tissue, for the eyes, the exposed genitalia, the open mouth. One learns that an open mouth can be used to make a specific point, can be stuffed with something emblematic; stuffed, say, with a penis, or, if the point has to do with land title, stuffed with some of the dirt in question. One learns that hair deteriorates less rapidly than flesh, and that a skull surrounded by a perfect corona of hair is a not uncommon sight in the body dumps.

All forensic photographs induce in the viewer a certain protective   7
numbness, but dissociation is more difficult here. In the first place these are not, technically, "forensic" photographs, since the evidence they document will never be presented in a court of law. In the second place the disfigurement is too routine. The locations are too near, the dates too recent. There is the presence of the relatives of the disappeared: the women who sit every day in this cramped office on the grounds of the archdiocese, waiting to look at the spiral-bound photo albums in which the photographs are kept. These albums have plastic covers bearing soft-focus color photographs of young Americans in dating situations (strolling through autumn foliage on one album, recumbent in a field of daisies on another), and the women, looking for the bodies of their husbands and brothers and sisters and children, pass them from hand to hand without comment or expression.

> "One of the more shadowy elements of the violent scene here [is] the death squad. Existence of these groups has long been disputed, but not by many Salvadorans. . . . Who constitutes the death squads is yet another difficult question. We do not believe that these squads exist as permanent formations but rather as ad hoc vigilante groups that coalesce according to perceived need. Membership is also uncertain, but in addition to civilians we believe that both on- and off-duty members of the security forces are participants. This was unofficially confirmed by right-wing spokesman Maj. Roberto D'Aubuisson who stated in an interview in early 1981 that security force members utilize the guise of the death squad when a potentially embarrassing or odious task needs to be performed."
>
> *—From the confidential but later declassified January 15, 1982 memo previously cited, drafted for the State Department by the political section at the embassy in San Salvador.*

The dead and pieces of the dead turn up in El Salvador everywhere,   8
every day, as taken for granted as in a nightmare, or a horror movie. Vultures of course suggest the presence of a body. A knot of children on the street suggests the presence of a body. Bodies

turn up in the brush of vacant lots, in the garbage thrown down ravines in the richest districts, in public rest rooms, in bus stations. Some are dropped in Lake Ilopango, a few miles east of the city, and wash up near the lakeside cottages and clubs frequented by what remains in San Salvador of the sporting bourgeoisie. Some still turn up in El Playón, the lunar lava field of rotting human flesh visible at one time or another on every television screen in America but characterized in June of 1982 in the *El Salvador News Gazette*, an English-language weekly edited by an American named Mario Rosenthal, as an "uncorroborated story . . . dredged up from the files of leftist propaganda." Others turn up at Puerta del Diablo, above Parque Balboa, a national *Turicentro* described as recently as the April–July 1982 issue of *Aboard TACA*, the magazine provided passengers on the national airline of El Salvador, as "offering excellent subjects for color photography."

I drove up to Puerta del Diablo one morning in June of 1982,   9 past the Casa Presidencial and the camouflaged watch towers and heavy concentrations of troops and arms south of town, on up a narrow road narrowed further by landslides and deep crevices in the roadbed, a drive so insistently premonitory that after a while I began to hope that I would pass Puerta del Diablo without knowing it, just miss it, write it off, turn around and go back. There was however no way of missing it. Puerta del Diablo is a "view site" in an older and distinctly literary tradition, nature as lesson, an immense cleft rock through which half of El Salvador seems framed, a site so romantic and "mystical," so theatrically sacrificial in aspect, that it might be a cosmic parody of nineteenth-century landscape painting. The place presents itself as pathetic fallacy: the sky "broods," the stones "weep," a constant seepage of water weighting the ferns and moss. The foliage is thick and slick with moisture. The only sound is a steady buzz, I believe of cicadas.

Body dumps are seen in El Salvador as a kind of visitors' must-   10 do, difficult but worth the detour. "Of course you have seen El Playón," an aide to President Alvaro Magaña said to me one day, and proceeded to discuss the site geologically, as evidence of the country's geothermal resources. He made no mention of the bodies. I was unsure if he was sounding me out or simply found the geothermal aspect of overriding interest. One difference between El Playón and Puerta del Diablo is that most bodies at El Playón appear to have been killed somewhere else, and then dumped; at Puerta del Diablo the executions are believed to occur in place, at the top, and the bodies thrown over. Sometimes reporters will speak of wanting to spend the night at Puerta del Diablo, in order to document the actual execution, but at the time I was in Salvador no one had.

The aftermath, the daylight aspect, is well documented. "Nothing 11 fresh today, I hear," an embassy officer said when I mentioned that I had visited Puerta del Diablo. "Were there any on top?" someone else asked. "There were supposed to have been three on top yesterday." The point about whether or not there had been any on top was that usually it was necessary to go down to see bodies. The way down is hard. Slabs of stone, slippery with moss, are set into the vertiginous cliff, and it is down this cliff that one begins the descent to the bodies, or what is left of the bodies, pecked and maggoty masses of flesh, bone, hair. On some days there have been helicopters circling, tracking those making the descent. Other days there have been militia at the top, in the clearing where the road seems to run out, but on the morning I was there the only people on top were a man and a woman and three small children, who played in the wet grass while the woman started and stopped a Toyota pickup. She appeared to be learning how to drive. She drove forward and then back toward the edge, apparently following the man's signals, over and over again.

We did not speak, and it was only later, down the mountain 12 and back in the land of the provisionally living, that it occurred to me that there was a definite question about why a man and a woman might choose a well-known body dump for a driving lesson. This was one of a number of occasions, during the two weeks my husband and I spent in El Salvador, on which I came to understand, in a way I had not understood before, the exact mechanism of terror.

Whenever I had nothing better to do in San Salvador I would 13 walk up in the leafy stillness of the San Benito and Escalón districts, where the hush at midday is broken only by the occasional crackle of a walkie-talkie, the click of metal moving on a weapon. I recall a day in San Benito when I opened my bag to check an address, and heard the clicking of metal on metal all up and down the street. On the whole no one walks up here, and pools of blossoms lie undisturbed on the sidewalks. Most of the houses in San Benito are more recent than those in Escalón, less idiosyncratic and probably smarter, but the most striking architectural features in both districts are not the houses but their walls, walls built upon walls, walls stripped of the usual copa de oro and bougainvillea, walls that reflect successive generations of violence: the original stone, the additional five or six or ten feet of brick, and finally the barbed wire, sometimes concertina, sometimes electrified; walls with watch towers, gun ports, closed-circuit television cameras, walls now reaching twenty and thirty feet.

San Benito and Escalón appear on the embassy security maps   14 as districts of relatively few "incidents," but they remain districts in which a certain oppressive uneasiness prevails. In the first place there are always "incidents"—detentions and deaths and disappearances—in the *barrancas,* the ravines lined with shanties that fall down behind the houses with the walls and the guards and the walkie-talkies; one day in Escalón I was introduced to a woman who kept the lean-to that served as a grocery in a *barranca* just above the Hotel Sheraton. She was sticking prices on bars of Camay and Johnson's baby soap, stopping occasionally to sell a plastic bag or two filled with crushed ice and Coca-Cola, and all the while she talked in a low voice about her fear, about her eighteen-year-old son, about the boys who had been taken out and shot on successive nights recently in a neighboring *barranca.*

In the second place there is, in Escalón, the presence of the   15 Sheraton itself, a hotel that has figured rather too prominently in certain local stories involving the disappearance and death of Americans. The Sheraton always seems brighter and more mildly festive than either the Camino Real or the Presidente, with children in the pool and flowers and pretty women in pastel dresses, but there are usually several bulletproofed Cherokee Chiefs in the parking area, and the men drinking in the lobby often carry the little zippered purses that in San Salvador suggest not passports or credit cards but Browning 9-mm. pistols.

It was at the Sheraton that one of the few American *desaparecidos,*   16 a young free-lance writer named John Sullivan, was last seen, in December of 1980. It was also at the Sheraton, after eleven on the evening of January 3 1981, that the two American advisers on agrarian reform, Michael Hammer and Mark Pearlman, were killed, along with the Salvadoran director of the Institute for Agrarian Transformation, José Rodolfo Viera. The three were drinking coffee in a dining room off the lobby, and whoever killed them used an Ingram MAC-10, without sound suppressor, and then walked out through the lobby, unapprehended. The Sheraton has even turned up in the investigation into the December 1980 deaths of the four American churchwomen, Sisters Ita Ford and Maura Clarke, the two Maryknoll nuns; Sister Dorothy Kazel, the Ursuline nun; and Jean Donovan, the lay volunteer. In *Justice in El Salvador: A Case Study,* prepared and released in July of 1982 in New York by the Lawyers' Committee for International Human Rights, there appears this note:

> "On December 19, 1980, the [Duarte government's] Special Investigative Commission reported that 'a red Toyota ¾-ton pickup was

seen leaving (the crime scene) at about 11:00 P.M. on December 2'
and that 'a red splotch on the burned van' of the churchwomen was
being checked to determine whether the paint splotch 'could be the
result of a collision between that van and the red Toyota pickup.' By
February 1981, the Maryknoll Sisters' Office of Social Concerns, which
has been actively monitoring the investigation, received word from
a source which it considered reliable that the FBI had matched the
red splotch on the burned van with a red Toyota pickup belonging
to the Sheraton hotel in San Salvador. . . . Subsequent to the FBI's
alleged matching of the paint splotch and a Sheraton truck, the State
Department has claimed, in a communication with the families of
the churchwomen, that 'the FBI could not determine the source of
the paint scraping.' "

There is also mention in this study of a young Salvadoran busi- [17]
nessman named Hans Christ (his father was a German who arrived
in El Salvador at the end of World War II), a part owner of the
Sheraton. Hans Christ lives now in Miami, and that his name
should have even come up in the Maryknoll investigation made
many people uncomfortable, because it was Hans Christ, along
with his brother-in-law, Ricardo Sol Meza, who, in April of 1981,
was first charged with the murders of Michael Hammer and Mark
Pearlman and José Rodolfo Viera at the Sheraton. These charges
were later dropped, and were followed by a series of other charges,
arrests, releases, expressions of "dismay" and "incredulity" from
the American embassy, and even, in the fall of 1982, confessions
to the killings from two former National Guard corporals, who
testified that Hans Christ had led them through the lobby and
pointed out the victims. Hans Christ and Ricardo Sol Meza have
said that the dropped case against them was a government frame-
up, and that they were only having drinks at the Sheraton the
night of the killings, with a National Guard intelligence officer. It
was logical for Hans Christ and Ricardo Sol Meza to have drinks
at the Sheraton because they both had interests in the hotel, and
Ricardo Sol Meza had just opened a roller disco, since closed, off
the lobby into which the killers walked that night. The killers were
described by witnesses as well dressed, their faces covered. The
room from which they walked was at the time I was in San
Salvador no longer a restaurant, but the marks left by the bullets
were still visible, on the wall facing the door.

Whenever I had occasion to visit the Sheraton I was apprehensive, [18]
and this apprehension came to color the entire Escalón district for
me, even its lower reaches, where there were people and movies
and restaurants. I recall being struck by it on the canopied porch
of a restaurant near the Mexican embassy, on an evening when
rain or sabotage or habit had blacked out the city and I became

abruptly aware, in the light cast by a passing car, of two human shadows, silhouettes illuminated by the headlights and then invisible again. One shadow sat behind the smoked glass windows of a Cherokee Chief parked at the curb in front of the restaurant; the other crouched between the pumps at the Esso station next door, carrying a rifle. It seemed to me unencouraging that my husband and I were the only people seated on the porch. In the absence of the headlights the candle on our table provided the only light, and I fought the impulse to blow it out. We continued talking, carefully. Nothing came of this, but I did not forget the sensation of having been in a single instant demoralized, undone, humiliated by fear, which is what I meant when I said that I came to understand in El Salvador the mechanism of terror. . . .

The place brings everything into question. One afternoon when   19
I had run out of the Halazone tablets I dropped every night in a pitcher of tap water (a demented *gringa*[1] gesture, I knew even then, in a country where everyone not born there was at least mildly ill, including the nurse at the American embassy), I walked across the street from the Camino Real to the Metrocenter, which is referred to locally as "Central America's Largest Shopping Mall." I found no Halazone at the Metrocenter but became absorbed in making notes about the mall itself, about the Muzak playing "I Left My Heart in San Francisco" and "American Pie" (". . . *singing this will be the day that I die . . .*") although the record store featured a cassette called *Classics of Paraguay,* about the *pâté de foie gras* for sale in the supermarket, about the guard who did the weapons check on everyone who entered the supermarket, about the young matrons in tight Sergio Valente jeans, trailing maids and babies behind them and buying towels, big beach towels printed with maps of Manhattan that featured Bloomingdale's; about the number of things for sale that seemed to suggest a fashion for "smart drinking," to evoke modish cocktail hours. There were bottles of Stolichnaya vodka packaged with glasses and mixer, there were ice buckets, there were bar carts of every conceivable design, displayed with sample bottles.

This was a shopping center that embodied the future for which   20
El Salvador was presumably being saved, and I wrote it down dutifully, this being the kind of "color" I knew how to interpret, the kind of inductive irony, the detail that was supposed to illuminate the story. As I wrote it down I realized that I was no longer much

1. foreign

interested in this kind of irony, that this was a story that would
not be illuminated by such details, that this was a story that would
perhaps not be illuminated at all, that this was perhaps even less
a "story" than a true *noche obscura*.[2] As I waited to cross back over
the Boulevard de los Heroes to the Camino Real I noticed soldiers
herding a young civilian into a van, their guns at the boy's back,
and I walked straight ahead, not wanting to see anything at all.

2. dark night

PATRICIA HAMPL

Prague

In May 1975, during the spring music festival that opens every   1
year with a performance of Smetana's "Ma Vlast" ("My Homeland"),
I went to Prague for the first time. The lilacs were in bloom
everywhere: the various lavenders of the French and Persian lilac,
and the more unusual—except in Prague—double white lilac.
Huge flat red banners with yellow lettering were hoisted everywhere
too, draped across homely suburban factories and from the subtle
rose and mustard baroque buildings of Staré Město (the Old City).

The banners were in honor of the thirtieth anniversary of the   2
liberation of Prague by the Soviet Army in May 1945. 30 *Let*, "30
years," it said everywhere, even on the visa stamp in my passport.
Many offices and stores had photographs in their windows, blow-
ups from 1945 showing Russian soldiers accepting spring bouquets
from shy little girls, Russian soldiers waving from tanks to happy
crowds. For the first time, I was in a city where the end of the
Second World War was really celebrated, where history was close
at hand. Prague was the first Continental European city I had seen
(I had come from London) and it was almost weirdly intact, not
modern. On the plane from America to London I had reminded
myself that London would be modern; *my* England was so much
a product of the nineteenth-century novels and poetry I'd been
reading all my life that I knew I would be shocked to see automobiles.
And in fact, nothing could prepare me for the slump I felt in
London: I wanted the city of Becky Sharpe, of Daniel Deronda,

Excerpted from Part III, "Prague," of *A Romantic Education* (1981).

even of Clarissa Dalloway, not the London of Frommer's guidebooks
and the thrill of finding lunch for 5 pence.

Prague stopped my tourism flat. The weight of its history and   3
the beauty of its architecture came to me first as an awareness of
dirt, a sort of ancient grime I had never seen before. It bewitched
me, that dirt, caught in the corners of baroque moldings and
decorative cornices, and especially I loved the dusty filth of the
long, grave windows at sunset when the light flared against the
tall oblongs and caused them to look gilded.

I had arrived in a river city, just as I had left one in St. Paul.   4
But the difference . . . On the right bank of the Vltava (in German,
the Moldau) the buildings were old—to me. Some of them were
truly old, churches and wine cellars and squares dating from the
Middle Ages. But the real look, especially of the residential and
shopping areas of Nové Město (New City—new since the fourteenth
century when Charles IV founded it), was art nouveau, highly
decorative, the Bohemian version of the Victorian. Across the river,
in Malá Strana (Small Side—Prague's Left Bank), the city became
most intensely itself, however; it rose baroquely up, villa by villa,
palace crushed to palace, gardens crumbling and climbing, to the
castle that ran like a great crown above it on a bluff.

The city silenced me. It was just as well I didn't know the   5
language and was traveling alone. There was nothing for me to
say. I was here to look.

My original intention in going to Prague was simple: to see the   6
place my grandparents had come from,[1] to hear the language they
had spoken. I knew Prague was Kafka's city, I knew Rilke[2] had
been born here, and I had read his *Letters to a Young Poet* many
times. I was a young poet myself. But my visit wasn't for them.
Mine was the return of a third generation American, the sort of
journey that is so inexplicable to the second generation: "What
are you going to *do* there?" my father asked me before I left
Minnesota.

That spring, the lines at the Prague Čedok office (the government   7
agency that runs tourism in Czechoslovakia) were dotted here and
there with young Americans looking for family villages. The young
couple in front of me in the line had come from Cleveland. The
man was asking a young travel agent, who was dressed in a jeans
skirt and wore nail polish the color of an eggplant, how he and

---

1. See "Teresa," *Dolphin Reader* pp. 818–25.
2. German novelist Franz Kafka (1883–1924) was born in Prague, as was German
lyric poet Rainer Maria Rilke (1875–1926).

his wife could get to a village whose name he couldn't manage to pronounce.

"There does not seem to be such a place," she told him. She ⁸ couldn't find a name on the map with a spelling that corresponded to the one the young man had brought from Cleveland on the piece of paper he was holding out to his wife. ("It's *his* family," she said to me. "I'm Irish.")

They decided to set out, anyway, for a village in Moravia that ⁹ had a similar spelling. "I guess that's the place," the young man said, without much conviction.

I asked my father's question: "What are you going to *do* there?" ¹⁰

"Look around," he said. "Maybe somebody"—he meant a rel- ¹¹ ative—"will be there."

My own slip of paper, which I'd brought from St. Paul, had the ¹² name of my grandmother's village ("spelling approximate," my cousin had written next to the name when he gave it to me), which was supposed to be near Třeboň, a small town in southern Bohemia. On the map, Třeboň was set among lakes (like Minneapolis, I had thought); here, the guidebook said, "the famous carp" were caught.

Suddenly, just then, as my turn came up, I had no heart for ¹³ the approximate name of the village, for the famous carp, the kind of journey the Cleveland couple had set for themselves. ("We're going to do the same thing in Ireland," the wife said.) I stepped out of the line, crumpled up my piece of paper, and left it in an ashtray. The absurdity of trying to get to Třeboň, and from there to wherever this village with the approximate spelling was supposed to be, lay on me like a plank. I felt like a student who drops out of medical school a semester before graduation; I was almost there and, suddenly, it didn't matter, I didn't want what I'd been seeking. Apparently I wanted something else.

"Do you want to get something to eat?" I asked the couple ¹⁴ from Cleveland.

But they didn't have time. "We have to split," she said. ¹⁵

"Yeah," said her husband. "It's a long way." ¹⁶

Perhaps, if you go to the old country seeking, as third or fourth ¹⁷ generation Americans often do, a strictly personal history based on bloodlines, then, the less intimate history of the nation cannot impose itself upon you very strongly. History is reduced to genealogy, which is supposed to satisfy a hunger that is clearly much larger.

But if you go on a journey like this not to find somebody, but ¹⁸ just to look around—then, in a country like Czechoslovakia (or

perhaps only there, only in Prague), the country's history is infused
with the urgency of the classic search for personal identity. The
country itself becomes the lost ancestry and, one finds, the country
is eloquent. Its long story, its history, satisfy the instinct for kinship
in a way that the discovery of a distant cousin could not. For it
is really the longing for a lost culture that sends Americans on
these pilgrimages.

It seems a peculiarly twentieth-century unhappiness, this lone-   19
liness for culture. The Russian poet Osip Mandelstam who perished
in one of Stalin's camps in 1938 was one of a group of poets
before the First World War who called themselves Acmeists. When
he was asked what, exactly, Acmeism was, Mandelstam said,
"Homesickness for world culture."

This impersonal loss and the desperation it creates often are not   20
appreciated in our psychological, personalized, society. "Masses
of people," Richard Sennett writes in his book, *The Fall of Public
Man*, "are concerned with their single life-histories and particular
emotions as never before; this concern has proved to be a trap
rather than a liberation." The reason Sennett suggests that "openness" and "being in touch with your feelings" and other such
catch phrases of supposed authenticity do not work is that "people
are working out in terms of personal feelings public matters which
properly can be dealt with only through codes of impersonal meaning." In Mandelstam's phrase, this is the inverted effect of homesickness for world culture.

Countries like Czechoslovakia—the small, squeezed countries   21
of Central and Eastern Europe—know this homesickness best.
The first words of the Czechoslovak national anthem are, "Where
is my home? Where is my home?" Strangely lost, elegiac words
for a national hymn. (Sir Robert Bruce Lockhart, the British journalist
and consular officer, thought it was the "least aggressive of all
national anthems.") They are the words of a small nation that
thinks of itself affectionately, as if it were a family. Except families
don't have to worry about sovereignty.

I put Třeboň out of my mind and spent the rest of the week   22
walking aimlessly around Prague. If I had answered my father's
question—what was I *doing*—I would have said I was sitting in
coffeehouses, in between long, aimless walks. A long trip for a
cup of coffee, but I was listless, suddenly lacking curiosity and I
felt, as I sat in the Slavia next to the big windows that provide
one of the best views of the Hradčany in the city, that simply by
staring out the window I was doing my bit: there it was, the castle,
and I was looking at it. I had fallen on the breast of the Middle
European coffeehouse and I was content among the putty- and

dove-colored clothes, the pensioners stirring away the hours, the tables of university students studying and writing their papers, the luscious waste of time, the gossip whose ardor I sensed in the bent heads, lifted eyebrows—because of course I couldn't understand a word.

In Vienna the coffeehouses—not all of them, thank God—lose   23 their leases to McDonald's and fast-food chains. But in Prague the colors just fade and become more, rather than less, what they were. The coffeehouse is deeply attached to the idea of conversation, the exchange of ideas, and therefore, to a political society. In *The Agony of Czechoslovakia '38/'68*, Kurt Weisskopf remembers the Prague coffeehouses before the Second World War.

> You were expected to patronize the coffeehouse of your group, your profession, your political party. Crooks frequented the Golden Goose, or the Black Rose in the centre of Prague. Snobs went to the Savarin, whores and their prospective clients to the Lind or Julis; commercial travellers occupied the front part of Cafe Boulevard, while the rear was the traditional meeting place of Stalinists and Trotskyites, glaring at each other as they sat around separate marble tables. The rich went to the Urban, "progressive" intellectuals to the Metro. Abstract painters met at the Union, and surrealists at the Manes where they argued with impressionists. You were still served by the black-coated waiters if you did not belong, but so contemptuously that you realized how unwelcome your presence was. The papers in their bamboo frames and the magazines in their folders, an essential part of the Central European coffeehouse service, were regrettably not available to intruders. If you went to the wrong coffeehouse you were just frozen out.
>
> But if you fitted in, socially, politically, philosophically, artistically or professionally, well, then the headwaiter and the manager treated you almost as a relative and you were even deemed worthy of credit.
>
> "Rudolf, switch on the light over the Communists, they can't read their papers properly," old Loebl, manager of the Edison used to instruct the headwaiter. "And see that the Anarchists get more iced water." Once you had ordered your coffee you were entitled to free glasses of iced water brought regularly by the trayload; this was called a "swimming pool."

The water was still brought, as I sat at the marble table of the   24 Slavia, though not by the trayload. Perhaps there were political conversations, even arguments: I couldn't tell. But the newspapers were the official ones of the Communist Party, including, in English, the *Daily Worker*. When I asked someone I'd struck up a conversation with, who was quoted as a source on American news, I was told, "Gus Hall," the president of the American Communist Party. "As a typical American?" I asked incredulously. "As the voice of the people," I was told. It struck me as funny, not sinister, although later I realized I was annoyed.

I walked around Prague, hardly caring if I hit the right tourist 25 spots, missing baroque gems, I suppose, getting lost, leaving the hotel without a map as if I had no destination. I just walked, stopping at coffeehouses, smoking unfiltered cigarettes and looking out from the blue wreath around me to other deep-drawing smokers. Everyone seemed to have time to sit, to smoke as if smoking were breathing, to stare into the vacancy of private thought, if their thoughts were private. I was in the thirties, I'd finally arrived in my parents' decade, the men's soft caps, the dove colors of Depression pictures, the acquiescence to circumstance, the ruined quality. For the first time I recognized the truth of beauty: that it is brokenness, it is on its knees. I sat and watched it and smoked (I don't smoke but I found myself buying cigarettes), smoked a blue relation between those coffeehouses and me. For this sadness turned out to be, to me, beautiful. Or rather, the missing quality of beauty, whatever makes it approachable, became apparent in Prague. I could sit, merely breathing, and be part of it. I was beautiful—at last. And I didn't care—at last. I stumbled through the ancient streets, stopped in the smoke-grimed coffeehouses and added my signature of ash, anonymous and yet entirely satisfied. I had ceased even to be a reverse immigrant—I sought no one, no sign of my family or any ethnic heritage that might be mine. I was, simply, in the most beautiful place I had ever seen, and it was grimy and sad and broken. I was relieved of some weight, the odd burden of happiness and unblemished joy of the adored child—or perhaps I was free of beauty itself as an abstract concept. I didn't think about it and didn't bother to wonder. I sat and smoked; I walked and got lost and didn't care because I couldn't get lost. I hardly understood that I was happy: my happiness consisted of encountering sadness. I simply felt *accurate*.

E. B. WHITE

Walden

Miss Nims, take a letter to Henry David Thoreau. Dear Henry: 1 I thought of you the other afternoon as I was approaching Concord doing fifty on Route 62. That is a high speed at which to hold a

Written in 1939, ninety-six years after Thoreau went to live at Walden Pond.

philosopher in one's mind, but in this century we are a nimble bunch.

On one of the lawns in the outskirts of the village a woman ² was cutting the grass with a motorized lawn mower. What made me think of you was that the machine had rather got away from her, although she was game enough, and in the brief glimpse I had of the scene it appeared to me that the lawn was mowing the lady. She kept a tight grip on the handles, which throbbed violently with every explosion of the one-cylinder motor, and as she sheered around bushes and lurched along at a reluctant trot behind her impetuous servant, she looked like a puppy who had grabbed something that was too much for him. Concord hasn't changed much, Henry; the farm implements and the animals still have the upper hand.

I may as well admit that I was journeying to Concord with the ³ deliberate intention of visiting your woods; for although I have never knelt at the grave of a philosopher nor placed wreaths on moldy poets, and have often gone a mile out of my way to avoid some place of historical interest, I have always wanted to see Walden Pond. The account which you left of your sojourn there is, you will be amused to learn, a document of increasing pertinence; each year it seems to gain a little headway, as the world loses ground. We may all be transcendental yet, whether we like it or not. As our common complexities increase, any tale of individual simplicity (and yours is the best written and the cockiest) acquires a new fascination; as our goods accumulate, but not our well-being, your report of an existence without material adornment takes on a certain awkward credibility.

My purpose in going to Walden Pond, like yours, was not to ⁴ live cheaply or to live dearly there, but to transact some private business with the fewest obstacles. Approaching Concord, doing forty, doing forty-five, doing fifty, the steering wheel held snug in my palms, the highway held grimly in my vision, the crown of the road now serving me (on the righthand curves), now defeating me (on the lefthand curves), I began to rouse myself from the stupefaction which a day's motor journey induces. It was a delicious evening, Henry, when the whole body is one sense, and imbibes delight through every pore, if I may coin a phrase.[1] Fields were richly brown where the harrow, drawn by the stripped Ford, had lately sunk its teeth; pastures were green; and overhead the sky had that same everlasting great look which you will find on Page

---

1. Throughout this essay, White is having fun echoing famous lines from Henry David Thoreau's *Walden*. This, for instance, is an echo of the opening line of the chapter titled "Solitude."

144 of the Oxford pocket edition. I could feel the road entering me, through tire, wheel, spring, and cushion; shall I not have intelligence with earth too? Am I not partly leaves and vegetable mold myself?—a man of infinite horsepower, yet partly leaves.

Stay with me on 62 and it will take you into Concord. As I say, it was a delicious evening. The snake had come forth to die in a bloody S on the highway, the wheel upon its head, its bowels flat now and exposed. The turtle had come up too to cross the road and die in the attempt, its hard shell smashed under the rubber blow, its intestinal yearning (for the other side of the road) forever squashed. There was a sign by the wayside which announced that the road had a "cotton surface." You wouldn't know what that is, but neither, for that matter, did I. There is a cryptic ingredient in many of our modern improvements—we are awed and pleased without knowing quite what we are enjoying. It is something to be traveling on a road with a cotton surface.

The civilization round Concord today is an odd distillation of city, village, farm, and manor. The houses, yards, fields look not quite suburban, not quite rural. Under the bronze beech and the blue spruce of the departed baron grazes the milch goat of the heirs. Under the porte-cochère stands the reconditioned station wagon; under the grape arbor sit the puppies for sale. (But why do men degenerate ever? What makes families run out?)

It was June and everywhere June was publishing her immemorial stanza; in the lilacs, in the syringa, in the freshly edged paths and the sweetness of moist beloved gardens, and the little wire wickets that preserve the tulips' front. Farmers were already moving the fruits of their toil into their yards, arranging the rhubarb, the asparagus, the strictly fresh eggs on the painted stands under the little shed roofs with the patent shingles. And though it was almost a hundred years since you had taken your ax and started cutting out your home on Walden Pond,[2] I was interested to observe that the philosophical spirit was still alive in Massachusetts: in the center of a vacant lot some boys were assembling the framework of the rude shelter, their whole mind and skill concentrated in the rather inauspicious helter-skeleton of studs and rafters. They too were escaping from town, to live naturally, in a rich blend of savagery and philosophy.

That evening, after supper at the inn, I strolled out into the twilight to dream my shapeless transcendental dreams and see that

2. See Thoreau, "The Fitness of a Man's Building His Own House," *Dolphin Reader* pp. 123–32.

the car was locked up for the night (first open the right front door, then reach over, straining, and pull up the handles of the left rear and the left front till you hear the click, then the handle of the right rear, then shut the right front but open it again remembering that the key is still in the ignition switch, remove the key, shut the right front again with a bang, push the tiny keyhole cover to one side, insert key, turn, and withdraw). It is what we all do, Henry. It is called locking the car. It is said to confuse thieves and keep them from making off with the laprobe. Four doors to lock behind one robe. The driver himself never uses a laprobe, the free movement of his legs being vital to the operation of the vehicle; so that when he locks the car it is a pure and unselfish act. I have in my life gained very little essential heat from laprobes, yet I have ever been at pains to lock them up.

The evening was full of sounds, some of which would have 9 stirred your memory. The robins still love the elms of New England villages at sundown. There is enough of the thrush in them to make song inevitable at the end of day, and enough of the tramp to make them hang round the dwellings of men. A robin, like many another American, dearly loves a white house with green blinds. Concord is still full of them.

Your fellow-townsmen were stirring abroad—not many afoot, 10 most of them in their cars; and the sound which they made in Concord at evening was a rustling and a whispering. The sound lacks steadfastness and is wholly unlike that of a train. A train, as you know who lived so near the Fitchburg line, whistles once or twice sadly and is gone, trailing a memory in smoke, soothing to ear and mind. Automobiles, skirting a village green, are like flies that have gained the inner ear—they buzz, cease, pause, start, shift, stop, halt, brake, and the whole effect is a nervous polytone curiously disturbing.

As I wandered along, the toc toc of ping pong balls drifted from 11 an attic window. In front of the Reuben Brown house a Buick was drawn up. At the wheel, motionless, his hat upon his head, a man sat, listening to Amos and Andy on the radio (it is a drama of many scenes and without an end). The deep voice of Andrew Brown, emerging from the car, although it originated more than two hundred miles away, was unstrained by distance. When you used to sit on the shore of your pond on Sunday morning, listening to the church bells of Acton and Concord, you were aware of the excellent filter of the intervening atmosphere. Science has attended to that, and sound now maintains its intensity without regard for distance. Properly sponsored, it goes on forever.

A fire engine, out for a trial spin, roared past Emerson's house, 12 hot with readiness for public duty. Over the barn roofs the martins dipped and chittered. A swarthy daughter of an asparagus grower, in culottes, shirt, and bandanna, pedalled past on her bicycle. It was indeed a delicious evening, and I returned to the inn (I believe it was your house once) to rock with the old ladies on the concrete veranda.

Next morning early I started afoot for Walden, out Main Street 13 and down Thoreau, past the depot and the Minuteman Chevrolet Company. The morning was fresh, and in a bean field along the way I flushed an agriculturalist, quietly studying his beans. Thoreau Street soon joined Number 126, an artery of the State. We number our highways nowadays, our speed being so great we can remember little of their quality or character and are lucky to remember their number. (Men have an indistinct notion that if they keep up this activity long enough all will at length ride somewhere, in next to no time.) Your pond is on 126.

I knew I must be nearing your woodland retreat when the 14 Golden Pheasant lunchroom came into view—Sealtest ice cream, toasted sandwiches, hot frankfurters, waffles, tonics, and lunches. Were I the proprietor, I should add rice, Indian meal, and molasses— just for old time's sake. The Pheasant, incidentally, is for sale: a chance for some nature lover who wishes to set himself up beside a pond in the Concord atmosphere and live deliberately, fronting only the essential facts of life on Number 126. Beyond the Pheasant was a place called Walden Breezes, an oasis whose porch pillars were made of old green shutters sawed into lengths. On the porch was a distorting mirror, to give the traveler a comical image of himself, who had miraculously learned to gaze in an ordinary glass without smiling. Behind the Breezes, in a sun-parched clearing, dwelt your philosophical descendants in their trailers, each trailer the size of your hut, but all grouped together for the sake of congeniality. Trailer people leave the city, as you did, to discover solitude and in any weather, at any hour of the day or night, to improve the nick of time; but they soon collect in villages and get bogged deeper in the mud than ever. The camp behind Walden Breezes was just rousing itself to the morning. The ground was packed hard under the heel, and the sun came through the clearing to bake the soil and enlarge the wry smell of cramped housekeeping. Cushman's bakery truck had stopped to deliver an early basket of rolls. A camp dog, seeing me in the road, barked petulantly. A man emerged from one of the trailers and set forth with a bucket to draw water from some forest tap.

Leaving the highway I turned off into the woods toward the 15 pond, which was apparent through the foliage. The floor of the forest was strewn with dried old oak leaves and *Transcripts*. From beneath the flattened popcorn wrapper (*granum explosum*) peeped the frail violet. I followed a footpath and descended to the water's edge. The pond lay clear and blue in the morning light, as you have seen it so many times. In the shallows a man's waterlogged shirt undulated gently. A few flies came out to greet me and convoy me to your cove, past the No Bathing signs on which the fellows and the girls had scrawled their names. I felt strangely excited suddenly to be snooping around your premises, tiptoeing along watchfully, as though not to tread by mistake upon the intervening century. Before I got to the cove I heard something which seemed to me quite wonderful: I heard your frog, a full, clear *troonk*, guiding me, still hoarse and solemn, bridging the years as the robins had bridged them in the sweetness of the village evening. But he soon quit, and I came on a couple of young boys throwing stones at him.

Your front yard is marked by a bronze tablet set in a stone.   16
Four small granite posts, a few feet away, show where the house was. On top of the tablet was a pair of faded blue bathing trunks with a white stripe. Back of it is a pile of stones, a sort of cairn, left by your visitors as a tribute I suppose. It is a rather ugly little heap of stones, Henry. In fact the hillside itself seems faded, brow-beaten; a few tall skinny pines, bare of lower limbs, a smattering of young maples in suitable green, some birches and oaks, and a number of trees felled by the last big wind. It was from the bole of one of these fallen pines, torn up by the roots, that I extracted the stone which I added to the cairn—a sentimental act in which I was interrupted by a small terrier from a nearby picnic group, who confronted me and wanted to know about the stone.

I sat down for a while on one of the posts of your house to   17
listen to the bluebottles and the dragonflies. The invaded glade sprawled shabby and mean at my feet, but the flies were tuned to the old vibration. There were the remains of a fire in your ruins, but I doubt that it was yours; also two beer bottles trodden into the soil and become part of earth. A young oak had taken root in your house, and two or three ferns, unrolling like the ticklers at a banquet. The only other furnishings were a DuBarry pattern sheet, a page torn from a picture magazine, and some crusts in wax paper.

Before I quit I walked clear round the pond and found the place   18
where you used to sit on the northeast side to get the sun in the fall, and the beach where you got sand for scrubbing your floor.

On the eastern side of the pond, where the highway borders it, the State has built dressing rooms for swimmers, a float with diving towers, drinking fountains of porcelain, and rowboats for hire. The pond is in fact a State Preserve, and carries a twenty-dollar fine for picking wild flowers, a decree signed in all solemnity by your fellow-citizens Walter C. Wardwell, Erson B. Barlow, and Nathaniel I. Bowditch. There was a smell of creosote where they had been building a wide wooden stairway to the road and the parking area. Swimmers and boaters were arriving; bodies plunged vigorously into the water and emerged wet and beautiful in the bright air. As I left, a boatload of town boys were splashing about in mid-pond, kidding and fooling, the young fellows singing at the tops of their lungs in a wild chorus:

> *Amer-ica, Amer-ica, God shed his grace on thee,*
> *And crown thy good with brotherhood*
> *From sea to shi-ning sea!*

I walked back to town along the railroad, following your custom. [19] The rails were expanding noisily in the hot sun, and on the slope of the roadbed the wild grape and the blackberry sent up their creepers to the track.

The expense of my brief sojourn in Concord was:[3]   [20]

Canvas shoes	$1.95	
Baseball bat	.25	⎱ gifts to take back
Left-handed fielder's glove	1.25	⎰ to a boy
Hotel and meals	4.25	
In all	$7.70	

As you see, this amount was almost what you spent for food for eight months. I cannot defend the shoes or the expenditure for shelter and food: they reveal a meanness and grossness in my nature which you would find contemptible. The baseball equipment, however, is the kind of impediment with which you were never on even terms. You must remember that the house where you practiced the sort of economy which I respect was haunted only by mice and squirrels. You never had to cope with a shortstop.

---

3. Thoreau kept, in his own *Walden*, a painstaking account of his expenses—down to the half cent.

JOAN DIDION

Marrying Absurd

To be married in Las Vegas, Clark County, Nevada, a bride must   1
swear that she is eighteen or has parental permission and a bridegroom that he is twenty-one or has parental permission. Someone
must put up five dollars for the license. (On Sundays and holidays,
fifteen dollars. The Clark County Courthouse issues marriage licenses
at any time of the day or night except between noon and one in
the afternoon, between eight and nine in the evening, and between
four and five in the morning.) Nothing else is required. The State
of Nevada, alone among these United States, demands neither a
premarital blood test nor a waiting period before or after the
issuance of a marriage license. Driving in across the Mojave from
Los Angeles, one sees the signs way out on the desert, looming
up from that moonscape of rattlesnakes and mesquite, even before
the Las Vegas lights appear like a mirage on the horizon: "GETTING
MARRIED? Free License Information First Strip Exit." Perhaps the
Las Vegas wedding industry achieved its peak operational efficiency
between 9:00 p.m. and midnight of August 26, 1965, an otherwise
unremarkable Thursday which happened to be, by Presidential
order, the last day on which anyone could improve his draft status
merely by getting married. One hundred and seventy-one couples
were pronounced man and wife in the name of Clark County and
the State of Nevada that night, sixty-seven of them by a single
justice of the peace, Mr. James A. Brennan. Mr. Brennan did one
wedding at the Dunes and the other sixty-six in his office, and
charged each couple eight dollars. One bride lent her veil to six
others. "I got it down from five to three minutes," Mr. Brennan
said later of his feat. "I could've married them *en masse*, but they're
people, not cattle. People expect more when they get married."

What people who get married in Las Vegas actually do expect—   2
what, in the largest sense, their "expectations" are—strikes one
as a curious and self-contradictory business. Las Vegas is the most
extreme and allegorical of American settlements, bizarre and beautiful in its venality and in its devotion to immediate gratification,
a place the tone of which is set by mobsters and call girls and
ladies' room attendants with amyl nitrite poppers in their uniform
pockets. Almost everyone notes that there is no "time" in Las

First published in *The Saturday Evening Post*, 1967.

Vegas, no night and no day and no past and no future (no Las Vegas casino, however, has taken the obliteration of the ordinary time sense quite so far as Harold's Club in Reno, which for a while issued, at odd intervals in the day and night, mimeographed "bulletins" carrying news from the world outside); neither is there any logical sense of where one is. One is standing on a highway in the middle of a vast hostile desert looking at an eighty-foot sign which blinks "STARDUST" or "CAESAR'S PALACE." Yes, but what does that explain? This geographical implausibility reinforces the sense that what happens there has no connection with "real" life; Nevada cities like Reno and Carson are ranch towns, Western towns, places behind which there is some historical imperative. But Las Vegas seems to exist only in the eye of the beholder. All of which makes it an extraordinarily stimulating and interesting place, but an odd one in which to want to wear a candlelight satin Priscilla of Boston wedding dress with Chantilly lace insets, tapered sleeves and a detachable modified train.

And yet the Las Vegas wedding business seems to appeal to   3
precisely that impulse. "Sincere and Dignified Since 1954," one wedding chapel advertises. There are nineteen such wedding chapels in Las Vegas, intensely competitive, each offering better, faster, and, by implication, more sincere services than the next: Our Photos Best Anywhere, Your Wedding on A Phonograph Record, Candlelight with Your Ceremony, Honeymoon Accommodations, Free Transportation from Your Motel to Courthouse to Chapel and Return to Motel, Religious or Civil Ceremonies, Dressing Rooms, Flowers, Rings, Announcements, Witnesses Available, and Ample Parking. All of these services, like most others in Las Vegas (sauna baths, payroll-check cashing, chinchilla coats for sale or rent) are offered twenty-four hours a day, seven days a week, presumably on the premise that marriage, like craps, is a game to be played when the table seems hot.

But what strikes one most about the Strip chapels, with their   4
wishing wells and stained-glass paper windows and their artificial bouvardia, is that so much of their business is by no means a matter of simple convenience, of late-night liaisons between show girls and baby Crosbys. Of course there is some of that. (One night about eleven o'clock in Las Vegas I watched a bride in an orange minidress and masses of flame-colored hair stumble from a Strip chapel on the arm of her bridegroom, who looked the part of the expendable nephew in movies like *Miami Syndicate.* "I gotta get the kids," the bride whimpered. "I gotta pick up the sitter, I gotta get to the midnight show." "What you gotta get," the bridegroom said, opening the door of a Cadillac Coupe de Ville and watching her crumple on the seat, "is sober.") But Las Vegas seems to offer

something other than "convenience"; it is merchandising "niceness," the facsimile of proper ritual, to children who do not know how else to find it, how to make the arrangements, how to do it "right." All day and evening long on the Strip, one sees actual wedding parties, waiting under the harsh lights at a crosswalk, standing uneasily in the parking lot of the Frontier while the photographer hired by The Little Church of the West ("Wedding Place of the Stars") certifies the occasion, takes the picture: the bride in a veil and white satin pumps, the bridegroom usually in a white dinner jacket, and even an attendant or two, a sister or a best friend in hot-pink *peau de soie*, a flirtation veil, a carnation nosegay. "When I Fall in Love It Will Be Forever," the organist plays, and then a few bars of Lohengrin. The mother cries; the stepfather, awkward in his role, invites the chapel hostess to join them for a drink at the Sands. The hostess declines with a professional smile; she has already transferred her interest to the group waiting outside. One bride out, another in, and again the sign goes up on the chapel door: "One moment please—Wedding."

I sat next to one such wedding party in a Strip restaurant the last time I was in Las Vegas. The marriage had just taken place; the bride still wore her dress, the mother her corsage. A bored waiter poured out a few swallows of pink champagne ("on the house") for everyone but the bride, who was too young to be served. "You'll need something with more kick than that," the bride's father said with heavy jocularity to his new son-in-law; the ritual jokes about the wedding night had a certain Panglossian character, since the bride was clearly several months pregnant. Another round of pink champagne, this time not on the house, and the bride began to cry. "It was just as nice," she sobbed, "as I hoped and dreamed it would be."

PAUL THEROUX

Sunrise With Seamonsters

The boat slid down the bank and without a splash into the creek, which was gray this summer morning. The air was wooly with mist. The tide had turned, but just a moment ago, so there was still no motion on the water—no current, not a ripple. The

First published, in a shorter form, in *Vanity Fair* in 1984, under the title "Rounding the Cape." Collected in *Sunrise With Seamonsters: Travels and Discoveries* (1985).

marsh grass was a deeper green for there being no sun. It was as if—this early and this dark—the day had not yet begun to breathe.

I straightened the boat and took my first stroke: the gurgle of   2
the spoon blades and the sigh of the twisting oarlock were the only sounds. I set off, moving like a water bug through the marsh and down the bendy creek to the sea. When my strokes were regular and I was rowing at a good clip, my mind started to work, and I thought: I'm not coming back tonight. And so the day seemed long enough and full of possibilities. I had no plans except to keep on harbor-hopping around the Cape,[1] and it was easy now going out with the tide.

This was Scorton Creek, in East Sandwich, and our hill—one   3
of the few on the low lumpy terminal moraine of the Cape—was once an Indian fort. Wampanoags. The local farmers plowed this hill until recently, when the houses went up, and their plow blades always struck flints and axe heads and beads. I splashed past a boathouse the size of a garage. When they dug the foundation for that boathouse less than twenty years ago they unearthed a large male Wampanoag who had been buried in a sitting position, his skin turned to leather and his bones sticking through. They slung him out and put the boathouse there.

Three more bends in the creek and I could see the current stirring   4
more strongly around me. A quarter of a mile away in the marsh was a Great Blue Heron—five-feet high and moving in a slow prayerful way, like a narrowed-shouldered priest in gray vestments. The boat slipped along, carrying itself between strokes. Up ahead on the beach was a person with a dog—one of those energetic early-risers who boasts "I only need four hours' sleep!" and is probably hell to live with. Nothing else around—only the terns screeching over their eggs, and a few boats motionless at their moorings, and a rather crummy clutter of beach houses and *No Trespassing* signs, and the ghosts of dead Indians. The current was so swift in the creek I couldn't have gone back if I tried, and as I approached the shore it shot me into the sea. And now light was dazzling in the mist, as on the magnificent Turner[2] "Sunrise, with a Sea Monster".

After an hour I was at Sandy Neck Public Beach—about four   5
miles. This bay side of the upper Cape has a low duney shore and notoriously shallow water in places. The half a dozen harbors are

1. Cape Cod, sandy peninsula in southeast Massachusetts.
2. Joseph Mallord William Turner (1775–1851), English landscape painter, famous for his visionary depiction of nature.

spread over seventy miles and most have dangerous bars. It is not a coast for easy cruising and in many areas there is hardly enough water for windsurfing. There are sand bars in the oddest places. Most sailboats can't approach any of the harbors unless the tide is high. So the little boats stay near shore and watch the tides, and the deep draft boats stay miles offshore. I was in between and I was alone. In two months of this I never saw another rowboat more than fifty yards from shore. Indeed, I seldom saw anyone rowing at all.

Sandy Neck proper, an eight-mile peninsula of Arabian-style 6 dunes, was today a panorama of empty beach; the only life stirring was the gulls and more distantly the hovering marsh hawks. A breeze had come up; it had freshened; it was now a light wind. I got stuck on a sand bar, then hopped out and dragged the boat into deeper water. I was trying to get around Beach Point to have my lunch in Barnstable Harbor—my forward locker contained provisions. I was frustrated by the shoals. But I should have known— there were seagulls all over the ocean here and they were not swimming but standing. I grew to recognize low water from the posture of seagulls.

When I drew level with Barnstable Harbor I was spun around 7 by the strong current. I had to fight it for half an hour before I got to shore. Even then I was only at Beach Point. This was the channel into the harbor, and the water in it was narrow and swiftly moving—a deep river flowing through a shallow sea, its banks just submerged.

I tied the boat to a rock and while I rested a Ranger drove up 8 in his Chevy Bronco.

He said, "That wind's picking up. I think we're in for a storm." 9 He pointed towards Barnstable Harbor. "See the clouds building up over there? The forecast said showers but that looks like more than showers. Might be thunderstorms. Where are you headed?"

"Just up the coast." 10

He nodded at the swiftly rushing channel and said, "You'll have 11 to get across that thing first."

"Why is it so choppy?" 12

His explanation was simple, and it accounted for a great deal 13 of the rough water I was to see in the weeks to come. He said that when the wind was blowing in the opposite direction to a tide, a chop of hard irregular waves was whipped up. It could become very fierce very quickly.

Then he pointed across the harbor mouth towards Bass Hole 14 and told me to look at how the ebbing tide had uncovered a mile of sand flats. "At low tide people just walk around over there,"

he said. So, beyond the vicious channel the sea was slipping
down—white water here, none there.

After the Ranger drove off I made myself a cheese sandwich,   15
swigged some coffee from my thermos bottle and decided to rush
the channel. My skiff's sides were lapstrake—like clapboards—
and rounded, which stabilized the boat in high waves, but this
short breaking chop was a different matter. Instead of rowing at
right angles to the current I turned the bow against it, and steadied
the skiff by rowing. The skiff rocked wildly—the current slicing
the bow, the wind-driven chop smacking the stern. A few minutes
later I was across. And then I ran aground. After the channel were
miles of watery shore; but it was only a few inches deep—and
the tide was still dropping.

The wind was blowing, the sky was dark, the shoreline was   16
distant; and now the water was not deep enough for this rowboat.
I got out and—watched by strolling seagulls—dragged the boat
through the shallow water that lay over the sand bar. The boat
skidded and sometimes floated, but it was not really buoyant until
I had splashed along for about an hour. To anyone on the beach
I must have seemed a bizarre figure—alone, far from shore, walking
on the water.

It was mid-afternoon by the time I had dragged the boat to   17
deeper water, and I got in and began to row. The wind seemed
to be blowing now from the west; it gathered at the stern and
gave me a following sea, lifting me in the direction I wanted to
go. I rowed past Chapin Beach and the bluffs, and around the
black rocks at Nobscusset Harbor, marking my progress on my
flapping chart by glancing again and again at a water tower like
a stovepipe in Dennis.

At about five o'clock I turned into Sesuit Harbor, still pulling   18
hard. I had rowed about sixteen miles. My hands were blistered
but I had made a good start. And I had made a discovery: the
sea was unpredictable, and the shore looked foreign. I was used
to finding familiar things in exotic places; but the unfamiliar at
home was new to me. It had been a disorienting day. At times I
had been afraid. It was a taste of something strange in a place I
had known my whole life. It was a shock and a satisfaction.

Mrs. Coffin at Sesuit Harbor advised me not to go out the next   19
day. Anyone with a name out of *Moby Dick* is worth listening to
on the subject of the sea. The wind was blowing from the northeast,
making Mrs. Coffin's flag snap and beating the sea into whitecaps.

I said, "I'm only going to Rock Harbor."   20
It was about nine miles.   21
She said, "You'll be pulling your guts out."   22
I decided to go, thinking: I would rather struggle in a heavy   23

sea and get wet than sit in the harbor and wait for the weather to improve.

But as soon as I had rowed beyond the breakwater I was hit   24
hard by the waves and tipped by the wind. I unscrewed my sliding seat and jammed the thwart into place; and I tried again. I couldn't manoeuver the boat. I changed oars, lashing the long ones down and using the seven-and-a-half-foot ones. I made some progress, but the wind was punching me towards shore. This was West Brewster, off Quivett Neck. The chart showed church spires. I rowed for another few hours and saw that I had gone hardly any distance at all. But there was no point in turning back. I didn't need a harbor. I knew I could beach the boat anywhere—pull it up over there at that ramp, or between those rocks, or at that public beach. I had plenty of time and I felt all right. This was like walking uphill, but so what?

So I struggled all day. I hated the banging waves, and the way   25
they leaped over the sides when the wind pushed me sideways into the troughs of the swell. There were a few inches of water sloshing in the bottom, and my chart was soaked. At noon a motorboat came near me and asked me if I was in trouble. I said no and told him where I was going. The man said, "Rock Harbor's real far!" and pointed east. Some of the seawater dried on the boat leaving the lace of crystalized salt shimmering on the mahogany. I pulled on, passing a sailboat in the middle of the afternoon.

"Where's Rock Harbor?" I asked.   26

"Look for the trees!"   27

But I looked in the wrong place. The trees weren't on shore,   28
they were in the water, about twelve of them planted in two rows—tall dead limbless pines—like lampposts. They marked the harbor entrance; they also marked the Brewster Flats, for at low tide there was no water here at all, and Rock Harbor was just a creek draining into a desert of sand. You could drive a car across the harbor mouth at low tide.

I had arranged to meet my father here. My brother Joseph was   29
with him. He had just arrived from the Pacific islands of Samoa. I showed him the boat.

He touched the oarlocks. He said, "They're all tarnished." Then   30
he frowned at the salt-smeared wood and his gaze made the boat seem small and rather puny.

I said, "I just rowed from Sesuit with the wind against me. It   31
took me the whole goddamned day!"

He said, "Don't get excited."   32

"What do you know about boats?" I said.   33

He went silent. We got into the car—two boys and their father.   34
I had not seen Joe for several years. Perhaps he was sulking

because I hadn't asked about Samoa. But had he asked about my rowing? It didn't seem like much, because it was travel at home. Yet I felt the day had been full of risks.

"How the hell," I said, "can you live in Samoa for eight years   35
and not know anything about boats?"

"*Sah*-moa," he said, correcting my pronunciation. It was a family   36
joke.

My brother Alex was waiting with my mother, and he smiled   37
as I entered the house.

"Here he comes," Alex said.   38

My face was burned, the blisters had broken on my hands and   39
left them raw, my back ached and so did the muscle strings in my forearm; there was sea salt in my eyes.

"Ishmael," Alex said. He was sitting compactly on a chair glancing   40
narrowly at me and smoking. " 'And I only am escaped alone to tell thee.' "[3]

My mother said, "We're almost ready to eat—you must be   41
starving! God, look at you!"

Alex was behind her. He made a face at me, then silently mimicked   42
a laugh at the absurdity of a forty-two year old man taking consolation from his mother.

"Home is the sailor, home from the sea," Alex said and imitated   43
my voice, "Pass the spaghetti, Mum!"

Joe had started to relax. Now he had an ally, and I was being   44
mocked. We were not writers, husbands, or fathers. We were three big boys fooling in front of their parents. Home is so often the simple past.

"What's he been telling you, Joe?" Alex said.   45

I went to wash my face.   46

"He said I don't know anything about boats."   47

Just before we sat down to eat, I said, "It's pretty rough out   48
there."

Alex seized on this, looking delighted. He made the sound of   49
a strong wind, by whistling and clearing his throat. He squinted and in a harsh whisper said, "Aye, it's rough out there, and you can hardly"—he stood up, banging the dining table with his thigh— "you can hardly see the bowsprit. Aye, and the wind's shifting, too. But never mind, Mr. Christian! Give him twenty lashes—

---

3. Job 1:16, spoken by a messenger telling Job of the massacre that has killed all the servants but himself. The line is echoed by Ishmael, narrator of Herman Melville's famous novel of the sea, *Moby Dick,* after all crew members of the *Pequod,* save himself, have perished.

   Throughout the next several paragraphs Alex quotes from, alludes to, or parodies other famous works about the sea, among them *Mutiny on the Bounty.*

that'll take the strut out of him! And hoist the mainsail—we're miles from anywhere. None of you swabbies knows anything about boats. But I know, because I've sailed from Pitcairn Island to Rock Harbor by dead reckoning—in the roughest water known to man. Just me against the elements, with the waves threatening to pitch-pole my frail craft . . ."

"Your supper's getting cold," father said.   50

"How long did it take you?" mother said to me.   51

"All day," I said.   52

"Aye, captain," Alex said. "Aw, it's pretty rough out there, what   53
with the wind and the rising sea."

"What will you write about?" my father asked.   54

"He'll write about ocean's roar and how he just went around   55
the Horn. You're looking at Francis Chichester! The foam beating against the wheelhouse, the mainsheet screaming, the wind and the rising waves. Hark! Thunder and lightning over *The Gypsy Moth!*"

Declaiming made Alex imaginative, and stirred his memory. He   56
had an actor's gift for sudden shouts and whispers and for giving himself wholly to the speech. It was as if he was on an instant touched with lucid insanity, the exalted chaos of creation. He was triumphant.

"But look at him now—Peter Freuchen of the seven seas, the   57
old tar in his clinker-built boat. He's home asking his mother to pass the spaghetti! 'Thanks, mum, I'd love another helping, mum.' After a day in the deep sea he's with his mother and father, reaching for the meatballs!"

Joseph was laughing hard, his whole body swelling as he tried   58
to suppress it.

"He's not going to write about that. No, nothing about the   59
spaghetti. It'll just be Captain Bligh, all alone, bending at his oars, and picking oakum through the long tumultuous nights at sea. And the wind and the murderous waves . . ."

"Dry up," father said, still eating.   60

Then they all turned their big sympathetic faces at me across   61
the cluttered dining table. Alex looked slightly sheepish, and the others apprehensive, fearing that I might be offended, that Alex had gone too far.

"What will you write about?" mother asked.   62

I shook my head and tried not to smile—because I was thinking: 63
That.

It had all been harmless ridicule, and yet the next morning I   64
got into the skiff at Rock Harbor and felt my morale rising as I rowed away. I thought about the oddness of the previous day: I

had ignored a Small Craft Advisory and had been tossed about in
a difficult sea; and then I had gone home and had a family dinner.
I had not been able to describe my rowing experience to them—
anyway, what was the point? It had been private. And in poking
fun at me, Alex had come crudely close to the truth—all risk-
taking has a strong element of self-dramatization in it: daredevils
are notorious egomaniacs. Of course it was foolish to be home
eating and bumping knees with the aged parents after such a day!
So, the next day, which was perfect—sunny and still—I went
out farther than I ever had and I rowed twenty-two miles.

It was my reaction to home, or rather to the bewildering jux- 65
taposition of this boat and that house. The absurdity of it all! I
was self-sufficient and private in the boat, but from this protection
at sea I had gone ashore and been half-drowned by the clamor
and old jokes and nakedness at home. Now it was satisfying to
be going—like running away. It was wonderful at last to be alone;
and if I had courage and confidence it was because I had become
attached to my boat.

"See you named it after a duck," a lobsterman called out as I 66
passed him that day. He was hauling pots out of the soupy water.

Goldeneye was carved on my transom and shining this sunny 67
morning, gold on mahogany.

"Killed plenty of them right here!" he shouted. "What with this 68
hot weather we probably won't see any until January!"

He went back to emptying his pots—the lobsterman's habitual 69
hurry, fueled by the anxiety that the poor beasts will die and deny
him his $2.70 a pound at the market in Barnstable.

But even in his frenzy of work he glanced up again and yelled, 70
"Nice boat!"

It was a beautiful boat, an Amesbury skiff with dory lines, all 71
wood, as well-made and as lovely as a piece of Victorian furniture,
with the contours and brasswork and bright finish of an expensive
coffin. Every plank, every separate piece of wood in a wooden
boat, has its own name. What you take to be a single part, say,
the stem, is actually the false stem, the stem piece and the breasthook;
and the frame is not merely a frame but a collection of supports
called futtocks and gussets and knees. We can skip this nomenclature.
Goldeneye is pine on oak, with mahogany lockers and thwarts, and
a transom like a tombstone. It is fifteen feet long.

Mine is the deluxe model. It has a sliding seat for sculling, out- 72
rigger oarlocks, and three rowing stations. It is equipped to sail,
with a dagger-board, a rudder and a sprit rig. I have three pairs
of oars and two spare thwarts. It is a very strong boat, with a flat
and markedly rockered bottom and the most amazing stern, tucked

high to prevent drag and steeply raked, tapering at the bottom, which makes it extremely sea-worthy for its size. The high waves of a following sea don't smash over it and swamp it but rather lift it and help it escape the swell.

"We used to make those for $35 each in Marblehead," an old 73
man told me in Harwichport. "That was years ago."

That certainly was years ago. This skiff cost me $4,371 at Lowell's 74
Boat Shop in Amesbury. I could have had it made for half that, or less, but I wanted the extras. Most good wooden boats are custom-made—no two are strictly alike. They are made for particular coasts, for a certain number of people, for the size and shape of the owner, for specific purposes. "If you were sea-mossing you'd say, 'Put on an extra plank,' " I was told by John Carter, curator of the Maine Maritime Museum. It was Mr. Carter who told me that this sort of boat had no business on Cape Cod. It is a North Shore boat, made for the waters off Cape Ann, where a shoal draft and a flat bottom are helpful in the tidal rivers. The dory style of boat wasn't a suitable fishing boat for the Cape; here, people fish farther out and often in very rough water.

Lowell's Boat Shop originated this skiff's design in the 1860's 75
and made thousands of them. It was a working boat—for hauling pots, handline fishing, and ferrying; and it was for river rowing on the Merrimack and also in protected harbors, like Salem. Rowing was one of the great American recreations, and the rowing age stretched roughly from the end of the Civil War until the invention of the outboard motor, in the 1920's. The outboard motor, which is one of the ugliest and most bad-tempered objects ever made, changed the shape of boats and made them also ugly and furiously turbulent. It is not very difficult for the average twin-engine cabin cruiser to swamp a thirty-foot sailboat. Motorboats are the rower's nightmare because the shoebox-shape creates a pitiless wake. I tend to think that only a motorboat can swamp a skiff.

My skiff had an old pedigree. It was based on the dory that 76
was designed by Simeon Lowell in the early eighteenth century, and it is related to the French-Canadian *bateaux*. There are family resemblances—and certainly connections—between it and the flat-bottomed boats you see in India, and the skiffs depicted in Durer engravings. There are sampans on the Karnafuli River at Chittagong in Bangladesh which are certainly skiff-like. John Gardner, who wrote a history of this style of boat, found an Amesbury skiff in "Big Fish Eat Little Ones" (1556) by Brueghel the Elder.

The shore had begun to look as featureless as the sea had once 77
done. The sea seemed passionate and enigmatic and the charts

showed the sea bottom to be almost comically irregular—here, at Billingsgate Shoal, miles from Rock Harbor, I could stand up; and farther on I could lean out of the skiff and poke crabs scuttling along the sand. I saw the shore as something shrunken and impenetrable. I had never expected to be indifferent to it, but I had grown impatient. It was the result of that awkwardness I had felt at going home. I rowed, and I stared at the receding shore as I had once stared at the brimming ocean. The shoreline was a smudged stripe: tiny boats, frail houses, timid swimmers—small-scale monotony.

A mile or so southwest of Billingsgate Light there was a large 78
rusty ship in the water. This was the *James Longstreet*, a Second World War Liberty Ship that had been scuttled here to be used as a target ship. I was told in Orleans to look for it. A few Cape Codders set themselves up in successful scrap businesses by sneaking out to the ship at night in the early days and stripping it of its copper and brass. During the Vietnam War, ARVN pilots flew up from Virginia and dropped sand bombs on it. It was big and broken, russet-colored this bright day, and listing from the weight of its barnacles.

I shipped my oars off Great Island—the Wellfleet shore—and 79
ate lunch. And then I made a little nest in the bow and lay there and went to sleep. It was hot and dead still and pleasant—like dozing in a warm bath, with a little liquid chuckle at the waterline. I was two miles out. I woke up refreshed, put my gloves on and continued, occasionally glancing at the long empty beaches and wooded dunes. My destination had been the Pamet River, but it was only two-thirty and I could see the dark tower of the Pilgrim Memorial where the top of Cape Cod hooked to the west.

Excited by the prospect of rowing so far in a single day, I struck 80
out for Provincetown. I found Pamet Creek and Corn Hill on my chart and calculated that I had only about seven or eight miles to go. A light breeze came up from the west and helped me. But water distorts distance: after an hour I was still off Pamet Creek and Corn Hill, and Provincetown looked no closer. I may have been about three miles from shore. I began to suspect that I had not made much progress, and that gave me a lonely feeling that I tried to overcome by rowing faster.

Just before four o'clock a chill swept over me. The sun still 81
burned in the sky, but the breeze had freshened to a steady wind. It was not the gust I experienced yesterday that pushed me back and forth; this was a ceaselessly rising wind that lifted the sea in a matter of minutes from nothing to about a foot, and then to two feet, and whitened it, and kept it going higher, until it was

two to four, and so steep and relentless that I could not keep the
boat straight for Provincetown. I thought of Alex saying: *The wind
and the murderous waves! Please pass the spaghetti, mother.*

I could only go in one direction—the way the wind was blowing   82
me. But when I lost concentration or rested on my oars the boat
slipped aside and I was drenched. I had no doubt that I would
make it to shore—the wind was that strong—but I expected to
be swamped, I assumed I would go over and be left clinging to
my half-drowned boat, and I knew that it would take hours to
get to the beach that way.

The discouraging thing was that I was nearer to Provincetown   83
than to the Truro shore. So I was turning away. I rowed for an
hour, pulling hard, and at times I was so tired I just yanked the
oars, keeping the high sea behind me. Every six seconds I was
smacked by an especially high wave—but even the sea's crude
clockwork didn't sink me, and it gave me a special admiration for
the boat's agility. The wind had beaten all the Sunfish and the
windsurfers to the beach at North Truro, but there were children
dodging waves and little dogs trotting along the sand, and people
preparing barbeques. I pulled the boat up the beach and looked
out to sea. Nothing was visible. That unpredictable place where
an hour ago I was afraid I might drown now looked like no more
than a frothy mockery of the sky, with nothing else on it.

"She was a hooker," the young man was saying. "She walked   84
into the place and said, 'I can take all you guys on.' Everyone
knew her—'Snowflake', they call her."

We were traveling on the coast road back to my Jeep. I had   85
had to hitchhike—there was no other way to go—and I was
picked up by two beer-drinking men in a jalopy. Their town was
in the news for being the location of a particularly notorious rape
trial.

"Then, after about eight or nine guys screwed her on the floor 86
of the bar she freaked out and went crying to the cops. 'They
raped me,' she says. But it wasn't rape—it was just a gang-bang.
You sure you don't want a beer?"

It was so sudden after my long empty day that it was as if I   87
were leading two lives—one on water and the other on land—
with nothing to connect them, even though they were only minutes
apart. This sort of travel made for a simultaneity that amounted
to surrealism.

I had come to dislike the disruption of going ashore. The following 88
day I rowed across the crook of the Cape to Provincetown, but I
did not beach the boat. I tied up to someone else's mooring and

had lunch on the water; and then I rowed towards Long Point
Light and around the harbor; and I feathered my oars and pro-
crastinated. Music and voices carried from the shore, the depressing
hilarity of vacationers, shrill all-male "mixers" and party-goers
queening it at the far end of Commercial Street; and glum couples
kicking along the sand; and sunbathers, leather freaks, whale
watchers, punks. At last, at sundown, I rowed in and blew up
my inflatable boat roller until it became a four-foot sausage, and
jammed it under the bow and wobbled *Goldeneye* up to a town
landing. I was watched by thirty-four men having a terrific time
on a hotel veranda.

"Come on up and have a drink, darling. We don't have AIDS!"   89
I was ashore once again.   90

That became the rhythm of this trip: skimming on the water   91
and almost hypnotizing myself with the exertion of rowing; and
then, at the end of the day, being startled by the experience of
touching land again. There was a serenity—something silken—
in the worst wind, and the behavior of water was always fascinating
and wayward. But this pretty skiff aroused a harrassing instinct
among bystanders. They shouted at me, they yodeled, they threw
stones.

Long-distance rowing in a wooden boat attracts attention. It is   92
one of those mildly frantic, labor-intensive activities, like operating
a spoke-shave or pumping a butter churn. It is difficult to indulge
in physical exertion and not seem like an attention-seeker—most
joggers are accustomed to being jakked at. Very few onlookers are
indifferent to someone getting exercise in public, and there is
something in the very sweat and single-mindedness of running or
rowing that inspires admiration in some people and ridicule in
others. An old square-faced hag in a motorboat nearly sank me
as she swerved past the tip of my oar in order to shriek, "Guess
you're not in a hurry!"

That was in Pleasant Bay. I had started at the top end of Meeting   93
House Pond and had rowed south down what they call The River
into Little Peasant Bay. I stayed on the outgoing tide and kept on,
past Chatham Light to the tip of Nauset Beach and into Stage
Harbor. Some of the worst Cape currents sweep between Nauset
and Monomy Island, but I could cope with them much better
than I could the inshore barracking of "Good exercise!" or "Faster,
faster!" or "One-two! One-two!" I got it from people in other
boats; I got it from swimmers and beachcombers; I got it from fat
facetious people at the boat ramps. It was usually well-intentioned,

but it was nearly always unpleasant. It was like having my bum
pinched.

And there were the kids in motorboats. When I was young the   94
roads of Massachusetts were full of hot rodders—pale pimply
adolescents in jalopies. In a general sort of way, a car represented
freedom, and driving—especially driving in a dangerous manner—
was a form of self-expression. *He wrapped himself around a tree*
was always said with a tinge of admiration. In those days, too,
sex was impossible without a car, and I doubt whether there are
many of my generation who didn't have their first sexual experience
in a car. We were the first generation of adolescents to drive cars
in any great numbers—Driver Training, with its leering instructors,
started when we were in high school. Driver Training was the
state's answer to hot rodders, and when the roads improved and
most of the main roads were highways, policing was stricter, drinking
laws were enforced, and the jalopy—useless on a highway—
became a thing of the past. At that point, hot rodding turned into
an aquatic sport.

Every year, off Cape Cod, swimmers are beheaded by kids in   95
motorboats; people wading have their feet chopped off, and other
unsuspecting souls are mutilated in even more grotesque ways.
There are spectacular collisions—boats ramming each other, or
plowing into docks, or flipping over. Often the engine dies and if
the boat is not swamped it is taken by the wind and the current
into the open sea. You need a driver's license for a harmless little
moped, but any twelve-year-old with a free afternoon is at liberty
to whisk himself around in the family motorboat: there is no law
against it, there are no laws at all about motorboating—there
aren't even rules. There is boating "etiquette", but virtually the
only people who observe it are people in sailboats.

I was on the southern side of the Cape. It is densely populated,   96
full of pretty harbors and ugly bungalows—and blighting the once-
charming towns are the fast-food places and the pizza parlors, the
curio shops, the supermarkets. On the bay side of the Cape there
are miles of empty beach and barren cliffs; but here the shore has
been entirely claimed by developers; the shoreline is a cluttered
wilderness of fences. Here and there are grand houses, even mansions, but there is little solitude. In a way, the mansions are responsible for the overdevelopment, for it was the boasting ostentation
of the newly rich that attracted the seedy developments. The pattern
is repeated all along the Cape, but it is at its ugliest at Hyannis
where the dynastic Kennedys—still breeding after all these years—
are the chief attraction. The Cape is a subtle landscape: there are

few places on it to which people naturally gravitate—no mountains, no valleys, only harbors. So the settlement has been based on social insecurity—people have planted their bungalows around the mansions of rich families (much as they have in Newport), proving once again that all classes have their snobberies.

And everyone there seemed to have a motorboat—especially   97
the teenagers. Boys in baseball caps, girls in bikinis, they went in circles, beating the ocean into a fury.

I rowed as fast as I could—dodging the sea traffic and the   98
shouters—from Stage Harbor in Chatham to Wychmere in Harwich. The prevailing southwesterly wind was always opposing my progress. I continued to Bass River, but this time did not go to my parents' house. I slept at my own house now, and my routine was to sneak the boat into the water early and head west. I rowed to Hyannis and was surprised by the strong current and the protruding rocks. The Cruising Guide said, "Out here, too, a brisk afternoon southwester blowing against an ebb tide can kick up a short breaking chop, unpleasant in any boat and possibly dangerous in a small open boat." But I stayed afloat. I crossed Lewis Bay. I rowed to Hyannisport and Wianno; and there, where overdressed people sheltered behind hedges, grimacing at the sea with expensive dentures, I stopped. Rowing around the Cape had become routinely pleasant. I needed another challenge.

I had been rowing through Nantucket Sound. It is a reasonably   99
safe stretch of water near the shore; but a few miles out it is another story entirely. It has been called the most dangerous water on the New England coast. There are shoals, tidal streams, stiff winds, sudden fogs. They are bad, but worse are the currents. The tide ebbs to the west and floods to the east—twelve separate charts in the Eldridge Tide and Pilot Book are needed to demonstrate the complex changes and velocity in the currents, and at their worst they surge at four knots, creating little maelstroms as they swirl past the deep holes in the floor of the Sound. It is like a wide wind-swept river, which flows wildly, changing direction every six hours; and the most unpredictable part lies just between Cape Cod and the northwest coast of Martha's Vineyard where, a bit lower down, the current has proven such a ship-swallower the waters are known as The Graveyard.

I decided to row across it in my skiff.   100

What had most impressed me about offshore rowing was how   101
alienating it could be. It really was like leading a double life: there was no connection between being in the rowboat and being on the Cape, and it was always somewhat disturbing to go ashore.

There was a pleasing secrecy in rowing this boat—or boating in general. It only seems like a conspicuous recreation; in fact, boating is a private passion—you are hidden on the ocean, which may be why boat owners are independent, stubborn, finicky, and famous for doing exactly as they please. There are few sea-going socialists.

I had never tried to explain my trip to anyone. It could not be   102
rationalized; it could only be stated. I said what I was doing but not why. *Must be good exercise,* people said. And then, when I discovered that things were different out here, and unrelated to life on land, I decided to keep it a secret. I began to understand the weekend sailor, the odd opinionated boat owner, the person urgent to set sail; I think I even began to understand those idiot kids in their motorboats. We were all keeping the same secret.

But in *Goldeneye* I believed I felt it more keenly: I was nearer   103
the water's surface, I was victimized more by the weather and the tides, I was moving under my own steam. These were all crucial factors in rowing across Nantucket Sound, where if I did not make careful calculations I would probably fail.

From the Eldridge Tide Table I determined that, for an hour or   104
so, four times a day, there was no current in the Sound. My idea was to find a day when this slack period occurred in the early morning, and then rush across, from Falmouth Harbor to Vineyard Haven. If the wind was light and visibility fairly good, and if I rowed fast, there would be no problem. A certain amount of luck was required, but that imponderable made it for me a more interesting proposition.

I chose the fourth of September, the Sunday before Labor Day: 105
Eldridge showed it to be just right from the point of view of the current, and the day seemed appropriate—it was regarded on the Cape as the last gasp of summer. The forecast was good—sunshine and light breezes. I was not confident about succeeding, but I knew that I would never have a better chance; conditions were as near to ideal as possible. Consequently, I decided to take my son Marcel with me. I liked his company, and he was strong enough to help with the rowing. If we made it he could take some of the credit; if we failed, I would take all the blame.

We left Falmouth Harbor in the early morning. It was a mile   106
to the harbor mouth, where the breeze was just enough to stir the bottom half of the American flag on the flagpole there. Once past the jetty it was too rough for the long oars and the sliding seat. I put in the extra thwarts, handed Marcel a pair of oars, and using the two rowing stations we headed into the mist.

The Vineyard was hidden in the haze of a hot summer's morning.   107
We pulled, talking a little at first, but in a short time fell silent.

It was hard rowing, it took total concentration; and we were both nervous—but each of us was at pains to conceal it from the other. The waves regularly hit us on the starboard side, and the spray on Marcel's back dried to white smudges of salt. Now the Cape shore had a veil of mist across it, and out of it came the ferry *Island Queen* with a bone in its teeth. It was just astern of us and then it changed direction. I knew it was headed for Oak Bluffs, so I could guess where Vineyard Haven was, in the mist.

About an hour after leaving Falmouth Harbor we were rowing   108
in the black water of the Sound, and neither the Cape nor the Vineyard was visible. In this misty isolation I felt a foolish thrill that was both terror and pleasure. I stopped rowing in order to savor it. Marcel said, "We'd better hurry." Another hour and we were off West Chop Lighthouse—the Vineyard had become gradually visible, like a photographic image developing on paper in a tray of water, acquiring outlines, then solidity, and finally color. A cabin cruiser went slapping past, and the bow of *Goldeneye* hit a four-foot curbstone of water, and we were drenched. But we had almost made it; and sheltered by the Vineyard, the water was flat enough for my long oars and my sliding seat. Marcel curled up on the stern locker and went to sleep as I rowed the two and a half miles to the head of Vineyard Haven harbor.

It had not been bad—I counted it as a small victory, and I was   109
so heartened by it that I decided to row back after lunch. It was an ignorant decision. I had forgotten about the currents; I didn't know that the rising afternoon winds on the Sound can be devastating; I did not realize how tired we were from the morning trip. And I had thought that West Chop was just another comic Cape name.

I soon learned. The current had begun to run west, and the   110
wind had picked up and was blowing to the east, fringing the three-foot sea with foam. About half a mile off the lighthouse we were powerless to resist the tipping wind, and the current took us into the chop—West Chop. The car ferry *Islander* went by, leaving vast corrugations on the water. We were no longer trying to get across to Falmouth; we were merely trying to stay afloat.

"Know what I think?" I said.   111

Bam went another wave, soaking us again.   112

"That we should turn back," Marcel said.   113

Immediately we turned the boat, and we rowed as hard as we   114
could; but it was two hours before we were back in the harbor and on a friendly beach. Now the fear was gone, and all that was left of my worry was exhaustion. And the experience of the day was so strange it could only be compared to the abruptness of a

nightmare—it was the experience of absurdity and danger, the surrealism of the unknown near home.

The next day the weather report was dire: a gale was expected, small craft warnings, heavy seas. Everything looked fine in Vineyard Haven, but I was unsure about a safe return to the Cape in the skiff. I decided not to risk Marcel's life and sent him back to the mainland on the ferry. As I felt I still had some time to spare, I rowed over to Bill Styron's dock.[4]

He was sitting on the porch of his house with his son Tommy. The sun high in the clear sky exaggerated with brilliance the whiteness of his house and the green of his lawn. We talked awhile over glasses of lemonade. Tommy praised my boat, and I urged him to row around the harbor.

"He works among homeless people in New York—waifs," Styron said, after his son had gone.

Styron is the friendliest of men. He is watchful but unsuspicious, and not in the least severe. He is so human, such an imposing physical presence, it is hard to think of him as literary, or even bookish. He is happy, apparently unmethodical and patient; he takes his time. I think of him as living a charmed life, having had everything he has ever wanted. Easy-going people who have intelligence are usually merciful: Styron is that way. It gives him tremendous grace.

"I must say," he went on, "I'm fetched by the idea of someone his age who doesn't want to go into banking."

Tommy in *Goldeneye* was dissolved in the intense glitter of the sun on the water. It was a perfect day.

"I've been to France three times since I saw you in Paris," Styron was saying. "I've had my fill of it for a while. One of the times I was on the Film Jury at Cannes. That was a real circus. The Soviet juror wanted to give the prize to Monty Python's *The Meaning of Life*. It seemed to me a silly film. But that's what the English are best at, isn't it? They're good at farce and low comedy. They're through with tragedies, I guess."

I said that to succeed at writing tragedy you had to take yourself pretty seriously, and the English didn't do that anymore. We Americans took ourselves very seriously indeed, which was why tragedy was so common in our novels and plays: it was an aspect of our innocence and our optimism. We were still interested in the texture of our character, still wondering about the future. The English had

4. William Styron (b. 1925), American novelist, author of *Sophie's Choice* and *The Confessions of Nat Turner*.

just about ceased to care. Their cynicism had turned them into bizarre jokesters.

Rose Styron, dressed for tennis, crossed the lawn and walked   123
onto the porch. We talked about bird watching, and India, and Northern Ireland. "Please stay for lunch," Rose said.

I said I had to row to Falmouth: I had set myself that task   124
today.

"We're having *sushi*," Styron said.   125

"You must get sick of people dropping in all the time," I said. 126

"We love it," Rose said. "I encourage people to drop in. Oh,   127
the other day my daughter said, 'Mother! Ricardo Montalban has just climbed up the dock—he's crossing the lawn!' I looked out and saw it was Senator Dodd on the grass!"

"Stay for *sushi*," Styron said.   128

But I said I had to go. We all walked down to the dock, as   129
Tommy brought the skiff back.

"Sure you don't want to go to Falmouth?" I said.   130

"Not today," Styron said. He clapped his hands on his belly.   131
"I'd just be extra weight."

"We'll both row," I said. "It'll take us three hours." I was getting 132
into the boat.

Tommy said, "With him rowing it would take four!"   133

They waved me off and I rowed, watching them walk down   134
their dock to lunch. It was one o'clock. An hour later I was at the buoy that marked the harbor entrance, and making no progress. I was pushed by the wind, pulled by the current. Within minutes I was in West Chop again, but much farther out than I had been the day before. I put in the short oars, but the chop was too fierce to row through—I couldn't row at all, I couldn't even steady the boat. The oars were bending and I thought it was likely that I might break one as I fought the current. Some boats passed me, riding high; they glanced at me and moved on. The wind was strong. Another hour went by: three o'clock—I was nowhere, still pulling. The Styrons had finished their lunch, and Bill was writing—he was an afternoon writer. He was working on a series of linked novellas, about the Marines. I thought of him saying, "I'm fetched by the idea . . ." I had never heard a northerner use that old word in that pleasant way. The waves thudded against my wooden skiff. "Stay for *sushi*." I'd said no. The Styrons had seen me go and probably said: That seems a good idea.

I was blown aside and tugged towards shore, and it was another 135
hour and a half before I got back to Vineyard Haven. Then I admitted to myself that I had almost been swamped—and it wasn't seamanship but only luck that had prevented it. I might have

drowned. I certainly had been frightened: they had been the worst waves I had seen all summer. But there was no link between anything out there among the seamonsters and lunch at the Styrons in this still harbor. It was almost six: I had spent half the day going nowhere. It would be dark soon—this sunset like the last hour of summer light for me.

I fretted in the harbor for a while, and then nerved myself and 136 asked a boat owner for a tow back to the Cape. "I'd be glad to," the man said, and tied *Goldeneye* to his cabin cruiser. I joined him at the wheel and he remarked on the high waves and strong wind. He wasn't bothered. He had a big boat and a deafening diesel engine: we were safe. I had been saved by the sort of boat I had been cursing all summer.

Goldeneye was crusted with salt again. Everything in it—the 137 charts, the tide tables, my food—was wet and had to be thrown away. I found the boat ramp at Falmouth clogged with rubbish— plastic bottles, some rope, a smooth swollen rat. I winched the boat onto the trailer and headed home.

"Here he comes," Alex crowed. There were ten people in the 138 dining room. "Big dramatic entrance! Look everybody, it's Ishmael! 'Aw, it was the schooner Hesperus that sailed the wintry sea!'" And then he took me aside. "What the fuck took you so long?" he said. "You were supposed to carve the turkey."

EVAN S. CONNELL

The Palace of the Moorish Kings

Often we wondered why he chose to live as he did, floating 1 here and there like a leaf on a pond. We had talked about this without ever deciding that we understood, although each of us had an opinion. All we could agree upon was that he never would marry. In some way he was cursed, we thought. One of those uncommon men who follow dim trails around the world hunting a fulfillment they couldn't find at home. Early in a man's life this may not be unnatural, but years go by and finally he ought to find a wife and raise children so that by the time his life ends he will have assured the continuation of life. To us that seemed the

From *St. Augustine's Pigeon* (1982).

proper pattern because it was traditional, and we were holding
to it as best we could. Only J.D. had not.

From the capitals and provinces of Europe he had wandered to
places we had scarcely heard of—Ahmedabad, Penang, the Sulu
archipelago. From the Timor coast he had watched the moon rise
above the Arafura Sea. He had slept like a beggar beside the red
fort in Old Delhi and had seen the Ajanta frescoes. Smoke from
funeral pyres along the Ganges at Varanasi had drifted over him,
and he'd been doused with brilliant powders during the festival
of Bahag Bihn.

Three hundred miles south of Calcutta, he had told us, is a 13th
century Hindu temple known as the Black Pagoda of Konorak
which is decorated with thousands of sculptured sandstone figures—
lions, bulls, elephants, deities, musicians, dancing girls and frankly
explicit lovers. Its vegetable-shaped peak, the *síkhara*, collapsed a
long time ago, but the *mandapa* is still there, rising in three stages.
It represents the chariot of the sun. This fantastic vehicle is drawn
by a team of elaborately carved horses and century after century
it rolls toward the Bay of Bengal. Nothing equals it, he said.
Nothing. The temple complex at Khajuraho is marvelous, but Konorak—and he gestured as he did whenever he could not articulate
his feelings.

What he was after, none of us knew. Seasons turned like the
pages of a familiar album while he traveled the byways of the
world. He seemed to think his life was uncircumscribed, as though
years were not passing, as though he might continue indefinitely
doing whatever he pleased. Perhaps he thought he would outlive
not only us but our children, and theirs beyond them.

We ourselves had no such illusions. We could see the clean   5
sweep of youth sagging. Not that we had considered ourselves
old, or even badly middle-aged, just that there was some evidence
in the mirror. And there was other evidence. Zobrowski's son, for
example, was in Asia fighting a war that had begun secretly,
deceptively, like a disease, had gotten inside of us and was devouring
us before we understood its course. We who had fought in the
Second World War had gone along confidently supposing that if
war broke out again we would be recalled for duty, but now the
government ignored us. It was somewhat embarrassing, as if we
were at fault. Young Dave Zobrowski did the fighting while all
we did was drive to the office. A boy hardly old enough for long
pants had been drafted.

The war offered a deep and bitter paradox. We had succeeded.
Beyond all possible question we had succeeded: we had defeated
the enemy, yet we had failed. Davy, too, attacked the riddle,

unaware at his age that an insoluble problem existed, just as it had existed for us and as it existed for our fathers after the war they called The Great War. Maybe young Dave was more conscious of this than we had been, because we were more knowing than our fathers; still, not much had been changed by our evident sophistication. One conflict ended. Another began. Awareness was irrelevant.

So, against this, we were helpless. We could only hope that our bewilderment and dismay were misplaced. The acid we tasted while listening to newscasts and hearing the casualty figures—"body count" the Pentagon secretaries chose to call it—we could only hope that these falsified and shameful statistics would soon be forgotten. During the Second World War we would have thought it degenerate to gloat over corpses. Now this had become official practice. Apparently it was meant to reassure and persuade us that the government's cause was just.

The slow spectacle of ourselves aging, a dubious war, the decay of our presumably stable nation—these matters were much on our minds when J.D. wrote that he had decided to stop traveling. He was planning to come home. Furthermore, he intended to get married.

We were, of course, astonished. At an age when his friends might become grandfathers he had concluded that perhaps he should stop amusing himself like a college boy in the summertime.

Our wives were not surprised. They considered marriage inevitable and they were relieved that J.D. had at last come to his senses. They were merely irritated that he had waited so long. They regarded his solitary wandering as some kind of pretext for taking advantage of women all over the world. If we were in charge, they seemed to say, he'd have been suitably married years ago. The news affected them quite differently than it affected Zobrowski and Al Bunce and the others who used to play football and marbles with J.D. in those tranquil days when it was safe to walk the streets, and the air in the city was almost as sweet as it was on a farm.

Then we didn't think of our city the way we do now. Sometimes in winter or when the earth was soft after a rain we would find deer tracks across a vacant lot, and occasionally we caught a glimpse of what we thought must be a strange dog vanishing into the shrubbery—only to realize that it was a fox. Now we go about our business in a metropolis. The sizeable animals have disappeared, nobody knows quite where; but we don't see them, not even their prints. Gray squirrels once in a while, some years a good many, but little else. Robins, jays, bluebirds, cardinals, thrashers—we used to sprinkle breadcrumbs on the snowy back porch just to watch a parliament of birds arrive. Today our luncheon guests are the ubiquitous sparrows who can put up with anything.

Smoke fouls the sky and we find ourselves constantly interrupted by the telephone. Billboards, wires, garbage. We have difficulty accepting these everyday truths. How can we admit that the agreeable past, which we thought was permanent and inviolable, has slipped away like a Mississippi steamboat? We like to think that one morning we will see again those uncultivated fields thick with red clover, streams shaded by cottonwood and willow, and butterflies flickering through the sunlight as clearly as illustrations in the heroic books we read when we were eight.

We used to discuss what we would do when we grew up. We made splendid plans. First, of course, we would be rich. Next, we would marry beautiful exciting women with names like Rita, Hedy or Paulette. We would race speedboats and monoplanes, become as famous as Sir Malcolm Campbell and Colonel Roscoe Turner, or perhaps become wild animal trainers like Clyde Beatty, or hunters like Frank Buck, or great athletes like Glenn Cunningham and Don Budge. There were jungles to be explored, mountain peaks that had never been scaled, cities buried in the sand.

One after another these grandiose ideas acquired the patina of dreams. We could perceive as we grew older that we had not been realistic, so it was natural for Bunce to stop talking about an all-gold motorcycle. Art Stevenson would laugh when reminded of his vow to climb Mount Everest. But there were less ambitious adventures which still seemed reasonable. It's not so hard, for instance, to visit the ruins of Babylon; apparently you can go by jet to Baghdad to hire a taxi.

All of us intended to travel—we agreed on that—just as soon   15 as matters could be arranged. As soon as we finished school. As soon as we could afford a long vacation. As soon as the payments were made on the house and the car. As soon as the children were old enough to be left alone. Next year, or the year after, everything would be in order.

Only J.D. had managed to leave. Surabaja. Brunei. Kuala Lumpur. The islands of Micronesia. He had sent us postcards and occasionally a letter describing where he had been or where he thought he might go next, so in a sense we knew what the world was like.

Once he had returned for a visit. Just once. He stayed not quite three days. We felt obscurely insulted, without being able to explain our resentment. He was not obligated to us. We had played together, gone through school together and exchanged the usual juvenile confidences, but no pacts were signed. We couldn't tell him to come home at Christmas, or insist that he stop fooling around and get a job. Nevertheless, we wished he would; bitterness crept into our talk because we knew he meant more to us than we meant to him. We suspected he seldom thought about us. He could guess where we would be at almost any hour; he could have drawn the outline of our lives day after day and year after year. Why should he think about us? Who thinks about a familiar pair of shoes?

Nor could we explain why we so often discussed him. Perhaps we were annoyed by his indifference toward our values. The work we did was as meaningless to him as the fact that our children were growing up. To us nothing was more significant than our jobs and our families, but to J.D. these vital proceedings had less substance than breadcrumbs in the snow. When he wrote, usually to Zobrowski, he never asked what we were doing. He considered us to have a past—a childhood involved with his own—but a transitory nebulous present and a predictable future.

During his visit we questioned him as if we might not ever talk to him again. We asked about Africa—if he had seen Mount Kilimanjaro. He said yes, he had been there, but you seldom see much of Kilimanjaro for the clouds.

Millicent asked if he had shot anything. He said no, he was not a hunter. But he had met an Englishman who did some sort of office work in Bristol and every year came down to hunt, and they had sat up all night drinking gin and talking while the clouds opened and closed and opened again to reveal different aspects of Kilimanjaro in the moonlight, and it sounded as though the lions were only a few yards away. This was as close as he had gotten to hunting the big game of Africa he told her with mock seriousness. Unless you counted the flies, which were savage brutes.

Nairobi, he said, was a delightful town, surprisingly clean, and the weather was decent. We had assumed that it was filthy and humid.

The Masai live not far from Nairobi, he said, and you can visit their compounds if you care to. They eat cheese and drink the blood of cattle and have no use for 20th century marvels, except for ceramic beads with which they make rather attractive bracelets and necklaces. Their huts are plastered with animal dung, yet you can tell from watching a Masai warrior that once they were the lords of this territory just as you see in Spanish faces the memory of an age when Spaniards ruled Europe. But it's embarrassing to visit the Masai, he said, because they start to dance whenever a tourist shows up.

I should guess they look forward to the tips, Zobrowski remarked.

They get paid, J.D. said, but you don't tip a Masai. And nobody needs to tell you.

Barbara asked how he liked Ethiopia. He said he'd been there but hadn't stayed long because of the cholera and the mud. He mentioned this Ethiopian mud twice. We thought it strange that his principal memory of such an exotic country should be something as prosaic as mud.

Nor did we understand why he chose to cross and recross a world of dung-smeared huts, lepers, starvation and cholera. No doubt he had seen rare and wonderful sights, he must have met a good many unusual people, and he had tasted fruits we weren't apt to taste. Granted the entertainment value, what else is there? His pursuit of ephemeral moments through peeling back streets struck us as aimless. He is Don Quixote, Zobrowski observed later, without a lance, an opponent or an ideal.

Perhaps J.D. knew what he wanted, perhaps not. We wondered if the reason for his travels could be negative—ridiculing the purpose and substance of our lives. In any event, we had assumed that he would continue trudging from continent to continent as deluded as Quixote until death overtook him in a squalid cul de sac. We were wrong.

He was planning to settle down. Evidently he had decided to emulate us. When we recognized this we felt a bit more tolerant. After all, what sweeter compliment is there? Then, too, it should be interesting to learn what the Black Forest was like. Dubrovnik. Kabul. Goa. The South Seas. At our leisure we would be able to pick the richest pockets of his experience.

Leroy Hewitt was curious about Moslem Africa and meant to ask if there were minarets and cool gardens, and if it was indeed true that the great square at Marrakesh is filled with storytellers, dancers, acrobats and sorcerers just as it was hundreds of years ago. Once J.D. had traveled from Marrakesh to the walled city of Taroudent, rimmed by dark gold battlements, and he had gone over the Atlas mountains to Tiznit and to Goulimine to the lost Islamic world of women wearing long blue veils and of bearded warriors armed with jeweled daggers.

From there we had no idea where he went. Eventually, from Cairo, had come a torn postcard—a cheap colored photo of a Nile steamer. The penciled message told us that he had spent a week aboard this boat and the afternoon was hot and he was drinking lemonade. How far up the Nile he had traveled we didn't know, or whether he had come down from Uganda.

Next he went to some Greek island, from there to Crete, and later, as closely as we could reconstruct his path, to Cyprus. He wrote that the grapes on Cyprus were enormous and sweet and hard, like small apples, and he had bought an emerald which turned out to be fraudulent, and was recuperating from a blood infection which he'd picked up on the Turkish coast. Months passed before we heard any more. He wrote next from Damascus. The following summer he was in Iraq, thinking he might move along to Shiraz, wondering if he could join a camel train across the plateau. He wanted to visit Karachi. What little we knew of these places we had learned from melodramatic movies and the *National Geographic*.

But what brought J.D. unexpectedly into focus was the Indo-China war. We saw him the way you suddenly see crystals in a flask of treated water. Dave Zobrowski was killed.

When we heard that Davy was dead, that his life had been committed to the future of our nation, we perceived for the first time how J.D. had never quite met the obligations of citizenship. During the Second World War he had been deferred because his father was paralyzed by a stroke and his mother had always been in poor health, so he stayed home and worked in the basement of Wolferman's grocery. Nobody blamed him. Not one of us who went into the service blamed him, nor did any of us want to trade places with him. But that was a long time ago and one tends to forget reasons while remembering facts. The fact that now came to mind most readily concerning J.D. and the war was just that he had been deferred. We resented it. We resented it no more than mildly when we recalled the circumstances; nevertheless we had been drafted and he hadn't. We also knew that we had accomplished very little, if anything, while we were in uniform. We were bored and sometimes terrified, we shot at phantoms and made absurd promises to God. That was about the extent of our contribution toward a better world. It wasn't much, still there was the knowledge that we had walked across the sacrificial block.

After the war we began voting, obeying signs, watering the grass in summer, sowing ashes and rock salt in winter, listening to the six o'clock news and complaining about monthly bills. J.D. had not done this either. As soon as his sister graduated from secretarial school and got a job he packed two suitcases and left. He had a right to his own life; nobody denied that. Nobody expected him to give up everything for his parents' comfort. But he had left with such finality.

Problems sprang up around us like weeds, not just family difficulties but national and international dilemmas that seemed to need our attention, while J.D. loitered on one nutmeg-scented island after another. Did it matter to him, for instance, that America was changing with the malevolent speed of a slap in the face? Did it make any difference to him that American politicians now ride around smiling and waving from bullet-proof limousines? We wondered if he had an opinion about drugs, ghettos, riots, extremists and the rest of it. We suspected that these threatening things which were so immediate to us meant less to him than the flavor of a Toulouse strawberry. And now young Dave was among the thousands who had been killed in an effort to spread democracy— one more fact that meant nothing to J.D. He was out to lunch forever, as Bunce remarked.

While we waited for him to return we argued uncertainly over whether or not it was a man's privilege to live as he pleased. Wasn't J.D. obligated to share with us the responsibility of being human? We knew our responsibilities, which were clear and correct, and hadn't disclaimed them. Maybe our accomplishments were small, but we took pride in them. We might have no effect on these staggering days, no more than we had affected the course of the war, but at least we participated.

We waited through days charged with electric events which simultaneously shocked and inured us, shocking us until we could feel very few shocks, until even such prodigious achievements as flights to the moon appeared commonplace. At the same time our lives continued turning as slowly and methodically as a water wheel: taxes, business appointments, bills, promotions, now and then a domestic squabble. This was why we so often found ourselves talking about J.D.—the only one whose days dropped from a less tedious calendar. He had gone to sleep beside the Taj Mahal while we occupied ourselves with school bonds, mortgages, elections, auto repairs, stock dividends, cocktail parties, graduations and vacations and backyard barbecues.

Because we had recognized adolescent fantasies for what they are, and had put them away in the attic like childhood toys, we felt he should have done the same. What was he expecting? Did he hope somehow to seize the rim of life and force it to a stop? Implausibly, romantically, he had persisted—on his shoulders a rucksack stuffed with dreams.

He drifted along the Mediterranean littoral like a current, pausing a month or so in Yugoslavia or Greece, frequently spending Easter on the Costa del Sol; and it was after one of these sojourns in Spain that he came back to see us. His plans then concerned the Orient—abandoned temples in a Cambodian rain forest, Singapore, Macao, Burma, Sikkim, Bhutan. He talked enthusiastically, youthfully, as though you could wander about these palaces as easily as you locate them on a map.

He had met somebody just back from the foothills of the Himalayas who told him that at Gangtok you see colors more luminous than any you could imagine—more brilliant, more hallucinatory than the wings of tropical butterflies. The idea fascinated him. We asked what sense it made, quite apart from the danger and the trouble, to go such a long distance for a moment of surprise. He wasn't sure. He agreed that perhaps it didn't make sense.

He'd heard about prayer flags posted on bamboo sticks, the waterways of Kashmir, painted houseboats, mango trees on the road to Dharamasala. He thought he'd like to see these things. And there was a building carved from a cliff near Aurangabad. And there was a fortified city called Jaisalmer in the Rajasthan desert.

Then he was gone. Like a moth that flattens itself against a window and mysteriously vanishes, he was gone.

A friend of Art Stevenson's, a petroleum engineer who was sent to the Orient on business, told Art that he happened to see J.D. sitting under a tree on the outskirts of Djakarta. He did not appear to be doing anything, the engineer said; and as he, the engineer, was pressed for time he didn't stop to say hello. But there could be no doubt, he told Art, that it was indeed J.D. dressed in faded khaki and sandals, doing absolutely nothing there in the baking noonday heat of Indonesia. He is mad, Zobrowski commented when we heard the story.

This, of course, was an overstatement. Yet by the usual standards his itinerant and shapeless life was, at the very least, eccentric; and the word 'madness' does become appropriate if one sits long enough beneath a tree.

However, some lunacy afflicts our own temperate and conservative neighborhood. We meet it on the front page every morning—a catalogue of outrageous crimes and totally preposterous incidents as incomprehensible as they are unremitting. What can be done? We look at each other and shrug and wag our heads as though to say well, suppose we just wait and maybe things will get back to normal. At the same time we know this isn't likely. So it could be argued that Zobrowski's judgment was a trifle narrow.

Anyway, regardless of who was mad, we waited impatiently for J.D. When he arrived we would do what we could to help him get settled, not without a trace of malicious satisfaction. But more important, we looked forward to examining him. We needed to know what uncommon kernel had made him different. This, ultimately, was why we had not been able to forget him.

Our wives looked foward to his return for another reason: if he was planning to get married they wanted to have a voice in the matter. They thought it would be foolish to leave the choice of a wife entirely up to him. They were quite in league about this. They had a few suitable divorcees picked out, and there were several younger women who might be acceptable.

We knew J.D. had spent one summer traveling around Ireland

with a red-haired movie actress, and we had heard indirectly about an affair with a Greek girl who sang in nightclubs along the Riviera. How many others there had been was a subject for speculation. It seemed to us that he amused himself with women, as though the relationship between a man and a woman need be no more permanent than sea foam. Leroy Hewitt suggested, perhaps to irritate the ladies, that their intricate plans might be a waste of time because J.D. probably would show up with a Turkish belly dancer. But the ladies, like Queen Victoria, were not amused.

We tried to remember which girls interested him when we were in school. All of us agreed that he had been inconstant. It was one girl, then another. And as we thought back to those days it occurred to us that he had always been looking for somebody unusual—some girl with a reputation for brilliance, individuality or beauty. The most beautiful girl in school was Helen Louise Sawyer. J.D. would take her on long drives through the country or to see travel films, instead of to a dance where she herself could be seen. This may have been the reason they broke up. Or it might have been because she was conceited and therefore rather tiresome— a fact which took J.D. some time to admit.

For a while he dated the daughter of a Congregational minister   50 who, according to the story, had been arrested for prostitution. Almost certainly there was no truth in it, but this rumor isolated her and made her a target. J.D. was the only one with enough nerve to date her publicly, and the only one who never boasted about what they had done.

His other girls, too, were somehow distinctive. Gwyneth, who got a dangerous reputation for burning her dates with a lighted cigarette at intimate moments. A cross-eyed girl named Grace who later became a successful fashion designer in New York. Mitzi McGill, whose father patented a vending machine that supposedly earned him a million dollars. The Lundquist twins, Norma and Laura. To nobody's surprise J.D. went out with both of them.

Rarities excited him. The enchanted glade. The sleeping princess. Avalon. We, too, had hoped for and in daydreams anticipated such things, but time taught us better. He was the only one who never gave up. As a result he was a middle-aged man without a trade, without money or security of any sort, learning in the August of life that he shouldn't have despised what might be called average happiness—3% down the years, so to speak. It wasn't exhilarating, not even adventurous, but it was sufficient.

Now, at last, J.D. was ready to compromise.

I've expected this, Zobrowski said. He's our age. He's beginning to get tired.

He's lonely, said Millicent. He wants a home.   55

Are we echoing each other? Zobrowski asked

On Thanksgiving Day he telephoned from Barcelona. He knew we would all be at Zobrowski's; we gathered there every Thanksgiving, just as it was customary to drop by the Hewitts' for eggnog on Christmas Eve, and to spend New Year's Day at the Stevensons'.

It was midnight in Barcelona when he called. Having gorged ourselves to the point of dyspepsia we were watching football on television, perfectly aware that we were defaulting on a classic autumn afternoon. Somebody in the next block was burning leaves, the air was crisp and through the picture window we could see a maple loaded like a treasure galleon with red gold. But we had prepared for the feast by drinking too much and by accompanying this with too many tidbits before sitting down to the principal business—split-pea soup, a green salad with plenty of Roquefort, dry heavy salty slices of sugar-cured Jackson County ham as well as turkey with sage and chestnut and onion dressing, mushroom and giblet gravy, wild rice, sweet potatoes, creamed asparagus, corn on the cob, hot biscuits with fresh country butter and honey that would hardly flow from the spoon. For dessert there were dense flat triangles of black mince pie topped with rum sauce. Nobody had strength enough to step outside.

As somnolent as glutted snakes we sprawled in Zobrowski's front room smoking cigars, sipping brandy and nibbling peppermints and mixed nuts while the women cleared the table. Embers snapped in the fireplace as group after group of helmeted young Trojans rushed across the miniature gridiron. It was toward such completed days that we had worked. For the moment we'd forgotten J.D.

His call startled us, though we were not surprised that he was 60 in Spain again. He had gone back there repeatedly, as though what he was seeking he'd almost found in Spain. Possibly he knew the coast between Ayamonte and Port-Bou better than we knew the shore of Lake Lotawana. He had been to Gijón and Santander and famous cities like Seville. He'd followed baroque holy processions and wandered through orange groves in Murcia. During his visit he spoke fervently of this compelling, strict, anachronistic land—of the apple wine *manzanilla,* fringed silk shawls, bloody saints, serrated mountains, waterless valleys, burnt stony plateaus, thistles as tall as trees lining the road to Jaén.

We remembered his description of goat bells tinkling among rocky Andalusian hills and we could all but feel the sea breeze rise from Gibraltar. One afternoon he ate lunch in a secluded courtyard beside a fountain—bread, a ball of cheese and some sausage the color of an old boot. He insisted he'd never eaten better.

He imitated the hoarse voices of singing gypsies—a strident

unforgotten East beneath their anguished music—and told us about a cataract of lavender blossoms pouring across the ruined palace of the Moorish kings at Málaga. As young as another Byron he had brought back these foreign things.

There's a town called Ronda which is built along a precipice, and he told us that when he looked over the edge he could feel his face growing damp. He was puzzled because the sky was blue. Then he realized that spray was blowing up the cliff from the river. It was so quiet, he said, that all he heard was wind through the barranca and he was gazing down at two soaring hawks.

He thought Granada might be Spain's most attractive city. He had told us it was the last Arab bastion on the peninsula and it fell because of rivalry between the Abencerrages and Zegris families—information anybody could pick up in a library. But for him this was more than a musty fact. He said that if you look through a certain grate beneath the floor of the cathedral you can actually see the crude iron coffins containing the bodies of Ferdinand and Isabella; or if you go up a certain street near the Alhambra you pass a shop where an old man with one eye sits at a bench day after day meticulously fitting together decorative little boxes of inlaid wood. And he liked to loiter in the Plaza España, particularly while the sun was going down, when swallows scour the twilight for insects.

He had ridden the night train to San Sebastián along with several members of the Guardia Civil in Napoleonic leather hats who put their machine guns on an empty seat and played cards, with the dignity and sobriety peculiar to Spaniards, beneath the faltering light of a single yellow bulb. Outside a station in the mountains where the train paused to build up compression there was a gas lamp burning with vertical assurance, as though a new age had not begun. Wine bottles rolled in unison across the warped floor of the frayed Edwardian coach when the train creaked around a curve late at night, and the soldiers ignored a young Spaniard who began to speak of liberty. Liberty would come to Spain the young man believed—even though Franco's secret police were as common as rats in a sewer.

From everything J.D. said about Spain we thought it must be like one of those small dark green olives, solid as leather, with a lasting taste.

He returned to Barcelona more than to any other city, although it was industrial and enormous. He liked the Gothic *barrio*, the old quarter. He enjoyed eating outside a restaurant called *La Magdalena* which was located in an alley just off the Ramblas. Whenever a taxi drove through the alley the diners had to stand up and push their chairs against the wall so it could squeeze past. Whores patrolled the *barrio,* two by two, carrying glossy handbags. Children who should have been at home asleep went from cafe to cafe peddling cigarettes. Lean old men wearing flat-brimmed black hats and women in polka dot dresses snapped their fingers and clapped and danced furiously with glittering eyes on cobblestones that were worn smooth when the Armada sailed toward England.

Flowers, apple wine, moonlight on distant plazas, supper in some ancient alley, Arabs, implications, relics—that was how he had lived while we went to work.

Now he was calling to us from a boarding house in the cheap section of Barcelona. He was alone, presumably, in the middle of the night while we were as surfeited, prosperous and unrepentant as could be. It was painful to compare his situation with ours.

So, Zobrowski said to him on the telephone, you're there again.   70

J.D. said yes, he was in the same boarding house—*pensión,* he called it—just off Via Layetana. He usually stayed at this place when he was in Barcelona because it had a wonderful view. You could understand Picasso's cubism, he said with a laugh, if you looked across these rooftops.

I'm afraid my schedule won't permit it, Zobrowski remarked.

What a pity, said J.D.

Zobrowski took a fresh grip on the telephone. It would appear, he said, that Spain continues to stimulate your imagination.

Actually no, J.D. answered. That's why I'm coming back.   75

Then he explained. He wasn't altogether clear, but it had to do with progress. With jet planes and credit cards and the proliferation of luxury hotels and high rise apartments you could hardly tell whether you were in Barcelona or Chicago. Only the street signs were different. It wasn't just Barcelona, it was everyplace. Even the villages had begun to change. They were putting television sets in bars where you used to hear flamenco. You could buy *Newsweek* almost as soon as it was published. The girls had started wearing blue jeans. There was a Playboy club in Torremolinos.

Years ago he had mentioned a marble statue of a woman in one of the Barcelona plazas and he had said to us, with an excess of romantic enthusiasm, that she would always be there waiting for him.

Zobrowski asked about this statue. J.D. replied that she was growing a bit sooty because of the diesel trucks and cabs and motorbikes.

He said he had recently been up north. The mountain beyond Torrelavega was completely obscured by factory smoke and there was some sort of yellowish chemical or plastic scum emptying into the river with a few half-dead fish floating through it.

The first time he was in Spain he had walked from Santillana   80

del Mar to Altamira to have a look at the prehistoric cave paintings.
There wasn't a tourist in sight. He had passed farmers with long-
handled scythes, larks were singing, the sky was like turquoise,
and he waded through fields of flowers that reached to his knees.
Now, he said, he was afraid to go back. He might get run over
by a John Deere tractor, or find a motel across the road from the
caves.

That bullfighting poster you had, Zobrowski said, the one with
Manolete's name on it. Reproductions of that poster are for sale
at a number of department stores.

You're flogging me, J.D. said after a pause.

I suppose I am, Zobrowski said.

However, I do get the point, J.D. said. Another decade and the
world's going to be as homogenized as a bottle of milk.

Millicent is here, Zobrowski said. She would like a word with   85
you.

J.D.! Millie exclaimed. How marvelous to hear you're coming
home! You remember Kate Van Dusen, of course. Ray Van Dusen's
sister?—tall and slim with absolutely gorgeous eyes.

J.D. admitted that he did.

She married Barnett Thomas of Thomas Bakery Products, but
things just didn't work out and they've separated.

There was no response. Millie seemed about to offer a trans-
Atlantic summary of the marriage. Separated was a euphemism,
to say the least. Kate and Barnett were in the midst of a reckless
fight over property and the custody of their children.

She's asked about you, Millie went on. She heard you might   90
be coming back.

I'm engaged, J.D. said.

We didn't realize that, said Millie without revealing the horror
that flooded the assembled women. We simply understood that
you were considering marrage. Who is she?

Margaret Hobbs, he said.

Margaret Hobbs? Millie sounded uncertain. Is she British?

You know her, J.D. answered. She's been teaching kindergarten   95
in Philadelphia.

Oh! Oh, my God! Millie said.

We had gone to grammar school with Margaret Hobbs. She was
a pale dumpy child with a screeching voice. Otherwise she was
totally undistinguished. Her parents had moved to Philadelphia
while we were in the sixth grade and none of us had heard of
her since. Her name probably hadn't been mentioned for twenty-
five years.

We met by accident last summer, J.D. said. Margaret and some other schoolteachers were on a tour and we've been corresponding since then. I guess I've always had a special feeling for her and it turns out she's always felt that way about me. She told me she used to wonder what I was doing and if we'd ever meet again. It's as though in a mysterious way we'd been communicating all these years.

How interesting, Millie said.

It really is, isn't it! J.D. said. Anyhow, I'm anxious for all of you to make her acquaintance again. She's amazingly well informed and she remembers everybody.

I think it's just wonderful, Millie said. We're so pleased. I've always wished I could have known Margaret better. Now here's Leroy.

Is that you, young fellow? Leroy asked.

Hello, said J.D. You don't sound much different.

Leroy chuckled and asked if he'd been keeping himself busy. J.D. said he supposed so.

Great talking to you, Leroy said. We'll have a million yarns to swap when you get home. Hang on, here's Aileen.

We look forward to hearing of your adventures, Aileen said. When do you arrive?

J.D. didn't know exactly. He was going to catch a freighter from Lisbon.

Aileen mentioned that last month's *Geographic* had an article on the white peacocks.

After a moment J.D. replied that the connection must be bad because it sounded as if she was talking about peacocks.

Have you been to Estoril? Aileen almost shouted.

Estoril? Yes, he'd been to Estoril. The casino was jammed with tourists. Germans and Americans, mostly. He liked southern Portugal better—the Algarve. Faro, down by the cape.

Faro, Aileen repeated, memorizing the name. Then she asked if he would stop in Philadelphia before coming home.

J.D. was vague. The freighter's first two ports of call were Venezuela and Curaçao. Next it went to Panama. He thought he might hop a bus from Panama, or maybe there would be a boat of some sort heading for British Honduras or Yucatán or maybe New Orleans.

Aileen began to look bewildered. She was sure that he and Margaret would be able to coordinate their plans and it had been a pleasure chatting. She gave the phone to Art Stevenson.

Art said a lot of water had flowed under the bridge and J.D. might not recognize him because he had put on a pound or two. J.D. answered that he himself had been losing some hair. Art proposed that they try to work out a deal.

Neither of them knew what to say next. Art gave the phone to
Barbara.

Barbara asked if he and Margaret would be interested in joining
the country club. If so, she and Al would be delighted to sponsor
them.

Not at first, J.D. said. Maybe later. Let me talk to Dave again.

He was thinking of buying a car in Europe because he had heard
he could save money that way, and he wanted Zobrowski's advice.
He had never owned a car.

Zobrowski suggested that he wait until he got back. Bunce's   120
brother-in-law was a Chevrolet dealer and should be able to arrange
a price not far above wholesale. Zobrowski also pointed out that
servicing foreign cars in the United States can be a problem. Then,
too, you're better off buying from somebody you know.

J.D. inquired about jobs.

We had never learned how he supported himself abroad. As far
as we could determine he lived from day to day. There have always
been individuals who manage to do this, who discover how to
operate the levers that enable them to survive while really doing
nothing. It's a peculiar talent and it exasperates people who live
conventionally.

A job could be found for him, that wasn't the issue. What
disturbed us was that he had no bona fide skills. Zobrowski was
a respected surgeon. Bunce was vice-president of the Community
National Bank and a member of the Board of Education. Art
Stevenson was director and part-owner of an advertising agency.
Leroy Hewitt was a successful contractor, and so on. One or another
of J.D.'s friends could find him a place, but there would be no
way to place him on equal terms. He could speak French, Italian,
Spanish, German and Portuguese well enough to make himself
understood, besides a few necessary phrases of Arabic and Swedish
and Hindi and several others, but language schools want instructors
who are fluent. He knew about inexpensive restaurants and hotels
throughout Europe, and the best way to get from Izmir to Aleppo.
No doubt he knew about changing money in Port Said. Now he
would be forced to work as a stock clerk or a Western Union
messenger, or perhaps as some sort of trainee competing with
another generation. The idea made us uncomfortable.

Margaret would soon find a job. Excluding the fact that Bunce
was on the Board of Education, she was evidently an experienced
teacher with the proper credentials. She could do private tutoring
until there was a full-time position. But J.D. in his coat of many
colors couldn't do anything professionally.

I have a suggestion, Zobrowski said to him on the telephone. 125
This will sound insulting, but you've got to face facts. Your capacities,
such as they are, don't happen to be widely appreciated.

I'm insulted, J.D. said.

Zobrowski cleared his throat before continuing: Fortunately, our
postmaster is related by marriage to one of the cardiologists on
the staff of Park Lane Hospital. I have never met this man—the
postmaster, that is—but, if you like, I will speak to the cardiologist
and explain your situation. I cannot, naturally, guarantee a thing.
However, it's my feeling that this fellow might be able to take you
on at the post office. It wouldn't be much, mind you.

Well, said J.D. from a great distance, please have a talk with
that cardiologist. I'm just about broke.

I'm sorry, Zobrowski said, although not surprised. You enjoyed
yourself for a long time while the rest of us went to an office day
after day, whether we liked it or not. I won't belabor this point,
but I'm sure you recall the fable of the grasshopper and the ant.

J.D. had never cared for lectures, and in the face of this we 130
thought he might hang up. But we all heard him say yes, he
remembered the fable.

If I sound harsh, forgive me, Zobrowski said. It's simply that
you have lived as the rest of us dreamt of living, which is not
easy for us to accept.

J.D. didn't answer.

Now, as we wait to greet him, we feel curiously disappointed.
The end of his journey suggests that we were right, therefore he
must have been wrong, and it follows that we should feel gratified.
The responsibilities we assumed were valid, the problems with
which we occupy ourselves are not insignificant and the values
we nourish will flower one day—if not tomorrow. His return
implies this judgment. So the regret we feel, but try to hide, seems
doubly strange. Perhaps without realizing it we trusted him to
keep our youth.

Thinking About Journeys

When Buttalius was vacationing in the Greek islands about 20 B.C., his friend Horace sent him a verse letter urging him to come to his senses and return home:

> Those who rush overseas change the constellations overhead,
>   but not their minds.
> We wear ourselves out with frantic leisure: In boats
> And four-horsed chariots we chase after the good life.
> But what you seek is here, in this humdrum town,
> If you have a tempered mind.

It may be that Horace was right. Larger philosophical issues aside, Roman travelers of his time thought Imperially, and were not likely to find in the provinces anything that would strike them as particularly remarkable. In this they probably resembled the great Victorian travelers, for whom travel was an opportunity to show a superiority to local circumstances. Mary Kingsley, who may have been the most remarkable of them all, used to burst into a clearing full of African cannibals, calling cheerily "It's only me, not to worry." Once, stranded on a tiny island with a huge hippopotamus, she forced the beast away by beating it on the snout with her umbrella—convinced, apparently, that God had made no creature large enough to withstand the will of an Englishwoman. The Victorian traveler is represented in this section by Anna Leonowens, whose memoir of her sojourn in Siam became the basis of *The King and I*.

The twentieth century has created its own form of Imperial traveler, one who treats the world as an amusement park, looking abroad only for better beaches and quaint natives. Travel agentry and packaged tours may encourage this attitude. As Walker Percy points out, the modern traveler, insulated from the journey itself by a series of climate-controlled vehicles, will too often arrive at a destination he finds slightly less interesting than the travel brochure in which he first saw it.

Sometimes, though, the traveler is open to the impact of the place. Lawrence Durrell says that ten minutes sitting receptively at Delphi can bring you nearer the spirit of ancient Greece than twenty years of academic labor. George Orwell journeying to Marrakech, Joan Didion to Salvador, and Patricia Hampl to Prague all find revelations that their pasts have both prepared them for and, fortunately, left them unbraced against. The impact of a place is not necessarily proportional to its distance from us. E. B. White's day trip to Walden is funny and sad because he carries with him a lifetime affection for Thoreau. Joan Didion, who lives a day's drive from Las Vegas, finds it more alien and provocative than some observers would find the Palace of the Dali Lama. Paul Theroux, by simply rowing in the familiar waters near his home, begins to see his neighbors and even his family with an alien's eye.

If we carried this line of thinking to its logical extreme we would end up saying, with Horace, that the best journeys are made in our hometown. Sometimes they are. But as Evan Connell's story reminds us, people who never stir from home envy the traveler as intensely as the homeless wanderer envies the householder. It is the encounter between our familiar domestic selves and the unfamiliar landscapes that makes the journey worthwhile.

QUESTIONS

1. What experiences have you had with travelers of the Imperial sort? Have you yourself traveled at times with a consciousness of your superiority to your surroundings?

2. What journeys have you taken that have made a strong impression on you? What sort of impression was it? Can you relate your journey to any of the journeys in this section?

3. What journeys have you taken that were worthless enough to illustrate Horace's thesis? Why were they so bad?

4. Is industrial tourism in fact a major obstacle to meaningful travel? What encounters have you had with the tourist industry?

5. As Paul Theroux points out, the same location can seem different when you see it as a voyager rather than as an inhabitant. Return to a familiar place and try to see it with a traveler's eye.

6. Does Horace's characterization of the Roman tourist apply equally well to the North American tourist today? What alternatives to frantic and mindless leisure exist for the contemporary traveler?

ABOUT WRITING

E. B. WHITE

Calculating Machine

A publisher in Chicago has sent us a pocket calculating machine 1
by which we may test our writing to see whether it is intelligible.
The calculator was developed by General Motors, who, not satisfied
with giving the world a Cadillac, now dream of bringing perfect
understanding to men. The machine (it is simply a celluloid card
with a dial) is called the Reading-Ease Calculator and shows four
grades of "reading ease"—Very Easy, Easy, Hard, and Very Hard.
You count your words and syllables, set the dial, and an indicator
lets you know whether anybody is going to understand what you
have written. An instruction book came with it, and after mastering
the simple rules we lost no time in running a test on the instruction
book itself, to see how *that* writer was doing. The poor fellow!
His leading essay, the one on the front cover, tested Very Hard.

Our next step was to study the first phrase on the face of the 2
calculator: "How to test Reading-Ease of written matter." There
is, of course, no such thing as reading ease of written matter. There
is the ease with which matter can be read, but that is a condition
of the reader, not of the matter. Thus the inventors and distributors
of this calculator get off to a poor start, with a Very Hard instruction
book and a slovenly phrase. Already they have one foot caught
in the brier patch of English usage.

Not only did the author of the instruction book score badly on 3
the front cover, but inside the book he used the word "personalize"
in an essay on how to improve one's writing. A man who likes
the word "personalize" is entitled to his choice, but we wonder
whether he should be in the business of giving advice to writers.
"Whenever possible," he wrote, "personalize your writing by directing it to the reader." As for us, we would as lief Simonize[1]
our grandmother as personalize our writing.

In the same envelope with the calculator, we received another 4
training aid for writers—a booklet called "How to Write Better,"
by Rudolf Flesch.[2] This, too, we studied, and it quickly demonstrated

---

First published in "The Talk of the Town" in *The New Yorker*, circa 1949, the year
in which Flesch's book was published.
1. To clean and wax a surface (from *Simoniz*, trade name for an automobile wax).
2. Austrian-American author (b. 1911) whose works all concern reading and writing;
he is perhaps best known as the inventor of the Flesch scale, a test for measuring
the readability of prose.

the broncolike ability of the English language to throw whoever leaps cocksurely into the saddle. The language not only can toss a rider but knows a thousand tricks for tossing him, each more gay than the last. Dr. Flesch stayed in the saddle only a moment or two. Under the heading "Think Before You Write," he wrote, "The main thing to consider is your *purpose* in writing. Why are you sitting down to write?" An Echo answers: Because, sir, it is more comfortable than standing up.

Communication by the written word is a subtler (and more   5
beautiful) thing than Dr. Flesch and General Motors imagine. They contend that the "average reader" is capable of reading only what tests Easy, and that the writer should write at or below this level. This is a presumptuous and degrading idea. There is no average reader, and to reach down toward this mythical character is to deny that each of us is on the way up, is ascending. ("Ascending," by the way, is a word Dr. Flesch advises writers to stay away from. Too unusual.)

It is our belief that no writer can improve his work until he   6
discards the dulcet notion that the reader is feeble-minded, for writing is an act of faith, not a trick of grammar. Ascent is at the heart of the matter. A country whose writers are following a calculating machine downstairs is not ascending—if you will pardon the expression—and a writer who questions the capacity of the person at the other end of the line is not a writer at all, merely a schemer. The movies long ago decided that a wider communication could be achieved by a deliberate descent to a lower level, and they walked proudly down until they reached the cellar. Now they are groping for the light switch, hoping to find the way out.

We have studied Dr. Flesch's instructions diligently, but we   7
return for guidance in these matters to an earlier American, who wrote with more patience, more confidence. "I fear chiefly," he wrote, "lest my expression may not be *extra-vagant* enough, may not wander far enough beyond the narrow limits of my daily experience, so as to be adequate to the truth of which I have been convinced. . . . Why level downward to our dullest perception always, and praise that as common sense? The commonest sense is the sense of men asleep, which they express by snoring."

Run that through your calculator! It may come out Hard, it may   8
come out Easy. But it will come out whole, and it will last forever.

JESSICA MITFORD

Let Us Now Appraise
Famous Writers

In recent years I have become aware of fifteen Famous Faces   1
looking me straight in the eye from the pages of innumerable
magazines, newspapers, fold-out advertisements, sometimes in black-
and-white, sometimes in living color, sometimes posed in a group
around a table, sometimes shown singly, pipe in hand in book-
lined study or strolling through a woodsy countryside: the Guiding
Faculty of the Famous Writers School.[1]

Here is Bennett Cerf, most famous of them all, his kindly, hu-   2
morous face aglow with sincerity, speaking to us in the first person
from a mini-billboard tucked into our Sunday newspaper: "If you
want to write, my colleagues and I would like to test your writing
aptitude. We'll help you find out whether you can be trained to
become a successful writer." And Faith Baldwin, looking up from
her typewriter with an expression of ardent concern for that vast,
unfulfilled sisterhood of nonwriters: "It's a shame more women
don't take up writing. Writing can be an ideal profession for women.
. . . Beyond the thrill of that first sale, writing brings intangible
rewards." J. D. Ratcliff, billed in the ads as "one of America's
highest-paid free-lance authors," thinks it's a shame, too: "I can't
understand why more beginners don't take the short road to publication by writing articles for magazines and newspapers. It's a
wonderful life."

The short road is attained, the ads imply, via the aptitude test   3
which Bennett Cerf and his colleagues would like you to take so
they may "grade it free of charge." If you are one of the fortunate
ones who do well on the test, you may "enroll for professional
training." After that, your future is virtually assured, for the ads
promise that "Fifteen Famous Writers will teach you to write
successfully at home."

These offers are motivated, the ads make clear, by a degree of   4
altruism not often found in those at the top of the ladder. The

First published in *The Atlantic Monthly,* July 1970.
1. They are: Faith Baldwin, John Caples, Bruce Catton, Bennett Cerf, Mignon G.
Eberhart, Paul Engle, Bergen Evans, Clifton Fadiman, Rudolf Flesch, Phyllis McGinley,
J. D. Ratcliff, Rod Serling, Max Shulman, Red Smith, Mark Wiseman. [author's
note]

Fifteen have never forgotten the tough times—the "sheer blood, sweat and rejections slips," as J. D. Ratcliff puts it—through which they suffered as beginning writers; and now they want to extend a helping hand to those still at the bottom rung. "When I look back, I can't help thinking of all the time and agony I would have saved if I could have found a real 'pro' to work with me," says Ratcliff.

How can Bennett Cerf—Chairman of the Board of Random   5
House, columnist, television personality—and his renowned colleagues find time to grade all the thousands of aptitude tests that must come pouring in, and on top of that fulfill their pledge to "teach you to write successfully at home"? What are the standards for admission to the school? How many graduates actually find their way into the "huge market that will pay well for pieces of almost any length" which, says J. D. Ratcliff, exists for the beginning writer? What are the "secrets of success" that the Famous Fifteen say they have "poured into a set of specially created textbooks"? And how much does it cost to be initiated into these secrets?

My mild curiosity about these matters might never have been   6
satisfied had I not learned, coincidentally, about two candidates for the professional training offered by the Famous Writers who passed the aptitude test with flying colors: a seventy-two-year-old foreign-born widow living on Social Security, and a fictitious character named Louella Mae Burns.

The adventures of these two impelled me to talk with Bennett   7
Cerf and other members of the Guiding Faculty, to interview former students, to examine the "set of specially created textbooks" (and the annual stockholders' reports, which proved in some ways more instructive), and eventually to visit the school's headquarters in Westport, Connecticut.

An Oakland lawyer told me about the seventy-two-year-old   8
widow. She had come to him in some distress: a salesman had charmed his way into her home and at the end of his sales pitch had relieved her of $200 (her entire bank account) as down payment on a $900 contract, the balance of which would be paid off in monthly installments. A familiar story, for like all urban communities ours is fertile ground for roving commission salesmen skilled in unloading on the unwary housewife anything from vacuum cleaners to deep freezers to encyclopedias to grave plots, at vastly inflated prices. The unusual aspect of this old lady's tale was the merchandise she had been sold. No sooner had the salesman left than she thought better of it, and when the lessons arrived she returned them unopened.

To her pleas to be released from the contract, the Famous Writers   9
replied: "Please understand that you are involved in a legal and

binding contract," and added that the school's policy requires a doctor's certificate attesting to the ill health of a student before she is permitted to withdraw.

There was a short, sharp struggle. The lawyer wrote an angry 10 letter to the school demanding prompt return of the $200 "fraudulently taken" from the widow, and got an equally stiff refusal in reply. He then asked the old lady to write out in her own words a description of the salesman's visit. She produced a garbled, semiliterate account, which he forwarded to the school with the comment. "This is the lady whom your salesman found to be 'very qualified' to take your writing course. I wonder if Mr. Cerf is aware of the cruel deceptions to which he lends his name?" At the bottom of his letter, the lawyer wrote the magic words "Carbon copies to Bennett Cerf and to Consumer Fraud Division, U.S. Attorney's Office." Presto! The school suddenly caved in and returned the money in full.

Louella Mae Burns, the other successful candidate, is the brainchild 11 of Robert Byrne and his wife. I met her in the pages of Byrne's informative and often hilarious book *Writing Rackets* (Lyle Stuart, 1969, $3.95), which treats of the lures held out to would-be writers by high-priced correspondence schools, phony agents who demand a fee for reading manuscripts, the "vanity" presses that will publish your book for a price.

Mrs. Byrne set out to discover at how low a level of talent one 12 might be accepted as a candidate for "professional training" by the Famous Writers. Assuming the personality of a sixty-three-year-old widow of little education, she tackled the aptitude test.

The crux of the test is the essay, in which the applicant is invited 13 to "tell of an experience you have had at some time in your life." Here Louella Mae outdid herself: "I think I can truthfully say to the best of my knowledge that the following is truly the most arresting experience I have ever undergone. My husband, Fred, and I, had only been married but a short time . . ." Continuing in this vein, she describes, "one beautiful cloudless day in springtime" and "a flock of people who started merging along the sidewalk . . . When out of the blue came a honking and cars and motorcycles and policemen. It was really something! Everybody started shouting and waving and we finally essayed to see the reason of all this. In a sleek black limousine we saw real close Mr. Calvin Coolidge, the President Himself! It was truly an unforgettable experience and one which I shall surely long remember."

This effort drew a two-and-a-half-page typewritten letter from 14 Donald T. Clark, registrar of Famous Writers School, which read in part: "Dear Mrs. Burns, Congratulations! The enclosed Test unquestionably qualifies you for enrollment . . . only a fraction of

our students receive higher grades. . . . In our opinion, you have
a basic writing aptitude which justifies professional training." And
the clincher: "You couldn't consider breaking into writing at a
better time than today. Everything indicates that the demand for
good prose is growing much faster than the supply of trained
talent. Just consider how a single article can cause a magazine's
newsstand sales to soar; how a novel can bring hundreds of thousands in movie rights. . . ."

There is something spooky about this exchange, for I later found   15
out that letters to successful applicants are written not by a "registrar"
but by copywriters in the Madison Avenue office of the school's
advertising department. Here we have Donald T. Clark's ghost
writer in earnest correspondence with ghost Louella Mae Burns.

Perhaps these two applicants are not typical of the student body.   16
What of students who show genuine promise, those capable of
"mastering the basic skills" and achieving a level of professional
competence? Will they, as the school suggests, find their way into
"glamorous careers" and be "launched on a secure future" as
writers?

Robert Byrne gives a gloomy account of the true state of the   17
market for "good prose" and "trained talent." He says that of all
lines of work free-lance writing is one of the most precarious and
worst paid (as who should know better than Bennett Cerf & Co.?).
He cites a survey of the country's top twenty-six magazines. Of
79,812 unsolicited article manuscripts, fewer than a thousand were
accepted. Unsolicited fiction manuscripts fared far worse. Of 182,505
submitted, only 560 were accepted. Furthermore, a study based
on the earnings of established writers, members of the Authors
League with published books to their credit, shows that the average
free-lance earns just over $3,000 a year—an income which, Byrne
points out, "very nearly qualifies him for emergency welfare
assistance."

What have the Famous Fifteen to say for themselves about all   18
this? Precious little, it turns out. Most of those with whom I spoke
were quick to disavow any responsibility for the school's day-to-
day operating methods and were unable to answer the most rudimentary questions: qualifications for admission, teacher-student
ratio, cost of the course. They seemed astonished, even pained,
to think people might be naïve enough to take the advertising at
face value.

"If anyone thinks we've got time to look at the aptitude tests   19
that come in, they're out of their mind!" said Bennett Cerf. And
Phyllis McGinley: "I'm only a figurehead. I thought a person had
to be qualified to take the course, but since I never see any of the

applications or the lessons, I don't know. Of course, somebody with a real gift for writing wouldn't have to be taught to write."

One of the FWS brochures says, "On a short story or novel you have at hand the professional counsel of Faith Baldwin . . . all these eminent authors in effect are looking over your shoulder as you learn." Doesn't that mean in plain English, I asked Miss Baldwin, that she will personally counsel students? "Oh, that's just one of those things about advertising; most advertisements are somewhat misleading," she replied. "Anyone with common sense would know that the fifteen of us are much too busy to read the manuscripts the students sent in." 20

Famous Writer Mark Wiseman, himself an ad man, explained the alluring promises of "financial success and independence," the "secure future as a writer" held out in the school's advertising. "That's just a fault of our civilization," he said. "You have to overpersuade people, make it all look optimistic, not mention obstacles and hurdles. That's true of all advertising." Why does the school send out fleets of salesmen instead of handling all applications by mail? "If we didn't have salesmen, not nearly as many sales would be made. It's impossible, you see, to explain it all by mail, or answer questions people may have about the course." (It seems strange that while the school is able to impart the techniques requisite to become a best-selling author by mail, it cannot explain the details of its course to prospects and answer their questions in the same fashion; but perhaps that is just another fault of our civilization.) 21

Professor Paul Engle, a poet who directed the Writers' Workshop at the University of Iowa, is the only professional educator among the fifteen. But like his colleagues he pleads ignorance of the basics. The school's admissions policy, its teaching methods and selling techniques are a closed book to him. "I'm the least informed of all people," he said. "I only go there once in a great while. There's a distinction between the *Guiding* Faculty, which doesn't do very much, and the *Teaching* Faculty, which actually works with the students—who've spent really quite a lot of money on the course!" Professor Engle has only met once with the Guiding Faculty, to pose for a publicity photograph: "It was no meeting in the sense of gathering for the exchange of useful ideas. But I think the school is not so much interested in the work done by the Guiding Faculty as in the prestige of the names. When Bennett Cerf was on *What's My Line?* his name was a household word!" 22

How did Professor Engle become a member of the Guiding Faculty in the first place? "That fascinated *me!*" he said. "I got a letter from a man named Gordon Carroll, asking me to come to 23

Westport the next time I was in New York. So I did go and see him. He asked me if I would join the Guiding Faculty. I said, 'What do I guide?' We talked awhile, and I said well it seems all right, so I signed on." How could it come about that the Oakland widow and Louella Mae Burns were judged "highly qualified" to enroll? "I'm not trying to weasel out, or evade your questions, but I'm so very far away from all that."

Bennett Cerf received me most cordially in his wonderfully posh   24
office at Random House. Each of us was (I think, in retrospect) bent on putting the other thoroughly at ease. "May I call you Jessica?" he said at one point. "I don't see why not, *Mortuary Management* always does." We had a good laugh over that. He told me that the school was first organized in the late fifties (it opened for business in February, 1961) as an offshoot of the immensely profitable Famous Artists correspondence school, after which it was closely modeled. Prime movers in recruiting Famous Writers for the Guiding Faculty were the late Albert Dorne, an illustrator and president of Famous Artists; Gordon Carroll, sometime editor of *Coronet* and *Reader's Digest*; and Mr. Cerf. "We approached representative writers, the best we could get in each field: fiction, advertising, sportswriting, television. The idea was to give the school some prestige."

Like his colleagues on the Guiding Faculty, Mr. Cerf does no   25
teaching, takes no hand in recruiting instructors or establishing standards for the teaching program, does not pass on advertising copy except that which purports to quote him, does not supervise the school's business practices: "I know *nothing* about the business and selling end and I care *less*. I've nothing to do with how the school is run, I can't put that too strongly to you. But it's been run extremely cleanly. I mean that from my heart, Jessica." What, then, is his guiding role? "I go up there once or twice a year to talk to the staff." The Guilding Faculty, he said, helped to write the original textbooks. His own contribution to these was a section on how to prepare a manuscript for publication: "I spent about a week talking into a tape machine about how a manuscript is turned into a book—practical advice about double-spacing the typescript, how it is turned into galleys, through every stage until publication." How many books by FWS students has Random House published? "Oh, come on, you must be pulling my leg— no person of any sophistication whose book we'd publish would have to take a mail order course to learn how to write."

However, the school does serve an extremely valuable purpose,   26
he said, in teaching history professors, chemistry professors, lawyers, and businessmen to write intelligibly. I was curious to know why

a professor would take a correspondence course in preference to writing classes available in the English Department of his own university—who are all these professors? Mr. Cerf did not know their names, nor at which colleges they were presently teaching.

While Mr. Cerf is by no means uncritical of some aspects of 27 mail order selling, he philosophically accepts them as inevitable in the cold-blooded world of big business—so different, one gathers, from his own cultured world of letters. "I think mail order selling has several built-in deficiencies," he said. "The crux of it is a very hard sales pitch, an appeal to the gullible. Of course, once somebody has signed a contract with Famous Writers he can't get out of it, but that's true with every business in the country." Noticing that I was writing this down, he said in alarm, "For God's sake, don't quote me on that 'gullible' business—you'll have all the mail order houses in the country down on my neck!" "Then would you like to paraphrase it?" I asked, suddenly getting very firm. "Well— you could say in general I don't like the hard sell, yet it's the basis of all American business." "Sorry, I don't call that a paraphrase, I shall have to use both of them," I said in a positively governessy tone of voice. "Anyway, why do you lend your name to this hard-sell proposition?" Bennett Cerf (with his melting grin): "Frankly, if you must know, I'm an awful ham—I love to see my name in the papers!"

On the delicate question of their compensation, the Famous 28 ones are understandably reticent. "That's a private matter," Bennett Cerf said, "but it's quite generous and we were given stock in the company, which has enhanced a great deal." I asked Phyllis McGinley about a report in *Business Week* some years ago that in addition to their substantial stock holdings each member of the Guiding Faculty receives 1.6 percent of the school's annual gross revenue, which then amounted to $4,400 apiece. "Oh? Well, I may have a price on my soul, but it's not *that* low, we get a lot more than that!" she answered gaily.

With one accord the Famous Writers urged me to seek answers 29 to questions about advertising policy, enrollment figures, costs, and the like from the director of the school, Mr. John Lawrence, former president of William Morrow publishing company. Mr. Lawrence invited me to Westport so that I could see the school in operation, and meet Mr. Gordon Carroll, who is now serving as director of International Famous Writers schools.

The Famous Schools are housed in a row of boxlike buildings 30 at the edge of Westport ("It's Westport's leading industry," a former resident told me), which look from the outside like a small modern factory. Inside, everything reflects expansion and progress.

The spacious reception rooms are decorated with the works of Famous Artists, the parent school, and Famous Photographers, organized in 1964.

The success story, and something of the *modus operandi,*[2] can be   31
read at a glance in the annual shareholders' reports and the daily stock market quotations. (The schools have gone public and are now listed on the New York Stock Exchange as FAS International.)

Tuition revenue for the schools zoomed from $7,000,000 in   32
1960 to $48,000,000 in 1969. During this period, the price per share of common stock rose from $5 to $40. (It has fallen sharply, however, in recent months.)

The schools' interest in selling as compared with teaching is   33
reflected more accurately in the corporate balance sheets than in the brochures sent to prospective students. In 1966 (the last time this revealing breakdown was given), when total tuition revenue was $28,000,000, $10,800,000 was spent on "advertising and selling" compared with $4,800,000 on "cost of grading and materials."

The Famous Schools have picked up many another property   34
along the way: they now own the Evelyn Wood Speed Reading Course, Welcome Wagon, International Accountants Society (also a correspondence school), Linguaphone Institute, Computer College Selection Service. Their empire extends to Japan, Australia, Sweden, France, Germany, Switzerland, Austria. An invasion of Great Britain is planned (the report warns) as soon as the English prove themselves worthy of it by stabilizing the currency situation. In the "market testing stage" are plans for a Famous Musicians School, Business Courses for Women, a Writing for Young Readers Course.

Summarizing these accomplishments, the shareholders' report   35
states: "We are in the vanguard of education throughout the world, the acknowledged leader in independent study and an innovator in all types of learning. We will continue to think boldly, to act with wisdom and daring, to be simultaneously visionary and effective." The schools, mindful of "the deepening of the worldwide crisis in education," are casting predatory looks in the direction of "the total educational establishment, both academic and industrial." The shareholders' report observes sententiously, "As grave times produce great men to cope with them, so do they produce great ideas."

From Messrs. Lawrence and Carroll I learned these salient facts   36
about Famous Writers School:

2. method of working.

The cost of the course (never mentioned in the advertising, nor   37
in the letters to successful applicants, revealed only by the salesman
at the point where the prospect is ready to sign the contract):
$785, if the student makes a one-time payment. But only about
10 percent pay in a lump sum. The cost to the 90 percent who
make time payments, including interest, is about $900, or roughly
twenty times the cost of extension and correspondence courses
offered by universities.

Current enrollment is 65,000, of which three-quarters are enrolled   38
in the fiction course, the balance in nonfiction, advertising, business
writing. Almost 2,000 veterans are taking the course at the taxpayers'
expense through the GI Bill. Teaching faculty: 55, for a ratio of
1,181⅘ students per instructor.

There are 800 salesmen deployed throughout the country (for   39
a ratio of 14⅗ salesmen for every instructor) working on a straight
commission basis. I asked about the salesmen's kits: might I have
one? "You'd need a dray horse to carry it!" Mr. Carroll assured
me. He added that they are currently experimenting with a movie
of the school, prepared by Famous Writer Rod Serling, to show
in prospects' homes.

I was surprised to learn that despite the fact the schools are   40
accredited by such public agencies as the Veterans Administration
and the National Home Study Council, they preserve considerable
secrecy about some sectors of their operation. Included in the
"confidential" category, which school personnel told me could not
be divulged, are:

   The amount of commission paid to salesmen.
   Breakdown of the $22,000,000 "sales and advertising" item
      in the shareholders' report as between sales commissions
      and advertising budget.
   Breakdown of the $48,000,000 income from tuition fees as   ·
      between Writers, Artists, Photographers.
   Terms of the schools' contract with Guiding Faculty members.

If Bennett Cerf and his colleagues haven't time to grade the   41
aptitude tests, who has? Their stand-ins are two full-timers and
some forty pieceworkers, mostly housewives, who "help you find
out whether you can be trained to become a successful writer"
in the privacy of their homes. There are no standards for admission
to FWS, one of the full-timers explained. "It's not the same thing
as a grade on a college theme. The test is designed to indicate
your *potential* as a writer, not your present ability." Only about
10 percent of the applicants are advised they lack this "potential,"
and are rejected.

The instructors guide the students from cheerful little cubicles   42
equipped with machines into which they dictate the "two-page
letter of criticism and advice" promised in the advertising. They
are, Gordon Carroll told me, former free-lance writers and people
with editorial background: "We never hire professional teachers,
they're too *dull!* Deadly dull. Ph.D.s are the worst of all!" (Conversely,
a trained teacher accustomed to all that the classroom offers might
find an unrelieved diet of FWS students' manuscripts somewhat
monotonous.) The annual starting salary for instructors is $8,500
for a seven-hour day, something of a comedown from the affulent
and glamorous life dangled before their students in the school's
advertising.

As I watched the instructors at work, I detected a generous   43
inclination to accentuate the positive in the material submitted.
Given an assignment to describe a period in time, a student had
chosen 1933. Her first paragraph, about the election of F.D.R. and
the economic situation in the country, could have been copied
out of any almanac. She had followed this with "There were
breadlines everywhere." I watched the instructor underline the
breadlines in red, and write in the margin: "Good work, Mrs.
Smith! It's a pleasure working with you. You have recaptured the
atmosphere of those days."

Although the key to the school's financial success is its huge   44
dropout rate ("We couldn't make any money if all the students
finished," Famous Writer Phyllis McGinley had told me in her
candid fashion), the precise percentage of dropouts is hard to come
by. "I don't know exactly what it is, or where to get the figures,"
said Mr. Lawrence. "The last time we analyzed it, it related to the
national figure for high-school and college dropouts, let's say about
two-thirds of the enrollments."

However, according to my arithmetic based on figures furnished   45
by the school, the dropout rate must be closer to 90 percent. Each
student is supposed to send in 24 assignments over a three-year
period, an average of 8 a year. With 65,000 enrolled, this would
amount to more than half a million lessons a year, and the 55
instructors would have to race along correcting these at a clip of
one every few minutes. But in fact (the instructors assured me)
they spend an hour or more on each lesson, and grade a total of
only about 50,000 a year. What happens to the other 470,000
lessons? "That's baffling," said Mr. Carroll. "I guess you can take
a horse to water, but you can't make him drink."

These balky nags are, however, legally bound by the contract   46
whether or not they ever crack a textbook or send in an assignment.
What happens to the defaulter who refuses to pay? Are many

taken to court? "None," said Mr. Lawrence. "It's against our policy to sue in court." Why, if the school considers the contract legally binding? "Well—there's a question of morality involved. You'd hardly take a person to court for failing to complete a correspondence course."

Mrs. Virginia Knauer, the President's Assistant for Consumer 47 Affairs, with whom I discussed this later, suspects there is another question involved. "The Famous Writers would never win in court," she said indignantly. "A lawsuit would expose them—somebody should take *them* to court. Their advertising is reprehensible, it's very close to being misleading." Needless to say, the debtors are not informed of the school's moral scruples against lawsuits. On the contrary, a Finnish immigrant, whose husband complained to Mrs. Knauer that although she speaks little English she had been coerced into signing for the course by an importunate salesman, was bombarded with dunning letters and telegrams full of implied threats to sue.

A fanciful idea occurred to me: since the school avers that it 48 does not sue delinquents, I could make a fortune by advertising in the literary monthlies: For $10 I will tell you how to take the Famous Writers' course for nothing." To those who sent in their ten dollars, I would return a postcard saying merely, "Enroll in the course and make no payments." I tried this out on Mr. Carroll, and subsequently on Bennett Cerf. Their reactions were identical. "You'd find yourself behind bars if you did that!" "Why? Whom would I have defrauded?" A question they were unable to answer, although Bennett Cerf, in mock horror, declared that the inventive mail order industry would certainly find *some* legal means to frustrate my iniquitous plan.

Both Mr. Lawrence and Mr. Carroll were unhappy about the 49 case of the seventy-two-year-old widow when I told them about it—it had not previously come to their attention. It was an unfortunate and unusual occurrence, they assured me, one of those slip-ups that may happen from time to time in any large corporation.

On the whole, they said, FWS salesmen are very carefully 50 screened; only one applicant in ten is accepted. They receive a rigorous training in ethical salesmanship; every effort is made to see that they do not "oversell" the course or stray from the truth in their home presentation.

Eventually I had the opportunity to observe the presentation in 51 the home of a neighbor who conjured up a salesman for me by sending in the aptitude test. A few days after she had mailed it in, my neighbor got a printed form letter (undated) saying that a field representative of the school would be in the area next week for a very short while and asking her to specify a convenient time when he might telephone for an appointment. There was something a little fuzzy around the edges here—for she had not yet heard from the school about her test—but she let that pass.

The "field representative" (like the cemetery industry, the Famous   52
Writers avoid the term "salesman") when he arrived had a ready explanation: the school had telephoned to notify him that my neighbor had passed the test, and to tell him that luckily for her there were "a few openings still left in this enrollment period"— it might be months before this opportunity came again!

The fantasy he spun for us, which far outstripped anything in   53
the advertising, would have done credit to the school's fiction course.

Pressed for facts and figures, he told us that two or three of the   54
Famous Fifteen are in Westport at all times working with "a staff of forty or fifty experts in their specialty" evaluating and correcting student manuscripts. . . . Your Guiding Faculty member, could be Bennett Cerf, could be Rod Serling depending on your subject, will review at least one of your manuscripts, and may suggest a publisher for it. . . . There are 300 instructors for 3,000 students ("You mean, one teacher for every ten students?" I asked. "That's correct, it's a ratio unexcelled by any college in the country," said the field representative without batting any eye). . . . Hundreds of university professors are currently enrolled . . . 75 percent of the students publish in their first year, and the majority more than pay for the course through their sales. . . . There are very few dropouts because only serious, qualified applicants (like my neighbor) are permitted to enroll. . . .

During his two-hour discourse, he casually mentioned three   55
books recently published by students he personally enrolled—one is already being made into a movie! "Do tell us the names, so we can order them?" But he couldn't remember, offhand: "I get so darn many announcements of books published by our students."

Oh, clean-cut young man, does your mother know how you   56
earn your living? (And, Famous Fifteen, do yours?)

The course itself is packaged for maximum eye-appeal in four   57
hefty "two-toned, buckram-bound" volumes with matching loose-leaf binders for the lessons. The textbooks contain all sorts of curious and disconnected matter: examples of advertisements that "pull"; right and wrong ways of ending business letters; paragraphs from the *Saturday Evening Post, This Week, Reader's Digest;* quotations from successful writers like William Shakespeare, Faith Baldwin, Mark Twain, Mark Wiseman, Winston Churchill, Red Smith; an elementary grammar lesson ("*Verbs* are action words. A *noun* is

the name of a person, place or thing"); a glossary of commonly misspelled words; a standard list of printer's proof-marking symbols.

There is many a homespun suggestion for the would-be Famous 58 Writer on what to write about, how to start writing: "Writing ideas—ready-made aids for the writer—are available everywhere. In every waking hour you hear and see and feel. . . ." "How do you get started on a piece of writing? One successful author writes down the word 'The' the moment he gets to the typewriter in the morning. He follows 'The' with another word, then another. . . ." (But the text writer, ignoring his own good advice, starts a sentence with "As," and trips himself in an imparsable sentence: "As with so many professional writers, Marjorie Holmes keeps a notebook handy. . . .")

Throughout the course the illusion is fostered that the student 59 is, or soon will be, writing for publication: "Suppose you're sitting in the office of a magazine editor discussing an assignment for next month's issue . . ." The set of books includes a volume entitled "How to Turn Your Writing Into Dollars," which winds up on a triumphal note with a sample publisher's contract and a sample agreement with a Hollywood agent.

In short, there is really nothing useful in these books that could 60 not be found in any number of writing and style manuals, grammar texts, marketing guides, free for the asking in the public library.

Thrown in as part of the $785–$900 course is a "free" subscription 61 to *Famous Writers* magazine, a quarterly in which stories written by students appear under this hyperbolic caption: "Writers Worth Watching: In this section, magazine editors and book publishers can appraise the quality of work being done by FWS students." According to the school's literature, "Each issue of the magazine is received and read by some 2,000 editors, publishers and other key figures in the writing world." However, Messrs. Carroll and Lawrence were unable to enlighten me about these key figures— who they are, how it is known that they read each issue, whether they have ever bought manuscripts from students after appraising the quality of their work.

The student sales department of the magazine is also worth 62 watching. Presumably the school puts its best foot forward here, yet the total of all success stories recorded therein each year is only about thirty-five, heavily weighted in the direction of small denominational magazines, local newspapers, pet-lovers' journals, and the like. Once in a while a student strikes it rich with a sale to *Reader's Digest, Redbook, McCall's,* generally in "discovery" departments of these magazines that specifically solicit first-person anecdotes by their readers as distinct from professional writers:

Most Unforgettable Character, Turning-Point, Suddenly It Happens to You.

The school get enormous mileage out of these few student sales. 63 The same old successful students turn up time and again in the promotional literature. Thus an ad in the January 4, 1970, issue of *The New York Times* Magazine features seven testimonials: "I've just received a big, beautiful check from the *Reader's Digest*. . . ." "I've just received good news and a check from *Ellery Queen's Mystery Magazine*. . . ." "Recently, I've sold three more articles. . . ." How recently? Checking back through old copies of *Famous Writers* magazine, I found the latest of these success stories had appeared in the student sales department of a 1968 issue; the rest had been lifted from issues of 1964 and 1965.

As for the quality of individual instruction, the reactions of 64 several former FWS students with whom I spoke varied. Only one—a "success story" lady featured in FWS advertising who has published four juvenile books—expressed unqualified enthusiasm. Two other successes of yesteryear, featured in the schools' 1970 ad, said they had never finished the course and had published nothing since 1965.

A FWS graduate who had completed the entire course (and has 65 not, to date, sold any of her stories) echoed the views of many: "It's tremendously overblown, there's a lot of busywork, unnecessary padding to make you think you're getting your money's worth. One peculiar thing is you get a different instructor for each assignment, so there's not much of the 'personal attention' promised in the brochures." However, she added, "I have to be fair. It did get me started, and it did make me keep writing."

I showed some corrected lessons that fell into my hands to an 66 English professor. One assignment: "To inject new life and color and dimension into a simple declarative sentence." From the sentence "The cat washed its paws," the student had fashioned this: "With fastidious fussiness, the cat flicked his pink tongue over his paws, laying the fur down neatly and symmetrically." The instructor had crossed out "cat" and substituted "the burly gray tomcat." With fastidious fussiness, the lanky, tweed-suited English professor clutched at his balding, pink pate and emitted a low, agonized groan of bleak, undisguised despair: "Exactly the sort of wordy stuff we try to get students to *avoid*."

The staggering dropout rate cannot, I was soon convinced, be 67 laid entirely at the door of rapacious salesmen who sign up semi-literates and other incompetents. Many of those who told me of their experience with the school are articulate, intelligent people, manifestly capable of disciplined self-study that could help them to improve their prose style. Why should adults of sound mind and resolute purpose first enroll in FWS and then throw away their substantial investment? One letter goes far to explain:

> My husband and I bought the course for two main reasons. The first was that we were in the boondocks of Arkansas and we truly felt that the Famous Writers School under the sponsorship of Bennett Cerf etc. was new in concept and would have more to offer than other courses we had seen advertised. The second was the fact that we had a definite project in mind: a fictionalized account of our experiences in the American labor movement.
>
> I guess the worst part of our experience was the realization that the school could not live up to its advertised promise. It is in the area of the assignments and criticism that the course falls down. Because you get a different instructor each time, there is no continuity. This results in the student failing to get any understanding of story and structure from the very beginning.
>
> My husband completed about eight assignments, but felt so intensely frustrated with the course that he could not go on. He couldn't get any satisfaction from the criticism.
>
> While the school is careful to advise that no one can teach writing talent they constantly encourage their students towards a belief in a market that doesn't exist for beginning writers. For us, it was an expensive and disappointing experience.

68 The phenomenal success of FWS in attracting students (if not in holding them) does point to an undeniable yearning on the part of large numbers of people not only to see their work published, but also for the sort of self-improvement the school purports to offer. As Robert Byrne points out, what can be learned about writing from a writing course can be of great value in many areas of life, "from love letters to suicide notes." For shut-ins, people living in remote rural areas, and others unable to get classroom instruction, correspondence courses may provide the only opportunity for supervised study.

69 Recognizing the need, some fifteen state universities offer correspondence courses that seem to me superior to the Famous Writers course for a fraction of the cost. True, the universities neither package nor push their courses, they provide no handsome buckram-bound two-tone loose-leaf binders, no matching textbooks, no sample Hollywood contract.

70 Unobtrusively tucked away in the *Lifelong Learning* bulletin of the University of California Extension at Berkeley are two such offerings: Magazine Article Writing, 18 assignments, fee $55; and Short Story Theory and Practice, 15 assignments, fee $35 ($5 more for out-of-state enrollees). There are no academic requirements for these courses, anybody can enroll. Those who, in the instructor's

opinion, prove to be unqualified are advised to switch to an elementary course in grammar and composition.

Cecilia Bartholomew, who has taught the short-story course by 71
correspondence for the past twelve years, is herself the author of
two novels and numerous short stories. She cringes at the thought
of drumming up business for the course: "I'd be a terrible double-
dealer to try to *sell* people on it," she said. Like the Famous Writers
instructors, Mrs. Bartholomew sends her students a lengthy criticism
of each assignment, but unlike them she does not cast herself in
the role of editor revising stories for publication: "It's the improvement in their writing technique that's important. The aim
of my course is to develop in each student a professional standard
of writing. I'll tell him when a piece is good enough to submit to
an editor, but I'll never tell him it will sell." Have any of her
students sold their pieces? "Yes, quite a few. Some have published
in volumes of juvenile stories, some in *Hitchcock Mysteries*. But we
don't stress this at all."

In contrast, Louis Boggess, who teaches Magazine Article Writing 72
by correspondence in addition to her classes in "professional writing"
at the College of San Mateo, exudes go-ahead salesmanship: she
believes that most of her students will eventually find a market
for their work. The author of several how-to-do-it books (among
them *Writing Articles That Sell,* which she uses as the text for her
course), she points her students straight toward the mass writing
market. In her streamlined, practical lessons the emphasis is unabashedly on formula writing that will sell. Her very first assignment
is how to write a "hook," meaning an arresting opening sentence.
What does she think of the word "The" for openers? It doesn't
exactly grab her, she admitted.

During the eighteen months she has been teaching the corre- 73
spondence course, several of her 102 students have already sold
pieces to such magazines as *Pageant, Parents, Ladies Circle, Family
Weekly.* She has had but six dropouts, an enviable record by FWS
standards.

My brief excursion into correspondence-school-land taught me 74
little, after all, that the canny consumer does not already know
about the difference between buying and being sold. As Faith
Baldwin said, most advertising is somewhat misleading; as Bennett
Cerf said, the crux of mail order selling is a hard pitch to the
gullible. We know that the commission salesman will, if we let
him into our homes, dazzle and bemuse us with the beauty, du-
rability, unexcelled value of his product, whatever it is. As for the
tens of thousands who sign up with FWS when they could get a
better and cheaper correspondence course through the universities
(or, if they live in a city, Adult Education Extension courses), we

know from reading Vance Packard that people tend to prefer things that come in fancy packages and cost more.

There is probably nothing actually illegal in the FWS operation, although the consumer watchdogs have their eye on it.   75

Robert Hughes, counsel for the Federal Trade Commission's Bureau of Deceptive Practices, told me he has received a number of complaints about the school, mostly relating to the high-pressure and misleading sales pitch. "The real evil is in the solicitation and enrollment procedures," he said. "There's a basic contradiction involved when you have profit-making organizations in the field of education. There's pressure to maximize the number of enrollments to make more profit. Surgery is needed in the enrollment procedure."   76

There is also something askew with the cast of characters in the foregoing drama which would no doubt be quickly spotted by FWS instructors in television scriptwriting ("where the greatest market lies for the beginning writer," as the school tells us).   77

I can visualize the helpful comment on my paper: "Good work, Miss Mitford. The Oakland widow's problem was well thought through. But characterization is weak. You could have made your script more believable had you chosen a group of shifty-eyed hucksters out to make a buck, one step ahead of the sheriff, instead of these fifteen eminently successful and solidly respectable writers, who are well liked and admired by the American viewing public. For pointers on how to make your characters come to life in a way we can all identify with, I suggest you study Rod Serling's script *The Twilight Zone,* in the kit you received from us. Your grade is D −. It has been a pleasure working with you. Good luck!"   78

JESSICA MITFORD

Comment on "Let Us Now Appraise Famous Writers"

This article gave me more pleasure, from start to finish, than any other I have written. Its preparation afforded the opportunity to apply everything I had thus far learned about investigative techniques. My efforts to get it published, a series of dizzying ups   1

First published in *Poison Penmanship* (1979).

and downs, gave me an insight into the policymaking process of magazines that I should never otherwise have acquired. The aftermath of publication filled my normally uneventful life with drama of many months' duration. It was also one of the few clear-cut successes, however temporary, of my muckraking career, so I pray forgiveness if an unseemly note of self-congratulation becomes apparent in what follows.

At first it was a mere twinkle in the eye. By some fortunate   2
confluence of the stars, the "Oakland lawyer" (who was in fact my husband, Bob Treuhaft) happened to tell me about his case of the aged widow vs. Famous Writers School on the very same day that Robert Byrne's excellent and amusing book *Writing Rackets* appeared in my mailbox. Lunching soon after with William Abrahams, then West Coast editor of the *Atlantic,* I regaled him with stories of the misdeeds of these Famous Frauds. Why not do a short piece for the *Atlantic,* suggested Abrahams, about seven hundred words, combining an account of the Oakland widow's unhappy experience with a review of Byrne's book? And so it was settled.

Here my publishing troubles began. The next day Abrahams   3
called up to say that Robert Manning, editor of the *Atlantic,* had second thoughts about the piece: while Manning agreed that the Famous Writers School advertising was "probably unethical," the *Atlantic* had profited by it to the tune of many thousands of dollars, hence it would be equally "unethical" for the magazine to run a piece blasting the school. I was aghast at this reasoning; would it not, then, be "unethical" for a magazine to publish an article linking smoking to lung cancer while accepting ads from the tobacco companies? I asked Abrahams. Well, yes, he saw the point. If Manning changed his mind, he would get back to me.

A week went by; no word from the *Atlantic.* By now adrenalin   4
was flowing (easily the most effective stimulant for the muckraker); those Famous Writers, I was beginning to see, were a power to be reckoned with if they could so easily influence the policy of a major magazine. Without much hope, I queried the articles editor at *McCall's.* She replied that *McCall's* would welcome a full-scale rundown on the school's operation, six to seven thousand words, no holds barred. This put the matter in an entirely new light; with *McCall's* lavish backing for a piece of that length, I could afford to go all out in pursuit of the story.

For weeks thereafter I lived in what turned out to be a fool's   5
paradise, traveling back East at *McCall's* expense to see the school in Westport and to visit its Madison Avenue advertising headquarters in New York, interviewing the Famous ones, poring over the

textbooks and the stockholders' reports. The finished article drew extravagant praise from the articles editor and her associates at *McCall's*, but when the editor-in-chief returned a week later from a trip out of town she rejected it. *Why?* I sternly asked her. "Well— I don't think it's very good," she answered, a comment to which there is, of course, no possible rejoinder. However, she promptly paid not only my large expense account but the full agreed-on fee, rather than the "kill fee" that is usual in such circumstances. Did she have a guilty conscience? Had the Famous Writers got to her? Yes, it turned out, but I only learned this much later.

Furious at this turn of events and in a black mood of revenge,   6 I submitted the piece to *Life*, whose editor immediately responded: he would be delighted to have it, photographers would be deployed to take pictures of the school and its Famous Faculty, it would be a major *Life* story. But the next day the editor happened to drop by the office of *Life*'s advertising manager, who mentioned that the school had contracted for half a million dollars' worth of advertising over the next six months. End of that pipe dream.

By now the article, Xeroxed copies of which were floating around   7 in New York publishing circles, had achieved a sort of underground notoriety; my editor at Knopf got a wire from Willie Morris, then editor of *Harper's*, saying he would love to publish it. I was on the point of turning it over to Morris when William Abrahams at last did "get back" to me: the *Atlantic* wanted it after all. Furthermore, Manning had canceled the magazine's advertising contract with FWS.

How does one go about researching such an article? My first   8 step, before laying siege to the Famous Faculty, was to accumulate and absorb every available scrap of information about the school, my objective being to know more about its operating methods than did the Famous Writers themselves—which, as I soon discovered, was not hard. Via the *Reader's Guide to Periodical Literature*, I found articles in back issues of *Business Week, Advertising Age*, the *Wall Street Journal* from which I was able to trace the school's phenomenal growth over the years. Robert Byrne lent me his vast file containing among other treasures the school's glossy promotional brochures, its annual financial reports, and the original correspondence between "Louella Mae Burns" and the "registrar."

Wishing to make contact with some live ones who had actually   9 enrolled in FWS, I hit on the idea of taking an ad in the *Saturday Review*'s classified columns, giving my name and a box number: "Wanted: Experiences, good, bad or indifferent, with Famous Writers School." I choose *SR* for the purpose because it seemed just the kind of middlebrow magazine whose readership might include likely victims. Nor was I disappointed; my ad drew several letters from dissatisfied students. Faced with the agony of selection from these, I decided eventually to use the one that seemed most representative—from the couple in "the boondocks of Arkansas," as they put it, conveying in authentic tones of frustration their earnest expectations of the school and their dashed hopes. (My Yale students, to whom I imparted this story, loved the idea of using the classified columns as a research tool. I was told that during my stint there as instructor, the advertising revenues of the *Yale Daily* soared as a result of ads placed by members of my journalism seminar.)

Thus prepared, I set about interviewing those of the Guiding   10
Faculty whose home addresses were listed in *Who's Who* and whose phone numbers I got from Information. Early one Sunday morning my husband found me at the telephone. "What are you doing?" "Dialing Famous Writers." He insisted I was wasting my time: "They won't talk to you, why should they?" "No harm in trying," I said. "Wait and see." He stood by fascinated as one after another they talked on interminably—it was hard to shut them up. Needless to say, their off-the-cuff comments—and their unanimously admitted ignorance of the school's operating methods—made for some of the most successful passages in the piece.

I was now ready to advance on the ultimate stronghold, the   11
school itself. Armed with my list of questions, carefully graduated from Kind to Cruel, I called the director, Mr. John Lawrence, and explained that Miss Faith Baldwin, Mr. Paul Engle, and other faculty members had suggested he could help me with an article I was writing about the value of correspondence schools. He immediately offered to pay my fare, first class, to New York where I would be put up at the hotel of my choice, and to set aside a day to show me around the school. (When I reported this to the articles editor at *McCall's*, she insisted that as a matter of principle *McCall's* should pay. I suppressed the fleeting and unworthy thought that I might collect the price of the fare from both.)

My day at the school was long, grueling, and on the whole   12
satisfactory. Late in the afternoon, having elicited through persistent questioning Mr. Lawrence's firm and unqualified assurance that *never* had the school demanded a medical certificate of ill health as the condition of a student's withdrawal, I sprung the final Cruel: Bob's file on the Oakland widow, which contained a letter stating, "It is the policy of the School that when difficulties such as yours arise that we require a statement from the physician in attendance attesting to the inability of the student to continue

on with studies. . . ." After listening to Mr. Lawrence's murky attempt at an explanation—"unfortunate occurrence . . . a slip-up"—I took my leave. There seemed to be nothing more to say.

I saved Bennett Cerf for the last. My interview with him in New   13
York went as described in the piece; the high point his illuminating remark about mail order selling: "a very hard sales pitch, an appeal to the gullible," which he immediately regretted and asked me not to quote.

How, then, could I justify quoting it? I have been asked this   14
many times by my students, and even by other working journalists. Was it not "unethical" of me? The technical answer is that at no time had Mr. Cerf indicated that his conversation was to be off the record, hence I had violated no agreement. Yet there is more to it than that. I can easily visualize interviewing an average citizen who is unused to dealing with the press, and acceding to his plea not to quote some spontaneous and injudicious comment. But— Bennett Cerf, at the top of the heap in publishing, television star performer, founder of FWS, who was cynically extracting tuition payments from the "gullible" for the augmentation of his already vast fortune? This hard heart felt then, and feels now, not the slightest compunction for having recorded his words as spoken.

We had one more brief encounter. I had just submitted the   15
finished article to *McCall's* and was showing a Xerox of it to a friend at Knopf, up on the twenty-first floor of the Random House building. We were giggling away about the Famous Writers when who should pop in but Bennett Cerf. The Random House offices are on the twelfth floor. What was he doing up here, I wondered— had somebody tipped him off to my presence? Genial as ever, Mr. Cerf took a chair and remarked jovially, "So HERE's the archvillain. I hope you're not going to murder us in that piece of yours."

"Murder you? Of course not," I answered. "It's just a factual   16
account of the school, how it operates, and your role in it."

"I don't like the look in your eye as you say that," said Cerf.   17
"Where are you going to publish it?"

Three possible answers flashed through my mind: (1) I haven't   18
decided, (2) I'd rather not say, (3) the truth. I reluctantly settled on the last. "If I tell you, do you promise not to try to stop publication?" I asked. Cerf made pooh-poohing sounds at the very suggestion. "It was commissioned by *McCall's*," I said. He sprang out of his chair: "*McCall's!* They're out of their mind if they think they can get away with this."

By the time the article had finally found safe haven at the   19
Atlantic, I was aglow with unbecoming pride which, as we know,

precedes a fall. It seemed to me I had diligently and fully explored every facet of the school's operation. The luck factor had been with me all the way; short of reading matter in a motel where I was staying, I had picked up the Gideon Bible, which miraculously fell open at the very passage in St. Luke's gospel quoted in the epigraph, "Beware of the scribes . . ." And somebody in Robert Manning's office had spotted and forwarded to me the postcard inserts in paperback books, an incomparable example of FWS's sloppy yet devious methods, which I use for the box, "Object Lesson."

The fall came after the piece was published, and it still gives   20
me nightmares. The *Atlantic* ran a letter from Cecelia Holland, a young novelist, who once when in financial straits had taken a job as instructor for FWS. She wrote: "Students are led to believe that each letter of criticism is personally written by the instructor. It is not. The instructor has a notebook full of prewritten paragraphs, identified by number. He consults this book and types out, not personal comments, but a series of numbers. Later, the paragraphs are written out in full by a computer-typewriter."

How could I have missed this stunning bit of chicanery which   21
so neatly epitomized the ultimate swindle perpetrated by the school? I shall ever regret not having set eyes on those automated typewriters, sincerely clacking out "This opening is effective. It captures the reader's interest. . . ." "I can see you made a try at writing a satisfactory ending, but you only partially succeeded. . . ." I had spent much of my day at the school watching the instructors at work—why had I not asked to see some of the "two-page personal letters of criticism and advice" promised in the advertising? Why had I not quizzed Mr. Lawrence as to whether I had been shown the entire premises—was there anything interesting in the basement that I might have overlooked? To this day it pains me to think of this lapse in my investigation, and I only relate it here as a solemn warning to the would-be muckraker to take nothing for granted, and never to be lulled into the assumption that one's research is beyond reproach.

Robert Manning scheduled the article for publication in July.   22
Once having taken up arms against the school, he proved himself a most effective ally. It was he who thought of the clever and apposite title, "Let Us Now Appraise Famous Writers," and who commissioned the brilliant cover cartoon by Edward Sorel, depicting Famous Writers William Shakespeare, Oscar Wilde, Samuel Johnson, Gertrude Stein, Voltaire, Ernest Hemingway, Mark Twain, Leo

Tolstoy, Edgar Allan Poe, and Dylan Thomas gathered to pose for their publicity photograph.

Before the July issue appeared on the newsstands, Manning 23 telephoned to say the *Atlantic* had already received fifty letters about the school from subscribers, who get their copies early. He was amazed—generally, he said, even a controversial article draws no more than a dozen letters during the whole life of the issue. (I can attest to this, having often published in the *Atlantic* on far more important subjects, such as the Spock trial and prisons, which generated maybe six to ten letters apiece. What sitrs up readers to the point of writing letters to the editor will ever remain a mystery to me.) Before the month was over, more than three hundred letters arrived, all of which were forwarded to me and all of which I answered. Most of them were from FWS students who felt they had been swindled and who wanted to get out of the contract. To these I replied, "Don't make any more payments and tell the school I advised this."

Developments now came thick and fast. Manning reported that 24 the July issue of the *Atlantic* had the largest newsstand sale of any in the magazine's history—which recalled to me a line in the "registrar's" letter to "Louella Mae Burns": "Just consider how a single article can cause a magazine's newsstand sales to soar. . . ." Both the Washington *Post* and the Des Moines *Register* ran the piece in their Sunday editions, the first and only time one of my magazine articles has been picked up and republished in a daily paper. It was subsequently reprinted in England and West Germany, both countries in which the school was trying to establish a foothold. The state universities of Washington and Indiana ordered reprints for distribution to all secondary-school principals and counselors, and all university directors of independent study. Television producers invited me to discuss the school on programs ranging from the *Dick Cavett Show* to ABC's *Chicago*.

As a result of all this, the controversy heated up in the most 25 exhilarating fashion, reaching an audience far beyond the readership of the *Atlantic*. I put up a map of the United States and began shading in the battle areas as they developed: D.C., Virginia, Maryland, covered by the Washington *Post*; Middle Western states, the Des Moines *Register*; and so on.

Soon the consumer watchdogs got into the act, and my map 26 filled up accordingly. Congressman Laurence J. Burton of Utah read the whole thing into the *Congressional Record* as a warning to the public. The Attorney General of Iowa filed suit to enjoin the school from sending its literature into that state, charging use of the mails to defraud. Louis J. Lefkowitz, New York State Attorney General, announced a crackdown on the school's "deceptive practices" and, adding injury to insult, ordered the school to pay $10,000 in costs. The New York City Department of Consumer Affairs demanded "substantial revisions" in FWS advertising and required the school to pay $3,000 to cover the cost of the investigation. The Federal Trade Commission launched a full-scale inquiry, sending investigators around the country to take depositions of the school personnel, the Famous Faculty, and disgruntled students.

Cartoonists merrily joined the fray. A drawing in *The New York* 27 *Times Book Review* portrayed an amply proportioned middle-aged lady writing a letter at her desk: "Dear Bennett Cerf and Faith Baldwin, Yes! I have a strong desire, nay, a *lust* to write. . . ." The *National Lampoon* ran a caricature of a disheveled Cerf, red pencil in hand, captioned: "Unlikely Events of 1971: Bennett Cerf Stays Up All Night Correcting Student Papers from the Famous Writers School." A *New Yorker* cartoon showed a scowling husband at the typewriter, saying to his smirking wife: "Go ahead, scoff. Bennett Cerf and Faith Baldwin say I have writing aptitude, and they know more about it than you do." *Screw* magazine ran a full-page ad for the Famous Fuckers School: "We're Looking for People Who Like to Fuck. Earn money at home. We know that many people who could become professionals—and *should* become professionals—never do."

The letters, the media interest, the cartoons filled me with nos- 28 talgia—they were so reminiscent of the response to *The American Way of Death,* published seven years earlier. So, too, was the school's counteroffensive, which was not long in coming, its opening shot a letter to the *Atlantic* saying that my article contained "at least twenty-three errors according to our latest count." Famous Writer Bergen Evans repeated this libel on the *Dick Cavett Show,* where he was given equal time to rebut my remarks. Pressed for what the errors were, Evans was unable to answer, nor were they ever revealed by the school; although *Time,* in its roundup of the story, said the list was "long but quibbling." The Evans effort drew a sharp comment from Harriet Van Horne, television critic for the New York *Post:* "One might have expected a professor of English to refute Miss Mitford objectively and efficiently. One expected wrong. Dr. Evans leveled a purely personal attack."

There was more of the same to come. In October, an outraged 29 employee of Congressman (later Senator) Lowell P. Weicker, Jr., of Connecticut sent me a Xerox copy of a letter to Weicker from John J. Frey, president of FWS. Drawing attention to the fact that

I had just been listed by Congressman Ichord, chairman of the House Internal Security Committee, as one of sixty-five radical campus speakers, Mr. Frey suggested that Congressman Weicker should read this information into the *Congressional Record* to counteract the damage done by Congressman Burton: "Most interesting is her association with the Communist Party, USA. We would like to visit you to discuss the nature and depth of damage to our reputation and with a suggestion that may set the *Congressional Record* straight. . . . We feel that this matter has assumed urgent proportions and would like to take counteraction quickly." (Weicker, the employee assured me, had no intention of participating in the "counteraction.")

Had Mr. Frey borrowed this idea from the undertaking fraternity,   30
whose response to *The American Way of Death* had been to get an ally in Congress, James B. Utt of Santa Ana, California, to read into the *Record* a lengthy report by the House Committee on Un-American Activities about my subversive background? In any event, it set me thinking about what undertakers and Famous Writers have in common: both promise their customers a measure of immortality, overcharge for it, and then fail to produce.

While all the attention lavished on the fracas in the popular   31
press and on television was most gratifying, even more so were accounts of the school's growing financial difficulties as reported in the daily stock market quotations, *The New York Times* financial pages, the *Wall Street Journal,* and *Advertising Age.* Having in the past been a resolute nonreader of stock market reports, I now swooped down on that page in the San Francisco *Chronicle* first thing each morning to see how the school was doing. For some months after my article appeared, FAS International stock declined consistently and precipitately, plunging from 35 to 5. But then it started creeping up again: $5\frac{1}{4}$, $5\frac{3}{8}$, $5\frac{1}{2}$ . . . I was in despair. "What can I *do?*" I wailed to my husband. When the stock reached 6, fearing perhaps for my mental well-being, he presented me with a certificate for ten shares of stock bought in my name as a special surprise: "That way, you won't mind so much if it does go up a bit," he said sympathetically.

In May, 1971, I was staying in Washington, doing research for   32
my book on prisons. One morning I got a telegram from my husband: "SORRY, YOUR FAMOUS WRITERS STOCK WIPED OUT. SUSPENDED FROM TRADING ON THE STOCK EXCHANGE." Later, he told me that when he had phoned in the telegram to Western Union, the operator had suggested, "Don't you think you should phrase that more

gently? Your wife might do something drastic—jump out of the window—if you tell her she's been wiped out."

Early the following year the school filed for bankruptcy. The final windup was reported in *More* magazine's Hellbox column for January, 1972: "Rosebuds (late blooming) to Jessica Mitford, whose devastating dissection of the Famous Writers School in the *Atlantic* has produced what all exposés aim at but so few achieve: tangible results. . . . The Mitford article and all the nosing around it prompted has staggered the school financially. Earnings dropped from $3,466,000 in 1969 to $1,611,000 in 1970. . . .

"A wilted rosebud should also go to the editor-in-chief of *McCall's*, who originally assigned the piece and then rejected it because, she explains, 'I did not want to offend Bennett Cerf at a time when *McCall's* was trying to improve the caliber of its fiction.' "

There is, however, a sad addendum: the Famous Writers School is creeping back.

I first became aware of this in 1974 when Justin Kaplan, the distinguished biographer and long-time friend of mine, sent me a letter he had received from Famous Writer Robin Moore inviting him to join the Advisory Board of the "new" FWS: "The emoluments are not inconsiderable," Mr. Moore had written. Justin replied, "I am interested in hearing more about the Advisory Board. I do need to find out how the new operation differs from the old, which as a friend of Jessica Mitford's I followed with more than routine interest." But answer came there none; on this matter, Mr. Moore "stood mute," as lawyers say.

More recently friends have clipped and sent me ads for the school—not the huge full-page clarion calls of yore, rather discreet columns headed "Are You One of the 'Quiet Ones' Who Should Be a Writer?"

Seeking to make a cursory check of the school's comeback, I asked a friend in San Francisco to write for the Aptitude Test. It arrived: the same old Aptitude Test. She sent it in, and within days a "Field Representative" appeared at her house: same old pitch, almost indistinguishable from the one I described in the article.

Some of the "Advisory Board" members listed in the current 1978 brochure are holdovers from the same old Guiding Faculty, although as a regular reader of the obit page I have noted that quite a few of these have gone to join the Famous Faculty in the Sky. I mentioned this circumstance to Cecelia Holland, who replied, "Oh—well, but surely you've heard of ghost writers."

DAVID BRADLEY

The Faith

One evening not long ago I found myself sitting on a stage in   1
front of a live audience, being asked questions about life and art.
I was uncomfortable, as I always am in such circumstances. Still,
things were going pretty well on this occasion, until the interviewer
noted that my father had been a minister, and asked what influence
religion, the church and the faith of my father, had had on my
development as a writer. After a moment of confusion, I responded
that since I had, at various times and with more than a modicum
of accuracy, been labeled a heretic, a pagan, a heathen, and a
moral degenerate, all things considered, the faith of my father had
had very little to do with my writing. Which was, depending on
how cynical you want to be, either a total lie or as close as I could
get to the truthful answer—which would have been: "Practically
everything."

The history of my relationship to religion cannot be stated so   2
simply as "My father was a minister." In fact, I am descended
from a long line of ministers. The first was my great-grandfather,
a freedman named Peter Bradley, who, in the early part of the
nineteenth century, was licensed to preach by the African Methodist
Episcopal Zion Church, one of two denominations formed at that
time by blacks who were tired of the discrimination they were
forced to endure in the regular Methodist Church. Peter's son,
Daniel Francis, followed in his father's footsteps and then went a
step further, becoming a presiding elder with administrative and
spiritual responsibility over a number of churches in western Pennsylvania and Ohio. Daniel Francis's son, David, followed his father's
footsteps, and then added a step of his own: he was elected a
general officer of the denomination (a rank just below that of
bishop), with the dual responsibility of traveling the country to
run conferences and workshops in Christian education and of
publishing the church's quasi-academic journal, the *A. M. E. Zion
Quarterly Review*, tasks he performed without interruption for nearly
thirty years. Since David was my father, it would seem reasonable
to expect that I would carry on the family tradition. That I did

First published in *In Praise of What Persists*, ed. Stephen Berg (1983).

not was a fact that was viewed with great relief by all those who knew me—including David senior. Nevertheless, my apostasy had its origins in the church. For because of my father's editorial functions, I grew up in a publishing house.

My earliest memories of excitement, bustle, and tension center 3 on the process of mailing the 1,400- or 1,500-copy press run of the *Quarterly Review.* The books came in sweet-smelling and crisp from the printer, were labeled, bundled, and shipped out again in big gray-green musty mailbags labeled with the names of far-off states, a process that was sheer heaven to a three- or four-year-old and sheer hell for everybody else, especially my mother, who did the bulk of the work and had to give up a chunk of her house to the process.

In fact, the work of publishing the *Review* took up the whole 4 house most of the time; it was just that work usually went on at a less frenetic rate. While my father was away, my mother, who was the subscription and shipping department, spent some time cleaning the lists (a constant task, since ministers, the main subscribers, were regularly being moved around) and typing names and addresses onto labels. When my father returned home, the tempo picked up. He spent a good bit of time in the study, writing to other ministers and prominent lay people to solicit articles and publishable sermons, and editing those that had already arrived. At that same time, he would be writing a bit himself, composing the two or three editorials that graced each issue.

The *Review,* while it was called a quarterly, was not published 5 every three months, but rather four times a year; my father took it to the printer when he was home long enough to get it ready, and when the printer had time to do the work. The date for that was sometimes fixed only a week or so in advance, and once it was set, the tempo became fairly furious; my father spent more and more time in the study, selecting cover art, editing the late-arriving articles, rewriting the press releases from the National Council of Churches that he used for filler. Then, on the date designated, with the copy in one hand, and my hand in the other, my father would go to the printer.

I looked forward to going to the printer with my father, in part 6 because of the printer himself, a venerable gentleman named George, the perfect image of a chapelman all the way down to his ink-stained knuckles and honest-to-God green eyeshade. The chapel over which he presided was no mere print shop, but the printing plant of the local daily, a dark cavern with an ink-impregnated wood floor and air that smelled of hot metal and chemicals, crowded with weirdly shaped machines. On the left a bank of linotypes spewed hot type and spattered molten lead onto the floor. On the right were machines to do the tasks that at home I saw done by hand—address labels, tie bundles, stuff envelopes. At the back, dominating the entire scene, was the great press on which the paper was printed, a big, black, awkward-looking thing that towered to the ceiling and descended into the bowels of the earth. Once George invited my father to bring me down at night to see the press roll, a sight that proved to be so exciting I could not tell if all the shaking was due to the awesome turning of the rollers or to the weakness in my knees; but usually we went to the printer during the day, and the big press was simply a silent presence.

During the visits to the printer, my father and George would 7 be closeted in the little cubbyhole that served as George's office, while I had the run of the chapel. It was on one of those occasions, I believe, that any chance I would follow in the family footsteps was lost. For on this one day, while George and my father muttered of ems and ens, one of the linotype operators paused in his work and invited me to write my name on a scrap of paper, and after I had done so, let me watch as he punched my name out in hot lead. I think that was the moment when my personal die was cast.

Of course, it might have had no lasting effect had not my father, 8 at about the same time, inadvertently introduced me to the corrupting pleasure of having written a book.

A few years before I was born, my father abandoned his studies 9 at New York University, where he had been working for a Ph.D. in history. Five years later, for no reason other than desire, he took up the writing of what would have been his dissertation: "A History of the A. M. E. Zion Church."

I do not remember what it was like being around him while 10 he wrote—I was, after all, less than five. I recall his methodology, which was to write a fairly detailed outline in a flowing longhand on lined paper, which he would store in a big loose-leaf binder until he was ready to turn it into a messy typescript which a typist—often my mother—later rendered as clean copy. (For one reason or another, this is the method I now use to write nonfiction.) I believe there was a certain heightening of tension during the time he was sending the typescript off to publishers; I know that he eventually entered into a cooperative arrangement with a press in Tennessee, a measure which forced him to take out a second mortgage—something I know he felt guilty about, since years later he would explain that we were not in better financial shape because of the book, but something he did not really regret, since he did it again in order to publish the second volume.

At the time the first volume was published, I was only six, but   11
already I was in love with books. I had my own card at the public library, and I had read everything they had that was suitable for a child my age, and a lot that was not. Moreover, I had reread much of it many times, and the characters and stories had become so familiar, that my imagination was no longer a participant in the process; as a result, I had taken to imagining the people behind the characters. I was not old enough for literary biographies (the biographies written for children at that time went heavy on Clara Barton and Thomas Alva Edison and the like, and concentrated on the time when they were children; I loathed the things). And so I made up my own, based on bits of story I had picked up here and there. I was fascinated with Herman Melville and Richard Henry Dana, Jr., both of whom my mother said had actually gone to sea. And I was captivated by Jack London, who, my father told me, had really gone hunting gold in the frozen Yukon.

But even though I was taken with these people, I felt removed   12
from them; they were not real—not as real, anyway, as the characters about whom they wrote. For I could imagine myself standing before the mast or trekking the frozen tundra, but I simply could not imagine myself writing a book.

But then one day a big tractor-trailer pulled up in the driveway   13
and began to unload cartons, and my father, normally not an impulsive or a demonstrative man, took the first carton and ripped it open and pulled out a book that had his name stamped on the front board in gold foil, and suddenly the men behind the books I'd read were as real to me as my father. And suddenly I began to see that slug of type, which I had kept safe, mounted and inked, imprinting my name on a book.

I have always been uncertain about the importance of some of   14
the things that have happened to me, suspecting that if one thing had not pushed me in the direction of writing, then probably something else would have. But I know the importance of that moment. For time and time again, people have said to me that the writing of a book is an impossible task, even to comprehend. For me, though, it was not only comprehensible, it was visible. And so, by the age of six or seven, I had firmly turned away from the family tradition. Ironically enough, at about the same time I began to discover the majesty and beauty of the Christian worship service.

When I was four or five, my father had started taking me with   15
him on some of his travels, usually in the summer, when his work
took him mostly to the Southeast. The first place I went with
him—and it became a regular trip—was Dinwiddie, Virginia, where,
in an aging ramshackle three-story building, the church operated
an "Institute"—a combination Christian education workshop,
summer camp, and revival meeting.

The Institute ran for three weeks—a week each for children,   16
teenagers (what the church called "young people"), and adults.
The format for all was basically the same: a day of classes punctuated
by morning and noon chapel services, an afternoon recreation
period, and three meals of good plain food—corn bread, grits,
chicken, pork, greens—and climaxed by evening worship. The
morning and afternoon worship services were short and pretty
plain affairs. The evening service was pageantry, if for no other
reason than that it was the focal point of everybody's day. My
father's involvement was primarily with the "young people," and
so I spent more time at the Institute when they were there. Evening
worship was important to them because it was the closest they
could get to a dating situation, and they made the most of it. It
was important to the ministers, who shared the various offices of
the service on a rotating basis, competing eagerly for the choice
assignments, preaching and praying. It was important to the people
in the community, who used the evening worship as a kind of
camp meeting. And it was important to me, because the Institute
was not equipped with a radio or a TV, and worse, had a limited
number of books. (I was so desperate for reading matter I practically
memorized the begats.) For me, evening worship was a source of
entertainment.

It began with the arrival of the audience, the scrubbed youths   17
and their chaperones, followed closely by the people from the
community: the older ladies in out-of-fashion but immaculate
dresses and toilet water; the men, seeming all of an age, with big
rough hands poking out of the cuffs of suit coats worn awkwardly;
the younger girls, in light dresses, casting flirtatious glances at the
young men at the Institute (who were usually from cities, and
therefore seen as sophisticated) and sharp challenging looks at the
Institute's young women (who were also usually from the city,
and therefore seen as probably a little wild). They would all troop
into the dilapidated auditorium, filling the rows of ragtag seating—
trestle benches, tip-up seats from abandoned theaters, folding chairs
mended with cardboard, even a couple of mismatched church
pews—and wait impatiently for the ministers.

The ministers entered from the front, moving more or less in   18
time to the sound that came from an off-key, beaten-up piano.
They were not unfamiliar figures—they were around all day, teaching
classes, arguing points of theology and church politics, and playing
Chinese checkers beneath the trees. Now they were solemn and
dignified in black suits and clerical collars, each intent on perfoming
his role, no matter how minor, with as much style as he could
muster.

Performance was the word, for the service was high drama,   19
from the solemnly intoned ritual invocation, to the rolling hymns
sung by a hundred people who needed no hymnals, in passionate
voices that overpowered the doubtful leadership of the gap-toothed
piano, to the hucksterish importunings over the collection plate,
as a minister would announce the total and then proceed to cajole,
shame, or bully the audience into bringing it higher. There was
no applause, of course, but the performance of each minister was
rewarded with responses from the worshipers; the preaching and
praying being applauded with a spontaneous chorus of "Amen,
amen," "Yes, yes, yes," and the ultimate accolade, "Preach on,
preach on." Which they did, sometimes until midnight.

I was overwhelmed by the worship services, not because I was   20
religious, but because there was something innately compelling
about the form and pacing and order of it: the slow, solemn
beginning, the rhythms of song and responsive reading, the spontaneous lyricism, the sense of wholeness and cohesion and abandon
when a preacher really got going, the perfection of catharsis when
the end of the service flowed swiftly and smoothly to the benediction.

I have often wondered why my initial emotional response did   21
not manifest itself as some kind of visible expression of faith—
why, while I sang the hymns and was moved by the pageantry,
I never gave myself over to witnessing or even made a journey
to the altar to accept Jesus as my savior. I believe this was due
to the example of my father, who found emotional religious
expression embarrassing, and took an intellectual approach to religion, to anything. In any case, my love of worship expressed
itself in an analytical way—I began to see it as a critical paradigm.
The order of service, with its variations in pacing and mood, its
combination of poetic and prosaic elements, of mysticism and
hucksterism, became, to me, the model of what a dramatic experience should be. This led to my development of a critical consciousness: I began to judge worship services as good, or not so
good. More important, from the point of view of a writer, I saw
enough services that were not so good to develop an editorial

sense, a feeling for when the prayer was becoming repetitive, when the hymn was wrong, when the minister failed to create a sermon that expanded upon the text. But more important than even that, I learned that the analytical, critical approach, while a useful means, was not, for me, an end.

For I had on a very few occasions seen a preacher, sometimes   22
not a usually good preacher, create, perhaps with the aid of divine inspiration, a service or a sermon that defied criticism. Once I saw it happen to my father.

The year was 1965. By that time, our summer travels had taken   23
my father and me beyond Virginia into North and South Carolina. Nevertheless, the format of the Christian education conventions we attended was the same as that at the Dinwiddie Institute. In one place, that year, they asked my father to preach.

I was not overly excited by the prospect, since I had heard him   24
preach two or three hundred times, and had always found his sermons to be rather dry, tending, as he tended, to focus on the head rather than the heart. The text was Isaiah 30:21: "And thine ears shall hear a word behind thee, saying, This *is* the way, walk ye in it," and as my father read it, I realized that I had heard the sermon he was beginning at least four times, liking it less each time. When he began to speak I expected the textual analysis and explication by definition that marked his style. But this night he abandoned that—something got hold of him. He followed the reading of the text with the telling of a tale.

He had, he said, been in high school, sitting in a classroom,   25
when a man had come to the school asking for volunteers to go up to fight a forest fire that raged on a nearby mountain. My father and some others agreed to go, and were taken up by wagon, then went on foot a mile or two farther, to a point where they had been told to dig a firebreak. The fire, my father said, seemed a long way away; not sensing the danger, they allowed themselves to become absorbed in their task. When finally they looked up from it, they found that the fire had swept about them—they were surrounded by flames.

They reacted as one would have expected. My father told of his   26
panic, how he had at first cried hysterically, then begun to curse, using words he had not realized he knew, had finally collapsed into desperate prayer, all, it seemed, to no avail. But then, when the smoke was at its thickest, when he was about to lose sight of his companions, when the very sound of their wailing was lost in the roaring of the flames, there came a voice calling to them to follow. They followed that voice, escaping with its guidance

through what must have been the last gap in the fire. Afterward they asked who it had been who risked himself to save them, but no one could tell them who it was.

From the tale my father moved to the obvious but eloquent 27 equation, exchanging that unknown savior for a known one, who called the same message, and who led all who followed him clear of the flames. And then, almost abruptly, and far sooner than anyone expected, he stopped. And he brought down the house.

That sermon shocked me. Because I knew my father, knew that 28 he had hidden that story for forty years, had kept it out of previous versions of the same sermon because he was the kind of man who hated to admit weakness, or indecision, or helplessness. I knew that to relive that time on the mountainside had cost him greatly, and to admit his own helplessness had cost him even more. But I realized that the sermon had been something beyond that which was usual for him, and I believed, for no reason I could express, but nevertheless believed, that it was the paying of the price that had made the sermon possible. I believed that in confessing his own weakness he had found access to a hidden source of power inside, or perhaps outside, himself—in any case, a source of power that was magical, mystical.

Until that night I had not understood what it meant to write. 29 I had known that the writer's goal was to reveal truths in words manipulated so effectively as to cause a movement in the minds and hearts of those who read them. But I had not understood that it would cost anything. I had believed that I could do those things while remaining secure and safe in myself—I had even believed that writing fiction was a way to conceal my true feelings and weaknesses. That night, I found out better. That night, I realized that no matter how good I became in the manipulation of symbols, I could never hope to move anyone without allowing myself to be moved, that I could reveal only slight truths unless I was willing to reveal the truths about myself. I did not enjoy the realization. For I was no fonder of self-revelation than my father, and though I knew I would love to do with written words what my father had done in speech, I was not sure I could pay the price. I was not sure I wanted to.

I do not know why my career as a writer did not end there. 30 All I know is that, in fact, it began there. For out of that night came the only idea I have that could truly be called an aesthetic standard: expensiveness. When I ask myself, as all writers do, whether to write something this way or that way, whether to keep this bit, or throw it away, I ask myself, along with all the practical, technical, editorial questions, Does it cost? Is it possible that someone

reading might discover something about me that I would rather not have him know? Is there something truly private here, something I would never admit face to face, unless, perhaps, I was drunk?

I would like to say that if the answer to those questions is No, I go back and dig down inside myself until I do find something it will cost me to say; the truth is I do not always do that. But I believe I should. And I believe that someday, when I am good enough, not as a manipulator of words and phrases but as a human being, I will. And I believe that each time I work, and make the effort, I get closer to that ideal. 31

I doubt that could be called a religious expression. That I act upon it is, however, a matter of faith. For I cannot prove that there is anything to be gained from writing with that sort of aesthetic in mind. I cannot show that my work will be read by more people, that my books will sell more copies, that I will make more money, get better reviews. I cannot truly say that the work is better—I believe it is, but I cannot prove it. Despite the fact that I cannot prove it, however, I believe this aesthetic of cost does make a difference in my writing and the reception of it. This belief is important. For without it I would not be able to pay the price of writing in the way that pleases me. I would write, but, by my standards, I would do it badly. Eventually I would give it up, or become a prostitute, in it only for the money. I need not fear this, because I do believe. The capacity for belief is something I acquired from being so much in contact with others who believed. This, perhaps, is the most important influence on me from the faith of my father. 32

GARRISON KEILLOR

Introduction to
"Happy to Be Here"

All but six of these stories appeared in *The New Yorker* between 1969 and 1982; all were written here in Minnesota, many of them in the front bedroom of an old stucco house in St. Paul, where I used to keep an unfinished novel. It lay on a shelf over the radiator, and next to it stood the typewriter stand, up against a window that looked out on an elm tree and a yellow bungalow with blue 1

First published in 1983.

trim, across the street. I assume it was an elm because it died that spring during an elm epidemic and the city foresters cut it down, but in fact there are only four or five plants I can identify with certainty and the elm is not one of them. I regret this but there it is: plant life has never been more to me than a sort of canvas backdrop. There was a houseplant in that bedroom, too, some type of vine or vine-related plant, and it also died.

I'd say that personal ignorance was the chief inspiration of that   2
poor novel, the shelf novel, and was the main cause of its lingering death that summer, including ignorance of plants. In a novel, characters shouldn't lean against "a tree"—it ought to be a specific tree (e.g., birch, maple, oak), just as when a character feels bad it ought not be a vague sense of uneasiness but something definitely *wrong* and the writer should say what. An impacted molar, too much beer at the ball game, fear of spiders, or *what*.

In my shelf novel, all the guys were marathon leaners. They   3
leaned against vague vegetation and felt vaguely ill and unhappy, probably the result of their getting no exercise and smoking so many cigarettes. They smoked cigarettes like some people use semicolons:

> "I'm not sure, not sure at all—" he lit a cigarette and inhaled deeply—"perhaps I never will."

After the elm died, the yellow bungalow was in clear view, and   4
I began to notice a fat boy who spent most of his sunny afternoons sitting on the front steps, smoking Marlboros and drinking Gatorade. He had long blond hair styled after Farrah Fawcett's, and weighed a lot. He was fourteen, a neighbor lady told me, and his name was Curtis. Every afternoon he hove into view and plopped down and proceeded to while away the hours watching traffic, and by June, when school ended and he added a morning appearance, he was getting on my nerves.

He was a nice boy, the neighbor said, was kind to children,   5
including my own, and had every right to take the load off his feet, and I had no right to expect he should run around with other boys who probably made fun of him, but I did wish he would do something. Read books. When I was fourteen, I was happy to read all day every day and into the night. I hid in closets and in the basement, locked myself in the bathroom, reading right up to the final moment when Mother pried the book from my fingers and shoved me outdoors into the land of living persons.

She was right to do that. If she hadn't, I would be four feet   6
tall, have beady little eyes and a caved-in chest and a butt like a bushel basket.

Boys stopped by the steps and talked to Curtis, he was no social
outcast. From the typewriter I noticed plenty of visits: skinny kids
in shorts, boys Curtis's age. At that age, kids are in constant motion
even when they stop and talk. They shift from foot to foot, pick
tufts of grass and throw them at each other, sit down, jump up,
poke each other, kick stones, but not Curtis, he was set in concrete.
The boys moved on, he stayed put, smoked his cigarettes, kept
his hair in place.

I could have moved the typewriter away from the window and
put Curtis and his problems behind me, and yet the novel in front
of me was no great shakes either and, in many ways, less interesting
than Curtis. Characters came into that novel, looked around for
a few pages, and jumped ship.

Suddenly he decided to go to France. He had never been to France.
France sounded pretty good to him. "Going to France," he said. She
lit a cigarette and inhaled deeply. "You said that before," she said
sardonically. But this time was different. This time he actually went.
She was really surprised, but there was no doubt about it. He was
in France. "I may never see him again," she thought, and she was
right. She never did.

Meanwhile, at the bungalow, Curtis's mom and dad emerged.
She was pretty and probably a terrific cook, by the look of things.
The dad was—how can you put this gracefully?—a real blimp, a
wide load, and the white polyester stretch-pants only emphasized
the cargo. He tapped Curtis on the head, and the three of them
got into their white Imperial. The adjustable steering wheel moved
forward, the dad slid in, and the car moved off like a dirigible
loosed from the mooring mast. I guessed they were going out to
eat and not to a restaurant with a lot of sunlight and plants and
spinach salads. A joint where the plates are like platters, where
the light is dim and a big person can take on a cow, no questions
asked.

I could have quit the novel and put it in a box; it was going
nowhere. In fact I quit the novel almost every day, put it in a
box, wrote more novel and put *that* in the box. I wished my
mother would come, rip the paper out of the carriage, and make
me go play tennis. What kept me beating on the novel was the
sheer size of it and of my investment in it; this was no birdhouse
I had screwed up but a genuine mansion, a three-story plaster-
of-paris mansion deluxe designed by me and propped up by
hundreds of two-by-fours; a fellow doesn't walk away from a
mistake that big, he likes to keep at it; he thinks that maybe the
addition of one more two-by-four will solve the problem.

Meanwhile, I wrote these stories.   11

I've been reluctant to collect them in a book because they were   12
written in revolt against a book and out of admiration for a magazine,
The New Yorker, which I first saw in 1956 in the Anoka Public
Library. Our family subscribed to *Reader's Digest, Popular Mechanics,*
National Geographic, Boy's Life, and *American Home.* My people
weren't much for literature, and they were dead set against conspicuous wealth, so a magazine in which classy paragraphs marched
down the aisle between columns of diamond necklaces and French
cognacs was not a magazine they welcomed into their home. I
was more easily dazzled than they and to me *The New Yorker* was
a fabulous sight, an immense glittering ocean liner off the coast
of Minnesota, and I loved to read it. I bought copies and smuggled
them home, though with a clear conscience, for what I most
admired was not the decor or the tone of the thing but rather the
work of some writers, particularly *The New Yorker's* great infield
of Thurber, Liebling, Perelman, and White.[1]

They were my heroes: four older gentlemen, one blind, one fat,   13
one delicate, and one a chicken rancher, and in my mind they
took the field against the big mazumbos of American Literature,
and I cheered for them. I cheer for them now, all dead except
Mr. White, and still think (as I thought then) that it is more worthy
in the eyes of God and better for us as a people if a writer make
three pages sharp and funny about the lives of geese than to make
three hundred flat and flabby about God or the American people.

I worked on the novel all summer. Curtis came out and sat on   14
the steps morning and afternoon during August, then school started
and he appeared only in the afternoon. Slowly it occurred to me
that I was only sitting around, and though a person would like
to think that ambition counts for something, the truth is that it
doesn't. There is no difference between a fat boy lounging on the
steps and a man at a typewriter turning out horseshit writing. No
difference at all. Not in this world or the next.

I kept the cardboard boxful of novel, thinking I wanted some   15
evidence in case there *is* a difference, then decided to throw it
away. I was in the midst of a divorce and was divesting myself
of all sorts of possessions, and threw the novel into the back of
a truck along with some other trash, and never thought about it
until thinking about this book.

1. James Thurber, A. J. Liebling, S. J. Perelman, and E. B. White were writers
whose tone, style, and view of the world helped shape the character of *The New
Yorker.* On White, see the introduction to *The Dolphin Reader,* as well as the several
essays by him reprinted in these pages.

Curtis has lost a lot of weight, the neighbor lady tells me, and   16
is doing quite well at the University of Minnesota where he is
majoring in plant pathology. He is married. My stucco house
is still there. My boy is twelve years old. This book is dedicated
to him.

RICHARD RODRIGUEZ

Mr. Secrets

I am writing about those very things my mother has asked me   1
not to reveal. Shortly after I published my first autobiographical
essay seven years ago, my mother wrote me a letter pleading with
me never again to write about our family life. "Write about something else in the future. Our family life is private." And besides:
"Why do you need to tell the *gringos*[1] about how 'divided' you
feel from the family?"

I sit at my desk now, surrounded by versions of paragraphs and   2
pages of this book, considering that question.

When I decided to compose this intellectual autobiography, a   3
New York editor told me that I would embark on a lonely journey.
Over the noise of voices and dishes in an East Side restaurant, he
said, "There will be times when you will think the entire world
has forgotten you. Some mornings you will yearn for a phone call
or a letter to assure you that you still are connected to the world."
There *have* been mornings when I've dreaded the isolation this
writing requires. Mornings spent listless in silence and in fear of
confronting the blank sheet of paper. There have been times I've
rushed away from my papers to answer the phone; gladly gotten
up from my chair, hearing the mailman outside. Times I have
been frustrated by the slowness of words, the way even a single
paragraph never seemed done.

I had known a writer's loneliness before, working on my dis-   4
sertation in the British Museum. But that experience did not prepare
me for the task of writing these pages where my own life is the
subject. Many days I feared I had stopped living by committing
myself to remember the past. I feared that my absorption with

Chapter 6 of *Hunger of Memory* (1981). See also Rodriguez's "Going Home Again:
The New American Scholarship Boy," pp. 394–405 of *The Dolphin Reader.*
1. Foreigners (particularly English or American).

events in my past amounted to an immature refusal to live in the present. Adulthood seemed consumed by memory. I would tell myself otherwise. I would tell myself that the act of remembering is an act of the present. (In writing this autobiography, I am actually describing the man I have become—the man in the present.)

Times when the money ran out, I left writing for temporary jobs. Once I had a job for over six months. I resumed something like a conventional social life. But then I have turned away, come back to my San Francisco apartment to closet myself in the silence I both need and fear.

I stay away from late-night parties. (To be clearheaded in the   5 morning.) I disconnect my phone for much of the day. I must avoid complex relationships—a troublesome lover or a troubled friend. The person who knows me best scolds me for escaping from life. (*Am* I evading adulthood?) People I know get promotions at jobs. Friends move away. Friends get married. Friends divorce. One friend tells me she is pregnant. Then she has a baby. Then the baby has the formed face of a child. Can walk. Talk. And still I sit at this desk laying my words like jigsaw pieces, a fellow with ladies in housecoats and old men in slippers who watch TV. Neighbors in my apartment house rush off to work about nine. I hear their steps on the stairs. (They will be back at six o'clock.) Somewhere planes are flying. The door slams behind them.

"Why?" My mother's question hangs in the still air of memory.   6

The loneliness I have felt many mornings, however, has not   7 made me forget that I am engaged in a highly public activity. I sit here in silence writing this small volume of words, and it seems to me the most public thing I ever have done. My mother's letter has served to remind me: I am making my personal life public. Probably I will never try to explain my motives to my mother and father. My mother's question will go unanswered to her face. Like everything else on these pages, my reasons for writing will be revealed instead to public readers I expect never to meet.

1

It is to those whom my mother refers to as the *gringos* that I   8 write. The *gringos*. The expression reminds me that she and my father have not followed their children all the way down the path to full Americanization. They were changed—became more easy in public, less withdrawn and uncertain—by the public success of their children. But something remained unchanged in their lives. With excessive care they continue today to note the difference between private and public life. And their private society remains only their family. No matter how friendly they are in public, no matter how firm their smiles, my parents never forget when they are in public. My mother must use a high-pitched tone of voice when she addresses people who are not relatives. It is a tone of voice I have all my life heard her use away from the house. Coming home from grammar school with new friends, I would hear it, its reminder: My new intimates were strangers to her. Like my sisters and brother, over the years, I've grown used to hearing that voice. Expected to hear it. Though I suspect that voice has played deep in my soul, sounding a lyre, to recall my "betrayal," my movement away from our family's intimate past. It is the voice I hear even now when my mother addresses her son- or daughter-in-law. (They remain public people to her.) She speaks to them, sounding the way she does when talking over the fence to a neighbor.

It was, in fact, the lady next door to my parents—a librarian— who first mentioned seeing my essay seven years ago. My mother was embarrassed because she hadn't any idea what the lady was talking about. But she had heard enough to go to a library with my father to find the article. They read what I wrote. And then she wrote her letter.

It is addressed to me in Spanish, but the body of the letter is in English. Almost mechanically she speaks of her pride at the start. ("Your dad and I are very proud of the brilliant manner you have to express yourself.") Then the matter of most concern comes to the fore. "Your dad and I have only one objection to what you write. You say too much about the family . . . Why do you have to do that? . . . Why do you need to tell the *gringos*? . . . Why do you think we're so separated as a family? Do you really think this, Richard?"

A new paragraph changes the tone. Soft, maternal. Worried for me she adds, "Do not punish yourself for having to give up our culture in order to 'make it' as you say. Think of all the wonderful achievements you have obtained. You should be proud. Learn Spanish better. Practice it with your dad and me. Don't worry so much. Don't get the idea that I am mad at you either.

"Just keep one thing in mind. Writing is one thing, the family is another. I don't want *tus hermanos*[2] hurt by your writings. And what do you think the cousins will say when they read where you talk about how the aunts were maids? Especially I don't want the *gringos* knowing about our private affairs. Why should they? Please give this some thought. Please write about something else in the future. Do me this favor."

Please.

---

2. Rodriguez's brother and sisters.

To the adult I am today, my mother needs to say what she 14
would never have needed to say to her child: the boy who faithfully
kept family secrets. When my fourth-grade teacher made our class
write a paper about a typical evening at home, it never occurred
to me actually to do so. "Describe what you do with your family,"
she told us. And automatically I produced a fictionalized account.
I wrote that I had six brothers and sisters; I described watching
my mother get dressed up in a red-sequined dress before she went
with my father to a party; I even related how the imaginary baby
sitter ("a high school student") taught my brother and sisters and
me to make popcorn and how, later, I fell asleep before my parents
returned. The nun who read what I wrote would have known
that what I had written was completely imagined. But she never
said anything about my contrivance. And I never expected her to
either. I never thought she *really* wanted me to write about my
family life. In any case, I would have been unable to do so.

I was very much the son of parents who regarded the most 15
innocuous piece of information about the family to be secret.
Although I had, by that time, grown easy in public, I felt that my
family life was strictly private, not to be revealed to unfamiliar
ears or eyes. Around the age of ten, I was held by surprise listening
to my best friend tell me one day that he "hated" his father. In
a furious whisper he said that when he attempted to kiss his father
before going to bed, his father had laughed: "Don't you think
you're getting too old for that sort of thing, son?" I was intrigued
not so much by the incident as by the fact that the boy would
relate it to *me*.

In those years I was exposed to the sliding-glass-door informality 16
of middle-class California family life. Ringing the doorbell of a
friend's house, I would hear someone inside yell out, "Come on
in, Richie; door's not locked." And in I would go to discover my
friend's family undisturbed by my presence. The father was in the
kitchen in his underwear. The mother was in her bathrobe. Voices
gathered in familiarity. A parent scolded a child in front of me;
voices quarreled, then laughed; the mother told me something
about her son after he had stepped out of the room and she was
sure he wouldn't overhear; the father would speak to his children
and to me in the same tone of voice. I was one of the family, the
parents of several good friends would assure me. (Richie.)

My mother sometimes invited my grammar school friends to 17
stay for dinner or even to stay overnight. But my parents never
treated such visitors as part of the family, never told them they
were. When a school friend ate at our table, my father spoke less

than ususal. (Stray, distant words.) My mother was careful to use her "visitor's voice." Sometimes, listening to her, I would feel annoyed because she wouldn't be more herself. Sometimes I'd feel embarrassed that I couldn't give to a friend at my house what I freely accepted at his.

I remained, nevertheless, my parents' child. At school, in sixth grade, my teacher suggested that I start keeping a diary. ("You should write down your personal experiences and reflections.") But I shied away from the idea. It was the one suggestion that the scholarship boy couldn't follow. I would not have wanted to write about the minor daily events of my life; I would never have been able to write about what most deeply, daily, concerned me during those years: I was growing away from my parents. Even if I could have been certain that no one would find my diary, even if I could have destroyed each page after I had written it, I would have felt uncomfortable writing about my home life. There seemed to me something intrinsically public about written words.

Writing, at any rate, was a skill I didn't regard highly. It was a grammar school skill I acquired with comparative ease. I do not remember struggling to write the way I struggled to learn how to read. The nuns would praise student papers for being neat—the handwritten letters easy for others to read; they promised that my writing style would improve as I read more and more. But that wasn't the reason I became a reader. Reading was for me the key to "knowledge"; I swallowed facts and dates and names and themes. Writing, by contrast, was an activity I thought of as a kind of report, evidence of learning. I wrote down what I heard teachers say. I wrote down things from my books. I wrote down all I knew when I was examined at the end of the school year. Writing was performed after the fact; it was not the exciting experience of learning itself. In eighth grade I read several hundred books, the titles of which I still can recall. But I cannot remember a single essay I wrote. I only remember that the most frequent kind of essay I wrote was the book report.

In high school there were more "creative" writing assignments. English teachers assigned the composition of short stories and poems. One sophomore story I wrote was a romance set in the Civil War South. I remember that it earned me a good enough grade, but my teacher suggested with quiet tact that next time I try writing about "something you know more about—something closer to home." Home? I wrote a short story about an old man who lived all by himself in a house down the block. That was as close as my writing ever got to my house. Still, I won prizes. When

teachers suggested I contribute articles to the school literary magazine, I did so. And when I was asked to join the school newspaper,
I said yes. I did not feel any great pride in my writings, however.
(My mother was the one who collected my prize-winning essays
in a box she kept in her closet.) Though I remember seeing my
by-line in print for the first time, and dwelling on the printing
press letters with fascination: RICHARD RODRIGUEZ. The letters furnished evidence of a vast public identity writing made possible.

When I was a freshman in college, I began typing all my as-   21
signments. My writing speed decreased. Writing became a struggle.
In high school I had been able to handwrite ten- and twenty-page
papers in little more than an hour—and I never revised what I
wrote. A college essay took me several nights to prepare. Suddenly
everything I wrote seemed in need of revision. I became a self-
conscious writer. A stylist. The change, I suspect, was the result
of seeing my words ordered by the even, impersonal, anonymous
typewriter print. As arranged by a machine, the words that I typed
no longer seemed mine. I was able to see them with a new appreciation for how my reader would see them.

From grammar school to graduate school I could always name   22
my reader. I wrote for my teacher. I could consult him or her
before writing, and after. I suppose that I knew other readers
could make sense of what I wrote—that, therefore, I addressed a
general reader. But I didn't think very much about it. Only toward
the end of my schooling and only because political issues pressed
upon me did I write, and have published in magazines, essays
intended for readers I never expected to meet. Now I am struck
by the opportunity. I write today for a reader who exists in my
mind only phantasmagorically. Someone with a face erased; someone of no particular race or sex or age or weather. A gray presence.
Unknown, unfamiliar. All that I know about him is that he has
had a long education and that his society, like mine, is often public
(*un gringo*).

2

"What is psychiatry?" my mother asks. She is standing in her   23
kitchen at the ironing board. We have been talking about nothing
very important. ("Visiting.") As a result of nothing we have been
saying, her question has come. But I am not surprised by it. My
mother and father ask me such things. Now that they are retired
they seem to think about subjects they never considered before.
My father sits for hours in an armchair, wide-eyed. After my
mother and I have finished discussing obligatory family news, he
will approach me and wonder: When was Christianity introduced

to the Asian continent? How does the brain learn things? Where is the Garden of Eden?

Perhaps because they consider me the family academic, my mother and father expect me to know. They do not, in any case, ask my brother and sisters the questions wild curiosity shapes. (That curiosity beats, unbeaten by age.)   24

Psychiatry? I shrug my shoulders to start with, to tell my mother that it is very hard to explain. I go on to say something about Freud. And analysis. Something about the function of a clinically trained listener. (I study my mother's face as I speak, to see if she follows.) I compare a psychiatrist to a Catholic priest hearing Confession. But the analogy is inexact. My mother can easily speak to a priest in a darkened confessional; can easily make an act of self-revelation using the impersonal formula of ritual contrition: "Bless me, father, for I have sinned. . . ." It would be altogether different for her to address a psychiatrist in unstructured conversation, revealing those events and feelings that burn close to the heart.   25

"You mean that people tell a psychiatrist about their personal lives?"   26

Even as I begin to respond, I realize that she cannot imagine ever doing such a thing. She shakes her head sadly, bending over the ironing board to inspect a shirt with the tip of the iron she holds in her hand. Then she changes the subject. She is talking to me about one of her sisters, my aunt, who is seriously ill. Whatever it is that prompted her question about psychiatry has passed.   27

I stand there. I continue thinking about what she has asked me—and what she cannot comprehend. My parents seem to me possessed of great dignity. An aristocratic reserve. Like the very rich who live behind tall walls, my mother and father are always mindful of the line separating public from private life. Watching a celebrity talk show on television, they listen for several minutes as a movie star with bright teeth recounts details of his recent divorce. And I see my parents grow impatient. Finally, my mother gets up from her chair. Changing the channel, she says with simple disdain, "Cheap people."   28

My mother and my father are not cheap people. They never are tempted to believe that public life can also be intimate. They remain aloof from the modern temptation that captivates many in America's middle class: the temptation to relieve the anonymity of public life by trying to make it intimate. They do not understand, consequently, what so pleases the television audience listening to a movie star discuss his divorce with bogus private language. My   29 father opens a newspaper to find an article by a politician's wife in which she reveals (actually, renders merely as gossip) intimate details of her marriage. And he looks up from the article to ask me, "Why does she do this?"

I find his question embarrassing. Although I know that he does   30
not intend to embarrass me, I am forced to think about this book I have been writing. And I realize that my parents will be as puzzled by my act of self-revelation as they are by the movie star's revelations on the talk show. They never will call me cheap for publishing an autobiography. But I can well imagine their faces tightened by incomprehension as they read my words.

(Why does he do this?)   31

Many mornings at my desk I have been paralyzed by the thought   32
of their faces, their eyes. I imagine their eyes moving slowly across these pages. That image has weakened my resolve. Finally, however, it has not stopped me. Despite the fact that my parents remain even now in my mind a critical, silent chorus, standing together, I continue to write. I do not make my parents' sharp distinction between public and private life. With my mother and father I scorn those who attempt to create an experience of intimacy in public. But unlike my parents, I have come to think that there is a place for the deeply personal in public life. This is what I have learned by trying to write this book: There are things so deeply personal that they can be revealed only to strangers. I believe this. I continue to write.

"What is psychiatry?" my mother asks. And I wish I could tell   33
her. (I wish she could imagine it.) "There are things that are so personal that they can only be said to someone who is not close. Someone you don't know. A person who is not an intimate friend or a relation. There are things too personal to be shared with intimates."

She stands at the ironing board, her tone easy because she is   34
speaking to me. (I am her son.) For my mother that which is personal can only be said to a relative—her only intimates. She makes the single exception of confessing her sins to a Catholic priest. Otherwise, she speaks of her personal life only at home. The same is true of my father—though he is silent even with family members. Of those matters too jaggedly personal to reveal to intimates, my parents will never speak. And that seems to me an extraordinary oppression. The unspoken may well up within my mother and cause her to sigh. But beyond that sigh nothing is heard. There is no one she can address. Words never form. Silence remains to repress them. She remains quiet. My father in his chair remains quiet.

I wonder now what my parents' silence contains. What would   35 be their version of the past we once shared? What memories do they carry about me? What were their feelings at many of the moments I recollect on these pages? What did my father—who had dreamed of Australia—think of his children once they forced him to change plans and remain in America? What contrary feelings did he have about our early success? How does he regard the adults his sons and daughters have become? And my mother. At what moments has she hated me? On what occasions has she been embarrassed by me? What does she recall feeling during these difficult, sullen years of my childhood? What would be her version of this book? What are my parents unable to tell me today? What things are too personal? What feelings so unruly they dare not reveal to other intimates? Or even to each other? Or to themselves?

Some people have told me how wonderful it is that I am the 36 first in my family to write a book. I stand on the edge of a long silence. But I do not give voice to my parents by writing about their lives. I distinguish myself from them by writing about the life we once shared. Even when I quote them accurately, I profoundly distort my parents' words. (They were never intended to be read by the public.) So my parents do not truly speak on my pages. I may force their words to stand between quotation marks. With every word, however, I change what was said only to me.

"What is new with you?" My mother looks up from her ironing 37 to ask me. (In recent years she has taken to calling me Mr. Secrets, because I tell her so little about my work in San Francisco—this book she must suspect I am writing.)

Nothing much, I respond. 38

I write very slowly because I write under the obligation to make 39 myself clear to someone who knows nothing about me. It is a lonely adventure. Each morning I make my way along a narrowing precipice of written words. I hear an echoing voice—my own resembling another's. Silent! The reader's voice silently trails every word I put down. I reread my words, and again it is the reader's voice I hear in my mind, sounding my prose.

When I wrote my first autobiographical essay, it was no coin- 40 cidence that, from the first page, I expected to publish what I wrote. I didn't consciously determine the issue. Somehow I knew, however, that my words were meant for a public reader. Only because of that reader did the words come to the page. The reader became my excuse, my reason for writing.

It had taken me a long time to come to this address. There are 41 remarkable children who very early are able to write publicly about their personal lives. Some children confide to a diary those things—

like the first shuddering of sexual desire—too private to tell a
parent or brother. The youthful writer addresses a stranger, the
Other, with "Dear Diary" and tries to give public expression to
what is intensely, privately felt. In so doing, he attempts to evade
the guilt of repression. And the embarrassment of solitary feeling.
For by rendering feelings in words that a stranger can understand—
words that belong to the public, this Other—the young diarist no
longer need feel all alone or eccentric. His feelings are capable of
public intelligibility. In turn, the act of revelation helps the writer
better understand his own feelings. Such is the benefit of language:
By finding public words to describe one's feelings, one can describe
oneself to oneself. One names what was previously only darkly
felt.

I have come to think of myself as engaged in writing graffiti.   42
Encouraged by physical isolation to reveal what is most personal;
determined at the same time to have my words seen by strangers.
I have come to understand better why works of literature—while
never intimate, never individually addressed to the reader—are so
often among the most personal statements we hear in our lives.
Writing, I have come to value written words as never before. One
can use *spoken* words to reveal one's personal self to strangers.
But *written* words heighten the feeling of privacy. They permit the
most thorough and careful exploration. (In the silent room, I prey
upon that which is most private. Behind the closed door, I am
least reticent about giving those memories expression.) The writer
is freed from the obligation of finding an auditor in public. (As I
use words that someone far from home can understand, I create
my listener. I imagine her listening.)

My teachers gave me a great deal more than I knew when they   43
taught me to write public English. I was unable then to use the
skill for deeply personal purposes. I insisted upon writing impersonal
essays. And I wrote always with a specific reader in mind. Nevertheless, the skill of public writing was gradually developed by the
many classroom papers I had to compose. Today I *can* address an
anonymous reader. And this seems to me important to say. Somehow the inclination to write about my private life in public is
related to the ability to do so. It is not enough to say that my
mother and father do not want to write their autobiographies. It
needs also to be said that they are unable to write to a public
reader. They lack the skill. Though both of them can write in
Spanish and English, they write in a hesitant manner. Their syntax
is uncertain. Their vocabulary limited. They write well enough to
communicate "news" to relatives in letters. And they can handle
written transactions in institutional America. But the man who

sits in his chair so many hours, and the woman at the ironing board—"keeping busy because I don't want to get old"—will never be able to believe that any description of their personal lives could be understood by a stranger far from home.

3

When my mother mentioned seeing my article seven years ago, she *wrote* to me. And I responded to her letter with one of my own. (I wrote: "I am sorry that my article bothered you . . . I had not meant to hurt . . . I think, however, that education has divided the family . . . That is something which happens in most families, though it is rarely discussed . . . I had meant to praise what I have lost . . . I continue to love you both very much.") I wrote to my mother because it would have been too difficult, too painful to hear her voice on the phone. Too unmanageable a confrontation of voices. The impersonality of the written word made it the easiest means of exchange. The remarkable thing is that nothing has been spoken about this matter by either of us in the years intervening. I know my mother suspects that I continue to write about the family. She knows that I spend months at a time "writing," but she does not press me for information. (Mr. Secrets.) She does not protest.

The first time I saw my mother after she had received my letter, she came with my father to lunch. I opened the door to find her smiling slightly. In an instant I tried to gather her mood. (She looked as nervous and shy as I must have seemed.) We embraced. And she said that my father was looking for a place to park the car. She came into my apartment and asked what we were having for lunch. Slowly, our voices reverted to tones we normally sound with each other. (Nothing was said of my article.) I think my mother sensed that afternoon that the person whose essay she saw in a national magazine was a person unfamiliar to her, some Other. The public person—the writer, Richard Rodriguez—would remain distant and untouchable. She never would hear his public voice across a dining room table. And that afternoon she seemed to accept the idea, granted me the right, the freedom so crucial to adulthood, to become a person very different in public from the person I am at home.

Intimates are not always so generous. One close friend calls to tell me she has read an essay of mine. "All that Spanish angst," she laughs. "It's not really you." Only someone very close would be tempted to say such a thing—only a person who knows who I am. From such an intimate one must sometimes escape to the

44

45

46

company of strangers, to the liberation of the city, in order to
form new versions of oneself.

In the company of strangers now, I do not reveal the person I   47
am among intimates. My brother and sisters recognize a different
person, not the Richard Rodriguez in this book. I hope, when
they read this, they will continue to trust the person they have
known me to be. But I hope too that, like our mother, they will
understand why it is that the voice I sound here I have never
sounded to them. All those faraway childhood mornings in Sacramento, walking together to school, we talked but never mentioned
a thing about what concerned us so much: the great event of our
schooling, the change it forced on our lives. Years passed. Silence
grew thicker, less penetrable. We grew older without ever speaking
to each other about any of it. Intimacy grooved our voices in
familiar notes; familiarity defined the limits of what could be said.
Until we became adults. And now we see each other most years
at noisy family gatherings where there is no place to stop the
conversation, no right moment to turn the heads of listeners, no
way to essay this, my voice.

I see them now, my brother and sisters, two or three times every   48
year. We do not live so very far from one another. But as an
entire family, we only manage to gather for dinner on Easter. And
Mother's Day. Christmas. It is usually at our parents' house that
these dinners are held. Our mother invariably organizes things.
Well before anyone else has the chance to make other arrangements,
her voice will sound on the phone to remind us of an upcoming
gathering.

Lately, I have begun to wonder how the family will gather even   49
three times a year when she is not there with her phone to unite
us. For the time being, however, she presides at the table. She—
not my father, who sits opposite her—says the Grace before Meals.
She busies herself throughout the meal. "Sit down now," somebody
tells her. But she moves back and forth from the dining room
table to the kitchen. Someone needs more food. (What's missing?)
Something always is missing from the table. When she is seated,
she listens to the conversation. But she seems lonely. (Does she
think things would have been different if one of her children had
brought home someone who could speak Spanish?) She does not
know how or where to join in when her children are talking about
Woody Allen movies or real estate tax laws or somebody's yoga
class. (Does she remember how we vied with each other to sit
beside her in a movie theatre?) Someone remembers at some point
to include her in the conversation. Someone asks how many pounds

the turkey was this year. She responds in her visitor's voice. And soon the voices ride away. She is left with the silence.

Sitting beside me, as usual, is my younger sister. We gossip. 50 She tells me about her trip last week to Milan; we laugh; we talk about clothes, mutual friends in New York.

Other voices intrude: I hear the voices of my brother and sister 51 and the people who have married into our family. I am the loudest talker. I am the one doing most of the talking. I talk, having learned from hundreds of cocktail parties and dinner parties how to talk with great animation about nothing especially. I sound happy. I talk to everyone about something. And I become shy only when my older sister wonders what I am doing these days. Working in Los Angeles? Or writing again? When will she be able to see something I've published?

I try to change the subject. 52

"Are you writing a book?" 53

I notice, out of the corner of my eye, that my mother is nervously 54 piling dishes and then getting up to take them out to the kitchen.

I say yes. 55

"Well, well, well. Let's see it. Is it going to be a love story? A 56 romance? What's it about?"

She glances down at her thirteen-year-old son, her oldest. 57 "Tommy reads and reads, just like you used to."

I look over at him and ask him what sort of books he likes 58 best.

"Everything!" his mother answers with pride. 59

He smiles. I wonder: Am I watching myself in this boy? In this 60 face where I can scarcely trace a family resemblance? Have I foreseen his past? He lives in a world of Little League and Pop Warner. He has spoken English all his life. His father is of German descent, a fourth-generation American. And he does not go to a Catholic school, but to a public school named after a dead politician. Still, he is someone who reads . . .

"He and I read all the same books," my sister informs me. And 61 with that remark, my nephew's life slips out of my grasp to imagine.

Dinner progresses. There is dessert. Four cakes. Coffee. The con- 62 versation advances with remarkable ease. Talk is cheerful, the way talk is among people who rarely see one another and then are surprised that they have so much to say. Sometimes voices converge from various points around the table. Sometimes voices retreat to separate topics, two or three conversations.

My mother interrupts. She speaks and gets everyone's attention. 63 Some cousin of ours is getting married next month. (Already.) And some other relative is now the mother of a nine-pound baby

boy. (Already?) And some relative's son is graduating from college
this year. (We haven't seen him since he was five.) And somebody
else, an aunt, is retiring from her job in that candy store. And a
friend of my mother's from Sacramento—Do we remember her
after all these years?—died of cancer just last week. (Already!)

My father remains a witness to the evening. It is difficult to tell   64
what he hears (his hearing is bad) or cannot understand (his
English is bad). His face stays impassive, unless he is directly
addressed. In which case he smiles and nods, too eagerly, too
quickly, at what has been said. (Has he really heard?) When he
has finished eating, I notice, he sits back in his chair. And his eyes
move from face to face. Sometimes I feel that he is looking at me.
I look over to see him, and his eyes dart away the second after
I glance.

When Christmas dinner is finished, there are gifts to exchange   65
in the front room. Tradition demands that my brother, the oldest,
play master of ceremonies, "Santa's helper," handing out presents
with a cigar in his hand. It is the chore he has come to assume,
making us laugh with his hammy asides. "This is for Richard,"
he says, rattling a box next to his ear, rolling his eyes. "And this
one is for Mama Rodriguez." (There is the bright snap of a camera.)

Nowadays there is money enough for buying useless and slightly   66
ludicrous gifts for my mother and father. (They will receive an
expensive backgammon set. And airplane tickets to places they
haven't the energy or the desire to visit. And they will be given
a huge silver urn—"for chilling champagne.")

My mother is not surprised that her children are well-off. Her   67
two daughters are business executives. Her oldest son is a lawyer.
She predicted it all long ago. "Someday," she used to say when
we were young, "you will all grow up and all be very rich. You'll
have lots of money to buy me presents. But I'll be a little old lady.
I won't have any teeth or hair. So you'll have to buy me soft food
and put a blue wig on my head. And you'll buy me a big fur
coat. But you'll only be able to see my eyes."

Every Christmas now the floor around her is carpeted with red   68
and green wrapping paper. And her feet are wreathed with gifts.

By the time the last gift is unwrapped, everyone seems very   69
tired. The room has become uncomfortably warm. The talk grows
listless. ("Does anyone want coffee or more cake?" Somebody
groans.) Children ae falling asleep. Someone gets up to leave,
prompting others to leave. ("We have to get up early tomorrow.")

"Another Christmas," my mother says. She says that same thing   70
every year, so we all smile to hear it again.

Children are bundled up for the fast walk to the car. My mother   71
stands by the door calling good-bye. She stands with a coat over

her shoulders, looking into the dark where expensive foreign cars idle sharply. She seems, all of a sudden, very small. She looks worried.

"Don't come out, it's too cold," somebody shouts at her or at   72
my father, who steps out onto the porch. I watch my younger sister in a shiny mink jacket bend slightly to kiss my mother before she rushes down the front steps. My mother stands waving toward no one in particular. She seems sad to me. How sad? Why? (Sad that we all are going home? Sad that it was not quite, can never be, the Christmas one remembers having had once?) I am tempted to ask her quietly if there is anything wrong. (But these are questions of paradise, Mama.)

My brother drives away.   73

"Daddy shouldn't be outside," my mother says. "Here, take this   74
jacket out to him."

She steps into the warmth of the entrance hall and hands me   75
the coat she has been wearing over her shoulders.

I take it to my father and place it on him. In that instant I feel   76
the thinness of his arms. He turns. He asks if I am going home now too. It is, I realize, the only thing he has said to me all evening.

PATRICIA HAMPL

Memory and Imagination

When I was seven, my father, who played the violin on Sundays   1
with a nicely tortured flair which we considered artistic, led me by the hand down a long, unlit corridor in St. Luke's School basement, a sort of tunnel that ended in a room full of pianos. There many little girls and a single sad boy were playing truly tortured scales and arpeggios in a mash of troubled sound. My father gave me over to Sister Olive Marie, who did look remarkably like an olive.

Her oily face gleamed as if it had just been rolled out of a can   2
and laid on the white plate of her broad, spotless wimple. She was a small, plump woman; her body and the small window of her face seemed to interpret the entire alphabet of olive: her face was a sallow green olive placed upon the jumbo ripe olive of her

The first twelve paragraphs comprise "First Piano Lesson," an unpublished memoir. This essay was written for *The Dolphin Reader* in 1985.

black habit. I trusted her instantly and smiled, glad to have my hand placed in the hand of a woman who made sense, who provided the satisfaction of being what she was: an Olive who looked like an olive.

My father left me to discover the piano with Sister Olive Marie   3 so that one day I would join him in mutually tortured piano-violin duets for the edification of my mother and brother who sat at the table meditatively spooning in the last of their pineapple sherbet until their part was called for: they put down their spoons and clapped while we bowed, while the sweet ice in their bowls melted, while the music melted, and we all melted a little into each other for a moment.

But first Sister Olive must do her work. I was shown middle   4 C, which Sister seemed to think terribly important. I stared at middle C and then glanced away for a second. When my eye returned, middle C was gone, its slim finger lost in the complicated grasp of the keyboard. Sister Olive struck it again, finding it with laughable ease. She emphasized the importance of middle C, its central position, a sort of North Star of sound. I remember thinking, "Middle C is the belly button of the piano," an insight whose originality and accuracy stunned me with pride. For the first time in my life I was astonished by metaphor. I hesitated to tell the kindly Olive for some reason; apparently I understood a true metaphor is a risky business, revealing of the self. In fact, I have never, until this moment of writing it down, told my first metaphor to anyone.

Sunlight flooded the room; the pianos, all black, gleamed. Sister   5 Olive, dressed in the colors of the keyboard, gleamed; middle C shimmered with meaning and I resolved never—never—to forget its location: it was the center of the world.

Then Sister Olive, who had had to show me middle C twice   6 but who seemed to have drawn no bad conclusions about me anyway, got up and went to the windows on the opposite wall. She pulled the shades down, one after the other. The sun was too bright, she said. She sneezed as she stood at the windows with the sun shedding its glare over her. She sneezed and sneezed, crazy little convulsive sneezes, one after another, as helpless as if she had the hiccups.

"The sun makes me sneeze," she said when the fit was over   7 and she was back at the piano. This was odd, too odd to grasp in the mind. I associated sneezing with colds, and colds with rain, fog, snow and bad weather. The sun, however, had caused Sister Olive to sneeze in this wild way, Sister Olive who gleamed benignly and who was so certain of the location of the center of the world. The universe wobbled a bit and became unreliable. Things were not, after all, necessarily what they seemed. Appearance deceived: here was the sun acting totally out of character, hurling this woman into sneezes, a woman so mild that she was named, so it seemed, for a bland object on a relish tray.

I was given a red book, the first Thompson book, and told to play the first piece over and over at one of the black pianos where the other children were crashing away. This, I was told, was called practicing. It sounded alluringly adult, practicing. The piece itself consisted mainly of middle C, and I excelled, thrilled by my savvy at being able to locate that central note amidst the cunning camouflage of all the other white keys before me. Thrilled too by the shiny red book that gleamed, as the pianos did, as Sister Olive did, as my eager eyes probably did. I sat at the formidable machine of the piano and got to know middle C intimately, preparing to be as tortured as I could manage one day soon with my father's violin at my side. 8

But at the moment Mary Katherine Reilly was at my side, playing something at least two or three lessons more sophisticated than my piece. I believe she even struck a chord. I glanced at her from the peasantry of single notes, shy, ready to pay homage. She turned toward me, stopped playing, and sized me up. 9

Sized me up and found a person ready to be dominated. Without introduction she said, "My grandfather invented the collapsible opera hat." 10

I nodded, I acquiesced, I was hers. With that little stroke it was decided between us—that she should be the leader, and I the side-kick. My job was admiration. Even when she added, "But he didn't make a penny from it. He didn't have a patent"—even then, I knew and she knew that this was not an admission of powerlessness, but the easy candor of a master, of one who can afford a weakness or two. 11

With the clairvoyance of all fated relationships based on dominance and submission, it was decided in advance: that when the time came for us to play duets, I should always play second piano, that I should spend my allowance to buy her the Twinkies she craved but was not allowed to have, that finally, I should let her copy from my test paper, and when confronted by our teacher, confess with convincing hysteria that it was I, I who had cheated, who had reached above myself to steal what clearly belonged to the rightful heir of the inventor of the collapsible opera hat. . . . 12

There must be a reason I remember that little story about my first piano lesson. In fact, it isn't a story, just a moment, the 13 beginning of what could perhaps become a story. For the memoirist, more than for the fiction writer, the story seems already *there*, already accomplished and fully achieved in history ("in reality," as we naively say). For the memoirist, the writing of the story is a matter of transcription.

That, anyway, is the myth. But no memoirist writes for long   14
without experiencing an unsettling disbelief about the reliability of memory, a hunch that memory is not, after all, *just* memory. I don't know why I remembered this fragment about my first piano lesson. I don't, for instance, have a single recollection of my first arithmetic lesson, the first time I studied Latin, the first time my grandmother tried to teach me to knit. Yet these things occurred too, and must have their stories.

It is the piano lesson that has trudged forward, clearing the haze   15
of forgetfulness, showing itself bright with detail more than thirty years after the event. I did not choose to remember the piano lesson. It was simply there, like a book that has always been on the shelf, whether I ever read it or not, the binding and title showing as I skim across the contents of my life. On the day I wrote this fragment I happened to take that memory, not some other, from the shelf and paged through it. I found more detail, more event, perhaps a little more entertainment than I had expected, but the memory itself was there from the start. Waiting for me.

Or was it? When I reread what I had written just after I finished   16
it, I realized that I had told a number of lies. I *think* it was my father who took me the first time for my piano lesson—but maybe he only took me to meet my teacher and there was no actual lesson that day. And did I even know then that he played the violin—didn't he take up his violin again much later, as a result of my piano playing, and not the reverse? And is it even remotely accurate to describe as "tortured" the musicianship of a man who began every day by belting out "Oh What a Beautiful Morning" as he shaved?

More: Sister Olive Marie did sneeze in the sun, but was her   17
name Olive? As for her skin tone—I would have sworn it was olive-like; I would have been willing to spend the better part of an afternoon trying to write the exact description of imported Italian or Greek olive her face suggested: I wanted to get it right. But now, were I to write that passage over, it is her intense black eyebrows I would see, for suddenly they seem the central fact of that face, some indicative mark of her serious and patient nature. But the truth is, I don't remember the woman at all. She's a sneeze in the sun and a finger touching middle C. That, at least, is steady and clear.

Worse: I didn't have the Thompson book as my piano text. I'm   18 sure of that because I remember envying children who did have this wonderful book with its pictures of children and animals printed on the pages of music.

As for Mary Katherine Reilly. She didn't even go to grade school 19
with me (and her name isn't Mary Katherine Reilly—but I made that change on purpose). I met her in Girl Scouts and only went to school with her later, in high school. Our relationship was not really one of leader and follower; I played first piano most of the time in duets. She certainly never copied anything from a test paper of mine: she was a better student, and cheating just wasn't a possibility with her. Though her grandfather (or someone in her family) did invent the collapsible opera hat and I remember that she was proud of that fact, she didn't tell me this news as a deft move in a childish power play.

So, what was I doing in this brief memoir? Is it simply an 20
example of the curious relation a fiction writer has to the material of her own life? Maybe. That may have some value in itself. But to tell the truth (if anyone still believes me capable of telling the truth), I wasn't writing fiction. I was writing memoir—or was trying to. My desire was to be accurate. I wished to embody the myth of memoir: to write as an act of dutiful transcription.

Yet clearly the work of writing narrative caused me to do some- 21
thing very different from transcription. I am forced to admit that memoir is not a matter of transcription, that memory itself is not a warehouse of finished stories, not a static gallery of framed pictures. I must admit that I invented. But why?

Two whys: why did I invent, and then, if a memoirist must 22
inevitably invent rather than transcribe, why do I—why should anybody—write memoir at all?

I must respond to these impertinent questions because they, like 23
the bumper sticker I saw the other day commanding all who read it to QUESTION AUTHORITY, challenge my authority as a memoirist and as a witness.

It still comes as a shock to realize that I don't write about what 24
I know: I write in order to find out what I know. Is it possible to convey to a reader the enormous degree of blankness, confusion, hunch and uncertainty lurking in the act of writing? When I am the reader, not the writer, I too fall into the lovely illusion that the words before me (in a story by Mavis Gallant, an essay by Carol Bly, a memoir by M. F. K. Fisher), which *read* so inevitably, must also have been *written* exactly as they appear, rhythm and cadence, language and syntax, the powerful waves of the sentences laying themselves on the smooth beach of the page one after another faultlessly.

But here I sit before a yellow legal pad, and the long page of 25 the preceding two paragraphs is a jumble of crossed-out lines, false starts, confused order. A mess. The mess of my mind trying to find out what it wants to say. This is a writer's frantic, grabby mind, not the poised mind of a reader ready to be edified or entertained.

I sometimes think of the reader as a cat, endlessly fastidious, 26 capable, by turns, of mordant indifference and riveted attention, luxurious, recumbent, and ever poised. Whereas the writer is absolutely a dog, panting and moping, too eager for an affectionate scratch behind the ears, lunging frantically after any old stick thrown in the distance.

The blankness of a new page never fails to intrigue and terrify 27 me. Sometimes, in fact, I think my habit of writing on long yellow sheets comes from an atavistic fear of the writer's stereotypic "blank white page." At least when I begin writing, my page isn't utterly blank; at least it has a wash of color on it, even if the absence of words must finally be faced on a yellow sheet as truly as on a blank white one. Well, we all have our ways of whistling in the dark.

If I approach writing from memory with the assumption that I 28 know what I wish to say, I assume that intentionality is running the show. Things are not that simple. Or perhaps writing is even more profoundly simple, more telegraphic and immediate in its choices than the grating wheels and chugging engine of logic and rational intention. The heart, the guardian of intuition with its secret, often fearful intentions, is the boss. Its commands are what a writer obeys—often without knowing it. Or, I do.

That's why I'm a strong adherent of the first draft. And why 29 it's worth pausing for a moment to consider what a first draft really is. By my lights, the piano lesson memoir is a first draft. That doesn't mean it exists here exactly as I first wrote it. I like to think I've cleaned it up from the first time I put it down on paper. I've cut some adjectives here, toned down the hyperbole there, smoothed a transition, cut a repetition—that sort of housekeeperly tidying-up. But the piece remains a first draft because I haven't yet gotten to know it, haven't given it a chance to tell me anything. For me, writing a first draft is a little like meeting someone for the first time. I come away with a wary acquaintanceship, but the real friendship (if any) and genuine intimacy—that's all down the road. Intimacy with a piece of writing, as with a person, comes from paying attention to the revelations it is capable of giving, not by imposing my own preconceived notions, no matter how well-intentioned they might be.

I try to let pretty much anything happen in a first draft. A careful 30 first draft is a failed first draft. That may be why there are so many inaccuracies in the piano lesson memoir: I didn't censor, I didn't judge. I kept moving. But I would not publish this piece as a memoir on its own in its present state. It isn't the "lies" in the piece that give me pause, though a reader has a right to expect a memoir to be as accurate as the writer's memory can make it. No, it isn't the lies themselves that makes the piano lesson memoir a first draft and therefore "unpublishable."

The real trouble: the piece hasn't yet found its subject; it isn't 31
yet about what it wants to be about. Note: what *it* wants, not what I want. The difference has to do with the relation a memoirist— any writer, in fact—has to unconscious or half-known intentions and impulses in composition.

Now that I have the fragment down on paper, I can read this 32
little piece as a mystery which drops clues to the riddle of my feelings, like a culprit who wishes to be apprehended. My narrative self (the culprit who has invented) wishes to be discovered by my reflective self, the self who wants to understand and make sense of a half-remembered story about a nun sneezing in the sun. . . .

We only store in memory images of value. The value may be 33
lost over the passage of time (I was baffled about why I remembered that sneezing nun, for example), but that's the implacable judgment of feeling: *this*, we say somewhere deep within us, is something I'm hanging on to. And of course, often we cleave to things because they possess heavy negative charges. Pain likes to be vivid.

Over time, the value (the feeling) and the stored memory (the 34
image) may become estranged. Memoir seeks a permanent home for feeling and image, a habitation where they can live together in harmony. Naturally, I've had a lot of experiences since I packed away that one from the basement of St. Luke's School; that piano lesson has been effaced by waves of feeling for other moments and episodes. I persist in believing the event has value—after all, I remember it—but in writing the memoir I did not simply re-live the experience. Rather, I explored the mysterious relationship between all the images I could round up and the even more impacted feelings that caused me to store the images safely away in memory. Stalking the relationship, seeking the congruence be-tween stored image and hidden emotion—that's the real job of memoir.

By writing about that first piano lesson, I've come to know 35
things I could not know otherwise. But I only know these things as a result of reading this first draft. While I was writing, I was following the images, letting the details fill the room of the page

and use the furniture as they wished. I was their dutiful servant—
or thought I was. In fact, I was the faithful retainer of my hidden
feelings which were giving the commands.

I really did feel, for instance, that Mary Katherine Reilly was   36
far superior to me. She was smarter, funnier, more wonderful in
every way—that's how I saw it. Our friendship (or she herself)
did not require that I become her vassal, yet perhaps in my heart
that was something I wanted; I wanted a way to express my feeling
of admiration. I suppose I waited until this memoir to begin to
find the way.

Just as, in the memoir, I finally possess that red Thompson book   37
with the barking dogs and bleating lambs and winsome children.
I couldn't (and still can't) remember what my own music book
was, so I grabbed the name and image of the one book I could
remember. It was only in reviewing the piece after writing it that
I saw my inaccuracy. In pondering this "lie," I came to see what
I was up to: I was getting what I wanted. At last.

The truth of many circumstances and episodes in the past emerges   38
for the memoirist through details (the red music book, the fascination
with a nun's name and gleaming face), but these details are not
merely information, not flat facts. Such details are not allowed to
lounge. They must work. Their work is the creation of symbol.
But it's more accurate to call it the *recognition* of symbol. For
meaning is not "attached" to the detail by the memoirist; meaning
is revealed. That's why a first draft is important. Just as the first
meeting (good or bad) with someone who later becomes the beloved
is important and is often reviewed for signals, meanings, omens
and indications.

Now I can look at that music book and see it not only as "a   39
detail," but for what it is, how it *acts*. See it as the small red door
leading straight into the dark room of my childhood longing and
disappointment. That red book *becomes* the palpable evidence of
that longing. In other words, it becomes symbol. There is no
symbol, no life-of-the-spirit in the general or the abstract. Yet a
writer wishes—indeed all of us wish—to speak about profound
matters that are, like it or not, general and abstract. We wish to
talk to each other about life and death, about love, despair, loss,
and innocence. We sense that in order to live together we must
learn to speak of peace, of history, of meaning and values. Those
are a few.

We seek a means of exchange, a language which will renew   40
these ancient concerns and make them wholly and pulsingly ours.
Instinctively, we go to our store of private images and associations

for our authority to speak of these weighty issues. We find, in our details and broken and obscured images, the language of symbol. Here memory impulsively reaches out its arms and embraces imagination. That is the resort to invention. It isn't a lie, but an act of necessity, as the innate urge to locate personal truth always is.

All right. Invention is inevitable. But why write memoir? Why not call it fiction and be done with all the hashing about, wondering where memory stops and imagination begins? And if memoir seeks to talk about "the big issues," about history and peace, death and love—why not leave these reflections to those with expert and scholarly knowledge? Why let the common or garden variety memoirist into the club? I'm thinking again of that bumper sticker: why Question Authority? [41]

My answer, of course, is a memoirist's answer. Memoir must be written because each of us must have a created version of the past. Created: that is, real, tangible, made of the stuff of a life lived in place and in history. And the down side of any created thing as well: we must live with a version that attaches us to our limitations, to the inevitable subjectivity of our points of view. We must acquiesce to our experience and our gift to transform experience into meaning and value. You tell me your story, I'll tell you my story. [42]

If we refuse to do the work of creating this personal version of the past, someone else will do it for us. That is a scary political fact. "The struggle of man against power," a character in Milan Kundera's novel *The Book of Laughter and Forgetting* says, "is the struggle of memory against forgetting." He refers to willful political forgetting, the habit of nations and those in power (Question Authority!) to deny the truth of memory in order to disarm moral and ethical power. It's an efficient way of controlling masses of people. It doesn't even require much bloodshed, as long as people are entirely willing to give over their personal memories. Whole histories can be rewritten. As Czeslaw Milosz said in his 1980 Nobel Prize lecture, the number of books published that seek to deny the existence of the Nazi death camps now exceeds one hundred. [43]

What is remembered is what *becomes* reality. If we "forget" Auschwitz,[1] if we "forget" My Lai,[2] what then do we remember? [44]

1. Polish site in World War II of the concentration camp Auschwitz-Birkenau, where more than a million prisoners, most of them Jews, were exterminated.
2. Incident in 1968 during the Vietnam war, in which American troops massacred unarmed Vietnamese civilians, including women and children.

And what is the purpose of our remembering? If we think of
memory naively, as a simple story, logged like a documentary in
the archive of the mind, we miss its beauty but also its function.
The beauty of memory rests in its talent for rendering detail, for
paying homage to the senses, its capacity to love the particles of
life, the richness and idiosyncrasy of our existence. The function
of memory, on the other hand, is intensely personal and surprisingly
political.

Our capacity to move forward as developing beings rests on a   45
healthy relation with the past. Psychotherapy, that widespread
method of mental health, relies heavily on memory and on the
ability to retrieve and organize images and events from the personal
past. We carry our wounds and perhaps even worse, our capacity
to wound, forward with us. If we learn not only to tell our stories
but to listen to what our stories tell us—to write the first draft
and then return for the second draft—we are doing the work of
memoir.

Memoir is the intersection of narration and reflection, of story-   46
telling and essay-writing. It can present its story *and* reflect and
consider the meaning of the story. It is a peculiarly open form,
inviting broken and incomplete images, half-recollected fragments,
all the mass (and mess) of detail. It offers to shape this confusion—
and in shaping, of course it necessarily creates a work of art, not
a legal document. But then, even legal documents are only valiant
attempts to consign the truth, the whole truth and nothing but
the truth to paper. Even they remain versions.

Locating touchstones—the red music book, the olive Olive, my   47
father's violin playing—is deeply satisfying. Who knows why?
Perhaps we all sense that we can't grasp the whole truth and
nothing but the truth of our experience. Just can't be done. What
can be achieved, however, is a version of its swirling, changing
wholeness. A memoirist must acquiesce to selectivity, like any
artist. The version we dare to write is the only truth, the only
relationship we can have with the past. Refuse to write your life
and you have no life. At least, that is the stern view of the memoirist.

Personal history, logged in memory, is a sort of slide projector   48
flashing images on the wall of the mind. And there's precious
little order to the slides in the rotating carousel. Beyond that
confusion, who knows who is running the projector? A memoirist
steps into this darkened room of flashing, unorganized images and
stands blinking for a while. Maybe for a long while. But eventually,
as with any attempt to tell a story, it is necessary to put something

first, then something else. And so on, to the end. That's a first draft. Not necessarily the truth, not even *a* truth sometimes, but the first attempt to create a shape.

The first thing I usually notice at this stage of composition is   49
the appalling inaccuracy of the piece. Witness my first piano lesson draft. Invention is screamingly evident in what I intended to be transcription. But here's the further truth: I feel no shame. In fact, it's only now that my interest in the piece truly quickens. For I can see what isn't there, what is shyly hugging the walls, hoping not to be seen. I see the filmy shape of the next draft. I see a more acute version of the episode or—this is more likely—an entirely new piece rising from the ashes of the first attempt.

The next draft of the piece would have to be a true re-vision,   50
a new seeing of the materials of the first draft. Nothing merely cosmetic will do—no rouge buffing up the opening sentence, no glossy adjective to lift a sagging line, nothing to attempt covering a patch of gray writing. None of that. I can't say for sure, but my hunch is the revision would lead me to more writing about my father (why was I so impressed by that ancestral inventor of the collapsible opera hat? Did I feel I had nothing as remarkable in my own background? Did this make me feel inadequate?). I begin to think perhaps Sister Olive is less central to this business than she is in this draft. She is meant to be a moment, not a character.

And so I might proceed, if I were to undertake a new draft of   51
the memoir. I begin to feel a relationship developing between a former self and me.

And, even more compelling, a relationship between an old world   52
and me. Some people think of autobiographical writing as the precious occupation of a particularly self-absorbed person. Maybe, but I don't buy that. True memoir is written in an attempt to find not only a self but a world.

The self-absorption that seems to be the impetus and embar-   53
rassment of autobiography turns into (or perhaps always was) a hunger for the world. Actually, it begins as hunger for *a* world, one gone or lost, effaced by time or a more sudden brutality. But in the act of remembering, the personal environment expands, resonates beyond itself, beyond its "subject," into the endless and tragic recollection that is history.

We look at old family photographs in which we stand next to   54
black, boxy Fords and are wearing period costumes, and we do not gaze fascinated because there we are young again, or there we are standing, as we never will again in life, next to our mother.

We stare and drift because there we are . . . historical. It is the
dress, the black car that dazzle us now and draw us beyond our
mother's bright arms which once caught us. We reach into the
attractive impersonality of something more significant than ourselves.
We write memoir, in other words. We accept the humble position
of writing a version rather than "the whole truth."

I suppose I write memoir because of the radiance of the past—   55
it draws me back and back to it. Not that the past is beautiful.
In our communal memoir, in history, the death camps *are* back
there. In intimate life too, the record is usually pretty mixed. "I
could tell you stories . . ." people say and drift off, meaning terrible
things have happened to them.

But the past is radiant. It has the light of lived life. A memoirist   56
wishes to touch it. No one owns the past, though typically the
first act of new political regimes, whether of the left or the right,
is to attempt to re-write history, to grab the past and make it over
so the end comes out right. So their power looks inevitable.

No one owns the past, but it is a grave error (another age would   57
have said a grave sin) not to inhabit memory. Sometimes I think
it is all we really have. But that may be a trifle melodramatic. At
any rate, memory possesses authority for the fearful self in a world
where it is necessary to have authority in order to Question
Authority.

There may be no more pressing intellectual need in our culture   58
than for people to become sophisticated about the function of
memory. The political implications of the loss of memory are
obvious. The authority of memory is a personal confirmation of
selfhood. To write one's life is to live it twice, and the second
living is both spiritual and historical, for a memoir reaches deep
within the personality as it seeks its narrative form and also grasps
the life-of-the-times as no political treatise can.

Our most ancient metaphor says life is a journey. Memoir is   59
travel writing, then, notes taken along the way, telling how things
looked and what thoughts occurred. But I cannot think of the
memoirist as a tourist. This is the traveller who goes on foot, living
the journey, taking on mountains, enduring deserts, marveling at
the lush green places. Moving through it all faithfully, not so much
a survivor with a harrowing tale to tell as a pilgrim, seeking,
wondering.

JOAN DIDION

Why I Write

Of course I stole the title for this talk, from George Orwell. One   1
reason I stole it was that I like the sound of the words: Why I
Write. There you have three short unambiguous words that share
a sound, and the sound they share is this:

I   2

I   3

I   4

In many ways writing is the act of saying *I*, of imposing oneself   5
upon other people, of saying *listen to me, see it my way, change your
mind*. It's an aggressive, even a hostile act. You can disguise its
aggressiveness all you want with veils of subordinate clauses and
qualifiers and tentative subjunctives, with ellipses and evasions—
with the whole manner of intimating rather than claiming, of
alluding rather than stating—but there's no getting around the
fact that setting words on paper is the tactic of a secret bully, an
invasion, an imposition of the writer's sensibility on the reader's
most private space.

I stole the title not only because the words sounded right but   6
because they seemed to sum up, in a no-nonsense way, all I have
to tell you. Like many writers I have only this one "subject," this
one "area": the act of writing. I can bring you no reports from
any other front. I may have other interests: I am "interested," for
example, in marine biology, but I don't flatter myself that you
would come out to hear me talk about it. I am not a scholar. I
am not in the least an intellectual, which is not to say that when
I hear the word "intellectual" I reach for my gun, but only to say
that I do not think in abstracts. During the years when I was an
undergraduate at Berkeley I tried, with a kind of hopeless late-
adolescent energy, to buy some temporary visa into the world of
ideas, to forge for myself a mind that could deal with the abstract.

In short I tried to think. I failed. My attention veered inexorably   7
back to the specific, to the tangible, to what was generally considered,
by everyone I knew then and for that matter have known since,
the peripheral. I would try to contemplate the Hegelian dialectic
and would find myself concentrating instead on a flowering pear
tree outside my window and the particular way the petals fell on
my floor. I would try to read linguistic theory and would find

First published in the *New York Times Book Review*, December 5, 1976.

myself wondering instead if the lights were on in the bevatron up
the hill. When I say that I was wondering if the lights were on
in the bevatron you might immediately suspect, if you deal in
ideas at all, that I was registering the bevatron as a political symbol,
thinking in shorthand about the military-industrial complex and
its role in the university community, but you would be wrong. I
was only wondering if the lights were on in the bevatron, and
how they looked. A physical fact.

I had trouble graduating from Berkeley, not because of this   8
inability to deal with ideas—I was majoring in English, and I could
locate the house-and-garden imagery in *The Portrait of a Lady* as
well as the next person, "imagery" being by definition the kind
of specific that got my attention—but simply because I had neglected
to take a course in Milton. For reasons which now sound baroque
I needed a degree by the end of that summer, and the English
department finally agreed, if I would come down from Sacramento
every Friday and talk about the cosmology of *Paradise Lost*, to
certify me proficient in Milton. I did this. Some Fridays I took the
Greyhound bus, other Fridays I caught the Southern Pacific's City
of San Francisco on the last leg of its transcontinental trip. I can
no longer tell you whether Milton put the sun or the earth at the
center of his universe in *Paradise Lost*, the central question of at
least one century and a topic about which I wrote 10,000 words
that summer, but I can still recall the exact rancidity of the butter
in the City of San Francisco's dining car, and the way the tinted
windows on the Greyhound bus cast the oil refineries around
Carquinez Straits into a grayed and obscurely sinister light. In
short my attention was always on the periphery, on what I could
see and taste and touch, on the butter, and the Greyhound bus.
During those years I was traveling on what I knew to be a very
shaky passport, forged papers: I knew that I was no legitimate
resident in any world of ideas. I knew I couldn't think. All I knew
then was what I couldn't do. All I knew then was what I wasn't,
and it took me some years to discover what I was.

Which was a writer.   9

By which I mean not a "good" writer or a "bad" writer but   10
simply a writer, a person whose most absorbed and passionate
hours are spent arranging words on pieces of paper. Had my
credentials been in order I would never have become a writer.
Had I been blessed with even limited access to my own mind
there would have been no reason to write. I write entirely to find
out what I'm thinking, what I'm looking at, what I see and what
it means. What I want and what I fear. Why did the oil refineries
around Carquinez Straits seem sinister to me in the summer of

1956? Why have the night lights in the bevatron burned in my mind for twenty years? *What is going on in these pictures in my mind?*

When I talk about pictures in my mind I am talking, quite specifically, about images that shimmer around the edges. There used to be an illustration in every elementary psychology book showing a cat drawn by a patient in varying stages of schizophrenia. This cat had a shimmer around it. You could see the molecular structure breaking down at the very edges of the cat: the cat became the background and the background the cat, everything interacting, exchanging ions. People on hallucinogens describe the same perception of objects. I'm not a schizophrenic, nor do I take hallucinogens, but certain images do shimmer for me. Look hard enough, and you can't miss the shimmer. It's there. You can't think too much about these pictures that shimmer. You just lie low and let them develop. You stay quiet. You don't talk to many people and you keep your nervous system from shorting out and you try to locate the cat in the shimmer, the grammar in the picture.

Just as I meant "shimmer" literally I mean "grammar" literally. Grammar is a piano I play by ear, since I seem to have been out of school the year the rules were mentioned. All I know about grammar is its infinite power. To shift the structure of a sentence alters the meaning of that sentence, as definitely and inflexibly as the position of a camera alters the meaning of the object photographed. Many people know about camera angles now, but not so many know about sentences. The arrangement of the words matters, and the arrangement you want can be found in the picture in your mind. The picture dictates the arrangement. The picture dictates whether this will be a sentence with or without clauses, a sentence that ends hard or a dying-fall sentence, long or short, active or passive. The picture tells you how to arrange the words and the arrangement of the words tells you, or tells me, what's going on in the picture. *Nota bene:*[1]

It tells you.

You don't tell it.

Let me show you what I mean by pictures in the mind. I began *Play It as It Lays* just as I have begun each of my novels, with no notion of "character" or "plot" or even "incident." I had only two pictures in my mind, more about which later, and a technical intention, which was to write a novel so elliptical and fast that it would be over before you noticed it, a novel so fast that it would

11

12

13

14

15

1. "Note well."

scarcely exist on the page at all. About the pictures: the first was of white space. Empty space. This was clearly the picture that dictated the narrative intention of the book—a book in which anything that happened would happen off the page, a "white" book to which the reader would have to bring his or her own bad dreams—and yet this picture told me no "story," suggested no situation. The second picture did. This second picture was of something actually witnessed. A young woman with long hair and a short white halter dress walks through the casino at the Riviera in Las Vegas at one in the morning. She crosses the casino alone and picks up a house telephone. I watch her because I have heard her paged, and recognize her name: she is a minor actress I see around Los Angeles from time to time, in places like Jax and once in a gynecologist's office in the Beverly Hills Clinic, but have never met. I know nothing about her. Who is paging her? Why is she here to be paged? How exactly did she come to this? It was precisely this moment in Las Vegas that made *Play It as It Lays* begin to tell itself to me, but the moment appears in the novel only obliquely, in a chapter which begins:

"Maria made a list of things she would never do. She would   16 never: walk through the Sands or Caesar's alone after midnight. She would never: ball at a party, do S-M unless she wanted to, borrow furs from Abe Lipsey, deal. She would never: carry a Yorkshire in Beverly Hills."

That is the beginning of the chapter and that is also the end of   17 the chapter, which may suggest what I meant by "white space."

I recall having a number of pictures in my mind when I began   18 the novel I just finished, A *Book of Common Prayer*. As a matter of fact one of these pictures was of that bevatron I mentioned, although I would be hard put to tell you a story in which nuclear energy figures. Another was a newspaper photograph or a hijacked 707 burning on the desert in the Middle East. Another was the night view from a room in which I once spent a week with paratyphoid, a hotel room on the Colombian coast. My husband and I seemed to be on the Colombian coast representing the United States of America at a film festival (I recall invoking the name "Jack Valenti" a lot, as if its reiteration could make me well), and it was a bad place to have fever, not only because my indisposition offended our hosts but because every night in this hotel the generator failed. The lights went out. The elevator stopped. My husband would go to the event of the evening and make excuses for me and I would stay alone in this hotel room, in the dark. I remember standing at the window trying to call Bogotá (the telephone seemed to work on the same principle as the generator) and watching the night wind come up and wondering what I was doing eleven degrees off the equator with a fever of 103. The view from that window definitely figures in *A Book of Common Prayer,* as does the burning 707, and yet none of these pictures told me the story I needed.

The picture that did, the picture that shimmered and made these other images coalesce, was the Panama airport at 6 A.M. I was in this airport only once, on a plane to Bogotá that stopped for an hour to refuel, but the way it looked that morning remained superimposed on everything I saw until the day I finished *A Book of Common Prayer.* I lived in that airport for several years. I can still feel the hot air when I step off the plane, can see the heat already rising off the tarmac at 6 A.M. I can feel my skirt damp and wrinkled on my legs. I can feel the asphalt stick to my sandals. I remember the big tail of a Pan American plane floating motionless down at the end of the tarmac. I remember the sound of a slot machine in the waiting room. I could tell you that I remember a particular woman in the airport, an American woman, a *norteamericana,* a thin *norteamericana* about forty who wore a big square emerald in lieu of a wedding ring, but there was no such woman there.

I put this woman in the airport later. I made this woman up, just as I later made up a country to put the airport in, and a family to run the country. This woman in the airport is neither catching a plane nor meeting one. She is ordering tea in the airport coffee shop. In fact she is not simply "ordering" tea but insisting that the water be boiled, in front of her, for twenty minutes. Why is this woman in this airport? Why is she going nowhere, where has she been? Where did she get that big emerald? What derangement, or disassociation, makes her believe that her will to see the water boiled can possibly prevail?

"She had been going to one airport or another for four months, one could see it, looking at the visas on her passport. All those airports where Charlotte Douglas's passport had been stamped would have looked alike. Sometimes the sign on the tower would say "Bienvenidos" and sometimes the sign on the tower would say "Bienvenue," some places were wet and hot and others dry and hot, but at each of these airports the pastel concrete walls would rust and stain and the swamp off the runway would be littered with the fuselages of cannibalized Fairchild F-227's and the water would need boiling.

"I knew why Charlotte went to the airport even if Victor did not.

"I knew about airports."

19

20

21

22

23

These lines appear about halfway through *A Book of Common* 24
Prayer, but I wrote them during the second week I worked on
the book, long before I had any idea where Charlotte Douglas
had been or why she went to airports. Until I wrote these lines
I had no character called "Victor" in mind: the necessity for mentioning a name, and the name "Victor," occurred to me as I wrote
the sentence. *I knew why Charlotte went to the airport* sounded
incomplete. *I knew why Charlotte went to the airport even if Victor
did not* carried a little more narrative drive. Most important of all,
until I wrote these lines I did not know who "I" was, who was
telling the story. I had intended until then that the "I" be no more
than the voice of the author, a nineteenth-century omniscient
narrator. But there it was:

"I knew why Charlotte went to the airport even if Victor 25
did not.

"I knew about airports." 26

This "I" was the voice of no author in my house. This "I" was 27
someone who not only knew why Charlotte went to the airport
but also knew someone called "Victor." Who was Victor? Who
was this narrator? Why was this narrator telling me this story?
Let me tell you one thing about why writers write: had I known
the answer to any of these questions I would never have needed
to write a novel.

JOHN KENNETH GALBRAITH

Writing and Typing

Nine or ten years ago, when I was spending a couple of terms 1
at Trinity College, Cambridge, I received a proposal of more than
usual interest from the University of California. It was that I take
a leave from Harvard and accept a visiting chair in rhetoric at
Berkeley. They assured me that rhetoric was a traditional and not,
as one would naturally suppose, a pejorative title. My task would
be to hold seminars with the young on what I had learned about
writing in general and on technical matters in particular.

I was attracted by the idea. I had spent decades attempting to 2
teach the young about economics, and the practical consequences

First published as "Writing, Typing, and Economics" in *Atlantic Monthly*, March
1978.

were not reassuring. When I entered the field in the early nineteen-thirties, it was generally known that the modern economy could suffer a serious depression and that it could have a serious inflation. In the ensuing forty years my teaching had principally advanced to the point of telling that it was possible to have both at the same time. This was soon to be associated with the belief of William Simon and Alan Greenspan, the guiding hands of Richard Nixon and Gerald Ford, that progress in this field is measured by the speed of the return to the idea of the eighteenth century. A subject in which it can be believed that you go ahead by going back has many problems for a teacher. Things are better now. Mr. Carter's economists do not believe in going back. But, as I've elsewhere urged, they are caught in a delicate balance between their fear of inflation and unemployment and their fear of doing anything about them. It is hard to conclude that economics is a productive intellectual and pedagogical investment.

Then I began to consider what I could tell about writing. My 3 experience was certainly ample. I had been initiated by two inspired professors in Canada, O. J. Stevenson and E. C. McLean. They were men who deeply loved their craft and who were willing to spend endless hours with a student, however obscure his talent. I had been an editor of *Fortune*, which in my day meant mostly being a writer. Editor was thought a more distinguished title, and it justified more pay. Both as an editor proper and as a writer, I had had the close attention of Henry Robinson Luce. Harry Luce is in danger of being remembered only for his political judgment, which left much to be desired; he found unblemished merit in John Foster Dulles, Robert A. Taft and Chiang Kai-shek. But more important, he was an acute businessman and a truly brilliant editor. One proof is that while Time, Inc. publications have become politically more predictable since he departed, they have become infinitely less amusing.

Finally, as I reflected on my qualifications, there was the amount 4 of my life that I have spent at a typewriter. Nominally I have been a teacher. In practice I have been a writer—as generations of Harvard students have suspected. Faced with the choice of spending time on the unpublished scholarship of a graduate student or the unpublished work of Galbraith, I have rarely hesitated. Superficially at least, I was well qualified for that California chair.

There was, however, a major difficulty. It was that I could tell 5 everything I knew about writing in approximately half an hour. For the rest of the term I would have nothing to say except as I could invite discussion, this being the last resort of the distraught academic mind. I could use up a few hours telling how a writer should deal with publishers. This is a field of study in which I especially rejoice. All authors should seek to establish a relationship of warmth, affection and mutual mistrust with their publishers in the hope that the uncertainty will add, however marginally, to compensation. But instruction on how to deal with publishers and how to bear up under the inevitable defeat would be for a very advanced course. It is not the sort of thing that the average beginning writer at Berkeley would find immediately practical.

So I returned to the few things that I could teach. The first   6
lesson would have had to do with the all-important issue of inspiration. All writers know that on some golden mornings they are touched by the wand; they are on intimate terms with poetry and cosmic truth. I have experienced those moments myself. Their lesson is simple; they are a total illusion. And the danger in the illusion is that you will wait for them. Such is the horror of having to face the typewriter that you will spend all your time waiting. I am persuaded that, hangovers apart, most writers, like most other artisans, are about as good one day as the next (a point that Trollope made). The seeming difference is the result of euphoria, alcohol or imagination. All this means that one had better go to his or her typewriter every morning and stay there regardless of the result. It will be much the same.

All professions have their own way of justifying laziness. Harvard   7
professors are deeply impressed by the jeweled fragility of their minds. Like the thinnest metal, these are subject terribly to fatigue. More than six hours of teaching a week is fatal—and an impairment of academic freedom. So, at any given moment, the average professor is resting his mind in preparation for the next orgiastic act of insight or revelation. Writers, by the same token, do nothing because they are waiting for inspiration.

In my own case there are days when the result is so bad that   8
no fewer than five revisions are required. However, when I'm greatly inspired, only four are needed before, as I've often said, I put in that note of spontaneity which even my meanest critics concede. My advice to those eager students in California would have been, "Don't wait for the golden moment. Things may well be worse."

I would also have warned against the flocking tendency of writers   9
and its use as a cover for idleness. It helps greatly in the avoidance of work to be in the company of others who are also waiting for the golden moment. The best place to write is by yourself because writing then becomes an escape from the terrible boredom of your

own personality. It's the reason that for years I've favored Switzerland, where I look at the telephone and yearn to hear it ring.

The questions of revision is closely allied with that of inspiration. There may be inspired writers for whom the first draft is just right. But anyone who is not certifiably a Milton had better assume that the first draft is a very primitive thing. The reason is simple: writing is difficult work. Ralph D. Paine, who managed *Fortune* in my time, used to say that anyone who said writing was easy was either a bad writer or an unregenerate liar. Thinking, as Voltaire avowed, is also a very tedious process which men or women will do anything to avoid. So all first drafts are deeply flawed by the need to combine compsition with thought. Each later one is less demanding in this regard; hence the writing can be better. There does come a time when revision is for the sake of change—when one has become so bored with the words that anything that is different looks better. But even then it may *be* better.   10

For months when I was working on *The Affluent Society,* my title was "The Opulent Society." Eventually I could stand it no longer; the word opulent had a nasty, greasy sound. One day, before starting work, I looked up the synonyms in the dictionary. First to meet my eye was the word "affluent." I had only one worry; that was whether I could possibly sell it to my publisher. All publishers wish to have books called *The Crisis in American Democracy.* The title, to my surprise, was acceptable. Mark Twain once said that the difference between the right word and almost the right word is the difference between lightning and a lightning bug.   11

Next, I would have stressed a rather old-fashioned idea—brevity— to those students. It was, above all, the lesson of Harry Luce. No one who worked for him ever again escaped the feeling that he was there looking over one's shoulder. In his hand was a pencil; down on each page one could expect, at any moment, a long swishing wiggle accompanied by the comment: "This can go." Invariably it could. It was written to please the author and not the reader. Or to fill in the space. The gains from brevity are obvious; in most efforts to achieve it, the worst and the dullest go. And it is the worst and the dullest that spoil the rest.   12

I know that brevity is now out of favor. The *New York Review of Books* prides itself in giving its authors as much space as they want and sometimes twice as much as they need. Writing for television, on the other hand, as I've learned in the last few years, is an exercise in relentless condensation. It has left me with the feeling that even brevity can be carried to extremes. But the danger, as I look at some of the newer fashions in writing, is not great.   13

The next of my injunctions, which I would have imparted with   14
even less hope of success, would have concerned alcohol. Nothing
is so pleasant. Nothing is so important for giving the writer a sense
of confidence in himself. And nothing so impairs the product.
Again there are exceptions: I remember a brilliant writer at *Fortune*
for whom I was responsible who could work only with his hat
on and after consuming a bottle of Scotch. There were major crises
for him in the years immediately after World War II when Scotch
was difficult to find. But it is, quite literally, very sobering to reflect
on how many good American writers have been destroyed by this
solace—by the sauce. Scott Fitzgerald, Sinclair Lewis, Thomas
Wolfe, Ernest Hemingway, William Faulkner—the list goes on
and on. Hamish Hamilton, once my English publisher, put the
questions to James Thurber: "Jim, why is it so many of your great
writers have ruined themselves with drink?" Thurber thought long
and carefully and finally replied, "It's this way, Jamie. They wrote
those novels, which sold very well. They made a lot of money
and so they could buy whisky by the case."

Their reputation was universal. A few years before his death,   15
John Steinbeck, an appreciative but not a compulsive drinker,
went to Moscow. It was a triumphal tour, and in a letter that he
sent me about his hosts, he said: "I found I enjoyed the Soviet
hustlers pretty much. There was a kind of youthful honesty about
the illicit intentions that was not without charm." I later heard
that one night, after a particularly effusive celebration, he decided
to return to the hotel on foot. On the way he was overcome by
fatigue and the hospitality he had received and sat down on a
bench in a small park to rest. A policeman, called a militiaman
in Moscow, came along and informed John, who was now asleep,
and his companion, who spoke Russian, that the benches could
not be occupied at that hour. His companion explained, rightly,
that John was a very great American writer and that an exception
should be made. The militiaman insisted. The companion explained
again and insisted more strongly. Presently a transcendental light
came over the policeman's face. He looked at Steinbeck asleep on
the bench, inspected his condition more closely, recoiled slightly
from the fumes and said, "Oh, oh, Gemingway." Then he took
off his cap and tiptoed carefully away.

We are all desperately afraid of sounding like Carrie Nation. I   16
must take the risk. Any writer who wants to do his best against
a deadline should stick to Coca-Cola.

Next, I would have wanted to tell my students of a point strongly   17
pressed, if my memory serves, by George Bernard Shaw. He said
that as he grew older, he became less and less interested in theory,

more and more interested in information. The temptation in writing is just the reverse. Nothing is so hard to come by as a new and interesting fact. Nothing is so easy on the feet as a generalization. I now pick up magazines and leaf through them looking for articles that are rich with facts; I don't much care what they are. Evocative and deeply percipient theory I avoid. It leaves me cold unless I am the author of it myself. My advice to all young writers would be to stick to research and reporting with only a minimum of interpretation. And even more this would be my advice to all older writers, particularly to columnists. As one's feet give out, one seeks to have the mind take their place.

Reluctantly, but from a long and terrible experience, I would have urged my class to recognize the grave risks in a resort to humor. It does greatly lighten one's task. I've often wondered who made it impolite to laugh at one's own jokes, for it is one of the major enjoyments in life. And that is the point. Humor is an intensely personal, largely internal thing. What pleases some, including the source, does not please others. One laughs; another says, "Well, I certainly see nothing funny about that." And the second opinion has just as much validity as the first, maybe more. Where humor is concerned, there are no standards—no one can say what is good or bad, although you can be sure that everyone will. Only a very foolish man will use a form of language that is wholly uncertain in its effect. And that is the nature of humor. 18

There are other reasons for avoiding humor. In our society the solemn person inspires far more trust than the one who laughs. The politician allows himself one joke at the beginning of his speech. A ritual. Then he changes his expression and affects an aspect of morbid solemnity signaling that, after all, he is a totally serious man. Nothing so undermines a point as its association with a wisecrack; the very word is pejorative. 19

Also, as Art Buchwald has pointed out, we live in an age when it is hard to invent anything that is as funny as everyday life; how could one improve, for example, on the efforts of the great men of television to attribute cosmic significance to the offhand and hilarious way Bert Lance combined professed fiscal conservatism with an unparalleled personal commitment to the deficit financing of John Maynard Keynes? And because the real world is so funny, there is almost nothing you can do short of labeling a joke a joke, to keep people from taking it seriously. A number of years ago in *Harper's* I invented the theory that socialism in our time was the result of our dangerous addiction to team sports. The ethic of the team is all wrong for free enterprise. Its basic themes are 20 cooperation; team spirit; acceptance of leadership; the belief that the coach is always right. Authoritarianism is sanctified; the individualist is a poor team player, a menace. All this our vulnerable adolescents learn. I announced the formation of an organization to combat this deadly trend and to promote boxing and track instead. I called it the CAI—Crusade for Athletic Individualism. Scores wrote in to *Harper's* asking to join. Or demanding that baseball be exempted. A batter is, after all, on his own. I presented the letters to the Kennedy Library.

Finally, I would have come to a matter of much personal interest, 21 one that is intensely self-serving. It concerns the peculiar pitfalls for the writer who is dealing with presumptively difficult or technical matters. Economics is an example, and within the field of economics the subject of money, with the history of which I have been much concerned, is an especially good case. Any specialist who ventures to write on money with a view to making himself intelligible works under a grave moral hazard. He will be accused of oversimplification. The charge will be made by his fellow professionals, however obtuse or incompetent, and it will have a sympathetic hearing from the layman. That is because no layman really expects to understand about money, inflation or the International Monetary Fund. If he does, he suspects that he is being fooled. Only someone who is decently confusing can be respected.

In the case of economics there are no important propositions 22 that cannot, in fact, be stated in plain language. Qualifications and refinements are numerous and of great technical complexity. These are important for separating the good students from the dolts. But in economics the refinements rarely, if ever, modify the essential and practical point. The writer who seeks to be intelligible needs to be right; he must be challenged if his argument leads to an erroneous conclusion and especially if it leads to the wrong action. But he can safely dismiss the charge that he has made the subject too easy. The truth is not difficult.

Complexity and obscurity, on the other hand, have professional 23 value; they are the academic equivalents of apprenticeship rules in the building trades. They exclude the outsiders, keep down the competition, preserve the image of a privileged or priestly class. The man who makes things clear is a scab. He is criticized less for his clarity than for his treachery.

Additionally, and especially in the social sciences, much unclear 24 writing is based on unclear or incomplete thought. It is possible with safety to be technically obscure about something you haven't thought out. It is impossible to be wholly clear on something you don't understand; clarity exposes flaws in the thought. The person who undertakes to make difficult matters clear is infringing on the sovereign right of numerous economists, sociologists and political scientists to make bad writing the disguise for sloppy, imprecise or incomplete thought. One can understand the resulting anger. Adam Smith, John Stuart Mill and John Maynard Keynes were writers of crystalline clarity most of the time. Marx had great moments, as in *The Communist Manifesto*. Economics owes very little, if anything, to the practitioners of scholarly obscurity. However, if any of my California students had come to me from the learned professions, I would have counseled them that if they wanted to keep the confidence of their colleagues, they should do so by always being complex, obscure and even a trifle vague.

You might say that all this constitutes a meager yield for a 25 lifetime of writing. Or perhaps, as someone once said of Jack Kerouac's prose, not writing but typing.

CYNTHIA OZICK

On Excellence

In my Depression childhood, whenever I had a new dress, my 1 cousin Sarah would get suspicious. The nicer the dress was, and especially the more expensive it looked, the more suspicious she would get. Finally she would lift the hem and check the seams. This was to see if the dress had been bought or if my mother had sewed it. Sarah could always tell. My mother's sewing had elegant outsides, but there was something catch-as-catch-can about the insides. Sarah's sewing, by contrast, was as impeccably finished inside as out; not one stray thread dangled.

My uncle Jake built meticulous grandfather clocks out of rose- 2 wood; he was a perfectionist, and sent to England for the clockworks. My mother built serviceable radiator covers and a serviceable cabinet, with hinged doors, for the pantry. She built a pair of bookcases for the living room. Once, after I was grown and in a house of my own, she fixed the sewer pipe. She painted ceilings, and also landscapes; she reupholstered chairs. One summer she planted a whole yard of tall corn. She thought herself capable of doing anything, and did everything she imagined. But nothing was perfect.

First published in *Ms.* Magazine, January 1985.

There was always some clear flaw, never visible head-on. You had to look underneath where the seams were. The corn thrived, though not in rows. The stalks elbowed one another like gossips in a dense little village.

"Miss Brrrroooobaker," my mother used to mock, rolling her 3 Russian *r*s, whenever I crossed a *t* she had left uncrossed, or corrected a word she had misspelled, or became impatient with a *v* that had tangled itself up with a *w* in her speech. ("*Vvv*en-triloquist," I would say. "*Vvv*entriloquist," she would obediently repeat. And the next time it would come out "*wi*olinist.") Miss Brubaker was my high school English teacher, and my mother invoked her name as an emblem of raging finical obsession. "Miss Brrrroooobaker," my mother's voice hoots at me down the years, as I go on casting and recasting sentences in a tiny handwriting on monomaniacally uniform paper. The loops of my mother's handwriting—it was the Palmer Method—were as big as hoops, spilling generous splashy ebullience. She could pull off, at five minutes' notice, a satisfying dinner for 10 concocted out of nothing more than originality and panache. But the napkin would be folded a little off-center, and the spoon might be on the wrong side of the knife. She was an optimist who ignored trifles; for her, God was not in the details but in the intent. And all these culinary and agricultural efflorescences were extracurricular, accomplished in the crevices and niches of a 14-hour business day. When she scribbled out her family memoirs, in heaps of dog-eared notebooks, or on the backs of old bills, or on the margins of last year's calendar, I would resist typing them; in the speed of the chase she often omitted words like "the," "and," "will." The same flashing and bountiful hand fashioned and fired ceramic pots, and painted brilliant autumn views and vases of imaginary flowers and ferns, and decorated ordinary Woolworth platters with lavish enameled gardens. But bits of the painted petals would chip away.

Lavish: my mother was as lavish as nature. She woke early and 4 saturated the hours with work and inventiveness, and read late into the night. She was all profusion, abundance, fabrication. Angry at her children, she would run after us whirling the cord of the electric iron, like a lasso or a whip; but she never caught us. When, in the seventh grade, I was afraid of failing the Music Appreciation final exam because I could not tell the difference between "To a Wild Rose" and "Barcarolle," she got the idea of sending me to school with a gauze sling rigged up on my writing arm, and an explanatory note that was purest fiction. But the sling kept slipping off. My mother gave advice like mad—she boiled over with so much passion for the predicaments of strangers that they turned into permanent cronies. She told intimate stories about people I had never heard of.

Despite the gargantuan Palmer loops (or possibly because of them), I have always known that my mother's was a life of—intricately abashing word!—excellence: insofar as excellence means ripe generosity. She burgeoned, she proliferated; she was endlessly leafy and flowering. She wore red hats, and called herself a gypsy. In her girlhood she marched with the suffragettes and for Margaret Sanger[1] and called herself a Red. She made me laugh, she was so varied: like a tree on which lemons, pomegranates, and prickly pears absurdly all hang together. She had the comedy of prodigality.

My own way is a thousand times more confined. I am a pinched perfectionist, the ultimate fruition of Miss Brubaker; I attend to crabbed minutiae and am self-trammled through taking pains. I am a kind of human snail, locked in and condemned by my own nature. The ancients believed that the moist track left by the snail as it crept was the snail's own essence, depleting its body little by little; the farther the snail toiled, the smaller it became, until it finally rubbed itself out. That is how perfectionists are. Say to us Excellence, and we will show you how we use up our substance and wear ourselves away, while making scarcely any progress at all. The fact that I am an exacting perfectionist in a narrow strait only, and nowhere else, is hardly to the point, since nothing matters to me so much as a comely and muscular sentence. It is my narrow strait, this snail's road: the track of the sentence I am writing now; and when I have eked out the wet substance, ink or blood, that is its mark, I will begin the next sentence. Only in treading out sentences am I perfectionist; but then there is nothing else I know how to do, or take much interest in. I miter every pair of abutting sentences as scrupulously as Uncle Jake fitted one strip of rosewood against another. My mother's worldly and bountiful hand has escaped me. The sentence I am writing is my cabin and my shell, compact, self-sufficient. It is the burnished horizon—a merciless planet where flawlessness is the single standard, where even the inmost seams, however hidden from a laxer eye, must meet perfection. Here "excellence" is not strewn casually from a tipped cornucopia, here disorder does not account for charm, here trifles rule like tyrants.

I measure my life in sentences, and my sentences are superior to my mother's, pressed out, line by line, like the lustrous ooze on the underside of the snail, the snail's secret open seam, its wound, leaking attar. My mother was too mettlesome to feel the

1. (1883–1966) American leader in the birth control movement.

force of a comma. She scorned minutiae. She measured her life according to what poured from the horn of plenty, which was her ample, cascading, elastic, susceptible, inexact heart. My narrower heart rides between the tiny twin horns of the snail, dwindling as it goes.

And out of this thinnest thread, this ink-wet line of words, must rise a visionary fog, a mist, a smoke, forging cities, histories, sorrows, quagmires, entanglements, lives of sinners, even the life of my furnace-hearted mother: so much wilderness, waywardness, plenitude on the head of the precise and impeccable snail, between the horns.   8

JOSEPH   WOOD   KRUTCH

No Essays, Please!

Every now and then someone regrets publicly the passing of the familiar essay. Perhaps such regretters are usually in possession of a recent rejection slip; in any event there are not enough of them to impress editors. The very word "essay" has fallen into such disfavor that it is avoided with horror, and anything which is not fiction is usually called either an "article," a "story," or just "a piece." When *The Atlantic Monthly*, once the last refuge of a dying tradition, now finds it advisable to go in for such "articles" as its recent "What Night Playing Has Done to Baseball" it is obvious that not merely the genteel tradition but a whole literary form is dead.   1

I am sure that the books on how to become a writer in ten easy lessons have been stressing this fact for a long time now. If *I* were writing such a book I certainly should, and I think that I could give some very practical advice. To begin with I should say something like the following: 2

Suppose that you have drawn a subject out of your mental box and you find that it is "Fish." Now if you were living in the time of Henry Van Dyke and Thomas Bailey Aldrich,[1] your best lead would be: "Many of my friends are ardent disciples of Isaac Walton." That would have had the appropriate personal touch and the requisite not too recondite literary allusion. But today of course   3

First published in *Saturday Review*, March 10, 1951.
1. Two genial American writers of the late nineteenth century.

no live-wire editor would read any further, not because this sounds like a dull familiar essay but simply because it sounds like *a* familiar essay. But "Fish" is still a perfectly usable subject provided you remember that salable nonfiction "pieces" almost invariably fall into one of three categories: the factual, the polemic, and what we now call—though I don't know why we have to deviate into French—*reportage*.

If you decide to be factual a good beginning would be: "Four 4 million trout flies were manufactured last year by the three leading sports-supply houses." That is the sort of thing which makes almost any editor sit up and take notice. But it is no better than certain other possible beginnings. The polemic article ought to start: "Despite all the efforts of our department of wild life conservation, the number of game fish in American lakes and streams continues to decline steadily." Probably this kind of beginning to this kind of article is best of all because it sounds alarming and because nowadays (and for understandable reasons) whatever sounds alarming is generally taken to be true. However, if you want to go in for the trickier *reportage* start off with a sentence something like this: " 'Cap' Bill Hanks, a lean, silent, wryly humorous down-Easterner, probably knows more about the strange habits of the American fisherman than any man alive."

Of course, no one will ever inquire where you got your statistics 5 about the trout flies, whether the fish population really is declining, or whether "Cap" Bill Hanks really exists. In fact, one of the best and lengthiest "Profiles" *The New Yorker* ever ran turned out to be about a "character" at the Fulton Fishmarket who didn't. Whatever looks like official fact or on-the-spot reporting is taken at face value and will be widely quoted. The important thing is that the editor first and the reader afterward shall get the feeling that what he is being offered is not mere literature but the real low-down on something or other—whether that something or other is or is not anything he cares much about.

Fling your facts around, never qualify anything (qualifications 6 arouse distrust), and adopt an air of jolly omniscience. Remember that "essays" are written by introverts, "articles" by extroverts, and that the reader is going to resent anything which comes between him and that low-down which it is your principal function to supply. "Personalities," the more eccentric the better, are fine subjects for *reportage*. Manufacture or get hold of a good one and you may be able to do a "profile." But no one wants any personality to show in the magazine writer, whose business it is to be all-knowing, shrewd, and detached almost to the point of nonexistence. This means, of course, that your style should have no quality which belongs to you, only the qualities appropriate to the magazine for which you are writing. The most successful of all the magazines functioning in America today seldom print anything which is not anonymous and apparently owe a considerable part of their success to the fact that nearly everything which appears in them achieves the manner of *Life, Time,* or *Fortune,* as the case may be, but never by any chance any characteristic which would enable the most sensitive analyst of style to discover who had written it.

The ideal is obviously a kind of writing which seems to have 7 been produced not by a man but by some sort of electronic machine. Perhaps in time it will actually be produced that way, since such machines now solve differential equations and that is harder to do than to write the average magazine article. Probably if Vannevar Bush[2] were to put his mind to the problem, he could replace the whole interminable list of editors, assistant editors, and research assistants employed by the Luce publications[3] with a contraption less elaborate than that now used to calculate the trajectory of a rocket. Meanwhile the general effect of mechanical impersonality can be achieved by a system of collaboration in the course of which such personalities as the individual collaborators may have are made to cancel one another out.

This system works best when these collaborators are divided 8 into two groups called respectively "researchers" and "writers"— or, in other words, those who know something but don't write and those who don't know anything but do. This assures at the very outset that the actual writers shall have no dangerous interest in or even relation to what they write and that any individuality of approach which might tend to manifest itself in one of them will be canceled out by the others. If you then pass the end-result through the hands of one or more senior editors for further regularization, you will obviously get finally something from which every trace of what might be called handwork has disappeared. One might suppose that the criticism of the arts would be a department in which some trace of individuality would still be considered desirable, but I am reliably informed that at least at one time (and for all I know still) it was the custom to send an "editor" along with the movie critic to see every film so that this editor could tell the critic whether or not the film should be reviewed.

2. American engineer and physicist (1890–1974); he invented one of the earliest forms of the computer and directed the development of the first atomic bomb.
3. Magazines published by Henry Robinson Luce (1898–1967), among them *Time, Life, Fortune,* and *Sports Illustrated.*

This disposed of the possibility that the review might in some way reflect the critic's taste.

Obviously, few publications can afford the elaborate machinery 9 which the Luce organization has set up. However, a great many strive to achieve something of the same effect by simpler means, and they expect their contributors to cooperate by recognizing the ideal and by coming as close to the realization of it as is possible for an individual to come. The circulations achieved by these publications seem to indicate how wise from one point of view their policy is. Those which still permit or even encourage a certain amount of individuality in their writers—even those which still offer a certain amount of nonfiction which is to some extent personal and reflective as opposed to the factual and the bleakly expository—must content themselves with relatively small circulations. Moreover, since they also print a good deal of the other sort of thing they create the suspicion that they survive in spite of rather than because of their limited hospitality to the man-made as opposed to the machine-made article.

No doubt the kind of essay which *The Atlantic* and the old *Century* 10 once went in for died of anemia. It came to represent the genteel tradition at its feeblest. No one need be surprised that it did not survive. But what is significant is the fact that, whereas the genteel novel was succeeded by novels of a different sort and genteel poetry by poetry in a different manner, the familiar essay died without issue, so that what disappeared was a once important literary form for which changed times found no use. And the result is that there disappeared with it the best opportunity to consider in an effective way an area of human interest.

Because the "article" is impersonal it can deal only with subjects 11 which exist in an impersonal realm. If its subject is not ominous, usually it must be desperately trivial; and just as the best-selling books are likely to have for title either something like *The World in Crisis* or *My Grandmother Did a Strip Tease,* so the magazine articles which are not heavy are very likely to be inconsequential. I doubt that anyone was ever quite as eccentric as almost every subject of a *New Yorker* "Profile" is made to seem; but if a topic cannot be made "devastating" the next best thing is "fabulous."

Perhaps what disappeared with the familiar essay was not merely 12 a form, not merely even an attitude, but a whole subject matter. For the familar essay affords what is probably the best method of discussing those subjects which are neither obviously momentous nor merely silly. And, since no really good life is composed exclusively of problems and farce, either the reading of most people today does not actually concern itself with some of the most important aspects of their lives or those lives are impoverished to a degree which the members of any really civilized society would find it difficult to understand. Just as genuine conversation—by which I mean something distinguishable from disputation, lamentation, and joke-telling—has tended to disappear from social gatherings, so anything comparable to it has tended to disappear from the printed page. By no means all of the Most-of-My-Friends essays caught it. But the best of them caught something which nowadays hardly gets into print at all.

Somehow we have got into the habit of assuming that even the so-called "human problems" are best discussed in terms as inhuman as possible. Just how one can profitably consider dispassionately so passionate a creature as man I do not know, but that seems to be the enterprise to which we have committed ourselves. The magazines are full of articles dealing statistically with, for example, the alleged failure or success of marriage. Lawyers discuss the law, sociologists publish statistics, and psychologists discuss case histories. Those are the methods by which we deal with the behavior of animals since animals can't talk. But men can—or at least once could—communicate, and one man's "familiar essay" on love and marriage might get closer to some all-important realities than any number of "studies" could. 13

No one is, to take another example, naïve enough to suppose that all the current discussions of the welfare state are actually as "objective" as most of them pretend to be. Personal tastes, even simple self-interest, obviously influence most of them but only insofar as they introduce distortions between the lines. Everybody who writes for or against the competitive society tries to write as though he did not live in it, had had no personal experience of what living in it is like, and was dealing only with a question in which he had no personal interest. This is the way one talks about how to keep bees or raise Black Angus. It is not the way either the bees or the Black Angus would discuss the good life as it affected them, and it is a singularly unrealistic way of considering anything which would affect us. Even the objective studies would be better and more objective if their authors permitted themselves freely to express elsewhere their "familiar" reaction to conditions and prospects instead of working in these feelings disguised as logical argument or scientific deduction. 14

All the sciences which deal with man have a tendency to depersonalize him for the simple reason that they tend to disregard everything which a particular science cannot deal with. Just as medicine confessedly deals with the physical man and economics 15 confessedly deals not with Man but with the simplification officially designated as The Economic Man, so psychiatry deals with a fictitious man of whom there would be nothing more to be said if he were "normal," and one branch of psychology deals with what might be called the I.Q. man whose only significant aspect is his ability to solve puzzles.

Literature is the only thing which deals with the whole complex 16 phenomenon at once, and if all literature were to cease to exist the result would probably be that in the end whatever is not considered by one or another of the sciences would no longer be taken into account at all and would perhaps almost cease to exist. Then Man would no longer be—or at least no longer be observed to be—anything different from the mechanical sum of the Economic man, the I.Q. man, and the other partial men with whom the various partial sciences deal. Faced with that prospect, we may well look with dismay at the disappearance of any usable literary form and wonder whether or not we have now entered upon a stage during which man's lingering but still complex individuality finds itself more and more completely deprived of the opportunity not only to express itself in living but even to discover corresponding individualities revealing themselves in the spoken or the written word.

That the situation could be radically altered by the cultivation 17 of the familiar essay I am hardly prepared to maintain. Its disappearance is only a minor symptom. Or perhaps it is just a little bit more than that. At least there are a number of subjects which might profitably be discussed by fewer experts and more human beings. They might achieve a different kind of understanding of certain problems and they might lead to more humanly acceptable conclusions. "Most of my friends seem to feel that . . ."

GEORGE ORWELL

Politics and the English Language

Most people who bother with the matter at all would admit 1 that the English language is in a bad way, but it is generally assumed that we cannot by conscious action do anything about

Written in 1946.

it. Our civilization is decadent and our language—so the argument
runs—must inevitably share in the general collapse. It follows that
any struggle against the abuse of language is a sentimental archaism,
like preferring candles to electric light or hansom cabs to aeroplanes.
Underneath this lies the half-conscious belief that language is a
natural growth and not an instrument which we shape for our
own purposes.

Now, it is clear that the decline of a language must ultimately   2
have political and economic causes: it is not due simply to the
bad influence of this or that individual writer. But an effect can
become a cause, reinforcing the original cause and producing the
same effect in an intensified form, and so on indefinitely. A man
may take to drink because he feels himself to be a failure, and
then fail all the more completely because he drinks. It is rather
the same thing that is happening to the English language. It becomes
ugly and inaccurate because our thoughts are foolish, but the
slovenliness of our language makes it easier for us to have foolish
thoughts. The point is that the process is reversible. Modern English,
especially written English, is full of bad habits which spread by
imitation and which can be avoided if one is willing to take the
necessary trouble. If one gets rid of these habits one can think
more clearly, and to think clearly is a necessary first step towards
political regeneration: so that the fight against bad English is not
frivolous and is not the exclusive concern of professional writers.
I will come back to this presently, and I hope that by that time
the meaning of what I have said here will have become clearer.
Meanwhile, here are five specimens of the English language as it
is now habitually written.

These five passages have not been picked out because they are   3
especially bad—I could have quoted far worse if I had chosen—
but because they illustrate various of the mental vices from which
we now suffer. They are a little below the average, but are fairly
representative samples. I number them so that I can refer back to
them when necessary:

> "(1) I am not, indeed, sure whether it is not true to say that the
> Milton who once seemed not unlike a seventeenth-century Shelley
> had not become, out of an experience ever more bitter in each year,
> more alien [*sic*] to the founder of that Jesuit sect which nothing could
> induce him to tolerate."
>
>   Professor Harold Laski (Essay in *Freedom of Expression*).
>
> "(2) Above all, we cannot play ducks and drakes with a native
> battery of idioms which prescribes such egregious collocations of voc-
> ables as the Basic *put up with* for *tolerate* or *put at a loss* for *bewilder*."
>
>   Professor Lancelot Hogben (*Interglossa*).

"(3) On the one side we have the free personality: by definition it is not neurotic, for it has neither conflict nor dream. Its desires, such as they are, are transparent, for they are just what institutional approval keeps in the forefront of consciousness; another institutional pattern would alter their number and intensity; there is little in them that is natural, irreducible, or culturally dangerous. But *on the other side,* the social bond itself is nothing but the mutual reflection of these self-secure integrities. Recall the definition of love. Is not this the very picture of a small academic? Where is there a place in this hall of mirrors for either personality or fraternity?"

Essay on psychology in *Politics* (New York).

"(4) All the 'best people' from the gentlemen's clubs, and all the frantic fascist captains, united in common hatred of Socialism and bestial horror of the rising tide of the mass revolutionary movement, have turned to acts of provocation, to foul incendiarism, to medieval legends of poisoned wells, to legalize their own destruction of proletarian organizations, and rouse the agitated petty-bourgeoisie to chauvinistic fervour on behalf of the fight against the revolutionary way out of the crisis."

Communist pamphlet.

"(5) If a new spirit *is* to be infused into this old country, there is one thorny and contentious reform which must be tackled, and that is the humanization and galvanization of the B.B.C. Timidity here will bespeak cancer and atrophy of the soul. The heart of Britain may be sound and of strong beat, for instance, but the British lion's roar at present is like that of Bottom in Shakespeare's *Midsummer Night's Dream*—as gentle as any sucking dove. A virile new Britain cannot continue indefinitely to be traduced in the eyes or rather ears, of the world by the effete languors of Langham Place, brazenly masquerading as 'standard English'. When the Voice of Britain is heard at nine o'clock, better far and infinitely less ludicrous to hear aitches honestly dropped than the present priggish, inflated, inhibited, school-ma'amish arch braying of blameless bashful mewing maidens!"

Letter in *Tribune*.

Each of these passages has faults of its own, but, quite apart 4 from avoidable ugliness, two qualities are common to all of them. The first is staleness of imagery: the other is lack of precision. The writer either has a meaning and cannot express it, or he inadvertently says something else, or he is almost indifferent as to whether his words mean anything or not. This mixture of vagueness and sheer incompetence is the most marked characteristic of modern English prose, and especially of any kind of political writing. As soon as certain topics are raised, the concrete melts into the abstract and no one seems able to think of turns of speech that are not hackneyed: prose consists less and less of *words* chosen for the sake of their meaning, and more and more of *phrases* tacked together like the sections of a prefabricated hen-house. I list below, with notes and examples, various of the tricks by means of which the work of prose-construction is habitually dodged:

DYING METAPHORS

A newly invented metaphor assists thought by evoking a visual [5] image, while on the other hand a metaphor which is technically "dead" (e.g. *iron resolution*) has in effect reverted to being an ordinary word and can generally be used without loss of vividness. But in between these two classes there is a huge dump of worn-out metaphors which have lost all evocative power and are merely used because they save people the trouble of inventing phrases for themselves. Examples are: *Ring the changes on, take up the cudgels for, toe the line, ride roughshod over, stand shoulder to shoulder with, play into the hands of, no axe to grind, grist to the mill, fishing in troubled waters, on the order of the day, Achilles' heel, swan song, hotbed.* Many of these are used without knowledge of their meaning (what is a "rift", for instance?), and incompatible metaphors are frequently mixed, a sure sign that the writer is not interested in what he is saying. Some metaphors now current have been twisted out of their original meaning without those who use them even being aware of the fact. For example, *toe the line* is sometimes written *tow the line*. Another example is *the hammer and the anvil*, now always used with the implication that the anvil gets the worst of it. In real life it is always the anvil that breaks the hammer, never the other way about: a writer who stopped to think what he was saying would be aware of this, and would avoid perverting the original phrase.

OPERATORS OR VERBAL FALSE LIMBS

These save the trouble of picking out appropriate verbs and [6] nouns, and at the same time pad each sentence with extra syllables which give it an appearance of symmetry. Characteristic phrases are: *render inoperative, militate against, make contact with, be subjected to, give rise to, give grounds for, have the effect of, play a leading part (role) in, make itself felt, take effect, exhibit a tendency to, serve the purpose of, etc., etc.* The keynote is the elimination of simple verbs. Instead of being a single word, such as *break, stop, spoil, mend, kill,* a verb becomes a *phrase,* made up of a noun or adjective tacked on to some general-purposes verb such as *prove, serve, form, play, render.* In addition, the passive voice is wherever possible used in preference to the active, and noun constructions are used instead of gerunds (*by examination of* instead of *by examining*).

The range of verbs is further cut down by means of the *-ize* and *de-* formation, and the banal statements are given an appearance of profundity by means of the *not un-* formation. Simple conjunctions and prepositions are replaced by such phrases as *with respect to, having regard to, the fact that, by dint of, in view of, in the interests of, on the hypothesis that;* and the ends of sentences are saved from anticlimax by such resounding commonplaces as *greatly to be desired, cannot be left out of account, a development to be expected in the near future, deserving of serious consideration, brought to a satisfactory conclusion,* and so on and so forth.

PRETENTIOUS DICTION

Words like *phenomenon, element, individual* (as noun), *objective, categorical, effective, virtual, basic, primary, promote, constitute, exhibit, exploit, utilize, eliminate, liquidate,* are used to dress up simple statements and give an air of scientific impartiality to biased judgments. Adjectives like *epoch-making, epic, historic, unforgettable, triumphant, age-old, inevitable, inexorable, veritable,* are used to dignify the sordid processes of international politics, while writing that aims at glorifying war usually takes on an archaic colour, its characteristic words being: *realm, throne, chariot, mailed fist, trident, sword, shield, buckler, banner, jackboot, clarion.* Foreign words and expressions such as *cul de sac, ancien régime, deus ex machina, mutatis mutandis, status quo, gleichschaltung, weltanschauung,* are used to give an air of culture and elegance. Except for the useful abbreviations *i.e., e.g.,* and *etc.,* there is no real need for any of the hundreds of foreign phrases now current in English. Bad writers, and especially scientific, political and sociological writers, are nearly always haunted by the notion that Latin or Greek words are grander than Saxon ones, and unnecessary words like *expedite, ameliorate, predict, extraneous, deracinated, clandestine, subaqueous* and hundreds of others constantly gain ground from their Anglo-Saxon opposite numbers.[1] The jargon peculiar to Marxist writing (*hyena, hangman, cannibal, petty bourgeois, these gentry, lacquey, flunkey, mad dog, White Guard,* etc.) consists largely of words and phrases translated from Russian, German or French; but the normal way of coining a new word is to use a Latin or Greek root with the appropriate affix and, were necessary, the *-ize* formation. It is often easier to make up

---

1. An interesting illustration of this is the way in which the English flower names which were in use till very recently are being ousted by Greek ones, *snapdragon* becoming *antirrhinum, forget-me-not* becoming *myosotis,* etc. It is hard to see any practical reason for this change of fashion: it is probably due to an instinctive turning-away from the more homely word and a vague feeling that the Greek word is scientific. [author's note]

words of this kind (*deregionalize, impermissible, extramarital, non-fragmentatory* and so forth) than to think up the English words that will cover one's meaning. The result, in general, is an increase in slovenliness and vagueness.

MEANINGLESS WORDS

In certain kinds of writing, particularly in art criticism and literary   8
criticism, it is normal to come across long passages which are almost completely lacking in meaning.[2] Words like *romantic, plastic, values, human, dead, sentimental, natural, vitality,* as used in art criticism, are strictly meaningless in the sense that they not only do not point to any discoverable object, but are hardly ever expected to do so by the reader. When one critic writes, "The outstanding feature of Mr. X's work is its living quality", while another writes, "The immediately striking thing about Mr. X's work is its peculiar deadness", the reader accepts this as a simple difference of opinion. If words like *black* and *white* were involved, instead of the jargon words *dead* and *living*, he would see at once that language was being used in an improper way. Many political words are similarly abused. The word *Fascism* has now no meaning except in so far as it signifies "something not desirable". The words *democracy, socialism, freedom, patriotic, realistic, justice,* have each of them several different meanings which cannot be reconciled with one another. In the case of a word like *democracy,* not only is there no agreed definition, but the attempt to make one is resisted from all sides. It is almost universally felt that when we call a country democratic we are praising it: consequently the defenders of every kind of régime claim that it is a democracy, and fear that they might have to stop using the word if it were tied down to any one meaning. Words of this kind are often used in a consciously dishonest way. That is, the person who uses them has his own private definition, but allows his hearer to think he means something quite different. Statements like *Marshal Pétain was a true patriot, The Soviet Press is the freest in the world, The Catholic Church is opposed to persecution,* are almost always made with intent to deceive. Other words used in variable meanings, in most cases more or less dishonestly, are: *class, totalitarian, science, progressive, reactionary, bourgeois, equality.*

Now that I have made this catalogue of swindles and perversions,   9

---

2. Example: "Comfort's catholicity of perception and image, strangely Whitmanesque in range, almost the exact opposite in aesthetic compulsion, continues to evoke that trembling atmospheric accumulative hinting at a cruel, an inexorably serene timelessness . . . Wrey Gardiner scores by aiming at simple bull's-eyes with precision. Only they are not so simple, and through this contented sadness runs more than the surface bitter-sweet of resignation." (*Poetry Quarterly.*) [author's note]

let me give another example of the kind of writing that they lead to. This time it must of its nature be an imaginary one. I am going to translate a passage of good English into modern English of the worst sort. Here is a well-known verse from *Ecclesiastes*:

> "I returned and saw under the sun, that the race is not to the swift, nor the battle to the strong, neither yet bread to the wise, nor yet riches to men of understanding, nor yet favour to men of skill; but time and chance happeneth to them all."

Here it is in modern English: 10

> "Objective consideration of contemporary phenomena compels the conclusion that success or failure in competitive activities exhibits no tendency to be commensurate with innate capacity, but that a considerable element of the unpredictable must invariably be taken into account."

This is a parody, but not a very gross one. Exhibit (3), above, 11 for instance, contains several patches of the same kind of English. It will be seen that I have not made a full translation. The beginning and ending of the sentence follow the original meaning fairly closely, but in the middle the concrete illustrations—race, battle, bread—dissolve into the vague phrase "success or failure in competitive activities". This had to be so, because no modern writer of the kind I am discussing—no one capable of using phrases like "objective consideration of contemporary phenomena"—would ever tabulate his thoughts in that precise and detailed way. The whole tendency of modern prose is away from concreteness. Now analyse these two sentences a little more closely. The first contains forty-nine words but only sixty syllables, and all its words are those of everyday life. The second contains thirty-eight words of ninety syllables: eighteen of its words are from Latin roots, and one from Greek. The first sentence contains six vivid images, and only one phrase ("time and chance") that could be called vague. The second contains not a single fresh, arresting phrase, and in spite of its ninety syllables it gives only a shortened version of the meaning contained in the first. Yet without a doubt it is the second kind of sentence that is gaining ground in modern English. I do not want to exaggerate. This kind of writing is not yet universal, and outcrops of simplicity will occur here and there in the worst-written page. Still, if you or I were told to write a few lines on the uncertainty of human fortunes, we should probably come much nearer to my imaginary sentence than to the one from *Ecclesiastes*.

As I have tried to show, modern writing at its worst does not 12 consist in picking out words for the sake of their meaning and inventing images in order to make the meaning clearer. It consists in gumming together long strips of words which have already been set in order by someone else, and making the results presentable by sheer humbug. The attraction of this way of writing is that it is easy. It is easier—even quicker, once you have the habit—to say *In my opinion it is a not unjustifiable assumption that* than to say *I think*. If you use ready-made phrases, you not only don't have to hunt about for words; you also don't have to bother with the rhythms of your sentences, since these phrases are generally so arranged as to be more or less euphonious. When you are composing in a hurry—when you are dictating to a stenographer, for instance, or making a public speech—it is natural to fall into a pretentious, Latinized style. Tags like *a consideration which we should do well to bear in mind* or *a conclusion to which all of us would readily assent* will save many a sentence from coming down with a bump. By using stale metaphors, similes and idioms, you save much mental effort, at the cost of leaving your meaning vague, not only for your reader but for yourself. This is the significance of mixed metaphors. The sole aim of a metaphor is to call up a visual image. When these images clash—as in *The Fascist octopus has sung its swan song, the jackboot is thrown into the melting pot*—it can be taken as certain that the writer is not seeing a mental image of the objects he is naming; in other words he is not really thinking. Look again at the examples I gave at the beginning of this essay. Professor Laski (1) uses five negatives in fifty-three words. One of these is superfluous, making nonsense of the whole passage, and in addition there is the slip *alien* for akin, making further nonsense, and several avoidable pieces of clumsiness which increase the general vagueness. Professor Hogben (2) plays ducks and drakes with a battery which is able to write prescriptions, and, while disapproving of the everyday phrase *put up with*, is unwilling to look *egregious* up in the dictionary and see what it means. (3), if one takes an uncharitable attitude towards it, is simply meaningless: probably one could work out its intended meaning by reading the whole of the article in which it occurs. In (4), the writer knows more or less what he wants to say, but an accumulation of stale phrases chokes him like tea leaves blocking a sink. In (5), words and meaning have almost parted company. People who write in this manner usually have a general emotional meaning—they dislike one thing and want to express solidarity with another—but they are not interested in the detail of what they are saying. A scrupulous writer, in every sentence that he writes, will ask himself at least four questions, thus: What am I trying to say? What words will express it? What image or idiom will make it clearer? Is this image fresh enough to have an effect? And he will probably ask himself two more: Could I put it more shortly? Have I said anything that is avoidably ugly? But you are not obliged to go to all this trouble: You can shirk it by simply throwing your mind open and letting the ready-made phrases come crowding in. They will construct your sentences for you—even think your thoughts for you, to a certain extent—and at need they will perform the important service of partially concealing your meaning even from yourself. It is at this point that the special connection between politics and the debasement of language becomes clear.

In our time it is broadly true that political writing is bad writing.   13 Where it is not true, it will generally be found that the writer is some kind of rebel, expressing his private opinions and not a "party line". Orthodoxy, of whatever colour, seems to demand a lifeless, imitative style. The political dialects to be found in pamphlets, leading articles, manifestos, White Papers and the speeches of under-secretaries do, of course, vary from party to party, but they are all alike in that one almost never finds in them a fresh, vivid, home-made turn of speech. When one watches some tired hack on the platform mechanically repeating the familiar phrases—*bestial atrocities, iron heel, bloodstained tyranny, free peoples of the world, stand shoulder to shoulder*—one often has a curious feeling that one is not watching a live human being but some kind of dummy: a feeling which suddenly becomes stronger at moments when the light catches the speaker's spectacles and turns them into blank discs which seem to have no eyes behind them. And this is not altogether fanciful. A speaker who uses that kind of phraseology has gone some distance towards turning himself into a machine. The appropriate noises are coming out of his larynx, but his brain is not involved as it would be if he were choosing his words for himself. If the speech he is making is one that he is accustomed to make over and over again, he may be almost unconscious of what he is saying, as one is when one utters the responses in church. And this reduced state of consciousness, if not indispensable, is at any rate favourable to political conformity.

In our time, political speech and writing are largely the defence   14 of the indefensible. Things like the continuance of British rule in India, the Russian purges and deportations, the dropping of the atom bombs on Japan, can indeed be defended, but only by arguments which are too brutal for most people to face, and which do not square with the professed aims of political parties. Thus political language has to consist largely of euphemism, question-begging and sheer cloudy vagueness. Defenceless villages are bombarded from the air, the inhabitants driven out into the countryside, the cattle machine-gunned, the huts set on fire with incendiary bullets: this is called *pacification*. Millions of peasants are robbed of their farms and sent trudging along the roads with no more than they can carry: this is called *transfer of population* or *rectification of frontiers*. People are imprisoned for years without trial, or shot in the back of the neck or sent to die of scurvy in Arctic lumber camps: this is called *elimination of unreliable elements*. Such phraseology is needed if one wants to name things without calling up mental pictures of them. Consider for instance some comfortable English professor defending Russian totalitarianism. He cannot say outright, "I believe in killing off your opponents when you can get good results by doing so". Probably, therefore, he will say something like this:

"While freely conceding that the Soviet régime exhibits certain   15
features which the humanitarian may be inclined to deplore, we must, I think, agree that a certain curtailment of the right to political opposition is an unavoidable concomitant of transitional periods, and that the rigours which the Russian people have been called upon to undergo have been amply justified in the sphere of concrete achievement."

The inflated style is itself a kind of euphemism. A mass of Latin   16
words falls upon the facts like soft snow, blurring the outlines and covering up all the details. The great enemy of clear language is insincerity. When there is a gap between one's real and one's declared aims, one turns as it were instinctively to long words and exhausted idioms, like a cuttlefish squirting out ink. In our age there is no such thing as "keeping out of politics". All issues are political issues, and politics itself is a mass of lies, evasions, folly, hatred and schizophrenia. When the general atmosphere is bad, language must suffer. I should expect to find—this is a guess which I have not sufficient knowledge to verify—that the German, Russian and Italian languages have all deteriorated in the last ten or fifteen years, as a result of dictatorship.

But if thought corrupts language, language can also corrupt   17
thought. A bad usage can spread by tradition and imitation, even among people who should and do know better. The debased language that I have been discussing is in some ways very convenient. Phrases like *a not unjustifiable assumption, leaves much to be desired, would serve no good purpose, a consideration which we should do well to bear in mind,* are a continuous temptation, a packet of aspirins always at one's elbow. Look back through this essay, and for certain you will find that I have again and again committed the very faults I am protesting against. By this morning's post I have received a pamphlet dealing with conditions in Germany. The

author tells me that he "felt impelled" to write it. I open it at random, and here is almost the first sentence that I see: "(The Allies) have an opportunity not only of achieving a radical trans-formation of Germany's social and political structure in such a way as to avoid a nationalistic reaction in Germany itself, but at the same time of laying the foundations of a co-operative and unified Europe." You see, he "feels impelled" to write—feels, presumably, that he has something new to say—and yet his words, like cavalry horses answering the bugle, group themselves auto-matically into the familiar dreary pattern. This invasion of one's mind by ready-made phrases (*lay the foundations, achieve a radical transformation*) can only be prevented if one is constantly on guard against them, and every such phrase anaesthetizes a portion of one's brain.

I said earlier that the decadence of our language is probably 18 curable. Those who deny this would argue, if they produced an argument at all, that language merely reflects existing social con-ditions, and that we cannot influence its development by any direct tinkering with words and constructions. So far as the general tone or spirit of a language goes, this may be true, but it is not true in detail. Silly words and expressions have often disappeared, not through any evolutionary process but owing to the conscious action of a minority. Two recent examples were *explore every avenue* and *leave no stone unturned*, which were killed by the jeers of a few journalists. There is a long list of flyblown metaphors which could similarly be got rid of if enough people would interest themselves in the job; and it should also be possible to laugh the *not un-*formation out of existence,[3] to reduce the amount of Latin and Greek in the average sentence, to drive out foreign phrases and strayed scientific words, and, in general, to make pretentiousness unfashionable. But all these are minor points. The defence of the English language implies more than this, and perhaps it is best to start by saying what it does *not* imply.

To begin with it has nothing to do with archaism, with the 19 salvaging of obsolete words and turns of speech, or with the setting up of a "standard English" which must never be departed from. On the contrary, it is especially concerned with the scrapping of every word or idiom which has outworn its usefulness. It has nothing to do with correct grammar and syntax, which are of no importance so long as one makes one's meaning clear, or with the avoidance of Americanisms, or with having what is called a

3. One can cure oneself of the *not un-* formation by memorizing this sentence: *A not unblack dog was chasing a not unsmall rabbit across a not ungreen field.* [author's note]

"good prose style". On the other hand it is not concerned with
fake simplicity and the attempt to make written English colloquial.
Nor does it even imply in every case preferring the Saxon word
to the Latin one, though it does imply using the fewest and shortest
words that will cover one's meaning. What is above all needed is
to let the meaning choose the word, and not the other way about.
In prose, the worst thing one can do with words is to surrender
to them. When you think of a concrete object, you think wordlessly,
and then, if you want to describe the thing you have been visualizing
you probably hunt about till you find the exact words that seem
to fit. When you think of something abstract you are more inclined
to use words from the start, and unless you make a conscious
effort to prevent it, the existing dialect will come rushing in and
do the job for you, at the expense of blurring or even changing
your meaning. Probably it is better to put off using words as long
as possible and get one's meaning as clear as one can through
pictures or sensations. Afterwards one can choose—not simply
accept—the phrases that will best cover the meaning, and then
switch round and decide what impression one's words are likely
to make on another person. This last effort of the mind cuts out
all stale or mixed images, all prefabricated phrases, needless rep-
etitions, and humbug and vagueness generally. But one can often
be in doubt about the effect of a word or a phrase, and one needs
rules that one can rely on when instinct fails. I think the following
rules will cover most cases:

(i) Never use a metaphor, simile or other figure of speech which
you are used to seeing in print.

(ii) Never use a long word where a short one will do.

(iii) If it is possible to cut a word out, always cut it out.

(iv) Never use the passive where you can use the active.

(v) Never use a foreign phrase, a scientific word or a jargon word
if you can think of an everyday English equivalent.

(vi) Break any of these rules sooner than say anything outright
barbarous.

These rules sound elementary, and so they are, but they demand
a deep change of attitude in anyone who has grown used to writing
in the style now fashionable. One could keep all of them and still
write bad English, but one could not write the kind of stuff that
I quoted in those five specimens at the beginning of this article.

I have not here been considering the literary use of language,   20
but merely language as an instrument for expressing and not for
concealing or preventing thought. Stuart Chase and others have
come near to claiming that all abstract words are meaningless,
and have used this as a pretext for advocating a kind of political

quietism. Since you don't know what Fascism is, how can you struggle against Fascism? One need not swallow such absurdities as this, but one ought to recognize that the present political chaos is connected with the decay of language, and that one can probably bring about some improvement by starting at the verbal end. If you simplify your English, you are freed from the worst follies of orthodoxy. You cannot speak any of the necessary dialects, and when you make a stupid remark its stupidity will be obvious, even to yourself. Political language—and with variations this is true of all political parties, from Conservatives to Anarchists—is designed to make lies sound truthful and murder respectable, and to give an appearance of solidity to pure wind. One cannot change this all in a moment, but one can at least change one's own habits, and from time to time one can even, if one jeers loudly enough, send some worn-out and useless phrase—some *jackboot, Achilles' heel, hotbed, melting pot, acid test, veritable inferno* or other lump of verbal refuse—into the dustbin where it belongs.

Thinking About Writing

Shoptalk, customarily forbidden at parties as too boring, can in fact be the most fascinating talk of all. Ask an architect what she is working on, and she may flatten out her napkin and begin to sketch the facade of a monastic chapterhouse. The round arch of the alcove, she says, looks like the entrance to a sheltering cave, and the benches inside it invite the footsore passerby to rest. At the same time, the alcove is a barrier between the actual door and the world, a reminder that on entering you cross the threshold into a place set apart. Nine napkins later, you have some notion of how extraordinary an architect's perception of space can be. Or ask a geologist what all these rumors about plate tectonics amount to, and you end up, half an hour later, with a vision of the earth's apparently solid surface divided into slippery bars of soap. The bedrock beneath you, you learn, slid in from Peru some millenia ago.

The essays in this section are all writerly shoptalk, and since our writers are talking about their vocation, they have sharp and sometimes controversial opinions. The standard advice in books of rhetoric, for instance, is that a writer should form a mental picture of the audience, discover its prejudices and its areas of knowledge and ignorance, and shape the essay accordingly. But E. B. White insists that the reader be treated as an equal partner rather than as a client or target: ". . . a writer who questions the capacity of the person at the other end of the wire is not a writer at all, merely a schemer." Richard Rodriquez has a picture of his audience when he writes:

> I write today for a reader who exists in my mind only phantasma-gorically. Someone with a face erased; someone of no particular race or sex or age or weather. A gray presence. Unknown, unfamiliar. All that I know about him is that he has had a long education and that his society, like mine, is often public (*un gringo*).

But this is clearly not the "analyzed" audience of many contemporary rhetoric books.

Like all artists and craftsmen, writers take a proprietary interest in their medium and are irritated when they see it spoiled. Thus George Orwell, "In Politics and the English Language," complains because the language, which should be "an instrument which we shape for our own purposes" is becoming inflexible: ". . . prose consists less and less of *words* chosen for their meaning, and more and more of *phrases* tacked together like the sections of a prefabricated hen house." Joseph Wood Krutch, one of the most successful informal essayists of the twentieth century, defends the essay with wit and style, but we can hear the molars grinding beneath the well-controlled face when he writes his parodies of contemporary "articles." Jessica Mitford's exposé of the Famous Writers School is especially funny because she knows the real difficulties of a writing career. John Kenneth Galbraith keeps his advice on writing quite light-hearted until he gets close to home and has to deal with the willful obscurity of many academic economists: "The man who makes things clear is a scab. He is criticized less for his clarity than his treachery."

Most interesting, perhaps, are the comments the writers make about themselves as writers, about their purposes and standards. Garrison Keillor's essay tells us how long he pursued what for him was a false scent, the trail of "the big Mazumbos of American Literature," and how he came to realize that what he needed to do was to make "three pages sharp and funny." Cynthia Ozick's goal is always the "comely and muscular sentence," and her attention is microscopic to a degree that she herself finds alarming: "I attend to crabbed minutiae and am self-trammeled through taking pains." David Bradley's standards are quite different. He looks, above all, for an honest report from the interior, and he knows that honesty is painful:

> When I ask myself, as all writers do, whether to write something this way or that way, whether to keep this bit or throw it away, I ask myself with all the practical, technical, editorial questions. Does it cost? Is it possible that someone reading might discover something about me that I would rather not have him know?

Patricia Hampl and Joan Didion, too, emphasize the element of disclosure in writing, but for them the issue is self-discovery. "Memoir must be written," Hampl tells us, "because each of us must have a created version of the past. . . . If we refuse to do the work of creating this past, someone else will do it for us." Didion's writing is like psychological detective work. She begins with "images that shimmer around the edges." She can't know the meaning of the images until she begins to write about them.

Didion's comments may sound like mystical claptrap to some readers, but what she says is echoed at some point by most of the writers in this section. Diverse as the writers collected here are, they all remind us that writing is not typing, that the mind is actively engaged by it—no holds barred. As Richard Rodriguez says, writing is not the act of recording knowledge, but "the exciting experience of learning itself." You think, at the top of paragraph one, that you are on solid ground. By paragraph three, you feel the bedrock shifting beneath you.

QUESTIONS

1. How consistent are the comments writers make in this section with the advice given in a college composition textbook?

2. When you write, how often do you think about your audience? How concrete is your picture of your reader or readers?

3. E. B. White, Richard Rodriguez, Cynthia Ozick, George Orwell, Joan Didion, Patricia Hampl, and Garrison Keillor all have selections placed in other sections of *The Dolphin Reader*. Examine the work of one of these writers. Does the writer's actual product match his or her professed goal?

4. David Bradley's aesthetic standard of "expensiveness" seems more obviously appropriate to a novelist or autobiographer than to writers on more public topics. Can it be applied to a political journalist like George Orwell, or a philosophical writer like C. S. Lewis, or an economist like John Kenneth Galbraith? Does "expensiveness" mean the same thing for them?

5. Have you, like Keillor, spent some time following a false scent as a writer? What sent you down the wrong trail, and how have your recovered? Have you fully recovered?

6. If you were, like Galbraith, suddenly made a professor of rhetoric—or a teacher of freshman composition—what practical insights about writing would you have to impart?

LIBERAL
KNOWLEDGE

JOHN HENRY NEWMAN

Enlargement of Mind

I suppose the *primâ-facie* view which the public at large would take of a University, considering it as a place of Education, is nothing more or less than a place for acquiring a great deal of knowledge on a great many subjects. Memory is one of the first developed of mental faculties; a boy's business when he goes to school is to learn, that is, to store up things in his memory. For some years his intellect is little more than an instrument for taking in facts, or a receptacle for storing them; he welcomes them as fast as they come to him; he lives on what is without; he has his eyes ever about him; he has a lively susceptibility of impressions; he imbibes information of every kind; and little does he make his own in a true sense of the word, living rather upon his neighbors all around him. He has opinions, religious, political, and literary, and, for a boy, is very positive in them and sure about them; but he gets them from his schoolfellows, or his masters, or his parents, as the case may be. Such as he is in his other relations, such also is he in his school exercises; his mind is observant, sharp, ready, retentive; he is almost passive in the acquisition of knowledge. I say this in no disparagement of the idea of a clever boy. Geography, chronology, history, language, natural history, he heaps up the matter of these studies as treasures for a future day. It is the seven years of plenty with him; he gathers in by handfuls, like the Egyptians, without counting; and though, as time goes on, there is exercise for his argumentative powers in the Elements of Mathematics, and for his taste in the Poets and Orators, still, while at school, or at least, till quite the last years of his time, he acquires, and little more; and when he is leaving for the University, he is mainly the creature of foreign influences and circumstances, and made up of accidents, homogeneous or not, as the case may be. Moreover, the moral habits, which are a boy's praise, encourage and assist this result; that is, diligence, assiduity, regularity, despatch, persevering application; for these are the direct conditions of ac-quisition, and naturally lead to it. Acquirements, again, are

Excerpted from *The Idea of a University* (1873). This essay was originally part of a series of nine lectures on university education delivered to the Catholics of Dublin in 1852.

emphatically producible, and at a moment; they are a something to show, both for master and scholar; an audience, even though ignorant themselves of the subjects of an examination, can comprehend when questions are answered and when they are not. Here again is a reason why mental culture is in the minds of men identified with the acquisition of knowledge.

The same notion possesses the public mind, when it passes on 2 from the thought of a school to that of a University: and with the best of reasons so far as this, that there is no true culture without acquirements, and that philosophy presupposes knowledge. It requires a great deal of reading, or a wide range of information, to warrant us in putting forth our opinions on any serious subject; and without such learning the most original mind may be able indeed to dazzle, to amuse, to refute, to perplex, but not to come to any useful result or any trustworthy conclusion. There are indeed persons who profess a different view of the matter, and even act upon it. Every now and then you will find a person of vigorous or fertile mind, who relies upon his own resources, despises all former authors, and gives the world, with the utmost fearlessness, his views upon religion, or history, or any other popular subject. And his works may sell for a while; he may get a name in his day; but this will be all. His readers are sure to find in the long run that his doctrines are mere theories, and not the expression of facts, that they are chaff instead of bread, and then his popularity drops as suddenly as it rose.

Knowledge then is the indispensable condition of expansion of 3 mind, and the instrument of attaining to it; this cannot be denied; it is ever to be insisted on; I begin with it as a first principle; however, the very truth of it carries men too far, and confirms to them the notion that it is the whole of the matter. A narrow mind is thought to be that which contains little knowledge; and an enlarged mind, that which holds a great deal; and what seems to put the matter beyond dispute is, the fact of the great number of studies which are pursued in a University, by its very profession. Lectures are given on every kind of subject; examinations are held; prizes awarded. There are moral, metaphysical, physical Professors; Professors of languages, of history, of mathematics, of experimental science. Lists of questions are published, wonderful for their range and depth, variety and difficulty; treatises are written, which carry upon their very face the evidence of extensive reading or multifarious information; what then is wanting for mental culture to a person of large reading and scientific attainments? what is grasp of mind but acquirement? where shall philosophical repose be found, but in the consciousness and enjoyment of large intellectual possessions?

And yet this notion is, I conceive, a mistake, and my present 4
business is to show that it is one, and that the end of a Liberal
Education is not mere knowledge, or knowledge considered in its
matter; and I shall best attain my object, by actually setting down
some cases, which will be generally granted to be instances of the
process of enlightenment or enlargement of mind, and others which
are not, and thus, by the comparison, you will be able to judge
for yourselves, Gentlemen, whether Knowledge, that is, acquirement,
is after all the real principle of the enlargement, or whether that
principle is not rather something beyond it.

For instance, let a person, whose experience has hitherto been 5
confined to the more calm and unpretending scenery of these
islands, . . . go for the first time into parts where physical nature
puts on her wilder and more awful forms, whether at home or
abroad, as into mountainous districts; or let one, who has ever
lived in a quiet village, go for the first time to a great metropolis,—
then I suppose he will have a sensation which perhaps he never
had before. He has a feeling not in addition or increase of former
feelings, but of something different in its nature. He will perhaps
be borne forward, and find for a time that he has lost his bearings.
He has made a certain progress, and he has a consciousness of
mental enlargement; he does not stand where he did, he has a
new centre, and a range of thoughts to which he was before a
stranger.

Again, the view of the heavens which the telescope opens upon 6
us, if allowed to fill and possess the mind, may almost whirl it
round and make it dizzy. It brings in a flood of ideas, and is rightly
called an intellectual enlargement, whatever is meant by the term.

And so again, the sight of beasts of prey and other foreign 7
animals, their strangeness, the originality (if I may use the term)
of their forms and gestures and habits and their variety and independence of each other, throw us out of ourselves into another
creation, and as if under another Creator, if I may so express the
temptation which may come on the mind. We seem to have new
faculties, or a new exercise for our faculties, by this addition to
our knowledge; like a prisoner, who, having been accustomed to
wear manacles or fetters, suddenly finds his arms and legs free.

Hence Physical Science generally, in all its departments, as bringing 8
before us the exuberant riches and resources, yet the orderly course
of the Universe, elevates and excites the student, and at first, I
may say, almost takes away his breath, while in time it exercises
a tranquilizing influence upon him.

Again, the study of history is said to enlarge and enlighten the 9
mind, and why? because, as I conceive, it gives it a power of

judging of passing events, and of all events, and a conscious superiority over them, which before it did not possess.

And in like manner, what is called seeing the world, entering   10
into active life, going into society, travelling, gaining acquaintance
with the various classes of the community, coming into contact
with the principles and modes of thought of various parties, interests,
and races, their views, arms, habits and manners, their religious
creeds and forms of worship,—gaining experience how various
yet how alike men are, how low-minded, how bad, how opposed,
yet how confident in their opinions; all this exerts a perceptible
influence upon the mind, which it is impossible to mistake, be it
good or be it bad, and is popularly called its enlargement.

And then again, the first time the mind comes across the arguments   11
and speculations of unbelievers, and feels what a novel light they
cast upon what he has hitherto accounted sacred; and still more,
if it gives into them and embraces them, and throws off as so
much prejudice what it has hitherto held, and, as if waking from
a dream, begins to realize to its imagination that there is now no
such thing as law and the transgression of law, that sin is a phantom,
and punishment a bugbear, that it is free to sin, free to enjoy the
world and the flesh; and still further, when it does enjoy them,
and reflects that it may think and hold just what it will, that "the
world is all before it where to choose,"[1] and what system to build
up as its own private persuasion; when this torrent of wilfull
thoughts rushes over and inundates it, who will deny that the
fruit of the tree of knowledge, or what the mind takes for knowledge,
has made it one of the gods, with a sense of expansion and
elevation,—an intoxication in reality, still, so far as the subjective
state of the mind goes, an illumination? Hence the fanaticism of
individuals or nations, who suddenly cast off their Maker. Their
eyes are opened; and, like the judgment-stricken king in the Tragedy,[2] they see two suns, and a magic universe, out of which they
look back upon their former state of faith and innocence with a

---

1. Milton's *Paradise Lost* ends with a picture of Adam and Eve leaving the Garden
of Eden after the Fall:

> *Some natural tears they drop'd, but wip'd them soon;*
> *The world was all before them, where to choose*
> *Thir place of rest. . . .*

2. In Euripides' *Bacchae*, King Pentheus of Thebes is the voice of reason and opponent
of the new god Dionysus. When he actually observes the Dionysian rites, he is
forced to admit that frenzy, passion, and sexual abandon are as powerful as reason.

sort of contempt and indignation, as if they were then but fools, and the dupes of imposture.

On the other hand, Religion has its own enlargement, and an enlargement, not of tumult, but of peace. It is often remarked of uneducated persons, who have hitherto thought little of the unseen world, that, on their turning to God, looking into themselves, regulating their hearts, reforming their conduct, and meditating on death and judgment, heaven and hell, they seem to become, in point of intellect, different beings from what they were. Before, they took things as they came, and thought no more of one thing than another. But now every event has a meaning; they have their own estimate of whatever happens to them; they are mindful of times and seasons, and compare the present with the past; and the world, no longer dull, monotonous, unprofitable, and hopeless, is a various and complicated drama, with parts and an object, and an awful moral.

Now from these instances, to which many more might be added, it is plain, first, that the communication of knowledge certainly is either a condition or the means of that sense of enlargement or enlightenment, of which at this day we hear so much in certain quarters: this cannot be denied; but next, it is equally plain, that such communication is not the whole of the process. The enlargement consists, not merely in the passive reception into the mind of a number of ideas hitherto unknown to it, but in the mind's energetic and simultaneous action upon and towards and among those new ideas, which are rushing in upon it. It is the action of a formative power, reducing to order and meaning the matter of our acquirements; it is a making the objects of our knowledge subjectively our own, or, to use a familar word, it is a digestion of what we receive, into the substance of our previous state of thought; and without this no enlargement is said to follow. There is no enlargement, unless there be a comparison of ideas one with another, as they come before the mind, and a systematizing of them. We feel our minds to be growing and expanding *then,* when we not only learn, but refer what we learn to what we know already. It is not the mere addition to our knowledge that is the illumination; but the locomotion, the movement onwards, of that mental centre, to which both what we know, and what we are learning, the accumulating mass of our acquirements, gravitates. And therefore a truly great intellect, and recognized to be such by the common opinion of mankind, such as the intellect of Aristotle, or of St. Thomas, or of Newton, or of Goethe, . . . is one which takes a connected view of old and new, past and present, far and near, and which has an insight into the influence of all these one on another; without which there is no whole, and no centre. It possesses the knowledge, not only of things, but also of their mutual and true relations; knowledge, not merely considered as acquirement but as philosophy.

Accordingly, when this analytical, distributive, harmonizing   14 process is away, the mind experiences no enlargement, and is not reckoned as enlightened or comprehensive, whatever it may add to its knowledge. For instance, a great memory, as I have already said, does not make a philosopher, any more than a dictionary can be called a grammar. There are men who embrace in their minds a vast multitude of ideas, but with little sensibility about their real relations towards each other. These may be antiquarians, annalists, naturalists; they may be learned in the law; they may be versed in statistics; they are most useful in their own place; I should shrink from speaking disrespectfully of them; still, there is nothing in such attainments to guarantee the absence of narrowness of mind. If they are nothing more than well-read men, or men of information, they have not what specially deserves the name of culture of mind, or fulfills the type of Liberal Education.

In like manner, we sometimes fall in with persons who have   15 seen much of the world, and of the men who, in their day, have played a conspicuous part in it, but who generalize nothing, and have no observation, in the true sense of the word. They abound in information, in detail, curious and entertaining, about men and things; and, having lived under the influence of no very clear or settled principles, religious or political, they speak of every one and every thing, only as so many phenomena, which are complete in themselves, and lead to nothing, not discussing them, or teaching any truth, or instructing the hearer, but simply talking. No one would say that these persons, well informed as they are, had attained to any great culture of intellect or to philosophy.

The case is the same still more strikingly where the persons in   16 question are beyond dispute men of inferior powers and deficient education. Perhaps they have been much in foreign countries, and they receive, in a passive, otiose, unfruitful way, the various facts which are forced upon them there. Seafaring men, for example, range from one end of the earth to the other; but the multiplicity of external objects, which they have encountered, forms no symmetrical and consistent picture upon their imagination; they see the tapestry of human life, as it were on the wrong side, and it tells no story. They sleep, and they rise up, and they find themselves, now in Europe, now in Asia; they see visions of great cities and wild regions; they are in the marts of commerce, or amid the islands of the South; they gaze on Pompey's Pillar,[3] or on the Andes; and nothing which meets them carries them forward or backward, to any idea beyond itself. Nothing has a drift or relation; nothing has a history or a promise. Every thing stands by itself, and comes and goes in its turn, like the shifting scenes of a show, which leave the spectator where he was. Perhaps you are near such a man on a particular occasion, and expect him to be shocked or perplexed at something which occurs; but one thing is much the same to him as another, or, if he is perplexed, it is not knowing what to say, whether it is right to admire, or to ridicule, or to disapprove, while conscious that some expression of opinion is expected from him; or in fact he has no standard of judgment at all, and no landmarks to guide him to a conclusion. Such is mere acquisition, and, I repeat, no one would dream of calling it philosophy.

Instances, such as these, confirm, by the contrast, the conclusion 17 I have already drawn from those which preceded them. That only is true enlargement of mind which is the power of viewing many things at once as one whole, of referring them severally to their true place in the universal system, of understanding their respective values, and determining their mutual dependence. Thus is that form of Universal Knowledge, of which I have on a former occasion spoken, set up in the individual intellect, and constitutes its perfection. Possessed of this real illumination, the mind never views any part of the extended subject-matter of Knowledge without recollecting that it is but a part, or without the associations which spring from this recollection. It makes every thing in some sort lead to every thing else; it would communicate the image of the whole to every separate portion, till that whole becomes in imagination like a spirit, every where pervading and penetrating its component parts, and giving them one definite meaning. Just as our bodily organs, when mentioned, recall their function in the body, as the word "creation" suggests the Creator, and "subjects" a sovereign, so, in the mind of the Philosopher, as we are abstractedly conceiving of him, the elements of the physical and moral world, sciences, arts, pursuits, ranks, offices, events, opinions, individualities, are all viewed as one, with correlative functions, and as gradually by successive combinations converging, one and all, to the true centre.

3. A gigantic column (88 feet high) in Alexandria, raised circa 300 A.D. in honor of the Emperor Diocletian.

To have even a portion of this illuminative reason and true [18] philosophy is the highest state to which nature can aspire, in the way of intellect; it puts the mind above the influences of chance and necessity, above anxiety, suspense, unsettlement, and superstition, which is the lot of the many. Men whose minds are possessed with some one object, take exaggerated views of its importance, are feverish in the pursuit of it, make it the measure of things which are utterly foreign to it, and are startled and despond if it happens to fail them. They are ever in alarm or in transport. Those on the other hand who have no object or principle whatever to hold by, lose their way, every step they take. They are thrown out, and do not know what to think or say, at every fresh juncture; they have no view of persons, or occurrences, or facts, which come suddenly upon them, and they hang upon the opinion of others, for want of internal resources. But the intellect which has been disciplined to the perfection of its powers, which knows, and thinks while it knows, which has learned to leaven the dense mass of facts and events with the elastic force of reason, such an intellect cannot be partial, cannot be exclusive, cannot be impetuous, cannot be at a loss, cannot but be patient, collected, and majestically calm, because it discerns the end in every beginning, the origin in every end, the law in every interruption, the limit in each delay; because it ever knows where it stands, and how its path lies from one point to another. It is the $\tau\epsilon\tau\rho\acute{\alpha}\gamma\omega\nu o\varsigma$[4] of the Peripatetic, and has the "nil admirari"[5] of the Stoic,—

> *Felix qui potuit rerum cognoscere causas,*
> *Atque metus omnes, et inexorabile fatum*
> *Subjecit pedibus, strepitumque Acherontis avari.*[6]

These are men who, when in difficulties, originate at the moment vast ideas or dazzling projects; who, under the influence of excitement, are able to cast a light, almost as if from inspiration, on a subject or course of action which comes before them; who have a sudden presence of mind equal to any emergency, rising with the occasion, and an undaunted magnanimous bearing, and an energy and keenness which is but made intense by opposition. This is genius, this is heroism; it is the exhibition of a natural gift, which no culture can teach, at which no Institution can aim; here,

---

4. "Foursquare." Aristotle's adjective for the person of solid virtue.
5. "To be astonished by nothing," to remain always calm, was the Roman poet Horace's ideal.
6. "Happy is he who can discern the causes of things and spurn all fears, inexorable fate, and the tumult of greedy Acheron" Virgil, *Georgics*. In greek mythology, Acheron is the river bordering hell.

on the contrary, we are concerned, not with mere nature, but with training and teaching. That perfection of the Intellect, which is the result of Education, and its *beau ideal*,[7] to be imparted to individuals in their respective measures, is the clear, calm accurate vision and comprehension of all things, as far as the finite mind can embrace them, each in its place, and with its own characteristics upon it. It is almost prophetic from its knowledge of history; it is almost heart-searching from its knowledge of human nature; it has almost supernatural charity from its freedom from littleness and prejudice; it has almost the repose of faith, because nothing can startle it; it has almost the beauty and harmony of heavenly contemplation, so intimate is it with the eternal order of things and the music of the spheres.

7. Model of perfection.

JACOB BRONOWSKI

The Creative Mind

1

On a fine November day in 1945, late in the afternoon, I was landed on an airstrip in southern Japan. From there a jeep was to take me over the mountains to join a ship which lay in Nagasaki Harbor. I knew nothing of the country or the distance before us. We drove off; dusk fell; the road rose and fell away, the pine woods came down to the road, straggled on and opened again. I did not know that we had left the open country until unexpectedly I heard the ship's loudspeakers broadcasting dance music. Then suddenly I was aware that we were already at the center of damage in Nagasaki. The shadows behind me were the skeletons of the Mitsubishi factory buildings, pushed backwards and sideways as if by a giant hand. What I had thought to be broken rocks was a concrete power house with its roof punched in. I could now make out the outline of two crumpled gasometers; there was a cold furnace festooned with service pipes; otherwise nothing but cockeyed telegraph poles and loops of wire in a bare waste of ashes. I had blundered into this desolate landscape as instantly as one might wake among the craters of the moon. The moment of

Chapter 1 of *Science and Human Values*. Originally delivered as one of a series of lectures at the Massachusetts Institute of Technology, in 1953.

recognition when I realized that I was already in Nagasaki is present to me as I write, as vividly as when I lived it. I see the warm night and the meaningless shapes; I can even remember the tune that was coming from the ship. It was a dance tune which had been popular in 1945, and it was called "Is You Is Or Is You Ain't Ma Baby?"

These essays, which I have called *Science and Human Values*, 2 were born at that moment. For the moment I have recalled was a universal moment; what I met was, almost as abruptly, the experience of mankind. On an evening like that evening, some time in 1945, each of us in his own way learned that his imagination had been dwarfed. We looked up and saw the power of which we had been proud loom over us like the ruins of Nagasaki.

The power of science for good and for evil has troubled other 3 minds than ours. We are not here fumbling with a new dilemma; our subject and our fears are as old as the toolmaking civilizations. Men have been killed with weapons before now: what happened at Nagasaki was only more massive (for 40,000 were killed there by a flash which lasted seconds) and more ironical (for the bomb exploded over the main Christian community in Japan). Nothing happened in 1945 except that we changed the scale of our indifference to man; and conscience, in revenge, for an instant became immediate to us. Before this immediacy fades in a sequence of televised atomic tests, let us acknowledge our subject for what it is: civilization face to face with its own implications. The implications are both the industrial slum which Nagasaki was before it was bombed, and the ashy desolation which the bomb made of the slum. And civilization asks of both ruins, "Is You Is Or Is You Ain't Ma Baby?"

2

The man whom I imagine to be asking this question, wrily with 4 a sense of shame, is not a scientist; he is civilized man. It is of course more usual for each member of civilization to take flight from its consequences by protesting that others have failed him. Those whose education and perhaps tastes have confined them to the humanities protest that the scientists alone are to blame, for plainly no mandarin[1] ever made a bomb or an industry. The scientists say, with equal contempt, that the Greek scholars and the earnest cataloguers of cave paintings do well to wash their

---

1. *Mandarin* is sometimes used to mean a person influential in intellectual or literary circles.

hands of blame; but what in fact are they doing to help direct the society whose ills grow more often from inaction than from error?

This absurd division reached its *reductio ad absurdum*, I think, when one of my teachers, G. H. Hardy, justified his great life work on the ground that it could do no one the least harm—or the least good. But Hardy was a mathematician; will humanists really let him opt out of the conspiracy of scientists? Or are scientists in their turn to forgive Hardy because, protest as he might, most of them learned their indispensable mathematics from his books?

There is no comfort in such bickering. When Shelley pictured science as a modern Prometheus[2] who would wake the world to a wonderful dream of Godwin,[3] he was alas too simple. But it is as pointless to read what has happened since as a nightmare. Dream or nightmare, we have to live our experience as it is, and we have to live it awake. We live in a world which is penetrated through and through by science, and which is both whole and real. We cannot turn it into a game simply by taking sides.

And this make-believe game might cost us what we value most: the human content of our lives. The scholar who disdains science may speak in fun, but his fun is not quite a laughing matter. To think of science as a set of special tricks, to see the scientist as the manipulator of outlandish skills—this is the root of the poison mandrake which flourishes rank in the comic strips. There is no more threatening and no more degrading doctrine than the fancy that somehow we may shelve the responsibility for making the decisions of our society by passing it to a few scientists armored with a special magic. This is another dream, the dream of H. G. Wells, in which the tall elegant engineers rule, with perfect benevolence, a humanity which has no business except to be happy. To H. G. Wells, this was a dream of heaven—a modern version of the idle, harp-resounding heaven of other childhood pieties. But in fact it is the picture of a slave society, and should make us shiver whenever we hear a man of sensibility dismiss science as someone else's concern. The world today is made, it is powered by science; and for any man to abdicate an interest in science is to walk with open eyes towards slavery.

My aim in this book is to show that the parts of civilization make a whole: to display the links which give society its coherence, and, more, which give it life. In particular, I want to show the

2. One of the Titans of Greek mythology, he gave humans the gift of fire.
3. William Godwin, Shelley's father-in-law, dreamed of a world of perfect personal freedom in small, self-sufficient communities.

place of science in the canons of conduct which it has still to perfect.

This subject falls into three parts. The first is a study of the   9
nature of the scientific activity, and with it of all those imaginative
acts of understanding which exercise "The Creative Mind." After
this it is logical to ask what is the nature of the truth, as we seek
it in science and in social life; and to trace the influence which
this search for empirical truth has had on conduct. This influence
has prompted me to call the second part "The Habit of Truth."
Last I shall study the conditions for the success of science, and
find in them the values of man which science would have had to
invent afresh if man had not otherwise known them: the values
which make up "The Sense of Human Dignity."

This, then, is a high-ranging subject which is not to be held in   10
the narrow limits of a laboratory. It disputes the prejudice of the
humanist who takes his science sourly and, equally, the petty view
which many scientists take of their own activity and that of others.
When men misunderstand their own work, they cannot understand
the work of others; so that it is natural that these scientists have
been indifferent to the arts. They have been content, with the
humanists, to think science mechanical and neutral; they could
therefore justify themselves only by the claim that it is practical.
By this lame criterion they have of course found poetry and music
and painting at least unreal and often meaningless. I challenge all
these judgments.

3

There is a likeness between the creative acts of the mind in art   11
and in science. Yet, when a man uses the word science in such
a sentence, it may be suspected that he does not mean what the
headlines mean by science. Am I about to sidle away to those
riddles in the Theory of Numbers which Hardy loved, or to the
heady speculations of astrophysicists, in order to make claims for
abstract science which have no bearing on its daily practice?

I have no such design. My purpose is to talk about science as   12
it is, practical and theoretical. I define science as the organization
of our knowledge in such a way that it commands more of the
hidden potential in nature. What I have in mind therefore is both
deep and matter of fact; it reaches from the kinetic theory of gases
to the telephone and the suspension bridge and medicated tooth-
paste. It admits no sharp boundary between knowledge and use.
There are of course people who like to draw a line between pure
and applied science; and oddly, they are often the same people

who find art unreal. To them, the word useful is a final arbiter, either for or against a work; and they use this word as if it can mean only what makes a man feel heavier after meals.

There is no sanction for confining the practice of science in this   13
or another way. True, science is full of useful inventions. And its theories have often been made by men whose imagination was directed by the uses to which their age looked. Newton turned naturally to astronomy because it was the subject of his day, and it was so because finding one's way at sea had long been a practical preoccupation of the society into which he was born. It should be added, mischievously, that astronomy also had some standing because it was used very practically to cast horoscopes. (Kepler used it for this purpose; in the Thirty Years' War he cast the horoscope of Wallenstein which wonderfully told his character, and he predicted a universal disaster for 1634 which proved to be the murder of Wallenstein.)

In a setting which is more familiar, Faraday worked all his life   14
to link electricity with magnetism because this was the glittering problem of his day; and it was so because his society, like ours, was on the lookout for new sources of power. Consider a more modest example today: the new mathematical methods of automatic control, a subject sometimes called cybernetics, have been developed now because this is a time when communication and control have in effect become forms of power. These inventions have been directed by social needs, and they are useful inventions; yet it was not their usefulness which dominated and set light to the minds of those who made them. Neither Newton nor Faraday, nor yet Norbert Wiener, spent their time in a scramble for patents.

What a scientist does is compounded of two interests: the interest   15
of his time and his own interest. In this his behavior is no different from any other man's. The need of the age gives its shape to scientific progress as a whole. But it is not the need of the age which gives the individual scientist his sense of pleasure and of adventure, and that excitement which keeps him working late into the night when all the useful typists have gone home at five o'clock. He is personally involved in his work, as the poet is in his, and as the artist is in the painting. Paints and painting too must have been made for useful ends; and language was developed, from whatever beginnings, for practical communication. Yet you cannot have a man handle paints or language or the symbolic concepts of physics, you cannot even have him stain a microscope slide, without instantly waking in him a pleasure in the very language, a sense of exploring his own activity. This sense lies at the heart of creation.

4

The sense of personal exploration is as urgent, and as delightful,   16
to the practical scientist as to the theoretical. Those who think
otherwise are confusing what is practical with what is humdrum.
Good humdrum work without originality is done every day by
everyone, theoretical scientists as well as practical, and writers and
painters too, as well as truck drivers and bank clerks. Of course
the unoriginal work keeps the world going; but it is not therefore
the monopoly of practical men. And neither need the practical
man be unoriginal. If he is to break out of what has been done
before, he must bring to his own tools the same sense of pride
and discovery which the poet brings to words. He cannot afford
to be less radical in conceiving and less creative in designing a
new turbine than a new world system.

And this is why in turn practical discoveries are not made only   17
by practical men. As the world's interest has shifted, since the
Industrial Revolution, to the tapping of new springs of power, the
theoretical scientist has shifted his interests too. His speculations
about energy have been as abstract as once they were about astronomy; and they have been profound now as they were then,
because the man loved to think. The Carnot cycle[4] and the dynamo
grew equally from this love, and so did nuclear physics and the
German V[5] weapons and Kelvin's interest in low temperatures.
Man does not invent by following either use or tradition; he does
not invent even a new form of communication by calling a conference of communication engineers. Who invented the television
set? In any deep sense, it was Clerk Maxwell who foresaw the
existence of radio waves, and Heinrich Hertz who proved it, and
J. J. Thomson who discovered the electron. This is not said in
order to rob any practical man of the invention, but from a sad
sense of justice; for neither Maxwell nor Hertz nor J. J. Thomson
would take pride in television just now.

Man masters nature not by force but by understanding. This is   18
why science has succeeded when magic failed: because it has
looked for no spell to cast over nature. The alchemist and the
magician in the Middle Ages thought, and the addict of comic
strips is still encouraged to think, that nature must be mastered
by a device which outrages her laws. But in four hundred years
since the Scientific Revolution we have learned that we gain our
ends only *with* the laws of nature; we control her only by un-

4. The cycle of heat and work exchanges in an ideal steam engine, conceived by
the nineteenth-century French engineer Sadi Carnot.
5. The rockets with which Hitler bombarded England in World War II.

derstanding her laws. We cannot even bully nature by any insistence that our work shall be designed to give power over her. We must be content that power is the byproduct of understanding. So the Greeks said that Orpheus played the lyre with such sympathy that wild beasts were tamed by the hand on the strings. They did not suggest that he got this gift by setting out to be a lion tamer.

5

What is the insight with which the scientist tries to see into nature? Can it indeed be called either imaginative or creative? To the literary man the question may seem merely silly. He has been taught that science is a large collection of facts; and if this is true, then the only seeing which scientists need do is, he supposes, seeing the facts. He pictures them, the colorless professionals of science, going off to work in the morning into the universe in a neutral, unexposed state. They then expose themselves like a photographic plate. And then in the darkroom or laboratory they develop the image, so that suddenly and startingly it appears, printed in capital letters, as a new formula for atomic energy. 19

Men who have read Balzac and Zola[6] are not deceived by the claims of these writers that they do no more than record the facts. The readers of Christopher Isherwood do not take him literally when he writes "I am a camera." Yet the same readers solemnly carry with them from their schooldays this foolish picture of the scientist fixing by some mechanical process the facts of nature. I have had of all people a historian tell me that science is a collection of facts, and his voice had not even the ironic rasp of one filing cabinet reproving another. 20

It seems impossible that this historian had ever studied the beginnings of a scientific discovery. The Scientific Revolution can be held to begin in the year 1543 when there was brought to Copernicus, perhaps on his deathbed, the first printed copy of the book he had finished about a dozen years earlier. The thesis of this book is that the earth moves around the sun. When did Copernicus go out and record this fact with his camera? What appearance in nature prompted his outrageous guess? And in what odd sense is this guess to be called a neutral record of fact? 21

Less than a hundred years after Copernicus, Kepler published (between 1609 and 1619) the three laws which described the paths of the planets. The work of Newton and with it most of our mechanics spring from these laws. They have a solid, matter of fact sound. For example, Kepler says that if one squares the year 22

6. Literary realists.

of a planet, one gets a number which is proportional to the cube of its average distance from the sun. Does anyone think that such a law is found by taking enough readings and then squaring and cubing everything in sight? If he does, then as a scientist, he is doomed to a wasted life; he has as little prospect of making a scientific discovery as an electronic brain has.

It was not this way that Copernicus and Kepler thought, or that   23
scientists think today. Copernicus found that the orbits of the planets would look simpler if they were looked at from the sun and not from the earth. But he did not in the first place find this by routine calculation. His first step was a leap of imagination— to lift himself from the earth, and put himself wildly, speculatively into the sun. "The earth conceives from the sun," he wrote; and "the sun rules the family of stars." We catch in his mind an image, the gesture of the virile man standing in the sun, with arms out- stretched, overlooking the planets. Perhaps Copernicus took the picture from the drawings of the youth with outstretched arms which the Renaissance teachers put into their books on the pro- portions of the body. Perhaps he had seen Leonardo's drawings of his loved pupil Salai. I do not know. To me, the gesture of Copernicus, the shining youth looking outward from the sun, is still vivid in a drawing which William Blake in 1780 based on all these: the drawing which is usually called *Glad Day*.

Kepler's mind, we know, was filled with just such fanciful anal-   24
ogies; and we know what they were. Kepler wanted to relate the speeds of the planets to the musical intervals. He tried to fit the five regular solids into their orbits. None of these likenesses worked, and they have been forgotten; yet they have been and they remain the stepping stones of every creative mind. Kepler felt for his laws by way of metaphors, he searched mystically for likenesses with what he knew in every strange corner of nature. And when among these guesses he hit upon his laws, he did not think of their numbers as the balancing of a cosmic bank account, but as a revelation of the unity of all nature. To us, the analogies by which Kepler listened for the movement of the planets in the music of the spheres are farfetched. Yet are they more so than the wild leap by which Rutherford and Bohr in our own century found a model for the atom in, of all places, the planetary system?

6

No scientific theory is a collection of facts. It will not even do   25
to call a theory true or false in the simple sense in which every fact is either so or not so. The Epicureans held that matter is made of atoms two thousand years ago and we are now tempted to say

that their theory was true. But if we do so we confuse their notion of matter with our own. John Dalton in 1808 first saw the structure of matter as we do today, and what he took from the ancients was not their theory but something richer, their image: the atom. Much of what was in Dalton's mind was as vague as the Greek notion, and quite as mistaken. But he suddenly gave life to the new facts of chemistry and the ancient theory together, by fusing them to give what neither had: a coherent picture of how matter is linked and built up from different kinds of atoms. The act of fusion is the creative act.

All science is the search for unity in hidden likenesses. The search may be on a grand scale, as in the modern theories which try to link the fields of gravitation and electromagnetism. But we do not need to be browbeaten by the scale of science. There are discoveries to be made by snatching a small likeness from the air too, if it is bold enough. In 1935 the Japanese physicist Hideki Yukawa wrote a paper which can still give heart to a young scientist. He took as this starting point the known fact that waves of light can sometimes behave as if they were separate pellets. From this he reasoned that the forces which held the nucleus of an atom together might sometimes also be observed as if they were solid pellets. A schoolboy can see how thin Yukawa's analogy is, and his teacher would be severe with it. Yet Yukawa without a blush calculated the mass of the pellet he expected to see, and waited. He was right; his meson was found, and a range of other mesons, neither the existence nor the nature of which had been suspected before. The likeness had borne fruit.

The scientist looks for order in the appearance of nature by exploring such likenesses. For order does not display itself of itself; if it can be said to be there at all, it is not there for the mere looking. There is no way of pointing a finger or a camera at it; order must be discovered and, in a deep sense, it must be created. What we see, as we see it, is mere disorder.

This point has been put trenchantly in a fable by Karl Popper. Suppose that someone wished to give his whole life to science. Suppose that he therefore sat down, pencil in hand, and for the next twenty, thirty, forty years recorded in notebook after notebook everything that he could observe. He may be supposed to leave out nothing: today's humidity, the racing results, the level of cosmic radiation and the stockmarket prices and the look of Mars, all would be there. He would have compiled the most careful record of nature that has ever been made; and, dying in the calm certainty of a life well spent, he would of course leave his notebooks to the Royal Society. Would the Royal Society thank him for the treasure of a lifetime of observation? It would not. The Royal Society would treat his notebooks exactly as the English bishops have treated Joanna Southcott's box.[7] It would refuse to open them at all, because it would know without looking that the notebooks contain only a jumble of disorderly and meaningless items.

7

Science finds order and meaning in our experience, and sets   29
about this in quite a different way. It sets about it as Newton did in the story which he himself told in his old age, and of which the schoolbooks give only a caricature. In the year 1665, when Newton was twenty-two, the plague broke out in southern England, and the University of Cambridge was closed. Newton therefore spent the next eighteen months at home, removed from traditional learning, at a time when he was impatient for knowledge and, in his own phrase, "I was in the prime of my age for invention." In this eager, boyish mood, sitting one day in the garden of his widowed mother, he saw an apple fall. So far the books have the story right; we think we even know the kind of apple; tradition has it that it was a Flower of Kent. But now they miss the crux of the story. For what struck the young Newton at the sight was not the thought that the apple must be drawn to the earth by gravity; that conception was older than Newton. What struck him was the conjecture that the same force of gravity, which reaches to the top of the tree, might go on reaching out beyond the earth and its air, endlessly into space. Gravity might reach the moon: this was Newton's new thought; and it might be gravity which holds the moon in her orbit. There and then he calculated what force from the earth (falling off as the square of the distance) would hold the moon, and compared it with the known force of gravity at tree height. The forces agreed; Newton says laconically, "I found them answer pretty nearly." Yet they agreed only nearly: the likeness and the approximation go together, for no likeness is exact. In Newton's sentence modern science is full grown.

It grows from a comparison. It has seized a likeness between   30
two unlike appearances; for the apple in the summer garden and the grave moon overhead are surely as unlike in their movements

7. Joanna Southcott (1750–1814) claimed to have transcribed divinely inspired messages concerning the Second Coming of Christ. At her death she left a locked box, instructing that it should be opened in the presence of all the bishops in a time of national emergency. It was opened, in the presence of one bishop, in 1928; nothing in it was deemed of interest, which further convinced the English religious establishment that she was merely a crank.

as two things can be. Newton traced in them two expressions of a single concept, gravitation: and the concept (and the unity) are in that sense his free creation. The progress of science is the discovery at each step of a new order which gives unity to what had long seemed unlike. Faraday did this when he closed the link between electricity and magnetism. Clerk Maxwell did it when he linked both with light. Einstein linked time with space, mass with energy, and the path of light past the sun with the flight of a bullet; and spent his dying years in trying to add to these likenesses another, which would find a single imaginative order between the equations of Clerk Maxwell and his own geometry of gravitation.

8

When Coleridge tried to define beauty, he returned always to 31 one deep thought: beauty, he said, is "unity in variety." Science is nothing else than the search to discover unity in the wild variety of nature—or more exactly, in the variety of our experience. Poetry, painting, the arts are the same search, in Coleridge's phrase, for unity in variety. Each in his own way looks for likenesses under the variety of human experience. What is a poetic image but the seizing and the exploration of a hidden likeness, in holding together two parts of a comparison which are to give depth each to the other? When Romeo finds Juliet in the tomb, and thinks her dead, he uses in his heartbreaking speech the words,

Death that hath suckt the honey of thy breath.

The critic can only haltingly take to pieces the single shock which this image carries. The young Shakespeare admired Marlowe, and Marlowe's Faustus had said of the ghostly kiss of Helen of Troy that it sucked forth his soul. But that is a pale image; what Shakespeare has done is to fire it with the single word honey. Death is a bee at the lips of Juliet, and the bee is an insect that stings; the sting of death was a commonplace phrase when Shakespeare wrote. The sting is there, under the image; Shakespeare has packed it into the word honey; but the very word rides powerfully over its own undertones. Death is a bee that stings other people, but it comes to Juliet as if she were a flower; this is the moving thought under the instant image. The creative mind speaks in such thoughts.

The poetic image here is also, and accidentally, heightened by 32 the tenderness which town dwellers now feel for country ways. But it need not be; there are likenesses to conjure with, and images as powerful, within the man-made world. The poems of Alexander Pope belong to this world. They are not countrified, and therefore readers today find them unemotional and often artificial. Let me

then quote Pope: here he is in a formal satire face to face, towards
the end of his life, with his own gifts. In eight lines he looks
poignantly forward towards death and back to the laborious years
which made him famous.

> *Years foll'wing Years, steal something ev'ry day,*
> *At last they steal us from our selves away;*
> *In one our Frolicks, one Amusements end,*
> *In one a Mistress drops, in one a Friend:*
> *This subtle Thief of Life, this paltry Time,*
> *What will it leave me, if it snatch my Rhime?*
> *If ev'ry Wheel of that unweary'd Mill*
> *That turn'd ten thousand Verses, now stands still.*

The human mind had been compared to what the eighteenth
century called a mill, that is to a machine, before; Pope's own
idol Bolingbroke had compared it to a clockwork. In these lines
the likeness goes deeper, for Pope is thinking of the ten thousand
Verses which he had translated from Homer: what he says is sad
and just at the same time, because this really had been a mechanical
and at times a grinding task. Yet the clockwork is present in the
image too; when the wheels stand still, time for Pope will stand
still for ever; we feel that we already hear, over the horizon, Faust's
defiant reply to Mephistopheles, which Goethe had not yet written—
"let the clock strike and stop, let the hand fall, and time be at an
end."

> *Werd ich zum Augenblicke sagen:*
> *Verweile doch! du bist so schön!*
> *Dann magst du mich in Fesseln schlagen,*
> *Dann will ich gern zugrunde gehn!*
> *Dann mag die Totenglocke schallen,*
> *Dann bist du deines Dienstes frei,*
> *Die Uhr mag stehn, der Zeiger fallen,*
> *Es sei die Zeit für mich vorbei!*[8]

I have quoted Pope and Goethe because their metaphor here is [33]
not poetic; it is rather a hand reaching straight into experience
and arranging it with new meaning. Metaphors of this kind need
not always be written in words. The most powerful of them all

8. "If ever I say to the passing moment: Stay a while! Thou art so fair! Then may
you cast me into chains. Then will I gladly perish. Then may the death-bell toll.
Then are you freed from my service. Let the clock strike and stop, let the hand fall,
and time be at an end."

is simply the presence of King Lear and his Fool in the hovel of a man who is shamming madness, while lightning rages outside.[9] Or let me quote another clash of two conceptions of life, from a modern poet. In his later poems W. B. Yeats was troubled by the feeling that in shutting himself up to write, he was missing the active pleasures of life; and yet it seemed to him certain that the man who lives for these pleasures will leave no lasting work behind him. He said this at times very simply, too:

> *The intellect of man is forced to choose*
> *Perfection of the life, or of the work.*

This problem, whether a man fulfills himself in work or in play, is of course more common than Yeats allowed; and it may be more commonplace. But it is given breadth and force by the images in which Yeats pondered it.

> *Get all the gold and silver that you can,*
> *Satisfy ambition, or animate*
> *The trivial days and ram them with the sun,*
> *And yet upon these maxims meditate:*
> *All women dote upon an idle man*
> *Although their children need a rich estate;*
> *No man has ever lived that had enough*
> *Of children's gratitude or woman's love.*

The love of women, the gratitude of children: the images fix two philosophies as nothing else can. They are tools of creative thought, as coherent and as exact as the conceptual images with which science works: as time and space, or as the proton and the neutron.

9

The discoveries of science, the works of art are explorations— more, are explosions, of a hidden likeness. The discoverer or the artist presents in them two aspects of nature and fuses them into one. This is the act of creation, in which an original thought is born, and it is the same act in original science and original art. But it is not therefore the monopoly of the man who wrote the poem or who made the discovery. On the contrary, I believe this view of the creative act to be right because it alone gives a meaning to the act of appreciation. The poem or the discovery exists in two moments of vision: the moment of appreciation as much as that

34

9. In Act III, scene iv of Shakespeare's *King Lear,* psychological, moral, familial, and political disorder all find a metaphor in the storm that batters these three vulnerable men.

of creation; for the appreciator must see the movement, wake to the echo which was started in the creation of the work. In the moment of appreciation we live again the moment when the creator saw and held the hidden likeness. When a simile takes us aback and persuades us together, when we find a juxtaposition in a picture both odd and intriguing, when a theory is at once fresh and convincing, we do not merely nod over someone else's work. We re-enact the creative act, and we ourselves make the discovery again. At bottom, there is no unifying likeness there until we too have seized it, we too have made it for ourselves.

How slipshod by comparison is the notion that either art or science sets out to copy nature. If the task of the painter were to copy for men what they see, the critic could make only a single judgment: either that the copy is right or that it is wrong. And if science were a copy of fact, then every theory would be either right or wrong, and would be so for ever. There would be nothing left for us to say but this is so, or is not so. No one who has read a page by a good critic or a speculative scientist can ever again think that this barren choice of yes or no is all that the mind offers.

Reality is not an exhibit for man's inspection, labelled "Do not touch." There are no appearances to be photographed, no experiences to be copied, in which we do not take part. Science, like art, is not a copy of nature but a re-creation of her. We re-make nature by the act of discovery, in the poem or in the theorem. And the great poem and the deep theorem are new to every reader, and yet are his own experiences, because he himself re-creates them. They are the mark of unity in variety; and in the instant when the mind seizes this for itself, in art or in science, the heart misses a beat.

WILLIAM G. PERRY, JR.

Examsmanship and the Liberal Arts: A Study in Educational Epistemology

"But sir, I don't think I really deserve it, it was mostly bull,   1
really." This disclaimer from a student whose examination we
have awarded a straight "A" is wondrously depressing. Alfred
North Whitehead invented its only possible rejoinder: "Yes sir,
what you wrote is nonsense, utter nonsense. But ah! Sir! It's the
right *kind* of nonsense!"

Bull, in this university, is customarily a source of laughter, or   2
a problem in ethics. I shall step a little out of fashion to use the
subject as a take-off point for a study in comparative epistemology.
The phenomenon of bull, in all the honor and opprobrium with
which it is regarded by students and faculty, says something, I
think, about our theories of knowledge. So too, the grades which
we assign on examinations communicate to students what these
theories may be.

We do not have to be out-and-out logical-positivists[1] to suppose   3
that we have something to learn about "what we think knowledge
is" by having a good look at "what we do when we go about
measuring it." We know the straight "A" examination when we
see it, of course, and we have reason to hope that the student
will understand why his work receives our recognition. He doesn't
always. And those who receive lesser honor? Perhaps an understanding of certain anomalies in our customs of grading good bull
will explain the students' confusion.

I must beg patience, then, both of the reader's humor and of   4
his morals. Not that I ask him to suspend his sense of humor but
that I shall ask him to go beyond it. In a great university the
picture of a bright student attempting to outwit his professor while
his professor takes pride in not being outwitted is certainly ridiculous.
I shall report just such a scene, for its implications bear upon my
point. Its comedy need not present a serious obstacle to thought.

From *Examining in Harvard College: A Collection of Essays by Members of the Harvard Faculty* (1967).

1. Logical positivists like Bertrand Russell insist that philosophical speculation be
tightly checked by reference to the "positive" date of experience. This position links
them to the psychological behaviorists.

As for the ethics of bull, I must ask for a suspension of judgment.   5
I wish that students could suspend theirs. Unlike humor, moral
commitment is hard to think beyond. Too early a moral judgment
is precisely what stands between many able students and a liberal
education. The stunning realization that the Harvard Faculty will
often accept, as evidence of knowledge, the cerebrations of a student
who has little data at his disposal, confronts every student with
an ethical dilemma. For some it forms an academic focus for what
used to be thought of as "adolescent disillusion." It is irrelevant
that rumor inflates the phenomenon to mythical proportions. The
students know that beneath the myth there remains a solid and
haunting reality. The moral "bind" consequent on this awareness
appears most poignantly in serious students who are reluctant to
concede the competitive advantage to the bullster and who yet
feel a deep personal shame when, having succumbed to "temptation," they themselves receive a high grade for work they consider
"dishonest."

I have spent many hours with students caught in this unwelcome   6
bitterness. These hours lend an urgency to my theme. I have found
that students have been able to come to terms with the ethical
problem, to the extent that it is real, only after a refined study of
the true nature of bull and its relation to "knowledge." I shall
submit grounds for my suspicion that we can be found guilty of
sharing the student's confusion of moral and epistemological issues.

I

I present as my "premise," then, an amoral *fabliau*. Its hero-   7
villain is the Abominable Mr. Metzger '47. Since I celebrate his
virtuosity, I regret giving him a pseudonym, but the peculiar style
of his bravado requires me to honor also his modesty. Bull in pure
form is rare; there is usually some contamination by data. The
community has reason to be grateful to Mr. Metzger for having
created an instance of laboratory purity, free from any adulteration
by matter. The more credit is due him, I think, because his act
was free from premeditation, deliberation, or hope of personal
gain.

Mr. Metzger stood one rainy November day in the lobby of   8
Memorial Hall. A junior, concentrating in mathematics, he was
fond of diverting himself by taking part in the drama, a penchant
which may have had some influence on the events of the next
hour. He was waiting to take part in a rehearsal in Sanders Theatre,
but, as sometimes happens, no other players appeared. Perhaps

the rehearsal had been canceled without his knowledge? He decided to wait another five minutes.

Students, meanwhile, were filing into the Great Hall opposite, 9 and taking seats at the testing tables. Spying a friend crossing the lobby toward the Great Hall's door, Metzger greeted him and extended appropriate condolences. He inquired, too, what course his friend was being tested in. "Oh, Soc. Sci. something-or-other." "What's it all about?"asked Metzer, and this, as Homer remarked of Patroclus, was the beginning of evil for him.

"It's about Modern Perspectives on Man and Society and All 10 That," said his friend. "Pretty interesting, really."

"Always wanted to take a course like that," said Metzger. "Any 11 good reading?"

"Yeah, great. There's this book"—his friend did not have time 12 to finish.

"Take your seats please" said a stern voice beside them. The 13 idle conversation had somehow taken the two friends to one of the tables in the Great Hall. Both students automatically obeyed; the proctor put blue-books before them; another proctor presented them with copies of the printed hour-test.

Mr. Metzger remembered afterwards a brief misgiving that was 14 suddenly overwhelmed by a surge of curiosity and puckish glee. He wrote "George Smith" on the blue book, opened it, and addressed the first question.

I must pause to exonerate the Management. The Faculty has a 15 rule that no student may attend an examination in a course in which he is not enrolled. To the wisdom of this rule the outcome of this deplorable story stands witness. The Registrar, charged with the enforcement of the rule, has developed an organization with procedures which are certainly the finest to be devised. In November, however, class rosters are still shaky, and on this particular day another student, named Smith, was absent. As for the culprit, we can reduce his guilt no further than to suppose that he was ignorant of the rule, or, in the face of the momentous challenge before him, forgetful.

We need not be distracted by Metzger's performance on the 16 "objective" or "spot" questions on the test. His D on these sections can be explained by those versed in the theory of probability. Our interest focuses on the quality of his essay. It appears that when Metzger's friend picked up his own blue book a few days later, he found himself in company with a large proportion of his section in having received on the essay a C. When he quietly picked up "George Smith's" blue book to return it to Metzger, he observed that the grade for the essay was A. In the margin was a note in the section man's hand. It read "Excellent work. Could you have pinned these observations down a bit more closely? Compare . . . in . . . pp. . . ."

Such news could hardly be kept quiet. There was a leak, and   17 the whole scandal broke on the front page of Tuesday's *Crimson.* With the press Metzger was modest, as becomes a hero. He said that there had been nothing to it at all, really. The essay question had offered a choice of two books, Margaret Mead's *And Keep Your Powder Dry* or Geoffrey Gorer's *The American People.* Metzger reported that having read neither of them, he had chosen the second "because the title gave me some notion as to what the book might be about." On the test, two critical comments were offered on each book, one favorable, one unfavorable. The students were asked to "discuss." Metzger conceded that he had played safe in throwing his lot with the most laudatory of the two comments, "but I did not forget to be balanced."

I do not have Mr. Metzger's essay before me except in vivid   18 memory. As I recall, he took his first cue from the name Geoffrey, and committed his strategy to the premise that Gorer was born into an "Anglo-Saxon" culture, probably English, but certainly "English speaking." Having heard that Margaret Mead was a social anthropologist, he inferred that Gorer was the same. He then entered upon his essay, centering his inquiry upon what he supposed might be the problems inherent in an anthropologist's observation of a culture which was his own, or nearly his own. Drawing in part from memories of table-talk on cultural relativity[2] and in part from creative logic, he rang changes on the relation of observer to observed, and assessed the kind and degree of objectivity which might accrue to an observer through training as an anthropologist. He concluded that the book in question did in fact contribute a considerable range of " 'objective', and even 'fresh'," insights into the nature of our culture. "At the same time," he warned, "these observations must be understood within the context of their generation by a person only partly freed from his embeddedness in the culture he is observing, and limited in his capacity to transcend those particular tendencies and biases which he has himself developed as a personality in his interraction with this culture since his birth. In this sense the book portrays as much the character of Geoffrey Gorer as it analyzes that of the American people." It is my regretable duty to report that at this moment of triumph

2. "An important part of Harvard's education takes place during meals in the Houses." An Official Publication. [author's note] Houses are dormitories for upperclassmen.

Mr. Metzger was carried away by the temptations of parody and added, "We are thus much the richer."

In any case, this was the essay for which Metzger received his honor grade and his public acclaim. He was now, of course, in serious trouble with the authorities. 19

I shall leave him for the moment to the mercy of the Administrative Board of Harvard College and turn the reader's attention to the section man who ascribed the grade. He was in much worse trouble. All the consternation in his immediate area of the Faculty and all the glee in other areas fell upon his unprotected head. I shall now undertake his defense. 20

I do so not simply because I was acquainted with him and feel a respect for his intelligence; I believe in the justice of his grade! Well, perhaps "justice" is the wrong word in a situation so manifestly absurd. This is more a case in "equity." That is, the grade is equitable if we accept other aspects of the situation which are equally absurd. My proposition is this: if we accept as valid those C grades which were accorded students who, like Metzger's friend, demonstrated a thorough familiarity with the details of the book without relating their critique to the methodological problems of social anthropology, then "George Smith" deserved not only the same, but better. 21

The reader may protest that the C's given to students who showed evidence only of diligence were indeed not valid and that both these students and "George Smith" should have received E's. To give the diligent E is of course not in accord with custom. I shall take up this matter later. For now, were I to allow the protest, I could only restate my thesis: that "George Smith's" E would, in a college of liberal arts, be properly a "better" E. 22

At this point I need a short-hand. It is a curious fact that there is no academic slang for the presentation of evidence of diligence alone. "Parroting" won't do; it is possible to "parrot" bull. I must beg the reader's pardon, and, for reasons almost too obvious to bear, suggest "cow." 23

Stated as nouns, the concepts look simple enough: 24

> cow (pure): data, however relevant, without relevancies.
> bull (pure): relevancies, however relevant, without data.

The reader can see all too clearly where this simplicity would lead. I can assure him that I would not have imposed on him this way were I aiming to say that knowledge in this university is definable as some neuter compromise between cow and bull, some infertile hermaphrodite. This is precisely what many diligent students seem to believe: that what they must learn to do is to "find the 25 right mean" between "amounts" of detail and "amounts" of generalities. Of course this is not the point at all. The problem is not quantitative, nor does its solution lie on a continuum between the particular and the general. Cow and bull are not poles of a single dimension. A clear notion of what they really are is essential to my inquiry, and for heuristic purposes I wish to observe them further in the celibate state.

When the pure concepts are translated into verbs, their complexities become apparent in the assumptions and purposes of the students as they write: 26

> To cow (*v. intrans.*) or the act of cowing:
> To list data (or perform operations) without awareness of, or comment upon, the contexts, frames of reference, or points of observation which determine the origin, nature, and meaning of the data (or procedures). To write on the assumption that "a fact is a fact." To present evidence of hard work as a substitute for understanding, without any intent to deceive.

> To bull (*v. intrans.*) or the act of bulling:
> To discourse upon the contexts, frames of reference and points of observation which would determine the origin, nature, and meaning of data if one had any. To present evidence of an understanding of form in the hope that the reader may be deceived into supporting a familiarity with content.

At the level of conscious intent, it is evident that cowing is more moral, or less immoral, than bulling. To speculate about unconscious intent would be either an injustice or a needless elaboration of my theme. It is enough that the impression left by cow is one of earnestness, diligence, and painful naiveté. The grader may feel disappointment or even irritation, but these feelings are usually balanced by pity, compassion, and a reluctance to hit a man when he's both down and moral. He may feel some challenge to his teaching, but none whatever to his one-ups-manship. He writes in the margin: "See me." 27

We are now in a position to understand the anomaly of custom: As instructors, we always assign bull an E, *when we detect it;* whereas we usually give cow a C, *even though it is always obvious.* 28

After all, we did not ask to be confronted with a choice between morals and understanding (or did we?). We evince a charming humanity, I think, in our decision to grade in favor of morals and pathos. "I simply *can't* give this student an E after he has *worked* so hard." At the same time we tacitly express our respect for the bullster's strength. We recognize a colleague. If he knows so well how to dish it out, we can be sure that he can also take it. 29

Of course it is just possible that we carry with us, perhaps from
our own school-days, an assumption that if a student is willing
to work hard and collect "good hard facts" he can always be
taught to understand their relevance, whereas a student who has
caught onto the forms of relevance without working at all is a
lost scholar.

But this is not in accord with our experience.

It is not in accord either, as far as I can see, with the stated
values of a liberal education. If a liberal education should teach
students "how to think," not only in their own fields but in fields
outside their own—that is, to understand "how the other fellow
orders knowledge," then bulling, even in its purest form, expresses
an important part of what a pluralist university holds dear, surely
a more important part than the collecting of "facts that are facts"
which schoolboys learn to do. Here then, good bull appears not
as ignorance at all but as an aspect of knowledge. It is both relevant
and "true." In a university setting good bull is therefore of more
value than "facts," which, without a frame of reference, are not
even "true" at all.

Perhaps this value accounts for the final anomaly: as instructors,
we are inclined to reward bull highly, *where we do not detect its
intent*, to the consternation of the bullster's acquaintances. And
often we do not examine the matter too closely. After a long
evening of reading blue books full of cow, the sudden meeting
with a student who at least understands the problems of one's
field provides a lift like a draught of refreshing wine, and a strong
disposition toward trust.

This was, then, the sense of confidence that came to our unfortunate section man as he read "George Smith's" sympathetic
considerations.

II

In my own years of watching over students' shoulders as they
work, I have come to believe that this feeling of trust has a firmer
basis than the confidence generated by evidence of diligence alone.
I believe that the theory of a liberal education holds. Students
who have dared to understand man's real relation to his knowledge
have shown themselves to be in a strong position to learn content
rapidly and meaningfully, and to retain it. I have learned to be
less concerned about the education of a student who has come
to understand the nature of man's knowledge, even though he
has not yet committed himself to hard work, than I am about the
education of the student who, after one or two terms at Harvard,
is working desperately hard and still believes that collected "facts"

constitute knowledge. The latter, when I try to explain to him, too often understands me to be saying that he "doesn't *put in enough generalities.*" Surely he has "put in *enough* facts."

I have come to see such quantitative statements as expressions   36
of an entire, coherent epistemology. In grammar school the student is taught that Columbus discovered America in 1492. The *more* such items he gets "right" on a given test the more he is credited with "knowing." From years of this sort of thing it is not unnatural to develop the conviction that knowledge consists of the accretion of hard facts by hard work.

The student learns that the more facts and procedures he can   37
get "right" in a given course, the better will be his grade. The more courses he takes, the more subjects he has "had," the more credits he accumulates, the more diplomas he will get, until, after graduate school, he will emerge with his doctorate, a member of the community of scholars.

The foundation of this entire life is the proposition that a fact   38
is a fact. The necessary correlate of this proposition is that a fact is either right or wrong. This implies that the standard against which the rightness or wrongness of a fact may be judged exists *someplace*—perhaps graven upon a tablet in a Platonic world outside and above *this* cave of tears. In grammar school it is evident that the tablets which enshrine the spelling of a word or the answer to an arithmetic problem are visible to my teacher who need only compare my offerings to it. In high school I observe that my English teachers disagree. This can only mean that the tablets in such matters as the goodness of a poem are distant and obscured by clouds. They surely exist. The pleasing of befuddled English teachers degenerates into assessing their prejudices, a game in which I have no protection against my competitors more glib of tongue. I respect only my science teachers, authorities who *really know.* Later I learn from them that "this is only what we think *now.*" But eventually, surely. . . . Into this epistemology of education, apparently shared by teachers in such terms as "credits," "semester hours" and "years of French" the student may invest his ideals, his drive, his competitiveness, his safety, his self-esteem, and even his love.

College raises other questions: by whose calendar is it proper   39
to say that Columbus discovered America in 1492? How, when and by whom was the year 1 established in this calendar? What of other calendars? In view of the evidence for Leif Ericson's previous visit (and the American Indians), what historical ethnocentrism is suggested by the use of the word "discover" in this sentence? As for Leif Ericson, in accord with what assumptions do you order the evidence?

These questions and their answers are not "more" knowledge. 40
They are devastation. I do not need to elaborate upon the epistemology, or rather epistemologies, they imply. A fact has become
at last "an observation or an operation performed in a frame of
reference." A liberal education is founded in an awareness of frame
of reference even in the most immediate and empirical examination
of data. Its acquirement involves relinquishing hope of absolutes
and of the protection they afford against doubt and the glib-tongued
competitor. It demands an ever widening sophistication about systems of thought and observation. It leads, not away from, but
through the arts of gamesmanship to a new trust.

This trust is in the value and integrity of systems, their varied 41
character, and the way their apparently incompatible metaphors
enlighten, from complementary facets, the particulars of human
experience. As one student said to me: "I used to be cynical about
intellectual games. Now I want to know them thoroughly. You
see I came to realize that it was only when I knew the rules of
the game cold that I could tell whether what I was saying was
tripe."

We too often think of the bullster as cynical. He can be, and 42
not always in a light-hearted way. We have failed to observe that
there can lie behind cow the potential of a deeper and more
dangerous despair. The moralism of sheer work and obedience
can be an ethic that, unwilling to face a despair of its ends, glorifies
its means. The implicit refusal to consider the relativity of both
ends and means leaves the operator in an unconsidered proprietary
absolutism. History bears witness that in the pinches this moral
superiority has no recourse to negotiation, only to force.

A liberal education proposes that man's hope lies elsewhere: in 43
the negotiability that can arise from an understanding of the integrity
of systems and of their origins in man's address to his universe.
The prerequisite is the courage to accept such a definition of
knowledge. From then on, of course, there is nothing incompatible
between such an epistemology and hard work. Rather the contrary.

I can now at last let bull and cow get together. The reader 44
knows best how a productive wedding is arranged in his own
field. This is the nuptial he celebrates with a straight A on examinations. The masculine context must embrace the feminine
particular, though itself "born of woman." Such a union is knowledge itself, and it alone can generate new contexts and new data
which can unite in their turn to form new knowledge.

In this happy setting we can congratulate in particular the Natural 45
Sciences, long thought to be barren ground to the bullster. I have
indeed drawn my examples of bull from the Social Sciences, and

by analogy from the Humanities. Essay-writing in these fields has long been thought to nurture the art of bull to its prime. I feel, however, that the Natural Sciences have no reason to feel slighted. It is perhaps no accident that Metzger was a mathematician. As part of my researches for this paper, furthermore, a student of considerable talent has recently honored me with an impressive analysis of the art of amassing "partial credits" on examinations in advanced physics. Though beyond me in some respects, his presentation confirmed my impression that instructors of Physics frequently honor on examinations operations structurally similar to those requisite in a good essay.

The very qualities that make the Natural Sciences fields of delight 46 for the eager gamesman have been essential to their marvelous fertility.

III

As priests of these mysteries, how can we make our rites more 47 precisely expressive? The student who merely cows robs himself, without knowing it, of his education and his soul. The student who only bulls robs himself, as he knows full well, of the joys of inductive discovery—that is, of engagement. The introduction of frames of reference in the new curricula of Mathematics and Physics in the schools is a hopeful experiment. We do not know yet how much of these potent revelations the very young can stand, but I suspect they may rejoice in them more than we have supposed. I can't believe they have never wondered about Leif Ericson and that word "discovered," or even about 1492. They have simply been too wise to inquire.

Increasingly in recent years better students in the better high 48 schools and preparatory schools are being allowed to inquire. In fact they appear to be receiving both encouragement and training in their inquiry. I have the evidence before me.

Each year for the past five years all freshmen entering Harvard 49 and Radcliffe have been asked in freshman week to "grade" two essays answering an examination question in History. They are then asked to give their reasons for their grades. One essay, filled with dates, is 99% cow. The other, with hardly a date in it, is a good essay, easily mistaken for bull. The "official" grades of these essays are, for the first (alas!) C "because he has worked so hard," and for the second (soundly, I think) B. Each year a larger majority of freshmen evaluate these essays as would the majority of the faculty, and for the faculty's reasons, and each year a smaller minority give the higher honor to the essay offering data alone. Most interesting, a larger number of students each year, while not overrating the second essay, award the first the straight E appropriate to it in a college of liberal arts.

For us who must grade such students in a university, these developments imply a new urgency, did we not feel it already. Through our grades we describe for the students, in the showdown, what we believe about the nature of knowledge. The subtleties of bull are not peripheral to our academic concerns. That they penetrate to the center of our care is evident in our feelings when a student whose good work we have awarded a high grade reveals to us that he does not feel he deserves it. Whether he disqualifies himself because "there's too much bull in it," or worse because "I really don't think I've worked that hard," he presents a serious educational problem. Many students feel this sleaziness; only a few reveal it to us.

We can hardly allow a mistaken sense of fraudulence to undermine our students' achievements. We must lead students beyond their concept of bull so that they may honor relevancies that are really relevant. We can willingly acknowledge that, in lieu of the date 1492, a consideration of calendars and of the word "discovered," may well be offered with intent to deceive. We must insist that this does not make such considerations intrinsically immoral, and that, contrariwise, the date 1492 may be no substitute for them. Most of all, we must convey the impression that we grade understanding qua understanding. To be convincing, I suppose we must concede to ourselves in advance that a bright student's understanding is understanding even if he achieved it by osmosis rather than by hard work in our course.

These are delicate matters. As for cow, its complexities are not what need concern us. Unlike good bull, it does not represent partial knowledge at all. It belongs to a different theory of knowledge entirely. In our theories of knowledge it represents total ignorance, or worse yet, a knowledge downright inimical to understanding. I even go so far as to propose that we award no more C's for cow. To do so is rarely, I feel, the act of mercy it seems. Mercy lies in clarity.

The reader may be afflicted by a lingering curiosity about the fate of Mr. Metzger. I hasten to reassure him. The Administrative Board of Harvard College, whatever its satanic reputation, is a benign body. Its members, to be sure, were on the spot. They delighted in Metzger's exploit, but they were responsible to the Faculty's rule. The hero stood in danger of probation. The debate was painful. Suddenly one member, of a refined legalistic sensibility, observed that the rule applied specifically to "examinations" and that the occasion had been simply an hour-test. Mr. Metzger was merely "admonished."

Thinking About Liberal Knowledge

"Now, what I want is, Facts. Teach these boys and girls nothing but Facts. Facts alone are wanted in life. Plant nothing else, and root out everything else. You can only form the minds of reasoning animals upon Facts; nothing else will ever be of service to them. This is the principal on which I bring up my own children, and this is the principal on which I bring up these children. Stick to the Facts, sir!"

Never has a philosophy of education been more succinctly stated than Thomas Gradgrind's opening lines of Dickens' *Hard Times.* It is, arguably, an inevitable philosophy in an industrial society where, as Thoreau says, men are so busy using their knowledge that they do not have time to remember their ignorance. It is certainly an enduring philosophy: one finds it in a somewhat diluted form in most attempts to define a "core curriculum" for primary, secondary, or college education. The Governor's Task Force on Basic Education (or some equally impressive body) will announce that every sixth-grader should be able to name the seven colors of the spectrum, left to right, and tests will be instituted to make sure that this happens. Whatever the defects of a curriculum based strictly on the learning of facts, it is easily implemented and monitored.

But to what end? Gradgrindism is the common target of the three essays in this unit. John Henry Newman, Jacob Bronowski, and William G. Perry all agree that the accumulation of facts is in itself simply beside the point. Bronowski retells a fable by philosopher Karl Popper:

> Suppose that someone wished to give his whole life to science. Suppose that he therefore sat down, pencil in hand, and for the next twenty, thirty, forty years recorded in notebook after notebook everything that he could observe. He may be supposed to have left out nothing: today's humidity, the racing results, the level of cosmic radiation and the stockmarket prices and the look of Mars, all would be there. He would have compiled the most careful record of nature that has ever been made, and, dying in the calm certainty of a life well spent, he would of course leave his notebooks to the Royal Society. Would the Royal Society thank him?

Of course it would not. The man would have produced what Perry calls pure "cow," data unconnected to a system of knowledge.

Neither Newman, Bronowski, Perry, nor the Royal Society is interested in "cow" unconnected with "bull." In fact Metzger, the protagonist of Perry's essay, is an unabashed bullster who, by an imaginative and audacious linking of the very few facts at his disposal, manages to get an A on an essay exam without attending lectures or reading the books. "In a university setting," Perry says with some admiration, "good bull is . . . of more value than 'facts,' which, without a frame of reference, are not even 'true at all'."

Taken together, the three essays present a view of education as clear as Gradgrindism, and almost as influential. In this view the merely diligent student, the empty vessel waiting to be filled with facts, is replaced with a livelier thinker, a tougher customer.

QUESTIONS

1. Is there a stage in learning a discipline when Gradgrindism is necessary, when the unquestioning accumulation of facts is the student's proper business? Is this stage complete by the time a student reaches college?

2. Are the views of Newman, Bronowski, and Perry elitist? Can they be applied in a country that assumes college education is everyone's birthright? Is Gradgrindism egalitarian? In what sense?

3. Describe and evaluate your experience with a teacher whose views were like Gradgrind's or like Perry's.

4. How would your college or university be changed if someone like Perry could reform it according to his ideas? Would it be a better or a worse place?

5. Are the views of our three essayists applicable only to education in the humanities? Are they incompatible with scientific education? Are they compatible with vocational training or with the specialized curriculum of students who are preparing to go into fields like medicine and engineering?

AUTHORS

ROGER ANGELL (1920–   )
lives in New York City. The stepson of the noted American essayist E.B. White, he was from 1946 until 1957 editor and writer for *Holiday Magazine*, and from 1957 until the present a regular contributor to as well as senior editor and fiction editor for *The New Yorker*, where he also writes a regular feature, "The Sporting Scene," noted for its insights into professional baseball. His works include: *The Stone Arbor and Other Stories* (1960), *A Day in the Life of Roger Angell* (1970), *The Summer Game* (1972), *Late Innings* (1983), and *Five Seasons* (1983).

JAMES BALDWIN (1924–   )
has been employed as a handyman, evangelist, errand runner, waiter, dishwasher, and author. He has been a resounding success as the latter. His work deals largely with the black experience in America and abroad, which has made him a spokesman for the Civil Rights movement in this country. His fiction includes: *Go Tell It on the Mountain* (1953), *Giovanni's Room* (1956), *Another Country* (1962), *If Beale Street Could Talk* (1974), and *Just Above My Head* (1979). His best-known and most highly charged works, however, are his two collections of essays, *Notes of A Native Son* (1955) and *Nobody Knows My Name: More Notes of A Native Son* (1961).

JOHN BERGER (1926–   )
is a Marxist art critic, essayist, translator, poet, novelist, playwright, and painter. His novels include *A Painter of Our Time* (1958), *The Foot of Clive* (1962), *Corker's Freedom* (1972), and *G* (1972). His essay collections include *Permanent Red: Essays in Seeing* (1960), *Toward Reality: Essays in Seeing* (1962), *The Moment of Cubism, and Other Essays* (1969), *The Look of Things: Essays* (1974), and *A Seventh Man: Migrant Workers in Europe* (1975).

ALICE BLOOM
lives in Mt. Vernon, Maine. She has taught in the departments of English at Washington University, St. Louis; the University of Michigan, Ann Arbor; the University of Maryland, Baltimore County; and is currently teaching at the University of Maine, Farmington. Her essays and reviews have appeared in *Hudson Review*, *Perspective*, *The Aegean Review*, *Puckerbrush Review*, *The Christian Challenge*, and *Yale Review*.

DANIEL JOSEPH BOORSTIN (1914–   )
has been described as an "anti-historian historian, a lawyer-in-academe," mainly because of his iconoclastic stances. *The Americans: The Democratic Experience* (1973) won him the Pulitzer Prize. Other works include: *The Decline of Radicalism: Reflections of America Today* (1969) and *The Republic of Technology* (1978).

DAVID BRADLEY (1950–   ),
contributor of articles, fiction, and reviews to periodicals, including *Signature*, *Savvy*, and *New York Arts Journal*. He has written two novels, *South Street* and the historical novel *The Chaneysville Incident* (1981), an account of the murder of thirteen runaway slaves who demanded liberty or death.

JACOB BRONOWSKI (1908–1974)
was born in Poland and came to America in 1964. A latter-day Renaissance man, Bronowski wrote on such

disparate subjects as William Blake and atomic theory. His most widely received work was *The Ascent of Man* (1973), a collection of essays drawn from a thirteen-part BBC production of the same name. His other works include *The Poet's Defence* (1939), *The Face of Violence: An Essay with a Play* (1954), *Science and Human Values* (1956), *The Western Intellectual Tradition: From Leonardo to Hegel* (1960), and *Magic, Science, and Civilization* (1978).

BRIGID BROPHY (1929–   ), novelist, essayist, and critic, lives in London, where, after reading classics at Oxford University, she was first employed in secretarial positions for a camera firm and a distributor of pornographic books. With the publication of *The Crown Princess and Other Stories* (1953) and *Hackenfeller's Ape,* which won the Cheltenham Literary Festival prize for best first novel in 1954, she commenced a writing career that has been as brilliantly incisive as it is prolific and diverse. Among her novels are *The King of a Rainy Country* (1956), *Flesh* (1962), *The Snow Ball* (1964), and *Palace Without Chairs* (1978). Her nonfiction works range from *Black Ship to Hell* (1962; a psychoanalytic study of humanity's self-destructive impulses) to *Mozart the Dramatist* (1964), *Fifty Works of English Literature We Could Do Without* (1968), and *Black and White: A Portrait of Aubrey Beardsley* (1970). A number of her witty and impassioned essays are collected in *Don't Never Forget: Collected Views and Reviews* (1966).

SUSAN BROWNMILLER (1935–   ), American author, journalist, and feminist. She is a contributor to, among others, *The New York Times Magazine, Esquire,* and *Newsweek.* In 1971 she published *Shirley Chisholm: A Biography,* the life of America's first black Congresswoman, but her prominence as a social historian came about primarily through *Against Our Will: Men, Women, and Rape,* in which she examines the history of rape through her thesis that rape is a political as well as physical assault, and a means employed for centuries of subjugating women. *Femininity* (1984) irritated many of Brownmiller's feminist read-

ers by surveying the concept of feminine allure with mixed sympathies.

PEARL S. BUCK (1892–1973) was born in West Virginia but spent her formative years living with her missionary parents in China. A noted humanitarian as well as prolific essayist, novelist, children's author, and poet, she is most famous for her Pulitzer Prize-winning novel *The Good Earth* (1931). Among her other works are *The Exile,* the biography of her mother; *Fighting Angel: Portrait of a Soul* (1936), her father's biography; and the two sequels to *The Good Earth, Sons* (1932) and *House Divided* (1935). She won the Nobel Prize for literature in 1938.

SHEILA BURNFORD (1918–   ) is best known as an author of children's novels about animals, *The Incredible Journey* (1961), *Mr. Noah and the Second Flood* (1963), and *Bel Ria* (1978), though her book of autobiographical essays, *The Fields of Noon* (1964), has been praised by critics. Her other works include *Without Reserve* (1969) and *One Woman's Arctic* (1973).

KENNETH CLARK (1903–   ) has come to be regarded as a sort of British national repository of knowledge of the fine arts from the classical period to the present. Perhaps best known for his BBC series *Civilization,* he has also written a number of influential books: *Leonardo Da Vinci: An Account of his Development as an Artist* (1939), *Looking At Pictures* (1960), *The Romantic Rebellion: Romantic Versus Classic Art* (1973), and *Animals and Men: Their Relationship as Reflected in Western Art from Prehistory to the Present Day* (1977).

EVAN S(HELBY) CONNELL (1924–   ) was born in Kansas City. From the publication of his first collection of stories, *The Anatomy Lesson and Other Stories* (1957), his work has won high acclaim. The title character of his first novel, *Mrs. Bridge* (1959), was deemed by some critics the "most fully-developed character in any post-World War II American novel." Among his other works: *Mr. Bridge* (1969), *The Connoisseur* (1974), *St. Augustine's Pigeon* (1980), and *Sun of* the Morning Star: Custer and The Little Bighorn (1984).

HARRY CREWS (1935–   )
teaches English at the University of Florida at Gainesville, is author of the regular column, "Grits," in *Esquire*, and a frequent contributor to *Playboy*. His novels include: *The Gospel Singer* (1968), *Naked in Garden Hills* (1969), *This Thing Don't Lead to Heaven* (1970), *The Hawk Is Dying* (1973), *The Gypsy's Curse* (1974), and *A Feast of Snakes* (1976).

CLARENCE DARROW (1857–1938)
was perhaps this century's most famous defense counsel. He received national recognition first through his defense of several notorious labor leaders in sensational cases. His two most famous defenses are of Leopold and Loeb (1924)—they were accused of murdering a young boy and managed to avoid the death penalty if not imprisonment—and of John T. Scopes, who broke Tennessee state law by teaching Darwinian evolution in a high school. His books include: *Crime: Its Cause and Treatment* (1925) and *The Prohibition Mania* (1927). His autobiography, *The Story of My Life*, was published in 1932.

JOAN DIDION (1934–   ),
one of the most acute observers of the times in which we live, is a novelist and essayist. Her stories and essays have appeared in many periodicals, among them *Vogue, Holiday, Harper's, The Saturday Evening Post, National Review*, and *The New York Review of Books*. Her novels include *Run River* (1963), *Play it as it Lays* (1970), *A Book of Common Prayer* (1976), and *Democracy* (1984). Her essays are gathered in two brilliant collections, *Slouching Towards Bethlehem* (1968) and *The White Album* (1979). An extended essay about her 1982 trip to El Salvador was published in 1983 as *Salvador*.

ANNIE DILLARD (1945–   )
achieved early success with her first published prose, *Pilgrim at Tinker Creek*, in which she follows Henry David Thoreau in examining nature with a metaphysician's eye, and which won the Pulitzer Prize for general nonfiction in 1974. She is a contributing editor of *Harper's*. Her other

works include *Holy the Firm* (1978), a collection of her poetry, *Tickets for a Prayer Wheel* (1982), and *Teaching a Stone to Talk* (1982).

JOSÉ DONOSO (1924–   )
was born in Santiago, Chile, and once worked as a shepherd in Patagonia. Today, however, he is regarded as one of the prime movers of the recent renaissance in Latin American fiction. His first book, *Summertime and Other Stories* (1955), was published only after Donoso had sold 100 copies through subscription; his first novel, *Coronation* (1957), was peddled by Donoso and friends on streetcorners in Santiago. His other works include *The Charleston* (1960), a collection of short stories; *The Major Stories of José Donoso* (1966); *Hell Has No Limits* (1966); *The Obscene Bird of Night* (1973); *The Boom in Spanish American Literature: A Personal History* (1977); a collection of novellas, *Sacred Families* (1977); and *A House in the Country* (1984).

W(ILLIAM) E(DWARD) B(URGHARDT) DUBOIS (1868–1963)
was professor of history and economics at Atlanta University and devoted his professional energies to the study of black history and socioeconomics. An opponent of Booker T. Washington's conservatism over racial issues, he founded the militant Niagra Movement in 1905 and was one of the early leaders of the National Association for the Advancement of Colored People. He left America in 1962 and became a citizen of Ghana, where he died. His studies include: *The Souls of Black Folk* (1905), *John Brown* (1909), *The Negro* (1915), *Black Reconstruction in America* (1935); his novels are: *Darkwater* (1920), *Dark Princess* (1928), and *The Black Flame: A Trilogy*; his autobiography, *Dusk of Dawn*, was printed in 1940.

LAWRENCE DURRELL (1912–   )
was born in India of Irish and English parents and worked at a variety of odd jobs—including jazz pianist, automobile racer, real estate agent, and public relations director for the British government in Cyprus during the 1950s—before moving to France in 1957 and taking up writing full time. He is an astonishingly prolific

writer of essays, poems, travelogues, and novels. Among his works are *Pope Joan: A Romantic Biography* (1954), *Bitter Lemons* (1957), *Tunc* (1979), *The Poems of Lawrence Durrell* (1962), and *The Spirit of Place: Letters and Essays on Travel* (1984). Durrell's masterpiece is undoubtedly *The Alexandria Quartet* (1957–60), four highly poetic novels which examine the intricacies of modern love.

GRETEL EHRLICH (1946–   ) was raised in Santa Barbara, California, "with horses," was educated at Bennington and UCLA, and spent a year in New York doing film editing. She has published two volumes of poetry, *Geode/Rock Body* (1970) and *To Touch the Water* (1981), and one of nonfiction, *The Solace of Open Spaces* (1985). She lives, with horses, in Shell, Wyoming.

LOREN EISELEY (1907–1977), sociologist, anthropologist, historian of science, archaeologist, and author, wrote popular scientific books with a poet's touch. Edward Hoagland describes him as "one of those transcendent imaginative thinkers who are not limited to one branch of science, nor to science itself." His works include *Darwin's Century: Evolution and the Men Who Discovered It* (1958), *Firmament of Time* (1960), *The Mind As Nature* (1962), *Francis Bacon and The Modern Dilemma* (1963), *The Unexpected Universe* (1969), *The Night Country* (1971), and *Darwin and The Mysterious Mr. X: New Light on the Evolutionists* (1979). His autobiography, *All the Strange Hours: The Excavation of a Life* was published in 1975; he also published several volumes of poetry, including *Notes of An Alchemist* (1972) and *All the Night Wings* (1979).

RALPH ELLISON (1914–   ) was born in Oklahoma City, Oklahoma. He attended Tuskegee Institute, where he studied musical composition; he has in his works demonstrated a lifelong passion for jazz. Ellison freely acknowledges another influence, that of Richard Wright, who introduced him to the works of Dostoyevsky, Joseph Conrad, and Henry James. He is best known for *Invisible Man* (1952) and *Shadow and Act* (1964).

JAMES FALLOWS (1949–   ) a Rhodes scholar, was President Jimmy Carter's chief speechwriter, and has served as writer and editor for *Washington Monthly, Texas Monthly,* and *The Atlantic.* His works include *The Water Lords* (1971), *Who Runs Congress?* (1972) [with Mark Green and David Zwick], and *National Defense* (1981). With Charles Peters he has edited *The System* (1976) and *Inside the System* (1976).

WILLIAM FAULKNER (1897–1962) was born in New Albany, Mississippi. His novels are often set in mythical Yoknapatawpha County, the nexus for his cyclical treatments of the rise and fall of various social strata in the South. Considered one of the great novelists of this century, he won the Nobel Prize in 1959. His major works include: *As I Lay Dying* (1930) *Sanctuary* (1931), *Light in August* (1932), *Absalom, Absalom* (1936), *The Hamlet* (1940), *Go Down, Moses,* (1942), *Intruder in the Dust* (1948), *The Town* (1957), and *The Mansion* (1959).

E(DWARD) M(ORGAN) FORSTER (1879–1970) was born in London. Novelist, critic, essayist, and librettist, Forster is best known for *A Passage To India* (1924), *Where Angels Fear to Tread* (1905), *A Room With a View* (1908), *Howards End* (1910) and the libretto for the opera *Billy Budd,* as well as two books of essays, *Abinger Harvest—A Miscellany* (1936) and *Two Cheers for Democracy* (1951).

ROBERT FROST (1874–1963) knew very little success until the publication of *A Boy's Will* (1913) made him a popular success in England. From this time on, Frost enjoyed a critical and popular success that few poets realize in their lifetimes. He won the Pulitzer Prize for poetry three times, for *New Hampshire* in 1923, *Collected Poems* in 1930, and *A Further Range* in 1936.

PAUL FUSSELL (1924–   ) was a professor of English and produced scholarly books on such subjects as 18th-century humanism, Walt Whitman, and prosody before he became a popularly successful author. With *The Great War and Modern Memory* (1975) he established himself as a popular modern historian of note, and he has gone on to write *Abroad: British Literary Traveling between the Wars* (1980); a collection of literary essays, *The Boy Scout Handbook and Other Observations* (1982); and *Class: A Guide Through the American Status System* (1983).

JOHN KENNETH GALBRAITH (1908–   ) is a noted Canadian-born economist and onetime American ambassador to India—and also a highly successful writer. His works include *The Affluent Society* (1958), *Economic Discipline* (1967), *How to Get Out of Vietnam: A Workable Solution to the Worst Problem of Our Time* (1967), *How to Control the Military* (1969), *The New Industrial State* (1971) and *Annals of an Abiding Liberal* (1979).

HARRY GOLDEN (1902–   ) was born Harry Goldhurst and is the founder of *The Carolina Israelite*, a bimonthly publication dealing with racism, trade unions, and civil rights. His moral stance has on more than one occasion inflamed his Southern neighbors, but Golden's wry touch often reduces angry cries to chuckles. His works include: *Jews in the South* (1951), *Only in America* (1958), *Enjoy, Enjoy* (1960), *Mr. Kennedy and the Negroes* (1964), *The Best of Harry Golden* (1967), *The Right Time: An Autobiography* (1969), and *A Bintel Brief* (1977).

NADINE GORDIMER (1923–   ) was born in Springs, South Africa, and her novels are devoted to apartheid, its practitioners and its victims. Because of their sensitivity to the plight of black South Africans, three of her works have been banned in South Africa. She is a contributor as well to American periodicals and literary magazines. Among her major works: *The Soft Voice of the Serpent, and Other Stories* (1952), *The Lying Days* (1953), *Six Feet of the Country* (1956), *Friday's Footprint, and Other Stories* (1960), *The Conservationist* (1975), *Burgher's Daughter* (1979), *A Soldier's Embrace* (1980), and *Something Out There* (1983).

PATRICIA HAMPL (1946–   ), poet and memoirist, was born in the "old city of saints," St. Paul, Minnesota, to parents of Czech and Irish descent. A profound and poignant sense of history, place, and beauty is the hallmark of her major work: two collections of poetry, *Woman Before an Aquarium* (1978) and *Resort and Other Poems* (1983); and, especially, her memoir *A Romantic Education,* which won the Houghton Mifflin Literary Fellowship in 1981.

GARRETT HARDIN (1915–   ), scientist, lecturer, and writer, is a professor emeritus at the University of California, Santa Barbara, and a contributor of more than 200 scholarly articles to various periodicals. He revels in cross-disciplinary investigations, claiming that "the iconoclastic work of the scholar who stands outside the various academic establishments is sometimes a bit lonely—but it *is* fun!" His works include *Biology: Its Principles and Implications* (1949), *Nature and Man's Fate* (1959), *Population, Evolution, and Birth Control* (as editor, 1964), *Exploring New Ethics for Survival* (1972), *Mandatory Motherhood: The True Meaning of "Right to Life"* (1974), *Managing the Commons* (as editor, 1977), *The Limits of Altruism* (1977), and *Promethean Ethics: Living with Death, Competition, and Triage* (1980).

NATHANIEL HAWTHORNE (1804–1864) was born in Salem, Massachusetts, site of the famous witch trials, and wrote tales and sketches as well as working as an editor until 1837, when his *Twice-told Tales* was published. In 1841 he lived on Brook Farm, the grand failed exercise in utopian socialism sparked by the Transcendentalist Club of Concord and Boston. From 1846 until his dismissal in 1849 he worked as the County Surveyor in the Salem County Custom House. In 1850 he published *The Scarlet Letter*, in 1851 *The House of The Seven Gables*, in 1852 *The Blithedale Romance*, and in 1860 *The Marble Faun*.

ERNEST HEMINGWAY (1899–1961) worked briefly as a reporter, then volunteered for service in an American unit in France during World War I; he was wounded in combat and, after the war, returned to journalism. This took him to Paris, where he immersed himself in the literary and artistic subculture he describes in *A Moveable Feast* (1964). He is best known for *The Sun Also Rises* (1926), *A Farewell to Arms* (1929), *Death in the Afternoon* (1932), and *For Whom the Bell Tolls* (1940).

EDWARD HOAGLAND (1932–   ), novelist and essayist, has said of himself that "writers can be categorized by many criteria, one of which is whether they prefer subject matter that they rejoice in or subject matter they deplore and wish to savage with ironies . . . I'm of the first type." A contributor to *The New Yorker* and *Esquire*, he has written a number of book-length works (usually dealing with his observations of animals and natural habitats), among them *The Courage of Turtles* (1971), *Walking the Dead Diamond River* (1973), *Red Wolves and Black Bears* (1976), *African Calliope: A Journey to the Sudan* (1979), and *The Edward Hoagland Reader* (1979).

JOHAN HUIZINGA (1872–1945) served as professor of history at the University of Leiden from 1915 until it was closed by the Nazis during the Occupation. An eclectic scholar, Huizinga treated the plastic arts of the Middle Ages and Renaissance in Western Europe in his major works, *The Waning of The Middle Ages* (1924), *In the Shadow of Tomorrow* (1936), and *Homo Ludens, A Study of the Play Element in Culture* (1950).

ALDOUS HUXLEY (1894–1963) was born into a remarkable family. Grandson of the noted English natural philosopher and essayist, Thomas Huxley, and son of Leonard Huxley, editor of the prestigious *Cornhill Magazine*, he achieved early success with three novels, *Crome Yellow* (1921), *Antic Hay* (1923), and *Those Barren Leaves* (1925). These were followed by three novels generally considered his best work, *Point Counter Point* (1928), *Brave New World* (1932), and *Eyeless in Gaza* (1936). *Brave New World* stands with George Orwell's *1984* in protest of the modern soulless disutopia. His *Collected Essays* was published in 1959.

JANE JACOBS (1916–   ) spent a year as a reporter for the Scranton, Pennsylvania, *Tribune*, then headed for New York City, where, after working as a stenographer, writer, and editor, she eventually became an associate and then senior editor of *Architectural Forum*. There she gradually became more and more critical of modern urban planning. Among her works are: *The Death and Life of Great American Cities* (1961), *The Economy of Cities* (1969), and *Cities and the Wealth of Nations: Principles of Economic Life* (1984).

RANDALL JARRELL (1914–1965) was a poet, critic, literary editor of *The Nation*, critic for *Partisan Review*, and contributor to, among others, *The New York Times Book Review* and *The New Republic*. He was an often vitriolic critic of poetry he felt lacking in sincerity or craftsmanship; poet Robert Lowell said of him in *The New York Times Book Review* that he felt "as much joy in rescuing the reputation of a sleeping good writer as in chloroforming a mediocre one." His works include: *Blood for a Stranger* (1942), *Losses* (1948), and a collection of essays and fables, *A Sad Heart at the Supermarket* (1962). His *Complete Poems* was published in 1968.

SAMUEL JOHNSON (1709–1784) began his literary career as a hack-writer and translator after a notably unsuccessful attempt at teaching. For over fifteen years he slaved for London publishers, producing essays, biographies, poetic satires, and covering Parliament for *The Gentleman's Magazine*. From 1747 until 1755 he worked on his monumental *Dictionary of the English Language*. To support himself while he worked on the *Dictionary*, he wrote essays twice weekly for a twopenny sheet he called the *Rambler*. He produced his landmark edition of Shakespeare's plays in 1765, followed by *The Lives of the Poets* in the years 1779–81. The man who wrote *Rasselas*, a moral tale of an Abyssinian prince, in one week (in 1759) to pay his mother's funeral expenses is buried in Westminster Abbey.

GARRISON KEILLOR (1942–   ) is host of American Public Radio's "A Prairie Home Companion," a nationally broadcast visit to the crackerbarrels of mythical Lake Wobegon, "where all the women are strong, all the men are good-looking, and all the children are above average." The show is a folksy smorgasbord of music and comedy, "sponsored" by ersatz sponsors like Ralph's Pretty Good Grocery ("if you can't find it at Ralph's, you can probably get along without it") and Powdermilk Biscuits ("Heavens they're tasty—and expeditious."). His fiction and features have been published in *The New Yorker* and *The Atlantic*; a collection of his humorous essays and stories, *Happy to be Here*, appeared in 1982, his *Lake Wobegon Days* in 1985.

MARTIN LUTHER KING, JR. (1929–1968)
was ordained a Baptist minister in 1947 and embarked upon a career of social activism. One of the catalysts for the Montgomery Movement, an early Civil Rights movement in the 1950s, he founded the influential Southern Christian Leadership Conference in 1957. A proponent of nonviolent civil disobedience, King won the Nobel Prize for peace in 1964. His published works include: *The Story of Montgomery* (1957), *Stride Toward Freedom: The Montgomery Story* (1958), *Letter From Birmingham City Jail* (1963), *Why We Can't Wait* (1964), and *Where Do We Go From Here: Chaos or Community?* (1968).

H(UMPHREY) D(AVY) F(INDLEY) KITTO (1897–1982),
professor emeritus of Greek at the University of Bristol, England, was throughout his career interested in recovering the cultural context in which works of the classical period and Shakespeare were written. Not surprisingly, he relied heavily upon Aristotelian forms in his analysis of literature, classical or not. His works include: *In The Mountains of Greece* (1933), *The Greeks* (1951), and *Form and Meaning in Drama: A Study of Six Greek Plays and of "Hamlet"* (1956).

JOSEPH WOOD KRUTCH (1893–1970)
was a literary scholar, drama critic, essayist, and naturalist. After teaching literature at Brooklyn Polytechnic Institute and Vassar, as well as journalism at Columbia University, he served as drama critic for *The Nation*; he also wrote a regular column in *Harper's*, "Easy Chair." Forced by

respiratory disease to move to Tucson, Arizona, he began his work as a social critic, interested primarily in the inroads technology and science have made upon nature and humans. His works include: *Comedy and Conscience after the Restoration* (1924), *Samuel Johnson* (1944), *Henry David Thoreau* (1948), *The Desert Year* (1952), *The Forgotten Peninsula: A Naturalist in Baja California*, and *If You Don't Mind My Saying So: Essays on Man and Nature*. His autobiography, *More Lives than One*, was published in 1962.

ANNA HARRIETTE LEONOWENS (1834–1915),
born in Wales, was governess to the family of the King of Siam. She drew on these experiences to write *The English Governess at the Court of Siam*, which was of course the inspiration for the long running musical *The King and I*. After leaving Siam, she came to New York, where she established a school for training kindergarten teachers. Her other works include *Romance of the Harem, Life and Travels in India*, and *Our Asiatic Cousins*.

C(LIVE) S(TAPLES) LEWIS (1898–1963)
was born in Belfast, Ireland, and distinguished himself as an essayist, a Christian apologist, a scholar of Renaissance and medieval literature, and an author of science fiction and children's novels. His works include: *The Problem of Pain* (1940), *The Screwtape Letters* (1942), *The Abolition of Man; or, Reflections on Education* (1943); his *Space Trilogy*, composed of *Out of The Silent Planet* (1938), *Perelandra* (1943), and *That Hideous Strength* (1945). Lewis's literary criticism includes *The Allegory of Love* (1936), *English Literature in the Sixteenth Century, Excluding Drama* (1954), and *The Discarded Image: An Introduction to Medieval and Renaissance Literature* (1964).

KONRAD LORENZ (1903–   )
was born in Vienna, Austria. He is considered the father of modern ethology (the study of characteristic patterns of animal behavior), largely because of his study of imprinting. His best-known works are *King Solomon's Ring: New Light on Animal Ways* (1952), *Man Meets Dog* (1955), and

Instinctive Behavior: The Development of A Modern Concept (1957).

RUSSELL LYNES (1910–   )
was managing editor of *Harper's* from 1947 until 1967, and has served as contributing editor since. He is author of several columns, including "The State of Taste" in *Art in America* (1969–72), "Russell Lynes Observes" for *Architectural Digest*, and "After Hours" in *Harper's*, and has published in various magazines. His essays and studies include: *Highbrow, Lowbrow, Middlebrow* (1949), *The Tastemakers* (1954), *The Domesticated Americans* (1963), *Confessions of a Dilettante* (1966), *The Art-Makers of Nineteenth Century America* (1970), and *Good Old Modern* (1973).

THOMAS BABINGTON MACAULAY (1800–1859)
served England as Commissioner of Bankruptcy, Member of Parliament, Secretary of War, and man of letters. In 1843 he published his *Collected Essays*; with the publication of the first two volumes of his *History of England* in 1848 he became a celebrity. The last two volumes of his *History* were published in 1855, and after resigning from Parliament in 1856 Macaulay was made Baron Macaulay of Rothley.

WILLIAM MANCHESTER (1922–   ),
journalist, novelist, and historian, is best known for his reconstruction of the events surrounding the assassination of President John F. Kennedy, *Death of a President* (1967). His other works include: *Disturber of the Peace: The Life of H.L. Mencken* (1951), *A Rockefeller Family Portrait* (1959), *The Arms of Krupp* (1968), *The Glory and the Dream: A Narrative History of America, 1932–1972* (1968), *Controversy and Other Essays in Journalism* (1976), and *American Caesar: Douglas MacArthur, 1880–1964* (1978). His memoir of of the Pacific in World War II, *Goodbye, Darkness*, was published in 1980.

GABRIEL GARCÍA MÁRQUEZ (1928–   )
was born in Aracataca, Colombia. He, as much as any author, is responsible for the renaissance of Spanish-language literature in this century. Although he has said that he is primarily a journalist, his best-known

work is *One Hundred Years of Solitude* (1970), a novel about the Buendía family of the mythical and often magical town of Macondo. His other works include *Leaf Storm and Other Stories* (1955), *No One Writes to the Colonel and Other Stories* (1961), *In Evil Hour* (1962), *The Autumn of the Patriarch* (1976), and *Chronicle of a Death Foretold* (1982) [dates of publication are for Spanish editions]. García Márquez won the Nobel Prize for literature in 1982.

PHYLLIS MCGINLEY (1905–1978),
the so-called "housewife-poet," is notable for her achievements as an essayist and writer of juvenile stories and novels, as well as her contributions to *The Atlantic, Good Housekeeping, McCall's, Vogue,* and *Reader's Digest*. She won the Pulitzer Prize in 1961 for her book of poetry, *Times Three*. Her other works include *On the Contrary* (1933), *One More Manhattan* (1937), *The Love Letters of Phyllis McGinley* (1954), and *Wonders and Surprises: A Collection of Poems*. Those interested in her work as an essayist should read *The Province of the Heart* (1959), *Sixpence in Her Shoe* (1964), and *Saint-Watching* (1969).

JOHN MCPHEE (1931–   )
is a contributor to virtually every magazine of stature in this country, including *Holiday, Playboy, The Atlantic,* and *National Geographic*; he has been a staff writer for *The New Yorker* since 1964. He has written on a diversity of subjects, from atomic energy to oranges. His works include: *A Sense of Where You Are* (1965), *The Headmaster* (1966), *Oranges* (1967), *The Pine Barrens* (1968), *A Roomful of Hovings and Other Profiles* (1969), *Levels of the Game* (1970), *Encounters with the Archdruid* (1972), *Wimbledon: A Celebration* (1972), *The Curve of Binding Energy* (1974), *Pieces of the Frame* (1975), *The Survival of the Bark Canoe* (1975), *Coming Into the Country* (1977), and *The John McPhee Reader* (1977).

MARGARET MEAD (1901–1978)
is noted for her studies of primitive peoples and complex contemporary cultures. Her graduate work led to her first major work, *Coming of Age in Samoa* (1928), a study of the way

Samoan culture conditions sexual behavior and concepts of self. This was followed in 1930 by *Growing Up in New Guinea* and *Sex and Temperament in Three Primitive Societies* in 1935. Her studies of modern cultures were devoted in no small part to matters of race and gender, particularly *Male and Female* (1949) and *A Rap on Race* (1971), coauthored by James Baldwin. The account of her early life, *Blackberry Winter*, was published in 1972. Her other works include: *Balinese Character: A Photographic Analysis* (1942), *Anthropology: A Human Science* (1964), *Continuities in Cultural Evolution* (1964), and *Culture and Commitment* (1970).

H(ENRY) L(OUIS) MENCKEN (1880–1956)
began his career as a journalist at age nineteen and by 1905 had achieved the editorship of Baltimore's *Morning Herald*. He was literary critic and editor of *The Smart Set* magazine from 1908 until 1924, when he founded and edited the lively *American Mercury*. His best-known work is *The American Language*, an immense yet readable study of what its title promises. From 1919 until 1927 he published his collection of essays, *Prejudices*, in six volumes.

JESSICA MITFORD (1917–   )
was born in England into an aristocratic (and eccentric) family. Her writings are usually exposés cutting right to the bone of certain institutions, professions, or rackets, revealing them for what they are. Her first popular success was *The American Way of Death* (1963), followed by *The Trial of Dr. Spock, the Rev. William Sloan Coffin, Jr., Michael Ferber, Mitchell Goodman, and Marcus Raskin* (1969), *Kind and Usual Punishment: The Prison Business* (1973), and *Poison Penmanship: The Gentle Art of Muckraking* (1979). Her autobiography, *A Fine Old Conflict*, was published in 1977.

NANCY MITFORD (1904–1973),
Jessica Mitford's sister, was an essayist, novelist, and playwright. In London her blue blood and literary skills served to introduce her to the English literary community. After World War II she moved to France; she was made Chevalier of the Legion d'Honneur and a Commander, Order of the British Empire, for her accomplishments as a woman of letters. She satirized the British aristocracy in two wickedly funny novels, *The Pursuit of Love* (1945) and *Love in a Cold Climate* (1949). Among her other works are biographies of Madame Pompadour (1954) and Frederick the Great (1970). *The Water Beetle* (1963) is a collection of her essays.

N. SCOTT MOMADAY (1934–   )
is a Kiowa Indian and teaches literature at Stanford University. Many of his works, including his Pulitzer Prize winning *House Made of Dawn*, deal with the culture and history of American Indians. His works include: *The Way to Rainy Mountain* (1969); a collection of Kiowa Indian folktales, *Angle of Geese and Other Poems* (1974); *The Gourd Dancer* (1976); *The Names* (1976), and the film script for *The Man Who Killed the Deer*, a novel by Frank Water. Momaday is often a reviewer for *The New York Times Book Review* on subjects concerning American Indians.

JAN MORRIS (1926–   )
was born James Humphrey Morris and was considered one of England's most resourceful journalists after he accompanied Sir Edmund Hillary's expedition and broke the news of Hillary's ascent of Everest in 1953. In 1964 began his transformation, through the use of female hormones and surgery, into a woman, a transformation chronicled in Morris's autobiography, *Conundrum*, published in 1974. Other works under the name Jan Morris include *Travels* (1976), *The Oxford Book of Oxford* (1978), *Spain* (1979), and *Journeys* (1984). Works under the name James Morris: *The World of Venice* (1960), *The Road to Huddersfield: A Journey to Five Continents* (1963), *The Outriders: A Liberal View of Britain* (1963), and a historical trilogy, composed of *Pax Britannica: The Climax of an Empire* (1969), *An Imperial Progress* (1973), and *Farewell the Trumpets: An Imperial Retreat* (1978).

ALICE MUNRO (1931–   )
is a Canadian-born writer of novels and short stories. Her works are often

set in small-town Ontario and examine what it is to be a woman in such a setting. Her works include *Dance of the Happy Shades* (1968), *Lives of Girls and Women* (1971), *Something I've Been Meaning to Tell You* (1974), *The Moons of Jupiter* (1983), and *The Beggar Maid* (1984).

JOHN HENRY CARDINAL NEWMAN (1801–1890)
took holy orders in the Church of England in 1824 and stood at the forefront of the Oxford Movement, a conservative movement to reestablish the authority and tradition of the Anglican Church. In 1846 he was ordained a priest in the Roman Catholic Church. As Pastor-elect of the proposed Catholic University in Dublin, Ireland, he delivered the lectures that were later to be published as *The Idea of a University* (1873). His most noted work is his spiritual autobiography, *Apologia Pro Vita Sua* (1864), also published as *History of My Religious Opinions*. He was created Cardinal in 1879.

MICHAEL NORMAN (1947–   )
is on the metropolitan staff of *The New York Times* and has done considerable freelance writing, much of it published by *The New York Times Magazine*. He has also worked as a reporter-producer for public television. An ex-Marine (but "the brass knuckles are teflon," he notes) and veteran of the Vietnam war, he is at work on a book about the lives of his fellow soldiers in the aftermath of Vietnam.

FLANNERY O'CONNOR (1925–64)
produced fiction dominated by her own brand of Southern Roman Catholicism—her characters often find themselves in a world understandable only through comically grotesque torments or penances. During her lifetime she had two novels published, *Wise Blood* (1952) and *The Violent Bear It Away* (1960), as well as a collection of short stories, *A Good Man is Hard To Find and Other Stories* (1955). *Everything That Rises Must Converge*, another collection of short stories, was published in 1965.

GEORGE ORWELL (1903–1950)
was born Eric Blair in Bengal, India. He worked in Burma as a police offi-

cer but returned to England and the Continent to travel and look for work. He worked as an investigative journalist in northern England and then covered the Spanish Civil War, where he was wounded in combat and about which he wrote *Homage to Catalonia* (1938). His best-known works are *Animal Farm* (1945) and *1984* (1949), in which he attacks totalitarianism savagely. Other works include: *Down and Out in Paris and London* (1933) and his *Collected Essays, Journals, and Letters* (four volumes) published in 1968.

CYNTHIA OZICK (1928–   )
is an essayist, poet, novelist, and short story writer. Her works include *Trust* (1966), a novel, and *The Pagan Rabbi and Other Stories* (1971); her poetry appears in *A Treasury of Yiddish Poetry* (1972). A collection of literary essays, *Art and Ardor*, appeared in 1983. Her poetry, essays, and translations have appeared in a number of periodicals.

DOROTHY PARKER (1893–1967),
essayist, editor, short story and movie writer, poet and critic, began her career as a member of the editorial staff of *Vanity Fair* and moved from there to *The New Yorker*, where she reviewed books and wrote the column "Constant Reader." She was a regular contributor to *The New Yorker* for most of her career. Noted for her barbed wit in conversation and in her printed assessments of her own and others' work, she nonetheless had a soft place in her heart for liberal causes; she was fined for taking part in a demonstration against the executions of Sacco and Vanzetti, and was cited by the House Un-American Activities Committee in 1951 for her connections with "Communist-front" groups. Omnibus volumes of her works include *Collected Stories* (1942), *Collected Poetry* (1944), *The Best of Dorothy Parker* (1952), *The Portable Dorothy Parker* (1973), and *A Month of Saturdays* (1971).

WALKER PERCY (1916–   )
was born in Birmingham, Alabama, and after graduating fom the Columbia University Medical School, embarked on a medical career. He

contracted tuberculosis, was confined to bed for two years, and suffered a relapse thereafter. He then decided to pursue a writing career. It is safe to say that his scientific bent and his conversion to Roman Catholicism have been two dominant influences on his writing. Among his novels are *The Moviegoer* (1961), *The Last Gentleman* (1966), *Love in the Ruins* (1971), and *The Second Coming* (1980). *The Message in the Bottle* (1975) is a collection of his essays.

NOEL PERRIN (1927–   )
teaches English at Dartmouth College and is a contributor to *The New Yorker*. His works include a collection of essays, *A Passport Secretly Green* (1961), *Dr. Bowdler's Legacy: A History of Expurgated Books in England and America* (1970), *Amateur Sugar Maker* (1972), *Vermont: In All Weathers* (1973), *First Person Rural: Essays of a Sometime Farmer* (1978), *Second Person Rural: More Essays of a Sometime Farmer* (1980), and *Third Person Rural: More Essays of a Sometime Farmer* (1983).

WILLIAM G. PERRY (1913–   )
has served with the Bureau of Study Counsel at Harvard University, where he teaches and publishes on the counseling of college students and the relation of education and personality. He is the author of *Forms of Intellectual and Ethical Development in the College Years: A Scheme* (1970).

PLATO (C. 429–437 B.C.)
was probably born in Athens and is regarded as the father of rationalist philosophy. Scholars are hard pressed to distinguish between Plato's thought and that of his mentor, Socrates, largely because of the form in which Plato lodges them. This form, resembling what we might call today a cross-examination, pits Socrates against an antagonist who is inexorably led to the point Socrates wishes to make. The question of whether Plato is faithfully recording the debate or putting words in the mouths of his "characters" cannot be answered. His other works include: *Gorgias, The Symposium, Timaeus*, and *The Republic*.

RICHARD RODRIGUEZ (1944–   )
was born in San Francisco, California, and lives there today. In his auto-

biography, *Hunger of Memory: The Education of Richard Rodriguez* (1982), he examines the loss of his ethnicity and his gradual alienation from the world of his Chicano parents, as well as his rejection of the system that offered him the fruits of a bilingual education and affirmative action.

DOROTHY SAYERS (1893–1957)
was one of the first women to earn a degree from Oxford. She was a novelist, playwright, Christian apologist, poet, translator of Dante, and essayist, though she is best known for her detective stories featuring the inimitable sleuth Lord Peter Wimsey. Among the best of them are *Strong Poison* (1930), *Murder Must Advertise* (1933), *Gaudy Night* (1935), and *Busman's Honeymoon: a Love Story with Detective Interruptions* (1937).

RICHARD SELZER (1928–   )
is a surgeon, professor of surgery, essayist, and author of fiction. He is a frequent contributor to popular and literary magazines, including *Madamoiselle, Redbook*, and *Harper's*. He won the National Magazine award from Columbia's School of Journalism in 1975 for his essays in *Esquire*. His book-length works include a collection of short stories, *Rituals of Surgery* (1974), and a collection of essays, *Mortal Lessons* (1977). His *Confessions of a Knife* appeared in 1984.

ADAM SMITH (1723–1790)
was born in the small Scottish fishing community of Kirkcaldy and at age four was stolen by gypsies, though he was recovered shortly thereafter. He was educated at the University of Glasgow, the center of the Scottish Enlightenment. After giving a series of public lectures on subjects as disparate as rhetoric, the classics, history, and economics, he took a post as professor of logic at Glasgow, though he soon moved to a position as professor of moral philosophy (a discipline including law, ethics, and theology) at that university. Given the nature of his studies, then, it comes as no surprise that his most famous work, *The Wealth of Nations* (1776), the first great study of political economy, is informed by a theory of human nature and social evolution gleaned from those wide readings.

JOHN STEINBECK (1902–1968)
was born in Salinas, California. After
an abortive attempt to establish himself as a writer in New York City, he
returned to California to a succession
of blue-collar jobs. He is best known
for his Pulitzer Prize-winning *The
Grapes of Wrath* (1939), *Of Mice and
Men* (1937), and a collection of short
stories, *The Long Valley*, which contains "The Chrysanthemums" and
"The Red Pony." In 1962 he won
the Nobel Prize for Literature and
published *Travels with Charley: In
Search of America*. Other works
include: *Tortilla Flat* (1935), *Cannery
Row* (1945), and *East of Eden* (1952).

**ROBERT LOUIS STEVENSON (1850–
1894)**
was born in Edinburgh, Scotland. At
an early age he became chronically
ill and turned to the cure usually
prescribed for lung disease in the
19th century—travel. His travels
stoked his talent for describing the
exotic, and, drawing on his experiences, he produced *An Inland Voyage*
(1878), *Travels With A Donkey in The
Cevennes* (1879), *The Silverado Squat-
ters* (1883), *Treasure Island* (1883),
Kidnapped (1887), and *A Footnote to
History: Eight Years of Trouble in
Samoa* (1892). He is also justly
famous for his portrayal of the struggle between the good and evil in
human nature in *Dr. Jekyll and Mr.
Hyde* (1886). In 1881 he published
Virginibus Puerisque and Other Papers,
a collection of essays.

JONATHAN SWIFT (1667–1734)
was born in Dublin, Ireland, but was
driven from Ireland to England by
James II's invasion in 1689. For ten
years he was attached to the household of Sir William Temple. He took
orders in The Church of England in
1684, and began his career as a sati-
rist in 1704 with *A Tale of a Tub* and
The Battle of the Books. He returned to
Ireland as Dean of St. Patrick's
Cathedral in Dublin and found himself, after publication of "The Dra-
pier's Letters" (1724–25) and "A
Modest Proposal" (1729), an Irish
national hero. His major work is of
course *Gulliver's Travels* (1726), often
regarded as the greatest satire in the
English language.

JEREMY TAYLOR (1613–1667)
was born in London and took holy
orders in the Anglican Church in
1633; he soon became chaplain of
King Charles I's household. Taylor's
reputation rests mainly on his *Holy
Living* (1650) and *Holy Dying* (1651).

PAUL THEROUX (1941–   )
contributes fiction, poetry, and essays
to *The Atlantic* and *Playboy*, to name a
few, reviews books for both the New
York and London *Times*, writes novels, and has spent a good part of his
working life in exotic places like Singapore and Uganda. His works
include *Waldo* (1967), *Jungle Lovers*
(1971), *Saint Jack* (1973), *V.S. Nai-
paul: An Introduction to His Work*
(1972), *Sinning with Annie and Other
Stories* (1972), *The Great Railway
Bazaar: By Train through Asia* (1975),
The Picture Palace (1978), *The Mosquito
Coast* (1982), *The Kingdom By the Sea*
(1983), and *Sunrise With Seamonsters*
(1985), a collection of essays.

LEWIS THOMAS (1913–   )
is a distinguished physician and professor of medicine, as well as a prolific contributor to such scientific
journals as *Science*, *Nature*, and *Dae-
dalus*. His columns, entitled "Notes of
a Biology Watcher" and published in
the *New England Journal of Medicine*,
were collected in *The Lives of a Cell:
Notes of a Biology Watcher* in 1974.
That book was applauded for
Thomas's optimistic view of man's
symbiotic relationship with nature
as was *The Medusa and the Snail: More
Notes of a Biology Watcher* (1979). In
1983 he published *Late Night
Thoughts on Listening to Mahler's Ninth
Symphony*.

**HENRY DAVID THOREAU (1817–
1862)**
was educated at Harvard, where he
heard "The American Scholar"
(called the "American intellectual
Declaration of Independence" by
Oliver Wendell Holmes), a lecture
delivered by his soon-to-be friend
and mentor, Ralph Waldo Emerson.
Smitten by Emerson's ideas, Thoreau
attended meetings of the Transcendental Club, which included Bronson
Alcott, Margaret Fuller, and, of
course, Emerson. Thoreau's major
writings include: *A Week on the Concord and Merrimack Rivers* (1849),

Resistance to Civil Government (1849), now known as *Civil Disobedience*, and *Walden* (1854), his best-known work.

MARK TWAIN (1835–1910)
was born Samuel Langhorne Clemens in Florida, Missouri. His career, as his writings indicate, was a varied one, for he served as a printer, journalist, riverboat pilot, and publisher. He is generally regarded as America's foremost humorist, and in *Huckleberry Finn* (1865) may have achieved the mythical "great American novel." His other widely read works include *The Innocents Abroad* (1869), *The Adventures of Tom Sawyer* (1876), *The Prince and The Pauper* (1882), *Life on The Mississippi* (1883), *A Connecticut Yankee in King Arthur's Court* (1889), and *The Tragedy of Pudd'nhead Wilson* (1894).

ALICE WALKER (1944–)
was born in Eatonton, Georgia, and spent the years immediately after her graduation from college helping in the Civil Rights movement, teaching in the Head Start program in Mississippi, and working for the New York City welfare department. Since 1968 she has taught and been writer-in-residence at various colleges and universities. Her stories, poems, and essays appear in a range of periodicals, including *Harper's* and *Ms.* Walker's fiction has eloquently revealed the nature of the lives of black women in contemporary culture. It includes two collections of stories, *In Love and Trouble: Stories of Black Women* (1973) and *You Can't Keep a Good Woman Down* (1981); and three novels, *The Third Life of Grange Copeland* (1970), *Meridian* (1976), and *The Color Purple* (1982), which won the Pulitzer Prize.

E(LWYN) B(ROOKS) WHITE (1899–1985),
after failing as a newspaper reporter, became the principal writer of short comments for "The Talk of the Town" section of *The New Yorker.* Ironic, amusing, and quick on its feet, "Talk" defined the magazine's style. White wrote longer essays for *Harper's* magazine, collected in *One Man's Meat* (1942). After World War II, his writing concentrated on peace and environmental safety. He also wrote children's books, including *Charlotte's Web* (1952), and contributed a memorable chapter to William Strunk, Jr.'s *The Elements of Style* (1959). Among collections of White's work are *The Essays of E.B. White* (1977) and *Poems and Sketches* (1981).

ROGER WILKINS (1932–),
the nephew of NAACP leader Roy Wilkins, has worked as a writer, lawyer, and U.S. government official. From 1969 until 1972 he was program director for the Ford Foundation, and from 1972 to 1974 he wrote for the *Washington Post.* He then joined the editorial board of *The New York Times,* where he was urban affairs columnist until moving to the editorial board of *Nation.* His autobiography, *A Man's Life,* was published in 1982.

TOM WOLFE (1931–)
is regarded as one of the leaders of "The New Journalism," a style characterized by techniques formerly associated with fiction: use of dialogue, shifting point of view, and close attention to setting, clothes, and character. His essays and studies include *The Kandy-Kolored Tangerine-Flake Streamlined Baby* (1965), *The Electric Kool-Aid Acid Test* (1968), *The Pump House Gang* (1968), *Radical Chic and Mau Mauing the Flak Catchers* (1970), *The Painted Word* (1975), *The Right Stuff* (1979), *In Our Time* (1980), *From Bauhaus to Our House* (1981), and *The Purple Decades: A Reader* (1982).

VIRGINIA WOOLF (1882–1941)
was born in London the daughter of Sir Leslie Stephen, the eminent biographer and critic. She became the linchpin of the "Bloomsbury Group," a coterie devoted to the arts and sciences, and, with her husband Leonard, founded the Hogarth Press. She is noted for her experimentation with "stream of consciousness," the attempt to reproduce thought in prose, in such novels as *Mrs. Dalloway* (1925), *To The Lighthouse* (1927), and *The Waves* (1931). Her distinctive voice characterizes virtually every page of her essays and studies, which are collected in, among others, *The Common Reader* (1925), *A Room of One's Own* (1929), *The Second Common Reader* (1932), and *The Death of the Moth* (1942).

BROWSER'S
INDEX

ON THE CONTRARY

Oscar Wilde said that Nature imitates Art, that before Whistler painted them there were no fogs along the Thames. If his statement were not false, it would not be witty. But to say that Nature imitates Art, when the Nature is human nature and the Art that of television, radio, motion-pictures, magazines, is literally true.

JARRELL, *A Sad Heart at the Supermarket*, p. 428

There are things so deeply personal that they can be revealed only to strangers.

RODRIGUEZ, *Mr. Secrets*, p. 996

It is far harder to kill a phantom than a reality.

WOOLF, *The Patriarchy*, p. 219

I don't take a night journey on a railroad for the sake of duplicating the experiences and conveniences of my own home: when I travel I like to get into some new kind of difficulty, not just the same old trouble I put up with around the house.

WHITE, *Progress and Change*, p. 135

The truth is that the city is a device for *reducing* stress—by giving humans a freer choice of escapes from the pressure (along with the weather) of their environment.

BROPHY, *The Menace of Nature*, p. 45

By and large it is only the very great who are not snobbish at all. They are the ones who are modest about their accomplishments because they have devoted their lives to achieving some kind of understanding and so have developed a deep tolerance for ignorance.

LYNES, *The New Snobbism*, p. 328

For the power of Man to make himself what he pleases means, as we have seen, the power of some men to make other men what *they* please.

LEWIS, *The Abolition of Man,* p. 186

This I believe to be a very common experience with women writers— they are impeded by the extreme conventionality of the other sex.

WOOLF, *The Patriarchy,* p. 220

But the fashion for reform, the drive to emasculate macho, has produced a kind of numbing androgyny and has so blurred the lines of gender that I often find myself wanting to emulate some of the women I know— bold, aggressive, vigorous role models.

NORMAN, *Standing His Ground,* p. 274

"Others merely live," he wrote; "I vegetate."

LYNES, *The New Snobbism,* p. 321

FAMILY

Amiable, ignorant, bovine women make much better mothers than neurotic college graduates.   BUCK, *America's Medieval Women,* p. 632

She is an open and trusting child, unprepared for and unaccustomed to the ambushes of family life, and perhaps it is just as well that I can offer her little of that life. I would like to give her more. I would like to promise her that she will grow up with a sense of her cousins and of rivers and of her great-grand-mother's teacups, would like to pledge her a picnic on a river with fried chicken and her hair uncombed, would like to give her *home* for her birthday, but we live differently now and I can promise her nothing like that.

DIDION, *On Going Home,* p. 408

And my mother. At what moments has she hated me? On what occasions has she been embarrassed by me? What does she recall feeling during these difficult, sullen years of my childhood?

RODRIGUEZ, *Mr. Secrets,* p. 997

For with the carefully prepared formula that maternal care has placed in its bottle the American child drinks in the admonition to succeed, to be the right weight, to learn to walk at the right time, to go up grade by grade in school, with good marks, to make the team, to make the sorority or clique, to be the one to be chosen by others for success.

MEAD, *Sex and Achievement,* p. 257

And that afternoon she . . . granted me the right, the freedom so crucial to adulthood, to become a person very different in public from the person I am at home.

RODRIGUEZ, *Mr. Secrets,* p. 999

The dictatorial father of Freud's time is virtually extinct. Once he roamed the land in vast herds, snorting virile snorts and refreshing himself in austere men's clubs walled with fumed oak, before thundering home to preside over his cave.

MANCHESTER, *In Defense of Snobs*, p. 350

Characteristically, the sister in America is the big sister, whose side the parents always take, who is so slick she always wins, who gets away with murder—that is, gets the same rewards with less effort—and the day-dream sister is the little sister, over whom one can win without effort.

MEAD, *Sex and Achievement*, p. 261

Children have never been very good at listening to their elders, but they have never failed to imitate them.

BALDWIN, *Fifth Avenue, Uptown*, p. 597

Such memories are not easy to shed, particularly since childhood, the time when people can best acquire a comradeship with animals, is also when they are likely to pick up their parents' fears.

HOAGLAND, *Dogs, and the Tug of Life*, p. 20

The notion that "nature" and "nature study" are somehow "nice" for children, regardless of the children's own temperament, is a sentimental piety—and often a hypocritical one, like the piety which thinks Sunday School nice for *them* though we don't go to church ourselves.

BROPHY, *The Menace of Nature*, p. 44

Her children or grandchildren and their children came every day to visit. Everyone talked to her, to each other, about what a nice place the nursing home was, how friendly the staff was, how clean the rooms were, how there were lots of people around to play cards with, and that the best part was that they could take her home anytime for dinners, picnics, holidays. And then they left, and hardly got out the front door before they burst into tears and cried aloud: why did their mother have to be there, in that nice, clean, friendly place?

HAMPL, *Teresa*, p. 820

Marriage is the classic betrayal.

DIDION, *On Going Home*, p. 406

FREEDOM

Under a government which imprisons any unjustly, the true place for a just man is also a prison.

THOREAU, *Civil Disobedience*, p. 696

There is no very great danger of a rich man going to jail.

DARROW, *Address to the Prisoners in the Cook County Jail*, p. 606

We know through painful experience that freedom is never voluntarily given by the oppressor; it must be demanded by the oppressed.

KING, *Letter from Birmingham Jail*, p. 710

"Freedom is the recognition of necessity"—and it is the role of education to reveal to all the necessity of abandoning the freedom to breed.

HARDIN, *The Tragedy of the Commons*, p. 785

A common and natural result of an undue respect for law is, that you may see a file of soldiers, colonel, captain, corporal, privates, powder-monkeys, and all, marching in admirable order over hill and dale to the wars, against their wills, ay, against their common sense and consciences, which makes it very steep marching indeed, and produces a palpitation of the heart.

THOREAU, *Civil Disobedience*, p. 696

When men mutually agreed to pass laws against robbing, mankind became more free, not less so.

HARDIN, *The Tragedy of the Commons*, p. 784

Policemen are not given nightsticks for ornament. They are given them for the purpose of cracking the skulls of the recalcitrant plain people, Democrats and Republicans alike.

MENCKEN, *The Nature of Liberty*, p. 723

Never before have I written a letter this long (or should I say a book?). I'm afraid that it is much too long to take your precious time. I can assure you that it would have been much shorter if I had been writing from a comfortable desk, but what else is there to do when you are alone for days in the dull monotony of a narrow jail cell other than write long letters, think strange thoughts, and pray long prayers?

KING, *Letter from Birmingham Jail*, p. 722

What it does mean to be spiritually androgynous is a kind of freedom.

PERRIN, *The Androgynous Man*, p. 270

I perceived in this moment that when the white man turns tyrant it is his own freedom that he destroys. He becomes a sort of hollow, posing dummy, the conventionalized figure of a sahib. For it is the condition of his rule that he shall spend his life in trying to impress the "natives," and so in every crisis he has got to do what the "natives" expect of him. He wears a mask, and his face grows to fit it.

ORWELL, *Shooting an Elephant*, p. 591

As American Negroes have discovered, to be officially free is by no means the same as being actually and psychologically free.

BROPHY, *Women*, p. 275

It's little wonder that, treated like slaves most of the time, the middle class lusts for the illusion of weight and consequence.

FUSSELL, *The Middle Class*, p. 333

That is, he wanted a woman who would contain herself docilely within four walls. And he could not have seen that an intelligent, energetic, educated woman cannot be kept in four walls—even satin-lined, diamond-studded walls—without discovering sooner or later that they are still a prison cell.

BUCK, America's Medieval Women, p. 626

No doubt the reason society eventually agreed to abolish its anti-women laws was that it had become confident of commanding a battery of hidden dissuaders which would do the job just as well.

BROPHY, Women, p. 275

Each new power won *by* man is a power *over* man as well. Each advance leaves him weaker as well as stronger. In every victory, besides being the general who triumphs, he is also the prisoner who follows the triumphal car.

LEWIS, The Abolition of Man, p. 186

HUMAN NATURE

Not only are the distinctions we often draw between male nature and female nature largely arbitrary and often pure superstition: they are completely beside the point. They ignore the essence of *human* nature. . . . What distinguishes human from any other animal nature is the ability to be unnatural.

BROPHY, Women, p. 279

"What," men have asked distractedly from the beginning of time, "what on earth do women want?" I do not know that women *as* women want anything in particular, but as human beings they want, my good men, exactly what you want yourselves: interesting occupation, reasonable freedom for their pleasures, and a sufficient emotional outlet.

SAYERS, Are Women Human?, p. 230

We might suppose that is was possible to say "After all, most of us want more or less the same things—food and drink and sexual intercourse, amusement, art, science, and the longest possible life for individuals and for the species. Let them simply say, This is what we happen to like, and go on to condition men in the way most likely to produce it. Where's the trouble?" But this will not answer. In the first place, it is false that we all really like the same things.

LEWIS, The Abolition of Man, p. 188

I believe that in all men's lives at certain periods, and in many men's lives at all periods, between infancy and extreme old age, one of the most dominant elements is the desire to be inside the local Ring and the terror of being left outside.

LEWIS, The Inner Ring, p. 301

Since scarcely anyone is so secure that his ego does not sometimes need a certain amount of external manipulation, there is scarcely anyone who isn't a snob of some sort.

LYNES, The New Snobbism, p. 316

Autobiography is only to be trusted when it reveals something disgraceful. A man who gives a good account of himself is probably lying, since any life when viewed from the inside is simply a series of defeats.

ORWELL, *Benefit of Clergy,* p. 482

This kind of thing makes one's blood boil, whereas—on the whole—the plight of the human beings does not. I am not commenting, merely pointing to a fact. People with brown skins are next door to invisible. Anyone can be sorry for the donkey with its galled back, but it is generally owing to some kind of accident if one even notices the old woman under her load of sticks.

ORWELL, *Marrakech,* p. 886

Wolf behavior prepared dogs remarkably for life with human beings.

HOAGLAND, *Dogs, and the Tug of Life,* p. 22

Aristotle made a remark which we most inadequately translate "Man is a political animal." What Aristotle really said is "Man is a creature who lives in a polis"; and what he goes on to demonstrate, in his *Politics,* is that the polis is the only framework within which man can fully realize his spiritual, moral and intellectual capacities.

KITTO, *The Polis,* p. 676

The normal and natural thing for human beings is not to tolerate handicaps but to reform society and to circumvent or supplement nature.

BROPHY, *The Menace of Nature,* p. 279

"The training makes our men interchangeable," an IBM executive was once heard to say.

FUSSELL, *The Middle Class,* p. 333

What we ask is to be human individuals, however peculiar and unexpected.

SAYERS, *Are Women Human?,* p. 228

The sum of all is this: that thou art a man, than whom there is not in the world any greater instance of heights and declensions, of lights and shadows, of misery and folly, of laughter and tears, of groans and death.

TAYLOR, *Holy Dying,* p. 800

KNOWING

Philosophy, in its more rigid sense, has been at the same work for ages; and after a myriad bald heads have wagged over the problem, and piles of words have been heaped one upon another into dry and cloudy volumes without end, philosophy has the honor of laying before us, with modest pride, her contribution toward the subject: that life is a Permanent Possibility of Sensation.

STEVENSON, *Aes Triplex,* p. 807

If truth is not to be found on the shelves of the British Museum, where, I asked myself, picking up a notebook and a pencil, is truth?

WOOLF, *The Patriarchy,* p. 613

Which would have advanced the most at the end of a month,—they boy who had made his own jackknife from the ore which he had dug and smelted, reading as much as would be necessary for this—or the boy who had attended the lectures on metallurgy at the Institute in the meanwhile, and had received a Rodgers penknife from his father? Which would be most likely to cut his fingers?

THOREAU, *The Fitness of a Man's Building His Own House,* p. 130

Seeing is believing; and if what you see in *Life* is different from what you see in life, which of the two are you to believe?

JARRELL, *A Sad Heart at the Supermarket,* p. 428

If we will risk seeming pompous or pedantic, we can say that the most important consequences of packaging have been epistemological. They have had to do with the nature of knowledge and they have especially had the effect of confusing us about what knowledge is, and what's real, about what's form and what's substance.

BOORSTIN, *Technology and Democracy,* p. 158

Yet it is in our idleness, in our dreams, that the submerged truth sometimes comes to the top. A very elementary exercise in truth.

WOOLF, *The Patriarchy,* p. 618

These ideas, which may seem a bit far-fetched to the modern reader, would not have troubled the men and women of the ancient world, for their notion of culture was one of psychic education, the education of the sensibility; ours is built upon a notion of mentation, the cramming of the skull with facts and pragmatic data which positively stifle the growth of the soul.

DURRELL, *Landscape and Character,* p. 879

If a liberal education should teach students "how to think," not only in their own fields but in fields outside their own—that is, to understand "how the other fellow orders knowledge," then bulling, even in its purest form, expresses an important part of what a pluralist university holds dear, surely a more important part than the collecting of "facts that are facts" which schoolboys learn to do.

PERRY, *Examsmanship and the Liberal Arts,* p. 1081

That night, I realized that no matter how good I became in the manipulation of symbols, I could never hope to move anyone without allowing myself to be moved, that I could reveal only slight truths unless I was willing to reveal the truths about myself.

BRADLEY, *The Faith,* p. 984

That only is true enlargement of mind which is the power of viewing many things at once as one whole, of referring them severally to their true place in the universal system, of understanding their respective values, and determining their mutual dependence.

NEWMAN, *Enlargement of Mind,* p. 1099

It still comes as a shock to realize that I don't write about what I know: I write in order to find out what I know. Is it possible to convey to a reader the enormous degree of blankness, confusion, hunch and uncertainty lurking in the act of writing?

HAMPL, *Memory and Imagination,* p. 1007

Truth doesn't change. Truth is one thing. It covers all things which touch the heart—honor and pride and pity and justice and courage and love.

FAULKNER, *The Bear,* p. 94

Art lies to us to tell us the (sometimes disquieting) truth. The Medium tells us truths, in fact, in order to make us believe some reassuring or entertaining lie or half-truth.

JARRELL, *A Sad Heart at the Supermarket,* p. 430

LANGUAGE

. . . and he used all sorts of steamboat technicalities in his talk, as if he were so used to them that he forgot common people couldn't understand them. He would speak of the "labboard" side of a horse in an easy, natural way that would make one wish he was dead.

TWAIN, *Old Times on the Mississippi,* p. 311

Once we killed bad men: now we liquidate unsocial elements.

LEWIS, *The Abolition of Man,* p. 193

Complexity and obscurity, on the other hand, have professional value; they are the academic equivalents of apprenticeship rules in the building trades. They exclude outsiders, keep down the competition, preserve the image of a privileged or priestly class.

GALBRAITH, *Writing and Typing,* p. 1026

The first step, he said, was to change nomenclature. Instead of *penetentiaries, guards,* and *convicts,* we must speak of *penal hospitals, psychiatric aides,* and *social patients.*

MANCHESTER, *In Defense of Snobs,* p. 344

Never use a foreign phrase, a scientific word or a jargon word if you can think of an everyday English equivalent.

ORWELL, *Politics and the English Language,* p. 1046

This is the man who tries so hard to be "natural," so hard to be "just folks," so hard to avoid having anyone else think that he is a snob, that he plays a game which (if I may be forgiven for being a Language Snob for a moment) is *faux naif.* He would not, for example, ever be caught using a foreign phrase. . . .

LYNES, *The New Snobbism,* p. 328

If sufficient people say, "I feel badly," or "It is me," then grammatical snobs are confounded: the error is accepted.

MANCHESTER, *In Defense of Snobs,* p. 351

Political language—and with variations this is true of all political parties, from Conservatives to Anarchists—is designed to make lies sound truthful and murder respectable, and to give an appearance of solidity to pure wind.

ORWELL, *Politics and the English Language*, p. 1047

Yet a writer wishes—indeed all of us wish—to speak about profound matters that are, like it or not, general and abstract. We wish to talk to each other about life and death, about love, despair, loss, and innocence. We sense that in order to live together we must learn to speak of peace, of history, of meaning and values.

HAMPL, *Memory and Imagination*, p. 1011

Such is the benefit of language: By finding public words to describe one's feelings, one can describe oneself to oneself. One names what was previously only darkly felt.

RODRIGUEZ, *Mr. Secrets*, p. 998

It is my regrettable duty to report that at this moment of triumph Mr. Metzger was carried away by the temptations of parody and added, "We are thus much the richer."

PERRY, *Examsmanship and the Liberal Arts*, p. 1078

The very words *death, danger, bravery, fear* were not to be uttered except in the occasional specific instance or for ironic effect.

WOLFE, *The Right Stuff*, p. 246

The "words" of various animal "languages" are merely interjections.

LORENZ, *The Language of Animals*, p. 29

LOVE AND FRIENDSHIP

If a dog really becomes a man's best friend his situation is desperate.

HOAGLAND, *Dogs, and the Tug of Life*, p. 19

One must be fond of people and trust them if one is not to make a mess of life, and it is therefore essential that they should not let one down. They often do.

FORSTER, *What I Believe*, p. 728

The artist who is seduced by mateyness may stop himself from doing the one thing which he, and he alone, can do—the making of something out of words or sounds or paint or clay or marble or steel or film which has internal harmony and presents order to a permanently disarranged planet.

FORSTER, *Art for Art's Sake*, p. 480

This is friendship. Aristotle placed it among the virtues. It causes perhaps half of all the happiness in the world, and no Inner Ringer can ever have it.

LEWIS, *The Inner Ring*, p. 306

Near the place where Oates disappeared they put up a cross with the inscription: "Hereabouts died a very gallant gentleman, Captain E. G. Oates of the Inniskilling Dragoons. In March 1912, returning from the Pole, he walked willingly to his death in a blizzard to try and save his comrades, beset by hardship."

N. MITFORD, *A Bad Time*, p. 176

Tradition decrees that after marriage real companionship between persons of opposite sex must cease except between husband and wife.

BUCK, *America's Medieval Women*, p. 634

. . . the country is a place where one is under the thumb of chance, constrained to love one's neighbour not out of philanthropy but because there's no other company.

BROPHY, *The Menace of Nature*, p. 45

We were both surprised. We looked at each other; I flushed but Myra did not. I realized the pledge as our fingers touched; I was panicky, but *all right*. I thought, I can come early and walk with her other mornings. I can go and talk to her at recess. Why not? *Why not?*

MUNRO, *The Day of the Butterfly*, p. 447

With them, love existed confined inside each individual, never breaking its boundaries to express itself and bring them together. For them to show affection was to discharge their duties to each other perfectly, and above all not to inconvenience, never to inconvenience.

DONOSO, *Paseo*, p. 69

Ron had stopped listening. He was staring across the room, with a quiet, faraway look on his face. Linda put her hand on his crossed left leg, just above the white part of his cutouts, and watched him with an expression of immense care and affection.

ANGELL, *In the Country*, p. 560

I must not assume that you have ever first neglected, and finally shaken off, friends whom you really loved and who might have lasted you a lifetime, in order to court the friendship of those who appeared to you more important, more esoteric.

LEWIS, *The Inner Ring*, p. 303

Personal relations are despised today. They are regarded as bourgeois luxuries, as products of a time of fair weather which is now past, and we are urged to get rid of them, and to dedicate ourselves to some movement or cause instead. I hate the idea of causes, and if I had to choose between betraying my country and betraying my friend, I hope I should have the guts to betray my country.

FORSTER, *What I Believe*, p. 728

MORALITY

Oscar Wilde, a really accomplished snob, said that "Morality is simply the attitude we adopt toward people we personally dislike."

LYNES, *The New Snobbism*, p. 319

Morality is both a public and a private matter, to be sure, and it is characteristic of the Moral Snob to put a good deal of ornamental fretwork on his public facade and let the private places of his personality be slovenly.

LYNES, *The New Snobbism*, p. 319

The methods may (at first) differ in brutality, but many a mild-eyed scientist in pince-nez, many a popular dramatist, many an amateur philosopher in our midst means in the long run just the same as the Nazi rulers of Germany.

LEWIS, *The Abolition of Man*, p. 193

It is a terrible, an inexorable, law that one cannot deny the humanity of another without diminishing one's own: in the face of one's victim one sees oneself.

BALDWIN, *Fifth Avenue, Uptown*, p. 603

It is not a man's duty, as a matter of course, to devote himself to the eradication of any, even the most enormous wrong; he may still properly have other concerns to engage him; but it his duty, at least, to wash his hands of it, and, if he gives it no thought longer, not to give it practically his support.

THOREAU, *Civil Disobedience*, p. 693

To nine out of ten of you the choice which could lead to scoundrelism will come, when it does come, in no very dramatic colours.

LEWIS, *The Inner Ring*, p. 304

Being naturally innocent and well-disposed and aboveboard, a member of the middle class finds it hard to believe that all are not.

FUSSELL, *The Middle Class*, p. 334

An ideal arrangement of ethical behavior in the United States would leave good works, those so-necessary good works, to widows and spinsters. . . .

MEAD, *Sex and Achievement*, p. 254

It is the very mark of a perverse desire that it seeks what is not to be had.

LEWIS, *The Inner Ring*, p. 305

Obscenity is a very difficult question to discuss honestly. People are too frightened either of seeming to be shocked or of seeming not to be shocked, to be able to define the relationship between art and morals.

FORSTER, *Art for Art's Sake*, p. 487

For of course, when promiscuity is the fashion, the chaste are outsiders.

LEWIS, *The Inner Ring,* p. 302

Great bodies of people are never responsible for what they do.

WOOLF, *The Patriarchy,* p. 622

This asocial gang-life of boys provides a basis for the adult criminal world in America.

MEAD, *Sex and Achievement,* p. 258

There is no such thing as a crime as the word is generally understood.

DARROW, *Address to the Prisoners in the Cook County Jail,* p. 603

THE PAST

We cling to a time and a place because without them man is lost, not only man but life.

EISELEY, *The Brown Wasps,* p. 56

I glimpsed what lay ahead—literally glimpsed it, for there was Mencken beside me—and deeply felt a profound sense of sadness for the irretrievable stamina of the receding past.

MANCHESTER, *My Old Man,* p. 835

We look at old family photographs in which we stand next to black, boxy Fords and are wearing period costumes, and we do not gaze fascinated because there we are young again, next to our mother. We stare and drift because there we are . . . historical.

HAMPL, *Memory and Imagination,* p. 1014

After all these years I can picture that old time to myself now, just as it was then: the white town drowsing in the sunshine of a summer's morning; the streets empty, or pretty nearly so; one or two clerks sitting in front of the Water Street stores, with their splint-bottomed chairs tilted back against the wall. . . .

TWAIN, *Old Times on the Mississippi,* p. 309

How can we admit that the agreeable past, which we thought was permanent and inviolable, has slipped away like a Mississippi steamboat?

CONNELL, *The Palace of the Moorish Kings,* p. 930

We stared silently at the tips of our rods, as the dragonflies came and went. I lowered the tip of mine into the water tentatively, pensively dislodging the fly. . . . There had been no years between the ducking of this dragonfly and the other one—the one that was part of memory. I looked at the boy, who was silently watching his fly, and it was my hands that held his rod. I felt dizzy and didn't know which rod I was on the end of.

WHITE, *Once More to the Lake,* p. 842

To write one's life is to live it twice, and the second living is both spiritual and historical. . . .

HAMPL, *Memory and Imagination*, p. 1014

I can no longer tell you whether Milton put the sun or the earth at the center of his universe in *Paradise Lost*, the central question of at least one century and a topic about which I wrote 10,000 words that summer, but I can still recall the exact rancidity of the butter in the City of San Francisco's dining car, and the way the tinted windows on the Greyhound bus cast the oil refineries around Carquinez Straits into a grayed and obscurely sinister light.

DIDION, *Why I Write*, p. 1016

Life disappears or modifies its appearances so fast that everything takes on an aspect of illusion—a momentary fizzing and boiling with smoke rings, like pouring dissident chemicals into a retort.

EISELEY, *The Brown Wasps*, p. 57

Every revolution which the sun makes about the world divides between life and death; and death possesses both those portions by the next morrow; and we are dead to all those months which we have already lived, and we shall never live them over again; and still God makes little periods of our age.

TAYLOR, *Holy Dying*, p. 801

PORTRAITS

At first the Crazy Lady appeared to be remarkably intelligent. She was older than the rest of us, somewhere in her thirties (which was why we thought of her as a Lady), with wild tan hair, a noticeably breathing bosom, eccentric gold-rimmed old-pensioner glasses, and a tooth-crowded wild mouth that seemed to get wilder the more she talked. She talked like a motorcycle, fast and urgent. Everything she said was almost brilliant, only not actually on point, and frenetic with hostility. She was tough and negative. She volunteered a lot and she stood up and wobbled with rage, pulling at her hair and mouth.

OZICK, *We are the Crazy Lady*, p. 409

When hardness surfaces in the very old we tend to transform it into "crustiness" or eccentricity, some tonic pepperiness to be indulged at a distance. On the evidence of her work and what she has said about it, Georgia O'Keeffe is neither "crusty" nor eccentric. She is simply hard, a straight shooter, a woman clean of received wisdom and open to what she sees. This is a woman who could early on dismiss most of contemporaries as "dreamy," and would later single out one she liked as "a very poor painter." (And then add, apparently by way of softening the judgment: "I guess he wasn't a painter at all. He had no courage and I believe that to create one's own world in any of the arts takes courage.")

DIDION, *Georgia O'Keeffe*, p. 467

Now that I can have her only in memory, I see my grandmother in the several postures that were peculiar to her: standing at the wood stove on a winter morning and turning meat in a great iron skillet; sitting at the south window, bent above her beadwork, and afterwards, when her vision had failed, looking down for a long time into the fold of her hands; going out upon a cane, very slowly as she did when the weight of age came upon her; praying.

MOMADAY, The Way to Rainy Mountain, p. 586

Toward all of us children he was very kind, and had the grace to be shy with us, which is unusual in grown-ups. He had great respect for my mother for she never held his drunkenness against him and would let us play with him even when he was about to fall in the fireplace from drink. Although Mr. Sweet would sometimes lose complete or nearly complete control of his head and neck so that he would loll in his chair, his mind remained strangely acute and his speech not too affected. His ability to be drunk and sober at the same time made him an ideal playmate, for he was as weak as we were and we could usually best him in wrestling, all the while keeping a fairly coherent conversation going.

WALKER, To Hell with Dying, p. 847

The loops of my mother's handwriting—it was the Palmer Method—were as big as hoops, spilling generous splashy ebullience. She could pull off, at five minutes' notice, a satisfying dinner for 10 concocted out of nothing more than originality and panache. But the napkin would be folded a little off-center, and the spoon might be on the wrong side of the knife. She was an optimist who ignored trifles; for her, God was not in the details but in the intent.

OZICK, On Excellence, p. 1028

Bradley has a few unorthodox shots, too. He dislikes flamboyance, and, unlike some of basketball's greatest stars, has apparently never made a move merely to attract attention. While some players are eccentric in their shooting, his shots, with only occasional exceptions, are straightforward and unexaggerated. Nonetheless, he does make something of a spectacle of himself when he moves in rapidly parallel to the baseline, glides through the air with his back to the basket, looks for a teammate he can pass to, and, finding none, tosses the ball into the basket over one shoulder, like a pinch of salt. Only when the ball is actually dropping through the net does he look around to see what has happened, on the chance that something might have gone wrong, in which case he would have to go for the rebound.

McPHEE, A Sense of Where You Are, p. 508

It was a bitter blow for the author of The American Language, and the worst of it was that he was fully aware of what was happening, understood the extent of the brain damage, and knew that his aphasia was incurable. In the Hopkins he had threatened to kill himself, but for all his thundering prose he had never been, and was not now, capable of violence. What actually happened was that he sank into a dreadful depression. He would stand in his study window, looking across at Union Square, on the opposite side of Hollins Street, saying almost inaudibly, "I wish this hideous existence would stop," saying, "How can anyone so stupid live," saying, "That a man like me, able to produce something, with the drive I had. . . . It's comic; it's just comic." In that first year of his disability he refused to allow anyone to read to him, refused to look at magazines with enlarged print, and wouldn't even listen to phonograph records. In one of his few remaining flashes of humor he hoarsely told me, "When I get to heaven, I'm going to speak to God very sharply."

MANCHESTER, *My Old Man: The Last Years of H. L. Mencken*, p. 831

I had been drawing a face, a figure. It was the face and the figure of Professor von X. engaged in writing his monumental work entitled *The Mental, Moral, and Physical Inferiority of the Female Sex.* He was not in my picture a man attractive to women. He was heavily built; he had a great jowl; to balance that he had very small eyes; he was very red in the face. His expression suggested that he was labouring under some emotion that made him jab his pen on the paper as if he were killing some noxious insect as he wrote, but even when he had killed it that did not satisfy him; he must go on killing it; and even so, some cause for anger and irritation remained. Could it be his wife, I asked, looking at my picture. Was she in love with a cavalry officer? Was the cavalry officer slim and elegant and dressed in astrachan? Had he been laughed at, to adopt the Freudian theory, in his cradle by a pretty girl? For even in his cradle the professor, I thought, could not have been an attractive child. Whatever the reason, the professor was made to look very angry and very ugly in my sketch, as he wrote his great book upon the mental, moral and physical inferiority of women.

WOOLF, *The Patriarchy*, p. 612

Her oily face gleamed as if it had just been rolled out of a can and laid on the white plate of her broad, spotless wimple. She was a small, plump woman; her body and the small window of her face seemed to interpret the entire alphabet of olive: her face was a sallow green olive placed upon the jumbo ripe olive of her black habit. I trusted her instantly and smiled, glad to have my hand placed in the hand of a woman who made sense, who provided the satisfaction of being what she was: an Olive who looked like an olive.

HAMPL, *Memory and Imagination*, p. 1003

The Greek woman is short and heavy, waistless, and is wearing a black dress, a black scarf pulled low around her eyes, a black sweater, thick black stockings, black shoes. She is stupendously there, black but for the walnut of her face, in the white sun, against the white space. She looks, at once, as if she could do everything she's ever done, anything needed, and also at once, she gives off an emanation of humor, powers, secrets, determinations, acts. She is moving straight ahead, like a moving church, a black peaked roof, a hot black hat, a dark tent, like a doom, a government, a force for good and evil, an ultimatum, a determined animal. She probably can't read, or write; she may never in her life have left this island; but she is beautiful, she could crush you, love you, mend you, deliver you of child or calf or lamb or illusion, bleed a pig, spear a fish, wring a supper's neck, till a field, coax an egg into life. Her sex is like a votive lamp flickering in a black, airless room.

BLOOM, On a Greek Holiday, p. 178

POSSESSIONS

The act of buying something is at the root of our world; if anyone wishes to paint the genesis of things in our society, he will paint a picture of God holding out to Adam a check-book or credit card or Charge-A-Plate.

JARRELL, A Sad Heart at the Supermarket, p. 421

Our inventions are wont to be pretty toys, which distract our attention from serious things. They are but improved means to an unimproved end, an end which it was already but too easy to arrive at; as railroads lead to Boston or New York.

THOREAU, The Fitness of a Man's Building His Own House, p. 131

As our common complexities increase, any tale of individual simplicity (and yours is the best written and the cockiest) acquires a new fascination; as our goods accumulate, but not our well-being, your report of an existence without material adornment takes on a certain awkward credibility.

WHITE, Walden, p. 901

The look that Mrs. Turpin and the pleasant lady exchanged indicated that they both understood that you have to have certain things before you know certain things.

O'CONNOR, Revelation, p. 359

The desire to belong, and to belong by some mechanical act like purchasing something, is another sign of the middle class.

FUSSELL, The Middle Class, p. 334

Indeed, I thought, slipping the silver into my purse, it is remarkable, remembering the bitterness of those days, what a change of temper a fixed income will bring about.

WOOLF, The Patriarchy, p. 622

Because most of the world is still what would be termed "poor," the more money you can spend, nearly anyplace, the more you are removed from the rich, complex life of that place. It is possible to buy everything that puts an average American life—taps that mix hot and cold, flush toilets, heating and cooling systems, menus in English—on top of any other existing world.

BLOOM, On a Greek Holiday, p. 182

If I pay you to carry me, I am not therefore myself a strong man.

LEWIS, The Abolition of Man, p. 184

Our society has delivered us—most of us—from the bonds of necessity, so that we no longer struggle to find food to keep from starving, clothing and shelter to keep from freezing; yet if the ends for which we work and of which we dream are only clothes and restaurants and houses, possessions, consumption, how have we escaped?—we have exchanged man's old bondage for a new voluntary one.

                    JARRELL, *A Sad Heart at the Supermarket*, p. 423

POTPOURRI

"Sincere and Dignified Since 1954," one wedding chapel advertises. There are nineteen such wedding chapels in Las Vegas, intensely competitive, each offering better, faster, and, by implication, more sincere services than the next: Our Photos Best Anywhere, Your Wedding on A Phonograph Record, Candlelight with Your Ceremony, Honeymoon Accommodations, Free Transportation from Your Motel to Courthouse to Chapel and Return to Motel, Religious or Civil Ceremonies, Dressing Rooms, Flowers, Rings, Announcements, Witnesses Available, and Ample Parking. All of these services, like most others in Las Vegas (sauna baths, payroll-check cashing, chinchilla coats for sale or rent) are offered twenty-four hours a day, seven days a week, presumably on the premise that marriage, like craps, is a game to be played when the table seems hot.

                    DIDION, *Marrying Absurd*, p. 908

I poked near the female's head with a grass; she was clearly undisturbed, so I settled my nose an inch from that pulsing abdomen. It puffed like a concertina, it throbbed like a bellows; it roved, pumping, over the glistening, clabbered surface of the egg case testing and patting, thrusting and smoothing. It seemed to act so independently that I forgot the panting brown stick at the other end. The bubble creature seemed to have two eyes, a frantic little brain, and two busy, soft hands. It looked like a hideous, harried mother slicking up a fat daughter for a beauty pageant, touching her up, slobbering over her, patting and hemming and brushing and stroking.

                    DILLARD, *The Fixed*, p. 64

We stand convinced today, at least those who remain sane, that lying and cheating and killing will build no world organization worth the building. We have got to stop making income by unholy methods; out of stealing the pittances of the poor and calling it insurance; out of seizing and monopolizing the natural resources of the world and then making the world's poor pay exorbitant prices for aluminum, copper and oil, iron and coal. Not only have we got to stop these practices, but we have got to stop lying about them and seeking to convince human beings that a civilization based upon the enslavement of the majority of men for the income of the smart minority is the highest aim of man.

                    DU BOIS, *Jacob and Esau*, p. 581

Women have served all these centuries as looking-glasses possessing the magic and delicious power of reflecting the figure of man at twice its natural size. Without that power probably the earth would still be swamp and jungle. The glories of all our wars would be unknown. We should still be scratching the outlines of deer on the remains of mutton bones and bartering flints for sheepskins or whatever simple ornament took our unsophisticated taste. Supermen and Fingers of Destiny would never have existed. The Czar and the Kaiser would never have worn their crowns or lost them. Whatever may be their use in civilised societies, mirrors are essential to all violent and heroic action. That is why Napoleon and Mussolini both insist so emphatically upon the inferiority of women, for if they were not inferior, they would cease to enlarge.

WOOLF, *The Patriarchy*, p. 620

"We shall next be told," exclaims Seneca, "that the first shoemaker was a philosopher!" For our own part, if we are forced to make our choice between the first shoemaker and the author of the three books On Anger, we pronounce for the shoemaker. It may be worse to be angry than to be wet. But shoes have kept millions from being wet; and we doubt whether Seneca ever kept anybody from being angry.

MACAULEY, *Francis Bacon*, p. 102

The Emperors, who weigh 6½ stone, look like sad little men and were often taken by early explorers for human natives of the South Polar regions, are in a low state of evolution (and of spirits). They lay their eggs in the terrible mid-winter, because only thus can their chicks, which develop with a slowness abnormal in birds, be ready to survive the next winter. They never step on shore, even to breed; they live in rookeries on sea-ice. To incubate their eggs, they balance them on their enormous feet and press them against a patch of bare skin on the abdomen protected from the cold by a lappet of skin and feathers. Paternity is the only joy known to these wretched birds and a monstrous instinct for it is implanted in their breasts; male and female hatch out the eggs and nurse the chicks, also on their feet, indiscriminately. When a penguin has to go in the sea to catch his dinner he leaves egg or chick on the ice; there is then a mad scuffle as twenty childless birds rush to adopt it, quite often breaking or killing it in the process. They will nurse a dead chick until it falls to pieces and sit for months on an addled egg or even a stone. All this happens in darkness and about a hundred degrees of frost. I often think the R.S.P.C.A. ought to do something for the Emperor Penguins.

N. MITFORD, *A Bad Time*, p. 170

But when she talked to me of ships her words did not evoke the hoarse sounds of ships' sirens that I heard in the distance on summer nights when, kept awake by the heat, I climbed to the attic, and from an open window watched the far-off floating lights, and those blocks of darkness surrounding the city that lay forever out of reach for me because my life was, and would ever be, ordered perfectly.

DONOSO, *Paseo*, p. 71

I believe in aristocracy, though—if that is the right word, and if a democrat may use it. Not an aristocracy of power, based upon rank and influence, but an aristocracy of the sensitive, the considerate and the plucky. Its members are to be found in all nations and classes, and all through the ages, and there is a secret understanding between them when they meet. They represent the true human tradition, the one permanent victory of our queer race over cruelty and chaos. Thousands of them perish in obscurity, a few are great names. They are sensitive for others as well as for themselves, they are considerate without being fussy, their pluck is not swankiness but the power to endure, and they can take a joke.

FORSTER, *What I Believe*, p. 732

SCIENCE

The serious magical endeavour and the serious scientific endeavour are twins: one was sickly and died, the other strong and throve.

LEWIS, *The Abolition of Man*, p. 194

Man masters nature not by force but by understanding. This is why science has succeeded when magic failed: because it has looked for no spell to cast over nature.

BRONOWSKI, *The Creative Mind*, p. 1066

Tolerance, good temper and sympathy are no longer enough in a world which is rent by religious and racial persecution, in a world where ignorance rules, and science, who ought to have ruled, plays the subservient pimp.

FORSTER, *What I Believe*, p. 727

All the sciences which deal with man have a tendency to depersonalize him for the simple reason that they tend to disregard everything which a particular science cannot deal with. Just as medicine confessedly deals with the physical man and economics confessedly deals not with Man but with the simplification officially designated as The Economic Man, so psychiatry deals with a fictitious man of whom there would be nothing more to be said if he were "normal," and one branch of psychology deals with what might be called the I.Q. man whose only significant aspect is his ability to solve puzzles.

KRUTCH, *No Essays, Please!*, p. 1034

Evidence cannot stand against him: if genetic research turns up new evidence of inherited characteristics, then geneticists are anti-democratic imposters.

MANCHESTER, *In Defense of Snobs*, p. 349

The stars lost their divinity as astronomy developed, and the Dying God has no place in chemical agriculture.

LEWIS, *The Abolition of Man*, p. 191

The very specialists in the forefront of finding out how animals behave, when one meets them, appear to be no more intrigued than any ordinary Indian was.

HOAGLAND, *Dogs, and the Tug of Life*, p. 25

We cannot reach social and political stability for the reason that we continue to make scientific discoveries and to apply them, and thus to destroy the arrangements which were based on more elementary discoveries. If Science would discover rather than apply—if, in other words, men were more interested in knowledge than in power—mankind would be in a far safer position, the stability statesmen talk about would be a possibility, there could be a new order based on vital harmony, and the earthly millennium might approach.

FORSTER, *Art for Art's Sake*, p. 478

The world today is made, it is powered by science; and for any man to abdicate an interest in science is to walk with open eyes towards slavery.

BRONOWSKI, *The Creative Mind*, p. 1063

WORK

There is some of the same fitness in a man's building his own house that there is in a bird's building its own nest. Who knows but if men constructed their dwellings with their own hands, and provided food for themselves and families simply and honestly enough, the poetic faculty would be universally developed, as birds universally sing when they are so engaged? But alas! we do like cowbirds and cuckoos, which lay their eggs in nests which other birds have built, and cheer no traveller with their chattering and unmusical notes. Shall we forever resign the pleasure of construction to the carpenter?

THOREAU, *The Fitness of a Man's Building His Own House*, p. 126

All people who work with their hands are partly invisible, and the more important the work they do, the less visible they are.

ORWELL, *Marrakech*, p. 884

It is all very well to say that women's place is the home—but modern civilisation has taken all these pleasant and profitable activities out of the home, where the women looked after them, and handed them over to big industry, to be directed and organised by men at the head of large factories.

SAYERS, *Are Women Human?*, p. 225

The right of the majority of mankind to speak and to act, to play and to dance was denied, if it interfered with profit-making work for others, or was ridiculed if it could not be capitalized.

DU BOIS, *Jacob and Esau*, p. 576

To this day, the choice of music or painting or poetry as a serious occupation is suspect for an American male.

MEAD, *Sex and Achievement*, p. 255

The cheapness of writing paper is, of course, the reason why women have succeeded as writers before they have succeeded in the other professions.

WOOLF, *The Patriarchy*, p. 217

... the American equation of success with the big times reveals an awful disrespect for human life and human achievement. This equation has placed our cities among the most dangerous in the world and has placed our youth among the most empty and most bewildered.

BALDWIN, *Fifth Avenue, Uptown,* p. 597

Even social workers, every hour of whose working day must, if they are to do their chosen tasks, be devoted to warm helpfulness, will defend their choice because it is interesting. . . . Only with apologies do they now admit to a simple desire to help human beings.

MEAD, *Sex and Achievement,* p. 255

Before that I had made my living by cadging odd jobs from newspapers, by reporting a donkey show here or a wedding there; I had earned a few pounds by addressing envelopes, reading to old ladies, making artificial flowers, teaching the alphabet to small children in a kindergarten. Such were the chief occupations that were open to women before 1918. I need not, I am afraid, describe in any detail the hardness of the work, for you know perhaps women who have done it; nor the difficulty of living on the money when it was earned, for you may have tried.

WOOLF, *The Patriarchy,* p. 622

In fact, there is perhaps only one human being in a thousand who is passionately interested in his job for the job's sake.

SAYERS, *Are Women Human?,* p. 227

AUTHOR/TITLE INDEX

Acknowledgments

(continued from p. iv)

ALICE BLOOM: "On a Greek Holiday," by Alice Bloom, excerpt from "On a Greek Holiday" by Alice Bloom. Reprinted by permission from *The Hudson Review,* Vol. XXXVI, No. 3 (Autumn 1983). Copyright © 1983 by Alice Bloom.

DANIEL BOORSTIN: "Technology and Democracy," from *Democracy and Its Discontents* by Daniel J. Boorstin. Copyright © 1974 by Daniel J. Boorstin. Reprinted by permission of Random House, Inc.

DAVID BRADLEY: "The Faith," by David Bradley. from *In Praise of What Persists* (Stephen Berg, ed., 1984). Copyright © 1984 by David Bradley. Reprinted by permission of Julian Bach Literary Agency, Inc.

JACOB BRONOWSKI: "The Creative Mind," from *Science and Human Values* by Jacob Bronowski. Copyright © 1956, 1965 by J. Bronowski. Reprinted by permission of Julian Messner, a division of Simon & Schuster, Inc.

BRIGID BROPHY: "The Menace of Nature" and "Women" from *Don't Never Forget.* Copyright 1966 by Brigid Brophy. All rights reserved. Reprinted by kind permission of the author.

SUSAN BROWNMILLER: "Prologue" from *Femininity* by Susan Brownmiller. Copyright © 1984 by Susan Brownmiller. Reprinted by permission of Linden Press, a division of Simon & Schuster, Inc.

PEARL BUCK: "America's Medieval Women." Reprinted by permission of Harold Ober Associates, Inc. Copyright 1938 by Pearl S. Buck. Copyright renewed 1965 by Pearl S. Buck.

SHEILA BURNFORD: "Pas Devant Le Chien" from *The Fields of Noon* by Sheila Burnford. Reprinted by permission of Harold Ober Associates and by permission of David Higham Assoc., Ltd., London. Copyright © 1962, 1963, 1964 by Sheila Burnford.

KENNETH CLARK: "Las Meninas," from *Looking at Pictures* by Kenneth Clark. Copyright © 1960 by Kenneth Clark. Reprinted by permission of Holt, Rinehart and Winston, Publishers, and by permission of John Murray (Publishers) Ltd., London.

EVAN CONNELL: "The Palace of the Moorish Kings," by Evan S. Connell. Excerpted from *St. Augustine's Pigeon.* Copyright © 1982 by Evan S. Connell. Published by North Point Press and reprinted by permission. All rights reserved.

HARRY CREWS: "Pages from the Life of a Georgia Innocent." Copyright © 1976 by Harry Crews. Reprinted by permission of John Hawkins & Associates, Inc.

JOAN DIDION: "Georgia O'Keeffe," from *The White Album* by Joan Didion. Copyright © 1979 by Joan Didion. Reprinted by permission of Simon & Schuster, Inc. "On Going Home" and "Marrying Absurd" from *Slouching Towards Bethlehem* by Joan Didion. Copyright 1967 by Joan Didion. Reprinted by permission of Farrar, Straus and Giroux, Inc. "Salvador" from *Salvador.* Copyright © 1983 by Joan Didion. Reprinted by permission of Simon & Schuster, Inc. "Why I Write" by Joan Didion. Reprinted by permission of Wallace Sheil Agency, Inc. Copyright © 1976 by Joan Didion. First published in *The New York Times Book Review.*

ANNIE DILLARD: "The Deer at Providencia" from *Teaching a Stone to Talk* by Annie Dillard. Copyright © 1982 by Annie Dillard. Reprinted by permission of Harper & Row, Publishers, Inc. "The Fixed," from *Pilgrim at Tinker Creek* by Annie Dillard. Copyright © 1974 by Annie Dillard. Reprinted by permission of Harper & Row, Publishers, Inc.

JOSÉ DONOSO: "Paseo" Reprinted by kind permission of Agencia Carmen Balcells, Barcelona, literary agent for José Donoso.

W. E. B. DUBOIS: "Jacob and Esau" by W. E. B. DuBois. From *W. E. B. DuBois Speaks, 1920–1963,* edited by Philip S. Foner. Reprinted by permission of Pathfinder Press. Copyright © 1970 by Philip S. Foner and Shirley Graham DuBois.

LAWRENCE DURRELL: "Landscape and Character" by Lawrence Durrell. *The New*